Donated
To The Library by

JOHN & CHERYL SIMMERLEY

Interior of Frederick County Clerk's Office when first impression
of the Washington Family seal was used
(Copy of this picture on file in National Library collection.)

Shenandoah Valley Pioneers and Their Descendants

A History of Frederick County, Virginia

(ILLUSTRATED)

Seal of Old County Court, Adopted 1758

From its Formation in 1738 to 1908

Compiled Mainly from Original Records of Old Frederick County, now Hampshire, Berkeley, Shenandoah, Jefferson, Hardy, Clarke, Warren, Morgan and Frederick

T. K. Cartmell
Clerk of the Old County Court

- Notice -

The foxing, or discoloration with age, characteristic of old books, sometimes shows through to some extent in reprints such as this, especially when the foxing is very severe in the original book. We feel that the contents of this book warrant its reissue despite these blemishes, and hope you will agree and read it with pleasure.

Cover illustration: from an engraving after a painting of George Washington by Charles Willson Peale

Facsimile Reprint

Published 1989 By
HERITAGE BOOKS, INC.
1540E Pointer Ridge Place, Bowie, Maryland 20716
(301)-390-7709

ISBN 1-55613-243-3

PRINTED BY
THE EDDY PRESS CORPORATION
WINCHESTER, VA.

PREFACE

The title of this volume should indicate to the reader, what he will find for his edification. Our County has never had her history published. Successive generations for one hundred and fifty years, were busy in their day making history; but no period produced the man who would turn aside from his daily avocations, to collate the facts and place them before the public in form for convenience and preservation. We had such men as Kercheval, Howe, Foote, Norris and several others, to publish many historical facts; but none of these writers ever gave us a history of Frederick County. Their treatment of historical facts was so general in character, that we gather very little from their attractive style, that can be utilized as county history. Our County had useful history; her subdivisions have the same. Much of it has been gradually hidden away in the accumulation of old files and old records of the county and the nine counties embraced in Old Frederick.

The State can best preserve her history through the labor and skill of the county historian. Some of the Virginia Counties have published histories, prepared by competent men.

The writer, many years ago, while County Clerk, discovered so much unpublished history of the Old County, that he was induced to adopt some plan to preserve its identity; and out of the multitude of memoranda, to secure a convenient hand-book of reference for his office. He had no intention to publish a history; knowing full well that much additional effort would be required to gather matter for a comprehensive history of the County. However, he hoped that some gifted son would appear and take up the matter, and in this way produce a volume of interesting facts. For twenty-five years he waited; but no one seemed inclined to undertake the task. In 1904, the opinion was so decidedly expressed that the Old Clerk was the proper one to use the matter collected, that he was induced to undertake the authorship of the volume he now presents to the reader. The descendants of the pioneers will find much to interest them; and the general reader will be astonished to see the valuable matter in easy form for his study. The author has avoided fiction, and traditionary history unless corroborated to his satisfaction. He has given much from his personal knowledge of facts, as they occurred during his long intercourse with the people of his native county. The work has been intensely interesting to him, though one of great labor. In the course of study, he has spent much time in all the clerk's offices of the Valley and other parts of the State. The State Library and Land Office were systematically examined, as only an old clerk could, to obtain matter to settle long-disputed questions pertaining to the history of Royal and Minor Grants. Such evidence was required to determine who were the pioneers and first settlers in the Valley. Old musty records were brought forth, that many had thought were destroyed in the evacuation of Richmond in the Spring of 1865; on which the author had spent several days in finding a clue, and then many more before he found the record. (These valuable records are now being indexed and will be more accessible to students). The History Building at the Jamestown Exposition contained much to show who hundreds of the pioneers were, and whence they came. Several weeks were profitably spent there. This induced the author to visit Maryland, Pennsylvania, New Jersey and New York, to follow clues. Ulster County, New York, has a mine of information concerning the early settlers in the Shenandoah. The Jerseys gave much that the author has used in various forms. From these sources, we have much matter not heretofore published. National and State Libraries, through efficient officers, extended rare courtesies. The War Department extended special privileges. Mt. Vernon was visited, where unusual privileges were given.

In addition to these sources of information, the author has been assisted in the preparation of his work by a careful study of the works of Washington Irving and Sparks' Life of Washington; Washington's Diary and Letters; Jefferson's Notes; Macaulay's History of England; Gabriel Muhlenburg's Life of General Muhlenburg; Meade's History of Old Families, Ministers and Churches; Hawk's History of Episcopal Church; Sprague's Annals of the Lutheran Church; J. F. Sachse's German Element of Pennsylvania; Herman Schuricht's Germans of Pennsylvania and Virginia; Max von Eelking's German Allied Troops, Hessians, etc.; (translated); Kirchner's History of Emmigrants; Bishop Asbury's Journal; Fithian's Journal; James R. Graham, D.D., Planting of Presbyterianism in the Northern Neck; Foote's Sketches of Virginia and North Carolina; Popp's Journal, Relating to Hessian Soldiers in Virginia; Stapleton's Huguenots; Bowman's History of the George Rogers Clark's Expedition; Hinke's German Reformed Colony in Virginia; W. T. Saffell's Records of the Revolutionary War, and 3rd Edition by Charles C. Saffell; Thirty Thousand Names of Emigrants, 1727—1776, published by Leary, Stuart & Co., Philadelphia; John Lederer's Discoveries of Wild Countries in Virginia and North Carolina; Hening's Virginia Statutes; Saml. Shepherd's List of Old Soldiers; W. G. and Mary M. Stanard's Colonial History; Keith's History of the Quakers; Calendar of Virginia State papers; Virgil A. Lewis' History of the Virginias; John P. Hale, Notes of Historical Society, West Virginia; Rev. Christian Streit's Diary; Drs. Krauth & Gilbert's Church History; J. A. Waddell's Annals of Augusta; J. L. Peyton's History of Augusta; W. W. Scott's History of Orange County; Crozier's Virginia Colonial Militia; Boogher, Nelson & Romaine, Genealogical Works in National Library; Henderson's Life of Stonewall Jackson; Dabney's Civil War; Col. William Allen on Valley Campaign; Alexander & Sorrell, Recollections of Staff Officers; Thomas Nelson Page's and J. Esten Cooke's Civil War Incidents; E. H. McDonald's Laurel Brigade; Generals Geo. H. Gordon & Carl Schurz, Histories and Sketches of Union Officers, Battles, etc.; oldest newspapers published in the Valley, and those of subsequent periods; Holmes Conrad (of Martinsburg) Letters and Notes; William G. Russell's Notes; William H. English's Conquest of the Northwest; Prof. J. W. Wayland's The German Element of the Shenandoah Valley; Standard Histories of Kentucky, Tennessee, Ohio, Illinois, Indiana, Missouri, and North Carolina.

The study of the history of the Old County and movements of the Shenandoah Valley pioneers, has been fascinating. The Colonial homesteads have been visited; many have been familiar to the author for a half century; following the descendants through many stages of development to the present, was instructive. The author has personal acquaintance with thousands of the present population of the Great Valley. For thirty years, the citizens of every community of Frederick County have been in close touch with him; he has enjoyed their friendship and confidence. This induced the numerous biographical sketches found in the volume. He is conscious of the fact that some families have been overlooked, as from his office-chair he scanned the County from memory.

The Old County, founded in 1738—once the home of the Redmen, with their tomahawk and scalping-knife, saw them subjugated; heard the tramp of Washington's and Morgan's men; witnessed the building of Fort Loudoun in the 18th Century, and the Star and other forts in the 19th, when she bared her breast for conflict between the armies of the North and South, marshalled by Stonewall Jackson and his dauntless leaders on the one side, on the other, by Banks, Sheridan and hosts of others;—witnessed the burning of the Valley by Hunter.

The history now offered, gives organization of first courts in all the counties in the Lower Valley; origin of the towns; sketches of their growth; the ferries, when and where established on the Shenandoah and Potomac; old and new roads, when, where and by whom opened; turnpikes, their charters and when first used; railroads, data in full; old homesteads and families; personal sketches of men of all classes; history of the princely estate of Lord Fairfax in the Northern Neck; sketch of the Fairfax family; history of Winchester from formative period to date; the old market and public square, that caused litigation of rights between the county and city; history of the celebrated suit and results; Indian, French, and Revolutionary Wars; study of military engagements in the Shenandoah Valley during the Civil War; location of battle-fields; dates of battles; lists of Valley Regiments; closing scenes at Appomattox; the John Brown raid; history of the churches, showing when and where the first was located West of the Blue Ridge; old courts, their officers, legal battles fought in their forums; history of the Fairfax & Hite suits, and many other notable suits and criminal trials; gleanings from old courts from their first organization.

The author commends his effort to the student of history or casual reader, who will find it a store-house of information, and a handbook of reference on all subjects pertaining to the counties of the Lower Valley.

"Ingleside," near Winchester,

December, 1908. T. K. C.

TABLE OF CONTENTS

LIST OF ILLUSTRATIONS

CHAPTER I

How and by Whom the Shenandoah Valley was Settled

The first families to settle in the Lower Shenandoah Valley, were generally known as the *sixteen families* who came with Joist Hite in 1732. None questioned this for many decades.

The Valley historian, Kercheval, and others following him, gave Hite credit as the first settler; and from this standpoint we introduce him as such. Though it may appear in the study of this question, that he had contestants, their claims will be treated later on.

Hite and his colony crossed the *Cohongoroota* River, where a village was started named Mecklenberg. Old records confirm this. The village bore this name for many years, until finally changed to Shepherdstown. Closely following Hite, Scotch-Irish Presbyterians began to settle in other sections within the boundaries of Old Frederick County, which then embraced all that is known now as Shenandoah, Page, Warren, Clarke, Jefferson, Berkley, Morgan, Hampshire and parts of Hardy and Rockingham Counties. The families who came with Hite, have caused untold trouble to the enquirer, as to who they were. Some have thought the record of their names and dates of arrival could be found in the records of Old Frederick County; and resorted to them, to be disappointed by not finding individual grants to these families. Hite held a grant to enter and locate *twenty* families, survey his tracts, and then give them his certificate, which the Colonial Council would ratify; and then, for the first time, the family name would appear. At the same time, just prior to 1734, we find many deeds to settlers who were not of the *sixteen* other families, who soon became landowners in the new settlements, as shown by court records. We may be pardoned in heading the list with the name of Fairfax as one of the actual inhabitants, though not the first.

One source of valuable and interesting facts, for which the author is indebted to Mr. Marion Bantz, concerning this family, is in his possession. He has quite a treasury of antiquities, kindly placed at the writer's disposal, of what can be termed Lord Fairfax's papers. Mr. B., a resident of Winchester, was present during the demolition of the well-known house on Piccadilly Street in Winchester, in which had been stored for many years relics of Fairfax's property. The new owner cared nothing for what he termed "rubbish;" and the original owner being long since dead, one of his surviving children, who had occupied the house during her entire life and only left it because of changed conditions, gave Mr. B. permission to search through the old wasting papers; and out of the wreck, he found the original "patent for the Northern Neck," and many other papers not recorded in *any* office. From these relics, the author will avail himself in the proper place, under the subject head of the Fairfax Family.

Next we might add the name of Washington,—*George* being the first member, coming as a stripling sixteen years old, (1748) "to measure out plantations for Thomas Lord Fairfax, the reputed owner of the northern neck." It was due to a desire on the part of Thomas Lord Fairfax, that young Washington became identified with Frederick County; for we find it recorded that in 1748 he visited his estates in Virginia, which he desired to "explore and lay out plantations." Lord Fairfax was not the first Fairfax to come to Virginia. Several of them lived in the section adjacent to the Mt. Vernon estate. An attachment between them was soon apparent to all; and none were surprised when his Lordship proposed to the stripling to undertake the work. Washington accepted, and together with an assistant, proceeded to Frederick County and took the buildings at Greenway Court for their headquarters, Lord Fairfax not yet having taken his abode at that historic and secluded place. His Lordship returned to England about this time, to prepare for his residence in the wilds of the new country; so we find him at Greenway Court in his mansion house in 1750, terming it " The Lord Proprietor's Office;" executing leases to many new settlers, and having same recorded in his own office.

The writer, in his experience among the old records of the County, found many traces to the history of the Northern Neck of Virginia. Many people have regarded the original grant for this proprietary, as from some crowned head in England to our Lord Fairfax, who bestowed upon him the title of Lord. We will have occasion to mention this more fully in a personal sketch of the Virginia Fairfaxes. The present object is simply to show where the family settled in Frederick County and what they settled on; to give the true history of this grant, and the reasons for Lord Fairfax's visit to England. His Lordship found his title in Virginia disputed by many persons, who produced what were distinguished as *Minor Grants.* He hoped to lay this matter before the Crown, and have his rights definitely settled.

The grant from King Charles II, March 12, 1664, to Lord Colepepper, was at an early day in the history of the Virginia Colony, and meant much for the settlers at Jamestown, and other places along and near the James, and York Rivers, and other streams that had confluence with the majestic Chesapeake. We are often asked, who was Lord Fairfax? Of course, the answer is promptly given: He was the proprietor of the Northern Neck of Virginia and Baron of Cameron in that part of Great Britain called Scotland, which answer is not sufficient in many cases. To one who by his education and association with historical events is already informed, these notes perhaps will convey no new knowledge; but the compiler hopes to place before all readers, facts that will easily answer such questions.

Lord Fairfax, as we will show later on, arrived in America for the first time in 1736, when he visited his agent, William Fairfax, who was located in the region later known as Mount Vernon, Virginia. William Fairfax, the agent, erected a house that became not only his residence, but also the Lord Proprietor's Office. His Lordship spent nearly three years at this court, which the owner called Belvoir; and then returned to England to present his grievances to the Crown. He desired fuller definition of his grant. During his stay in England, he learned the conditions of the *Colepepper Grant,* which became one of the holdings of the *Baron of Cameron.*

Lord Fairfax was born in England. His father was Thomas Fairfax, who married Lady Catharine Colepepper, the daughter and only heir of Lord Thomas Colepepper, who was last surviving heir of the Lord Colepepper to whom King Charles granted "all of the country known at that time as the Colony of Virginia; excepting therefrom such other grants theretofore made" and *"other reservations,"* boundaries of which were set out and required to be entered in the record of the infant colony at Jamestown, and subsequently at Williamsburg. Though many of the old records were destroyed, the writer now has in his hands the original Colepepper Grant, found among the old papers previously mentioned. Our Thomas, however, was the Seventh Fairfax to inherit the title of Lord Cameron, a title of which he ever seemed proud, and never failed to mention in all his papers relating to his holdings in America.

As has been stated, there were special grants for certain parts of Virginia; but Lord Fairfax believed he was the owner of all. The King had reserved for himself certain quit rents, not only from the special patents, but also from Colepepper. The latter, however, exercised arbitrary rule and power in his proprietary, collecting rents and gathering much from the parish allowances. This tyrannical treatment aroused the American blood; and petitions went to the King; and in consequence, the Great Grant was limited to the Northern Neck. (See boundaries elsewhere: also Hening's Statutes, 1748, pp. 198-9, confirming smaller grants to settlers.)

So far as known, Lord Thomas Colepepper had but one brother, Alexander, who was joint heir in the great grant. But the two brothers had an agreement that Thomas was to take in his name the entire grant, and then convey to Alexander a certain interest in the vast territory embraced in the original grant. But Thomas, the father of Catharine, died before this conveyance was completed; so this explains the sweeping conveyance made to Alexander Colepepper by Catharine Fairfax, sole heir of her said father, "reserving to herself what she termed the Northern Neck in the Old Dominion of Virginia in America." This deed of conveyance, dated 1710, contained some reliable history concerning the early settlers. She recites many things that throw light on the holdings of many families in large tracts of lands all over Virginia. Our valley settlers have the history of their grants fully set out therein. It was held at one time, that the first settlers had poor title to their homesteads; but this voluminous deed, starting out to convey a large and well-defined territory in the Tidewater country to her uncle Alexander, explains the case fully. Lord Fairfax, having possessed himself with this knowledge, was content to take his grant for the Northern Neck, understanding that the *minor grants* must be respected. He returned to America, as already stated, in 1748; and, upon his arrival, proceeded to Greenway Court, a point 12 miles southeast from Winchester, Virginia, where he established his home and offices. There he lived and there he died, according to reliable information, in 1782, at the advanced age of 92 years—not in Winchester, in 1781, as so often stated in magazine articles.

We are indebted to Mr. William C. Kennerly, whose grandmother lived at Greenway Court at that time, for his inimitable reproduction of what she related to him: "The hearse was brought from Alexandria. The cortege was composed of relations and friends from Fairfax County, and his neighbors from every settlement along the Shenandoah, and proceeded to Winchester with considerable pomp. His remains were placed in the Episcopal Church Yard on Loudoun Street, now the site of the business block on east side of the street, north of the corner of Water and Loudoun streets." When Christ Church (Episcopal) was erected on the corner of Water and Washington Streets, his remains were removed and buried 'neath the chancel of that church.

The boundaries of the Northern Neck, as reserved by Catharine, the mother of Thomas Lord Fairfax, are as follows—(actual survey too lengthy to be given): Beginning on the Chesapeake Bay, lies between the Potomac and Rappahannock Rivers, crossing the Blue Ridge, or rather passing through the Gap along the Potomac at Harpers Ferry, then with the "Cohongoruta" to its source in the Alleganies; then by a straight line, crosses the Great North Mountain and Blue Ridge to the head waters of the Rappahannock, wherever that might be.

We will find the closing up of the boundary lines resulted in serious trouble to Fairfax, for at that point he runs against the large grants to the VanMeter brothers, Carter, Hite and others. As previously stated, the Fairfax conveyance recognizes the rights of certain inhabitants, sparsely settled throughout the Virginia domain. In many cases, names are given (See Call. 4, 42), stating that many persons had acquired rights to hold vast tracts by reason of special grants from the Crown at different stages in the history of the country, so as to encourage emigration to the New World, when it was found desirable for England to enter in and possess the land, and no longer allow the Plymouth and Jamestown Colonists to feel they had any right except such given and granted them by the Crown. And thus we have such settlers, with special grants, for slices out of what had already been embraced in the original grant to Lord Colepepper for Virginia, Lord Baltimore, for what is now Maryland and Delaware, the Duke of York for all the territory lying between the Connecticut and Delaware Rivers. The last named was James Duke, of York, and brother to King Charles II, who, growing tired of his wild and far-away estates, conveyed his entire interest in what is termed the Territory above the Hudson and Delaware Rivers, to John Lord Berkeley and Sir George Carteret, with the approval and confirmation of the King.

Some digression is usually allowed all writers; and as Virginia was to become the home of many inhabitants of numerous Maryland and Jersey grants, it is well to give brief mention of certain conditions prevailing in those sections.

King Charles II, March 12, 1664, saw his opportunity to parcel out in the New World, large estates for his nobility; and, as already stated, the grants referred to soon grew to be powerful aids to his plan of making a *New England* on this side the Atlantic. This encouraged emigration, not only from England, but from Ireland, Scotland and France. The Dutch, Swedes and Hollanders soon sought homes in the new world —the last named landing on the Jersey coast; the former, chiefly looking for those who had settled along the Maryland, Virginia and Carolina Coasts, found homes among the early settlers. Now began a new trial. These settlers desired titles to their homes; and much confusion arose. We find King Charles in the latter part of his reign, and James II, who ascended the English throne in 1685, making special grants to families who had become permanent settlers in Lord Colepepper's dominion, but declining to do so in the domains of Lord Baltimore and the Duke of York. The Duke of York adopted the plan of subdivision of his grant, and conveyed to Lord John Berkley and Sir George Carteret what was above the Hudson and Delaware Rivers. This appears to have been at the suggestion of the King; for the Duke seemed displeased, and pleaded with the King to know "what he did own in America." Accordingly we find in 1674, Charles renewed his grant to the Duke for the remainder, who was "to hold under such terms as he prayed." Lord Berkley and Sir George Carteret soon divided their grants into what they termed East and West Jersey, and a boundary was established between them which shows its line of monuments to this day. Then was formed the *Proprietor's* government,—to own and control the soil without taxation, so long as they held in their own right, or their heirs, but not so with any *purchaser,* under whom it became taxable by the State. This proprietary ownership and government of vast tracts in America, was extended not only to those of Jersey and York, but to Lord Baltimore in Maryland and Delaware, and to Lord Colepepper in Virginia. Lord Berkley offered inducements to immigrants. One, John Fenwick, induced Lord Berkley to allow him to establish a colony,—which was then and is now known as Fenwick Colony. The deed was recorded at old Salem by John Fenwick, March 1, 1682, for a moiety of his Proprietary which he originally purchased from Lord Berkley. This deed of conveyance is to Governor William Penn for this moiety, reserving for himself the said John Fenwick, all the tract called Fenwick Colony, supposed to contain 150,000 acres. Mention is made in these pages of this Fenwick Colony, by reason of its having furnished many emigrants to the Valley of Virginia in the early part of the Eighteenth Century, when its discovery had been made by Governor Spottswood—he of the Golden Horseshoe Expedition. What he saw filled his party, not only with wonder and admiration, but a desire to hastily return and spread the news, inviting immigration from the settlement lying along the Jersey coast and the more thickly settled parts of Pennsylvania. These Northern settlers soon began to seek the wonderland; and at this point we must state, many of these settlers were beginning to feel oppression from the Lord Proprietors. And as they had learned through Governor Penn, that King William III, during his reign from 1638, for thirteen years, had offered grants to a certain number of families who wanted to go into Virginia and make homes out of the forests, Mary II joined the king in this new effort to people the new lands. This was carried into effect; and good Queen Anne, in her reign of fourteen years beginning 1701, confirmed all such grants, and promised to protect them. So we find about 1725, many persons in those northern settlements seeking information how they could obtain grants in the new country. The tide set in about 1730; some crossing the Potomac East of the mountains, and a few families crossing the Cohongaroota West of the mountains. The latter made a settlement in 1732 near the river, and called it Mecklenberg. As has been stated, others followed the Opecquon Creek, and settled about thirty miles further South; others at the confluence of the two rivers, Potomac and Shenandoah. Some writers on the subject of the first settlement in the great Valley, think it was at the latter place where Robert Harper and others in 1736, stopped and built log cabins, and a ferry boat to accommodate those who were still coming and often found no way to cross over. Now we have come to the point, who were these people who came from the cold North? We have recorded evidence of their courage, ambition, energy, skill, good morals and sufficient means to develop the newly discovered valley; so that it was possible for its hills and dells to become renowned for their fertility, and afford homes for the thousands who fill every avenue of life; and its history shows who were jurists, statesmen and professional men of every class, and whose farmers have in trying times, made it possible for armies to subsist and recruit their depleted stores, while her artisans and inventors furnished other sinews of war. These will ever be recognized as equal to any other people; and as for the warriors, who have won fame from friend and foe, beginning with the invincible Morgan, and coming on down through every military exploit of the country, to Stonewall Jackson and his *foot-cavalry*—none suggests the thought that their fame will ever fade or be forgotten by succeeding generations.

The reader will excuse such digressions as may seem too often to creep in, as we attempt to lead him along through the various phases of the history of Old Frederick County.

Joist Hite has had the credit given him by other writers, of being the first white man to settle in the Lower Valley, which was then known as Spottsylvania. In 1734, Orange was formed from Spottsylvania. In 1738, an Act of the House of Burgesses directed two new counties to be formed, one to be Frederick and the other Augusta, and taken from Orange, as was stated in the opening of these sketches. Hite also has the credit of bringing sixteen families with him; but since no court was organized until Nov. 11, 1743, we have no record of the *minor grants* referred to in the records of Frederick County prior to the first court. Many were recorded in old Spottsylvania and also in Orange. We will for the present, treat this as the first immigration, and endeavor to name them all and locate them in the sections of the County where they began their work as pioneers. It must be borne in mind, that so soon as they crossed the Potomac at what is Harpers Ferry, or at some point West of the Blue Ridge, they entered the country to be known as Old Frederick County. We must not forget that these first pioneers had entered the proprietary of the Colepepper grant, which at this coming had descended to the Fairfax, who was to bring contention and confusion to many whom our Lord Thomas found, as he thought, squatters in his realm. So having this understood, we will start with the Hite settlers. Some of the sixteen families were Joist Hite's immediate family, for he had several sons of full age and three married daughters. Thus we have four out of the sixteen within his own circle, which enabled him to assert a right to rule and direct the movement of his new colony. His sons inter-married with the other families.

Hite speaks of his sons-in-law, Paul Froman, George Bowman and Jacob Chrisman.

While Hoge, Allen, Wilson, White and others, represent in part the English contingent, and Van Swearingen, Van Meter and others, represent the sturdy Dutch, Germans, Swedes and Hollanders, a more extended notice will be given in this work of all the families referred to and their descendants, in a chapter on schools and churches. Our attention at present must be given to the location of the sixteen families, and what they had in their hands to give them a legal right to enter at will the new country, and possess the land and build a log cabin. So, as has been previously stated, William Penn had pointed the way. He it was and the good John Fenwick, who had secured from the English rulers the *minor grants* referred to; and when they started out for their new home, Joist Hite carried with him the "parchments," granting rights to such families as could find suitable location; then to survey their homestead, describing accurately and erecting monuments of boundaries, so that it could be shown the king who the actual settler was and his name. And the crown recognized these in treating with Lord Thomas Fairfax. (Hen. Statutes, 1748, p. 198).

As has been intimated, many of these grants gave Fairfax much trouble later on, and annoyance to the settlers. Many ejectment suits were instituted by his Lordship, availing him nothing, however, in any claim against the settler, where he had fully complied with the provisions of the grant. But where he failed to set out fully his boundaries, so that his lines could be fully established, then he suffered loss. Many of the ejectment suits of Fairfax against the settlers in the Valley and elsewhere, grew out of the leases that had been made by William Fairfax as the agent of the actual heir and owner of the Colepepper grant, so far as it applied to the Northern Neck. Many such leases had been made by him and other agents previous to the time of vesting the title in our Lord Thomas. And be it remembered, the latter emanating from the Fairfax family, were only temporary leases to run for a term of years, mostly twenty years, yielding to the proprietor "On each recurring Lady's Day one Pepper Corn." The lessee to use his tract as he saw, to his own interest: the object being to encourage settlement and offer inducements for substantial development of much of the trackless waste. Some of these short leases were renewed by Fairfax when he landed at the Greenway Court and took control in 1750; the other leases mentioned were the stumbling blocks to the new Proprietor; for when he, with his youthful surveyor, began to make surveys for tracts to persons to whom he was making leases for a term of one hundred years, and to be renewable under certain complied conditions, he found other claimants who had long before become actual settlers and standing on their "Clearing" beside their own "Log Cabins," as they exhibited their leases bearing unmistakable evidence of authority, not only from the Colonial authorities, but with the stamp and approval of the reigning Monarch of England. Fairfax could not have been unaware of the legality of the last-named leases for in his inheritance of the Northern Neck, he took what his mother, Catharine Colepepper, had under the great Colepepper grant, with its provisions: the King reserving the right to make grants within the territory to settlers, requiring in each case that proof should be given the government that such person had settled on his great tract with so many families, and that the tract had been subdivided, and surveys of the subdivisions actually made and conveyance made to an actual settler on his part. Such grants were to be perpetual, and not to be interferred with by Fairfax or his heirs.

The original plan of the King, "ordained for the purpose of planting colonies in America," worked well, and was the cause of large development of many sections of Virginia. So this condition of the settlement should not have surprised Fairfax; but it apparently did; for he treated such as squatters on his soil, who must yield to him a rental and take his lease, and be subject to his demand or vacate. This meant much to these families who had felled the forest for the good homes they had planted, with virtually the rifle in hand, to protect the settlement from the powerful tribes of Indians, who were disputing every effort to make white settlements. We find when this demand was made by Fairfax through his agents, he met opposition. He was confronted by men who knew they were right; who, in full faith in their claims, had not only builded their homes and reared sturdy families, but had organized churches and schools, which at that period were flourishing. Many things occurred to mar the peace of his Lordship. He soon found litigation on his hands. In his surveys to lessees, he found monuments marking boundaries of large and extensive areas, such as were claimed by Joist Hite and his settlers, and those of Van Meter, Russell and Carter; the latter resulting in the most famous legal battles fought to a conclusion in the early history of the Virginia Colonies.

As this chapter is intended to mention Hite and his colonies, we will dispose of Hite's claim as the first settler, and then give names, so far as we know, of the families who came with him. We may appropriately state here that Hite, in failing to comply with his agreement made through Governor Penn, suffered much annoyance in holding to his claim when attacked by Fairfax. For when it was developed that he obtained his grant, stipulating that twenty families was to be the number, while he could only show sixteen, he at once began repairing his weak points. Being a man of great nerve, and of no small ability as a lawyer without the profession, he at once undertook to cure in part the mistake he had made, and to fortify against the attacks of Fairfax. Thus we find him recognizing the Van Meter grants to be, not only better than his, but ante-dating his. The writer is well aware how this statement will be received by many readers; but he must endeavor to state facts in this history of the early and first settlers of the Lower Valley; and if it detracts from the glory of Hite, who has always had the credit of being the first white man to plunge into the unexplored forests of the Old County of Frederick, even before its formation in 1738, it must be done; though the writer was tempted to pass it by, desiring this old pioneer should have all the glory. He believed he *was* the first to confront the savage tribes on their native soil; and over many "Clearings" did he and his neighbors contend with the warriors of "Opekenough"—he who held sway along the streams of his own naming, which afterwards the white man abbreviated to what we have to-day—"Opeckon"—a stream to become famous, not only for struggles made by the Redmen in protecting his wigwams and hunting grounds from the White invaders, but in later years when the descendants of these invaders were compelled to take their stand in battle array along its historic banks to stem another invasion from the same country from whence the first invaders came, and in their peculiar way accomplished the object sought—both being for subjugation:—the first driving before them the wigwam and tomahawk, to result in subjugation only after nearly two hundred years of steady warfare and treaties;—the new invasion requiring only four years of terrific carnage and bloodshed to devastate the Lower Valley, ultimately resulting in the subjugation planned from the first. How strangely differing the causes of the invasions and their results! The former came to do their part in developing a continent in the wilds of America, offering an asylum for liberty-loving people from every clime and nation, to be one of the mighty host sweeping Westward, to some day land upon the shores of the Pacific Ocean, leaving marks of civilization in their wake, as the states and cities with their teeming millions were ever attesting the wisdom of the first invader. Not so with the last! They swept the land with a besom of destruction—they leveled homes as well as forests; but never builded homes and cities. They invaded for desolation! And in their wake, as they pressed southward and westward, left ashes and ruin. But the descendants of those grand old first settlers, followed the example of Joist Hite, and made the best of their mistake. Hite had underestimated the strength of his contestants. And when he found his position, the wily old chief used his diplomacy and held his ground. Referring again to Hite and the Van Meter grants, we will state here that Hite obtained by purchase forty thousand acres of the Van Meter grant, and immediately began to make deeds for tracts of land to the many settlers who were now, in 1734, seeking homes; and having located many who had come subsequent to the arrival of his colony, thus showing his good intentions to carry out his agreement to locate at least forty families. Then he turned his attention to the Hite grant, as it has been called,—to have it renewed, so as to protect those of the sixteen families he had located before Fairfax raised his point for ejectment. Many suits followed, as has already been stated; and Fairfax prevailed in some of the latter class; so that some of the sixteen will not appear in the list of those who owned their own land.

Lest there be confusion in regard to the holdings of Hite, the author deems it best to give a condensed statement at this point. Hite, through the influence of Governor Penn, received a conditional grant from the Virginia Council in 1730, for one hundred thousand acres of land, to be located West of the Great Mountains, not therefore granted,—upon which he was to locate forty families, within a certain time. This number was reduced to twenty families—and not sixteen, as has been so often stated by tradition. Finding the Van Meter grant in his way, he purchased from them, and proceeded to comply with the conditions,—which required the Van Meters to locate one hundred families. This seemed a prodigious undertaking; and he went to the Governor's Council for an extension of time. This he obtained. He now had virtually about two hundred thousand acres of land. He saw his chance to comply. Immigrants had followed in his wake, seeking land

Old Joist Hite Fort, near Bartonsville; erected 1750

for homes. Hite at once located many families on the previously surveyed tracts of forty thousand and thirty thousand acres, known to him as the Van Meter tracts; and then proceeded to complete his survey for the one hundred thousand acres, and also for an additional twenty thousand acres South of the North fork of the Sherando River. Later on it will be shown to whom he parceled out this vast territory; and this will give the location of his Great Grant. Joist Hite continued to look after the interests of his colony—and helped his sons and sons-in-law to build their homes, which were substantial, and surrounded by some of the richest and best located lands in the County. Several well built stone houses on these tracts were erected during Hite's lifetime.

There is something peculiar about the elder Hite in the way he managed his estates and business. He died comparatively a poor man—as will be seen by his will; while his children grew rich, and continually increased their holdings. As has been stated, Hite lived and died in Frederick County. He changed his residence frequently; living at one time where he first stopped at Shepherdstown,—then moving to the Opecquon Creek, at what is now Bartonsville. There he built a stone house on the West side of what is the Valley Turnpike. At the same time, he and other settlers built a stone fort due East from what was to be his residence, the ruins of which can be seen to-day on the East side of the said pike. Later on, 1753, one of his sons, Col. John Hite, aided by his father, built the splendid stone house now occupied by Mrs. Harry Hack (Mrs. Arbuckle). Joist Hite lived for some years in his stone house,—and lent aid to the settlement of the Opecquon Valley. This will have fuller mention with other families. We find Hite once more building a large house and living with his son Isaac Hite, near the Shenandoah River, known as "Long Meadows." He then changes his residence, and is found living at Shepherdstown, and making deeds to purchasers for small tracts of land in that section, and part of (as he recites) the Patent Deed. We locate him there as a resident, at least temporarily; for, in his acknowledgment of these deeds, the certificates are signed by Justices of the Peace living at and near Shepherdstown. We find him again at the Old House on the Opeckon; and there seems to be no doubt that he died there, the exact date not fully shown; but, as his will is dated April 25th, 1758, and was probated at a County Court held 7th day of May, 1761, it is very evident that his death occurred a short time before 1761. Where the old worn-out man was laid to his final rest, has often been the subject of enquiry. Some have it that he was buried near his old Home at Bartonsville, in a family "graveyard," which for a long time, from its close proximity to the Valley Pike on the East side and North of his son's residence, was calculated to fix that as his burial place. A few old slabs mark several graves. No one ever saw the name of Hite on any.

During the writer's experience as Clerk of the County Court, he was drawn into a correspondence with Hon. William H. English, of Indianapolis, Ind.,—he being President at the time, of the National Historical Society. He will be remembered by many as the candidate for vice-president on Hancock and English ticket at the Presidential election. Mr. English was a lineal descendant of Joist Hite, and desired some information about the question of the "last resting place of his old ancestor." This correspondence resulted in his visit to the writer in 1895. His son, Hon. William E. English, accompanied him,—and we spared no effort to settle the question. Evidence was obtained that Hite was strongly attached to the Opeckon Church, with its five acres,—part of which had been in use for years as the burial place for early settlers,—this being almost in full view from Hite's home: Such proved conclusively that Hite was buried at the old Churchyard. This *Yard* was occupied by the church, one large graveyard in the northeast corner, and by two small plots lying on the North and South end of the church. These plots had substantial stone walls to protect them, and remained intact until the battle of Kernstown, when they were somewhat battered, and later on the stones were carried into Gen. Sheridan's camp and used as chimneys for winter quarters. Then the grave marks were soon destroyed. This occurred in the case of the large cemetery in the northeast corner of the five acre lot. It was well remembered by many, that the Plot on the North end was used by the Hite family,—and slabs at one time marked their graves. The writer well remembers his early visits to this far-famed spot, and had often related incidents occurring during these boyhood visits. It was the custom, as well as the rule, in that day for the families in the surrounding country to attend that church; and on one of the occasions, the writer saw and heard many things to make lasting impressions on his young mind. One touched him closely; and it was while his father, in company with Dr. William Hill, the pastor, Col. John Gilkeson, and several others just before service, stood leaning over the stone wall of the Plot on the North end of the church that the boy's quick ear caught much to interest him,—for Dr. Hill remarked: "There is the grave of the wonderful man, the old German, Yost Heite." This had a double interest for the boy,—for he often heard strange stories at home, in the old negro cabin, where the old Auntie, who had been a slave in the Hite family, had become the property of the writer's grandfather, when he married the granddaughter of Joist Hite. So on his arrival at home, he soon rushed to the old cabin to startle the old Auntie with his story. She received it calmly,—and replied that she knew that; and also, that right by his side her *Mistus* was buried in 1792. Such incidents often give such strength to traditional history, that the student finds it more reasonable and correct than many of the compendiums of data and chronology through which he has spent much time to settle the question. Much comment on the old man's name has been made by many writers—it being spelled differently. This may be accounted for by different ideas of translation of the German he wrote; for no writing of his has been seen in all the writer's research of the records, where he ever wrote English. So when making records of his writing in English, the Clerk, if not acquainted with the German, would call upon some one for its translation, and they differed in their version,— so this no doubt accounts for the name appearing in print in so many different ways. The writer in his early life never heard his name called but the one way, and that Joss Hite. But the translations referred to, make it appear frequently as Yost Hite—Yoist Heite, Joss Haite, Joist Heighte, Just Heite; but in the latter part of his career, the record was chiefly made by the same clerk, and it was invariably written in a large hand *Joist Hite.*

Joist Hite, Anna Maria his wife, and their children John, Jacob, Isaac, Abram, Joseph, his sons; daughters: Mary Bowman, Magdelena Chrisman, and Elizabeth Froman, and their children will receive fuller notice elsewhere. Hite's wife died in 1738. He married again in 1741, the marriage contract follows at this point.

"IN THE NAME OF JESUS

WHEREAS, WE, two persons, I Just Heite and Maria Magdalina Relict, and widow of Christian Nuschanger, according to God's Holy Ordinance with the knowledge and consent of our Friends and Children and Relations are going to enter into the Holy State of Matrimony. We have made this Nuptial part one with the other. First promise to the aforesaid Maria Magdalina all the Christian Love and faithfulness. Secondly, as neither of us are a moment secure from death so I promise her that my House shall be her Home or Widow Seat so long as she lives and the Heir to whom the said House shall fall shall provide her necessary Diet and Cloathes and of that do not please but that she rather desires to have her commendations in any other place, so shall the aforesaid Heir to the House yearly pay her Six pounds ready money and this is my well considered desire.

JOST HITE.

And Likewise wife I, Maria Magdalina promise the aforesaid Just Hite, First all Love and Obedience, Secondly I am designed to bring with me to him some Cattle, money, household stuff which in an Other Agreement with Attested Witnesses shall be Described and should I die before the said Hite so shall the said Hite have the half thereof and the other half shall be delivered back again to my heirs and this is allso my well considered desire Thirdly and Lastly, whoever of the aforesaid persons shall die forst the half of the portion the Woman brings with her shall go back again to her heirs.

her
MARY X MAGDALENA.
mark

JOHN HITE.
JACOB HITE.
ISAAC HITE.
JOSEPH HITE.
his
JACOB IN NISSWANGER.
mark

In the Contract of Just Hite and Mary Magdalena his wife, married persons made the 10 of November, 1741, the following goods were brought in to-wit:

1. In ready money twenty-two pounds, Seventeen Shillings and four pence.

2ly. Two mares one colt of the value of fourteen pounds.

3ly. Two drawing steers value three pounds, ten shillings.

4ly. To Course Bed Cloathes in all three pound, Sixteen Shillings and six pence. And the said money is adjudged to be in Virginia Currency the 16th of November, 1741, also one horse mare Six pound.

Witnesses: JUST HITE.

PETER STEPHENS
LEWIS STEPHENS
his
JACOB IN NISWANGER
mark

Translated and Copied from the German original by JAMES PORTEUS.

At a Court held for Frederick County on Tuesday the Third day of September, 1745.

Jost Hite in Open Court acknowledges these his Articles of Agreement made between him and Maria Magdalena his wife before marriage, which on his motion is admitted to record together with an account of goods brought by the said Maria Magdalena Endorsed on the back of said Articles.

TEST: THOS. WOOD, *Cl Cur.*"

The original is in German, signed in German; was recorded first in Orange County, then in Frederick, 1744. We find no evidence of any children born by this marriage.

The reader will excuse this extended notice of the famous Joist Hite, since he was the chief figure in the early settlement of the Lower Valley; and also excuse the brief notices in the following pages of many other settlers who became far more famous in their lives, as they struggled to plant the colony under so many adverse circumstances

Having thus briefly disposed of the Hite family, we will turn attention to some of the other families who came with Hite. We mention merely the names of those who settled upon tracts of land that Hite set off for them from the original grant to him for himself, and the twenty families he was to locate. We find William Hogue on the Opecquon, John White on Hogue Creek, Nathaniel Thomas at the head of the Opecquon, Benjamin Borden near Shepherdstown, "binding with its western line on the Bullskin Run," David Vaunce on the Opecquon, Stephen Hansbella, Christian Nisewanger, etc., (fuller mention later on.)

Hite located the Irish immigrants on the Opecquon. This was known as the Irish immigrant party that arrived between 1737 and 1740. This is somewhat misleading; for the ships' lists show the English, Irish, French, Scotch and Welsh made up the list; and those who sought homes in the Shenandoah under the guidance of Hite's son, were John Bruce, Patrick Berry, Denis Dough, Patrick Daugherty, Thomas Doster, John Littler, John Fitzsimmons, ... O'Guillon, and three Riley families representing the Scotch, English and Irish, the Morgans from Wales; Louis Dumas and his two sons, Charles and Thomas, the French;—many more of this class, eighty in all: not a German among them.

CHAPTER II

The Minor Grants

In the preceding pages, mention has been made of *Minor Grants.* The author finds in unravelling many incidents of the early settlement of Frederick County, that so much inconsistency is revealed in writings claiming to be historical facts that it becomes necessary to give the history of these minor grants, and thus prove who were the first settlers. It must be remembered that the reigning English Monarch always claimed the right to create colonies in the New World; and form colonial governments, and did so exercise this right; and Virginia being the colony with which we are now treating, these notes apply to this colony. Large grants emanating from the Crown direct, were chiefly to that part of the colony known as *Tidewater.* One large grant, known as the Colepepper Grant, embraced what is generally called the Northern Neck. As already stated, the Crown always reserved the right to make special grants to certain companies or individuals who could give some assurance of becoming actual settlers; and when this was shown, such persons were even allowed to enter the domain of the large grants. There had to be some tribunal in the colony to regulate this: so at an early day, the Governor was associated with certain gentlemen to be known as his *council*; and persons desiring to locate in the new country, must secure from the Governor and Council an order to have surveyed for settlement, a certain number of acres of land, stating the locality; and this order required that families should be located within a specified time; and when so proven to the Governor and Council, a grant or deed should be made to the applicant or his assigns, or such persons as he would name. These individual grants or deeds were known as the *Minor Grants.*

We find that Isaac and John Van Meter assigned their order, dated 17th of June, 1730, to Joist Hite in 1731, who was required to seat his requisite number of families; and when this was done, Hite filed his surveys with the Secretary of the Council, and a list of persons to whom he desired patents, deeds or grants to issue; and thus we have a number of such grants, that will receive fuller mention later on: Hite had grants made to himself for many thousand acres; and from these tracts he made many deeds himself to certain families. A list of such will be given later on. In executing the order of Governor and Council, Hite was not required to locate his surveys and families in one tract of forty thousand or one hundred thousand acres, but allowed to make selections from Cohongoruta on the North, southward through the Shenandoah Valley. There were large intervening tracts, left as ungranted land, afterwards granted by Lord Fairfax to other immigrants, after 1744. We now approach an interesting period in the history of the early settlers, for when Hite entered upon the subdivision of his grant of one hundred thousand acres of land, to be entered by actual settlers on tracts not heretofore granted in the special grants already mentioned, for be it remembered, Hite held no such grants as has often been stated by persons not fully informed, "that he had a grant of one hundred and fifty thousand acres in one body, and this had as its southern boundary the Shenandoah river." This is mere fallacy; yet many believe it. He found obstacles that were almost as troublesome to the pioneer as the Indian. He found "blazed trees," planted monuments, and other marks, in the forests and along rivers and creeks, which indicated to him at once, that some surveyor had been on the ground before his entry. This was appalling to Hite and his people, but he was equal to the occasion; and as stated in the early part of this subject of Hite and his grants, we find him diligently at work repairing his fortune. He soon found from other immigrants coming in, who had run these strange lines; for these new people carried with them deeds from Isaac Van Meter, for tracts of land to be measured out of his grant. Hite at once saw from recitals in these deeds, that some one had the prior right; and when he saw that Isaac Van Meter was the man to deal with, he knew what course to pursue. He had known Van Meter back in old Salem, New Jersey, where Isaac was a prominent resident. How, when, or where Hite had his first interview with Van Meter as to what was apparent to him: (A dispute over their titles), is not known. Sufficient for our purpose, however, we can assert they had an interview in some way; and as evidence of this, we find a compromise settlement between them in 1731, by which Hite became the purchaser of the celebrated grants, which he takes in regular conveyances from the Van Meters, and also assignment for grants to issue from the Governor and Council, and enters them for record at Williamsburg and Orange Courthouse, seven years before the court of record was organized in Frederick County. Hite, in order to carry out his original plans, began the work in 1736 of making deeds to certain of the settlers who either came with him in 1732 or soon followed in his wake. Such deeds are to be found recorded in the Clerk's Office of old Orange, thus giving the names of many of these first settlers which will appear in these pages, so as to show clearly who many of the people were who first settled West of the Blue Ridge and North and West of the Sherando River. We have stated, under the head of Hite and his family, that he found it necessary to purchase the Van Meter Grants. In the next Chapter, we will show what these grants were, and more fully prove that Hite was not the first white man to plant his foot on the soil.

CHAPTER III

The Van Meter Grants, their History and the Proof that Van Meter preceded Hite — as the First White Man to Cross the Potow-mack

The records of the two grants of forty thousand acres each, to John and Isaac Van Meter, as will be seen in this Chapter in the original grants to both are dated 17th June, 1730, and are of record on page 363 of the Mss. Journal of the Governor and Council of Virginia, 1721-1734. Isaac Van Meter at this time lived in Old Salem, New Jersey, (as heretofore stated), while his brother, John Van Meter, was living on a tract of two hundred acres granted him by Lord Baltimore, November 3rd, 1726, which he located at or near what is now Monocacy Junction, near Frederick, Maryland. Lord Fairfax's grant from the crown ante-dated these and all other grants; but at that date it was supposed that the great Colepepper Grant, which had been curtailed to the Northern Neck, then Fairfax's grant, did not extend beyond the Blue Mountains, and that the *Potow-mack* River was wholly East of these mountains; and it was not until about 1736-7, that Lord Fairfax, the father of our Lord Thomas through his agents, discovered by survey that his grant covered an empire, more than he supposed. This will be better understood by a study of his map made at that time, a photo copy of which the writer has and hopes to have appear later on. From a careful study of this question, the writer has no doubt but that the Van Meters well knew what Lord Fairfax and Governor and Council of Virginia did not know at that time, as to what was the extent of the Fairfax Grant; hence Van Meter resorted to what would be called to-day "sharp practice," by transferring his entire grant into the possession of an innocent third purchaser, Joist Hite, and then to become holders of such portion as they desired for themselves by transfer and purchase from Hite. This became later, as Van Meter no doubt anticipated, a subject of litigation,—and it was not finally settled until after principals and their children had been dead many years. The courts sustained Van Meter, and confirmed title to all assigns for interest in the Van Meter grants purchased from "Jost Heitd," the legal battles were fought to a finish in 1800, which the author hopes to treat fully if space will admit. There are many details in this transaction that could be more fully set forth in this work, which would lend a tinge of romance to this interesting period, but we must avoid romancing, and try to state facts in a brief and plain way. But, inasmuch as Van Meter is to be proven an actual first settler, though it has often been asserted that Van Meter never lived on his grants, it might be well to sketch his movements at this point, trusting to give them more prominence in another Chapter. John Van Meter was an interesting character he and his family,—his own ancestry and his descendants, will make a most interesting chapter, giving the details of his life, leading as they do from Marbletown, Ulster County, New York, where he was born in 1683, following his removal down through New Jersey into Maryland in 1726, and his final settlement in the Valley of Virginia soon after 1730, where he died in 1745. "Jost Heyt" is also traceable in like manner, almost year by year, with such minute detail as to show conclusively that he followed John Van Meter, who led him into this land of promise.

(Here follows the copy from the original Van Meter Grants). MSS Journal of the Governor and, Council of Virginia, session 1721-1734, page 363.)

"On reading at this board the petition of John Van Meter setting forth that he is desirous to take up a tract of land in this colony—on the west side of the great Mountains for the settlement of himself and eleven children and also divers of his relations and friends living in the government of New York are also desirous to move with their families and effects to settle in the same place if a sufficient of land may be assigned them for that purpose and praying that ten thousand acres of land lying in the fork of the Shenado River including the places called by the names of Cedar Litch and Stony Lick and running up between the branches of said river to complete the quantity and twenty thousand acres not already taken up by Robert

Carter and Mann Page, Esqus. or any other lying in the fork between the river Shenado: and the river Cohonguroota and extending thereto to Operkon and up the South branch thereof—may be assigned for the Habitation of himself his family and friends.

The Governor with the advice of the Council is pleased to give leave to the said John Van Meter to take up the said first mentioned tract of ten thousand acres for the settlement of himself and family; That as soon as the petitioner shall bring on the last mentioned tracts twenty families to inhabit: or that this board is satisfied so many are to remove thither: Leave be and it is hereby granted him for surveying the last mentioned tract of twenty thousand acres within the limits above described in so many several Dividends as the petitioner and his partners shall think fit; and it is further ordered that no person is permitted to enter for or take up any part of the aforesaid Land in the meantime: Provided the said Van Meter and his family and the said twenty other families of his Relations and friends do settle thereon within the space of two years according to his proposal."

("MSS: Journal of the Governor and Council of Virginia, 1721-1734, page 364.)

"Isaac Van Meter of the Province of West Jersey having by petition to this Board set forth that he and divers other German families are desirous to settle themselves on the West side of the Great Mountains in this colony; he the *petitioner has been to view* the lands in those parts and has discovered a place where further such settlement may conveniently be made and not yet taken up or possessed by any one of the *English Inhabitants* and praying that ten thousand acres of land lying between the lands surveyed for Robt. Carter, Esq., and the fork of the Shenado river and the river Operkon in as many several tracts or Dividends as shall be necessary for the accommodation and settlement of ten families (including his own) who proposes to bring to the said Land:

The Governor with the advice of the Council is pleased to order as it is hereby ordered that the said Isaac Van Meter for himself and his partners have leave to take up the said quantity of ten thousand acres of Land within the limits above described and that if he bring the above number of families to dwell there within two years; Patent be granted him and them for the same in such several tracts or Dividends as they shall think fit and in the meantime the same be referred free from entry of any other person: Dated at Williamsburg, 17th June, 1730."

These Van Meter grants in themselves prove that they preceded Hite and his colony. Since the best we can do for Hite is, that he started from his last stopping place in Pennsylvania in 1731, and as the grant to Isaac Van Meter recites conclusive proof, the Council sitting at Williamsburg from 1721 to 1734 expressly sets forth in their order dated 17th June, 1730, that Isaac the Petitioner *had been to view the lands in those parts*—"those parts"— are described in the survey made within the two years—as lying along both sides of the Shenandoah—one to John and one to Isaac. And these surveys embrace forty thousand acres each, and were confirmed to these *brothers,* May 12th, 1732—(See old files in State Library, Richmond, Virginia). John must have spied out the land about the time of its first discovery by the Spottswood expedition,—for in tracing John from Ulster County, New York to his stop on the Monocacy River in Maryland, the writer finds him in 1727, over in Old Spottsylvania, lending his advice to the German settlers at Germania,—"skilled artisans" who had come in answer to the scheme adopted by the Governor. And it is barely possible that John, in his desire to roam and find new places, was tempted to try the summit of the Blue Mountain lying to the West, and see what was beyond. Tradition tells us that he blazed his way through the dense forests, so as to point his way of return to the Germana settlement; and, as he and Isaac represented to the Council afterwards, that they viewed the lands. They surveyed their lands chiefly from the forks of the Shenandoah (near Front Royal) westward; thus showing that they entered the valley through the gaps of the Blue Ridge at that point, hugging the line forming the northern boundary of the Robt. Carter and Mann Page grant. This settles the question as to whether he or Hite was the first white man to visit the country South of the Cohongoroota; so while giving Van Meter credit for this honor, it leaves the impression, then, that Hite was the first man to cross the Potomac. We would be glad to give him this honor without further question, but, as we are trying to state facts in relation to these old pioneers, all bent upon finding the promised land, the writer must confess that in all his investigations and careful study, he finds some circumstantial evidence that almost settles the questions. We have seen that Hite purchased large portions of the Van Meter grants, and the records show that Hite in 1734 conveyed land to purchasers for tracts in the vicinity of Shepherdstown, and recites that the lands conveyed by him were parcels embraced in the Isaac Van Meter Patent; thus showing that Van Meter's grant also embraced land near the Potomac,—and the question naturally arises, how did Van Meter first reach that point—Did he cross the Potomac West of the Blue Ridge in the vicinity of Shepherdstown, and there locate part of his patent? If so, he crossed the Potomac before Hite; thus leaving Hite with a doubt as to whether he is entitled to what we hope to give him,— the credit of being the man who first stood on the South banks of the Potomac West of the Blue Ridge. And may we not pass this and record it as a fact; for we have this language in the survey of Isaac Van Meter's grant: "Survey extended from the north bank line of the Sherando river northward to the Operkon river then following its flow embracing the land and prairies, forests and streams and their sources lying betwixt thereof—said Operkon and ye said Sherando: Both lines showing monuments for courses and measures." This certainly is the patent referred to in Hite's first deed to settlers; and we may conclude that when the Van Meters entered the Valley at the forks of the Shenandoah, that Isaac proceeded northward to lay off his patent; and ultimately found himself on the Potomac near the site of Shepherdstown, having "followed the flow of the Operkon river." As already stated, it has been the desire of the writer to settle this moot question; but to do so and give sufficient proof, required the most diligent search and investigation, with the assistance of old Virginia Clerks, Librarians of several states, Secretaries of Historical Societies, and welcome access to the files of the colonial days. And these aids, helping to verify the hundreds of incidents recorded in various forms in the old County Clerk's office, where the writer has spent more than a quarter of a century, is his reason for submitting the foregoing to the casual reader, or to the student of history of this part of the Valley known as Old Frederick County, as satisfactory proof as to who should have the credit for blazing the first tree in the Virginia forests or crossing the Potomac. While many may feel disappointed that the case has been so proven against the claim so long made for Hite, we hope they will find in these pages full proof that he was ever at the front, and did more than any one in planting colonies and bringing civilization out of the newly discovered country; and to prove this, we will now proceed to state who composed his colonies, starting with those whom he first located on land through the deeds he executed.

We find in the old records of Orange County, that Hite started the work of parceling out to the families who claimed to belong to his colony, tracts of land all located West of the Blue Ridge, making forty-six conveyances, and all admitted to record in March, 1736. Some refer to his own grants, dated June 12th and Oct. 3rd, 1734; some to his grants through his Van Meter purchase, dated 17th June, 1730; in the proper place, will appear names and location of families who came with Hite and also those who followed and entered the Country about that time, and awaited grants to come through him, no grant being made to any one prior to 1734, at which time Hite and the Van Meter Grants having matured, the seating of the one hundred families and even more, is fully proven by the records.

We must take it for granted that many of these conveyances were made to the sixteen families so often spoken of as coming with Hite; as it was understood by the terms of Hite's grant that he would be required to locate twenty families and convey to them the tracts of land they could select and have surveyed, and as this was done, the same must be certified to the general Council at Williamsburg.

The first deed from Hite referred to, was to one of his German friends, Stephen Hansonbella (afterwards written in the Frederick County Records, Hotsinpeller) and four hundred and fifty acres near head of Opecquon Creek, next to Christian Nisswanger, four hundred and thirty five acres to Thomas Wilson for one hundred and sixty-seven acres on Operkon Run to John Van Meter for four hundred and seventy-five acres, being the lowermost part of that tract whereon John Lilburn resided on Operkon Creek, part of the Van Meter Grant; to Thomas Chester one hundred acres on North side of North River; to Louis Stuffey for three hundred and thirty-nine acres on West side of Sherando River near head of Crooked Run to Robt. Desarfe for three hundred acres near place called Long Meadows adjoining Isaac Hite, son of Joist Hite, to Christian Blank, for sixty acres on North side of North branch of Sherando River, "being within the bounds of ten thousand acres granted to John Van *Metre* on June 6th, 1730, and sold to Hite, Oct., 1734;" from Hite to Hendery Hunt for one hundred and twenty acres on West side of Sherando River "being part of the forty thousand acre grant purchased by Hite from John Van Meter, (Note: part of the sixteen families and Hite's six families and the full number of sixteen is obtained.) This brief mention of the conveyances by Hite at that period, is given here for two reasons: it settles one point, that Hite actually purchased the Van Meter grant which ante-dated his by four years, and that he also found it necessary to use the same to give title to his fellow-colonists. As has been stated elsewhere, the specific terms of the original Hite grant required him to make a settlement in the new country of not less than twenty families; and having this accomplished, he must allow them to make selection for their habitations such parcels of land *not theretofore granted to actual settlers,* and then convey to them, out of his grant, good title for their home. When some of these selections were made and reported to the Council at Williamsburg for approval, Hite was informed that his grant could not embrace many of these tracts,—as they were either within the Van Meter grants already surveyed, or they were parts of tracts leased by agents of the Fairfax estate. These leases were to run twenty years in most cases; and just at that point began the question of who was owner. Some of the colonists preferred to take their chances with the Fairfax claim; and held on to their selection, and became what was known after as *squatters;* and they and their descendants were at law with Lord Fairfax after his arrival in 1749. Many of these suits were pending in our courts after Lord Fairfax's death, many of them losing their homes.

The names of the grantees from Hite, as has been stated, were familiar in that day, and are given to show who composed the twenty families. No record was ever made by Hite, who his colonists were, except by such conveyances mentioned; and we have sufficient of these to prove that he had more families on the ground as settlers in 1736,—and they West of the Blue Ridge than his grant required,—most of them taking their deeds through the Van Meter Grant, the conveyances to Christian Blank and Hendery Hunt were dated and admitted to record in February, 1739. These conveyances disclose to us some interesting facts. Several writers on the subject of the coming of Joist Hite and, as they stated it, "with his sixteen families, fixed his settlement on the Opequon in the vicinity of Bartonsville and Kernstown; and this seemed reasonable enough. As we have already shown, Hite and many of the people coming to the Valley about that period, settled on land along the Opequon Creek principally towards its source. This, then, would embrace the Cartmell and Glass family with their large grants of land lying on either side of the stream, beginning at the head and following its course eastward to the Bartonsville neighborhood, where Hite had chosen his home. But we cannot claim that Hite settled the two last named families in 1735,—the emigrant, Samuel Glass, and his family coming direct from the North of Ireland,—and Nathaniel Cartmell and his large family coming from Westmoreland County, England, who at once entered upon their lands and were entirely independent of the Hite emigration. But it must be admitted that they followed in the wake of Hite. Glass secured a *minor grant* through Hite for nine hundred acres of land at the head springs of Opecquon Creek; Cartmell relied upon his entry, and was never disturbed but once by suit of ejectment by Fairfax, and then won the case. The conveyances referred to show where the families were located, extending from the junction of the North and South branches of the Shenandoah, near the present site of Front Royal,—westward towards the Little North Mountain and along the Opecquon towards its mouth near Shepherdstown. This indicates that the twenty families were not settled in close proximity for mutual protection from attacks from Indians, but they were locating in good sections on good lands, and willing to take their chances with the denizens of the virgin forests, whether wild animal or Redskin. It is fair to claim, however, that the first conveyances made by Hite in March, 1736, and recorded in the old Orange court, were made to his colonists, who comprised his twenty families; and for this reason the names of the grantees have been given. We will give the names of the grantees at this point who subsequently received deeds for their tracts, as their surveys had been reported to the Governor and Council; they having made their selections and reported that they "were seated." All of the following deeds were recorded in the Orange Court prior to the holding of the first term of court in Frederick County, and are from Joist Hite:

Oct. 26th, 1737, to John Seaman for one thousand acres adjoining Benj. Borden—James Wood April 25th, 1738, for one hundred acres on West side of "Opequon run."

William Williams, April 27th, 1738, for two hundred and twenty-five acres on "Opequon run."

Louis Stevens, April 28th, 1738, for three hundred and thirty-nine acres—Crooked run.

Peter Writtenhouse, May 21st, 1740, for four hundred and fifty acres adjoining Long Meadow.

Jacob Christman, May 14, 1740, for seven hundred and fifty acres.

John Hite, May 21, 1740, for five hundred and sixty-eight acres, part of Hite's grant and also one hundred acres adjoining, purchased by Joist from Richard Pendall on "Opequon."

William Reed, May 14, 1740, for two hundred

and ten acres on southwest side of "Opequon run," part of Hite's grant—1734.

John McCormick, May 26, 1740, for three hundred and ninety-five acres adjoining the Borden, Griffith and Hampton, etc. tract of eleven hundred and twenty-two acres. This grant was for land north of the point where White Hall village stands.

Samuel Walker, May 21st, 1740, for one hundred acres on "west side of Sherrando river."

Chas. McDowel, July 20, 1740, for six hundred acres.

James Burns, May 24, 1741, for one hundred and twenty-eight acres on "west side of Sherando."

Robert Allen, May 21, 1742, for six hundred and eighty-five acres on "south side of Opequon run." This tract was west from the Bartonsville section.

John Harrow, May 19, 1742, for two hundred and ninety acres on "north side of Opequon run."

Abram Wiseman, June 23, 1734, for one hundred and seventy-two acres on "west side of Opequon run"—part of the five thousand and eighteen acres Hite Grant. It will be seen that some of the descriptions fix the North, South and West side of Opecquon. It must be remembered the Opecquon flows nearly due East from its source for about four miles, and along this course lie the tracts described as on the North and South side; then the general course is North, and this accounts for certain tracts mentioned that lie on the East, North and West sides of the Opecquon.

"James Vance, June 25, 1742, for two hundred and fifty acres on both sides of small meadow near Opequon Presbyterian meeting house."

Peter Make, June 23, 1742, for one hundred and sixty-eight acres on "Opequon run."

David Vance, May 20, 1742, for one hundred acres on both sides of the "Opequon run."

James Hoge, May 26, 1742, for seven hundred and sixty acres. This was near the present site of Kernstown, lying West—and was part of Joist Hite's grant for thirty-three hundred and ninety-five acres, known as the Springdale Settlement, where Col. John Hite lived.

Jacob Hite, October 20, 1742, for twenty-six hundred and sixty-eight acres on "south side of Opequon."

John Pentz, Oct. 20, 1742, for one hundred and eighty-nine acres on "north side of Sherando river."

Thomas Brown, Oct. 20, 1742, for eight hundred and eighty-two acres on west side of Sherando river.

Samuel Glass, Nov. 26, 1742, for nine hundred acres on the head of Opequon on west side of said creek, meaning south at that point.

David Logan, Nov. 26, 1742, for eight hundred and sixty acres on "west side of Bufflow Meadow"—known for years as Buffalo Marsh.

Paul Froman, Nov. 22, 1742, for one hundred and twenty acres on North fork of Sherando river, adjoining Thomas Chester.

Emanuel Grubb, Aug. 26, 1742, for two hundred and fifty acres on north side of Shenandoah river.

John Grubb, Aug. 26, 1743, recorded same day, for two hundred and sixty-five acres on "north side of S. river."

Thomas Ashby, Feb. 1, 1742, for two hundred acres on north side of Shenandoah river.

Robert McKay, from Just Hite, William Duff and Robert Green, June 28, 1744, for five hundred acres on Linvell's Creek, being part of a grant to Robert McKay, Just Hite, William Duff, and Robt. Green for seven thousand and nine acres, dated March, 1736.

This makes it appear that part of this grant was located in the lower and western part of Rockingham County,—before the Augusta line was established. The larger part of this grant embraced the vicinity of Front Royal. The grant made as late as 1739, was peculiar in its provisions, in that this company had a grant for land wherever they could locate a survey on land not theretofore located. Several other small tracts were afterwards surveyed and conveyed by the company to purchasers; but it does not appear that the company ever fully complied with the terms, which were, that as they found unsettled lands and a settler to take tracts, to report the survey to the Council, and then the Company to make deeds; until they thus used up the seven thousand and nine acres, for which the order was made. A number of *minor grants* were issued to the Shepherd, Morgan, Swearingen, Stephen, Boyd, Dark, Harper, Porterfield, and other families, as early settlers, on the South side of Cohongoroota River, now embraced in the Counties of Berkley and Jefferson, while Joliffe, Lupton, and others, in the north end of Frederick; Helm, Calmes and others, along the Shenandoah; Wood, Rutherford and others near Winchester, had their experience with the "Minor Grants," and as the first settlers will receive fuller notice in this volume.

CHAPTER IV

Old Frederick County

To write the history of Frederick County in Virginia, which at one time embraced so much of the territory lying East of the Blue Ridge, the writer finds its early history so closely interwoven with Tidewater Virginia, that he can scarcely make it complete, without introducing much that may appear at many stages as an attempt to give the history of Lower Virginia.

The reader must at the outset rest assured, that incidents are only mentioned when they connect the two sections, so that the formation of the new County of Frederick could become a fact. Tidewater Virginia referred to, must not be considered as only the territory embraced in the original creation of the first colony, which included all of North America between Nova Scotia on the North to Florida on the South, and for many years after the first English landing, was known as Virginia.

Indeed, it may be said this title dates from the discovery of the Carolina coasts by Sir Walter Raleigh; for we have English history recording the pleasure afforded Queen Elizabeth when Raleigh gave his report of that celebrated seagoing expedition, when he had named that great territory Virginia, in honor of the Virgin Queen. This was in 1585. The failure of Sir Walter to colonize the Carolina shores, and the mysterious disaster to what was known as the "Roanoke Colony"—a disappearance so complete, that no ray of intelligence has ever thrown light on their fate—chilled the spirit of adventure. Other efforts of the Virgin Queen to colonize the shores of America, were dismal failures; and it remained for James I to successfully plant the first English colonies. The Virginia Company of London, obtained a charter in 1606, for one hundred miles square of the territory lying between Hudson River on the North, and Cape Fear River, North Carolina. The Virginia Company of Plymouth, obtained a charter for one hundred miles of territory between the Potomac River on the South and Nova Scotia on the North. Of course, the geographical lines were destined to overlap, and produce contentions between the chartered companies. On this, we have no comment to make here. The first named companies developed Tidewater Virginia, and discovered the country West of the Blue Ridge, some of which became Frederick County, the subject of the present study. The author deems it proper to outline the first steps of this Company. The first settlement made at Jamestown, May 13, 1607, was attended with difficulties, privation and destitution, until about 1620. The London Company seemed determined to secure a foot-hold; and obtained a second charter in 1609, extending their holdings for two hundred miles North and South from Point Comfort—"up into the land throughout from sea to sea; west and northwest; and also all the islands within one hundred miles along the coasts of both seas." The general reader knows this Company never extended its rights from sea to sea. The immigration that subsequently sought homes in the new world, pushed slowly westward and southward, until the tide not only reached the great mountains, but swept over them shortly after 1732. That tide, which extended into the northwest territory, untimately gave to Virginia what was called *The Northwest*, which Virginia soldiers penetrated, and founded the Ohio and Illinois country under the leadership of Col. George Rogers Clark, who planted the Virginia standard on the border posts; and reported to Patrick Henry, Governor of the Colony, the result of his expedition.

It will be shown in other chapters what was acquired, and what was ceded to the Government in 1784, after reserving what would be necessary to satisfy the officers and men, for their services. This is more fully treated in chapters on the Valley Men during the Colonial wars; where it will appear who many of the men were, and amounts of land granted by the Colony.

In Vol. I, p. 224, Hening's Statutes, we have the first legislation in reference to a subdivision of the Virginia Colony into counties, enacted in 1634. "The country was divided into eight Shires, which were to be governed as the shires in England, and Lieutenants to be appointed the same as in England; sheriffs to be elected as in England, to have the same powers as sergeants and bailiffs needs require." The list of shires, or counties, formed in 1634, viz.:

James City County, Warwick, Elizabeth City County, North Hampton, Isle of Wight, Henrico, York and Mecklenburg, is inserted here to lay the foundations for subdivisions that made it possible to create counties one hundred years later West of the Blue Ridge. It may be of interest, as matter of reference, to trace the dismemberment of the old Colony, starting with York County, from which New Kent was erected in 1754:

Old Rappahannock from Lancaster.. 1656
Essex from Old Rappahannock 1692
King and Queen from New Kent.. 1691
King William from King and Queen 1710
Spottsylvania from Essex, King Wm., and King and Queen 1720
Orange from Spottsylvania 1734
Frederick and Augusta from Orange.. 1738

Referring again to Hening's Statutes, Vol. IV, p. 450, we quote from Act of General Assembly, 1734, the following, to define the boundaries of Orange so far as it relates to the territory so soon to be known as Frederick and Augusta: "Bounded northerly by grant of Lord Fairfax; and westerly by utmost limits of Virginia, to be called and known by the name of Orange." And as Frederick in her first formation, embraced the country comprising all of the Shenandoah Valley from the Augusta line, which crossed the Valley near the site of Harrisonburg, we must treat all of the Valley thence northward to the Potomac, and then westward to the French boundary, to give a history of Old Frederick; this would include the history of a large part of West Virginia. This volume will not claim to be a complete history of Old Frederick to its western boundary. Only a few incidents will appear which connected that section with the Lower Valley. The writer is well aware that some reader will regard the statement as infringing upon the rights of the West Augusta District. This, however, will be fully explained. Much conflict of authority appeared between Augusta and Frederick, all of which was amicably determined by legislation when the dividing lines were defined.

When we come to chronicle many incidents in the development of the Lower Valley, the writer may often appear as writing the history of the Lower Shenandoah Valley, so attractively written by J. E. Norris, 1890. The writer knew Mr. Norris well; and was associated with him for more than six months, giving him the benefit of his long experience in the old clerk's office, as he prepared his work, regarded by many as valuable for any library. To aid Mr. Norris in his effort to give us a history of the Lower Valley, the writer freely gave him the use of a large collection of notes he had constantly made, as they would be unfolded to him in his daily routine of searching titles to estates, or for incidents of interest to correspondents; and thus in this gradual way, he possessed the chief material used in his History of the Lower Valley. The writer since that day found much unwritten history, which will be embraced in these pages. Some incidents may differ from those given by Mr. Norris; but we must use many of the original notes in this work; and if the reader should feel that we fail to credit Mr. Norris as our authority, he should remember that Mr. N. seldom referred to his authority in using the notes of his author. The writer has in his hands a letter from Mr. Norris, written from Texas, where he died shortly after, stating that a large collection of the notes furnished by the writer, was in his trunk at Hagerstown, Md., and that his son would return them to the author. With this explanation, we will now proceed to condense incidents, and so weave them into a book of reference. The public feels the need of a volume that will quickly answer the many questions daily asked concerning the formation and development of the county, so it may be a ready hand-book for all.

By an Act of the House of Burgesses, Nov., 1738, Old Orange County, which embraced so much more territory than we can comprehend, was divided into three counties—viz.: Orange, Frederick and Augusta, Frederick being named for Frederick, then Prince of Wales; Augusta for Princess Augusta, the wife of the Prince, who was the oldest son of George II, but died before his father.

"Owing to some delay of the population in these parts, not being able to report a sufficient number of competent men able to officer the new County," the Courts for all this section were held at Orange C. H., until Nov., 1743, when the first Court was held for Frederick County; and as this was an important feature in the organization of Frederick County, embracing (as will be more fully shown elsewhere) the territory afterwards subdivided into the counties of Rockingham, Shenandoah, Jefferson, Berkley, Morgan, Hampshire, part of Page, part of Hardy, and finally Clarke and Warren Counties. And when we remember that only a few settlements were to be found at that time, and they considerable distances apart, we need not be surprised that the "population" was slow in reporting a sufficient number of men from these settlements for Justices and other officers, and preferred to attend court at Orange C. H. for five years after their formation. We give the authority for holding this first court, as entered at that time in the old records of the county; and as it was beyond any doubt the first record made in the courts of Frederick County, it is well worthy a place in this work, in all the style of that period and apparent dignity of the occasion; and we can readily imagine the Gentlemen Justices who appeared at that time in answer to the distinguished authority, exhibited much dignified solemnity in assuming the judicial control of the growing population. The record is in the hand writing of one who became familiar in the history of the State, and is well preserved in a well bound volume, with the simple words on the cover: "Order Book No. 1, 1743." This order book, comprising 480 pages, is altogether in the handwriting of James Wood, the Clerk. He dignifies his first entry by using the large size letters, sometimes called "German Text."

FREDERICK COUNTY *Sct*

"Be it Remembered, That on the eleventh day of November, Anno Domini, MD,CCXLIII-1743.

A commission of the Peace dated the twenty-second day of October, MD,CCXLIII, under the hand of the Honorable William Gooch, Esq., His Majesties Lieutenant Governor and Commander in Chief of the Colony and Dominion of Virginia, and the seal of this Colony; Directed to Morgan Morgan, Benjamin Borden, Thomas Chester, David Vaunce, Andrew Campbell, Marquis Calmes, George Hoge, John White, and Thomas Little; Gents, and a Dedimus for administering the oaths to said Justices being read, the said Morgan Morgan and David Vaunce, pursuant to the said Dedimus, administered the oaths appointed by Act of Parliament to be taken instead of the oaths of allegiance and Supremacy, and the oath of abjuration unto the said Marquis Calmees, Thomas Rutherford, William McMahon, Meredith Helms, George Hoge and John White, who severally subscribed the Test and then said Morgan Morgan and David Vaunce administered the oaths of a Justice of the Peace and of a Justice of ye County Court in Chancery unto the said Marquis Calmees, Thomas Rutherford, William McMahon, Meridith Helms, George Hoge and John White, and afterwards the said Marquis Calmees, Thomas Rutherford, William McMahon, Meridith Helms, George Hoge and John White pursuant to the said Dedimus, administered all and every the said oaths unto the said Morgan Morgan and David Vaunce, who severally subscribed the Test and were sworn in the Commission accordingly."

Court Proclaimed

At a Court held for Frederick County on Friday the Eleventh day of Nov., 1743.

Present:

Morgan Morgan,
David Vaunce,
Marquis Calmees,
Thomas Rutherford,
William McMahon,
Meridith Helms,
George Hoge,
John White.

Gent Justices.

A Commission to James Wood Gent under the hand and seal of the Hon. Thomas Nelson, Esq., Secretary of Virginia, bearing date twenty-second day of October, MD,CCXLIII, to be Clerk of County Court of this county being produced and read in Court the said James Wood having taken the oaths appointed by Act of Parliament to be taken instead of the oaths of allegiance and supremacy, and the oaths of abjuration made, and subscribed the test, was sworn Clerk of this court accordingly;"

And the Court being thus organized by "all of the Justices then present taking their seats," proceeded to qualify court officers as provided for in the Commission from the Governor; James Wood was sworn Clerk of this Court, Thomas Rutherford—High Sheriff, and George Home, County Surveyor. As it may be of interest to many, the names of the first Lawyers to appear in the court to practice their profession will be given at this point, though they will appear in their proper order in the list of attorneys of the county Court throughout its history to the present date: James Porteous, John Steerman, George Johnston, and John Newport—strange names to the people of this day. These gentlemen appeared and "being duly qualified to practice the art of the law," desiring that privilege be entered in the minutes of the court that they be granted the use of the courthouse to attend to legal wants of such persons who may desire professional service." Some will enquire where and what was the Courthouse mentioned in this order! This will be treated under the head of the Courthouse and Market Place.

The business at the first term was confined chiefly to making orders to put the government in motion. The clerk was ordered to procure books for the purpose of keeping a minute of the proceedings—and to enter orders of court and this rule held for fifty years of keeping two separate books for the court, one called "Minutes," and the other "Court Order Book." Many enquiries have been made of the writer as Clerk, to explain this; and much of the unpublished history of the early days is found, in the Minute book —We will have occasion to quote frequently, incidents from their musty leaves. Few persons have ever seen them; for one hundred years they were packed away, out of sight and out of use. The Clerk was directed to "employ a suitable person to fetch the law books from the house of Mr. Parks for the use of the Justices;" and this order was entered "that no constables or overseers of the poor be appointed at this term, but those who have been serving as such officers of the Orange Court as it extended within the limits of Frederick County, be continued in their respective offices until another term of this court." We will use some space in producing copies of other orders, that doubtless will contain matter of interest to some readers who may chance to read these pages. The reason will appear satisfactory, when we consider that only about ten years had passed since the first settlements were made;—and the reader of the old "minute book" of that period will be astonished to see how many names appear—some to reveal the fact, for the first time, to many a far-away descendant, whose ancestor was prominent in the organization. Some names within a few decades entirely disappeared from the "population;" others became still more prominent in the affairs of their State as artizans, statesmen, soldiers, etc. Taking this order entered at this term, we find names then prominent—some afterwards more so—but to-day not one of the names are to be found in our records as citizens of the county, except the well-known Robinson family. One name, however, that of McNamee is now known in the county as a resident, but not on any record; and it seems strange that this name is represented in the person of a widow, connecting the incidents with this late day. The minute shows it to be the first will probated in Frederick County; "The Last Will and Testament of Bryant McNamee, dec'd., was presented into court by Elizabeth McNamee, Executrix therein named, who made oath thereto according to law, and being proved by the oaths of Israel Robinson and William Richie, two of the witnesses thereto, the same admitted to record; and the said Israel Robinson and William Richie also further made oath that they saw Edward Hughes, another witness to the said will, sign the same as an evidence—and on the motion of the said executrix her performing what is usual in such cases, certificate is granted her for obtaining a probate thereof in due form; and the said Elizabeth McNamee together with Evan Watkins and William Richie her securities, acknowledged their bond for the said Elizabeth McNamee's faithful and true administration of the estate of "said Bryant McNamee dec'd, which Bond is admitted to record."

The next order was a grant of Letters of Administration to Elizabeth Seaman, on the estate of Jonathan Seaman, "she being the widow and relict of the dec'd, with John Denton as security." The appraisers named for the McNamee estate are Morgan Bryan, Richard Beason, Edward Hughs, and Israel Robinson—all new names to this generation except the numerous families of the last named.

The next minute—"Abram Pennington in open court acknowledged his Deed of Lease for land to Christopher Beeller"—no such names in Frederick at this date.

At the December Term of this court, held on "*Fryday* the ixth day of December, MD,CCXLIII," four of the Justices were present: Morgan Morgan, Wm. McMachen, David Vaunce, and George Hoge. It will be observed the clerk learned how to spell the name of McMachen, the name will appear later on as McMickin. The writer had a personal friend many years ago—Mr Samuel McMicken of Moorefield, West Virginia, and he claimed his line of descent from the old Justice.

First minute at this Term is the filing of a petition by John Wilcox and others for a Road from John Funks mill to Chesters Ferry—and from thence to where the road takes out of Chesters Road to Manassas Run. Viewers were appointed. Many readers will have no difficulty in locating the route for this new and first road asked to be opened. Starting from what was soon known as Funkstown, now Strasburg, and the heading for the celebrated Gap in the Blue Ridge to the historical "Manassas." How many old comrades can be named who are survivors of many weary marches over this well known road! Few realized its importance when it was "marked" and laid off by "Thomas Chester, John Wilcox and Jacob Funk." Observe how careful the Court was in the selection of the viewers, starting with Thomas Chester at one end, coming to the forks of the Shenandoah River near Front Royal, and then to West end of Funks Mill. This road was used in various ways by the contending armies during the Civil War. Other mention of this road will appear in Chapter on Battlefields. The next minute should be of interest from the fact that the principal features relate to the first settlers near Shepherdstown. The next minute shows that the last will and testament of Benjamin Borden was presented by his widow, Zeruiah, and Benjamin Borden—his son—who it will be seen was then, in 1743, of lawful age. The father without doubt being the Benjamin Borden who followed the Hite Colony. This will should have been read and studied by historians of Augusta County. The celebrated Burden Grant located on the "upper" James River, is disposed of by the testator, and settles many errors in relation to this grant. At this Term, James Porteous was named as King's Attorney—"until his honor, the Governour's pleasure is known." At the January Term (13th) the following order is entered "Ordered that the Surveyor of this county run the dividing line between this and Augusta county, according to the Act of the Assembly, from the head springing of Hedgeman river to Pattersons Creek." Referring to the "Act of Assembly," we find very little to determine either its starting or terminal points. Many persons differ as to what is the head springs of a river. Sufficient for our purpose, however, that the spring mentioned was in the mountains East of the Luray Valley, and point of Pattersons Creek, West from Moorefield,—while supposed to be a straight line and "marks erected," many are confounded when they consider certain high mountains encountered, some summits of which had not been scaled until in recent years.

We find in the minutes of this Term, evidence of settlements on Capon River,—this one entry being sufficient: "On petition of Noah Hampton and others for a road from Noah Hampton's mill into a road on Great Ca-Capon near James Coddy's *Ftt,* ordered that Jonathan Coburn, Isaac Thomas, Peter Kuykendall and James Delheryea, or any two of them, view, mark and lay off the road petitioned for by the said Hampton &c., and make return of their proceedings to this court." When we consider in this day of rush and bustle, the brief period since Governor Spottswood proclaimed to the world what he had discovered beyond the Great Mountains,—we must be impressed with the quick attention people gave to his glowing description of the wonderful land, abounding with game, studded with virgin forests, and watered with mountain streams. They seemed to be settling everywhere. On the Great Ca-Capon—we find they had a mill, and needed roads for a growing settlements, and mention Coddy's Fort, standing to this day—a suitable fortress—Nature's own formation—which answered well their purposes as a place of safety in defending the settlements from frequent attacks of roving tribes of Indians. This historical Rock, known to-day as "Coddy's Castle," offered nothing as a place of safety from other hands during the Civil War. At same term, James Wood presented a bill for plank he bought of Isaac Perkins for use of the court.

We also have in evidence the first appearance of a "Pedlar," in Frederick County; and it might be well to give a copy of the order: "John Dooues on his motion is permitted to Trade as Pedlar in this Colony, he having paid the Governor's fee and together with Thomas Rutherford Gent, his security entered into Bond according to law and acknowledged the same, the said Bond is admitted to record." The *Pedlar* in that day was a much needed trader in the Colony—and most likely, as he sold his wares, he proved very often an interesting visitor; for he travelled from settlement to settlement; and no doubt his news of the distant neighbors, as he imparted it, was of much interest to his willing listeners. At the same court, License was granted for the first Ordinary—or House of Entertainment, in the county. "On the petition of William Hoge, Jun. for leave to keep Ordinary at his House in the County, License is granted him for one year, he having paid the Governor's fees, together with James Wood Gent, his security, entered Bond according to law." Where this first "Ordinary" afterwards called "Tavern" was located, we only have to find he was located and is shown in his deed, as being about where Kernstown now stands, and very near the old Opeckon Church.

Second day of same term, January, 1744, Patrick Riley, was granted a similar license, also Tomas Hart, Lewis Neil, Andrew Campbell, and Morgan Morgan were granted licenses to keep Ordinaries at their respective houses, all located in the county, and were required to "furnish lodgings and food and Liquors at prices fixed by the court."

We have more attorneys appearing at this term, offering their services, viz.: William Russell, John Quinn and Gabriel Jones,—having taken the oaths, took their places at the Bar. On another day of the same term, William Jolliffe and Michael Ryan appeared and having taken the oaths, took their places at the bar; one Constable was appointed for each Justice—Benjamin and Robert Rutherford qualified as Deputy Sheriffs. Business for Lawyers and Constables came very fast;—many petty depredations complained and actions to recover from some fleeing debtor,—all small amounts, however. No crime of any importance. When these cases were examined by the court "and evidence being sufficient," the defendants were committed to Jaoil until they could furnish security for their appearance "before His Magestys Court holden at *Wms* Burgh." No trial of felony by the new court. The first Coroner for the new County was qualified, he having produced his Commission from the Governor, dated Oct., 1743. At this Term, we have this about the first Ferry—the County Court takes interest in. Such grants may have been made by the Court at Orange: "John Kersey by his Petition set forth that by an order of Orange county Court he had leave to keep Ferry over Sherandoe river near the wagon Road where he liveth, and Prayed leave to continue the said Ferry; Its ordered that same be continued accordingly." Upon enquiry, we are led to believe that this Ferry was below Front Royal. However, we will let some descendant of the enterprising Mr. Kersey follow this out. Another road is requiring attention of the Court,—thus showing that the settlements were desirous of opening communication with each other,—bringing about much intercourse and trade; and to locate these sections for the reader of to-day, we give a few orders of Court, which show in some cases a little light that may do much to answer inquiries from so many persons to know. "If the old Plantation still stands on the old wagon Road from Winchester to other parts; that their ancestors had often told them of such old places they left behind them when they sought new homes in the West."

"On petition of John Wood, it is ordered that John Hardin, Samuel Timmons, and Edward Rogers, or any two of them, view the Road from Blue Ball to *Ashbies* bent branch and make Report." "On petition of Patrick Riely, its ordered that the Road be cleared from the head of the spring by The *Chappel* to Johns Evans, as it has been formerly laid off by order of Orange Court," where this Chappel was in '1743, (We will treat this under the head of Churches, etc.)

"On petition of Thomas Province and others for a Road from John Frost's mill to the main road between John Littlers plantation and John Millburns"—Ordered John Littler, William Dillon, and Joseph Burchham—lay off the same &c."

An order was made at this term requiring Ordinary keepers to sell "Liquors" at same rating granted by the Orange court—to continue until a rating is fixed at the next Mch ct. Richard Morgan moved the court to "discharge him from the bond as surety for Elizabeth Perkins, as she was squandering away the estate of her Father," the bond having been given in the Orange court—The case was continued to next term,—when we find the Court repremanding Mr. Morgan for having made statements to the court without first ascertaining what the Orange Court would show, and confronted him with a copy of a satisfactory accounting by said Elizabeth—of her administrators estate, and that he be adjudged to pay all costs of this enquiry. At the next term, Feb., 1744, we find another road is needed. The minute is copied to show the locality, "Ordered that George Bowman, Andrew Falkenborough and Robert McKay Junr—view and lay off the road from John Funk's mill across Cedar run Creek ford, to the said Robert McKay's junr and to Branston's Gap, according to the petition of Jacob Teeters." At the next term we are informed of the localities through which this road passes. This minute is entered; George Bowman and Robert McKay, jur.—made their report for viewing and laying off the road from John Funks mill,—"have laid off the road from John Funks mill back of George Helm's, and from thence to Cedar Creek ford and Robert McKays, thence Gregories' ford upon the River." "George Dellener, (Dellinger) Robert McKay, and George Bowman, appointed Overseers." In the report of commissioners to open the road from Funks Mill to Chester's Ferry, to where the road takes off to Manassas Run,—Jacob Funk, overseer, seems to be another road, heading from Cedar Creek Settlements towards the Manassas Settlements, than the road petitioned for in the first minute given. At the February term we find a long order, directing John Littler—the Yorkshireman and Wm. Dillon to lay out the road from John Frosts Mill to the main road between Littlers and Millburns, in these words:—"We have laid off the road from Captain Frosts mill thence to *Buffler*-lick, thence to the Backside of John Bossers' field, thence to David Shringers, thence to the usual ford, thence on east side of Wm. Frosts' Plantation, thence along a good Ridge by a course of marked trees to Matthias Elmores, thence along said Elmores creek to the head—the best *convenienst*s way that can be had by widow Dillons, by the said marked trees to the main road leading to Rappahannock—between John Littlers and Millburns." This road started from the settlements along Red Bud and that part of Opecquon Creek, passing them, and now found on the two streams in that section, crossed the Opecquon at Dix's Ford, at the farm now owned by Lucien Carr, of Winchester, and thence along the main road leading to one of the gaps in Blue Ridge. We think it well to take some space along the line of opening roads,—because in this simple way we locate many families, giving their names in the petitions and orders; and may thus awaken enquiry and such investigation along such lines, that will tend to unravel many mysteries surrounding the old ancestors regarding their homes, etc. The road asked for at a former term,—to run through the Ca-Capon country, is heard from again at this term. The Report, which was confirmed,—says "that a road from the north Branch of Ca-Capon to *James Cody's* is needed."

Here is authority shown by the Court in the matter of handling Liquors. It seemed to be much needed in that day so that the retailer of the beverage should be regulated to suit the resources of those who cared to indulge in a social glass; the long order will be abbreviated. The court fixed a price on every class of drinks; and a very important rule was made: the beverages must be pure, and were to be inspected regularly. We may infer that the honorable Justices placed this burden on themselves; for they failed to name the inspector, possibly one of the attorneys relieved them; for it will be seen later on that Gabriel Jones and his lusty friend of the Emerald Isle were concerned about the welfare of those who handled the *spirrits;* Heavy bonds were required for a full compliance with the law.

February 11, 1744, Gabriel Jones was recommended as Kings Attorney, and proceeded to prosecute—Dooues for assault and battery on one Samuel Isaacs; the first trial in the new court. March Court, 1744—Henry Munday was admitted to practice law. The Clerk was directed to procure from England setts of standard weights and measures. One of the new attorneys, Michael Ryan, was debarred the practice of law for two months, for "drunkenness." At this term, March 10, Gabriel Jones presented his commission as Kings attorney for this court; and having taken the oaths of office—which were very binding and impressive—we soon find him busy prosecuting every offender of the law, and became such a successful prosecutor,—that page after page of the old minute books for a long time are taken up in recording who the offenders were, nature of the offense, and ultimate results of many interesting trials. The efficient Kings Attorney not only changed the order of the transgressors living, but had the court adopt the new style for computing time—or at least the change was made, and from that time courts began the year on the first day of January instead of the first day of April. At the April term, 1744, we have the first mention of a Jury, which was called to actually try a "charge" of Commonwealth versus Michael Ryan, for assault and battery. The minute reads thus: "This day came the parties by their attorneys, and a Jury also came, to wit: James Hoge, foreman, (no other Jurymen named) who being *Tryed* and sworn to try, &c., &c., one of the Indictments for a Felony, etc." At this term occurs an incident that will be of interest to many, as it meant much to the whole "Population," as we have occasion to treat more fully under head of Churches, etc.

"Ordered that the Clerk of this court write to his Hon., the Governor, for a power to Choose a Vestry for the Parish of Frederick, in this County."

The Court having in their first experience found the Jury system some relief in deciding questions of facts,—the Hon. Justices to pass upon the law points—we find them ever ready to call a Jury. At another day of this term we have for the first time the names of a Jury, and give them here as a matter that may be of interest to some; .... Edward Rogers, Robert Allan, Thomas Cherry, Thos. Berwick, Morgan Bryan, John Bruce, Peter Woolfe, John Olford, George Hobson, Colbert Anderson, Gerge Martin, James Bruce, James Hoge, Robt. Smith, John Linzey, John Hite, Francis Ross, Samuel Isaacs, Robert Willson, William Davis, Jno. Frost, and John Richardson; they were all land owners. This gives the reader the names of families then resident of the county, and he may get a clue to his old ancestor.

"At the May term (11) 1744, a Commission from Governor Gooch—was presented to the court by the Clerk. This was the appointment of the Justices for ensuing year, the old Justices being reappointed and others newly commissioned. We give the names of the new Justices: Thomas Little, John Linzy, Jacob Hyte, Thomas Swearingen, Israel Robinson, Solomon Hedges. The first Grand Jury for the county was summoned for this term. Their names and their findings, are given in full and show many new names coming to the front to make history for the county:—John Hardin, foreman; Robt. Allan, George Hobson, James Vance, John Wilcox, Peter Woolfe, Isaac Pennington, David Logan, Robert Worth, Joshua Hedges, Robt. Willson, Samuel Norris, Hugh Parrell, James Hoge, Jacob Niswanger, Charles McDowell.

The following persons were indicted "for selling liquors without License: Robert Craft, James Findley, Shinn, and Cuthbert Harrison, and James Burns, a Constable, for swearing oaths and otherwise disturbing the peace and dignity of the Community; Jonathan Curtis, for plowing on Sunday;" the old Justices seemed determined to maintain a rigid observance of the Sabbath. Noah Hampton, who succeeded at a former term in having a road opened from his mill on Great Capon, was presented for taking more toll from his customers than the law allowed. One other deserves special mention, and the minute is copied: "We present Coll. James Wood for getting drunk and swearing two oaths within six months." It is surmised, the Clerk was then reformed, as in his long service after, he was noted for his dignity and decorum.

"June term—8,—" Duncan Oguillion was granted a license to keep an Ordinary, and since he was awarded the contract for building the jail, we may assume he was a resident of the village. It appears later on that Duncan partook too freely of his refreshments; for we find him imprisoned in the jail he had recently built. At this term we find the Sabbath-breaker, Jonathan Curtis, in deep trouble. He was indicted for writing and publishing several articles against the Established Church. Evidently this Quaker was not willing to be governed in his new field of freedom. At the same court we have this incident: Rev. Wm. Williams was fined 4 pounds and costs, to pay for "joyning in the holy bonds of matrimony, several persons, he being no orthodox minister," the minute shows that he resented the unjust action of the court, and he was fined 26 shillings for "behaving indecently before the court." Doubtless he was a visiting Presbyterian minister, and joined in wedlock some of the Scotch-Irish in the vicinity of "Old Opeckon" meeting house. The Church of England at that time recognized no Ministers other than those ordained by that Church; as by reference to chapter on churches is more fully explained. On the same day, two Attorneys incurred the displeasure of the justices,—the court fined James Porteous and John Quinn for "indecently behaving and swearing before the court;" caused by disagreement of the attorneys over the trial of a case. At this term, the first naturalization papers were granted; Peter Mauk, a German, being the first. He was one of the Adam Mueller Settlement in the "Massanuttin" region, fully treated elsewhere. Not long after this act of the old settler, quite a number of Protestants appeared and subscribed to the oaths prescribed by Acts of Parliament. Some of their names are given; Philip and Michael Boucher (afterwards written Boogher); Henry and George Lough Miller, Valentine and Christopher Windle, John Harman, George Dellinor, John Frederick, V. Helm. One of the minutes of this term must be given by reason of the significant allusion to where the first Courts were held: The court laid the first Levy at this term and specified how the same should be distributed:

To James Wood, Clerk, extra services tobacco	1248 ℔
as per account	2015 "
" same for four record books and one law book from Wm-burgh 8 shillings or	128 "
" James Wood, 6 Webbs Justices for use of county £3, 5s. or	1040 "
" Mr. Secretary Nelson	670 "
" James Wood, for use of Court house, £4, or	1280 "
" Thomas Rutherford, Sheriff—extra services	1248 "
as per account	20923 "
" Isaac Perkins for 526 feet of plank for use of court house	315 "
" Gabriel Jones as Kings attorney	2000 "
" John Bruce, for building the Stocks & Pillory	1840 "
" John Harrow, for iron work on Stocks & Pillory	320 "
" James Porteous, for public services	1000 "
" Andrew Campbell, pay for three men going to South Branch concerning Indians	960 "
" John Jones, constable	211 "
" James Wood, for standard weights and measures	5440 "
" George Home, for running dividing line	24416 "
By 1283 tithables at 59 lbs, Tobacco per poll	75697 "

This minute is a valuable record, showing the number of persons who had been found by diligent officers and required to pay the poll tax. The number 1283 shows the county to be sparsely settled; for it must be borne in mind, the old County had not yet been subdivided, then again that Tobacco was a staple crop, and also a legal tender. The minutes will repay careful reading and study. The minutes of court for several subsequent terms contain many interesting incidents. We will add this minute, "Mr. James Wood produced his commission as Surveyor, signed by the President and Masters of William and Mary College." At this term George Home surveyor of the county, made return of his report. "That he had run the county line according to an order of this court, marking the Augusta line, same is admitted to record." The writer has been unable to find this record. The original was returned to Williamsburgh and later destroyed by fire in Richmond. This court for the first time made an order for having personal property "Listed for Taxation;" and certain of the Justices to take these "Lists." Later on, the office "of Comr. of the Revenue" was created.

—but we find Justices continued to perform this service—of course they were not required by Statute to perform it. They seemed to treat the office as one of the emoluments of the Hon. Court. This was the case in the office of High Sheriff; the senior Justice always being named by the Governor for this office after the Justices had formally recommended one of their number for appointment. This gave the court the right to pass upon the fitness of their President. We find the court asking the High Sheriff to recommend several persons for Deputies; the court would then appoint one of the Justices who seemed willing to help along, for many were needed to serve processes in the sparsely settled country:

At the October Term, 1745, we have this minute to show how work on the public buildings is progressing:

"Levied to James Bruce for mending the seats in the Court house to be paid in Tobacco .... 64 pounds
To John Littler for plank for prison.. 890½
" Marquis Calmes for iron work on the Prisons .... 3200 "
" Duncan O'Guillon for work on Goal, tobacco .... 6400 "
" Hugh Campbell for digging the Dungeon of the Prison .... 1120 "

We are unable to account for the distinction between the Prison and Goal, doubtless the one building embraced both. From the next item, we infer the Justices were fortifying their judicial positions;

"Levied to Giles Chapman for bringing to the court 13 Acts of Assembly.'' The foregoing minutes clearly indicate a completion of the Jail or prison just prior to this term. Norris in his History, gives the date of completion September 8th 1748, (an error;)

The Court held Monthly terms; and from this period each term indicated new settlements springing up, to receive attention from the courts. The tide of immigration had turned towards the famed country lying South of the "Cohonguruta," where families were seeking homes West of the Blue Ridge. As has already been said, petitions for opening roads were pouring in at every term; and the ten years succeeding this term from which the last minutes were gathered, witnessed enormous development, A full list of roads opened prior to 1753, is given in chapters on the topography and physical features of the County. The court was also granting mill rights on the various streams. A number of superior mill sites were soon appropriated; and rude, but useful structures sprang up in all sections. We will try to locate the more prominent as this study progresses. The nucleus for villages being formed will be located—Churches or Meeting Houses were going up which will be found in Chapters on Churches. The Field notes of Washington show many surveys for tracts of land which were returned to Court, and ordered to be recorded or filed. Deeds were then made to many settlers at various places, extending from the Shenandoah to Great Capon, and along South Branch, Some were located in what is called, "Washington's Pattersons Creek Survey," embracing many thousand acres. Many found homes in what was known as "South Branch Manor," the old surveys are very instructive. They locate the tracts, names of grantees, and dates of entry. As it may serve to show who many of the arrivals were, brief notices of the names and regions where they settled about 1749-50, will be given, though some doubtless had erected the *squatters cabin* several years previously, and waited for some Lord of the Manor to come and give them title. Some names appear with surveys, who had other tracts and resided on such as the very earliest settlers. Andrew Campbell, one of the Justices, lived in the vicinity of the Baths northwest of Winchester; George Wm. Fairfax, survey for land on Long Marsh, John Anderson on same,—Captain Thos. Ashby on Shen. River above Burrells Island, Henry and Robt. Ashby on the Fairfax Road, Jas. Blackburn lived on his land on Long Marsh, Capt. George Neavill had survey on Long Marsh, Thos. Colston's survey on same, John Cozen's on same, Richard Carter for several large tracts on same, Isabella Jump, survey on same, John Vane and John Madden at Joe's Hole on Long Marsh, Saml. Isaacs and Isaac Pennington on Long Marsh, Thos. Johnston owned land on same, adjoining Col. Blackstone; George Smith, on the same; Jeremiah Wood, Patrick Rice, Nathaniel Daugherty, John Loftin, Hannah Southerd, Maj. L. Washington, had surveys on Long Marsh made by Washington and his chain carriers. Long Marsh has ever been noted for its fertile soil and Colonial Homesteads, and is today the name of one of the Magisterial Districts in Clarke County. The Bullskin Creek offered attractions for the following named persons, who were settling in that section, and the Washington surveys, embraced them. Henry Bradshaw, Lawrence Washington, Marquis Calmes, the Justice; Richard Stephenson, Wm. Davis; G. W. Fairfax; Joshua Haynes, George Johnston (in another tract he is mentioned as Capt. George Johnston) Thos. Lofton, & Dr. James McCormick are mentioned as "abutting owners" to

Capt. Johnston's tract. Johnston sold his tract to George Washington. Patrick Mathews was on the South side the Bullskin; Capt. Isaac Pennington, mentioned as a resident, on the Bullskin:—Washington in his notes says, "I lodged there, the first night in first survey campaign," and Anderson Pitts had been previously on his patent, also Capt. Thos. Rutherford "was seated and desired no survey," likewise Nathaniel Thomas, also Saml. Walker (written in notes Waker,) Robt. Worthington was on a large grant. The following surveys were along the Shenandoah River; Robt. Fox, Edward Musgrove, George Neavill, adjoining Wm. Vestal who owned the Vestal Iron Works at base of Blue Ridge; Saml. Knisman, Henry Enoch, John Newton; Henry Harris's survey near the "Manor Line," "John Vestall, previously seated on Pattent." The following named persons had surveys made them on the South Branch. Washington, says John Collins had settled in the Manor—near the Indian Village (North of site of Moorefield,) and that he and Mr. George Wm. Fairfax spent the night with Collins. This note also appears "James Rutledge was settled about seventy miles above mouth of South Branch, where they spent a night. Michael Stump, Henry Venable, need surveys, for lands settled on prior to 1748. This note is dated April, 1758. The young surveyor evidently made one mistake in his life; for at that date, Col. Washington was in the *Fort Duquesne campaign,* and also interested in his election campaign on his return in June. This survey must have been made in 1753, while on his surveying expedition. In same note book this appears: "surveyed a tract of land——acres for William Baker on Lost River, November 10, 1749, which adjoins Barnaby McHandry," John Kinson had his survey on Lost River, several surveys are mentioned. Jonathan Arnold and David Woods on North River of Ca-Capon, Darby McKeever, Sen., for survey on Ca-Capon River, and several others; Abram Johnston and others were on Pattersons Creek in 1748, supposed to have come from Penn, via, Fort Cumberland. That was dangerous ground at that period, for many immigration trains were attacked by roving bands of Indians, as will be shown later on. Washington and Fairfax name their chain carriers and markers for each tract, and this will furnish some names that will not appear elsewhere. The list is given for reference. Frequently he selected men who were adjoining owners; the following represent several sections; John Anderson, Henry & Robt. Ashby, Capt. M. Calmes, markers on their own lands, Francis & Thos. Carney, Joshua Haynes, Henry Henricks, Tos. Jones, John Keith, Timothy McCarty, Thos. McClanahan, Dr. James McCormick, John Miller, Jno. & Ned Musgrove, Hgh. Rankin, Ruben Rutherford, Stephen Sebastian, Richard Taylor, Lewis Thomas, Owen Thomas, Jno. Urton, Alexander Vance, Wm. Wiggons, Jeremiah Wood, and Worthington. For much interesting matter relating to surveys, the old deed books deserve careful study; and for personal matter relating to Surveyor Washington—see Field Notes, among the *Washington Papers,* and especially, one marked "A Journal of my Journey over the Mountains." His companion in this "Journey" was George Wm. Fairfax. There is some evidence that he was Senior Surveyor in this work, begun in *1748,* one year prior to Washington's appearance with Lord Fairfax. One other field book and journal, contains notes indicating that Washington's first appearance as a surveyor was in 1749, where he continued in the work until 1753. We offer this for no speculation, but simply quote from old Washington papers, as matter that must interest the reader.

CHAPTER V

Boundaries of Old Frederick County

The last Chapter, with gleanings from Old Courts, brought us to 1750;—and as settlements were rapidly forming over the vast territory, the author deems it wise to suspend notices of the proceedings of the Court, and endeavor in this Chapter to give more definite description of the old County. The importance of this will be seen in the study of the following Chapters. The settlements were already harrassed by Indian raiders, and the time drawing near when the old County was to be the scene of Indian Wars; and soon came what were known as the French and Indian Wars.

A considerable digression may be instructive to the reader, whose ancestors probably were on the frontier in 1750; Chapters on these wars will follow in proper order. Frederick County, at its formation in Nov., 1738, was distinguished in the Act, as "Everything west of the Blue Ridge—north of a certain line." This always seemed so indefinite, and has occasioned much confusion even in the experience of the author,—that he felt it his duty in preparing these pages, to give a more definite boundary to the great Territory embraced within the limitations of the County,—or more strictly speaking her limits on the East, North and South. As to her western limits—which seemed to have *no* limit, much speculation has been written and said concerning it; some insisting that it only ended at the shores of the Pacific Ocean. Others were willing to confine it to the territory East of the Mississippi River; while others gave the Ohio River as the western boundary, and still others fixed the Allegany Mountains, as the western line. Of course all these geographical questions have been laid open to the eye of the student who has informed himself of these boundaries. But neither the general reader, nor the school children ever meet with the matter so condensed, as to give any satisfactory settlement of the question. As has been stated elsewhere in this work, the boundary on the East is plainly defined by the line of mountains or range of hills, called the *Blue Ridge*, the northern boundary followed the Potomac River to a point in the "High Mountains,"—meaning a point beyond Cumberland,—then in a straight line to the "Great Waters," meaning the Ohio River at a point above Wheeling. To understand what this meant, one must see the Map of that section and follow this straight line, and he will find many encroachments on what is Maryland and Pennsylvania. At that time the lines between the three States had not been fully determined; and, we might add, never have been settled to the satisfaction of the incredulous. Not all the solemnity and dignity attaching to the "Mason and Dixon" line could fully please everybody. The Congress, Courts of Justice and State Legislatures, have worked over it, and still the line in some measure is incomplete. Recent legislation in the three States sustains this claim. A Commission has been, and is now, engaged in erecting monuments of division line.

The Author had his curiosity aroused years ago by contact with officials and citizens of several border counties of Pennsylvania,—finding among the files and records of those Counties, the final disposition by the District Court, of suits litigated in what was in that day regarded as Virginia territory, of course within the bounds of Frederick County, and what was at one time regarded as West Augusta District. Of course, this was interesting; but it was perplexing, and the question arose, how came those papers there? The answer is, the old border Counties along the supposed Pennsylvania and Virginia line, embraced much Pennsylvania territory, which was regarded as being within the jurisdiction of our District Courts; and when the line was run to determine the question in 1776-1785, the territory lying on the Pennsylvania side, within those Counties continued to hold the "Files," etc. of old suits, which more nearly affected the Pennsylvania citizen than those on the Virginia side. The running of this line suddenly stopped all suits pending between Fairfax and the squatters on his *"Northern Neck."* He discovered that his "Neck" must be confined to Virginia. Some interesting history is connected with those squatters on the Pennsylvania side,—requiring many Acts of the State Legislature, and even the Congress, to determine their rights, but of their history, this work need not further treat. We will now follow the line westward, as then claimed by Frederick County from its point on the Ohio above Wheeling, extending northwestward to the Great Lakes, until a point is fixed on the line of Longitude 87 degrees West from Greenwich (now 10 degrees West from Washington) West and North of the present site of Chicago, thence South to the 37th degree of Latitude; the point on the Lakes, and the line South, being along the boundaries of the "French Possessions," questions then unsettled—and only determined later on by the capture of "Old Fort St. Vincent"—now "Vincennes," by the celebrated Clark's French and Indian Campaigns. Then it became desirable to move the line further West, so as to include the latter point, so the Frederick and Augusta County line was extended to the 89th degree of Longitude;—and this latter was adhered to for many years,—and was frequently the subject that Congress felt called upon to enact some unwarranted laws governing the Virginia territory of the Great West. It will be seen on our present Maps, that these lines embraced nearly all of Ohio, all of Indiana, and about half of Illinois. Following the line from about where Cairo on the Mississippi River is to-day, eastward, we take nearly all of Kentucky. It was believed at that time, to be all of that territory, and the question was not raised;—but subsequent claims of West Augusta County,—so-called—resulted in a division line being established between the *Magisterial Districts* of Tennessee, and Kentucky,—which resulted in Frederick County losing a portion of the "dark and bloody battle ground." We now have the geographical position of Old Frederick County, including part of Augusta;—and for many years her authority was respected within this vast territory; frequent mention being made in old records of her jurisdiction in her "Kentucky Magisterial District," and of her Colonies in the "Ohio portion," and those at "St. Vincent." Old Order Books show that processes were served on "dwellers in the Ohio portion," and those within the Illinois District." Frequent orders appear in the old Minute Books of the old Justices' Court, continuing Court from day to day, to await the arrival of the Justices from the Kentucky District, who had been delayed by reported high waters," or of Indian hostilities. Often additional Deputy Sheriffs were appointed by the Court and ordered "to proceed to render such aid as might be required to escort the honorable Justice to this Worshipful Court." Investigations clearly prove that the Justices mentioned, did not live in Kentucky proper; they resided somewhere in Western Virginia, and their jurisdiction was supposed to embrace the regions referred to. Augusta County exercised similar jurisdiction. This produced confusion, and was cured finally by the General Assembly defining the lines of the Districts. When the line entered Virginia from the Kentucky region at a point on the Kanawha River, it intersected the boundary line of Augusta County through the mountains, to a point on the South Branch, below the present site of Moorefield in Hardy County, then following an unsettled line between the two counties,—"to a head Spring of Robinson river east of the Blue Ridge." This answered the purpose for awhile. There seemed to be a desire for an established line between the Counties,—and that Augusta should extend her terminal point on the Ohio River to a point up that stream a greater distance, as is shown by extracts from the MSS Journal of the House of Burgesses. We find in 1744, an Act directing the Courts of the two counties to have their County Surveyors run and establish the line. So, as already stated, at the January term of the Frederick co. ct. 1744, the order was promptly entered; but as will be seen, this order directed the Surveyor to run the dividing line between this and Augusta County—from the Head spring of Hedgeman river, to Pattersons Creek; and a report later on shows this line to have been run. Nothing to show of any effort to run the line through the unsettled mountains "beyond the power of man to penetrate and scale." Some years later, these difficulties were overcome; and the line was established,—even changing the point on Pattersons Creek; and starting from that point higher up the stream, found a new point on the Ohio, and the new territory taken from Frederick was styled and recognized as West Augusta District. Soon this vast territory was opened up for White settlers; and Colonists appeared on Pattersons Creek, and other water courses, and "grew strong along the Ohio river," and formation of new Counties desired. So we find the first lopping process, to reduce the size of Old Frederick took place in May, 1753, when an Act of the Assembly at Williamsburgh, directed a new county to be formed, and to take it from the western parts of Frederick & Augusta, and named it Hampshire. Doubtless many of the good people of that section were thinking of their "Hampshire Hills" in England—from whence many of the Colonists came, chiefly preferring to locate among the hills and mountains that constantly reminded them of the appropriateness of the name for their new county. We find in their Petition, many English names of the actual citizens,—requesting the name of Hampshire be given their new County. As this is an important event in the history of Frederick

County, and certainly of Hampshire, we give a copy of the Act relating to this matter.

In the General Assembly Of Virginia, November, 1753, 27th yr. of the Reign of George II.

"An Act for adding part of the county and parish of Augusta that lies within the territory or tract of land, called the Northern Neck belonging to the right honourable Thomas Lord Fairfax, Baron of Cameron, and it will be more convenient, if the dividing line between the said territory, and the other part of the said county be added to the county and parts of Frederick, and, whereas, the said county and parish of Frederick are of a very long and large extent, and inconvenient to the inhabitants thereof,—

"II. Be it enacted by the Lieutenant Governor, Council and Burgesses, of this present General Assembly, and it is hereby enacted by authority of the same, That on the first day of May next ensuing, all that part of the county of Augusta which lies within Northern Neck, be added to, and made part of the county of Frederick; and that from and immediately after the said first day of May, the said county of Frederick and the said part of the county of Augusta so to be added to, and made part of the county of Frederick, as aforesaid, be divided into two counties; and all that part thereof, lying to the westward of the ridge of Mountains, commonly called and known by the names of the Great North Ca-Capon mountain and *Warin* Spring mountains, extending to the Potomack river, be one distinct county, and called and by the name of Hampshire; and all that other part thereof, lying to the eastward of the said ridge of mountains be one other distinct County, and retain the name of Frederick;—"III. And for the due administration of justice in the said County of Hampshire, after the same shall take place. Be it enacted by the authority aforesaid, That after the first day of May, a court for the said county of Hampshire, be constantly held by the Justice thereof, upon the second Tuesday in every month in such manner as by the laws of this Colony is provided, and shall be by their Commissioners directed, IV. And be it further enacted by the authority aforesaid, That all that part of the parish of Augusta in the county of Augusta, which after the division aforesaid, will be within the said counties of Frederick and Hampshire, shall be added to, and made part of the parish of Frederick.

"V. Provided always, That nothing herein contained shall be construed to hinder the sherriffs or collectors of the said counties of Augusta and Frederick, or the collectors of the parish of the county of Augusta, as the same now stands intire and undivided, from collecting and making distress for any public dues or officers fees, which shall remain unpaid by the inhabitants of that part of the county of Augusta to be added to the county of Frederick, as aforesaid, and the inhabitants of the said county of Hampshire, respectively, at the time the same shall take place; but such sherriff or collectors, respectively, shall have the same power to collect and distrain for the said fees and dues, as if this Act had never been made.

"VI. Provided also, That the courts of the said counties of Augusta and Frederick, shall have jurisdiction of all actions and suits, both in law and equity, depending before them, respectively, at the said division shall take place, and shall try & determine such actions and suits, and issue process and award executions against the body or estate of the defendant in any such action or suit, in the same manner as if this act had not been made, any law usage or custom to the contrary.

"VII. And be it further enacted, That from and after the first day of May, which shall be in the year of our Lord, one thousand, seven hundred and fifty-six, the said parish of Frederick shall be divided into two district parishes, by the line dividing the said county of Frederick, from the said county of Hampshire, and that all that part of the said parish of Frederick, which, after such division, will be within the said county of Frederick, shall retain the name of the parish of Frederick; and all the other part thereof, shall be called and known by the name of the parish of Hampshire;

"VIII. Provided always, That nothing herein contained shall be construed to hinder the officers the benefit of the law as herein provided,———;

"IX. And be it further enacted by the authority, aforesaid, That the freeholders and housekeepers of the said parish of Hampshire, shall meet at some convenient time and place, to be appointed and publickly advertised at least one month before, by the sherriff of the said county of Hampshire, before the first day of July, 1756, and then and there, elect twelve of the most able and discreet persons of the said parish to be vestry men thereof, which said persons so elected having in the court of the said county of Hampshire, taken and subscribed the oaths appointed, to be taken, by an act of Parliament, made in the first year of the reign of his Majesty King George the first, "intitled" An act for the further security of his Majesty's person and Government and the succession of the crown in the heirs of late princess Sophia, being Protestants, & for extinguishing the hopes of the pretended prince of Wales, and his and secret abettors, and taken and subscribed the oath of abjuration and repeated and subscribed the test, and also subscribed to be conformable to the doctrine and discipline of the Church of England shall to all intents and purposes be deemed and taken to be vestrymen of the said parish;—X. And be it further enacted by the authority aforesaid, That upon the death, removal or resignation of any of the said vestrymen, the remaining vestrymen, shall be, and they are hereby impowered to choose and elect another vestryman, in the room of such vestryman, so dying, removing or resigning—;—This act was not fully applied to Hampshire county until 1756—when the new county organized its Court—and proceeded to execute its orders and judgments without the aid of the Frederick county sheriff &c. The county seat was established by an act of the Assembly in 1762, and chartered as the borough of Romney. Reference has been made to some confusion about Courts on the Pennsylvania border. In the construction of Augusta and Frederick, the line between the two counties was not understood by them. Augusta construed the northern line to be, that it took a straight course due northwest from the head springs of Hedgeman River to the Ohio, and claimed her terminal was on the river at a point above Pittsburgh; while Frederick was described in her northern line, as extending to the Great water beyond the Ohio. Of course this was confusion; the territory of one overlapping the other; and as both courts had coexistent legal rights along the Pennsylvania border, this is why orders of both courts appear as above mentioned. This was all cured when the line was finally run; when the Augusta line terminated far down on the Ohio, while the Frederick Territory beyond the Ohio was not affected;—

In 1772—Frederick was called upon to lop off more of her vast territory. We find the Genl. Assembly entertaining petitioners from both the southern and northern borders, resulting in an act to form the County of Berkley on the North, and the County of Dunmore (Shenandoah) on the South, Dunmore embraced the territory South of Cedar Creek and the North Fork of the Shenandoah River from its junction with Cedar Creek, to its junction with the South Fork, near the site of Front Royal, (this line was in dispute several times, but finally settled by legal survey.) A change of name was made in 1777, on motion of one of the members of the House of Burgesses, under peculiar circumstances—Lord Dunmore was regarded as a *Tory,* so offensive to the loyal citizens of Virginia, who had grown weary under his tyranical usurpation, that before the moving member could take his seat, his resolution was adopted, and the name of Dunmore, ordered to be obliterated from the records, and substituted Shenandoah in its stead, giving the county a name after the historic river passing through it. The town of Woodstock which had been established in March, 1761, by Act of the Genl. Assembly, was chosen as the county seat, and the county government was soon under way.

Berkley embraced what is now Berkley, Jefferson and Morgan Counties,—the boundary line defined by survey. No such natural boundaries of water courses or mountain ranges, as was the case in other subdivisions of the old county.

Martinsburg was a small town at this formation, being laid out by Adam Stephen, and was adopted as the county seat. Clarke County was formed from Frederick in 1836; the Blue Ridge forming its eastern boundary, and the Opecquon mostly its western boundary, giving it an area of 17 miles in length and 15 miles wide; the Shenandoah running along and near its eastern boundary. Berryville was the county seat.

Warren was formed in 1836, from Frederick, taking in a portion of Shenandoah to give it an area of 20 miles in length by 12 miles in width. The Shenandoah River runs through it at the base of the Blue Ridge, and takes in its course the waters of the north fork coming out of Shenandoah County. Cedar Creek runs through its northern border. Front Royal, established in 1888, on 50 acres of land taken from the Van Meter Grant, became the county seat.

Having briefly given the boundaries of Old Frederick, as well as the subdivisions, thus reducing the Old County to its present area,—26 miles in length and 22 miles for its mean width, Winchester being the county seat, a distinction she has held for 165 years, we may now regard the geographical position settled, and proceed in the next chapter to dwell at some length upon many of her celebrated physical features.

Pack Horse Ford, near Shepherdstown

CHAPTER VI

Physical Features of Frederick County

The reader must not expect to find in this effort a description of the vast territory of *Old* Frederick County, as this would detract seriously from the value of this work, as the author has endeavored in all cases to confine himself to simple facts, that may make it useful to the enquirer when seeking information concerning historical incidents of the county. Be it remembered that, since the county's early history, great States have been formed out of her territory. Behold Ohio, Indiana, Illinois and Kentucky, and, can we add without regret, West Virginia, with their teeming populations, the original stock of which planted their homes in the undeveloped country, having received their love for adventure in their mother State, Virginia. Regard the phenomenal progress in development,—not only in the rise of great cities, her arts and sciences, agricultural results, places of learning,—her product of scholars, statesmen and heroes, but actually lining up at every opportunity to supply the whole country—not with corn, but with the Chief Magistrates of the Nation! So with these intimations of our intention to let others tell of Old Frederick's northwest territory, with its accumulating millions of money and citizens, we will confine the effort to a more contracted part of her original domain, only briefly touching upon the rapid development of Western Virginia.

It was known to the early settlers that the "Great Waters," so frequently mentioned by Acts of the old House of Burgesses, promised in that early day, wonderful systems to utilize the resources of the mountain sections. Much money and effort was spent along this line; but not until within the memory of the writer did the hidden wealth begin to reveal itself. Some discoveries of coal and valuable iron ores were made in the early days; but seekers of wealth had not yet learned the way of converting the limitless forests of finest varieties of lumber into easy money. Nor did it seem possible that the successive mountain ranges could ever be made to yield up the coal and ores of which they were largely composed; but such has been done; and to-day, who can enumerate the coal, oil corporations and private enterprises of this class, or the immense lumber companies. All of these enterprises soon found the bold mountain streams inadequate to move the new products into the commercial world, ever waiting for more supplies. This soon attracted the railway capitalists who, after they saw the demand for increasing transportation, had their experienced men on the ground to trace out ways for the massive locomotives that must come to the help of the natural waterways. Take a railroad map of to-day, and we find railroad lines threading their ways along the valleys and through the mountains, until we have such a network of railroad systems, that we are unable off-hand to estimate their number, much less their miles of trackage. All this has resulted in untold wealth; and makes West Virginia hardly second to any State in the iron and coal belt in the country. West Virginia has made herself well known to the world since the Dismemberment Act; taking her place in the halls of national legislation; assuming the duties and share of the higher judiciary of the nation; furnishing on demand men capable to take high rank in the Supreme Court, who are rendering useful service as wise and fearless judges. Her students and scholars are commanding recognition. Her rapid advance is witnessed in her growing colleges and university seats of learning, well known now to the world at large. Not to make invidious distinction, we find one of the wonders of the age in Elkins College, an institution rising in splendid form among the mountains, as a result of the endowments of Senators Davis and Elkins, whose munificent gifts and fostering care of the young plant, made it shine forth as a gem in what only a few years ago was a wilderness. The College, with its possibilities, has been offered by these gentlemen to the "Winchester Presbytery" not for any special religious or denominational control, but to place it under the benign influence of this well-known Church government. No uncertain plans surround its future work. Success must attend its further efforts.

Coming still nearer to Old Frederick, the Institution for the "Deaf, Dumb and Blind" at Romney, has a national reputation for not only a beautiful location, splendid buildings, but proficiency in the system of educating a helpless class of boys and girls, so as to make them enjoy useful lives. Much good will result to visitors who may chance to look in upon this "Institution," seeing for themselves what has been done in our nearby Hampshire Hills.

At this point, we may as well continue a notice of Old Frederick. The reader must remember the warning heretofore given, that no attempt will be made to give even a condensed history of what became Hampshire—nor even since that period. We have no need of such effort; for West Virginia has supplied this want through her Historical Society, giving to us several histories of her physical features. We must be content with a partial description of the old County, lest we weary the reader, who maybe has scaled her mountains for game or pleasure, or hooked the trout from the hidden streams, and knows more about the surface of that country than the writer. So we will compromise by giving just enough, not to weary the one, but gladden the heart of the other. As already stated, the larger part of Hampshire is of that mountainous character peculiar to all of West Virginia; and many thousand acres of the high mountain land has never been brought into cultivation, indeed, never can be. The eastern boundary is a range of hills of considerable altitude, known as Big Timber Ridge, though in truth, they are properly the ranges of the Great Ca-Capon Mountains, that run about North and South, at whose base flows the stream from which the mountain takes its name. This rugged river flows through the county and into the Potomac. West of these are mountain ranges with local names—Big Sandy and other ranges. Passing through these, we enter the North River Valley, through Blue's Gap, over the Northwestern Turnpike, passing almost under the Hanging Rock. Crossing soon the North River, with its narrow Valley, and through to Capon and its rugged Valley, we have left Bear Garden Mountain and "Tear Coat,"—the latter a dangerous and turbulent stream in rainy seasons. The celebrated turnpike wends its way through other mountains, over North River, Little Capon, and Jersey Mountains, until we suddenly emerge from their wilds into the hospitable and attractive town of Romney, well known for its location on the South Branch of the Potomac. Running just West of the town at the base of the South Branch Mountain, of peculiar attractions, is the fast flowing river. Here the tourists and seekers of pleasure find cool nights in summer, and glowing hearthstones in winter; wild game in the mountains for winter sport, and abundant fishing in the far-famed river. Certainly, no sportsman can be found who is in ignorance of the "Branch" and its stories. We are now in the heart of natural beauty, and the picturesque locality of historic Romney. Overlooking this lovely river, as viewed from "Yellow Banks" or "Indian Mound Cemetery," where its broad sweep of water at this point, slowly moves away northward to the Potomac, through those rich alluvial South Branch bottoms, as they are called, cover in some places with waving harvests, in others, fine herds of *short-horns* enjoying the rich pasturage peculiar to the lowlands of this river. From source to mouth, from these points, the tourist has a sweeping view of the river. Four miles below are the famous *hanging rocks;* about the same distance above is seen the "Trough," where the river has torn its way through high mountains. The scenery here becomes so entrancing, that the tourist hesitates whether to detour or proceed through Mechanicsburg Gap, and penetrate still further the mountain wilds. One tourist did thus hesitate, while in reverie, and was aroused by one who drew his attention away from the lovely scene, to behold a face that has left its picture in memory's cabinet since that day. Standing there before him, was one who had been long regarded as the inflexible judge; but here he cast off the ermine of his high office, and stood on these "Banks" free from his daily routine, a pure, noble man—(James W. Armstrong). Plans were soon settled. He drew the young tourist away and into his own hospitable home; and the familiar faces found there, and the intellectual, cordial and happy hours spent under that roof-tree, repaid him with memories that can never be effaced.

The scenery of the river must be taken first. The passage of the river from Moorefield through the Trough, where the river has for ages with its swirling waters, made but little change through this narrow gorge, for the same old rocky walls are there. Following the river in its flow, the tourist sees the great hanging rocks, where the river grows bold and turbid as it washes the rocky shores, until in the sweep of centuries, the walls have been worn away, and we have the rocks hanging in majestic wonder,—forming a canopy of mountain granite along its base. Along the river's rim, skillful engineers have given to the traveller a good driveway and tracks for the railroad from Green Spring Station on the B. & O. Railroad to Romney. These highways have opened up the resources of South Branch Valley to the markets of the country. From Romney Station, herds of export cattle are shipped averaging 2,000 lbs. Other natural wonders attract our attention. We now cross the river over an iron bridge, where the Northwestern Turnpike enters Mechanicsburg Gap—the first step of the Alleganies. True, all other mountains which we have left behind us, are known as the Allegany Ranges. This gap shows that the mountains round about us, must have met with some terrible flood of pent-up waters away back of the memory of man, cutting the mountain in twain, and leaving perpendicular sides of gray granite and mountain sandstone, strange to the eye of the geologist, to remind the traveler that nature has been subjected to enormous convulsions,—doubtless for the use of man. Here the road leaves the mountain walls for a short space, to enter the approaches to Pattersons Creek Valley. From here, a highway leads to Moorefield in Hardy County, and also to a point on the B. & O. Railroad. We follow this Northwest Turnpike into and up the narrow Pattersons Creek Valley for miles, when we gradually reach the base of the Alleganies proper; then for a climb of several hours. Once on the summit, we find a great sweep of table-land, stretching out in every direction for miles around. This is the renowned "Glades,"—an oasis in the mountain wilderness, affording most abundant pasturage for' thousands of cattle. On, and still further into other mountains—on, towards Cheat River and the multitude of mountains around and about in confusion of both location and names. In the early days of Old Frederick, the mountain country was but little known to the outside world; but to the bold mountain dwellers in their rude cabins, who hewed their way, and whiled away the days in hunting for the furs that gave them good returns. Their patient waiting brought marvelous returns to many of their descendants, who to-day possess their wealth in the mine, oil-well or forest.

We must now return and take a glimpse at what lies East of the South Branch:—Lost River, in the southern part (now Hardy County), the Ice Mountain to the North, and other natural curiosities that deserve special mention. Taking Lost River as a starting point, which for a long time was regarded as a distinct stream, but later on it was discovered that it became part of the Great Ca-capon River, flowing along the base of a mountain for many miles. Lost River has its source in the mountains South of the point where its name is changed to Ca-Capon, distant about twenty miles, starting from the "divide" of the waters of the Shenandoah and the Potomac, heading near the head springs forming the stream, running on through Brocks Gap to the North fork of the Shenandoah River in Rockingham County. Along this Lost River are many interesting natural features, such as Cold Spring Cave, which is at the base of Lost River Mountain, about twelve miles below the source of the river. Many grand mountain views are to be seen from the river, as it runs through the narrow but fertile valley, winding up with its wonderful disappearance under Lost River Mountain (Timber Ridge), to reappear as Capon. One must view this struggle between river and mountain, to appreciate this natural wonder. It is stated by those who have so viewed and investigated this freak of nature, that this passage is fully three miles from entrance to outlet. This river and many large springs form the first we see of what is called Capon River. About four miles from this New River, as it was once called, there is a cove in the western side of Great North Mountain, of wondrous grandeur, celebrated for its cool atmosphere in summer. Within this cove are clusters of springs, gushing from the base of the mountain, some of which have become famous for their medicinal qualities. It was claimed at one time that these springs were the head springs of Capon River; and to fix their location they were called "Capon Springs" by some enterprising gentlemen who had formed a company for their development and improvement. The writer was informed many years ago by Mr. Westphall Frye, then a large landowner and resident of Wardensville, that his father Henry Frye had some prior claim of discovery and ownership, and called them Frye's Chalybeate Springs. The contest for ownership between the new claimant and Frye, resulted in the State retaining an interest in the "Medicinal Springs," and denying grants to both parties. Frye relinquished his claim, and a grant was made to the trustees of Watson-Town (See Hen., 1787) for a number of acres surrounding the springs, reserving the springs for the use of the general public. Cabins were erected. Soon a small establishment was erected for the accommodation of visitors. From this small beginning, changes were rapid, and more accommodations required, until the place became so famous, that it was found necessary to erect what was known for many years as the "Mountain House." Then it was this mountain resort attracted great crowds every summer; some of the most distinguished statesmen seeking its attractive inducements. In more recent years, the Mountain House became the central figure of a great group of attractive cottages; and through the skill, taste and lavish expenditure of effort and money by its owner, Capt. Wm. H. Sale, the place has become so renowned, as to need no further description. Its present owner and proprietor, Charles F. Nelson, son-in-law of our deceased friend, Capt. Sale, is successful in maintaining its enviable reputation as one of the best summer resorts to be found in the Virginia mountains. We must pass on to other features, from this attractive place, for a stop at the celebrated "Ice Mountain," already alluded to. This is a veritable mountain, and is found on North River a branch of Ca-Capon, about 27 miles northwest from Winchester, ten miles north of Capon Bridge, and is entitled to mention as a natural curiosity. The reader must not be incredulous. While it is not an "iceberg," it is entitled to the name borne by it for generations. This mountain is composed chiefly of loose mountain rock, rising to a height of about 800 feet from its western base on the river. From this point we have the best view of this wonder. By its peculiar shape and general formation, with but little shrubbery or vegetation on its rocky sides—nearly perpendicular on the river side, one is reminded of Old Storm King Mountain on the Hudson above West Point. The stupendous grandeur of both, impresses the beholder. Some good climbing is required to scale the steep sides and be rewarded by discovering actual ice in mid-summer. Upon removing some of the loose, heavy sand, and gray granite stones, you will find this strange, natural phenomenon—pure and perfectly formed pieces of ice, weighing often several pounds. As might be supposed, a very strong spring of cold water gushes from near the base of the mountain, where doubtless at this day is an ideal place for picnic parties. The writer remembers several such parties that he joined in the long ago. It is easy to recall these incidents in his life, but not so easy to find the survivors of that company. He knows of but three of that party of forty who enjoyed the day at the Ice Mountain!

Another natural curiosity of Hampshire is found about two miles above the forks of Capon, and it is known to-day as Caudy's Castle. Strange stories are told of this real curiosity, which stands out independent and alone from other mountains scattered around. Its eastern base rests upon the river, and, similar to the Ice Mountain, is a solid mass of granite, perpendicular to the height of at least 500 feet. Kercheval gives it this description: "A line drawn around its base, would probably not exceed one thousand or twelve hundred yards. From its western side, it may be ascended by a man on foot to within about ninety or one hundred feet of the summit; from thence the rock suddenly shoots up something in the form of a comb, which is about ninety or one hundred feet in length, eight or ten feet in thickness, and runs about North and South. On the eastern face of the rock from where the comb is approached, a very narrow undulating path is formed, by pursuing which, active persons can ascend to the summit." On this table rock several feet square, and from this point, the author was informed by several venturesome mountain climbers, that the view of the little valley, the winding river and broken mountain ranges, can only be surpassed in beauty by similar scenes in the great mountains of *New* Hampshire. We find in Kercheval's study of Caudy's "Castle" he treats it as a tradition. Can it be possible that so painstaking a compiler of interesting incidents of the early history of Old Frederick, which then included this very wonderful *castle,* could have mistaken actual fact for tradition! as the records of the Old County have revealed to the writer of these pages. If the reader will refer to the chapter on the organization from Orange, he will find a copy of the order of our County Court held Dec., 1743, directing that a road be opened on the petition of Noah Hampton, James *Coddy &c.,* from Hamptons Mill into a road, *&c.* near Col. Coddy's Fort, &c. Later on we find the House of Burgesses and the General Council of Virginia, voting him a grant of his tract of land, in consideration of his founding and maintaining a post of protection on Ca-Capon at Coddy's Fort. This establishes beyond any doubt the connection between Caudy's Castle and "James Coddy's *Ftt.*"

We will now briefly touch upon the development of the County, as it relates to towns, villages, highways, minerals, etc. As already stated, Romney was the county seat, located in the heart of the County on the eastern bank of the South Branch, forty-three miles distant from Winchester, by way of the Northwestern Turnpike. Other towns in the county that started in its early history, were Frankfort, Springfield, Cold Stream Mill (Bloomery in later years) and Paddy Town—none of which have grown in importance, hindered doubtless by the innumerable cross-roads' stores found in every section. In later years, quite a village started at Capon Bridge, where the Northwestern Turnpike crosses Capon River over the wooden-covered bridge. Several stores—one owned by Samuel Cooper—the post office, stage office, shops, etc. made it a village offering inducements to a traveler to stop and rest; and this he was sure to get in the early days at old Mag. Bell's Tavern; still later on, at the delightful hotel owned by our old friend John A. Smith, the stage-line man from Winchester to Romney. The traveler would forget his weariness while

Mr. Smith recounted his experiences as an old stage driver; in more recent years this Hotel has undergone changes that make it a real home for the guest who stops with Mrs. Smith and her estimable daughters. Many other places of interest along the line of development of this large county could be mentioned. Local historians have covered the ground in this respect; and the author can well afford to trust to their fuller description, and not cumber these pages with what is familiar to many. However, it may be well to make a note of the comparatively new industries. Large veins of Bituminous coal have been found, and are receiving the attention of miners who hope to reap fortunes for themselves and work wonders for the population of that section. Some years ago, Mineral County was formed from the northwestern part of Hampshire and its wealth of ore and coal deposits are fast becoming famous. The Hampshire County Fruit Growers' Association—have for several years enjoyed the distinction of having converted many of the Hampshire hills and mountain tracts of land into a wonderful network of orchards,—where the peach, plum and similar fruit has been produced in abundance. Having thus briefly sketched the outlines of the topography of the first county formed from old Frederick, along with glimpses of its development. We will treat the remaining portion of old Frederick as a whole in the following chapter.

To write an outline of the natural features of *The Valley*—embraced in old Frederick County, is no light task;—but to write an intelligent and comprehensive description of the physical features of this immense territory,—her surface so diversified with river, mountain, valley and glen, is a prodigious task—and the author makes the attempt with misgivings. To many of our readers, this part of his work will appear unnecessary—for everything is familiar to their eyes and they have no need to search these pages for a description of the scenes about them. But we must not forget, that if this effort to produce a history of this historic section is even a partial success, we must recognize the fact that these pages will be searched by many readers, more for a description of the land than of the men who have developed the resources of the County. So understanding this as a duty imposed on author and reader, an effort will be made to point out and briefly describe many such natural features, presenting the topography of the country—in simplicity of statement. One needs no spur to the imagination, to picture scenes of wonder, as we behold the natural points of interest from some well selected point; and when this point is found, no pen can describe the scenes that lie before him in quiet grandeur; nothing short of the talent found in a gifted landscape painter, could do justice to the vision presented to one who may chance to try the summit of *Massanuttin,* or the cone of the old Round Hill, northwest from Winchester—both presenting views North and South. Is it any wonder then, when one who has no such talent for painting pictures,—find himself on the summit of the Blue Ridge—looking over the picture that filled the soul of the chivalrous Spottswood and his knights of the Golden Horseshoe with awe, wonder and gladness,—hesitating for fear of failure, and retiring to his former place in the valley—as those spirited knights and bold Leader returned to their places in *Tidewater,* to exclaim "Too wonderful to describe, is that country beyond the mountains!" we who have never known any other place as home but the home our ancestors, located in some delightful spot out yonder in the Valley—find pleasure and profit in lingering on this summit of the celebrated Blue Ridge. From this summit can be seen the four grand boundaries of the county—the summit of this Ridge being the dividing line between old Orange and Fairfax, on the East side southward lining up to the summit, are Madison, Rappahannock, Fauquier and Loudoun; these four having been formed from the two first named;—Loudoun 1757, Madison, 1792, Fauquier, 1759, Rappahannock, 1831. Orange and Fairfax are mentioned as the counties from which the present neighboring counties were taken to make them join old Frederick along this summit. It must be remembered that Prince William and Spottsylvania had a claim to this boundary long before Orange and Fairfax, Madison and Green brings us to the old line between Augusta and Frederick; Loudoun resting on the Potomac, makes the North and East corner of Old Frederick in the vicinity of Harpers Ferry; the river thence westward for the North boundary, with the State of Maryland to the line of old Hampshire, about 40 miles distant; thence along mountain and stream to form the western line in the distance between Hampshire and Frederick. This chain of mountains, sometimes called Big North, Big Sandy, and other misapplied names. Big Timber Ridge being more properly the accepted name, as the divide of waterways that flow East and West—those on the West to Great Capon, and those on the East forming Back Creek flowing into the Potomac many miles away—while on this mountain boundary we find the *four Knobs,* between this point and Paddy Mountain are two coves, one noted for its walled mountains on every side, except the narrow entrance on the North, within which natural enclosure are hundreds of acres utilized by the owners for grazing purposes. The other cove further South is a complete fastness, and affords a home for sturdy hunters, many of whom will be mentioned in another chapter. The county line continuing South along another range of mountains called the Divide, extends to the old Augusta line. This water-shed sending its streams into Cedar Creek and North branch of the Shenandoah. On the West side, the waters find their way from the divide to Lost River.

Having thus given the grand outlines of the old county, we will now locate and describe some of the natural points within these lines, that can be seen from the Blue Ridge summit. Looking southward along this eastern line, the eye takes in a chain of mountains forming the western line of what is known as Page—or Luray valley, extending upwards of forty miles to a point called Swift Run Gap, thence southward, to the *Port Republic Battlefield,* where we find the Old Augusta line. Keeping now within this line, we have enough in the Page Valley to fill much space. The chain of mountains—has been known to some as the Fort Mountains—to others as the Massanuttin Range; locally it has several names. At its eastern base, flows the South River for about fifty miles. The Blue Ridge Range, forming the eastern line are mountains with many local names,—well known for rich deposits of mineral ores—some of which have been converted into iron by the prosperous smelting furnaces in that vicinity. This Valley is of rare beauty, with its fertile river bottoms—flowing streams, famous springs and clustered mountains. Following the western side of this valley,—the mountain range seems to have been thrown into great confusion at sometime in their history;—many groups of high mountains rising from the plain to bewilder beholders. This range of mountains abruptly terminates on the North bank of the Shenandoah where it flows eastward, soon to unite near Front Royal with South River. The Massanuttin and Fort mountains, mean all the mountains in the main valley lying southeast of the North Fork, where it flows down the valley East of Woodstock and Strasburg. Of course this chain has its local names, chief of which must be Massanuttin, as it is seen from every point in the Valley, rising in abrupt grandeur to an altitude of nearly two thousand feet at several points—breaking off to the right and left into strange and peculiar formations presenting a scene that tempts the imagination to fix a cause for this sudden ending of the great range. It may be that in some great upheaval of nature, the cluster of mountains was formed by the displacement of the regular range, and the ponderous masses torn from their original lines, were deposited in other places nearby, and thus the change covered a plain with new creations of nature—which have become one of the wonders of the Valley. We can easily fall in with this opinion, so often expressed by scientists, and sometimes by amateur geologists, who have at different times studied the formations of the entire Valley,—and given as their solution of such natural features and the soil strata of the Valley as it extends northward to the Potomac. The distinct lines are sharply drawn, as we follow the flow of the river and smaller streams—the general formation being Limestone. This limestone formation does not extend from the Shenandoah flowing along the base of the Blue Ridge to the mountain ranges to the West; but, as stated, this surface is broken by the distinct lines mentioned. Following the course northward from the Massanuttin cluster, we find a most singular slate formation; in some places, several miles wide, ending on either side of the *Opeckon Hills* with the limestone formations; the soil having but little natural fertility. This peculiar feature is found on both sides of the Opeckon Creek, where it flows northward into the Potomac, upwards of forty miles away. A study of this slate formation tempts the searchers to follow this up to the base of its abrupt ending of the mountains. There they discover that the base is of slate formation, while the mass of mountains, piled up in such confusion, are of the mountain sandstone and Granite formations, that compose the regular chain which so suddenly terminates at this point. So they have argued, that at some time,—may-be before our Centuries began their numbers—the mountain proper was swept from its base—possibly by a remnant of the great flood as its waters receded to the Ocean,—and as they swept forward,—the chain that once rested on the slate base was washed way,—leaving the almost barren slate bed to mark the place where the mountains once extended northward,—leaving Old Massanuttin a solitary sentinel to mark the spot where the floods, and upheavals of nature, changed the formations from what they must have been in the dim past—to what they have been for ages. This change caused a gate-way for waters of the Upper Valley to pass out and onward forever, under the brow of this broken mountain. While the grandeur of these mountains impress us, and we stand in admiration as we view their outlines—and the *Fort* of Nature's own making, and slake our thirst from sylvan streams threading their way through vale and dell,—perhaps we dwell too long on the beautiful picture as we beheld it from our perch on the Blue Mountains.

Looking off to the West, we see gleaming in the evening sunlight, many silver threads, as it were, appearing and disappearing among the hills and dales lying between our great boundaries, until with anxious rapture, we grow impatient to have an explanation, and with a strong field glass find they are the mountain streams coming on from their distant sources, to form the swirling river that rushes along at the base of this mountain. The music of its torrents, bursting over its rocky bed, is echoed far up in the mountain; and while the eye feasts upon the transcendent loveliness of the Valley stretching out far away in every direction, the ear feels the effect of the river's song as it rushes on forever; and so, impressed with both, lingers and soliloquizes, too long perhaps for the reader, who is enquiring about the sections of most interest to himself. Looking again westward and southward from the sources of those shining streams —Cedar Creek, coming from the Big Divide, at least thirty miles to its mouth,—Hawks Bill,—North River coming out of the Upper Valley from its source near Staunton, where South River has its source. Trout run is seen in the distance, as a silver thread only at one point, and then empties into upper Cedar Creek. Dry River, with its broken lines, only traceable by the dim outlines now and then, on its course to the river. Narrow Passage Creek is seen with a strong glass,—but no glass can reveal the lovely stream "Linville Creek" as it flows through *Edom Valley*,—hidden from view by a range of hills, running not far away from the Big North Mountain, West of New Market. Only a glimpse is seen of the beautiful valley bordering on this stream,—that will ever have a strange interest to the writer; for it was when charging with his Cavalry Battalion, the battle line of Stoneman's Cavalry,—that he, with several comrades, were thrown by the shock of battle headlong into this same stream, and there lay for several hours,—resulting in an injury felt now after a lapse of forty-five years. Deprived of a glimpse from this summit,—he must be content with the recollections. This digression was not intended—too much reverie!

In looking over those shining streams, the eye falls upon such a multitude of landscapes—that it is difficult to make any selection to touch with the pen, in order to give an idea of the natural topography of the outstretched valley. In the distance we take in the Big North and Capon Mountains, running in broken lines southward, to form the boundary line on the West;—passing through the big cove—under the shadow of Paddy Mountain along the meanderings of Cedar Creek, we pass through the lower rim of the Little Cove, out upon a mountain running southerly to and beyond the Augusta line. Tradition, as given from father to son, has it that Washington surveyed this boundary line, while in the employ of Lord Fairfax prior to 1755. The Acts of the House of Burgesses, enacted a law in 1752, directing a survey to be made "through," to the Augusta line, and define the same by suitable monuments, etc.,"—thus verifying the statement of the mountaineers that the line was run just prior to 1755. This shows their memory good as to dates. May it not be just as good as to who was the surveyor? In this region for miles in length, are to be found the most lofty mountains East of the Alleghany Range. Some of their summits have never been scaled, but in their sides and their base extensive iron workers have found it profitable to reduce the rich ores. Large tanneries have used up thousands of acres of fine chestnut oak bark found throughout the mountain region. No valley is found of any value between these mountains. Many places of abrupt ending and broken ranges, with independent high mountains,—seemed to have tumbled over and closed some of the valleys at many points; thus forming the Coves—affording good homes for the large game that has always abounded and is much hunted in these parts. Sportsmen recount wonderful stories of their experiences, not only of the chase for the game—but of other strange beings found in such mountain fastness. The mountaineer, in all the primitive style of dress and general living habits. These strange but necessary characters will receive fuller notice in the proper place; for they and their ancestors did their part in the great development of the old county.

While we endeavor to point out some of the mountains in this northwestern section of the county, as found within the boundary line referred to,—it is well to state that in the subdivision of Frederick, when Hampshire was formed, and from which Hardy was formed in 1786, Dunmore from Frederick in 1772, a grand corner was established. In more recent surveys by the County Surveyors of the four counties, when they fixed well defined monuments furnished by each county, planted them on the summit of the "highest point of the group, locally known as the *'Four Knobs.'*" This group is often called Capon Mountain, and we may add that residents mention it as at the head of the Big Cove, or Vance's Cove,—the name of a family now in this cove,—descendants of one Samuel Vance, who has left through family tradition, graphic accounts of the early days. The old settler along with others of his venturesome spirit knew of several Indian battles and massacres. From this group of high points, can be seen many other mountains—such as the "Three High Heads,"— Tea Mountain—and "Cupola Mountain" of rare grandeur. As already stated, their summits are but little troubled by lumbermen. Fairly good, rough wagon roads have made these places accessible, through the combined efforts of the furnace men, tannery and Lumbermen, the Iron furnaces, known as the Vanburen & Newman furnaces, are found in this rich ore belt, (idle at this time). Much of the brown Hematite ore is found, and one mountain, the Cupola—has been distinguished among this extensive group—as the "Manganese mountain," many predictions are made of what this mountain and ore belt will yield when the long expected occurs—the railroad that must come some day from the Coal Fields of West Virginia to this mountain country and thence to the Virginia Seaboard. The area comprised within the mountains referred to in the western part of Shenandoah County extending far up the valley is an agricultural belt, although broken by ridges and hills—having local names. This belt is noted for its extensive river plantations, studding the north branch of the Shenandoah on either side with splendid homes. Much wealth abounds, and the country is in a high state of cultivation.

CHAPTER VII

Topography of Old Frederick North of the Line Between Shenandoah and Frederick

The lower or northern portion of the old County, is void of the mountain grandeur found throughout the upper portion briefly treated in the last Chapter; and this being so evident from a glance at the territory towards the North, we deem it best to describe it briefly in a separate Chapter. The reader must not be deceived by the intimation given, that no landscape beauty presents itself as the undulating section rolling off to the Potomac is viewed from the same summit of the Blue Ridge; for while we miss the great range of mountains to the South, and northwest of this point, and the groups of lofty and unscaled tops of those gigantic sentinels—we still have sufficient mountain scenery along the western border, to attract the beholder. For in that steadfast, unbroken range of the Big North unbroken, in so far that no independent mountains appear along this range, the seeming impenetrable fastness is broken in several places by the waterways that drain the contiguous sections—these breaks, or *Gaps*, as they are commonly called, afford an outlet for nature that her gushing springs demand,—as their individual rivulets wind through hill and dale to mingle with similar outpourings, forming bold streams, to rush on through the defiles of that apparently impenetrable mass "THE Big North" it must be remembered is not a dividing line all along the western border, the line going South along its summit at a point just East of Capon Springs; then following the divide to the corner of the four counties mentioned in the last chapter. The line running South from the summit on the Big North follows this summit for several miles, then leaving it to run eastwardly over the High Knobs, crossing Paddy's Creek twice before it first touches Cedar Creek at a point one mile southwest from Star Tannery, then taking the boundary of western Shenandoah, going southwardly within the angle formed in The Cove, within which is found the "Half Moon Mountains," and Paddy's Range with its High peaks and corners, East of Capon Springs, the line falls away abruptly, crossing the head spring streams of Back Creek—to find the watershed along the summit of Big Timber Ridge for a few miles, to Little Timber Ridge, leaving it at a point near, Acorn Hill P. O., then in a straight line over Big and Little Sandy Ridges through to the old Berkley line (Morgan), on to the Potomac, the old northern boundary. Flowing along the western base of the Big North is Back Creek; and of a truth it is a *back creek* —hidden from view for miles—hemmed in on one side by the rock-ribbed mountain, on the other by hills of many names—the foot hills, as it were, of Big Timber Ridge. To see this mountain stream in all its natural attractions, one must follow its bed for about ten miles over the public highway leading from Capon Springs, by Rock Enon, out into Back Creek Valley, where the Northwestern Turnpike Crosses this creek eleven miles from Winchester. The public road, in following this creek until recent years, crossed and re-crossed it seventeen times in traveling this nine miles. Its clear water and rocky fords, gave the stream a peculiar interest to the many persons coming from crowded cities, seeking the celebrated mountain resorts found in this section. West of this creek and tributary to the same watershed, are Isaacs, Sleepy, and Brush Creeks. They flow through Timber Ridge—a queer formation in many places. Sandy soil seems to be the character of a large area between the North Mountain and the Capon Range,—suddenly running into blue and yellow slate formations, giving a surface soil for cultivation, far superior in many respects to other slate surfaces found in the eastern part of the county. Suddenly the blue and grey Limestone ridges crop out, with a soil similar to Limestone regions. Then, again, appears a red sandy loam—known as Red-lands,—distinguishing it from all other sections. Sturdy and prosperous people have for many years occupied and tilled this fertile section. Around and in full view of Red-lands, are groups of mountains off to the North and West, that have much local history. It was through this section that Braddock, Washington, Morgan and others marched, who were identified with the French and Indian Wars, and roadways made and cut —by the soldiers of their respective commands, have kept their individuality to this day. No modern engineer ever felt he could improve a plan mapped out by young Washington. Tradition gives many interesting incidents of those marchings, and road-makings, some of which are fully sustained by our old records.

Having followed the western boundary to the point where we joined Maryland, we follow the Potomac River to Harper's Ferry. From Harpers Ferry, we follow the summit of the Blue Ridge to the point where the two counties of Augusta and Frederick cut the Valley in twain. As their boundary line was established, the line from Harpers Ferry southward was the eastern line of all this territory. To the East of this line are the subdivisions of the older counties already mentioned.

We will now point and locate some of the most prominent natural features of the old County, seen plainly in some instances, and dimly in others, from the same point on the Blue Ridge; Kercheval, in his description of the surface of the old county—says, "That from two points on the Blue Ridge—the observer can see Harpers Ferry—all of the northern boundary, nearly all of the western and southern boundaries, and the chief features distinguishing one locality from the other, and thus have a good understanding of the geography of the country, without visiting the various sections, and that was proven by his personal visits to every section embraced within the boundaries." The writer has enjoyed the same experience. Some interesting features seen from the points referred to, are the *Gaps* in the Blue Ridge, as they are commonly called. The first to the South is known as Swift Run Gap. Other gaps appear, but of not much importance, until we reach the region of Chesters, Thoroughfare, and Ashby's Gaps in the vicinity of Front Royal. At these points, we find mountain roads leading over and beyond, to Rappahannock and Fauquier Counties. "Happy Creek" has found its way through the *Ashby's-Bent Pass,* and was once the scene of the bivouac of great armies—as well as fierce struggles at other times between contending factions. The remembrance of those incidents, forced the writer to conclude that its name should be changed; but a glimpse at the peaceful homes seen along its way, changed the impression; and doubtless it is best to let this stream retain its name for the distance it flows, on its happy way through this gorge in the mountains, to be swallowed in the river. The next Gap of importance is Berry's Ferry Gap, affording a road-way through the Blue Ridge to enter Fauquier County. On the summit of the pass, almost in touch is the "Big Poplar," the corner of the four counties—Loudoun and Fauquier on the East side, and Clarke and Warren on the West. This point is on a TABLE LAND stretching far to the North and South. Approaching from either side, the first impression made—is, that we are not at the summit of a mountain—but on the ridge of some elevated plain—for around on every side are farms, and the grazing lands for which this section is famous. But gradually impression changes—as we gaze around toward every point of the compass—the great Piedmont Country, stretching out to the East, the nearby eastern slopes revealing many villages—partly hidden by the broken hills of forest glens—yet we can locate Upperville, Paris, Middleburg, Leesburg, Aldie, and other well known towns: Looking to the West and North, we have a comprehensive view of the great Valley of Virginia. The effect of the altitude is soon felt. While not great, it is sufficient to give a commanding view embracing many counties, with their splendid population. Following the line of vision along this Ridge are the passes or gaps. Off to the North the first of importance is Snickers Ferry Gap, now commonly called Castleman's Ferry Gap—so named from the Ferry over the Shenandoah, 15½ miles from Winchester. The pass then leads on through many defiles, and over the mountain benches—until finally we emerge on to high and extended plains—the traveller has to be told that he has attained the summit of another point on this Ridge—five and a half miles of climbing from the Ferry. Here again he beholds the country on either side. Many changes appear along this route over the mountain. The demands of progress required the removal of the historic Ferryboat, and in its stead the river is crossed at this point on the modern Steel Bridge, erected in 1904-5. On the summit the U. S. Government has taken advantage of this conspicuous elevation, and erected during the last five years suitable buildings for the Weather Bureau's Signal Station. South from the road-way can be seen the Bluemont Hotel, of considerable attractions to guests in summer months. At the eastern base of the mountain where the road descends to Loudoun County, is the Village of Bluemont, (formerly Snickersville), terminal of the Washington and Ohio Railroad, (Old Loudoun and Hampshire). No other gaps appear to the North, of sufficient importance to notice here until we arrive at Harper's Ferry, the point of confluence of the two Rivers, one flowing from the West, draining the Allegany Ranges—the other from the South hugging the base of the Blue Ridge in its course, draining the Upper Valley. Both of these rivers in their approach to this confluence, as might be supposed, become rugged mountain rivers, coming as they do from opposite directions, gathering their forces from mountain and glen—draining a vast area. It might be supposed they would become deep, navigable streams at their exit from such a great valley. Not so, however. They grow broader and more turbulent as they approach each other for the final struggle for an outlet through the mountains. These approaches are over the rock-ribbed channels forming through the Centuries. The blue limestone formations of both the upper and lower stratas of this region offer impregnable barriers to navigation—especially is this true of the river coming from the South. In its approach to this Gap, the bed of the river at low water, reveals a picture of the under strata of this section wonderful to behold—ledges, tables, cones and piles of huge limestone formations projecting themselves through the splashing, surging, tumbling torrents, forming wonders of creation only to be found in the ending of the *Shenandoah.* While no attempt has ever been made to convert this river into a navigable stream to suit modern times, the author remembers distinctly—when the old *log rafts* found their way from the Upper Valley in times of high water, loaded with products of that section, to find the markets of Georgetown and Alexandria. Some day, however, the raft with all its cargo, would go to pieces by accidentally colliding with some submerged reef. The hopes of the owners were dashed to ruin; and the swirl of waters sometimes swallowed up members of the venturesome crew. These rivers, now familiarly known as the Potomac and Shenandoah, seem to have had many struggles in establishing their names. For many years the Potomac was known from this point westward as the Cohongoroota, as the continuation of the "Quiriough," alias "Powtowmack,"—to the Head Springs in the Alleghaney Mountains (see Colonial Statutes 1736), receiving in its flow through the mountains the waters of "Wappacomo," the Indian name of the South branch. The name was used in the Colonial statutes, long before Fairfax raised his contention with Maryland regarding the boundary of his Grant, Maryland holding that *Wappacomo,* was the *Cohongoroota;* Fairfax holding, as did the Colonial Government, that the Wappacomo was the South branch of the Cohongoroota (Potomac), River which extended nearly due West to its source in the mountains beyond Cumberland. This stream was sometimes designated the North branch of Potomack. Diligent search of old statutes,—and a full review of Reports made to the Colonial Assembly,—as well as those subsequently made up to 1832, establishes fully that the North Branch, so called, was and has become the Potomac proper; the name Cohongoruton and Cohongoruta often appears in this connection. During all these contentions, the river from Harper's Ferry running eastward, bore many names which, though queer, seem preferable to the Indian name Quiriough—and thus we have Pawtaw-mak, Pot-O-Make, Po-co-moke, Po-to-Moke, Pot-ow-moke,—and several others too numerous to mention. Why these odd names should be used by the Crown or the Colonial government to distinguish the historic stream we know not. All must have been happy when all contestants settled down to *Potomac,* as the name to dignify the far-famed river, on its way from mountain to Sea—gathering from its tributaries a force of waters sufficient to float many Navies,—and a water-way for commerce from Washington to the sea-board. The *"Sherando"* also had its share of names. For instance—Gerando-Gerundo, Shendo, Sherundo Shennandow—at last we find the euphonious *Shenandoah.* This Indian name, according to traditions, had its origin with the old Iroquois tribe when they held sway in the celebrated *Hunting Grounds.* A thrilling story is told of war between "Opeckenough" and the Iroquois chief "Gherundo." The former, in one of his annual forays for game, found a small band of warriors West of the mountains, who proved to be part of the Iroquois tribe. After the hunt was over, Opeckenough returned to his villages on the *Chickahominy* below Williamsburg, but left his son *Shee-Wa-a-Nee* and a band of warriors to watch the *hunting grounds.* It was not long until the main body of the Iroquois returned and gave battle, and Gherundo drove the chief East of the mountains. Opeckenough left the lowlands as soon as he was informed by *runners,* and within a few days he came with a large force and fell upon Gherundo in great fury; defeated and drove him from his *Sherando,* never to return from his home on the New York Lakes. Shee-Wa-a-nee was left again in charge; and from that day the *Shawnee* Tribe held the Sherando Valley until driven out by white settlers. The pioneers found the Shaw-a-nese tribe clinging to the Opeckenough name for the Creek that has become famous. The tragic ending of the old blind Chief in his "Lowlands" is matter for general history. Having traced the rivers from their sources to their confluence, we should give some special notice to their exit from the Shenandoah Valley. As the new stream the Potomac, magestically sweeps through this gap—made in the world's history by the pent up waters of the great Valley lying South and West; looking up from the river side to the jagged ends of the broken mountains, the head grows dizzy in the effort to take in the points of interest. Fully 1200 feet above this point on the river—looking to the North or South, are beheld many objects that have attracted thousands, as they were suddenly confronted with this grand creation of nature. Many points of view present themselves, —from which the sublimity of the scenery stands out so prominently; one or two are conspicuous above all others. From the Maryland side of the river a stupendous rock overhangs the Potomac, claimed to be a striking likeness of Washington. After much gazing, a semblance is formed by the gradual development of the nose, lips and chin, until an admirable picture is formed, which being hard to discover, is harder to efface from gaze or memory. While the statue is of large proportions and magestic in its location, it fixes an impression that you can see a mildness of feature, so familiar to all in every picture by the artist of the great man. The other point of special interest is *Jefferson's Rock* on a hill overhanging the river. From this rock one not only has a rapturous view of the grand scenery—but may gather scraps of unwritten history told by accommodating "habitants" of the Village nearby. The top of this rock, as seen by the author many years ago, is flat and about twelve or fourteen feet square. Its base which does not exceed five feet in width, rests upon the top of a larger rock, its height not quite six feet. The whole so well balanced, that slight effort with an ordinary lever, causes it to vibrate perceptibly. On this rock we are told there was another rock of smooth surface which attracted the attention of Mr. Jefferson when visiting this place, and it was on this rock where he inscribed his name—the writer had often heard of this incident in Mr. Jefferson's life, and of course was disappointed in not finding the name; and upon enquiry, was informed that the capstone referred to, that bore the inscription, had at one time been hauled from its place; and thus the name was gone. For an explanation of this, we were told that it was the act of some vandal,—an enemy of Jefferson, who hoped to destroy the name of a statesman that will never be forgotten while America has a history. The name of the vandal could not be obtained then,—but the story has been confirmed long since,—for in a study of the legislation of the new State prior to and embracing the period of 1800, we find that the General Assembly was called upon by some enthusiastic friend of Mr. Jefferson—to take some action to show that "Virginia resented an act of discourtesy shown one of her sons, offered by the unwarranted conduct of a Federal officer, by the name of Henry." It was then easy to find an explanation of the incident. In the political and exciting "presidential" campaign of 1798-9, between the Federal and Democratic parties, a Captain Henry, who was stationed at this place with a squadron of U. S. Troops, headed a band of his men, all being federalists, no doubt,—rolled off this capstone that contained the inscription; and thus put out of sight a name from his political standpoint that was detestable,—Jefferson's name will never be disassociated from this rock, and sight-seers still hunt for the name. The lone rock on the mountain side will ever bear his name—while the name of the "Henry," (who bore no trace of kin to the immortal Patrick) would be forgotten except for this vandal act. Mr. Jefferson so immortalized the scenery of this break in the mountains, affording passage for the Rivers, that we give a portion of his eloquent description, as seen by him from a point on the Blue Ridge overlooking the whole picture—Gap, Rivers and Valley. We are told, as he stood on this high point, he gave to the world his graphic reasons for such creations. Here is what he said: "The passage of the Potomac through the Blue Ridge, is perhaps, one of the most stupendous scenes in nature. You stand on a very high point of land. On your right comes the Shenandoah, having ranged along the foot of a mountain a hundred miles to seek a vent. On your left approaches the Potomac, in quest of a passage also; in the moment of their junction, they rush together against the mountain, rend it asunder, and pass off to the sea. The first glance of this scene hurries our senses into the opinion that this earth has been created in time, that the mountains were formed first; that the rivers began to flow afterwards; that in this particularly, they have been dammed up by the Blue Ridge of mountains, and have formed an ocean which filled the whole Valley; that, continuing to rise, they have at length broken over at this spot, and have torn the mountain down from its summit to its base. The piles of rock on each hand, particularly on the Shenandoah—the evident marks of their disrupture and avulsion from their beds by the most powerful agents of nature, corroborate the impression. But the finishing which nature has given to the picture, is of a very different character; it is a true contrast to the foreground; it is as placid and delightful as that is wild and tremendous; for the mountain being cloven asunder, she presents to your eye, through the clefts, a small catch of blue horizon, at an infinite distance in the country, inviting you, as it were. Here the eye ultimately composes itself; and that way, too, the road happens actually to lead. You cross the Potomac above the junction, pass along its side through the base of the mountain for three miles, its terrible precipices hanging in fragments over you, and within about twenty miles, reach Frederickstown, and the fine country round that. This scene is worth a voyage across the Atlantic; yet here, as in the neighborhood of the Natural Bridge, are people who have passed their lives within half dozen miles, and have never been to survey these monuments of a war between rivers and mountains, which has shaken the earth itself to its center."

The first impulse of the writer after reading and studying this comprehensive description given us by this great genius, who had studied works of Nature as well as arts and sciences, is to withdraw quietly from the scene, and leave the reader to dwell over the rapturous picture given us; but we are reminded that all this creation has had its practical side,—and as we make this effort in the direction of describing the natural creations, it is plainly our duty to see what man has accomplished; though he waited long, to take advantage of some of these natural features. And it was thirty years after Mr. Jefferson's visit, before the pass was used for the great highways of traffic now so familiar to the visitor: The Baltimore & Ohio Railroad and the Canal hard-by,—with the McAdamized turnpike threading its way over the bridge and along the base of the broken mountains struggling to maintain their rights—all crowded to supply the demand made by man to transport the products of a country where nature has been so lavish in her formations, and man so boastful of what he has done to open the store-houses of nature—and rush away the wonders of her bosom, as well also, to give the world an opportunity to partake of the products of a soil well tilled. This point will be more fully treated under the head of Railroads, Towns, etc. Proceeding from this point, to locate the northern boundary—we need only follow the course of the "Cohongoruta" westward, into the great mountains. The Valley lying between the Blue Ridge and the Great Mountains is cut in twain by this river; the section to the South being the Shenandoah Valley—that to the North, has been known for many years as the Cumberland Valley. The river for twenty-four miles—air line—performs some peculiar movements across the valley—hesitating, as it were, which course to pursue,—whether to lop off at many points sections for either valley;—plunging often to the North,—then South,—then East, making so many changes in its tortuous course, that the distance is about doubled, as it fixes the line between Virginia and Maryland. And, if one takes a position on the first mountain going West—he will have a view of the winding river that presents a picture of apparently several rivers, running in much confusion along the eccentric bends and turnings, are alluvial soils. The region at some points appears as a valley, and again, a hill country with its suggestive features, generally, however, the country on either side impresses the beholder with a wealth of agriculture. The river in many places is broad and beautiful, giving an idea that it is a navigable stream; and, as will be shown in this volume, was navigable, for experiment, once.

We find on its southern banks Shepherdstown, 12 miles above Harper's Ferry, which not only marks the point alluded to, but also the *old Mecklenburg crossing of the river by the first settlers.* West from this point, the river describes many forms and shapes in its course; passing Williamsport, we approach the mountain gorges and winding ways; reach later on, the elevations leading past Paw-Paw,—Greenspring,—Sir Johns Run,—crossing South Branch, and up to Cumberland—where the altitude is very perceptible. For the purpose of defining the northern boundary we need go no further West.

CHAPTER VIII

Natural Points of Interest of Old Frederick County

In treating the topography of this great section of the Lower Valley, the author may at times make some departure from his scheme; the intention being to keep separate the creations of nature from those of man; and having disposed of the natural features, then to take up the attractive development of this wonderful surface. We may at times find a blending of the two; but in this chapter we hope to avoid as much as possible any mention of the development other than to aid in distinguishing some locality, by mentioning the name of a town or other prominent feature.

The surface of this great section is broken by mountains, hills and bold streams. Of the former, the Big North along the western border, has already been mentioned as forming part of the western boundary. This mountain is in full view from so many points in the valley, that we naturally conclude it is entitled to its name. Its splendid proportions are not its chief attractions; for it affords inexhaustible supplies of lumber of many varieties; and has been the base of supply of the celebrated chestnut-oak bark, which has made several large tanneries famous for their superior products. In the early days it afforded shelter for large game—bear, panther, wolf and deer. Family traditions have been given the writer to study—the hope being he would in some way weave into his work many exploits of the forefathers, who not only reveled in the chase, but found much profit in gathering *pelts* from these animals, which, in the early days, was their stock-in-trade; as orders of court show that rewards were offered and liberal premiums paid for the destruction of such animals. The pelts found sale at good prices. The fur dealer in that day made frequent shipments of his *packs*. The courts, however, required the packs to be inspected. No explanation of this that the writer has ever seen, but in one instance. The Sheriff reported one *condemned pack,* he having discovered that "the pelts were overlaid with the brown Tobacco leaf," the pack was ordered to be sold at publick auction in front of the jail on the Publick Lotts!" The traditions mention combats with Indian hunters, who claimed the first right to use the *trails* and *crossings.* Generally these Indian hunters at that period were *peace* Indians. They never hesitated to claim their rights, and this resulted in many sharp fights. In other pages, some account of these hunters' battles may appear. The writer reluctantly omits giving them further mention here, as they abound with much to show the character of those early mountain settlers which would furnish names of many, whose descendants have become noticeable factors in the political history of the county. On the eastern slopes of the Big North, many famous springs are found; some noted for the strength and gush of the fountain, others for their medicinal qualities. Among the latter, is found the cluster of springs in the Cove section; and while in that section, coming down the eastern slope, we must mention *The Gravel Spring,* now owned by G. Wash Pifer, Esq. This spring is truly one of the gems of the mountain. Pembroke-Springs, still further North are susceptible improvements, which should give them prominence as a mountain resort. We pass on now to find the head streams of a famous creek known as Hogue Creek (pronounced Hog). In tracing the Pioneers to their settlements on the various streams, the origin of this name will be given. This is a real mountain stream, drawing its supplies from the East and West. Wolf Spring away up on the slopes of the North Mountain and numerous springs on the eastern slopes of Little North, all wend their way to form Hogue Creek, which, ere its ford is reached, where the Northwestern Turnpike crosses it, six miles West from Winchester, becomes very often a mountain torrent with destruction in its way, not only to fencing and growing crops, but it has swept away within the writer's recollection, human lives and teams of horses. Such disasters should encourage the authorities to erect bridges over this and Back Creek. Certainly Frederick County, with all her resources, should be able to pay for bridging the principal streams, since she has never been called upon to expend a dollar for this purpose in a hundred years.

Some of the springs on the eastern slope of the Little North are found within three and half miles of Winchester. Some flowing to the Potomac *via* Hogue Creek, and others sending their streams to the same river *via* Opecquon Creek.

Following the streams flowing to Hogue Creek from the point named, the course is now followed over the Northwestern Turnpike and through a gap in these Little North Mountain ranges, that from the earliest time in its history has been known as *Hoop-Petticoat Gap,* so dubbed by reason of the "lasses" of that section adopting the hoop skirt and making their hoops from the hickory poles found in that section. Some wag applied the name in jest, never dreaming of its duration. The hoop skirt became popular at a subsequent period, when not only the lasses of the Gap adopted the style, but all the social realm. The writer remembers the charms of this style, modernized by the crinoline skirt about 1850 and used for a considerable time thereafter. This Gap is entitled to its old name. Records speak of roads being opened to the Great Road leading through *Hoop-Petticoat Gap;* and deeds for land in that region describe boundaries etc., in this Gap. Hogue Creek flows generally in a northeasterly course, going through some good sections. The bottom lands are narrow and subject to overflow. Some productive farms are seen along its banks, principally in the vicinity of Pughtown. Near this point, the creek receives the waters of *Indian Hollow.* The country along Hogue Creek, where it empties into Back Creek, at a point three miles East of Pughtown, is hilly and broken; and in some places nature seemed inclined to make a mountain range to fringe its banks. Returning from the creek region to the mountain range, within four miles West of Winchester, we find what is locally known as Chambers Mountain, so called as being a section of mountain land granted to John Chambers by the Governor and Council. Chambersville post office is named for this man. The Gap passes along the abrupt ending of the mountain leaving off to the northeast nearby what was once the extension of this mountain, a conical-shaped mountain, called Round Hill. This spur rises majestically at the North end of the first valley seen as you emerge from the mountains over the *Great Road* leading from the Ohio to Winchester. The traveler, so accustomed to mountains of every form, height, grandeur and confusing ranges, over turbulent creeks and rivers, has the mountain scenery and pictures of nature so suddenly transformed by this other work of nature, that he is brought to a halt, impressed with this wonderful change. Back of him are the mountains, miles upon miles of them. At no moment in all the travel for days, whence so ever he came or whither he went, had he a glimpse of an open country. Now in full view, without an effort, he beholds the open country. Not even the lines of the Blue Ridge are seen from this point. No, nothing but table land lying under the eastern shadows of the Little North, (Chambers) fringed on the East by strips of woodland, with gently undulating ridges of limestone, just enough to draw distinctive features, forming a line between this and the great valley. Looking to the South, the eye rests upon a fringe of the mountain forests, extending along a slight eminence scarcely perceptible, but sufficient to shut off the view of the upper valley; while on the North, rising gradually from the road-way is old Round Hill, to shut off the northern view; and thus the vision is confined to this soothing scene of this first open country. The area is not great; only about two thousand acres of land can be seen from the first point of observation. Several homes of prosperous farmers are seen to the East and South. Directly in front are seen two brick churches, situated on either side of the Great Road leading to Winchester; the one off on the green hillock in a grove of forest trees, is the Presbyterian Church, with a small cemetery hard-by. Off to the North, and nestling under the shadows of Round Hill, is the M. E. Church, South. The country store and post office of Chambersville at the forks of the Roads are new features, and belong to the period known as "Since the War." Lying off to the South, in the midst of many acres of luxuriant meadow lands a half mile away, is a prominent homestead, a veritable *Colonial Home,* the domain of which extends from the horizon on the South, to the Northwestern Turnpike, from which the traveler is taking his view, *Old Retirement* is the name by which it has been known since 1782, when the writer's grand sire, Nathaniel Cartmell, took it as his allotment of the large Cartmell grant. Here several generations of this family first saw the light, the author being one of the second generation. Little North Mountain is a range of mountains, starting in its first distinctive formations, far up towards the southern boundary to be broken in twain by Cedar Creek, and again by a smaller stream, tributary to this creek, forming Fawsett's Gap, in early days Carr's, and later, as Longacre's Gap. From this gap no other break is made in this range for five miles. Passing Round Hill, the range is much broken leading northward. Now and then are spurs and ridges, the character so changed, that following its course, the mountain features are so blended with the hill country, that one would suppose that we have a lost mountain. Soon, however, as we approach the Potomac at a point above Martinsburg, we find this range again taking on strong mountain features. Here a high point is seen, distinguished now as North Mountain Depot, a station on the main line of the B. & O. R. R.

The country between the two mountains, may be styled the Hill Country, broken, as it is, for many miles. One never feels that it could be distinguished as a valley, though it is natural that those unacquainted with the country would conclude that it is. Very many prosperous farmers are found throughout this region, giving evidence that there is much fertility in the slate and mountain soil, when intelligent labor is bestowed. Though the section is not regarded as generally favorable to agriculture, the land not commanding the prices found in the section East of the Little North, much was done in former years for the development of some of the mineral resources found in the upper section, such as smelting furnaces. One feature of this section, worthy of notice is a cataract found near the *Old Furnace,* near the eastern base of the Big North Mountain, locally known as Mountain Falls. We find this beautiful cataract but little known to the outside world, though only about fourteen miles southwest from Winchester. *The Falls* as they are called, are formed by a beautiful little mountain stream, coming from a large spring near the summit. The stream grows very restless and bold, as it finds its way through a mountain gorge and through a glen between the mountain and Falling Ridge, running in a northerly course for more than a mile from the mountain spring, where it suddenly swings to the East for its first plunge over a solid mountain granite rock, about one hundred feet high. At this point it is about twenty feet wide; then a second plunge is made. The last water-fall shoots entirely free from the perpendicular wall of granite; more than one hundred feet in length is the granite bed of the stream, which falls away in slopes for a final plunge, thence it passes with gradual descent, and at once becomes a smooth and quiet stream, supplying Mr. R. M. Cooper's farm with abundance of water. The mist rising from the base of the fall and many other features, impress the beholder. Reader, go see this *Niagara in miniature!*

CHAPTER IX

The Lower Valley—Old Frederick in the Early Days

The observer should occupy points on the Blue Ridge in the morning, and on the Little North in the evening. The morning view being heightened by the early sunbeams rising over the Blue Mountains on which he stands, and watches their rays gradually seeking out and disclosing to view the many little valleys, hill tops and rolling surface, and marking the tiny rivulet and babbling brook, shining like silver threads. And, as the eye endeavors to follow their tracings,—the little lines often lost to sight as they wind their way along the base of some hill, showing that the surface of the placid picture is broken by ridge and dell. Though looking down upon the scene from the mountain point, the first impression is that the surface is smooth; but in watching the changing scene revealed by stronger rays of sunshine, the markings become distinct. The rivulets have found their way around the hills and through the vales, and enter the larger streams; and as they gather all their silver threads into the larger line, the sheen of waters is so increased, as to be dignified with names. Some of them have become historic for a thousand reasons. The most prominent of these water lines has now become so well defined by its flashing and rushing waters, that it deserves first mention. The Opecquon, as it is called at this writing, is so well defined in its tortuous course, that it can readily be traced to the Potomac; though sometimes the unpracticed eye confuses the many broad gleams of water, and the impression is given that several distinct streams are forming a confluence. Not so, however; it is the same distinct stream from head to flow. So many enquiries have been made of the writer as to the source of the Opecquon Creek, that it is well to give it at this point. And as the source has always been familiar to him, he may be pardoned for giving the location so plainly, that no question need arise hereafter to cast a doubt. The head springs forming this creek, are found at the base of the Little North Mountain, about four miles (air line) southwest from Winchester. Off in the vale below this base, are many springs within a radius of five hundred yards; and this cluster of springs was for many years regarded as the head springs, and were designated as the Cartmell and Glass Springs; thus called by reason of their grants of land lying on either side of the stream which embraced all these springs. The stream formed a line between their grants for a mile of its eastern course. These springs afforded such water power, that the stone mill, only a few hundred yards below (still standing), was erected by Mr. Glass. Following the early period, it was claimed that the large springs were on the side of the smaller stream coming from the mountain. To set at rest the point so often raised, it was found that other springs above were entitled to recognition. These were embraced in the grant also, and owned in the early days by same owners. They were for many years known as the Cartmell and Tavenner Springs, more recently the property of Levi G. Miller and John H. Cochran. But even above these springs, is found one other, and the only one. It is noted for its cold and delightful water, and is owned by the author.

The Opecquon from its source, for three miles flows due East, and continually receives the waters given out by the wealth of springs in its course; so that it becomes a formidable stream 'ere it passes from the limestone belt into the slate section at Bartonsville, six miles South of Winchester, where the Valley Turnpike crosses it on, or rather through, an old historic wooden bridge. The creek from this point runs through the slate belt, which extends from the Massanutten to the Potomac, and finds so many obstacles in the strongly-marked slate ridges and deep veins, that many changes occur in its course. Sometimes we trace it flowing South; then suddenly curving one of the ridges, it flows northward; then, as suddenly, due East; then northeast. By this time it has made the point where it was once marked by a large mill (Parkins), where the Front Royal Turnpike crosses, five miles from Winchester. From this point, it plunges boldly into a thickly wooded country, called the Pine Hills. The growth, generally stunted, here gives evidence of weaker soils than the alluvial limestone lands found along its first three miles. Its devious way through these hills is interesting to behold, so many difficulties are encountered in its apparent struggle to reach the Potomac. The writer has often wondered why this creek did not find an outlet to the

Shenandoah, which seemed to be the natural outlet for all this water; and how it should have turned from what seemed its natural course, to seek an outlet to the Potomac many miles away, breaking through those formidable slate ridges, was a mystery only to be explained by the demands of Nature. When we, however, find that this bold creek heads for the Potomac in a more northerly course, the problem is partly solved. Some such water-way was required to drain and water this peculiar slate section, otherwise it would have been a glaring waste, extending far through this rich Valley. Without it much of the Lower Valley would never have received its grandeur. Nature's formation of this great slate belt, separating these two limestone sections, must have been no accident. At any rate, the once barren slate belt has been transformed. Whether it will ever become as fertile as its limestone neighbors, is doubtful. But the transformation has ever offered attractions to those who have followed its course, seeming to prefer them to others on either side. This creek, where it starts on its northerly course, is crossed again by the Millwood Turnpike, six miles from Winchester. Later on, it is crossed by the Berryville Turnpike, at a point known as Spout Springs. This spring is on the eastern bank, where the traveler from Winchester to Berryville slakes his thirst, and watches the movements of the *hydraulic ram,* sending a goodly supply of cold water to the home of Mr. Daniel T. Wood on the West side, where his large flour mill is situated on Redbud. This stream, one of the three tributaries of the Opecquon, flows from the West. Abrams Creek and Ash Hollow Run, form their junction near this mill, emptying into the Opecquon just below this Spout Spring Ford and Redbud Run—a strong stream flowing from its head springs along the base of Applepie Ridge, and finding its way into the Opecquon below this ford. Redbud has become historical in the part she played when armies lined its banks awaiting the shock of battle.

The Opecquon for several miles from a point below the Parkins Mills, forms the boundary of Clarke County, and continues as such to the three Counties of Frederick, Clarke and Jefferson. From this Spout Spring Ford, the creek takes as its general course a northeast direction, picking up on its way the small streams coming from either side—those from the West being Lick Run, flowing through the grounds of the Jordan White Sulphur Springs; Littler's Run and Turkey Run flowing through Brucetown.

The Opecquon has here become quite a majestic little river; many places presenting rugged scenery, as she rushes through overhanging cliffs; then falling away into broad, placid basins, where her bosom grows broader, and presents the idea of miniature lakes; then, as if longing to get away and reach the Potomac, the swirls again appear, and a turbulent creek is seen forcing its way through many formidable slate ridges. The Old Charlestown Road, often called the old Baltimore Road, crosses this creek northeast from Winchester. In tracing the meanderings of this stream, the reader will observe that at none of the road-crossings mentioned, do we find the Opecquon at a distance exceeding six miles from Winchester. In its tortuous course, every point of the compass seems to woo its waters;—describing in these courses, a crescent around Winchester, from whence all of her great roads leading out in every direction, except due West, must, within six miles, cross this historic stream.

In tracing the Opecquon from source to flow, mention is made of Abrams Creek. This stream is entitled to fuller description, while treating of the waterways of the County. The creek, doubtless, is entitled to the name tradition has given it. One of the first settlers of this section was Abram Hollingsworth, who located himself at a large spring southeast from the original site of the Borough of Winchester, but some time before it was thus known. The spring has ever been known as Hollingsworth Spring; and at this writing, in part the property of the family of that name and the City of Winchester. Why this family should have preferred naming the stream Abram rather than the family name, might raise some question for speculation. This stream comes from springs West of the City of Winchester, the most notable being, of course, what is known as the Town Spring near the suburbs, and on the roadside of the Northwest Turnpike. From this spring, Winchester drew her water supply for more than a century. Still to the southwest, about a mile distant, is the cluster of springs on the properties now owned by James B. Russell and Jacob E. Baker, on the main course of the creek. Still further to the northwest are found three other springs, immediately on the *divide* of the watershed between Hogue Creek and Opecquon. The first is at the home of Dr. John S. Lupton, two miles from Winchester on the northwest side of the Turnpike; the others are near the eastern base of the Round Hill—one of them on the very summit of the divide, on the property owned for many years by the Hodgson family. From this spring can be seen the stream flowing westward to form Hogue Creek—all within three miles of the first cluster mentioned; and from that point on, it is known as Abrams Creek,—a stream noted for its splendid mill sites, where factories and mills were erected in the early part of the Nineteenth Century. The first was the large stone mill erected by Isaac Hollingsworth in 1827 near the Valley Turnpike, one mile South from the Courthouse. A short distance below on the East side of the Pike, was the Nathan Parkins Mill. Below this and in full view are three other mills—the first for many years the property of Jonathan Smith;—next the Kern's Mill; then the Swartz Mill, near the South side of the Front Royal Turnpike, now the William Brothers' Woolen Mill. Up to this point, the course of this stream was first southeast; then East; then due South for a short distance; then due East to the last named mill. At this point, it abruptly turns its course North for a quarter of a mile, where it meets the town run near the Abram Hollingsworth Spring, where David Hollingsworth for many years maintained a prosperous mill. In after years, about 1870, it became the property of Ober & Sons, who used it as a phosphate, or fertilizer, factory under the management of U. L. Dorsey. Then in 1884, it was used as a creamery or dairy plant for the manufacture of butter—E. R. Thatcher and John V. Tavenner proprietors. Falling into disuse in a few years, it became the property of the City of Winchester, to form a basis for additional water supply. Below this point, the stream flows northeast through a hill country. Other mills appear. The first was the property of James McCallister, but was abandoned many years ago. One other, just below, was also the property of the McCallister family, who gave it the name of Greenwood Mills.

The reader will see that Abrams Creek is entitled to distinction, as an important factor in the interests of Winchester, and for the country many miles around. It should be mentioned here, that the Winchester Paper Mill Company became the owners of the Jonathan Smith Mill property in 1874, erecting large and suitable buildings for the manufacture of strawboard paper. The enterprise was successful. It is now owned by the American Strawboard Company—known as the Trust. The plant is operated now to its fullest capacity. The subject of mills and factories will be treated under their own particular head and not continued here. The digression made in the case of Abrams Creek, was deemed necessary to give it some prominence, owing to its relation to the old county seat. Having pointed out the course of the Opecquon and some of its tributaries, further mention of the waterways of the country will be postponed for the present; and some of the highways that have been made as the country developed, will be treated in the next chapter.

CHAPTER X

Old County Roads and Turnpikes—Their Charters, &c.

The author has bestowed much time and labor in his endeavor to give some intelligent understanding of the important highways of the County, showing their markings in such way, that the reader may trace them to and from the many settlements; and even beyond the boundary lines, where such roads enter adjoining counties. Much of this matter was given in the chapter on the organization of the first courts, as the court orders related to the petitions presented to the court, asking for the right to open roads through the county; so some repetition may occur.

A careful description is given in Chapter I, of the important roadways opened by order of court for the first two years, the orders of court being copied in full.

Several roads from the Valley passed through gaps in the Blue Ridge over to Orange Courthouse, and other points East of the Blue Ridge; others from the settlements of the "Bullskin" and Cohongoroota, and from settlements on the Opecquon near Shepherdstown to the county seat, and then along Great Capon, and along Pattersons Creek, do not require mention here. As the settlements were made in many sections and population rapidly increased, a demand was made for roads at every monthly term; and the courts were very prompt in complying with the requests of the petitioners. Very soon the settlements had ways of intercourse, and also roads to attend monthly courts as litigants, jurors or witnesses.

In order that the reader may see briefly what progress the new settlers were making along this line, the author will give a list of many of the roads laid out in the county, embracing every section within its boundaries; giving names of many persons, and suggesting localities that, if he cares to do so, he may examine the old order books of the court for the first ten years, even before the town of Winchester was established by law in 1752,—and he will find much of interest in every order. But let him take warning, lest some important matter escape his attention. For be it known, that those old courts, through their clerk being more economical with the space in their books than with language employed to express their meaning, much is so closely written and interspersed with other minutes of the terms; and not being indexed, are only found after careful reading of every page. The writer has spent many hours and even days, to make it possible to place before the reader the following list. We take them in their order:

From the Courthouse to Morgan Morgans.
" the meeting house at the Gap of the Mountain above Hugh Paul's to Warm Spring.
" Courthouse to Littler's old place.
" Smith's to John Littler's.
" Parkin's Mill to Jones' Plantation.
" Sturman's Run to Johnson's Mill.
" John Milton's to John Sturman's.
" Cunningham's Chapel to the River.
" Hite's Mill to Chrisman's Spring. (Old Camp Meeting Ground).
" the County Road to the Chapel and to McCoy's Spring (McKay).
" Opecquon to the Courthouse.
" Cedar Creek to McCoy's Run.
" Spout Run to John Sturman's.
" Opecquon to Sherando River.
" Geddings' plantation to Littler's Mill, (later Wood's mill).
" Hite's mill to Nation's run.
" Mill Creek to Littler's old place. (Old Tavern stand).
" Ferry to the County Road.
" Stephen's Mill to McCoy's Chapel.
" Wm. Hughes plantation to Jeremiah Smith's.
" Simon Linder's to Old Lloyd.
" Branson's Mill to Gregory Ford.—(Shenandoah County).
" Cunningham's to Borden Springs.
" Capt. Rutherford's to Potomac.
" " " to John McCormick.
" Howel's Ford to the top of the ridge.
" David Lloyd's to top of Blue Ridge at Vestal Gap.
" lower part of Patterson's Creek to the wagon road.
" the mouth of Patterson's Creek to Jobe Pearsell's.
" Watkins Ferry to Falling Waters.
" Hite's Spring to Middle of Swamp in Smith Marsh.
" Gap on Little Mountain to Kersey's Ferry.
" Littler's old place to Opequon.
" stone bridge to Parker's on the North River of Cap Capon.

From Richard Sturman's to Cunningham's Chapel.
" the Courthouse to Ballinger's plantation.
" Funk's Mill to Cedar Creek.
" Funk's Mill to the Augusta line—(route of the Valley Turnpike).
" the town to Dr. Briscoe's (evidently Stephensburg).
" bridge near Lindsey's to Cunningham's Chapel.
" Stover's Mill to Gabriel Jones' plantation.
" Frederick Town to mouth of South Branch.
" Long Marsh to Vestal's Iron Works.
" Wm. Frosts' to John Frosts' Mill.
" Hoop Peticoat Gap to Hite Mill.
" Branson's Mill to Hite's Mill.
" Ross's Fence by the great road to Opequon.
" Johnson's house to road to Fairfax County.
" Caton's house to Jacob Hite's.
" Watkinson's Ferry to Vestal's Gap.
" John Ratchlies to John Fossetts.
" Stephens Mill to Mary Littler's.
" Chester's to Branson's Mill.
" North River to Great Capon.
" Cunningham's Chapel to Neill's Ford.
" Cedar Creek to Cross Roads at John Duckworth's.
" John McCormick to main road to town.
" On the river side from Long Marsh to Vestal's.
" Sleepy Creek to Widow Paul's.
" Morgan's Chapel to Opequon.
" Lloyd's crossing at the river to top of Ridge.
" Burwell's Mill to Fox Trap point.
" Kersey's to the Ferry Road of Sherando.
" river at Edge's Ford to Francis Carney.
" the head of the pond in Sherando to Wormley Quarter.
" bridge to head of great pond on Sherando.
" Sturman's Bridge to Burwell's Mill.
" Nation's Run to Capt. Hite's.
" Town to the Opecquon.
" head spring of Stribling's to Cunningham's Chapel.
" Mark Harman's Mill to Isaac Hollingsworth.

Many of the roads mentioned in the foregoing list are worthy of more extended notice than others; and referring to the first chapters of this work, will be seen sufficient description of the important Highways to readily locate their route, and also give the names of the landowners through which the proposed road passes. If any should desire to follow the description more fully; they would do well to select the names of the land owners and resort to the deed books of that period, for the deeds for the lands in the section;—and they will find satisfactory evidence to verify all statements briefly made as to the location, etc.

One of the roads mentioned in the foregoing list was destined to become famous;—but in the order of court receives the usual attention: no mention made for the necessity for the highway other than to afford communication between outlaying settlements and the county seat. The petitions simply ask for the cutting out and open a way "from Frederick Town the county seat, to the Mouth of the South Branch." This evidently was the first direct road opened from the county seat to the settlements beyond the great Mountains;—though on several occasions the settlers on the South Branch had petitioned the court for roads in their section. Same in the case of Great Capon and Patterson's Creek. Some came to court from those sections. Processes had been served on the inhabitants of all those "outlying settlements"—and the attendances at court show that they found some route to travel,—but no evidence given to locate the way of their coming. Those outlying settlements were not off-shoots from the Shenandoah Valley Settlements, but were independent settlements,—made by persons and families following the course of the Cohongoroota, seeking a valley no doubt which would equal the Shenandoah. And as they found the upper Potomac unpromising for settlement, owing to the rugged country along its course—they eagerly looked for some better country;—and in the Valley extending up the Great Capon and South Branch and Patterson's Creek they entered upon what they called the "Tomahawk" or "Squatters Right," and began to settle up those promising sections; and lived by their own community laws. They, however, were soon discovered;—and "hunters and trappers" gave glowing accounts of the new country and new people. They were within the jurisdiction of the Frederick County government; and we find them often at the county seat, asking for aid to build "Forts," open roads, and for appointment of Dep. Sheriffs, etc. This new roadway to those settlements is easily traced from the Courthouse in a northwest direction to the head of "Indian Creek" ("Indian Hollow") to "Hog Creek," then out to the "Sand Mountains"—along "any accessible Valley to the Gap in the great mountain," and beyond this to the mouth of Great Capon—No mention is made of any landowner after leaving Back Creek, until the route touches the entrance to Capon Valley. From the Courthouse to Back Creek, the names of land owners are given, so that the route is easily located. From Great Capon westward, no name appears. But mention is made of certain settlements through which the route is to take,—to end at the mouth of South Branch, where it passes through the lands of Garret, Reese and others, to where the road leaves the river ford (meaning the Potomac) going out to the southwest. Having thus briefly touched the general direction of this new road,—we may add that this direction was followed by those who opened the way for better communication between the lower valley and those sections West of the Great mountains. By reference to the minutes of the Courts subsequent to the first order made to open this road—we find within three years the report from the Commissioners shows the road opened, and allowances made in Tobacco to the Commissioners and other persons for their services. No landowner coming for damages. It appears this new road was of such use when opened, that its fame as an important highway was soon established. We find that George Washington was in Winchester 1753, on his way to the French Authorities along our western boundaries,—enquiring for a way to reach the vicinity of "Will's Creek," that would be more direct than the route North of the Cohongoroota. Fortunately the youthful Washington was much given to writing notes—not only of surveys he made—but of himself and the many incidents occurring on such expeditions he was then making. Throughout his eventful life, he was ever ready with his pen to note much that has become historically interesting. Washington's "Journal" fixes the date of his arrival in Winchester on the occasion of the incident mentioned; and from it the author will collect much to explain the object of his seeking. The Journal of the Governor's Council, and Acts of the old General Assembly of that period,—afford much more information on the necessity of this expedition. As mentioned in a former Chapter, the English Government claimed the country from the Atlantic to the Pacific;—and Virginia claimed within her boundaries the territory West of the Potomac; and Old Frederick claimed a large portion of the western country. The Journal of the Council shows that many persons asked for an incorporation of the "Ohio Company" authorizing them to locate on lands West of the Ohio. The petition was denied;—but a grant was secured from the Crown for the location of settlements on any lands between the Ohio and Mississippi River not to exceed 700,000 acres; as settlers were located, same to be reported to the General Council at Williamsburg, where proper record was made in what we to-day would call the Land Office. The "Statutes at Large" refer to these grants, and mention Acts of the Assembly creating laws for their government. Prior to this period, it was well known that the French from their seat of Colonial Government in Louisiana, were pushing up the Mississippi Valley, and making treaties with the notable Indian tribes, enabling them to fix strong outposts at St. Louis and along the Lake region. England began to resent these encroachments of the French; and empowered the Governor of Virginia (Dinwiddie) in 1752, to take the proper course through the Councils of the Virginia Colony, to notify the French settlers and commandants of their outposts if found, within her boundaries,—that England's claim had not been surrendered to any of the territory in question; and such settlers would be subjected to the laws of the Colony of Virginia; and that all armed forces must immediately withdraw, together with all Indian allies,—excepting such tribes as chose to make peace Treaty with the Governor and his Council,—subject to approval of his Majesty King of England, etc. So we find the General Assembly of Virginia diligently at work in the next session, considering plans to protect the frontier people. The fur traders filed complaints of depredations of the French and Indians on the Virginia settlement. The Assembly promptly authorized the Governor to send by proper persons, formal notice to the French outposts, of the Acts of the Assembly. The governor entrusted this important work to young George Washington, who held a commission as Major of Militia in the Virginia lines. To Major Washington's Journal, we are indebted for information of dates, etc. "We started from Williamsburg the last day of Oct., 1753, came to Alexandria and thence to Winchester where horses were supplied and baggage and other needs were packed." This was considered at that period the "outposts" of the Virginia villages. The Redman still held out for his rights in mountain regions to the West; and it was natural that the youthful Envoy should enquire of those who might know, the easiest and safest route leading from Winchester to Will's Creek Station, then a trappers fort or Lodge. We find the expedition fully made up at Winchester, and ready for their start on this hazardous work. This entry is made in the Journal;— "On Ye 17th day of Ye Month of Novemo,—the party consists of one guide and *packer,* one Indian interpeter, one French interpeter, and four *gentlemen."* Strange to say no mention in this entry in his Journal appears of the names of any of this party. Later on, before the completion of this expedition, he mentions frequently—"Gist, and "Van-braam" as the guide and French "interpeter," while he was at the French fort holding Council with the Commandant "M.de St. Pierre." This Mr. Gist was the guide certainly at the French fort, and on his return down the river to Venango after six days hardships, and further on to the Alleghany River, must have been the guide from start to finish. Who composed the expedition no mention is made. Tradition has it, that young Dan Morgan had just arrived in town from the western settlement on the South Branch—as a driver of a pack for the *fur men* offered his services to Washington as a guide, and was accepted,—and it was on this perilous journey that the future Generals saw in each other the traits that made strong ties between them when they encountered more perilous times. The author will postpone further mention of the expedition for succeeding Chapters. He only presents the aforesaid incidents, to show the wisdom of those who selected the route to the outlying settlements. Washington frequently mentioned certain points seen on his way to the mouth of the South Branch, and the easy crossings of the Sandy Mountains, and safe fords over the mountain streams. He was pleased to note in his Journal that "the skill of the engineer manifested itself along the entire route." He makes a note in his Journal while at Will's Creek Station, "that a goodly number of very sturdy settlers are building houses at this point, and that this should be encouraged by better protection in the erection of a fort with stockades; as Indian tribes were crossing this way from the 'Susqeuhannas' to the Hunting grounds on the upper waters, and in case they would attack the settlements without this protection they would have no means of escape, and must suffer massacres." Fort Cumberland was erected at this point within the following year, through the joint efforts of Maryland and Virginia. This road became useful in transporting supplies to the Militia who occupied this fort. The Companies being made up at Winchester, marched over this road, which later on was known as Braddock's Road, by reason of his army taking their line of march to meet the foe, and returning by the same road after their disaster on the Monongalia. This road was intersected by the Pack Horse Road, just before its entrance of the Gap leading to Great Capon, and known at this writing as Bloomery Gap, Pack Horse Road is still pointed out, and became what was afterwards called the Old Baltimore Road. The Old Braddock Road in time had its general course changed somewhat by the construction of the North Frederick Turnpike, which was Chartered in 1854, one of the principal changes being near Winchester, where the new route abandoned the "Indian Hollow Route to Hog Creek"—to afford facilities of access to the markets of the better and more thickly settled section. Thus we find historic Indian Hollow as sparsely settled at this writing, as it was one hundred and fifty years ago; and very few of the good dwellers of that section ever think of the stirring events that one time made the place more famous than any other section.

The author has given this roadway more prominence than can be given to many others. It seems appropriate, however, to mention another roadway—leading from the county seat to the southwestward. At the March term, 1745, an order was entered, appointing Samuel Glass, Nathaniel Cartmell, Vance Marks, Paul Froman and others "to lay out the best and nearest route to the County seat, and mark the way through the big timbers, said road to commence at Froman's Run on Cedar Creek, pass by the Cartmell Springs at the head of Opequon,—and thence to the County seat." At a subsequent term, the report from the Commissioners was confirmed. This report mentions a road being made "on the Trail from the head of Cedar Creek across the mountains to the heads of the South Branch;" and recommends that a juncture should be made between the two, the Court makes no minute but the simple order confirming the report. Whether this juncture was formed then is not known; but in after years the two sections were connected by these roads; and armies marched over them as they did over the road to the mouth of the South Branch. The fact is established by the language of the Commissioners in reports in both cases, that settlers at both ends of the South Branch were seeking a way through the mountains to the county seat of the old County about the same period. The old road established by the order 1745, leading from Winchester to the upper Cedar Creek Country, was for many years called the Cartmell Road. It never became a highway noted for its smooth surface; but had some renown for its long stretches through shady forests and over clear streams coming from the nearby mountain springs. In 1851 the Cedar Creek Turnpike Company was chartered, granting them the right to construct a turnpike from a point on the Valley Turnpike two miles South of Winchester, to Cedar Creek. Their engineers followed very closely the old route laid out in 1745,—thus showing that the early settlers possessed considerable knowledge for locating roads. This applies to hundreds of other roads, many of the best public roads travelled to-day are over the very routes laid out one hundred and fifty years ago. For instance, the roads leading from the center valley to the gaps in the Blue Ridge, can be traced over the exact old route for miles. As the population increased, there was demand for more roads; and as they became so numerous, —the author will group them, giving name of new road—and in some cases names of overseers.

of old roads. These references can be followed up easily by those who may look into the route taken from localities named, and may thus identify some that have peculiar interest. As will be seen in the grouping of these roads, the spirit of improvement prevailed to a great extent. The list shows the number of roads opened in the early part of the Eighteenth Century to have been very great; and then in the latter part of the same century, beginning with the period of the trying time of the Revolutionary War, and during the reconstruction period thereafter, the same spirit is seen. Beginning at the March term 1788, closing Oct. 1789—a little over eighteen months, about fifty new and difficult roads were opened and put in condition for travel, and no complaint of high taxes or burdens. This is in marked contrast with this period where we have not an average of two new roads in any year; and there seems to be more discussion, and effort made to keep the roads in repair, than the fathers spent in the Eighteenth Century to construct them in the first instance. They had no road plows, stone crushers, or any other road machinery. They had to hew their way through the virgin forests, make fords over difficult streams—sometimes erecting rude bridges. They knew nothing of the vast resources enjoyed by the succeeding generations. We will see later on that the fathers not only excelled in making roads to open communication with all the settlements, but they developed the country along other great lines. While studying the question of roads of the Eighteenth Century it may be well at this point to mention another class of roads made in the early part of the Nineteenth Century. Two great thoroughfares are shown in this class, both of which are replete with historic interest, both applying for charters about the same time, 1830-31; the one sweeping through the great valley with its McAdamized track,—forming a cemented bed, the limestone on either side throughout its entire length of one hundred miles, furnishing material for the concrete. This was called the Valley Turnpike. However, this road was shut off, as will be seen, and required to wait for several years. Its name has gone into every Hamlet in every State in this broad land. This was the way the Southrons came, when their army was organizing at Harper's Ferry in 1861. Battalions and army corps, marched and counter marched along this great highway, until its name became familiar in a million homes. This Turnpike was not authorized by law until March 24th, 1838, though the charter for its right to construct the road was in the batch of public improvements when the charter was granted the N. W. T. P. March 17, 1831; so we find this Charter slept for seven years in the dusty files of bills and petitions in the Secretary's office.

The long preamble accompanying the petition sent to the General Assembly recites, "that the proposed route for the Pike would take the general course of a great Stage Road running from Winchester via Staunton to the Tennessee Roads. This "Big Road," having been the travel way for a great many years for the wagon line of commerce from Baltimore to Knoxville and other points in Tennessee," previous to the Valley Turnpike period, this "Big Road" as it was generally called, had local names for its long stretches. The first, from Winchester, ended at Stover's or Funkstown (latterly Strasburg), crossing the Opecquon at Col. John Hite's plantation;—crossing Cedar Creek at Major Briscoe's lower ford, and the Shenando River at the ford to Funk's Mill, and was called the Briscoe Road. (Let the reader look for further explanation at old Court orders to find who the *tihtables* were along this road,—who were required to work four days during the year to keep up repairs. There he will find names of land owners who peopled this section and will also be able to follow the exact route.)

From the Stoverstown point, the old road was called the Funkstown and Branson's Mill Road, and the overseer for eleven miles was George Bowman, who held his important office for many years. From Woodstock the old roadway held to the high ground; and from the best information obtained on this point, old residents claim that the Pike followed the old route to Mt. Jackson. At this point, some material changes were made to gratify the owners of the celebrated river bottom land. Information on this point may be obtained by examination of the records of Shenandoah County. All the way to this river point, the roadway has held to the most fertile part of the Valley, bridging streams from the Opecquon—over Cedar Creek—winding its way along the river and over "Fisher's Hill," through the "Narrow Passage." The whole route affords interest to the traveler. Tourists from other States have enjoyed the traverse of this far-famed road since the war period; and at this writing no summer day passes that the Automobile is not seen on this Pike, whirling along—passing the front gate of the author's home.

The other great thoroughfare, is the highway leading from Winchester, northwesterly to the Ohio River. It secured a Charter March 19, 1831, after many years had been frittered away in efforts to defeat this measure. The first effort to secure a Charter was made in 1819, when a general law was enacted defining the limitations and restrictions of the proposed company. The plans were so unsatisfactory to the western counties, by reason of a failure to secure sufficient aid from the State, that the project was held up for several sessions; renewed in session of 1827; and not until the session of 1830-31, was the effort fought to a finish. Then the Charter was encumbered with certain provisions, not entirely satisfactory. Some interesting incidents relating to that period were revealed to the writer in his study of the House Journal of the General Assembly which granted the charter for these two great highways. The Western Virginia Counties through their state senators and delegates, had been making themselves heard on the subject of "Internal Improvements" for some years;—claiming that the section beyond the Valley counties was not receiving their share of the State revenues, in making public improvements; and for several sessions this subject occupied the closest attention of the *Tidewater Statesmen,*—lest they would lose some coveted prize—such as new roads, and bridges, and additional expenditures of money on canal projects, etc. Plans had been forming for several years, to have the state make a great road from the Potomac River through the Shenandoah Valley, to cross the headwaters of the James far South in the Valley. The burning issue between the parties in every campaign was "Internal Improvements," and this at the expense of the State. Statesmen sprang from every section, either to combat or favor this measure; and when the plans matured for the General Assembly to grant a Charter for the Valley Turnpike, it was found the improvement party was strong enough to carry it through—and when the matter was taken up, a new and unexpected feature presented itself. The western counties held the balance of power. They came to the Legislature pledged for internal improvements at the state's expense; and when their wily and astute Delegates announced their position, great consternation fell on all; and for a while the party of economists felt sure that all would fall through and the State treasury would escape depletion for another session. But the old politicians of Western Virginia took advantage of their opportunity, and agreed to carry the Valley Turnpike Charter through,—provided a public improvement be made from the Great Valley to some point on the Ohio River. The valley people could have their road to the headwaters of the James, but Western Virginia must have a road from the eastern counties, through the mountains to the Ohio. The whole session was alive with these tremendous questions; and when the western counties found they could control Legislation,—they secured all they asked for,—and even more. The committees in charge of these enterprises, reported only one of the bills—the one for the construction of the Northwestern Turnpike from Winchester westward to the Ohio. The overwhelming expenditures necessary to construct two such roads at the same time, and the promoters of the Northwestern Road knowing that frequent calls would be made on the State for money to conduct the work, adopted a scheme to secure this aid by holding up the Valley Turnpike for several sessions; during this time securing appropriations from the State—or rather using her credit to affect loans. We find the Road well on the way before the Valley Company was granted a charter,—and when their charter was granted March 3rd, 1834, and then amended March 24, 1838, the northwestern people secured an Act April 7th, 1838, providing for *the completion* of the Northwestern Turnpike to *Parkersburg.* So, as has been stated,—these great thoroughfares were struggling to appear before the public at the same time, though the Valley was held in check by what might be termed sharp practice. We find both roads in traveling conditions to their respective terminals at almost the same time. The magnitude of the undertaking to make a passable road from the Valley to the Ohio must have been appalling. The Acts of the Assembly Feb. 6th, 1834, authorizing the company to "borrow on credit of the Commonwealth from time to time such sums of money not exceeding the total of $86,000.00 was sufficient no doubt to keep the enterprise from lagging. We find again by an Act of the Assembly dated March 30, 1837, the company was again authorized to use the credit of the State for an additional sum of $50,000.00. An Act passed April 7th, 1838, placed the *unfinished* section of the Northwestern Turnpike under the direction of the Principal engineer; the whole road now being under the general control of the Board of Public Works,—through the President and Directors of the said road. Tolls were fixed by law for "Road travel and special rate for Bridge travel." The Bridge across the South Branch near Romney, was erected and put into service in 1837—and the Act of the Legislature April 7th, 1838, provides for the "rebuilding of the bridge which was *recently erected and destroyed;* and that the sum required therefor be paid from the tolls that may be received on said road." The Valley Turnpike Company was organized as a joint stock company. The State, through the Board of Public Works, to subscribe to three-fifths of the shares of stock,—and the private stockholders two-fifths of the stock, until the sum of $300,000.00 was subscribed;—which was to be divided into shares of $25.00 each; and when this sum was subscribed, the President and Board of Directors of said company were authorized to construct the road. Beginning at Winchester and to end at Staunton. Books for subscriptions were to be opened at Winchester, Woodstock, Harrisonburg and Staunton. Winchester was authorized to subscribe for 400 shares of the stock on behalf of the Corporation. The General Assembly by several Acts, designated the persons to receive subscriptions to the stock, and named the places where such stock could be taken for the two roads. It would be interesting to some, no doubt, if the names of all such were given here, but as they can be seen by referring to Acts of Assembly we will pass them by.

It must be understood stock was taken in the Northwestern Road, subscribed by individuals upon the faith and credit of the State to be redeemed by the State. This was done; and the great road became strictly a state road; and thus the western counties secured a prize well worth their shrewd legislation. The Northwestern Turnpike was, and is yet, a much traveled highway, for many years connecting Ohio and our own western counties with the country seat east of the great mountains.

The Board of Public Works long since relinquished control of that portion West of the Hampshire County line, and finally Feb. 26, 1884 released that part within Frederick County, and placed its management under the control of the Board of Supervisors of said County. The road is still maintained by moderate tolls. To appreciate the work of making a turnpike from Winchester to Parkersburg one should travel over its well graded bed,—follow its devious ways over the streams,—cross the mountains,—penetrate the *Glades* and great timber and coal belt, and witness the results of the engineer's skill, and, standing somewhere on the Alleghany Ranges, he will have some conception of the great work. The writer, in his day, has seen Emigrant trains pass out of sight into the mountain country over this old road, as they went seeking new homes beyond the Ohio; and also has seen droves and droves of cattle, horses and sheep, wending their way over this same road, seeking the eastern markets. All this traffic has ceased; for the railroad has diverted it their way. There are those of the long ago who still look for the bellowing herds and the Emigrant's old covered wagon. The whistle of the Locomotive denotes progress, —but the memory of those *"drovers"* soothes the spirit, akin to the feeling of him, who "drank from the old Oaken Bucket."

The General Assembly by an Act April 7, 1838, granted a charter for a turnpike to be constructed from Moorefield to the Northwestern Turnpike at Chas. Blue's in Hampshire County, by the name and style of "The North River and Moorefield Turnpike Company." This road was completed; and is maintained in good condition to this writing.

Another important Turnpike in the Valley is "The Martinsburg and Winchester Turnpike." A charter was granted this company March 24, 1838, "with all the rights, powers and privileges, and subject to all the restrictions and liabilities herein given to and imposed upon the Valley Turnpike Company," the state giving same aid as granted the Valley Turnpike Company. This road is too well known to need any description; it being a continuation of the Valley system. It is managed and controlled by its own President and Directors. The route is through one of the most highly cultivated sections of the Valley—gorgeous scenery to the right and left;—and the great Valley lying to the south gives the traveler full satisfaction in his effort to study the landscapes so well known to thousands, who once in the line of duty marched over this Pike; when the armies of the North and South frequently used this highway. It has been estimated that more than a million soldiers marched over this road within the space of three years—with attendant artillery and army trains; that fully one hundred thousand horses, wagons, etc., also traveled it. The close of the war found it in bad condition. The company, however, rallied to their work, and had the Pike pass through its reconstruction period, long before the U. S. Government allowed the county government to pass beyond that period in her affairs.

Three other Turnpike Companies were granted charters subsequent to those mentioned, to construct roads from Winchester to other places, to-wit: the Berryville and Winchester Turnpike Chartered first 1831, under the general law, and amended March 30, 1839. The Front Royal Turnpike was chartered March 27, 1848. Then the Millwood Turnpike. The North Frederick Turnpike chartered Feb. 24, 1851, along with the Hampshire and Morgan Turnpike Company. These are all useful highways, affording easy travel to the Courthouse and the Winchester markets. Mention has already been made of the North Frederick Turnpike. The State had an interest in this road; and Feb. 16, 1901, granted this to the Board of Supervisors. An Act of the General Assembly authorized the Board to use the surplus fund arising from tolls to purchase the private stock. This was done, and the Turnpike formally turned over to the Board of Supervisors for their management and control. Tolls are still collected for repairs.

Mountain House, Capon Springs

The Berryville road is in good condition, and repairs maintained from the tolls received. This road, although chartered for years, never commenced work on extension from Berryville to Winchester until 1846. (Acts of Assembly March 5, 1846).

The Front Royal Turnpike has had a struggle from its beginning. The first four miles out from Winchester was originally intended to be a "Plank Road." Contracts were made with Messrs. Louis and Joel Lupton to furnish from their saw mill, two inch boards twelve feet long—and sills to be laid on the newly graded road bed, this was all done and the new device for road making looked well; but when the teams and heavy loaded wagons started in to enjoy the smooth surface on some rainy and sleeting days, much disappointment came. The teams had no footing on the many hills;—and the wagons could not be held to the track. Some were gliding into each other, and some off the track altogether. Of course, the plank road held on for several years but very unsatisfactorily; the boards rotted and the foundation became dangerous—until the change was made back to the earth bed. Then a long struggle to attempt the "McAdam" plan. The war coming on to interrupt repairs, the road was virtually abandoned by the company; and Sept. 25, 1874, they sold their franchises to Edmund Purcell—a former contractor, who was a creditor. The new owner gave the road such repairs as to justify tolls being charged. He finally was prevailed upon by the patrons of the road to sell his interest to private individuals. This he did, with the understanding that a deed should be made to Albert Baker who, on the part of all concerned, would abandon the road and then the County would be required to keep up repairs. (See Acts of Assembly Feb. 28, 1898, authorizing the Company to sell all its franchises and corporate stock and that of the private stock. This deed was made June 10, 1898). At the Nov. term 1898, of the County Court orders directed the Road Boards of Shawnee and Opequon Districts to assume control of the road and put the same in proper repair. This plan has worked well and the road is in fair condition.

The Millwood Turnpike, running from Boyce Station on the Norfolk and Western R. R. due West from Millwood, crosses the Opecquon and follows the general route and direction of the old stage road through the Pine Hills. It intersects the Front Royal Turnpike one mile from Winchester, a distance of nine and one half miles.

Two other Turnpikes have had their day in the County: one being the Frederick and Hardy Grade,—or Moorefield and Winchester Turnpike (See Acts of Assembly March 8, 1846 and March 1847 amended Feb. 22nd, 1848 and March 15, 1849) Charter was granted to "construct a turnpike from Moorefield via Wardensville, to enter Frederick County at a point near Cold Spring, and to intersect the Northwestern Turnpike about five miles west from Winchester," the State was called upon for aid, which was given to the extent of three-fifths of the capital stock $33,000.00, and together with private subscriptions, the road was made ready for travel, and for a number of years it was used as the route to Capon Springs, a mountain resort attracting hundreds of faraway city people—who would take stage lines at Winchester over the new road, making the first halt at the popular hotel under the brow of the Big North, where the genial host Mr. James A. Russell, gave his guests such hearty welcome, that a few survivors to this day delight in recalling his entertaining anecdotes and traditions of his mountain country. "Pembroke Springs" also is on this route. A new hotel, kept by Dr. William Keffer, and "Cold Springs," were other places where the travelers could be refreshed. Just above Cold Spring, a mountain road led off from the Pike to take stages over the Big North and down into the cove on the West side, where the Capon Springs "Mountain House" suddenly loomed up before the smoking teams, announcing their sudden approach by blasts from the stage horns. The writer recalls many such scenes; but those that impressed him most as a boy, was the passing of those stage lines along the Northwestern Turnpike, in full view of his old home near the Round Hill. Here he often saw four stages, each drawn by four fine horses—(two competitive lines)—sweeping into the Hoop Peticoat Gap, where they soon entered the new graded road for Capon. Stages full of passengers—many on the outside with the driver to better enable them to enjoy the lovely landscape;—stage horns blowing, whips cracking, in the hands of good lusty fellows; horses all aglow with excitement and foam, gave a charm to the rapidly passing picture repeated every day through the "Spring's season."

Another Turnpike is worthy of mention: The Cedar Creek and Opequon Turnpike, chartered March 24, 1851, which provided that the cost of construction was not to exceed four hundred dollars per mile, starting from Cedar Creek at a point commonly called the Old Forge, following the route or road bed previously mentioned as the Cartmell Road, to the head of the Opecquon. There quite a change was made; leaving the old road bed to the North, but soon running parallel with it for a mile; then in a more direct line to a point on the Valley Turnpike (Hillman's Tollgate)—distance being twelve miles. Running as it did through limestone ridges, the grade was difficult and expensive to construct; the Company was unable to adopt the plan fully, and succeeded partly in paving the road. The company had an expensive road to maintain; and after keeping up repairs from tolls and no surplus to pay the stockholders,—the road was abandoned in 1873; when the County court appointed overseers, and the road was maintained at the expense of the County. From that time to present writing,—the road is in better condition now, than at any time in its existence.

The Welltown Turnpike fills a long needed want of the fine sections through which it passes, from the village of Welltown North from Winchester to its intersection with the Winchester and Martinsburg Turnpike. This Pike is maintained by moderate tolls, under the management of the Winchester and Martinsburg Turnpike Company.

Another road, though not a chartered one, is known as the Apple Pie Ridge Road. This has been a noted thoroughfare for many years; and is becoming more prominent among the roads of the County by reason of the great fruit belt through which it passes, from its intersection with the North Frederick Turnpike two miles from Winchester, to connect with the Berkeley County roads. This old road is always expected to furnish its usual number of snow blockades in winter. It was opened by an order of court about the middle of the Eighteenth Century, and called the Ridge Road—"to lead from the Braddock Road into the Quaker settlement to the Northward." The road is kept in good repair by the District Road Board. Another old County road not chartered is the Middle Road,—and might be termed a ridge road, for it follows partly the extension of the Apple Pie Ridge southward from Winchester, leaving the Valley Turnpike near Hillman's Tollgate; running thence about southwest along this ridge for a number of miles, to ultimately terminate at Old Forge. As its name denotes, it runs about midway between the Valley and Cedar Creek Turnpike, for about eight miles: then it and the Cedar Creek Road gradually converge to the same terminal—Old Forge. This road is much traveled by the many prosperous farmers living in the rich section through which it passes.

The foregoing sketches of the turnpikes and other public roads, embrace such roads chartered and opened subsequent to the subdivision of the old County. It must be remembered at this period the other counties, once part of Frederick, were busy with their improvements, and had up to that time accomplished such wonders of development, that the author deems it best not to embrace their roads and Turnpikes in this Chapter.

The demand for Turnpikes in this territory comprising old Frederick was astonishing. When the great movement was started by the Valley, and Northwestern Turnpikes, this spirit caught hold upon all of these subdivisions;—and soon they were clamoring for Pikes, for Hampshire, Berkeley, Jefferson, and Shenandoah Counties. And in a study of the Acts of the General Assembly for years after, the various sections found the State was giving aid to such enterprises. Every session was deluged with petitions for charters for turnpikes; and it looked at one time, the state would become bankrupt unless this flood were cut off. We find that the old State was tossing on such billows that no party was strong enough to rescue her from financial ruin. Millions of dollars of a bonded debt, piling up year after year;—so that nothing but the war period could call a halt. Many who may read these sketches will recall the "Readjuster history" of this great bonded debt; and how many innocent holders of such bonds felt the shrinkage of their value. To give some idea how eagerly all sections were dipping into the Public Crib, we will mention the charters granted to the territory of Old Frederick at the session when the last Turnpike was chartered, to-wit: the short session of 1851, when the following Turnpike Companies received charters. Their names will enable the reader to locate them, and be able to identify them with our Counties:

New Market and Sperryville Turnpike Company.
Luray and Front Royal " "
Cross Roads and Summit Point " "
Jefferson and Frederick " "
North Frederick " "
Morgan and Frederick " "
Cedar Creek and Opequon " "
Hampshire and Morgan " "
North River " "
Potomac " "
Berkeley and Hampshire " "
Hedgesville and Potomac " "
Harpers Ferry and Hillsboro " "

All of these in one session, besides many appropriations made to aid the weak companies who held older charters, and had suspended work for lack of funds to complete their roads.

CHAPTER XI

Railroads, Charters, Locations, Etc.

The last chapter having disposed of the sketches and location of old county roads and turnpikes, the author deems it best to treat the subject of the other great highways in this chapter.

The old county was well abreast of the times with the railroad and its early history. One of the first railroads to make successful an effort to make it possible for the new idea to prevail and attract capitalists, to bring the products of the interior country to the seaboard, was the Baltimore and Ohio. In its infancy, it saw the great possibilities of connecting the western country with the eastern, and that with an interchange of products, a great commercial era would be created. So we find the new company of capitalists feeling their way towards the Ohio, before the smoke had cleared away from the first trial locomotive near Baltimore. There seemed to be no way to the Ohio but through Virginia. We find in the early history of the B. & O., many plans were proposed; and as success crowned the undertaking on the first section near Baltimore, the people of that enterprising city became enthused, and pressed for an extension, of their line; little dreaming of the success which ultimately crowned their efforts and made it possible for their little city to rise in grandeur and become the great commercial city of to-day. The projectors of the extension, favored striking Virginia at some point West of the Blue Ridge, then taking as direct a route as possible through the mountains, to some point on the Ohio River, near the mouth of the Kanawha River. The engineers never gave encouragement to this route, but favored one entirely through the State of Maryland to Wheeling on the Ohio. Then came the first dissension; and for several years progress was delayed. Finally a compromise was made, and the route chosen to enter Virginia at Harpers Ferry, from that point to take the most accessible way to Wheeling. For present purposes it may be added, this plan was adopted; and charters secured from Maryland and Virginia for the route to be located. So we find the northern boundary of the Old County was taken, through Jefferson, Berkley, Morgan and Hampshire Counties leaving the last named at Greenspring to enter Maryland, and again entering Virginia between Cumberland and Keyser; and thence through Virginia to the Ohio at Wheeling. After years developed the fact, that those who once favored a route to some lower point on the Ohio, were wise in their view; for the well known route to Parkersburg, made later on by the B. & O., proves the wisdom of the Company in adopting the original suggestions. In the General Assembly of Virginia, Session 1826-7, we find the first mention of the Baltimore & Ohio Railroad. The caption of the Act is here given, to establish the date of the charter granted by Maryland: "An Act to confirm a law, passed at the present session of the General Assembly of Maryland, entitled, "An Act to incorporate the Baltimore and Ohio Railroad Company." Following is the Virginia Act—passed March 8th, 1827—Preamble: "Whereas, An Act has passed the Legislature of Maryland, entitled an Act to incorporate the Baltimore & Ohio Railroad Company, in the following words and figures, viz.:"

The Act then proceeds to give the full text of the Act passed by the Maryland Legislature, much of which would interest the reader, but our space forbids its entry here. The second section of the Act employs this language—That "the Capital Stock of the said Baltimore and Ohio Railroad Company, shall be Three Millions of Dollars in shares of One Hundred Dollars each, of which ten thousand shares shall be reserved for subscription by the State of Maryland and five thousand for the City of Baltimore." The twenty-second section reads thus: "That if this road shall not be completed in two years from the passage of this Act, and shall not be finished within this State in ten years from the time of the commencement thereof, then this Act shall be null and void."

The Virginia Act is embraced in one section, and in part reads thus: "Therefore, be it enacted by the General Assembly. That the same rights and privileges shall be and are hereafter granted to the aforesaid Company within the territory of Virginia, as are granted to them within the territory of Maryland. The said Company shall be subject to the same penalties and obligations imposed by said Act, and the same rights, privileges, and immunities which are reserved to the State of Maryland or to the citizens thereof, are hereby reserved for the State of Virginia, and her citizens. That the said road shall not strike the Ohio at a point lower than the mouth of the Little Kanawha on said river."

The work on this road was soon under way, after the charters were granted; engineers making surveys. The Company adopted some and rejected others—contractors submitting bids for work, etc.

Harpers Ferry was soon chosen as a point to cross the Potomac River; where work was begun to span the river with a bridge. The route westward from this point followed very nearly along the northern boundary of the Old County.

The General Assembly of Virginia, session 1831, was confronted with a peculiar situation regarding the new idea,—*The making of railroads.* There seemed to be much rivalry between the Valley people; for we find that an Act was passed the 22nd of March, 1831, to "Incorporate the Staunton and Potomac Railroad Company." The provisions indicate that the object was to make Staunton and Martinsburg the terminals. Strong men were named in the Act, representing Staunton, Harrisonburg, Woodstock, Winchester, Charlestown and Martinsburg, to receive subscriptions to "the Capital Stock of One and one half Million Dollars." Whether this Act suggested the movement for a railroad from Winchester to Harpers Ferry is not shown. At the same session, by Act passed April 8th, 1831, a charter was granted to the *Winchester and Potomac Railroad Company.* The projectors of this railroad, seemed to have faith in their ability to secure the capital for the enterprise. The Act named John R. Cooke, Alfred H. Powell, Alexander S. Tidball, John Gilkeson, Henry W. Baker, M. B. Cartmell, Joseph H. Sherrard, Henry M. Brent, John Brome and John Heiskill, for the purpose of receiving subscriptions to the amount of "Three Hundred Thousand Dollars in twelve thousand shares of 25 Dollars each, to constitute a joint Capital Stock, for the purpose of making a railroad from the town of Winchester to some convenient point on the Potomac River, at or near Harpers Ferry." The first of these two Acts which provided a plan for subscription to the first railroads in the Valley proper, was slow of movement, and failed to materialize, while the second Act, was eagerly accepted by the promoters of the W. & P. R. R., and subscriptions were rapidly made; and all the initial steps taken to secure the right to make the road, etc. They were before every session of the General Assembly for years—March 1832—January, 1833, and February, 1834. This is the preamble of the Act passed Feb. 6, 1834: "Whereas, it is represented to the General Assembly of Virginia, that the President and Directors of the Winchester and Potomac Railroad Company have placed under contract nearly the entire line of the road, from Winchester to the Potomac, upon terms highly advantageous to the Company, to the community at large, and to our State, the latter holding an interest of two-fifths of the stock; that the work is now rapidly and actively prosecuted; that the installments due from private stockholders have been promptly paid, and that owing to the vigor with which the work has been conducted, the number of laborers employed, and the consequent heavy demands upon the Company, the funds of the private stockholders are nearly exhausted." This shows the promptness of the promoters of this road to press their progress to completion. The State at this session, under same Act, made it the duty of the Board of Public Works to proceed at once to take steps to furnish the State's quota of her installment, and thus enable the Company to continue their work without embarrassment. The Stockholders must have been remarkable in their faith in the enterprise, and their compliance with the terms of their subscription; for it will be seen by the statement made in the preamble, that they paid their installments promptly. The writer has in his hands the original list of the stockholders, and the amount of stock subscribed; and it has been an interesting study. The list comprises the names of many of the leading citizens of that day, prominent actors in the drama of life during that period, representing every class of business. To-day many of those names are not to be found in the population of this section; their places of business long since closed; while others appear in the business affairs of the county; and not a few of their descendants have been prominently before the public as politicians, lawyers, merchants, farmers and tradesmen, some of whom in the same family names have enjoyed the advantages of this railroad from its completion to the present time. Wonderful revolutions have occurred in railroad-making, since the arrival of the first railroad car in Winchester. The Writer has before him, the reports of the President and Directors of this Company, one dated Aug. 1st, 1835, signed by John Bruce, President, setting forth fully how the rail track was made—differing entirely from the *cross tie* and *steel rail* of to-day. The President congratulates the stockholders and the county at large upon the great improvement nearing completion; mentions several reasons for delay at the Harpers Ferry terminal; says the Company was hindered by the general government not acting promptly, to grant the right of way through the public property at Harpers Ferry, increased the difficulties, always considerable, of carrying the work over the only rugged path, through that village, left by nature for the passage of such an improvement." The report says: "A very small portion of the gradation yet remains unfinished at Harpers Ferry." There was some trouble to form a junction with the Baltimore and Ohio Road. The two Companies finally agreed to jointly construct a viaduct, to transmit the trade of the two improvements. It appears, however, that the B. & O. constructed the viaduct and provided accommodations for the expected business. Mr. Bruce in his report says: "We have derived much good counsel and encouragement in many ways from this enterprising Baltimore Company." He further says: "Nearly two-thirds of the railway have been laid—and materials are gradually deposited and in a state of rapid preparation along the remaining portion of the line." This was given in the report dated Aug. 1st, 1835, yet the Author in seeking some incident of the opening of the line into Winchester, has been told by several old men that they remembered when the first train came into the Winchester Station in the Spring of 1835. Such statements have made him very chary in accepting tradition as his authority in the preparation of this work, that there was no station at Winchester at that date. The President says: "A large and substantial depot in the vicinity of Winchester is in progress, and will be ready in time to accommodate the trade of the Company and provision has been made for the construction of burthen cars, as well as those for passengers." The report fixes another matter of interest in the history of the two Railroads, and is of sufficient importance to justify this transcript: "Already have our farmers and merchants enjoyed a foretaste of the advantages to be justly expected from the improvement in which we are engaged, since the opening of the Baltimore and Ohio Railroad to Harpers Ferry in December last (1834)." This event stimulated the Winchester Company, as it was generally called during that period; and we find the B. & O. anxious to assist the *Valley Branch* of the system in many ways, her engineers affording the necessary aid in locating the terminal for intersection of the main line. The arrival of the Baltimore road at Harpers Ferry made that the shipping point of the Lower Valley. The report referred to, mentions this as the chief reason for an early completion, so that the Winchester and Potomac could make Winchester the shipping point; and estimates the traffic by the wagon trains to be immense—that these trains will seek the nearest shipping point of the Railroad, that shippers have learned of the lessened expense; and another great feature to be considered is the passenger traffic. That since Harpers Ferry has become the station on the Baltimore road, two daily lines of stages were required to accommodate the traffic from that point to Winchester—all of which was so enlivening to the communities along their way, that the stockholders should take much comfort in the prospect of their road securing this from its first opening. Winchester being the shipping point, commanded control of trade in a far reaching sense. The hundreds of tented wagons, coming from Southwest Virginia and Tennessee, were glad to make Winchester their discharging and receiving depot. This required additional accommodation—warehouses had to be built to care for the wares changing transportation; wagon yards and tavern stands were to be found in various places in town, offering inducements to the incoming wagon trains—the Valley Turnpike and Northwestern Road were pressing every point to attract the wagon trains over their highway when completed; so that Winchester between 1830 and 1840 had much promise from the three great highways struggling through that period to make her their terminal. All three of these highways became important factors in the development of the Country for miles around. Business men in Winchester became prominent, and grew prosperous. The agricultural interests were stimulated and products from the splendid farms found a cheaper way to reach the distant markets. For many years the railroad used the primitive *burthen* cars—and passenger coaches drawn by a locomotive that, at this writing would be a curiosity to attract attention, as it was to those who first beheld the iron horse puffing and snorting into the old station over the old flat rails, more than three score years ago. As time wore on, the old engine was laid aside with the old *burthen* and queer-looking passenger cars, and the "T" rail substituted for the old flat rail, that so often sprang from its bed and penetrated the floor of the coach, much to the discomfort and safety of the passengers, as well as to the inconvenience of the conductor and his crew. The new style of rail, secured to cross ties, with the improved car wheel under better and larger cars, brought a great change in the road both for speed and comfort. A day came, however, when still greater changes occurred. In the early sixties, the writer saw hundreds of these rails taken from both the B. & O. and W. & P. Roads, together with several of the locomotives, and hauled away with great teams to the southward, this was considered a *war measure*. The Confederate government needed such sinews of war, to be used on other railroads for transportation of government supplies; and if the Union armies needed these broken places to be repaired, the U. S. Government had unlimited resources to draw from. Some of this war measure business proved to be a serious inconvenience to this section for several years after the war closed; for the gap or break extended from Winchester to Stephenson's Station, five miles North of Winchester. Stages and wagons filled this gap; and traffic soon started in this way. The rebuilding of this road in every respect was a burden on the Company; but the day came when the road was in working order, and new life given the old Company. Steel rails found their way to supplant the iron; but we regret to say that at this writing, very little improvement in the car service. The B. & O. Company leased the road after the war, rebuilt what was necessary, and continued to run the line as the Valley Branch of the main line. In recent years the B. & O. Company purchased the stock and became the real owners, but have not changed the name. It is needless to add, the dividends now are very satisfactory to the new stockholders. The B. & O. abandoned the old passenger station, and erected the one now in use, corner of Piccadilly and Kent Streets, which is an attractive building well supplied with modern improvements and more accessible than the old. The B. & O. Road being on the border line of the contending sections North and South, suffered heavily during the war by frequent raids from the Confederate side; the object being to tear up the track, destroy the rails and cross ties, and thus delay the transportation of armies to different points; cut off supplies, and if any train could be captured, carry needed supplies back to the main army. The writer witnessed several of these dangerous exploits. The line was struck at some point generally West of Greenspring and Cumberland Stations; the rails were rapidly torn up; cross ties piled in heaps, and great fires made. On these, the rails were thrown and soon mis-shapen and useless iron rails were tumbling around. Then the troopers would jump into their saddles again, and move rapidly to another point and await the arrival of the long freights, so rich with the things the soldiers needed; and in the rear of this train at a safe point, more track would be torn up, and the raiders waited for the big freight to hurry back from the scene the *Rebels* had so lately made for them. On their backward movement, they would run into the break last made, and while the train men were in confusion, the cavalry boys dashed up with yells and pistol firing that demoralized the B. & O. crew. But these dashing cavalrymen sometimes caught a surprise, by picking up a Government train heavily guarded; and sometimes they would make some show of resistance; and skirmishing would ensue that made it best for the raiders to go elsewhere. Sometimes the Confederate leader was a man of more valor than prudence, and occasionally one of these dashing fellows would get the stray bullet; and this marred the pleasure of the raiders. These raids changed the plans of several great battles. Reinforcements were delayed, and a new order of battle planned. This will be mentioned again in the war periods of Old Frederick. The B. & O. was equal to the emergency, and with the aid of the Government soon got their road bed in shape, but too late to deliver reinforcements and supplies on time. This road was a great loser in one sense by the war, but she was also a great gainer. It was in constant use, the Government paying millions for the transfer of shifting armies from East to West. Oftener, however, from West to East, to recruit the great army of the Potomac. When the war closed, the B. & O. had a worn-out track; but she was fortunate enough to have the U. S. Government to re-imburse her for her war claim for damages; and thus with these millions she soon put her splendid highway in such condition, that it is now the popular route from the East to the West and vice versa.

Manassas Gap Railroad

This Railroad incorporated by an Act of the General Assembly, March 9th, 1850, amended by Act of Feb. 10, 1851, while not originating in old Frederick County, soon becomes of special interest to two of the subdivisions of the Old County. Starting from Alexandria, passing through Fairfax, Prince William and Fauquier Counties, on through Manasses Gap in the Blue Ridge into Warren County, in the vicinity of Front Royal; thence through Warren County, crossing the Shenandoah at Riverton, running near the boundary line between Warren and Frederick, crossing the North fork of the Shenandoah below Strasburg—it entered Shenandoah County and made Strasburg its southern terminal for several years. Then the road was extended to Woodstock, and on to Harrisonburg. This road was in active and profitable operation from Alexandria to Strasburg at the outbreak of the war, when the Valley trade was interrupted. The road was used at various times by both armies; the Valley end extending to Harrisonburg being of great service to the Southerners. The line from Strasburg to Harrisonburg was stripped of its rolling stock by General

Jackson, when falling back from Gen. Banks' army in 1862. The battles of Bull Run and Manassas were fought along its line—places familiar to many old "Vets" of both armies. At the close of the war, the road was ready for the Valley trade, and received a large portion of it, flowing from points South of Strasburg. This road has been for several years, merged in the Southern Railway System, and controls a large traffic; its carrying trade going *via* Washington City, and on to the sea board.

Alexandria, Loudoun and Hampshire Railroad

While Frederick County was, and is yet, interested in this railroad; aided in securing its charter, and promised a large subscription to the stock of the company when the road entered the county from some point in the Blue Ridge—all that has been seen of this road West of the Blue Ridge was the markings of a well defined route, passing through Frederick and on to the coal fields of Hampshire. When that genial-hearted man and accomplished engineer, Maj. Blythe, with his competent corps, in the early fifties came to locate a route through Frederick, the writer recalls many incidents connected with their work. Land owners were fearful their farms would be cut in twain, and damages result that could not be repaired, and many suffered anxiety concerning their crops, fearful they could not save them from the pick and shovel brigade which they looked for every day to appear in their midst. No need to worry over such prospects, they were often told. Some, glowing with hope that the Locomotive would soon come puffing from some gap in the Blue Ridge, were also told to be patient. Alas, for many human fears and hopes! Nearly all of those who were thus affected by the new enterprise, have long since passed from our midst; and we who survive are still looking for the locomotive. We may add, that in recent years this road now known as the Washington and Ohio, has reached the eastern base of the Blue Ridge, and at old Snickersville has its "Bluemont Station."

Winchester and Strasburg Railroad

A charter was granted by the General Assembly April 23, 1867, to this Company to construct a railroad from the town of Winchester to the town of Strasburg, with authority to connect the same with the Winchester and Potomac and Manassas Gap Railroads. We find by an Act of the General Assembly passed Feb. 26, 1877, some interesting matter relating to the connection at Strasburg; and as much controversy has arisen in recent years concerning the inconvenience given the passenger and shipper, it is considered proper to give the leading features of this last Act. The Act reads: "Whereas, the said Winchester and Strasburg Railroad Company have constructed and completed under provisions of said Act a Railroad from the said town of Winchester to a point on the Manassas Gap Railroad near the town of Strasburg, and by means of the use of the track of the said Manassas Gap Railroad are willing to run, or procure to be run, by its lessee or other person, or corporation operating its said road, trains to said town of Strasburg at or near the Capon crossing, and is willing to treat and regard the said depot when so erected as a regular station on its road, for such trains as are accustomed to stop at stations of a similar character and dignity on its own road—." Other provisions of this Act, when accepted by the W. & S. Company, fixed the responsibility upon this company to provide proper accommodation for the patrons of this road, and save them from the annoyance that so frequently occurs at Strasburg in making transfer of passenger and freight traffic. It is unfortunate that the railroad system in the valley is so broken. The B. & O. operating the W. & S. from Winchester to Strasburg—the Southern from Strasburg to Harrisonburg, and the B. & O. from the latter town to Staunton—and all this on a single track through this great Valley. The Winchester and Strasburg Road has one of the best tracks in the country, and rolling stock ample to carry the increasing business.

The Martinsburg and Potomac. (Cumberland Valley Railroad)

This railroad was incorporated by an Act of the General Assembly July 9th, 1870, and the enterprising Company, under the management of Mr. Thomas B. Kennedy, President of the Cumberland Valley R. R. from Hagerstown to Harrisburg, Pa., secured prompt support from Frederick County and City of Winchester in 1881. Many citizens subscribed liberally to the stock; thus giving an earnest of their support to the movement. The road was soon constructed, and opened for use 1885, and with full equipment of cars and other rolling stock, won plaudits from its patrons, affording the passenger many railroad comforts, as he sped his way out of the Shenandoah into the Cumberland Valley to enjoy the attractive features of both valleys as seen from the well conducted train. The coming of this road was hailed with delight by people of all classes. It meant cheaper coal! This great agricultural section had felt the need of a competing line to get their products to the great markets. Freights were high, and profits on close margin. The advantage of competition was soon felt by the community, better facilities were offered the public, and cheaper rates soon produced larger shipments. We only voice the Lower Valley when we add, this new railroad has been a success from the day it entered this section. New and increasing agricultural and horticultural industries, have made it an actual necessity; for as will be seen in other pages of this work, both railroads were taxed to their utmost capacity to handle the products of 1905. Frederick County subscribed $30,000.00 and City of Winchester $20,000.00 to the capital stock, all of which was paid promptly, and in return, they received certificates that were purchased by the Cumberland Valley Railroad Company in 1905 at a discount on their par value. Private stockholders sold their stock at the same rate. Both County and City have used the money, received from sale of their stock enough to retire the most of their bonds. This closes the data of the railroads as now found in operation within the present bounds of the County.

Shenandoah Valley Railroad Company.

We should be interested in this great improvement sweeping through four subdivisions of old Frederick. A brief sketch will be given at this point. The company was incorporated by Act of the General Assembly Feb. 23, 1867, the prospective route surveyed, and numerous routes proposed. Many Winchester people felt sure that this new railroad must make her a point on its line. A few prominent business men, however, opposed it; arguing that if this road touched Winchester, it would detract from the prosperity of this section, and there was danger that the growing little city might become a way station. These same business men saw the day when the city in a great measure lost a large volume of Clarke County trade that had always sought this market.

This railroad starting from Hagerstown, crosses the Potomac River at Shepherdstown, passing entirely through Jefferson County, crossing the W. & P. R. R. at a point South of Charlestown, running thence in nearly a straight line to enter Clarke, making Berryville a prominent station on its line. Next important station, Boyce near Millwood; then into Warren County, crossing the Manassas Gap R. R. (The Southern) and Shenandoah River West of Front Royal; then into Page County, through the Luray Valley. Beyond this point the road soon passes over the original boundary between the two old Counties Augusta and Frederick. The work of construction commenced in 1872. The road was completed and opened for business from Hagerstown to Berryville first day of October, 1879. This railroad has been operated for several years by the Norfolk and Western system; which has made it one of the great competitive Southern lines of commerce.

These brief sketches of the railroads mentioned, are given as matter of reference to those who would like to answer the question so often asked the writer: When was some one of these railroads chartered? when constructed, and where located?

Next to the railroads, came another development somewhat akin to the railroad system; for without it they would be practically helpless; and for this reason we think it might be of interest to many to mention the "Telegraph System." Very few persons are able to give an intelligent answer relating to questions asked about the first appearance of the "Telegraph" in the Valley of Virginia; (and if in operation elsewhere in Virginia, let some one answer when and where). It must be remembered that the B. & O. and W. & P. Railroads were the first railroads operated in Virginia; and that the B. & O. Company claims the honor of being the pioneer in this wonderful public improvement. Alongside of the B. & O. was the old Winchester and Potomac Railroad; and it was but natural that they should encourage the infant enterprise, so urgently pressed by the inventor, Samuel F. B. Morse. To this end, they gave aid to the inventor when he appeared before the General Assembly of Virginia in the sessions 1848-9, when he presented the plan of his great work. The General Assembly passed an Act January 17, 1849, "authorizing Samuel F. B. Morse and John F. Pickeral and their associates, who have or may become owners of Morse's Electro-Magnetic Telegraph, to put up and maintain a line of said Telegraph from Harpers Ferry to the Ohio River—through the territory of this State upon the ground of the Baltimore and O. R. R. Company so far as it extends." A charter was granted them to incorporate this proposed line, under the name and style of the Western Telegraph Company "for the purpose of building and managing said line of Telegraph." At this session we find the W. & P. Company too, seeing the need of the Telegraph for their business, gave their aid for the formation of a company to secure the right to use the telegraph. An Act was passed March 12, 1849, granting a charter to Jacob Baker, Henry M. Brent, John Bruce, Geo. W. Hammond, Joseph H. Sherrard, Wm. L. Clark, Sen., and their associates, "who have acquired from Samuel F. B. Morse and others the right to construct and carry on the Electro-Magnetic Telegraph, invented and patented by said Morse, from the town of Winchester to Harpers Ferry—the charter name being The Valley Telegraph Company.

It will be seen the old Railroad Companies were dealing with Morse in person. Few if any of those old actors ever dreamed of what their initiative steps were destined to do with the great net-work of Electro-Magnetic currents encircling the globe, and enlivening the life of millions of hamlets and villages throughout the universe; even transmitting intelligence on waves of atmosphere and light between distant points, unseen from each other.

The Western Telegraph Company and Valley Telegraph Company were later on gathered up into the folds of the great monopoly, *The Western Union* which has covered America with her lines. The B. & O. and all other great railroads, have for many years operated their independent lines, strictly for railroad purposes. We find in addition to the enterprises and public improvements embraced in the foregoing accomplished facts, another enterprise occupying the attention of the public-spirited men of that period; and this, too, when it was regarded that railroad construction was so stupendous an undertaking, that only great capitalists could hope to accomplish it. But here we had a class of men composed of farmers, tradesmen, lawyers and mechanics, undertaking a work then new to the world and actually working it out. This, too, during its infancy. Others had conceived the idea that the Shenandoah Valley should have an enterprise similar to the one fast approaching the Potomac border of the Old County. Before the Chesapeake and Ohio Canal was fully completed to Harpers Ferry, many public-spirited men were agitating the building of a canal from Harpers Ferry, along the Shenandoah River, to some point far up the Valley. We find an interesting account of the first meeting of the promoters of this scheme, held in Winchester as early as 1831—the full account published in the Winchester Republican. Strong reasons were given not only why a canal should be made, but that one could be made. Steps were taken to secure the opinions of experts, such as the engineers who had entered largely into the work of the Chesapeake and Ohio Canal. The President and active men of that corporation, were in close touch with the proposed enterprise. We find a very satisfactory paper from Hon. Charles F. Mercer, President of the Canal Company then seeking its way from Georgetown to Cumberland (who was Member of Congress from this District) in which he makes very plain the possibility of the plan, and the consequent profits resulting to a country so resourceful as the Shenandoah Valley. The promoters became so encouraged, that we find them before the General Assembly, 1831, attracting such attention, that the whole Valley delegation was in solid line to not only secure the charter then granted, but to secure aid from the State. Later on, we find surveys were made for the section of five miles near Harpers Ferry, and reports made by such engineers as Fulton and Latrobe—men of national reputation, and also by the State engineers of the entire river. Mr. Mercer became so enthused, that he introduced a bill in Congress asking for an appropriation to deepen the channel of the river and make the Shenandoah navigable for *better boating*. Congress made an appropriation to pay the cost of survey—but none for the great work of deepening the channel. This seems to have satisfied the projectors of the proposed canal, who, doubtless thought what the U. S. Government proposed to do would answer the demand for a water highway; and their project was never agitated again. The Hon. James G. Blaine, related to the writer many interesting incidents concerning this U. S. Government undertaking; and stated that after the reports were made of these preliminary surveys, Congress took the matter up again, and the Omnibus Bill asking for appropriations, had the Shenandoah River named as one of the places to spend Government money; but by some work of the Committee, Shenandoah and many other rivers and harbors were stricken out. The U. S. Government was freely spending money at Harpers Ferry, where the U. S. Armory and National Arsenal were maintained.

CHAPTER XII

Public Ferries

It may be of interest to some readers to learn how and when the great waters were crossed in the early days of the first settlers.

The House of Burgesses at a very early day made provisions for ferries to be maintained at designated points on the waters East of the Blue Ridge. We find that in 1736 the Colonial Government had been apprised of the necessity for ferries along the Shenandoah River; and by an Act, provided for the first ferries over this river. The first being "for a ferry from the land of William Russell on Sherando to cross into the fork or cross main river, be established and maintained by the Justice's Court until the Ferrymen receive sufficient tolls to pay his time." This Ferry was located near the site of Front Royal. The Second, "On Sherando River from the land of William Russell next above the mouth of Happy Creek, in the County of Orange across into the fork—the price for man three pence, and for one horse three pence, or across the main river the same; and that the courts of the several counties wherein such ferries shall be kept, shall have power to appoint proper boats to be kept at the said ferries for the convenient transportation of coaches, wagons and other wheel carriages." This very significent language, conveys the impression that wagons and other wheel carriages were in use between settlers on West side of the Blue Ridge and the sections on the East side—and this, seven years before the first court was held in Frederick County, and two years before its erection as a County, less than four years after the first appearance of Joist Hite as a settler in the Shenandoah Valley, the lands of William Russell lay altogether on the South and East side of the main river and South Fork, and were part of a grant to him. He was of the number of settlers of the immigration from the East side of the Ridge, who found other settlers in the Valley desiring intercourse with the East side, and especially so with the County seat at Orange Courthouse, and needed some way to cross the rivers with their wagons etc. We must remember that this was only about sixteen years after Governor Spottswood proclaimed the Valley a wilderness of grandeur unknown to the white man. The first settlers seemed to be as eager to possess the new country and remain on the ground, as the Oklahoma settlers have exhibited in their efforts in recent years. There can be no doubt about the Russell Ferry being the first ferry established over any river West of the Blue Ridge. Tradition has it that ferries were established at Harpers Ferry and Shepherdstown about this period. This claim is not sustained by any record evidence; and as will be shown later on, no such ferries existed as early as 1736. At this point it is well enough to show in part one of the reasons why the new County of Orange was formed in 1734. The House of Burgesses had the matter presented to them, that settlements were being made on the West side of the Great Mountains, and should have greater attention than could be given by Spottsylvania County; that it was desirable to erect a new county, and have a county seat nearer the new settlements. Orange County was formed from the latter. In one of the sections of the preamble; this language is used to show the concern the Colonial Government had for the new settlements: Section 3, "And for the encouragement of the inhabitants already settled, and which shall speedily settle on the westward of Sherando River; Be it enacted, that all the inhabitants which shall be settled there the 1st day of January, 1735, shall be free and exempt from the payment of public, county and parish levies, by the space of three years, from thence next following."

The House of Burgesses, 1748, passed a general law declaring the streams as part of the general domain, and that no rights existed in any inhabitant to convert any such streams to their private or for public use. The Justices' courts were instructed to take jurisdiction and control in the several counties; and to either grant or restrict the uses, when not in conflict with the right of general control vested in the Governor's Council. So the court put itself in evidence, that the right should be guarded. In the case of John Kersey, the Orange Court gave him the ferry right over the "Sherando" River, 1736, and Frederick County confirmed this by an order January 13, 1744. The land at the Kersey Ferry was owned by Thomas Ashby, of Prince William County, who conveyed it to Joseph Berry in 1757; and very soon it was called Berry's

Ferry. Berry was then a resident of Prince George County. Joseph Berry secured fuller rights to run this ferry, by an Act of the General Assembly Dec. 11, 1790. Up to that time, he had conflict with the ferry established by the Court, and tradition says that two ferries were operated there.

The first ferry established on the Potomac, West of the Blue Ridge, was in 1755, and this was near what was then known as Mecklenburg. Thomas Swearingen upon his application, endorsed by quite a number of settlers on the South side of the *"Cohongoluta,"* was granted the right to establish a ferry over said river from his land to a point opposite in the Province of Maryland.

Robert Harper was granted a right to establish and maintain a ferry March, 1761, "to cross the "Powtomack" from the point in Frederick County to the land of said Robert Harper on the opposite side—being in the Province of Maryland." This would indicate that Robert Harper did not start this ferry from his land on the South side, to land on his land on the Maryland side. This led the Author to search carefully for Harper's deed for land on the Virginia side, hoping to be able to determine what point on his land on the South side was the starting point. Assuming that he would start from some point on his land and not on the land of another, and thus settle the question of a ferry being in use at or near the confluence of the Powtomack and Shenandoah. Strange to say, however, no such deeds can be found; and no evidence appears that Robert Harper owned any land in Frederick prior to 1780. This casts a shadow over the claim that Harper's ferry was the oldest ferry West of the Blue Ridge. Some have argued that the ferry could not have been from the point now known as the Village of Harper's Ferry (as there was not sufficient water at that point) and that it was below the confluence that the ferry was established. This is not true; for the Act says it is from a point in Frederick County, etc., and the boundaries of this county did not extend far enough East to make it possible for the provision to apply. Others give good reason for a point up the river where sufficient water was found; and this is sustained by the evidence that Harper owned land on the opposite side from the last named point; while there is no evidence that he owned land on either side, below the union of the two rivers, where sufficient water could have been found.

October, 1755, Thomas Shepherd was given the right "to erect and maintain a ferry from the town of Mecklenburg in Frederick County—from his land to cross the Cohongoroota and find suitable landing on the Maryland side." This right he did not enjoy long, for we find that in November, 1766, this grant was withdrawn and the ferry discontinued, in the following language, "The Ferry is discontinued—found unnecessary—same being at a very small distance from a ferry already established from the land of Thomas Swearingen—crossing the Cohongoroota from a convenient point over to the Maryland side."

We also find that Abraham Shepherd in 1778, secured a charter for a ferry from Shepherdstown over the "Potowmack" to the land of Thomas Swearingen on the opposite side in Maryland. This Act was repealed in 1779. This shows that Swearingen was ever ready to control the Shepherds whenever they appeared on his preserves. The records show Swearingen owner of land at this point in 1748, on both sides of the river. The old court records show that a road was opened in 1744 from Shepherd's Ferry to the Bullskin; so some Shepherd was there with a ferry at an early day.

1792, Edward McSheary, in the County of Berkley secured ferry rights across the Potomack, to the Iron works on the Maryland side.

Snicker's Ferry on the Shenandoah River where one of the old county roads leads from Frederick County through the Blue Ridge to connect with roads to points East of the Ridge, was laid out by order of Court at a very early day. "A ferry being needed for the much increasing travel"—the court granted ferry right, at that point, 1766.

1789, Charles Buck, by an Act of the Assembly, erected a ferry in Frederick County across the North Fork of Shenandoah River, at the mouth of Passage Creek, to the land of Isaac Hite on opposite shore. Thomas Buck at the same time secured ferry rights across the North fork of Shenandoah River, to the lands of George Hardin and Rowley Smith.

The Charles Buck mentioned above was before the court June term, 1767, for insulting the court, and the Sheriff was ordered to put him into the "Stocks" and keep him there a half hour. Same punishment was meted out to Thomas Martin for like offense. The old Justices were firm men, and some times severe.

1784, Ralph Humphreys was granted right for public ferry from his land in Hampshire County across the South Branch of "Potowmack."

1789, Luther Martin was granted a charter for a public ferry from his land in the County of Hampshire across the "Potowmack" River, at the confluence of the North and South Branches thereof.

1790, George Glaize was granted ferry rights

by General Assembly, from his land in County of Hampshire across the South Branch of the Potowmack, to the land of Conrod Glaize.

1790, by an Act of Assembly, John Chenowith, secured a right for a public ferry from his land in Hampshire County across Great Ca-Capon Creek, to the opposite shore.

1790, Rees Pritchard by Act of Assembly, erected a ferry across the North Fork of Great Ca-Capon to his land on opposite shore.

Having briefly pointed out some, if not all, the highways, including ferries, the author deems it of sufficient importance to notice the question of mills in a separate chapter.

CHAPTER XIII

Mills and Other Developments

We find in studying the first settlers, they were in direst straits for several years, while the important provision was being made to supply the wants of the whites with meal and flour. On the arrival of the pack horse train, this necessary of life was amply cared for; but such tedious modes for supplying the settlers with breadstuffs, soon became too uncertain. The original stock once consumed, their old pack trains expected to come with other settlers, seldom if ever arrived in time to relieve their wants. Many families were not to be disconcerted. They resorted to the Indian mode of preparing cornmeal—the *mortar* and *pestle* became a necessary part of the household effects. This old mortar was generally of stone, hollowed out to receive the corn; then the pestle was vigorously used, and the corn reduced to meal. The author saw one of the old mortars many years ago, carefully guarded and retained as a relic of the early days. The increasing demand, caused enterprising men to seize the natural power found in so many creeks; and rude grist mills were erected as one of the first developments. Old orders of court previously mentioned relating to roads, revealed the location of the first mills. It will be seen that Funk's Mill, Hite's, Frye's, Friend's and others were on Cedar Creek and the North fork of the Shenandoah; while the Opecquon kept the wheels running for many famous mills. Samuel Glass, the emigrant, erected a stone mill near his house about 1736, using water from two large springs. This building is now used as a residence for the Steck family's tenant, a photograph of which will appear in this connection.

Lower down, Marquis and Allen had mills. Van Horn also erected a mill. This was in after years known as Neill's mill (Huck's). One of the first mills was erected by Joist Hite and his son, Col. John, and occupied a space known as *Stockade,* hardby the site of the Bartonsville property now owned by L. R. Dettra. This was built of stone, and served as an impromptu fort, which has been mentioned elsewhere.

The two mills on Cedar Creek near Marlboro are successors to very early grist mills. Frequent notice to parties concerning roads, locate these and give names of owners. Lower down the creek, a very large mill was erected by Valentine Rhodes, occupying the site of the Col. Briscoe Mills.

The mills owned at this writing by Mr. Daniel T. Wood are on the same foundation where a mill and distillery were operated in 1767. Several mills were on other streams flowing into the Opecquon at that point, notably the Greenwood mills, erected about 1785 by John and James McCalister, who had a large business in Winchester. John built a substantial house at that point and lived there. The mills along the North Mountain stream were erected at an early day. Maj. White had two mills on the drains of Hogue Creek; the one near his old residence remains in fairly good condition, but not running. The Russell and Richard's mills were famous in their early days. In another chapter, a number of mills are mentioned. Abram Hollingsworth started one of the first mills near Winchester, at his large springs now the city water power. The Milltown Mills erected by Isaac Hollingsworth in 1827, took the place of one erected by Isaac Perkins prior to 1756.

A reference to order of Court found in a previous chapter, shows that Noah Hampton had a mill on Capon, 1744, known as the old Stackhouse mill.

The old time country water mill has virtually become a thing of the past. The new process for making flour by the "Roll System," where the grain is conducted through a succession of rollers, instead of the old *burr millstone* process, has revolutionized the mill business to such an extent, that nine-tenths of the old style have become poor investments and have gone into disuse. Many old mill owners grappled with the new style and were driven out of the lucrative business they previously enjoyed. The milling business is now confined to very few persons, who are men of means; and by concentrating capital with an intelligent handling of the new system, it proves a good investment. There are several in the County, one known as the Keckley Mill on the Valley Turnpike near Winchester; one at Bartonsville; one near Middletown, known as the D. J. Miller mill; one at Marlboro, the owner, Dorsey Brill; one at

Gravel Springs, Luther Brill, owner; one at Brucetown; one at Whitacre.

The mill near the head of Opecquon owned now by Salem E. Cooper, who succeeded Casper Rinker, was erected by permission obtained from the County Court March 3rd, 1812, to-wit: "On petition of Joseph Glass stating he was desirous of erecting a water Grist mill upon the "Opeckon" Creek in this County, the lands at that point on both sides belonging to him," granted with usual restrictions. This mill was the cause of much litigation with a co-terminous owner. Mr. Glass made the tail-race near the line of Martin Cartmell, owner of Homespun. On the Cartmell land was a famous spring and dairy. The spring stream was cut in twain by the deep tail-race; the spring supply ceased. Cartmell demanded damages. Glass failed to respond. A suit was instituted, which was on the docket for ten years. Cartmell lost, upon the ground that he had signed Glass's petition, with an understanding that Glass should cut his race of such depth as would prevent overflow of waste water. The useless old stone dairy remained intact until about 1890, when Mr. Miller, the owner removed it.

CHAPTER XIV

Gleanings From Old Courts, Continued

The author in his promised digression has probably wandered too far from the period where the minutes of court were drawn upon for the incidents given in former chapters. He deemed it best to follow out the development of the country by the numerous county roads, and in the same connection dispose of the railroads and ferries, so there would be continuous narration throughout; and passed over the stirring years from 1750, and into the Nineteenth Century. During that time, the Old County was girding herself for tremendous events in her history—preparation for the Indian Wars, and following this closely, came the Revolution in 1775, and her transformation from a Colony to one of the great States of the New Union.

The new order of government, demanded the action and counsel of wise men. The old courts continued to record many incidents that are of exceeding value as part of our historical life; some of which may find place in these pages, if space permits. We must now retrace our investigations, and disclose some of the stirring acts of the courts. Sept. 4th, 1753, this minute is made at this term. "A Treaty between the Indians is in progress; It is ordered by the Court, for preventing disturbance during the Treaty with the Indians at the town of Winchester, that no Ordinary keeper, or other person presume to sell or give to the Indians, strong Liquors of any sort, unless those persons who shall be appointed to supply them with what shall be thought necessary."

Five Great Chiefs with a small following, spent many weeks near the town trying to work a scheme to have the white settlers vacate their territory West of the Great Mountains. This was refused; but a treaty was made to allow the Indians to remain in their villages on the Ohio River undisturbed, and that they should have the right to sell land on their reservation to peaceable white settlers. This treaty was basely violated by unscrupulous adventurers; and a bloody war was the result. (See French and Indian War sketches in this Volume.)

As will be seen in chapter on Winchester, the town was fully established when Maj. Washington appeared before the court in Jan., 1756, with his authority to organize the Militia, and announced his plans. He needed officers to form companies for his expedition against the Indians; and after stating the emergency, the Court, upon this recommendation, designated the following men to serve as Captains in the Virginia Regiment; George Mercer, Robert Stewart, Thomas Cocke, William Bronaugh, Joshua Lewis, John Mercer, William Peachy, and David Bell. Walter Stewart, John Williams, and Augustine Brockenbraugh, were Lieutenants; and Charles Smith, Lehaynsius DeKeyser, and William Crawford, Ensigns. This is more fully treated in the sketch of the French and Indian War. All took the required oath to His Majesty the King of England.

The sudden disclosure to the Justices caused consternation; and as stated elsewhere, they ordered an adjournment to the house of Enoch Pearson. The Grand Jury failed to appear, owing to the Indian forays in the mountain sections to the West; they *were excused*. Following November Court, Captains Thomas Swearingen, William Cocke, John Funk, Cornelius Ruddell, and William Vance presented claims before the Court for public services for themselves and detachments sent under their command—on an expedition to protect outlaying settlements. The court promptly allowed their payment. Some of the officers mentioned here figured in the Revolution.

The following year, the Court makes an entry of the expenses of the election, and required Washington and other candidates to file a report of what their *outlay* had been, and for what purpose.

June Court, 1755, "Ordered that Isaac Perkins, Gent. the Representative from this County attending House of Burgesses, be allowed pay for eleven days in June and nineteen days in August, 1755."

Nov. 3rd, 1756, "Ordered that Hugh West and Thomas Swearingen be allowed pay as representatives from this County to House of Burgesses in 1756." This shows that each county paid their representatives for serving them in the General Assembly.

March Court, 1758. "Ordered that William Miller do procure a Silver Seal for the County court, to be about the size of an English Half

Crown with words, 'Frederick County,' engraved thereon, and the Arms of Virginia."

(This will be more fully mentioned in closing order of the County Court about two years ago.)

At this term John Hite, Robert Allen and Samuel Pritchard, were ordered, "To mark a road from Col. Hite's through the town out on Lewis Stephen's plantation."

Col. Washington had his tithables entered on tax lists Oct. 4, 1757—preparing them for his election campaign.

Nov. 4, 1757, "Sheriff ordered to get furniture for Courthouse and other fixtures."

Feb. 3rd, 1758, Special term held "to examine etc., Edward Doyle, charged with having destroyed part of the nose of Joseph King."

October, 1758, "Ordered that stone steps be placed up the hill to the courthouse."

1758 "Ordered that the Court be moved to the town of Winchester from Stephensburg on account of Smallpox."

August, 1757, "Ludwig Castleman charged with the murder of James Haines, a soldier; committed for Grand Jury."

Thomas Speak, Gent., Captain of Company of Militia, Marquis Calmes, Captain; John Hardin and Bayliss Earle, Lts. took the oaths. James Littlepage was recognized to appear at next term. Henry Spear, Captain, and Wm. Morgan and Archibald Ruddell, also appeared at the Nov. Term and were qualified.

James Keith, who was soon to be the Clerk of the Court, was admitted to practice law. Thomas Melbourne was paid one pound, five shillings, for services as guard in taking criminal to Williamsburg jail—less than six dollars for the long and uninteresting journey. The Sheriff and guards of to-day by improved modes of travel, would require about $20.00.

This next minute shows the Justices were uncertain whether their records and scalps were not equally in danger. "The Clerk is ordered to remove the records to Fort Loudoun there being imminent danger from the enemy—or elsewhere as the case may require; and the Justices do seek a place of safety for further sessions of the Court."

Isaac White, a bold mountain man, was added to the list of constables at this term, doubtless to give extra service to his Lordship Thomas Lord Fairfax the presiding Justice. This was October 5, 1757, and it determines the question as to when the Fort was completed. Some writers claim that Col. Washington was not in Winchester when the Fort was built; that he was with his command in the Fort Duquesne campaign. This command was in active service in the summer and fall of 1758—one year after the order was entered Oct., 1757. This is fully shown in chapters on that war. The authority for erecting Fort Loudoun is fully given in chapters relating to Winchester, also the style of the fort when first used by the Virginia Regiment.

Passing over this period for several sessions of the Court without comment, we find a minute entered at the Feb. term, 1760, which is given here as a matter of reference: "The last will and testament of James Wood, late Clerk was produced and proved by Thomas Wood, who deposed that he saw James Porteous and Katharine Fitzsimmons sign their names as witnesses, said will is ordered to be recorded."

Archibald Wager had been appointed by Deputy Secretary Nelson, acting for the Governor, Clerk of the Court; and we find that James Wood, the son was, qualified as Deputy May 7, same year. For reasons that do not appear, Wager's term was terminated when James Keith on the 4th of May, 1762, produced a commission as Clerk from the Secretary, and was duly sworn and qualified. Further notice will be given these old Clerks in the proper place.

The Old County Court from 1757 for about eight years, was continually called upon for assistance to protect outlying settlements. The Indians in every foray approached nearer the county seat, and the exposed places were calling for aid to build rude forts and stockades. The Governor and his military aids responded; and as will appear elsewhere, protection was given, but massacres continued to occur. The reader can well imagine from the character of the brief minutes already given, that the Court was much disturbed for its own safety. We must remember too, that the old Justices were thinking of their homes in the various sections. They were well apprised of the frequent battles along the Great Capon and South Branch, and what had occurred in the settlement North of Woodstock; but when the roving bands appeared on Hogue Creek and on Cedar Creek, and carried away not only many scalps, but many prisoners, we can well see why they were anxious to seek Fort Loudoun for safety to the *old records,* also their friends and families in peril. If space can be given for brief accounts of some of the Indian raids and massacres, the author will gladly lay them before the reader, so as to show how the old settlers struggled to maintain a foothold. Some of these settlers had been in this struggle for more than twenty years; and often whole families were swept away by the torch and tomahawk without a moment's warning; and reader, it may be we will name some who suffered who were your ancestors.

There is abundant evidence to support the course pursued by the justices, in relation to the Indians and their expected depredations. As stated already, they were duly apprised of such depredations, which had become too frequent to pass unnoticed. One of the roving bands was led by their Chief, the notorious "Killbuck." This chief survived all the wars, and was visited by several citizens of Great Ca-Capon, South Branch and Patterson's Creek settlements. He lived to a great age. He was a Shawanese savage, mentally strong, and brutal in his instincts. We are indebted to Kercheval for the reliable incidents he has so carefully preserved. He relates in detail conversations had with "Killbuck" long after all treaties had been signed, and when the Old Chief was living in the Indian villages in Sciota Valley, Ohio. The men who visited "Killbuck," were sons and kinsmen of those who had been massacred; and from the Old Chief they gathered much information relating to who had been killed and who carried away captives. The Shawnee tribe knew every foot of the country mentioned. They resented the encroachments of the Whites, and when they had apparently abandoned the country East of the Alleganies and moved their villages, and professed to be peaceful, yet they frequently recrossed the Alleganies, and suddenly descended upon the settlers to murder and pillage. Col. Vincent Williams, Benj. Casey, two of the Weltons, Van Meter and several others composed the party seeking this information. They relate the old Chief's conversation in full, but we lack space to include them here. However, we mention briefly that much light was given concerning the murder of Mr. Williams on Patterson's Creek in 1756; how Williams had killed five out of the seven of the warriors in the first attack and he, "Killbuck" with another band, approached the house in rear, lifted a warrior high enough to shoot through a crevice between the logs and thus killed the old hero who had withstood similar assaults. He was then quartered, and a quarter hung on each corner of the house. Mr. Williams left children that distinguished this family in the development of Hardy County. One grandson James, lived at the scene of the murder on Patterson's Creek, one hundred years subsequent to the tragedy. One son, Mr. Edward Williams, was Clerk of Hardy County 1830, being then an aged man.

Much has been told through tradition of the Indian battle of *The Trough.* Killbuck told much about their attack on the small fort about seven miles above Romney. The whites were defeated in an open engagement, but held the fort; the Indians committed deviltry on the unprotected, lower down the river. The remains of the old fort were standing near the home of the old Daniel McNeil place on the river. Old logs and other material used in this blockhouse, were well preserved when the author last saw it. There was another fort not far away on the Van Meter land: This was Fort Pleasant. Traditions concerning the battle of the Trough are treasured among the families in that section. There was a fort on Big Capon near the Northwest Turnpike, that relics have been taken from in recent years. This was "Edward's Fort." Capt. Mercer was stationed there in 1757, and his report of the disaster corroborates all that "Killbuck" told of his wily attacks. The Indians entered the Ca-Capon Valley in small parties to take observation. Killbuck's party of forty warriors visited a mill and killed the two men found there They carried away meal and corn and passed along a stream at the base of a high mountain, strewing meal in several places on the route, to lure the whites in their pursuit. Killbuck selected a high point for his ambuscade, and awaited the arrival of the garrison from the Fort. Capt. Mercer, with forty-five men followed the trail; and supposing the scattered meal indicated disorder and haste in the Indian band, the whites rushed on and suddenly received a most destructive fire from the Indians. Sixteen of Mercer's men fell dead; and as the others made hasty retreat, they were pursued by Killbuck and slaughtered. Only six men got back to the fort. Kercheval says that Mr. George Smith, residing on Back Creek, told him in 1833 that one of the men escaping death from the Indians in the battle, was desperately wounded but succeeded in making his way over the mountains to his neighborhood, and he knew him for years. The Valley historian gives us some other interesting matter relating to this fort. He says Mr. William Carlisle, now 95 years old (1833), who lived near the battle ground, removed and settled on Capon soon after the battle was fought. The garrison was strengthened, for it was well known the Indians would return with larger forces and endeavor to destroy the fort. Some color is given a tradition that credits Daniel Morgan with being present at the next assault on the fort; for we find the Court allowed payment to Daniel Morgan and others for claims produced for supplies taken by them to the settlers on Great Ca-Capon. The same old Mr. Carlisle states further that he had frequently heard that "Dan" Morgan was in the battle that soon followed the first. This time two Frenchmen accompanied the Indians; the garrison defeated this force, causing great slaughter, with slight loss to the whites. The failure on the part of those reporting the battles with the Indians to give details is greatly to be regretted. Had they done so, many descendants to-day could point with pride to the old pioneer fathers and give their names; but we must remember that this custom is practiced in all reports of battles—nothing more said than some field officer lost, and the number of privates fallen or captured.

Just previous to the battle of The Trough, some depredations on the South Fork by a band of warriors led by Killbuck were also mentioned by the old Chief, which Dr. Charles A. Turley reduced to writing. He says the first attack was upon a well fortified dwelling of a Mrs. Brake, when she and a Mrs. Neff were carried away. The former was Tomahawked and scalped. The latter escaped and gave the alarm, and a body of men from "Buttermilk Fort" led by John Harness, (Great-grandfather of Col. William Henry Harness of the Laurel Brigade). This pursuit led to the battle at The Trough. About this period, Indian bands raided the neighborhood of Gerardstown; killed a man by the name of Kelly and several of his family, and carried away several women and children. George Stockton and Isabella, his sister, were of this number. Charles Porterfield about 20 years old, was killed in a running fight with the band. A man named Cohoon, made his escape; his wife was killed. The Stocktons were carried far North, but both finally returned to their former home. Similar bands about this time which were in the vicinity of Winchester, killed a man named Flaugherty and his wife. Several members of the MacCracken family on Back Creek, twelve miles from Winchester, were killed, and two of his daughters carried away captives. After an absence of four years, they found their way back to their former home, and related their experiences to Mr. Neill, who related these facts to Mr. Kercheval. Jacob Havely and several of his family were killed near Mountain Falls, about fifteen miles southwest of Winchester. Dispennette and several of his family were killed, and Vance and his family. It appears from the collection referred to, that the same marauding band appeared in the neighborhood of Belle Grove, the residence of Maj. Isaac Hite, and attacked the family of a Mr. Nicholls composed of eighteen persons, killing most of them, and carried away the remainder to meet a worse fate. At that time, there was a small fort near the present site of Middletown. Many persons were saved by taking refuge there. In 1758, a band of fifty Indians and four Frenchmen, entered the neighborhood of Mill Creek about nine miles South of Woodstock. The people took refuge in the house of George Painter. Painter was killed and the other whites surrendered. Four infants were torn from their mothers, and were hung up in trees and brutally shot, and left hanging. The Indians then moved away with forty-eight prisoners, among whom were Mrs. Painter, five daughters and one of her sons; a Mrs. Fisher and several of her children. Two of the Painters escaped capture. One young man ran over that night to Powell's Fort, fifteen miles distant, and to Keller's Fort, and secured the services of a body of well mounted men; but they failed to overtake the savages, who escaped to their villages West of the Allegany mountains. There they burned young Jacob Fisher at the stake. After an absence of three years, Mrs. Painter with her son and two of her daughters and Mrs. Smith with *her Indian son,* Fisher, and his surviving sons, and several other prisoners returned home. Three of Mrs. Painter's daughters remained with the Indians; two never returned. Many later on returned with Michael Copple, they were afterwards married and raised a family. She always conversed with her husband in the Indian language, that both had acquired while prisoners. Mr. Kercheval says Mrs. Rebecca Brinker the daughter of George Bowman, son-in-law of Joist Hite, lived to a great age in the neighborhood where the atrocities last named occurred, and related the incidents to him, she having personal knowledge of their occurrence.

In 1758, the Indians killed a number of people in the Hawksbill settlement: John Stone, Jacob Holtman's wife, and her children. The house of John Brewbaker was burned; Stone's wife and child about eight years old, and George Grandstaff, about sixteen, were carried away. The Indians murdered Mrs. Stone and her infant on the South Branch Mountain. Grandstaff returned in about three years. It was about this date that word came to the Justices' Court, that the Indians were at the old Zane Iron Works, and had entered the house of a man named Young, killed several of his family, and carried away two of his daughters.

NOTE: On the 10th day of April, 1908, Mr. Aiken Robinson found five skeletons on his farm a mile South of the old Zane Furnace, two were adults and three smaller sized. It is fully substantiated in several ways, that the skeletons represent the massacred Young family mentioned. Mr. Robinson, prepared a vault near by, and in presence of many neighbors, removed the skeletons to it and erected a slab with suitable inscriptions to mark the spot.)

Kercheval says that Lieut. Samuel Fry raised a force of about forty men and overtook the band on Short Mountain, a spur of the Allegany, and recaptured the prisoners; killing several Indians. Mr. Kercheval tells us that in 1753, William Zane and several of his family were taken prisoners on the South Branch and carried away. Isaac Zane, one of his sons, remaining during his life with the Indians; and that he saw this Isaac Zane at Chillicothe in the autumn of 1797, and had conversations with him upon the subject of his captivity. He stated that he was captured when about nine years old; was four years without seeing a white person, had learned the Indian *Tung* quite well, but never lost his knowledge of English. That when he grew up to manhood, he married a sister of the *Wyandott* King, and raised a family of eight children. His sons were all Indian in their habits. The daughters married white men and became civilized, and their progeny doubtless became prominent Ohio citizens. This man was instrumental in effecting desirable treaties of peace. The United States Government granted him a patent for ten thousand acres of land. He was a near relative to Gen. Isaac Zane of Frederick County.

There were two forts on Lost River, one on the land afterwards owned by Jeremiah Inskeep called "Riddles Fort" where a man name Chester was killed; the other was Warden's Fort, where William Warden and a Mr. Taft were killed and the fort burned. So it appears the little forts were not always an assurance of safety. In 1756 the Indians made a brutal attack upon a party of harvesters near Petersburg, West Virginia, when Jonathan Welton, and a man named Delay were killed after a desperate encounter. Jobe Welton received a fearful wound from a tomahawk, severing several ribs. He was left as dead, but later reached the little fort. Three of the whites were butchered; a Mr. Kuykendall escaped by remaining in the camp. In 1758, a band of Indians surprised Fort Seybert, located near the site of Franklin in Pendleton County. The bloodthirsty Killbuck was the Chief; he demanded surrender. Seybert, after a parley with the savage, agreed to surrender on terms that all would be spared. The savages violated every promise, and murdered all except a young man named James Dyer, who made a miraculous escape, and returned to live on South Fork, where the writer saw some of his descendants several years since.

In the study of Indian wars and the forts needed to protect the settlers, the writer was astonished to find the remains of an old Fort on Patterson's Creek near the present site of Frankfort, known as Ashby's fort; and he was impressed with the coincidence that in the Civil War, Dick Ashby, one of the Ashby brothers, was killed in its vicinity. Capt. John Ashby owned the property and a great many traditions belong to this fort. Near it Charles Keller was killed. His descendants were numerous in Hampshire County a few years ago, and possessed much historical matter. Logan, the renowned Indian warrior, killed Benj. Bowman in a hand-to-hand encounter near this fort, and took his companion, Humphrey Worsted prisoner. Thomas Higgins, one of the first settlers on the Cohongoroota, erected his cabins near Bath Springs; but was driven out by Indians, and settled near Gerardstown; and there his home was looted by Indians and three of his sons were taken away prisoners. Nothing was ever heard from them; and it is likely they perished at some unknown point. Two men of this name were living on the upper Cohongoroota in the early part of the Eighteenth Century; they were related to this family. There is a tradition that one of the sons was seen at Wheeling after the Dunmore War; and some have thought the two referred to, were the sons, but nothing has been found by the writer to verify this.

The Maj. White Fort was on the West side of Hogue Creek about seven miles from Winchester. This place was known for more than a century as the White Homestead. Dr. White, son-in-law of Wm. Hogue, had settled there as one of the first settlers. In 1763 Maj. Robt. White, son of the Doctor, lived there, and for the safety of the many families who had settled along the Big North Mountain, he had erected a small fort and stockade around his residence. At the July term of that year, the Major appeared in person before the Justices. He was then a Justice himself—and startled his brethren by announcing that Indians had appeared in his neighborhood the day previous, but disappeared without molesting anyone; and that he also had been informed that a large band was marauding the settlements on Great Ca-Capon. The Court was moved to convene and take steps to protect the settlements. No action was taken, and the Major returned to take charge of the situation himself. He warned the families, and went along the mountain for fully six miles as far as Owen Thomas's home, and advised all to come to his Fort. As this raid involved families and neighborhood so near to Winchester, it is well to give the narrative as related by Maj. John White a son of the owner of the Fort property. Some little confusion as to dates appears. One statement gives July, 1763, as the time; another June, 1764. This may have occurred by two raids, having been made, for we have evidence that Indians raided that settlement twice. Some of the families took no heed to the warning. Owen Thomas being one, saying he could not leave his harvest, and then rode to his neighbor Jacob Keckley, who had several sons, to propose that they arm themselves and work together at their harvest. He was shot dead on this trip. This was certainly the next day after Major

White had visited the Justices. In June, 1764, Maj. White went again to warn the people that they had better come to the Fort; that he was reliably informed that a large band was on the war path. Now the narrative becomes intensely interesting to many people who live in Frederick County to-day, and especially in that section. This warning was heeded, but the families moved slowly. Mrs. Thomas, the widow, Mrs. Jones, and a man named Clowser started with their families, but stopped at the house of a man named Lloyd, two miles from the fort, and spent the night, the next morning at an early hour they resumed their journey, and before they were out of sight of the house, the Indians attacked them, and killed, wounded or took away as prisoners twenty-three persons. A young son of Owen Thomas who had been killed in the previous raid, ran back into the house and hid himself, and escaped detection, although the Indians brought his mother and sister back into the house bound, and kept them there while they fried bacon and ate breakfast. They then set fire to the house and moved off. The boy managed to escape from the fire and the Indians, although he rambled about for two days before he found any person to whom he could tell his direful story. The families had fled to the Fort, Lloyd and several of his children, David Jones and wife, two old people, some of the Thomas family also, Henry Clowser and two of his sons were killed; Mrs. Clowser and four of her daughters taken away captives. The youngest child about two years old, was horribly butchered while crossing the North Mountain, the band heading for the South Branch. They halted one night near Furman's fort; the men at the fort fired upon them. The next morning they moved away, and while crossing the river, which was dangerous fording, Mrs. Thomas escaped, and lived for many years, to tell her neighbors thrilling stories. The wounded who were left near Major White's were gathered up after the departure of the Indians and carried to the Fort, where they were cared for. Out of the seven so found, only one survived. This was Hester Lloyd, who had two scalps taken from her. A Dr. McDonald attended her; he trepanned her head and she recovered, and lived many years. Kercheval says that Gen. Smith, Maj. R. D. Glass, Mrs. Susan Glass, Mrs. Shultz, and Mrs. Snapp severally stated to him that they frequently saw this woman after she recovered from her wound. Mrs. Thomas's daughter and Mrs. Clowser and her three small daughters were taken to the Indian town, and after an absence of about six months were released from captivity and all returned home safely. There is something in Kercheval's narrative about the three Miss Clowsers, who were prisoners at the same time. They were aged respective 10, 7 and 5 years. After their return they grew up in their old neighborhood; were married, and raised families of children, and they were all three widows when Kercheval knew them, and lived not more than five or six miles apart; two of them were Mrs. Shultz and Mrs. Snapp, who lived about one and a half miles from his residence, and a third, Mrs. Frye, not exceeding six miles. Such history must be accepted as entirely reliable. Descendants of all these families reside in Frederick County at this writing. Major White reported a list of those killed and obtained assistance from the Court to relieve the wants of the wounded and helpless.

The writer finds the name of Thomas appearing in some traditionary history that is confusing in one respect. He is given the name of Evan, Owan, and Ellis Thomas, evidently confounding him with some other than the man Maj. White reported as being killed in the first raid.

In 1764, William Furman and Nimrod Ashby left the Furman fort near the Hanging Rock below Romney and crossed the country to hunt deer in the Jersey Mountain. They were overtaken by a band of Delawares, and both were killed. This was the band which had been in Frederick County, and penetrated as far as Cedar Creek. On their way through Hampshire County, they Killed Oliver Kremer, and took his wife prisoner. The band divided; one undertook the settlements under the base of the North Mountain, and the others started for Cedar Creek. The latter neighborhood was saved by a singular incident: A woman who was fleeing from the white settlement, ran South for about eight or nine miles, and thus kept in advance of the Indians. She met two brothers named Fawcett, near their homes, and told them what had happened. They gave the warning to others, and the families hastened to Stephen's Fort, where Old Forge was afterwards started by Zane. The Indians found the people prepared, and turned away and joined the other party, after plundering some vacant houses. It has often puzzled many persons to find a reason why the Indians did not burn every house. It might be, the various tribes expected to gather enough strength and combination to some day utterly destroy the whites, and then they would occupy the deserted houses.

In 1765, a roving band attacked a settlement on Narrow Passage Creek, not far from Woodstock, killing an old man named Geo. Sigler. In 1766, they tried the Narrow Passage settlement again, this time killing two men named Sheetz and Taylor. The same year, the Powell's Fort was visited, but passing on, they went to the residence of John Gatewood on South River and there murdered a *Menonist preacher* named John Roads, and also his wife and three sons. The other children were made captives. The Court made an allowance for these children. This is supposed to have been the last massacre East of the North Mountain. Many more well established incidents of Indian warfare and sufferings of the early settlers could be given, but want of space forbids further notice. Some names of the settlers who were conspicuous, that have not been mentioned, may receive notice in other pages. We must close this chapter of such stirring events, so that we may introduce to the reader the old settlers in their new role, as enlisted soldiers, to fight battles with the Indian and his French allies. In the next chapter it will be seen that the fearful visitations to Frederick County related in the foregoing chapter, were during the French and Indian War, and the massacres were committed by roving bands of savages, who, skulked regular war-fare, and chose one of murder and pillage.

CHAPTER XV

The Indian and French War

The reader will remember that it was in 1752 that Governor Dinwiddie arrived in Virginia to assume control of the infant colony that had for some time been threatened with invasion from the French, who claimed all territory wheresoever the French standard was planted. France had at that time a line of forts from New Orleans to Quebec. In this line was the famous Fort du Quesne on the Ohio River, the site of the City of Pittsburg. Of course, all the forts were garrisoned, and communication kept open along the whole line.

The French made their first appearance in North America in 1534, forty years after the landing of Columbus with his Spaniards. Entering the St. Lawrence River, Jacques Cartier, commanding the expedition, laid claim to all the territory for France. In 1608 Quebec was founded by the French. Large immigrations encouraged advances through the country to the West and South as far as the Great Waters—meaning the Gulf of Mexico on the South and the Pacific Ocean on the West—so far as they knew. In June, 1673, the upper Mississippi was discovered by Marquette, a Monk of the Franciscan order. Six years later, La Salle made other explorations by way of the Great Lakes. Entering a river on Lake Michigan, he finally sailed down the Illinois River and erected a fort at a point where Peoria now stands, calling it Crêve Coeur, signifying "broken heart," his difficulties had been so hopeless. In 1682, La Salle pushed his expedition to the Gulf, by way of the Mississippi River, claiming all territory on either side. He named the vast claim Louisiana, after his royal master Louis XIV. The garrisons and all French officers and soldiers from the St. Lawrence to the Gulf, adopted every measure needed to make friends with the Indian tribes. They taught them that the French would protect their rights and drive out their natural enemy, the British. The French were well informed of the frequent conflicts between the colonists and the Indians, all of which went to show oppression and cruelty on the part of the British invader, who had no regard or respect for the rights of the Aborigines. The Indians had shown some evidences of open hostility, and were ready to form the alliance proposed by the French. Then it was that the Indian villages and towns were gradually moved towards the French lines, having learned of the approach of a friendly power from the West. They were always careful, however, to not abandon their villages entirely; always sending bands of warriors to the hunting grounds beyond the great mountains. The lowland tribes had friendly relations with the colonists, and never voluntarily left the tidewater section. The great valley lying West of the mountain range called the Blue Ridge, extending through from Georgia, the edge of North Carolina, Virginia, Maryland and Pennsylvania, was regarded by colonists and the savage tribes as the hunting grounds of the natives, extending through the Seventeenth and far into the Eighteenth Centuries.

There had been many treaties between the Virginia colonists and the Indians, both at home and abroad, that the whites were to make no encroachments on the rights reserved for the use of any tribe who chose to hunt or range in this territory. Some of the agreements and stipulations were very severe, to-wit: If any strange Indian was found hunting or roaming in the country East of the Great Mountains, "he could be killed or captured and sold as a slave:" and if any white man was found in the section West of the Big Mountains, he should not appeal to the Colony of Virginia for redress in case he suffered at the hands of the Indians. So it can be safely stated, that no white settlers ever ventured to enter the forbidden country until about 1728, being about twelve years after Governor Spottswood announced to the world that the great hitherto unknown country was now open for settlement.

It must be understood that all the tribes had some kind of understanding between themselves; that certain regions with imaginary lines, were claimed by the individual tribes as their domain, until some breach occurred between them when bloody encounters often destroyed such rights; and in several instances were exterminated. As the more powerful increased in strength, it was but natural that they should dominate in royal fashion in their respective sections. The author has with much difficulty discovered who the tribes were, of interest to this section; and where they were located. The following list is given to preserve their history. Consulting the best authorities on the Aborigines, we find these tribes had a common language; and while their dialects differed somewhat, yet they could communicate with each other. The tribes here mentioned made regular forays from about 1710 to 1734, with their bands of hunters, into what was then known as the *Indian Country*, which embraced everything West of what was called the Big Mountains—the Blue Ridge Range.

I. The Shawanese (Shawnee), the most powerful and warlike of all, claimed all the hunting ground between the Blue Ridge and the Alleganies, and as far South and West as the Mississippi. They had three large villages in this section: one near where Winchester now stands, one on the North River, now Shenandoah County, and one on the South Branch below the present site of Moorefield. The Shawanese were ever ready for bloodshed; but they allowed other tribes to visit them, demanding tribute from them in their expeditions. The Valley country was regarded as the battle ground for many visiting tribes. All writers agree that the French movement along the western boundary, resulted in relief to the colonists. This tribe (Shawanese) gave untold trouble to the first settlers, while they moved their villages towards the West, as the white immigration rapidly increased after 1736. The outlying settlements suffered from many attacks; the settlers finding it necessary to erect numerous small forts and stockades. Sometime prior to 1753, the French kept in close touch with all the tribes; and particularly did this apply to the Shawanese. The prospect of bloody wars on the colonists, supported by their French neighbors, attracted their attention towards a new settlement on the Ohio River.

Kercheval says: "In the spring of 1754, the Indians suddenly and unexpectedly moved off, and entirely left the Valley."

II. The next tribe was the "Tuscaroras." Their villages were near the Cohongoroota—now Berkley County. The Creek and Church bear the name of this tribe to this day.

III. The Senedos, who occupied the village on the river in Shenandoah County, was an offshoot from the Shawanese, one of the young chiefs having colonized at that point. In 1732 the Cherokees from the South exterminated them.

IV. The Catawbas, were South Carolina Indians, having several villages on the Catawba River.

The Delawares, had their villages on the Susquehanna River, Pennsylvania.

VI. The Susquenoughs, who have been confounded with the Susquehanna River tribes, was a large and friendly tribe. They were first found along the Chesapeake Bay; but the warlike Cenela tribe drove them from the tidewater section. They finally settled along the Upper Potomac. Many evidences of their villages are to be seen at this day.

VII. The Cenelas, also moved westward; and they too started villages on the upper Potomac.

VIII. The Pascataway tribe, remained on the head waters of the Chesapeake.

IX. The Cherokees, who had villages on the Tennessee River, and in certain sections of Carolina, Georgia and Alabama, were noted for their great stature, in complexion resembling the white race. This tribe made annual forays to the upper Valley. They were part of the Six Nations of the South, having for their central tribe the "Muscogulges;" the Seminoles, Chickasaws, Choctaws and Creeks forming the Nation, as the organization was called.

The nine tribes mentioned were regular visitors to the Valley country up to 1740, as also were hunters from the five Nations (often called the Six Nations in treaties), who had their villages scattered along the rivers and lakes of middle and Western New York: The Mohawks, Oneidas, Onondagas, Cayugas and Senecas. As previously mentioned, the Indians who claimed the right to hunt in the territory West of the Blue Ridge, had a language common to all the tribes. The French have several interesting histories, descriptive of the French expeditions in North America prior to the Revolutionary War. From studies of these histories, much has been learned concerning the Indian, both as to his traits and dialect—the latter being styled by the French writers as the "Algonquin" language, who assert that it was in common use by all Indians between the Carolinas and Massachusetts.

We have well written traditions, entitled to credit for accuracy, that confirm the above statement; and many proofs that the colonists, having learned the language from Powhatan, had but little difficulty in understanding the language of the other tribes. The reader will readily see that when the white settlers began to assert and maintain their rights under grants from the Colonial government, they found numerous bands of roving Indians to contend with; and consequently many collisions occurred, resulting in death to the settlers and also to many Indians. For although the savages were stubborn and vengeful, and yielded slowly to the encroachments upon their favorite hunting grounds, the old pioneers had come into the promised land to stay; and every new arrival of immigrant trains pressed farther West; so the old denizens of the wild regions had many wrongs to redress. They believed they were the natural and lawful owners of the soil, and the British had no right to wrest it from them by right of discovery or settlement of her people—though they might by conquest have a claim. But the Indian had now become fully aroused, and was ready to meet the issue. And thus was inaugurated the first Indian war. Supported by the French, a bloody and cruel war continued from 1754 until 1766. At no time during the twelve years, could the border settlers feel safe from massacre. Many occurred; whole settlements were driven back from the Allegany region whither many had penetrated; whole families frequently disappeared forever,—the victims of the tomahawk and scalping knife. The Colonial government took prompt action; raised an army, and placed at its head Col. Fry and Lt. Col. Washington. We gather from the Washington notes, that this army numbered three hundred good and tried frontiersmen. The march was made from the village of Winchester, through the mountains to what was then known and is still, as Great Meadows. Near this point, Lt. Col. Washington opened the war in earnest, by surrounding an encampment of the French, killing the commanding officer and several others and capturing the remainder of the force. Capt. Fry having died shortly after this capture, Washington made Great Meadows his base; built what he called Fort Necessity, and then advanced with his main force toward the French Fort Duquesne. Ramsey, in his biography of Washington, gives a complete and graphic account of this first failure of Washington to accomplish a victory. His retreat to Fort Necessity before the advancing French, the attack on his garrison and capitulation to the French commander, securing terms for the safe return of "his army to the inhabited parts of Virginia" are historical facts too well known to require further mention.

This movement against the French, produced a sensation. The French and their Indian allies grew desperate. The British government in 1755, hastened Genl. Braddock with two regiments of regulars across the ocean and on to the struggling colonists. Braddock arrived at the mouth of Chesapeake Bay, Feb. 20, 1755. Genl. Craighill in his exhaustive work on the movements of Genl. Braddock, says: "Two regiments of British troops arrived at Hampton Roads about the same time, and were sent at once to Alexandria, and there quartered. Sir John St. Clair arrived about six weeks before Braddock, and assumed the office of Quartermaster General and Engineer of Roads, and made a reconnoissance of the country as far West as Cumberland, in company with Gov. Sharpe of Maryland. Fort Cumberland, then called Fort Mt. Pleasant, had been built in 1754; and they found it occupied by the Virginia, Maryland and South Carolina troops. The Pennsylvania troops that had been promised, failed to put in their appearance. St. Clair returned to Williamsburg by way of Winchester, traveling over and inspecting the road that Col. Washington had previously opened from Winchester to Wills Creek and Forks of Capon; and having had a conference with Washington, proceeded to Williamsburg to meet Genl. Braddock. (See the Washington letters and Diary). The governors of the several colonies were in convention at Alexandria early in April, and tendered Braddock and his staff a noted reception, and—doubtless, offered some good advice. Winchester was selected as the base of operations, and the point for letters to be sent to the General. Ten days after the convention, Braddock was at Frederick, Maryland, and there had interviews with Washington and Franklin; and it was there that Washington (who had previously resigned his commission as Colonel) was offered a place on the General's staff; though Sparks says "Braddock marched into the interior and was joined by Washington at Winchester, when the latter assumed the duties and station of aide." The Washington letters state that he rode from Winchester and overtook the General at Frederickton May 5, 1755, and then returned to Winchester. Sargeant's History says: "By St. Clair's advice, the army was to start from Alexandria in two divisions: one regiment and a portion of the stores to Winchester, Virginia, whence a new road was nearly completed to Fort Cumberland; and the other regiment with the remainder, by way of Frederick, Maryland.

On the 8th and 9th of April, the Provincials and six companies of the 44th regiment under Sir Peter Halkett, set out for Winchester, and Lt. Col. Gage and four companies remained to escort the artillery. April 18th, the 48 regt. under Col. Dunbar, set out for Frederick, Md. The Maryland Governor and many Maryland citizens urged the General to move the whole force through Maryland, knowing a road would be opened to Fort Cumberland or Wills Creek; and as this was impracticable, causing too much delay, Col. Dunbar on May 1st, headed his division for the Potomac, so as to enter Virginia and strike the road already opened. Washington in a letter dated May 14th, says: "Col. Dunbar's regiment recrossed at Connogogee and came down within six miles of Winchester to take the new road to Wills Creek." Irving says that Braddock went from Frederick to Winchester; that the road on the Maryland side had not been made. Returning to the division under Sir Peter Halkett, when he left Alexandria, Genl.

Craighill says their first day's march took the command to old C. H. (Fairfax) 18 miles, then to Colemans 12 miles—Nourse's 15 miles—Thompsons, 12 miles—Keys 17 miles—to Winchester 23 miles; crossing the Shenandoah at Keys Ford and the mountain at Keys Gap; stopping near the site of Charlestown, and then to Winchester. So many erroneous impressions being held regarding Braddock's march to Winchester, the author deemed it wise to give the matter space for a brief statement of facts. It must be added here, that the British government urged all the American colonies to adopt measures for mutual protection, and to be prepared to act in concert with the British troops under British generals. A union was formed in 1754. We will only mention what was done by Virginia as a result of this agreement; and keep in view that this work is intended to show the connection the old Frederick County and the upper Shenandoah settlers had with the Indian and French War. Virginia was ready with eight hundred volunteers to support Braddock on his arrival at Alexandria. This force was divided into eight Companies, all officered by experienced Indian fighters, who were familiar with Indian warfare, and the force composed of settlers who had been constantly alert for years defending their homes from Indian forays. It is to be regretted that no authentic list of that eight hundred was preserved. The writer will in succeeding pages; give the names of quite a number who were certified by the old county court as soldiers entitled to a liberal bounty that the Virginia government granted them in land along the Ohio River, for their service in the Indian Wars.

The following are the names of the captains of the nine companies: Stephen, Mercer, Lewis, Waagener, Stewart, Hogg, Peyronny, Poulson and Cocke. The three first named became distinguished generals with Washington in the Revolution against Great Britain, 1776-00. General Braddock on his arrival in the village of Winchester, headed a formidable army, as it appeared to the Valley settlers. The regular troops were well equipped; and they with the Virginians as guides and skirmishers, together with Maryland's quota, gave hope that the Indian war must soon end. The British General, however, failed to rely on the troops the colonies offered him; and used them as rear guards and laborers to make the roads suited to his lofty ideas of his line of march into the Monongohela country, where he arrived and crossed the river July 9th, 1755, with his army of about 2,000 men.

Before leaving Winchester, Braddock detached one of the Virginia companies, with Capt. Thomas Lewis, for the purpose of making a forced march to the Greenbrier country, and there building block houses and stockades, to intercept the movements and raids of the Indians, who Col. Washington had learned were then moving from the Ohio River villages toward Staunton. We must not attempt a description of the disaster and utter defeat that overwhelmed Braddock and his army, after they crossed the Monongohela on that fateful day. The ambuscade was complete. Braddock disregarded the opinions of experienced frontiersmen such as Washington, Stephen, Stewart and many others; and madly rushed on, to fall mortally wounded in the midst of 700 of his army who fell dead in the first terrific attack. The remainder were put to flight. The General was carried off the field of carnage in his own silk sash, which was converted into a hammock. Tradition says that this hammock was fastened to the pommels of two saddles, and the General carried between the troopers' horses. Another account is, that his British officers, by relays, carried him in his sash the entire distance, except when crossing the river, he was placed in a wagon.

The Braddock sash incident deserves fuller notice, by reason of its close association with the historical events of the County. The sash, which was large and of perfect weave, carefully preserved as one of the many relics of this disastrous war, was presented to Genl. Zachary Taylor in 1846, when he was engaged in the Mexican War, with the understanding that he should present it to the bravest man in the army. The General, however, never understood it that way, and deemed it best to retain and endeavor to preserve it. At this writing it is in the possession of his daughter Mrs. Bettie Dandridge (formerly Mrs. Maj. Bliss). The Author has seen it; and feels safe in pronouncing it the sash used on the occasion mentioned.

Genl. Braddock died July 13th, at 8 P. M., near the Great Meadow Fort. He was buried in the middle of the road, and the troops and wagon trains passed over the grave, so that it could not be found to disturb and mutilate his remains.

The tragic end of this man gave the event such notoriety, that each succeeding generation of the Valley people handed down the oft repeated story of Braddock's defeat, until it has become part of the history of the Old County and her subdivisions.

Some writers have described him as desperate in his fortunes, brutal in his behavior, obstinate in his sentiments, but withal a capable captain.

He has been called a gallant bull-dog. Another says he was profligate, arrogant, and a bigot to military rules.

Washington's coolness and experience succeeded in making a retreat that became as famous as the defeat. The withdrawal of the British army left all the western borders of Virginia and Pennsylvania exposed to untold cruelties perpetrated by the Indians, who had become more infuriated than ever before. The French were willing allies in much of the devastation that swept over that region. Indians in great numbers forced their way into the Valley at several points. Many settlers in the exposed places fled from the Valley over into eastern Virginia. War between England and France was the result of this defeat. Great Britain declared war against France May 9th, 1756. This put an end to what was known as the French and Indian War; and opened what has been distinguished by historians as the British and French War for the conquest of North America. The poor colonists were in trying straits; and when the great need for men on the border, was the daily cry, they were called upon for soldiers, to protect their settlements from the savages. The French soon discovered that their Indian allies must be used in regular warfare, and not for the butchery of women and children; and this new movement by the French, gave relief eventually to the outlying settlements. Virginia furnished 1,600 men for the new army. Washington was made Colonel, Adam Stephen Lt. Col., and Andrew Lewis, Major. England was alarmed at the successful campaigns of the French along the entire border line. The dark days seemed to portend the end of England's claim. The French and Indians had glowing prospects of conquest of all North America, which were not diminished until 1758, when the scales began to show the weight of the Colonists and British forces; and when 1760 dawned upon the country, victory shone upon the British arms, resulting finally in England's conquest of Canada, after a struggle extending over 150 years. The French were driven from the Ohio Valley, and their Indian allies were left to bear the brunt of vengeance that the old settlers were now ready to wreak upon them, wherever found.

The treaty of peace between England and France was signed at Fontainbleau, 1762.

Returning to the defeated and retreating Braddock army, we find them dispirited. The British regulars followed Col. Dunbar to Fort Cumberland, thoroughly demoralized. Although their flight was rapid, they would have been overtaken by the pursuing enemy and doubtless destroyed, had it not been for the coolness and experience of Washington, who headed the Virginians, all of whom were accustomed to Indian warfare. They made frequent stands during that terrible retreat of one hundred and twenty miles through the mountains, and from ambush hurled many of the advancing bands of murderous savages to their death; and thus their retreat was covered. Many of the Eight Hundred were left strewn along this line of retreat. The troops under Washington, knew what it meant to their homes in the Great Valley, if the French and Indians were allowed to reach their home country. So we find the "Washington Notes and Diary" full of the most pathetic statements concerning the valor and desperation the Valley soldiers displayed along the line of march. Dunbar never halted to render any aid. Sir Peter Halkett is mentioned as on two occasions having rallied his Hibernians, and fought them valiantly. Dunbar having sent his supply train to the front, the rear-guard never saw this train or received any rations until they arrived at Fort Cumberland. Hunger and hardship depleted the ranks of the dauntless Eight Hundred as badly as did the pursuing foe. The names of many who fell by the wayside on this retreat, were years afterwards presented to the old Frederick County court by the survivors, asking that their widows and children should receive aid from the Court, which promptly made provision for this class. Many descendants of this noble band have no knowledge of the service their ancestors rendered in those trying days. The Author in some cases has been able to locate some such descendants, from whom he received grateful acknowledgments. More than one Colonial Dame owes her membership in her Society, to such accidental information. And, reader, it might be well for you to some day enquire of a successor of the old Clerk who now incidentally mentions these facts, and learn from him if your ancestors can be traced to this Spartan band which saved the Great Valley in the middle part of the Eighteenth Century, from untold horrors.

Col. Dunbar left the wounded and sick at Fort Cumberland, exposed to the enemy, and with the remnant of his Royal Regiments, marched away to Philadelphia. One of Washington's letters says that St. Clair, who was in the village of Winchester, in charge of the base of this military movement, also moved towards Philadelphia, claiming that he had not received orders from Col. Dunbar. Washington, who was only a staff officer on this expedition, was without authority to further act, and leaving the Virginians, South Carolinians and the remnants of two

Maryland companies, to be governed and used as the surviving company officers should determine, returned to Winchester; and there wrote two characteristic letters to Gov. Dinwiddie, which resulted in his going to Williamsburg during the latter part of the Winter of 1756. There he reported to the Governor. He received a commission from the Colonial Government as Colonel, and was given the command of all the Virginia forces then in the field and others who were to make up Virginia's quota, for the great struggle rapidly approaching between France and England.

Col. Washington returned to Frederick County; and once more assumed command, making Winchester his base. As previously stated, his associate officers were Lt. Col. Adam Stephen and Major Andrew Lewis. Here he organized his army. The old border companies were recruited and mustered in to serve during the war. So once more, the Valley people felt secure. Fort Loudoun was built; and other forts and stockades were hastily erected all through the settlements, and preparations made once more for renewed hostilities. This time desperation seized the whole country. This brutal war was to be terminated. An active campaign was conducted by the British and Colonists. Washington once more started on his march to Fort Cumberland in July, 1758, with 2,000 men in his division. There he was to form part of the army of 6,000, with Genl. Forbes in command.

We have the inclination but not the space to recount the disasters of this army, in their intended attack on Fort Duquesne. Washington, however, on November 25th, with about 1,000 men, succeeded in capturing the Fort, which was demolished by the retreating enemy.

November 25th, 1758, Fort Duquesne passed from the French to the English. On the 26th, Genl. Forbes wrote William Pitt, who had been instrumental in supplying reinforcements to assist the Virginian Colony in repelling the savages and their French allies, of the fall of the fort and retreat of the enemy down the Ohio. The General found the fort burned; but he changed the name to Pitt, and built a new fort on the site. He also announced another important incident, that on this day, being Sabbath, Rev. Mr. Beatty, a Presbyterian Chaplain, preached a Thanksgiving sermon.

Owing to bad generalship on the part of Forbes, heavy losses to his army occurred in his preliminary movements. The reader will remember this was the third campaign made by Washington and his Valley companies; and must be reminded at this point, that Washington found time during this period, to be a candidate for election to the House of Burgesses, when he was defeated; again a candidate in 1758, while in active service, and was elected; again in 1761, was re-elected. (This is more fully treated elsewhere.)

In recounting the occurrences of this last movement against the French—known as the Forbes Expedition—the reader, if he be a student of history, will remember that the British also moved against the fortified lines of the French from the St. Lawrence, Niagara, and the Ohio, at the same time, with well equipped armies; and although reverses fell to the lot of the British and Colonial troops in all these preliminary movements, the French lines were broken when Fort Duquesne was captured by the army that had Winchester for its base of operations. A similar attack was made on forts lower down the Ohio, after great struggles in the mountain regions, the Indian allies pursuing their mode of warfare of skirmishing from ambush. The army under Genl. Forbes often wavered, and suffered severe losses. Whole companies were destroyed or captured; and before the French finally gave way and abandoned the country, the British army had suffered such losses, that at the close of the long and bloody campaign, it lacked the spirit and efficiency to pursue and destroy the retreating foe.

The Indian tribes, then known as the Six Nations, and the Shawanese and their neighboring tribes who had been drawn into the war, concentrated their forces and retired to what was known as the Big Woods, across the Ohio opposite the point known as Point Pleasant, soon to become famous for one of the last great battles the Indians fought. In the Big Woods were many Indian villages. There the Indians sullenly waited further movements; and stubbornly contested every advance made toward the country they held as their own. The confederated tribes were governed and controlled by great warriors, as Cornstalk (a Shawnee chief), Blue Jacket, Red Hawk (a Delaware) and chiefs of the Mingo tribe, and Wyandottes, and the celebrated Logan of the Cayugas. The Colonists and British generals were anxious to treat with these great warriors, and have the inhuman war to close. England was too much engaged in her war with France, to send further aid to the Colonists, to protect them from the warring tribes; and while the Colonists, especially the Virginia border settlers West of the Blue Ridge, were unable to wage successful warfare across the Ohio, they succeeded in holding back in great measure any heavy advance into the outlying settlements. But it must not be concluded that the Indians were inactive; for we have many authentic accounts of massacres occurring during the period prior to the Fountainbleau Treaty of Peace. The Indian warriors were often wily enough to penetrate far into the settlements both in the upper and lower Valley, on hunting expeditions, and to plunder the country, and carry back not only horses and provisions for their villages, but many white prisoners.

Finally, the day came when the British made peace with France, and could aid the colonies; and the Indians, seeing their French allies had deserted them, were ready to make peace. But the terms they offered, were regarded by the Colonial governments as too objectionable to be considered; and concessions demanded of the tribes, once more aroused them to frenzy; and all the savagery of their wild nature blazed forth in alarming symptoms. The long looked-for peace had not come to the border people; the great war-like tribes would not yield. They regarded the white man as the invader of their soil and the murderers of their women and children. They were alarmed by the determined encroachments of England. All the old French forts were manned with British troops; and new forts built far out along the great lakes, formed lines in their rear. So it was, that these renowned warriors felt that a great effort must be made to exterminate the whites and drive them beyond the Great Mountains, leaving to the old owners of the Great Valley, hunting grounds and all to the West, including their Big Woods territory beyond the Ohio. The time had come for them to defend their rights and recover them from the whites, or be driven out and become wandering tribes forever. History is so full of the destructive war these tribes plunged the country into, 1764-65, that we cannot give space for more than a brief mention, to show the connection of the Lower Valley with another Indian war. The object was now to recover all the country from the Lakes to the Carolinas. Hostilities were opened by wholesale murders of the Indian traders, only two out of 120 escaping. Whole garrisons along the great Lakes, were slaughtered. Furious attacks were made on Fort Pitt. That garrison was reinforced, and held out, though they suffered a loss of over one hundred in killed and wounded. We may briefly add here, that it was during this war that the Wyoming massacre occurred, and many settlements were desolated on the Susquehanna.

Several battalions of Virginians—men of the Valley region—were engaged in this new and most destructive of all the Indian wars; which terminated in the Autumn of 1764, after more than a year of butchery along the entire border settlements, which was especially destructive to the western sections of the two Valley counties, Frederick and Augusta. A peace was effected that was to leave all the territory embraced in the two counties, forever free from the Indian claim. The Indian Confederacy entered into a treaty with the British and Colonists. This treaty, the chiefs endeavored to have their tribes live up to, and no more enter the white man's country. Some excursions were made, but only to hunt and wander over their old haunts; and they were very peaceably disposed for several years. But in 1773, some white men who desired revenge for the murder of their wives in the wars previous to this period, killed several Indians. The Indians retaliated, and made preparations for an uprising. This brings us to what has been called Dunmore's War. He was then Governor of Virginia; and regarding the situation as one requiring his personal attention, he called for volunteers from the Valley counties—Frederick and her three new offsprung counties, Shenandoah, Hampshire and Berkley, and also Augusta. Very soon, Col. Andrew Lewis had a force of 1,000 men moving from Augusta towards the Ohio and Kanawha Rivers; while the Governor with ten companies from the lower counties, proceeded towards Fort Pitt, where there seemed to be some conflict of authority. In the spring of 1774, Kercheval says: "Daniel Morgan and James Wood, commanded two of the companies." The names of other officers of the ten companies may appear later on, under the head of "Sketches of certain families." Several prominent men on the frontier have been held responsible for this unfortunate event. Chief among them were Capt. Michael Cresap, commanding the port at Wheeling, and Col. Croghan and his nephew, Dr. John Connolly, both ambitious and strong men—true and loyal to Virginia concerning her claim as to certain disputed territory around Pittsburg, then unsettled between Virginia and Pennsylvania, (which subject will be fuller treated in other pages of this work). Connolly took possession of Fort Pitt, and partly razed and dismantled it, and then built one to his own liking on the old foundation, calling it Fort Dunmore.

Capt. Cresap was a willing ally of Connolly's in his independent war on the Indians. He had not believed in sparing life, so far as concerned the Indians, and now exhibited desire to exterminate the race if possible. A careful study of the causes and instigators of this Dunmore War, will repay the reader, and enable him to place the blame where it rightfully belongs. This war resulted in great loss of life, principally in Col. Lewis's command, in his marches through the mountains and frequent ambuscades, finally ending with great loss of life at Point Pleasant, October 10, 1774—a memorable day. Some of the survivors have left recorded facts relating to *the* deperate fighting on both sides. The far-famed Shawnee Chieftain Cornstalk, commander-in-chief; Logan, renowned as well for his oratory as for his adroitness as a captain in battle and other chiefs, supported by brave Red warriors on the one side; and the Lewis brothers with their famous captains and the White heroes of the other wars, on the other, made this final struggle along the Ohio, one that has become famous the world over. Col. Lewis won a victory and drove the Tribes across the Ohio; pursued them some distance, and was overtaken by Dunmore with his Lower Valley Companies, and was informed that he, the Governor, had already effected arrangements for a new treaty.

Viewing this final struggle of the Cresap-Connelly-Dunmore War, as we see it now, shorn of all prejudice and hatred between the races, we are forced to the conclusion that it was precipitated by the Cresap-Connelly Confederation for no other motives than greed and revenge; their ambition being to plant new colonies on captured territory regardless of all treaties, and secure from the complaisant Governor grants for thousands of acres of the Ohio country, and then parcel it out to the new settlers at their own price and terms. Dunmore frustrated their plans by his treaty; thus securing the friendship of the hostile tribes so far as he was concerned, but leaving bitterness and discontent between the Colonists who had been drawn into the war. Dissensions soon arose between Lewis's branch of the service and the Cresap factions; and the border was again inflamed with fearful results. The brave Lewis and his whole force believed that Dunmore had deliberately planned for the annihilation of the gallant little army that had crossed over from the Greenbrier country, to aid the settlers along the Ohio to repel invasions from the Redmen. More than one writer has charged Dunmore with duplicity with the Cresap-Connolly factions, to incite feuds and jealousies between the Colonists, to blind them to his British master's oppressions, by whom the rights of the struggling colonists were disregarded. But his plans were broken by the terrible battle of the Point. Lewis and his noble survivors emerged from that conflict to become household words through succeeding generations, for their heroism, while the name of Dunmore was expunged from the records of the Valley for his perfidy and brutality. That there was discontent among the settlers along the Ohio, there can be no question of doubt. The line between the two colonies of Virginia and Pennsylvania, had not been fully determined. The conflict of ruling authority in the territory adjacent to Fort Pitt, was giving much concern. The two Colonial governments were at wordy war; and when Dunmore marched with his army to Fort Pitt, with the declared purpose of aiding the Cresap-Connolly factions to suppress the Indian uprising, he, immediately upon his arrival, sanctioned what Connolly had done, in usurping the claim to all the country around Fort Pitt and to the West. This he had claimed as within the jurisdiction and control of Virginia, ignoring all claims of Pennsylvania, whose citizens were made prisoners and punished for their refusal to recognize him as the *Assistant* Governor of Virginia. This question grew so serious, that the Congress in session at Philadelphia in 1775, was appealed to by many settlers along the Ohio, to carve out another State and recognize their grants. The members of that Congress from Pennsylvania and Virginia, issued an address to the complaining sections of the western border, and urged them to abandon all contentions and animosities, and devote their united efforts to sustaining the country in the great struggle for independence, and save the infant Republic from British rule.

This address was signed by P. Henry, Richard Henry Lee, Benjamin Harrison, Thos. Jefferson, John Dickinson, Geo. Ross, B. Franklin, Jas. Wilson and Charles Humphreys.

dated Philadelphia, July 25th, 1775.

This patriotic effort failed to quiet the claims of the border people; but the love of country drew their attention to the impending conflict between the colonies,—now States, and England; and the disputed claims were allowed to rest until the close of the great Revolution: of which, more anon.

Returning to the treaty effected by Dunmore at Camp Charlotte, on the Ohio River, the Governor immediately set out for Williamsburg, the seat of Government, leaving behind him Cresap and Connolly bitter enemies—each bent upon the overthrow of the other. Genl. Lewis, chagrined at the domineering conduct of the Governor, who showed no appreciation of the terrible sacrifices made by the Point Pleasant heroes, obeyed the order to return to Greenbrier and there disband his forces.

Of the treaty something should be said: The principal chiefs and warriors assembled in grand council, to consider Dunmore's offers. Many were sullen, and not disposed to yield to Long Knives, as they called the White commander. Cornstalk, the Shawanese Chief and acknowledged King of the Northern Confederacy, had given his word that peace could be effected with his people. He had in battle given his orders, which were implicitly obeyed; but in this council, his warrior tribes had to be dealt with by argument; and being gifted with eloquence, he had great power over them. One of Dunmore's staff officers, Col. Richard Willson, in his interesting history of the Dunmore expedition, speaking of the august attitude of the great chief, pending the many discussions of the articles of peace, says: "I have heard the first orators in Virginia, Patrick Henry and R. H. Lee, but never have I heard one whose power of delivery surpassed that of Cornstalk."

Cornstalk succeeded in obtaining consent from nearly all the tribes of his confederacy. The other chief, of equal renown, was Logan. He refused to leave his tent to take part in the peace proceedings—He had no faith in the border White settlers. He believed they were bent upon the complete overthrow and destruction of the Indian—He had agreed to more than one treaty, broken by the Whites. Their villages had been destroyed, and many peaceable men of his tribe had been recently murdered; and he was sore in heart. The loss of his forest home, to be taken by the White stranger, his kindred all killed. No wonder that he hesitated to enter into treaty with the same people. The Governor knew the importance of securing this Chief's assent to the peace settlement; and commissioned several of his officers to visit Logan in his tent and use every effort to have him come before the council. He declared he would not oppose the treaty made by Dunmore, but refused to meet the Whites in council. We are indebted to one of these officers for preserving an incident in this warrior's life, that gave him more fame, perhaps, than any other Redman ever attained, for the pathetic picture he drew of the Race and their traits. It will be remembered that it has been shown that the Tribes composing this Northern Confederacy, spoke a language that had become somewhat familiar to the Colonists. So we need not be surprised to learn from one of these officers, that Logan impressed him so much with his statement of the wrongs he had suffered from the White man in his onward march westward, and what he had offered to the friendly settler when he went his way, that they understood every word he uttered, and gave his speech in his reports of the treaty.

Mr. Jefferson, the gifted orator of Virginia, in his celebrated notes on the Indian Wars, speaking of his treaty, says: "I may challenge the whole orations of Demosthenes and Cicero, and of any more eminent orators, if Europe has furnished more eminent, to produce a single passage superior to it." Doubtless this oration has often been repeated by the reader, when a school boy; and here it is to remind him of an era he may have forgotten:

"I appeal to any White to say if he ever entered Logan's cabin hungry, and he gave him not meat; if ever he came cold and naked, and he clothed him not. During the course of the last long and bloody war, Logan remained idle in his cabin, an advocate for peace. Such was my love for the Whites, that my countrymen pointed as they passed and said: 'Logan is the friend of the White man.' I had even thought to live with you, but for the injuries of one man. Colonel Cresap the last Spring, in cold blood and unprovoked, murdered all the relations of Logan, not even sparing my women and children. There runs not a drop of my blood in the veins of any living creature. This called on me for revenge. For my country I rejoice at the beams of peace; but do not harbor a thought that mine is the joy of fear. Logan never felt fear. He will not turn on his heel to save his life. Who is there to mourn for Logan; not one."

It is a matter of history that the two distinguished warriors mentioned, were faithful to the terms of the treaty, though some writers charge them with treachery and a return to deeds of butchery. This is not sustained by facts.

We have traditional history to acquaint us with their lives during the next three years; but it is not of material interest to relate. They were friendly with the Whites, and lived on peaceful terms with all the border people. Cornstalk often related how the warlike tribes were in a state of discontent, and felt that the Whites were disregarding the terms of the treaty, and claimed that his powerful tribe, the Shawanese, were not disposed to redress their wrongs except by the mode the treaty provided. It must be remembered that the country was on the threshold of the Revolutionary War. England held the captured army posts lying beyond the Chillicothe Indian villages, all manned with regular British troops. She had viewed with anxiety the spirit of independence manifested in the colonies; and hoping to allay this spirit, encouraged the discontented Indians to resist encroachments made along the border, principally along the Ohio River settlements. So when the spring of 1777 came, the Indians were looking to the British officers for help; and refused to further treat with the colonists. Cornstalk viewed this state of affairs in the Indian encampments, with so much uneasiness, that he and Red Hawk visited the Point Pleasant Post, then held by the

Virginians under Capt. Arbuckle, an old Indian fighter who had been the celebrated guide for Genl. Lewis's expedition three years previous. Cornstalk told the Captain that all the nations had joined the English except himself and the Shawanese, and that unless they were protected by the Whites, "they would have to swim with the stream." Capt. Arbuckle blundered in his decision. He determined not to allow Cornstalk and his friends to return, but held them as hostages for the good conduct of his powerful tribe. This was unfortunate: Cornstalk felt that the post had violated the rules of war. They came with good intentions, and he virtually as the accredited agent for his tribe; and he should have been allowed safe return; and more than likely the friendly relations might have been maintained; and the influence of this powerful tribe on the other nations, might have resulted in beneficial changes in the next few years. It was natural that the Shawanese people grew anxious when their chief and his people failed to return. His son and two young warriors grew suspicious, and came to the opposite side of the river; and the son succeeded in attracting the attention of some of the garrison who rowed over and brought the son over to see his father. He too was made a prisoner upon his arrival at the Fort; and it is related that Cornstalk then said he had been betrayed; and if the Whites desired to kill him, to do so; that he was not afraid to die. To be fair in this statement concerning the affair, it must be mentioned that the two warriors who remained on the other side of the river, killed a man named Gilmore, a returning hunter from the Indian reservation. His body was found and brought over to the Fort. Then the cry was heard: "Let us kill the Indians in the Fort." The party was led by one, Capt. Hall, a man who had boasted of his triumphs in many personal encounters with Indians. They rushed into the fort and poured deadly volleys upon the unprotected and helpless Cornstalk and his six companions. This was no triumph for Hall to boast of. More than once has his name been mentioned in condemnation of the man who instigated the cold-blooded murder of a warrior, far superior to himself in prowess of arms, as well as honor. This brilliant Indian warrior had in more than one foray, other than regular warfare, been the leader in atrocious massacres of innocent settlements in the great Valley and the mountains; but we must remember, this mode of savage warfare was practiced to overcome the Whites and drive them back from their hunting grounds, as well as to glut their vengeance. Their grievances were hard; and fearfully did this chieftain avenge them; tragically did he atone for his misdeeds. It may be added that Logan met a similar fate at the hands of trusted friends later on. These occurrences closed the friendly relations between the two races that had existed for about three years; and the Indians became the useful allies of the British wherever they could be used to harrass the colonies. The dusky warrior was once more in the field so attractive to him. All their natural instincts were for war. But the Indian wars with the Colonies that had been ruthlessly conducted for nearly thirty years, had now ceased; and the war of the Revolution was upon the war-stricken Valley.

The Author has already taken too much space to show the connection of the Valley people with the celebrated Indian Wars; and realizes that he has left untold many interesting and historic incidents of the great struggle for supremacy between the two races, in his meagre account of the general engagements. Later on he will recount more fully some of the Indian battles and massacres, in which the names of the victims may be given, and also the habits and customs prevailing among the Redmen of the Eighteenth Century.

Having previously shown the trials, privations and losses to the Shenandoah Valley settlements, in their struggles to make good their gradual conquest of territory from Indian tribes; doubtless the reader will conclude that warfare was the prime feature in the life of the first settlers; and having apparently returned to their peaceful avocations, that they were content to know war no more. But their history reveals them as ever alert to redress a wrong, coming from whatsoever source; and we are prepared to accept what has been told of their readiness to investigate the grievances complained of against their own government. Strange rumors were afloat concerning the situation around Williamsburg. The Royal Governor of Virginia had for some time been regarded with suspicion. His actions along the Ohio border were well remembered; and it was known that he had determined to oppress and overawe the colonists, and force them to submit to increasing demands made by the Crown. Dunmore knew the discontent engendered by the act of the British Parliament in 1764, taxing certain articles imported for American consumption, and disapproved by them. They regarding it as a tax without their consent. The Colonies grew indignant, but no act of rebellion occurred. Dunmore was preparing for any move made by the Virginians. In the following year when the celebrated Stamp Act was passed, a general revolt of the Americans was disclosed. Virginia in the most pronounced manner, declared her position through the Patrick Henry resolutions, which were supported with such fervor and zeal by the distinguished men who composed the General Assembly, that their adoption became a matter of warning to the British Crown. The people of Virginia were anxious to avoid a conflict, and seemed unwilling to declare any intention that could be construed into a desire to become independent of the mother government. England misconstrued this apparent loyalty; and believed that the Colonies through fear of chastisement and oppression, would never resort to arms to defend their rights. And, aside from this, the Royal Governors were loyal to the Crown, and could keep in subjection those who were inclined to rebel. Being thus deceived, England was led to commit the overt act, when her Parliament adopted the notorious Boston Port Bill, and prepared to enforce the collection of the tariff tax on the cargoes of tea then afloat in that harbor. Then it was that the fires of Rebellion were kindled in every hamlet. The Continental Congress in 1776, as it is well known, declared for Independence; and the call went out for volunteers to defend their action; and thus the old Valley was again drawn into a war that taxed their patriotism as well as their resources. How they responded will be shown later. We must follow the Virginia Governor; and see if he developed the infamous traits of character that Genl. Lewis and his followers had charged. Dunmore acting in concert with Genl. Gage, who was in command at Boston in the spring of 1775, by strategem undertook to carry out the order sent him by Genl. Gage; and the reader need not be surprised that the trusted messenger was Connolly of the Dunmore War notoriety. The object was to secure all the gunpowder in the Virginia colony, and thus prevent the colonists from supplying the soldiers who might arise in rebellion; so that without ammunition, they could be suppressed. Accordingly, the Governor contrived to have several English war-ships in easy call: One was sent up York River and anchored near Williamsburg. On the 20th of April, 1775, Dunmore seized the powder. This was done in the night. The English ship's captain with an army of soldiers marched from the landing over to Williamsburg and easily secured every keg of powder in the magazine and carried them to his ship. The next day, the Governor was openly charged with connection with the scheme; and to escape vengeance, answered that he feared an uprising of the slaves and was preparing for such an emergency. The people soon realized the extent of his dastardly work, and were aroused from mountain to sea. The volunteer companies hastened towards Williamsburg. Patrick Henry at the head of one body of men, boldly marched upon the Governor and offered him battle unless he returned the powder. To avoid a conflict, the Governor offered money in lieu of powder, which was accepted. He then had troops to land from the ships, to come and guard his palace. The Virginians never halted. They were there for revenge; and the Governor, being a coward, fled from the scene of his recent perfidy and the palace where he had lived in regal splendor for years; and with his family hastened aboard one of the English ships, and with other ships that he gathered from the Chesapeake Bay, sailed into the Norfolk port, a town of about 7,000 people. From that point he sent messengers through the surrounding country, to urge the negroes to insurrection, and aid him to destroy the rebellious population. Many slaves joined his army. His wanton destruction of property and brutal treatment of helpless citizens revealed his true character. A battle was fought at a place called Great Bridge; and after a desperate fight, the English fell back to Norfolk. The Governor was compelled to seek shelter in his ships once more. The Virginians fired upon the ships. Dunmore then fired upon the town, which resulted in the total destruction of the beautiful little seaboard city. Dunmore then sailed away to become a terror to other towns along the Chesapeake. He once sailed up the Potomac as far as Mount Vernon. After several other battles with the Colonial troops along certain shores, he sailed away with his fleet, carrying much plunder, and, as has been said by several historians, took with him about one thousand of the poor deluded slaves and sold them to the West Indies' planters. His case seems fully proven. His infamy and treachery to the Virginians was complete; and as already stated, the Old Dominion did what she could to obliterate his name from her records, leaving only enough to tell of his double dealing.

Had Dunmore forsaken his Royal master and been true to the Virginia Colony, he would have been her largest land owner. He had procured grants of land in many sections for many thousand acres. He had five tracts in Hampshire County, viz.: 400 acres on both sides of North River and Great Ca-Capon; 229 on Little Capon, 100 on Short Mountain; 284 on drains of South Branch; 129 on South Branch on the Great Wagon Road. These tracts were regarded as vacant after the Revolutionary War, and titles given to actual settlers. The 400 acres, after frequent changes, finally became the property of John A. Smith of Capon Bridge in 1879. In one of the deeds from Fairfax, he says: "This is one of the tracts surveyed by George Washington," lying on East side of North River.

CHAPTER XVI

Gleanings from the Old Courts, Succeeding the Revolutionary War

In the preceding chapters relating to the wars, which terminated with American independence for the colonies, it is appropriate in this chapter to once more refer to the court proceedings and place in evidence the prompt recognition of the valued services of some of the old soldiers of the colonial period,—we do this to not only give the names of those recognized, but also to give dates of court orders as a reference where, by diligent search, others may be found not named in this limited list. It was during the Indian Wars that the General Assembly appointed Genl. James Wood, Capt. John Hite and Robert Rutherford, commissioners for Frederick County, to settle the accounts of troops for their services in the Colonial Wars and to persons for damages done by the Indians, and for supplies furnished the Continental Line Soldiers. A list was partly made and submitted to the Court; but before their work was completed, Col. Wood died. This list was not fully taken up until after peace was declared, though a few cases were considered during the Revolutionary War. We find this matter taken up by the Court in 1788, when these and similar minutes appear at different Terms for several years:

"Lieut. Col. George Muse is allowed pay for services in the 1st Va. Regiment prior to 1758."

"James Jack allowed pay in Colonial Wars prior to 1758."

"James MaGill, allowed pay in Colonial Wars prior to 1758."

"Sept. 7, 1779, Francis Austin proved he was a Sergeant in the 1st Old Ills. Regiment."

"Rebecca Shanks, wife of Samuel Shanks, a soldier, is with two children allowed 25 pounds for her support for the ensuing year."

At the Court held in 1780, old minutes contained the following, that may prove of sufficient interest to some reader as to induce him to examine those old records for traces of his ancestors. The minute submitted is to show what was required by the Virginia laws to obtain proof of services in the Continental Line and Colonial Wars:

"Feby. 2, 1780, David Kennerly proved in Court his military service in Continental Army; was Quartermaster in Light Horse Troop in the Company of Capt. Robert Stewart in 1755, and was commissioner under Dr. Thomas Walker to the Troop on the Va. frontier; in 1758 was Q. M. to Va. Regiment commanded by Col. George Washington, and also Ensign; and in 1762 served in Regiment command by Col. Adam Stephen; appointed Lieut. and served as Q. M. and asked for certificate for obtaining a Land Warrant."

"March 8, 1780, Adam Stephen appeared in Court; made oath that in 1754 he was appointed eldest Capt. in Col. Fry's Corps, and that upon death of Col. Fry, he was promoted to rank a Major in said Corps, and was at the battle of the Meadows: and with Genl. Braddock as Lieut.-Col. of The Virginia Regiment. and served under Col. Washington and then under Col. Bird; and was in command of the Regt. in the Spring of 1762 when disbanded, and has had no land except the 5,000 acres gotten by the King's proclamation of 1763."

"March 8, 1780, Gabriel Throckmorton proved he was Sr. Lieut. in Col. Byrd's Regiment in 1758, and that in 1759 served as Captain in Battalion commanded by Col. Peachy, for protection of the frontier, and had never received but 3,000 acres." (The old warriors placed high estimates on their service, or very low on the thousands of acres they received as Indian fighters.)

At the same Court, "James McCallister proved that in May, 1763, he was a Lieut. in the Penn. Regiment, and served during the French War, and produced his commission under the hand of James Hamilton, Lieut. Gov. of Pennsylvania; and that he is an inhabitant of Virginia and has been for four years past."

"George Rice proved that he had served as Captain on Staff in Brigade of the Pack-Horse War in Col. Boquet's expedition in 1756 to the westward, in the late War between Great Britain and France."

"James Anderson proved he was Captain of the Jersey Blues in 1756 commanded by Col. Johnston, and that he has been an inhabitant of this State for the eight years past."

"Daniel Hunsicker proved that in the year 1763 he served as Lieut. in Col. French's Penn.

Regiment, and that he is now an inhabitant of Virginia."

"Mary Beatty whose husband is a soldier in the Colonial Army and has three children and unable to support them—is allowed 5 bushels of corn and 50 lbs. of bacon."

"Nov. 2, 1779, on motion of Major Genl. Chas. M. Lee, it is certified that he served as a Lieut. in the British Army in America in the year 1755. (Note: This was the Genl. Lee who became Washington's enemy. Of him we will further speak.)

"Sarah Mounts, widow of Richard Mounts, a soldier in the Continental Line, allowed pension."

"Francis Austin, Sergeant in the first Old Regiment, assigned his interest to Bryan Bruin."

Feby. 29, 1780, we have a soldier receiving the attention of the Court: James Lane, arraigned for stealing a sum of money was adjudged guilty—and that the prisoner (being a soldier) be taken to the Public Whipping Post, and that the Sheriff do there give him thirty-nine lashes on his bare back, and Roland Baker, his accomplice, for like reason be given the same punishment. These soldiers escaped a worse fate through the leniency of the stern Justices."

"March 18, 1780, Christopher Fry proved he was a non-commissioned officer in 1756, and served in Col. Byrd's Regiment."

"April, 1785, William McMullin proved that his son John was a soldier in the Continental Line, and died in service, and never married—was allowed pay, etc."

"John Smith, James Smallwood and George Calames—allowances made for flour, etc., for use of the troops, and to Isaac Hite for one horse."

"Charles Magill and Francis Whiting qualified as attorneys at law."

"Jany. 1786, Edward McGuire, President Justice, was recommended by the Court as appointment for Sheriff."

The minutes of the Court from 1781 to 1784 contain similar orders.

"Nov. Court, 1784, Joseph Holmes produced his commission as Lieut. Col., and at the May Court, 1785, was sworn as Sheriff."

"June Ct., 1785, Isaac Hite Jr., sworn as Major.

"Nov., 1784. John Kercheval Jr., and Samuel Kercheval and Wm. Taylor sworn as Deputy Sheriffs."

1788-89 Minute Books of County Court.

"Ordered, That the Sheriff pay to Andrew Dent eight pounds, it being the amount of his Pension the last year, agreeable to a certificate from, under the hand and seal of his Excellency the Governor,—he having made oath according to law."

"Ordered that it be certified that Mary Cook, a pensioner, continues an inhabitant of this County and in indigent circumstances, and the widow of Wm. Cook, deceased."

"Ordered that the Sheriff do pay unto Leonard Cooper the sum of Fifty Pounds, it being the amount of his pension the last year."

"Ordered that the Sheriff do pay unto George Hite the sum of Forty Pounds, it being the amount of his pension the last year."

"Ordered that the Sheriff do pay to Catherine Helphinstine the sum of Twenty Pounds in full for two years Pension due to her on the 12th day of June last, 1788, as per certificate."

"Ordered that it be certified that Catherine Helphinstine a pensioner, is still living in this County, in indigent circumstances and continues a widow."

"Ordered that the Sheriff do pay unto Robt. Sherrard, agt., of John Wilson and Francis Wilson, Orphans of John Wilson, deceased, the sum of Twenty Pounds, it being the amount of their Pension the last year."

"Ordered that the Sheriff do pay unto Margaret Kreamer Eight Pounds, it being the amount of her pension the last year, agreeable to a certificate.

"April Court: Ordered that the Sheriff do pay to Hannah Crawford One hundred and thirty-five Pounds, being the amount of her Pension the last year., etc."

"Ordered the Sheriff pay William Rodering Twelve Pounds the amount of his Pension.

"Ordered the Sheriff do pay George Hite Forty Pounds, it being amount of his Pension."

"Ordered the Sheriff pay Arthur Dent Eight Pounds, it being the amount of his Pension the last year."

"Ordered the Sheriff pay Peter Rust Ten Pounds, the amount of his Pension the last year."

"Ordered the Sheriff pay to James Keeling Eight Pounds, it being the amount of his Pension the last year."

"Ordered the Sheriff do pay unto Mary Cook Twelve Pounds, it being the amount of her Pension the last year, etc."

"Ordered the Sheriff pay Leby Hellion,........ ......it being the amount of her Pension the last year."

"Ordered that John Hockman be recommended to be appointed Capt. of Militia of the County, Solomon Van Meter his Lieutenant, and Argyle Ashby his Ensign."

"Ordered that Wm. Elzey be recommended to be appointed Capt. of the Militia." (These are given as samples of many orders of Court entered in reorganizing the military establishment under the laws of new State.)

CHAPTER XVII

Roads Opened and Overseers Appointed 1788–89

Order Book—1788-89

	PAGE.
From Haynes's tan yard to Crooked Run—Joseph Haynes, overs'r	1
" Newton to Christman's Spring—John S. Williams, overs'r	37
" Kendrick's Upper Ford to Bucks Ford—John S. Williams, overs'r	38
" Wiley's sawmill to Ashby's Gap—John S. Williams, overs'r	38
" Brown's Lower Mill to Newton—John S. Williams, overs'r	40
" Battletown to Lewis Lower Mill—John S. Williams, overs'r	84
" From Lewis Neill's Mill to the road leading to Snicker's Ferry—William Tyler, overs'r	84
" Newton to Chesters—William Tyler—overs'r	86
" Colvin's Ford to Shenandoah River—Isaac Hite, Jr., overs'r	90
" Hite's Mill to Fry's Gap—Isaac Hite, Jr., overs'r	104
" Stephensburg to Williams fence—Henry Stephens, overs'r	150
" Winchester to Berrys Ferry—Henry Stephens, overs'r	151
" The New Road to Berkley line and to Brices—Henry Stephens, overs'r	152
" The top of Little Mountain to Marlboro Forge—Henry Brill, overs'r	154
" Brown's tanyard to Newton—Jacob Leonard, overs'r	154
" The Blue Ball Tavern to Berkley line—James Bruce, overs'r	159
" Brown's Ferry to Front Royal—James Bruce, overs'r	170
" Island Ford to Morgan's Ford—James Bruce, overs'r	171
" Stephensburg to Chesters Gap—James Bruce, overs'r	173
" Capt. Steads to the Warm Spring Road—Isaac Smith, overs'r	185
" Zane's Forge towards Stover Town—Martin Haggy, overs'r	187
" Buck Marsh Bridge to Old Chappel—Thos. Byrd., overs'r	187
" Helms Mill to the Main Road—Thos. Byrd, overs'r	226
From Stephensburg to Chester Gap—Thos. Byrd, overs'r	226
" Gregory's Ford to the forks of Manassas Run, William Hood, overs'r	233
" Browns Lower Mill to Stephensburg,—William Hood, overs'r	241
" Stephensburg to Williams—Discow, overs'r	242
Through George Braxton's Plantation, Ord.	311
" Langley's Spring to the Chappel Road—John Colvin, overs'r	312
" Helm's Mill to the Main Road—John Colvin, overs'r Ord.	321
" Philip Carpers to David Brown's New Mill—Ord.	321
" Buffaloe Lick to the road from Brown's Mill, Ord.	326
" Livingstone's Lane to Hite's Mill—Edward Howe, overs'r.	326
" Neills Mill to the Little North Mountain, Ord.	327
" Colvin's Ford to Hites Ford—Isaac Hite, Jr., overs'r.	330
" Parkin's Mill to Redd's Ford—Robt. Allen, overs'r.	330
" Opecquon to the Forge—John Allan, overs'r.	331
" The Forge to Cedar Creek—Martin Haggy, overs'r.	331
" The Berkley line to Littlers Run—Abraham Branson, overs'r.	334
" The School House in Stephensburg to Sutherlands field, Ord.	406
" Philip Carpers to David Browns New Mill, Ord.	409
" Stephensburg to Myers Mill, Ord.	409
" Widow Coopers to Browns Mill—Ord.	409
" Christopher Becks to Henry Lewises' Ord.	414
" Lextons Mill to Josiah Ballingers Ord.	415
" The Road to Chesters Gap, to Manassa Gap—Wm. Vanort, overs'r	426
" Battletown to Snickers Ferry—Mathew Wright, overs'r.	502

The full minutes entered relating to the foregoing roads, describe the route taken, and give names to land owners affected by the new roads.

August Term, 1788:

This list of Grand Jurors at this Term is given to show some of the old families serving the War, and ready to serve their country in a civil capacity:

Thos. Byrd, Foreman; Francis Stribling, Jacob Grapes, Lewis M. Shaver, Jacob Roher, Jacob Bowen, Vance Bush, David Wilson, James Henning, John Emmitt, Henry Catlett, Joseph King, Stephen Pritchard, Mabra Madden, Joseph Anderson. Seven of this number have entirely disappeared from our records, though the descendants, under other names, are residents of the Lower Valley at this writing.

The Grand Jury presented several persons for various offences: several overseers of roads for not keeping their roads in repair. One is given to show the interest old Courts took in requiring good roads to the meeting houses: This appears at the November Term, 1788:

"The Overseer of Road from Capt. Samuel Glass to Opecquon Meeting House presented, and indicted for not keeping said road in repair."

March Ct., 1789.

"Alexander White, Esq., having been elected a member of Congress in the United States, which under a late Act of Assembly, it is the opinion of this Court vacates the office of Deputy States Attorney for this County, Whereupon the Court proceeded to the appointment of a person to act in that capacity, when Charles Magill, Sr. was unanimously appointed, and thereupon took the oath accordingly.

It will be observed that the minutes of the Court, briefly given, embrace the entire period known as the War period. Although British rule was changed to that of Independent States, and a new order of government was gradually taking place, and fully inaugurated when the first Constitution was adopted by the Thirteen Colonies, the Colonies having in joint convention in Philadelphia, 17th day of September, 1787, fully established and ordained the celebrated Constitution and submitted it to the States for ratification, unavoidable delays occurred. Several States could not act promptly, owing to conflicting opinions. Virginia, however, soon had her government conform to the Articles of Union and Confederation; and under her own Constitution, adopted June 29th, 1776, the courts had been recognized. But without any interruption so far as related to Frederick County prior to this radical change, the Courts were held in accordance with the spirit and authority of the Declaration of Independence. The only perceptible change appearing to the casual reader, would be the disappearance of the usual opening Order: "By the Grace of God and of our Lord and Sovereign King, etc.;" and, taking its place. "By the Grace of God and authority of the *Commonwealth* of Virginia"—the Court was opened without comment. The first Court to convene after the Colonies had declared for Independence, was August 6th, 1776; and it may be well to enter here who composed this first Court, and what was presented for action: Present, John Hite, Isaac Hite, Chas. Mym Thruston, John McDonald, John Smith and Edward Taylor.

"An Ordinance of the Honorable, the Convention of the Commonwealth of Virginia, directing that the different members named in the *former* Commission of the Peace, should continue to act in the said office, upon their taking the oath prescribed in the said Ordinance:"

"Whereupon Isaac Hite and Chas. Mynn Thurston administered the oath to John Hite; who took and subscribed the same, and then the said John Hite administered the said oath to all the aforesaid members, who took the same as Justices of the said Commonwealth."

"James Keith took the oath as Clerk of Court—Henry Peyton took the oath as Deputy Clerk—Angus McDonald took the oath as Sheriff—Nathaniel Cartmell Jr., took the oath as Dep. Sheriff—Gabriel Jones, Alexander White, George Roots, Dolphin Drew, John Magill and Henry Peyton, Jr., took the oath as attorney." Such men deserve special mention, their patriotism being fully emphasized by this prominent action. The infant Republic had arrayed herself against the Mother Government; and to many doubtless, the declaration meant ruin for those who so boldly avowed their rebellion. Lord Fairfax, who had been the Presiding Justice and County Lieutenant under the Colonial Government, was noticeably absent.

At a subsequent Term, the Court discovered that quite a number of the old Justices declined to appear and take the oath; and in order to complete the list of Justices, the following gentlemen were named in this order:

"Ordered, That Marquis Calames, Robert Wood, Wm. Gibbs, Philip Bush, Robt. White, Joseph Holmes, Thomas Helm, Edward McGuire, and Edward Smith be recommended to his Excellency, the Governor of the Commonwealth of Virginia as proper persons to be added to the Commission of the Peace for this County."

William Booth, Warner Washington and Thomas Bryan Martin, three of the old members, declined to serve.

During the War period, a number of persons were arraigned before the Court, charged with treason to the new Government. Fines were imposed, and in some cases jail sentences were executed. In consideration of the fact that many descendants of the *Tory element* were fully identified as loyal supporters of the cause of Freedom, names of such are omitted. Owing to this state of affairs, the Court proceeded to execute the law in relation to the loyalty of citizens; and at the November Term, 1777, we find this order:

"Ordered, that Edward McGuire is appointed to administer the Oath of Fidelity, prescribed by law, to the inhabitants of Winchester, pursuant to the directions of an Act of the Genl. Assembly," (Dec., 1775, May, 1776).

Thomas Helm, to administer oaths, etc., in the Districts of Captains Barrett, Ball and McKinney.

Joseph Holmes in the Districts of Captains Gilkerson, Nisewanger and Barron.

Robert Throckmorton, in the Districts of Captains Wilson and Longacre.

Wm. Gibbs, in the Districts of Captains Reynolds and Baldwin.

Robert White, in the Districts of Captains Babb and Rinker.

Edmund Taylor, in the Districts of Captains Farron and Catlett.

John Hite in the Districts of Captain Helm.

The law provided punishment for any who refused the oath. Fuller mention will be made about this Tory element. The reader will recognize a singular coincidence of places and names in the following. Kercheval in his History of the Valley, says: "That while Genl. Morgan was taking a little needed rest near Winchester, after defeating Tarleton at the Battle of the Cowpens, the General was informed of a *nest of Tories* holding out in some force, on Lost River and South Fork in Hardy County, and was requested to lead an expedition to that section and quell the rebellion. The old warrior was soon on the march; arriving in the Lost River Valley, he found that John Claypole and his two sons were defying the authorities of that County. They were suppressed; and the expedition then proceeded to the stronghold of the other insurgents on the Fork, about fifteen miles above Moorefield, where they found John Brake, a well-to-do German well fortified and determined to resist an attack. Brake and his insurgents had previously withstood several attacks from the Militia, and had become very bold, and his band had increased in numbers. But they were now confronted by men who had come to subdue and not to parley. The house was surrounded; many Tories escaped to the woods, however, and were not captured; but the moving spirit, Brake, capitulated, and Morgan and his little army feasted on the products of the old Tory—farm, mill, distillery, beeves, pigs, lambs and poultry—while their horses enjoyed the unmown meadows, oat fields, etc.

Coincident with the foregoing, is the following, which occurred eighty-one years subsequent to the period referred to: It was while Genl. Turner Ashby was enjoying a needed rest after his arduous achievement, guarding and protecting the rear of Genl. Jackson's Army, as he slowly fell back from Banks' advance on Winchester in the Spring of 1862. The Valley Army was in camp in the vicinity of Lacey Springs, North of Harrisonburg. Ashby was informed that it was important to the Service to send a small force of Cavalry to Moorefield and take observations of any Federal columns moving from West Virginia points towards the Valley; and while on this expedition, to discover certain parties in that section that had been reported to Jackson as enemies who secretly reported every movement of the Confederates to the Washington Government; and that when discovered, the system must be destroyed. Ashby proceeded at once to select men who were by their residence familiar with the country. For this service the author's Company was detailed—Company B, of the 17th Battalion, Ashby's Brigade, W. H. Harness, Captain. The officers and men were enjoined to avoid engagements with the enemy. The Company, by circuitous marches, crossed the mountains and Lost River; thence over the mountain via Howard's Lick, and halted at *Gunpowder Springs* near Moorefield, fully obscured from view either by citizens or the Federal troops then occupying the Moorefield Valley. The next day the Company was divided into three detachments, to reconnoitre the Post. Information had been obtained from trusted persons that there was a nest of *Swamp Dragons* far up on South Fork, on Brake's Run, and that they must be the men we were expected to capture. Capt. Harness was too well known in that section to take the lead; and he detailed the writer to head the detachment, composed of as wary and brave men as ever bestrode a horse. They started out well aware that prudence was the better part of valor. It was well known the Federal scouts wore grey uniforms and it was deemed best to approach the house and play the *Jesse Scout* trick of war. This was regarded by some as reckless, as the detachment might be ambushed. The writer was allowed to try the experiment of deception. The few men found in the house readily accepted the situation, and eagerly told what they knew about Rebels, expressing a desire that we would some day capture that Captain Harness, Samuel Alexander, Jim Lobb and several others, members of our Company. They had just returned from the Federal Camp and had heard this scouting party had gone in that direction, and were fully prepared to expect their arrival any hour. This was a bit of news that had to be heeded: and the party was preparing to move off, when Brake the owner of the property insisted the boys must have dinner. This was hastily taken by a few, the remainder standing guard to give notice of the approach of Federals. Brake was informed that he and his party must accompany the detachment to camp and there be identified as loyal and true; which was agreed to. Brake, his son-in-law, Pope, and several others were soon on the trot, marching towards Moorefield, but when within three miles of the camp, our little column filed to the right, crossing the mountains to Lost River, and thence to the Valley Headquarters, where the prisoners were interviewed by Genl. Jackson. It is needless to say they soon discovered the trap they had fallen into. They were kindly treated by our party; and when a squad of Co. A, of Ashby's Command, made a dash to take them from our guards while resting at Cootes' store in Shenandoah County, Captain Harness and the writer and one Guard, Jim Cunningham, had bullets to pass through our clothing, and a man named Mason of Co. A, one of the attacking party, was badly wounded in the foot. This Co. A recognized two of the prisoners as members of a gang that had killed one of their men. This digression must now end. The author hopes some survivors of the old Company may read these incidents and be able to recall the hardships of that expedition. Fuller notice may be given this expedition later on.

The incidents narrated above, suggested to the writer another, in which Tarleton, the notorious British Colonel that Morgan had defeated, made himself famous in his effort to capture Mr. Jefferson, the Virginia Governor, and the General Assembly then at Charlottesville. We have several versions of this exploit of the Colonel—one from Howe, p. 166, and one from Tucker's Life of Jefferson. We will take the liberty to draw from both:

In May, 1781, when Cornwallis invaded Virginia, the Legislature adjourned from Richmond to Charlottesville, as a place of greater safety. In June, Tarleton was detached to Charlottesville, with 180 Cavalry of his legion and 7 mounted Infantry, with directions to surprise the General Assembly, seize the person of Jefferson, then the Governor, and do such other things as the partizan Colonel chose. A gentleman who was in the neighborhood of the British Army, suspected Tarleton's object and was able to give Jefferson two hours' notice. Quite a commotion occurred; the Governor hastened to make his escape, but took time to adjourn the Assembly to re-assemble on the 7th of June at Staunton. All escaped capture except seven members. Tarleton entered Monticello, Jefferson's mansion, ten minutes after the Governor had gotten away with his family. The British soldiery perpetrated the most wanton acts of destruction, pillage and robbery—cattle and horses driven off, and unbroken horses killed, barns and fences burned, and growing crops of corn and tobacco destroyed. The surrounding country for miles suffered. Tucker says: "Thirty thousand slaves were taken from Virginia by the British in these invasions, of whom it is computed twenty-seven thousand died of the small-pox, or camp fever. The whole amount of property carried off and destroyed during the six months preceding Cornwallis' surrender, has been estimated at 3,000,000 pounds sterling." Similar wanton destruction occurred in later years, conducted by such demons as David Hunter. Tarleton entered Charlottesville on the 4th day of June; Mr. Jefferson's Term as Governor expired four days after. Ex-Governor Patrick Henry had been the Governor's guest during the session, but now hastened towards Staunton to join the General Assembly. Mr. Henry has been distinguished for many enviable traits; but here is an incident that has not been told so often that it may not be repeated. Governor Gilmer has left many interesting stories relating to the dispersion of the statesmen at Charlottesville. One is that Mr. Jefferson concealed himself in Carter's Mountain, and that Patrick Henry, in his flight to Staunton, met Col. Lewis in one of the streets, to whom he related the adjournment and flight of the Legislature, then on their way to Staunton. Col. Lewis, not knowing who the stranger was, said to him: "If Patrick Henry had been in Albemarle, the Birtish Dragoons never would have passed over the Rivanna River."

The legislators were badly demoralized; for we find they felt Staunton was unsafe, and dreaded Tarleton might suddenly appear in their midst. Quite a number left during the night, and sought the hospitable home of Col. Geo. Moffett, near which there was a cave that would afford a safe retreat. During Mr. Henry's hasty changes, he had the misfortune to lose one of his boots. While partaking breakfast the next morning, the hostess, Mrs. Moffett, who was an enthusiastic Whig, remarked: "There was one member of that Legislative body she knew would not run." The question was asked by one of the party: "Who is he;" Her reply was "Patrick Henry." At that moment a gentleman with one boot colored perceptibly. The party soon left, and after their departure a servant rode up with the lost boot and enquired for Mr. Henry, stating that Patrick Henry had left Staunton in such haste that he had forgotten his boot. Of course, Mrs. Moffett knew at once who it was *the boot fitted.*

The foregoing incidents serve to show the frenzied condition of the period which we now treat of, 1776-1788.

The Fathers of the Revolution possessed many traits that we fail to appreciate at this late day; and it might be well to briefly state their situation, when they wrote the memorable words: *"The regal government is totally dissolved."* No other form of government had then been adopted. Henning tells us: "The militia laws had been suffered to expire; the revenues of the Crown were in the hands of its late officers, from which they were not extracted until a late period; and when they dared that hazardous enterprise of Revolution, found themselves without a government—without men—and without money. Indeed, they had nothing to support them in the awful contest, but their own virtue and talents, and a firm reliance on the Sovereign Disposer of all events." But there was no halting—Onward was their slogan in Council or in the armies. The wheels of government could not turn without money, and many schemes were adopted to husband the products of the farms and mills; Committees of Safety were created; stringent laws enacted by all the Colonies to prevent waste of supplies, and to encourage economy in all things but *brain and muscle.* The Continental Congress saw the need of issuing paper money, which they styled continental money. It became necessary to resort to the scheme five times during the War. The dates and amounts of issue were as follows, and its value at certain periods:

1775, June 22, issued $2,000,000, and together with other issues to 1781, $2,000,000, were issued, and of this none redeemed.

1777, January, paper currency 5 per cent. discount; in July, 25 per cent., and before the end of the year $3 in paper would not purchase one in silver.

1778, April, $4 in paper to one dollar in coin.

September, $5 to one in coin, and in Dec., $6.50 to one in coin.

1779, Feby., $8.50; May $12; Sept., $18 to one in coin.

1780, March, $1 in paper three cents; May, two cents; and Dec., $74 in paper was worth one dollar in silver.

This worked havoc among the soldiers at Valley Forge and elsewhere. Old Confederate soldiers will see from the foregoing similar trials experienced by the soldiers of Lee in the Winter, 1864-5.

The Prohibitionists of the present day, in their sweeping efforts to suppress traffic in intoxicating beverages, may be surprised to learn that their movement is not more radical than measures adopted by the State one hundred and twenty-nine years ago. The Act of Assembly speaks for itself:

"October, 1778—3rd year of the Commonwealth—

Whereas the *great quantity of grain* consumed in the distilleries, will increase the present alarming scarcity, Be it enacted by the General Assembly, That *no* kind of spirituous liquors shall be distilled from Indian corn, wheat, rye, oats, barley, buckwheat, meal or flour, within this Commonwealth, between the fifteenth day of February next and the fifteenth day of October next." Severe penalties were provided for all violators of the law. This was regarded as an emergency act. The law was repealed in 1779, whether by reason of a surplus of grain obtained by the prohibitive Act, or because the legislators became alarmed at the scarcity of spirits around their base of operations; for be it remembered that lawmakers then, as now, were cautious concerning their individual wants.

The General Assembly, during the trying War period, was confronted by grave issues that emanated from the States of Maryland and Pennsylvania. These had to receive much attention; and as Frederick County was directly concerned in those issues, brief mention will be given: The issue was the *Cession of the North-West Territory,* that Frederick and Augusta had fought singly and alone to wrest from the grasp of the Redmen and their French allies, and had maintained their supremacy over, up to the time when the two States objected to such claims of Virginia. They hesitated in signing the Articles of Confederation between the States, until Virginia should yield her rights (which the two States denied she had), and cede her pretended interest in all territory West of the Ohio River. Maryland was a stumbling block to confederation, refusing to take any step until a guaranty was given that all the States should have joint interest in the territory through the United States Compact. The situation was perilous. British statesmen watched the controversy with increasing interest. One of the statesmen, in a familiar address to Parliament, predicted that the jealousies and discord between the States would result in disruption and internal strife, and that the cause of American freedom must become a myth, and for this reason if for no other, war should be waged more vigorously. Virginia had patriotic statesmen who were willing to make greater sacrifices, if need be, to secure a compact between the States; and has left in evidence her acts and her reasons. The Genl. Assembly, Jany. 2, 1781, after exhausting all plans for settlement, finally yielded and published the following: "The General Assembly of Virginia, being well satisfied that the happiness, strength and safety of the United States depend, under Providence, upon the ratification of the Articles for a Federal union between the United States, heretofore proposed by Congress for the consideration of the said States, and preferring the good of their country to every object of smaller importance—

Do Resolve, That this Commonwealth will yield to the Congress of the United States, for the benefit of said United States, all right, title and claim that the said Commonwealth hath to the territory northwest of the river Ohio, upon the following conditions, to-wit: That the said territory so ceded shall be laid out and formed into States containing a suitable extent of territory, and shall not be less than one hundred nor more than one hundred and fifty miles square." * * *

Other provisions were made to protect persons already seated in the territory, and West Virginia Soldiers in locating their land warrants, especially those of the Col. George Rogers Clarke expedition. The Articles, being ratified after this Act of Virginia, harmony prevailed; and the United Colonies laid aside their internal dissensions, and gathered renewed strength to overcome the invaders and secure peace.

During the War period, church dissensions had increased; and the element known as *Dissenters* had become prominent throughout the Colony for their patriotism and zeal in the Cause of Freedom, while the established church exhibited such a luke-warm interest in the Cause, that many of the ministers who had received support from the State, deserted their standard and also refused assistance to the Cause. This produced such intense feeling as to require notice by the Assembly. Beginning in 1776 with remonstrances, the clergy were notified that dissenters would not be required to contribute to their support. This allayed in part the feeling of discontent; but this measure once inaugurated, other demands were made, and the subject threatened disaffection. Many good churchmen were in active service, and felt agrieved at the Acts of the legislative body, while the dissenters demanded that the Church and State should separate, and let all religious bodies have an equal right. So we find these issues agitated the body politic to such an extent that various compromises were tried. None, however, would satisfy the dissenters, who now had become a power in the land, but an adherance to their demand. The ministers of the Established Church must depend upon their parishioners for their support The Assembly hesitated to repeal the law, and continued from session to session to *suspend* payment; and thus it continued until the close of the War. The wedge had entered, however, and the time was approaching when this tower of strength, the Established Church had clung to so tenaciously, must be riven from base to cone. These and other dissensions not mentioned, often gave serious admonitions. The zeal and patriotism of the masses prevailed, and the Glorious Independence was finally achieved.

During the great struggle, the State was compelled to resort to a most trying plan to recruit the depleted regiments; the militia was thoroughly organized, and the scheme for *drafting* men that has always dampened the ardor of many *quasi* supporters of war, was regarded as a burden, and rigorous measures were adopted. Commissions were created in every County, which were required under penalty to list the able-bodied men and draw therefrom, as the exigencies required. At first it was every twenty-fifth man; then the twentieth; finally resorting to every tenth. The counties were required to equip the new levies, who were hurried away to the Continental Line. The Quakers and Menoists were required to furnish substitutes, and their societies compelled to pay what was agreed upon by the Commission. All of this was harrassing, and produced distress. We are glad to say that the Draft fell lightly on the Valley section. Her citizens seem to have been soldiers and patriots; for we find Frederick had furnished her quota by volunteers, while in some counties the Draft exceeded one hundred men.

During this period, the General Assembly found it uncomfortable to remain at Williamsburg; so we find that body in May, 1779, passed an Act to remove the Capital to Richmond, and provided that six whole squares should be secured for the public buildings, and accommodations found as soon as practicable for the sessions to be held at that town. The Fathers were more expeditious in those days than now; for we find at their next session, about twelve months after they passed the above Act, this language. "At a General Assembly begun and held at the Public Buildings in the Town of Richmond on Monday the first day of May, 1780." This indicates their fitness for those stirring times. We must add, however, that Henrico County placed her Court House at the disposal of the Assembly, and in the *Public Building* the sessions were held.

CHAPTER XVIII

Revolutionary War Period (Continued) — Officers and Enlisted Men From Old Frederick

The author has been frequently asked who were the Shenandoah Valley men to render service in the dark days of the War 1775-83; and desiring to give some answer, submits the following, which doubtless will be disappointing, because of its incomplete list. Efforts have been made by hundreds of chroniclers to find dates pertaining to that period, all of whom acknowledge their inability to collect such desirable information, owing to the irregular records of the official army reports that found their way to what became in after years the *Bureau of Military Records*. It is a reasonable conclusion that many of the old leaders were not as efficient in making military reports as they were in making battle against their English foes; consequently many branches of the service have no place in the records. Seekers for such knowledge are embarrassed often, and fail to obtain what they had good reason to believe was obtainable. Many old files and rosters of troops give nothing but the surname of enlisted men, without reference to the section of country from which they enlisted; while whole regiments are only mentioned by numbers, without giving the names of officers or men. And as the commissioned officers and enlisted men aggregated many thousands during the Seven Years' War, the reader will appreciate the difficulty presented, when the confused and unsatisfactory mass is laid before the student of such history. The enlistments were made in different sections, *en masse,* and not generally by Companies; they were marched away from their sections in squads—called Companies—and on their arrival at the several military posts, were assigned to the various regiments. Many Virginians were found in S. Carolina, New Jersey, Maryland and Pennsylvania regiments. Thus their individuality was broken. Captains from Frederick and other counties, did not in all cases enlist men and organize companies. Captains received their commissions from their respective Colonies or States, and were authorized to procure men for the service. Colonels were likewise commissioned, but in many cases were authorized to *raise Regiments;* and when the requisite number was raised by Companies, Captains would be assigned by the Colonel, and he would assume command and report for duty. Sometimes the Colonel procured a sufficient number to comprise two regiments. We find, for instance, Daniel Morgan appearing in Winchester in the spring of 1777, with a commission and authority from the American Congress to enlist and organize two regiments of riflemen, to be known as the Eleventh and Fifteenth Virginia Regiments. Enlistments were quickly made; for we find him with the two regiments on the march May 31st, 1777, and reporting the following as the line officers:

Daniel Morgan, Col.
Abram Buford, Sec'd. Col., (succeeded Morgan May 15, 1778).
John Cropper, Lieut. Col.
Geo. B. Wallace, Lieut. Col.
David Stephenson, Major.
Philip Slaughter, Capt. and Paymaster.
Saml. Jones, Lieut. and Paymaster.
Albudyton Jones, Adjutant.
Robt. Porterfield, Lieut. and Adjutant.
John Barnes, Lieut. and Q. M.
Mace Clements, Surgeon.
Joseph Davis, Surgeon.
John Crute, Q. M.'s Sergt.
Wm. Death, Q. M.'s Sergt.
Chas. Erskine, Sergt. Major.
Thos. Pollock, Sergt. Major.
Robt. Sharman, Fife Major.

Col. Morgan also reported twelve regular Companies and their company officers; and also names of captains of four independent rifle companies of his same command. The Companies were designated by numbers (not by letters as now).

Company No. 1.

James Calderhead, Capt. (One citizen by this name living now in Frederick County).
Thos. Lucas, Lieut.
Thos. Burd, Lieut.
Wm. Hood, Ensign.
Elijah Reffey, Sergt.
James Weir, Sergt.
Wm. Karns, Sergt.
John Foster, Drummer.
John Shields, Fifer.

Company No. 2.

Chas. Gallagher, Capt. (Died May 24, 1777).
Joseph Davis, Lieut.
Robt. Young, Lieut.
Chas. Tyler, Ensign.
Thos. Roberson, Sergt.
Francis Langfelt, Sergt.
John H. Johnson, Sergt.
Robt. Mills, Sergt.
Richard Marshall, Corporal.
John Quint, Corporal.
Aquilla Naval, Corporal.
Yelverton Reardon, Corporal.
John Farrell and Robt. Shannon, Drum and Fife.

Company No. 3.

Wm. Johnston, Capt. (Everard Meade, assigned as Capt., March 1, 1778).
Wm. Powell, 1st Lieut. (Jas. Wood, 1st Lieut. Mch. 1, '78—Keith, 2d Lieut.)
Robt. Porterfield, Lieut.
John Townes, Ensign.
Peyton Powell, Sergt.
Archibald Botts, Sergt.
Wm. Oldrid, Sergt.
Michael Logsett, Sergt.
John Means, Corpl.
Wm. Palmer, Corpl.
Shadrick Reader, Corpl.
John McCart, Corpl.
John Harris, Drummer.

The list of privates of this Company bears the names of old Frederick County men: Peyton—Graham—Thomas—Rutherford, etc. The Company is mentioned Nov. 1, 1778, as the "Light Horse," and gives the name of:

John Crittendon and Timothy Feely as now *Lts.*

John Bruce and John Lyon as Sergts.

Company No. 4.—June 1, 1777.

Chas. Porterfield, Capt.
Thos. Tabbs, Capt.
John Blackwell, Capt.
Peyton Harrison, Lt.
Valentine Harrison, 2d Lt. (Assigned Apl. 1, '78).
Wm. Edmondson, Sergt.
Geo. Greenway, Sergt.
James Dunbar, Sergt.
Sol. Fitzpatrick, Sergt.
Duncan Meade, Fifer.

This Company, composed in part of privates detailed from other Companies, to-wit: Beckett, Davis, Viol, Duncan, Crown, Anderson, Roundsifer, Clevenger, Stump, Bartlett, Ray, Adams, Robinson, Middleton, Groves, Hopewell, Giles, Jacobs, the following year, December 1, (1778) had suffered severely in loss of men, and was recruited with 48 men—many of them being familiar Valley names: Jno. Wood, Augustus Berry, Clement Richards, Adam Sheets, Jas. Holmes, Jas. Noland, Ed. Clevenger, Jno. Kelly, Geo. Wolf, Wm. Roe, Thos. Lee, Jno. Bell, Robt. Green, Lewis Stump, Jno. Philips, Wm. Beason, Wm. Hicks.

(*Note.* For full list of officers and men comprising the Morgan Regiments, Eleventh and Fifteenth, See Saffell's "Men of the Revolution," Cong. Library.)

Company No. 5.

Wm. Smith, Capt. (Apl. 1, '78, Robt. Powell, Capt.
Isaiah Larks, Lt.
Thos. Lomas, Ensign, (Apl. 1, '78 Roy Ensign).
Isaac Brown, Sergt. (Apl. 1, '78, Thos. Keane, Sergt.
Jno. Owsly, Sergt.
Thos. Owsly, Sergt.
John Bruce, Corp. (Apl. 1, '78, Jas. Armstrong, Corpl.
Randall Morgan, Corp.
Mathew Byram, Corp.

Privates Jno. Miller, Richard Lee, two Richard Jones. No other familiar Valley names in list of privates.

Company 6.—June 1, '77.

Thomas Blackwell, Capt. (Apl. 1, '78, Reuben Briscoe, Capt.
John Marshall, Lt.
James Wright, 2d Lt.
Thos. Randall, 3d Lt. (Apl. 1, '78, Thornton Taylor, Ensign.
John Morgan, Sergt. (Apl. 1, '78, Peter Bonham, Sergt.
Saml. Philips, Sergt.
John Anderson, Sergt.
Joseph Garner, Sergt. (Apl. 1, '78, Jno. Sidebottom, Corp.

This enlistment for this Company was from East of Blue Ridge.

Company No. 7.—June 1, '77.

Peter Bryn Bruin, Capt.
Geo. Calmes, Lt.
Chas. Magill, 2d Lt.
Timothy Feely, Ensign.
James Dowdall, (Cadet).

The list of privates shows the following as Valley men: Bowen, Blair, Hill, Handshaw, Glass, Legg, Crum, Sparks, Thompson, White, Lovell, Meade, Black, McGuire, Vance, Davis, James Gamble, Moore, Wm. and Jno. Holmes, Jno. White, and many other Valley names.

Company No. 8.—Nov. 30, '78.

Thos. Willis, Capt. (Feb. 14, '78, Phil. R. R. Lee, Capt.)

Luke Cannon, Lt. (Saml. Love, Lt.)

Saml. Love, Sergt.

Privates: A. Foster, Jno. Russell, Peter Larue, Henry Webb, Jno. Young, Henry Russell, R. Abbott, Ward, Robt. White, And. Harrison, Stephen Ham, Elisha Hawkins—all Valley names.

Company No. 9.

Geo. Rice, Capt.

James Wright, Lt.

John Barnes, 2d Lt.

Richard Marshall, Sergt. Major.

(This Company was composed of Eastern Virginians.)

Company No. 10.

Samuel Booker, Capt.

Lance Butler, Lt.

Daniel Vasser, Sergt.

Wm. Cook, Sergt.

James Ryalls, Corp.

Saml. Ryals, Corp.

John Lewis, Drummer,

No Valley men for privates.

Company No. 11.

James Gray, Capt.

Saml. Jones, Lt.

Thos. Davis, Ensign,

Robt. Craddock, Sergt.

Willis Wilson, Sergt.

Spratley Simmons, Sergt.

Richison Booker, Sergt.

Henry Tillar, Sergt.

Holt, Sublett, and Trent, Corporals.

No Valley names in list of privates.

Company No. 12.

John Gregory, Capt.

David Mason, Lt.

Thos. Holt, Lt.

Louis Best, Sergt.

Wm. Pryor, Sergt.

The four Independent Rifle Companies of Morgan's Command report names of the four captains, to-wit:

Capt. Gabriel Long, (Phil. Slaughter, Lt.)
Capt....... Shepherd, (James Harrison, Lt).
Capt. ...... West, (Reuben Long, Ensign).
Capt. ...... Bradys.

The four captains were evidently Valley men.

Col. Alexander Spottswood commanded a Virginia regiment from Jany. 1, to June 1, 1777—Number of regiment not given.

Richard Parker, Lt. Col.

Benjamin Day, Adjt.

Ambrose Madison, Paymaster.

Robt. Bell, Q. M.

Many changes in the personnel during the year.

The Third Virginia Regiment was commanded by Col. Wm. Heth. Col. Tom Marshall was with the regiment, but soon detailed for other service.

James Hansbrough, Q. M.

David Griffith, Chaplain and Surgeon. Some Valley names in this regiment.

A Virginia regiment—number not given—composed of five companies, was commanded (1777) by Col. Nathaniel Gist. Jno. Gist Capt. of 1st Company, Strother Jones, Capt. of one of the five companies; Thos. Bell, Capt. of one (No. 3). Names of other officers not familiar West of the Blue Ridge. Some Valley men privates in Col. Gist's Regiment were David Luckett, Arch Bartlett, Jos. Nail, Thomas Griffin, and Saml. Bent.

There was another Virginia Regiment, the Eighth, composed chiefly of Valley men, a majority of whom were of the German stock, that had settlement from the Potomac to the Augusta line, and had been conspicuous in the formation of the new counties taken from old Frederick. Rev. Peter Muhlenberg, the historic Gospel preacher at Woodstock, had been recognized by the Colonial Government as a man of war-like spirit. He had fanned the spark of patriotism for more than twelve months; and no surprise was expressed when the flame suddenly burst forth in the Winter of '76, with their preacher fully uniformed and with his commission of Colonel, authorized to enlist men and organize a regiment to serve in the "Virginia Line." Some strange fatality followed this regiment, so far as the records show. Except for letters (not official), that Genl. Muhlenburg addressed to the Genl. Assembly of Virginia in 1777, when he had been commissioned Brigadier Genl.—wherein he mentioned some of the "efficient officers fitted to command the Eighth Regiment,"—we would have no evidence who any of the officers were. He only mentions a few as in the line of promotion: Capt. Abraham Bowman, Capt. Peter Helfenstein, and Capt. Philip Slaughter. Capt. Bowman was commissioned Colonel in Jany. 1777; Peter Helfenstein, Major. From some cause, the Eighth Regiment has no muster roll in existence. Men were detailed from this regiment in 1778, to recruit the Rifle Companies; and thus we have the names of many which will appear later on, if space permit. Only one Company roll has been preserved, so far as the records show. This was known as Buck's Minute Men. The Company was composed of Valley men, and mustered into service at Woodstock by Col. Muhlenburg in 1777. Thos. Buck was Captain, and filed the original muster roll in the Pension Office in Washington when Congress passed the first law to issue bounty land warrants to soldiers of the Revolution. The list bears the certificate of County Lt. Joseph Pugh, dated Sept. 16, 1777.

List of Officers

Thomas Buck, Capt.
John Crookshank, 1st. Lt.
Lionel Branson, Ensign.
Wm. Reed, Sergt.
Jacob Lambert, 2d Sergt.
Jno. Steel, 3d Sergt.
Jeremiah Philips, 4th Sergt.

List of Privates

Fredk. Honaker, Wm. Hoover, Jno. Bently, Wm. Black, Valentine Lock Miller, Philip Smith, Martin Gay, Gasper Lutz, David Piper, C. Sapington, Martin Miller, Abram Gable, Wm. Morelock, Jno. Middleton, Geo. Lockmiller, Wm. Bagnall, Geo. Miller, Henry Shumaker, Herbert Stockbridge, Wm. Copeman, Christian Boseman, Andrew Copeman, Michael Setsar, R. Bizant, Jno. Snider, Jno. Somers, Saml. Dust, John Hoover, Elijah Aadell, Conrad Hansberger, Wm. Harris, Thos. Price, Zachariah Price, Jno. Marshall Taylor.

We find good reason given why this Company was mustered into service without the requisite number—sixty-five—"provided for" by former Acts of the Virginia Assembly, in the formation of the Virginia regiments: At the sessions held in the Spring of 1777, provision was made to form militia companies of not less than 32 nor more than 58 in number. These companies were to be supplied with suitable accoutrements. Non-commissioned officers and privates to carry rifle and tomahawk, good firelock and bayonet with pouch and horn, or cartouch, and with three charges of powder and ball." (See Henning's Statutes, May 5, 1777) and required to assemble weekly for drill and other exercises. The enlistments mentioned were in compliance with an Act of the Assembly, Oct. 18, 1776, providing for six new battalions of Infantry, strictly for Continental Service, and also provided for the completion of the nine battalions previously raised to constitute the regular regiments, which were offered additional bounty, etc. (See American Archives, 5 series, Vol. 2, p. 1112.) Under this Act of Oct. 18, we have the following names appear as Colonels whose commissions are dated Nov. 15, '76: Edward Stevens, Daniel Morgan, James Wood, Saml. Meredith, Charles Lewis, and David Mason. (See Am. Archives, 5 series, Vol. 3, p. 695).

There is some confusion of dates in this connection, for it will appear in the chapter relating to Daniel Morgan, that he and his riflemen were in the Autumn of 1775 on their march from Massachusetts to Canada—ending at Quebec with his capture. Yet we find him in Virginia the following November organizing a rifle regiment, to reinforce Genl. Gates in his campaign against Genl. Burgoyne, and fighting the battle that resulted in the surrender of the latter 17th October, 1777. We must conclude that Genl. Morgan was not in Virginia in the Autumn of 1776, on his mission to raise rifle regiments, but in the Spring of 1777. The Author finds several historians in their treatment of the incidents of the Revolutionary War, give conflicting dates as to the Morgan Campaign; and he has most studiously endeavored to collect facts; and is indebted to officials having custody of the War Archives in the War Dept. in Washington and those in the Virginia State Library, and had the personal aid of such experienced compilers as Mr. Chas. E. Kemper, Geo. H. Saffell, W. F. Boogher and others.

CHAPTER XIX

Morgan and His Men. George Rogers Clark Expedition Old Justices, Marriages, etc.

In the foregoing chapter, reference is made to Capt. Daniel Morgan and his Company, who marched from Winchester, Virginia, in the Summer of 1775, with orders to report at headquarters of the Northern Army, then being organized at Boston by the Commander-in-Chief, Genl. Washington, who, having received his commission June 15, 1775, proceeded to select men who were known to him for their efficiency, and have them commissioned to raise rifle companies as they were called, and hasten to the Northern border where war was well established by the British at all forts.

Daniel Morgan of Frederick County, Va., was the first to receive a Captain's commission,—at least, he was the first to respond from Virginia. Tradition gives him the credit of raising his company within ten days after receiving his commission. The men who undertook that march were imbued with patriotism surpassed by none. They were not called upon to remain in their own Valley, and conduct a warfare against the savages who had troubled their mountain settlers, and to defend their own homes. This new service meant a severance of ties and endurance of hardships that would have appalled many brave men. Then, too, they were to form part of the "Continental Line," liable to service anywhere and everywhere. Unfortunately, no evidence in our County records shows who composed this Company; and for more than a century, all that is known to the Valley people concerning the *Ninety-six* Riflemen and the famous "Dutch Mess," who marched to Quebec and suffered defeat, was that transmitted from father to son. The author in his researches, found among the files of the State Department at Washington, matter of much interest concerning the campaign in Canada in the Winter of 1775-6. As is well known, Benedict Arnold was in command of the invading army, Genl. Montgomery conducting the unsuccessful attack upon the British garrison at Quebec. Montgomery was killed after gallantly storming and carrying the outer walls. His detachment suffered severely, and fell back. Arnold then appeared; and under his rally, the Continental lines achieved temporary victory. At this juncture, Arnold was severely wounded and carried from the front. Capt. Morgan then assumed command, and made a desperate charge; but he and his gallant Virginians were overpowered and forced to surrender, leaving over 100 of the 800 Continentals dead, lying in the snow around the ramparts. 300 men, including Maj. Morgan, were prisoners; the remnant escaped capture, and undertook a straggling retreat through the snow and forests of Maine, resulting in untold suffering to all and death nearly half their number. We must conclude that of the latter, were several of the Winchester Company; for as will be seen later on, only about 65 are accounted for of the 96 that tradition fixes as the number that started from Winchester July 14, 1775, and bivouaced the first night at the "Morgan Springs" near Shepherdstown. The files referred to become valuable at this late date, because they reveal the names of many of this old Company that have never been mentioned within the memory of the oldest inhabitant of the Lower Valley. We can afford to accept the list here given, for Major Morgan aided the British officer in obtaining a description of all the dead, wounded and prisoners, so far as related to his own Company.

The U. S. Government record shows that on the 4th day of January, 1776, Col. Allan Maclean, of the 84th Regiment of "Royal Emigrants" inspected the prisoners, and with the aid of officers, took their names and places of nativity. Those of British birth were required to enlist in his regiment, under the threat of being sent to England and tried as traitors. Under this threat, many enlisted. Inasmuch as the Valley people are especially interested in the Morgan Company, these pages will not be encumbered with the names of the heroes from other sections than Old Frederick.

List of killed, wounded and prisoners of Capt. Daniel Morgan's Company of Riflemen at Quebec, Canada, 1775-6.

Killed:

Lt. John Humphrey, Wm. Rutledge, Cornelius Norris, David Wilson, Peter Wolf, John Moore, Mathew Harbinson, Richard Colbert.

Wounded:

Benjamin Cackley, Solomon Fitzpatrick, Daniel Anderson, Spencer George, Daniel Durst, Hezekiah Philips, Adam Heizkill (Heiskell) John McGuire, Jesse Wheeler.

Prisoners:

Capt. Daniel Morgan, Lt. Wm. Heath (or Heth), Lt. Bruin (slightly wounded), Sergt. Wm. Fickhis, Sergt. Charles Porterfield, Sergt. John Donaldson, John Rogers, Corporal; Benjamin Grubb, corp.; John Burns, John Connor, Solomon Veal, Jacob Sperry, Adam Kurtz, John Shoults (Shultz), Chas. Grim, Peter Locke (Lauck); John Stephens, David Griffith, John Pearce, Benjamin Roderick, Thomas Williams, Gasper De Hart, Benjamin McIntire, Jeremiah Gordon, Roland Jacobs, Daniel Davis, John Brown, John Oran, John Maid, John Harbinson, Jedediah Philips, Jacob Ware, Absolon Brown, Thomas Chapman, Charles Secrists, Jeremia Riddle, Wm. Flood, William Greenway, Robert Mitchell, George Merchant, John Cochran, Curtis Bramingham, Timothy Feely, Conrad Enders, Patrick Dooland, Christopher Dolton and Robert Churchill. Seven of the number closing this list, enlisted in the King's service, while George Merchant, who had been captured on picket and, attired in his rifleman's uniform, was sent to England for exhibition as a specimen of the troops of the Colonies. He was liberated and sent home the next Summer.

The traditions of Winchester have always mentioned the following as well-known members of the Rifle Company who started to Quebec with Capt. Morgan, to-wit: 1st Lt. John Humphrey, 2d Lt. Wm. Heth, 1st Sergeant Geo. Porterfield. Privates: George Greenway, Wm. Greenway, Seth Stratton, John Schultz, Jacob Sperry, Peter Lauck, Simon Lauck, Frederick Kurtz, Adam Kurtz, Charles Grim, George Heiskell, Robert Anderson, Wm. Ball and Mark Hays. We observe some discrepancy in the name of George Porterfield as 1st Sergeant. Charles Porterfield was the 1st Sergeant of this Company; George Porterfield "was a sergeant" in a company enlisted in Winchester by Col. Morgan in the Spring of 1777. We also notice that Morgan did not report to the British officer the names of George Greenway, Seth Stratton, Simon Lauck, Frederick Kurtz, George Heiskell, Robert Anderson, Wm. Ball and Mark Hays; so we must conclude that these eight men of the remnant who escaped capture and ultimately arrived in Winchester, and were regarded by the prisoners on their return as part of their old company: or, it may be, they were confounded with the enlistment in the Spring of 1777, for the rosters of the two regiments organized then by Col. Morgan, show their names; and it may be added here that Timothy Feely either escaped after his enlistment in the King's service, or was soon exchanged, for he appears in the Summer of 1777 in Capt. Charles Porterfield's Company. This was Sergeant Charles Porterfield, a native of Frederick County, Va., mentioned by Genl. Arnold in his report to Genl. Washington as the first man to scale the walls at Quebec, and recommended by him for promotion. When exchanged, he received a commission as Captain, and recruited a company from the Lower Valley and equipped it at his own expense. He was killed at Camden, S. C., while leading a regiment, as Lt. Col. of the Virginia Line. His brother George was Sergeant in his Company, afterwards Captain by promotion for gallant conduct.

A scrap of local history can appropriately be mentioned here. It appears that some of the survivors of the Rifle Company, very soon after the Revolutionary War, organized a society styled the "Dutch Mess,"—thus perpetuating a title bestowed upon certain members of the Company by their companions during their Northern campaign. How many composed the original organization, none can tell; though regular observance of the anniversary of the Quebec campaign and capture, continued for a half century, no record appears to show who they were. Doubtless those familiar with the association in the early days, had no dreams of its perpetual observance and recognition; and though the old heroes have long since answered the final roll-call, the memory of the Dutch Mess is retained at this time by one or two old citizens of Winchester. The Author for many years during his boyhood period, had recounted to him many incidents connected with the annual celebrations, and heard much that would interest the reader now; but possibly some would not be inclined to accept such traditionary incidents. Fortunately, however, it is a well established fact that some of the Old Mess were well remembered by quite a number of intelligent elderly citizens towards the close of the Nineteenth Century, and would frequently mention the names of the survivors; and thus we are enabled to give a partial list. At this point it may be well to give authority for the foregoing statement. Mr. Wm. G. Russell, noted for his fund of information, when an old man twenty years ago, derived much pleasure in recounting to the writer many incidents of historical value; and he stated that he knew many of the old 96 Riflemen, and had vivid recollection of such anniversaries. Mr. Russell's statement, however, confined the Society or Mess to a membership of six, viz: John Schultz, Jacob Sperry, Simon Lauck, Charles Grim, ... Heiskell, and Peter Lauck, some of whom he had known intimately; and from his knowledge of the Society, the old soldiers only intended to keep up the associations formed on the march and in the camp; that they were well known as the Dutch Mess during the campaign. Mr. Russell also stated that as the number grew less, many citizens would be in line on the recurring anniversary, and did much to show their appreciation of the distinction given the old heroes. Should any reader feel inclined to learn something concerning the fate of other troops than those given as the Morgan Company, he is referred to "The Invasion of Canada in 1775;" by Edward Martin Stone, published at Providence, R. I., which is to be found in the National Library. He may there see that his ancestors were among the unfortunate invaders.

The Genl. George Rogers Clark campaign to the Illinois Forts in 1778, should be of sufficient interest to the Old Frederick County's history, to entitle it to mention here. As is well known to many readers, there were two forts on the frontier occupied by British officers and their Indian allies, that became a burden to all settlers in the territory eastward and along the Ohio River. Genl. Clark was chosen to command the expedition fitted out to capture those forts. We will briefly state that this little army equipped for light marching, was composed of men who had endured hardships and were fully acquainted with Indian warfare. We will only mention that two of his companies were commanded by Captain Joseph Bowman of Frederick County, and Leonard Helm, of Fauquier County, and will only give the names of other officers and privates that may be familiar to Valley people. Many of their names appear in the records of the Old County prior to her subdivision; many of their descendants are to be found in the Counties from Shenandoah to the Potomac River. The enlistments were made in the dead of Winter, January, 1778; and when the expedition encountered the hardships of the march and the warfare needed to capture Old Fort St. Vincent and Kaskaskia, they stamped themselves heroes, and received from the government substantial recognition for their services by grants of land in the captured country:

Company Officers

Capt. Joseph Bowman, Capt. Leonard Helm; 1st Lt. Isaac Bowman; 2d Lt. Abram Keller; 1st Sergt. Daniel Dust; 2d Sergt. Isaac Keller; 2d Sergt. Jacob Speers; Sergt. Buckner Pittman; Sergt. Wm. Rubey; Sergt. Saml. Strode; Sergt. John Breeden.

Privates

Abraham Miller, Wm. Slack, Thomas Perry, Robt. McClanihan, Thomas Cartmell, Edward Bulger, Abram James, Barnaby Walters, Thomas H. Vance, George Millar, Patrick Doran, Nathan Cartmell, Isaac McBride, Edward Murrey, Joseph Simpson, Van Swearingen, Isaac Vanmeter, John Bender, Lewis Bender, Robert Bender, Christian Bowman, Christopher Coontz, Jacob Detering, Geo. Hite, Barney Master, John Setser, John Bentley, Henry Honaker, Fred. Honaker, Henry Funk, Alex. McIntire, Wm. Berry (1) Wm. Berry (2), Philip Long, George King, Zebeniah Lee, John Isaacs, Wm. Myers, John Peters, Geo. Shepard, Peter Shepard, John Sitzer, Peter Brazer, Richard Breeden, John Bush, John Conn, Francis Haller, Fredk. Sowers.

The foregoing is not a complete list of the men in the two companies. It is intended only to preserve the evidence that the Valley was called upon, and her sons responded; and when the campaign closed with the Northwest Territory virtually as their trophy, the survivors were discharged in August, 1778. Many of their number never returned. Capt. Bowman died at a fort in the Summer of 1779; a number were killed in battle and found graves on the wilds of the frontier, Thomas Cartmell being one, and was buried at St. Vincente (now Vincennes). The Author has a fac-simile copy of his signature to a paper written prior to his death, the original being on file with the State Historical Society of Indiana. The Author is indebted to the Hon. Wm. H. English, President of the Society for many years, and also the author of the comprehensive and interesting history, "The Conquest of the North-West," for many courtesies.

In the Winter of 1781, the Congress was petitioned for reinforcements for the northwest forts. The Valley again responded. Virginia, in supplying her quota, recruited two companies from the "State Line," and the men were assigned to Capt. Benjamin Biggs and Capt. Uriah Springer's Companies. Only the familiar Valley names are given here: Wm. Barr, Richard Carter, James Smith, Jacob Conrad, Samuel Osburn, Wm. Bailey, Michael Kairnes (Kerns), Robert Crawford, John Lockhart, James Lockhart, David Clark, John Morrison, John Connor, Chas. Morgan, John Bean, John Daugherty, Jacob Rhodes, Jacob Rinker.

Genl. George Rogers Clark, who commanded the Western expedition already referred to, died Feby. 18, 1818.

Capt. Wm. Goodman of Berkley County, one of his officers, died July 10, 1825.

Capt. Wm. Sommerville, one of his officers, died March 18, 1826.

Lt. Nathaniel Henry, of Frederick, one of his officers, died Jany. 14, 1824.

Capt. Robt. White, of Frederick, one of his officers, died July 26, 1828.

Capt. Thomas Cartmell, of Frederick, one of his officers, died in the campaign.

Lt. Wm. Eskridge, of Frederick, one of his officers, died Oct. 9, 1830.

Ensign Reese Pritchard, of Hamp., one of his officers, died Sept. 25, 1824.

The following were some of the Valley men who suffered at Valley Forge, and gave such signal service to Genl. Washington in that trying Winter, that Congress recognized them in Special Act. They were members of an Artillery Company recruited at Winchester:

Capt. John Dandridge, commissioned Feby. 1, 1777.

Capt. Nathaniel Burwell, Aide to Genl. Robt. Howe.

Capt. John Blair.

Lt. William Campbell.

Lt. Wm. Stephenson.

Capt. Anthony Singleton.

Capt. James Pendleton. Several Maryland officers and men mentioned.

The celebrated Legion of Cavalry commanded by Lt. Col. Henry Lee (Light Horse Harry) was raised East of the Blue Ridge. Major Henry Peyton recruited men from the Valley, however. The following are given, thinking they may be connected with the reader:

Maj. Peyton (died in service), Maj. Jos. Eggleston; Lt. and Surgeon Alexander Skinner, Wm. Winston, Adjt., and Lt. Patrick Carnes, Capt. Mathew Irwin, Surgeon Michael Rudolph, Capt. George Handy, Lt. Wm. Lewis, Robt. Powers, Albion Throckmorton, Wm. B. Harrison, Clement Carrington, John Champe. A number of cadets were taken from the military school and distributed among the following companies, to drill the men: Captains, Johnson Oliver Towles, Thomas Patterson, Wm. Gregory, Saml. Hopkins, Saml. Cabell, Thos. Ruffin, Thos. Massie, Thos. Hutchins and John Jones. (See Military Archives, War Dept., Washington, D. C.)

At the December Term, 1796 of the County Court, Henry Beatty and many others were recommended for appointment as officers in the *Virginia Line* of Militia.

The reader doubtless feels that we have lingered long in our story of the Revolutionary War period. This effort required many weary days of travel and search; and out of the mass of records and historic collections, we submit the following chapters with as much brevity as possible in condensing incidents that apply to Frederick County. Many more could be narrated from the thousands now in hand; but the patience of the reader and our limited space must be considered.

The Court, 1784, directed the Clerk to record all marriages returned by ministers who had *performed marriage rites.* This was pursuant to an Act of Assembly, 1784, requiring all such persons to make a list of marriages they had solemnized and return same to clerk's office. The old marriage record is in the County Clerk's Office. Previous to the Revolution, the Established Church kept a register of all marriages. Dissenters were required to make return to that church. The marriage record is an important County record.

For other gleanings from the County Court records, subsequent to the close of the Revolutionary War, the reader is referred to the chapter pertaining to the history of Winchester.

The following is given as a list of Justices composing the Court from 1795 to 1813, inclusive:

John Smith, Wm. Vanmeter, Cornelius Baldwin, Wm. Snickers, James Singleton, Wm. Lynn, Jno. B. Tilden, Dolphine Drew, John S. Ball, Isaac Hite, Robert Berkley, George F. Norton, Bushrod Taylor, Chas. Smith, Jacob Heironimus, Joseph Baker, Thos. Buck, James Ware, Nathaniel Burwell, Mandley Taylor, Geo. Blakemore, Chas. Brent, Joshua Gore, Beaty Carson, Robt. C. Burwell, Edward McGuire, Lewis McCoole, Moses Russell, Griffin Taylor, James M. Marshall, Philip Nelson, John Bell, Joseph Gamble, Jno. Jolliffe, Robt. Vance, Edward Smith, Elijah Littler, Wm. McCoole, John Bell, Thomas Stribling, Saml. Baker, Benj. O'Rear, Jno. McCoole, Joseph Tidball, Wm. Castleman.

Order Books for the period mentioned, record the date of appointment, and much matter of interest.

CHAPTER XX

The War of 1812-14

The author has made strenuous efforts to secure sufficient data to produce a brief sketch of the part Frederick County had in this war; but owing to the carelessness on the part of those who could have preserved much to interest succeeding generations, we have very little in our home records to show who were the moving spirits to respond to the appeals made for volunteers to redress wrongs that Great Britain had perpetrated on the high seas and to our coastwise mercantile interests. Mr. Jefferson, during his term as President, remonstrated with the British Government, protesting against the outrages upon American vessels, and the impressment of American citizens into unwilling service in British fleets; and endeavored to avoid another war with England. But the British lion shook his mane in defiance, and England proceeded to maintain her claim as mistress of the seas; and when President Madison virtually declared war, a majority of the American people were ready when the call came for each State to furnish her quota. James Barbour then Governor of Virginia, called for volunteers. Winchester immediately became the scene of war preparations. Recruiting stations were established in the Lower Valley; and in a short time companies were organized, and marched away. This we know from tradition and clippings from newspapers of that period; but no record was made by this County of who her sons were that so quickly responded; and what the Author offers now has been taken from the Military Archives at Washington, where much confusion confronts the student in his efforts to secure a list of those who enlisted in Frederick County. We are able to state, however, that several companies were accredited to this section, and Winchester named as the recruiting station for companies commanded by Capt. Willoughby Morgan, Capt. Thos. Roberts, Capt. Wm. Morris, Capt. Henry Beatty, and Capt. Michael Coyle. From the military files the writer, so far as he could, arranged the lists in the following order:

The First Infantry Company was recruited by Capt. Morgan, who was promoted, and entered the regular Army. The Company was then reorganized and used as Mounted Infantry, and became known as Cavalry Company Number Four.

Officers:

Capt. Thos. Roberts. No other officers named. *Members of Company,* as the record says:

Thomas Roberts, Wm. Roberts, Alexander Holliday, Wm. Ball, William Campbell, James Campbell, Solomon Heister, Wm. C. Holliday, Jacob Baker, Charles Conrad, Nicholas Burwell, Augustus Streit, Peter Bowers, Jno. Bowley, James Bennett, Joshua Reed, John Denny, Andrew Bush, Presley Hansbury, James Vance, Sandy Hutchinson, Jno. M. Magson, Richard Beckwith, James Barr, Stewart Grant, Isaac Lauck, Jno. Sloat, James Meredith, Philip Sherer, John Foster, Philip Hoff, John Price, Isaac Kurtz, John Miller, Richard Holliday, Philip Bowers, James White, John Carter, George Rice, Jno. C. Clarke, Robert Jack, Geo. Swallum, Solomon Spengler, Jonas Ashby, Wm. Kane, Lewis Beatty, John Everly, John W. Miller, Alexander Newman.

Artillery Company (No Number).

Officers: Capt. Wm. Morris; 1st. Lt. Geo. W. Kiger; 2d Lt. Isaac Lauck; 3d Lt. Wm. Streit; 4th Lt. Jno. Poe; 1st corporal Wm. Van Horn; 2d Corp. Wm. Young; 3d Corp. Nathan Parkins; 4th Corp. Wm. Macfee; Fifer, John Day; Drummer John Everly. Privates: Danl. Gray, Jno. Allen, Thomas Austin, Wm. Barnes, Levi Booker, Francis Beckwith, David Cather, John Cooley, Louthan Cochrane, Jos. Kremer, Robt. Davidson, Wm. Dalby, John Fenton, Jno. Farmer, Thomas Foster, Roger Fulkerson, Richard Gibbs, Jno. Hoffnagle, Samuel Herdsman, Wm. Hutchison, George Heinrick, John Johnson, John Haas, Jno. Hoffman, John Hesser, Asa Joyce, Richard Jones, Daniel Kiger, John Keeler, John Klyfustine, Thos. Lafferty, Jno. Miller, John Morris, James McCann, Craven Shaw, John Schultz, George Schreck, Elisha Winn, Henry Young.

Infantry Company No. 5.

Officers: Michael Coyle, Capt.; Wm. Throckmorton, 1st. Lt. Privates: Michael Copenhaver, Jacob Copenhaver, Henry Sloat, Jacob Mesmer, Robert Long, Isaac Russell, Jacob Lauck, ... Brill, Daniel Brown, Frederick Aulick, Benjamin

Scrivner, Jno. V. Brown, John Magson, Henry Crebs, John Coyle, S. Hester, Wm. and Stephen Jenkins, J. Foster, John Jenkins.

The files show other names, but none appear as familiar names in this section; therefore are left out. A few names listed, are in doubt as to their residence. All the Companies named were sent to Norfolk and Point Comfort. Some of the Frederick County men died of yellow fever,—one being James Campbell, who was promoted to 1st Lt. in Co. 4. Lt. Campbell was a son of Wm. Campbell and uncle of the Author. Some other fatalities from the same fever. No other Frederick County men reported. It is known that other companies were raised in this section. Judge Henry St. George Tucker recruited a cavalry company and marched to Norfolk. No list, however, appears. The following are to be found on the pay-roll, but their names are not connected with the Winchester Companies. They were what was known as Emergency Soldiers, enlisted for ninety days—what we would now term Reserves. We find that Simeon Hillman, Simpson Touchstone, Henry Glaize, Zachariah Crawford, Evan Thatcher, Richard Jones, James Welch, Simon Owen, Jackson Ryan, Nat. Ryan, Nicholas Perry substituted for Abner Hodgson, a drafted man. Many more of the latter class, but not familiar names in this section. The Author knew quite a number of those mentioned, and knew some who secured pensions under Act of Congress in 1846, whose widows were continued on the pension roll for many years: Two notable cases being Mrs. Charlotte Hillman, widow of Simeon, and Mrs. Eliza Russell widow of Isaac,—they being the last survivors to receive pensions. The former died about 1896, the latter 1900. The reader will readily connect many of our present-day business men with the old patriots who answered their country's call nearly one hundred years ago: For instance, Jacob Baker who was Quarter Master for his Company; whose carefully kept accounts, as such, are in possession of his daughter, Miss Portia Baker. Mr. Baker was founder of the house of Baker & Company, whose sons succeeded him for many years, while his grandsons and great-grandsons are daily seen at the old stand, pursuing the same methods established by their illustrious sire. Mr. Isaac Russell transmitted to his sons James B. and Isaac W. Russell his thrift and integrity, who are prominent business men. Many others will be recognized by many citizens as men who in their day discharged their duties faithfully in their various avocations. Many of the names sound strange in the ear to-day, for time has worked many changes. Some families have become extinct, and the places they once filled, others now occupy; but it would be well for us to remember their deeds and virtues. If they had their faults and failures, we have none to tell them now. Peace to their ashes!

The author has on his table at this writing the Discourse of Rev. Wm. Hill, D.D., which he delivered in the Presbyterian Church in Winchester, Feby. 20, 1815, the occasion being a day set apart by common consent as a day of "Thanksgiving" by the Citizens of Frederick County for the Peace just concluded between this country and Great Britain. Dr. Hill's oratory and graphic arraignment of Great Britain for causing the war which resulted in loss of life and wanton destruction of property by the British, including the capitol at Washington, and many valuable records, is a literary gem, rare indeed. Every word of the sermon would edify the reader; but lack of space forbids further notice. Its brief mention is made to show the feeling of the Valley people as they once more rested under the banner of Peace. The sermon was published by Mr. John Heiskell, Editor of one of the newspapers of the town.

The Author is indebted to Miss Laura Gold, daughter of Mr. Wm. H. Gold, deceased, (who, in his day had many valuable collections of this character), for use of the pamphlet and other interesting publications.

CHAPTER XXI

The Old Justices' Court

From 1743 to 1776, the old Justices' Court was the only court holding jurisdiction in the territory embraced in Old Frederick. From 1776, there were two courts of Law and Equity in the State, which had jurisdiction in this section of the Valley. In 1802, the Court was increased from two judges to three, and Districts apportioned. In 1809 another change occurred; and the "Superior Courts of Law," known as the Old Law and Chancery Court, was set in motion. One judge to hold terms twice a year in every County, superceding what was the old District Court—virtually the same court, but the records kept at some central point in the District. Winchester for many years was this point, being chosen by Act of Assembly in 1811; and old Order Books of this Court, now in the county clerk's office, are interesting to study. The District embraced among other counties, Loudoun County. Full minutes of the Chancery trials for the counties appear in these records. The first judge to preside in this court was Judge Robert White, succeeded by Judges Wm. Brockinbough and John Scott. They were not regularly assigned. The General Assembly, Apl. 16, 1831, established a Court of Law and Chancery in each of the counties. Hon. Richard E. Parker, Judge of the General Court, was assigned to this Circuit. After his death in 1836, Hon. Isaac R. Douglas was appointed Judge of this Circuit. After his death in 1850, Hon. Richard Parker, son of the former Judge of this name, was appointed for the Circuit. Gleanings from this Court give us some matters which will show the jurisdiction of this Court. The trial of Commonwealth cases changed from the County Court. At the November Term, 1844, the Grand Jury presented Daniel Anderson for perjury at the election held in Newtown: witnesses G. L. White, R. W. Barton and J. L. Johnson. John M. Mayson, Conrad Kremer and Peeter Kreemer constable, for "abase" of their office by influencing voters. Joseph Long, a tavern keeper in Newton, for partiality as Comr. of Election, etc., and twelve other persons presented for stoning Bushrod Taylor's tavern in Winchester, and for riotous conduct on night of election, Nov., 1844. David G. Danner was keeper of the tavern. This was the exciting election of Franklin Pierce for President. Whigs and Democrats waged a memorable campaign; and the victors were too jubilant to suit the temper of the defeated Whigs, who presented the cases before the Grand Jury.

The first clerk to the first chancery court was John Peyton, 1793—Daniel Lee, 1804.

In 1809, Circuit Courts were substituted for District Courts, and one judge of the General Court assigned to each Circuit. This system prevailed for many years, the sessions held in April and September in Frederick.

By an Act of the General Assembly, the first Term of the Superior Court of Chancery to be held in Winchester, was on the 7th of July, 1812, Hon. Dabney Carr, Judge; Daniel Lee, Clerk,—Judge Carr's long service continued until another change was made in the circuit, when Hon. Henry St. George Tucker presided from 1824—Daniel Lee, Clerk—until 1831, when another change was made in the Districts; and, as has been shown, Judge Richard E. Parker appeared and was Judge until 1837. It was during Judge Carr's term that a celebrated criminal trial occurred. This was known as the Doct. Berkly murder case. Three of his negroes, one woman and two men, committed the horrible murder in the Spring of 1818. His body was boiled and reduced to a mass, then burned, together with his clothing. His brass buttons were found in the ashes; and through the efforts of his overseer, Robinson, the negroes were brought to trial and convicted, and hung in July of same year. The other slaves were transported to the Dry Tortugas. Berkly's home passed to John Rust. This was in the section now Warren County.

The clerks were Joseph Kean, W. G. Singleton. Since the latter's term closed by the Civil War, the courts were reorganized: E. S. Brent, Clerk, 1865; James B. Burgess, 1871; J. A. Nulton, 1881; Wm. L. Clark, Phil H. Gold.

The judges of the Circuit Courts under the constitution of 1850, appointed a Commonwealth's attorney for their Districts, who attended the Judges around their circuits. The Old Justices Court appointed same officer generally to serve in their courts.

This Circuit Court tried many famous cases during the term of Judge Douglas. The old minutes afford interesting reading and study; but want of space forbids their mention here.

After Judge Parker's appearance in 1851, one of the cases tried by him in Nov., 1851, was known on the docket as Bennett Russell vs. Negroes Juliet, etc. This case had tortuous course through the courts—many hearings, and was not closed until Feby. Term, 1856. The plaintiff was the son of Bennett Russell, who by several clauses in his will, provided for the emancipation of a large family of his slaves. Russell lived in Clarke County; the case was ably conducted on both sides; the legal lights from Clarke and Frederick attracting large crowds of people at every trial, and was one of the most hotly contested cases heard in our courts. The Russell heirs sought to annul the will, while the negroes through their able counsel, met the issue in a determined way, holding that the will plainly indicated what the jury should do. The case was started in the Clarke Court, but by agreement was transferred to Frederick. The Court ruled that the jury should pass upon the facts relative to certain clauses of the will, and no more. Counsel for plaintiff strove to prove the clauses were too vague and indefinite, and should not be regarded as binding upon the executors. Counsel for defendants urged the execution of the intention of the testator. The jury, after many days of patient attention to testimony, and the able arguments of counsel, rendered a verdict favorable to the negroes. They considered the emancipation clauses sufficiently plain, and the will should stand. The Court ordered the will to be recorded in Clarke County, and let the case rest. The executors resorted to delays, and the negroes waited long for their freedom.

The trial of Thomas Cain for rape, which started in 1850, and was concluded before Judge Parker, was a famous case and created much feeling in the community. Men of to-day well remember the epithet Wicked Cain, that was applied to this man, who expiated his crime by a term in the penitentiary.

At the June (15) Term, 1856, the famous murder trials of Spurr and Copenhaver was before the Court. The Grand Jury indicted Wm. H. Spurr and Andrew Jackson Copenhaver for the murder of Isaac Smith. Smith lived at the mill property South of Winchester now owned by the paper mill company. On his visit to Winchester on a certain night, he entered the old Massie Tavern, just South of the Presbyterian Church on Loudoun Street, where he met the accused men. There was some drinking, and then a quarrel, which resulted in the killing of Smith. Spurr stabbed him fatally, and Copenhaver, using brass knuckles, struck the blow that felled their victim. They then rushed from the house; Spurr disposed of the dirk, which was afterwards found, while Copenhaver flung his knuckles on the roof of J. B. T. Reed's residence on opposite side of the street. The only witness to the tragedy was Jacob W. Kiger the young bartender. Through him it was learned who committed the fatal act. The two men were apprehended and promptly brought before the Court. They were arraigned and the same day indicted for the murder. They waived all technical delays and elected to be tried separately; and, strange to say, the case was called the next day. Spurr was tried first; he had secured the services of Mr. Robt. Y. Conrad and his partner, J. Randolph Tucker. Fred W. M. Holliday was Commonwealth Attorney. The jury in the box were the following well known men: John Cather, George Kern, Solomon Pitman, Alfred Clevenger, Jas. W. Sibert, James Lewis, Alfred Garrett, Robt. B. Smith, Jeremich D. Smith, Jno. W. Muse, Martin B. Muse and Henry Crumly. Intense excitement prevailed everywhere. All could see that the young attorney for the Commonwealth was impressed with his responsibility. Ambitious, courageous, possessed of remarkable mental and physical ability, and with a strong case, he was well aware the contest was to be one that required all he had. He knew the able counsel for the defense, Mr. Conrad, was acknowledged by all to have no superior, and perhaps no equal, for the conduct of such a serious case. The quiet demeanor of this able lawyer was enough to disconcert an enthusiastic prosecutor like Holliday; and when his eye rested upon the brilliant Tucker then in his prime, he knew he had to contend with weighty strokes from Conrad and the marvelous eloquence of Ran Tucker. The recollection of this trial enables the writer to recall the picture vividly; the handsome figure and manner of young Holliday attracted attention from all. The court room was crowded in every conceivable way—the bar full of the men who made the Winchester bar famous for so many years. The pathetic side to the picture were the venerable fathers of the prisoners and the murdered man. Mr. Spurr sat near his boy, and old Mr. Jonathan Smith sat with bowed head near the man who was expected to convict the slayer of his son. Smith was noted for his towering form and warm temperament. The sympathy of the people was with the father of such a son, stricken down in the prime of such remarkable manhood. At the close of the first day's trial, the Sheriff, Wm. D. Gilkeson, and his three deputies, Robt. M. Cartmell, Wm. D. Gilkeson, Jr., and James Gilkeson, were sworn to take the jury in their custody and return them to court the next morning, and not allow them to hold communication with any person. Every day, then, until the conclusion of the trial, there was no abatement of interest. The weapons and bloodstained clothing were all arrayed before the jury in Holliday's dramatic style. The spectators were aroused; intense feeling prevailed, requiring constant vigilance of the officers to restrain. As may be supposed, the argument was the great feature; and seldom if ever had the old court room heard such eloquence. The impressions made on the youths of that day as they watched the parries and thrusts of the skillful trio and heard the pathetic pleadings of counsel for the prisoner, laid the foundation for the reputation that Ran Tucker had as an orator, which never left him.

June 21st, 1855, the jury handed in the verdict: "We, the jury find the prisoner guilty of murder in the second degree and fix his punishment at 18 years in the penitentiary.

(Signed) John Cather, *Foreman.*"

Andrew Jackson Copenhaver was put upon his trial for same offence immediately at the conclusion of Spurr's. A jury was in waiting; additional counsel employed by old Mr. Smith to assist the Commonwealth. Senator James M. Mason appeared in the case, and Mr. Philip Williams appeared with Conrad and Tucker for the prisoner. The following persons composed the jury: Moses Nelson, H. B. Pitzer, Daniel Carver, Samuel Roland, Solomon Glaize, Wm. Frieze, Elijah Shull, Geo. H. Lewis, Martin Frieze, Thos. S. Sangster, Martin M. Adams and John Ewing.

The case was conducted along the same lines as the one just closed; the two new lawyers—both distinguished for their legal ability, ably assisted in the trial, which continued for eight days. Mr. Conrad and Senator Mason had many legal tilts on admissibility of evidence; and it was remarked by many that Mr. Conrad gained rather than lost ground. Mr. Williams made himself famous in his cross-examination of the witness Kiger, and wrung from him an admission that Copenhaver had some degree of provocation. These great lawyers were attractive in every line of the case; and when the jury returned the verdict late in the evening of the 29th of June, none were surprised at this finding: "We, the jury find the prisoner guilty of murder in the second degree and fix his punishment for the term of 15 years in the penitentiary."

The prisoners were sentenced on the 2d of July, and hurried away to Richmond. The Court named two guards to assist Deputy Sheriffs Cartmell and Gilkeson to conduct the prisoners safely to the penitentiary. Some one may ask, did the prisoners serve their terms which would extend through the War that ended in 1865. We answer no. There has always been some mystery about the sequel of these celebrated cases. Mr. Tucker was soon called to Richmond as Attorney General for Virginia, Henry A. Wise being Governor; and during his term, he granted a pardon to both prisoners. Spurr and Copenhaver became useful citizens during the remainder of their lives, which terminated a few years ago. All the jurors, officers of court and every member of the Winchester bar living at that period, have long since passed beyond earthly tribunals.

The Circuit Court had concurrent jurisdiction with the Justices' Court in what was called Naturalization of Aliens. This occasioned much confusion, and often men lost their right to vote because their names did not appear in proceedings of the County Court. The majority of such cases were disposed of in that Court, and it was natural some politicians would conclude it was the only court where evidence could be found to sustain the claim. The writer deems it desirable to give the names of a few well-known citizens in their day, of this class. At the Nov. Term, 1851, Robert Hamilton and Patrick Brady, natives of Ireland, and Henry Kinzell, native of Darmstadt, Germany; and May 1, 1852, John Kater of Scotland, Patrick Moore, Dennis and Michael Saunders of Ireland, James Donaldson and Thos. Dixon of England, and Andrew McCarthy of Ireland.

At the June Term, 1855 are several interesting minutes of this character: John Kerr of England, Robert Steel of Scotland, James Tipping of Ireland, Samuel Hardy of Great Britain (son of Charles, was born in Britain), John Wild of Bavaria. Of this number, Robert Steel proved that he declared his intentions in the Justices' Court May 15, 1839; John Kerr satisfied the Court that he many years previous declared his intentions to become a citizen, but the evidence of the date could not be produced: the Court, however, finally admitted him to full citizenship. James Tipping produced proof that his declaration was entered Nov. 2, 1840; Samuel Hardy proved that he was a minor when he arrived in America and he was now 36 years of age.

At the Nov. Term, 1855, Alexander Steel of Scotland and Michael Hassett of Ireland received their papers. This may suggest to some reader one mode to discover something about his ancestor that would be of interest.

At the June Term, 1858, we find the Circuit Court spending many days over the trial of another murder case. This was the notable case of James Catlett alias Jim Wells, a well known negro of the County, who killed Sam

Brock an inoffensive and much esteemed negro of the town. Catlett was found guilty of murder in the first degree, and sentenced June 26th to be hung. Lewis A. Miller, Sheriff, and his deputy John G. Miller, erected the gallows in the jail-yard and executed the order of court August 6, 1858.

At this Term the Grand Jury indicted quite a number of free negroes for remaining in the State without lawful permission. At that time a law on our statute books required all free negroes to report to the Clerk for registration, and then to obtain certificates from the court to remain for one year only, when they were required to repeat the process. If they could prove good character and were in the employ of some responsible person, they were allowed to remain. In the southern end of the County there was one family that gave much trouble from their influence among the slaves. Mundy Robinson and his large family were indicted, and this led to the indictment of many others. These cases remained on the docket until the Civil War virtually closed all proceedings.

At the June Term, 1859, John McVicar was naturalized. This man became a noted scout for Stonewall Jackson, as will be more fully shown. At this Term we find that Powell Conrad, Lewis N. Huck and Charles L. Ginn were admitted to practice law. Margaret Lucas, a free negress, as the minute reads, was convicted of murder in second degree.

In the Spring of 1861, the Court tried —— Robinson for murder. She was one of the Mundy Robinson free negroes mentioned above. This woman was employed by Benjamin Cooley, who then lived at Belle Grove. She murdered Mrs. Cooley while the two were in the meat house, using a meat cleaver. The woman was promptly tried; the verdict was "guilty of murder in the first degree." The prisoner was remanded to jail without being sentenced. Her counsel, Col. Richard E. Byrd, moved the court to set aside the verdict. During the same Term, the prisoner was brought into Court. As sentence was being pronounced, Col. Byrd raised a point of law that brought the Court to a standstill and every member of the bar to their feet. Col. Byrd announced to the court that the prisoner raised no objection to the verdict of the jury; but did object to any judgment of the Court that would endanger the life of the unborn child. Col. Byrd's law was sound, but evidence must be produced to the Court that such conditions existed. Old authorities were produced; and the Court being satisfied as to what course to pursue, ordered a jury of eight women to be summoned by the Sheriff to appear forthwith in court, to be sworn to visit the jail and enquire into the prisoner's condition, and report their verdict to the court. When the writ *de ventre inspiciendo* was issued, old attorneys declared it was the first to issue in Virginia; and the author has never found in any court in the State any record of such issue. Our old friend John G. Miller was sheriff. With his usual promptness, he proceeded to execute the strange writ, while the Court and anxious spectators awaited results. Mr. Miller returned after an hour's absence, greatly excited, declaring he could find no woman who would obey his summons, and that some of the Potato Hill women threatened him with bodily harm. He was informed by the Court that he and his deputy must execute the order at once. Mr. Miller stated that his deputy, James B. Russell, was out of town, and that he would resign before he would endure another experience. The Court announced that his resignation would not be accepted until he had executed the writ; the jury was summoned, and after due deliberation returned their verdict: whereupon the prisoner was remanded to jail without sentence; and we may add, she was never executed. Pending the occupancy of the town by the first Federal troops, this prisoner disappeared.

At the November Term, 1858, Washington G. Singleton made first appearance as Clerk of this Court.

November 16, 1860, this minute appears and is given as a sample of the action of Court relating to this class of persons:

"Mary Phelps a free negro woman," filed her petition to be reduced to slavery. Notice was posted at the front door of the court house for one month, that she would move the Court to direct that she and her children become the property of the wife of John Avis. The emancipated slaves were required to remove to some free State; failing to do this from choice, by reason of their attachment to the white family who had been their owners, they selected some member of that family and secured permission to return to their former state of slavery. This indicates how the old slaves regarded their owners,—prefering to remain with those they loved rather than enjoy the boon of freedom in a strange land where the people did not understand the relations between master and slave.

At the Nov. Term, 1861, James Shipe was tried for the murder of Henry Anderson, of Winchester, Va. The murder occurred in an old stone house on the farm near the old Gold homestead now the property of Phil. H. Gold. Anderson was fatally stabbed with sheep shears. Dr. G. L. Miller informed the writer that this was his first case, and he used a knife to cut the weapon from the body. Shipe was sentenced to 18 years in penitentiary.

CHAPTER XXII

Banks, Etc.

The financial panic experienced by Virginia during the Revolutionary War and for several years subsequent thereto, caused the business men and statesmen to consider the subject, so as to avoid a repetition of such troubles to the commercial life of the State. Much time and several sessions of the Assembly were frittered away before a solution of the difficulty found favor. At last, in the Winter of 1804, the General Assembly settled upon the plan of having their first *Bank*, styled The Bank of Virginia, to be established at Richmond; capital stock not to exceed $1,500,000.00, divided into shares of $100 each. Subscriptions to be opened at Richmond the first Monday in May next, in Norfolk, Petersburg, Fredericksburg, Winchester, Staunton and Lynchburg on same day, each point being limited in number of shares—Winchester's quota being Five hundred and twenty-five shares. Commissioners were named to superintend the issuance of the shares: Hugh Holmes, Edward Smith, Robt. Mackey, Adam Douglas, Wm. Davidson, John Ambler, Archibald Magill and John Milton were named for Winchester. This stock was quickly taken and the scheme was satisfactory. The infection seemed to spread rapidly, for we find the Farmers Bank of Virginia was incorporated Feby. 13, 1812 (during the war period, it will be observed); Richmond to be the place of location; shares to be $100 each, paid in gold or silver coin. Winchester was allowed to take sixteen hundred and sixty-six shares in this second Bank; the commissioners appointed to issue stock being Gerard Williams, Edward Smith, Chas. Magill, Beattie Carson, Edw. McGuire, Daniel Lee, Daniel Gold, Isaac Baker, Joseph Gamble, Abraham Miller, Peter Lauck, Henry St. George Tucker, Alfred H. Powell, Lewis Wolfe and Lemuel Bent. This Bank was incorporated so that the capital should be distributed among the several towns named as follows: to Richmond one-fourth; to Norfolk one-fourth; Winchester one-eighth, and same to the other three towns. This, then, was the origin and establishment of the Farmers Bank of Winchester, —being a branch of the mother bank.

The Valley Bank was chartered 1817, to be located at Winchester, under the name of *The Bank of the Valley in Virginia.* Provision was made in the charter that the stockholders of said bank might appoint places of deposit and discount in the counties of Jefferson, Berkley, Hampshire and Hardy, and one in either Loudoun or Fauquier, to the amount of $100,000, to be known as the branch banks of the mother bank. The board of directors of both The Farmers, and Bank of the Valley, were required to visit each branch at semi-annual periods and make full settlements, etc. The writer remembers well those interesting visits. They were notable events; much rivalry was maintained in each town, when lavish hospitalities were dispensed. They were occasions for universal entertainment. Romney and Moorfield seem then to have been favorites with the Board of Directors; there was something in the mountain air perceptibly exhilarating. Both banks grew to be influential institutions, presided over by men in every locality, competent to wield influence and to maintain the credit and marvelous success they achieved. Nothing seemed powerful enough to disturb them; and only the Civil War, with its four years of disastrous work, could cause them to close their doors. This they did, and moved their effects South to escape destruction. The old Farmers Bank could never rally; the Bank of the Valley was placed in the hands of a receiver named Fant; and if he ever received anything by virtue of his office, there is no evidence of it in these parts. The writer, while gathering data for this notice, conversed freely with officers of one of the banks now doing business on the same site; and learned that the books, papers and old bank notes remained in the old Valley Bank building for years. Out of the debris of this wrecked bank, many relics of former days were rescued. Mr. W. Douglas Fuller, now Cashier of the Farmers and Merchants Nat. Bank of Winchester, presented the writer with three of the old bank notes. One, of the denomination of $20.00, was issued at Winchester May 7, 1856, and reads: The Bank of the Valley in Virginia will pay on demand twenty dollars at its Banking House in Leesburg to J. Janney or Bearer. No. 218-C H. M. Brent, Cashier; T. A. Tidball, President.

This shows how the mother bank at Winchester managed her branch banks in other towns.

The Bank of Winchester

This banking institution was in successful operation when the Civil War made it necessary to close its doors and secure its funds and papers. The writer has been informed by one acquainted with the circumstances, that the money and papers were securely placed in boxes and buried in the cellar of Doctor William Miller's residence; and when peace was declared and it was safe to reproduce the effects of the bank, Mr. Robt. B. Wolf, the youthful cashier, was able to account for every dollar; the result being that the stockholders were in a much more comfortable situation than could be expected. This bank was started as a savings institution—with Mr. Robert Y. Conrad, president, and Robert B. Wolf. cashier. They first occupied the building on West side of Loudoun Street, nearly opposite Court House Avenue. From there they went to the building cornering on Loudoun and Water Streets, now the property of S. Hable; from there to the law office of Mr. Conrad, several doors South of the Evans Hotel. Vaults were there made, with other changes, that converted the first floor into a comfortable banking room; and there the Bank closed about 1862, and has not since resumed business.

The capital stock was estimated at $100,000.

There are three banks of deposit and discount now doing business in Winchester.

The Shenandoah Valley National Bank, having obtained a charter, with capital stock of $130,000, which was promptly taken, the Board of Directors purchased the old Valley Bank property, and opened its doors and vaults for business in January, 1866: Mr. Philip Williams, president, Henry M. Brent, Sr., cashier. This institution continued to use the old property until about 1900, when it was decided the volume of business and profits justified the erection of the magnificent palace now seen on the old site, northwest corner of Loudoun and Piccadilly Streets. The building is complete in all its equipments—modern business offices, vaults, etc., adorn the interior. The affairs of the bank are perfectly handled by the efficient corps of officers and clerks. Mr. S. H. Hansbrough, president; John W. Rice, cashier, J. Few Brown, assistant, G. G. Baker, teller, T. Walter Gore, clerk. The capital stock has been increased to $200,000.

The Union Bank of Winchester obtained a charter as a banking institution with the capital stock of $50,000, and opened its doors on West side of Main Street, March 30, 1870. Wm. L. Clark, president; Robert B. Holliday, cashier. For many years after Mr. Holliday's death, M. H. G. Willis was cashier. Jas. B. Russell, Esq., has been president for many years; Lee R. Grim, Esq., is cashier, succeeding Mr. Willis after his death. This bank has always maintained a safe and profitable management of its affairs, and ranks high among banking institutions, stockholders and depositors. The efficient young clerks Summers and Cooper.

Just across Loudoun Street is the other bank: The Farmers and Merchants National Bank. The imposing building attracts the eye; and the visitor beholds magnificence in its architecture and style. The interior has every modern device for comfort and safety. This bank was started Jany., 1902, with capital stock of $100,000, fully taken, being organized as follows:

R. T. Barton, president, John Keating, vice-president; H. D. Fuller, cashier; Lewis N. Barton, assistant cashier. Directors: Daniel Annan, Dr. W. P. McGuire, Wm. C. Graichen, German Smith, Jno. M. Steck, S. M. Chiles, E. D. Newman, Perry C. Gore, Jas. W. Rhodes, Thomas M. Nelson, H. H. Baker, M. M. Lynch, W. E. Barr, J. S. Haldeman. Mr. Gore and Mr. Nelson having since died and Mr. Smith resigned, the Board continues as organized. The corps of clerks and assistants are Randolph McGuire and T. Y. Kinzel, tellers; J. H. Cather, note clerk, Frank G. Walter, bookkeeper; Eugene Chiles and Clinton Haddox, clerks.

The success of this enterprise has been marvelous, exceeding the expectations of its most sanguine promoters.

The brief notices given of the banks might properly belong to the sketch of Winchester, where only a reference is made to their existence.

CHAPTER XXIII

Revolutionary War Heroes

The Congress by the Acts, 1832-1834, voted certain allowances to soldiers of the Revolutionary War who could produce sufficient proof of service to the courts of their respective counties; and upon the certificate of such courts, the soldier to receive what was termed bounty land warrant, graded as to rank of officers, and privates of the rank and file. Acting upon this, many old soldiers appeared before the County Court of Frederick, and had their applications considered. We give the following as matters that may interest the reader and induce him to read the minutes 1834-1838, and he may find his ancestor was of the noble band.

June Ct., 1835, Cecelia Archer, wife of Wm. Archer, proved she was the only child of Wm. Morrell deceased, who was a soldier in Genl. Anthony Wayne's Army, and was killed in expedition against the Indians.

Darius Grubb proved his service. Wm. Pennybaker proved he was the heir of Conrad Pennybaker a deceased soldier. Francis Brown proved by heirs. His son died 1833. See list of children, Ann Bartlett, wife of Joseph C. Bartlett, being one.

Carter B. Chandler proved his service.

Col. John Smith proved his service. His certificate secured a pension in money of $600 yearly. He died 1836, when his children made an unsuccessful effort to secure land warrant; for the Colonel had accepted his grant in money, and not in land, which ceased at his death. He left no widow. This was Col. John Smith of Hackwood. Daniel Cloud's service was proved by his heirs, he having died Feby., 1815. Names of the heirs given would be interesting to this family. (See p. 215 O. B., 1835).

Samuel Wright proved his service, Oct., 1836.

George Wright's service proved by heirs. He died Feby. 3, 1832. Names of children given.

The Marple, Elliott, Wright and Chrisman families in western part of Frederick given as his children.

Sept., 1838, John Williams proved his service and mentions his wife Susannah.

John B. Tilden an aged Revolutionary officer, proved that Robert Chambers of Kentucky, Joseph Chambers of Cincinnati, Mary wife of John Cain of Philadelphia, Catherine wife of Wm. Nichols of Philadelphia, and Jane deceased wife of Jno. B. Tilden, were brothers and sisters and only heirs of Annie McKnight of Berkley County, widow and devisee of Doct. Humphrey Fullerton of Fredk. County, a soldier of the Revolution. Jno. Bell Tilden died July 21, 1838 —Was a pensioner of $26.66 per month. His children, Martha Reed, Mary A. J. Victor, Jno. B. Tilden, Asburyna T. Phelps, Ann B. McLeod, Eltha Tilden and Richard, appeared in Court May 6, 1839 and produced proof as to age, etc.

At the May Term of the County Court, 1835, the following persons were granted Barroom License: To Michael Fizer at his house in Petticoat Gap; John Beemer, Kernstown; Henry Swann at the Forge Works; James Seevers at Littler's mill; David Rhinehart, Pugh's Town; Treadwell Smith at Battletown; Sarah Chapman, Capt. Joseph Long, Newtown; David Davis at his house; John Wm. Morrison, his house; Abram Watson, his house.

At the November term, 1838, a very remarkable trial occupied the attention of the Court for several days. The Court required the evidence to be entered in the Minute book, where is shown a complete history of the celebrated case, which the writer will briefly mention: The murder of William Brent, a well known gentleman of Winchester,—by a runaway slave, was an oft repeated story during the boyhood days of the writer. Mr. Brent was the son-in-law of the venerable Robert Long, who lived on the corner of Washington and Amherst Streets, where for many years he conducted a popular school for young men. Mr. Brent lived with Mr. Long; he left home in the morning of Nov. 2nd, 1838, to hunt through the forests northwest of the town. Later in the day he was found by Robert Affleck in the woods near the Pughtown road, suffering from several fatal wounds, having been stabbed with a knife. Brent related the incidents of the attack. He had found a strange negro man in the woods partly covered with leaves, and asked the man to give an account of himself. He answered that he was on his way to Pughtown, and asked for directions. Brent told him to follow him and he would show him the road. They had proceeded but a few steps, when the negro seized the muzzle of the gun, and with the other hand plunged an ugly dirk knife into his body several times; then hurried away with the gun. He soon met a negro boy and questioned him about the road. This interview resulted in his identification with the murder. Brent was taken to Mr. Affleck's home nearby; Drs. Hugh McGuire and Stuart Baldwin were summoned, but could not save his life. He gave a clear account of the tragedy. On the 9th, he died. Several days after, Sylvester Monroe, of Hampshire County, arrested a negro man whom he regarded as a *runaway slave;* and while in the Romney jail, he was visited by two officers of Frederick County, George Kreemer, Jr., and Henry Daniel. They felt sure he was the murderer, and securing a writ, the prisoner was brought to Winchester and placed in custody of Robert Brannon, the Jailor. The prisoner was indicted and tried on the 19th of Nov.; found guilty, and sentenced to be hung on the 28th day of Dec., next. The boy had no trouble in recognizing the man he met on the road. The prisoner in his confusion, differed somewhat with the statement of Brent; the negro claiming he did the killing to prevent his return to his master, Benjamin Lillard of Rappahannock County. The murderer's name was Benjamin Pulley. He was hung on the Commons near the site of the "Sacred Heart" Catholic Cemetery.

Mr. Brent's widow married Mr. John Cooper, who is still living. Mrs. Cooper was the mother of the well known Cooper-Brothers of Winchester. Wm. Brent was the son of Innis Brent, brother of Henry M. Brent, Sen.

Extracts from Minutes of County Court from 1850 to 1856.

List of Justices elected under the new Constitution—the first time magistrates were elected by the people—Formerly they were appointed by the Governor and Genl. Assembly:

Jas. P. Riley, Sr., James Brooking, Wm. A. Bradford, Jos. E. Payne, A. Nulton, M. B. Cartmell, Robert J. Glass, Henry P. Ward, Daniel Hinckle, Daniel Collins, Felix Good, James Cather, Jacob Senseny, Andrew Kidd, Jos. S. Davis, Henry W. Richards, Isaac Russell, Jno. B. McLeod, David L. Clayton, Robt. L. Baker, Wm. J. Roland, Henry H. Baker, Joseph Brumback, Mager Steel, Robt. C. Bywaters, Edward R. Muse, Joseph Richard, Annanias D. Russell, Jno. S. Magill, Isaac Hite.

Three vacancies occurred during the period. Dr. W. A. Bradford removed to Clarke County; Henry P. Ward, resigned. David L. Clayton died, and David Timberlake elected in 1854. These were representative men of that period; all were men of intelligence, and owners of good property. The County Court, with such justices on the Bench, reflected credit upon the County.

The County officers to qualify at the first term, 1850 were: T. A. Tidball, clerk, Fred W. M. Holliday, Commonwealth's Attorney, Mahlon Gore, County Surveyor (father of our late Sheriff Perry C. Gore), Chas. H. Barnes and A. A. Robinson, commissioners of the Revenue (appointed by the Court).

Sept. Term, 1850—

The iron picket fence enclosing the courthouse yard and courthouse, was ordered to be erected. John Bruce, Jacob Baker and John S. Magill were appointed commissioners to execute order. The kind of fence and boundary lines were well defined. The fence was completed the following Summer. Since the War, several sections near the courthouse, including three gates, have been removed.

Jany. Court, 1851. The Sheriff was ordered to hire out a list of delinquent free negro taxpayers, 46 in number—names all given. This was in accordance with an Act of Assembly provided for by the Constitution. The Sheriff at a subsequent term, reported to Court that he had offered the negroes for hire, but had not received bids offered, and asked for instructions.

At this Term, Dr. Robert T. Baldwin who was recommended to the Governor for appointment as Sheriff, he being the Senior Justice, produced his commission and was duly qualified.

Nathaniel M. Cartmell, sworn as Deputy.

Joseph Tidball, qualified as Attorney for Commonwealth.

Oct. 6, 1851, Wm. L. Clark, Jr., was granted certificate, to present himself before the Supreme Court for examination and for license to practice law.

Thos. S. Sangster and Joseph O. Coyle were appointed commissioners of the revenue for the County. It will be seen this power was vested in the Justices under that Constitution.

November, 1851—

Elections held to elect members of Congress. The following were the only voting places at the time:

Winchester Courthouse, Gainsboro, Newtown, Brucetown, Swhiers's Tavern, Middletown.

Same Term, the heirs of Rev. Joseph Glass deceased. On motion, the estate was relieved from payment of taxes and levies on "Cuff" an aged and infirm negro man. This is given as a sample of what was done in many similar cases.

March 1, 1852—William Wood produced his commission as sheriff from the Governor of Virginia—N. M. Cartmell and Wm. D. Gilkeson sworn as deputies.

Wm. McKay (McCoy) a well known Irish citizen of Back Creek, was granted his naturalization papers; and to the knowledge of the writer, he was always an enthusiastic voter.

May, 1852, the following persons were licensed to keep private entertainments. This meant that *grogs* of liquors could only be dispensed to those who *took lodgings.*

To David L. Clayton, David Dinges, Susan Carter, Zachariah Kerns, B. Ridgeway, and Philip Carper.

August, 1852. All the Justices assembled and elected Jno. S. Magill presiding justice. The justices were apportioned for the various terms of court,—three gentlemen justices to sit with the president.

The Court also established new precincts or voting places, viz.: at Winchester, the Courthouse, Grim's Tavern, Engine House on Cork Street. (This was the Old Friendship) Hoover's Tavern.

In the County, Coe's School House, Anderson's Tavern on Back Creek (known as No. 6) Russells (Old *Dumb-Furtle*).

At stated terms, the Justices assembled to pass upon all claims presented against the County. This included allowances for keeping roads in repair. These occasions always brought a crowd of claimants and spectators. Those were the halcyon days of the Old Justices Courts. Hundreds of the country people could be seen on the Green and in the old Market Square, where politicians renewed acquaintances and freely patronized the old taverns. No saloons then— No such scenes are witnessed now. A vast majority of the population never know when courts are held, under our new system.

Jany. Court, 1855. Evan R. Thatcher was made jailor; Samuel Coe was qualified as justice in place of Daniel Collins, resigned.

John R. Cooke, a former distinguished member of the Winchester Bar, died recently in Richmond. Resolutions of respect entered.

June Court, 1855, Luke Riely a native of Ireland, was naturalized. Mr. Riely made his home with the writer's father for 13 years—a conscientious man.

June 2, 1856, F. W. M. Holliday, who had been elected Commonwealth's Attorney in May, took oath, etc.

Jno. M. Magson appointed Superintendent of Courthouse, etc.

June 30, 1856, Wm. D. Gilkeson sheriff for several years, required to give new bond and allowed to hold his term until January, when he would be required to settle. N. M. Cartmell, R. M. Cartmell and Jno. W. Correll appointed deputies to collect the taxes for him. Gilkeson failed and his sureties suffered seriously,—several of them made bankrupt.

Richard W. Burton, new justice, sworn; also the following constables qualified: James Z. Smith, Geo. H. Keiter, Jno. M. Magson, Thos. O. Clark, E. H. Scrivner and Saml. Williams.

August 5, 1856, Thos. A. T. Riely elected clerk in May, qualified—Jas. P. Riely his deputy.

October 6, 1856, Michael Ryan, native of Ireland, naturalized. He was well known for many years for his integrity. At same Term, resolutions of respect were entered for Mr. L. J. C. Chipley, member of the Bar, who had recently died in Newtown.

Nov. 21, 1856. Lewis A. Miller, who had been elected sheriff, qualified, with John G. Miller as Deputy. The latter is living at this time and active, at the age of eighty-four.

Patrick Dolan, native of Ireland, naturalized.

CHAPTER XXIV

Gleanings from Old Justices' Court from 1862 to the First Court under the Underwood Constitution.

Judges, Officers, Criminal Trials.

The Order Book used by the County Court up to the evacuation of Winchester by Genl. Jackson March 11, 1862, was mislaid or stolen. This is the only record book of the old office lost. This has been a source of inconvenience, for it contained minutes of the Court for about four years. Many important orders, therefore, will not appear in this connection. Under the disturbed condition, the Court found considerable embarrassment at the Term held March 31, 1862, for it will be remembered by some that Stonewall Jackson and Commissary Banks were contending for supremacy over this section. This Term was held with Hon. Jno. S. Magill president, "pro tem," J. R. Bowen and R. J. Glass on the bench. This order speaks for itself:

"Ordered that the Sheriff do summon the magistrates of the County to appear at the next term, to consider the propriety of changing the place for holding court. All cases on the Docket continued. Jno. S. Magill, Pro tem."

June 2, 1862. Court convened again, and entered a long order describing the sanitary condition of the courthouse and courthouse yard, requesting the town authorities to have same cleaned, limed, etc., and bring bill to the court for payment. The courthouse and hall had been in constant use as a hospital: Robt. L. Baker, Pro tem, etc.

No other term held until Oct. 6, ('62).

Hon. Geo. W. Ward, presiding justice.

T. E. McCoole and R. L. Baker, justices.

This order appears: The Court being informed by the Clerk that the records of this office which were conveyed for safe-keeping to the office of the court of Page County, had been partly destroyed by Federal troops, that what remains of them may be damaged by further invasions. He is ordered to take such measures as may be necessary to remove the said records back to the county or otherwise to dispose of them for safe keeping * * * and for him to confer with Messrs. Barton & Williams in reference to the proper course, etc.

We will say now, that all the records were removed by the clerk, by order of court, at the suggestion of Genl. Jackson a few days previous to the evacuation, through the writer, who was then Acting Provost Marshal.

December 1, 1862, the court makes this significant order: "Jno. M. Miller, W. B. Walter and J. H. Kemp are appointed Salt Agents for this County, who shall pay out of the fund hereafter provided, and receive the County's quota of salt from the Salt Agent for the 10th Congressional Dist. as provided by the Governor's proclamation, and have it transported from Staunton to some convenient and safe place near this County, and then distribute it among the inhabitants of the County, viz.: seven pounds of salt to each member of a family, and to collect 6 cts. per pound, etc. * * * H. M. Brent, Philip Williams and H. B. Streit appointed comrs. to borrow $7000.00 to pay State Agent for same, said sum to bear interest at 6 per cent. until Jany. 1st, 1866. August 31, 1863, same Commissioners were directed to borrow $12,000.00 on same terms, so as to secure more salt. This gives some idea of the conditions then prevailing—County records out of County, and unsafe, and people without salt.

Nov., 1863, the Court requested all the justices that could be found to appear and consider what should be done as to the support of many families, where husbands and sons were in the army, and also to consider the question of protection of crops, where much fencing had been destroyed.

Feby. 24, 1864, the Court entered an order for W. G. Singleton, Deputy (J. Chap. Riely the Clerk being absent) to collect the scattered records and return them to the clerk's office. At the June Term ('64), Mr. Singleton reported that he collected part of the records and had placed them in the vault of the Bank of Winchester, in back part of Bank. Sheriff was directed to pay Mr. S. $20.00 in Virginia Bank money, *if convenient.*

Sept. 5, 1864, Court adjourned to meet at the house of W. G. Singleton in Winchester, until otherwise ordered. Robt. L. Baker, pres. The Court convened several times after this term and admitted wills to probate.

In the Spring of 1865, when Peace was declared, an election was held in pursuance of the Proclamation by the Pierpont State Government, then seated at Alexandria. At this election, none but well known Union or Loyal men could be voted for. Voters at this election could be none other than well-known Union men. This meant Carpet Bag Citizens and the few Union men in this section. The vote was light, but the new officers were recognized by the Military Governor Schofield, and ordered to organize courts, etc., under what was known as the Iron Clad Oath. The newly-elected officers were notified to assemble at the courthouse; and we find the whole number present on July 3, 1865. George W. Ginn, who had the ear of the new government, was master of ceremonies; and under his supervision, the following justices *were sworn into office*: George W. Ginn, J. Fenton Jackson, Daniel T. Wood, Alfred Seal, Geo. B. Diffenderffer, Thos. McCardell, Samuel R. Atwell, Jos. S. Denny, Henry B. Pitzer, David Lupton, Geo. Y. Fries, Wm. Brown, Isaac DeHaven, John Lamp, Wm. Cather, Jonathan Jenkins, Edward Eno, Wm. R. Smith, Jr., James Bean, Moses R. Richard, Alfred Williams, Jno. S. Magill, Jno. N. Meade and D. J. Miller.

Mr. Wood and Mr. Smith are the only survivors of this list. No shadow of doubt existed as to the loyalty of a large majority of the men named. Some were well known for their radical sentiments, and were regarded by the helpless citizens as unfit to sit as a court to try issues that might be joined between Confederate soldiers and the Union element of the County. The minutes of that meeting do not show that any were questioned as to their loyalty. The oath of office they were required to take should settle that point; but when the writer enquired of one who was present, how several of the list could pass inspection of the lynx-eyed manager, the answer was given that several of them were severely criticized and pronounced by several leaders as sympathizers of the South. Much bitter feeling and inflammatory language flowed; and it seemed at one time that at least three of the list would be rejected, but a vote was taken and a majority voted that all should be allowed to serve. It may be asked, what right had any of the Justices to determine who was eligible. Answer can be given that the men who assumed that right were so violent in their actions regarding Southern sympathizers, that they had no regard for consequences, knowing full well that the bogus government would sustain any act of theirs, and, if need be, *the military was within easy call.*

Mr. Ginn informed the justices they must elect the presiding justice, and moved the vote be by ballot. George W. Ginn was appointed teller. The vote being thus cast, the teller discovered that Geo. W. Ginn was elected president.

C. W. Gibbens, who was elected clerk at May election, was duly sworn, etc.

Samuel Trenary—sworn as sheriff.

Edwin S. Brent, who was elected clerk of circuit court, was sworn.

Frederick Gross and Stacy J. Tavenner, comrs. of the revenue, were sworn.

Jas. P. Riely and L. N. Huck, first attorney to appear, and sworn to practice law. W. G. Singleton also allowed to practice law, all having taken the Amnesty oath.

The Court directed the Clerk to send some trustworthy person to Luray to collect all books and papers he could find belonging to Frederick County, and return them to the office of this County.

During the Term, Robt. T. Barton granted certificate to appear before the Supreme Court for examination to practice law.

Court then adjourned, to meet in the court house at the next term.

July 31, 1865, John Pollock appeared with a certificate from the Ohio court, and moved to be admitted to practice law in this Court—Granted. He was then, at the suggestion of the president, appointed to act as Commonwealth's Attorney, being the first *carpet bagger* to take office. He soon gave promise of the unpopularity that shone forth in his many hostile acts. He was a *shyster* lawyer of the lowest order. His efforts to force litigation against a helpless people, did more to secure what was known as the Stay Law, than any other agency. The General Assembly was powerless without the sanction of the military governor; and he was induced to adopt this remedy. This was one redeeming trait in the character of Genl. Schofield. Pollock, having succeeded in fleecing a number of his faithful friends, skipped out one day, leaving his clients to mourn over their loss; while others rejoiced at his departure.

This Stay Law afforded relief to hundreds of impoverished people. The order issued by the Military Governor, December, 1868, operated as a stay of executions relating to sale of personal property until Jany. 1, 1869. June 29, 1869, Gen. Canby, by this order, No. 80, extended the time to Jany. 1st, 1870. This order also required, when real estate was sold under decree of court, no sale to be valid where the bid was less than two-thirds of its last-assessed value. This rule prevailed as to real estate for many years. Persons regarded it as safe practice.

This order was signed by command of Brevet Major Genl. Canby, attested by Lawrence E. Bennett, Capt. 17th Infty. U. S. A., Military Comr. Dist. of Va.

At above Term, Wm. L. Clark, Jr., and Col.

L. T. Moore and Joseph S. Carson were admitted to practice law. Chas. H. Kamp produced his commission as notary public, signed by Gov. Geo. H. Pierpont.

Court ordered repairs to courthouse, and adjourned to meet in the clerk's office.

Sept. 4, 1865. Robert Y. Conrad, Uriel Wright, U. L. Boyce, Andrew G. Kennedy, R. T. Barton, T. T. Fauntleroy, Jr., ... Watrous (a carpet-bagger) appeared and took the attorney's oath, and were admitted to practice law. Many wills and estate accounts were produced to the court, probated, and entered for record,—quite a number having been held by parties until there was some assurance of safety in bringing them forth.

Overseers for nearly all the roads were appointed.

Sept. 5—Chas. L. Ginn, son of the president, appeared as the Commonwealth's attorney by appointment of the military.

August 31, 1868, C. M. Gibbens produced his commission as clerk of court to fill the vacancy occasioned by the death of his father C. W. Gibbens,—the commission signed by the Major Genl. commanding Military Dist. of Virginia.

Similar minutes appear in the courts for the years intervening between this date and the Spring of 1870, when the Old Justices Court system disappears (Chap. 25.). In accordance with the New Constitution, the General Assembly elects judges for County courts. Joseph S. Carson was elected April 2, 1870, to serve Frederick County Court. We find that as soon as he took and subscribed the oaths of office, his first official act was a vacation order dated April 22, 1870, when he appointed the first registrars for the County, preparing for an election to be held in May, when county and district officers were elected.

At this first term, J. Vance Bell, the one-armed Confederate soldier, who was appointed sheriff for his term of office, to take effect at the adjournment of the May court, was duly qualified, also his deputies, Chas. B. Hancock, Perry C. Gore and Robt. I. Kurtz (who became jailor).

Joseph H. Sherrard qualified as clerk, having been elected at the May election.

Judge Carson's service on the bench terminated suddenly. Stricken with apoplexy while horseback riding up Water Street, he was judge less than one year, as the following minute in the order book of the county court shows:

April 6, 1871. The court failed to meet today, pursuant to the adjournment, because of the sudden death of Judge Jos. S. Carson on Tuesday evening April 4, 1871, after the adjournment of court.

TEST: Jas. P. Riely, *Clerk.*

Joseph H. Sherrard received the appointment as Judge from the Governor, to fill the vacancy. He held his first term May 1, 1871. No other change in court until Judge Sherrard resigned the office, to take effect after the adjournment of the December court, when he signed the adjourning order December 3, 1883. The Judge had been troubled for several years with impaired eyesight; in fact, was totally blind for one year. The writer guided his hand when affixing his signature to court papers in many cases for the last year of his term.

William L. Clark was appointed by the Governor to fill out Judge Sherrard's unexpired term. His first appearance on the bench was December 31, 1883. His term, which terminated December 14, 1891, was noted for the number of criminal trials. For six years the criminal docket was never cleared of trials for every kind of felony; it being frequently remarked that an epidemic of crime had fastened its fangs upon the hitherto peaceful section. But the stern and energetic efforts of this Judge, aided by his faithful officials, and especially by the skill and ability of the youthful attorney for the Commonwealth, Richard E. Byrd, who unceasingly bent every effort to successfully ferret out the suspected violators of law, and ultimately brought men to the bar of court to give an account of the misdeeds with which they were charged. And there the accused and others learned that this young representative of the Commonwealth, shielded none by subterfuge and compromise; and thus the Docket eventually appeared in its normal state. Some of these trials will be briefly mentioned.

After disposing of such cases as arson, burglary, housebreaking, plundering country stores, and in several cases church property, two murder cases, one near Brucetown and one in northwest part of the County, the guilty parties paid the penalty by terms in the penitentiary. There was a lull in such activities for awhile; and officers and court enjoyed the change. In the Autumn of 1886 the Commonwealth was informed of a crime that had been committed several miles East from Newtown. This was a mysterious case. The body of young Andrew Broy was found in the woods of Mr. S. Ridgeway; an investigation made, resulting in a coroner's inquest; and a verdict rendered that death was caused by pistol shots dealt by persons unknown to the jury. The case was submitted to Mr. Byrd, who soon had a chain of circumstantial evidence started, with but one or two links missing. The evidence pointed to Ashby Ridenour as the slayer. He had been seen in company with the murdered man on the morning of the day that young Broy had been seen alive. They had been close friends; and it was asked what motive induced the killing. Mr. Byrd discovered that Broy held the bond of the suspected Ridenour, and a search of the body failed to produce this bond; but in the same woods, the bond was accidently found by the searching party. Mr. Byrd's theory was that the murderer had secured the bond, and in his flight from the body, had hidden it in a ravine and accidently lost it among the leaves. This was the motive relied on. The arrest of Ridenour was ordered, and a special grand jury ordered for January court. A number of witnesses were summoned, and Jany. 4, 1887, a true bill was returned by the grand jury, fixing the murder upon the accused, signed by David B. Dinges, foreman. This was the first step towards the célebrated trials of T. Ashby Ridenour, running through the court for more than two years. The prisoner secured the services of the talented young criminal lawyer Wm. R. Alexander, who, from the start, made the most determined defence to save the prisoner's neck.

The two young rival lawyers, realizing at once that reputation was to be made in the case, measured up the work. Their skill in handling their respective sides of the case, was eagerly watched by their many friends. As the preliminary steps were taken for the trial, each side needed delays. The Commonwealth had to fill the missing links in its chain, while prisoner's counsel hoped such delays would allay excited prejudice. Finally, on the 4th of April, 1887, both parties announced to the Court they were ready for trial. 140 witnesses had been summoned; a jury was secured who were found free of prejudice, and the first trial opened. For seventeen days of strenuous effort on the part of the counsel, patience of the worn jury, and active services of the officers, and dignified rulings of the august court, the multitude of spectators heard the reading of the verdict by the clerk when the jury had taken their seats, after having spent the day in their room considering their verdict, at last, in the afternoon of April 21, 1887,—"We the jury find the prisoner guilty of murder of the first degree, C. E. Graves, foreman." Mr. Alexander moved for a suspension of judgment and for new trial, and for an appeal. The whole Summer was used up by taking the case to the Court of Appeals. A new trial was granted, which was started Jany. 2, 1888, with a jury from Shenandoah County, it being impossible to secure one from Frederick. This trial continued for nineteen days, when the jury returned from their room on the evening of Jany. 21st, with the verdict: "We, the jury find the prisoner guilty of murder in the first degree. (Signed) E. NISEWANNER, *Foreman.*"

Mr. Alexander felt his disappointment equally as much as the prisoner. Very few young or old lawyers would have made further effort. Not so with young Alexander. He promptly asked for a new trial, and for his bill of exceptions to be examined and signed by the Judge preparatory to an appeal; and, the writer will add, this exceeded in the number of exceptions any bill he has ever handled in his long experience. Officers, prisoner, members of the bar and spectators were dismayed at what seemed to be a futile attempt to save the prisoner from the gallows. In due course, however, the Clerk was called upon for a copy of the record. This seemed a burden too heavy to bear a third time. The record now amounted to about five hundred pages; and he had never received a cent for the other copies. At this juncture, Chas. B. Rouss sent his check to Mr. Alexander to aid him in the Appellate Court. The Clerk, however, failed to get his portion of the generosity of Mr. Rouss—all was required for other purposes. The case was handed down just in time to have the third trial Jany. 1st, 1889. This trial required seventeen days. A jury was summoned from Loudoun County, and resulted in this verdict, that surprised many people:

"We, the jury find the prisoner *not guilty* as charged in the indictment.

(Signed) CHAS. P. MCCABE, *Foreman.*"

During these trials, of course, the lost bond was an important feature. This bond was signed by T. A. Ridenour, and the other writing altogether in the hand of Broy. Experts were produced by the Commonwealth to prove Ridenour's handwriting. The defence met this by experts to prove the contrary. The former stated positively that the bond was signed by Ridenour, comparing his signature with other well-known writings of his; while the latter expressed grave doubts on the subject. Alexander used some sharp practice on the expert for the Commonwealth. He secured the services of an expert penman, and had him make a clever copy of the bond,—imitating the entire form of the writing; discolored the paper, and had it resemble the original in every point. The day he recalled the expert to cross-examine him as to one or two points in the handwriting, he asked the Clerk for the bond, which was handed him. He contrived to make exchange, holding the original and handing the imitation to the Washington expert, who then had become very dignified and important. He had so fully and learnedly *dissected* the writing already, that he declined to answer questions; but the Court directed him to answer. Mr. Alexander asked him to examine the bond carefully and then say if he was positive that the writing was in the hand of Broy and the "T. A. Ridenour" was that of the prisoner at bar. After a careful examination, his answer was "I say now what I said when examined touching this writing, that Broy wrote the note and T. A. Ridenour wrote the signature." Mr. Alexander then handed him the original and asked witness "Who wrote that note and the signature?" The Court demanded explanations from counsel, while the expert was covered with confusion. The Court censured the practice but declined to censure counsel. The incident produced its effect on the jury doubtless. But the jury, after the trial, told the clerk that one link in Mr. Byrd's chain had been broken by the defense; and this was the pivotal link. One witness, Miss Mamie Birmingham, who never hesitated in the former trials to state she saw the two men pass her door and finally enter the woods together, and said she had no doubt as to who they were. On cross-examination in the last trial, Mr. Alexander plied her carefully with the question of absolute certainty. She began to waver; and when told she must say she had or had not a shadow of doubt, she admitted that *she might have been mistaken.* The case rested at this point; and the argument began, which became famous for many years. The two rivals received the plaudits of the crowd, while the prisoner wandered around in his freedom, bewildered at the change.

CHAPTER XXV

The First Lynching in The County

Wm. M. Atkinson, a member of the Winchester Bar, was elected by the General Assembly to succeed Judge Wm. L. Clark. Judge Atkinson's first term was held Jany. 4, 1892. Nothing more than the ordinary business of courts occupied the attention of the new Judge for several terms. Several misdemeanors were tried by his Honor, which plainly indicated his ability to try graver offences when brought into his court. The June Term, 1893, was to bring the Judge's attention to one of those kind of cases that produce excitement with all classes: William Shorter, a young negro about 19 years old, had been arrested charged with an attempted rape upon a highly respected young white girl in the vicinity of Stephensons station. At this term the case went before a special grand jury, which resulted in indictment for the heinous offence. Upon his arraignment the same day, it was discovered that a mob was forming to take the law in their hands and save the Court this trouble. This was the 5th of June. The officers of the court after consultation with the Judge, advised that the prisoner should not remain in the jail while the usual crowds of people would be in town and next day observing the Sixth of June Memorial, etc. The Judge ordered the Sheriff, Perry C. Gore, Esq., to take the prisoner to Staunton and confine him in that jail until a jury could be secured and preliminaries arranged for trial. Every precaution was used to secure the prisoner a fair trial, the day fixed for trial being June 13th. The jailor, Adam Forney, was sent the night before, so that he might have the prisoner in court the next morning by 10 o'clock. When that hour arrived, the court was in session, awaiting anxiously the appearance of the jailor and his prisoner. It was not long before wild rumors were in the air. The train had arrived in Winchester, and passed on schedule time. The writer and Judge were seated near each other at the Clerk's desk endeavoring to account for the non-appearance of the jailor. At this juncture several persons came to the desk and under great excitement stated: The prisoner had been taken from the train at Kernstown and lynched by a mob. This was a surprise; some fears had been entertained that some reckless persons might be at the station in Winchester on the arrival of the train, and that an effort would be made to do the prisoner bodily harm, and the sheriff planned to have the train halt at Water Street and land the prisoner there, and then hurry him to the court room. The waiting judge and clerk would not have been surprised to hear that the sheriff met trouble on his way to the courthouse. As soon as possible, Mr. Byrd and Mr. Gore were dispatched to Kernstown to investigate the situation. There was no telephone communication at that time with Kernstown, and the mob had cut the telegraph lines. For nearly two hours the surging crowds around the courthouse exhibited intense excitement. The negroes were seen in groups sullenly discussing the case, which increased the intensity of feeling. The writer, at the request of the Judge and many citizens, approached the crowds of excited men and urged them to disperse so as to avoid a collision with the excited negroes. Passing on to Main Street, he recognized two men riding up and down the Street in the most defiant manner. He called them to the curb and urged them to leave the Streets and tell others to do the same, and pointed out the danger. They promptly disappeared; he then approached several groups of negroes that were favorably known to him, and told them plainly they must go to their homes and keep quiet, that this was the only thing that would prevent a wholesale massacre of many good negro citizens by the frenzied crowd,—that one word from them now would precipitate riot, and bloodshed would follow. The sober-thinking negroes acted promptly, and for several hours they prudently withdrew from the streets, and few persons knew at the time the narrow escape Winchester had made from the horrors of a reign of terror. The sheriff on his arrival at the Kernstown railroad station, acquainted himself with the fact and returned with his report for the Court, which was virtually the following: That when the train neared the station, several strange men signalled the engineer to stop. The engineer was guarded, while others of the party boarded the train and proceeded to rescue the prisoner. The resistance by Adam Forney the jailer was remarkable. He had Shorter handcuffed to his arm, and refusing to release his prisoner, the lynching party resorted to rough means, when Forney was overcome and the prisoner, with rope fasted around his neck, was dragged from the car and across the station yard to the West side of the Valley turnpike to a stunted locust tree. He was soon hoisted to a limb to dangle in the air, while some of the party fired several shots into the writhing body. The work was quickly done; the lynchers, having wreaked their vengeance on the miserable wretch, hastily moved away, taking the various roads leading from the place, and none could aver whence they came or whither they went. The party was composed of about thirty quiet but resolute men. No riotous conduct and no confusion of plans. The Commonwealth's Attorney, R. E. Byrd being present, ordered a coroner's inquest, which was delayed several hours. Their verdict was "that the death was caused by persons unknown to the jury." The court promptly ordered the arrest of all suspected persons; the sheriff returned his writs with no arrests; the excitement gradually subsided; and for some time the community felt that the tragedy would be wholesome to certain classes. This was the first and only case of Lynch Law in the County. It may be shown in other pages that soldiers were lynched during the Civil War.

The natural conclusion would be that the prompt discovery of the crime and terrible retribution, with all its abhorrent details, was sufficient to appall all evil-doers and deter them from indulging in similar fiendish acts. Not so, however, for in less than two years we find the court once more confronted with an outrage committed near Middletown. This was the case of Thornton Parker, a negro of that locality. He was arrested, taken before Justice Wm. Davison, who found the charges well sustained, and promptly turned the prisoner over to the County Court. A special grand jury was called for March 11, 1895. An indictment was returned to court, charging Parker with assault and vicious attempt to commit rape upon a married woman living a little West of Middletown. The court ordered a *venire facias* to issue, summoning a jury for the 15th to try the case. Every precaution was taken to avoid a repetition of the unlawful proceedings witnessed in the case of Shorter. The Governor ordered Col. James C. Baker, commanding the 2d Virginia Regiment, to detail the Woodstock Company to proceed to Winchester, to aid the Sheriff in protecting the prisoner. Col. Baker and Capt. Magruder promptly arrived with the Company and assumed the responsibility, to quell any uprising or disorder. The trial was quiet and orderly in every respect, though intense excitement prevailed outside the court room. Guards were doubled, and the court room scene was one long to be remembered—the bristling bayonets of infantry, the testimony of the outraged lady, and that of witnesses who detected and ran down the brutish creature who now sat in the dock, guarded by the jailor. The attentive jury in the box, the scathing prosecution by Mr. Byrd, the just judge on the bench and breathless crowds eagerly listened to catch every syllable uttered for or against the prisoner, grew intense. Some relief came when the jury were handed the papers, as the sheriff conducted them to the jury room. In twenty minutes they filed slowly back, and taking their seats in the box, were asked by the clerk if they had agreed upon a verdict. The answer was yes, and the verdict handed to the writer, who read this finding:

"We, the jury find the prisoner guilty as charged in the indictment and fix his punishment with death by hanging."

(Signed) Jno. W. Harper, *Foreman*."

The judge promptly sentenced the prisoner, and fixed the day of execution between the hours of 8 and 10 o'clock in the morning of the 19th of April next. The outraged people seemed satisfied that the forms of law had been observed, and the prisoner was remanded to jail, guarded by the military. He soon was in the cell and surrounded by a death-watch. When the 19th of April came, Mr. Gore and his deputies were fully prepared to execute the sentence. At 9 o'clock Mr. Gore detailed James W. Stottlemyer, a prominent constable from Stonewall District, to spring the trap; and in twenty minutes, one more of this wretched class of criminals was a dead carcass, ready to be carted away. It may be asked was this the only retribution? We cannot answer. The effect of this judicial execution must have been greater than the other mode, for thirteen years have passed without a repetition of this crime in the Lower Valley.

The court disposed of the usual number of misdemeanor cases for the remaining term of Judge Atkinson. No more death penalties. The reader would be interested in a patient study of the court proceedings. Many incidents of much interest to the County have long since been forgotten. Indeed, in his recent re-study of them, the writer was astonished to see the volumes of matter once familiar to him and written out by his own hand. We have arrived at that point in this disjointed narrative, when another change was to occur to the County Court. This will receive attention in the next chapter.

CHAPTER XXVI

Old County Court Abolished

The reader will notice that the County Court was known as the Justices' Court until the Spring of 1870, when it ceased to exist by virtue of the provision in the Underwood Constitution framed in 1867-68.

The Justices during the colonial period were often called Justices of the Crown, signifying their mode of election or appointment; the Crown, through representatives at the capitol, creating the first bench of justices in each county; and as vacancies occurred, this bench would recommend some suitable gentleman for appointment, when commissions were issued from the Governor and his Council. And thus the Justices Court, comprised of the choice gentlemen of their respective counties, produced a court renowned for their judicial acts. As already shown, some of the justices could not subscribe to oaths required after 1776; and for several years, the remaining justices composed the courts. After the new State framed and adopted its first Constitution, justices were elected by the General Assembly until 1851, when a sweeping change was made, and another Constitution framed by what was known as the great Reform Convention. This Convention met for the purpose of revising the Constitution framed in 1829-30; and the revision cut the old instrument so rudely, that it could not be recognized by its friends. To use the language of W. W. Scott, historian of Orange County. "The old Constitution was utterly cast aside, except that George Mason's Bill of Rights was retained almost word for word." The right of suffrage was extended to every white male citizen 21 years of age; all officers were made elective by this class of new voters; so the Justices were elected by the people from 1850, and as such, composed the County Court until 1870, when Justices or Magistrates as they were termed, no longer composed a bench of Justices, but acted in judicial capacity to a limited extent in their respective Districts. The office is void of emoluments, and none seek the office, though generally some good men are found who will accept it. For any service rendered, they receive a mere pittance.

The County judges, elected by the General Assembly for terms of six years, received small salaries. The judge for Frederick County was paid $350.00 annually. He was also Judge of the Corporation Court of Winchester, with a salary of $500.00.

About the year 1900, another Convention craze struck the country through the mouthpiece of some ambitious politicians. Their lamentations over the evils of the Underwood Constitution, found lodgment with many good people, who were pursuaded to believe they had borne the burden long enough. The fact was patent to many older men who had borne the brunt of political strife, that such burdens had been removed by healthy amendments, and the chief objection to that Constitution was the name. The people had become accustomed to the Judge system, and really had no desire for change; but appeals came to the Valley counties, for aid to have a Convention that would virtually eliminate the objectionable negro vote that was the cause of corrupt elections. The Valley people reluctantly yielded; and the Constitution was not only framed by the Convention but *proclaimed,* and refused to be submitted to the people for ratification. This was in violation of sacred pledges. Well, it is true the negro was eliminated; but in doing this, thousands of old white voters were offended by the provisions, and have become indifferent to results; and many are of the opinion the Democratic party has lost good ground which is being occupied by the Republicans. The lack of enthusiasm in both parties is evident; while a new and third party is gathering up the discontented, preparing to sweep the State from mountain to sea. This is called the Anti-Saloon party.

When the change came for the Judge of the Circuit Court to try all causes, the County Court clerks did in most cases become the County Clerk and also Clerk of the Circuit Court until 1906, when the office would be filled by the clerk elected at the general election held in Nov., 1905. The writer thus became the new clerk, with Phil. H. Gold as Deputy, who had been Clerk of the Circuit Court.

When the time approached for the County Court to cease, universal regret was felt. The sentiment was expressed tenderly. The old landmark established in the Eighteenth Century, now to be obliterated in the Twentieth, produced reflections that threw new light on the shadowy past. The last term was held in January, 1904. Every member of the Winchester bar then in the city, by common sentiment, was in the court room. Mr. R. T. Barton, in well chosen remarks, made the motion that the bar be allowed to adopt suitable resolution touching the last hours of the Court, at whose bar his and perhaps ancestors of other members present, had appeared from its foundation through its long life. The resolutions were ordered to be spread on the minutes. All the attorneys, by request, signed the record; the Clerk was then requested to produce the old seal of court, which had been in constant use since its adoption in March, 1758; the Court directed the writer to certify to the signatures and acts under seal of Court; and on that page of the Order Book the reader will see the last legal impression of the old seal, which by motion of the bar, the Court committed to the custody of the writer, to hold subject to order of the proper authorities of the County. The old Court was finally adjourned January 30, 1904, Judge Atkinson signing the orders.

The Circuit Court, with its new jurisdiction, convened Feby. 1, 1904, with Judge Thos. W. Harrison Judge of the Circuit on the bench, and the writer at the desk as clerk. During the Summer of 1903, the clerk's offices were transferred from the old building; the County Court records placed in the Court room, while those of the Circuit Court occupied the room in the city building known as the Circuit Clerk's office. This change was made to enable the Board of Supervisors to fire proof the Clerk's Office building and rearrange it for convenience and safety.

The first minute of this First Term, noted the filing by the Judge his commission, and the fact of his having taken and subscribed the oaths of office; and that T. K. Cartmell, ex-officio-clerk of the Circuit Court, announced that he had assumed charge of the Clerk's Office of said Court, and appointed Phil. H. Gold deputy.

The Court appointed Wm. M. Atkinson, Jno. M. Steck, Robt. M. Ward, R. E. Byrd, H. S. Larrick commissioners in chancery—all members of the bar, and also D. S. Glaize and Robert Worsley—the two last not attorneys.

R. E. Byrd was appointed Examiner of Records for this 17th Judicial Circuit.

At this term Briscoe C. S. Shull and Julian W. Baker were appointed to re-assess lands and lots for Frederick County.

The County Clerk was clothed with new powers by the new constitution, being given concurrent jurisdiction with the Judge in fiduciary matters. Provision made for probate of wills by the Clerk in his office; to appoint and qualify executors, administrators, etc.,—was required to keep what is known as "The Clerk's Fiduciary Order Book," wherein he should record all such proceedings. The first entry made in this book was the proof and orders pertaining to probate of the will of Mr. Henry Stephenson, Feby. 22, 1904.

By the Constitution, the Board of Supervisors was constituted a court to try all road cases. This applied to new roads or alterations, with power to award damages. This being a new feature with the Board, the Clerk was expected to give it the benefit of his experience. All road cases had been tried in the old County Court.

Thus it will be seen the Clerk virtually held four offices: County Clerk (who is custodian of all County records); by virtue of this office he is Clerk of the Circuit Court, Probate Judge, and also Clerk to the Board of Supervisors. All these duties imposed upon one man great responsibility, and onerous mechanical work. The proper care of Court papers ever ready for production of the proper file, is perplexing; the minutiae of all the departments requires patience, skill and ability; the nervous strain becomes dangerous. Despite all this, the writer, in a retrospect of the many years service rendered in all these departments, takes rapturous delight in his recall of pleasant intercourse with the splendid people of old Frederick.

It will be seen elsewhere in this work, that the Board of Supervisors have entire control of the Northwestern Turnpike and North Frederick Turnpike to the Hampshire line. This branch of their service requires much time and thorough knowledge of the needs of such useful thoroughfares. This chapter must close without fuller notice of proceedings of the Court and Board of Supervisors.

CHAPTER XXVII

City of Winchester, 1743-1850

Winchester may well be called the historic City of the Shenandoah Valley—made so by incidents full of interest to the actors in the great drama, through all the stages of her prolonged life. She has always been the county seat of Frederick County since its "erection." Beginning with the first court in 1743, her life has been interspersed with many changes that sound strangely in our ears of to-day. During her infancy, the name of "Fredericktown" and "Opeckon" frequently appear in the minutes of the first courts, to designate the place for holding court. James Wood, the first clerk of this court, saw the necessity for organizing a town where the court was being held; and asked permission of the court on the 9th day of March, 1744, (new style) to allow him to dedicate a number of lots of land, to be taken from his home farm for the use of the County; but at the same time informed the court that his title to the tract where he resided, was not completed, as some question had already arisen that the grant he had obtained from the Governor and Council of Virginia, might conflict with the old grants to the Fairfax family. The Justices of the Court were cautious enough to take from their clerk a bond for one thousand pounds to indemnify them against damage or loss. This bond was executed with due formalities, and is here given: "Know all men by these presents that I, James Wood, of Frederick County, am held and firmly bound unto Morgan Morgan, Thomas Chester, David Vance, Andrew Campbell, Marquis Calmes, Thomas Rutherford, Lewis Neill, William McMachen, Meredith Helm, George Hoge, John White and Thomas Little, gents, Justices of the said County and their successors, To the which payment well and truly to be made, I bind myself, my heirs, executors and administrators firmly by these presents, sealed with my seal, and dated this 9th day of March 1743. (old style).

"The condition of the above obligation is such that whereas the above bound James Wood having laid off from the tract of land on which he now dwells at Opeckon, in the County aforesaid, twenty-six lots of land containing half an acre each, together with two streets running through said lots of the breadth of thirty-three feet, as will more plainly appear by a plan thereof in the possession of the said Morgan Morgan, Marquis Calmes and William McMachen, and whereas the said James Wood, for divers good causes and consideration of the sum of five shillings current money to him in hand paid, the receipt whereof he doth hereby acknowledge, Hath bargained and sold, on the conditions hereafter mentioned, all his right, title, interest, property and claim, to twenty-two of the said lots to the aforesaid Morgan Morgan, etc., His Majesties Justices of the said County, for the time being and their successors, to be disposed of by them for the use of the said County as they shall judge most proper, the said lots being numbered in the before mentioned plan as follows: Nos. 1, 2, 3, 6, 7, 8, 9, 10, 11, 12, 14, 15, 16, 17, 19, 20, 22, 23, 24, 25, and 26, on the following conditions, viz.: that they the justices or their assigns, shall, within two years from the day of the sale of the said lots, build or cause to be built on each lot one house either framed work or squared logs, dovetailed, at least of the dimensions of 20 feet by 16, and in case any person in possession of a lot or lots fail to build within the time limited, the property of the said lot or lots to return to the said James Wood, his heirs or assigns. Now if the said James Wood, his heirs, executors and administrators, shall from time to time at all times hereafter maintain, protect and defend the said Justices, their successors and assigns, in the peaceable and quiet possession of the before mentioned lots of land from all persons whatsoever, Thomas Lord Fairfax, his heirs, or any other person claiming under him *only excepted,* And further if the said James Wood, his heirs, etc. shall hereafter obtain either from His Majesty by patent or from the said Thomas Lord Fairfax or his heirs, etc., shall within one year, if required, make such other title for the said lots to the said Justices or their successors, as their counsel learned in the law shall advise so far forth as his own title shall extend. Now if the said James Wood, his heirs, executors, and administrators, shall well and truly perform all and singular the above conditions then this obligation to be void, other-

wise to be and remain in full force and virtue.
Sealed and delivered in the J. Wood.
presence of:
Wm. Jolliffe,
Jno. Newport,
Thos. Postage.

At a court continued and held for Frederick County, on Saturday the 10th day of March, 1743 (old style) (new style 1744), James Wood, gent, in open court, acknowledged this his bond to his Majesties Justices which is ordered to be recorded. TEST: J. Wood, *Cl. Ct.*"

The reader will observe that the Justices in accepting the offer made by James Wood, were fully aware of the difficulty that might arise concerning the title to the land; and while they required Wood to indemnify them, they made an exception to the Fairfax claim. It must be remembered that *our* Thomas Lord Fairfax had not arrived in America, but was represented here by his agents and attorneys; and they doubtless were well informed of the regular demands made by these agents of the Fairfax family, upon those who had settled upon lands granted them by the Governor and Council of the Colony of Virginia. All of which being within the domain of Fairfax, must some day result in litigation. And the Justices were not willing to ignore the Fairfax claim. No doubt they felt that if Mr. Wood could make good his generous offer, that Lord Fairfax might either confirm the Wood transaction, or himself would be pleased to set off a portion of his land for public uses. As will be seen later on, Fairfax not only recognized the James Wood dedication, but added to it in a substantial way.

Mr. Wood was hindered in securing his title for several years, owing to contentions raised between the Lord Proprietor's agents and all the settlers of that period. The settlers in many cases—Wood being one yielded to these demands for yearly rents—some stoutly held out and refused to recognize any claim as better than what was known as the *Minor Grants* (already explained in the first chapters of this work). And this explains in part the delay in securing a charter for the town of Winchester until 1752—eight years after the lots had been surveyed and offered by Mr. Wood. As stated previously, Lord Fairfax arrived in America in 1749; and very soon appeared in the vicinity of the county seat with the youthful Washington, to make surveys, etc. Mr. Wood being an English gentleman of prominence in the new County that was to become the future home of his Lordship, it was natural that some social relations existed between these gentlemen relative to the development of the country. Mr. Wood was owner of a grant from Lord Fairfax for land on the South side of Opecquon Creek, located near the point where Stephensburg was laid off by Lewis Stephens. For some reason, Lord Fairfax desired to become owner of this tract of land. He and James Wood effected a settlement of these claims, and Wood sold his Opecquon tract to Fairfax, giving him a "quit rent title to any other land the said James Wood had had previously surveyed to him the said Wood." Fairfax took every occasion in all his conveyances, quit rent deeds, or any other writing, to style himself "the Lord Proprietor;" and that he still held the fee in all the land, as the British Crown had transferred it to him; and that he must be consulted as to the propriety of making towns, etc. So we see him appear in the House of Burgesses, in sessions of 1751-2, to direct the provisions in the proposed charter. Strange as it may appear, it is nevertheless true, that although Fairfax had settled the claims between himself and James Wood—giving him a quit-rent title—he never granted his fee to Wood; and we find him with such influence—not only with Wood who virtually was the owner of the land—as to have him submit to the acknowledgment that the Lord Proprietor had the right to determine upon a plan for the town, but he also had the wording of the Act of the General Assembly made to satisfy him. The County Justices also were impressed with the importance of this right; and whenever they took action in regard to this new town, were careful to say "subject to the approval of his Lordship the Right Hon. Thomas, Lord Fairfax, etc.". The charter, as has been stated, was granted in 1752; and because of its importance, and to take its place in this book of reference, and for the language used to define the Fairfax relation to the town,—we give an exact copy: "An Act for establishing the town of Winchester, and appointing Fairs therein, February, 1752.

"I. Whereas it has been represented to this General Assembly that James Wood, gentleman, did survey and lay out a parcel of land, at the Court House in Frederick County, in twenty-six lots of half an acre each, with streets for a town, by the name of Winchester, and made sale of the said lots to divers persons, who have since settled and built, and continue building and settling thereon; but because the same was not laid off, and erected into a town, by Act of Assembly, the freeholders and inhabitants thereof will not be entitled to the like privileges, enjoyed by the freeholders and inhabitants of other towns in this Colony.

"II. Be it enacted by the Lieutenant Governor, Council and Burgesses, of this present General Assembly, and it is hereby enacted, by the authority of the same, That the parcel of land lately claimed by the said James Wood, lying and being in the fifty-four other lots of half an acre each, twenty-four thereof to be laid off in one or two streets on the East side of the former lots, the street or streets to run parallel *with the street already* laid off, and the remaining thirty lots to be laid off at the North end of the aforesaid twenty-six, with a commodious street or streets, *in such manner as the Proprietor thereof, the Right Honorable Thomas Lord Fairfax shall think fit be,* And is hereby constituted, appointed, erected, and established, a town, in the manner already laid out, to be called by and *retain* the name of Winchester, and that the freeholders of the said town, shall, for ever hereafter, enjoy the same privileges, which the freeholders of other towns, erected by Act of Assembly enjoy.

"III. And whereas allowing fairs to be kept, in the said town of Winchester, will be of great benefit to the inhabitants of the said parts, and greatly increase the trade of that town. Be it therefore enacted, by the Authority aforesaid, That for the future two fairs shall and may be annually kept, and held, in said town of Winchester, on the third Wednesday in June, and the third Wednesday in October in every year, and to continue for the space of two days, for the sale and vending all manner of cattle, victuals, provisions, goods, wares, and merchandizes, whatsoever; on which fair days, and two days next before, and two days next after, the said fairs, all persons coming to, being at, or going from same, together with their cattle, goods, wares and merchandizes, shall be exempted, and privileged, from all arrests, attachments, and executions, whatsoever, except for capital offences, breaches of the peace, or for any controversies, suits, or quarrels, that may arise and happen during the said time, in which case process may be immediately issued, and proceedings had, in the same manner as if this act had never been made, any thing herein before contained, or any law, custom, or usage, to the contrary thereof, in any wise, notwithstanding.

"IV. Provided always, That nothing herein contained, shall be construed, deemed, or taken, to derogate from, alter, or infringe, the royal power and prerogative of his Majesty, his heirs and successors, of granting to any person or persons, body politic and corporate, the privileges of holding fairs, or markets, in any such manner as he or they, by his or their royal letters patent, or by his or their instructions, to the Governor, or Commander in Chief of this domain, for the time being, shall think fit."

This may sound strange to some of our patriotic readers; but we must not forget that the Colonies were still wearing the yoke of their Royal Master without daring to murmur. Indeed, if one takes the trouble to study the phraseology of any Act of the Governor's, Councils, General Assembly, or courts—he will be impressed with feelings akin to disgust. Mark the abject humility of a people who had sought the wilds of America, hunting some spot where they could cherish the idea of freedom! While they submitted for the time and acknowledged the power of the Royal George II, the spark of freedom never entirely died out—as his successors gradually learned!

The custom of holding fairs in all the towns of the Colony, was one that followed the English settler to America. He had enjoyed the privileges of fairs in his old country. We have record evidence, such as orders of court, sheriff's returns, etc., to show that the fairs provided for in the charter, were regularly held for many years, conflicting often with the sessions of court —Litigants, officers and witnesses claiming the immunities saved to them by the law in relation to fairs. These fairs were a necessity in the early days of the country. The increasing population required some scheme to enable them to dispose of their surplus, such as horses, cattle, etc.—the mechanic coming in for his share of benefits. People came from the surrounding country in such numbers, with their animals, products, wares, etc., that the Court—or Justices —were frequently called upon to give aid for the accommodation of those *who came illy provided.* And often Deputy Sheriffs were appointed to *assist the Superintendents,* to keep good order, etc. The increased sales of property, and exchanges of same between the people as they thus assembled twice yearly, brought about an intercourse with the outlying settlements that proved of great advantage. No telegraph; no regular mails in the border country. Letter writing was rare; and letters generally sent by some friend or by some person "intending shortly to visit certain parts." These fairs contributed largely toward developing the new town of Winchester. Her many vacant lots were rapidly purchased by visitors; and thus the town became the central market for the lower section of the Valley. The old deeds from Wood and Fairfax show that persons came from all the settlements to start some kind of business; and we find quite an increase of licenses for the "Ordinary Keeper"—and other enterprises. When

Winchester was founded by Mr. Wood in 1744, we have no evidence that any foundation for a village had been laid. The whole country for miles around was in virgin forest. Indeed, early orders of Court make mention of the impenetrable forests, and make careful orders that certain commissioners shall proceed to cut a roadway *through the dense forests out to the grass land both to the North and the South* from the county seat. But in many cases these continuous forests were of great advantage to those who were building the new village, furnishing the rude material for the log-cabins. The court had already appointed persons to *clear* the ground for the courthouse—saving such logs as would be suitable for a substantial building. So we have it fully settled that the first courthouse was a log structure; and so also was the jail. Instructions given that the logs so used should be uniform in size and the building so constructed, *the corners should have each and every log dovetailed in to add strength to the same.* The old deeds reveal to us some interesting features regarding the young village. In most cases, the lots remote from the "marshy ground" were the first to be made habitable, with their log-cabins; but very few in the North and South ends of the survey were built on until about 1748, when orders of court *extend to the houses* at the South end of Loudoun Street "recently erected;" the owners thereof notified that they had not complied in building such chimneys as required of settlers who erect houses for dwellings on the town lots. Outlying lots excluded from this requirement. These outlying lots were a feature in the plan of the town, to provide every purchaser of a lot *down town,* with lots ranging from three to five acres on the South and North ends of the town; to furnish ground for gardens, pasturage for stock, etc., and these lots as they passed to the villager, were enclosed. A great many of the outlots remained open for a number of years, and were called the "common," where village cows were expected to roam at will; and the boys of that period had no limitations to their sports, when once on the "common." No fears of interference from the "cops" from down-town. For there were no such useful officers in the early life of Winchester. As the population increased, the boys waxed warm; and tradition furnishes glowing accounts of the battles royal, fought to a finish on the old Common. The Common on the South was for many years unenclosed. Indeed, at least ten acres was not embraced in any grant or in the plan of the town, though within the boundaries; and because no owner appeared, it was known as the Common for more than one hundred and twenty years; and was designated by the Courts as the place for public executions. It was the place for holding general muster of the militia. The Common on the South was generally called Sheep Hill; and became so well known, that an order of court directs the sheriff to erect a "suitable building on Sheep Hill Common to be used for the *safe keep* of persons sick with the smallpox."

This Hill or Common must not be confounded with that part of the town proper, which has had for many years its local distinction "Potato Hill." Many old citizens of to-day relate incidents told by the fathers of the origin of this name.

The North Common was distinguished as Fort Hill,—by reason of the erection of Fort Loudoun there in 1756-7. The North end of the town was not laid off into streets at that time. No street North of Piccadilly, or rather Fairfax Lane. James Wood conveyed parcels of land, ranging from five to twenty acres, to be taken from his tract where it adjoins Rutherford's grant. One such five acres was conveyed to Robert Craik. The survey fixes this as adjoining the lots laid off for town lots, and adjoins the town lots previously conveyed to said Craik and Enoch Pearson. (Town lots not be confounded with "Public Lots.")

This survey was once part of the stockade of the Fort. Being all of Loudoun Street at that point, and extending eastward toward present tracks of the W. & P. R. R. When Col. Washington surveyed and laid out the plan of the Fort, he evidently had an informal grant from James Wood, and the consent of the Lord Proprietor Fairfax, to erect a fort on the site he had selected. For be it remembered that while James Wood's grant embraced the land where Winchester now stands, Fairfax always claimed his yearly rents, and the right to locate sites for towns within his dominion. He doubtless exercised the same right in relation to the erection of forts. Be that as it may, Washington was not embarrassed by any claimant; the welfare of the public demanded this protection; and doubtless, the entire population endorsed his adoption of what was known as the *North Common* for the site of his fortification. He was fully empowered by an Act of Assembly March 17, 1756. In Henning's Statutes, Vol. 7, p. 34, we find this clause of the law: "And whereas it is now judged necessary that a fort should be immediately erected in the town of Winchester, County of Frederick, for the protection of the adjacent inhabitants against the barbarities daily committed by the French and their Indian allies; be it therefore enacted, that the Governor or Commander-in-Chief of the Colony for the time being, is hereby empowered, and desired to order a fort to be built with all possible dispatch, in the aforesaid town of Winchester; and that his honor give such orders and instructions for the immediate effecting and garrisoning the same, as he shall think necessary for the purpose aforesaid." The Act appropriates £1,000. ($5,000) for carrying the provisions into effect. This fort was called Fort Loudoun, in honor of Lord Loudoun who had been appointed Commander in Chief of the British armies, then in America. The Virginia Historical and Philosophical Society, many years ago, had an engraving made of the old fort, which shows it in a good state of preservation, showing it to have been a field work, or redoubt, having four bastions, whose flanks and faces were each 25 feet, with curtains 96 feet. When Loudoun Street was extended beyond Piccadilly, going North, it was necessary to cut through the South and North walls, leaving the larger part containing the old well, on the West side. A small part of the two walls, with the two eastern bastions and end wall, was lèft on the East side of the street. We have reliable tradition that Col. Washington had his own Regiment, then stationed at Winchester, to throw up the earthworks and sink the well, through a solid rock to the depth of 103 feet, which afforded an ample supply of good water. (The well at this writing is in a good state). The fort embraced a half acre; many of its embankments and mounds are to be seen, and have been carefully preserved. Howe says: "The fort contained a strong garrison; and, as was stated by one of the oldest inhabitants of Winchester in 1843, that he had been informed by Washington's officers, that Washington marked out the site of this fort, and superintended its erection; that he bought a lot in Winchester; and had a blacksmith shop erected on it, and brought his own blacksmith from Mt. Vernon to make the necessary iron work; and when the work was completed, Washington had it mounted with six 18-pounders, six 12-pounders, six 6-pounders, four swivels and two howitzers." This fort doubtless, was much needed to afford protection to the inhabitants of outlying districts. The French and Indians had combined to destroy the settlers in those districts; and they were compelled to flee for safety. So Winchester at that early period became a great rallying point. The Blue Ridge at that time was considered the frontier line; and settlers to the West of that line stood in great danger from the frequent incursions from the French forts along the Ohio, etc. So we can readily see that a well-equipped fort, with Col. Washington on the ground, was the initial step toward the making of the western empire. Ever after this event, the desire to go still deeper into western wilds, seemed to become part of the ambition of many Valley settlers; and later on their emigrant trains passed over the mountains and across the Ohio into the country that was to afford homes to Virginia families, whose descendants are now continuously returning to see the birth places of their ancestors.

After the town was extended by reason of the demand made by persons who had received grants from Fairfax for certain of the eighty lots he had set apart in 1752, as an addition to the town lots, previously surveyed by James Wood the founder of the town,—there were misunderstandings, existing to-day, concerning both Wood and Fairfax, in relation to the laying out of the town —much difference of opinion regarding the question of priority. We are frequently asked how much land did Lord Fairfax *give* to the peoplè for a town; and when did Wood give his addition; and where were the boundaries thereof? Briefly answered, Lord Fairfax never gave the town anything! He seized the opportunity; and made the most of it. But fairness to the reader, as well as the performance of a self-imposed duty in compiling the history of the town, requires a statement of facts that may grate harshly on sentiment, and leave some to grieve over a wrong impression. We know that many of the present inhabitants of the old town have had handed down to them the belief that Lord Fairfax actually sliced off from his immense holdings a sufficient quantity of land, and gave, or dedicated, it for the use of the citizens of the County for the purpose of a county seat, that eventually developed into the far-famed Valley City. Such impressions are wrong; and should have been corrected years ago. To prove this, the reader need only study record evidence,—disregarding all traditions relating thereto in the town's history—the records of the County and of the State, the Acts of the General Assembly, and files and reports of District and Appellate courts for a period of thirty years prior to 1808, and he will have revealed to him a litigant, who was unceasing in his efforts to disturb and destroy the first settlers in the Valley of Virginia, by his exactions in collecting his rents, etc.

As has already been stated, Lord Fairfax made his first appearance in Frederick County in 1749, though he had previously made himself well known through his agents. Chief of these were Robert Carter and William Fairfax (a cousin). They had powers delegated them to lease lands to settlers, and in many cases to make actual grants—all to be ratified by the proprietor, or to be annulled. Many of these leases and grants were held by inhabitants of the vicinity, where the little village had been founded by James Wood. The courthouse and jail were already erected on what was known as the public lots (or public square), having its boundaries well defined—Loudoun Street on the West, Boscowan (Water) Street on the South, Cameron on the East, and private lots on the North (Court House Avenue now being latter boundary). Lord Fairfax on his arrival in Frederick County, established his court and recorder's office at Greenway Court; and at once opened his office to transact business with his retainers (as he often termed them), who were making the wilderness a habitable country. About this time, he frequently visited the county seat; and soon joined Wood in his efforts to enlarge the town. His Lordship took possession of the situation, and had an addition surveyed, to be laid off in lots of a half acre each, eighty in number, together with eighty out lots of five acres each, with streets. This addition is the same mentioned in the charter of 1752. The map, or diagram, of this addition, together with the charter, was kept in the Lord Proprietor's office until after his death, when it was found by Mr. Robert Mackey, who produced it in the county court at the December Term, 1794, it being fully proven, and ordered to be recorded; and was entered in Deed Book 24 (No. 2) on page 91. Every effort was made to find some evidence in the proprietor's office, of his dedication, or a deed for the public lots to the County; but none were ever found. He had made deeds or grants for all of the eighty lots in the new addition, and had them on file and on record in his office. Many of them were never seen until after his death. They were removed from his office in 1797 to the Office of the Register of Land, at Richmond, Va.

To show the spirit animating his Lordship, when undertaking to relieve Wood in his second effort to build the old Winchester, the author feels it necessary to give space for a copy of one deed. All are alike in description, requirements, consideration, etc. These grants were the subject of much litigation by Fairfax, his heirs and assigns; therefore it is well for the reader to see the relations between the holders of the town lots and Fairfax. Some references will be made to the suits waged against the lot-holders, to compel them to pay the stipulated rents. The inhabitants of the town in some cases denied the right of Fairfax to collect his annual rent of five shillings and, in some cases, quit rents. As will be seen by the terms of the grants referred to, and fully set forth in the grant to James Wood for Lot No. 1, a copy of which is introduced here, the grantees were liable to ejectment suits. Some of the inhabitants had enjoyed quiet possession of tracts of land contiguous to the newly laid out town, under grants and leases formerly made them by the Colonial Government, requiring them to pay to the Lord Proprietor an annual rent of one shilling for every 50 acres; and where the grant was from Fairfax for tracts of land, one shilling sterling money for every 50 acres, regarded as *quit rents;* and it was very reasonable for such grantees to refuse compliance with this new order of things; for it will be seen that Fairfax by his ruling, ignored the Crown grants—sometimes called Colonial or Minor Grants, and arbitrarily required the lotholder to pay him the yearly rent of *five* shillings sterling money for the half-acre lot in the town proper, including the five acre lot out on what Fairfax called the "Common." Although in every deed or grant, he says he had set apart a tract of land containing 439 acres as a common, here we find persons required to pay excessive rents for the use of lots on the Common, when Fairfax says he had *given* this land on the Common, for the use of the town—or, if they had free use of the lot on the Common that always went with the lot down town, then the latter was charged five shillings for the ½ acre, while only required by the Crown Grants to pay at the rate of one shilling for every fifty acres.

Injustice and unfairness seemed to be apparent in this new scheme of Fairfax's for adding to the town that Wood had founded eight years before. These conditions were calculated to engender bad feeling between the Lord Proprietor and the town's people. And as the years went by; and the spark of freedom had been kindled into a flame that burst forth all over the land in 1776, it is not to be wondered at that old Frederick County, including Winchester Town, was ready to throw off the yoke of the British Lord, and refuse to pay any kind of rent. This, of course, resulted in almost endless litigation, which will be treated more fully in the Chapter on The Fairfax Suits. In the following grant, the reader has the exact language of all other grants for the eighty lots, by changing name of grantee.

"The Right Honourable Thomas Lord Fairfax, Baron of Cameron in that part of Great Britain called Scotland, Proprietor of the Northern Neck of Virginia; To All to Whom This present Writing shall come sends greeting: Know ye that for good causes for and in Consideration of the Rents and Covenants hereafter reserved and expressed, I have given, granted and confirmed, and by these presents for me, my heirs, and assigns, do give, grant and confirm unto Mr. James Wood of the County of Frederick and Colony aforesaid, a certain Lott or half acre of Land heretofore waste and ungranted, scituate, lying and being in the Town of Winchester in the said County, Numbered (1) and bounded as in the survey and plat of the said town made by Mr. John Baylis. Also one other Lott or Tract containing five acres of Land Num. (53) heretofore waste and ungranted scituate in the County aforesaid, contiguous to the said Town being part of and included in a Tract of land containing (439) acres, given by me as a Common for the use and benefit of the Inhabitants of the Town aforesaid and is bounded as by a plat of the said Common made by the said Baylis.

To Have and to Hold the said two recited Lotts of Land, together with all and singular appurtenances unto the said James Wood, his heirs and assigns forever, upon the conditions following (to-wit:) That the said James Wood, his heirs, etc., shall not build or cause to be built on the Lott No. (1) in the Town aforesaid, any dwelling-house, whose dimensions shall be less than sixteen by twenty feet, with a chimney thereto of brick or stone; neither shall the said James Wood his heirs, etc. erect or build, or cause to be erected or built any dwelling house, storehouse, warehouse, or other buildings of any nature or kind so ever, upon the said Lott (No. 53) in the Common aforesaid nor by any Act or Deed of his the said James Wood, his heirs, etc., or his or their last will and Testament in Writing, suffer or permit the said Lott No. (53) in the Common aforesaid, to be separated or divided in property from the said Lott No. (1) in the Town aforesaid, but that the same shall be kept with; and whenever the property of the said Lott No. (1) is altered, by Bargain, Sale, Gift, Mortgage, Execution, Will, or otherwise, pass, descend and go with the same, as parcel of, incident to and as an appurtenant thereof forever, for the benefit and advantage of the said Town, and shall be subject to the same Rules and Orders that other Lotts in the Common aforesaid are subject to; Furthermore, yielding and paying to me, my heirs, etc., the yearly Rent or Sum of five shillings sterling Money, for the aforesaid two Lotts; provided also that if the said annual Rent should be behind and unpaid by the space of thirty days next after the same is become due and payable in any year and no sufficient distress upon the premises can be found, whereof the same may be levied, Then and in case the said Lotts shall become forfeit and vested again in me, my heirs, etc. In Witness Whereof I have hereunto sett my hand and seal. Dated this fifteenth day of May, in the twenty-sixth year of the Reign of our Sovereign Lord George the Second, etc. Dmi. one thousand seven hundred and fifty-three.

Mr. James Wood Deed For
Lott No. (1) in the Town } FAIRFAX."
of Winchester

In the foregoing grant to James Wood, it will be seen that Lord Fairfax describes the Lot No. 1 as "part of and included in the Tract of Land containing 439 acres, given by me as a Common for the use and benefit of the Inhabitants of the Town aforesaid." As already stated in previous pages, Lord Fairfax never made a grant to the Borough or Town of Winchester in any form. While he says he designates the certain tract of 439 acres for the use of the inhabitants of the town, he had his surveyor John Baylis in 1752 to survey and lay off his *addition* of 439 acres to the town into 80 lots, from No. 1 to 80 inclusive, and into streets and alleys; and to each lot he added an "out-lot" of five acres—requiring 400 acres to comprise the out-lots, that he designated as the Common. As each of the town lots proper contained one half acre, they would require forty acres—altogether 440 acres instead of the 439, for the lots alone; and nothing for streets and alleys. And as Fairfax granted his lots to persons and required them to pay exhorbitant rentals annually, it is clearly seen that the assertion that Lord Fairfax never gave the town of Winchester any part of his vast domain, is borne out by the simple statement of facts. The ground occupied by the Episcopal Church and graveyard, fronting on Loudoun and *Boscawan* Streets, was embraced in the original grant from Wood to the *Justices for a County Seat.* No record in any office, county, State or the Lord Proprietor's of any such grant. Strange to say, Fairfax made but one grant other than those to individual purchasers, and this was to the "Reformed Calvinists," dated May 15, 1753. It will be noticed this grant bears same date as the grant to James Wood, and to the following persons,—the list of whom is given to show who many of the lot-owners were at that date. It is proper, however, to state that some were not residents of the town:

NAME	LOT NO.	COMMON LOT NO.
.... Lemon	2	46
Alexander McDonald	3	19
.... Wood	4	10
.... Wood	5	31
.... Weitreit ..	6	71
Henry Brinker	7	47
William Cocks	8	77
Thomas Woods	9	59
.... Hope	10	67
....	11	..

Name	Lot No.	Common Lot No.
....	12	..
.... Parkins	13	65
William Cockran	14	25
Isaac Perkins	15	22
Marquis Calmes	16	15
Lewis Neill	17	42
Thomas Bryan Martin	18	63
....	19	..
James Pilcher	20	51
John Jones	21	80
.... Caldwell	22	76
George Bruce	23	61
John Jones	24	9
John Howard	25	21
Thomas Ryan Martin	26	59
....	27	..
....	28	..
....	29	..
John Hite	30	69
John Hite	31	30
....	32	..
Samuel Earle	33	68
....	34	..
....	35	..
....	36	..
....	37	..
....	38	..
James Lemon	39	25
Merder Palb	41	13
....	40	..
....	42	..
....	43	..
....	44	..
Capt. Geo. Mercer	45	..
David Stephens	46	66
Andrew Fretley	47	52
John Steward	48	78
Lodowick Castleman	49	48
....	50	..
Lewis Stephens	51	..
Lewis Stephens	52	..
Lewis Stephens	53	..
John Feif	54	..
....	55	..
....	56	..
William Cochran	57	36
Tobias Otto	58	..
....	59	..
John Greenfield	60	50
Edward McGuire	61	4
....	62	..
....	63	..
....	64	..
....	65	..
.... Bush	66	70
Thos. McCloun	67	2
Robt. Craigen	68	58
Jesse Bratten	69	3
Godfrey Hambert	70	60
Martin Bostin	71	17
John Steward	72	..
....	73	..
John Carlyle	74	34
John Harrow	75	29
John Greenfield	76	18
George Washington	77	16
Christopher Wetsell	79	5
Peter Sperry	80	74

The foregoing list was copied from the record and files of the Land Office, Richmond, Va. The blank spaces show no names or numbers on the record that can be filled, owing to their illegible state. It embraces every grant made by Lord Fairfax for any land within the boundaries of the Town of Winchester.

The present populace will be searched in vain for any of the names on this old list. All have disappeared from the archives of the town with the exception of three—McGuire, Wood and Jones.

The author at this point deems it consistent with his plan, to follow the foregoing line of vested titles, by a brief reference to the change wrought by the Revolutionary War, so far as relates to Lord Fairfax, who barely survived the War. By his will, of record in the Old County office 5th of March, 1782, he constituted his nephew, Rev. Denny Martin, then a citizen of England, the heir to his title and the remnant of his possessions in the Northern Neck. The point was raised at once that he, being a British subject, could have no legal rights in America; and the estate so devised by Lord Fairfax was subject to escheat laws, as will be more fully treated elsewhere. We simply add that this claim was dropped. Denny Martin—afterward Denny Martin Fairfax—being an old man of 71 years, with no desire to change his residence from England to America; and his American possessions needing his personal attention, which he could not give, and "for divers other good causes and valuable considerations," he, by his deed of Aug. 30, 1797, (of record in the Genl. Court at Richmond) conveyed to James M. Marshall "all and every of those divers tracts, pieces and parcels of land, being part and parcel of the proprietary of the Northern Neck of Va., with all beneficial right and interest of whatsoever nature the same may be." Of course, this embraced all the claims for rent then remaining unpaid for a number of years. Mr. Marshall the new American owner of the remnant of the once great

Northern Neck, guided by his legal knowledge, his glowing patriotism, and his high regard for equity, discovered that no legal title was vested in Frederick County and the town of Winchester, for what has been designated the Public Lotts, or court house and market square—the Public buildings, consisting of the Court House, *two* jails, clerk's offices, market house, public warehouse, etc., having had the uses thereof since 1744, when Wood laid out the ground for this purpose as the county seat. Mr. Marshall acted promptly; and brought the status of this case before the General Assembly in 1799, suggesting a plan by which a legal title could pass. And the General Assembly by an Act authorized him as the holder of the legal title, to make conveyance thereof to such persons designated by the Act to receive the title. And as there is but little known by the public generally relating to this transaction, we deem it best to give the full copy at this point:

(Thomas Lord Fairfax, Will. Book No. 4, page 583.)

"IN THE NAME OF GOD AMEN I, The Right Honorable Thomas Lord Fairfax, Baron of Cameron, in that part of Great Britain called Scotland and Proprieter of the Northern Neck of Virginia, do make and ordain this my Last Will and Testament in manner following, that is to say, I do hereby subject all my real and personal estate to the payment of my debts and legacies give and devise all that my undivided sixth part or share of my lands and plantations in the Colony of Virginia, commonly called or known by the name of the Northern Neck of Virginia, with the several advowsons right of presentations thereto belonging or appurtaining I have therein with ye Messuages and Tenements buildings hereditaments and all other the appurtenances thereto belonging, all or any part whereof being formerly the estate of the Honourable Alexander Culpeper Esquire, deceased together with all other lands and tenements. I have am possessed of, or have a right too in the said Colony of Virginia, to the Rev. Denny Martin, my nephew now of the County of Rent in Great Britain to him his heirs and assigns for ever if he the said Denny Martin, should he be alive at the time of my death, but in case he should not. Then I give and devise the same and every part and parcel thereof to Thomas Bryan Martin, Esquire, his next brother now living with me to him his heirs and assigns forever and in case of his death before me, I give and devise the same and every part and parcel thereof to my other nephew Philip Martin, Esquire, brother to the aforesaid Denny and Thomas and to his heirs and assigns forever provided always and upon this condition, that the said Denny Martin if alive, at the time of my decease, or in case of his death, the said Thomas Bryan Martin, if he should be alive at the time of my death, the said Philip Martin, if he should be alive at the time of my decease, shall pay or cause to be paid to my nieces Frances Martin, Syvella, and Ann Susanna Martin, and to each and every of them that shall be living at the time of my decease an annuity of one hundred pounds sterling during their and each of their natural lives and further that he the said Denny Martin, or he to whom the said sixth part of the said Northern Neck shall pass by this my will shall procure an act of Parliament to pass to take upon him the name of Fairfax and Coat of Arms and whereas I some time since gave to aforesaid Thomas Bryan Martin, the Plantation or tract of land I purchased of John Borden, containing upwards of six hundred acres which gift I hereby confirm, and ratify to him his heirs and assigns forever I also give and bequeath to him the said Thomas Bryan Martin, all the stock of cattle, sheep, hogs, implements of husbandry household goods and furniture now or shall be at the time of my decease, on the farm or plantation whereon I now live called Greenway Court. I give devise and bequeath to my aforesaid three nephews or such of them that shall be alive at the time of my decease, to-wit Denny Martin, Thomas Bryan Martin, and Philip Martin, all my negro slaves that I shall die possessed of to be equally divided between them share and share alike, and whereas I did in a late will now cancelled give a considerable pecuniary legacy to my brother the Honourable Robert Fairfax, Esquire, which sum of money at his earnest desire and request I have since paid him therefore I now only give him the further sum of five hundred pounds sterling as memorial of my affection and to buy him mourning. I also give and bequeath to my sister Francis Martin, five hundred pounds sterling to buy her mourning. All the rest and residue of my estate both real and personal not hereinbefore disposed of I give devise and bequeath to my elder nephew the aforesaid Rev. Denny Martin, his heirs and assigns forever AND LASTLY I do nominate and appoint my said nephew Thomas Bryan Martin, Peter Hog, and Gabriel Jones, both of the County of Augusta in the Colony of Virginia, my executors fully relying on their fidelity and integrity to see said trust hereby reposed in them faithfully and truly executed. I do hereby give and bequeath to each of the said Peter Hog, and Gabriel Jones the sum of five hundred pounds current money of Virginia, apiece, and do direct that my executors aforesaid give no other security to the Court where this my will shall be proved but their own bonds and that they shall not be liable for each others transactions but only for their own nor be liable for any unforseen casualties or unavoidable accidents but only for willful negligence and malfeazance I likewise direct my estate may not be appraised but only inventoried.

In witness that this my last will and testament containing two sides and part of a third of a sheet of paper, I have hereunto set my hand and affixed my seal the eight day of November one thousand seven hundred and seventy-seven. FAIRFAX, (SEAL).

Signed sealed and published by the testator the Right Honourable Thomas Lord Fairfax as and for his last will and testament in the presence of us, who in his presence and in the presence of each other, have hereunto set our names as witnesses:

JOHN HITE,
ANGUS MCDONALD,
RICHARD RIGG,
JOHN SARGEANT,
THOMAS SMYTHER.

5th October, 1778, Republished by the Right Honourable Thomas Lord Fairfax in the presence of Isaac Zane, Daniel Field.

WHEREAS since the making of my last will and testament dated the eight day of November, 1777, which I hereby confirm excepting the alterations herein after mentioned in this instrument of writing which I intend as a codicil and to be taken as such and as part of my said will First That the negro slaves left in my said will to be equally divided between my nephews Denny Martin, Thomas Bryan Martin, and Philip Martin, Esquires, shall be divided into four equal parts instead of three one-fourth part thereof I give and devise to Bryan Fairfax, Esquire, my intent and meaning being that he shall have an equal share or part of my said negroes with my aforesaid three nephews AND WHEREAS in my aforesaid will I have bequeathed an annuity of one hundred pounds sterling to each of my three nieces Frances Martin, Syvella Martin, and Ann Susannah Martin, during their several lives I do hereby devise and bequeath that upon the death of Francis Martin her annuity of one hundred pounds sterling be given and continued to the second child of the aforesaid Bryan Fairfax, during his or her natural life and that upon the death of Syvella Martin, the annuity of one hundred pounds sterling bequeathed to her be given and continued to the third child of the aforesaid Bryan Fairfax, during her or his natural life, and further upon the death of my other niece Ann Susannah Martin, the annuity of one hundred pounds sterling bequeathed to her be given and continued to the fourth child of the said Bryan Fairfax, during his or her natural life, and further and lastly I do hereby direct the sum of five hundred pounds sterling money of Great Britain to be paid to each of my two executors mentioned in my said will instead of the sum given them in current money.

In witness that this codicil is to be annexed and taken as part of my aforesaid will, I have set my hand and affixed my seal this 27th day of November, 1779. FAIRFAX, (SEAL).

Signed, sealed and published by the testator The Right Honourable Thomas Lord Fairfax, in the presence of us, the subscribers as a codicil to his last will and testament and annexed thereto.

ROBERT MACKY,
PETER CATLETT,
JOHN S. WOODCOCK,
JOHN HITE.

At a Court held for Frederick County the 5th day of March, 1782. This last will and testament of the Right Honourable Thomas Lord Fairfax, deceased, was proved by the oaths of John Hite, Richard Riggs, Thomas Smyther, witnesses thereto and the codicil thereunto annexed was also proved by the oaths of Robert Macky, Peter Catlett, John S. Woodcock, and John Hite, witnesses thereto are ordered to be recorded and upon the motion of Thomas Bryan Martin, and Gabriel Jones, surviving executors therein named who made oath according to law, certificate is granted them for obtaining a probate thereof in due form whereupon they entered into and acknowledged bond conditioned as the law directs.

By the Court, JAS. KEITH, *C. C.*"

"THIS INDENTURE made the second day June in the year of Our Lord One Thousand Eight Hundred and One Between James M. Marshall of the City of Washington in the District of Columbia in the United States of America and Hatty, his wife, of the one part, and Charles Mynn Thruston, John Smith, Robert White, Sen'r., Edward McGuire Sen'r., James Gam'l. Dowdall, Joseph Longacre Sen'r., John S. Woodcock, David Kennedy, Thomas Massie, Robert Macky, Thomas Buck, Goviard Briscoe, John Kean, Isaac Hite, Jun'r., Rawleigh Colston, Matthew Wright, Cornelius Baldwin, Nathaniel Burwell, Thomas Parker, John Hickman, George F. Norton, James Singleton, Strother G. Suttle, Meredith Helm, George Blackemore, Charles Smith and Daniel Conrad, Gentlemen Justices now in the commission of the peace in and for the

County of Frederick in the Commonwealth of Virginia, and Henry Beatly, Mayor, Lewis Wolfe, Recorder, William Davison, William Ball, Joseph Gamble and Peter Lauck, Aldermen of the Corporation of Winchester of the other part, Witnesseth Whereas the General Assembly of Virginia on the thirty first day of December in the year of our Lord one thousand seven hundred and ninety nine passed an Act concerning the Public Square in the Borough of Winchester (reciting therein that it had been represented that James M. Marshall is willing to convey to such persons as may be empowered by the General Assembly of Virginia to take a conveyance, all his right, title and interest in and to the public square in the Borough of Winchester in the County of Frederick except that part on which the church stands and the church yard annexed thereto) and thereby enacted that any Deed of Conveyance made and executed by the said James M. Marshall for the public square as aforesaid to the Justices of the County aforesaid, the Mayor and Aldermen of the said Borough of Winchester and their successors (to and for the use of the said Borough of Winchester and County of Frederick) shall be as good and valid in law as if such conveyance had been made to an individual.

"NOW THIS INDENTURE WITNESSETH that the said James M. Marshall and Hatty his wife, in pursuance of the will heretofore expressed and of the said Act of Assembly in this particular case made and provided Have Bargained, Sold and Conveyed unto the aforesaid Justices of Frederick County and the said Mayor and Aldermen of the said Borough of Winchester and their successors to and for the use of said Borough of Winchester and County of Frederick all the right, title and interest of them the said James M. Marshall, and Hatty his wife, either in Law or Equity in and to the public square in the Borough of Winchester in the County of Frederick except that part of which the Church stands and the Church yard annexed thereto which said Public Square of Ground contains four Lots and each Lot is one hundred and nineteen feet in front and one hundred and eighty-nine feet nine inches deep and said Square is bounded by Loudoun on the Westward, by Lots No. 19 and 26 on the Northward, by Cameron Street on the Eastward and by Bocowan Street on the Southward, on which said Public Square stand a Court-House, Market-House, two Jails, two Engine-Houses, a black-smith shop and the Protestant Episcopal Church and Church-Yard annexed thereto (which part of the said ground on which the said Church stands and the Yard annexed thereto enclosed by a stone wall is expressly excepted out of this conveyance) TO HAVE AND TO HOLD the said Public Square of Ground with the buildings and improvements thereon and all other the appurtenances (except as before excepted) unto the aforesaid Justices of Frederick County and the Mayor and Aldermen of the said Borough of Winchester and their successors (to and for the use of the said Borough of Winchester and County of Frederick) forever according to the true intent and meaning of the Act of Assembly before in part recited. And the (said) James M. Marshall and his heirs the land and other premises hereby conveyed unto the Justices of Frederick County and the Mayor and Aldermen of the Borough of Winchester and their successors to and for the use of the said County and Corporation against them, the said James M. Marshall and Hatty, his wife and their heirs and all and every other person and persons claiming or to claim by, from or under him, them or any of them shall and will warrant and forever defend by these presents. IN WITNESS whereof the said James M. Marshall and Hatty, his wife have hereunto set their hands and seals the day and year first hereinbefore written. J's. M. MARSHALL, (L. S.).

(L. S.).

Signed, sealed and delivered
in the presence of:
J. PEYTON,
GRIFFIN TAYLOR,
OBED WAITE."

It must not be forgotten that James Wood, by an Act of the Genl. Assembly, 1758, laid off other lots as an addition to the town founded by him in 1744 and added to by the Fairfax Addition in 1752. That portion referred to in the Act of 1758 comprised 106 acres taken from his other land contiguous to the town of Winchester. This is properly called Wood's Addition and lies in western part of the City, through which the streets and alleys, running at right angles, are shown in the plat of the town,—now part of the files of the Corporation Clerk's office.

Having given much space to show fully the topography of the town, whose boundaries thus established, continued without change. No more additions (Two others to be hereafter mentioned, one in 1782; the other 1905). The area and plan well adapted to any demand made for any class of trade or business, as well as for the palatial residences that adorn the city of to-day. We must now show as briefly as possible, how this territory or parcel of land was used; and who many of the users were. As already stated, the old Justices Court appropriated quite a large space in the central part as early as 1744 in accepting the offer of Col. Wood, and proceeded to erect the necessary buildings required for a county seat. They evidently chose the site themselves; and from that date on through many years, the court made frequent orders concerning the proper management and control of their "Public Lotts." These orders are replete with valuable historic incidents—too numerous, however, to make it desirable to include them in this work. Proper reference will be given, however, to show authority for statements hereafter made.

To the present inhabitants of Winchester, the Public Lotts mentioned in the old court minutes, means the courthouse square and what was once the old market square—the former containing the Court House and clerk's offices, for the use of the county; the latter adorned by the handsome and spacious building with frontage on Cameron Street (Market), known as the Rouss Memorial, for the use of the City. This much would doubtless be sufficient for the present, but as our office is to write history, the reader will see the necessity for more explicit description, and future generations will expect us to have compiled incidents in such form as to give ready answer to such enquiries as are now being continually made in relation to the subject matter now being treated. The writer has been deluged with such enquiries for the last quarter of a century—many so simple, yet difficult to answer. For instance, how few there be who could answer the oft repeated questions: When was your court house built? Is it the first that was used by the courts? What is the history of the old building? While such questions may have quick answer from an old Clerk of court, grown familiar with such incidents, he is astonished to find the general lack of information on this and similar subjects. And so the author feels it his duty to compile in this work much matter for reference, gathered from time to time from out of the musty records of by-gone periods. As elsewhere stated, the early courts took the first steps toward the county seat buildings by plain orders, directing certain persons to *clear* the ground for the erection of a "log-house," and report to court; then the site selected, and dimensions of the court house given into the hands of several of the Justices, to proceed to build, etc. This log-house for the court was erected on the ground now occupied by the West end or vestibule of the present court house. The length must have been forty feet, for in the instructions to the persons executing the order, is this language "The logs must be 40 feet with even dimensions and well shapen on two sides" and as no other lengths were given, it is safe to assume that the building was square. Those virgin forests must have had "tall timber" to furnish the Justices' bill. The first court house faced South. Orders of court show the anxiety to have the space *in front* of the court house to Boscowan Street (Water) cleared of all obstructions. One minute shows the impatience of the court, requiring the Justices who had charge of this improvement, to report the cause of delay in *removing the stumps*, so as to afford better entrance to the court house from Boscowan Street. Later on report was made that the court's order had been executed. The committee reported the new jail ready for occupancy. This building was located towards the southeast of the court house front, toward Water Street, and "44 feet from the line thereof," "with an enclosure for jail-yard in the rear;" the site being about 40 feet South from the entrance to the city hall from the *plaza*. No report as to the clerk's office for several years; mention being made at some terms of the court about the records being in the court house. Tradition has it that Mr. Wood, the clerk, kept the office at his own house near the town,—the property now owned by Col. W. W. Glass. The site for the first office had been selected, however, and this was to be near the southwest corner of the foundation of the court house and 11 feet distant therefrom. This must have embraced part of the ground occupied by the West end of the present clerk's office and the two law offices now owned by Mr. Bantz. As will be shown later on, the Public Lotts embraced all ground between the present court house yard and Water Street No building of any kind on that space until 1762, when a stone building was erected fronting on Loudoun Street, ten feet distant from the Loudoun Street corner. This stone building was for a number of years the home of the Episcopal Church of Winchester, (of which fuller mention will be given under the head of churches, etc.) Sometime prior to the erection of this edifice, a considerable space directly South of the old Clerk's Office was used as a burial ground for a number of persons—the whole corner lot receiving some sort of dedication from Lord Fairfax. No one doubting his authority to do what his Lordship desired in his own proprietary. So, doubtless, the townspeople and authorities were cognizant of his act—it may have been but the wave of his magic hand; sufficient, however, to settle the question. And the Court no more concerned itself in relation to that part of what had been called the "Public Square," except, however, on several occasions, the court had its attention called to the fact that some encroachments were being made on the "burial ground" from the extension of the clerk's office. Then it was that the line was determined between the county property and the corner lot referred to. A stone wall was erected, running from Loudoun Street to the clerk's office, which afterwards became the subject of much attention from the court. No mention made of who paid the cost of erection; but the court ever afterwards kept this wall in repair, and protected it from the raids of the village boys, who seemed to enjoy feats so gymnastic in their character, as to bring condemnation on the wayward youths. The reward offered for their apprehension and conviction produced a profound sensation. The court making orders to pay cost of needed repairs, etc.

The North wall of the present Bantz building, was built on the foundation of the old party wall, by Jacob Senseny; he appearing in court, and securing permission to remove the old wall and to erect his building wall on the same foundation. Only a portion of this wall was removed at that time; the remainder continued unbroken for many years, when it also gave way for the erection of the law offices which now join the West end of the clerk's office; Mr. Bantz securing permission from the Board of Supervisors of the county to use this foundation and to make openings on the court yard, under same restrictions imposed on Jacob Senseny by the County Court, June 3, 1828. From the southeast corner of the old clerk's office, a stone wall was extended to Boscowan Street, thus enclosing the whole of the lot then being used as the "grave yard," and the church lot adjoining.

The first old log clerk's office was reported to court frequently as being inadequate for the increased demand for the "transaction of business and proper and convenient care of the books and court files." The court took no action until 1780, when "complaint was laid before the court that the clerk's office was in bad repair." Action was promptly taken, and commissioners appointed to report a plan for a one-story brick building of suitable size and probable cost: This office building occupied the ground due West from the old log office, and was strictly a brick building, walls, floor and roof—the chief object being to make a fire-proof office: The building afforded a safe place for records—but not popular with officers and persons who were required to spend much time within its cold, damp walls; and frequent efforts were made to have the court make many changes suggested. But the court gave no heed to the appeals. The writer was informed by a gentleman who spent fourteen years prior to 1827 with Mr. T. A. Tidball, Dep. Clerk of the County Court, while Judge Keith was Clerk, that the only attention the court gave to the complaints concerning the discomforts of the brick vault, as it was then termed, was when Mr. Tidball produced several of the old record books, badly mildewed, to the court, showing the old office to be unsuited for records. This was in 1827. The court at once took steps to build the third clerk's office. This was erected on a new site, being the present building known as the County Clerk's Office. This was finished during the Autumn of 1832. (At June Ct., 1832, $974.50 was appropriated to pay for completing office.) The new office was two-storied; the lower floor occupied by the Clerk of the County and Circuit Court—the room on the East end used by the County Court, the one on the West by the Circuit; the two large rooms on second floor used by the officers respectively for storing old records. This large building was ample in every way for many years; but the accumulation of papers, books, etc. taxed its capacity, and in 1886 large brick vaults were added to the South side, and afforded fire-proof rooms for a large amount of the valuable records, etc. The author was then serving his first years as clerk; and finding the danger the records were in, presented the case to the Board of Supervisors, who very promptly complied with his request, and erected the annex on the South side, which is still in use. The whole building was thoroughly remodeled in 1904-5. The two lower rooms were thrown into one office, to conform to the change made by the New Constitution,—to be known as the County Clerk's Office; the Clerk to be ex-officio Clerk of the Circuit Court. The building was made fire-proof; the upper floor to be in two rooms, the East room for old records, the West room fitted up for the Board of Supervisors to hold their meetings in. At the present writing, the county has an office building sufficient to accommodate the increasing business for several decades.

The present court house was erected on the site of the first log structure which was used for many years, fronting on Boscowan Street. In the Spring of 1826, the old log building was remodeled and repaired. Then it was that the front was changed to open toward Loudoun Street, with only a small vestibule "20 by 20 feet square, and the outside walls to be covered with boards neatly nailed on; and interior walls to be covered with hardened mortar, with white lime finish." During the Spring terms, held monthly, orders of court were made, directing certain of the Justices to superintend the changes being made; court being held in the same court-room until the July term, when the order appears: "It appearing to the court that it will be impracticable to hold the sessions of this court in the court house of this county during the time it is undergoing repairs, it is ordered

Frederick County Court House; erected in 1840

that the sessions of this court and the superior court of law for the county be held in the court house of the corporation of Winchester, which has been tendered to the court until said repairs shall be completed." (The Corporation court-room was in the new Market Hall, on second floor).

"Ordered that the commissioners appointed to superintend the repairs of the courthouse, do enlarge the steeple, so as to receive a town clock, provided such enlargement can be made at an expense to the county not exceeding one hundred dollars." Much delay occurred in completing the changes ordered by the court. The Justices were much divided in their views as to the improvements ordered. Some favored an entirely new structure—"using limestone for walls." The final report by the sheriff of the money he had paid, upon order of the commissioners for "changes to the court-house," shows payment for "staying the roof;" for plastering the walls; for front doors, and large porch," for furniture, including two desks for the Justices and District Courts; and for the "stand for the Justices seats;" for "stairway, and seats for the grand jury room on the stairs." Nothing said about the outside walls, where boards were expected to be neatly nailed. Doubtless the old "well-sharpened logs" remained unchanged,—no reference being made in subsequent orders of court relating to the steeple for the town clock. An ordinance of the town council, dated July 12, 1826, appropriating $750, "for the expense of procuring and erecting a town clock, to be placed in the steeple now erecting upon the County Court House," seems to be conclusive that a town clock was in the steeple of the old court house; and further evidence is shown in an ordinance of the town council, dated June 10, 1828, providing for proper person to take charge of the town clock, "who shall regulate and adjust and keep same in order." The writer found tradition and records at variance in this case. Some old citizen asserting that the first town clock was placed in the steeple of the present court house this embarrassment occurs in many similar cases relating to buildings erected on the "Public Lotts," and used for public purposes. They were known as the county jail, the golden temple, engine house, tobacco warehouse, ducking stool, the market house, fire engine house with watch tower in second story, also a corporation clerk's office. We are fortunate in having record evidence in these cases, to determine their location and uses. The fathers seemed determined to make full use of the "Public Lotts." In addition to the eleven buildings in use at the period mentioned (1828), the unused spaces East and South of the county court house and clerk's office, were used by the public as "wagon stands" on the regular market days, and as a hitching place for horses. At the period mentioned, the county and town authorities vied with each other in offering and affording ample accommodations to the country visitors, whether patrons of the various businesses prospering in the old town, or the large crowds attending the courts. Special care had been observed for many years that hitching posts should be provided for the "Justices' horses." But as early as 1801, an order was made by the court "for the erection of additional hitching posts." As the reader of to-day sees the old court house, clerk's office, and the imposing city hall,—there is no vestige of the many buildings referred to. Nothing to indicate that the market, wagon stand or "hitching posts" ever adorned or utilized any of the space. Not even the music of the neighing horse is heard as he stands on "Frederick Plaza" and surveys the scene; and as he beholds it, a thrill of joy stirs him; but his thrill bears no comparison to those that stirred the souls of them who once deemed the "Old Market Space" the mecca for all the generations who in the far-away past gathered there for traffic or pleasure. The writer deems it best at this point to locate the buildings mentioned. The first of the class referred to was the jail, which, as stated elsewhere, was a log cabin fronting on Water Street, nearly opposite the southwest corner of the city hall, erected in 1744. The "Ducking Stool" received attention at the December Term, 1746. One of the Justices was directed "to erect a ducking-stool according to the model of that at Fredericksburg. This was a *pitt* 7 feet deep and 6 feet square in the clear, and walled with stone, with roof. This occupied the space near the large window of the basement of the city hall opening on the Plaza for unloading coal. It was used chiefly to punish unruly females; but sometimes to sober the drunken men of the day. The custom prevailed for many years. No evidence when its use was discontinued. In 1790 the last order appears in reference to this old-time mode of punishment. The county "goal" erected in 1744, was rude in structure, and served a good purpose in its day. Many incidents are mentioned in the minutes of court that would be interesting to many readers, but limited space forbids mention. As evolution progressed, the class of prisoners varied. The insolvent debtors law being then in force, many names appear. Lt. Geo. Washington applied to the court for permission to imprison some of his unruly soldiers. This was denied, and the young officer erected a military prison on his own lot, on West side of what was afterwards called Loudoun Street, North of the Shen. Valley Bank corner. During this period, some Indians were captured South of the town and sentenced to prison for violation of a treaty. Then the Hon. Court made formal call upon Col. Washington to furnish guards for protection of the county jail and the prisoners. The guards were supplied, and they ever after acted in concert with the military. It was found desirable in 1758 to enlarge the jail. We find in 1760, the Sheriff was allowed compensation for the stone addition to the jail. This style of jail continued up to and during the Revolutionary War. In 1790 the jail was reported to Court by the sheriff as being unsafe, and that the prisoners should be transferred to a place of safety. No steps were taken to assist the sheriff; and here appears a lack of the usual system, adhered to by the courts through the preceding years, when very full minutes were made in reference to buildings. Only a brief order appears in 1792, when two commissioners are directed to confer with the sheriff in regard to the procurement of a suitable house for the prisoners. The next order in reference to the jail appears at March Term, 1803, to-wit: "Ordered that the sheriff in connection with the Corp. of Winchester, do expose to public sale for ready money the stone and other materials in the Old House on the Public Square, lately occupied as a Goal." Among the old files, vouchers were found showing full settlement with the sheriff for expenses in the erection of the jail. Stone as building material, predominated; all the work apparently was completed in 1790, so far as ascertainable from the original orders. This new stone building was erected immediately North of the site of the old log *Goal.* The old jail wall was repaired; and once more the prisoners found a new home for many years. This wall extended from along Water Street to Market, to a point 12 feet South of the West end of the "public scale of weights and measures;" "thence to the point of beginning on Boscowan Street." This settles the location of the jail and also the old hay scales, about which there has been frequent disagreement. Fire damaged this building in 1821. Tradition gives loss of life by this fire—not sustained by record evidence. Temporary quarters were provided for the prisoners; and within six months, the building was restored at a cost of $180.00. No other such interruption discomforted the sheriff and his prisoners until the 12th January, 1843, when the entire jail building was destroyed by fire. Many prisoners were confined within its walls; but the fire occurring at the Noon hour, they were hurried from danger. Thus ended the jail on the public square. Feby. 6, 1843, this order appears in the minutes of the county court: "The jail of this county having been destroyed by fire since the last term of this court, it is ordered that the Justices of the county be summoned to Saturday next to take into consideration the subject of building a new jail * * * "Ordered that Jacob Baker, John W. Miller and George R. Long be appointed a committee to procure a suitable building for a jail of this county until a permanent jail is erected."

The Justices at the March Term following, decided to purchase a site elsewhere (which will receive fuller notice later on). The next of the eleven buildings erected on the Public Lotts, was the Tobacco Warehouse. This was a large building fronting on Water Street "distant from the jail wall 24 feet in the clear." April 6, 1825, the following appears in the minutes of the County Court, to-wit: "Upon the petition of Joseph Holmes, Gent. and others, merchants in the Borough of Winchester, that they may have a portion of public ground assigned them for the purpose of building a Tobo. Warehouse, Ord., that J. G. Dowdall, Robert Mackey and John McKean, Gent., be appointed to lay off on the public Lot adjoining Water Street 100 feet square for the purpose aforesaid, and that the said land is vested in Joseph Holmes, John Smith and Ed. Smithers, Trustees for the purpose aforesaid; * * * and shall cause to be erected within 12 mo. a warehouse for the purpose aforesaid. This building was not only to receive and store all tobacco changing hands, but for other storage. During that period, tobacco was preeminently chief of all crops raised in the country. Inspectors assessed a tax upon all packages, and fixed its value; and thus tobacco continued to be used to pay taxes, salaries to officers, and frequently was regarded as *good currency.* The Colonial Government had, by legislation, made it a legal tender; and it so continued for many years under the new State government.

The next building in order, was the "Market House," erected on a site where the North end of the City Hall now stands. Cameron (or Market) Street had not yet been fully opened and graded. The site selected had been occupied for many years by a rough stone house. There is some foundation for the tradition that it was used at one time as a magazine to store munitions of war. The old court order directs "The old fort house to be removed and the surface levelled for a foundation for the new Market House." Tradition fixes this old stone house as an old market house for many years. For several years prior to 1820 there were two market places. One was a large yard in front of the Lutheran Church on Water Street, and the other was known as the Brannon or Rust Yard, near the courthouse. The latter is now occupied as law offices; and the remainder of the large yard North of the offices in use by the city. We have no record evidence to determine what was on the space long known as the Market Square, so far as a market house appears, until June 6, 1821. Then a record appears in the minutes of the county court, to-wit: "A resolution of the Common Council of the Corporation of Winchester passed on the 1st day of June, 1821, calling upon the court for aid in erecting the *New* Market House in said Corporation, was produced * * * Same was declined." This language would imply that the *new* market house was substituted for an older one. The ordinances of the council, entered of record by the council, fail to state that they were erecting a new market house. The building was in use during the Summer of 1821. We find an ordinance of the city council dated June 15, 1821, sets out fully how the market shall be conducted, showing that it was ready for use. While the County Court declined to aid the Town in building the new market house, we find by an order of that court in 1822, $300.00 was appropriated to reimburse the town for expense incurred in reducing the rock-ribbed hill on which the old stone house stood, and grading it to the level of Cameron Street. The writer was informed by Mr. Wm. G. Russell during his lifetime—he then being of great age—but with intellect untouched by the usual infirmities of age, that the old stone fort house stood on the same hill, extending from Major Conrad's residence to the old court house; and that what was afterwards Cameron Street, was not opened until 1819; and that teamsters had a driveway through the old Rust wagon-yard around the base of the limestone ridge, crossing what was for three-fourths of a century afterwards the market square, entering Water Street at the West end of the old jail wall. Mr. Russell's statements were so clear on all such facts pertaining to the early history of the town, as to attach no doubt to his numerous statements. The author availed himself of the opportunity, and has copious notes from which he has drawn much that is given in these pages; and desiring to gather other incidents not mentioned by his venerable friend, he has frequently interviewed many of the oldest citizens, and been surprised several years ago by old persons who gave interesting accounts of how the "old hill" had been removed, and "they had earned their first money as boys working about the quarries, receiving *six pence* per day for their services;" thus confirming the minute statement made by Mr. Russell.

The market house extended from Court House Avenue, along Market Street to a point about opposite the window of the police station "lock-up:" it being two stories of brick. The walls of the ground floor were in large arches on the two sides, the arch-ways being closed with lattice work, affording light and ventilation to the whole of the first story, used exclusively by market people—butchers stalls and blocks; stands or tables, to display the fresh vegetables from the farms adjacent to the town, and also from the celebrated gardens operated at the West end of the town by the two well-known Scotchmen, Robert Steele and Thomas Allen. The floor of this building was paved with good brick; annexes were extended from each end westward, to supply the demand for more space. The first erected on the North end in 1840; the South end in 1848. After the old Hay scales were moved to near the County Clerk's office, an open court way was left, which was enclosed with an iron railing. Within this court, live poultry, pigs, lambs, etc., were exposed for sale; and it was within this court or open space that Charles Broadway Rouss, when a boy, sold pins and needles to those who attended market. The friendships formed in those days were never forgotten; and the millionaire Rouss delighted to renew his acquaintances during his periodical visits to the scenes of his early life; and often did he request the writer to point out "the old timers," as he called them. Later on will be shown more fully his unflagging interest in the town. For the present, we are trying to locate the market-house and space, which by such incidents have become sufficiently historic to justify this extended description. The second story was approached by a stairway from the broad pavement on Market Street. From the stair landing above, entrance to the three rooms on that floor was made under some restrictions: The large room at the North end was always known to the rising generation as a very mysterious place, it being for many years the home of the "Blue Lodge;" and those old Masons jealously guarded the interior so well, that perhaps no boy ever had a glimpse of the *queer* found therein, until he some day found himself "A free and Accepted Mason." The two rooms in the South end were used for many years; the first entered being known as the Town Hall, where the Corporation or Recorders Court was held; and the room in the extreme South end, as the Council Chamber. The latter was used by the Council for a long time after the markets were abolished. The old building proper survived the ravages of the Civil War—at least, it was not destroyed. The annexes, being wooden buildings, disappeared by degrees. For the first two years of the War, all the building except the Masons Room, was used for quarters for troops, guard-houses, etc. To anticipate any question arising as to the occupancy by troops of the market house during the war, the author gives the following extracts from the minutes of the common council: "March 17, 1862, On motion of H. S. Baker, Resolved that a Committee be appointed to wait upon the proper Federal military authority and endeavor to get the military to vacate the market house or a portion of it. So that it may be used for market purposes; and thereupon the President appointed H. S. Baker, P. Williams, Geo. Keller and Wm. L. Hollis, Committee." The Federals referred to as taking such liberties, were of Genl. Banks' Army, doubtless; for the writer remembers well that Genl. Jackson evacuated Winchester on the 11th of March, 1862, and the Federals promptly moved in. During the whole of that Winter, the writer, while Provost Marshal of the Post, used part of the market house—the town hall upstairs and the northern annex, for his provost guard quarters; and no protest ever came from the citizens' council. The only evidence we can give that the Federals vacated the market house, is furnished by the reports made to Genl. Jackson, that the writer's command had captured a large lot of small arms and military stores and some prisoners in the market house, and were guarding the same, and asked for orders. The General, by his surprising march, had given Banks no time to hear and receive the Committee from the Council; and our happy band for two days had no intimation from the Council that they were unwelcome occupants of the market house.

We give the following, to show the condition of the old building towards the close of the War July 30, 1864:

"On motion of Wm. H. Streit, it is ordered, that the Committee on Market and Market-house, be and it is hereby authorized to take down the middle portion of the market house, using such materials as they may need, and sell the remainder at public sale for current Bank or Corporation money and that the police keep special watch on said remainder until sold."

Sept. 12, 1864. "The Committee on Market and Market House who were directed to sell the middle portion of the Market House, reported that before any sale was made the *South Wing* of the Quadrangle had fallen down, and that it was believed that the other wing would be destroyed. * * *."

"Ordered that the Committee sell the brick in the pillars of the wings of the market house * * * Same Committee is ordered to have the doors and windows of the West and North sides of the second story of the market house planked up."

As already stated, the old building's annexes, or wings, were badly damaged, but not entirely destroyed. The following extract from proceedings of the town council, after peace was declared, may be of sufficient interest to justify its appearance in this connection.

Oct. 30, 1865. "The Bill for appropriating money for the repairs of the Market house *proper,* was taken up as the unfinished business of the last Council, and after it was discussed, on motion of Dr. McCormick, the blank was filled with two thousand dollars and on motion the bill was read a third time * * * and the Committee on Markets and Market House, to-wit: That said Committee proceed forthwith to cause said Market House proper (the brick structure as it now stands) to be well and permanently repaired * * * And if said committee deem it expedient to do so, they are instructed to cause to be erected a shed on West side of said Market House to its full extent during the present fall and ensuing winter. The records show that the improvements were made as fast as the strained Treasury would justify. A long and substantial wing was built from the North end along Court House Avenue, furnishing ample accommodation for years.

We find the "Blue Lodge" survived the shock of war. The following extract from the Common Council's records may be of sufficient interest to some readers to justify entry here:

Dec. 7, 1865. "A communication was received from J. B. T. Reed, John Kerr and Wm. R. Denny, on behalf of the Order of Free Masons, having reference to the improvement of the Market Square, and erecting buildings thereon, etc. Referred to Committee."

Jany. 8, 1866. The Committee for Improvement of the Market Square, etc., made their report: "The Committee of Council and the Committee on behalf of the Masonic Fraternity of Winchester have met and have had a free, full and harmonious conference." This resulted in the Council agreeing to build pillars and place girders under the North end of the old brick building, and then under certain conditions, the Masons were to construct their hall on the arches, and thus have a new home on the old site. These agreements were complied with by the parties concerned; the market house put in good order; and the Masons occupied their new lodge room until the Masonic Temple "On Loudoun Street," was dedicated July 22, 1868, the corner stone was laid May 29th, 1867. The old lodge room was not abandoned, however, until the old market house was condemned, to give place to the city hall erected on part of the old site. The Council again occupied their renovated quarters on the second floor. The market continued for about fifteen years, gradually falling off in patronage by producer and consumer; the market regulations relaxed, and the retail business found its way to shops, etc. in different sections of the town. The old abandoned market space was used by county people as a hitching yard. The old building, from disuse, became an object of derision for years; the city using it—partly for police quarters, in the South end; the remainder occupied by farm implement dealers, sheds, etc. for the debris, wood, etc., for the city's uses. This occupancy was much criticized and censured; and all were glad to see the old walls and rubbish disappear during the Spring and Summer of 1900, to give place for a building that would adorn and benefit the town. The average citizen who desired the change, often delighted in recounting the incidents that belonged to the old market house and space. Nearly all the old actors on that stage where the Old Market Drama was enacted semi-weekly, have passed to the great beyond. The survivors are growing few, and ere another decade, there will be none to tell of the interesting history of the Old Winchester Market.

The engine houses referred to, are next in order. The common council at a meeting held Oct. 28, 1825, passed an ordinance, appointing Beaty Carson, John Bell and Saml. H. Davis a committee to erect an engine house fronting on Water Street, in the corner formed by the walls of the Episcopal Church yard and the court house yard—the said walls to form part of the building, and the new walls to be of brick. This doubtless occupied the ground where the Bantz shoe store building now stands, inside of the church yard wall on Main Street to Water Street corner; "the space from the engine house to be gravelled to Water Street," and was the first engine house erected by the town. The first fire engine was stored for several years prior to this date in other buildings, the owners receiving rent for same. This ordinance provides for the erection of a *new* engine house. Tradition has it that the first engine house occupied some other point—location, however, not fixed. Mr. Russell thought the engine house built in the Church yard in 1825, was the first. This building was removed in the Summer of 1829 to accommodate Jacob Senseny, who had become the owner of the old church yard, and desired the space for his new buildings. We have record evidence for this in Ordinance of Council, Oct. 1, 1829, from which the following extracts are taken: "Mr. Heiskell, Mr. Sherrard, Mr. Bell and Mr. Gold appointed to superintend the erection of house of the dimensions of twenty-one feet by twelve at the southwest corner of the jail wall, for the reception of the fire engine, and there be erected upon the same an additional story of the height of eight feet, with three windows to be well secured with iron bars, which said additional room shall be used as a watch house, or place of temporary confinement for all vagrants or other disorderly persons, who may be legally taken up by patrols * * *; and the said committee to ascertain from competent workmen the expense of erecting a house of similar construction and dimensions of the *one lately occupied as an engine house* which was removed for the accommodation of Jacob Senseny, and to receive from the said Senseny the amt. ascertained to be the value of said building." This new building occupied twelve feet of the space between the old jail wall and the tobacco warehouse, leaving an alley way from Water Street to the Market Square, 12 feet in width. This building is not mentioned in the records as an engine house again until 1843, when it is designated the "watch-Tower" building, in payment of incidental expenses, such as fuel and furniture. Mr. Russell and several other well-informed old men stated that the "Sarah Zane" engine, when changing its domicile on the Senseny lot referred to in the foregoing pages, was taken to the ground floor of the new engine house near the jail. Mr. Russell thought this use was of short duration, until other quarters could be prepared.

By a resolution adopted by Council Feby. 18, 1843, it was "Resolved the Fire Engine called the 'Star' Engine be put under the charge of Edward S. Anderson, Captain of the Star Fire Company, and the said Company be allowed to occupy the *room in the house on Water Street* adjoining the jail wall, to keep their engine in." It will be observed that the Council does not speak of it as the Engine house; and it is reasonable to conclude that part of the building, if not all, was used by Council for such public purposes, until they later on erected another and a larger building. To dispose of the house on Water Street, see Minutes of Council, July 6, 1844. "The President of Council is directed to sell for the best price that can be had, the brick engine house near the remains of the old jail * * *." A short life! The order for its erection Oct. 1, 1829, and for its removal July 6, 1844.

We notice next a building that was famous in its day, and a subject for contention between the town and county authorities throughout its entire existence, and of much criticism from nearby property owners—generally called the "Golden Temple." The first record concerning this building will be found in proceedings of Town Council, Spring of 1832; and in County Court, June 4, 1832. An application was made by the Council to the County Court for permission to erect a building on the northwest corner of the court house square, "to be used for containing a fire engine." This was promptly granted. There seemed to be no exception taken to this building, as it was intended for the *new fire engine* purchased just subsequent to this action. The county court made an appropriation towards the purchase of this engine. Council became slightly inflated by the good start. Exhibited some extravagant ideas at their meeting June 25, 1832; and decided to erect a building for many purposes. Appointed commissioners, to contract for and superintend the erection of a building on the northwest corner of the public square, of the following dimensions: 23 feet on Loudon Street, in a line with the present wall which encloses the public square, and running back forty-one feet with the avenue leading from Loudon Street to the market house, and running back 23 feet into the court house yard. To be two stories high, and to be built of brick." This plan was changed by Ordinance of July 11, 1832: "The building to be 38 feet long, and 30 feet wide." This building had two rooms of equal size in the lower story, both fronting on Loudoun Street, with a door leading into each room. These rooms became the engine houses for the two fire engines until 1849. A gate was made in the wall of the court house yard, "fronting the Isaac Hoff building (now Farmers and Merchants Bank) to admit entrance of engines into Ct. House Yd. for protection to Ct. House in case of fire." It seems strange the gateway was not enlarged at the main entrance from Loudoun Street to the court house. The change of plan provided for a portico to be erected on the South side of the building, with stairway from the ground floor to the second floor of the portico; and the second story divided into two rooms, with doors entering same from the portico. The order provides that one of the upper rooms *shall* be used for a clerk's office. The records show that the room in East end, on the second floor, was in use as the office for the corporation clerk, and also contained the records of the town in 1840; and had been so used for several years. We find this record in the county court, June 4, 1838: "Ordered that Jacob Senseny and Daniel Gold ...... a committee to confer with the corporate authorities of the town * * * about the removal of the brick building on the public square now used as a clerk's office for the Corporation Court, and to take such measures, etc." This building, which was erected 1832-3, soon became troublesome to the county court. Frequent notices for several years, how objectionable it had become, on account of its "general uses and prominence on the court of the court house grounds." The Council had evidently exceeded the limit for space granted them by the county court, to build an engine house. The room fronting on Loudoun Street had been converted into a hatter's shop—and other purposes. One of the rooms on the first floor was reserved for the engine; and the other rented to some parties, who soon converted it into an objectionable place—using it as an eating house, bar-room, etc. Several ordinary keepers (who were afterwards hotel men in the town) protested to the court and urged its discontinuance. The Court was so goaded, that finally an order was taken at the August Term, 1840—just seven years after the building was erected—which shows the mood of the court: "Ordered that Taliefero Stribling, Joseph G. Gray, and Robert T. Baldwin be appointed a committee to examine the records of this court and ascertain upon what authority the Yellow brick building on the northwest corner of the public square was erected by the corporate authority of the town and report to first day of next court." This committee made a report that shows the position of the Council. They refused to take any steps toward removing the Yellow building. The court added Wm. Stephenson and Richard W. Barton to the committee, with instructions to enforce the court's order. Council stood upon the right granted them by the court in 1832, and continued the uses objected to. On July 19, 1841, Council, by a resolution adopted, shows the authorities had troublesome tenants, to-wit: "Resolved, That the Treasr. do take such measures as may be deemed necessary to collect or secure the rent of the house on the Northwest corner of the public square, which was rented from the first day of January last to John P. Bentley, and to employ one or two attorneys, if necessary * * *." On Dec. 31, 1841, action was taken as follows: "Resolved that the Treasurer be a committee to rent out on tomorrow at public renting for one year the building on the N. W. cor. of the public square, commonly called the Golden Temple * * *." Later on the committee reported the building rented; and it appears that up to this time, the rooms intended for the fire engines had not been used for that purpose; but that all the building had been rented except the room used by the Clerk of the corporation court. The friction between the authorities continued for many years; the county court insisting through its committees that Council did not need the building for engines, as they were not yet moved from the Tower House on Water Street near the jail wall. The Council at their meeting, March 12, 1842, for the first time took action for the removal of the engine; appointed a committee "to have such alterations made in the *Southern room* of the building on the northwest corner of the public square, for the safe-keeping of the Sarah Zane engine and hose carriage and such other apparatus as may be convenient to deposit there." It will be remembered that the Tower House was used in part as an engine house until 1844, when it was made untenable by the burning of the old jail in January, 1843. A change of the Council in 1845, brought about a better state of feeling between the authorities. A new committee from the Council, to-wit: Jos. H. Sherrard, Geo. R. Long, and Wm. G. Russell, conferred with the committee from the court; and they determined upon the removal, and so made their reports in harmony. Council, at their meeting June 23, 1845, directed the Treasurer to notify *all* the tenants in occupancy of the Yellow building, that their tenancy as tenants and sub-tenants would cease on the first day of Jany. next (1846). On June 29, 1846, Mr. Sherrard asked leave to introduce an Act to remove the brick building on the northwest corner of court house square, and to cause two engine houses to be erected. Then again Sept. 24, 1846, the Act to remove the brick building in front of the C. H. was again taken up; then a committee appointed to select a site for the erection of two engine houses. The county court during this time was not idle; and often had their committees to appear before Council, and urge the removal of what had become a nuisance to the public—the court going so far as to offer another space for fire-engine house strictly. After repeated failures to have the obnoxious building removed, Council at a meeting held Oct. 26, 1847, decided to move the building, and to erect two fire engine houses. We find at their meeting Dec. 9, 1847, Mr. Logan asked leave to introduce an Act to repair the engine house building on corner of Ct. H. Square. The county court became very impatient; and at the Feby. Term, 1848, when Mr. Streit made his report, showing that Council would remove the building when suitable houses could be obtained for the fire engines, the Court accepted the proposition. Council, at a meeting Mch. 11, 1848, appointed a committee "to see no harm was done to their fire engines from any quarter claiming a right to the ground upon which the engine house now stands * * *." The old Golden Temple was nearing its close. Council offered as one reason for holding on to the building, because they had no place for a clerk's office. So we find Council in their meeting April 22, 1848, answering a communication from the county court in reference to this building, and appointing a committee to confer with committee from the court upon the subject of procuring a site for the corporation clerk's office. The court, at its March Term, had offered the site referred to. At the June term, the court extended the time agreed upon for removal until Sept. 15 next (1848), and leave given Council to erect suitable buildings for fire engines on any part of the public square, except on the West or northwest of the courthouse. It may be added here, that the building was not removed by the 15th Sept. It was still standing at the March term, 1849. During that Spring, the records of the court were placed in an office near the extreme East end of the Farmers and Merchants Bank, then occupied by Mr. W. L. Bent. There the corporation clerk's office remained until in 1850, when the Council purchased an office, of one story, on courthouse avenue; and the office was continuously kept there until the new office was prepared in the city building. Mr. James B. Russell purchased the then old office, and on its site erected his present one.

The author offers a word in explanation of the extended notice given the old brick buildings formerly occupying the ground known as the Public Lotts. This pen picture of the old public property, as it appeared prior to 1850, has been given at the request of many citizens of Winchester, hoping thereby to secure a brief history of it. Careful and patient perusal will show the reader, that every building and site here treated, answers numberless questions asked the author and others in these latter years, which could only otherwise be answered accurately by reference to the hundreds of minutes entered in the records of the public offices. The facts are briefly given, and the rough draft of the picture is submitted, in the hope some readers may be enlightened, and learn the value of the old records, preserved by the painstaking fathers who, having performed their duties, trustingly committed their records to succeeding generations.

We must mention another fact in connection with the old court house yard, which has always been enclosed. A stone wall formed its protection for nearly fifty years. It was changed to more modern style in the Fall and Winter of 1829, when Jacob Senseny, desiring to improve his property adjoining the square, entered into a contract with the court, to remove the old wall which had been in bad condition for several years, and substituted a brick wall two feet high, with a wooden railing thereon, all the timbers of which were to be of locust. He also secured permission to widen the pavement on Loudoun Street, falling back from the old wall seven feet,—thus accounting for our wide pavement. Then it was that gates were placed on the front, and in the wall between the East end of the court house and the old graveyard wall. The wall on the South side was removed, to allow the first brick building erected by Senseny, to occupy the foundation for his North wall. This is treated more fully elsewhere. This wall, Mr. Russell informed the author, was very ornamental, and Mr. Senseny's work was highly approved. (See orders of county ct., Aug. term, 1829). This wall was in time removed, to give place to the present iron fence seen on the three sides. It was erected prior to the Civil War.

CHAPTER XXVIII

Water Supply, Etc., Gas, Electricity, Manufactures, Etc. Some Criminal Trials, Etc.

The next matter of interest may be styled, the water supply of the village of the Eighteenth Century and city of the Nineteenth and Twentieth Centuries.

As may be supposed, the village had abundant water for the half century of its existence, drawn from numerous springs and wells. The former became objectionable, by reason of their natural drainage interfering with the streets; and frequently the old courts curtailed many privileges, which were finally willingly abandoned. There were several public wells sunk by order of court. Four were carefully guarded for many years, and stringent rules enforced for their protection. One of these wells was near where the Kerr school building now stands, and was called the Helphenstine well; one was on a vacant lot South from the old jail, which afforded supply of water for the public buildings. This received special attention, as also did the one on Piccadilly Street, near what was known for many years as the Dunbar corner. One, William Miller, who lived on the spot, exercised some control in 1756, and enclosed it with his lot. The court, upon complaint of many citizens, promptly ordered the enclosure torn away, and fined Mr. Miller for encroaching on the street. The writer was shown many years ago the location of this well, which was in the pavement, just West of the corner. The other was near the old wagon yard between Braddock and Main Streets, and South of the town run. There was a private well near the old tavern that stood near where the law offices now are due North of Market Square. Then there was the famous well at Fort Loudoun, sunk by the soldiers in 1756. As the population increased, the inhabitants had their private wells. We have no record of when water pipes were laid to conduct water from the springs, to supply the town. The late Mr. John N. Bell told the writer many years ago, he remembered that when the pipes were laid in Water Street in 1840, workmen found old logs, that were formerly used to convey water from the springs; and old men told him that these logs were first laid about 1810; and that an ancestor of the late Oliver Brown used some new device to bore them. (*Note*: Mr. Russell fixed the date as 1808.) The court records show that Council directed commissioners to "allow the public hydrants to run constantly *to overcome the foulness complained of.*" This was in 1826. Then in 1829, John Heiskell, A. S. Tilball, John Bell, Wm. L. Clark, and Henry M. Brent were appointed commissioners to purchase iron pipes of six inch diameter to be laid from the spring to the jail, and other sizes for the streets. This afforded an ample supply, doubtless, for several years; in fact, no other mention is made on this score until 1836, when a question was raised about the purchase of the Tidball Spring. Some delay, from some cause, occurred in completing this purchase,—one being the necessary legislation to empower council to issue bonds, etc. In 1840 we have the following record in the old County Office: Deed from T. A. Tidball, dated June 15, 1840 "To the Mayor and Commonalty of the Town of Winchester" for the spring and house, Tidball to forever have ½ inch pipe of water from same spring, etc. (Deed Book 68, p. 407). From that date the town was secure in her water supply, receiving an abundance of water by gravity system, for all purposes; and no one of that period in the history of the town, ever imagined the day would come when the Old Tidball spring would prove inadequate to supply the demands of succeeding generations. They little dreamed it would be necessary to resort to the expensive system now used to supplement the old. Of this new system, we will now speak, though somewhat in advance of other subjects to be given, that occurred at an earlier period. About 1890, Charles B. Rouss offered to the city a proposition to increase the water supply that the modes of modern living demanded. That he would donate $30,000 for the purpose, if the City would appropriate a similar sum. The city accepted the liberal offer, and proceeded to first find a good source of supply. After many efforts, the old Hollingsworth Spring was selected, and purchased at a high price, and then began the outlay and reckless expenditure of money to convey the water to a reservoir, on a hill West of the town. This was finally accomplished; engines and pumps were installed at the Spring; pipes laid through the city; and in a short time, the town was enjoying an overflow of water. After several years experience, it was found new and more powerful engines were needed, and of course, expense of running increased; and at this writing, the city is casting about to find soft water in the mountains West of it. If this be done, the gravity system can be used, and thus the cost of maintaining the present water supply, reduced. Some one was to blame in the adoption of the plan now in use. Ex-Governor Holliday, who was the confidential friend of Mr. Rouss, advised against any plan offered, that would prevent the purchase of the spring. So many well-informed men were compelled to yield, or abandon the project and thus lose Mr. Rouss's liberal offer. The water tax derived from the new system, is sufficient to pay all running expenses; but there is a demand for soft water that will be heeded, doubtless, by the city fathers. The present abundant supply of water has induced enterprising men to locate here,—two mills already enjoying its advantages. The first was the large knitting mill on Kent Street; and then the Woolen mills, a little to the East. The large ice plant North of the B. & O. R. R. station, enjoys unexcelled facilities on this account.

Since the introduction of this new supply, the question of sewerage has agitated the public; and at this writing, an engineer has been engaged to make surveys and measurements; and upon his favorable report, the council may proceed to supply a much needed luxury to the inhabitants. It will be a desirable change from the cess-pools and surface drainage—the former a constant menace to health; the latter a trial to pedestrians.

In this connection it will be well to say that, as far back as 1813, the town authorities had some negotiations with Mr. Edward Smith, who owned a tract adjoining the western suburbs of the village, where the C. V. R. R. station now stands. This tract adjoined James Wood on the West. Smith sold 4½ acres of this land to Major Wm. Davidson and John Richardson, and mentioned that in their use of the spring at this point, they should observe contracts made by him with the mayor, and also certain private owners. Smith and Richardson erected a mill and distillery at that point, and made provision for the private owners to convey water by pipes through their lots *on the run below.* In 1819, Hugh Holmes and Joseph C. Baldwin purchased the 4½ acres together with the mill and distillery thereon, subject to the contracts previously made. Holmes conveyed his interest to Baldwin, who continued as owner until his estate was settled in 1826, when Nicholas Fitzsimmons, trustee, sold it to James Stackhouse. The deed describes accurately the 4½ acres and the buildings, consisting of a ***grist mill,*** distillery, stables, dwelling, etc. Mr. Stackhouse added his cabinetmaker's shop, lathes, etc., and must have discontinued the distillery, for nothing further is said about it in subsequent transactions with coterminous owners, relating to water pipes. All speak of the mill-race. James Stackhouse was succeeded by his son Stephen, who sold the entire property to the railroad company. He then had removed to Florida. It will be seen that other writers have erred in stating that Col. Wood erected the first mill during the Colonial period, and that it was the first mill in operation in this locality. Col. Wood's grant from Fairfax embraced this mill site. The provision for securing water from the spring at that point for the inhabitants of the town, are fully set out in the grant dated 1753; and when Mary Wood and her son Robert in 1797, conveyed 37 acres of their land including this mill-site, the same reservations are recited in the deed to Edward Smith. (These may be found in Deed Books of the old District Court, county clerk's office).

About the year 1850, Chas. Welch and George Legg erected a large mill known as the "Steam Mill." This was on West side of Market Street near the town run, and was in successful operation until destroyed by Federal troops during the War. The firm succeeded in securing a rail track down Market Street, connecting their mill with the W. & P. R. R. depot. The next mill is that on North Market Street, established by Wm. B. Baker since the War and popularly known as the mill of Baker & Co. Mr. Baker's two sons, Messrs. Albert and Alexander Baker, inherited the property, and have for many years maintained its reputation.

Illuminating Gas Introduced into Winchester

The Winchester Gas Company was a prosperous corporation organized by Act of Assembly, March 2, 1853; capital stock $60,000; shares $50. The gas house on East Water Street was and yet remains the generating power-house. The stock was purchased 1905-6 by a new corporation, known as the Winchester Gas & Electric Light Company. The streets are now lighted by electricity furnished by a corporation which, a few years ago, built great dams across the Shenandoah, and from their immense power-plant near Millville, are able to turn the wheels of large factories, mills, etc., and are now arranging preliminary plans for an electric car-line to connect Winchester with Washington City.

In 1827, a *Medical College* was inaugurated in Winchester, continuing only a few years. It was again, under a new charter, put in operation in 1847, and remained in successful operation until the beginning of the Civil War. In 1862, its buildings, which stood on the northwest corner of Water and Stewart Streets, were burned by the Federal army, because the college contained the dissected body of the son of John Brown of Harpers Ferry notoriety. Mr. Chas. L. Crum purchased the lot and erected the handsome residence seen there now, occupied by his widow and her two daughters. The faculty of the college, as it existed in 1859, was: Hugh H. Mc Guire, Prof. of Surgery, Bushrod Taylor, Prof. of Materia Medica, J. Philip Smith, Prof. of Medicine and Obstetrics; Hunter H. McGuire, Prof. of Anatomy, etc.

At a very early period in the history of Winchester, we find special attention was given to the fur trade. The pelts of animals received such treatment by the *old skin dressers,* that won preference in the far-away markets. This was a noted place for the tanning business; and for one hundred and fifty years, the town could boast of one or more tanneries. They were landmarks of the town. Streets were opened to the tan yards, and surveys to lots made respecting the rights of the tan yards along the old town run. The old bark mill and vats were curiosities to school boys, and proved very remunerative to the owners and operators. We could name several who amassed what was in those days considered fortunes. All have disappeared; and at this writing not a vestige remains of the once lucrative trade. Glove making has, for many years, been quite a feature in the town. The large factories of W. C. Graichen on N. Market Street, the F. A. Graichen factory on Water Street opposite Frederick Plaza, and D. H. Anderson on South Main Street, are successors to those who were here early in the 19th century, when Seemer, Brown, and others laid the foundation for the reputation which the products of the present operators still enjoy. The output from these factories is immense; the W. C. Graichen Company being called upon to supply the demand from the home and abroad, with its foreign trade steadily increasing.

For many years prior to 1900, the manufacture of boots and shoes on a large scale, attracted the attention of local capitalists; and the Winchester Boot & Shoe Company was organized. Business was started in the large brick building, corner Main and Cork Streets; but the project was not remunerative. Competition was too strong; and after many fitful struggles, it was sold to private parties, who later on reduced the force. The owner finally closed his doors, sold his lasts, and entered Government service, receiving a lucrative salary in his declining years. We allude to Henry Schneider, who is still a resident of Winchester.

The manufacture of stoves, plows and mill machinery, was successfully conducted prior to the War by George W. Ginn, who amassed quite a snug property, and supplied a great home demand. His cook-stoves and the old *ten-plate* were his specialties. The writer remembers well when the first cook-stoves were sold in the surrounding country, through which *Daniel Chapman,* with his wagon loaded with the new device for cooking, could be seen frequently, using great persuasion to induce the good housewives to take one on trial. The old-time colored cooks rejected the stove for a long while, preferring the old fire-place, with its *spit* and ovens.

The Snapp family of Winchester for many years conducted similar works. They own the only foundry now in Winchester.

Clippings from the Winchester Virginian, published by Robinson & Hollis, March 5, 1834.

Election Notices. Notice is hereby given that an election will be held on Monday the 30th June inst. at the several places appointed by law in Frederick County, to choose three fit persons to represent the County of Frederick in the next House of Delegates, viz: at Winchester, under direction of Sheriff, at Berryville, Middletown, Stephensburg, at Geo. Ashby's, Pughtown, and Moses Russell's. THOMAS BUCK, *Sheriff.*

The candidates were Maj. James Gibson, Richard W. Barton, Jno. B. D. Smith, Jacob Heironimous, Wm. Castleman and Dr. James Hay. The county then included Clarke and Warren territory.

Lewis Eichelberger advertises his Angerona Institute, as a young ladies' boarding and day school.

A. C. Smith has a lengthy advertisement of Smith's Seminary for boys and girls—all branches taught. Jacob Senseny, trustee, offers for sale a coach-makers shop, blacksmiths shop, coach house, and, in Wood's addition, lot No. 7 on South side of Water Street. Lloyd Logan offers 50,000 Spanish segars for sale, and Tidball's mixture snuff. Geo. and Tilden Reed say they had just covered the new dwelling house of Col. Joseph Tuley with tin. Brome and Ball offer a piano and suitable music for sale. Stewart Grant has general merchandise, hardware, china, etc. Isaac Pennington manufactures bar iron at his works on Capon River 28 miles from Winchester, for sale at $100.00 per ton, delivered at any point within 60 miles from his forge. J. Harrison & Company are one door South of Taylor Hotel, and have clothes, etc. Thos. Philips & Co., Brome & Bell, and Wm. Miller have garden seeds.

J. Kean, C. C., has a number of legal ads. The old Massie Tavern offered for sale by Isaac S. Lauck. Danner's Hotel and Stage Line Office, adjoining Middletown, offer inducements to the traveller,—just opened. Trustee's sale in front of Taylor's Hotel of tract of land 2 miles East of W. & P. R., near Seever's Tavern. James Castleman, trustee, will sell in front of court house several valuable likely negroes. James Haney has his tailoring establishment in front of court house. This paper contains a spirited correspondence between Col. Josiah W. Ware and citizens of Winchester, in relation to a division of the county, so that a county should be formed East of the Opecquon. This controversy was brought about by what was presented to the General Assembly in the form of petitions. The citizens of Winchester resented the action of Col. Ware, and published what they styled *a manifesto*. Col. Ware, in defending his position, charged the town justices with unlawfully and unjustly using the county levies to pave the *market square* and represents that the sections of the county remote from this market, should not be taxed to improve the town of Winchester; and that the section East of the Opecquon, where he lived, received no benefits. This culminated in bitter feeling, that increased; and that section waged a fight for the new county, and succeeded in having the county of Clarke taken from Frederick. This feeling found its way to the country people, and for years the contention between town and county continued. Both corporations were confused as to their respective rights and obligations. The town authorities generally appeared before the County Court, and secured *permission* to erect certain buildings and lay certain pavements on the "public lotts." The court, as shown in the first pages of this sketch, never relaxed its control. The contention existed, however, for many years. As time wore on and the town became stronger, the council felt constrained to take action in regard to her public improvements, that often savored of a disregard for the county's jurisdiction. Such, however, were always settled to the satisfaction of the County Justices. The Civil War coming on in 1861 obliterated for a time all rights, and contentions subsided. The entire population was too much absorbed with the sweeping devastation of both private and public rights and property, to advance any claims as to who should rule. The first few years subsequent to the War were full of trials to an impoverished people; and all struggled together to repair the waste places. The writer recalls with sincere pleasure his recollections of the harmony of effort manifested by the survivors of the great conflict. Then the social life began to revive; and while all struggled to get a firm footing once more, he has never known so much social intercourse to exist in the community. But new constitutions and new laws came that wrought many changes. The Pierpont government assumed the right to take possession of the State buildings in Richmond, in the Spring of 1865. Military Government asserting control, the Civil government had little to do. The Military re-organized the courts. Then followed the celebrated Underwood Constitution, with sweeping changes. The old courts gave way to the County and Corporation Judge system.

Court Trials

In the range of litigation, Winchester has had her full share; and several very important and interesting suits could be mentioned, if space permitted.

Winchester derives much comfort and many advantages from the enterprises that were ushered in with the Twentieth Century; notably, the Winchester Ice Plant, has filled the place of the natural ice-dealers, Geo. W. Hillyard & Sons, who for many years in stentorian notes apprised the citizens that Summer had come and along with it also their ice. This old-style luxury has been supplemented by the large crystal blocks of ice. Added to this plant, just North of the B. & O. R. freight station, are cold storage buildings, where fruit and food stuffs are preserved for months, awaiting better prices, etc.

The telephone system came earlier, but not so satisfactory, until the Bell System was inaugurated about eight years ago. The United and Bell companies now supply the city with wonderful advantages, both in business and social ways; while both systems have connections throughout the Valley.

The Winchester Creamery, located on South Kent Street, Jacob W. Haldeman, owner and manager, makes butter by the most modern methods, producing this table delicacy in large quantities and in most attractive styles; the farmers for many miles around supplying rich fresh milk, which being treated by large separators, gives the creamery a daily supply of cream unsurpassable.

We may properly mention at this point a charitable institution, that was established by the county and town as a home for indigent persons. This was called the *Poor House,* and stood boldly out on the western suburbs. A lot of five acres was conveyed to Richard K. Meade and others. Overseers of the Poor for Frederick County and the Corporation of Winchester by Christopher Fry, Nov. 6, 1793. The recital in this deed says "For a lot at the West end of Piccadilly Street, on the West side of the Warm Spring Road, being an out-lot containing five acres, adjoining the land of Genl. Wood. On this lot was erected a large brick building to accommodate the destitute poor and insane persons. This building was used for this purpose until 1821. In 1820 an Act of the Genl. Assembly passed Feby. 9th, empowered the Overseers of the Poor to sell this property, and reinvest the fund for similar purposes. The property was sold to Fleet Smith for $4,000; the overseers having purchased from Fleet Smith, of Loudoun County, two tracts of Land, which he conveyed by deed dated Jany. 1820, to the Overseers of the Poor, viz: David Ridgway, Philip Burwell, Wm. Campbell, Bennet Hall, Robert Bryarly, Obed Waite and others, Overseers of Poor of Frederick County and Corporation of Winchester. The two tracts of land were near the Round Hill, adjoining Weaver, Glaize and Campbell, containing in the aggregate 321½ acres. This land was formerly owned by Wm. Holliday, deceased; his heirs, Robert, Wm. M., James W. Holliday and Wm. Davison and wife, having conveyed their undivided interest to Fleet. On this land the overseers erected the brick building used at this writing, on what has been called the Parish Farm, at a cost of $4,000. In the Summer of 1821, the inmates of the *Angerona Poor House* were removed to their new quarters; and from that time the property has been continuously used for charitable purposes; presided over by a superintendent and matron. Some of the superintendents have been John Harman, Caspar Rinker, Findley Geo. W. Chrismore, James H. Canter, M. H. Albin, and the present incumbent James H. Affleck, with his efficient wife as matron. In 1828, Wm. Daniel conveyed to the Overseers of the Poor, 51½ acres of wood land West of the Poor House.

The Angerona building, erected in 1794, forms part of the handsome mansion now occupied by Thomas Cover.

CHAPTER XXIX

The Newspapers of Winchester

The first newspaper published in the Shenandoah Valley was shown the author several years ago, from which he made many notes that afterwards appeared in the history written by Mr. J. E. Norris. The paper referred to was the "Virginia Gazette and Winchester Advertiser." The first number bears date July 11, 1787, with the announcement that the proprietors Henry Wilcox & Co. will supply the "latest information from the seats of government, statements of the markets, etc.," and offers it columns for correspondents to furnish the public with reliable news." The editor announces to his readers, that he is prepared by experience in the foreign cities to give the readers such publications as will win their respect and support. The lengthy and forceful "salutatory" declares for such style and principles as would ornament some periodicals of today. Doubtless the survivors of the Revolutionary struggle needed strong food; for the country had not recovered from the direful effects of the war. Just why the Gazette changed its firm name, we are not told; but we find that August 29th Bartgis & Wilcox announce the change. Bartgis seemed to be an enterprising publisher, for we find in a notice Jany., 1788, the firm is Bartgis & Co. The success of the Gazette encouraged a similar enterprise; for April 2, 1788, Richard Bowen & Co. issued their first number of the Virginia Centinel. The rivalry that existed between these newspapers, furnish interesting matter for sensational readers; but we have not space to justify a copy of many notes in the writer's hands. An advertisement appears in one of the *Weekly issues,* that we can afford to enter, which indicates the spirit of the period. The full text will not be given as it appeared May 4, 1786. After giving the authority granted by Act of the Genl. Assembly to certain citizens of Winchester for holding a public lottery, for the purpose of raising a sufficient sum to furnish the German Lutheran Church in Winchester, two thousand tickets at $3.00 apiece were offered for sale, and the names of the managers given to-wit: Col. Chas. M. Thruston, Mr. Edward Smithy, Maj. Thomas Massie, Col. Joseph Holmes, Col. James G. Dowdall, Mr. John Peyton, Rev. Christian Streit, Mr. Lewis Hoff, Mr. Philip Bush, Mr. Geo. Kiger, Mr. Harry Baker, Mr. Adam Heiskell, Mr. Geo. Linn, Mr. Peter Lauck, Mr. Frederick Haas—all representative men regardless of denomination. Note how they regarded the undertaking! Part of the advertisement reads: "It is hoped the pious purpose of this lottery, will be a sufficient recommendation, and the friends of all Religion, of all denominations, will cheerfully help to promote it by becoming adventurers." The result must have proven satisfactory. The following appeared in the issue of the Centinel of May 14, 1788: "Last week we had the pleasing satisfaction to behold the old roof of the English Lutheran Church, in this town, taken off for the purpose of replacing it with a new one. This was much wanted, as divine service could not, for sometime past be performed there without endangering the safety of the congregations. While we congratulate our fellow-citizens on the prospect they have of worshipping their creator in this commodious edifice, we are happy in pronouncing that the public spirit in this town, tho' *situated in the woods,* is equal to that of the most populous towns or cities on the Continent."

The Gazette of July 23, 1788, has this advertisement "The subscribers for the purpose of building the Presbyterian Meeting House in the town and borough of Winchester, are requested to meet at the house of Mr. John Donaldson, on Saturday next, the 26th inst. precisely at 3 o'clock P. M. in order to adopt and fix upon a plan for erecting the same, where all persons of undertaking to build said church will please attend with their plans and estimates.

William Holliday,
James Holliday,
Robert Sherrard,
Managers."

The foregoing, aside from showing when the first newspapers were published, is of interest to the present citizens of Winchester, as it establishes and corroborates dates and incidents, mentioned in sketches of the churches, which were obtained from other sources by the author.

The two newspapers were favored with numerous and somewhat varied advertisements. For instance, the Methodists' Society gives notice in the Centinel August 26, 1788, "that they had established a Quarterly Meeting, which would be held at the house of John Milburne, on Saturday and Sunday 30 and 31st of August at 11 o'clock, each day."

The Gazette of Nov. 23, 1787, had this announcement: "Notice is hereby given that the **Winchester Dancing Assemblies** will commence on Wednesday, the 28th inst. at the house of Mr. Edward McGuire."

(Signed) CORNELIUS BALDWIN,
JOHN PEYTON,
JOHN CONRAD,
PHILIP DALBY,
CHAS. MCGILL,
JAMES ASH.

One other notice appears that "Mr. J. Moriarity informs the ladies and gentlemen that he will teach Dancing in the Modern Method of Europe at Mr. McGuire's Ball Room.

The Gazette in its issue October 12, 1787, contains the following card, so significant, that it is deemed best to have it in full.

"Messrs. Printers: As the welfare of the borough of Winchester in a great measure depends on the exertions of its inhabitants, in guarding against the most dangerous of elements, by forming a *Second Fire Company,* in this place; it is earnestly requested, that those who wish to become members, will meet, at Mr. Edward McGuire's tavern, on Saturday the 13th inst., at 5 o'clock in the evening, to propose rules and regulations for the government of the same.

Winchester, Oct. 9, 1787. CIVIS.

This card clearly shows that one other Fire Company was organized and already using its best efforts to protect the citizens; and it has been settled by investigation, that the first company was supplied with ladders and buckets; and did not have an engine. A minute in the old order book, 1784, shows they were allowed space for *ladders and buckets* in a shed adjoining the old jail. The engine is spoken of in two other issues of the newspapers in the Summer of 1788; and doubtless this was the engine we have alluded to in connection with the old engine house. Who gave it the euphonious name of "The Goose Neck," the writer cannot say. Succeeding fire companies will be mentioned later on. We will dispose of other publications while the old newspaper notes lie before us.

Judging from the following advertisements of places of business, "The Tavern" branch of enterprise claims considerable space. Edward McGuire leads the list, "offering his *services* and his *capacious tavern house* for patronage to *none other than gentlemen and ladies;* that his hostelry was open for "assemblies" and societies on notice, and his spacious *Ball room* at the disposal of dancing committees approved by him." This hotel or tavern occupied the site where the Taylor Hotel now stands, and most probably erected just prior to 1770. It was once known as the Heth Tavern, Mr. McGuire succeeding Heth as lessee about 1765, when the house was remodeled and enlarged, and grew famous under McGuire's control until about 1800.

Thomas Edmonson appears in the Centinel with his announcement that his new and modern tavern "has unsurpassed accommodations for travellers and other visitors," standing on his lot opposite Fort Loudoun, sign of the Big Ship. He also offers his *ball table* for the use of his guests "who are players of the ball and stick." "The Black Horse tavern" kept by John Walters on the "Marsh" (supposed to have been Water Street) presented his sign. So also Philip Bush with his "Golden Buck" sign, on Cameron Street South of Water. This famous house occupied a large space on West side of Cameron Street, South of the Town Run or Marsh, as it was then called, adjoining the property now the residence of Mr. Baetjer and others, formerly known as the Wm. Streit property. (The Streit property was the home of Rev. Christian Streit. Danl. Morgan and wife conveyed this property to Rev. Streit Feby. 17, 1787, and is described as on New or Cameron Street.)

When this property was yet owned by Mr. Bush's estate, the County Court secured quarters in a portion of the old building, to house the prisoners taken from the jail that had been destroyed by fire; and later on the Presbyterian congregation used it for Divine services, pending the building of the Loudoun Street Presbyterian Church. It was at this hotel or tavern that the incident occurred between Prince Louis Philipe of France and Landlord Bush that caused the latter to cut down the sign of the Golden Buck. (This tradition may receive further notice, if space permit.)

Philip Dalby in same paper, gives notice of his tavern, which stood on East side of Loudoun Street, below Cork, with the sign of the house in a rude picture at the head of his advertisement.

Many odd advertisements appear in both papers, and show who many of the business men were immediately after the Revolutionary War. And for this reason, they are entitled to brief notice: James Ridley had a factory "to manufacture stays (corsets) for ladies to suit any figure."

The Winchester Hemp and Flax Factory was started on Piccadilly Street, and able to furnish linen threads, ropes and bolting cloths.

Jonah Hollingsworth and George Mathews offer their *fulling mill,* at Abraham's Delight southeast from Winchester, for work in their line. Bookbinders were operated in connection with one of the newspapers. Archibald Magill has large *assortment* store, among many articles mentioned—"a large stock of patent medicines."

Philip Bush Jr., at the sign of the Golden Urn, opposite Mr. William Holliday's dwelling house, was jeweler and goldsmith. Robert Wells advertises to make watches and repeating eight-day clocks. The following is suggestive. Who can locate the mills mentioned? Richard Gray "wants all kinds of country produce, and will receive all grain delivered at fifteen mills, in the surrounding country, viz.: Morgan's Brown's, Helm's, G. Bruce's, Hite's, Perkins', Stroop's, Gibbs', Lewis', Bull's, Snicker's, Wormley's, W, Helm's, and Wilson's. Daniel Norton & Co. offer "Fall goods just imported in the "Dado," Capt. James Grayson, Master." This store was on the corner of Loudoun and Piccadilly Streets. Miss Maria Smith offers her services to teach English studies and "Dresden Embroidery." John and James McAlister opened a store at the sign of the Tobacco Hogshead opposite the bridge in Winchester. This was one of the largest stores in town, and aside from their regular grocery business, bought largely "leaf tobacco, genseng, deerskins, military certificates." They also secured privilege to erect a building South of the old clerk's office for a nail factory. Court required them to make it of "heavy stone and shun risk for fire." Doubtless the old building can be seen at East end of alley where it enters the county property. The court ordered the old stone shop called McAllister Nail Factory to be removed many years ago. The order was never executed. Subsequently it was used for a bakery house by Mr. Ganslen. They were Revolutionary soldiers. The late Peter Kurtz possessed the bound copies of the old papers, from which these notes are taken. On the inside cover was written "This binding is the property of James McAllester." Query. Where is now the old "binding?" John Hite, Jr., advertises his "new and elegant mill on the Opeckon." J. G. Dowdal, a merchant, offers, silks, linens, rum, wine, bar-iron and steel. Robert Sherrard's new store "offers a beautiful assortment of spring goods." Col. John Peyton orders a muster of the Militia of Frederick County. Thomas Eagan offers for sale "a valuable and convenient stone house opposite the Church on Loudoun Street." (The Episcopal Church) J. H. Jones "thanks the public for patronizing his school so liberally. William Holliday offers for rent "his elegant two story stone house," and in same adv. offers for sale "a likely Negro woman, with two children and a sign for a tavern keeper." Adam Kiger reduced his price "for making suits of clothing to twelve shillings." Archibald Magill had a fine grocery, liquor and hardware on corner of Loudoun and Piccadilly Streets. Adam Hockman puts himself up "as post rider from Winchester to Staunton—Will carry letters and packages and deliver to Newtown, Stovers Town, Millers Town, (Woodstock) New Market, Rockingham Town, Keesel Town, etc. Fifty-nine letters remained in the Postoffice held for postage—twenty-five cents due on each," and person receiving required to pay postage.

Meshach Sexton established an oil mill and hemp mill, 1788; Daniel Miller and Hank Calvert offer to make suits of clothing for twelve shillings; John Kean offers merchandise at his store adjoining McGuire's tavern. Rewards are offered by Hamilton Cooper for the return to him of his servant man Dennis Wheelen. James Rumsey, inventor of the first steamboat, describes several of his runaway servants, one of whom, Francis Murray, had his eyebrows shaved and wore an *iron collar.* The next advertisement appeared at the same time, which may startle some readers:

"Just received from Cork, and to be disposed of for ready cash, or crop of tobacco on short credit,

A few healthy men and women who have from three and one half to four years to serve under indentures. Among the men are laborers, waiters, weavers, shoemakers, taylors, whitesmiths, coopers, plasterers and tilers, hair dressers, shiners and breeches makers. The women are washers, seamstresses, etc. HOOE & HARRISON.

Alexandria, Oct. 23, 1788."

Since the "startled reader" may be perplexed for an explanation of this, we add at this point, that this peculiar condition of domestic affairs of the old settlers, prevailed throughout the entire colony, and found necessary in the development of the Country, was sanctioned by the Crown at a very early period, and a record kept by the Colonial government. And we find the *State* of Virginia, after the Revolutionary War, recognized the trade in *indentured servants.* So far as the custom relates to the Old County, our old records furnish the proof. And the reader is referred to the old Court Order Book for brief mention of the fact of such importations. And if he be curious and patient enough to learn who composed the class of citizens arriving, to become in later years in many cases useful and even prominent citizens, let him open some of the mouldy files of that period, and see many names that are familiar in our population now—the descendants of many of whom the author has had occasion to trace. No disgrace should be attached to the class referred to. They had heard of the *Liberty over in America;* and being without means to pay their transportation, were willing to endure the terms required by men and masters of the sailing craft, and thus work out their own freedom. Lack of space and other reasons forbid insertion of their names in these pages.

The following is given as a matter of reference: Order Books, Oct. 5, 1779: "James Wilson came into court and made oath that he in partnership with Samuel McChesney, Imported into this State twenty-seven Indentured Servants in the year 1771. Said *list to be recorded;* And same Ct. James Wilson and James Kelso and Samuel McChesney Imported into this State twenty-one Indentured Servants in 1772; and James Nelson and James Kelso Imported into this State One Hundred and Thirty-Six Indentured Servants in years 1772-3-4 and '75." Same Ct. James Kelso came into court and made oath that he in the year 1777 brought into this State his family consisting of twelve persons in number; Same ordered to be recorded."

The Kelso family have it settled in the brief minute, the date of their arrival in Frederick County. They became citizens of Hampshire County. The author was once called upon to show, if possible, the date of their arrival, and gratified one of the descendants, then a resident of Wyoming, with a copy of the minute.

The two old newspapers give extended notices and editorial comment on an election held in Winchester on Tuesday, March 4, 1788, the only voting place for all the county, embracing what is now Frederick, Clarke and Warren. The County was entitled to two delegates to the Convention which was to convene in Richmond, to consider the ratification of the First Federal Constitution. Four candidates were in the field; ratification was in the air; 541 votes were polled, and resulted in John S. Woodcock receiving 191 votes, Alex. White 162, Charles Mynn Thruston 71, John Smith 117. The first two were favorable to ratification. The Gazette notes in its issue July 2, 1788, that delegate White had sent a letter to Frederick by the hands of Col. R. Humphreys and Col. E. Zane, informing his constituents that Virginia had ratified the Constitution. It then devoted several columns to its report of the demonstrations that followed. Capt. Heiskell's Company of Infantry joined in a parade with the citizens and the organized societies of the place, all under the marshalship of Maj. Mc Guire; and the McGuire tavern gave supper to representatives of all organizations, where toasts were drunk to the number of thirteen, in honor of the thirteen States forming the first Federal Union. And it would seem that all had indulged in sufficient demonstration to give the Union a start on its future course. But the Centinel, in its issue of July 9, 1788, gives an account of the Ratification and Fourth of July Celebration, and says the Village could not satisfy the demand for hilarity: "That all the crafts of the town, the citizens and Military commanded by Capt. Heiskel, with Maj. McGuire, Chief Marshal, marched in procession through the streets to the *Federal Spring* at Genl. Wood's home, and there, were served with a *Barbeque* dinner."

The newspapers furnished much that would show many features of society and mode of living in that day; and we have endeavored to make a few selections that help to picture the old Town in that day, showing who were then in active life, and some of their vocations. But we must lay aside such old notes and take up another line from the old records of the county, and show what others did.

The old records referred to have been drawn upon to furnish matter in preceding pages, which brought us to the period mentioned in the old newspapers. Lack of space forbids much more that could have been added.

The Court had never up to that period been confronted with trial of murder cases. Though crimes of grave character were disposed of by the Old Justices with deliberation and promptness, it was not until 1791, that they were called upon to pass the death sentence. At the August Term, 1790, James Medlicot was tried for the murder of William Hefferman on the night of July 29th. His trial was brief. He was convicted of murder in the first degree, and sentenced to be hung. The sentence was executed after some delays, occasioned by the efforts of counsel for prisoner, to obtain a new trial. The day of execution cannot be given. An order of court in Spring of 1792 appears for the Sheriff to pay Edward Smith and Isaac Miller £1.10.0 each for erecting the gallows, showing that the execution took place shortly prior to that court.

The second murder trial in the old county court, was called at the June term, 1798, for the trial of Ralph, a negro man slave, the property of James Strother, for the murder of said James Strother and Elizabeth his wife, on the 5th of May last "by administering to them the seed of a certain Noxious and Poisonous Herb called James Town Weed." The Court was composed of Charles Mynn Thruston, James G. Dowdal, Thomas Buck, Gerrard Briscoe, Matthew Wright and Charles Smith, Gentlemen, Justices. Mr. Archibald Magill was assigned as counsel. The prisoner was found guilty and condemned to be hung on the 20th of July next, at the usual place of execution. This sounds as if there had been executions more than one; but as no evidence appears of but the one, we must conclude the court adopted the language found in the old *book of forms.* This matter is entered in connection with notes on Winchester, because the executions occurred within its jurisdiction.

The newspapers published in Winchester may properly here receive notice again. The two rival sheets, referred to, passed under the control of Richard Bowen, who started the Centinel. And he for many years just prior to and after 1800, published one paper, The Gazette. The office was on Water Street in the old stone building (second floor) corner of Water Street and Lutheran Church Alley. He was succeeded by Mr. Collett, and he successively by John Haas, John Heiskell, Freeland, Eichelberger and several others. John Foster and James Caldwell published the Constellation about 1810, and also conducted a book-publishing house. The Constellation passed into the hands of several successors; Mr. Cashell, J. G. Brooks, S. H. Davis, then to Gallagher and Towers. Peter Printz issued first copy of the Winchester Republican in 1824. Joseph H. Sherrard (Judge Sherrard) started the Virginian in 1827, which appeared weekly. During this period Lewis F. Eichelberger was editor from about 1834 and for several years thereafter, when E. C. Bruce became the owner, and later sold out to J. J. Palmer, the last owner. This was always a Jeffersonian Democratic paper. The Republican changed owners several times; Geo. E. Senseny being the accomplished Whig editor for a number of years. He was succeeded by Nat. B. Meade a year before the Civil War, and was the owner when Banks' soldiers destroyed the plant in 1862. For three years during the War, Winchester had no one willing to venture on the news line. In the Summer of 1865, Geo. R. Henry, and P. L. Kurtz, practical printers, with H. K. Pritchard as editor, started the Winchester News, and conducted a useful weekly until 1888, when the plant was purchased by Bailey & McAuliffe. During that period, Mr. E. Bruce gave much interest to the paper through his attractive editorials. In 1888, Dr. J. F. Ward and Robt. M. Ward purchased the plant, and started a book-bindery enterprise in connection with the News. They had several associates as managers and local editors: B. M. Wade, then John M. Silver, and C. H. Purcell. The plant changed hands and continued for several years by G. F. Norton. On Jany. 12, 1895, the City was surprised by the appearance of the first daily newspaper—the Evening Item, a sprightly single sheet, launched by John I. Sloat, who sold his interest to the Ward Bros. They sold the entire outfit to Mr. Norton, who gave it a start as the Winchester News-Item. Mr. Sloat, July 4, 1896, started the Evening Star. This proved a success; and the two dailies flourished for several years.

The Winchester Times first appeared in 1865; Goldsborough and Clark editors and owners. Clark soon sold his interest, and Goldsborough and Russell became owners. Maj. Robt. W. Hunter succeeded to the control of this paper, and produced an attractive weekly. Henry D. Beall, afterwards of the Baltimore Sun, purchased one-half interest, and for several years Hunter and Beall conducted a strong Democratic organ, and continually sounded keynotes for the rally of the party that reconstructed the country. Capt. E. G. Hollis succeeded Beall, and with Hunter and Hollis, many remember the excellent paper issued by them, and can recall many interviews had with the genial Hollis. Hunter afterwards sold his interest to T. W. Harrison (now our circuit Judge). R. E. Byrd purchased a half interest, and Wm. Riely became manager and local editor. In 1883, the Winchester Times Publishing Company was established; and with R. E. Byrd as editor, gave the public such additional newspaper advantages as no other point in the Valley enjoyed. In 1902, the Times purchased the Evening Star; and then a lively contest continued between the dailies, much to the edification and amusement of the many readers. This contest ended in 1907, when the Times Publishing Company purchased the News and Item plant and good will from Mr. Norton. The latter continued his job press work, and added a large stationery supply business, which he conducts in the old Star office—the old stone building on Water Street, opposite the clerk's office.

The first Republican paper to issue in Winchester was called "The Journal," A. M. Crane, editor. This also started in 1865. It was short-lived, and sold in 1869 to N. B. Meade, who started the Sentinel, a Democratic paper. After about two years circulation, publication suspended. A third paper was too much for the community. In 1884, T. H. Goshorn started another Republican paper called the Leader. It continued for a few years, under the editorship of E. D. Root, and then succumbed for lack of support.

The Republican newspaper project has never been a success here.

The City of Winchester, since the merger of the News-Item with the Times and Evening Star, has but one paper and that "The Evening Star," H. F. Byrd, manager, D. B. Conrad, local editor. This is a Democratic paper, bold and aggressive, receiving spice and stimulus from the brain and pen of Richard E. Byrd, now Speaker of the Virginia House of Delegates. The Star enterprise is successful, the paper having an immense circulation for an interior city. The plant has been fully equipped, with every up-to-date appliance for a first class daily. The paper is now (1907) firmly planted in the large brick building on Water Street opposite the City Hall.

The old Virginian was once published on same street west of this point, and also on the second floor of the old Senseny building, now the Bantz property, and the old Republican and Winchester News on second floor of the Henry Kinzel building, on corner of Main and Courthouse Avenue, occupied now by the Farmers and Merchants Bank.

CHAPTER XXX

Educational Developments in Winchester. Fire Companies

As briefly stated heretofore, the question of education received attention prior to 1787. We have evidence of the successful management of a classical school firmly established on Boscowan Street near Cameron, at that time; and so many conclude that it was the nucleus of the Winchester Academy. Certain it is that steps had been taken then to establish the Academy. An Act of the Genl. Assembly, passed Dec. 9, 1789, seems to settle this. The language of the Act is given as a matter of proof:

Sec. 1. "Whereas it is represented to this present Genl. Assembly, that the mode directed by law for appointing trustees of the *Winchester Academy* is *found from experience* highly inconvenient," etc. The Act then provides that the Trustees of the Winchester Academy holding office on the first Monday in Feby. next, "shall be and remain trustees of said Academy until they shall be removed by death, resignation; inability or refusal to act." * * * and for the better support of said Academy." Then the Act goes on to set apart certain school lands for that purpose, 1st, a certain lot or half-acre of ground in town of Winchester of which a certain Adolph Strole died seized—a tract of land in the County of Frederick, 200 acres that James Hamilton died seized, etc., and one other tract of 520 acres, late the property of Thos. Spear. This land was directed to be sold and proceeds to be used by the Trustees "most conducive to the interest of the Institution." Several places were pointed out to the writer many years ago where the "Institution" or Academy conducted its course of learning for the youths of that day, until its establishment on what was familiarly called for half a century "Academy Hill." This was an old landmark until the Civil War terminated its further use. The old foundation is to be plainly seen on the hill West of the Winchester Hospital, and on the North side of that street, once called Academy Lane. The old building was an imposing structure of brick and stone.

From this school went men thoroughly equipped for the many places of trust they afterwards filled: The writer can recall the names of hundreds—honored in all the professions: the ministry, law, medical and surgical, fine arts,—statesmen and jurists; whose voices and acts have made history, interesting for the whole land. The present populace of Frederick County and the City of Winchester shows many of the Old Academy boys holding places in the esteem and confidence of their fellow citizens. The writer recalls many of his old class of 1855-8, who went down on the battle-ground, hard by the Old Academy hill.

A few years after the War, the property once owned by Bushrod Taylor, now the site of the Winchester Inn, was used as the Winchester Academy, principal A. Magill Smith, later on by Dr. Minor and Jas. B. Lovett. Mr. Richard A. Robinson, of Louisville, Ky., a native of Frederick County, devised a sufficient sum to endow what is now the Shenandoah Valley Academy, located on a still higher point to the Northwest, on the same ridge. A provision was made by Mr. Robinson, that Professor James B. Lovett should be principal; and that Frederick County and the City of Winchester should always be entitled to a limited number of scholarships,—all of which have been complied with; and the Academy is in a flourishing condition. The feature of uniforming the students and requiring military drills, was inaugurated in 1907.

There were several other schools in the early part of the Nineteenth Century, justly entitled to special attention; but old notes have been mislaid, and the author will pass them by for the present. Rev. Joseph Baker, a Baptist Minister, conducted a young ladies seminary on Fort Hill until about 1845.

The York School for young ladies, was on Market Street (the same building after the War was known as Fairfax Hall). S. P. York, the principal, by his strong Union sentiments and utterances in the early part of 1862, was induced to hastily abandon his school.

The Winchester High School was instituted and conducted by a Mr. Thorpe, at the West end of Piccadilly, then called "Angerona." It was very successful for several years until closed by the opening of the Civil War. Mr. Thorpe was succeeded by two other principals. The school never rallied after the War.

A young ladies seminary was successfully conducted in the old Fort Loudoun property, subsequent to the War, under the management of Rev. James B. Avirett, D.D., for several years. He was once Chaplain of the Fourth Ala. Regiment. His marriage to Miss Mary Williams, daughter of Mr. Philip Williams, identified him with influential families. He was not only a successful educator but an eloquent preacher.

Fairfax Hall was founded by Rev. Silas Billings and his daughters, in 1869. This school was ably conducted by these principals for many years; its reputation attracted a large attendance of pupils from distant sections. It was popularly known as a denominational school,—Rev. Mr. Billings being a distinguished Presbyterian Divine. After his death, his daughters, the Misses Cornelia and Mary Billings, continued the school for many years. These accomplished ladies left the impress of their work and skill on the community, that outlasts their useful lives. They were assisted by their brother-in-law, Prof. Geo. C. Shepard, who finally succeeded them; and together with his well-trained and highly esteemed daughter, Miss Nina Shepard, maintained the high character of Fairfax Hall, until in 1902, inducements were offered Prof. Shepard to remove to the Winchester Inn, where the school was continued for several years, and then discontinued, regretted by many.

The Episcopal Female Institute was started in 1874 by the Rev. J. C. Wheat, D.D., as principal. This was an incorporated school. The Lloyd Logan mansion-house and grounds attached, on corner of Braddock and Piccadilly Streets, was purchased by the corporation. Dr. Wheat became famous as an educator; and worked the seminary up to a high standard. Mr. A. Magill Smith succeeded him, and for several years, assisted by Mr. Wm. Marshall and a competent corps of teachers, maintained its high standard. Mr. Smith, retiring several years thereafter to private life on his farm in Fauquier County, Mr. Marshall continued the system adopted by his predecessors; and thus by his peculiar fitness, is successfully conducting the institution at this writing.

One other school that grew famous as a ladies seminary, was started in 1866. Mrs. Ann Magill and her accomplished daughters, Miss Mary T., and Miss Eva, conducting it as a private enterprise of high order, they soon attracted the attention of influential families, and it rapidly attained a reputation that crowned their efforts with gratifying success. The school was started in the large brick building on corner of Main and Cork Streets.

This first effort was simply to provide means of support—the fearful consequences of the War having wrought such changes, that Mrs. Magill, like so many of the old families of Virginia, saw the necessity of taking up the burden; and by efforts never known to many of her class, this energetic and saintly woman was strengthened for her new trails. She lived to enjoy success in her undertaking; and her many pupils have risen at the mention of her name, in this writing, to call her blessed. The writer recalls with sincere pleasure, his impressions when viewing this body of pupils led by Mrs. Magill, as they entered the precincts of the old Kent Street Church on each recurring Sabbath morning; and can record here the feeling that others have experienced, that the sanctity of the place was heightened by the presence of this remarkable woman. Her birth, education and associations fitted her for any high station. Daughter of Judge Henry St. George Tucker, one of the most distinguished men of his day; and her husband, Dr. Alfred T. Magill, the peer of any! The school was later removed to Angerona. After her death, her daughters continued the school, until failing health required a cessation. Miss Mary Tucker Magill became the author of the history adopted by the Schools of Virginia. Other productions from her pen are well known.

The Valley Female College, which had its beginning at old Angerona, with Prof. Arbogast, principal. Dr. Hyde succeeding him, removed the school to Fort Hill, occupying the large property known as Fort Loudoun. Dr. Jno. P. Hyde, the principal having secured the fostering care of the Methodist Conference, it became very prosperous in its new quarters; and for many years Dr. Hyde was instrumental in securing a large patronage from his own church. While it was regarded as denominational in character and name, much liberality was shown, and substantial support came from other quarters. Dr. Hyde's failing health, warned him to heed the advice of his physician, and he virtually closed the college. One or two efforts were made by others to continue the work; but it was soon evident the master mind and hand had been withdrawn, and the college had to succumb. Dr. Hyde enjoys the honor, not only of being Chaplain of Turner Ashby Camp, but Grand Chaplain of the Grand Camp of Confederate Veterans of Virginia,—an office he fills with credit to himself and satisfaction to his old comrades. The affliction of impaired eyesight never prevents his attendance on all re-unions.

Winchester of to-day has another seminary that has become marvellously successful in its short history. This is *Fort Loudoun Seminary.* Two young ladies—graduates of old Fairfax Hall, and other colleges—Miss Glass and Miss Gold, inaugurated this school in 1905; and chose the old Fort Loudoun property for their first efforts. Success attended every step; a liberal patronage was enjoyed the first session. Miss Katherine Glass, one of the principals, purchased the property, and proceeded to fit up the capacious building according to her own plans and ideas. Her experience in other institutions noted for their equipment, qualified her for the task of producing an attractive home for young ladies. These accomplished principals, with vigorous womanhood to aid them, soon had a circle of instructors equal to any, and an increase in attendance at each session. The high class of culture observed, and location, gives this seminary many advantages, and increasing hope for a brilliant future. It may be observed, so far as Miss Glass is concerned, she may properly attach some sentiment to their location. Her ancestors started the town, James Wood, her maternal grandsire, being the first clerk of the county; and later, her other kinsman James Wood, Jr., was stationed at Fort Loudoun as a Colonel of the Virginia Line, and was afterwards Governor of Virginia. From the old bastions and parapets of the Fort, one views a full sweep of the Lower Valley, as he casts his eye along the horizon, where the outlines of seven counties can be traced; while in closer touch, the beautiful landscape—revealing the old homesteads, fertile valleys, green ridges and blue hillocks, a restful feeling pervades the soul of the beholder, and the exclamation comes, what a wondrous place Fort Loudoun seems for tutor and pupil!

The Public Schools

In treating of this branch of education in Frederick County, the writer feels called upon to offer some explanation of what is often called the Free School System in Virginia; and to endeavor to correct erroneous impressions formed from what other writers have given to the public. For instance, one writer says: "Until the close of the Civil War, Virginia had no public school system. All were select schools, except here and there a school for the very poor known as the 'charity' school. These 'charity' schools were sometimes kept up at the expense of the city or town where located, and sometimes established through the generosity of an individual; and none but extremely poor parents ever thought of sending their children to them, they being patronized mostly by orphans of very indigent persons." This is an unfortunate misrepresentation of the case. The writer can state there never was any such plan, or a "charity" school in Frederick County, for the education of the class referred to. And a careful inquiry reveals none such in the State prior to the Civil War. The General Assembly, by Act passed February 25, 1846, laid the foundation for Free Schools in such counties as chose to avail themselves of the right. This law provided for the election in any county; when the qualified voters could decide for or against the free school, for said county: if in favor, the taxpayers to be assessed with a school tax equal to not more than fifty per cent. on the aggregate amount of the State revenue, county levy, etc. Free persons of color not to be assessed. When such fund was acquired, the school commissioners to open schools in the districts, where all children between six and twenty-one years, could enter and be educated at the expense of said fund, when in the judgment of the commissioner, they were so entitled. Those not entitled, would be required to pay six cents for each *school day*. This law was never in force to any great extent in the State. Clarke County tried it successfully for several years. Other counties objected; and as it was not compulsory, four-fifths of them never tried the experiment.

There was no occasion for the Charity School. The class mentioned was provided for by another scheme; and children of the poor were never ostracized and shut off from other schools and society, as this writer emphatically states; and no such stigma should be allowed to pass unnoticed. It is true that the children of indigent parents were provided for, as we will show. The State of Virginia had in her treasury what was known as the "Literary fund;" and from this fund all the counties annually received their respective quotas, to be ascertained by what was known as the School Census, taken by a Commissioner holding office in each county, who also was treasurer of the county fund. His report had to show the probable number of children that would require its use. There never was any discrimination made in any of the schools. All children attended the neighborhood school; and very seldom did any pupil know who would receive benefit from the Literary Fund. This was a matter between the teacher and the commissioner, the former being paid a fixed sum for each day such pupils attended school. Joseph S. Carson was the commissioner for many years up to and prior to 1862. We must add also, what constituted this Literary Fund. The foundation was laid just subsequent to the Revolutionary War; and it is noticeable that the Civil War virtually ended the scheme. In consideration of Virginia ceding to the United States a large slice of her Western territory, the General Government was to pay annually a certain sum to the State, which she, by an Act of the General Assembly prior to 1811, constituted the Literary Fund—said fund to be used for certain well-defined educational purposes. To this fund was added all revenues arising from sales of escheated lands and town lots, or personal effects of any estate liable as escheat. This Act was passed February 9th, 1814. The fund increased rapidly, and afforded a satisfactory method for the education of the class mentioned. The Act of Assembly of 1819 provided that such children "shall with the assent of parents or guardian be sent to such school as may be convenient, to be taught reading, writing and arithmetic." This appears to have been a pretty liberal provision. We may add that it was in the same year 1819, that the University of Virginia was established, and $15,000 of this fund was used for erecting buildings, etc.

When the Civil War closed, the changed conditions of the State, with her new Constitution, provided for a free school system through special taxation. We may endorse freely the principle, though we condemn much of the mismanagement, throughout the State; but in late years the subject has received more careful attention by our legislators; and rapid strides are now being made in this laudable work.

The Public School in Winchester is a model in its work; and from its introduction, it has made a good record.

The first school was in the basement of the Braddock Street M. E. Church, with Capt. J. C. Van Fossen as principal. The attendance justified combining the schools for boys and girls, and for several years it was conducted at Fort Loudoun.

The Public School of Winchester at this writing is conducted in the large four-story building on the corner of Market and Cork Streets—with the several departments on each floor crowded. This building was erected in 1883, costing $20,000; and is known as the John Kerr School for White Children. Mr. Kerr donated about $10,000 for its erection, provided the city would supplement it with an equal amount. By the liberality of Mr. Kerr, it became possible for the city to possess the handsomest school edifice in the Valley; and under the efficient management of a Board of Trustees, the city enjoys unusual advantages under the Public School System. This school has the credit of graduating young men who have taken prominent places in the commercial life of the country; some becoming popular practitioners of the law, and others engaging in various pursuits. Capt. Van Fossen continued as principal, until death terminated his useful life a few years ago.

The public schools of the county will be mentioned in connection with chapters on Frederick County developments.

Fire Companies

Winchester has a national reputation for its well-equipped fire department, surpassing many large cities in the State in this respect. This was effected through the liberality of Charles Broadway Rouss, who always had a tender regard for his old home town. The three companies: Union, Friendship, and Sarah Zane, through this source, own their own splendid steamers; while the Union and Friendship can also boast of engine houses that would adorn any city. The Union, on corner of Water and Braddock Streets, has a commodious hall on second floor, where Mr. Rouss's birthday is annually observed on the 11th day of February, with an elaborate banquet, and orations from distinguished speakers.

The Friendship has its home on Cork Street, opposite the Baptist Church. It also has a fine hall for the use of its large company.

The Sarah Zane Company is located on corner of Main and Fairfax Lane. This company handles its steamer with a pair of fine horses.

In addition to these efficient engine companies, are the Hook and Ladder Company, on Water Street, and the South End Hose Company located on Monmouth Street between Braddock and Main Streets. Considerable rivalry has always existed between the three engine companies, not only as to service but as to priority of organization. The Friendship fixes 1831 as the time when they first responded; the Union 1833, and Sarah Zane 1840. The several companies are referred to notes on Winchester in preceding pages. They will see that, as far back as 1787, efforts were made to organize a "Second Fire Company."

CHAPTER XXXI

Old Taverns and Streets. Mayors from 1804

From old court records and other reliable sources, we find much that relates to *ye olden times.* The author is often in a quandary what to relate that would be desirable for these pages.

The names and locations of many of the old taverns in Winchester, that secured license after 1800, is briefly given, to preserve the names of owners who were active in early part of the 19th century. We find Daniel Linn opposite McGuire's; Wm. Van Horn, corner of Loudoun and Fairfax Lane. The old printer, Peter Kurtz, on Main Street South of the Marsh Run; Henry Bush, son of Philip, on Loudoun Street, where the Presbyterian Church now stands; Elisha E. Russell John C. Clark, Mrs. Edmund Pendleton and John Pitman succeeded Bush for the next twenty years. On Potato Hill, corner Loudoun and Monmouth Streets, the "Wagon and Four Horses" was kept by Elijah Walker, Benj. Richards, and Wm. Hurr respectively. This place became famous as the *Negro Traders' Jail.* The author recalls some memorable scenes there. Opposite, on West side was Philip Amick (now the home of Mrs. Spotts). L. T. F. Grim, Henry Fridley and Robert Brannon had their place on East side of Cameron Street, and Grim, Brannon and Haymaker kept a famous old tavern on the North side of Market Square, occupied now by the Holliday office buildings. In the rear were extensive wagon yards. This old house was first occupied by Conrad Kreemer; then by A. Rust. Kreemer was an old Revolutionary soldier who had deserted from the British. He was the father of the John and Conrad Kreemer families. The Kremer Bros., grocerymen, are of this line.

Peter Lauck's Red Lion on the corner of Loudoun and Cork Streets, was famous in its day. He was succeeded by popular landlords in their time—Edmund Pendleton, James Bryarly, Col. James Kiger and Josiah Massie. This old building passed to John Fagan, and is partly the residence of one of his descendants, Mr. Haines. Mr. Wm. G. Russell related many incidents of great interest concerning these gentlemen and the popular hostelry, which extended from the corner of Cork to the other tavern just North; and there was great bustle and rivalry, when the old stage coaches came in from distant points. Edward McGuire owned a stage line in connection with his tavern; and contention arose who should entertain the guests. Bushrod Taylor purchased this line when he succeeded McGuire in the tavern, and continued to wage war against the other taverns. Mr. Taylor was widely known as the proprietor of the old Taylor Hotel. He had the rare opportunity of entertaining many of the most distinguished men in their day. After the old McGuire building was destroyed by fire, it was rebuilt as it now appears. This also was badly damaged by fire several times. Mr. Taylor being discouraged, felt inclined to abandon the place, but was prevailed upon to organize a joint stock company for the purpose of strengthening the enterprise. This was accomplished in 1846. The house was remodeled, with Mr. Taylor manager, but his death occurred shortly thereafter. The settlement of his estate showed he owned 88 shares of stock valued at $3520.00, and owned all the furniture valued at several thousand dollars.

Geo. W. Seevers succeeded Taylor. The house was successfully run by such proprietors as Geo. W. Hammond (Mr. Taylor's son-in-law), N. M. Cartmell, and P. C. L. Burwell, until Genl. Banks took possession of it for a hospital in the Summer of 1862. Stonewall Jackson had his headquarters in the house for a short time. Then Genl. Banks, Sheridan and others. The old building has now been closed for several years. Prior to the War, the Union was a rival hotel, situated on the corner of Market Street and Fairfax Lane, where the Glaize lumber yards and planing mills now stand.

Philip Hoover had the tavern on the corner of Fairfax Lane and Loudoun Street, when the Civil War came. The old house is in good repair at this writing, and kept by Steve McDonald.

Some strange fatality attended the proceedings of the town government of Winchester, from the day of its incorporation as a town in October 1779, until 1804. No record can be had of the acts of the Common Council, neither the minutes of any court held by the mayor. Nothing, in fact, to show who composed the august body, the common council. Neither do we find who filled the office of mayor until 1804. Consequently, we must conclude the record was kept, but lost in some way now unaccountable. The existing record is well preserved, embracing the period from 1804 to 1811. Then another break. The records are well arranged in the fire-proof vaults of the City Hall, and so accessible, that we will not attempt to enumerate many details of the Acts of Council and Court, but refer the curious reader to the city clerk's office.

The Corporation authorities have always zealously watched over the affairs of the town. At an early day in the 19th century, the engineer had to solve two street problems: one was to drain the marshes and confine the water to one channel, to make the streets passable. Loudoun Street was opened as a road from Cork to Piccadilly in 1761—through what they termed quagmire, and which required a lottery scheme to accomplish. It was not until after 1842 that Loudoun Street was extended from Fairfax Lane North and through the stockade on Federal Hill. A roadway had been cut through the timber and hill, but the road or street received its first overseer and work in 1843. The street from Cork to Piccadilly was filled with stone and drained on each side. The other problem referred to, was the limestone ridges, from North to South, on a line immediately East of the court house, as has been stated elsewhere in these pages. In many places they were higher than the site of Major Conrad's residence. The removal of the ledges of limestone is more fully mentioned elsewhere. The lottery scheme was authorized by an Act of Genl. Assembly December 7, 1791. Geo. Kiger, Edward Smith, Joseph Tidball, John Kean, John Peyton, Lewis Huff and Isaac Stitler were authorized "to raise by one or more lotteries a sum not exceeding two hundred pounds, to be by them applied towards defraying the expenses of paving the Main street in borough of Winchester." Considerable delay followed this; and it was more than twelve years before the court passed the final order to accept the paved street and appoint an overseer, etc. The council proceeded cautiously for many years subsequent to the opening and paving Loudoun Street. The next street to receive the paving treatment was Boscowen, which was often called the Water Street, by reason of the frequent overflows from floods. There were numerous springs through the marshy section out as far as the Wood plantation. Finally a scheme was adopted to drain the marsh; and then it was the old town run became a landmark (more fully shown under head of Water Supply to the Town).

Mayors of Winchester from 1804—date of the first record, to 1811, and from 1843 to 1907:

Lewis Wolf 1804; Chas. Magill 1805; Wolf again 1806; Chas. Brent 1807; Beatty Carson 1808; Brent again 1809; Carson 1810; Joseph Gamble 1811. The records from this date to 1843 are not to be found.

Jas. P. Riely, Mayor 1843; next Geo. W. Seevers held office to 1847; Joseph H. Shearard held the office until 1865, when Robt. Y. Conrad was elected. He was succeeded by Geo. W. Ginn 1868; Capt. Lewis N. Huck 1870; J. B. T. Reed from 1872 to 1876; Wm. L. Clark to 1884; then John J. Williams until 1886.

F. A. Graichen 1886; Wm. Atkinson 1888; Wm. R. Alexander 1890; T. N. Lupton 1891 to 1896; Jno. J. Williams 1896-98; R. T. Barton 1899 to 1902; Wm. C. Graichen 1902; Harry H. Baker, June 14, 1904.

Criminal Trial

The writer has been requested to include in these notes a notice of the trial of two men for murder. Two young negro men Westley Honesty and Tabby Banks, were indicted at the November Term, 1884, for causing the death of .... McFall. They had been charged with conspicuous misbehavior during a memorable Democratic celebration of the recent victory gained by the Party in the election of Grover Cleveland, Nov., 1884. The streets were full of jubilant processions; noisy bands joined in, regardless of party lines; and all the surging crowds of people, hundreds mounted on prancing steeds —plow-horses or what not—were supposed to be in uninterrupted enjoyment of the night hours. Not so, however. Some of the processions were stoned from several dark alleys; and quite a number of persons had been injured before it was generally known. When once discovered, many of the visiting bodies declared that the guilty parties should suffer. The negroes were charged with everything, and the tumult grew serious. One of the assaults occurred nearly opposite the Taylor Hotel. Several persons saw two young negroes hastily enter the stable yard of the Haddox Building. Others who were in the yard dimly saw through the darkness, two men scale the fence; and just at this time, others on the street saw a young white man in a dazed condition. Friends hastened him to his room, without knowing what caused his trouble. Physicians called in, found his skull fractured; and the man unable to say more than that he had been struck by a brick. This incident was not generally known until the crowds dispersed. This saved the town from bloodshed, for the masses of offended white men could not have been restrained. The young man ....McFall was well known for his quiet demeanor and good habits. His death demanded that the guilty parties should be found and brought to trial. Quite a number of young negroes had been arrested for disorderly conduct. Of this number, Honesty and Banks were suspected as the murderers. Further investigations pointed clearly to them; witnesses appeared to identify them as the two men seen fleeing through the stable-yard. Others saw them in a scuffle with a young white man near the spot where their victim was found. The case coming on for trial at the December Term, of the corporation court, Banks was tried first. Judge Richard Parker appeared for the prisoners, and ably defended them. Banks was found guilty of murder in the first degree, and day fixed for execution. A stay of execution was granted, and case went to Court of Appeals. Honesty, on his trial, met the same fate. Judge Parker got both cases before the Appellate court, by reason of several strong legal points which the court sustained, though Wm. R. Alexander, prosecuting attorney, ably combatted every point raised,—Major Holmes Conrad assisting in the prosecution. The cases were not called in Corporation Court until March 18, 1886, when the opinion of the Appellate court was handed down and made part of the proceedings of the March Term. The Appellate court sustained the judgment of the lower court; whereupon the court passed sentence upon the prisoners, fixing the 4th day of June, 1886, as the day of execution for both. The execution was in the jail-yard—Westley Honesty and Tabby Banks were the only murderers hung under judgment and sentence of the Hustings court of Winchester. Several other murder cases have been tried, resulting in long terms in the penitentiary.

Opeckon Memorial Church

CHAPTER XXXII

Churches — When and Where Planted, and by Whom Established

The author will not undertake to write a history of the Pioneer Churches. This has already been done to some extent, by eminent men better equipped than he—they writing of their particular denominations, with church records to draw from for more than a hundred years, must, as a matter of fact, give better history than one who treats the subject in a general way. Such church historians as Doctor Wm. H. Foote, in his Sketches of Virginia, 1855; and Bishop Meade, 1857; "Old Churches, Ministers and Families of Va.," Sprague's "Annals of the Lutheran Pulpit," Wolf's "Lutherans in America," Semple's "History of the Early Baptists in Virginia," Rev. James R. Graham, D.D., "The Planting of Presbyterianism in The Northern Neck of Va.," 1904, and many others. A study of any of these carefully prepared histories, or even a glance at their interesting pages, would have discouraged the writer in an attempt to take up the theme and write history of the church in its early planting. He has never entertained any intention of the kind; but in writing history of the Old County and its early settlers, and of the development of the country, it would be impossible to make these pages what they should be, unless the Church, with its far-reaching influence, become a matter of frequent and extended notice. And while the author hopes to collate dates, incidents, and matter relating to the early churches, no effort will be made to gather incidents from every church erected in every locality, which would require a volume in itself, to contain such matter gathered by him from hundreds of sources. Much interesting unwritten history follows every church and its people, through all the pioneer life, and later on, by Dissenters, and mistaken governmental control—mingling of Church and State authority. With the dawning of the Revolution, 1776, came a new era, and the great Christian Church in Virginia was freed from the prejudice and misrule of those in high authority, who claimed the right to control all the Parishes of the Established Church, as well as all "dissenters, those calling themselves Presbyterians, Baptists, and any other Protestants." As all this applied to the Valley, as well as to other sections of Virginia, the writer refrains from giving any incidents that would startle the quiet and peaceful denominations found in Frederick County in recent years. While the writer may draw largely from the works of the distinguished authors referred to, he may at times in presenting his view of the early history of the Church in this section, differ with them in so far as it relates to the church antedating the church records. The writer has for years gathered from every source at his command, all data possible that would settle the question; at what point and date, was Divine Worship first held by the early settlers. In his searches, it was plain that one of the first things to be done in a new settlement, was to "fix" a place of *Worship*, and along with the erection of their rude dwellings, the log-meeting house, and school-house found a prominent place. This being the case, some settler would donate the lot and define its boundaries. If not set out in his conveyance to the *Meeting House* trustees, some subsequent conveyance would recite the fact; and thus lend much aid in fixing the location and date. So catching this idea, he has carefully examined old records for every locality from the Potomac to the Upper Valley, where claimants have arisen to claim the honor for their respective localities, as being the place where the first church was erected. He has given willing ear to tradition, which is often valuable history. Along both these lines much appears to strengthen several claims. Old Chapel, Opecquon and Tuscarora are three close contestants. Opecquon being a claimant for the whole period of its history, it is reasonable that much traditionary history attaches to it; and these traditions descend from generation to generation in such close and unbroken connection, that the author determined to test their accuracy by record evidence. A conveyance was found dated 1737, for a lot of land, with this recital: "Adjoining the Presbyterian Meeting House tract at the Opeckon." (See Orange County records.) The records of Donegal Presbytery, 1736, contain this: "Mr. Gelston is appointed to pay a visit to some new inhabitants near Opeckon in Virginia who have been writing to Mr. Gelston, and when he was over the river, desired a visit of this kind; and he is to spend some time in preaching to said new inhabitants according to discretion." Here we have both Church and County records of the place and date of this first claimant—*Opecquon Presbyterian Church.*

The next claimant is Tuscarora Church, founded on tradition and fully set forth in Howe's "Historical Collections of Virginia," page 192. Dr. Graham in his carefully prepared work on Presbyterianism in the *Northern Neck,* disposes of this claim in the following language: "Long ago it was current in Berkley County, that the spot where Tuscarora Church now stands, is the first place where the Gospel was publickly preached west of the Blue Ridge. But while the claim of Tuscarora to a very early origin is doubtless well founded, tradition of itself is not sufficient to determine a historical fact; something more reliable must be advanced if we would set aside the long accepted conclusions of Dr. Foote and others." Dr. Graham says "The name of Tuscarora in Virginia does not appear in existing Ecclesiastical Records until April 1760." The author has resorted to the public records for evidence of this claim of Tuscarora, and would gladly furnish such, for she has a grand history and is entitled to all we could give to distinguish her from the sister churches. Old records give nothing to encourage a claim prior to 1763.

Old Chapel has much recorded evidence to sustain a claim of priority, as will be seen in Chapter I, of this volume, in giving details of the first Courts. December 1743, it was ordered that a road be cleared and opened from the head of the Spring by the *"Chappel* to John Ewans," as it had been formerly laid off by Order of Orange County Court. This is evidence that a Chapel was a chief feature on this road, and must have been a place for preaching the Gospel, as its name denotes; and it was there in 1743, and how much longer before this date, made it an interesting feature in trying to settle the question of priority. Of course, the original order of the Orange Court was anxiously examined to see if the name Chappel appeared in the order referred to. The route of the road is described as "intersecting a Road from the Opecquon Ford to the big spring, thence through the big timber, to the river and into the road leading to Rappahannock." The petition was signed by Patrick Riely and others, thus connecting the two orders of court; but nothing is said about a "Chappel" in the Orange order; so we must infer that this *"Chappel"* must have been erected subsequent to the date of the first order, but prior to the date of the latter. The author hoped for much in reading Bishop Meade's Old Churches, etc., thinking if Old Chapel of the present day was entitled to distinction of this character, the Bishop would gladly give it. Speaking of the five different divisions of Frederick Parish, he says: "After itself had been reduced by Acts of Assembly, I proceed to mention the new churches built since the Revolution. Among the first things done by the Frederick Parish, after its reorganization in 1787, was the adoption of measures for the building of a Stone Chapel where it was designed to erect that one which failed through the disagreement of the people and Vestry, just before the Revolution, viz, where that called Cunningham's Chapel stood. The land having now come into possession of Col. Nathaniel Burwell, the same two acres for a church and burying-ground, which were offered by Col. Hugh Nelson before the war, were now given by Col. Burwell, and the present Stone Chapel ordered to be built in 1790."

It will be seen from this quotation, that Bishop Meade fixes no date for the building of the original Chapel, nor does he tell who the Cunningham was, whether he was minister or layman; and no mention that it stood there on the old site in 1743. Upon the evidence submitted, it is hoped that the conclusion is reached, leaving no doubt that it was the Old Opecquon Meeting House, where the Gospel was first preached West of the Blue Ridge. Assuming this to be true, we will proceed to give some incidental history of the churches of Old Frederick, starting with Old Opecquon. Doctor Foote in his "Sketches of Virginia," says: "About three miles from Winchester, on the paved road to Staunton, on the western side of the road, near a little village (Kernstown) is a stone building surrounded by a few venerable oaks. That is Opecquon Meeting House, and between it and the village is the Grave Yard, in which lie the remains of some of the oldest settlers of the Valley. This house is the third built on this site for the worshippers of the Opecquon congregation to this date, 1855." Says Dr. Graham in his work: "The first Presbyterian Minister west of the Blue Ridge, of whose history and fields of labor we have *distinct* and *unquestioned knowledge,* was Rev. Samuel Gelston, who preached at Opecquon in 1735. He was born in Ireland in 1692. He came in 1735; the next year application for his ministerial services was made to New Castle Presbytery, from both parts of *Opekon* and Cedar Creek, which two churches for nearly a hundred years were associated in one pastoral charge. Rev. James Anderson visited same field in 1737; and during this visit he organized the Opecquon Church. And it was this Mr. Anderson who was chosen by the Dissenters West of the Blue Ridge to bear their complaints to the Colonial Government, setting forth the persecutions made by the Established Church, and praying for relief. Gov. Gooch was then acting Governor; and it was through his influence that the Dissenters were allowed greater privileges than those of the Tide-water sections; and doubtless this was why the Scotch-Irish and other Presbyterians flocked to the Valley of Virginia during the 18th century." Mr. Anderson leaves no record of his pastorate. Dr. Foote says "That in 1739 Mr. John Thompson, as an evangelist, preached at Opecquon and the new settlements on the frontiers of Virginia, and that Mr. Wm. Robinson, on his long-to-be-remembered tour through Virginia and North Carolina, repeatedly preached at Opecquon in 1742." The Presbyterial Records of Old Donegal Presbytery furnish the names of Rev. John Hindman, Samuel Caven, Wm. Bertram, —— Linn, and Alexander McDowell, as frequent visiting Ministers from their Presbytery to do Missionary and Evangelistic work at Opecquon, Cedar Creek, and elsewhere. This was continued at intervals until 1754, when we find Opecquon with her first Pastor, who was Rev. John Hoge, grandson of Wm. Hoge (Hogue), who gave the land on which the first Meeting House was built. Mr. Hoge's pastorate continued for eighteen years. The Presbytery records show that his salary was scarcely adequate. He made complaints of privations and great labor while he rendered efficient service to the early settlers, and that he did not receive sufficient support from the two churches to justify his further service in this field. This last statement to his Presbytery, produced prompt action in that body, for this language appears: "Mr. Hoge is released from his pastoral charge on account of non-payment of salary." We find these churches for some years after the withdrawal of Mr. Hoge, were supplied by Revs. Vance, McKnight, Thompson, Slemmons, Craighead, Balch, Linn and others who had pastorates in other sections. We have evidence of Mr. Hoge being a resident of the Opecquon Valley up to 1775. In 1781, Rev. John Montgomery received a call from three churches—the Opecquon, Cedar Creek and Winchester. In 1789, Rev. Nash Legrand succeeded Mr. Montgomery, and continued his acceptable service until 1809. Dr. Graham says: "Legrand was never installed in the Opecquon field, though he continued his labors for nineteen years, when impaired health compelled him to resign." Dr. Graham further says: "Mr. Legrand died in 1814, while on a visit to his old friends in Frederick County, and his unmarked grave is in the burying-ground of his old Stone Church in Winchester."

Unfortunately no church records were preserved for many years; and this state of affairs narrows the history of the church to either tradition or Presbyterial reports. After Mr. Legrand's ministry closed, the church was supplied by many distinguished ministers: A. A. Chapman, John Lodor, David H. Riddle, J. D. Mathews, Dr. Wm. Hill, Mr. Kilpatrick and others. The church in Winchester increased as the population grew, and exercised some kind of control; and the congregation received attention from the Winchester Church. Especially was this the case after the organization of the New School Church (Loudoun Street), under the pastorate of Dr. A. H. H. Boyd and by Rev. Silas Billings from Cedar Creek. The old church was never without regular preaching, the congregations however diminishing as removals occurred, and disposition on the part of many families to attend the Winchester churches, though the old Opecquon was never closed until the Battle of Kernstown, with its attendant devastations, which put the old stone building in such condition, that services were discontinued until the close of hostilities. Then it was soon overhauled by Rev. Wm. A. Crawford, who had recently become a resident of the neighborhood, and through his efforts, aided by his accomplished and saintly wife, converted one end of it into a habitable place. Sunday School and Gospel Services were eagerly enjoyed by the neighboring families, irrespective of *Creed;* and for several years regular services were held. However, a day came when fire destroyed the old temple. For many years thereafter, the walls were tumbling in, and the old graveyard so long neglected, was at last hidden out of sight by bush and briar. All lost hope of restoring the old place, excepting Mr. Crawford and his family. At last the day came, when the descendants of the old ancestors, whose graves were hidden in the wilderness, agitated the subject, often discussed, and as often abandoned it. Finally it was suggested that an effort be made to erect a Memorial to the first settlers of the Lower Shenandoah Valley. Plans were at once adopted; the author was made chairman of the "Church-Erection Fund." He immediately addressed a circular letter to the descendants of the old families, whose names were found on the monuments and broken slabs in the old graveyard, stating the object. The descendants alone were expected to contribute funds to reclaim the old place, and erect a suitable memorial on the foundation of the old church. This circular was sent to the Middle West, Northwest and other States, to the newspapers in many cities and towns. Contributions were to be sent direct to the cashier of the Shenandoah Valley National Bank at Winchester, to be placed to the credit of the *Church Erection Fund;* the sender to notify T. K. Cartmell, Clerk of Frederick County Court. Interesting and encouraging letters, with liberal contributions, came from every section. This first step was taken in January 1896, and in the Spring the work of cleaning away the old foundation began; and soon new walls were started on part of the old foundation, which was 60 feet in length and 45 feet in width—the Memorial Building to be much smaller. The committee chose the foundation on the West and South sides, Workmen and committees worked cheerfully, and in a short time, the blue limestone walls were run up to a point where the *Corner-Stone* was to be laid; and quoting from The Evening Star, a Winchester daily, we have the following notice written by some visitor:

"*Corner Stone Laid.*—Accepting the invitation of some friends, the writer joined a party to visit the Old Opecquon Church yesterday afternoon, where we found quite an assemblage of interested persons, irrespective of sect or creed, the occasion being to place the corner stone in position. The Memorial Building, which is rapidly going up, is a most artistic piece of work, the limestone rock from the old ruin being used as far as practicable. The services yesterday afternoon were intended to be informal. Rev. Henry M. White, D.D., pastor of Loudoun Street Presbyterian Church, read appropriate Scriptures, also a paper prepared by him recounting some incidents of the early history of the church, as well as the names of the ministers who have from time to time preached in the old Church, and also matters incident to the present effort to erect this Memorial to the departed people. Mr. C. G. Crawford, Ruling Elder of the present Church, read a list of the membership, and also the names of the contractors and workmen engaged on the new work. Rev. Wm. A. Crawford offered a most impressive prayer; Mr. T. K. Cartmell next announced a list of the contents of the box, which included copies of the Star, all placed in the Stone by Master Frank Crawford, then the Willey Brothers, contractors, laid the Corner-stone to the satisfaction of all present; the inscription on the stone being:

"Organized about 1738——Built 1790——Rebuilt 1870—73——Rebuilt 1896.

VISITOR."

Work proceeded steadily until the structure with its walls of hewn stone, unique tower—home for the sweet toned bell—(a special memorial) gothic style of architecture, memorial windows, etc., fully completed in October 1897. The dedication service October 30th, was a memorable event. Descendants from far and near, were early on the ground, members of Winchester Presbytery from various churches were present. Dr. Jas. R. Graham opened the services with an invocation; Rev. A. C. Hopkins, D.D., of Charlestown, in a happy address, presented the keys of the church to Elder C. G. Crawford; prayer by Rev. Wm. A. Crawford. Dr. F. M. Woods, of Martinsburg, preached the sermon, after which luncheon was served on the grounds. In the afternoon Dr. H. M. White, who has had the pastoral care of the Opecquon Congregation for several years, made an address full of historical events relating to the Old Opecquon. Dr. Jas. P. Smith, editor of the Central Presbyterian, well known to many as Stonewall Jackson's Aid and Chaplain, was the bearer of a letter from Rev. Moses D. Hoge, D.D., addressed to the writer, chairman of the finance committee. This letter contained a liberal contribution to be used in the memorial to his ancestors; and the writer was requested to read the letter to the audience. Rev. A. G. Link, of Strasburg, Cedar Creek, and Cedar Cliff churches, Rev. W. Mc. White, of Lewisburg, were present. Ministers from other denominations were present and entered into the services with great cordiality. One pleasing incident of the day occured when one of the Winchester artists appeared on the grounds, and desired views of the scene. He was fortunate in securing several of these. The old graveyard, recently reclaimed and with its old grave-stones in better position than they had been for a number of years, and the *sacred acre* enclosed with a wrought iron fence on the West, South and East sides, on the North end with a limestone wall formed from the remnants of the old yard fence, supplemented by rocks from the old church walls, presented a picture that was inviting to the eye of the artist; so he soon adjusted portions of the crowd, to give in the photograph a picture of the church, the old graveyard, and also those who were prominent in the day's services. Many of these photographs found their way into many distant homes. The old graveyard was visited during the day by many visitors. About the center of this plat stands a rude and odd-shaped sand stone, bearing marks of time, as the crumbled edges show, caused by bullets during the battle that once surged through the grounds, or from atmospheric influences. Whatever be the cause, the stone itself attracts attention from its jagged edges and rude appearance. But the strange inscription is startling. The writer many years ago, made a fac-simile copy, so that it could be preserved before further defacement would destroy its history; and to better preserve it, gives this space. On one side is the following:

Opeckon Graveyard

"John Willson
Intered here The Bodys of
His 2 Childer & Wife Ye Mother
Mary Marcus, Who Dyed Ag'st The 4—1742
Aged—22 Years

On the opposite side are these letters:

"FROM
IRL,AND
July Vi, th 1737
Co y Arg ma
G H"

Dr. Foote in "Sketches of Virginia" (1855) says: "This stone was the first reared in the Valley of Virginia to mark the resting place of an emigrant, and the inscription should be preserved; the stone was erected by the husband who inscribed the letters himself, to be a memorial to his young wife and children, and tradition also says he was the School-Master."

On the North side of this yard, we find much space occupied by the Glass family, and a limestone monument tells its own story. "Erected to the memory of Samuel Glass and Mary Gamble his wife, who came from Ban Bridge, County Down, Ireland, taking their abode on the Opecquon in 1736." (See Glass Family Sketch.) In the plat surrounding this Glass monument lie several generations of this family, some marked by simple marble slabs bearing names and dates. Dr. Foote in his Sketches, gives place for a poem in connection with his visit to this monument, written by a young lady who had so often charmed the worshippers in the Old Church with the melody of a voice that ever softened the heart and fastened impressions upon the memory of all, of the lovely life that was so soon to close, and she to take her place by the ancestors. One simple slab bears the name of Miss Sarah A. Glass, the authoress of the poem;. We give the first and last lines of this lengthy poem:

"Hear you not the warning sigh
On the breeze that passes by;
Lingerers near this solemn ground,
To our silent home ye're bound."

"Lingerers! idle not your day;
Fly and seek Him while you may."

Another monument attracts attention, standing directly South of the Glass shaft. On this white marble shaft, we read that it was erected in memory of the Gilkeson family. On one side is "John Gilkeson died June 1793; Sarah Gilkeson died March 1810." On the other side—"Col. John Gilkeson Sept. 15, 1783——Feby. 27, 1856. Sarah L. Gilkeson Aug. 21, 1781——May 30, 1847." Around this monument are many slabs marking the resting places of several generations of this large and influential family. The writer will mention here that the Col. John mentioned, was the father of Mr. John Gilkeson who so liberally contributed to erect the Memorial Church; and also by the generous efforts of his widow, the Church bell and graveyard fence were their joint memorials. The Church bell deserves special mention here, lest it be forgotten. Mrs. Gilkeson wrote the author that she desired a bell to be made according to her own plan, and entirely at her expense; that she would have her husband's friend, who had been his secretary for thirty years, proceed to Albany N. Y. and carry with him valuable jewels that were valued highly by her and her husband, and have the founder fuse them into the molten mass, which was to be cast into this Memorial bell. The finished work was carefully brought to the writer, with letters from Mrs. Gilkeson requesting "That we bear in mind that if any accident occurred in fitting it in its home, a broken bell meant a broken sentiment."

Our committee was greatly rejoiced and relieved when the cords were drawn and the sweet tones of this memorial were heard twelve miles away. Its music is now heard on each recurring Sabbath, reverberating among the Opecquon vales and dells. The writer trusts that readers of these lines will pardon this digression. Such sentimental incidents are often forgotten, and told in after years, would be as mere tradition, with none to vouch for the real incident. East of the Gilkeson shaft, are marks of the resting places of many others. Mention of any of the names in the group will interest the reader—Willson, White, Hoge, Vance, Marquis, Hite, Davis, Simerall, Chipley, Ashby, Ashley, McAuley, Massie, and many others who represent pioneer classes, whose names will more fully appear in other pages. The old Cemetery has been considered filled many years ago; many graves have no marks now, their old markings destroyed; for war devastates the most sacred of all places; and now much of the old place will forever remain a blank.

Bullskin Church

According to the most reliable information obtained from old county and church records and other sources, we find this church entitled to recognition as one of the old places of public worship. Dr. Graham says "The name of Bullskin Congregation appears in the old Donegal Records for April 1, 1740, and that Mr. Caven is directed to visit Bullskin and that he should preach at *'Upekin,'* the Friday before going to Bullskin." The church stood near the headspring of Bullskin Creek. This spring is nearly a mile South from Summit Point, in Jefferson County, W. Va., near a turnpike road to Berryville. Many evidences are to be found that this church was well supplied by able Ministers for many years; but to-day, strange to say, not a vestige of the old church remains, and very few of the old residents can recall anything connected with it. The name seems to have disappeared from among the Presbytery records very soon after 1795. Dr. Graham also says Mr. Legrand was there in 1791, and that Dr. Archibald Alexander (then a licentiate), accompanied him from Winchester, and they held services in the Old Church on the hill; and that services began to be held at other and more central points, which gradually drew away the members from the old place. Dr. Wm. Hill was called by the Charlestown and Smithfield Churches to be their pastor, and doubtless this hastened the abandonment of the old church; for Dr. Hill at that time was attracting wide attention."

South Branch Church

We have evidence of the existence of a Presbyterian preaching place at some point in the South Branch Valley, as shown in the church records of Donegal Presbytery, Dec. 11, 1740, and again May 30, 1741. Old county records show that several settlements were petitioning the court for roads, etc. The location of this church is not known at this writing. It is well known, however, that there were several preaching places near the mouth of South Branch River in the early days, but no regular churches. Dr. Graham says no such church was ever organized.

Cedar Creek Church

This old Church deserves special mention. The writer has been familiar with that section of the county and the incidents of the church history throughout his entire life; and the many traditions told in his hearing as a child, verified by repetition in later years, all led him to believe that the antiquity of this old stone church, standing near one of the grandest springs in all the country, on the edge of the *Glebe Lands,* antedated all other churches excepting Opecquon. But we must yield to Dr. Graham's Church History, and have Cedar Creek come in as number 4, though so many things have occurred in the relations between Opecquon and Cedar Creek, that we still hold to the belief that the Opecquon pastor preached at this point. In the very early records of the Old County, may be found a reference to the Meeting House lot near the Big Spring. In Deeds for lands surrounding this place, this language is used in one to define the boundary: "On the south end of the Meeting House property near the Big Spring." This deed was dated 1736, and recorded in 1745; so we see there was a Meeting House there in 1736. This date corresponds with one tradition, which was, that when the first meeting house was built, *it was before there was a Frederick County.* The stone church building now in use was the one that was rebuilt since the Civil War, and on the site of the old stone church erected prior to the Revolutionary War. The front was changed. It will be observed this was not the site of the old Meeting House which stood northwest about one hundred yards distant. There is a deed dated 1762, made by Lord Fairfax, in which he conveys 100 acres of land to Wm. Vance, Wm. Evans, James Colville, James Hogg and Andrew Blackburn, elders of the Presbyterian Congregation of Cedar Creek, for the purpose of building a meeting house thereon.

The writer recalls many delightful seasons in the history of this church, especially so when Rev Silas Billings was Pastor of the Woodstock Church. He also served this church so acceptably, that many of the older residents take delight in recounting incidents of the old *Protracted Meetings* Mr. Billings often held. It was an ideal place in the Summer months for such services. The fine spring near-by, the rocky cliffs well shaded by the old forest trees, the woodman's axe had spared, all lent a charm to the place; and good cheer came when heavy baskets were carried to the many rock-brakes, where natural rock tables were found, to spread the lunch that so bountifully served the many couples under the boughs of the oaks. Mr. Billings was not only a good preacher, but renowned for his splendid church music. His voice strong and well trained, was so full of melody of the *old time singing,* that listeners never grew tired. At those meetings could be seen many people from Round Hill, and the head of Opecquon and other sections. The Hoge family lived in that section at one time, when Rev. John Hoge was pastor of this church. This church is near Marlboro Post Office, in the South end of the county, distant from Winchester about twelve miles.

Tuscarora Church

The author at one time was much concerned in relation to a claim set up by friends of this old church. It was when engaged in working out the history of Old Opecquon, he received a letter from a friend, the scholarly writer of "Sketches of West Virginia," announcing that he had discovered the point where the Gospel was first preached West of the Blue Ridge, and that the point so found was where the old Tuscarora church stood, arguing that it was one of the earliest settlements in the Valley, with many good reasons given to sustain the claim, and referred to Howe's History of Virginia. His "Sketches of Virginia" gives the reader many pleasing incidents; and the Tuscarora incident is one. We give in full what he says: "Many of the early settlers of Berkly County were Scotch-Irish who were Presbyterians," and then adds: "It is said the spot where Tuscarora Meeting House now stands, is the first place where the Gospel was publicly preached and Divine Service performed West of the Blue Ridge. This was and still remains a Presbyterian edifice." Howe gives no other explanation. He gathered his information in the usual way—from interviews with residents of the sections he visited in 1843. No mention made of county or church records. This presented a question that to be settled in a more authentic way. The records of the county and church were studied, but revealed nothing to sustain the claim. Old county records refer to church property in 1764, in certain deeds conveying lands on Tuscarora Creek from Beeson and others, one of the recitals being, "The parcel or lot of land for the Meeting House is hereby excepted." It is fair to assume that the meeting house was the old Presbyterian Church, known as *Tuscarora,* and has been so regarded in all these years. Old Church records fail to give a word concerning Tuscarora until 1760; and here we quote Dr. Graham, who says: "The name of this church does not appear in any existing Ecclesiastical Record until 1760. This will excite some surprise, as the accepted local tradition is that its existence precedes that date by at least fifteen, if not twenty years." Dr. G. also says: "Supplications from 1762 until 1771 were made regularly for supplies for Tuscarora at nearly every stated meeting of the Old Donegal Presbytery," and that the following ministers were sent as supplies—for a number of years, viz, Messrs. McGann, Roan, Hemmons, Cooper, Craighead, Alexander, McCreary, Hoge, Balch, Lewis, Lang, Vance, Thompson, Duffield, and Rhea. For sketches of the pastorates of these ministers, see Dr. Jas. R. Graham's "Planting of Presbyterianism in the Northern Neck." This Church had a large membership when the Winchester Presbytery was organized in 1794. This membership lost much of its strength in after years, as the Martinsburg church grew in strength. The church is one of the country appointments of Rev. Dr. F. M. Woods, Pastor of the Martinsburg Church. The present old stone building was erected about 1811 and is the third building erected at this point.

Back Creek Church

From church records, this is an old church, receiving attention from the old Presbytery at same period that Tuscarora first appears, 1760. It is located in a rich valley about eight miles West of Martinsburg, and about four miles southwest of Hedgesville. The large stone building now in use by this rich and prosperous congregation, stands on the West side of the Creek, near the celebrated *Tomahawk Spring,* and was erected more than a hundred years ago. This church had for its pastors such men as Hoge and Vance. (It was once called Vance's Meeting House.) The author has in his possession part of the Diary of "Fithian," a man remarkable for his Evangelistic work among the early churches of Virginia and North Carolina. This diary has been carefully preserved by the family of Rev. Joseph Glass, who for many years labored in that section. Mr. Fithian was sent out by the Donegal Presbytery to do special work; and being thoughtful enough to keep a diary of his travels, and what churches he visited, his notes can be regarded as reliable and very useful. His Presbytery so regarded it; and from this source the author is aided in these sketches. We give one of his notes in full, to show his brevity and accuracy. This was several years after his first great *"Rambles through Virginia and Carolina."* "Sunday, June 18, 1775, over the North mountain I rode to Mr. Vance's Meeting House at Back Creek. The Sacrament was administered, Ninety-three communicants, vast assembly. The North mountain is very high, at the top it is almost bare. The view below on each side is rich and beautiful, on each side we see ridges of hills, and ridges on ridges still succeed until you cross the Alleghaney."

Ca Capon Church

Says Dr. Graham, "This Congregation asked the old Presbytery to give them a separate Organization in 1768, and Mr. Hoge was appointed to supply the Forks of *Cape Capon."* Tradition has it that a Presbyterian church was maintained at this point, but was abandoned in the early part of the 19th Century; and the membership drifted to the Bloomery Church about four miles from the *Forks.* The Bloomery Church barely exists at this writing.

Falling Waters Church

This old Church has a history very familiar to the Presbyterians of the Lower Valley. For some reason its record places it as the ninth church in point of date to receive recognition by the Donegal Presbytery. However, it has such traditionary history as makes it very reasonable that the Irish settlers who were there in 1745, organized a church at what is known as Lower Falls. Old county records show that a large colony of Irish and Scotch immigrants settled near the "Ford," on the South side of the Potomac, and were there in 1744, contending for titles to their "preempted lands." Says Dr. Graham, "The name of this church appears for the first time in Church records, April 28, 1762. But the first appearance proves that this church was strong, and had evidently enjoyed ministrations of the Gospel for a long time; and when Presbytery appointed ministers to give this church attention evidence appears that this congregation tendered a liberal support. Mr. Fithian says, "In 1775 Mr. Andrew Hunter and myself visited this church—having crossed the Potomac May 19th—on our way from Hagers Town and arrived among Mr. Hunter's relatives, and was introduced to Mr. Hunter's Mother, sisters and brothers." Mr. Fithian gives this interesting note: "Sunday, May 21 (1775), Mr. Hunter and I preached at Falling Waters Meeting House. It stands on the Potomake, is well situated, and I am told is a numerous society. The people gave good attention, sang the Scotch, or as they called them David's Psalms. The congregation is chiefly made up of country Irish and half Scotch, most of them Presbyterians. We dined at one Bowland." The Church records show that the ministers who were preaching at several of the churches heretofore mentioned, were the "Supply" for this church until about 1792. Subsequent to this period, Dr. Graham says the following named ministers were pastors: Jno. B. Hoge, 1811-1822; Jas. M. Brown, 1834; J. E. Woodbridge, 1835-36; Lewis F. Wilson, 1837; Henry C. Brown, 1875-1877; J. H. Gilmore, 1878-89; S. M. Engle, 1891-94; Edward R. Leyburn, 1895-1902; J. C. Leps, 1902.

Pattersons Creek Church

The Scotch-Irish settlers on the Pattersons Creek Manor in their conveyances at an early day, mention the *Meeting* House property,—nothing to show what sect or society. By reference to Dr. Graham, we are able to say the Presbyterians occupied a church on this creek in 1768, and had a prosperous congregation in 1781, and that Rev. Mr. Waugh was their first Supply. The first regular pastor, Rev. Thaddeus Dodd, was there in 1777-1779. Dr. W. H. Foote was Pastor 1846-1860, while he had the field embracing Romney and Springfield. M. W. Woodworth, 1865-1887; J. M. Duckwall, 1889; I. N. Campbell, 1891-93. Other Ministers supplied this Church at various times.

Shepherdstown Pres. Church

This Church has many claims for distinction, one being that they entertained the Virginia Synod in 1799. They also claim it to be the oldest Church Organization in the Valley of Virginia. This has often been discussed by other claimants. No record evidence can be found to support the claim. Dr. Graham gives some strong reasons in support of the claim. He says, however, "that it was in 1768 the name first appears in the old Donegal Presbytery records, and from this date to 1783, the church had no regular pastor, but was supplied no doubt by such men as Rev. John McKnight. This continued to 1787, when Rev. Moses Hoge settled there and ministered to this church as their Pastor for twenty years." Next came Rev. John Mathews, 1808-1830; E. C. Hutchinson, 1830-33, also John D. Mitchell, 1830-31, both being "supply;" John T. Hargrave, 1834-39; Joseph M. Atkinson, 1845-49, pastor; A. C. Heaton (supply), 1851-54; Henry Mathews, 1853-60; Robt. L. McMurran, 1860-66; E. W. Bedinger, 1867-70; Henry C. Brown (supply), 1873-74; Jas. A. Armstrong, 1880-83; Charles Gheislin, 1883. Under his pastorate this church enjoys great prosperity.

Elk Branch Church

This Church is located at what is known as Duffields Station on B. & O. R. R., about six miles West of Harpers Ferry. The building is on the North side of Elk Branch. This place had some notoriety in the early days. A small fort was there, and the stockade enclosed the large spring and it was at this point where the first Church stood. For convenience of site, the congregation erected the present building, which is about a half mile East. Church history says this Church first appears 1769. Tradition gives a much earlier date, and many accept the latter as reliable. Dr. Graham says, "The same Ministers supplying other churches in the Lower Valley, were supplies of Elk Branch." John McKnight was the first pastor, 1776, served until 1782. No other church records of this church until 1833. Since then the church has prospered under the pastoral care of Rev. Silas Billings, 1858-1869; John A. Scott, 1870-90; Robt. B. Woodworth, 1891-93; J. E. Triplett, 1893.

Hopewell (Smithfield) Presb. Church

This is the name given to the Smithfield Church in Jefferson County. The writer was much confused several years ago while collecting these notes—two Hopewell Meeting Houses in Quaker settlements in same county—the old stone

Hopewell house a few miles North of Winchester, on East side of Apple-pie Ridge, and the Hopewell Church mentioned in the old Presbyterial records, raised the question if the Hopewell (now Smithfield) might not have been a Quaker Meeting House. But a careful investigation cleared the atmosphere around this old Presbyterian point. With a few exceptions, this church has been regularly supplied, and has prospered. Its first record is 1773; the first stated supply was Rev. Jas. Martin and John Hoge, 1780. Dr. Wm. Hill served this church during his eight years ministry at Charlestown and Bullskin, 1791. Other Ministers supplied the church for several years, covering the ground until Rev. Wm. C. Walton came, 1818-23; J. M. Atkinson, 1845-49; Edwin L. Wilson, 1875-93; Chas. R. Stribling, 1893-97; R. Ashlin White, 1897.

Springfield Church

This church is in Hampshire County. The record does nothing more than to reveal the fact that a church was at this point in 1792, when Rev. John Lyle served the church for fifteen years, living at that point. Dr. Foote says Mr. Lyle was ordained by the Presbytery of Lexington, at Springfield, Nov. 30, 1793. His permanent residence until his death was at Springfield, dividing his time between Springfield, Romney, and Pattersons Creek. That he established a classical school at Springfield, which attained great celebrity. Mr. Lyle married a sister of Rev. Joseph Glass, a granddaughter of Samuel Glass the emigrant. Other ministers serving this church as pastors, were Dr. Wm. H. Foote, 1845-1860; George W. Finley, 1870-91; Carson W. Hollis, 1893-94; G. A. Gilbortzer, 1895-1902; Edward A. Snook, 1902.

Romney Presb. Church

For more than a hundred years this church has been prominent in the records of the Winchester Presbytery, always presenting features of strength and influence in the Hampshire County Ecclesiastical field. Composed of men of zeal, wealth and intelligence, the membership in general being above the average; supplied with ministers of marked ability, the impression was easily made that the Romney Church ranked with the oldest churches West of the Blue Ridge. The writer was astonished and confused, when investigating the origin of this church, that no early record could be found—either church or county—to throw any light on the subject. It was well understood that no county record was expected to be found concerning the town itself earlier than its incorporation as a town in 1762, as the county seat was elsewhere. Therefore the first public record of the town, gave no encouragement that a search of the court records would reveal anything relating to the Romney Church prior to this date; and indeed quite a long time elapses after that date before mention is made of it. Tradition has a church organization on the South Branch at a very early day; and that, too, within the bounds of what was afterwards Romney, the county seat. The first Church record is to be found in the Minutes of the Old Donegal Presbytery, October 1781, when this Presbytery was requested to send an Ordained Minister to assist the congregation in completing an Organization, and to ordain Elders. And in this request, this congregation was joined by the congregation of Pattersons Creek. This indicates that both places were occupied by Presbyterian congregations at a period much earlier than this Presbyterian Record shows. The author not being able to find more, thought it wise to consult such authority as Dr. Foote, and finds in a work styled by him "The Sessional Records of Mount Bethel Church," the following statement: "Until the year 1833, the members of the Presbyterian Church in Hampshire County were all with the exception of those living convenient to Bloomery, enrolled in one church under one Eldership. During the year 1833, according to the direction of Presbytery, the necessary steps were taken for the division of the church, and in the Fall of 1833, the Presbytery divided the church at Mt. Bethel and directed four new ones to be organized, one on the Jersey mountain, one on the North River, one in Springfield, and one on Pattersons Creek, the church in Romney not requiring an organization. The reason for this division was, that the members had become so numerous, that in their scattered situation the church was unwieldly." Mt. Bethel is mentioned by Dr. Graham who throws additional light on the division mentioned by Dr. Foote, viz, the following minute found in the Winchester Presbytery for October 17, 1812: "Mr. Black informed Presbytery that the Congregations heretofore known on these Minutes by the names of Springfield and Romney, having become disorganized, have been by him organized into one congregation, hereafter to be known by the name of *Mt. Bethel.*"

Dr. Graham also gives a list of pastors of the Romney Church: Rev. John Lyle, 1793-1807; James Black, 1812-1833; Robt. B. White, 1836-1844; Dr. Wm. Henry Foote, 1845-1860; George W. Finley, 1870-1891; E. D. Washburn, 1893-1905. Dr. Frank Brooke is the Pastor at this writing. He succeeded Dr. Washburn after the latter's lamented death.

CHAPTER XXXIII

Winchester Presbyterian Church

In giving a sketch of Presbyterianism in Winchester, the writer is confronted with much that would be tedious to the general reader, and embarrassing to others, who may be descendants of the Presbyterians who in the early part of the 19th Century had many conflicts in the old Stone Church, erected in 1790 at the East end of Piccadilly Street. Some of the conflicting opinions entertained by the large and influential congregation, were too often expressed by the old Scotch-Irish members, in manner and language that frequently threatened ruptures between Pastor and people. Much of this has become familiar to the writer in his study of the history of this Church; but he sees that no good can result from rehearsing it in this connection; and will endeavor to give matter for useful reference only.

Much has been said in the sketch of Old Opecquon, relating to this church. There it will be seen that Winchester Presbyterians were members of the parent Church—(Opecquon) from its first establishment; and continued to attend church services there for many years after the town was incorporated in 1752. About this period, the Ministers serving Opecquon and Cedar Creek churches, occasionally preached at some place in the Winchester village; and later on, preached by regular appointments. The congregation increasing as the Town grew, a demand was made for an independent organization; so that they might be supplied with a regular pastor. The Old Presbytery in 1781 has this minute: "That Winchester be added to the Opecquon and Cedar Creek churches, and that the Minister appointed to supply the latter, give an equal part of his time and service to Winchester." We find this was done for about ten years. It appears that Rev. John Montgomery was the Minister during this period; and his service so acceptable, that the church increased not only in numbers, but also in its desire to have independent Organization, and a new house of worship. The records show that both movements were well on towards completion in 1790, when Rev. Nash Legrand was called and began his celebrated pastorate in the new stone church. This stone building, now about 118 years old, can be seen to-day in fairly good condition. Says Dr. Graham—"The old Church no longer used for Presbyterian worship, is a building of unusual historical interest. Besides the distinguished men who as pastors, have occupied its pulpit—Legrand, Hill, and Riddle, nearly all the famous Presbyterian Ministers of our country from 1790 to 1834, have preached within its walls. It was honored by a Meeting of the General Assembly of the Presbyterian Church, 1799—the only place out of Philadelphia (with a single exception) in which for a period of almost fifty years, that venerable Court had ever met. The Synod of Virginia has met in it Eleven times,—more frequently than in any other Church whatever. In it Oct., 1791, during a session of the Synod, the Rev. Archibald Alexander was licensed to preach the Gospel. In it also the Presbytery of Winchester was Organized in 1794."

Truly this old Church has a history that should be preserved. It is now occupied by the "Colored Public School." The Presbyterians in 1834 sold the old stone building, together with ten feet of ground at each end, and fifteen feet in the rear, to the Baptist Church for their church purposes, for the term of 500 years, who sold it in 1858 to the Colored Baptist Church, who continued their use until broken by the Civil War 1863, when it was used as a stable by Federal troops. At the close of the War, it was leased to the School Board of Winchester for the use of Colored Schools. The School Board made repairs required, and proceeded to use the old Church property at variance with the privileges granted in the first deed. Some encroachments have been made in converting this property to the present uses. In the old Graveyard, that once was part of the Church lot, many old families buried their dead; immediately East of the Church. The ashes and bones of many noble men and women repose beneath the play-ground of this School. Neither the remains of the dead nor the scholars are disturbed by the change that less than one hundred years has wrought in this noted place. For several years prior to the sale of the old Stone building, dissensions arose in the old Church, some having their origin between Pastor and people, some between the Official body and people and Pastor combined. Suffice it to say, however, there was a rupture in 1826, forboding no good to the Presbyterians. Steps were taken to build a new church, which was completed in 1827, and called Kent Street Presbyterian, taking its name from the street at its intersection with Water Street. David H. Riddle, a young licentiate, preached for the new congregation for several months, and was ordained Pastor Dec. 4, 1828. The other fraction adhered to the old name and continued services in the Old Stone Church until 1832, when a union was made between the factions. This union produced harmony, and they then became known as The Presbyterian Church of Winchester. The united church continued its joint services in the Old Stone Church until in 1834, Dr. Hill the Pastor resigned; the Church called Rev. John J. Royall, who served until 1838. Rev. Wm. M. Atkinson succeeded him; and it was during his pastorate that the division occurred in the Presbyterian Church, designated *Old* and *New Schools*. .This division found its way into the Winchester Church, resulting in the withdrawal in 1839 of four Elders and forty members from the old organization, who organized what was known as the Loudoun Street Church. They purchased the northern half of lot number 14 on southeast side of Loudoun Street, receiving a deed from Joseph Neill, dated Nov. 9, 1839. The board of trustees to whom this lot was conveyed, was so changed that in 1848 it became necessary to reorganize; and the following were appointed by the Court, Dr. Wm. Hill, A. H. H. Boyd, Geo. W. Ginn, Geo. Keller, Wm. D. Gilkeson, R. M. Campbell, Jas. P. Riely, David Russell, and M. B. Cartmell. The New School branch received the ministrations of Dr. Hill for several years. In 1842, Rev. A. H. H. Boyd was called. His ministry was noted for the acceptable service rendered, endearing him to the children of the third and fourth generations. His pastorate terminated at his death, Dec. 16, 1865. Jonah W. Lupton succeeded Dr. B—, serving until 1867; George L. Leyburn, pastor from 1867 to 1875; then Dr. Henry M. White, 1875 to Nov. 21, 1899, when he resigned on account of failing health. During the early ministry of Dr. Boyd, the two churches, Round Hill three and a half miles West from Winchester, and Hayfield about eight miles West from Winchester, were erected. The latter stood on the Northwestern turnpike, where the residence of Boyd P. Ramey now stands. The building was badly damaged during the Civil War, and was rebuilt on the South side of the pike. The neat brick church is in good repair; but owing to changed conditions and removals of Presbyterian families, services are discontinued. The Round Hill Church was erected 1845-6, in a beautiful grove of virgin oaks, on ground dedicated by M. B. Cartmell, (the author's father). This place was long famous for the *Annual Protracted Meetings* held in the old Grove, large congregations spending the whole day on the grounds, attending services rendered by many of the most distinguished Ministers of their day. These Annual meetings were largely attended by families from every section of the county. The generous supply of refreshments served by the hospitable membership of this Church, continuing for more than a week, made these occasions memorable to all. Fain would the writer digress here, and pen many of his personal recollections of that interesting period in his life; but the line of duty calls his attention to the Kent Street Church where we left Dr. Atkinson in charge in 1846. Rev. Beverly Tucker Lacy, an eminent and forceful preacher, succeeded him in 1846, was installed June 19, 1847, served until 1851; then Rev. Jas. R. Graham came in Oct., 1851. His long service in this Church ended March 20, 1900, in the Union of the two Churches, with Dr. Graham as *Pastor-Emeritus,* but chosen to render such service to the new organization as would be agreeable to him. Kent Street Church suffered heavily during the Civil War; but was fortunate in having Dr. Graham as its shepherd. His faithful service has become an interesting part of the history of Winchester. It was in this Church where Stonewall Jackson worshipped when stationed at Winchester. The Presbyterians in the Southern States were firmly cemented by the events of the Civil War; and when the opportunity came in 1865, Old and New School Churches in the Southern General Assembly obliterated their lines of difference. Thenceforth the two Town Churches pressed their work with perfect harmony; and continued their relations as separate organizations. When the resignation of Dr. White's long pastorate of twenty-four years was tendered, his congregation was seriously affected, and endeavored to secure a plan that would continue the relations of Pastor and people. Dr. White's pastorate had not only been dear to his own large congregation, but useful in its influence to the entire community. When his Church finally submitted, and the pulpit became vacant, the congregation decided to confer with Kent Street Church in relation to a union of the two Churches. After many preliminary conferences, both congregations entered into the necessary details, resulting in a union under one Pastorate. This was effected March 20, 1900, after a separation of sixty years. Rev. Julian S. Sibley was called in Sept., 1900, and served until July, 1904, when he resigned. The church was without a regular Pastor until the

Autumn of 1905. Dr. Graham filled the pulpit until Rev. J. Horace Lacey, D.D., entered upon his work with marked unanimity of feeling from the large congregation.

At this union of the two Congregations all the church property was merged and placed in hands of new trustees. Dr. Wm. S. Love, George W. Kurtz, Jas. B. Russell, Loring A. Cover, Wm. H. Smith, and T. K. Cartmell. The new Organization elected as Ruling Elders: Dr. P. W. Boyd, W. W. Glass, T. N. Lupton, George C. Shepard, George W. Kurtz, and T. K. Cartmell; and as Board of Deacons, W. S. White, Wm. H. Smith, Henry S. Baker, M. Lohr Capper, John W. Myers, Henry Moling, Harry C. Baker, and Jno. E. Padgett.

The Church is now in a flourishing condition. The old edifice was remodeled, the large and comfortable Sunday School building seen in the rear of the main building, takes the place of the old basement, and the Sabbath School and Wednesday-night services are conducted there. The floor of the church building was lowered, and the auditorium, with its attractive changes, was completed in the spring of 1908. The cost of all the improvements amounted to about $28,000.

The old Kent Street building and lot was sold, and is now occupied by The Winchester Laundry.

The Round Hill Church

The reference made to this church in preceding pages, embraced its history while a branch of the Loudoun Street Church; and for convenience, this mention will now be made. During the pastorate of Dr. White, he preached regularly at Round Hill and Hayfield in the Sunday afternoons, and found the Congregations desired separate organizations. With his assistance, this object materialized in 1879, when a separate organization was accomplished, and steps taken to call a pastor. Rev. Alexander Sprunt, a young licentiate, came as an Evangelist in 1879 (Rev. W. H. Wood was assistant to Dr. White prior to this). The first regular Pastor was A. S. Moffett from January, 1881, to Dec., 1884. He was succeeded by Rev. L. E. Scott, from May, 1886, to May 10, 1892, who was highly esteemed by the congregation. Robert W. Carter was in charge from 1893 to Sept., 1898. He was succeeded by Rev. John J. Fix, whose service was very effective in alleviating some of the unfortunate trials this congregation had so recently endured. His resignation was reluctantly accepted the latter part of 1902, to enable him to accept a call to the Church at Manchester near Richmond, Va. Since then this Church has had the service of Dr. White, pastor of Opecquon Memorial.

Gerardstown Church

Dr. Graham says: "This Church was an established Church in 1783, and was known for many years as Cool Spring, and was about five miles from Gerardstown, on what is known as the Runny-Meade farm, which has been owned by Mr. Wilson Coe for a half Century." No date is given when Presbyterian Worship was first conducted; but being an established Congregation in 1783, it is evident that services had been regularly conducted there for a considerable time, for in their appearance in Presbytery at that date, they asked that the services of an eminent minister be appointed a supply, with a view to his being called as the pastor. This request coming from Cool Spring and Bullskin, proves that this church was well on the way to the success it attained within the next ten years. We have evidence in hand that having secured the services of eminent Ministers, many advances were made in the church work. About 1793, the church was removed to the growing Village of Middletown, afterwards changed to Gerardstown. This change, however, pending the erection of the first church in the Village, and the death of Rev. Thomas Poage, the promising young minister who had been called to the new Church, must be the reason why this church was without a pastor for the next six years. In 1799, the Church took front rank among her sister churches when the Rev. Joseph Glass received the call, and at once entered upon his notable service, terminating 1817. He also served the Back Creek Church during this pastorate. This first church building was large, being brick and in the old style of architecture. The attractive edifice recently erected on the site of the old church, surrounded by extensive grounds and picturesque old Village Graveyard near-by, lends an interest to this historic place, that impresses every visitor, very dear to descendants of the old families who laid the old corner stone, and buried their loved ones in the long ago. This Church has had distinction in the able Ministers serving faithfully in all these years. The first Ruling Elders were Wm. Wilson, Mathew Rippey, and Samuel McKown. The venerable Lewis F. Wilson was their pastor 1837-1853, and his son, Rev. E. L. Wilson, served this church from 1874 until 1893. He was succeeded by Rev. R. Ashlin White, son of Rev. George White, D.D.

Charlestown Church

This is one of the old churches in Old Frederick County. The Presbytery records show that in 1787 the congregation was calling for help, in the order of a "Minister to Supply them service." This was answered, and soon the supply came, and a small building was erected on a lot purchased from Charles Washington. In the early part of the 19th Century, a large stone building was erected, which was used until 1852, when the present handsome church was erected on the original site. The first Pastor was Rev. Wm. Hill. Charlestown has always been regarded as one of the strongest Churches in the Winchester Presbytery, gaining much renown in late years for having its distinguished and universally esteemed Pastor, Rev. A. C. Hopkins, D.D., who experienced hardships and service as soldier and chaplain through the entire struggles of the Stonewall Brigade, 1861-1865. This church, after Dr. Hill's resignation, for some unaccountable reason, had no regular pastor until 1825, when it was reorganized. Rev. Wm. C. Walton, pastor from 1825 to 1827, then Rev. Septimus Tustin, 1833-37; Thos. W. Simpson, 1838-41; Warren B. Dutton, 1842-66; A. C. Hopkins, D.D., Dec., 1866. During the preparation of this work Oct. 7, 1906, the 40th anniversary of Dr. Hopkin's pastorate was celebrated with appropriate services, not only by his own congregation, but by the entire community; thus showing the appreciation of his fellow citizens for the faithful service he has rendered them.

Berryville Presbyterian Church

This Church was organized June 10, 1853, starting out with a small membership and no church building. Some embarrassment might be expected in the progress of this weak Presbyterian plant, nurtured in a community previously held by the Episcopal and Baptist Churches, both having large memberships. The first house of worship was dedicated in the summer of 1854, Rev. Charles White being the first Pastor. This active and beloved pastor rendered service to the Harpers Ferry and White Post congregations until 1875, when he accepted a call to a Church in West Hanover Presbytery. Rev. C. S. Lingemfelter pastor from Nov. 1875 to 1880; Rev. A. B. Carrington, from 1881 to Jany. 1, 1884, then Rev. J. Harry Moore came from a strong church in Louisville, Ky., and took charge in Nov., 1885, and served until the summer of 1890. During this pastorate, he revived the old Stone Chapel congregation. Mr. Moore had spent his early life in the Counties of Jefferson and Clarke, and to the manor born, was very successful in his work. Rev. Charles R. Stribling came in the spring of 1891, and his pastorate closing Jany. 18, 1897, together with his faithful ministrations to the weak churches at Stone Chapel and Smithfield, are recalled by his many friends with much pleasure. Rev. David H. Scanlon, the present active and faithful pastor, entered upon his work Nov. 18, 1900. He also supplies the pulpit in the recently remodeled Stone's Chapel, and has organized a church near Stephenson's Station. This Congregation erected a neat church edifice near Clear Brook. Since Dec. 8, 1901, Mr. S. preaches at this point regularly.

Front Royal Presbyterian Church

No Church record is full enough to fix definitely the date of this organization; it must have been about 1800. Some evidence of this is found in old county records, when the Church lot was conveyed to trustees. Following the trend of Dr. Graham's Sketch of this Church, it was known in 1796 as South River, at which time the Winchester Presbytery was in session, and adjourned to hold an afternoon session "at the School House in Front Royal." A few years later the name of South River disappears from the Church records, and that of Front Royal takes its place.

The first Pastor was William Williamson, his pastorate beginning in 1794. At this date, he established an English and Classical School at Front Royal, this being his home; and for many years he preached at all points in the surrounding country where his service could do good, from Woodstock on the West to Middleburgh and Warrenton to the East. In 1841, Rev. Robert S. Bell was installed, and served until 1845. We are unable to show whether Mr. Williamson was the only pastor from his installment to the time of his death, which occurred about the time of Mr. Bell's appearance. Rev. Jas. E. Hughes was stated supply from 1850 to 1855; Rev. T. Berry came in 1856, Rev. S. M. Loughhead being for one year; Rev. Henry Hirdie was there from 1859 to 1861, as supply, and same for Woodstock church. No church record gives the name of any pastor for this church from 1861 until 1876, when Rev. Carson W. Hollis, was installed; he resigned Sept., 1893. Rev. A. F. Laird was installed Oct. 7, 1894, resigned 1901. Rev. Jas. A. McClure installed June 12, 1903. This Church is no longer a weak member of the Winchester Presbytery, but has been very unfortunate in the many vacancies in her pulpit.

Martinsburg Presbyterian Church

The early Church records are generally sought for reliable information regarding organization of the many churches through the entire Valley, though sometimes we are disappointed. Such is the case now before us. The Presbytery records give only vague notices prior to 1800; consequently, it must be accepted as a fact, that the Martinsburg Village Presbyterians attended Old Tuscarora, two miles West. Some organization must have had a home as early as 1807, for the Church record shows that Rev. John Mathews was preaching regularly, 1807-'08. In 1808 and 1830 he was at Shepherdstown, and also at Charlestown 1809-1827, seeming to be in demand. In 1827, he returns to Martinsburg and is the Pastor until latter part of 1830, when succeeded by W. C. Mathews for six years. In 1837, Rev. Peyton Harrison came and served the church successfully for seven years. He was succeeded by Rev. Jno. Boggs in 1845, remaining but one year. Rev. W. H. Love seems to have been on the ground before Mr. Boggs left for S. Carolina, which was the 5th of May, 1847, while Mr. Love's call was extended to him first of Jany. same year. The latter was pastor until 1849. Rev. Robt. T. Berry came in 1850, as stated supply, and remained in charge until 1859. We now have a minute in the church record that is fuller of interest than the entry indicates to the casual reader of church history. Rev. A. C. Hopkins was installed as Pastor Dec. 6, 1860; his pastorate terminated Sept. 1, 1865. Nothing in the record to show he had been given his extended leave of absence during the War period of 1861-65. This youthful Parson heard his country's call; folded his church vestures, and laid them aside to don the gray uniform and soon became a faithful soldier, to follow the new *Banner* as it was carried to victory or defeat. The author several years ago, while taking a vacation from his office, enjoyed the delightful companionship of this Rev. gentleman, spending a vacation from his Charlestown Church. We were in the foothills of the Alleganey Mts., at the hospitable home of mutual friends. Old war experiences were related; the atmosphere of that lovely lawn was laden with the aroma we both had enjoyed in the monotonous life of a soldier in Winter quarters. No rude summons broke the momentary enchantment—no sudden ending of furloughs or leave of absence. However, we answered a familiar summons where we were expected to not only enjoy the viands on the hospitable board waiting for us inside, but to join a party who represented so much in each of our lives,—two of them daughters of the distinguished Minister, Dr. Foote, one, the companion of our mutual friend—who bore the title *The Just Judge*. His genial spirit no longer gave us cheer; the dark mantle had fallen across his pathway and left a pall of sadness over this home. Around that board were others, forming a party possessed of more than average intelligence. All had enjoyed more than the usual advantages and were well equipped with interesting incidents and events belonging to the *long ago,* one of the ladies being a daughter of Dr. Wm. M. Atkinson, once a distinguished pastor of several Presbyterian Churches; another, member of the party being the granddaughter of Rev. Joseph Glass. The author trusts to the charitably-inclined for an excuse for this digression.

Returning to the subject of the Martinsburg Church, which had been without a regular pastor during the war period, when the church suffered greatly from the distracted conditions of a border town, many differences arose in the congregation. Lines were sharply drawn between Unionists (as they were called), and the families who were represented in the Southern Cause. Many husbands and sons in peril on the firing line; many of whom found rest in a hero's grave. This accounts for the long silence. At last, however, in June, 1866, Rev. Jas. E. Hughes came from Baltimore and undertook the arduous task of healing dissensions, and had made a fair start, when death closed his efforts Sept. 23, 1867. Then came Rev. David H. Riddle in the Spring of 1868, and continued a useful pastorate which ended May 25, 1879, caused by failing health. He was succeeded by the Rev. Frances M. Woods, who was installed Pastor Oct. 15, 1879, and has continued with success in all these years, he being the present pastor, full of vigor, endowed with splendid intellectual powers, grace of manner and dignity of style—eloquent of speech, fervid and zealous in his pastoral life, fully imbued with the doctrine of his Master whom he serves. His labors have been richly rewarded. A few years ago, he and his harmonious congregation succeeded in remodeling the old church, and produced a handsome edifice.

Woodstock Presbyterian Church

Some surprises came while investigating the early history of this Church. As early as 1794, we find references to the services of certain Ministers, but no light thrown on the Organization until a much later period. Church records fail to establish dates until 1820, when a record is made. Rev. Wm. Henry Foote was located there as Stated Supply, and continued as such until 1827. During this time he also served the Strasburg Church. During the years 1824-1830, Rev. John Lodor served this church in the same capacity. Rev. Lewis F. Wilson appears as the first regular Pastor Dec. 13, 1834; and continued as such until Oct., 1836. In 1837, Rev. Silas Billings was installed pastor and served the church for several years—how long is not stated. Daniel G. Mallory was there 1855-56; Robt. Gray, 1858-59. From 1859 to 1861, Henry Hardie was pastor. Rev. John M. Clymer accepted a call Nov. 25, 1860, and had a prosperous pastorate to 1871. In 1871 Thos. E. Converse was pastor to 1875.

Rev. Robt. H. Fleming was installed pastor July 29, 1876; continued as such until Nov. 11, 1886. He was succeeded by T. P. Epes Oct. 29, 1887; served until 1890. Then came Geo. E. Henderlite 1890; resigned 1893 to enter Foreign Mission field in S. America; Rev. P. D. Stephenson, D.D., accepted a call 1895 and is the present popular Pastor.

Cedar Creek Church

This Church has had frequent mention in connection with the Old Opecquon Church, having been grouped at different times with the churches of Strasburg, Woodstock, Opecquon and latterly with Cedar-Cliff. Rev. Nash Legrand served this Church from 1790 to 1809; Andrew Shannon, 1810-1818; John Lodor, S. S., 1836. Wm. H. Woods came in May, 1878; resigned Nov. 3, 1887. He served the group. A. G. Link, the present popular Pastor, was installed for this group Oct. 13, 1889 (Strasburg and Cedar Cliff), at Cedar Creek, July 1, 1904. Rev. Mr. Clymer also preached at Cedar Creek 1860. Rev. Silas Billings frequently preached there during the years his Seminary was in operation in Winchester. Dr. A. H. H. Boyd conducted several protracted meetings at this church for several years prior to the Civil War. A number of other churches within the bounds of Winchester Presbytery might properly receive notice in this connection. Many such are in the territory of Old Frederick County, they being the prosperous Churches of Piedmont, Keyser, Davis, Gormania, Moorefield, Petersburg, and elsewhere; but this allotted work will not admit of fuller sketches. Doubtless, some readers will think that the Presbyterian Church has had fuller notice than necessary. This may be explained. It was well equipped with a record from the establishment of its first place of Worship at Old Opecquon; and with its claim as the oldest Organization in the Shenandoah Valley, it seemed to be a necessary part of this work. In the treatment of other Churches in this connection, every effort has been exhausted by the author to obtain data from all the Churches, without respect to *Creed;* so that a condensed history may be had in this compilation, affording a reference to the student who may be in search of the matter now offered him.

CHAPTER XXXIV

The Episcopal Church in Old Frederick County

The author, in introducing this subject to the reader, confesses to some hesitancy in presenting this Church next in priority of organization to the Presbyterian Church. This hesitancy is natural, when the reader will consider that one of the very oldest church organizations in our New World was the Centenary Reformed Church. This Church, represented by a bold and determined body of Reformed Calvinists, that braved the waves of the Atlantic, leaving their German homes and kindred, to land on the shores of a land they believed would be an asylum of peace, or a grave of rest from persecution. Tradition and reliable historians have placed them in an organized body in America in the earliest days; and indeed, tradition locates this devoted sect in the Shenandoah Valley prior to 1738. But inasmuch as no record appears to substantiate this claim, and as it is well known the Episcopal Church was regarded as the Established Church, wherever the white settlers founded their homes, it is fair to conclude that the latter was strongly in evidence, when the first County Court was opened; for we find the Court taking steps to secure a Vestry, and an order entered and certified at a subsequent (April) Term, 1744.

"Ordered that the Clerk of this Court, write to his honor the Governor for a Power to Choose a Vestry for the Parish of Frederick in this County." The Frederick Parish was created, and boundaries defined, by Act of House of Burgesses when the County was formed. Vestrys were chosen by qualified voters resident of the Parish, after being duly notified of the day for an election. None but freeholders and housekeepers were allowed to vote. The law provided for the election of "twelve of the most able and discreet persons of the Parish," who when elected, must appear before the Court and take the oaths required by Act of Parliament. The Vestrymen so instituted and installed, were authorized to collect the assessments for the support of the Established Church; to erect suitable houses of worship, etc. The first Vestry was so chosen after the Court received the order of the Governor in answer to the Court's order. There is much evidence that the "freeholders and housekeepers" made an unfortunate selection; for after eight years in office, the House of Burgesses placed upon its statute books a severe condemnation of the entire body, charging them with oppressive and corrupt practices—"That they had collected upwards of fifteen hundred pounds sterling, on the pretence of building and adorning Churches in their parish." A remarkable fact is presented in the study of this case. Although this body of supposed able and discreet persons had in their hands, a sum equal to nearly $8,000.00 they were unable to point to a single log cabin that had been erected by them. Bishop Meade in his criticism of the first Vestry in Frederick Parish says "The Churches of that day were log houses costing from thirty to fifty pounds. There must have been much *mis*spending of money." The old Legislators were not so charitable. The Act contains their language—"They have misapplied or converted the same to their own use." Aside from the wrong done the Church and the oppression inflicted on the tax-payers, the Episcopal Church lost its opportunity to make history during the interesting period embracing the early settlement of old Frederick County. Had it not been for the unfaithful acts of the persons claiming the high honor of being Vestrymen the Church to-day could point with pride to more than one edifice and be assured that they stood on ground made sacred by the "Chappel" erected there in the early days of the Colony. This starts the enquiry, what is known of these "Chappels," so often mentioned? Tradition locates three, McCoy's, Cunningham's and Morgan's. Some writers differ as to location and date of erection, and even assert that several more are found at prominent points. The question must be raised here, that if such are facts, and if the *Chappels* were in use prior to 1755, why is it that the old Vestry records do not show the fact? It is well known that the Established Church was noted for its record of events, such as marriages, deaths, baptisms and births, and an annual report of the support given the minister. Taking the history of nearly every Episcopal Church in the old Colony East of the Blue Ridge, such reports were not only required, but actually made. The officiating minister and church wardens were able to show church records so replete with the history of the Colonial period, that the student must ever regret that, so much unwritten history is folded away in the musty files and records of those old Parishes. Not so with Frederick Parish;—no church record to be found prior to 1764, to give in detail the important incidents constantly occurring in the life of the Church.

An act of the General Assembly, Feby. 1752, authorized an election to be held, "At some convenient time and place to elect twelve persons able and discreet, to serve as Vestrymen for the Parish, this election to be held before the 15th day June next." At this election the following persons were chosen; Thomas Lord Fairfax, Isaac Perkins, Gabriel Jones, John Hite, Thomas Swearingen, Charles Buck, Robert Lemmon, John Lindsey, John Ashby, Jas. Cromley, Thomas Bryan Martin, and Lewis Neill. This new body put in motion a spirit of Church enlargement, at least evidences spring up from several sections; and the parishioners scattered over the large Parish, seem to have taken their first and only start to erect places of worship. No trouble to find several of these through the proper channel,—the Church record. Bishop Meade says, "The Vestry book commences in 1764." The question might be asked, what were the Vestrymen doing in this Church during the twelve years they had served? While they failed to preserve a record, they doubtless were at work. Evidences found in the old court order books, show their diligence to provide necessary means to support the ministry and to care for the poor. Some are named as trustees to hold the ground at the various places where Church buildings were going up, commencing at Winchester in 1752-3, Mecklenburg and Mill-creek. Later on, we have Bunker-Hill (or Morgan's) and one in a small village, afterwards Charles-Town; and when the new Vestry was formed in 1764, the foundation was laid for quite a number of churches in Frederick Parish. As matter of interest to some readers who may not see it elsewhere, a list of this famous Vestry is given here. List of Vestrymen instituted in 1764: Isaac Hite, John Hite, John Greenleaf, Thomas Rutherford, James Keith, John Neville, Charles Smith, James Wood, Jacob Hite, Thomas Wadlington, Burr Harrison, Thomas Swearingen, Van Swearingen, Angus McDonald, Philip Bush, Frederick Conrad, George Rice, Alexander White, James Barnett, Marquis Calmes, John McDonald, Edward Snickers, Warner Washington, Joseph Holmes, Benjamin Sedgewick, Edmund Taylor, John Smith, and Samuel Dowdal. It will be remembered that Vestrymen were elected at special elections, by Acts of the General Assembly, the Courts to fix the dates and places of election. At that time the country was mentioned as *The Settlements*; and each settlement was expected to select one or more persons to be voted for in that settlement, "to serve in the Vestry of Frederick Parish." So the list was composed of representatives from every Settlement. The Winchester settlement, or church, had John Hite, James Wood, White, Holmes, Conrad, Bush, Rutherford, Keith, and John Smith; while Jacob Hite the two Swearingens, Wadlington and Charles Smith, were in the North end of the parish, serving as trustees and church wardens for the churches at Mill Creek (Morgan's) Sheperdstown and Martinsburg. Warner Washington and the two McDonalds came from the Charles Washington Village. The line of this district extended to within seven miles of northern limit of the Winchester district. For the Burwell Chapel (Old Chappel), Calmes, Neville, Barnett and Snickers; For Cedar Creek and Long Meadows embracing McCoy's Chapel and Leith's Ferry, the latter being near the forks of North and South rivers (Front Royal vicinity). We have Isaac Hite, Greenleaf, Taylor, Sedgewick, Rice and Dowdal in the district embracing the settlements South of the Opecquon Creek, to the river boundary South and East. Several of these Vestrymen must have resigned after a short service, for their names appear in church records of other denominations; James Barnett being a promoter of the Baptist Organization, called Old Zion, near Nineveh Village; Bush and Conrad trustees for the Reformed Calvinists. This Vestry, with the exceptions mentioned, continued their services until 1780. The Revolutionary War brought a new order of things in the Church life. The new General Assembly enacted laws that were not only embarrassing to the old Vestrys, but declared all Vestrys dissolved; and defined the restricted powers of the new Vestrymen, who were to be chosen by their respective parishioners, or members of the Protestant Episcopal Church, and no more to be elected by all the freeholders and housekeepers. The church had been shorn of support from direct taxation. Surely this was a new order of things. All religious sects, denominations or churches placed on equal footing and "could be supported by their respective Congregations." Many good churchmen allowed their zeal to waver in 1776, when an Act of The General Assembly suspended payment of salaries to their ministers by special taxation. But when another Act in 1802, confiscated their Glebe lands, many succumbed and seemed to give up in dispair, and allowed a gloom of inertness to settle over the Episcopal Church that was deeply regretted. Many years of trial were required to get the Church accustomed to its changed conditions. What was regarded then as disastrous to the Church, proved to be a blessing; for new men with new aspirations appeared on the threshold of the new Church in Virginia; and the first decade marked a comforting change. *The Old Establishment* was gone, and the firm foundation laid for the magnificent history this church has made in the land, upholding the tenets of the new *Establishment,* her eminent ministry and conscientious laymen have marked the continent with monuments of success in her new policy of religious freedom to all.

The old Vestrymen who ended their service in 1780, became distinguished in their day as statesmen, soldiers and citizens; and left descendants to follow lines marked out which led many to even greater distinction than the fathers ever attained.

In taking up the work of the individual churches in Frederick Parish, it is proper to state that the earliest date found in any record, fixes the Burwell Chapel, (sometimes called the Spring Chapel, and finally *Old Chapel*), as the first place of worship set up in Old Frederick Parish for Episcopal services. We have abundant proof of this. As shown elsewhere, there was a "Chappel" on a road that was opened in 1743, passing by the Burwell Spring, and as the name *Chappel* was given by the Episcopal Church for the small place designed for Gospel services, it should be accepted as an Episcopal Church "point." Later on, the Court records refer to Cunningham's Chappel, in the vicinity of the Big Spring. It has been thought by many that some Cunningham erected the Chappel referred to in the order of Court. The county records show the Cunningham name frequently as owners of land at two points on the Opecquon Creek at a very early day. The same records reveal the fact, however, that one of the name was not a good churchman, though he may have erected the little *Chappel*; for he is found in open court 1745, defending a charge brought by his wife for abuse and ill treatment. The Case being proved, the court adjudged him guilty, a fine of 20 pounds, assessed-bond given for good behaviour, and he required to give his injured wife separate support. The church records show that the Vestry in 1772 decided to build a church on land of Charles Smith, at some point near the site of the Village of Berryville, and several hundred pounds were promised as building fund. In 1773, the Vestry for some reason changed their plan, and decided to build the church at Cunningham's Chappel, where two acres of land had been dedicated by Col. Hugh Nelson, of York, owner of the large tract afterwards known as the Burwell tract, or Carter Hall tract. Bishop Meade says, "The plans for this building failed and no such church was built." This incident is narrated to show the connection of the *Chappel* and *two acres,* mentioned as the Col. Nelson dedication, subsequently known as the *Burwell Graveyard and Old Chapel*—identically the Cunningham Chappel mentioned in the order of court in 1743. Still further evidence is given of the identity, as will be seen in Deed book 28, in old Frederick Clerk's Office. The following extract is given:

"May 10th, 1791, By request of Mr. Samuel Baker, agent for Col. Nathaniel Burwell of James City County, Va, I surveyed two acres of land on Chappel Run, etc.

John Cordell,
surveyor."

The object of this survey is shown in a Deed dated Nov. 25, 1792, from Nathaniel Burwell of James City County, to the Minister and Vestry of Frederick Parish, "as Trustees for the benefit of the Protestant Episcopal Church in said Parish, for two acres of land lying on both sides of Chapel Run, (signed) Nathaniel Burwell. Winesses

Philip Nelson
Samuel Baker
Walter Burwell
Ludwell Grymes."

An interesting incident may be mentioned in this connection. Two lineal descendants of Samuel Baker, who had the survey made in 1791 for Col. Burwell Madison H. Baker and his sister Miss Lelia Baker, own and occupy the *Chappel Green* homestead adjoining the Old Chapel Cemetery.

The Old Stone Chapel as seen to-day was built in 1793. The foregoing statement may seem tedious to many readers; but when it is considered that much contention has arisen in regard to what was meant in the original Order of Court touching this first "Chappel" of "which" there is any evidence, and this contention made by strong testimony that one other Chapel had priority over all others for date of erection and use in the Old Parish. The writer was compelled to take this course to collate facts found in both Church and County records, and submits them for the reader to determine if the case is fully proven. It is well to mention in this connection, that several writers on this subject and several historians have given Morgan's Chapel as the first building erected for public worship in the territory West of the Blue Ridge, and that Richard ap Morgan, a devout Welchman, had the distinction accorded him by tradition, as being the first white man to settle in this territory, and that he erected his log Chapel in 1726, on his grant near the Potomac River. Some locate him at Old Mecklenburg; some on Mill Creek, and others at Morgan's Spring. Some fix the date of his grant in 1730, and state it for a fact, as being the first grant for land in the Shenandoah Valley. Hawks, in his History of the Episcopal Church in Virginia, falls into the grave error that many church historians have

Old Chapel, near Millwood

made accepted traditions too often, and neglected to search the public records for facts to fix dates and incidents relating to the first settler *and on what he settled.* This is unfortunate, for it often misleads the inquirer. Take this one point in his treatment of the *Morgan Settler.* He says, "Morgan Morgan in the year 1726, removed to what is now Berkly County and built the first log Cabin on the South side of the Potomac West of the Blue Ridge"; and that in the year 1740, "he associated with Dr. John Briscoe and Mr. Hite, and erected the first Episcopal Church in the Valley of Virginia." This is most unfortunate. It comes as a shock to the history reader, for doubts and shadows are cast over his splendid work. The question must arise, where could this information have come from? Certainly no one can produce proof of this, while the contrary is shown in both County and State records, which are well preserved. The author of this work will produce this proof in his sketches of the First Settlers. What is still more astonishing is that Norris in his History of The Lower Valley, falls into the same error. No excuse for him, which we can give the *Church historians.* Mr. Norris came to the Valley to collect data from old County Clerks and old records, so that he could give a historical account of the first settlers, that would be accepted as *absolutely correct.* He was allowed free use of the voluminous notes the writer had collected in his long experience; and while many of these notes were transferred to his work in many cases, *verbatim.* His completed work shows that he went astray in many cases, and accepted *tradition* as his authority. Generally speaking, all find tradition captivating and a writer is apt to be drawn aside by the allurements of romance, where the naked facts can be laid aside and pen pictures appear to gratify and entertain but seldom enlighten.

As will be shown later on, neither Dr. Briscoe nor Mr. Hite could possibly have been associated with Morgan in 1740, and no such Grants were or could have been made in 1726 and 1730. The Author deemed it necessary to settle this priority for the old Cunningham, Nelson, Burwell, Old Chapel question, before proceeding to show what the Parish work was from its first planting in Winchester. Before entering upon this branch of the subject, the reader's attention is called to the following transcript from the records of Frederick County, in explanation of the Nelson dedication referred to;

"November 10th, 1773.

"I do give Liberty to the Vestry of the Parish of Frederick County to build a Church on any part of two acres of my land on and about the part where the *Old Chapel now stands,* including the Spring and the 2 acres above mentioned for a burial ground,

Attest, HUGH NELSON"

JOHN KERCHEVAL

(see deed book 16, p. 474)

It can be seen that Col. Nelson was impressed with the fact that an *Old Chapel* already occupied part of the two acres. It will be remembered the Vestry formed plans in 1773, and had funds in hand, to build a Church at this point; but doubtless deemed it useless to execute the plans, as the old Chapel afforded them a satisfactory place for Church services. Who the ministers were who ministered to the old Chapel Congregation, we are fortunate in having such authority as Bishop Meade to guide us. He says, "The Rev. Mr. Gordon was the first Minister; when his ministry commenced and ended not known." Lay readers were named for the different Chapels, during the period ending 1780, viz: John Ruddle, James Barnett, John Barns, Henry Nelson, James Graham, Henry Frencham, Morgan Morgan, John James, Wm. Dobson, Wm. Howard, John Lloyd. "The next Minister, Rev. Mr. Meldrun, withdrew in 1765, by reason of a law suit between him and the Vestry. Rev. Mr. Sebastian receiving his orders from the Bishop of London, came in 1766 remained only two years; then came Rev. Mr. Thruston in 1768, and undertook the work for seven places in Frederick Parish, Winchester and Shepherdstown being the two most important points. He resigned in 1777 and entered the army, and soon won his commission as Colonel in the Revolutionary war." The Church records show no minister in charge until 1785, when the new Vestry, R. K. Meade, G. F. Norton, John Thurston, Edward Smith, Raleigh Colston, Girard Briscoe, John Milton, Robert Wood, Thos. Massey, elected Rev. Alexander Balmain as the Parish Minister. Mr. Balmain had served in the Virginia Regiments as Chaplain. The Church at Winchester had at the coming of Mr. Balmain attained such prominence, and the town was so attractive, that the new Minister chose Winchester as his home. It must be of interest to all, when, where, and how the first Episcopal Church in Winchester was located. Tradition fixes the N. W. Corner of the Public Square as the site of the first Church, and that Lord Fairfax in 1752, made a deed of conveyance to the Vestry for the large lot lying between the Court House Yard and Water St., extending East along Water to a point opposite the N. E. Corner of the present Court House. This is in the main correct. There is no record of any such deed, however, County and State records have been diligently searched, as well as all known papers of The Lord Proprietor's Office, in vain, to find such paper; and it must be concluded that Lord Fairfax when at the County Seat, as Justice and County Lieutenant, claiming proprietary rights over all the domain around him, and seeing that part of this Corner lot had already been appropriated for a burial ground, and as this remaining space was well adapted for church purposes, gave his approval in some way, and a building was erected. In the Sketches of Winchester, in other pages of this work, can be seen an extended description of this lot, which will not be repeated here. We have no evidence among the Court records as to the exact location of the first church, or date of erection. The first building erected on what can be called the Church Lot, was in 1762-3, when a stone building was erected fronting on Loudoun St., 10 feet distant from the *Boscawen* St. Corner and was used and controlled by the Vestry. This is shown by frequent notices to the Court, of infringements on the rights of the church property. Complaints were filed "For abuse and damage to the walls surrounding that property, and wanton and reckless *roamers* over the graves in the rear of the Church." What service, and who conducted the same, in this first church for the first decade, none can tell. No church records. Doubtless, some lay readers or some pious vestrymen conducted the service. No public record shows when the second church building was erected on this lot. Tradition has it, that a larger building was there a few years before the Revolution in 1776, immediately North of the first edifice, but owing to the changed conditions brought upon the Episcopal Church, this new structure was never in use until Rev. Mr. Balmain's arrival as the Minister to take control of the changed conditions a suitable man for this work, as was proven by his long and successful ministry of thirty years. Bishop Meade says, "I was his assistant during a number of the last years of his life"; and his tribute to the worth and faithful service of this co-worker, touches responsive chords in many hearts of those who have studied the life of the old Soldier-Minister. Following Mr. Balmain, came Rev. Mr. Bryan and Mr. Robertson, and so far as known closed the services in the Old Church on Loudoun St. In 1827 *Christ Church* was organized, and was known as "Of the Frederick and Winchester Parish." Rev. J. E. Jackson was the first Minister to take charge of the work that had developed a large Congregation of many of the most noted persons of that period. Mr. Jackson undertook the work of building the new home for this Congregation, which resulted in the large and comfortable church edifice on the corner of Water and Washington Streets, well remembered by the author as a point of local interest.

The Sabbath School in the *Basement,* where youths were well trained by faithful men and women prominent in the affairs of their church as well as of the town. Looking over this Congregation now, which is large and in superb quarters, the old building remodeled and comfortable. Chapel East of the Rectory, we see a change that is impressive. The elderly ones have long since passed out of sight, and but few youths of that day are seen in the pews of the *Fathers.* Mr. Jackson was succeeded by Rev Mr. Rucker in 1842, he resigned in 1847, to be succeeded by Rev. Cornelius Walker, whose ministry continued to the close of 1860, to whom the author is indebted for much matter comprised in this sketch. During Dr. Walker's ministry, the tower-belfry was erected in 1855. Rev. Wm. C. Meridith came in 1860 and except the four years spent as a soldier and Chaplain continued until 1875, honored and esteemed by all. The writer knew him as a personal friend, and spent many days with him in the near-by mountains, seeking recreation and *game.* During the absence of Mr. Meridith in the Confederate Army, services were seriously interrupted. No Minister to give pastoral care to the remnant of the large congregation that had been depleted by the quick response of men of all ages, answering Virginia's *call* for her sons to lay aside their peaceful avocations, and take firm stand upon her border, and stem the tide of Coercion rushing from the North. Some of the brave youths going out from this congregation, never returned. Some returned with marks of the maimed hero. The empty sleeve and wasted forms were much in evidence, as they sought their accustomed places. The faithful Minister also returned to take up the work of reconstruction. Several visiting Clergymen during the War, present as Chaplains in the army, ministered to the congregation, Rev. Jas. B. Avirett being one. Rev. Magruder Maury spent some time in such service. Mr. Meridith was succeeded by Rev. Jas. R. Hubard, whose pastorate continued to 1887, when Rev. Nelson P. Dame in a short time came, and throughout his long and eminent service accomplished much in his Church. His resignation in 1904, left the Church without a regular rector nearly one year, when the Vestry was fortunate in securing the Rev. Wm. D. Smith, the present Pastor.

During the early life of the Winchester Church, the ministers were giving their attention also to several other points in the old parish. Subdivisions set in very early after the Winchester Parish was set off. Bishop Meade says, "It resulted in five subdivisions," the second being Wickliffe and Berryville, with Rev. Richard Wilmer as the first Rector, in 1834. He was succeeded by Mr. Peterkin, then Mr. Whipple. This Parish was fortunate in receiving service from such faithful and distinguished men, who later on were elevated to the

Bishoprick. The division of the old parish in 1769, resulted in the three parishes, with Beckford on the South, Frederick, comprising several chapels and other places in the Central division; the other was Norborne, and embraced nearly all that territory now comprising Berkeley, Jefferson and Morgan Counties. Very few churches were found in this parish until after the Revolutionary War. It seems the first church was built in Martinsburg, then a small village; though several Chapels were in use from 1755, and probably the Morgan Chapel once known as the Mill-Creek Chapel, was in use in 1752. (This is mentioned in the road order, referred to elsewhere). The Martinsburg Church was regarded as an old, unsafe building in 1835. However the new church was not completed until 1843, when it was solemnly dedicated by Bishop Meade. He mentions the Clergymen present as assistants: Revs. Alexander Jones and J. Chisholm of Virginia, and James A. Berck and Theodore B. Lyman of Maryland. There seems to have been very few ministers in this parish for a number of years. Either the Church records are at fault for not recording the names and terms of service of the Ministers—if any were in the large field, or the Ministers were too indifferent concerning such matters that now appear of great interest in all the Churches; the demand being to keep a strict record of every event in the churches. The conclusion must be that there was a scarcity of clergymen. This is well known to have been the case from 1785 to 1820 owing to the severe changes brought about by the War with England. However after 1785, the names of Veasy, Wilson and Page frequently appear as very active in their work. Bishop Meade, speaking of these Ministers, says, "They were deeply pious, zealous and far beyond the ministerial standard of the Parish." For a few years after 1800, Heath, Price, and Allen seem to be the only active clergymen. From 1816, more activity is discernible, and parish records give the names of the following ministers, who seemed to distribute their work all over the parish, starting from Martinsburg, which had at the latter date become quite prominent by reason of many distinguished citizens then resident there. The first Rector at Martinsburg in 1816 was Thos. Horrell, then Enoch Lowe, and Edward R. Lippit to 1823; John T. Brooke to 1826, Jas. H. Tyng to 1830, Wm. P. Johnson to 1832, Cyrus H. Jacobs to '36, C. C. Tallefferro to '37, Jas. Chisholm to '42, D. F. Sprigg to '50; Richard T. Davis to '55; W. D. Hanson to '60; John W. Lee to '75; Robert D. Roller to '79; Henry Thomas to '88.

It is difficult to determine the dates of erection of the several old church buildings in Norborne Parish. At Shepherdstown as early as 1785, the County records show that a church lot was there and location of a division line between a *coterminous owner and the new Episcopal Church lot.* This evidently was Trinity Episcopal Church, as it was called, in 1840, when it was removed and a larger edifice was erected on same ground, and finished with great taste and care. The question arises, was this the church that was consecrated April 5th, 1859, by Bishop Johns? Did it require nineteen years to complete this splendid building? Dr. Charles W. Andrews was Rector at the time. The same ministers whose names have already been given as those of Norborne Parish, were Rectors of this Church. Rev. John P. Hubard was there from 1875 to 1880; Rev. L. R. Mason came in 1881. Over in Jefferson County can be seen to-day the ruins of the most noted church structure in Norborne Parish, and possibly the oldest of them all. No record to tell. Even Tradition is silent as to definite dates. Old men have said it was built before the Revolutionary War, but unable to give dates. Bishop Meade says, "It was a ruin when I was a boy," and places the date of its erection between 1760 and 1770—giving no reason for this conclusion, however. This ruin has always been known as *Old St. George's Chapel,* and stands on natural limestone foundations in a rock-bound spot, in an open field on the farm of Col. Davenport, one mile from Charlestown. This was supposed to have been the most costly church building in the Parish, and it is unfortunate that no record can be produced to unfold its interesting history, which would show who of the old families are buried in the *old burial ground* hard-by all of which has long since been abandoned, and none to tell whose dust is beneath the surface. Who can tell what the cycles of time have in store for many more of the sacred places found in our midst! A Century is a great leveler. The writer has witnessed in his day the passing out of sight of several sacred spots, so dear to some of the old Ancestors.

Zion Episcopal Church, Charlestown, cannot be regarded as an old church, but has been one of importance; second building replaced the first church in 1817. From this date, churches at Harpers Ferry, Bunker Hill, Smithfield and Hedgesville have all advanced in their work, receiving attention from the ministers of neighboring churches, all being called parishes. The subdivisions of the old parish can scarely be named. Bishop Meade says, "Rev. Mr. Allen exercised his ministry at twelve points included in the Parishes." He was succeeded by Rev. B. B. Smith as Rector of Zion Church Alexander Jones was also there. The old Church was destroyed by fire, and then rebuilt and dedicated in 1852. Rev. Dr. W. H. Meade grand-son of Bishop

Meade, became Rector of this Church in 1867. The building suffered from use and wanton abuse by Federal soldiers during the Civil War. The Church repaired the losses, and has also an attractive chapel in Charlestown, Rev. Dallas Tucker succeeded Dr. Meade April, 1883.

For many years the *"Old Chapel"* was the principal place of worship for that section of old Frederick embraced now by the Wickliffe, Berryville and Millwood Churches. Mr. Treadwell Smith and Genl. Thomas Parker undertook the work of establishing a convenient place of worship for the neighborhood known as Wickliffe, and succeeded. A stone building was erected, and services held there for several years. Owing to the unsafe condition of the walls, a very handsome brick building was erected in its stead. Later on, the Church at Berryville was erected, to accommodate the increasing membership; thus lopping off gradually the services at Old Chapel, which had long since not only become too small for the large congregations, but inconvenient, the roads being impassable during inclement seasons. In 1834, there seems to have been a well arranged plan to abandon the Old Chapel altogether; and a movement made to have a church near the attractive village of Millwood. Mr. George Burwell, of Carter Hall, offering a site for the building. All went well until a canvass was made in the congregation for sufficient funds to erect the more modern and commodious edifice known now as the Millwood Parish Church. It was soon found that too much sentiment lingered around the Old Chapel and its grounds, hallowed by the incidents of nearly a Century; for be it remembered, Old Chapel and its graveyard had been the most prominent point mentioned in the Old County records relating to Frederick Parish; and it was natural for the descendants of the long buried Ancestors to oppose its abandonment. A compromise was effected, both points to receive equal attention from the Minister. As time wore on, the services at Old Chapel became less frequent. Finally an agreement was effected, that continues to this day: there should be an annual pilgrimage of the two congregations, when interesting services were held. To many this was a sacred day, hallowed by the memories revived. After a few decades, the links between the past and the present dropped out of the chain one by one, until the service is now one of duty. The old burial ground found there during the last two Centuries, with its many unkept graves on both sides of the "Chappel-run," has undergone a magic change. Family plats of ground in regular order, marked by either the simple slab and simple inscription, or the imposing shaft and massive monuments, with brief histories of the many noted persons, are seen on every side, as the visitor stands 'neath the bending bough of the great forest giants, as they cast their shadows over this romantic and historic spot. The State and Church are well represented here. Men of four war periods lie under this sod. Family records note the burial place of some who have no mark at the grave to tell who the hero was. In recent years, the people of the adjoining communities honored themselves and their country by erecting a suitable monument to the gallant Clarke soldiers who fell at their respective posts during the War between the States 1861-65; their names and branch of service artistically inscribed upon the sides of this shaft of honor—many of them well known to the author. On this shaft is the name of one that brings vividly to him a scene of carnage never to be effaced from the memory of those who witnessed it. This was Capt. Wm. N. Nelson, who carried marks of the bullet that passed entirely through his breast, entailing lingering years of weakness and suffering. Many were dazed at his survival of the ghastly wound. The gallant, gentle chieftan, saintly man, warm hearted friend, has answered the last call. While his comrades say peace to his ashes, all have fresh memory of his glorious deeds.

In Beckford Parish, in South end of Old Frederick, the brick Church in the Village of Middletown was erected through the efforts and liberality of such distinguished men as Strother Jones, Senr., and the three Hite Families living in that vicinity. This Parish was supposed to be distinct from other parishes, but for many years the White Post Meade Memorial, Zion, and one other point formed a separate Parish; all these points ministered to by the same Minister. In recent years Middletown and Stephens City have been under the care of Christ Episcopal Church, or properly speaking, Winchester parish, as Mission points.

CHAPTER XXXV

Parish of Hampshire

The Episcopal Church had opportunities afforded it by the Colonial Government in this Parish at a very early day. The Parish was formed in 1753, and every step taken to support a ministry in that hill country. The *tithes* were laid and collected, and the church fund was ready, but Ministers failed to respond. In 1771-72, three men were ordained in England for this work in Hampshire Parish, viz: Ogilvie, Manning, and Kenner. Bishop Meade says, "Mr. Manning alone ever reached there, the others settling in Parishes below the Ridge." Rev. Mr. Reynolds seems to have been the first Episcopal clergyman to officiate in marriage ceremonies in the parish, and this chiefly in that part later known as Hardy County; old family records show this. Later on, the names of Revs. Norman and Sylvester Nash celebrated marriages in the Episcopal form, as shown by family records. So these three seem to have been the only Ministers of the Established Church that made the venture to plant churches among the numerous Dissenters who held the hill country. The church records are without reference to the work of these Ministers, except that during the time of Mr. Nash's labors, he succeeded in building two log churches in the parish—no mention however of their location. Tradition fixes Romney as one point. Mr. Sylvester Nash is accredited with having been instrumental in building a brick Church at Romney in the place of the log church, and that his services were appreciated, but the interest waned, and he retired, and for many years other Ministers went into this Parish and failed to accomplish much. Rev. Dr. Walker says in an article he was kind enough to send the author, "I held mission services in the Romney Church prior to the Civil War, and it seemed to be uncertain who had the rights of use, the Presbyterians or my Church, for I had been informed that the building was the property of the Episcopal Church, thus showing that very little had been done by the Episcopal Church prior to the mission work." The author has been informed by old citizens of Romney, daughters of Dr. Wm. H. Foote, that the brick church mentioned, was beyond a doubt the property of the Episcopal Church, and at the time Dr. Walker held his mission services, the Presbyterians owned and used their own Church property, and never had any need for the use of the Episcopal Church building; but the Methodists used it for many years as their preaching place, and have always had the use of it. A Mr. Hedges and also Mr. Irish made efforts to keep alive the Episcopal services after Mr. Nash left the parish. Bishop Meade says, "Their efforts were unsuccessful; and we will not dispair of seeing her old bare walls clothed again with garments of praise, and a crown once more on her head." The Saintly Bishop never had his hopes realized, so far as the old brick building goes; but through *some sublime mode,* he may know that his sacred Episcopacy is enjoyed in the attractive church erected since the War in the old town in the vicinity of the Public Institution, and has for years worn the crown he prayed for.

Moorefield has its mark of progress for the Church, in its comfortable church property and increase of membership.

Beckford Parish, heretofore mentioned as comprising the Southern sections of the old Frederick Parish, embraced all of the country known as Shenandoah County. In the study of the origin and progress of the Episcopal Church in the Shenandoah section of Beckford Parish, the author has found much confusion. There is very little doubt as to the location of the first church. All writers agree that Woodstock was the central point for more than one Congregation of Protestant Christians, a large Congregation of German Lutherans being the chief, differing somewhat from what was known about that period as the Swedish Congregation. The country adjacent for many miles had been settled by what was generally supposed a sturdy class of Germans; but along with this German immigration came quite a number of Swedes, not differing materially from the Germans. So the Settlement was regarded as the German Settlement. In 1772, a number of persons had formed an independent Society and made an effort to have trustees appointed by the old Justices Court, to hold property for the use of the "Swedish Congregation," as they styled their organization. No differences between the two Congregations appear, all worshiping in the same building. This state of affairs existed until the dark clouds of the Revolution appeared on the horizon. The old German Lutherans adhering strictly to their form of worship, the Swedes making some departure, and were holding separate services, observing the ritualistic forms. Just at this juncture, before any friction occurred in the large Congregation, there appeared in their midst one of the most remarkable men of that period, Rev. Peter Muhlenburg, a man equal to any emergency, as will be seen later on, a German, possessing all the peculiar traits that characterized the German settlers with whom he was to mingle; and also equipped with the rites and forms of worship that captivated the Swedish contingent. Nothing more is heard of a separate organization. This young Minister had received a training that fitted him for the critical condition existing in this Congregation. A student of German Lutheran Theology, ordained as a Minister by his own father, he had ministered to a Lutheran Church, and knew the needs of the German Lutherans. Without forsaking his Creed, he had also been ordained to the Ministry by a Bishop of the Established Church in England; and he had the right given him to return to America and conduct the Episcopal services. Thus equipped, he entered upon his memorable ministry at Woodstock. His strong character was soon felt; and it is no wonder that he grasped the situation, and laid the foundation for the first Episcopal Church in Shenandoah County. Still, some confusion exists in relation to this Church. Episcopal Church writers always mention it as the Muhlenburg Swedish Episcopal Church, and the Lutheran Church writers never show any reason why it could in any sense be other than Lutheran. Prominent descendants of the old Swedes have held tenaciously to the tenets of their fathers, and aided by other Episcopalians, succeeded after many failures, in placing the Church of their ancestors on a firm foundation in that part of Old Beckford Parish. It seems strange, however, that while all other denominations made marvellous advances throughout all that region, that this branch of the church should fail in its efforts to plant churches in the section where the old Swedish Church had laid the foundation. Howe in his History of Virginia, mentions it as a fact coming under his own observation. "There was no Episcopal Church in that section in 1843, and the Town of Woodstock had only three Churches at that date, German Reformed, Lutheran and Methodist." Whatever the contention may be between the Lutherans and Episcopalians, in regard to the old Church in Woodstock, and whatever claim either may advance as to the Muhlenburg Ministry, a perusal of the Deed for the Lots numbers 113 and 114, found recorded in Shenandoah County Clerk's Office, bearing date Sept. 27, 1774, should settle the question of vested title to the church property—the *grant* being expressed in unmistakable language: "Doth by these presents alien and make over to the said Vestrymen of the said Parish of Beckford and their successors in office, on behalf of said Parish, * * * and for use and purpose of building and supporting a Church for public Worship." And as to his ministry, whether Episcopal or Lutheran, his biographer, Dr. Henry Muhlenburg, whose wife was a granddaughter of Genl. Muhlenburg, and himself a grand-nephew, he should be accorded credit for what he writes of this Minister, over whom the contention arose. He says, "That in hunting for a Minister who could speak German, the name of a young Lutheran Minister, Peter Gabriel Muhlenburg, was suggested, and that the members of the Vestry of the Episcopal Church of Winchester, and Dr. Peters, of Philadelphia, offered to pay the expenses of young Muhlenburg to England if he would be ordained an Episcopal Minister. Hugh Mercer and James Wood (the latter afterwards Governor of Va.), were the Vestrymen of Winchester who made the offer." The present church building is on the original site; was erected in 1882, and was consecrated while Rev. Wm. Walker was Pastor. Succeeding him in the following order were Rev. J. T. L. Hynes, Dr. James Grammar, Dabney C. C. Davis, and Wm. H. Darbe, the present Minister. The membership is small. The Parish embraces St. Andrews Church and Mt. Jackson, Va. As a matter of reference, the following is entered here in connection with the Episcopal Church. In other pages of this volume, the subject of Glebe Lands is fully treated. The Winchester Parish owned tracts of land from which the Minister received the rents and profits. Jany. 12, 1802, the Genl. Assembly directed the Overseers of the Poor to sell certain of the Glebe Lands. Pursuant to an Amendment 1821, the Overseers of the Poor sold to David Castleman and Chas. McCandless, trustees, one of the Glebe tracts, on Feb. 4, 1822, containing 156 acres, price $3,930. This recital appears in the deed, "Whereas said tract had become vacant by death of Rev. Alexander Balmain, D.D., which took place 16th June, 1821." This land had been held by the Minister, Church Wardens and Vestry for many years.

CHAPTER XXXVI

The Lutheran Church

The Planting of Lutheranism in Old Frederick County, Va., presents a subject of no ordinary interest to any writer who desires to embody in a brief sketch an outline history of its first appearance with the white man in the wilderness West of the Blue Ridge. In the very earliest court records, petitions came up from certain German Lutheran Settlements for the opening of roads. Two of these Settlements seemed so remote from each other, that the conclusion often forces itself upon the gleaner of incidents from the old records, that they had but little intercourse with each other. Indeed, it often appears that they entered the Valley from different points, one of these being Funk's Settlement near the site of the present town of Strasburg. They were struggling to have a road from their Settlement to Orange Court House; and later for a ferry across Sherando River, and also a road to the county seat of Frederick County. Strange coincidences here. Borden's Settlement in the North end of the county wanted a road from Operkon Creek to the ferry on the Cohongoruta River, and also from their settlement, crossing Mill Creek to the county seat of Frederick County. Tradition fixes no very early date for church services at either of these Settlements, and the county records show the names of Funk and Borden to be of the very first persons holding land as *Homesteads* in the new County; and same records show their signatures in German. So it plainly appears that these German settlers planted their religious creed along with their log cabins; and so thoroughly lived their religion that they were easily distinguished as German Lutheran Settlements. No county record reveals the name of any minister at that early day conducting Gospel services in these Settlements. As to who they were, the author must rely upon such authority as the Church affords, in its own irregular history covering the latter half of the 18th Century. The writer, in his effort to compile historical events relating to this church, makes no claim to present anything new to the clergy or even to the laity, for it is well known that much has been written and said by those competent in every way to present details of the rise and progress of the Lutheran Church, much of it in most attractive form; but the writer was much embarrassed in his effort to obtain details, to learn that only a few persons could produce the reliable sketches, written by Rev. Drs. Gilbert and Krauth, that were so full of information concerning the church they had served so faithfully in various fields. Their ministry and their brief attractive sketches go hand in hand, and should be revered as treasures for their church. The author could have rendered satisfactory service to the church and the country by reproducing the memorable discourses of the ministers just mentioned and thus have them preserved in this publication, and probable circulation. The records of the Lutheran Synod of Virginia, are not as full and satisfactory as they should be;—indeed, such records give evidence of carelessness and a lack of knowledge concerning the importance of preserving church history. This does not simply apply to the old fathers who were making history for the population of all these counties, but it applies in a great measure to these generations. They have learned to know the value of preserving historical events, yet they fail in many cases to record incidents that will be sought for by those who follow us.

Consulting Sprague's Annals of the Lutheran Pulpit, we have some light thrown on an important feature in the history of this Church. It appears that the Lutheran Church was not only planted in the North end of the Old County at New Mecklenburg, but had a house of Worship there in 1760, and a regular pastor in 1776, in the person of Rev. Mr. Bauer. This was about the time the German Lutheran Church was established in Shenandoah County, which had been part of Frederick. No evidence that either of these points had the services of a regularly ordained minister. The church records observe complete silence when any reference is made to Lutheran Congregations, as to who the ministers were, and except for the contents found in the old corner-stone of the old Lutheran Church in Winchester, none would know who laid the foundations of the historic old Stone Church. And strange to say, no other church record shows the name of the minister who officiated on that occasion. The Synodical record shows that a

German Lutheran Congregation was in an organized state in 1762 at Winchester, and makes a brief note, stating "that upon their application they were received into regular Synodical connection with the Synod of Pennsylvania." This Synod *was the only Lutheran Ecclesiastical body in the Country.* The records of this Congregation—found in the Corner-stone,—may have mentioned many things of interest relating to the planting of this Church in the Village of Winchester. None have been preserved so far as known, except the valuable document which gives in full the names of the founders of the church they proposed to build, and also the date of the beginning of this great work, as well as a declaration of their principles as fearless and determined men holding the faith of Martin Luther. This document which has been so carefully preserved in all these years, is given at this point in full in the English translation; the original is written in *Latin,* and not in German, as has been stated by several writers.

"In the name of God the Father, Son and Holy Ghost, Amen.

The foundations of this Temple, by the Grace of God, were laid in the year of Christ 1764, on the Sixteenth day of April. The Hearers and Founders of this Temple are all and each members of the Evangelical Lutheran Church, at this time residing in this *City* of Winchester, to-wit: Thomas Schmidt, Nicholas Schrack, Christopher Henockel, David Deitrick, Christopher Wetzel, Peter Helfenstein, George Michael Laubinger, Heinrich Becker, Jacob Braun, Stephen Franckel, Christopher Altrilk, (this name was afterwards Aldrich and Eldridge, as old records show) Tobias Otto, Eberhard Doring, Andreas Friedly, Christopher Heintz, Imanuel Buger, Donald Heizel, Jacob Trautvein, Joh Sigmond Haenh, Johannas Lemly, Johannes Lentz, Christian Schumacher, Michael Roger, Michael Waring, Christopher Lambert, Samuel Wendel, Michael Gluck, Julius Spickert, Balthaser Po, Jacob Koppenhaber, (Copenhaver) Heinrich Weller, under whose care and inspection and at whose expense this Temple is built.

At that time bore rule George III, King of Great Britain, Our most Clement Master, and his Officers and Governors in Virginia, Francis Fauquier in Williamsburg, presiding with highest authority, and Thomas Fairfax Chief Magistrate of this whole District, at that time residing not far from this City, who has given to us gratuitously and of good will two lots of ground, embracing one acre, for Sacred uses.

This Temple has been Consecrated to the Triune God and to the Evangelical Lutheran Religion alone; all sects whatever name they may bear and all others, who either dissent from or do not fully assent to our Evangelical Lutheran Religion, being forever excluded:

As a permanent record of which to our posterity this paper is here placed, and has been deposited for everlasting remembrance in this Corner-Stone;

Drawn up in Winchester April 16th MDCCLXIIII.

Johann Casper Kirchner, At that time Minister of the Evangelical Lutheran Church,

Scribe LUDWIG ADAMS,

ANTHONY LUDI, School-Master in City."

Efforts have been made to discover what relation Rev. Kirchner bore to this Congregation, whether he was regular Pastor, or only a visitor requested to attend these special services. No church reveals anything more than his signature to this document. Dr. Gilbert says in his pamphlet on the "Fathers of the Church," that he was Pastor of the first Lutheran Church in Baltimore in 1762, and that he died in 1773. Dr. Gilbert adds "I am unable to produce any other record of this Minister, whose name is given as the first Lutheran Minister to appear in the Shenandoah Valley. It will be enquired by some who may chance to read these pages, how were the old Congregations maintained by any regular service, so as to preserve their Organization and be able to enjoy the Gospel service of the Faderland? No Minister to give a Shepherd's care in all these years! Yes, this sounds strange to the Churches of to-day. Not many could survive the peculiar conditions existing in those old Congregations for thirty years. It must be remembered, however, that wherever a Lutheran Congregation was found, there was their cherished "Augsburg Confession," and like the *"Shorter Catechism and Confession of Faith"* has been to the Presbyterian in his exile, it was a guide to them for all things. The Lutheran Church had in its old Constitution, ample provision for the *School-Master* of the Settlement, in the absence of the Minister, to conduct Gospel services and perform duties in the burial service. He was also "enabled for proper observance of Worship at stated times;" and when accessions were made to their membership, there is but little doubt that such men as are named in the record found in the cornerstone of the old Stone Church on the eastern side of the little "City," in 1764, were fully capable of testing the fitness of all who desired to become one of their number. And may it not be accepted as a fact, that all these Lutheran Congregations that preserved their Organizations for so many years without the pastoral care of any minister were bands of Christians well worthy the service of such men as Bauer, Streit and Muhlenburg when they came with regular Church Orders, to accept Calls made for their services. Bauer at Mecklenburg, 1776; Muhlenburg at Woodstock, and Streit at Winchester, 1785. Between the years 1770 and 1776, some missionary work was done in the Lower Valley by Rev. J. C. Hartwick, Henry Moeller, and C. F. Wildbahn. County records show that Trustees held a lot in Stephensburg 1770, for the use of the German Lutheran Congregation; and Church notes show they had a log house on this lot. Old deeds show that adjoining lot owners had lines to adjoin the *graveyard;* and church records show that a brick church was erected on the old site in 1813. Some may enquire at this point, who were these regular pastors who came to these congregations, and what did they do to distinguish them from many other men? The names of Muhlenburg and Streit have grown familiar to each succeeding generation; and the writer hopes to make them more so to the readers of this volume in other chapters. At this point it is proper to set forth what the ministers found awaiting them at their respective locations. Mr. Bauer, when he took charge at Shepherdstown in 1776, found the Congregation well organized and worshiping in their peculiar way without a regular minister, in a building comfortable and suitable for church purposes, which the new Pastor and Congregation dedicated for church services. Services were conducted in this church by succeeding pastors until 1795, when the corner stone for a new church was laid with imposing ceremonies. Rev. David Young having assumed the pastors work, labored acceptably for several years. He died in 1801, after a protracted illness. His ministrations were strictly to the English style which became popular; perhaps some of the good old German Lutherans felt the effect too much; and this may account for the appearance among them in 1802 of a new pastor with the unmistakable German form of worship, if the name is any index to his view of what service this Congregation should have to cure what disaffection had crept in through the English form; so Rev. Mr. Gausinske undertook to give his lessons in German. But the little English leaven was too much for him to overcome; his short stay only fanned the flame that had started, and he soon left the field. The Church suffered with these useless dissensions for years. During this time, Rev. Mr. Rabonack, another German, tried the field for about two years; he gave way to a Mr. Kehler, who combined the English and German, but failed in less than one year. Fortunately on the first day of July, 1819, Rev. C. P. Krauth, whose reputation as a sublime Christian Minister had long since been known to this Congregation, accepted their call and preached an effective sermon in pure English; and his daily contact with the people soon won their confidence, and gradually the storm abated and good fellowship prevailed, and for the eight years of his service, the Church took new life; the English service was fully established, and has been maintained to this day. After Dr. Krauth's retirement in 1827, the Church has prospered under the ministry of Revs. Medtart, Weir. Martin, Speecher, Seiss, and several others. The Church is considered strong in the Virginia Synod of to-day.

The next in order of the trio of Ministers mentioned, is Rev. Peter Gabriel Muhlenburg. He arrived at Woodstock when the church to which he had been called—like the country, had some unrest that bordered on dissensions. As we have seen in the sketch of the Episcopal Church, there were two distinct sects in the Congregation—the Swedish being one, and the German Lutheran the other; the former desiring more ritualism in the service. Both had certain forms; and a disinterested observer once remarked, "It was plain they had a distinction, but he failed to see the difference." There was a difference however, which was being felt by this large body of people, with no shepherd to take oversight. Just at this juncture came Muhlenburg, fully equipped to meet the emergency. Doubtless he was a Lutheran like his father, but he had conceived the idea that he could be more effective in his ministry if he had church orders bestowed on him by the Established Church;—at least he would not be embarrassed or hindered in his service by any Vestry, who seemed to think in that day that their duty was to annoy other churches, instead of devoting themselves to their own and exercising proper influence over the struggling membership, and providing suitable edifices for their own people to worship in. Mr. Muhlenburg was not disturbed by any Vestry. He knew the wants of the German Lutherans, and was well fitted to serve the Swedish faction. He proved himself able to cope with the conflict, and all went well, differences subsided, and his brief ministry has been a wonder and a puzzle to many,—how he could lay the foundation for an Episcopal Church, and serve the Lutherans so acceptably. From the time he laid aside his church vestures and donned the uniform of an officer in the great struggle for freedom from British tyranny, he has been claimed by both Churches as their Minister; and as he never returned to the ministry when hostilities ceased, none will ever know what he was. The Congregations at Woodstock and other points in Dunmore County, had great reverence for his good deeds and useful and successful ministry. The churches, of course, suffered loss during the Revolutionary War, with no pastor for any of the neighboring churches. Many of the best members entered their country's service; many of them never returned. In 1790, Rev. Paul Henkel came from his native State, North Carolina, and began a ministry in several vacant churches. Beginning where New Market was soon to become a village, Mr. Henkel seemed to have the whole of Shenandoah as a mission field for several years. No regular minister had charge of the Woodstock Church until 1829, when the first Convention was held that year. Dr. Gilbert says this was August 10-11th, and mentions Rev. J. Nicholas Schmucker, of the Woodstock and Strasburg Charge, also the Laity was Jacob Ott, of Woodstock, and Lawrence Pitman, of Mt. Jackson. Nov. 5th, 1838, Rev. J. B. Davis was ordained at Strasburg. Dr. Gilbert says that Messrs. D. F. Bittle and Isaac Baker had been recommended as suitable persons for licensure and obtained the same. According to the best Church records, the churches in Shenandoah during all the years prior to 1850, received very irregular service, very few ministers appearing in the churches, and no record to show any Stated Pastor. For more than forty years the Church has prospered throughout the Shenandoah section, seeming to take new life after the Civil War. The next of the trio is Rev. Christian Streit, who had settled in Winchester on the 19th day of July, 1785, according to Wolfe in his interesting work, *The Lutherans of America*. Mr. Streit had seen service in the Revolutionary War as Chaplain, and was taken prisoner by the British while he was pastor at Charleston, South Carolina. Mr. Streit in his new field, assumed the pastoral oversight of a large congregation of sincere and devoted Lutherans, but of such admixture of German and English, that he was confronted with grave responsibilities, and was embarrassed somewhat by lack of proper place of worship; for standing out in bold relief were the massive bare walls of the new Stone Church, whose cornerstone had been laid 16th day of June, 1764; and now full 21 years had passed and the building was unfinished. No adornments, not even windows or doors. The unfinished building indicated a state of affairs in this Congregation that was enough to discourage some men. Mr. Streit at once set to work to know the cause of this long delay of completion. One good reason was the six years of war that had unhinged everything in the country,—even the power of King George. The building had been used as barracks for soldiers, as they occasionally assembled at Winchester for formation of the new regiments. (The Author will say at this point, this building could not have been used as barracks for Genl. Braddock's Regiments, as claimed by some writers, going so far in one case as to say, "Genl. Braddock was attracted by its peculiar location, situated on an eminence that commanded a view of the surrounding country, he appropriated it for his Head Qrs.; and in this building he and Col. Washington planned the march and details of the campaign which was to end in his death and disaster to his splendid army,"—all of which must of course be nothing more than the fanciful touch of a reckless pen for magazine articles. As is well known, the foundation of this building had not been selected, even, when Braddock was in the village in 1755).

The spirit that prompted the old Germans in '64, to lay the foundation of the massive structure, seemed lacking in the people that Mr. Streit found in '85; and he was compelled to preach his first sermon as Pastor on Sunday, July 25th, 1785, in the old log church on the same hill, the building which had for years been used alternately by the Reformed Calvanist and German Lutheran Congregations. Mr. Streit soon learned that the former were the real owners of the property; and he at once stirred a lively spirit in his congregation; the result being that all sprang to the work of completion, and together with a *Lottery scheme* provided for by an Act of the Genl. Assembly, 1788, they secured funds sufficient, not only for the completion and adornment of the church, but to justify an order for two bells to be cast in Germany; and later on in 1793 the spire went up; and in 1795, an organ was purchased. Mr. Streit had his congregation comfortably seated 1789 in what has been known for more than a Century as the *Old Stone Church on the Hill.* All this proved his wonderful efficiency; and his long pastorate made it possible for this church to attain the prominence it has held for the last century. It must be remembered that Mr. Streit had all the requirements needed for his great work, his learning, piety, energy, and youthful vigor, together with his supreme integrity, secured the devotion of his entire congregation. He preached able, sincere and often eloquent sermons, either in the German or English, as seemed to him desirable—which marked him as a man who commanded the respect and esteem of all, regardless of creed or social status.

His pastorate continued until his death, which occurred 10th March, 1812, lacking a few months to make it 27 years, that he had served this congregation. His *old diary* shows that he preached 386 times during the first three years—156 at Winchester, 58 at Stone's Chapel, 52 at Newtown, 26 at Strasburg, 28 at Old Furnace, 26 at Pine Hills, (Bethel) 6 at Capon, 4 at Warm Springs, (Whitehall) and 30 at various places in Virginia, Maryland and Pennsylvania. The author as Clerk of Court, was often called upon to give certificates of marriages of the old ancestors, and name of the minister celebrating the ceremony. The name of Christian Street appearing so often, he has recently taken the trouble to find how many marriages were solemnized by him. The first marriage was that of Wm. Law and Mary Peterson, Oct. 5th, 1785. The last marriage was that of Adam Haymaker and Sally Grim, Dec. 25th, 1811. During that time he officiated at 617 marriages.

Rev. Abram Reck succeeded Mr. Streit Jany. 1st, 1813. During his pastorate, the church building had many changes. The old style high pulpit which occupied the East side like a high loft, or miniature tower, was reduced in height and set up on the South end. The spire was then found to be in the wrong place and it was rebuilt in 1821. The church provided for a manse for their pastor, by converting the old stone school-house which for many years had stood on the northwest corner of the church lot, into a comfortable dwelling. Here Mr. Reck resided during the remainder of his ministry, which terminated in 1827. The church was much disturbed during his ministry by reason of his inability to convince many of his members of the wrongs they were charging to others. Counter charges prevailed; and the Pastor found it best to resign. They needed a Streit at the helm. The disaffection was afflictive, but since it was an affair of this church, and not that of this generation, there is no need of giving any reasons for their trials. While they were grievous and hard to bear, there came a man in 1828—Rev. Lewis Eichelberger, who succeeded in bringing the church back to its safe moorings; and for years his good counsel and faithful service not only renewed the life of the old Congregation, but tightened the cords and strengthened the stakes of every Lutheran point in the county. In 1833 he resigned his charge of the Winchester Church, so that he might give more time to the other charges, with whom he laboured for many years. Many persons still living, can, and do, recall his successful work in this field, from mountain to river.

Rev. N. W. Goertner having accepted a call from this Church, became the Pastor, preaching his first sermon Feby. 1st, 1834. While his sermons were good and his service faithful, there was an apparent lack of harmony between pastor and people. Perhaps his doctrine was more Calvinistic than Lutheran; and discovering this himself, he resigned in 1836, and later on connected himself with the Presbyterian Church. Rev. Mr. Stork, a young man of much promise, preached his first sermon as pastor of this church Oct. 9th, 1837. Rev. J. R. Keisee succeeded Mr. Stork in 1843, serving as pastor during 1843, when he resigned. The church had become strong both financially and numerically. A strong feeling had shown itself for several years among a certain class of the congregation, to make changes, to accommodate a sentiment for a *down town* church. This was objected to, of course, by the older members who had an equally strong sentiment to cling to the Old Stone Church on the Hill. Compromises, however, were made, and the Council decided to provide a lecture-room at some convenient place down town to be used for night services, Sunday school, etc. Before proceeding to erect the room for lecture service, it became apparent that the demands for a change of location must be met; and the congregation decided in the latter part of 1839 to purchase the lot on Water St., where the present church now stands. On this lot work was started in the summer of 1840 to build a lecture-room. The trustees received further instructions from the congregation and the original plans were changed, and one adopted that would give a building suitable for all church purposes. During the erection of the new church, the older members were becoming reconciled to the change; and when the day came for the dedication of the new church home that had cost the congregation nearly $7,000; it was stated in a local newspaper of that date, "The entire congregation was present and gave evidence of their approval of the great change they had made." Rev. F. W. Conrad preached the dedicatory sermon on the first Sunday in Jany. 1843. No record shows who filled the pulpit in the new church during the following Spring and Summer. Rev. J. Few Smith was installed Nov. 1, 1843. He was a man of ability; and his ministry was fruitful of much good. After nearly five years service, he resigned, much to the regret of the congregation, who spread upon their minutes their appreciation of his pastorate. Mr. Smith entered the ministry of the Presbyterian Church, and was noted for his eloquence and power. The new church was now at that point where she entered upon her great career, which she has maintained to this day. April 9th, 1848, Rev. C. P. Krauth became their Pastor and remained as such until in the Autumn of 1855. Mr. Krauth's successful services to this church were such as could be expected from a man of his endowments. His learning and devotion to the duties of his sacred office, gave him a hold upon the affections of the congregation which never lost its influence. It was during Dr. Krauth's ministry—1850, that many costly improvements were made to the edifice—an imposing bell-tower was erected for the old bell which was brought from the old stone building, and there it is in use at this writing. The writer remembers well when the new pipe organ gave forth its first volume of music to the large waiting congregation. It was quite an event at that time for a church to invest the large sum of $1,000. for such purposes—total expenditures about $3,000. The following year the church continued its evidence of prosperity, in the purchase of a home for their pastor on Loudoun St., due West from the Jail.

The year 1854 was one of historic interest to the Lutheran Church of Winchester. She seemed to have almost reached the zenith of her glorious progress. The large congregation had come up through many tribulations, and were happy and prosperous in their new home on Boscowan St., well equipped for every service. Their faithful pastor, after years of anxiety and service, was safely housed in the comfortable Manse; pastor and congregation enjoying their occasional pilgrimages to the old Stone Church on the Hill, which had furnished a home for the fathers and succeeding generations, through many well remembered episodes. Their cup of joy was well nigh full,—the old stone bulwark standing as it were a sentinel, to not only give watch over the new edifice and assembling congregations on each recurring Sabbath, as her old bell sent forth her musical call for service, but also as the guardian and keeper of the sacred grounds where their loved ones had been gathered for their eternal sleep. The glare of the mid-day sun and tornado storms produced no change in the old guardian. Dwellers in the town below grew to feel that it was an imperishable land-mark dear to all; little dreaming that the hour was near at hand when sombre clouds would cast their shadows over not only this happy congregation, but the entire community would be aroused to a sense of irreparable loss. The night of Sept. 27th. 1854, became memorable as the time when from some unknown cause, the old stone land-mark was destroyed by fire. The great stone wall crumbled on the North, South and East sides, leaving the West wall to mark the spot where sacred services were held, and where sacred ashes had lain for a half Century. The entire population was so stirred over their loss, that Dr. Krauth made the incident the subject of a discourse on the third Sabbath in Oct., 1854, so full of pathos, eloquence, and reflex of the feeling of the assembled community, that it has been treasured through all the passing years. At the earnest solicitation of the people of every Creed through their representatives, as will be seen in the following correspondence. The Address was published in pamphlet form, Dr. Krauth chose as his Text—"Our holy and beautiful house, where our Fathers praised Thee, is burned up with fire,—Isaiah LXIV, 11."

"CORRESPONDENCE.

WINCHESTER, VA., Oct. 25th, 1854.

REV. C. P. KRAUTH,

Dear Sir, We desire to express the pleasure which we in common with a very large audience, derived from the instructive and beautiful discourse delivered by you on Sunday last and suggested by the burning of the venerable edifice to which every citizen of our town has been attached by strong ties from infancy. We but express a general wish, when we ask that you would place in our hands a copy of your discourse for publication. It is the more proper that you should comply, from the fact that such an event deserves to be made memorable, and such a building, with so many hallowed associations clustering about it, should not perish without the perpetuation of its history in a form durable and worthy of the theme. We say no more than it merits, when we add that your discourse was eminently worthy of the subject,

We are, with high regard, your friends,

WILLIAM MILLER — J. R. TUCKER
JACOB BAKER — JO. TIDBALL
THOS. B. CAMPBELL — H. J. MESMER
ROBT B. HOLLIDAY — J. S. CARSON
F. W. M. HOLLIDAY" — T. A. TIDBALL.

"LUTHERAN PARSONAGE, WINCHESTER, VA.

J. R. TUCKER ESQ., AND OTHERS,

Gentlemen—I am not less willing to commit the discourse you so kindly ask for publication, because I feel that your estimate of it is one of the heart and not of the judgment. I meant but to lay a garland on an Altar, and I thank you that your reverence of the memories to which I meant to do homage, has given value to so inadequate an offering,

I am truly and gratefully yours

CHARLES P. KRAUTH.

The author is indebted to the publication referred to, for much valuable data as his guide

Ruins of old Lutheran Church, Winchester

in constructing this sketch, feeling assured that coming from one in such close touch with that period, that his information can be relied on. Want of space alone prevents a reproduction of the notable address. Dr. Krauth says that the old church had not been abandoned; but that occasional services were held there, and at various times Bishop Meade administered the Holy Communion in this Church; and the German Reformed had the use of it repeatedly. The Episcopal Congregation worshipped there for some time; and during the Summer of 1854, it was placed under the control of the Methodist Church during their temporary privation of a place of worship. In one of the aisles, near the pulpit, the brick pavement was removed for the grave of Rev. Christian Streit, and here his remains were interred with most solemn services. When the old church was reduced to ashes and dust, it was befitting the time that his tomb should be undisturbed. It lies under the ashes of the old Tabernacle. A monument has in recent years been erected near-by, with suitable inscriptions. Mr. Streit was born 1749, according to tradition, in West Jersey. His first wife died shortly after his arrival in Winchester; he then married Susan Barr 1789. She was the mother of William, Evalina, Henry B., Philip B., Emily, wife George Baker, and Frances A., wife of John Baker White, Catherine daughter of the first wife, married Jacob Baker. Mr. Streit lived and died in the old stone house on Market St., Winchester, now the home of Henry Baetjer, Esq., once the property of Genl. Morgan (see deed from Daniel Morgan dated Feby. 17th, 1787, for "certain Lotts on W. side of New or Cameron St., adjoining Philip Bush's store-house," etc.) Tradition gives this as Morgan's first residence in Winchester.

Dr. Krauth resigned as Pastor of the Winchester Church Oct. 1855, to take charge of the First English Lutheran Church at Pittsburg. After a short pastorate, he entered the University of Penn. He also, later on, became a prominent Professor of Theology in the Lutheran Theological Seminary. Succeeding Dr. Krauth were the following Ministers: Rev. A. Essick, Mr. Baum, Rev. Mr. Dosh in 1862, who continued pastor until 1871. Dr. D. M. Gilbert came in 1873; when he resigned, Rev. Lewis Miller was called, and when he resigned, Mr. Seabrook succeeded to the pastorate. Rev. George S. Bowers was called after Mr. Seabrook resigned. Mr. Bowers entered as Pastor in 1902 and is the present pastor, filling all the demands of this large and influential congregation.

St. Johns Lutheran Church in Martinsburg has an old church record dated 1779. There is evidence of two Congregations worshiping together in the same building, the Reformed Calvinist and the Lutherans. Their first services were held in 1776. The first building used by them, was a large log structure. In 1829-32 an imposing building was erected and dedicated by the Lutherans, which they used until the Civil War, when it was taken for a hospital. The Government in great haste appropriated $1,000, in 1868, for damages,—a majority of the congregation being loyalists.

The Lutheran Church at Shepherdstown has been mentioned in the first part of this sketch, showing Rev. Mr. Bauer was there in 1776. It has been well established that a Congregation of Lutherans worshipped there in about 1760. This Church was in much trouble from 1795, when the building was erected for Worship; the Germans and English disagreeing as to forms of worship. In 1819 Dr. Krauth took charge; and the dissensions were healed. They now have a modern edifice, and the Church is prosperous.

The period from 1702 to 1730 was marked by large accessions to the Lutherans of America, seeking an asylum from persecution. Large numbers of Germans came in 1711-17 and the years ensuing. On June 3, 1710, as many as 4,000 landed in ten vessels at New York, after a voyage of frightful hardships, from which several hundred had perished on the way. These were fugitives from the *Palatinate,* for whom the sympathies and munificence of Queen Anne had not only provided shelter, clothing and food in England, but also free transportation to the New World, with subsistence on the way, and princely domains for their occupation. These Palatinate refugees were the first Lutherans whom religious persecution drove to these shores. Their history is one of tragic interest. Within a single generation, their beautiful country,—one of the fairest and most fertile regions of Europe, had been thrice devastated by the armies of Louis XIV, who laid claim to the succession on behalf of his brother the Duke of Orleans. The country was overrun by barbarous soldiery who knew no pity for old or young; and when it was found impossible to hold what had been conquered, Louis gave command to have the Country, turned into a desert. Macaulay says "The French Commander announced to near half a million of human beings, that he granted them three days of grace. Soon the roads and fields which then lay deep in snow, were blackened by innumerable multitudes of men, women and children, flying from their homes. Many died of cold and hunger; but enough survived to fill the streets of all the cities of Europe with lean and squalid beggars who had once been thriving farmers and shopkeepers. Meanwhile the work of destruction began; the flames went up from every market-place, every hamlet, every parish church, every country seat within the devoted Province. The fields where the corn had been sown were ploughed up, the orchards were hewn down. No promise of a harvest was left on the fertile plains where once had been Frankenthal. Not a vine, not an almond tree was to be seen on the slopes of the sunny hills round what had been Heidelberg."

These atrocities swept on and over the whole Rhine region. Germany was frenzied; all Europe was horrified, and protested—but no avail. Butchery and devastation swept on until thousands were driven to some haven of peace. America was pointed out to them by the humane English Queen; which may answer in part why the German element became so numerous in the Shenandoah Valley within a few years after its discovery.

CHAPTER XXXVII

The German Reformed Church in Frederick County

This Church in the early settlement of Old Frederick County, was known as the "Reformed Calvinists Congregation." Old Orders of Court and other public records, mention no other name for this Church; and the Church records mention them as the *Reformed Calvinist Ministry* from the *Palatinate,* Germany. Their local Church record shows that their first Gospel services were held *in* the *Opeckon,* where at that time, 1743, was forming a nucleus of a village known as *Opecquon,* for many years—certainly as late as 1770. In the immediate vicinity, quite a number of Presbyterian families were there as early as 1736. Mr. Hoge conveyed them a lot (as shown elsewhere) of ground to erect a Meeting House on, and soon thereafter conveyed a lot for the *"Graveyard"*—the boundaries being given, "That it adjoins the lot whereon the Meeting House now stands." No record to show that the Reformed Calvinists had any claim upon this or any lot in *"Opecquon."* Tradition has always shown that they worshipped where the Presbyterians worshipped—Indeed, it was the same place where the Quakers had quarterly meetings for years and continued to meet until the points of Hopewell and Crooked Run, were adopted as place for *"Meetings."* It is unfortunate that the reckless writer will appear so often on such interesting subjects, which leads to confusion and misapprehension. Quoting the language found in a publication bearing the date 1890, the reader will have before him what is termed "An historical fact about this Church:" "The crumbling foundation of the little Stone Church near Kernstown is supposed to be the locality where this Congregation Worshipped. The Church was abandoned in 1753-4 when a Presbyterian Congregation occupied it, and by long occupation by them it has since been known as a Church of that denomination." If the reader will turn to the sketch of the Presbyterian Church in this volume he will find facts derived from the most reliable records, concerning the origin of the *Old Opeckon Church*—and a description of the old grounds, *graveyard,* etc. In the article just quoted, the writer deals in supposition; and is in error when speaking of the "little stone church." If he had seen the foundation of those crumbled walls, he never could have made this statement. The marks of the old foundation are plain at this writing. There he could have seen where the largest stone church in all the region, had stood for ages. Such statements do injustice to the noble band of Christians known as the Reformed Calvinists, who have ever maintained their reputation for integrity, sincere and unvarnished religion, and devotion to their methods. This Church has never wavered in her march through all the past; never at any time having a large Congregation, but always able to preserve their individuality among her sister Churches, with whom cordial relations existed at all times. The Fathers in the early lays worshipped at several other points in the Old County, one being at what is now called *Old Furnace,* St. John's where for many years they and the German Lutherans had joint ownership in a lot of ground near the site of the present church at that point. The place was then called "Zane," and the lot long since has formed part of the cemetery lot adjoining. Another point was Stone's Chapel, which was for many years prior to 1793 known as Jacob's church, and supposed to have been the property of the Reformed Calvinists and Lutherans. The deed says "To the Calvinists and Lutheran Societies." The Presbyterians and Calvinists were regarded by all as the same body of Christians; and when the deed was found by the writer, the Reformed Calvinists yielded, and have not raised the point since. The first evidence of this Congregation having Church services in Winchester, was very soon after 1753; for it was in that year they secured a deed from Lord Fairfax for the ground forming the site of their first church building which conveyance is dated May 15, 1753, and for Lots No. 82 and 83. This seems to be the only Deed that can be produced by any Church in the Lower Valley in which Lord Fairfax was grantor. The author has instituted search through every available source—county records as well as State and Church, and has had the aid of competent and experienced persons. The old records kept by Lord Fairfax at Greenway Court, were removed to the Office of Register of Lands in Richmond after his death, and there they have been carefully filed and preserved, and special effort was made to find deeds to other church property, and none could be found. As this is the only one found, it is well to have it appear in this connection. Why the trustees named should have been more fortunate than their neighbours, is not shown. Some have claimed that his Lordship was one of the Reformed Calvinists, and this is why he singled them out. Fairfax was not inclined to make such instruments; he preferred to appear as the Lord Proprietor, and where he allowed privileges of this character, he refrained from dealing with Church sites, burial grounds, etc., as he did with individuals. The latter were required to show his papers, or be ejected.

"The Right Honourable, Thomas Lord Fairfax, Baron of Cameron in that part of Great Britain called Scotland Proprietor of the Northern Neck of Virginia, To all to whom this writing shall come sends Greeting. Whereas Messrs. Philip Bush, Daniel Bush, Henry Brinker, Jacob Sowers, and Frederick Conrad of Frederick County, having set forth to my Office in behalf of the Reformed Calvinists, that Lotts Numbered (82) and (83) in the addition to the Town of Winchester in the Said County are conveniently situated for erecting and building a Meeting house for the use of the said Congregation, Know ye that for the causes aforesaid for and in consideration of the annual Rents and Covenants herein after reserved and Expressed I have given, granted and confirmed and by these presents for me, my Heirs and Assigns, Do give, grant and confirm unto the said Philip Bush, Daniel Bush, Henry Brinker, Jacob Sowers and Frederick Conrad, as Trustees appointed by the said Congregation the said recited Lotts of land for the use aforesaid and for no other purpose whatsoever as bounded by a survey and Platt of the said addition made by Mr. John Bayliss as follows, on the Southern side by Philpott Lane, on the Westw'd end by East Lane, on the Northern side by Abbchurch Lane, on the Eastw'd end by the East line of the said addition—To have and to hold the said Recited Lotts of land No. (82) and (83) Together with all and singular the Appurtenances thereunto belonging. To them the said Daniel Bush, Philip Bush, Henry Brinker, Jacob Sowers and Frederick Conrad and Successors for ever they the said Philip Bush, Daniel Bush, Henry Brinker, Jacob Sowers and Frederick Conrad and their Successors appointed Trustees as aforesaid, therefore yielding and paying to me, my Heirs and Assigns or to my certain Attorney or Attorneys Agent or Agents or to the certain Attorney or Attorneys of my Heirs or Assigns, Proprietors of the said Northern Neck yearly and every year on the feast day of St. Michael the Archangel the fee rent or sum of Ten Shillings Sterling money for the Said Lotts of land, Provided that if the Said Philip Bush, Daniel Bush, Henry Brinker, Jacob Sowers and Frederick Conrad and their Successors shall not pay the said Reserved annual as aforesaid, so that the same or any part thereof shall be behind or unpaid by the space of thirty days next after same shall become due if Legally demanded, that then it shall and may be lawful for me, my Heirs or Assigns, Proprietors as aforesaid, my or their certain Attorney or Attorneys, Agent or Agents into the above granted premises to Reenter and hold the same so as if this Grant had never passed. Given under my hand and Seal, Dated the fifteenth day of May in the twenty-sixth year of his Majesty King George the Second Reign, A. D., one thousand seven hundred and fifty three. . . . .

Registered in the Proprietors Office
In Book L folio 75

Fairfax."

No record has been found to give the exact location of the first building erected on the lots. Tradition, and Church records fully establish the fact, that the first building was in the most primitive style, and was in use by the Reformed Calvinists and Lutheran Congregations as early as 1758. By reference to the sketch of the Lutheran Church, it will be seen—Rev. Mr. Streit preached in this church in 1785; and it was known at the time as the Old Log Church, not far away from the unfinished structure known afterwards as the *Old Stone Church*. The location of the lots is easily found by reference to the records, situated on the eastern part of the Village of Winchester, bounded by Philpot Lane and East Lane. Who the Ministers were who preached for this Congregation from the erection of the log Meeting-House to about 1790, is not known to any of the membership of the present congregation. It is well established that Missionaries of this faith preached at various times throughout the Valley for many years after the first settlement. Such traveling ministers were careful to keep note of their work and travels in pocket diaries. These have been preserved by the Church in some way, but are not always accessible. A prominent Minister of this Church related "To the Author" many interesting incidents embraced in those notes, pertaining to the early life of the Reformed Calvinists along the waters of the *Sherando* River, that prove entertaining to the reader; but inasmuch as his informant had never seen these valuable "pocket diaries"—these pages need not be cumbered with what may appear doubtful to some readers.

The Winchester Church from about 1790, undertook through the efforts of several enterprising ministers, to preserve a record of the church, and some of the recorded incidents would be interesting to all. Rev. G. M. Schneyder seems to have been the first regular Pastor, at least the record kept by himself or Rev. Willey for the years 1790 and 1800 inclusive indicate this. Some have thought that a succeeding Pastor, Rev. Dr. John Brown, wrote the whole up to 1804. From this date, nothing is recorded to show that this Congregation continued services; indeed, but little mention is made other than to maintain evidence of ownership of the property. Notes appear that permission had been granted the Baptists to preach in the old Church. The name of Robert Sedgewick appears as a Baptist Minister in charge for a number of years. The most diligent enquiry of Officers and laymen of this Church, resulted only in the answer, that they had no authentic record covering the period of at least twenty-five years prior to 1840. Just previous to 1840, an effort was made to repair the old log Meeting-House, that had withstood the ravages of time for nearly one hundred years. An appeal was made to the Synod, comprised of this and other Congregations in Virginia, Maryland and Pennsylvania, for aid. To this appeal, a generous response was given; and that influential body advised the Congregation to erect a Memorial edifice, one to commemorate the *"One hundreth anniversary* of the Organization of the Reformed Calvinist Church in the Shenandoah Valley. This was a happy thought, one that filled the struggling band with inspiration. Their new zeal manifested itself to such an extent, the whole community was stirred with generous emotions; and it became possible for this revived remnant of the noble band, that had been scattered for so many years, to rally under their old banner, and when once planted on their new position, they began at once to fortify it. With aid from the Synod, and indefatigable efforts of the faithful men and women, the walls went up and a bulwark was soon offered for the little fold. Their beautiful Memorial received the name of the "Centenary Reformed Church." For twenty years they were undisturbed. Standing on the corner of Market and Cork Streets, it became a prey to the legions of Banks, Milroy and Sheridan—Federal Generals—who always encouraged wanton destruction of Church and private property. This little monument of so much zealous Christian effort, was first converted into a hospital, and then a stable for officer's horses—resulting in total destruction of all the adornments of the Memorial. The bare walls and a shattered roof alone, marked the spot where the Centenary Reformed Church had stood. The same old zeal which shone out from the fathers, caught hold of the survivors. So soon as the first sad days of a *Peace that can never be forgotten,* settled over the land that had been torn asunder, and with great sacrifice and untold effort, the little Church on the Corner, received such repairs as it was possible to give, and the scattered Congregation once more entered their sacred portals. Many additional repairs were made from time to time. The great strong Government at Washington was appealed to for redress, to cover the damages the church had sustained. No heed was given to constant effort. At last, however, when nearly all of the participants in the havoc of destruction had sunk out of sight, along with much of the animosity that existed so long between the two sections North and South, there came a day when new rulers and almost a new people recognized the justice of the claim for damages, that went up not only from this church but from similar Organizations. The Government had taken strong measures to redress in part such terrible wrongs. This Church in 1904-5 was allowed a reasonable sum for damages. The Congregation decided to erect an entirely new building on the old site; and to-day as you pass the old corner, you will observe this congregation has made good use of their opportunity, and spent their money and labor in a judicious way. The beautiful modern edifice is attractive to the eye, and gives great comfort to this deserving band of faithful men and women. Long may they be sheltered within its walls, and neither they nor their generations to follow, be ever again driven out from its sacred precincts, by any foe, be he *Man or Devil.*

The Church has been faithfully served since 1840, by the following named Ministers: Rev. Geo. A. Leopold came then and was succeeded by Rev. D. H. Bragonier, Robert Douglas followed him and assumed the work of several Churches; in 1845 he became sole Pastor; in 1847, Rev. G. W. Willard entered as pastor, and was succeeded by the Rev. J. O. Miler in 1850, who was succeeded by Rev. Seibert Davis in 1854. He remained until 1857; and was succeeded by a Mr. Fentzell, whose pastorate ended in 1861. Just as the War clouds appeared along the horizon, he hastened to a more congenial clime. In 1862, the church was closed for church purposes and occupied by Union Soldiers. After its renovation in 1866, Rev. Hiram Shaull became the Pastor, serving until 1873; Rev. Chas. G. Fisher came in 1874, and resigned in 1880; when Rev. A. R. Krener came and remained four years; S. L. Whitmore came next; and was followed by Mr. Shontz and others, as visiting supplies. Rev. J. B. Stonesifer was installed as regular Pastor May 1st, 1892, whose ministry was productive of much good. His resignation Dec. 29th, 1900, was regretted by his many friends. The present Pastor, Rev. T. K. Cromer has made his pastorate very acceptable, not only to his own Church, but to the community in general. To him is given the credit for untiring zeal in creating the handsome edifice. Some one may be interested in the Old Log Meeting House that was left on the hill, when the new church was erected down town in 1840-1, and will enquire what was its end. Answer is given by quotation from a Newspaper published on 14th Febry., 1844. "Last night, the whole population was aroused to behold a spectacle so alarming, so weird and full of grandeur, that its like may never appear again, though for quite a long time the stoutest heart was affected. A strange light filled the dark Eastern sky; then the whole heavens were illuminated, from flaming light ascending from the *Old Graveyards* on the hill. This proceeded from the burning of the Old Log and frame house, for many years the former home of the German Reformed Church, the peculiar scene was heightened by the reflection of the fire light on every house-roof in town all covered with many inches of snow."

Around this old building the dead of many generations had been buried; and the *Lots* deeded by Fairfax have for many years been used as a burial place for the dead friends of this Church, which continues its control.

CHAPTER XXXVIII

The Methodist Episcopal Church

The first Methodist Church building erected in Winchester was in 1793, on Cameron St., between Water and Cork Sts. The lot was purchased in 1791. Where the Methodists held Church services prior to this date is not positively known. It is well established that Ministers of this Faith frequently preached in various sections of the Lower Valley as early as 1788, but no building is recorded as their property or place of worship. The lot purchased was owned by Wm. Beaty, and by reference to this deed, will be seen the exact location. Winchester Church was one of a large Circuit—the Congregation must have been very small for years. No ministers were stationed at Winchester until about 1825; after 1830, it was continued on the list as a Station and the minister resided in the town—but preached over a large Circuit. The Methodist Church has made astonishing strides within the last Century. The first appearance of the Methodists in America was about 1770; and we are told by Rev. Francis Asbury in his Journal that when he arrived in Philadelphia, from England on 27th Oct., 1771, there were Methodists all told in America not exceeding Six hundred, who were unorganized. He also says, "the Conference was held in Phila., July 14th, 16th, 1773—the first held in America." At this Conference ten ministers reported being present and eleven hundred and sixty members of the "Society" were reported by the Ministers. This Journal shows that Mr. Asbury visited Frederick County, Va., during the summer of 1772 as Missionary, to spy out the land for this great Society; so that they could come over and possess the promising field. A special note is made that he was in the Village of Winchester, Tuesday Nov. 24, 1772—and "preached in an unfinished house, the rain beating in upon me, the people beheld the stranger with great astonishment." He records this important fact, that there were not one hundred Methodists in Virginia at that time. When we consider that this young man afterwards became the distinguished Bishop Asbury, whose reputation knew no bounds, his name and service being familiar in the Original Thirteen States, the notes he made of the progress of Methodism in this section of Virginia, should be interesting to all readers. In his Journal, the following entry is made, "Saturday June 21, 1783, preached to a few people in Winchester; For seven days past I have had to ride the whole day, and preach without eating until five or six o'clock in the evening, except a little biscuit; this is hard work for man and horse, this however is not the worst, religion is greatly wanting in these parts. The inhabitants are much divided; made up, as they are of different nations, and speaking different languages; they agree in scarcely anything, except it be to sin against God." This great and good prelate in his effort to plant his Church in Old Frederick County, came at a time when Winchester was the theatre of Church work memorable for the harmony that existed between the Episcopalians, Presbyterians, Reformed Calvinists, German Lutherans, Baptists and even the Roman Catholics, all on the ground moulding character and principles for the noted men and women of that day. And doubtless the good man was appalled at the remnant of the population with whom he had to deal. Wickedness in this class did not deter his *Society* in their great work. The history of this Church shows that their ministers, as the grand old Circuit riders of the long ago, sought this class; and by their marvelous work from their first appearance, rode their Circuits extending from the Blue Ridge to the Alleganies and secured a foothold for Methodism, that made it possible to produce astonishing results. Behold her numerical strength of today, outstripping all other denominations, and to be reckoned with now as a power in the land! Grand, glorious Soldiers of the Cross! the World salutes you this day, as you have attained the summit from which you can see on every hand the mighty work of your dauntless hosts; Your Asbury had his day of despondency; but he never wavered, for we find an entry in his Journal dated July 21, 1784 when he seems encouraged about the Winchester people. He says, "We had many to hear at Winchester; they appeared to be orderly and solemn, and I hope it will appear that some were convicted;" The Bishop must have had great concern for the *mixed* population, for we find him in Winchester Sunday, June 4th, 1786, he says in one note, "The Lutheran Minister began a few minutes before I got into Winchester; I rode leisurely through the town, and preached under some spreading trees on a hill, on Joshua XXIV,

19, to many white and black people. It was a solemn, weighty time; all was seriousness and attention." At this point the author is reminded of many incidents in the lives of the old *slaves* with whom he was on familiar terms in the *happy past.* Some of these incidents may find place in these pages. One that he recalls may be appropriately entered here; doubtless it had its origin in the sermon preached under the *spreading trees.* It is well known by a few persons of to-day that among the large number of slaves owned by Rev. Joseph Glass, there was a woman of powerful stature, and one of the original Africans, known far and near as "Aunt Chloey," whose African dialect was so peculiar that no attempt will be made to imitate it. She had many traits that marked her as a woman of strong mental capacity, showing her knowledge of the habits and customs of the people she knew in her early life. She was communicative on such subjects only to those for whom she had the highest respect and regard. Her young mistress, Miss Anne Glass, asked her on one occasion if she remembered General Washington when he was in Winchester? Quickly came the answer, "No honey, I never see Gen'l Washington, but I see that other great preacher, Bishop Asbury." Aunt Chloey lived to a great age—109 years. She died in 1856.

The Bishop was determined to see that the people of Winchester should have good counsel. We find this note, "On Sunday, August 23, 1789—having made a tour of the Berkeley Circuit, I came to Winchester. We had alarming Words from Ezekiel XXXIII, 11, I feel the worth of souls and their disobedience gives me sorrow . . . . . " He records another incident and it is given as a reference for answer to the question, When was the first Methodist Church in Winchester erected? "Winchester, June 6th, 1793, They have built an excellent house, and we have better times than I expected; here nothing would do but I must preach, notwithstanding the lanes and streets of the town were filled with mire, owing to the late rains." Again in May 1794, he records his arrival in Winchester. He continued his visits to Winchester, and at last the Church records show in 1805, that he had been no idler in the wild Vineyard since his first appearance in 1783. The 22 years had produced wonderful results as shown by the Church record.

"Saturday, March 30th, 1805—Bishop Asbury came to Winchester to hold the Conference—Monday, April 1st, We opened the Baltimore Conference, sitting five days in very great order and peace, We had Seventy-four Preachers present." This is the first great event in the history of this Church. Within the writer's memory differences arose in the Methodist Church which resulted in separation into two Conferences. In 1844 the first step was taken; of which we will not now speak.

Returning to the first Church on Market St., this was sold in 1818 to Peter Ham. The second church was built on a lot on same side of the street and was used until 1852, when it was sold; and the Female Seminary conducted by S. P. York was in successful operation until the War clouds in 1861 drove Mr. York out of business. After the War, Rev. Silas Billings and Daughters reopened the place for a young Ladies' Seminary. In 1853, Sept. 12th, the corner-stone of the magnificent building on the Corner of Market and Cork streets—diagonally opposite the Centenary Reformed church—was laid with imposing ceremonies. The congregation had then become so large, that it required a building of large dimensions. Some of the most distinguished Methodist Divines have swayed great audiences assembled there, with a style of oratory well remembered by the writer. How easy it is to recall the impressive Norval Wilson, who won the esteem of all, and John S. Martin with his overwhelming arguments that brought conviction to many hearers; And the inimitable Tom Sewell—with his flashes of oratory, that stirred emotions which could be done only by this popular speaker. From the day this church was dedicated, the congregation was fortunate in having such strong men to minister to them; and it was mainly due to their influence that the disturbing questions were held in check for several years. The Methodists had been struggling with the Slavery question since 1844—when there was an agreement in the General Conference upon a plan of separation. Two Organizations were created to be known as the Methodist Episcopal Church, and the M. E. Church South. The Southern membership was slow to become too distinctive, desiring to cling to the old Mother Church for many reasons; and this is why we find the one Church in Winchester until a year or two before the impending *Crisis* came. While it was well known for many years, that differences existed in the Winchester congregation, no overt act occurred to produce a separation. All were disposed to worship together; but it finally became apparent that harmony was affected, and although many regretted the necessity, yet all felt there was a principle to stifle if this condition continued. At last the momentous step was taken, when on July 5th, 1858, thirty members withdrew from the Market street church, and were granted Certificates "As being persons of good report, and consistent members of the M. E. Church." The movement was headed by the late Col. Wm. R. Denny; (whose son, Rev. Collins Denny, D.D., has been for several years a distinguished member of the Faculty of the Vanderbilt University—Nashville.)

This band of thirty, who stood for the principles as they viewed the situation, were no laggards—they proceeded to organize as a separate Church, and on the 24th of the same month, Rev. W. W. Bennett, Presiding Elder of the Washington District duly organized them as a Congregation under the Virginia Conference, M. E. Church South. The writer remembers the reception given their first Pastor, Rev. George H. Ray, when he came the following November, and held his first services in the Court House Hall. No other man could have suited the critical period so well as did Mr. Ray. His success in shaping the course of this new congregation was marvelous. He commanded the respect of the community and was highly esteemed by all. The site for the new building was selected on Braddock Street, and a neat and comfortable edifice was soon erected. The following Christmas, the building was far enough on the way, to make the basement possible to have their Christmas services held in it. The work was pressed, and the church was completed by July, 1859, and dedicated. Rev. John C. Granberry, D.D., conducted the services. This Church enjoyed a few years of remarkable progress—Organized two Missions outside the Town. Mr. Ray conducted a series of services far out in the country, at a well known point Lamp's School House—where there is a noted Spring and an inviting grove of forest trees. Here Mr. Ray, aided by some of the old time Class Leaders of that section, held the first *Bush Meeting* held in the memory of the writer. The distinction beween this and what was once out-door "Grove Meetings" was, that the former had a few tents on the ground, not of sufficient number to entitle it the distinction of the Old time Camp meeting. At this Bush Meeting, Mr. Ray was instrumental in giving the large crowds who daily assembled, a good time, though he may have failed to make all his hearers good Christians. Succeeding Mr. Ray, came Rev. E. M. Peterson, P. F. August, Lester Shipley, all members of the Virginia Conference. Mr. Shipley while Pastor, entered the Confederate army and the Church was without a Pastor during Gen'l Banks' *stampede* through the town in the Spring of 1862. This renowned Genl. had seized the church upon his arrival in Winchester, and converted it into a hospital. The Union army always used it when the town was in possession of the Federals, and was so badly wrecked by such use, that it required years of stint and labor after hostilities ceased, to put the building in condition for Church services. The present handsome Braddock St. M. E. Church South, with its Annex for Sunday school work, is now the home of the revived Church, the main building was greatly improved and enlarged in 1898-9, and when the U. S. Government made allowance of $2,560 for damages, in 1904, the Church erected their annex. Since the close of the Civil War, the following Ministers have successively rendered effective service to this church: Rev. Norval Wilson served as Pastor until Conference could make the regular appointment. During his ministry this Church was greatly strengthened by accessions from the Market Street Congregation. Quite a number of the old congregation had felt the effects of an atmosphere engendered by the episodes of the war, causing a desire to seek what was more congenial to their feelings; and thus the old Market Street Church looked desolate for several years. Some very strange sights were presented the old citizens on Sabbath mornings for the first year or two after the war. A few men from almost every other church in the town, were seen wending their way to the old corner where they had heard so much that was congenial to their lacerated feelings, not from sorrow that the Union had been saved, but that so many Rebels had been spared to return and re-enter *their* old churches. It looked strange in that day to see Elders and Deacons, Stewards and good lay members, seeking the recesses of the Northern Methodist Church—where they could unburden their woes, and remember the *Boys in Gray*, who were fit subjects for their special pleadings. Rev. R. S. Hough was appointed by the Baltimore Conference of M. E. Church South, and came as pastor in Spring of 1866. Succeeding him, came I. R. Finley, J. E. Armstrong, T. R. Carson, Samuel Rodgers, J. S. Gardner, H. H. Kennedy, J. W. Shoaff, W. P. Harrison, D. M. James, S. S. Martin, G. T. Tyler, T. E. Carson, (second term), J. N. McCormack, W. H. D. Harper, S. R. Cox, W. H. H. Joyce, Chas. D. Bulla, and D. H. Kern, present pastor.

The Market Street Church has had the following Ministers since the Civil War: Revs. Crever, Ward, Welsh, Gardner, Courtney, Fergusson, France, Bishop, Koontz, Eldridge, West, Weed, and the present Pastor Mr. Beale. The congregation has increased in the last few years; but it is doubtful if the old Tabernacle will ever see the old time crowds that assembled there in the long ago, and heard with rapturous delight Rev. Ben. Brooke, when at his zenith as an Orator. The old Church has witnessed many interesting events; being the largest Church edifice in Winchester for many years, it was frequently used to accommodate large bodies, where addresses on religious subjects were delivered by renowned Orators. During all the years through which the Winchester Methodist Churches were forging their way up to the present point, it must not be forgotten that in the country many churches were seen to arise from the Potomack on the North, to the sections South and from the Blue Ridge to the Green slopes of the Allegany. All this great territory was once in one circuit; and for many long weary years the lone horseman had been seen wending his way in and out, through the settlements, and later on the primitive village and remote places, to disseminate the doctrines of *Free Salvation*. The old circuit-rider rendered service, not only to his own church, but was largely instrumental in keeping the sparsely settled country in touch with the outer world; and thus his influence grew. His appearance among the rugged mountaineers was hailed with delight, for he was their mail-carrier and news gatherer. They were men of great courage, as well as energy. In this way, the frontier and destitute regions were taught Methodism pure and unadulterated. The little Meeting-houses soon became the important place among these people. As the interest increased, others came to share the labours; and in a few decades the territory abounded with working Methodists; and in all the regions round, evidences sprang up to show that they were gradually possessing the land. One of the oldest preaching places for the Methodists, was Stephensburg. The Family record of Col. John Hite's family tells of his daughter Elizabeth and her husband, Rev. Mr. Phelps, building the first Methodist church at that point as early as 1794. The substantial brick structure now used by the Methodists at that place, stands on the old site. In the graveyard found in the rear, are buried the remains of the founders of this church, the grand-daughter of Joist Hite and her husband Mr. Phelps. A Congregation of Methodists had a preaching point at Senseney Town (Middletown) at a very early day, and worshipped in the single Meeting-house, where other denominations had joint use. As the Methodists increased at this point, and at such places as Funkstown, McKay's (Nineveh) and Stephensburg, the circuit-rider was taxed to serve so many other points remote from those named. It was but natural that he should devise some plan for contracting the work and have the scattered Congregations rally at some point, where closer ties could be formed by continued conferences with each other, where ministers from neighboring circuits could come, and there enjoy the *Love-feast* that was promised. There was no suitable building at any point in the circuit, nor accommodations for the assembling Congregations. These conditions in the large Circuit increased as the zeal of the Minister increased, as he traveled from point to point; all of which was to culminate in the primitive Camp-Meeting. There was an ideal place near the centre of the "Upper Circuit" for such an assemblage. No Meeting-house could be selected, lest that point be regarded as more favoured than others. The place, above all others—well known in the circuit—was "Chrisman's Spring," known as such since 1735, taking its name from Jacob Chrisman, son-in-law of Joist Hite. The former and his descendants owned the vast tracts adjoining, on which was the old homestead, where liberal hospitality was offered to Ministers of the Gospel. The famous spring and adjacent forests were freely offered by this generous family. The oldest inhabitant to-day has no recollection of the first Camp-Meeting, with the old tent wagons on the ground and roughly improvised annexes, to offer shelter to the families who had come well provided with food. The scanty sleeping accommodations were sufficient to induce the *Campers* to remain on the "Grounds" for about ten days. Who can tell of or measure the results of this first "Love-Feast" in the Lower Valley. The impetus given the work of the Methodists, had its first wave of progress to start from this first assembly of Congregations. Their conferences created strong ties between them, and from that day, coming on down to the period when the writer, with thousands of the population for miles around annually, in the Month of August—repaired to the Camp-Meeting at Christman's Spring. Then it was when the *modern Camp* had come to take the place of the *primitive*. The appearance on the ground of a half hundred tents, with luxurious appointments, standing in village style—streets and alleys—the old tented wagon there—but in the rear of the tent lines, supplies for the multitude. The hollow square, amply supplied with seats fronting the *Preacher's Stand*, always crowded with respectful audiences during services—day and night, formed an arena, that in itself was enough to inspire the preacher, as he stood before the people to tell the Old Story of the Cross. In addition to this, there were the grand old Oaks with their goodly boughs, the growth of Centuries casting their shadows over the multitude that waited upon his words; people and preacher felt the influence of the scene that was thus produced in what had been the solitude of a great forest. Whatever the source of inspiration, the good and holy men never failed to impress the audience with their marvelous eloquence. Kercheval says, "The first Camp Meeting held in the Valley in my memory, was at Chrisman's Spring, about two miles South of Stephensburg, on the Great Highway from Winchester to Staunton; this was probably in the month of August 1806." He adds that he travelled through the Southwest Counties in 1836, and often saw where Camp-meetings had been held.

The Methodist Church of the present day need

not rely upon the primitive plan for gathering accessions from remote places, or the hedges and highways. In the early efforts the camp-meeting plan was regarded as a necessity. Many people were slow to attend formal church services. There was something about the solemn church building, and the congregations in Sunday attire, and the minister with his pious dignity, that was not inviting to the class who preferred spending Sunday, the day of *rest,* in a way more congenial to their view of the Sabbath, consequently this large body of non-church goers was becoming an object of concern to the itinerant preacher; and when he had once evolved the plan for gathering in this class, the success of this Church was assured. The careless and indifferent were attracted by the novelty, and found their way to the Camp-ground, where many attractions were offered to encourage his attendance and stay; and ere many years had passed with this great experiment, the non-church-goer was as much in evidence at the camp-meeting, as the most devout class-leader, and every one of these great seasons of special effort, marked the date of conversion of many ungodly men, who from that day experienced a new era in their lives. Many of the brightest lights of the Church saw the first flash of the new existence at the old time Camp-meeting. Towers of strength they were in Evangelizing the land. We must say, however, that abuses crept in unawares during these great gatherings, for it is well known that many were drawn thither from no other motive but pleasure; and often gave trouble; but that august "Committee" seemed to possess the mysterious power of omnipresence. The refined pleasure-seeker, as well as the turbulent fellow, suffered rebuke; and good order prevailed. The ten days spent on those old camp-grounds, in some old forest near some noted spring, surpassed all the ocean-resorts of the present day for genuine pleasure and lasting memories. It might be said that the life of this great work, that loomed up on the horizon of the 19th Century, gradually faded away after an experience of three score years. The Civil War period made quite a break in this out-door service; but very soon after the restoration of peace, the hosts assembled again annually; and for twenty years much enthusiasm prevailed in favor of this form of worship. But the Church no longer felt the need of such auxiliaries; and it is a rare thing now in the Lower Valley. To-day every village and hamlet is supplied with regular church service in neat edifices, of modern style; and in most cases, congregations are there to receive the message with as much formality as other churches.

The Middletown M. E. Church South is of such design and architecture, as to attract the attention of all admirers of beautiful church buildings. It is an ornament to the Country; and one must conclude that Methodism at the old "Senseney-town" had been strengthened by its contiguity to the original camp-meeting. The point has attracted several Superanuated Ministers and their families, to make permanent homes there; and the visitor to this attractive little gem of the Lower Valley will be well repaid by the courteous reception by the townsfolk, and enjoy interviews with the grand and good men who, worn out in the service of their Church, are now waiting the summons that must soon come. In such society, many delightful hours can be enjoyed as reminiscences are unfolded, and here you will find men who had been faithful to the trust of conducting the oldest camp-meetings, ever ready to entertain you with thrilling incidents in the life of the old Circuit-rider. This could and should fill a volume of interesting reading. Doubtless some one will preserve notes of the *past,* relating to such men, and in some way give to the public what the writer cannot properly do in this volume.

Stephensburg Methodist Church.

The little Village of Stephensburg was one of the earliest places in old Frederick for the *New Sect,* called Methodists, to make an effort to organize for church work. Long before her neighbouring town, Winchester, ever dreamed of the approaching Methodists, this little village had been visited by such men as Richard Owings and John Hagerty in 1775, and Francis Asbury in 1778, itinerant preachers of that period. In the notes on the M. E. C., at Winchester, the reader will see quotations from the Journal of Bishop Asbury, to confirm the claim made for Stephensburg and also in the sketch of Col. John Hite and family, where it will be seen his daughter Mrs. Phelps, and her brother John Hite, jr., have the credit of building the first Methodist Church at Stephensburg. Taking this in connection with Church history and reliable traditions, it is shown that very soon after the appearance of the "two Strangers" that Kercheval mentions as being there in 1775, "preaching their strange doctrine of free Grace." Mr. Asbury was there 1778, and preached in an unfinished church. This was the first church built there, and was where the first church was organized by the following persons viz, Rev. Elisha Phelps and wife, John Hite, Jr., John Taylor and wife, Lewis Stephens, sen., and wife, and several others. We find in the record of Col. John Hite's family, that Mr. Phelps and his wife lived and died near the village and both were buried in the rear of the little church of their founding. We have the proof of this on the Slab found in the Churchyard showing the grave of Elisha Phelps and Elizabeth, his wife, bearing date 1815. Mrs. P. lived just North of Newtown. The Chipley family lived for years on the property.

The Methodists steadily increased at Stephensburg, and while many trying ordeals have fallen to the lot of the little town on the Valley's great highway, the Church at Stephens city of to-day, is one that has a place of honor in the Conference to which it belongs. Many godly men have arisen to high places in the Church at large, who had their beginnings here. The writer recalls several local preachers of great power, who took delight in recounting incidents of the early history of this Church. One was "Father Walls," as he was generally known; starting in the latter part of the 18th Century and receiving new impulses in the dawn of the 19th. He was an actor on the stage of that wonderful era; and his life and work were given wholly to the cause he had espoused. His grandson, Dr. Wm. Walls, and the writer had many experiences in the class-room of the old Winchester Academy, wrestling with "Euclid" the school-boys horror. Rev. John Allemong, of more recent memory, was a man of "good report." His life was of that exemplary kind that leaves a good impression on the community in which he had a long and useful ministry, beginning in 1820, ending in 1872. Prior to 1827, the congregation worshipped in their original log church—loth to give it up. About this time, the brick church was built on the old site—with many modern appendages, such as the high pulpit, bellfry-galleries, etc. This building suffered much unnecessary damage during the Civil War. The brick parsonage was burned, as a retaliation for some imaginary wrong done to Hunter's army. In 1882, the church building became unsafe and was removed from its foundation, and the present large and attractive church was erected on the old site. The congregation extended its borders, and through the joint efforts of Rev. F. A. Strother two new churches were built—one at Relief, and one to the S. E., called Lost Corner. This old Winchester Circuit was supplied by noted men in its day, such as John S. Martin, Wm. G. Eggleston, David Bush, Wm. Wheelright, and others. They were some of the grand old itinerants of the by-gone days. The Winchester Circuit was divided into what has been called two charges—Stephens City and Middletown. This change occurred in 1891.

The next M. E. C., in order as to date within the bounds of the old County, is found at Brucetown, where there has been for many years a large and prosperous Congregation. Gainesboro has maintained a strong standing in the Circuit to which it belongs. The old Greenspring Church has a good history, which may receive fuller notice. On Timber-Ridge in the Western part of the county, are several churches doing good work,—Rock Enon M. E. church on Back-Creek, was built to supply a long felt want in that neighbourhood.

The Round Hill M. E. Church, standing on the north side of the Northwestern Turnpike, is not the original building, it being virtually the third house erected on that site. In 1844-5 the first building was erected on the lot purchased from Elijah Hodgson (see deed dated June 1st, 1844 to M. E. C. trustees). The first church had an interesting history when Methodism had become a factor for good in every neighbourhood, it was found desirable to organize a church at this point. This was to be associated with organizations in several other places, notably the little preaching point—known in that day as Lamp's School-house. Living in that neighbourhood was a man but little known to the outside world, but was destined to take place among the prominent Methodists in his day; but he always desired his work should be confined to his own *Hills;* this was "Henry Milhon," the founder of the M. E. church at Round Hill, from his own Pine forests came the huge logs for that first building, hewn and shaped by himself with the utmost precision, every one in perfect dress; and when the day came to *raise* the building, the writer was there as a boy spectator. The tall, gaunt, wiry man was at every point, and with willing neighbours, his first church went up; and before the winter came, this strange man as the *Local* preacher, conducted a successful meeting. His rugged but sincere sentences were rounded out with such zeal and originality, that his hearers seemed transfixed. This man was then in his prime—was a convert of the old Camp-meeting, and received such inspiration, that he never faltered in his work, telling others of the "story about the Cross," which had changed his reckless life. Without the advantage of the simplest rudiment of education, he set about by the aid of his wife, who could read, to learn suitable scriptures and hymns, and from such studies, the knowledge came that he never forgot. He was always ready with appropriate "Texts," from which he gave his hearers the most exhaustive explanations. While no orator, his original ideas were moulded into expressions that alarmed, and then soothed the convicted sinner. Let it be told, he grew famous among the many persons that were awakened by his strange power. He was known far and near as Father *Milhorn,* tho' never more than the Local Preacher—all Methodists know what this title implies! However, his services were in demand all over the

Circuit. It was during the close of his career, that his little church was damaged by fire (1860). Such men as Wm. Hodgson, A. W. Hodgson, John and Chas. Hawkins, Jacob Spillman, Wm. Milhon, and others promptly aided Father Milhon in repairing the building. His son-in-law, Rev. Wm. Hodgson, had then become a local preacher, and he for many years gave his life's best work to this service; and it may be added that during the life-time of Father Milhon, Mr. Hodgson was generally mentioned as the "Little Preacher." During the four years of the Civil War, his services were in demand and freely rendered to many of the destitute places in the surrounding country, while Mr. H. was one of the non-combattants, he was well known to the Southrons, as one in full sympathy with their cause; and many returning Confederates at the close of the war felt the grasp of his strong hand, that told of his sympathy. The writer knew him well. The second building was destroyed during the winter of 1864-5. A portion of Gen. Sheridan's Cavalry Corps wintered in the vicinity of this church and soldiers during that severe winter carried it in pieces to their camps —for winter quarters, as they did all the outbuildings from the adjoining farms, with the notable exception of a few families who were spared by reason of their *loyalty to the Union.* After a few years had passed by, the Methodist congregation, which had use of the old Presbyterian church in full view, outgrew some of the bitter feeling that War had engendered, and quickened the emotions that existed with some of the old members to return to their old place of worship. This resulted in the erection of the present brick church on the old site. The congregation has never attained its old prestige for Church work; the old church leaders are no longer at the helm. Some have answered the great summons, and some have removed beyond the bounds of the old Circuit.

CHAPTER XXXIX

The Baptist Church

This Church has been unfortunate, in that no church record can be produced that relates to the first appearance of this denomination of Christians in Frederick County. The first Baptist Meeting House of which any record appears, was at a point now the site of Gerardstown. There was a small Congregation at that point as early as 1773. No evidence of any pastor. Doubtless services were conducted in the Meeting-House by visiting ministers. The sect was called Old School, and sometimes Hardshell Baptists. One of this class was reported to the Justices' Court for disorderly conduct. This case went to the Grand-Jury. Upon investigation, it appeared that the offence most complained of, was his effort "to hold meetings in the *Night time* and in a boisterous manner, violating the Act of Parliament, to the great annoyance of the Established Church." The old Grand-Jurors failed to see that the complaint was such as to justify punishment. About this period a Congregation of this society secured a deed for land near a point, now Nineveh, near the Warren County line. There they had a house of worship, and always maintained an Organization, and were regarded throughout the last Century as Primitive Baptists in reality.

Winchester was slowly recognized by this Church as congenial to their creed. Other church records show that the Baptists had a preacher to stop in Winchester in 1790, who preached in the Lutheran and Presbyterian churches. Many years later, they procured use of an abandoned schoolhouse, and held regular services. The Congregation was composed of zealous people, but increased slowly in numbers. Many years would intervene between regular pastorates; but they never disbanded. Rev. Joseph Baker who conducted a large and successful school on Fort Hill, where Fort Loudoun Seminary is located, was a Baptist minister. He was instrumental in securing the Old Stone Presbyterian church in 1834, for the use of the Baptist Church, "Lease to extend said uses for 500 years." Mr. Baker drew around him some very active church workers, which resulted in accessions to this Church. This denomination had its intervals of discouragement. Frequently the church had no regular pastor. The field was visited by an accomplished young man in 1854, Rev. Mr. Ryland, who was very active in his ministry, preaching at Winchester, Cedar Creek, Back Creek, Head of Opecquon and other points. The congregations increased and the Church was being revived, when the Civil War broke in upon such work. Mr. Ryland entered the Confederate Army. After the War, the Baptists made another effort through Rev. Mr. Willis; and from that time, this Church has held its renewed position. Mr. Willis for several years conducted a young ladies' seminary in what was called the "York" building, formerly the old Methodist church; and while thus engaged, gathered the denomination together and succeeded in building a church, nearly opposite, on Market Street; and there for several years preached to increasing congregations. Later on Mr. Willis removed to another field; the church building was sold to the "Disciples" Sect; and once more the Baptists were forced to find another home. Securing a lot, they located their church on South side of Cork Street, between Main and Market. The neat little church where they now worship was erected 1885; the first Pastor, Mr. Davison, was succeeded by D. Clark, Jackson and Murdock; Rev. Mr. Northern is the present Pastor. The Church has sustained serious losses in the deaths of such men as M. H. G. Willis, P. C. Gore and others, and is struggling to maintain its work.

The Baptists have a strong Church in Berryville, which has been fortunate in securing such a pastor as the distinguished Divine, Dr. Broaddus, who has so acceptably ministered to this congregation for many years, his pastorate covering a longer period than that of any other Minister of this Church in the Lower Valley, so far as known to the writer. Other points in Clarke County are within his field. The Berryville Church was what might be called an off-shoot of the old Buckmarsh Church, where the Baptists had worshipped for at least sixty years. In 1840, the Congregation for several good reasons, changed their place of worship to Berryville, where they had erected a suitable building, and changed the name from Buckmarsh to that of Berryville. The Church grew much stronger, and has always maintained a strong position with her sister churches of other denominations. The handsome church building now in use, situated so prominently, as an ornament to the town, was erected 1885. Everything in its appointments—Minister, people, edifice and situation, indicate prosperity.

The Baptists who first appeared in the lower part of Frederick, now Berkeley County, never made much progress in that section. In their principal town, Martinsburg, their first organization was not effected until 1858 or '59. A small congregation held services in an old unoccupied building, until they very soon purchased a lot on King Street and expected to build their church: but the war of 1861-65 checked all their ardor; and it was not until 1869 that another impetus was given by starting the new building. The weak, struggling congregation was fully five years erecting the present suitable church. The membership steadily increased, and they have had the services of some eminent men.

There has never been advanced by any Baptists authorities, any good reason for the slow progress made by their denomination in the country West of the Blue Ridge. No such progress as is shown by other Churches. The history of this Church is one of success in many sections of Virginia. Eastern Virginia, especially, fairly teems with large congregations and costly churches. Not so in the Shenandoah Valley, although they appeared and seemed co-existent with the formation of Frederick in 1743, then they came with a large "immigrant train" from New Jersey, and settled at the Gerardstown point, when Rev. John Gerard organized them. Semple's history, *Early Baptists*, says they came from Maryland. One other immigration came from Maryland later on, and joined a large number from New England, and settled on Capon River in 1754, where they purchased land and soon gave considerable impetus to their church movement. The leader, Mr. Stearns, however, became dissatisfied, and together with a large number of the society removed to North Carolina, where he joined the well known Baptist movement, which resulted in marvelous success. However, this very success gave them serious trials. At that time, the Established Church adopted strong measures to repress the "noisy dissenters," and with the aid of the courts, succeeded in checking their advance. Prosecutions followed persecution; many distinguished leaders were imprisoned "as disturbers of the peace." Had Mr. Stearns and his friends remained on Capon, where no such prosecutions occurred, and made the same efforts for the propagation and spread of their doctrines, who can tell what the results might show to-day. It must not be understood that those who remained in the Shenandoah section were unmolested; for it is well known to many what befell the Rev. James Ireland, the Scotch Baptist preacher, who became so famous for his eloquence and zeal, that he attracted crowds of people. He also attracted the attention of many who became his persecutors. Fighting over every effort he made, he was the object of special concern to the Established Church. While the persecutions never assumed the character of those shown in Eastern Virginia, other methods were employed to drive him and his Sect out of the Country; but the old Scotchman met every such effort in the same spirit that characterized his people wherever found, whether in the Motherland, or in the Virginia Valley.

Extract from the Winchester, Va., Gazette, published June 17th, 1806. "Departed this life on the 5th, ult., in his 58th year, Elder James Ireland, Pastor of the Baptists Congregation at Buck's Marsh, Happy Creek and Water Lick in Frederick and Shenandoah Counties, Va." "On Sunday the first inst., a suitable and affecting discourse was delivered at Buck's Marsh Meeting-house, the place of his interment." James Ireland's church work from 1780, was chiefly West of the Blue Ridge. In his work East of the Ridge, he was hindered by persecutions, suffered imprisonment and insult from several ministers of the Established Church.

The United Brethren Church.

This Denomination for many years maintained several churches in the surrounding country, but not until 1873 were they sufficiently strong in Winchester to venture a separate Organization. This was accomplished, however, by Rev. G. W. Howe, and by his energy and perseverance, aided by the country Brethren, a Congregation was formed for the great work of building a suitable house for Public Worship, and for support of a Station Pastor. This was successfully accomplished in 1873; the work has steadily increased, and at this writing, the congregations are large and composed of that class who enjoy the progress this church has made. Many families who lived in the outlying field, have purchased homes in the city, and are strong supporters of this church, which is located on the East side of Braddock St., between Piccadilly and Peyton Streets. The ministers who have served this church were Revs. G. W. Howe, Mr. Crowell, Mr. Skelton and Mr. Wine.

Several points in the County have been occupied by the *Brethren* for many years, and a number of good families are prominent and active members of this Church. The well known Hott family has furnished several ministers to serve this church. The Parlett and Fries families have also furnished men who have become widely known for their pastoral services and educational work. The Western part of the county can show several attractive buildings. There the U. B. Congregations have made large accessions. At and near Stephens City this Church has supported its regular Pastor. The U. B. Church has had its share of dissensions, growing out of divisions in their Church at large, and for several years, very unfortunate differences have arisen in two or three congregations, concerning their vested rights in Church property. What these differences are, and who to blame for this interruption of harmony in three of the Congregations, need not be discussed in this sketch.

The Christian or Disciples Church.

This Denomination several years ago occupied the old Baptist Church on Braddock St. Rev. Mr. Pirkey, a very popular preacher of Strasburg, preached in Winchester for several years and organized a Church at a point in the county known as Welltown, and through his efforts and the generous aid of Jas. T. Clevenger, Jno. W. McKown and others, that congregation was able to erect its neat church building, (Galilee), and have maintained Church relations that resulted in much good to the community. The denomination has four other churches in the County, built within the last twenty years—Ebenezer on Timber Ridge, near Whitacre; Rock Enon, Jubilee on Front Royal Pike, near Winchester, and one at Bartonsville. The Church name properly is "The Disciples." The old Christian Church, which has for many years maintained a place of Worship in the Western part of the county, is still in existence. These denominations differ as to Creed and discipline, and are entitled to distinction, though they are regarded by the uninformed as the same denomination.

The Christian Baptists.

This Church has often been called the Tunkard denomination. This is erroneous. We have two places of Worship in the county under the control of the Christian Baptists, Salem Church, near Vaucluse was organized in 1866, Elders Daniel Baker and Daniel Brindle. Mr. Baker donated the site. The other Church, Peach Grove, is about two miles East of Winchester, built in 1892. Prof. N. D. Cool is the Minister in charge of these Churches. Prof. Wayland of the University of Virginia, and L. R. Dettra, of Frederick County are Ministers in this Church. The membership is small in this section, but they have large Congregations in the Upper Valley.

Old Hopewell Meeting House

CHAPTER XL

The Society of Friends

The *Quaker* has been so prominent in the Shenandoah Valley from its earliest settlement, that to write a sketch of this Society that would portray the relations and historical incidents of their peculiar life, would result in reproducing a history of the old county. Many interesting traditions concerning the Quakers, have been handed down through the generations in such order, that many have been accepted as reliable history.

Organized in about 1760, they have been systematic in recording their history, and adopted plans to preserve the same. Prior to, and during the period, so interesting to the people of the Shenandoah Valley, these silent people in answer to enquiries relating to that period give the one answer: "The records of our Society were destroyed." How or by whom, they say not. Fortunately, the old County records have revealed many things of value, so far as it relates to data which determines the location of their first *Meeting-house*; for by reference to Deed-Book No. 2, page 354, it will be seen they have a deed from Alexander Ross, dated April 3, 1751, for ten acres of land, where they had a Meeting-house. This afterwards became "Hopewell." This deed shows the presence of Quakers in old Frederick sometime prior to the date of the deed from Ross. This deed is not to trustees—but to Evan Thomas, Evan Rogers and others; and in describing the location of the ten acres, an important fact is mentioned, that a Meeting-house was already there. Taking this record in connection with the most reliable history obtainable, we have the date almost established when that Meeting-house was built. Samuel Janney in his "History of Friends," says, "Alexander Ross about the year 1732, having obtained a Grant for One hundred thousand acres of land in the Colony of Virginia, situated near Opequan Creek a tributary of the Potomac; a settlement was soon after begun there by Alexander Ross, Josiah Ballenger, James Wright, Evan Thomas and other Friends from Pennsylvania, and Elk River in Maryland. Under authority of Chester Quarterly Meeting they established in *1744* a Monthly Meeting, called Hopewell, which thus became a branch of *Phila. Yearly Meeting.*" It is safe to assume that shortly thereafter, Ross and other Friends erected their Meeting-house without receiving a deed for the lot, and subsequently it was apparent to the Organization that they should have a deed for the land where they had put their house. Then the deed of 1751 appears for the ten acres. This must determine their first appearance in the old County, as well as the date of their first organization.

The Quakers have a peculiar history, one that cannot be given here for want of space. However, a brief sketch may be given, that may lead some reader to study their peculiar traits. They had their persecutions beyond a doubt; and it may be asked, did their conduct or peculiar doctrine or religious Creed provoke their persecutors to single them out for the many trials through which this sect has passed? The British Government, in the 17th Century gave them warning, time and again, that their "False doctrines and practices were inimical to the good government offered them." They were so oppressed by the exactions demanded by the authorities, that they were virtually driven out of that country; and the tide of their emigration headed for America. Many landed on the upper Atlantic Coasts, and settled in small colonies in Jersey and Pennsylvania. Some landed on the Carolina Coasts and pushed their way into Virginia; and strange to say, they very soon attracted the attention of the Virginia authorities, because of their "Practices and teachings," which must have been very offensive; for the old Statute-books of 1760 have severe laws relating to their suppression. The full text will not be given; the Preamble of the Acts will be sufficient to show the temper of the old Burgesses, and also enumerate a few of the poor "silent Man's offences."

"An Act for Suppressing the Quakers."

"Whereas there is an unreasonable and turbulent sort of people, commonly called Quakers, Who Contrary to the Laws do *Dayly* gather together unto them Unlaw-ll assemblys and Congregations of people, teaching and publishing lies, miracles, false visions, prophecies, and doctrines which have influence upon the Communities of men, both *Eclesiasticall* and Civil, endeavouring and attempting thereby to destroy religion, laws, communities, and all bonds of civil Societies leaving it *arbitrarie* to *everie Vaine and Vitious* person Whether men shall be safe, laws established, and Governours rule, hereby disturbing the *Publique* peace and just interest; to prevent and restrain which *Mischeif,* It is Enacted, etc."

This Act goes on to provide for their arrest and punishment, and forbids any Captain of any vessel to land any Quaker on the Shores of Virginia. That no person be allowed to consort with or entertain them; No person allowed to publish any of their books, or sell the same . . . . . , (see Henning's Statutes at Large, Vol. 1, pp. 532-3).

Here again in their new home they incurred the displeasure of the Colonists to such an extent, that their life might seem a burden. Not so, however. They plodded on in their quiet way, acquired comforts, and even wealth in many cases; and it may be said this is characteristic of the Quaker—they are frugal, enconomical, resourceful, and helpful to each other. Poverty is a stranger to their families. They have ever claimed exemption from service as Soldiers—being opposed to war; and have been recognized by State laws, as non-Combatants and required to do no act in conflict with their conscience. The question may now be asked, has he always adhered to this rigid rule? History gives an answer that throws doubt on the whole subject, and places the sect in an attitude never assumed by any other class. While their position has been that of the non-combatant during every war period in his old home from which he had been driven to the wilds of America, where he proclaimed his desire to be allowed exemption from participation in any struggle in his adopted country, they were accorded the exemption; and thus they were regarded as conscientiously opposed to conflicts and litigation. Historians who have traced the Quaker through his wanderings, show that he had emotional periods similar to other classes, and that he was not, strictly speaking, *non-partisan* in the war periods through which he passed—never emerging from them without incurring the displeasure of the combatants. He is found suffering privation and punishment, for the aid and sympathy he freely gave to his old British oppressors, when that power sought to subjugate American patriots. If he had remained neutral, and stood on his *creed of perpetual peace,* he could not have been criticised, for in his adopted country the new populations fought for one of his principles, *"That conscience should dictate all actions."* But it seemed impossible for the silent and peace loving Quaker to be passive when the upheavals of War had encompassed hamlet and town. The oppressive rule of Britain, so sorely felt in the Colonies, made it necessary for patriots to defend their sacred rights. The Sect knew the sting of British rule; they had suffered persecution from every officer in the Colonies who executed the edict of Royalty. And it would have been perfectly natural for the persecuted Quaker to extend his sympathy to the struggling patriots who had undertaken to shake off the oppressive yoke. None would have required him to forsake his creed, and participate in the bloody strife to which they were so averse. Strange to say, however, he was so pronounced in his views regarding the Revolution, that he became an object of wonder, not only to the American soldiers, but also to the British invaders, the latter regarding him with suspicions of doubt, because of his unstinted aid; and the former because of his unreasonable hostility to their cause. No writer has succeeded in clearing this mystery.

While the Patriot Army in the early part of 1777, had its Battalions and Regiments occupying many important points in Pennsylvania, it was discovered that these silent and peaceful people, (opposed to war in every form) had become secret enemies of the cause of Freedom and Independence. The most damaging service they could render was discovered; their communications to the British Commanders were intercepted and implicated many prominent Quakers in the surrounding country, and also in Philadelphia. This discovery enraged the Colonists, for the Quaker was found to be more dangerous than whole Battalions of Redcoats. Posing as a peace-loving citizen within the Patriot camps, yet taking the most offensive part as a partisan. Their removal or extermination must be prompt, else wholesale destruction would soon come from the enemy who had thus learned the secrets of the American forces. It was decided that their removal to some distant point would accomplish better results than their *execution as spies.* Writers of much force have written extensively and exhaustively on this episode; and all agree that the"Offense would have been punished with death, had it been committed by any other class." The Military took the matter in hand and placed a number of those who were fully proven to be the offenders, under arrest. A few suspected persons were included in the squad of prisoners. The following named persons comprised the principal offenders: Joshua Fisher, Abel James, James Pemberton, John James, John Pemberton, Henry Drinker, Israel Pemberton, Samuel Pleasants, Thomas Wharton, Thomas and Samuel Fisher. It has always been a matter of speculation as to the number of prisoners that were sent out of Pennsylvania, under guard. Some have given the number as many as thirty; others twenty, and others fifteen. No military report gives the number. They were marched through Maryland and into Virginia, and confined at the Army-post near Winchester, where several hundred of the captured enemy were confined. They were delivered to Col. John Smith who had command of this District. Col. Smith in his reports concerning the Prison under his control says, "I deemed it proper to parole the prisoners other than soldiers, but the Civilians refused any terms offered them." One report shows that quitea number grew sick and were placed in a building in the town, for treatment. No mention made of any deaths—though tradition says that several of them died while imprisoned. Tradition says the Quaker prisoners were confined along with three hundred Hessian prisoners in a building in the southern part of Winchester, which was standing unchanged about fifteen years ago. This seems too unlikely to be true. No such building of sufficient size to hold over three hundred prisoners, stood in the southern part of the old town in 1777. During the confinement of the civilian prisoners, they appealed to a distinguished Lawyer of that day, Alexander White, Esq., to aid them in securing their release. After the British evacuated Philadelphia, and the Patriot army changed positions, Mr. White secured their release upon their affirmation that they would henceforth live by their Creed *and be at peace with all men.* Of course, the Society of Friends was sorely tried during the remainder of the war; and were the subject of malignant ridicule for many years. The Society had, before the period alluded to, made permanent settlement in Frederick County, and many families became useful and highly respected citizens, forming part of some successful enterprises. Many of this Sect settled on the most productive lands in the county, and enjoyed the distinction of prosperous farmers, persons of wealth and influence. The Quakers of old Frederick bore none of the names of the Pennsylvania prisoners; nor did they ever seem to depart from their creed of peace, or meddle with any of the conflicts attending the forward movement of a great country. But strange to say in later years the same old spirit which animated the Philadelphia Quakers to step aside and enter silently into war's terrible experiences, wooed some of these non-combatants to seize the first opportunity to enter into intrigue with the devouring foe, and sacrifice those who had been companions and neighbours. The most notable of this small number who forsook the tenets of their faith, throwing the peace creed to the winds, was a young Quakeress, who secretly offered herself as an emissary between the contending armies—to supply the Federals with such information that would enable the Commanding General to take the struggling Southrons unawares (for many of whom she still professed an ardent affection) which resulted in carnage appalling to all, except the *silent* damsel, who so ignominiously endeavoured to sacrifice human life. Was it for love of her departure from the doctrines of her grand old fathers, or was it for the promised reward offered her by Gen'l Sheridan, which she afterwards received? (a gold watch and chain). The writer knew this young woman, and was familiar with this incident when it occurred. She is now a resident of Washington. The writer refrains from giving her name in consideration of the respect he has for her many relatives. It can be truly said, this was an exception. None can point to a single other member of this sect who carries the odium of such an act. Doubtless many of this highly esteemed class, known as the *Friends,* were the most loyal Union men in all the regions around; none however can be found willing to give approval to such a departure from their faith.

The author familiar with the Quaker, and his peacefully disposed life, can recall many pleasant and interesting incidents, as they occurred during his unbroken intercourse with them, from his childhood to the present writing. Their friendship has often been a comfort. On one occasion, however, this friendship resulted in much embarrassment. It was during the war period in the Winter of 1861-2 that the Confederate Army under command of Genl. Jackson (Stonewall) lay in Winter Quarters for miles around Winchester. The author was then Acting Provost Marshal for the Army Post with office located in what was then called the Senseney building (now Bantz's). Col. Lawson Botts of the 2nd Virginia Infantry, was Commandant of the Post. The duties of the Provost were well defined by Genl. Jackson in his general orders, as well as in a personal interview, when the Genl. called his attention to the General Order, forbidding persons to pass beyond the lines without a *Pass* from the Provost Marshal—whether civilian or soldier; stating that too much freedom was accorded citizens to pass beyond the lines, that the U. S. troops were then on the border line, along the Potomack, and he had been informed that quite a number of persons, whose loyalty to the Confederate cause had been doubted, were allowed to enter his lines from that quarter and allowed to return in the evening; that it must be understood that no person should be given a pass unless his *loyalty to the South* was beyond question; and where suspicion existed, the person must have some loyal friend to vouch for his conduct; (this was a special order) and no soldier to have the office pass, unless he could produce regimental pass. The closing of that first day brought untold numbers of people to the office—soldiers and citizens. A majority of the former were refused passes. Of the civilian class, very few appeared that were not favorably known at the office, and they were readily disposed of. At this juncture, the young *Provost* was brought to a stand-still by the appearance in the door-way of a Man of striking figure, whose garb, style and language were sufficient to mark him a quaker. His quiet demeanor denoted a strong will. The writer easily recognized this dignified quaker as one of the many *Friends* from whom he had always received tokens of kindness and esteem. Embarrassment seized both; it was known that there in that door-way stood the only man in Frederick County who had voted for Abraham Lincoln; this Friend was Joseph N. Jolliffe, whose home lay about six miles due North from the army lines. He saw the situation and quietly met the issue, simply saying: "Friend, thee will give me a pass to return to my home," the Officer still embarrassed, made no answer until his demand was repeated. There was no request for the pass; simply a *demand.* His attention was called to the General Order posted on the walls of the Office. He quietly remarked that it could not apply to him; that he was non-partisan. Then the question was asked, are you loyal to the *Confederate cause?* His reply was "Neither loyal nor disloyal; the uprising forbodes evil; I refuse to take part, and wish to be governed by my own conscience." He was then asked if the vote he had cast for Lincoln, who had declared war against the Southern States, would not justify the Provo in refusing him a pass, until he was vouched for by some loyal friend. Then for the first time his eye flashed fire, drawing his tall form to its most dignified height, he replied—"Then thou art not my friend," and suddenly left the office; but returned in a few minutes with his friend, T. T. Fauntleroy, Esq., (afterwards Judge Fauntleroy) who desired to know "why his friend Jolliffe was deprived of his liberty." The Genl. order was shown Mr. F., who hastily said he would apply to Genl. Jackson in person, and together they went to Headquarters; the Genl. told them the Order should not be changed, and that nothing but a pass signed by the Provo would pass persons through the lines. Mr. Jolliffe remained in Winchester that night. The next morning, Mr. F. appeared again, and with changed manner asked that a pass be given, and that he would endorse Mr. J. The reply was, that the *Special order* was, that he must *vouch for his loyalty.* This he refused in his characteristic style, creating a breach in the relation of two friends that required years to heal. Several years after the War, Mr. F. moved by impulses that could be awakened only in such impulsive men, generously offered apologies, and declared that the performance of the duty imposed on the officer, was an act he would ever admire, and nothing could affect his friendship again. Mr. Jolliffe never mentioned the incident, though the writer understood the meaning of the warm grasp of hand during the closing years of his life. Mr. Jolliffe was never molested by the Confederate authorities. He survived the war, the Reconstruction period, and lived to see his country re-united; going down to his grave respected and esteemed by all who knew him. This digression may be allowable, when it is considered that it shows an incident of the times when the silent quakers who lived by their creed, were accorded the privilege of non-combatants, and were never called upon to render military duty, and received as much protection from the Confederate army as from the Union.

The impartial reader in his study of the creed of the Society of Friends, may conclude that the motives of the Quaker prisoners were greatly misunderstood; that they meant to impress both powers with the enormity of guilt resting upon those who had gone to war, and that they intended no harm to befall the Patriot soldiers, though they condemned the "uprising of the people." The Quaker prisoners were humanely treated by the Virginians, who were in no sense responsible for their arrest and exile. To their own State, Pennsylvania, the friends of the prisoners must be cited, to learn that their own *State Supreme Executive Council* refused to consider their remonstrance, and directed the President of the Council to write to the Congress and let them know that "The Council has not time to attend to that business, in the present alarming Crisis." *"Exiles in Virginia"* gives interesting incidents concerning the Quaker prisoners, from which we take the following: "On the 11th of Ninth Month 1777, the prisoners started on their march by Waggon train seventeen being quakers, three being persons suspected of treason." The list is given at this point, though it may include the names of some already given;

James Pemberton, Edward Pennington, Henry Drinker, Mrs. Fisher, Wm. Drewet Smith, Elijah Brown, Samuel Pleasants, Charles Eddy, Wm. Smith (broker), Thos. Gilpin, Israel Pemberton, Thos. Wharton, Samuel R. Fisher, John Hunt, Charles Jarvis, Owen Jones Jr., Thos. Pike, Thos. Afflick, John Pemberton, Thos. Fisher.

We learn from the diary of one of the prisoners, James Pemberton, that John Hunt and John Pemberton frequently held Meetings at their lodgings in Winchester. This makes it appear that the Quakers had no Meeting-house in Winchester at that date. Same diary says they held Meetings at Hopewell during their exile; and then records that John Hunt and Thos. Gilpin died during their exile and were buried at Hopewell. The writer has carefully examined the Hopewell graveyard, and finds no slabs to mark graves of those who were buried there prior to 1800.

On the 16th of March 1778, the Congress, then sitting at Yorktown, passed a resolution to deliver over to the President and Council of Pennsylvania, the prisoners sent from the State of Virginia. They were, after some delay, brought to Pottsgrove in Pennsylvania, and there discharged, (see Janney's History of the Friends).

It has been claimed as a well settled fact these many years, that the quakers were opposed to slavery, and had never been guilty of the crime of owning slaves. This however, is not true. For, consulting several authorities, it can be seen that the Friends of Chester Quarterly Meeting, held 1730, made this minute, "The Friends of this Meeting resuming the proposition of Chester Meeting, relating to the purchasing of such Negroes as may hereafter be imported; and having reviewed and considered the former minutes in relation thereto . . . . . Are of the opinion that Friends ought to be very cautious of making any such purchases for the future."

The Friends for many years maintained three Meetings, and for some reason they were all designated as Hopewell Meeting; the first being Hopewell on Apple-pie Ridge, one at Pugh's town (Gainesboro), and one on Crooked-run, (East of Stephens City).

Old Hopewell is and has been for many years a massive stone building, accommodating large crowds at the yearly Meeting; drawing members of the sect from other counties, and even States, while Frederick and near-by counties sent throngs. The day was regarded as a meeting place for every class; and abuses of the privilege was practiced by the thoughtless. This condition prevailed to such an extent, that a change was desirable, and the Yearly Meeting was transferred to Winchester, where the Society has a large house and grounds, Cor. Piccadilly St. and Fairmont Ave.

The Hicksites and Orthodox branches, however, hold one Yearly meeting for one day at Hopewell, while only the Hicksites own and occupy Centre Meeting-house in Winchester. Two other Meetings were held on Apple-pie ridge—one at the *Ridge* meeting-house, and one in the vicinity of White-hall. For many years there was a *Meeting* at what was known as the Quaker School-house on the Cedar Creek turnpike, near Fawcetts Gap, which was abandoned many years ago. The Meeting at "Pughstown" was well attended for many years; but the Methodist Church has gradually strengthened its Congregation by accessions from the families of the old Society who were once numerous on Back-creek. There is an old gravyard adjoining this place that contains the remains of many of the pioneers. Crooked-run Meeting has been abandoned so long, that very few young quakers of to-day are aware that a large Meeting was once a part of that section. Prior to the Civil war the quakers had a Meeting-house in the South end of Winchester, which is mentioned in notes on Cemeteries. This was known as Centre Meeting. The Meeting-house was on the West side of Washington Street, corner of Stewart, German and Monmouth Streets. A whole square was conveyed by Sarah Zane of Philadelphia to Joshua Lupton, Samuel Brown and Samuel Swayne in 1814, "for the purpose of erecting a Meeting-house thereon, and for a burial ground on part thereof for use of the Friends society." The site is now occupied by residences.

The quakers of to-day are reduced in numbers to such an extent, that their Meetings are slimly attended. Some families adhere to their faith more than to the old time customs. In the olden time they were easily distinguished from other classes by their quiet demeanor and peculiar style of dress; but we never see the broad brimmed hat, or the shad-belly coat in these days.

The Mennonist Society.

Very few readers of these Sketches are aware of the early appearance of this Sect. They were in small groups—South of the North-fork of the Shenandoah River—alongside the first Lutherans, extending up the Luray Valley and also South up the main Valley, towards Harrisonburg, where they also had the Tunkers for neighbours. This sect was certainly represented in the Massanuttin region, but no evidence of Meeting-houses. They were found by German Evangelists and Moravian Missionaries. The Shenandoah County section, and Rockingham have had small settlements for many years. In recent years this Society had several preaching places in Frederick County, and until within the last five years, maintained a church near Kernstown Railroad station. This has since closed, and the property sold to S. M. Chiles, who converted it into a tenant-house. All the members of this Church, known to the writer, were exemplary Christian citizens. Many of them men of means. They came into this section chiefly from Pennsylvania, since the Civil war. A Menonist preacher lived near Massanuttin, and was killed by the Indians about 1760 (see reference in War notes).

CHAPTER XLI

The Roman Catholic Church

In writing a history of the Catholic Church in the territory of Old Frederick, the author approaches the subject with many misgivings, knowing this Church has a history; but the records showing what part this Church had in the development of this county are so meagre, that justice cannot be done her. Where such limited knowledge prevails, many incidents of self sacrifice which the first Catholic settlers endured, may never be told. We know they were here in the forming of the county; they were land owners, good citizens, and as loyal to American institutions as they ever were to their Mother Church. They, too, had their struggles. Deprived of the accustomed ministrations of their Church, they never faltered, but waited for the time when a service of *Matins* and *Vespers* might be enjoyed.

The Shenandoah region had a strange infatuation for emigrants. Hastening from the seaboard landings, through sections of country equal in soil and climate, and more congenial to their religion, they crossed the Cohongoruta; erected their log-cabins and—we may say, their altars too, in what was a wilderness. Pennsylvania offered inducements to the German Protestants; Delaware and Jersey to Scotch-Irish Presbyterians, and Maryland to the Catholics. We have endeavored to show in preceding pages, what the former did in the new country; we will now try to show what the latter did in his new environments.

We have evidence that several Priests visited this section prior to 1800; and that Mass was said at Richard McSherry's Jr. at his homestead called "Retirement farm"; and that it was a well-known stopping-place for Priests. Wm. McSherry who lived near Martinsburg, was also a devout Catholic; and Mass was said in the house of John Timmons, a resident of Martinsburg. There was no church at that date; and the visiting priests came from Maryland—Revs. Denis Cahill, Frambach, Gallitzin and others are named. It is well established that there were no resident priests prior to 1840 in all this section. We find Rev. Richard Whelan and Rev. Jos. S. Plunkett visited all the towns in Frederick, Berkeley, Jefferson, Hampshire, Hardy and Shenandoah. There must have been a regular place of worship in Martinsburg as early as 1820, for the church record kept by Rev. James Redmond, has several entries in it as early as 1820. This appears "In the chapel room 1820," Father Redmond married a couple in this chapel on that date. It has been asserted by some writers that he started the building of what was known as the old stone church, doing much of the work himself. The following named priests served this church until 1840: Rev. John Mahony, Geo. Flautt, F. B. Jamison, Richard Wheelan, Jos. Strain, P. Danaker; and from 1842 to 1856, Revs. John O'Brien, Jos. H. Plunkett, and Andrew Talty. It is more than likely the church proper was erected about 1830. We find by frequent reference to the work of Mr. John T. Reily, that about fifty Catholic families lived in Martinsburg at the time, who aided in the erection of the church, as did also "many Protestant friends." The church was located on the ground of the present cemetery, at a cost of $4,000. This was known as St. Joseph. The present imposing church property, with its parochial school, was completed in 1883. Mr. Reily says the Laity's Directory, 1822, has this entry: "The Catholics of Martinsburg, Winchester, Bath and Shepardstown were formerly attended by priests from Maryland, but in future would be in charge of the priest stationed at Winchester." This corroborates the statement made by old Catholics to the author many years ago, that there was a church in Winchester long before 1800. This church was at the East end of Piccadilly Street, North of the old Presbyterian Church. Near it was the consecrated yard that contained their dead. This old place has been mentioned in chapters on Cemeteries. When the War closed in 1865, the little church was in ruins; and the old yard contained many defaced and broken slabs—evidence that vandals had been there in the garb of soldiers. The first services were held in Michael Hassett's house. About this time came Rev. J. J. Kain, who ministered and worked in his congregation with such zeal, that it became possible to erect the imposing edifice now the home of many Catholics. Standing on South Loudoun Street, it is an ornament to the city; and offers many inducements to members of this church to change their country homes for homes in the city. Father Kain was the distinguished Bishop of his Church soon after leaving Winchester. Father Van De Vyver came next and succeeded in completing the edifice. The church was dedicated by Bishop Kain, 1875, under the special patronage of the *Sacred Heart of Jesus*. They now were ready to enjoy the services of their first resident pastor. Up to this time, Winchester was an out-mission under the care of the Harpers Ferry Church. Rev. J. Hagan came first; a comfortable home for the priest was built, and also the towering steeple for the ponderous bell, whose tones are so strong and withal so melodious, the entire city feels a just pride in the sonorous tones it daily wafts over every home. The next pastor was Rev. D. J. O'Connell, D.D., who for many years was Rector of the American College at Rome. In 1883, Rev. J. B. O'Reilly came. Under his pastorate, the site for the new cemetery was purchased; and removals made from the old graveyard. It may be proper to say that several old tombs were not disturbed. Quite a number of the graves were unmarked; and the unknown tenants remain in blissful ignorance of the abandonment of the old graveyard that had been consecrated a century ago. Certainly the dust of the donor of the ground, Edward McGuire, was left; the marks that once distinguished the spot where he had lain so long, were obliterated; and the writer was informed by Father O'Reilly that it would have been impossible to identify the remains of such; and he deemed it best to level the surface and turn it over for other purposes. Genl. Denver protested against the removal of his grandfather Patrick Denver, and requested the writer to present his views; but Mr. O'Reilly was unyielding, and insisted upon the removel of all found in graves that were marked.

Rev. Father McVerry is now pastor of Sacred Heart Church, and a most consistent and devout priest, held in high esteem by all who know him. The writer appreciates his courtesies.

The Catholics in 1889 erected a church property in Charlestown. Harpers Ferry for many years before the War had a prosperous church, and the priests resided there.

Shepardstown was slow in establishing a church at that point, though there is one there now, which has gathered strength since 1890.

The Catholic Church at Harpers Ferry escaped destruction during the Civil War; and has had reasonable success. Priests of note have celebrated Mass in the old church. It was in this old church where the author many years ago, first saw the Crucifix, the Virgin Mary and the Holy Child—figures of worship occupying a place near the chancel. His youthful impressions remain to this day. The church occupies one of the most prominent and picturesque heights of that hilly town.

Front Royal and Strasburg were early mission fields for the Catholics. Not even a nucleus for churches was formed, however, until after the Civil War. Front Royal has had for several years a growing church. An incident associated with this church is worth relating: It was during the Civil War, that a young soldier of the Confederate Army, a member of the celebrated Maryland Line, was disabled and languished for many weary days in the home of a friend in Front Royal. He was tenderly cared for by a lady whose name cannot be recalled, but she was a devout Catholic, and so was the young soldier, Carroll Jenkins, whose life was slowly ebbing away, far removed from his luxurious home in Baltimore. His grateful acknowledgment for the attentions given him by his Catholic nurse, and the ministrations of such church rites as she could render, prompted him to give substantial evidence of his appreciation. He informed his newly-made friends that he was the son of Mr. Thomas C. Jenkins of Baltimore, who was well known for his wealth and association with the Michael Jenkins family of that city; and he directed that after his death, when communication was open with Baltimore, that his father be informed and requested, that he desired of whatever estate he possessed, or that his father intended he should share had he lived, that a sufficient sum should be appropriated for the purpose of erecting a memorial church in Front Royal, and on the spot where he had succumbed to the fate of war. The church now in Front Royal stands as the memorial to the young soldier. The father and family had complied with his wishes. The membership is small. The church is under the care of the Sacred Heart Church of Winchester. Father McVerry ministers the Holy Sacrament to this mission.

It may be added, that the same Jenkins family contributed liberally to the completion of the Sacred Heart Church in Winchester.

In closing the sketches of the various churches found in Old Frederick County and her subdivisions, the author submits their perusal and study to the indulgent reader of this volume, trusting that he may find many historical incidents of value, and be compensated for his time; and thus understand why so much space has been devoted to this part of the development of the great territory the fathers found West of the Blue Ridge in the early part of the 18th Century. In this the 20th Century, but few if any readers can afford to entertain a thought that the church development was not a necessity; and, indeed, it must be conceded that it was necessary; for without it, the far-famed Shenandoah Valley would have presented a spectacle of chaos, and even barbarism, that is beyond the ken of man to comprehend. Each and every denomination carrying the banner of the Christian faith, has had its part in the great drama; and to-day as they take the retrospective along with the prospective view, they must feel emboldened in their efforts to press the work forward, encouraged by the hope that the Church will ultimately triumph over all other creations. It is the only institution to survive the upheavals of time. Its first appearance indicated no such results. Founded at a period in the world's history; few indeed could appreciate its origin, and only a few were present at its birth. The humblest of a mighty nation, stood awed by the demeanor and language of a young Hebrew who, standing in their midst, made the most fearless and unequivocal announcement ever made by man; and though only spoken in the presence of the humble, and that in an obscure place, the utterance has never lost any of its power:—"Upon this rock I will build my Church, and the gates of hell shall not prevail against it." This was Jesus of Nazareth; and how well the Church to-day attests the fulfillment of that astounding declaration. No scheme of destruction has ever been devised by man to destroy or overcome the Church. Every atom of creation perishes; nations, and their thrones, have been extinguished; generations come and go; the mighty law of change and decay will ultimately remove the earth and its firmament; but time in her cycles is giving proof that the Church thus founded, will survive all the wreck of matter. History marks the rise and fall of many civilized powers. She also marks the increasing power of that church. She also marks the rise of false religions, only to show their final overthrow. She also marks an era, when philosophy offered its tenets of false reason, that perished in the using.

This Church was founded at a time when the world's population had full knowledge that obliteration and decay stood boldly out in every known land, to prove that nothing was imperishable. Perhaps they pointed to a few exceptions, to be seen in the massive columns some of the mighty rulers had builded, and to their pyramid-monuments on the borders of an Egyptian desert. All other creations had vanished under the hand of the universal destroyer. No wonder, then, that the announcement of this stranger should be received with doubt and derision. All civilized nations to-day acknowledge that the strange Hebrew was the Christ; and the Institution he founded has defied, and will forever to the end defy all destructible agencies. And on this foundation, all the denominations treated in the foregoing sketches, openly declare there is where their banner has been planted; and under it they are making rapid strides to encircle the earth. The benign influence of this great development has become an integral part in the development of Civilization of the Universe, resulting in the Christianizing of the untold millions.

CHAPTER XLII

The Cemeteries

In the olden time, the villagers knew nothing about the necessity of providing some general place where the whole community could dedicate some appointed spot for the burial of their deceased friends, which would be under some systematic control. The church yard was deemed sufficient; and as the several churches had sufficient space, the members of the different denominations appropriated this space. And thus the old church-yard gradually filled to over-flowing. For instance, as previously stated, the old graveyard in the rear of the first Episcopal Church, corner of Loudoun and Boscawen Streets, was found at an early day, inadequate to meet the wants for this purpose. Many removals were made to a new plot of ground southwest from where the hospital now stands. The old ground was converted to other uses. The old Lutheran and German Reformed Churches on the hill had ample space adjacent to the churches. There we find the early settlers resting undisturbed; while to the North, the old Presbyterian Church at the East end of Piccadilly Street continued the use of their adjoining lot until 1840. The graveyard was carefully guarded for many decades. Some of our most noted persons rested there for a century undisturbed; some removals were made to Mt. Hebron about the middle of the 19th Century; the monuments and enclosures yielded to the ravages of war, and tombs lost all evidence of their identity. A recent visit to this once sacred place impressed the writer with the feeling that the descendants had forgotten the ancestors who will soon be in nameless graves; the old slabs have been displaced in many instances; and some slabs bear inscriptions that would startle many of our busy men and women if they realized the inexcusable neglect. Go, reader, some day to this place, and take warning, lest you receive at the hands of your descendants similar neglect of a righteous duty! The once gifted Rev. Nash LeGrand, and many others of his class, lie beneath that sod without the vestige of a marker. The invincible Daniel Morgan was buried here in July, 1802. Genl. Roberdeau, the Powells, Magills, Beatty, Smiths, Whites, Holmes, Baldwins, Grays and others were laid to rest here. Some were removed to Mount Hebron. Just to the North are other plats, one where the Roman Catholic Church had a consecrated place for their dead; but the limits of the Eastern suburbs of the City pressed on, until this, too, was abandoned; and, maybe, all that remained of the old pioneers of this Church, were gathered up and carried to their new cemetery at the South end of Market Street. The Methodist congregation, for many years, interred their dead in the other lot. Some were removed to Mt. Hebron. The Friends had their graveyard near their old Meeting House that stood between Stewart and Washington Streets. Some removals were made prior to the Civil War. During the War, hundreds of Confederate soldiers were buried on the same lot, in the Episcopal graveyard, and afterwards removed to Stonewall Cemetery; likewise, many Union soldiers were buried there. The Society of Friends for many years interred many of their dead in the two graveyards South of Winchester, one on the Valley Pike near the Hollingsworth Mill property, and the other N. W. from the paper mill.

It was found desirable about the year 1840, that there should be some common place of burial, provided and maintained on some legal plan. Steps were taken to organize a company to provide the necessary funds. This being assured, The Mount Hebron Cemetery Company was chartered; and when the present location was adopted, a large lot was purchased adjoining the old Lutheran and Reformed Calvinists graveyards on the East. The grounds having been suitably laid off in plats and driveways by an accomplished landscape engineer, Mount Hebron was ready for dedication June 22, 1844. The impressive services were conducted by Rev. Dr. A. H. H. Boyd, pastor of Loudoun Street Presbyterian Church, with an introductory address, reading of Scriptures by Rev. Dr. Wm. Rooker, rector of Christ Church, and dedicatory prayer by Rev. Dr. Wm. M. Atkinson; address by Wm. L. Clark, Esq., concluding prayer by Rev. Wm. B. Edwards; Rev. D. H. Bragonier read one paper.

After the singing of three hymns, Rev. Joseph Baker pronounced the Benediction. The first interment was made August, 1844, the wife of Dr. Atkinson. The newspapers of that date gave extended notices of the dedication services. Dr. Foote, in his sketches, says: "The first interment in the graveyard was the body of Mrs. Atkinson, wife of Rev. Wm. M. Atkinson, D.D., pastor of the old school Presbyterian Church, Winchester." The lots were sold at a reasonable price; and 'ere long, the removals from the old graveyards produced the appearance of a cemetery of long standing. The transfer of old slabs and monuments with old inscriptions, gave the impression often felt by visitors, that Mt. Hebron started with the 19th Century. Genl. Daniel Morgan, and the Huguenot General Roberdeau, were removed from their old places and became part of Mt. Hebron history; and as the century closed, nearly all the participants in the dedication had been laid to rest in the various lots. Previous to this, however, every lot had been taken, and other additions required to meet the increasing demand. The original plans were extended to new purchases; and before the Twentieth Century was ushered in—less than sixty years since the first interment—the Cemetery embraced thirty-five acres. The first addition, lying between the original plat and Stonewall Cemetery, started about 1870, has long since been well filled with imposing monuments, and simpler slabs, that speak to the passer-by volumes for reflection. The silent city is increasing in numbers that may soon equal the living city, that nestles so beautifully between the hills a few hundred yards West. (The number of interments are 4,485 at this writing). The site was well chosen for this city on the hill, the elevation being sufficient to command a view of the entire lower Valley. To the East is that transcendent prospect, the Blue Ridge, at whose base one can outline the turbulent Shenandoah, hastening on to meet the Potomac at Harpers Ferry; out on that Western horizon are the foot-hills of the Alleganies; and to the South the inimitable scenery of the Alps of America, the *Massanutton* peaks and ranges. The skill of man has done much to bring out the attractions that Nature had founded. The sighing evergreens and waving foliage of towering trees, enhance the lines of beauty; and the quiet visitor strolls 'neath the overhanging boughs, and really learns to enjoy the impressive solitude. The sacred place, with each succeeding year, becomes the mecca of many new visitors, seeking communion of kindred spirits, where so many hallowed memories cluster, that can never be imparted to others.

The Mount Hebron Cemetery comprehends the entire grounds now enclosed by an iron fence, the gift of Mr. Rouss. This incloses Stonewall and also what is generally known as the Old Lutheran Graveyard, with the ruins of the old Lutheran Church standing near the centre, a description of which will be found in the sketch of the church, elsewhere in this volume.

Stonewall Cemetery.

Immediately to the East and adjoining Mt. Hebron, is Stonewall Cemetery, beautiful in situation, and sacred by reason of what it contains. Here are entombed the Confederate soldiers who succumbed to disease or went down in the shock of battle on the fields lying in full view in every direction. This has the distinction of being the first Memorial offered to the soldiers who perished in the Civil War; and the noble women of this section are entitled to the honor, for they sank not when the Banner was furled; they who had been in camp and hospital, and cheered the marching columns, scarcely allowed the smoke and din of War to pass from the Valley, before they rallied to their support willing helpers, to gather together the thousands of fallen brave; and succeeded after untold trials, in transferring all to this plat of ground secured for that purpose, until, with continued perseverance, they produced the impressive picture seen to-day. The unknown dead were consigned to one great mound. Eight hundred and twenty-nine of the Boys in Grey were found without a vestige to tell their name, regiment, home or kindred. All knew what they were. Their remains were laid away with imposing ceremonies; and the lofty marble shaft standing in the centre of their mound, attests the devotion of those who performed the service. On the base of the monument is read "Who they were none know; what they were all know." A sentiment that will be held in reverence as long as time spares the marble from destruction. This magnificent shaft is 48 feet high, crowned with the life-sized figure of a Confederate infantryman, in full uniform, with rifle and accoutrements. The imposing monument impresses all beholders with its grandeur. The writer has never in his varied travels, seen any that approached its impressive effect. All the Southern States have large sections in the cemetery, including Maryland and Delaware. Nearly every grave is now marked by marble headstones; while several States have imposing monuments in their respective sections, where several thousands of their gallant sons are sleeping the years away—now almost a half-century since they yielded up their lives. This cemetery was dedicated October 9, 1866; Ex-Governor Henry A. Wise the orator. Language fails in attempting to describe the scenes of that day. The country far and near fairly poured forth the entire population, who participated in the ceremonies with so much solemnity, that its impressions are felt to this day by those who witnessed the great concourse, as it wended its way through Mt. Hebron, and finally massed itself in the hallowed grounds.

Beyond all doubt, the first step taken to organize memorial associations of this character, was in Winchester in the Spring of 1865, shortly after peace was declared. The writer, to preserve the evidence, gives it here, knowing the circumstances and being made familiar with the facts at the time:—Mrs. Williams, wife of Mr. Philip Williams, the renowned lawyer, visited Dr. A. H. H. Boyd early in May, 1865, and related an incident that deeply interested the persons there present in Dr. Boyd's room, who was an invalid. Mrs. Williams stated that a farmer had told her that while plowing in one of his fields for corn, he had turned up the bodies of two Confederate soldiers, and believed that many more such things would occur; and suggested that something should be done. It was determined then in that room, that Mrs. Williams and Mrs. Boyd would make the effort to get the ladies of the town and country to join them in what soon became a prodigious undertaking. The organization, known ever after as the "Ladies Memorial Association" was effected, with Mrs. Williams as president and Mrs. Boyd vice-president, with numerous committees. As the result of their efforts, we have but to examine the records of the Society, which shows that June 6, 1865, witnessed an outpouring of people assembled on the grounds, where hundreds of Confederates had been re-interred, and the foundation laid for the first Confederate cemetery in all the land. There was a floral offering on that day, and addresses by popular speakers, and, informally, the Stonewall Cemetery became a fact, which, as already said, was formally dedicated in October, 1866. The scenes of that day can never be effaced from the memory of those who witnessed it. Thousands of people came with evergreens and flowers; processions of small girls arrayed in white, wearing sashes, formed on the grounds; and then the floral offerings began. We must mention, however, that a large concourse of people first visited the Confederate graves in the Episcopal graveyard, and also the lot adjacent called the Quaker Lot—both these places receiving floral tributes. A considerable sum of money was collected that day through various agencies, to aid the ladies in their laudable work. Of course, every surviving Confederate was anxious to aid them. Word went out through various channels, what the Ladies Memorial Association desired to do. The far-away Southern homes caught the sound echoing there everywhere; and soon substantial answer came. Alabama was the first State heard from in January, 1866. She sent by the hands of Capt. —— Roy, twelve hundred dollars. This was by private contribution from what was regarded an impoverished people; and all funds were so skillfully handled, that by the next 6th of June, the work of re-interment had been completed. Since that day, however, other bodies were found and placed in the cemetery. People of this day will never know what was required for this work. The whole country was searched for burial places; and when the bodies were found, came the difficult task of identification. It was desirable to not only learn the name, but the Company, Regiment and State, so they could be appropriately buried in their respective places; and the mound in the center attests the fact that many gallant men must be unnamed. There has never been any cessation from this ceremony on each recurring Sixth of June; and as the years pass away, the attendance increases; so that at this writing, the Sixth of June has become the most notable day in the year.

The National Cemetery is located due North from Stonewall, and separated by a narrow County road. It contains about five acres, and was dedicated in 1866. Several thousand Union soldiers, slain in battle, were gathered from various places within a radius of twelve miles and buried here by the U. S. Government. A large expenditure of money was required for this purpose, and for building a stone wall as enclosure. The Superintendent's Lodge on Valley Avenue, forms the entrance to the grounds, which was laid out in sections, forty-eight in number. Interments generally were divided between the States represented. We find here a section for unknown dead, the number being 2,382, while the known dead with headstones number 2,098. A number of handsome monuments have been erected by different organizations, who have visited Winchester quite often. The Veteran associations are always cordially entertained by Turner Ashby Camp of Confederate Veterans.

The Catholic Cemetery.

This cemetery was located on the South end of the City, and has been handsomely laid out and adorned with trees and shrubbery. It was to this cemetery that the removals from the old graveyard referred to, were taken. Among those removed here, were many who emigrated from Ireland prior to 1800. Of this emigrant list was Patrick Denver and his wife. He was the Grandfather of Genl. Denver for whom the city of Denver is named.

This promises to be the chief Catholic burial place of the lower Valley. The location is unsurpassed; and many imposing monuments mark graves of well-known persons. The writer had personal acquaintances with many, and warm, friendly relations with others—John Fagan, the pioneer Catholic, Hassett and Rhyan—splendid specimens of the Emerald Isle. Patrick Reardon who one time won laurels with the famous squadrons of Mosby's Rangers; and later on, enthused Turner Ashby Camp with poesy, songs and story; Maurice Lynch, robust and vigorous after years well spent, noted for his integrity. Many more could be named. Reader, go read their epitaphs, and learn who have gone to form another city of our dead.

In *The Old Lutheran Cemetery,* commonly so called found within the enclosure known now as Mt. Hebron, seen on the West side, immediately to the left from the main entrance, the visitor soon finds himself among those who were part of the Eighteenth Century. Old Revolutionary heroes are here! Tread softly; and be patient to decipher many strange inscriptions, and you will gather bits of history that have been well preserved. Morgan's Sharpshooters are scattered here and there. Some are easily found and recognized by their epitaphs. Here we find some of the Dutch Mess—Lauck, Sperry, Grim, Kurtz. A little westward we find a white marble, upright slab, that tells the simple story of the fifth member: "In memory of John Schultz who departed this life 5th day of November, 1840, in the 87th year of his age." The sixth, Heiskell, found his grave in Romney. Men may safely say the last of the soldiers of Quebec lie here; while just on the edge of Mt. Hebron, the broken slab tells where their General, Morgan, has lain for years. In the old churchyard you will find the Millers, Hoffs, Bakers, Singletons and many others; and hard by the old ruin, we stand by the grave of Streit, the founder of the English Lutheran Church. A substantial monument has been erected on his grave; but the old Church walls seem to have been spared all destroying elements, to lend pathos to the spot. May it be spared for other generations!

The main entrance to Mt. Hebron is appropriate; and impresses the visitor with its unique and solemn grandeur. Mortuary chapel on the left, and lodge for superintendent on the right, connected with an arched span, and heavy iron gates to bar the entrance, when required. Both chapel and lodge built of heavy cut, blue limestone,—the architect and builders have furnished a monument to their skill and workmanship. This, too, was a gift from Mr. Rouss, the Cemetery Company supplementing an equivalent. Mr. James Hamilton, an old Confederate soldier, has been the faithful superintendent for many years, and has grown familiar with all the tombs and inscriptions found within the enclosure.

Thus having briefly described the Silent City, we must again turn our attention to the city under the hill, in the next chapter.

Old Market, Winchester, Va.

CHAPTER XLIII

Transformation From Town to City Government

The Market Square Suit

The City of Winchester, under its city charter of April 2, 1874, received its initiation with Judge Sherrard's first term, held April 22, 1874, with R. Wm. Walter, clerk. This new order of government, superceding the old Justices court, was required by what is generally termed the "Underwood" constitution, framed by a convention held in Alexandria, 1867-8. This was the beginning of the carpet-bag government, that distracted the State for several years. If there was a delegate from Winchester, he was there without the sanction or knowledge of his constituency. We need not mention his name; and doubtless he lived long enough to regret his association with the "Black and Tan" crowd he found there, illegally fastening a yoke on the necks of Virginians. Fuller notice of this will appear under the County Court proceedings.

The City of Winchester recovered rapidly after she was organized. As we have shown, the damaged buildings were repaired; streets and other public places receiving a full share of attention. The county and city had some friction as governing bodies, relating to the court house, market square, etc., but nothing occurred to mar the harmony between them. Occasionally the city exercised certain control, that was questioned by the new county government. The Board of Supervisors was jealous of its rights, and perhaps were over zealous to preserve such rights. As time wore on, the city felt the importance of radical changes on the market square, and gradually encroached upon the sacred rights of the county people, in restricting certain spaces, that had theretofore been regarded by country visitors as convenient for standing their vehicles and hitching horses. This, as may be supposed, increased the irritation; and while the city for a time heeded the remonstrances, and held up their plans of improvement, the meaning of the proposed improvement soon developed. The city had for several years agitated the question of building a court house, with council chamber, public offices and an opera house, on the site occupied by the old market house; and this idea caught the attention of Charles B. Rouss. He very soon gave evidence of his desire to see this accomplished in his day, and of his sentimental attachment to the old market space, where he had trafficked with the market people in his younger days; and now the desire seized him to erect a memorial on this spot—not to himself alone, but to the "old timers," as he so expressed himself to the writer on several occasions. The city became intensely interested, and hastened to adopt plans that would be agreeable to all parties—Committees from the council frequently appeared before the Board of Supervisors, to confer with them; for it was conceded by all that the consent of the county must be obtained before any plans could mature. All this meant a change of the uses of the public space. The county people realized the necessity for some change, so long as it did not infringe upon the space so long used as a *hitching yard.* After many such conferences, an agreement was verbally made, between the Board of Supervisors and committee from the council with Mr. Wm. H. Baker, chairman, that the city could appropriate the space occupied by the old market house, extending from court house avenue along Market Street, to about where the South end of the city hall now stands, minus the space occupied by the present council chamber and police court room; and extend their space West to where the line of hitching posts stood;—not to disturb the public water trough and hydrant on this line—this West limit being the West line of the present building. The question seemed settled; and all waited for further developments. Pending this waiting, new forces were at work. Mr. Rouss had to be consulted with; and besides, the architect in his plan, needed 4 feet additional over the West line. Mr. Baker confronted with this barrier, called upon the writer, who was clerk of the board of supervisors, explained the dilemma; and requested that a meeting of the Board be called. They were notified, promptly assembled, and considered the grave question. They pointed out to the committee that it would be better to change the building plan, than to disturb the Western limit and remove the line of posts. To this the committee offered no serious objection, but the incorrigible architect would not yield: The committee retired. Mr. Rouss had been heard from; and he insisted the line of posts must be removed entirely; and that if horses were hitched on the remaining space, they must be far removed from the building. To this the county people seriously objected, and the Board declined to make such changes. Up to this time, the relations between the council and board of supervisors had not been strained. It is true, individuals were found here and there who discussed the subject vehemently; and it was natural that the differences between the two bodies should be misunderstood; and prejudices prevailed to some extent. During this apparent lull of action in the city council, they were advised by an attorney, acting as their counsel. at their June meeting, 1885, to at once assert the right to control the uses of the market square. The Council adopted the proposition made by their attorney, and enacted an ordinance at that meeting, so radical in its terms, that it would be well for the reader to see it for himself in the record, want of space not permitting its entry here. We have now arrived at the first step in the great suit. The next morning, when the writer arrived at the clerk's office from his home in the country, he was astonished to behold a member of the council in charge of a gang of hands, rushing the work of tearing up the stone pavement on that part of the square now known as Frederick Plaza. The writer approached the councilman, Mr. Washington G. South, and requested an explanation. He abruptly replied that the city would at once remove the pavement and hitching posts, and plant trees on the ground, and convert it into a park. A protest was entered; the writer sought the attorney who advised this rash step, and requested a delay until he could summon the Board of supervisors. His reply was that the work would be completed before the day ended, if possible. The writer took the responsibility (there being no other countrymen in town at that hour, to consult) to take prompt action by injunction. He was disconcerted to some extent by members of the bar declining to take such a hopeless case. While in this predicament, he called upon Judge Wm. L. Clark who had been judge since Judge Sherrard resigned, Dec. 17, 1883; stated the case, and asked for a restraining notice until the injunction papers were prepared. The Judge enquired by what right I had to bring such action, and in whose name. Answer was promptly given that the suit would be in behalf of T. K. Cartmell and all other citizens of Frederick County. His answer was, this could only be done when the parties proved their right as owners of the ground in question. Answer was given that proof of ownership could be given. He answered that he had frequently heard of this claim, but it had always been regarded as a myth. The answer to this was that the writer knew there was a deed on record in his office, and he could furnish a copy within an hour. The Judge's reply was that he would await the production of the copy. The writer realized that he was surely alone in this attempt, the Judge himself standing upon technicalities, while the county was suffering loss every moment. During the preparing of the copy, Richard E. Byrd, the young attorney for the commonwealth, appeared in the office, to whom the situation was briefly stated. He was requested to act for the county, and readily consented to do so. At that time, he and T. W. Harrison (now Judge of the circuit ct.) were law partners. The writer requested the firm to take the case. Both were young men of ability, but without experience in legal battles—ambitious and courageous, however; and being conscientious, they undertook what they believed a good cause. From that moment, they won, not only the confidence of the county people, but their unstinted esteem and affection, which has never wavered; and the positions they hold to-day attest the continued confidence of the people they have faithfully served. Arrayed against them, were the brilliant lights of the Winchester bar, Hon. Holmes Conrad and Robert T. Barton. Every honorable legal effort was made by opposing counsel, from start to finish, to save their clients; the injunction was granted after bond was given by the writer, with Jno. G. Miller surety. During the day, as country people came to town and became acquainted with the startling affair, a score of them rushed to the clerk's office and offered their support. The day was filled with excitement; and all saw that an unfortunate battle was on. The city strove to dissolve the injunction, but failed. The case came on to be heard on its merits, before the circuit court, Judge Robert Turner, presiding. In preparing for trial, both parties ransacked old records for evidence to prove who had controlled the uses of the property. Scores of depositions were taken; and when the case was heard, counsel on both sides were well prepared with evidence, and with forceful argument, presented the case. Every munition of forensic warfare was exhausted during the trial. The youthful attorneys for the county, felt the stimulus of the crowded court room, where every vale and hillside was represented. They were nerved by this presence. All knew the giants standing forth in their power. It was a battle royal. After several days of heroic effort, counsel rested their case. Then the stern, inflexible Judge announced his opinion—adverse to the County. The writer at once requested counsel to move for an appeal to the Supreme Court of the State. A heavy bond was required, and a score of enthusiastic county men stepped up to the clerk's desk, requesting they be entered as surety on the writer's bond. The following day, June 9, 1885, the board of supervisors were in session, and an ordinance entered on their records. They pledged the support of the county, and assumed all responsibility for the suit. Counsel for both bodies, prepared for the appellate court. Judge Robinson, of Lexington, Va., was employed to assist Harrison & Byrd in that court. The court met in Staunton in the Spring of 1889; the case was ably argued; and when that august body handed down their opinion, it was in favor of the county. The order made the injunction perpetual, giving the control of all uses of all the public property to the Board of Supervisors and County court. Of course, the result was accepted by the county with jubilant feelings, but in no oppressive spirit to the city. The case had been in litigation for three years, and all parties were tired out. And now, when the smoke of conflict had cleared, both parties once more opened negotiations for some compromise, whereby the city might enjoy her much needed buildings. All propositions coming from the city, which affected the hitching yard question, were promptly turned down by the Board;—they seemed to bank strongly on the opinion handed down by the Court of Appeals. Perhaps this action was regarded by the city as an assumption of a right not given by the decree, in which it was clear enough the city should enjoy a just proportion of the public space; and the Board never denied this. They did, however, deny the right of the city to remove the hitching-posts. They accorded to the city the proper right of sanitary regulations and police jurisdiction. They also accorded them the right to remove the market house, and to erect on the site such municipal buildings as the city needed. But the city was anxious to secure the assistance Mr. Rouss had offered; and this meant obliteration of the hitching yard. This condition of affairs continued several years, much to the annoyance and discomfort of all parties concerned. The city being deprived of what she thought her just rights, and the Board perplexed and embarrassed, when called upon to consider propositions that affected the convenience and declared rights of the county people when called to the city to attend court or to transact business, to be driven from the place which for generations had been used as their common heritage. We need not be surprised at the refusal of the Board of Supervisors, to compromise on any plan that would deprive the people of this right. Finally it was suggested by representatives of the city, that they should have some control, and that a convenient place might be found to take the place of the old square, and used to accommodate the country people. This seemed a most reasonable proposition; and the Board became deeply concerned, and felt this plan was the solution to the difficulty. Then the question was raised, could the settlement be made without legislative or judicial action. Counsel for the Board advised against hasty action. For several months previous to this, Mr. Alex. R. Pendleton had been requested to act as associate counsel with Mr. Byrd; Mr. Harrison had been elected by the Genl. Assembly as Judge of this circuit. The last proposition from the city, was presented to the Board in July 1897, which the Board regarded as one not clear as to the rights the county should retain in the public square. This was resented by the city, and Council prepared to bring suit to determine the respective rights. It must be remembered, that while the two bodies were making and rejecting propositions, there was one factor requiring constant attention. This was Charles Broadway Rouss, who had $30,000 to lay down on the market square, so soon as the warring factions in his old county furled their flags and proclaimed peace. And the records of the Board of supervisors of that period, show many of his letters. The correspondence between Mr. Rouss and Mr. Barton is worth study (see B. of S. Book, No. 3, p. 183). There are seen the characteristics of the man. The writer was induced to visit Mr. Rouss at his New York place, to interview him on the subject. We had always known each other, and the visitor was received cordially. The subject was discussed. Mr. Rouss stated his plan, that his desire was to see a memorial building on the old square, but the Board of supervisors would not allow it to be done. The writer told him if he would put $50,000 into the building, provide a court room and clerk's office for the circuit court, and allow the horses to occupy the old places on the square, that the board of supervisors would grant all the right they had in such portion of the square, as the city would need; and, that if this was done, he would not see a horse on the square at the end of five years; that the people would of their own volition, cease to stand their vehicles around the fine memorial building he proposed to erect to his *old-timers.* He assented to this plan, and arranged to meet the Board at the residence of Mr. Marrion Bantz in Winchester, and there learn what their views were. He was told that the Board knew nothing of this the writer's visit, and when he met the supervisors, he could make this proposition, and the writer believed they would accept it. In a short time he came; and

Mr. Bantz very quietly entertained the party. At the table, he was requested to ask each supervisor if he would agree to such a plan. All answered affirmatively; and all parties separated, feeling the work was done. Had this plan been carried out, the city would never have been called upon to appropriate $9,000 for the purpose of purchasing the Grim property for a hitching yard for the county. Before leaving for his home, Mr. Rouss had interviews with several prominent city gentlemen, that resulted in a change of his views which, as will be shown, was unfortunate for the city. Mr. Rouss probably would have erected the entire building at his own cost, whether it required $50,000 or more; and as was pointed out to him by the writer in the interview referred to, the memorial would be strictly his own, without aid from either city or county. After his return to New York, he authorized the purchase of what was known as the Jacobs lot; and August 7, 1899, Mr. Barton notified the board of supervisors, then in session, that the city had a new proposition to offer, the substance of which was, that the parties should agree to a division of the market square; the city to build on her portion, and the county abandon the square as a hitching yard,—the city to furnish the Jacobs lot for hitching yard, etc. This the Board rejected, giving as reason, that the said lot was not suited for such purposes; that its location in rear of the law offices on court house avenue, and its close proximity to the Baker residences on Market Street, would become a nuisance, that in a short time would have to be abated, and the result would be the county would lose the hitching yard that she had so tenaciously held on to so long. The Board suggested that if a suitable place could be found, they were not averse to such plan. This occasioned some delay, which the city regarded as a hardship, and became alarmed; fearing Mr. Rouss would repudiate the whole transaction, and withdraw his generous offer. Several citizens, representing both sides, held conferences on the subject, which resulted in another proposition presented by a committee from the council to the board of supervisors, Oct. 5, 1899, in substance this: that the city would pay the county $8,500 in consideration of the removal of all hitching posts thirty feet distant from the West line of the proposed building, partition to be made of the square, and the agreement to be incorporated in a consent decree. This was accepted by the Board, and the agreement signed by E. Holmes Boyd, Dr. Wm. P. McGuire and Chas. A. Heller, committee from the city, and by Wm. H. Dinges, chairman of the Board, duly attested by T. K. Cartmell, clerk. This settlement was submitted to Mr. Rouss, who immediately wrote Mr. Barton another characteristic letter, which was presented to the Board Oct. 7, ('99), Mr. Rouss opposed any settlement that tolerated hitching horses and standing wagons, etc., on any part of the square, excepting the small portion immediately South of the clerk's offices. Of course, this annulled the agreement. The parties on both sides realized that the horse must go—or the city would not receive aid from the millionaire who could dictate terms. The Board agreed to consider other plans promptly, and we find the committee before the Board again on the 11th October, '99, with a proposition that was agreed to, which was: The City to pay the county $9,000; pave the plaza, and erect water closets, etc., in rear of the clerk's office; to erect the stone wall from the corner of said office to Water Street—the plaza to be 61 feet in width from the East end of the court house; and the county not to be hindered in any way in purchasing the Grim lot and using the same for a hitching yard. This lot had been conditionally purchased by the Board. To this all parties agreed; and the final transaction was solemnly executed in the presence of counsel for both sides—R. E. Byrd, A. R. Pendleton and Wm. H. McCann for the county, and Robert M. Ward, for the city.

This agreement was signed by E. Holmes Boyd, Dr. Wm. P. McGuire, and Chas. A. Heller, committee for the city, attested by Geo. H. Kinzel, City Tresr., with the corporation seal; Wm. H. Dinges, chairman of board of supervisors, attested by T. K. Cartmell, clerk of Board, with seal of County.

All the members of the Board standing near, to-wit: James Cather, Clark Cather, H. P. Whitacre and Thomas E. Morrison, a good photograph was secured of the scene, which now adorns the wall of the board of supervisors' room over the clerk's office. There was great rejoicing over the happy ending. Mr. R. E. Byrd tendered the entire party a formal reception at his residence the same evening, where all enjoyed every feature of that memorable banquet.

A decree of court was soon obtained, confirming the settlement; partition deeds were executed and recorded in both offices. (Deed Book No. 119, pp. 405-6-7, County clerk's office).

The tearing down of the old market house was started during the Winter. By Spring a large force of workmen were preparing the foundation; while the County proceeded to convert the Grim property, purchased for $10,000, into the hitching yard now in use, corner Water and Market Streets. All parties enjoyed the changes,

City Hall, Winchester, Va.
(Market Street Entrance)

as they progressed; and as the magnificent building gradually unfolded its attractive features, under the hands of skillful architects and workmen, the passer-by would invariably stop to admire the new order of things. The corner-stone exercises were imposing; Mr. Rouss and friends present; visiting masonic and other fraternities joined hands in seeing *the corner-stone well laid.* No need of an attempt to describe the building. Its massive walls and attractive style stand prominently forth to speak for themselves; and will be there doubtless for many a cycle after author and this work will have been forgotten. The court-room, offices for circuit and city court, the handsome council chamber in the South end, with offices on either side for city treasurer and comr. of revenue. On the ground floor, office for superintendent of streets, police court room and station-house with lock-up. On the third floor, an auditorium that will compare favorably with high-class opera houses in larger cities. The building is heated by steam and lighted with electricity and gas. The green-sward surrounding the edifice, and Frederick Plaza, make such a transformation of the scenes of twenty years ago, that one feels bewildered at the change. It has already been shown what changes occurred in the old court house and offices. During all the foregoing struggles, Capt. E. G. Hollis was the efficient clerk of the council, and also the writer's deputy. These positions he held to the entire satisfaction of the contending parties.

CHAPTER XLIV

Principal Towns of Old Frederick, When Created, Where Located and Brief Notice of Progress

Having devoted much space to Winchester in preceding chapters, it is well to mention other towns at this point. No effort will be made to furnish the history of the towns and villages, which followed the old county seat, as part of the development of the county. The dates of formation, showing priority of establishment, will be sufficient to conform to the scheme of this work. The names of promoters will be given to show who were conspicuous actors in the respective settlements.

Stephensburg

The *New Town of Stephens,* as it was distinguished in the application of Lewis Stephen for the charter to erect a town, was not founded by Peter Stephens. This is contrary to the statement made by Kercheval, the Valley Historian, whose lack of accuracy is seldom questioned. Tradition says that Peter Stephens, one of the Hite immigration, built his first cabin on ground where the town was established,—this being prior to 1834. There is very little doubt but that the village was being formed gradually for several years prior to the Act granting a charter to erect and lay out a town. The language of the Act indicates this clearly; and it was no doubt regarded by many that Peter was founding a town, and a nucleus was there when the charter was granted. On May 2, 1755, Peter conveyed to Lewis a tract of four hundred and twenty-four acres, and described by a survey that locates it on Crooked Run, and evidently timber land; and further says it is part of 674 acres granted by patent to the said Peter. The language of the Act indicates further that the town was on another tract, one of *nine hundred* acres. A copy of the Act is herewith appended:

"Act of Assembly, 1758.

"An Act for erecting a town on the land of Lewis Stephens in the County of Frederick, For enlarging the Town of Winchester, and for erecting a town on the land of Nicholas Minor in Loudon County.

1. Whereas it hath been represented to this present General Assembly, that Lewis Stephens being seised and possessed of *Nine* hundred acres of land near the Opeacon, in the County of Frederick, hath surveyed and laid out forty acres, part thereof into lots of half acre each, with proper streets for a town, and hath caused a plan thereof to be made and numbered from one to eighty, inclusive, and hath annexed to each of said lots, numbered 26, 27, 28, 29, 30, 31, 32, 33, 34, 35, 46, 47, 48, 49, 50, 51, 52, 53, 54, 55, five acres of land, and to each of the remaining sixty lots ten acres of land, part of the *Nine* hundred acres; all of which lots with the lands annexed thereto, *are purchased* by different persons and are now settling and building thereon, and humbly desire that the same may be by an Act of Assembly erected into a town.

* * * Therefore be it enacted by the Lt. Governor, Council and Burgesses, * * * That the Right Hon. Thomas, Lord Fairfax, Thomas Bryan Martin, James Wood, Lewis Stephens, Gabriel Jones, John Hite, John Doe, Isaac Parkins, Robert Rutherford and Philip Boush, gentlemen, be constituted and appointed trustees of said town of Stephensburg and Winchester, and they or any five may * * ."

This Act entitles Stephensburg to the credit of being the second town chartered in the Shenandoah Valley. Lewis Stephens followed the example of founders of other towns. He dedicated a certain lot or square, located within the corporate limits, to the said town, or freeholders thereof, for public purposes. This square or lot has been used as the public square or a Common for public purposes. At one time the citizens of the town erected upon part of the public square, a large brick school building; and when it was destroyed by Federal troops during the Civil War, they afterwards erected another school building on part of the common. Then in 1874, they set apart another portion for Green Hill Cemetery (white). In 1880, the citizens laid off on same common, the Colored Cemetery. This old Common was used for the militia in general muster, prior to the War. The old Stephensburg gained considerable notoriety as a manufacturing point. It grew famous for the Newtown Stephensburg wagon that was in great demand by the teamsters who once traversed all roads leading to the South and West, transporting merchandise to faraway sections. The writer was told an incident relating to this make of wagon: An old Forty-Niner said, when his company started on that great expedition to the gold fields of California, they equipped the company with the best supplies procurable; and that the only wagon that survived the six months' usage, was the one marked Newtown Stephensburg. Germans composed the population, and held to the use of their language until about 1800. Kercheval says his first acquaintance with the town was in 1784; and the German language was generally used. The Stephens family was German. Peter always signed any paper he executed in German; Lewis likewise for many years. The town is located on high ground, so that the scenery of all the mountains on the border land, is so varied in its beauty, that the eye can always find new objects to admire within the scope of vision. The surrounding country is populated with frugal, well-to-do farmers. The town has always maintained a reputation for its stores, shops and taverns. In ye olden times, there were several of the latter; and often the court was called upon to restrict the management, especially on the *Big Muster* days. These taverns were well-known stopping places for the old *covered wagon,* and fine teams. Then and there the villagers would gather to hear the news from Alexandria or Tennessee; and the flowing bowl was patronized freely. That was Newtown a half century and more ago. The Stephens City we find there now, knows nothing of the old transportation system. The railroad passes her station about one-fourth of a mile to the West, carrying all supplies for the increased volume of business. No flowing bowl there any more—no old-time tavern. An attractive hotel takes the place of the old land-mark. In another chapter will be shown who some of the population were, then and now. The subject of churches has been treated fully under the head of "Churches." The town was incorporated in 1879, and has a good municipal government. The many smoke-stacks near the station, mark the place of the great lime kilns, where many thousand barrels of pure lime are burned yearly, and find a market in the Southern States.

The tranquil life of this beautiful little city was much disturbed for some time by one of the citizens of the town securing a patent from the State of Virginia, to appropriate that portion of the *Common* that had not been theretofore taken by the town for public uses; his claim when he got the grant in August, 1906, being, that it was for waste and ungranted land. Having received his deed, he proceeded to sell lots. Then the descendants of the old Indian fighters, got out their war-paint, and the battle royal opened. A wise judge soon disposed of the claim when the case got into his hands: "The common must remain as the founder intended, for use of all, for *public purposes.*" So quiet again prevails, without fear of similar attacks in the future.

Woodstock.

The old German, Jacob Miller, who had settled on the land where Woodstock now stands, must have entertained large ideas of his new country. He had resided at this point for nearly thirty years; had gathered around him many of his kindred and friends, who had erected houses on both sides of the main road leading North and South, securing deeds from Miller for the sites; and for many years it was described in old conveyances as Mueller's (Miller's) Town, or Muellerstadt. In March, 1761, Miller secured an Act to establish his town under the name of Woodstock. It appears from the language of the charter, that he had great expectations, for we find he laid off twelve hundred acres for his town, subdivided into 192 building lots, 96 into half-acre lots for this purpose, the remainder into streets, alleys, and a number of five-acre lots known as the out-lots. By referring to Sketches of Churches, it will be seen that the German language and customs prevailed, and rigidly controlled affairs, with no change in this respect until the appearance of Rev. Peter Muhlenburg. Woodstock was well located to attract the business of the increasing population. Being on a well travelled road, it grew and waxed strong, and was a town of considerable proportions. When Dunmore county was taken from Frederick in 1772, Woodstock was with unanimous approval, chosen as the county seat. The citizens at their first court adopted a resolution endorsing the administration of Lord Dunmore. We find the citizens in October, 1777, adopting a resolution, condemning this Dunmore, and instructed their Burgess to secure an Act to change the name from Dunmore to Shenandoah, after the bold and beautiful mountain stream passing through the two valleys, lying East and West of the Massanutten Range.

The town is almost due South from Winchester, 30 miles distant. It was famous during the Colonial period, as the rendezvous of the brave men who met and fought the Indians in their numerous visitations; and in the Revolutionary War period, her name is prominent in the annals of that War. It will be seen in notes on the two periods mentioned, who many of her citizens were, who rallied under Muhlenburg and Morgan. Woodstock has always been prominent in the educational feature, leading off with noted schools, and coming to the front with her "press" work—men of adaptability in charge, who helped shape her interesting history. Strong men they were who lived in Woodstock in the early days, of whom we hope to speak in other pages.

Woodstock of to-day presents the appearance of a quiet little city, supplied with all that is needed for the splendid population of the place and vicinity, by up-to-date mercantile houses. —The Massanutten Academy, and Public Schools —one of the best weekly newspapers published in the country, under the editorial control of an old Confederate veteran, who followed Col. Lige White through many noted campaigns—Capt. Jno. H. Grabill, is doing good service for his prosperous section. The reader should take time to drive down to the Shenandoah about a mile distant, and enjoy the river and mountain scenery; and then extend his observations and visit the Massanutten Fall, a cataract of about 50 feet of perpendicular descent, distant about two miles to the Eastward. The town has a fine water supply. The several denominations of Christians have beautiful, modern church buildings, the Episcopal being on very historic ground, —virtually the site of the first church edifice erected in Woodstock about 1773, when the German Lutheran and Reformed Calvinist congregations worshipped together. This is more fully set forth under head of Churches.

The author adds the following note as a desirable reference; inasmuch as the foundation for all land titles of Woodstock, is in the old Frederick county clerk's office. As late as 1791, Henry Ott, executor of Jacob Miller, executed deeds to many persons who had failed to secure conveyances from Miller in his lifetime, for their lots in Woodstock; and such deeds are recorded in Frederick County. This may remove the difficulties found in tracing title and boundaries of the lots, as the author well knows.

Strasburg

This was the next town established by law in the Lower Valley, and for many years before its erection, was called *Staufferstadt*, in honor of its founder Peter Stover. In Nov., 1761, Stover applied for and received his charter; and then it was the name was changed to Strasburg, bearing the name of his birthplace in the *Faderland*. The trustees were William Miller, Mathew Harrison, Jacob Bowman, Valentine Smith, Chas. Buck, Peter Stover, Isaac Hite, Leonard Baltice (Balthis) John Funk, and Philip Huffman. This Act forbade *stick* chimneys for houses. Here also the Germans controlled their affairs, and held tenaciously to their language and customs. The town made slow growth until within the last few years. Her citizens are refined and well-to-do. The stores and schools are of good type. She boasts of a hospital superintended by Dr. Bruin, and an up-to-date hotel, the Chalybeate House, presided over by an ex-Confederate, Mr. McInturff, who takes delight in teaching his guests to angle for the finny tribe in the River hard-by, and he also does in providing for the whetted appetite. One of the first mills operated West of the Blue Ridge was Funk's Wheat and Corn Mill, located near the site of the present town.

Romney was not known to fame or name when Hampshire County was taken from Old Frederick in 1754; for we have no evidence that the small cluster of houses found there when the Indian battles of The Trough and Hanging Rock were fought, was dignified by a name. Some traditions fix the place as Furman's Fort; one gives it as Wappatomka Village. There was a village of the latter name on the South Branch, formed by the first settlers in that Valley when the River bore the Indian name of Wappa-To-Ma-Ka, signifying the hunting regions of the Delaware Chief Wappa, who was supposed to have obtained this right by his prowess in wielding his tomahawk;—and from this was derived the name Wappatomahawk, subsiding finally to the name given by the Whites of the village they had formed on the banks of the stream, as they huddled their families together for mutual protection. We have evidence that a number of squatters were there when Lord Fairfax decided to establish a town. Washington, his surveyor, reported this fact to his Lordship, in his field notes. So we find by an Act of the General Assembly, Nov., 1762, Fairfax "laid off fifty acres into streets and lots of half-acre each." The Act then prescribes rules to govern the same, through trustees, and the town was named Romney. This was eight years subsequent to the formation of the County. It is not known that the county seat was at this village prior to its establishment by law. Some writers have fixed the place lower down the river, while some have gone so far as to fix the vicinity of Springfield as the place for holding the first courts. Certain it is that Romney has been the county seat since 1762. It can justly claim the title bestowed by a sketch writer "The Mountain City." Though it can boast of little increase in population, yet it has been distinctive as a seat of learning—the home of Dr. Wm. Henry Foote, who gave us volumes of sketches of Virginia and North Carolina. The Deaf, Dumb and Blind Asylums of West Virginia, have formed part of its history for the last thirty years. The Northwestern Turnpike forms its Main street. Its mercantile interests and other business of the town have been enhanced by the railroad to Greenspring Station on the Main line of the B. & O. R. R Other mention of the town will be found in notes on the Romney Church.

The Indian Mound Cemetery derives its name from the Indian mound found within its enclosure. This mound indicates the existence at this point of an Indian village, when the Delawares held sway.

Mechlinburg was established by law November, 1762. The town was laid off by Capt. Thomas Shepherd. The little village once bore the name of "Pack Horse Ford," signifying the place on the Cohongoroota, where the pack-horse trains crossed the river, and also where the pack-horses were relieved of their burdens. All orders of court speak of the village as "Pack Horse," to and from which, roads were opened to the county seat at Winchester and to neighboring settlements. While the village was also called Shepherdstown for many years, it was legally known as Mecklinburg until 1798, when by an Act of Assembly it was given the name of Shepherds Town, in honor of its founder, at which time additions to the town were made; and the town assumed all the rights of incorporation granted Mecklinburg by Act of Assembly Dec. 2, 1793. The trustees elected in accordance with this Act were Abraham Shepherd, Henry Bedinger, Conrad Byers, Jacob Haynes, John Morrow, Henry Line, and Wm. Chapline. the names suggesting that the German element was in this section, although it has been frequently stated in sketches of the place, that the Welch and Scotch-Irish were the first settlers. We have shown elsewhere who were the first settlers along the Cohongaroota and its tributaries, date of their grants, etc. The reckless statement made by one writer that Mecklinburg antedated Winchester by twenty years, and the settlement made there prior to 1727, can be attributed to his willing ear, eager to catch the vaporings of some enthusiasts whose imaginations must be gratified. His utter fallacy is easily proven by public and private records, and by other traditions existing in the same section to-day. We offer no word to detract from the credit of the splendid citizenship of the New Mecklinburg settlement; but they were not the first settlers. None were better, though; they have left their records to posterity, and we must not allow ourselves to misrepresent them. The growth of the town justified the enabling Act of Genl. Assembly, secured Feby. 18, 1820. This Act provided for an election of Mayor, Recorder, Aldermen and Common Council. To this new body of rulers, was given the name of The Common Hall of Shepherdstown. This town has the distinction that no other in the Valley can claim: At one time a conspicuous village in Frederick County, an incorporated town in Berkeley County, and for more than one hundred years an important town in Jefferson County,—the latter being formed in 1801. Its development was slow; but to-day, the attractive little City on the Potomac, about twelve miles above Harpers Ferry, shows what has been done by its population. She boasts of her splendid churches, as shown in other pages,—eight in number: one Lutheran, one Protestant Episcopal, two Methodist (white) one old Reformed, one Presbyterian, one Roman Catholic, two colored churches, Baptist and Methodist. The Shepherd College, one of the populous schools of the Lower Valley, has been for many years conspicuous. A branch of the State Normal Schools has been successful in this connection, and a Graded School of high order. Several private schools also are found. The newspaper interests have kept stroke with the town's progress. The first to be published in town was the American Eagle in 1815, by Maxwell & Harper; The Journal in 1823, by John Alburtis; The Register, by Hardy & McAuly, in 1849, who were succeeded by capable men; it finally becoming one of the most attractive papers published in the Valley, with H. L. Snyder at the helm. With the Shepherdstown Bank, numerous lines of mercantile interest, and all trades represented, the little city is justly entitled to the good name she bears.

Bath has an interesting history, inasmuch as the site was selected by Lord Fairfax; and it was on his motion that it received its charter and name by an Act of the General Assembly, Oct., 1776, antedating the establishment of other and larger towns in the Valley. It was known then. as the Warm Spring tract, part of a large tract known in the surveys made by Washington as the Swan Pond tract. The medicinal waters of this Spring had already attracted the attention of several families who erected cabins and resorted there. Fairfax felt the necessity of preserving the springs for use of the public. He laid off fifty acres into streets and lots, adjoining the springs. The charter describes the location as being part of a larger tract of land the property of the right honorable Thomas, Lord Fairfax, or other persons holding grants from him. The trustees appointed were Bryan Fairfax, Thomas Bryan Martin, Warner Washington, Rev. Chas. M. Thruston, Robert Rutherford, Thomas Rutherford, Alexander White, Philip Pendleton, Samuel Washington, Wm. Elzey, Van Swearingen, Thomas Hite, James Edmunson, and James Nourse, Gents. It must not be concluded that the trustees were citizens of that section; for it is a well-known fact that they were not. Pendleton and Elzey owned land in the Western part of Berkeley at that time, and both families became prominent in that section later on. The Pendletons from that period have been well-known owners of large landed estates. The State of Virginia exercised control of the Springs, and several times passed laws to govern the free use of the water. When Morgan County was formed from Berkeley and Hampshire in 1820, the place was soon designated as the county seat, and the name changed to Berkeley Springs. In recent years, the place has grown in importance. Several fine hotels, court house and large mercantile houses, churches, schools and manufacturing plants in the vicinity, make it a town at the present writing, of considerable notoriety. Distance from Washington 94 miles, Harpers Ferry about 45 miles, and 41 miles N. W. from Winchester.

Lexington and Moorefield were established in October, 1777. These towns do not properly belong to the section treated in this chapter, and are only mentioned for the reasons following: The Act establishing Lexington, contains a specification so peculiar, that we think well to mention, since the town has become so famous as a seat of learning. This extract from the Act, speaks for itself: "And be it further enacted that at the place appointed for holding court in the said county of Rockbridge, there shall be laid off a town, to be called Lexington, thirteen hundred feet in length, and nine hundred in width." Then the Act provides payment to the owners of the land so taken, etc.

Moorfield is mentioned to show who were freeholders on the Upper South Branch, while it was part of Hampshire County. The Act reads: "Whereas it hath been represented to the Genl. Assembly, that the establishing a town on the lands of Conrad Moore, in the County of Hampshire, would be of great advantage, &c. * * * Be it therefore enacted &c. That sixty-two acres of land belonging to the said Conrad Moore, in the most convenient place for a town be and the same is granted to Garret Vanmeter, Abel Randall, Moses Hutton, Jacob Read, Jonathan Heath, Daniel McNeill and George, freeholders, Trustees, to be by * * * laid out into lots &c. Which shall be and the same is established a Town, by the name of Moorefield, etc."

Martinsburg, the prosperous city of the present day, has a history so varied with important events, that a brief sketch of her rise and progress cannot do her justice; and the author deems it best under the circumstances, to confine himself to a few simple facts. Her history has been attractively written by historians well equipped with traditions, and recorded facts. To such we refer the reader. We gather from copious notes now before the writer, that a nameless village was in existence there, while that section was yet in Old Frederick. Orders of court define a new road leading through a village to Stephens' Mill, before Berkeley was erected in 1772; and the same Stephens and others had some contention in court about water rights, several years previous. License was granted for an ordinary at the same time. In 1778, Martinsburg was established by law. The Act of Assembly says: "Whereas, It hath been represented to this present Genl. Assembly, that Adam Stephen Esq., hath lately laid off 130 acres of land in the County of Berkeley, where the *Court House of said County now stands,* in lots and streets for a town, and hath made sale of several of said lots to divers persons, some of whom have since settled and built thereon, etc." The language determines the fact that the court house was built and in use some time previous to the date of charter. Quoting from the Order Book of the Court at its first session, we give the following extract: "Berkely County, S.S.

"Be it remembered that at the house of Edward Beeson the 19th day of May, 1772, a Commission of the Peace and a Commission of Oyer and Terminer, from his excellency Lord Dunmore, dated the 17th day of April in the year aforesaid, directed to Ralph Wormley, Jacob Hite, Van Swearingen, Thos. Rutherford, Adam Stephen, John Neville, Thos. Swearingen, Samuel Washington, James Nourse, Wm. Little, Robert Stephen, John Briscoe, Hugh Lyle, James Strode, Wm. Morgan, Robt. Stogdon, James Seaton, Robert Carter, Willis and Thos. Robinson." The Justices were duly sworn, and proceeded with the duties of their first term. William Drew was the first clerk, Adam Stephen, sheriff, Saml. Oldham, Depty., Alexander White, Depty. Kings Atty; James Keith (Clerk of Frederick Co.) John Magill, Geo. Brent, Geo. Johnston, Philip Pendleton and Alexander White, attorneys, were admitted to practice. The gentlemen whose names are mentioned, are entitled to fuller notice, which the author hopes to give in biographical sketches. The minutes of the court clearly indicate that sessions of court were held in the Edward Beeson house, until the following November, at which time Adam Stephen produced authority from the Secretary's Office, to adjourn the court to Morgan's Spring. The court then adjourned to meet where directed by the writ, and held court in the house of John Mitchell, where sessions were held until 1774, when court adjourned to the house of Isaac Taylor. Traditions are rife with mystery relating to this place of holding court. The "Morgan Spring" mentioned in the writ, has never been located near this village. There were then, as now, several springs, and *branches* bearing the name of

Morgan, but none near where John Mitchell lived. The name, therefore, is calculated to disturb some readers; but this is very plain, the court was held in the village for several years, and was there when the first court house was ready for use, the latter part of 1779. Kercheval says there was serious contention between Stephen and Jacob Hite, who was a large land-owner in Berkeley, concerning the location of the county seat; and when Stephen prevailed, Hite became disgusted and left the country. (See sketches of the Hite family.) During this period, the country had become involved in revolution against the oppressive rule of England. Then it was that strong men were needed to direct affairs in the Valley; and Berkeley County furnished her full quota. Of these we will speak later. Col. Samuel Washington, who was County Lieut., resigned to enter the Continental Army. One of the files of the old court contains the will of Major Genl. Charles Lee, once famous as an avowed enemy of Genl. Washington. The old document savors of the man's peculiar and sordid temperament. After many bequests of the large estate owned by him in Berkeley County, he closes with the following: "I desire most earnestly that I may not be buried in any church or church-yard, or within a mile of any Presbyterian or Anabaptist Meeting house, for since I have resided in this country, I have kept so much bad company when living, that I do not chuse to continue it when dead. I recommend my soul to the Creator of all Worlds and all Creatures, who must from his Visible Attributes be indifferent to their modes of Worship or Creeds, whether Christians, Mahometans or Jews, whether instilled by education or taken up by reflection, whether more or less absurd, as a weak mortal can no more be answerable for his persuasions, notions or even skepticism in Religion than for the color of his skin."

The American Cause of Freedom suffered no loss from his relations to Genl. Washington, that forced him into private life. (Further notice may be given this strange character.)

The Press was to the front at an early day. *The Berkeley and Jefferson Intelligencer and Northern Neck Advertiser,* published by John Alburtis in 1902, indicates from bills paid by court for legal advertisements, that this was not its first appearance. *The Martinsburg Gazette* was also dispensing news prior to 1811. About 1830, Mr. Edmund P. Hunter, combined the *Gazette* with the *Public Advertiser;* and thenceforth the country around Martinsburg witnessed lively scenes in the newspaper business. The Press kept well abreast of the times, up to the present writing. The first daily made its appearance in 1907.

The Martinsburg Academy was in successful operation prior to 1812, with Rev. Jno. B. Hoge as teacher of languages. The churches have always been a feature in Martinsburg life (more fully treated under head of churches). For many years the B. & O. Railroad had extensive shops there, the principal portion of which has been removed in recent years to Brunswick, Maryland. The city of to-day can show the visitor several manufactories in successful operation—the large Knitting Mills being one. Berkeley developed other towns: Darkesville, Hedgesville, Falling Waters, Bunker Hill, Shanghai, and several others of more or less note, will not be mentioned further now. The city is noted for its large commercial interests. Merchants, tradesmen and professional classes are in evidence in their fine business places.

Hedgesville, about 7 miles Northwest of Martinsburg, near the North Mountain B. & O. Railroad station, was a recognized village 150 years ago. A prominent family, named Hedges, settled there about 177—; and for several years it was spoken of as the Hedges Villa. The married members of the family gradually added new buildings, and thus the village grew apace. The town of to-day shows but little to mark it as one of the towns of the Valley, yet it has its attractions—good society and beautiful location. (The family who founded it will receive fuller notice.)

Darkesville, situated on Mill Creek in Berkeley County, and on the Martinsburg Turnpike, had many struggles to secure its well-accepted name. Genl. Buckles owned a fine estate near this point. Many people in the section often called it Buckles Town; but this name gradually gave way; and for many years, the little village holds to the name given it in honor to Genl. Wm. Darke of Revolutionary War fame.

New Market. This town located in Shenandoah County, on the Valley Turnpike, was the next to receive a charter. This is traditionary, however. The statement made by Howe in his History of Virginia, fixes the date 1784. The author fails to find the Act of Assembly verifying this statement, but submits it without further comment. The town has a national reputation, by reason of the valor displayed by the Cadets from the Military Academy of Lexington, in a hard-fought battle on the plains of New Market, during the Civil War.

Charlestown was established by an Act of Assembly in October, 1786, upon the application of Col. Charles Washington, brother of Genl. Washington. (Charles had acquired a large tract in that section through the knowledge of the surveyor, his brother.) He was authorized by the

Act to lay off eighty acres of his land, in such manner as he might deem best "into half-acre lots, with convenient streets, which shall be and is established a town, by the name of Charles Town." The trustees in the Act to hold the said lots, etc., were John Augustine Washington, Robt. Rutherford, Wm. Darke, James Crane, Cato Moore, Benjamin Rankin, Magnus Tate, Thornton Washington, Wm. Little, Alex. White, and Richard Ransome—most of whom had rendered distinguished services, and others become famous, in their several careers as public men. They were of that splendid type of citizens, that have held sway in the grand county of Jefferson to the present day.

Charlestown became the county seat of Jefferson County upon its erection from Berkeley in 1801. The first court was held Nov. 10, 1801, in the house of John Mines. Here again we have an array of men who were the Justices comprising the first court. Their names indicate they were peers of the founders of the town: George Hite was their first clerk, Wm. Little, sheriff, John Baker was qualified as Deputy Atty. for the Commonwealth. Wm. McGuire, Edward Christian, Lewis Elsey, Mathew Whiting, John Dixon, Samuel Reed, Elisha Boyd, Wm. Tate and Hugh Holmes were admitted to practice the law. At the December Term, Archibald Magill was an attorney also admitted to practice. The first court house was built in 1807-8. In 1836-7 a second court house was built. This was the building where the celebrated John Brown trials were conducted. This was destroyed by soldiers during the Civil War. Charlestown has had its history written so often and so attractively, by reason of its fame where Brown and his confederates were so justly tried and condemned; and later the scene of the orderly and perfectly conducted executions, though the entire country was stirred to its depths. Charlestown has had the benefit of sound doctrine taught her citizens through her press, schools and churches. Of these sources of education, much has been said under head of churches. The Press was first represented in 1808, when the Farmers Repository appeared. *The Virginia Free Press* was published by John S. Gallaher in 1827. This able paper was edited in later years by his sons. The paper had taken an active part in the early days of the Civil War, in its dissemination of Southern principles. The entire plant was destroyed by some fanatics who came as Federal soldiers. *The Spirit of Jefferson* appeared in 1844, famous as a Democratic paper. One or two other papers have at times been published.

The schools of learning have always been fostered and well supported by the citizens of the town. We have evidences of the Classical School having been well patronized more than one hundred years ago, and a seminary for young ladies in 1810. Charlestown was one of the *boom* towns, during the period which stirred the people of the Valley from the Potomac to the James, some years since. Speculative citizens laid out an addition, started manufactories; built a large and handsome hotel, etc. In recent years, the latter was converted into a college. This school has also flourished. In the organization of West Virginia, Charlestown was chosen for holding one of the United States District Courts, and from this distinction has received material support. Two railroads skirt her suburbs, affording many advantages.

Gerrards Town was the next town in the Lower Valley established by law. This was in 1786. It had been previously known as the village Middletown in the County of Berkeley. Rev. David Gerrard, a Baptist Minister, Wm. Henshaw, James Haw, John Gray, Gilbert McEwan (McKown) and Robert Allen were appointed Trustees.

Frankfort was chartered in 1787. The little village in Hampshire County was conspicuous at a much earlier date. The trustees appointed by the Assembly were: John Mitchell, Andrew Cooper, Ralph Humphreys, John Williams, Sr., James Clark, Richard Stafford, Hezekiah Whiteman and Jacob Brookhart. 139 acres of land, owned by John Sellers, was taken for the site.

Front Royal was established by an Act of the Genl. Assembly, 1788. From the language of the Act, we have the evidence before us of the existence of a village there prior to that time. As mentioned in a previous chapter, the village must have been formed by a number of families for mutual protection some time prior to the Revolution, locating their houses on land purchased from the original owners Solomon Vanmeter, James Moore, Robert Haines, Wm. Cunningham, Peter Halley, John Smith, Allen Wiley, Original Wroe, Geo. Chick, Wm. Norres and Henry Trout,—be laid out into lots and streets. Trustees were appointed to hold and control said town, subject to the requirements of the Act. This control continued for many years, enlarging its borders as population increased; and when Warren County was erected in 1836, it was chosen as the county seat, and has remained as such to this day. The location is one to attract the visitor—the lofty mountain peaks, fast-flowing river,—"Laughing Waters"—formed by the South and North Rivers and their tributaries,—presents a stream picturesque and sublime. The work of spanning the water ways in the vicinity by the railroads, and other causeways for general county use, has been a serious problem to the authorities responsible for providing crossings of the rushing waters when at flood tide.

Churches, schools and general business give an appearance of a prosperous town. We hope to say something of the men who have figured in the upbuilding of Front Royal. We may add that, agreeable to some interesting traditions, the old village enjoyed several names, to distinguish her from other villages formed in Old Frederick. Some readers have heard of the incident of the "Royal Oak," once a landmark; and of the Militia Captain giving his famous order to one of his companies to *"about face and front the Royal Oak,"* and that waggish bystanders caught the spirit of the day and, abbreviating the military order, laid the foundation for the present name. Their cry was "Front the Royal." Judge Giles Cook's father related this incident to the writer, stating that his father was a member of the Company and remembered the incident well.

The town is situated about 18 miles Southeast from Winchester, within a mile of the Blue Ridge. It may be well to add here, that Shenandoah County once embraced a strip of the territory in the vicinity of Front Royal; and the titles to many tracts of land South of the North River are traceable through the records of that county; and when Warren County was formed, the new county included this section and, together with the strip taken from Frederick County on the North side, produced some confusion, as her land titles are to be found in three counties. The writer, as clerk of Frederick, has experienced this inconvenience. Many of the present-day people are unaware that the Shenandoah courts contain such records, covering the period from 1774 to 1836.

Front Royal is becoming quite an educational centre. The Randolph Macon Academy, whose imposing building on elevated ground, adds much to the attraction of the place. The Eastern College and graded schools under the supervision of Mr. Roy, the well-known superintendent of public schools offer advantages to every class. The six white and two colored churches seem to emphasize the fact that the beautiful town has many features to recommend it as a home for the cultured.

Riverton so nearby, with its population of about 3,000, teeming with enterprise, might be considered part of the city gradually forming at the confluence of the two mountain rivers. The Hagerstown Division of the Norfolk and Western Railroad, and the Manassas Division of the Southern system, afford unlimited facilities for present needs and greater development.

Middletown is situated in the Southern part of Frederick County, twelve miles from Winchester, on the great Valley Turnpike. It has become so prosperous and prominent in recent years, that very few persons stop to enquire of its early history. As a village, it was known for years as Senseny Town. Dr. Peter Senseny being owner of a large tract of land in the vicinity, applied for a charter to lay out a town as early as 1796, called *Middleton;* and in 1878 it was regularly incorporated, and is governed by a mayor and common council.

The old town is entitled to recognition as a manufacturing point. Clocks made at Middletown as far back as 1786, were noted timekeepers, and were in demand far and near. Quite a lucrative business resulted from this single trade. The old wooden wheels were first used; then brass was introduced, and the artisans were able to produce the eight-day clock in attractive pattern. Some are in use to-day. The same enterprising clock makers also controlled the watch trade for many years; and strange to say, manufactured outfits for surveyors, producing a compass that gained enviable reputation. Doubtless the reader will be astonished to learn that the present County Surveyor, A. J. Tavenner, Esq., uses a compass manufactured by Jacob Danner at Middletown. Mr. T. purchased this old compass at a public sale several years since as a curiosity; and when he needed a new compass, sent this old instrument to an expert in a distant city, to have him determine its value. He was informed that the compass was of the type that had become rare, and was valuable, and the reputation of the maker was well established, and that the Surveyor could secure none better. This evidence of what the little town did in other years, is deemed worthy of preservation.

The first successful effort to produce a machine to supplant the *flail and threshing floor,* to thresh wheat from the straw in this county, had its start in the same town. Some old men of to-day remember the one manufactured by James Ridings, about 1817; and then the McKeever. These inventions were wonders in their day. When it was discovered that it was possible to *beat* out one hundred bushels of grain in one day, farmers grew suspicious. Such threshing instruments served their day well. The writer remembers their marvellous work; and has watched this line of progress up to the time when the steam thresher has made it possible to separate wheat from straw—the former ready for the mill, and the latter perfectly ricked by an automatic ricking attachment. We might enquire what may not happen in this branch of industry 'ere the first half of the 20th Century is passed.

The progressive spirit has worked in her citizens through many decades; and that was the cause of the entire community becoming enthused a few years ago (1889) to such an extent, that projectors of schemes were numerous. The town borders had to be enlarged, to admit of the possible developments.

New Middletown was laid out on the Western suburbs. Lots, streets, parks and other public places appeared on the greensward and in cornfields. People from far and near subscribed for shares of stock, purchased corner lots, and watched the coming of the "plants." And as the foundation was laid for the proverbial Hotel, and the carriage manufacturing plant, stockholders watched eagerly the progress of the great building down near the station. The staid business men of the village elbowed with the sturdy and prosperous farmer, all bent upon rapid work, to make ready for the throngs then wending their way thence from the frozen North. The home people hurriedly organized, and soon all were stockholders, presidents, secretaries, directors, bankers, treasurers. All had lucrative offices in prospect. All waited for the crowds. No matter if the crops did suffer. No time now for anything but development of the New Town. Alas, however! Some one pricked the bubble; and many of us have been seeking amid the debris of this explosion, for the returns promised by the *promoters.* This was a strong term then; and even now some feeling prevails among those who know, that it is desirable the term be no more applied to the *Middletown Boomers.* With the explosion, went the many wild schemes; and to naught went the accumulations of years of toil. Prosperous farmers saw their fine farms pass beyond their grip; and men who had enjoyed comfort and even affluence for a generation, bent under their weary load, and their last days were not as the former. But we are able to say that the old town has come to the front again; and the desert will soon again blossom as the rose. The churches have been mentioned in another chapter. General business is in a healthy condition; her stores are above the average found in county towns. Wagons, carriages and other vehicles are made to order by such competent men as Wm. H. Everly.

Middletown is situated on an elevated plain, from which one has full view of the great mountains. The scenery is surpassing in grandeur. The historic battle-field of Cedar Creek is yonder to the West; and old citizens will point out places where Sheridan, Early, Wright and Rosser, with their battalions, strove to win the day.

CHAPTER XLV

Towns in Frederick County (Continued)

Gainsboro, the attractive little town, about 10 miles Northwest from Winchester, with its several enterprises, stores, shops and homes of good citizens, has its streets and churches. In the long ago it was known as Pughtown. In about 1770, it was founded by Job Pugh when a nucleus of a village was formed near the old Quaker Meeting House, then called a branch of Hopewell. The plat and charter of Pugh Town was dated Jany. 12, 1797; it was surveyed by order of Job Pugh. George Ruble of Frederick County and Jesse Pugh of Winchester were appointed trustees. The houses were required to be not les than 16 feet square, with brick or stone chimneys. The order was made in a Superior Court held at Winchester for the counties of Berkeley, Frederick and Shenandoah. Adams Street is the main street. Other streets named by Job were Washington, Lewis, Stephens and South Streets. It became one of the voting places many years ago; and politics waxed warm in those days. Old Whigs and Democrats had many drawn battles. In that day, the *rum counter* played a strong part in her local politics. Many years ago there came a change; and quiet elections are now held. The interest has subsided along with the rum. Some of the oldest settlers made their homes on Back Creek near this little town, of whom something will be said in Personal Sketches.

White Hall, or Loop, as it was once called, is found on Applepie Ridge, 8 miles North of Winchester. This, too, has been a voting place for many years. Surrounding this village is the celebrated "apple belt." A good country road running Eastward, takes the traveler through Well Town (now Grimes post office), a small village of much local history. To reach this from Winchester, take the Martinsburg Turnpike, and then the Well Town Turnpike. Going East from the village, we pass Clearbrook, a station on the C. V. Railroad, on the way to Brucetown, a large village noted for its flour mills, and Jobe's Woolen Mills, formed there many years ago and successfully operated.

Neffstown is a Northern suburb of Winchester. The McVicar carriage and wagon shops are located there, on East side of the Winchester and Martinsburg turnpike.

In the Western part of the county are the promising little villages of Whitacre, Cross Junction, Shockeysville. The North Frederick Turnpike penetrates that section, and affords an outlet for the villagers to the Winchester markets.

Traveling West over the Northwestern Turnpike, the store and postoffice 3½ miles from Winchester, marks the place of Chambersville. Eight miles out, we come to Hayfield, a thriving and beautiful settlement at the foot of the Great North Mountain. On Back Creek, twelve miles from Winchester, following the same road, is found the village of Gore, made famous as the location of "Valley Home" a mountain resort for city folk, who enjoyed the hospitality of Mrs. S. S. Gore. A half century ago, this vicinity was distinguished as Lockhart's Tavern, a noted hostelry in the early part of the 19th Century. Of its founder, Genl. Lockhart, fuller notice will be given. Parishville, further West, on same road, at the eastern base of Big Timber Ridge, owes its origin and growth to Mr. Geo. W. Parish, the enterprising merchant, stock-dealer, etc.

The village of Mountain Falls to the South, near the eastern base of the Big North, has much local history. A central point, where good farms, good flouring mills, a *Fuller's Mill*—type of the first settler, now, like the spinning-wheel—stands silently watching progressive events. Lying out towards the mountain, can be found the remains of the once prosperous Taylor Furnace, started in the long ago by Genl. Zane and Maj Bean. To Capt. A. J. McIlwee must be given the credit for much that is seen at the present village. His large distillery plant and up-to-date store, were successfully handled by him for years subsequent to the Civil War period. The former he abandoned several years since, and the latter with its lucrative trade, has passed to his son-in-law Mr. S. B. Pifer. This is and has been a famous voting place, now known as Russells Precinct. Away back in the last century, politicians spoke of it always as a Dumb Furtle; and around this precinct many notable contests occurred. Then it was the tactics used by Col. Washington in his election, were adopted and worked for all that was in them. As time wore on, another village was created several miles South. This has been known as Star Tannery. Near this point, which is on Upper Cedar Creek, the voting precinct of Dry Run was established; and the leading spirits of that vicinity soon threw down the gauntlet to the old Dumb Furtle chieftains, showing a disposition to divide honors with the old bosses, as to who should control Back Creek Magisterial District. The challenge was accepted; and from that day, the Cover mountain sides have been called upon to send their dwellers to the polls—their great Captain well equipped with munitions, and supported by stern mountain men, soon gained a reputation for well-fought battles, for victory often perched on his banner. A pleasant rivalry still exists, though the old Captain and his old hosts are only observers now of the younger set, as they keep up the rivalry. Star Tannery, as may be supposed, derived its name from the largest tannery ever operated within the present limits of Frederick County. This enterprise grew rapidly under the skillful control of Mr. Thomas Cover, who, with his associates, found a dilapidated tan-yard there a few years subsequent to the War, and discovered its advantage of location, being in the center of the greatest chestnut-oak bark region then known in these parts. The success of the new tannery was assured. The little village gradually arose, and for many years during the lifetime of the plant, was noted for its thrift and prosperity. A few years ago, the bark supply was exhausted, and the beautiful little mountain village felt her days were numbered. The splendid institution finally closed its doors, but the citizens did not succumb; they rallied on the firm foundation made by their philanthropist and capitalist, and are maintaining the good name of "Star Tannery."

Following Cedar Creek in its Eastward course, we find on the North side, several miles away, the village of Marlboro, near the site of the famous Marlboro Iron Works, commonly called *"Old Forge."* Here Isaac Zane, the iron-founder as he was called, manufactured many articles useful in families, such as the old ten-plate stove, and plate castings for the large open fire place common in those days, a sample of which can be seen in the hall of the Sarah Zane Fire Company. That large plate once formed the siding to an old fire-place in "Homespun," the ancestral home of the Cartmell family, the home of Mathias Miller since 1854, near head of Opecquon, and now the property of his nephew, Dr. A. D. Henkel. Mr. Miller, in changing the interior of the old stone house many years ago, removed the plate from one of the fire places, and later presented it to the Sarah Zane Company. The mill, good country store, post-office, a few good residences in close proximity to two churches, and it being the voting place Old Forge, the place is mentioned with some license as Marlboro.

Kernstown. This town should be treated distinctively. It has been mentioned by magazine writers as a small town lying East of the Old Opecquon Presbyterian Church. It is mentioned in old court records as *Hogue's Ordinary,* being the place where William Hoge conducted his tavern, or ordinary. About the Revolutionary period it was mentioned as Karnsville, in reference to opening a road. Later on it received its present name Kernstown. Several families of this name owned land comprising the site. This town was celebrated in early days as a tavern-stand. Two taverns were successfully conducted there for half a century or more. The old covered wagons traveling the Valley Pike, which is its only street, made the place famous as their stopping place. The taverns did not always maintain the good reputation they once enjoyed. Many violations of the law, by the hilarious, were duly noticed by the old courts,—names of the offenders given and offense named. Owing to the too frequent occurrence of such disturbances, the tavern license was revoked; and from that period the town has been noted for its decorum. Notwithstanding the large distillery started there by L. E. Savage, about thirty years ago, and conducted since his death by his son Joseph H. Savage, under whose skill and management the great plant is not known to encourage use of its products in the village, the passer-by fails to discover the objectionable features usually found around common distilleries. Three-fourths of a mile further South on the same road, is the Kernstown railroad station and postoffice. At this point also the village store is kept.

Berryville. This is one of the towns established many long years previous to the erection of Clarke County. It was then known as Battletown, a name given it as the tradition goes, because of frequent altercations between boisterous gangs who had imbibed too freely; and the story has it that Daniel Morgan deemed it his duty to quell all such, and frequently took a hand in the game. The future general soon won distinction; and was regarded as the man to bull the bully. His fame went abroad, and more than once he was called upon to measure strength with some of the hardy toughs from the *Ridge* settlements. . The Old County Court of Frederick examined into several of those battles. Daniel sometimes had the fines to pay. Later on the town was granted a charter Jany. 15, 1798, and incorporated and named Berryville for its founder Benjamin Berry. Twenty acres of land, the property of Benjamin Berry and Sarah Strebling, was taken. Clarke County was formed March 8, 1836; Berryville was chosen as the county seat, where the first court was held March 28th. The Justices who were appointed by the Governor, were duly qualified to sit and hold the terms of the county court. They were John W. Page, Nathaniel Burwell, Francis McCormick, Frances B. Whiting, Edward J. Smith, David Meade, James Wiggenton, Philip Smith, Geo. H. Norris, John Hay and Jacob Isler. John Hay was elected Clerk of the Court; John E. Page was chosen Commonwealth's Attorney; George H. Norris was first Sheriff. Many members of the Winchester Bar were present and admitted to practice law. Order made to purchase lot and provide for erection of necessary public buildings. The lot chosen was owned by Geo. S. Lane. The court provided ample space for prison bounds—ten acres, and planned to embrace the Hotel of Treadwell Smith. This may appear significant to the *no-license* town of Berryville to-day. David H. McGuire succeeded John Hay as clerk in 1852, holding the office until 1865. Lewis F. Glass was elected, and held office for about four years, when his son George was appointed by the Military government. Served until 1870, when he was appointed by Judge White, who was the judge elected by the General Assembly under the new constitution. Major Saml. J. C. Moore was chosen Commonwealth's Attorney, and Robert P. Morgan sheriff. John E. Page succeeded Judge White in 1872, the latter having resigned. Judge R. A. Finnell elected in 1880; Judge Giles Cook, Jr., in 1886. The first circuit court was held July 30, 1836, Judge Richard E. Parker, presiding, Hugh Holmes Lee being Clerk. Since his retirement in 1852, the county clerk performed the duties of both courts. In 1875 Capt. John M. Gibson began his long term as county clerk. He was succeeded Jany. 1, 1906, by Mr. Samuel McCormick, Capt. Gibson becoming deputy. In January, 1882, the charter was amended—limits extended.

Berryville has always taken front rank in every effort to promote the interests of the growing town—her citizens are intelligent and ambitious. She has been well supplied with churches and schools, to afford proper culture and training. Grace Episcopal Church having received the special care of Bishops Meade, Wilmer, Peterkin and Whittle. The Presbyterian, Baptist and M. E. Church South, are all attractive places for worship. (See Church Sketches for fuller notices.) Three Colored Churches—Free Will Baptist, African M. E. Church and one other—

The public school system adopted by the State 1869-70, has received cordial support from the town and county. The public schools of Berryville soon offered unrestricted facilities to all classes. The Shenandoah University School, so ably conducted by Capt. Wm. A. McDonald for many years, offered a high course of education for young men, and was well patronized by them. Able and competent instructors continued the school for many years. The Graded School Department of the Public Schools, superceded the private institution. The Shenandoah Female Academy is in a prosperous condition. Several secret societies have good working lodges in Berryville,—the Masons, Red Men and Good Templars being prominent.

The Bank of Clarke County was organized Jany. 22, 1881. With sufficient capital and good officers, it affords accommodation for the large business interests of the place. The Phœnix Carriage Works, established 1867, was successfully conducted for many years by Mr. Geo. C. Thomas. The planing mill was once a feature of considerable interest for years. The firm of Ogden and Thomas had such successors as Wm. Baker, L. R. Dettra and others. The town was always noted for the old-time tavern, with such proprietors as Smith, Castleman, and others—all now virtually succeeded by a large, modern hotel, the Battletown Inn.

Berryville is an important shipping station on the Norfolk & Western Railroad, 40 miles South of Hagerstown, 60 miles N. W. from Washington City, 10 miles East from Winchester.

Millwood was one of the old Colonial villages, where the Burwell family owned fine estates. One of the oldest mills in that section was started by the family; though tradition gives Daniel Morgan credit for building the first, nothing can be found to sustain this. Evidence has been found that a mill was located at Burwell's Spring prior to 1760. The old warrior was more given to riots at that period than to mill building. The churches of the village have received notice in other pages. The female seminary, conducted by representatives of old Clarke County families, has been prominent for years. Millwood has always been distinguished for its high-class society. Surrounded as it is by rich and influential *land-barons,* the Colonial homesteads are numerous, and will receive fuller notice under proper head.

The railroad village of Boyce, a short distance West on the N. & W. Railroad, has attracted a large volume of the business that Millwood once enjoyed. Boyce is the shipping point for this highly improved section; and the village presents a scene of activity. Several excellent stores, farm-implement ware houses, etc., attract the attention of every visitor. Mr. John Sprint, one of the old land-marks of that section, has entertained many distinguished visitors in his day, and more than once the author has enjoyed his fascinating reminiscences. The reader should visit this interesting character, and learn much more of the olden times of the far-famed little Clarke County before it becomes too late, Mr. Sprint being now an old man.

White Post. This little village derived its name from a post that Lord Fairfax erected during his sojourn at Greenway Court. Many of his Lordship's visitors were often confused concerning the roads through the virgin forests leading in the direction of his *Court;* and this guide-post was erected and painted white, with directions to plainly indicate the direct route. The post has been renewed several times by some persons who desired to perpetuate the idea of the old Baron. Its use as a guide-post was long since abandoned, except to point out the place of the straggling little village, where good residences, two churches and stores are found nestling in part of the yet virgin forest. White Post village is about 12 miles S. E. from Winchester.

(This closes notices of the towns found in that section of Frederick. We will return to other sections of the Old County, beginning with those of Jefferson.)

Harpers Ferry. This famous town was distinguished in Legislative Acts from other villages on the Potomac, as the "Village at the Falls," and thus was styled "Shenandoah Falls, at Mr. Harper's Ferry." This continued until after the Revolutionary War, when the Potomac Improvement Company was chartered. As was well known, the Robert Harper Ferry was a point on the River, and was supposed to be above the Falls; and as the point affected by the Legislature was near the confluence of the two rivers, it was necessary to designate this point; and we find the name Sherando appears frequently. But the villagers adhered to their familiar name; and later on the town was incorporated as *Harpersferry,* March 24, 1851. It was of slow growth. The site was not inviting—the hillsides too steep to offer inducement to builders of homes, and the narrow low grounds uninviting because subject to overflow. When the U. S. Government selected the place for the manufacture of army muskets, owing to its natural water power, the General Assembly of Virginia granted permission for its location. 125 acres of land was purchased, and options on two other tracts obtained; and the work of erecting suitable equipments for an armory was started in 1796. During 1799-1800, the place was used as a camp of instruction and drill for a body of troops concentrated there. On the table-land overlooking the armory, Genl. Pinckney established *Camp Hill.* The place has retained its name, and became a place of note during the Civil War. One of the officers of that Command, Capt. Henry (mentioned in another chapter) being a political enemy of Mr. Jefferson, was guilty of an act that connects his name with the place. The first superintendent of the Armory was ——— Perkins. He was succeeded by Capt. James Stubblefield in 1810, and held the position many years. Succeeding him was John H. Hall, the inventor of a breech-loading gun. He was put in charge 1819. A Col. Dun succeeded him in 1830. He was killed by one of the artisans named Ebenezer Cox. The poor fellow, from all accounts, was justified in the eyes of his friends, but the law made him pay the penalty. He was executed August 27, 1831. Genl. George Rust then became superintendent, and held the position until succeeded by Edward Lucan, in 1837. His successors were Maj. Craig, Maj. Symington, Col. Huger and Maj. Bell. In 1854, the system of management was changed from the military rule to the Civil. Mr. Chas. J. Faulkner then in Congress from this District, secured the Act of Congress; when Henry W. Clowe, an expert mechanic, secured the position. Under his skill, the armory obtained its best results, until politics appeared and brought the appointment of Alfred M. Barbour. His office was close by the property. Falling into the hands of Virginia in 1861, the Arsenal was seized, and arms and machinery were removed South, under the management of Mr. Clowe, who proved himself useful to the Confederate Government. Col. Clowe spent his years in Winchester, and died highly respected by his numerous friends. In 1869, the Government having abandoned the uses of an arsenal at this point, the property was sold to an unknown syndicate. Mills were to appear, but none came; and the property finally became absorbed by the B. & O. Railroad Company and private persons. All has given way to the progressive age. John Brown's famous fort is marked by a shaft. The Railroad occupies the ground with improved tracks and station houses. A massive steel bridge spans the river far above high water-mark; and no longer does the railroad suffer damage from floods that annually wrecked the old bridges. Harpers Ferry was a great sufferer by the War; but the waste places are no longer seen. Handsome churches and good residences, with good stores, produce an agreeable change. The Catholic, St. John's Episcopal, Presbyterian, Lutheran, and two M. E. Churches have good congregations. The Storer College up on Old Camp Hill, for the education of negroes, has flourished for many years. It was endowed by two citizens of Maine, Storer and Cheney. This school is principally used to educate and prepare negroes as teachers in schools of the South, for their race. Congress granted the ground and such buildings located thereon, formerly used for government purposes.

The destructive floods at this place have been numerous and disheartening, resulting in loss of life and property. The citizens have always rallied, and in time rebuilded. From authentic sources, we give dates of some notable cases. One in 1804, again in 1815; one in 1837; while that of 1852 is well remembered for the sweeping away of mills, houses, bridges, railroad tracks and canal property. The Summer of 1870 wrought untold horrors. This was caused by a sudden rise in the Shenandoah. The loss from Harpers Ferry along the river, as far as Front Royal, in life and property, can never be fully estimated. This was repeated in 1889—caused by floods in both rivers. Persons who witnessed the havoc, mention it now with horror-stricken countenances. In recent years the destruction has not been so great. As will be seen in chapters relating to the Civil War, scenes were enacted there that have become renowned throughout the continent; and thousands of tourists visit the place to gaze upon historic spots, and never cease to admire the quaint little town and its wonderful environments. With this partial description, we pass to the other towns of Jefferson, not already mentioned.

Bolivar. This might properly be considered a suburb of Harpers Ferry, being about a mile distant from the river. It is an incorporated town, however, with less than 500 inhabitants; and for this reason it was embraced in the former sketch, being part of Camp Hill.

Halltown is a small village on the road to Charlestown. The Virginia Paper Mills are located here.

Duffields Depot on the B. & O. main line, is six miles West from Harpers Ferry—Churches, stores, etc., good residences and enterprising citizens, make it a village worthy of note. Leetown is noted for the remarkable spring of water found there, and as the home of Genl. Charles Lee, of whom more will be said. Kabletown, 7 miles South of Charlestown, is on the Bullskin. While it is surrounded by some of the most productive farms in the County, it has made but little growth since Daniel Kable founded it in the 18th Century. Rippon is about six miles from Charlestown. This, too, is a small village, situated on the Bullskin. The Episcopalians and Presbyterians have good churches there. Summit Point is on the Winchester & Potomac Railroad, five miles South of Charlestown. This is a growing village.

Middleway—(Smithfield). This town has quite an interesting history. Some confusion exists as to its name. It is better known as Smithfield to many persons, and to many others as Wizard Clip. It was laid out by its founder, John Smith, in 1794. Previous to this, the quaint little village, located in a rich section of country, attracted many settlers from other sections. And now came the beginning of trouble to some of its citizens. One of the newcomers was Adam Livingston, who purchased desirable property in the vicinity of this village, and established his home there a few years before the town was laid out as Smithfield. The notice given this man and an incident in his life, by several writers, gives the impression that the quiet villagers were much disturbed at the occurrences, which savored strongly of witchcraft. We give the story for what it is worth, showing that even at that time, the old superstitions were not entirely extinct. Livingston is reputed to have been an exemplary protestant, and a man of strong mental character; but had a few grains of prejudice towards the Romish Church; and none were surprised when he refused shelter to a stranger after discovering that he was a Catholic. No inducement by reason of sickness of the belated stranger, could remove the prejudice; and under protest he took him in only for the night. The sick stranger, being conscious of his extreme condition, requested the services of a priest. Livingston was horrified at the thought of his house being converted so suddenly into a confessional. So he informed the dying man that there was no Catholic priest to be had—none in his region; and besides, no priest could cross his threshold. No importunities offered by the faithful Romanist could move the bigoted Protestant; and amid such gloom, the unshriven soul of the stranger was launched into the great Beyond. The dead stranger was released from his earthly woes, while his host was left to encounter the woes that resulted in the destruction of his earthly home, and perhaps weakened his faith relating to his future. Strange scenes are chronicled, as they appeared to some who were keeping watch over the bier. Flickering and disappearing lights, mysterious footsteps and mournful noises, awakened emotions that could not be suppressed, and the watchers had all their superstitions aroused. Each succeeding night brought new wonders—the steady tramp of horses around the house; the furniture displaced by unseen hands, warnings from strange voices, soon affected the stalwart Livingston; but he firmly held out in his denunciation of all evil spirits. When the strange visitors, however, introduced their *clipping* programme, the old Englishman weakened when he beheld the destruction to his clothing and bedding, all in ribbons, the tails of his animals clipped, and nameless other woes. Other persons suffered similar losses, until, driven to despair, he was apprised of a mode of relief, revealed to him in a dream: He must seek help from one who could stay the mysterious work of the *spirits.* He called on Father Cahill, a Catholic priest who was then at Shepherdstown. The priest was a willing listener; and proceeded at once to the scene of all this woe; and by faithful prayers and free use of *holy water,* the wizard was appeased and driven out of Smithfield, as good St. Patrick once drove the snakes out of Ireland. Then it was the new name appeared; and from that day, it was known as the Wizard's Clip, abbreviated sometimes to Clip; but the generations as they came and went, heard the story; and the present generation shows a few who wag the head when the subject is mentioned, and relate much more than the writer has given concerning this story of the last appearances of wizards in the Lower Valley. The writer has seen extended notices carefully prepared by intelligent Catholics, who credit the work of Father Dennis Cahill.

The present thriving and beautiful town is well supplied with churches, schools and mercantile wares, and is noted for its sociability.

Jefferson has other villages well founded and deserving of special mention, if space permitted; but several towns in the two old counties of Shenandoah and Hampshire should have place among the towns of Old Frederick.

Three places in Hampshire may be mentioned. Taking Bloomery at the North end of the County, we find a straggling village now. The writer remembers the place as one of activity, with its flour mill, woolen mill, and an iron furnace famous for its pig iron, operated by the Pancoast family, who only closed down about 1856. One of the largest stores in the country was to be found there. A large landed estate was owned and operated on an extensive scale by the Genl. Sherrard family. Bloomery is mentioned in early records; was the scene of battle during the Civil War, between the old militia and U. S. Troops. It is on the old North Frederick and Hampshire Turnpike, about 30 miles N. W. from Winchester.

Capon Bridge is a village on Big Capon, 19 miles from Winchester, where the Northwestern Turnpike crosses this stream over an iron bridge. For many years the old covered wooden bridge was a distinguishing feature in all that section. About twenty years ago, a tannery was started on the West side of the river by Mr. Zepp, passing from him to Thomas Cover & Son, who enlarged it considerably and derived much profit from the investment. Ownership changed again, when Cover, Drayton & Leonard operated it, until, with other tanning interests owned by them, it was sold to the American Leather Trust, at fabulous prices. The town is growing, with several large stores, good hotel, kept for many years by the John Smith family; shops, etc., which give the place an air of exceeding prosperity.

Watson Town—Capon Springs.

This place is so well located and so popular as a mountain resort, that it needs no notice here. In former chapters, it is mentioned for its location. It was chartered in 1787, as Watson Town, and trustees were appointed to protect the property and collect a tax from visitors, to aid in the improvement of the place. A lottery scheme was authorized by the Act of Assembly, 1830, to secure funds to make a road from the Springs to a point on the East side of the Big Mountain. This was accomplished in time; and for years a good mountain road has offered easy access from the Valley on the East. Capon Springs is 22 miles S. West from Winchester. In addition to the hotels and cottages, there is a Union Church, large store, post-office, etc. In the Act of 1830, the name of Capon Springs Baths first appears, as being in the town of Watson. Skipping over the mountains to the Southward, we will briefly notice several towns in Shenandoah that have not received special mention.

Edinburg is situated on the Valley Turnpike, 5 miles S. W. from Woodstock. Stony Creek, passing the place, affords many advantages for manufacturing plants. The churches, mercantile houses, schools, etc., indicate prosperity on the part of her citizens.

Mount Jackson. This town is in the heart of a wonderful agricultural and fruit section of the Valley. Situated on the great Valley thoroughfare, the visitor will find much of interest. While not so old as New Market, she has become her rival, with many attractive features. Some celebrated river farms near by, have always supported the enterprises of the town.

Hawkinstown and *Quicksburg* are towns South of Woodstock; while North, on the Valley Pike, we find two towns: Toms Brook and Maurerstown—both prosperous towns and no longer villages. Of the former, we mention a fact that may not be familiar to her citizens. This is much older than many other similar places. The writer, in tracing the first road extending from the Potomac to the County seat of Frederick, was interested in its continuance South. This route called for certain well known places, such as mills and homesteads of settlers. Crossing Cedar Creek at a mill, thence South through lands of well known settlers, crossing *Thomas's Brook,* disclosed the fact that one Thomas owned the land where Toms Brook now stands. This road was laid out in 1764; and the Valley Pike was required to follow as nearly as possible the old roadway from Winchester South through the Valley—at all times to pass the old tavern and wagon stands.

West from the last named places, are several villages: Lebanon Church located on the Back Road, running South from Marlboro, is a thriving village. A little further West, we find Cotton Town and "Snarrs"—the scenes of battle between Jackson and Freemont. In the beautiful little valleys, hugging the mountain section, are found such places as Columbia Furnace, Tannery, etc.

Orkney Springs, about 18 miles S. W. from Woodstock, has quite a reputation as a health resort. The medicinal waters found gushing from several strong springs, possess properties highly beneficial to some invalids; while the mansion house and its cluster of attractive cottages, give it the appearance of a prosperous village. For many years, Orkney received a liberal patronage.

Seven Fountains, known in early days as Burners Springs, located in the Massanutten range of mountains, romantic from its peculiar environments, as well as for its approaches through Powells Fort Valley and over the high mountain going out from Woodstock, it attracts quite a number of families from the busy sections, where refreshing mountain air and the chalybeate and other waters are found in profusion.

CHAPTER XLVI

Notabilities of Old Frederick County. The Fairfax Families.

A cleaving interest will always adhere, perhaps, to perpetuators of the surname which Lord Fairfax eternified in the nomenclature of Virginia. Here within our borders this interest naturally inheres in the well known native cohesion of our State-folk. To those that live at a distance, however, it vaguely looms as a sentiment. Indeed there prevails an idealization of our Virginian Fairfaxes, who are fancifully regarded as the heritors and living symbols of Lord Fairfax's fame in history.

Romantic writers are responsible for this illusion; and because the Fairfax family name has become involved with the traditions of Lord Fairfax, it is thought that an interesting inclusion of these chronicles would be an outline of the ramifications of the two families of Fairfax in Virginia. The progenitors of both these family lines in America were sprouts from the same ancestral tree in England which sent forth Lord Fairfax as the head of one of its Junior branches.

And though they both—these Fairfax ancestors—antedated Lord Fairfax as Colonists, neither of them immigrated originally to Virginia, this has been shown elsewhere in this volume.

At the beginning of the Eighteenth Century, John Fairfax had established himself in the Province of Maryland. Later on in 1717, William Fairfax appeared in America and settled himself amidst the Puritans in the Colony of Massachusetts. This William was a near by cousin of Thomas Fairfax who, in 1710, had succeeded his father as sixth Baron of the Scotch title; Baron of Cameron. When quite a young man, William Fairfax had ventured to sea and served in the navy under a kinsman of his, a captain Fairfax. William Fairfax was twice married; firstly, in 1717, to Sarah Walker whose father, Maj. Thomas Walker, was stationed at that time in the island of New Providence. Fourteen years later, Sarah Fairfax died at Salem, Mass. William Fairfax's second marriage was with Deborah Clarke of Salem Mass. Several years prior to the time we are now considering Lord Fairfax had heired, in right of his mother, the vast proprietary estate of Lord Colepeper in Virginia. Lord Fairfax had never crossed the Atlantic, however, when, in 1732, the death occurred of Robert Carter who had long served as Steward of the proprietary under Lord Colepeper. This placed the new proprietary in an awkward quandary. His sole knowledge of his vast domain which, at that time was mostly a wilderness, was the vague inception derivable from his parchments as we have already shown his grant embraced specifically enough, the whole intervening country between the head-waters of the Rapahannock and the Potomac rivers and the Chesapeake Bay, but where were those "Headwaters"? No surveyor had yet attempted to follow this inquiry and, without official definement of the proprietary limits, a large area was being granted away as already stated by the Crown in a region which Lord Fairfax insisted to be a part of his patented possessions. Such was the new proprietaries plight when he wrote to his American kinsmen, William Fairfax, of Massachusetts, and proposed to him to go to Virginia and undertake the management of his northern Neck proprietary. This offer was accepted and William Fairfax moved with his family to Virginia in 1733. He settled upon a leased plantation in the County of King George. It was something in the nature of a problem then to obtain a cleared plantation in northern Virginia, because the Colepeper proprietary grant had retarded the development of that district among the foremost planters there then were the Washingtons, and of that family there were several members residing in the counties along the Potomac.

In 1739, William Fairfax purchased of Edward Washington a plantation recorded then as in the County of Prince William. Three years thereafter, however, this part was taken away from Prince William to form a new County, and this county was called in honor of the new proprietor—Fairfax. Near by this Edward Washington plantation was the "Hunting Creek" plantation of Augustine Washington—father of our Immortal George; and that which was then known as "Hunting Creek" plantation is to-day the World-famed, if not the World-revered, Mt. Vernon. It was just at this time, 1739, that Lord Fairfax crossed the Atlantic to institute a survey, under Crown authority, to establish his boundary limits. While on this visit it appears that plans were made for the erection upon William Fairfax's plantation of a substantial house to serve, not alone as a residence, but as well for a place of security for the custody of the records of the northern neck Proprietary; as shown elsewhere this house was called Belvoir. In 1741, William Fairfax was elected a member of the House of Burgesses, he retained the management of the Northern Neck estate until his death in 1757. From both his marriages there were children. By Sarah Walker there issued two sons; George William, who married Sarah Cary, daughter of Col. Wilson Cary, and Thomas who died unmarried. There were also two daughters; Anne, who married Lawrence Washington, and Sarah, who married Maj. John Carlyle. George William Fairfax became assistant with his father in the management of Lord Fairfax's property. It will right much misunderstanding to mention here that it was George William Fairfax who, while "agent for Lord Fairfax" (To use George Washington's own words) who gave the first remunerated employment to the youthful Washington. Lord Fairfax knew nothing whatever of Washington until the boy's own survey report commanded his attention. The comprehensive field notes of Washington were so unmistakably trustworthy that the boy was instructed to report himself to "His Lordships Quarters over the mountains."

Another correction of legend is, that George Fairfax and George Washington, while next door neighbors, were not "boy companions together," as often represented. George Fairfax, the full grown man employed George Washington, the boy, and scarcely more than a child was Washington just 16 years of age. At the death of William Fairfax in 1757, his son George William succeeded him to the Proprietary stewardship. A few years theretofore, however, Thomas Bryan Martin, a nephew of Lord Fairfax, had come out to Virginia and established himself in his bachelor uncle's home. Three years had hardly elapsed since the death of William Fairfax, when information reached George William's ear that Martin was contriving to influence his Uncle into making a change in the Proprietary management. Shortly thereafter, the whole land Office outfit was transferred from the Belvoir House to a depository built for its purpose on his Lordship's manor, Greenway Court. The bitter feeling created in George William Fairfax by Martin's influence over his lordship, is shown through letters of the former which have been published by Edward D. Neill. In 1773 George William Fairfax went with his wife to England where both of them died, there was no issue from their union. From William Fairfax's marriage with Deborah Clarke the issue: Bryan, William Henry and Hannah. William Henry died unmarried. Bryan Fairfax, the older of the two, was married twice; firstly, to Elizabeth Cary, sister to his half-brother George's wife, and secondly, to Jennie Dennison. In 1754 Bryan Fairfax was appointed Deputy Clerk of the County of Fairfax.

At the death of Lord Fairfax, the Northern Neck proprietary as shown in his lordship's will (as heretofore shown) to his nephew, the Rev. Denny Martin, who thereafter assumed the surname of Fairfax. The new proprietary appointed as his manager his brother Thomas Bryan Martin and Gabriel Jones. In consideration, however, of back claims upon Lord Fairfax's estates rendered by William Fairfax as his manager, prior to 1757, (And which were thus a quarter of a century over due at his Lordship's decease), Denny Fairfax revoked the above appointments and appointed Bryan Fairfax alone in lieu of them. The document that effected this transposition was dated at London, Sept. 21, 1784. By it, Denny Martin was to be absolved from all back-claims whatsoever by the heirs of William Fairfax, for the stipulated consideration of Bryan Fairfax's substitution from Martin and Jones in the stewardship of Denny Fairfax's Proprietary. In the following year, however, the Legislature of Virginia practically obliterated the Northern Neck Proprietary and as shown elsewhere ordered all records, books, documents, etc., pertaining to lands within that district, to be removed from proprietary custody and placed in the State Land Registrars Office in the City of Richmond. Bryan Fairfax was a man of profound piety. Although belonging to the military of the Colony, he declined to take up arms against the Crown in the Revolution. His letters reveal that during his military service he was wont to spend whole hours at night on his sentry post in prayer. In 1789, when in the 57th year of his life, he became a minister of the Protestant Episcopal Church, "having accepted the moderate Calvinistic interpretation of the 39 articles." From 1789 until 1792, he preached at old Falls Church in the County of Fairfax; subsequently, he became a "visitor of parishes" in his district.

On the death of Lord Fairfax, in 1782, the latter's title passed to his brother, Robert, in England. Robert, seventh Lord Fairfax, died without heir in 1793; and now the barony of Camron fell in abeyance. Five years later—in 1798—the Rev. Bryan Fairfax went to England to test the validity of a claim for himself to the heirship of the Cameron title. He addressed a petition to his Majesty King George III, and this found its way to a committee of the House of Lords under the headship of Lord Walsingham. On May 6, 1800, this committee submitted its report, which declared: "in favor of the petitioner." As this incident has supplied inspiration for many erroneous publications, the interest of intelligent readers would benefit by its clearification as a fact. The Rev. Bryan Fairfax's petition prayed for his resignation as heir to the succession to the title. But the granting of that petition did not, *per se* constitute the petitioner a baron of Cameron, nor did he himself assume that he did. The instrument merely secured to him and to his heirs thenceforward, the right to assume the title subject to the legal exactions imposed, the Rev. Bryan Fairfax never exercised for himself his right to qualify for the title. On the contrary, he is on record as having declared that he had "no ambition to bear an empty title." His will, which is filed in Fairfax County, attests to the fact that he was known as and designated both at and after his decease, as simply Bryan Fairfax.

It is only due to the honored descendants from the Rev. Bryan Fairfax, to mention here, that no bearer of his surname has ever been responsible for any publication which tended to sentimentalize the "Lords" Fairfax of Virginia. The Rev. Bryan Fairfax died in 1802, leaving two sons and two daughters, Ferdinando, his second son, married Elizabeth Cary; he lived as a planter in Jefferson County, and left many descendants. The oldest son, Thomas, who was heir in line to the title was married three times; firstly, to Mary Aylett; secondly, to Louisa Washington; thirdly, to Margaret, daughter of William Herbert. From this third wife there issued all of his ten children of whom six were sons; Albert, Henry, Orlando, Raymond, Ethelbert and Reginald. Henry Fairfax, his second son, married Caroline Herbert, of Maryland, and conducted at his home, "Ash Grove" in Fairfax County, a well known boarding school for young ladies. He was Captain of a volunteer Company in the Mexican war and died in 1847, leaving several children. Orlando, the third son, married Mary Randolph Cary, he was a well known family physician in Alexandria in early life, and subsequently he practiced in Richmond, where he died leaving a large family.

Raymond, Ethelbert and Reginald, the fourth, fifth and sixth sons of Thomas Fairfax, all died unmarried. Thomas Fairfax spent his life as a planter in Fairfax County and died at his home, Vaucluse, in 1846, at the age of 84.

The oldest son, Albert, died before his father, in 1835.

Albert Fairfax married Caroline Eliza, daughter of Richard Snowden of Maryland, and left by her two sons, Charles Snowden and John Contee. At the death of Thomas Fairfax, in 1846, Charles Snowden Fairfax, his grandson, became, by birth-right, the heir to the Barony. He was among the pioneers to California and, four years after the admission of that State to the Union, he was elected to its House of Delegates. In 1857, he was made Clerk of the California Supreme Court, he married Ada Benham of Cincinnati, Ohio, and died in 1869 without issue. The heirship to the title reverted then to his brother, John Contee, of North Hampton, Prince George's County, Maryland. John Contee Fairfax studied medicine and practiced it in his home county in Maryland. He married Mary, daughter of Col. Edmund Kirby, of New York, an officer of the U. S. Army. Dr. John Contee Fairfax died at his home in Maryland in 1900, leaving three daughters, Caroline, Josephine and Charlie; and two sons, Albert Kirby and Charles Edmund. Albert Kirby Fairfax, the eldest son had attained the distinction of being the first of Rev. Bryan Fairfax's descendants to seek recognition of the heirship of the Barony of Cameron.

When preparations were making for the coronation of King Edward VII, an application was made to the Earl Marshall of England for a Barons summons to Albert Fairfax to appear at that ceremony. He was accordingly "Commanded." And although prevented from attending that function, he was personally addressed as Lord Fairfax by the Lord Chancellor, which recognition alone invested him with the courtesy right to "walk" as the Baron of Cameron. It yet behooves him to bear the title in actuality to legalize his signatureship of it, to renounce his American citizenship and formally declare his allegiance to the British Crown.

As much that is apocryphal has been written of the prerogatives of this title, intelligent interest will approve the recitation here of facts which will explain them.

In the British realm, whatever privileges are possessed by a peer, belong to the peer as a member of Parliament only, and thus, where membership in Parliament is hereditary, Peerage privileges are also, but then only.

All peers of England, absolutely, and all peers of Scotland, down to the title of Baron, were constituted, at the union of England and Scotland, as peers of Great Britain. The Barons of Scotland remained, as they were peers of Scotland only, and the one possibility of their entering the House of Lords is through election. For each and every Parliament of the United Kingdom there are 16 Scottish representative peers elected; and the right to vote, at the Parliamentary elections, is the only hereditary privilege that inures to a baron of Scotland, and consequently to the Baron of Cameron. In the Scottish sense, that a barony implies a free hold of property, the Barony of Cameron is not indeed a Barony at all. It is a patent of baronial dignity which Charles I created, in 1627, and which he conferred in a manner not unusual to the Stuart King, for the consideration of a fee to the royal Exchequer. Albert Kirby Fairfax is, as yet, unmarried so is his brother Charles Edmund, and thus the primogenital line of descent from the parent colonists, William Fairfax, may be said to pause with an interrogation. In order that no entanglement may remain in the lines of the two Fairfax families, we shall now hark back to John Fairfax, in Maryland, who, although anterior to William Fairfax as a colonist, had no descendant in Virginia until their third generation. This line of Fairfaxes did not cross the Potomac until after the Revolution and therefore they were not in Virginia during the time of Lord Fairfax. The reader may recall that, in the original grant of Maryland Cecilius Calvert, the second Lord Baltimore, was given a palatinate or quasi-royal authority over that province. The Calvert family were Catholics. And, notwithstanding that Lord Baltimore established in his colony the first freedom of religious worship in America, there subsequently developed in Maryland such bitter hostility to zelots of the Romish faith that, from 1692 to 1715, the Crown suspended the Charter rights of the Baltimores and abrogated their palatine authority. It was during this period of "suppression of papas rule" in Maryland that John Fairfax appeared in that Colony. He himself was a papist, and of that faith was the primogenital vein of the English Fairfaxes, the Viscounts of Emley—the Lords of Fairfax of Gilling Castle in Yorkshire. The first record of moment pertaining to John Fairfax, is the prosecution by him of trespassers upon his property in Charles County. He is found recorded repeatedly as sponsor and surety for his co-religionists, and various pleas of "*compassion* for those Catholics who have truly scrupulous consciences," are peep-holes through the imaginative mind may picture the tribulations endured by the then faithful adherents of the Church of Rome. John Fairfax married Catherine, daughter of Henry Norris of Maryland, and to the former's only son, John Fairfax II, there descended the Norris homestead. John Fairfax II, of Charles County, Maryland, married Mary, daughter of Edward Scott of Baltimore County. In 1720, nine years before there existed *a Baltimore Town,* Mary Scott Fairfax possessed her parental plantations "Scott's folly" on Elk Ridge, then in the County of Baltimore John Fairfax II died at his Charles County home in 1735, leaving four daughters and one son, William. William Fairfax of Charles County, Maryland, married firstly Benedicta Blanchard, to whom there were three daughters; and two sons; Jonathan and Hezekiah. William Fairfax's second marriage was with Elizabeth, daughter of Peyton Buckner of Virginia, and by this union there issued two more sons; John and William, and three daughters. William Fairfax, the senior, was a planter of considerable possessions in Maryland and although he, and both of his older sons, were qualified for the military service, all three of them, as did the Fairfaxes in Virginia, stood loyal to the British Crown in the Revolution. In 1789, William Fairfax disposed of his Maryland plantation and invested in properties in Virginia whither he moved in 1791 and made his home at Occoquan. He died at his Occoquan home in 1793. Jonathan Fairfax, the oldest of William's four sons, remained for life a Marylander. His home, "Goose Bay" was near old Port Tobacco in Charles County, and there he died in 1787 having predeceased his father by six years. He married Sarah, daughter of Richard Wright, by whom there issued four daughters; Lewesta, Sarah, Anne Booker and Elizabeth; and five sons, Richard Wright, Walter, John, Henry and Peter. Hezekiah Fairfax, the second of William Fairfax's sons married Margaret Calvert. He made his home in Prince William County, Virginia, and left four sons, John Hezekiah, Minor, Thompson and Sanford, the descendants of whom we lack space to follow.

William Fairfax II, married Anne, daughter of Silas King of Va., and, having heired his father's home at Occoquan, he died there in 1845. John Scott Fairfax, this second William's oldest son, married Anne, daughter of Peyton Mills of Virginia, and settled in Kentucky, where John Peyton Fairfax, his eldest son, is now well known. John Fairfax, the third son of the senior William Fairfax, was the first of this family line to cross the Potomac and become a Virginian. Notwithstanding that this family were Tories, and further more that they were not even Virginians, Gen. Washington, in 1783, just after resigning his command of the army, sent to Maryland for young John Fairfax and offered him the position of assistant to his nephew, Lund Washington, in the management of his extensive properties. John Fairfax, who was but 19 years of age, accepted the offer and went forthwith to Mount Vernon. Within two years, Lund Washington received an appointment in the public service and John Fairfax succeeded him. For seven years he remained with Gen. Washington, and letters now in the family well preserved attest to the regard in which he was held by the Father of his Country.

The realty holdings of Washington, at his death, aggregated something like 55,000 acres, a fact which conveys an intelligent understanding of John Fairfax's responsibilities.

Just as Washington profited by acquiring garden-spots that he found while surveying the domain of Lord Fairfax, so profited young Fairfax by his knowledge of Washington's holdings in the rich natural meadows of Mongalia County, known as the Glades. John Fairfax bought an extensive tract in the Monongalia Glades and, in 1790, resigned his position with Washington and went thither to live. In 1794, he was appointed by Gov. Brooke a Justice of the Court, later he became the presiding Justice. Three times he was elected to the Legislature of Virginia and, prior to and during the War of 1812, he was Col. of the 104th Virginia Regiment. Col. Fairfax died in 1843, having, throughout his entire manhood, occupied official positions of trust and responsibility. Persons still living, who heard Col. Fairfax's own account of it, allege that Gen. Washington told him he was actuated in befriending him by a recognition of the great debt which he, (Washington) himself, felt that he owed to a Fairfax. Let it be remembered that Lord Fairfax died in 1782, on the year before this John Fairfax appointment, and he, who is memorable in history for his patronage to the young surveyor, is said to have declared, upon his death bed, that he should never look into the face of the Conqueror of Lord Cornwallis—and he never did! Was, or was not, this plaint of his old patron, a thorn in the heart of Washington which pained and rankled? And did he, when that mighty sword was hung up in the hall of Mount Vernon, did he feel that he was making atonement by giving his favor to young Fairfax, just as the kind old master of Greenway Court at one time favored him? Col. John Fairfax was married twice; firstly, to Mary, daughter of Samuel Byrne of Virginia; and secondly, to Anne Lloyd, daughter of Frances Boucher Franklin of Maryland. Two sons, William and Buckner, were born of the first marriage and two more sons, Frances Boucher Franklin and George Washington were born of the second. Both Franklin and George Washington Fairfax, held commissions as Colonel in the military service and all four of these sons attained official prominence by State appointment. Buckner Fairfax, in particular, was a man of leading. In 1849, the Legislature of Virginia appointed him Brigadier General of the third Military District. General Fairfax was elected to the Legislature of Virginia five times, four terms in the Lower House and one in the Senate.

Returning to the vein of seniority in the family, Jonathan Fairfax who died in Maryland in 1787, left five sons and four daughters. Of these five sons, who have already been named, Henry, alone, survived the maturity of manhood. Henry Fairfax embarked in business with a foreign shipping house in Baltimore, and, profiting by his experience, he went to the then prosperous Port of entry Dumfries, Virginia, and became one of the leading shipping merchants of his time. His vessels contributed aid to the Government in the war of 1812, and he himself held the rank of Captain in the 36th Virginia Regiment during that War. Apart from his Dumfries concerns, Henry Fairfax was interested in a banking house in Baltimore and, at his death in 1847, he left a fortune. He was married three times; firstly, to Sarah Triplett, daughter of William Carter of Dumfries; secondly, to Sophia, daughter of Jesse Scott of Dumfries; and thirdly, to Elizabeth, daughter of Thomas Lindsay, of The Mount, in Fairfax County. From the first marriage there issued five daughters, and a son, Henry. Henry Fairfax, the second, married Jane Parks Price, grand-daughter of Colonel Stephen Rex Price, of the British Army under Cornwallis in the Revolutionary War. Dr. Edwin Fairfax, now living in Missouri, is his oldest son. From the senior Henry Fairfax's marriage with Elizabeth Lindsay there issued two children, Martha Lindsay, who married Bowling Robertson of Petersburg, Virginia; and a son, John Walter. John Walter Fairfax, in the ante-bellum period, was a leading social figure in northern Virginia. He owned, among other valuable properties, "Oak Hill," the former country seat of President Monroe, at Aldie, which was his family home. He married Mary, daughter of Col. Hamilton Rogers, from which marriage there issued four sons and a daughter. Hon. Henry Fairfax, the oldest son, and present owner of the Monroe estate, married Eugenia Tennant of Richmond, Va. Hamilton Rogers Fairfax married Eleanor Van Rensselaer of New York; John Walter Fairfax, the second of New York, is unmarried; Lindsay Fairfax married Grace Bradford of Lennox, Mass., and Mary Elizabeth married Col. Charles G. Ayres of the U. S. Army.

In 1861, John Walter Fairfax espoused the cause of the Confederacy, as did every Fairfax of Virginia—with but one single exception. A single allusion to the record of Col. Fairfax in the Civil War, will serve as an index to the quality of his manhood, he became the ranking officer on the staff of Gen. Longstreet; and by his knightly gallantry—his dashing defiance of danger and contempt for fear—he came to be characterized by the troops in the field of battle, as "Longstreet's Fighting Aide." Col. Fairfax died in March 1908, at the former home of his father, on the Potomac—Leesylvania.

At the end of his four score life, it was written of him, and justly, that few men of his time had sustained so distinctly as had he, the traditional standard of the old school Virginia gentlemen.

Fairfax Peerage.

The claim established No. 17, 1908.

The London Daily Telegraph, dated Nov. 18,

1908, contained several columns, giving in full the proceedings in determining the question of title to the Barony of Cameron. The Committee for Privileges of the House of Lords, by whom all peerage claims are determined, met Nov. 17, 1908, and arrived at a conclusion, admitting the claim of Albert Kirby Fairfax to the title, honour and dignity of Lord Fairfax of Cameron, in the Peerage of Scotland.

The Committee was composed of the Lord Chancellor, Lord Ashbourne, Lord Robertson, and Lord Collins; the Earl of Onslow presiding as chairman of the Committee. The case was fully heard; the Attorney General being present, was questioned by the Committee concerning the proof produced. The Earl of Onslow propounded the question, "Have you anything to say, Mister Attorney?"

The Attorney-General, "I have no observations to offer; the only points which occurred to me for criticism have been cleared up."

The Lord Advocate, "The point on which there was any doubt in my mind was with regard to the decease of Charles Snowden Fairfax, the tenth Lord Fairfax, without issue. That point seems to be completely cleared up."

The Lord Chancellor, "I move that your Lordships resolve that the petition has made out his claim to the title, dignity, and honour of Lord Fairfax of Cameron."

"The motion was put and agreed to, and the proceedings terminated."

CHAPTER XLVII

George Washington, Surveyor, Citizen, Soldier, Legislator and President

George Washington, the young surveyor for Lord Fairfax, and his two brothers, Samuel and Charles Washington, may be very properly classed with the early settlers of Frederick County. George acquired title to certain large tracts of land from Lord Fairfax. Some are designated the Bullskin surveys. One contained 550 acres, several other tracts were purchased from lessees of Fairfax. While Lawrence purchased several tracts in 1747, he was not a resident of the county. Samuel and Charles settled on this land, and continued as residents of the Valley. Samuel lived on a tract near the site of Charlestown, Jefferson County. Charles owned the site, and laid out the town, and the village took his name (see notes on Towns). Their homesteads were established prior to 1750, and maintain individuality to this day. Harewood, a large stone structure, still standing in good repair, was built in 1749-50 by Col. Samuel Washington. Large families were reared on these historic plantations. Many of the name became prominent both in the civil and military life of the Shenandoah Valley. The last male member of the family, Captain Bushrod C. Washington, removed the remnant of his family to the State of Washington during the preparation of these notes. Col. Samuel was a member of the old Justices' Court in 1771, and a Vestry man of Norborne Parish.

Augustine Washington owned large tracts in Frederick County in the vicinity of Old Hopewell Meeting House. Part of this land became the property of George Fayette Washington, born 1790, died 1867. His son, Maj. Burwell B. Washington (known as Bird), born 1830, died 1868, married Miss Buchannan. She and their only child, Miss Birdie B. Washington, are all that are left in the Valley bearing the name, the old Homestead "Waverly" is owned by them, though they reside in Washington, D. C. Augustine Washington executed a deed for several tracts. His signature was attested by George Washington and others. The family seal was used; the originals are in the Old Clerk's office at this writing, bearing date June 19, 1752.

This fact became known to the State Department at Washington; and it is regarded as the oldest impression of the Washington Seal found on record. The Government secured a lithographic copy of the original Deed and the Seal, and also one of the interior of the old Clerk's Office, a copy of which appears in this volume.

George Washington executed several deeds for tracts of land; the originals are on file in this Office; he also purchased several tracts during the time he made the surveys for Fairfax. One was from George Johnston, a member of the Winchester Bar. The Agreement for this purchase shows that it was executed in Winchester, and in the law office of Mr. Johnston. This office was used by Washington while in the town, when plotting his surveys. This office was located on the corner of Braddock Road and Cork Street; and tradition fixes the old stone and log building at that corner as "Washington's Headquarters." Whether this meant his Military or Surveyors Office is not known. Lieutenant Washington spent some time at a Tavern near this corner, while in command of the "Out Post." Whether it was the one located on Braddock Street, near the site of the M. E. Church, where he had a stockade on the opposite side for his soldiers, is not known. This lot was then owned by Edward Cartmell, who produced a certificate from the young Commander, for his allowance for rent. The Commissioners approved the claim, which was paid by Act of the House of Burgesses, 1758. This lot being directly North of the Johnston Office, it is fair to assume the Lieutenant had his office with his friend George Johnston. Several traditions point to Philip Dalby's Tavern on Main Street, near Cork, as the place where Washington was quartered. This must be taken with due allowance, for Dalby was not a tavern-keeper at that time; and minutes of Court, show that Washington filed complaint before the Court, charging the tavern-keepers on Loudoun Street with unlawful sale of rum to his Soldiers, and moved the Court to rescind the license of Jno. Linndsey and Philip Bush, Jun. This the Court denied. It seems doubtful that his Soldiers would frequent the tavern where he was quartered, and on this ground we may assume he was quartered at Heth's Tavern on Braddock Street, near his soldiers' barracks. (This street or road was then often designated as Second Street) and had his Office on the Corner above. George

Washington's Headquarters, Winchester

was not so easily turned down. He announced himself a candidate for election to the House of Burgesses, and entered the arena of politics as a temperance candidate; opposing tippling houses and general drunkenness; going so far as to "flog his own men for being found drunken with Liquors." In this election he was defeated by Capt. Thomas Swearingen, who received 270 votes, Hugh West, 271, Washington, 45. The friend of the tavern-keepers was elected. The young officer learned some lessons by his defeat, saw the peculiar mode adopted by his opponents; and in 1758, he was up again and used the political tricks of his former enemies. In this election, he was supported by such good politicians as Col. James Wood and Gabriel Jones, *King's Attorney*. It is no wonder then that Washington received 310 votes, while Thos. Bryan Martin received 240, Hugh West had 199, and Thos. Swearingen 45. But the Burgess elect had the *Liquors* to pay for. The law required him to produce his sworn statement of kind and cost, this amount was given, £39 6s, for following items—A hogshead and barrel of punch, thirty-five gallons of wine, forty-three gallons of strong cider, and dinner for his friends. The County then embraced all of the Lower Valley, including Hampshire County, and only one Voting place. This was Winchester.

As shown elsewhere, Col. Washington was with his command West of Fort Cumberland; and it is fair that his friends should stand for his election and also for the distribution of the liquids. Washington being with Genl. Forbes in the Fort Duquesne campaign, may account for his absence from his seat in the Assembly. The House Journal shows that he was present as a member of the House of Burgesses until 1760, and was represented by proxy in the person of Col. James Wood (according to tradition, the father of the Clerk). Col. Washington, on his return from his military campaign, was married to the widow Martha Custis, January, 1759, in New Kent County, Virginia. On May 18, 1761, Washington was elected over two opponents, when he received 505 votes; Capt. Geo. Mercer 399, and Col. Adam Stephen 294. By reference to appendices, the certified copy of List of Burgesses, gives Washington's term of service 1758-1765. This closed all claims that Frederick County has to his citizenship. His subsequent residence at Mt. Vernon, and his services as military hero, First President of the United States, and his death in 1799, belong to National History. Elsewhere will appear when and how he built Fort Loudoun.

CHAPTER XLVIII

Joist Hite, the Pioneer

In the foregoing pages Joist Hite appears as the first white man to settle for habitation in the almost boundless territory known as Old Frederick County. So notable a character is entitled to more definite notice than the writer intended in this history of the early settlement of the *Lower Valley*. As already stated, the object will be to give brief sketches of the first settlers and not cumber this work with matters that might only be of interest to a few readers. But it has been suggested by many correspondents as well as personal appeals from many descendants of the Hite family, that from the voluminous notes the author has in hand touching the life and movements of this remarkable, historic man, that he turn aside from his defined plan and place before the reader the only complete and accurate history of the man—from facts gathered from family, State, County, and Church records.

"Herman Schmichts" valuable work on the German settlements of New York and the Jerseys, gives "Heighte" prominent notice—though not as one of the earliest Dutch emigrants who colonized a large section of that section of America. He states that "He settled with his company of emigrants on the Hudson River." The Court records at Kingston, New York, show that he "was" at Kingston on the Hudson River in 1710. In the early records, his name appears as "Hans Jost Heydt," written in German; very often in the translation written "Yost"—"Joist" and "Jost." Soon after his arrival he ceased to use the name Hans (which means John) in affixing his signature to documents. It has not been definitely settled as to the place of his birth or the exact date. It is well established that he came direct from Strasburg, Germany, with his wife Anna Maria DuBois, and a daughter Mary. While living at Kingston as members of that Dutch settlement, we have from the records of the old Dutch Reformed Church of Kingston, the names of two other daughters born to them, Magdalene and Elizabeth; also dates of their baptism. Traditionary history gives him the title of Baron Jost Hite. The author has exhausted every plan to verify this, but no evidence of such title has been found in his native country. Doubtless from his appearance in several settlements, both in New York, Pennsylvania and Virginia, with his ability to not only purchase land, but to lead and control a number of emigrating families, he acquired a complimentary title. The name of Yost Heite appears frequently in the files of the Court of Old Salem, New York, and also in New Jersey, during the seven years of his residence in the Dutch settlement. He was a fur trader and trafficked in the settlement; and in the list of the population he reports as his family, himself, Hans Just Heyt, wife, Anna Maria, daughter Mary, son John, daughters Magdalene and Elizabeth. These lists were written in English in the handwriting of a practiced penman. Hite and his party made no purchases of land during his stay on the Hudson. In 1717, they are found settled on a large tract of land above Philadelphia, where Germantown was laid out. Some questions arose concerning the titles to these lands. Hite was led to believe the "Fenwick Grant" from Lord Berkley extended along the Delaware River as well as in the "Old Salem proprietary"; but finding that one survey was on the Schuylkill River, he exchanged his holdings at the Germantown settlement for a large tract on this river and removed to the mouth of "Perkimer Creek"—now written Perkomen. There he built a mill and opened up farms, and sold land and made other purchases, becoming prominent in the affairs of the sections around the many settlements. Some of these transactions were with William Penn. In 1729, he learned from John VanMeter that a new country had been discovered in the Virginia Colonies, hitherto unknown to the white settlers, but occupied by numerous tribes of Indians, and that Governor Spottswood was offering great inducements to immigrants. Then it was that Hite became interested by conferences with Governor Penn, and secured what he thought was a grant from the Virginia "Governor and Council,"—his first grant to land in the Shenandoah Valley. He sold his lands on the Schuylkill, and started with what he thought the requisite number of families, to become actual settlers in the new country, so that his grant could be made secure. He is found by record evidence in the Virginia Colony in 1732, struggling to fortify himself against all claimants. This is fully treated in a former chapter of this work under the head of the Van Meter Grants. It may not be regarded as digression to mention in connection with the above statement, that Gov. Penny-

Homestead of Col. John Hite; erected 1753

packer is the present owner of a tract of land that Hite sold when he left Pennsylvania; and the title is traceable to Hite. When Joist Hite arrived in Virginia—a trackless territory lying West of the Blue Ridge, it was within the jurisdiction of old Spottsylvania County; and as Hite and his families were required to settle on the grants he had purchased from John and Isaac VanMeter, who had obtained them from the Colonial Government 17th of June, 1730, Hite's purchase was dated the 5th of August, 1731, and again on October 31st, 1731, Joist Hite and Robert McKay obtained an order of the Governor and Council at Williamsburg, to have surveyed to them 100,000 acres on the West side of the Great Mountain, on conditions of settling one hundred families thereon within two years. During that year, Hite removed to and settled on that land. He afterwards obtained an extension of time for compliance to December 25th, 1734.

On 12th of June, 1734, an order of Council was made stating that Hite had made due proof of compliance with the terms of the grant to the Van Meters, and had settled on the land the regular number of families, and directed patents to issue to him or his assigns, upon the surveys returned to the Secretary. By the conditions to the two Van Meters, there should be forty families seated to get the 40,000 acres. Hite had settled 54 families on this land "by Christmas 1735." Records in the Register of Lands office fully prove the foregoing statement. This matter of settlement is fully set out in the celebrated suit of Hite et als. vs. Fairfax et als., in report of the cases heard in the Courts held to determine titles to and in the Northern Neck. (See 4 Call 42). There the student, if he so desires, will find the high authority of the Court of Appeals settles the question of Hite's arrival and settlement on his grants in 1731. The author will state here that the Hite family tradition is that it was in the Spring of 1732.

Hite and his settlers soon found the Court at Spottsylvania too remote to afford such control as the new settlements required; and he is found at the front to secure the erection of a new County. In 1734 Orange County was taken from the old county and a Court organized. He was appointed by the Governor as one of the justices forming the Court, but he never qualified. Again we find him pressing for a Court to be located in his increasing settlements West of the Blue Ridge. In 1738 Orange was divided into three counties—Frederick and Augusta to be formed in the territory West of the Great Mountains. This period finds the Hite family locating in places that generally served as homesteads for many years. Mention has already been made in other pages of this work, of some members of this noted family; but the writer complying with the request referred to, will give at this point a more extended notice of the Jost Hite family.

Briefly stated, the family on their arrival in Virginia, consisted of the elder Hite and his wife, Anna Maria, (she died in 1738), daughter Mary and her husband George Bowman, Elizabeth and her husband, Paul Froman, Magdalena and her husband, Jacob Chrisman, John Jacob, Isaac, Abraham and Joseph. Hite was a busy man from the time his grants were ordered until they were confirmed. He had numerous surveys made and reported to council, and secured the *Minor Grants* from the Council by direction from the Crown, and thus was enabled to seat his own family favorably.

George Bowman, Paul Froman and Jacob Chrisman, his sons-in-law, were allowed to make their own selection; and grants or deeds were given them for the large tracts so selected for their homesteads. These homesteads and their families will be more fully treated in the succeeding pages of this work. John, the eldest son, married Sara Eltinge of Frederickton, Md., in 1737. She was a daughter of Cornelius Eltinge and Rebecca Van Meter. They lived near Kingston, New York, but later on owned land on the Monocacy in Maryland. The reader will notice in the former pages, that the old pioneer John Van Meter on his explorations, spent some time on his own land on the "Monocacy." John Hite became very prominent in the early settlements; held many offices of trust; was honored and esteemed by his own County, trusted with distinguished positions by the Colonial Government; and rewarded by the British Crown. His children were, Anna Maria Hite, born Dec. 25th, 1738; Rebecca married Chas. Smith; Margaret married Isaac Brown; Elizabeth married, first, Maj. Hughes, second, Rev. E. Phelps—John born June 25th, 1751.

Col. John Hite who, as he was known by this title, will be mentioned as Colonel in this sketch, settled with his father on the Opecquon six miles South of Winchester, where the Great Road crossed that stream. The father erected a stone house on the West side of the road, also a small mill, and built a stone fort on the East side near the first residence erected by his son. The families occupied separate homes, but held the land, mill and forge in common. Many neighboring settlers found refuge in the stone fort. In 1747, John had litigation with workmen for failure to complete his barn. In 1753, he built the fine stone residence near the old fort, and occupied it as his residence with his family during the Colonial period in true colonial style. He was a large slave-holder. His father owned slaves who were artisans; and together they made the Spring Dale settlement hum with the development of this rich section. The tract of land containing about 2,000 acres, embraced a picturesque landscape, and has always been noted for the fertility of the soil. Many productive farms were sliced off in after years; and new owners erected new homes. The original tract was reduced in size, but the substantial and original stone buildings, 150 years old, are in good condition. The old stone house occupied by Douglas Lockwood's family was the one used by Joist Hite as his residence immediately after his second marriage in 1741. His first wife, the mother of all his children, died in 1738 at "Long Meadows," the home of his son Isaac. Elsewhere will be given a copy of the marriage contract between Hite and his second wife. Near this house was a stone mill erected, the only one in that section for many years.

The present Springdale Mill, or Bartonsville Mill, was erected on the site of the old mill, with forge and small fort; which stood near where the present Turnpike bridge spans the Opecquon. The Col.. John Hite residence is now owned and occupied by the family of Mr. Harry·Hack, deceased. Mention will be made later on of others who occupied this celebrated homestead.

Col. John Hite appears in evidence as a man of prominence during his entire life. Old Court records show that he was appointed surveyor of roads in 1747; was a Justice in 1748; Assemblyman in 1752, 1772-1780; was on a Court Martial in 1755 as Captain; was Major in 1756; Lieutenant Colonel 1757; and Colonel in 1760, and President of the Court Martial. This Court Martial inquired into delinquencies of the soldiers of the French and Indian War, and reported their findings to the Court. He was Trustee for the town of Winchester in 1758; was one of the New Court in 1776, and was made County Lieutenant in place of Lord Fairfax. The family records give brief mention of visits from "surveyor Washington" in 1784; and later "from Col. Washington." He died in 1792; his daughter's second husband, Mr. Phelps, was a Methodist minister of the old style, and preached at Stephensburg. John Hite jr., only son of Col. Jno., married Susana Smith, and rebuilt the mill near his father's in 1788. He afterwards moved to Rockingham County, and had for a second wife Cornelia Reagan. His family record shows that he had 20 children. It is not known what became of the twenty children, beyond a knowledge of their migration to other States. Several remained in the Valley. Only a small number reached the age of maturity. Jacob, a son of John Hite, Jr., married Sally Scales of North Carolina, daughter of Maj. Nat. Scales. A daughter by this marriage, Mary Scales Hite, married John Laidley of Scotch descent. His father, Thomas Laidley, came from Scotland in 1774; he served as a soldier in the Revolutionary War. After the War, he settled on the Monongalia River. He was in the Virginia Convention in 1788. His son John was a lawyer; he served in the War of 1812; practised law in Cabell County, Va., and was in the Virginia Convention of 1829-30. John Laidley's son, Hon. W. S. Laidley, is an eminent lawyer in Charleston, West Virginia, and in active practice at the age of seventy.

Jacob Hite, second son of Joist Hite, chose for his homestead a large tract of land in the northern part of Frederick County, where he erected substantial buildings for his own family—and also numerous buildings for several other families who joined him—and also "quarters" for his slaves. It was not long before his settlement acquired the name of Hite's town; but later on, when Berkeley County was formed, and the County seat to be chosen, Hite felt secure in his claim that his village was the most central and offered to dedicate land for a Court House and Public buildings. Martinsburg was then a village and entered the contest. The rivals for the prize were led by two men of pronounced ability, Gen. Adam Stephen for Martinsburg, and Jacob Hite, for his village (Now Leetown). Stephen and his followers secured the selection of Martinsburg. Hite always claimed that fraud had been practiced, and proved his case, but too late to serve his purpose. He then sought relief before the House of Burgesses, and endeavored to have another County carved out of the Eastern part of Berkeley and a slice from Frederick, but when he found this formation would leave his village in Berkeley County, the project was abandoned. Jacob was very prominent in the early settlement. He is found with his father, the elder Hite, before the Governor and Council, seeking cause of delay in confirming the *Minor Grants* to the families who were erecting their homesteads on the original grant. Then he is found before the Courts of Orange, assisting his father to secure the services of the County Surveyor to "lay out roads," in the Southern part of what was afterwards Frederick County. The family records and tradition show that he visited Ireland in the interest of the infant Colony, that his father was planting in the Sherando Valley, and was successful, returning with quite a number of Scotch-Irish families who soon became helpful in the development of the country. On this return voyage he made the acquaintance of Catherine O'Bannon whom he married. She only lived a few years, leaving three sons who became distinguished men in their day, Capt. John, and Col. Thomas Hite, and Jacob O'Bannon Hite. Jacob's second wife was Mrs. Frances Madison Beale.

Her father was Ambrose Madison, descendant of the emigrant who settled in Gloucester County, 1653. It was through this line that we find James Madison Sr., son of Ambrose Madison and Frances Taylor, who married Nellie Conway 1749. Their son James became President of the United States. By the O'Bannon marriage Jacob had two daughters, viz. Mary Hite married Rev. Nathaniel Manner and had for a second husband Rev. Busby, and Elizabeth, her sister, married Col. Lawrence Beale. The children by Jacob's second marriage were a son and daughter, George and Eleanor.

The marriages of Jacob's children is given briefly: John married Sarah ——————— and had three daughters, Mary married Edward Grant, Catherine married Thodoric Lee, Sarah married Alex. P. Buchanan, Second, Thomas Hite, born 1750, married Frances Beale in 1772. He lived in the house built near Lee town and called it New Hopewell; was a member of the House of Burgesses. His two children were, (1st), Frances M. Hite, married Carver Willis in 1798. (2nd), James Hite, born 1776, lived at the old homestead during his entire life and died there in 1855, married three times, first wife Juliett Baker 1798, children by this marriage, Frances Conway, married Dr. Wm. Waters, Juliett Wood, married Dr. Thomas Briscoe, Thos., born 1805, died 1883; Mary Ann, married Jacob Grove in 1806. He married his second wife in 1813, their children were Eleanor Briscoe, married Isaac S. Bowman, Elizabeth S., married Dr. W. D. Hale, Charles J., married Rebecca Bowman. James, the fifth child, known as Col. James Hite, married Lydia Peterson, only one child by this marriage, named Peter Yost Hite, born in 1832. Here we have the pronunciation of the elder Hite's name as the family regarded it in that day.

George Hite, son of Jacob by second marriage with Frances M. Beale, grandson of Joist Hite, married Debora Rutherford. He served as Captain of Volunteers in the Revolutionary War, and in 1801-1817 was County Clerk of Jefferson County, Va., their children being Robt. C. Hite, married Courtney A. Briscoe, and was Clerk of Jefferson County; Frances Madison, married James L. Ranson, Susan Rutherford, married John R. Flag; Mary E., married Richard B. Beckwith; Margaret entered a convent. Jacob O'Bannon Hite, mentioned as the third son of Jacob, was killed by Indians in South Carolina. The mention of this incident very properly introduces the very dramatic incidents in the life and death of Jacob, the father of the last named son. After his unsuccessful effort to secure the location of the County seat of Berkeley County on his land, he became dissatisfied with his surroundings and sold the larger portion of his land in Berkeley County, and prepared to move his family to South Carolina. Before leaving, however, he made ample provision for such of his family as desired to remain in Virginia. His son Thomas and his Daughter, Mrs. Willis, and his son George, as the family tradition gives it, endeavored to dissuade their father from this removal, he would not yield. Thomas and Mrs. Willis were given large tracts of well improved land not far away from their old homestead, and George was placed at William and Mary College; and then in 1786 he started on his southern journey with his wife and younger children and his slaves, and a few neighboring families migrated with him. Kercheval says, "He had not been long settled in his new home in S. C. before the Indians murdered him and several of his family in the most shocking manner"—then adds—"before the bloody massacre took place, an Indian squaw who was much attached to Mrs. Hite, called on her and warned her of the intended massacre, and urged her to remove with her little children to a place of safety. Mrs. Hite immediately communicated this intelligence to her husband who disbelieved the information, observing "the indians were too much attached to him to do him any injury." The next morning, however, when too late to escape, a party of Indians armed and painted in their usual war dress, called on Hite and told him they had determined to kill him. It was in vain that he pleaded his friendship for them, and the many services he had rendered their nation. Their fell purpose was fixed, and nothing could appease them but his blood and that of his innocent and unoffending wife and children, they barbarously murdered Hite, his wife, and several of their children. After this terrible massacre they took two of his daughters, not quite grown, and all his slaves as prisoners, and carried off much plunder and booty." When we recall that Jacob Hite with his father spent the greater part of their lives with several Indian tribes, and were on friendly terms and understood Indian habits, customs and Indian treachery, it is strange that he allowed his delusion to overcome his caution and thus be sacrificed. Kercheval in his narrative concerning this massacre states that he obtained his information from Jacob's son, Col. James Hite, and then adds, "Mr. Hite kept a large retail store, and dealt largely with the Creek and Cherokee tribes. It is said a man by the name of Parrish who went to Carolina with Hite and to whom Hite had been very friendly, growing jealous of Hite's popularity with the Indians, instigated the savages to commit the murder, and then adds that about the year 1784 or 1785, he saw the late Capt. George Hite (Who had been an officer in the Revolutionary Army), who had just returned from an unsuccessful search after his two young sisters, who were taken captives at the time of the murder of his father. He had traversed a great part of the southern country among the various tribes of Indians, but could never hear anything of them. Capt. Hite, a short time after the war of the Revolution, recovered part of his father's slaves who had been taken off by the Indians, and states that one of these slaves was owned by Maj. Issac Hite of Frederick County. This woman brought home an Indian son. Kercheval adds that he frequently saw this son, who had all the features of an Indian; and that part of Hite's slaves remained with the Indians and were kept in rigorous slavery; and that in the winter of 1815-16 he fell in with Col. Wm. Triplett of Wilkes County, Georgia, who informed him that in the Autumn of the year 1809 he was traveling through the Creek country, and saw an old negro man who told him he was one of Jacob Hite's slaves, taken when his master and family were murdered in S. C. He further informed Col. Triplett that there were then 60 negroes in possession of the Indians, descended from slaves taken from Hite, the greater number of whom were claimed by the little Tallapoosa King." It is a well known fact that when the Creek, Cherokees, Chicasaws, Choctaws and other tribes were colonized in their reservation of what has since been known as "Indian Territory," beyond the Mississippi River, they carried with them a large number of negroes and half-breeds, that no persuasion or force on the part of the Government could induce them to leave behind them in the States, so this accounts for a large number of negro slaves owned by these tribes at the outbreak of the Civil War; and why the tribes were so intensely Southern in their sentiments; many of whom were gallant private soldiers and even officers in the Confederate army. The writer while U. S. Marshall in Texas prior to the war, had occasion to visit the territory, and was astonished to see the great number of negro slaves held by the Indian planters, and upon inquiry learned that the original stock had been captured from the whites in S. C., Miss., Fla., etc., before the tribes were removed to their reservations. Doubtless many of those seen by him were descendants from the slaves of the Hite family. They could speak no language but the tribe's, with whom they lived.

The writer has additional traditionary history relating to the capture of the Hite daughters and slaves, which may be regarded as authentic, considering the source; and as it presents a pathetic coloring to the sad picture drawn by the old historian Kercheval, the writer will give it here as well as he can recall from memory the incident as related to him in the long ago. After the capture of the two young girls, the chief of the Creek tribe chose Eleanor for his squaw wife, and guarded her with great care and concern while the marauders were retreating from the scene of the massacre. At that time the Indians were allies with the British, and the retreat was towards the nearest British Army post. It was during this retreat that Eleanor and a negro girl made their escape. Eleanor was recaptured, but the negro girl, who succeeded in securing a fleet pony, was not overtaken. After the Indians reached the British Army, one of the officers saw the young captive Eleanor, and succeeded in buying her from the chief. He took her to the Florida sea-coast, and there wooed and won the affections of the young Eleanor; but owing to her broken health, as a result of her hardships of her capture and imprisonment with the band of savages, she died at Pensacola upon her arrival there. George Hite, the son, who had been placed at William & Mary College by his father, hearing of the awful calamity that had overtaken the family, immediately started upon a search for his sisters. He found some of the old slaves who enabled him to trace his sister Eleanor to Pensacola. He learned enough to satisfy him that his sister had experienced severe hardship, but no maltreatment, and that she had been cared for by a British officer named Johnson; and in after years he learned of the attachment between him and his sister. George Hite found the negro girl who had escaped and brought her back to Virginia. She soon after gave birth to an Indian boy. In after years, this boy became the father of a notable negro woman, who became the property of Maj. Isaac Hite, of Belle Grove, and was a faithful servant to his family through several generations, always known as aunt Nellie, and was certainly about 100 years old at her death. Jacob Hite, Sr., was Sheriff of Frederick County during his residence in that part of Frederick, afterwards Berkeley County. This office in that day, required the Sheriff to collect the taxes and disburse the same; so this explains the order of Court, Nov. 10, 1749, when Jacob Hite, Sheriff, executed his bond to Court, with James Wood as his surety in penalty of 48,610 pounds of tobacco—"the said, Jacob the Sheriff being required to collect the assessments in kind." He again, Nov. 1750, executed bond as Sheriff, with John Hite as his surety, in penalty of 78,452 pounds of tobacco under such conditions as the Court imposed. The first land upon which Jacob settled, was one of the *Minor Grants* that Jost Hite made to him for 2,668 acres on what he describes "as known as Hopewell Run, in the Northeastern part of Frederick County." From this tract Jacob conveyed to this brother Joseph in 1751, 1,168 acres lying along Hopewell run.

It was on the original tract, that the Hopewell residence was created as the homestead for some member of Jacob's family for many generations.

Isaac Hite, the third son of Joist Hite, was born May 12, 1721 (One family record gives it as 1728), married Eleanor Eltinge, sister to Col. John Hite's wife. He was evidently regarded by his father with much favor. One of the first selections made by the elder Hite as homesteads for his immediate family, was designated by him as Long Meadows, consisting of 900 acres of alluvial soil and beautiful landscape. This he had surveyed, and in his report to the Council at Williamsburg he recites "that it shall become the Homestead of my son Isaac Hite," but e Joist to hold the survey in his name until his said son was seated thereon. This was done in 1737, while Isaac was a minor. The father sold and conveyed from this original tract several small tracts, and in each case he recites that the land so conveyed is part of his son, Isaac's, tract. Isaac spent his entire life upon this fine estate and enjoyed the rural life of a country gentleman. His skill as a planter; his close application to the development and improvement of this celebrated homestead, resulted in comfort and elegance to the owner and his large family, and from his caste of intellect and well disciplined life, his offspring imbibed the principles and traits of character that distinguished many of his descendants as prominent in social and public life, whose influence was felt throughout Virginia and even beyond her borders. The author has had intimate acquaintance with this numerous line; and is inclined to give much space in following up the various lines from their ancestor of Long Meadows; but must confine this sketch to brief mention. Isaac and many of the Hite family and connection, as they ceased from their earthly life, were interred in old Long Meadows Graveyard. Some graves are marked; many were allowed to rest under the sod near their kith and kin, with no distinguishing marks as to who or what they were. But tradition gives pathetic stories concerning some who have slept the years away. Isaac, the subject of this chapter, was married April 12, 1745, died September 28, 1795. His wife Eleanor died November 10, 1792.

The old Long Meadows family graveyard just alluded to, was not far away from the mansion house, and in the Meadow near the yard fence. Here Mrs. Buchanan (Ann Hite), the parents of Isaac and Eleanor, and most of their descendants with a few close friends of the family, were buried up to the time of the Civil War. Federal troops were frequently in camp on and around the beautiful grounds of the old homestead, and consequently as was their custom, destroyed nearly every grave mark, leaving only three old granite slabs to mark the spot where Isaac and wife and daughter, Mrs. Buchanan, had peacefully rested, until this horror swept over the hallowed spot. Long Meadows passed into the hands of Col. George Bowman, a descendant of Joist Hite. In 1845, Col. Bowman pulled down the old house, and erected on the site the modern brick building that has passed into the hands of strangers. The Long Meadows tract, embracing at one time several thousand acres, has long since been subdivided, leaving at this writing the brick house and several hundred acres well cared for by its present owner, Mr. Andrew Brumback, a native of Frederick County. It may be interesting to this line of the Hite family to have a carefully and well formed list of the children of Isaac and Eleanor Eltinge Hite appear at this point for preservation, also of their descendants, all of which in its condensed form has been reduced to accuracy, requiring much time and research. Nothing but reliable authorities have been accepted. (The author has a list of dates of births and deaths).

1. Ann Hite, born Jan. 8, 1746, died Aug. 9, 1816, married James Buchanan of Falmouth, Va. No issue.

2. Mary Hite (Aug. 25, 1748—Jan. 2, 1798).

3. Eleanor Hite (Oct. 27, 1750—Oct. 24, 1781). Married Maj. John Williams.

4. Rebecca Hite (Jan. 19, 1754, married Gen. Wm. Aylett Boothe).

5. Isaac Hite, Jr., (Feb. 7, 1758—Nov. 24, 1836). Married (first) Jan. 2, 1783, to Nellie Conway Madison, daughter of James Madison, Sr., married (2) Dec. 1, 1803 to Ann Tunstall Maury, daughter of Rev. Walker Maury and Mollie Grimes. Issue of Isaac Hite, Jr., by his first wife. 1st. Nellie Conway Hite (Married Dr. Cornelius Baldwin. 2nd. James Madison Hite, married Caroline M. Irvine. Issue of Isaac Hite, Jr., by his second wife Ann Tunstall Maury, 1st, Ann Maury Hite, married Philip Williams. 2nd. Isaac Fontaine Hite, married Maria Louise Davison, daughter of Maj. William Davison and Maria Smith. 3rd Mary Eltinge Hite, married John S. Bull Davison, son of Maj. William Davison. 4th. Rebecca Grymes Hite, married Rev. John Lodor. 5th. Walker Maury Hite, married Mary Eleanor Williams, daughter of Isaac Hite Williams and Lucy Coleman Slaughter. 6th. Sarah Clarke Hite, married Judge Mark Byrd, son of George Byrd and Hannah Allen. 7th. Penelope E. Hite, married Raleigh Brooks Green. 8th. Hugh Holmes Hite, married Anne Randolph Meade. 9th. Cornelius Baldwin Hite, married Elizabeth Smith, daughter of Col. Augustine Charles Smith and Elizabeth Dangerfield Magill. 10th. Matilda Madison Hite, married Dr. Alexander McDonald Davison, son of Maj. William

Davison. Issue of James Madison Hite and Caroline M. Irvine, (1) Isaac Irvine Hite, married Susan Burwell Meade, daughter of Col. Kidder Meade of Lucky Hit, Clarke County, and Rebecca Green of Fredericksburg; his second wife was Mrs. Ann Maria Cutler, only child of Dr. Arthur Hopkins; no children by the second marriage, and of the six children by the first, but three lived to maturity, William Meade was listed in the Confederate Army at the age of 16 and was killed in his first battle, Mary Meade Hite and Susan Randolph Hite, who married brothers, Messrs. Baker, and moved to Florida. 2. Caroline Matilda Hite, married Maj. Alexander Baker of Clarke County, son of James Baker of Stone Bridge, son of Samuel Baker, agent and private secretary of Col. Nathaniel Burrell, who donated the land for Old Chapel; The issue of Alexander Baker and Caroline M. Hite, (1) Maria Ingram, married Dr. Thomas Lewis, had one child—George—mother and son long since deceased. 2. Nannie Hite, married Dr. Cockey, now of Texas. 3. Caroline M. died in the bloom of her beautiful life when about 28 years of age. 4. Alexander, Jr., died as he attained his early manhood. 5. Lelia Hite. 6. J. Madison Hite Baker, both unmarried and reside near Old Chapel. 3. James Madison Hite, Jr., married Harriett Green Meade, daughter of Col. Meade of Lucky Hit—they left one child, Drayton M. Hite who lives unmarried in Baltimore. 4. Ann Eliza Hite, married Julian Skinker of Stafford County. Issue, 1. Thomas J. Skinker, married Nannie B. Rose, daughter of Fontaine Rose and Bettie Maury. 2. Margaretta Skinker. 3. John Calhoun Skinker. 4. James H. Skinker. 5. Mary J. Skinker. 6. John H. Skinker. 7. Cornelius Hite Skinker and 8. Hugh G. Skinker. Issue of Thomas Julian Skinker, 1. George M. 2. Bessie Rose. 3. Irvine Hite. 4. Anne Eliza. 5. John. 6. Thomas. 7. Howard. 8. May Scott. James H. Skinker married 1st Maria Carr, daughter of Judge Carr of Roanoke, no issue; he married second 1886 Annie May Kennerly, daughter of Capt. Joseph McC. Kennerly and Josepha Beale of Greenway Court, Clarke County, Va. Issue, (1) May Clotilde, (2) Dorothy Ann. Cornelius Hite Skinker married Minnie L. Grany of Missouri. Issue, 1. Howard G. (2) Cornelius H. (3) Lois E. Hugh G. Skinker married Ann Lee Rucker. Issue, 1. Hugh Garland. 2. Julian Hampson. 3. Susan Hite. Dr. Cornelius Baldwin married Nellie Conway Hite, issue 1. Eleanor Conway, married Edward J. Davison, Issue 1. Cornelia. 2. William Smith, 3. Edmonia Louise Davison was left an orphan at the age of two years, was adopted by her aunt Mrs. Hay, at whose house in Athens, Greece she died at the age of seven. 2. Mary Briscoe Baldwin went as a missionary of the Episcopal Church to Athens, Greece, and Jaffa, Syria; at the latter place she died and is buried there in the English cemetery. 3. Dr. Isaac Hite Baldwin was a Surgeon in the U. S. Navy. 4. James Baldwin, 5. Ann Maury Baldwin married Isaac Hay, U. S. Consul at Jaffa, had one child, John Baldwin Hay, U. S. Consul Gen. at Constantinople.

Issue of Philip Williams and his first wife, Ann Maury Hite, 1. Philip C. Williams married Mary C. Whitridge, he was for many years a prominent physician in Baltimore, they had four children, 1. John Whitridge married Margaritta S. Brown, he is a physician of Baltimore, issue, 1. Margaretta W. Mary Cushing, Ann W., Mary Cushing Williams married Wm. T. Howard of Richmond, Va., issue, Mary C., Philip W., William W. Williams, Dudley Williams and he married Mary I. Jones, Ann Hite Williams married Thomas T. Fauntleroy, Issue, Philip Williams Fauntleroy, married Miss Battle of Mobile, Ala., is now rector of Mt. Calvary Episcopal Church, St. Louis, Mo., and has six children, Madeline, Frank Battle, Thomas Turner, Philip Williams, Nettie Battle, Zadie Faunteroy. Issue of Thomas Turner Fauntleroy and his second wife Elizabeth Hite, Thomas T., Cornelius, Robert R., Dr. Joseph F., Ann, her sister married Edward J. Willis. Griffin Fauntleroy, Mary, Catherine. Issue of Isaac Fontaine Hite and Maria Louis Davis, Anna J. Hite, married John W. Wright, issue, Maria Louise Wright, married W. S. Cooley, issue, Anna M., Jaquelin S., Louise F., William A., Jane Hite, Davis H.

George Butler Wright married Eltie Canter, daughter of Rev. John Canter, issue Nora, Edgar, Charles E., Maude, Leonore, Howard B., Mattie S.

Isaac Fontaine Hite enlisted in the Confederate Army at the age of 17 under Col. William Morgan, killed at Beverly, W. Va.

Issue of John Bull Davison and Mary Eltinge Hite, Anna M., married Robert H. Turner, and had six children, Lucy E., who married Charles C. Marshall, son of Capt. James Marshall, Anna Davison married Dr. Geo. Wm. Carter, Smith Davison Turner married Julia Cook, Henry A. Turner married Lelia N. Orison, Cornelia Hite Turner married Geo. W. Adams, Philip W. Turner married Mary L. Daniel, Sarah Jaquelin Davison unmarried, she was born in 1829, Virginia A. Davison unmarried, John Smith Davison married Mary E. Bowman, daughter of Isaac S. Bowman and Eleanor Briscoe Hite, daughter of Col. James Hite (Grandson of Jacob, the son of Joist Hite); Issue by this marriage, John S. Davison, unmarried, Mary Jaquelin, Francis A., married Henry H. Olmstead, a great-granddaughter of Col. James Hite, Maury W., Raleigh

B., Walker M., Louise Fontaine, married Rev. Robt. Baker of Winchester, Va., issue, J. Christian Baker, Mary E., Robert Magill, Maury D., Edward S., Catherine S., married Charles A. Stewart, Louise Fontaine, Henry Ball.

Bessie Byrd Davison, seventh child, unmarried, Cornelia Hite Davison, William Davison, married Sallie R. Watson, daughter of William Howard Watson of Greenville, S. C., graduated in medicine at the University of Maryland and practiced in Middletown, Va., now dead, Issue, William W., Jessie B., Nannie D., Mary Eltinge Davison, Alexander J. Davison married Hester M. Marshall, daughter of Capt. James Marshall of Happy Creek, issue, James M., married Mary A. Streepy, Fontaine Hite Davison, William, Cary Ambler, Ludwell B., Charles M. and Alexander J.

Issue of Rebecca Grimes Hite, (daughter of Isaac Hite, Jr.), married Rev. John Lodor, issue, Louise Ann Lodor, married Benjamin Brinker, issue, George Eltinge Brinker, married Olin Brinker, her cousin, Madison Brinker.

Eltinge Lodor married George Hinkley, Rebecca Hite Lodor married Dr. Joseph Lacy, John Shepherd Lodor.

Dr. Walker M. Hite graduated at the University of Virginia in 1832, married Mary E. Williams, daughter of Isaac Hite Williams, issue, Isaac Williams, Camilla Thornton, issue Mary Louise Hite, Isaac T. Hite.

Fontaine M. Hite, George Smith Hite enlisted at the outbreak of the Civil War in Pickett's brigade, wounded near Richmond June 27, 1862, died ten days later in Chimborazo Hospital. Mary Walker Hite married Frederick S. Longfield. Walker Hite married Betty F. Coleman, issue, James Floyd, Lucy Williams, George Smith, Eliza Williams, married Geo. S. French, issue Eleanor Williams, Richard Gibson, Mary E., David Milton, George McComas.

John J. Williams Hite.

Issue of Judge Mark Bird and Sarah C. Hite, Mark Bird and Elizabeth Green Bird who married Judge K. B. Stephenson of Parkersburg, issue, Lucy L. who married Judge Frank S. Tavener, Woodstock, Va., issue, Mary E., Walter S., Chas. Wade, Mark Bird Stephenson married Alice Bolts of Rappahannock County.

Ann Hite Bird, Mary Louise Bird, married Hon. Smith S. Turner, son of Col. Robert Turner, issue, Sallie Bird, Robert Henry, Lucy Green, she married Dr. Edward Browning, issue, Smith Turner Browning.

Mark Bird Turner, Isaac Hite Bird married Lelia Zirkle, issue, Catherine C. and Warren Hite.

William Maury Bird married Miss Culver of Iowa, where he resides.

George H. Bird, Eltinge F. Bird, Sarah Madison Bird married William Twyman Williams, son of Samuel C. Williams, Grandson of Philip Williams and Sarah Croudson, issue, William Twyman Williams, Anna Hite, Philip, and Clayton E., Cornelia Walker Bird.

Issue of Hugh Holmes Hite and Anna Randolph Meade, Hugh S. Hite, he enlisted in the 17th Virginia regiment under Gen. A. P. Hill, and was mortally wounded near Williamsburg, May 5, 1862, and died three days later.

Kidder Meade Hite married Susan Fitzhugh Voss.

Lucy Meade Hite married Charles Shirley Carter, issue, Nannie Carter married Robert Dulaney, issue, Shirley Carter, Marian, John Hite and Virginia L.

Cornelius Randolph Hite married Elizabeth Catherine Stark.

William Fowler Hite married Isabella F. Love.

Henry Bird Hite married Caroline Rose Bird, issue, Henry Bird, Mary Bird, Randolph M., and Preston Bird.

Lewis F. Hite married Abbie James, he is a minister in Boston, Mass. Ludwell Bolton Hite, Haden DuBois Hite, and Maury Grymes Hite.

Issue of Cornelius Baldwin Hite and Elizabeth E. Smith, Cornelius B. Hite married Lewis Marshall, Elizabeth S. Hite married Judge Thomas T. Fauntleroy, fully recorded in sketch of T. T. Fauntleroy.

Matilda Madison Hite married Dr. Alexander Davidson, issue, Annie Maury Davidson and she married Dr. M. Powell, son of Capt. Thomas Powell; McDonald Davidson, John Smith Davidson, Cornelia Hite, Wm. Armstrong married Anna M. Kinbrough, Louise Fontaine Davidson married Col. Mark J. Leaming. Dr. Davidson's second wife was Mary C. Powell, they had six children.

Abraham Hite.

This son of Joist Hite was born May 10th, 1729, married Rebecca Van Meter, Dec. 3rd, 1751; Abraham died Jan. 17, 1790. The Hites and Van Meters were kindred through the first wife of Joist Hite, whose maiden name as fully shown in the foregoing was Dubois, one of the Huguenot families driven out of France; and as will be shown elsewhere, the Van Meters settled on the South Branch of the Potomac River. It was natural for Abraham Hite to visit the Van Meter relatives, and there became acquainted with Rebecca, a daughter of Isaac Van Meter, whom he married in 1751, this is proven in several ways, one of which is interesting and reliable; thus showing the value of County records. Isaac Van Meter in his will, dated Feb. 15, 1754, probated in '57, recorded in the old County Clerk's Office at Romney, W. Va., devises certain lands to Abraham Hite, "husband of my daughter Rebecca." Abraham was a man of much prominence in his day, as will be shown later on. He lived in Hampshire County, and at one time was a large land-holder; represented the County in the Virginia House of Burgesses. The children of Abraham and Rebecca: 1. Isaac Hite, born 1753, baptized by Rev. Zable. 2. Abraham, Jr., born 1755 and baptized by the Rev. Andrews, died in Louisville, Kentucky, in 1832. 3. Joseph, born 1757, baptized by the Rev. Meldren. In the old Orange Court there is of record a deed from Joseph Hite (brother) to Abraham for a tract of land in Frederick County; this tract Abraham subsequently conveyed to Richard and Fielding Lewis (1755). The Hampshire County records of 1763 show conveyances of land to Abraham Hite, and later on show that he was a member from Hampshire County in the House of Burgesses 1769-1771, also 1772-1774; his residence was near Moorefield, on South Branch, and when Hardy County was formed, taking part from Hampshire on the North and Augusta on the South. In 1776 he was a member of the Virginia Convention and chosen by a resolution July 4th, one of a commission to take evidence in regard to claims for lands purchased from Indian tribes. In 1776 he and James Wood (son of the Clerk afterwards Gov. Wood) became sureties for Maj. Charles Seymour for $14,800.00 County money, with which to raise a battalion of soldiers for the Revolutionary War. His military career is interesting and will be briefly given here. He was commissioned Lieutenant of the 8th Virginia Regiment by John Jay, President of the Congress at Philadelphia; May 20th, 1779, he was commissioned Captain in the same regiment; Nov. 23, 1779, he was Paymaster of same Regiment to May 12, 1780, when he was made a prisoner at Charleston, S. C. No one was appointed in his place, and his services were accredited to him until peace was declared. It is well to state here that some confusion has occurred in the family traditions in relation to the incident just related. Some descendants claim that the Paymaster was Abraham, Jr., while others claim that the father while prisoner endured such hardships that his death which occurred Jan. 19, 1790, was the result of his prison life. The writer concludes however that in as much as the father was in active service and always in line of promotion, it was natural that he is the Abraham mentioned in the War records of that period; and had it been the son, his name would appear as Abraham Hite, Jr. Doubtless the son saw service in the war, but it nowhere appears; he and his brother were in Kentucky in 1773, only 18 years old, shows his disposition for adventures, and army life might have had its allurements, as it has for so many young men. But it is likely those brothers saw border warfares in Kentucky; they were in Kentucky in 1775, and settled finally in Louisville after the war, "forming a part of the Bowman and Hite company," who about that period purchased large tracts of land and for years conducted a large business, resulting in great profit to all parties concerned. During the period referred to, Kentucky was treated as Majesterial District of Old Frederick County; and this continued in part until 1778, when it was set off and designated as the County of Kentucky in the State of Virginia. But in the Colonial period, many legal questions were adjudicated in the Justice's Court of Frederick County (See Court Minutes, 1763-68). In 1781, the County of Kentucky was divided into three counties and known as Fayette, Jefferson, and Lincoln Counties. Abraham Hite and his wife Rebecca in their old age left Hampshire County, following their children to Kentucky, and died there. The Hites, Bowmans and Clarkes had at that time become very prominent. A brother of George Rogers Clarke, Jonathan, had married a Hite, daughter of Isaac Hite of Long Meadows, and removed to the Falls of the Ohio, afterwards Louisville. No record of the marriage of Isaac, son of Abraham Sr. Abraham Hite, son of Abraham Sr. permanently settled in Kentucky and married Miss Wynkoop, issue Catherine, born June 20, 1793, James, born June 1, 1794, George, born March 18, 1795, Hannah, born July 3, 1796, Rebecca, born Dec. 18, 1797, Abraham Isaac, born Nov. 18, 1799.

Joseph, the youngest son of Joist Hite was born 1731. Old conveyances are executed by Joseph and Elizabeth, his wife. This is all that has been learned of his marriage, and as he and his wife died prior to 1758, leaving young children, this may be accepted as a good reason why his family record was not preserved. The will of his father is dated 1758, and Joseph is mentioned as his deceased son, so this is conclusive; this will mentions but three of Joseph's children, though other records show that he had four, Joseph, Jr., being one, and he being the oldest child, inherited his father's estate and thus it is known that the children of Joseph and Elizabeth were Joseph Jr., born 1753, was Lieutenant of the 8th Virginia Regiment in 1778, resigned 1780; John, born 1754; William, born 1756, died 1828; Ann, born 1757. Joseph Jr. owned land in old Frederick County until 1815, when he removed to Kentucky. In 1761, Jacob Hite was appointed Guardian of Joseph, in 1774 Joseph Jr. made deeds for land to Thomas Hite, consideration 380 pounds; in 1776, he conveys land to John Hite, and also in 1778 when for the first time his wife joins in the deed. John Hite, second son of Joseph, was a merchant in Shepherdstown and a trustee in 1796. William, the third son, went to Kentucky and had a large family to survive him. No effort will be made to show who composed this family; this will be found in works of other writers on early settlers of Kentucky. Ann, the only daughter of Joseph Hite Sr., married Thomas Cartmell and moved to Kentucky. Joseph Hite Sr. and Jacob owned a large tract of land in the North end of Frederick County. Jacob conveyed a large tract to Joseph in 1746; he was overseer of an important road in that section; on the 27th of Feb,. 1757, Joseph's widow and Jacob Hite were appointed by the Justices Court to administer on the estate of Joseph Hite "now recently deceased;" in the inventory of his estate returned by them to Court, they list: "two Dutch books—a bible, a psalter, testament, prayer-book, money scales, and 14 gallons of rye liquor"; all these articles were used by this family doubtless just as the occasion demanded.

The Bowman Line

Having to a considerable extent given sketches of the sons of the elder Hite, as was stated in the preceding pages, there were three sons-in-law of Joist Hite who formed part of the first immigration, viz, Bowman, Chrisman and Froman, and a fuller mention would be given their families later on. Mary Hite, the eldest daughter of Joist and Anna Maria, married George Bowman prior to 1731, exact date not ascertained. He was beyond any doubt a German; his signature appears among the old County records legibly written in German. Scribes for several years twisted it out of all appearance to the name popularly adopted by the family, to wit, Bowman. He chose for his homestead a heavily timbered section located on the North branch of the Sherando River; where he built a substantial house which continued to be his home during his life. They reared a family of thirteen children, nearly all of whom grew to be men and women, and most of them were settled by their father on choice tracts of land, chiefly in Frederick and Dunmore Counties. Several went farther up the Valley, going as far as Augusta County (now Rockingham). The first child, John George Bowman, was born prior to their arrival in the new country. Joist, the applicant for his order to have the surveys made for the numerous families, mentioned these married daughters and mentions the number composing the family to arrive. The Bowman's were accredited with one male child. Several statements have appeared that this first child was born in 1732 and died in 1749; the youngster may have arrived during the journey of the emigrant train at some point North of the Cohongoruta; at any rate, it must be accepted that he was a member of the family that his grandfather stated was to arrive and settle on his surveys. John Jacob, second son, born December 2, 1733, was killed in battle at Remson's Mill June 20, 1780. He was prominent in Kentucky, not only for his encounters with the Indians, holding the rank of Captain; but was the first County Lieutenant of Kentucky County before it was made a State; he married Grizel Greenlee. Emma Maria Bowman, born 1735; Elizabeth Bowman, born 1737, married Isaac Rudell, an officer under Gen. George Rogers Clarke; Johannes Bowman, born 1738, Sarah Bowman, born 1741, Regina Bowman, born 1743; Rebecca Bowman, born 1745, married George Briscoe; George Bowman, ninth child, born 1747; Abraham Bowman, tenth child, born Oct. 16, 1742, was Colonel of the famous 8th Virginia Regiment, known as the German regiment in the Revolutionary War. Joseph Bowman, born 1752, Maj. and second in command to Gen. George R. Clarke in the Vincennes Expedition, died at Vincennes of wounds, Aug. 14, 1779. His important and interesting journal of this Expedition, is in possession of the Kentucky Historical Society, from which the writer has derived much information; Catherine Bowman, born 1757, died 1826 (twin). Isaac Bowman, born April 1757 (twin); he was in the Clarke Expedition and captured by Indians in Nov. 1779, afterwards escaped and later on returned to the old Bowman home, near Strasburg, Va. Many interesting incidents of his severe trials, told by himself, have been preserved and would find place here, but for want of space; he married Elizabeth Gatewood, issue, Philip, married Isabelle Richardson, moved to Indiana and left a large family; Abraham married——— Overall; Catherine married Dr. Henry Richardson; Susan, married Dr. John Richardson, issue, of Isaac Bowman by his second wife, Mary Chinn. Joseph, married Elizabeth Bowman, a cousin; John, married Miss Williams; Eliza, married Joseph Fauntleroy, Isaac Sydnor Bowman, married Eleanor B. Hite (See Jacob Hite's line); George Bowman, married Elizabeth Hupp; Robert, married Phillippa Glasscock; Mary, married Dr Brinker; Washington, unmarried; Rebecca Bowman, (See Jacob Hite's line).

The Chrisman Line

Magdalene Hite, daughter of Joist, was baptized at Kingston, N. Y., 13th Sept., 1713 (Age not given). She married Jacob Chrisman, a German, and it is highly probable that their bridal trip was a part of the emigrant train that the elder Hite headed for the Colony of Virginia, in 1730. It has been well established that his train composing about 20 families, were on the road from Schuylkill to the wild country West of the Great Mountains in Virginia; that they spent about one year near Shepherdstown, and awaited the order for Joist to have surveys made. When this order came, Jacob Chrisman had selected a tract for his survey at a great spring, which spring was known in 1735 as "Chrisman's Spring," and to this day is one of the land-marks of the county. A large body of land was surveyed for this homestead and boundaries fixed, report made to the Governor and Council at Williamsburg and a grant ordered to be issued. References in old deeds, describe this tract as "the grass land, prairie." Boundaries are "on the no timber line"; and much more to prove that for several miles surrounding this Spring tract, there was no timber suitable for buildings. Chrisman purchased from George Bowman "some acres out of his large timber." Since that day, succeeding generations of this Chrisman family saw great forests spring from this treeless section; and ever on to this writing, this and all contiguous tracts of fine land have been well supplied from the new forests. Issue of Jacob Chrisman and Magdalene Hite, first Abraham, born October 15, 1733; Sarah, born Sept. 23, 1734; Ann Maria, born 9, Nov. 1735; Isaac, born 9 Nov., 1736; Johannes, born 9 March, 1739; Jacob, George, Henry, Rebecca. Of this family much could be said of many of the children who survived the parents. The writer hopes to give more extended sketches of several of the members who became prominent in the development of the old County. Consulting war records of the old Vincennes Expedition, the name of Henry Chrisman appears as a private in Capt. Joseph Bowman's company. The family record shows that a Chrisman married a daughter of Joseph McDowell of "Quaker Meadows," Frederick County, Va., (She had a brother Gen. Charles McDowell who married Grizzie Greenlee, widow of Capt. John Bowman). It is believed this Chrisman was Henry mentioned above; two sons of this marriage, Hugh and Joseph Chrisman, lived and died in Kentucky. The two sons seemed to be attached to the McDowell family, for it is shown that Hugh's daughter Betsy Chrisman married Samuel, son of Maj. John McDowell, and Joseph married a daughter of Caleb W. McDowell, of North Carolina. One daughter of Joseph married a son of Joseph McDowell Lewis, another daughter married Hon. Marcus Cruikshank of Alabama.

The family record grows confusing at this point. Doubtless the McDowell and Lewis families have one that will enable them to trace their lines back to the emigrant.

Joseph's son, George, married Celia McDowell, daughter of Col. Joseph McDowell of "Quaker Meadows." A daughter by this marriage became the wife of Gov. L. E. Parsons, of Ala.; another married Jordan Scott, of Jasemine County, Kentucky; Lewis Chrisman married Miss Lyle of Fayette County, Ky., two sons of this marriage were prominent citizens of Jasemine County, Ky. Polly Chrisman married Samuel McDowell, leaving a son and daughter, William and Sarah McDowell, well known residents of Jasemine County, Ky.

Paul Froman.

Elizabeth Hite, daughter of Joist Hite, married Paul Froman, who was known to belong to the Quaker society. They, like the Bowman and Chrisman sons-in-law, were married before the arrival of the Hite family in Virginia. The old Court records of Kingston, N. Y., show she was baptised on the 4th of Nov., 1711; the tradition of the family is such as to justify the statement that this daughter Elizabeth was the first Hite born in America. Paul Froman selected for his homestead a large tract of land on the North side of Cedar Creek. This tract of land embraced a large scope of country, extending down the Creek to what was afterwards Zane's Forge then extending far North, embracing what was known for many years as Winter Hill. The Brent homestead, in more recent years, the home of Mr. Casper Rinker, now that of his daughter, Mrs. N. B. Clagett. Froman chose for his home a point not far West of Winter Hill, where famous springs abounded, flowing from the base of rugged limestone ridges, which have been called the Little North Mountain. One of his first habitations was made in the form of a block house or fort, which was near the Creek as it flows through some low ground, two acres of which was enclosed by a stockade picket fence, all of which was intended as a place of safety for several other families, who had settled northward and further up the Creek. Froman gave to James Colville and William Bayliss a joint interest in the stockade, in consideration of their good service in rendering the same safe from roving Indians. This grant was understood later on to be an interest in the land, but Mr. Colville's heirs failed to make their claim good. This stockade and first block-house, was for many years the home of the Moss family, now owned by J. W. Cleaver. Froman built a substantial house later on at one of the springs mentioned, for his private use, which was his home in 1743, when he appears in Court and asks for "A road to be opened from the county seat to his house and the settlement on Froman's run—a branch of Cedar Creek." It will be seen in former pages, where and how this road was opened. Dr. Isaac Hite Baldwin owned this homestead and a remnant of the larger tract during his life-time. Since his death it has become the property of J. W. Cleaver. Family tradition fixes 1751 as the date when Froman built the mansion house, and that the house at the stockade was the house referred to in the Order of Court. If that be true, 1751 was an early day for the colonists to build stone houses. The records show that Joist Hite conveyed land to Froman—500 acres using this language, "To adjoin on the side of Froman's survey." This conveyance is recorded in the Orange County Court, before Frederick had a Court of record. Paul Froman and Elizabeth Hite had five children, viz, 1. Sarah Jane, born Nov. 15, 1732, died about 1750; it is well established and claimed by the family that she was the first white child born in the Valley, the writer has vainly searched for evidence to disprove this. The statements made by others in newspaper articles, that two other families claim this distinction, that their family records proved that a child of their family antedated this birth date by several years. They were called upon to prove their claim. One proved the date of one child in 1732, but could not show by any record where or when this child was born. Court records are silent as to whether this family were actual residents in the new territory at that date. It does appear that they were grantees in a deed for land in the North end of the County in 1736. (2) John Paul Froman, Jr., born Oct. 16, 1734; (3) Maria Christina, born March 1, 1736; (4) Elizabeth, born May 8, 1738, married Nathaniel Cartmell and died at their home, "Retirement," about four miles due West from Winchester, (See notes on Cartmell family); (5) Jacob Froman—no record of age—found he accompanied his father, Paul, and family when he removed to Pittsburg where he purchased land; the whole family seemed full of adventure, and were ever ready so seek some new land. Jacob proceeded to look for a better country, and floated down the Ohio on a raft, and landed on the Kentucky shore and became a prominent man in the new State; his brother, John Paul, Jr., soon followed; and the father, with a remnant of his family sold his property at an advance, and thus furnished with a considerable fund, removed to Kentucky; and invested his money in such manner as to result in a wealthy estate for his family at his death. He died an old man. John Paul married a Miss Cartmell, daughter of one of the two brothers who had gone from Virginia to Kentucky; John Paul had the distinction as being on same jury with Daniel Boone, John Bowman and others at Lexington, Ky., in 1784, to decide whether Alexander McKee and John Conelly were British subjects, on inquest of Escheats, etc. Jacob Froman was a member of the Kentucky Convention in 1792. The name of Froman appears several times in the Journal of the General Assembly of Kentucky, during the trying period of the new State. A daughter of Paul Froman Sr. married John Overall (see Overall sketch).

The author has unhesitatingly given Hite the credit of being the first white man to settle in the Shenandoah Valley on the North and West side of the North branch of the Shenandoah River. This has been done deliberately after the most untiring effort to secure facts; fully aware that other historians have written fully on the subject, fixing the date so far in advance of the Hite settlement, that it became necessary to exhaust every conceivable avenue of information to secure facts to prove the date of the first settlement. It soon appeared, however, that the Hite and VanMeter grants had priority over all others, so far as it related to that part of the Valley referred to; and the actual presence of Hite in the country on the Opecquon Creek with his requisite number of families in 1732, which is so well established. The records of the State, Legislative, Executive and Judicial, confirm this. As already stated, the records of the Council show that Hite had complied with the order issued in 1730, and had a record made of his survey for thousands of acres of land, embracing the tracts settled on by the twenty families. The House of Burgesses mention it as a fact in its Journal, that Yost Heite had already made settlements beyond the Great Mountain, and the Governor directed the Minor Grants to be made to such settlers for the land that Hite had filed his surveys for in 1732; and as has been previously stated in these pages, when the Fairfax and Hite suit was pending in the Supreme Court, that judicial body entered an order, stating that it had been fully proven that Hite and a sufficient number of families were actual settlers in 1732; and there is no record evidence that any other person had settled in the Great Valley—certainly not in the Northern part, embraced in what was known in 1738 as Frederick County. Other writers give the names of families who lived at a very early date in the old Mecklenburg neighborhood near the Potomac River, and mention grants to certain families, ante-dating any given to Hite or even the order for Isaac VanMeter to make a survey. This doubtless was taken from tradition long drawn out. Descendants of such old pioneers as Morgan, Shepherd, Van Swearingen and others, could easily be misled in regard to dates. No doubt exists as to their early appearance along the Potomac, but they were not there prior to 1734; and no record from any source can be produced to prove any such claim. The writer, in order to satisfy an enquiry from one of the families who had faith in the tradition, made a second personal examination of every record relating to such incidents, that can be found in the State Library, Land Office, Judicial Reports at Richmond, and had the assistance of the experienced officers in charge, who were eager to give the information for the work in hand. To Maj. John W. Richardson, Register of the Land

Office, the writer and the reader of these incidents are under lasting obligations. His earnest desire to find matter relating to the early history of his State, that would finally determine this important question of the first settlement, coupled with his long experience and intellectual endowment, made it possible for the author to announce who the first legal settler was in the country West of the Blue Ridge, and where he settled.

It must be kept in mind that the first order for settlement in old Frederick County, was issued to Isaac and John VanMeter in 1730, and others whose holdings will be treated later on; and that Hite purchased the VanMeter right to enter and make survey. In 1732, he returned his surveys for numerous tracts; and the first actual deed or grant for land in the lower Valley was to Hite, August, 1734, which is more fully treated in former pages. The author in consideration of the patience of the reader of these pages, feels inclined to close the matter; and only suggests to the student of history, that he will find publications, full of romance, supported by such interesting tradition, founded on recorded facts, that he will be startled by such revelations, but warns him not to accept all such as actual historical fact, until the case is more fully proven. The writer had such startling sensations during the years of his study of this question, when called upon to read and study a carefully prepared paper placed in his hands by Dr. John P. Hale, President of the West Virginia Historical and Antiquarian Society. This paper was prepared for and became part of the records of that Society in 1899. Any student of history will justify the action of the writer regarding this paper. Statements were made that seemed reckless to one whose only aim was to lay before future generations simple facts, to establish beyond all question how, when and by whom this settlement was made. Dr. Hale's attention was called to apparent inaccuracies. His reply only heightened the writer's interest; giving, as he did, his sources of information. He quoted familiar traditionary history, long since disproven by available records; the claim being that one John Smith was in the Shenandoah Valley in 1729, and that he secured a grant for 4,000 acres of land from Gov. Gooch and that there were no land titles until 1729, when Gov. Gooch inaugurated a scheme to give title to settlers. This sounds strangely, when presented as a historical fact. The records are full of grants from all the former governors for at least three-fourths of a century; while there is no record from Gov. Gooch, or any other governor, for land West of the Blue Ridge until 1734. If the numerous grants quoted by Dr. Hale, have no more foundation than this Smith grant, then the paper is valueless as history. The able and accomplished President of the West Virginia Historical Society, referred the writer to two historians who had bestowed much time and effort to secure historical incidents for publication, and stated that he relied on their work for much he had given: One was J. E. Norris, who wrote the History of the Lower Valley in 1889, and Aler's History of Martinsburg; and stated that these gentlemen have fixed a very early period for the first settlement. The author was very familiar with the Norris history; but examined it again to see if it was possible to have proof of the claim made. Norris says that Mr. Howell Brown, surveyor of Jefferson County, informed him that Mecklenburg was settled in 1728; and this, Mr. Norris proclaims as a historical fact, that the old historian Kercheval's idea that the Valley was first settled in 1732 was an exploded idea. The writer has found in his effort to produce facts, that it is safe to keep within the scope and sphere of the first Valley historian, who possessed rare and valuable knowledge, and his statements have been verified by carefully collated facts in our records, so often referred to in this work. Norris says Mr. Brown said, Germans settled at the Pack Horse ford in 1728, and speaks of Richard ap Morgan as a ***German*** of means, education and refinement, and with a large family. This was a mistake. Richard ap Morgan was a Welshman, and more than once he is referred to as a native of Wales. He grew wealthy and prominent in his section, and sold land to many families. This Morgan never had a grant from the government for land. Hite sold him part of his large Hopewell tract in 1735, then Morgan made conveyances—all of which show for themselves. In 1734, grants were made to Morgan Morgan and Thomas Shepherd for land "upon the application and survey filed by Joist Hite." These last mentioned were part of Hite's original 100,000 acre grant, and not of the 40,000 acre grant, often mentioned in the Land Office as the VanMeter survey. In deeds from Morgan and Shepherd to others, this language is used several times that, "the land is part of the original survey," which meant the survey to Hite. The writer has in his possession a certificate from the Register of Land Office in Richmond, that there is no record or any other evidence, that the Morgan or Shepherd grants bear any dates prior to 1734. Mr. Aler's History of Martinsburg is of peculiar interest to that historic town. He does not in any way give proof of any settlement at Mecklenburg in 1726 or 1727; he only writes from tradition. Mr. Holmes Conrad, for many years a resident of Martinsburg, and one of the best informed men concerning incidents of the Lower Valley in the long ago, wrote of this Morgan and others, as coming into the Valley "several years after Hite's Germans had opened the way for settlement." If this could convince the reader from the standpoint of Dr. Hale, and the brief references given by the author, to disprove the claim set out in Hale's paper, we could afford to rest the case, and not pursue a study of other proofs offered by Dr. Hale, to sustain a claim for a much earlier date than any ever offered; and this comes in such unique form, that it is well to give it place, and let it stand for what it is worth. This is popularly known as the "Tombstone incident." Dr. Hale carefully uses the following language, and has it become part of the collected incidents for the Historical Society of which he was President. He says: "There is a tombstone in a churchyard at Duffields, five miles South of Pack Horse Ford, on which is inscribed the name of Catrina Bierlin, born 1687, died 1707." Then adds: "the inscription on which is still legible, erected to the memory of a Christian woman, and bearing date 1707, must be taken as certain proof of a white settlement at that point at least as early as that date. The grave of a woman carefully marked can mean no less." This, if true, would as a matter of course, be conclusive proof that Germans were on the ground prior to 1707; and there could be no end of speculation regarding the matter. The writer will show further on, the impossibility for white people to live in a country absolutely owned and rigidly guarded by savages. No friendly tribes dared go West of the Blue Ridge from the low lands of Virginia, nor come from the North and cross the Cohongoruta into the forbidden country on hunting forays, knowing full well that such savage tribes as the "Shawanees" would either exterminate or be exterminated. John VanMeter is the only white person of whom there is any well founded evidence of entering the forbidden country prior to 1725. VanMeter accompanied the Delawares through the Lower Valley in quest of big game; they met the Catawbas coming from the South. Both tribes disputed the right of entry; a terrific battle occurred, the Delawares suffering a crushing loss. VanMeter barely escaped; the whole tribe would have been annihilated, had it not been for the return of the Shawanees from their big annual hunt on the South Branch of the Potomac. They encountered the Catawbas on Cedar Creek and overwhelmed them with such slaughter, as to gratify the remnant of the Delaware band; and John VanMeter's traditionary history of the battles and his venture, has been carefully preserved and handed down through succeeding generations. VanMeter saw no white people. The reader will observe that Dr. Hale dealt with circumstantial evidence to sustain his claim for an earlier settlement of the Valley; and the author uses circumstantial evidence to off-set same. He felt it his duty to test this claim, and if possible, establish this early date, and thus show to the World that Gov. Spottswood and his chivalrous knights, were not the first to discover the world West of the Blue Ridge Mountains. He addressed a letter to the Hon. W. S. Laidley, a prominent lawyer of Charleston, W. Va., with whom the writer had enjoyed friendly relations for several years. Knowing Mr. Laidley had spent much effort for years as an antiquarian, he felt that he might possess some information that would be desirable to embrace in this work. A prompt reply announcing that he was a member of the Historical Society, the correctness of whose statements I had questioned, as found in the papers prepared by Dr. Hale, their President, was gratifying. Mr. Laidley stated that he was also prepared to assist the writer in reconciling the differences arising from the "Tombstone Incident." Later on, Mr. Laidley furnished the following statement: "The stone was secured by Dr. Hale and is now in the rooms of the Historical Society. The reason it was obtained is, that it was being walked over by cattle and pigs; and to preserve it, it was secured." He adds: "There may have been a church yard some years ago, but it is not the church yard at Duffield at this date. There may have been some dates that were once legible on said stone, but they are not so now. When the Doctor wrote his piece, he had not seen the stone; he knows now that he never saw a report of the stone that had even the name of the woman correctly reported; and we have never seen anyone who ever saw the stone when said dates were legible. The stone says, "Hier Ruet Catrina Beirlin," and says she was born 1687, with considerable doubt on the 6 and 8; then follows a verse, expressive of the faith of the woman in Jesus; after which there is supposed to be a place for the date of her death, and it has been said to have been "1707," but it is not there now. The final figure 7 is to be seen, but no more figures in front of it; and that from the best inspection that can be had, this date may have been 1747 or 1757 or 1767, but could be no other, because by the manner in which the letters and figures are made, the end of every line has a deep dot, hole or depression, by which we may determine figures or letters where we cannot see the lines; and just before the final 7, there is a dot or hole which makes some figure, not a round one, but one which ended as a four, or five, or a six, might, and which no other could; and that no jury, after hearing the evidence of witnesses competent to testify, would render a verdict for 1707 as the date of the woman's death." Mr. Laidley adds, "We cannot believe that this woman lived and died at this place at that time, or there must have been others there with her, and many of them also. To have had monuments there, there must have been considerable civilization, and considerable settlement, with quite a town and quite a people. It was unknown to any one in Virginia, and the Assembly in 1722, by its treaty with the Indians, authorized them to kill all the whites found West of the mountains."

The reader doubtless will agree with the author, that had there been such a hamlet or neighborhood as Mr. Laidley mentions, that it must necessarily have been at that point when the treaty was made. Then it is more than likely the ferocious savages exterminated the entire settlement; but it is not likely that a town or settlement of this class was so totally destroyed and nothing left to tell the awful story of their existence and total destruction, except this tombstone marking the grave of a woman who had died 15 years before their utter annihilation. There certainly would have been some recital around the camp-fires of the Indians who must have glutted themselves in such a massacre, for it is a well known fact that the Redman always delighted to transmit to posterity eloquent accounts of his bloody deeds, but never those of his reverses and lost battles. No, we must agree with all the circumstances, and accept the view taken by Mr. Laidley, that the West Virginia Historical Society did not prove its claims; and we must conclude that there is nothing but imagination in the 1707 date. Later on, other matter will be introduced in treating other subjects, that will prove beyond a doubt that the Colonial government was compelled, as a measure of protection to the Colonists East of the Blue Ridge, to make such treaty in 1722, as was so rigidly enforced, as to preclude the possibility for white men to enter the forbidden ground. Then we have the unvarnished statement of Samuel Kercheval, in his valuable historic collection. He says: "From the most authentic information which the author has been able to obtain, Hite and his party were the first immigrants who settled West of the Blue Ridge, and they were soon followed by others, viz, Jacob Stover, who came in 1733, Allen, Moore, White, and others, in 1734; Richard W. Morgan obtained his grant in 1734, Thomas Shepherd, Van Swearingen, Ed. Lucas, John Lemen, Robert Buckle, Robert Harper, and others, were among the first settlers on the Potomac. Kercheval says, "I devoted much time and research to the question of the settlement of the Valley, and placed the first in 1732." There is one incident connected with the Tombstone referred to, that should be mentioned in this connection, so as to avoid confusion to the reader when he chances to see and read the inscription on a tombstone near Duffield Station on the B. & O. R. R., Jefferson County, W. Va. This stone was erected by Dr. J. P. Hale, President of the West Virginia Historical Society, in the Spring of 1900. This was to replace the original, then in the possession and keeping of said Society. The inscription on the old stone was in German, and required many words to express the sentiment animating those who first erected it. Efforts were made by two prominent German scholars many years ago, to produce a correct translation. They differed as to the name, date of birth, and language of the stanzas. Dr. Hale in a letter dated August 23rd, 1900, which was published at the time, says he corresponded with the Rev. Dr. John Scott, and obtained from him a translated copy of the old inscription, which differs as to name and date of birth; Dr. Scott giving the name for the first time simply "Katrina Beirlin," "Born 1686." Dr. Hale accounts for the difference in date, because the stone might not have been perfectly seen; and adds that "a photograph was taken of the old stone when removed, and the photograph brought out the figures plain enough to show the 1686, and that the entire inscription can now be made out except the last line, *"Died in 1707."* This was near the bottom of the stone, more exposed to the damp, and may have been in softer stone; and is now nearly obliterated, only the terminal figure 7 of the date being distinct." This explanation sounds strange when we recall the lapse of time from 1707 to 1887—180 years; the statement of Dr. Scott being, that they found a German inscription plainly preserved in 1887; yet we have Dr. Hale's statement referred to above—in his public letter of August 23rd, 1900—that there was nothing on the last line but the figure 7. Some will say, if the figures were so well preserved in 1887, how could they have been effaced by dampness in 13 years, the time being 1900 when Dr. Hale says the 1707 could not be drawn out by a photograph?

The writer has been tedious in his long drawn-out statement concerning this matter, his excuse being that it has been done at the request of many persons who have differed in their view of the case; and knowing that it is a question that will be mentioned by others who will succeed us, thinks it best to give all readers the benefit of his careful research and study of all matter that could be found to throw any light upon the strange old monument. His conclusion is that there never has been a time within the last 100 years, when any translator of the German could have made an absolute correct writing from that rough old sandstone, showing all the figures, language and dates. No two persons who have tried within the last 50 years, have produced the same results. And reader, go into any of the old churchyards and examine the rude old sandstones with their inscriptions in English, and you will be astonished at the formation of the old figures. Many dates can only be settled by conjecture. While there is unmistakable evidence that quite a number of families came into the Valley with the "Heydhdt" emigration or soon thereafter followed, and became squatters, claiming what was called the Tomahawk Right; and then waited for title to issue from the Colonial government; many of this class were compelled to purchase from Hite, Fairfax, Ross and others, who had proceeded in an intelligent way to secure title for immense tracts of land. Then later on, they sold their surveys of the sub-divisions, to the families as they made their selection.

It must be borne in mind that although Hite was the first legal settler in the northern part of the Shenandoah Valley, he was not the first to secure an order from the Colonial government to make survey, and locate families West of the Blue Ridge. In many conveyances from Hite for land in that section, the description locates the grant; and mentions the Isaac VanMeter grant which he purchased, and from which many of the farms lying along the South side of the Opecquon embracing the vicinity of both Stephens City and Middletown, were taken. One grant, so often mentioned by magazine writers, called the "King Carter Tract," deserves attention here because of the date given for its entry, 1729. This kind of history is very misleading, and gives endless trouble to the student of history. The claim is, that this grant was for 50,000 acres and embraced the large area on the West side of the Shenandoah River, composing all the Southern part of Clarke County. Col. Robert Carter was a large land owner in that section at an early day, but he obtained all his holdings through the Culpeper or Fairfax grant, and not through the medium of Colonial government grants; and it should not be accepted as a fact that "King Carter's grant" was classed with those granted to emigrant families desiring to settle on the West side of the Great Mountains. The confusion naturally occurs—Col. Robert Carter had Royal grants from the Crown for large tracts of land, but these grants embraced sections altogether East of the Blue Ridge but as is well known to many, Carter represented the Culpeper grant at one time, and was a faithful agent, for we find him as early as 1728, entering caveats in the Court of the Governor and his Council, in the interests of the Proprietors of the Northern Neck, to stay the issue of patent grants to many persons applying for orders for surveys, some of whom had already invaded the Fairfax proprietary. Col. Carter was rewarded for his service by receiving a lease from the Fairfax estate for many thousand acres of land, to run 100 years, "and renewable forever." (Fuller mention of this sketch of Col. Carter). The lease was not obtained until litigation was instituted, to ascertain the rights of a company composed of Russell, Chew et als. This company had filed an application for order June 6, 1728, to survey 50,000 acres, and locate families between the Great Mountain and the Sherando River. This evidently was intended to take the section on the South and East side of the river in the vicinity of Front Royal. This company was granted 10,000 acres by the decision of the Court; and during the sessions of the Council, 1733-4, William Russel and Larkin Chew received their grant; (See MS. files, Land Office, Richmond, Va.). We must not suppose that Hite had no rivals in his early efforts to make settlement of the Valley; for we find an order in Manuscript Journal of the Council, dated June 17, 1730, giving permission to Jacob Stover to survey two tracts of land of 5,000 acres each, not heretofore granted to settlers, that may be found West of the Great Mountains; one tract of 5,000 to be surveyed and laid off on both sides of the South Fork of the "Shenando river; one tract of 5,000 to be surveyed and laid off on the South side of the North fork of the Shenando river." The old Spottsylvania County records show that Jacob Stover received grants for the two tracts named in his order; both grants dated Dec. 15, 1733, and as they bear an earlier date than any other in the Shenandoah Valley, a brief description is here given of both tracts: Tract No. 1, On the West side of the Great Mountains, beginning, etc., on the Sherando River, at the foot of the Great Mountains, thence, etc., to the foot of Naked Mountain at the upper end of large island in the river, as per survey filed of 5,000 acres of unclaimed land,"—2nd tract, "Lies on the west side of the Great Mountains, on the South fork of the Sherando river, beginning, etc., above the mouth of Hawk-bill's Creek over against a high mountain, as per survey filed for 5,000 acres of unclaimed land." One of these tracts embraced the region where Strasburg now stands, known for many years as Stover's Town, and included what is now called Massasnutten section. The other certainly embraced much of the country extending up into what is known as the Luray Valley. Some writers claim that a large German settlement had been seated in the *Massaniting* region for several years previous to the date of Jacob Stover's application; and that Adam Miller and others contested the application of Jacob Stover. It will be observed, however, that the language used in the Stover grants expressly states that it was unclaimed land. According to Kercheval, Stover was compelled to adopt dangerous methods in order to secure his grant, being required to seat the requisite number of families. It seems strange that if Adam Miller and his neighbors were on this tract, that Stover would have taken such desperate chances to secure his grant. Kercheval says that when his petition was presented to the King, he had the requisite number of persons on the land, he having given human names to every horse, cow, hog and dog he owned," which he represented as heads of families; and some may wonder why Adam Miller and his associates did not interpose some objection. We find Miller with a petition dated 1733, urging the Council "to take up a claim that he and 51 other inhabitants at Massanitting are anxious to present in a complaint that Jacob Stover, having secured a grant for the land on which they had settled, refused, or was unable to make them good deeds." The magazine articles and traditionary history relating to this Mueller (or Miller) settlement, reveal much of interest, and entitled to consideration. A careful study proves that Stover had associates in his effort to settle the country South of the North Fork of the Shenandoah River; and this study reveals a class of persons entirely distinct from the Hite immigration which crossed the Cohongoroota, entering the Valley from the North. Gov. Gooch in a proclamation issued 13th of March, 1742, recognizes Adam Miller as a citizen of the Sherando Country, and accepts proof that he had so resided in that section for 15 years; and upon such evidence he was naturalized, by subscribing the oaths of renunciation and allegiance; and if he was there, we must take it for granted that others had joined him.

The author has in his experience in the study of the early settlements, found much to enlighten as well as to confuse the student; and this incident is prominent in this class. The document referred to as the Gov. Gooch paper, has been carefully preserved in printed form by the William & Mary College Quarterly, Vol. IX, No. 2. pp. 132-33. But whence came this Miller and Stover party? We will endeavor to show this fully in sketches of families, etc. At this point, however, the author will mention that if any reader so desires, he will find in the State Library at Richmond a paper signed by the settlers at the Massasanutten, referred to above; which being in the form of a petition addressed to Gov. Gooch complaining of the injustice shown them by Jacob Stover, who represented himself as owner of vast tracts in the Massaniting country, and had induced them to settle on the land, but was not the legal owner, etc., which petition unfortunately is not dated. But we must conclude that it was presented by the signers prior to its entry in the Calendar of State Papers, which was dated 1733. The petitioners state that they had four years previously purchased 5,000 acres of land from Stover, and had seated their families. This implies that Stover and those families were on the ground in the vicinity of Strasburg and Massanitting region in 1729. The following named persons are the signers:

Adam Mueller,
Abraham Strickler,
Mathias Selzer,
Philip Lang (Long),
Paul Lung (Long),
Micheal Rinehart,
Hans Rood,
Micheal Kaufman,

It will be observed by some readers, that the names of all signers became prominent in that part of the Valley in the development of old Frederick County; and it may also be observed that all their descendants were inclined to remain South of the North Fork of the Shenandoah River for more than 100 years.

The author knows that traditions have been kept in several families, which indicate rivalry between the two immigrations of the Opecquon and Massanutting; and the river flowing from the upper Valley passing Strasburg and the Massanutten, is mentioned frequently as the dividing line between the sections.

We find another competitor for Hite to contend with, appearing in the same year with the VanMeter brothers, John and Isaac, before the Governor and Council, with a petition to allow certain families to enter and survey tracts of land on the Opecquon Creek in the country West of the Sherando River. This petition was signed by Alexander Ross and others, whose names will appear later on. The order was made on the 28th of Oct., 1730, granting Alexander Ross and his joint petitioners the right to survey and lay out contiguous tracts not exceeding 100,000 acres. from such waste land not embraced in any order heretofore made for the seating of families on the West side of the Great Mountain. This is the most general and liberal order made by the Council; and only required families to be seated on well defined surveys, but not limited as to time, and when so seated, the proper deeds of conveyances should issue. Much confusion has arisen about deeds, grants, etc. Very often writers have confounded Acts of the Council. The first act of Council was an order entered upon the petition filed; the next act being a grant to the principal petitioners—one or more— proof being shown that families had been seated. The next act would be for deeds to be made to such families for the tracts upon which they were actually seated, same as found in the grant to the principal. This helps to explain why references are so often found in the first deeds for land in the new country West of the Blue Ridge, many such deeds being recorded in Spottsylvania County until 1735, then in Orange County, until 1743, when they first appear in Frederick County Court records. For the reason stated, some writers have been led into error in their statements that grants were issued to Stover, Hite, Carter, Ross and others, by the dates of the order for survey, the order reading, "An order of survey is granted, etc." But it must be remembered, that the surveys had to be filed in the Governor's office before the grant was issued for the petitioner to hold the tract; and also that many orders granting the right to survey large tracts and seat families thereon were never further heard from.

Alexander Ross and his settlers were slow in securing their grant for the large tracts. The first appears Nov. 22, 1734, for 2,373 acres. This tract lies North of Winchester. Ross sold and conveyed from this tract 214 acres to Joseph Bryan, one of his original petitioners. This is the first deed from Ross recorded in Frederick County, executed April 13, 1744. The description, as shown in the record, will repay some descendants of the parties and show where their ancestors made their first homes. The 2,373 acre tract referred to was part of the 40,000 acre tract Ross surveyed and laid off and sub-divided into tracts or homes for the Quaker families drifting from Pennsylvania, Delaware, and other points North in 1734. This immense body of land was the country extending from the Opecquon to and including the Apple Pie Ridge section, extending his survey North along the Opecquon. Of course, Ross found obstacles in the form of what is generally known as the Joist Hite grant. Hite had obtained his order through John Van-Meter in 1730, to make similar surveys for the families that followed him, and Ross found not only monuments describing the boundaries of Hite's sub-divisions, but found families already seated and building their cabins. Some such surveys Ross disregarded, which ended in caveats from the Hite settlers. Ross lost out on this. However, he found a vast territory unclaimed, though his surveys never aggregated the 100,000 acres he expected to find North of the North branch of the Sherando River. It may be added here, that pending the controversy, Ross lost many of the Quaker families, some of whom took titles from Hite and became so firmly seated, that for more than a century the land remained in the family names.

CHAPTER XLIX

Daniel Morgan, Colonial Soldier, Revolutionary War Hero and Citizen

Although much has been said of General Morgan in other pages of this volume, as a hero of the Revolutionary War period, the writer has been urged to embody in this work all matter discovered by him in a study of this remarkable man. It must be admitted that much has been found relating to Morgan's life that has never hitherto been published. Interest may attach to some incidents gathered from the mass of notes collected by the author. Several books and historical sketches have been written relating to his military life. This need not be repeated here. It may interest some readers to learn something of the birth and parentage of the man of so many parts.

In numerous tracings through every avenue offering a clue, we discover that Daniel Morgan's parents lived in New Jersey in 1752. The Morgans, several in number, were known as Welsh Iron Workers; and were induced to emigrate to America at the instance of Allen and Turner, founders and owners of the celebrated Union Furnace Iron Works and Plantations in West Jersey and Pennsylvania. Some evidence of their residence at Durham, Penna. The history of Bucks County, Penna., contains many statements relating to this family, pointing out the birth-place of Daniel Morgan; and identifies the youth of that period and section with the Daniel Morgan who appeared in Virginia as Captain of Militia, in 1771. This was the young Morgan who appeared in Court May 3, 1758, at Winchester, Va., to answer the charge of assault and battery. Tradition fixes an earlier date, that of 1755, and that his parents lived near what is now the village of Nineveh, Warren County; and that young Morgan was with Braddock's Army at its defeat.

Howe in his statements relating to this expedition, gives quite a sensational account of young Morgan being court-martialed for "drubbing an English Officer." Morgan was sentenced to receive five hundred lashes. After receiving four hundred and fifty, Morgan fainted, and escaped the other fifty. The author finds many conflicting statements connected with this tradition. Once he was informed that Morgan received this punishment in South-West Virginia; and that "the oak tree that served the purpose of a whipping-post, was carefully guarded, and is now in good condition."

There seems to be no necessity for belief of this incident, to give notoriety to the young man. Old court proceedings give evidence of his presence at Winchester, attending court, during the time of Braddock's War. The old records also reveal the fact that he rendered service with the Minute Men several times during the Indian incursions on Great Cacapon and South Branch; and had his allowance for services certified. This has been more fully mentioned elsewhere. The New Jersey and Pennsylvania historical notes show that Daniel and his parents disappeared from that section in 1754; one writer stating that doubtless the parents had died, and Daniel alone sought a place in Virginia.

The young man was not averse to rough amusements; and more than once was haled before the Court, for "assault and the disturber of the Peace on public occasions." His experience gradually wrought a change in his life; for after ten years thus spent, we find him listed with taxable property and taking his place among a better class. The court appointed him Overseer of a road in 1766. This seemed to stimulate him. The following year, he received a premium for raising 728 pounds of hemp; and gives a list of horses, cattle, etc., for taxation. Sept. 10, 1773, the Justices entered this order in the proceedings of that term: "It is ordered that Daniel Morgan carry Timothy Ragan, a felon who broke the jail at Anne Arundel County, Maryland, and deliver him to the Sheriff of said county, and bring in his account of expenses, at laying of the County levy." In October, he was allowed £6 2.8 for same.

The same year he gave a mortgage on a tract of land, and included several negroes. The young Captain borrowed the sum to pay an old debt on the farm. From this date he prospered. Old records show that Capt. Morgan was accumulating property; securing possession of valuable tracts of land. One of these he desired to improve, and establish a home for his family. He had then married his only wife. This was Abigail Bailey. (The name has been written *Agazail* in several transactions.) This tract contained 255 acres; and upon this he built the famous Saratoga Stone Mansion, during the time when he was enjoying his leave of absence from his command. He had been requested to recruit the regiments referred to. This virtually made him commandant of the Military District. He found the condition of the prisoners, confined in stockades near Winchester, deplorable; and adopted a plan to separate them, and provide for their employment. He made several large details, and set them to work repairing roads in the vicinity of Winchester. One detail of 84 men he took under his own supervision, and undertook the work of quarrying stone for his own house. The men found it a healthful exercise; and no word of complaint came from them. But one of the officers of the Virginia Regiments, preferred charges against him for unjust and unauthorized treatment of the "Dutch prisoners." Morgan was requested to make his report to the War Office. The examination of this report and his straightforward statement together with affidavits made by some of the prisoners, exonerated Morgan; and he was allowed to control all the prisoners in his district. This met the approval of Joseph Holmes, the Deputy-Commissioner General of Prisoners. (See archives of War Dept., Class A, Convention Prisoners.) His house was completed about 1782. His settlements with workmen in 1783, reviewed by the court, give itemized accounts of work done, for which they obtained judgment against the General. It is thought he spent about ten years at Saratoga, where his children were born. He was in Winchester in 1796, and is found about that time in the house on Ambler Hill, which in after years became the property of Rev. A. H. H. Boyd, D.D., now known as the home of the late Judge Joseph H. Sherrard. It was there he spent the remainder of his life; died there in 1802; and by his will it will be seen he left a large estate. This was executed 17th March, 1801, and witnessed by John Walton, Jacob Harmer, and Obed Waite. To this he added a codicil, 17th March, 1802, witnessed by Obed Waite, Hamilton Cooper, and John Kingan. His will is recorded in the Old District Court, and now on file in the County Clerk's Office of Frederick County. We may add a few of its provisions, to show briefly the extent of his estate and names of his family. He declares, "his faculties of mind are good"; but being weak in body, expresses "an abiding faith in the atonement of my Blessed Lord and Savior, Jesus Christ." The first devise states he had executed two trust deeds on the same day, for "the place called Saratoga, containing 255 acres, also 407 acres adjoining the lands of Thomas Bryarly, the heirs of John Bell, deceased, Richard K. Meade, which was purchased of N. Ashby; also 311 acres adjoining Saratoga, purchased of Nathaniel Burwell, Esq., late of Isle of Wight County, deceased, also 100 acres, purchased of N. Burwell, Esq., of Frederick County, adjoining Saratoga, all of which is in Frederick County, Virginia, also all the stock, slaves, household stuff, and furniture of the said place called Saratoga, and in the mansion house thereon, to hold in trust for my daughter Betsy Heard, wife of James Heard." This additional provision appears: "I now give, devise, to my said daughter Betsy Heard all my land in the State of Kentucky, whether granted for military services, or otherwise * * * * computed to be about ten thousand acres, to her absolutely. * * * * Five thousand acres in Tennessee, on Crow Creek, purchased of Major Armstead for five thousand dollars." A codicil changes this; and provides for his daughter during her life, and at her death, the several large tracts so devised, to pass absolutely to his grandchildren Matilda Heard, Nancy Morgan Heard, Daniel Morgan Heard, and Morgan Augustus Heard. This daughter seems to have touched the old General's sensibilities by the free use of his name. We may properly say here, that the son-in-law, Major James Heard, became a man of national prominence; and his children are freely mentioned in Kentucky history.

A liberal devise is made to his "Beloved wife Abigail, a farm of 278 acres and appurtenances absolutely." "And all the rest, residue and Remainder of my estate, real personal or mixed, I give, devise * * * * unto my wife Abigail, for and during the term of her natural life, and after her decease to my well beloved daughter Nancy Nevill, wife of Presley Nevill."

He also makes this "All my military lands in the Northwestern Territory I give, devise * * * to Presley Nevill, my son-in-law, to be disposed of at his discretion, to him, etc., forever."

The Morgan house in Winchester was erected by Genl. Morgan and has attached to it some traditions that may attract attention, one being that Hessian prisoners were employed in its construction. This has been proven untrue; since the erection of the edifice was about nine years after the prisoners had been released. It is barely possible that some of the prisoners who preferred to remain in Frederick County, were employed by Morgan, as there were men of this class who were skilled workmen. The original building embraced what is known as the Western half of the present structure. Alex. Tidball purchased the old place after the widow's death, from Nancy Nevill and others. The widow died at the home of her daughter near Pittsburg. Tidball made some additions; and Dr. Boyd, when he first occupied the property, completed the change. During Dr. Boyd's tenure, Morgan's two old military chests were stored in the old attic, and left in the house by the Boyd family when they vacated for Judge Sherrard. One of the chests later on was turned over to relic-hunters; and it is said that it became the property of one of his descendants, the wife of Admiral Robeley D. Evans. Genl. Morgan was buried in the old Presbyterian Churchyard. Over his grave was placed a large marble slab bearing this inscription:

"Major General Daniel Morgan
departed this life
on July 6th, 1802,
In the 67th Year of his age
Patriotism and Valor were the
prominent Features of his Character;
And
the honorable services rendered
to his Country
during the Revolutionary war
Crowned him with Glory, and will
remain in the hearts of his
Countrymen
A Perpetual Monument
to his
Memory."

Dr. Foote in his visit to this old Churchyard, while collecting incidents for Foote's Sketches of Virginia, gives this pathetic expression to his emotion, as he stood by this tomb: "Here, then, beneath this slab, the man whose voice could make soldiers tremble with his hoarse shoutings, lies as quiet as that infant there. What a man! A day laborer in this Valley some eighty years ago, a volunteer against the Indians, and marked by his commander as an officer for his enterprise and courage. A wagoner and an abused Colonial Militia-man in the service of his King. An officer of the Riflemen at the storming of Quebec with Montgomery, and at the battle of Saratoga, A major General in the Continental Army, * * * Around him here are the ashes of talent, learning and refinement, a congregation of youth and age."

Rev. Wm. Hill, D.D., Pastor of the old church, officiated at the funeral service, conducted in the old stone church.

During the Civil War, many depredations were made by Union soldiers. The Morgan slab suffered from such acts; pieces of which were broken off and carried away as relics. It was during the Summer of 1865, that an effort was made by some New Jersey visitors to even remove the slab and remains of the old hero to New Jersey. This was forestalled by the prompt and resolute action of Col. Wm. R. Denny and several other citizens of Winchester. They removed the old broken slab to a safe place; disinterred the remains in the night, and buried them in Mt. Hebron, in the lot the Cemetery Company had in the original plan reserved for Genl. Morgan's tomb. The spot has become historic now; the old slab was brought from its hiding and placed over the new grave, and there it remains, the only monument to this truly great man. Many efforts have been made to erect an imposing shaft on this large plot, to preserve and perpetuate a memory of his noble deeds. A grateful Nation may some day atone for this neglect.

In the Old General Court held by Judges Richard Parker and James Henry, at Winchester, Sept. 29, 1797, we find a record of the last public service rendered by Genl. Morgan: He was appointed foreman of the grand jury, which returned several indictments, one being against his friend, Samuel Washington, for assault.

Gabriel Peter Muhlenberger,
Minister, General in War 1776.

The author has many enquiries from persons interested in the life and character of such men as Genl. Muhlenberg; and answering same, will briefly touch upon matter taken from reliable sources.

Pennsylvania Archives of History, substantiates much that has been said of this man, who flashed as a meteor in the Shenandoah Valley, and apparently disappeared.

The Sketch of the Lutheran Church in this work, gives what the writer deemed sufficient at the time; but enquiries show the contrary. Gabriel Peter Muhlenberg was ordained a Minister of the Evangelical Lutheran Church in 1768; served several years with churches in New Jersey; married Anna Barbara Meyer, 6th Nov. 1770, in New Jersey. New fields were opening in Virginia that offered him inducements. In order to serve as pastor in Virginia, he must be ordained by a Bishop. The Swedish branch of the Lutheran, or Reformed Church required this. This branch had always retained bishops; and their discipline required their pastors must be ordained and consecrated by a bishop—and to receive the benefit of the tithes in Virginia, he must be ordained by an English Bishop; so he resigned his charge in New Jersey, and, quoting from his journal: "We sailed March 2, 1772"; and states that he and two other Americans were ordained at the same time, 23rd April, 1772, at Kings Chapel, St. James, by the Bishop of London, Mr. Braidfoot and Mr. White being the two others. On his return to America, 1772, he took charge of the Woodstock Church, as shown in the Church Sketches. On the 21st March, 1776, Col. Muhlenberg marched his 8th Regiment to Suffolk, Va. Subsequent to this, he and his Regiment served in the Carolinas. After this, he returned to the Valley and other places in Virginia, to recruit for the Virginia Regiments. April 1st, 1777, we find him at the head of a Brigade formed from the regiments he had organized. They were the 1st, 5th, 9th, and 13th regiments. They were marched to New Jersey. The German Regiment,

8th, was assigned to a German Colonel. Genl. Muhlenberg was engaged in the campaigns of the North. At the close of the War, he proceeded to the falls of the Ohio, (Louisville), and located his land warrant for 13,000 acres of land. He stood for election for the Third Congress of the United States; was accorded a seat in that body 1793; and served several terms; was elected U. S. Senator from Pennsylvania in 1801; resigned to accept the appointment of Collector of Port at Philadelphia, which he held until his death at his home near that city, Oct. 1st, 1804.

CHAPTER L

Colonial Homesteads and Those of the Nineteenth Century

The writer in his study of old historic events of the County, always derived pleasure in any information that could designate the location of some of the homesteads of the old settlers, and date of erection; and for this reason, he will take some space to reproduce not only these, but also such as he discovered by close investigation. It may prove interesting to readers 'ere this Twentieth Century closes.

Kercheval, in his history of the Valley, mentions quite a number of fine houses he had seen, but fails to mention any belonging to the Colonial period, and only one prior to the year 1800. This seems very strange; for it is well established that several good stone houses were built between 1750 and 1770, and the owners were well known to the Valley historian. As already shown in sketches of the Hite family, Joist Hite and his son John were building stone houses in 1747; and in 1753 the splendid stone house now owned by the family of Harry Hack, was built.

The old Cartmell stone house was built in 1771, known as *Homespun,* now the property of Dr. Henkel. The date can be seen in the South gable. About 1810 Martin Cartmell added to the original a stone structure, which he called the Ball-room addition. The first floor was called the drawing room, while the second floor was the ball-room. This building grew unsafe, owing to faulty foundation, as affirmed by the owner, while others hinted that its dedication had somewhat to do with its fate. After standing about forty years, it was thrown down, leaving the original building, which from present appearances, may be seen in good condition a hundred years since.

Greenwood

On the Opecquon, from the head spring down to the stone buildings erected by Hite, can be seen several remnants of original Colonial houses. The Grenwood homestead, now owned by the Steck family, where Samuel Glass, the emigrant, settled in 1736, where he erected a large log building for his residence. To this was added a wing by his descendants; and still later, about the year 1800, the log structure was covered with wide plank nailed on with nails made by negro slaves of the family. Later still, in the 19th Century (1850) the old planks were removed and more modern style adopted to cover the old log-house. It was during this change, the writer saw the huge logs of the original building, and learned much concerning its history from two old negro women then supposed to be over 100 years of age, slaves of the original owner. The old logs contained many markings of the workmen, indicating the date of erection, and time table of carpenters, etc. The whole structure perfectly sound. To this, the present owners have added many improved conditions, but in no other way have disturbed the old emigrant's building. Greenwood was the home of Mr. James Carr Baker and his family. Here he reared his four children. The writer, by his alliance with this family, became part of the old homestead. Memories too tender to mention in this volume, cluster there still. His two children were born under the old roof-tree!

Belleville, now the property of John Cochran, and for many years owned respectively by L. G. Miller, Stacy J. Tavenner and Wm. R. Campbell, was the home of Mr. Becket, a son-in-law of emigrant Glass. His first house was the log cabin which served for his home until 1774, when the present stone house was in process of building, not finished, however, until after the Revolutionary War.

Cherry Meade, lower down the stream, now the property of John G. Miller, was founded by David Glass, son of the emigrant. The house was a large log building. The original structure remains, with some additions made by subsequent owners. The old logs are no longer in view. Thomas Kramer succeeded Mr. Beckett and held it until 1840, when R. Madison Campbell made it his home until about 1873. Some of the tenderest memories of the writer are indissolubly linked with Cherry Meade while it was the hospitable home of Mr. Campbell.

Long Meadows, now the property of Robert J. Glass, was settled by Robert Glass, son of the emigrant. The family name has always retained ownership of this magnificent homestead. At one time the estate embraced 920 acres of the most fertile land on the Opecquon. Several large tracts were sold off subsequent to the Civil War, thus reducing Long Meadows to its present boundaries. The stone house now seen is on the original site built prior to 1800; adjoining it on the West is the old stone building used by the neighborhood as a Fort during Indian forays. Around this old building a stockade was erected in 1755. Major Glass was commissioned by the County Court to summon Minute Men to assist in fortifying against Indians. The General Assembly voted him an allowance for supplies furnished his little garrison.

Colvin's Fort, lower down the stream, was erected by the settlers—a stone building—and remains in fair condition to this day. This now is the farm owned by the Jones Brothers. Joseph Colvin, who first settled near the site of this fort, removed his family to a place on upper Cedar Creek and there built a small fort. This has caused some confusion. Colvin became a prominent citizen of that section, as stated in previous chapters.

Several old stone houses built along the Eastern base of the North Mountain during the Colonial period, are yet in good condition. The one occupied for many years by the widow Richard and her family, near Mountain Falls, P. O., was supposed to have been erected by Isaac Zane. One other to the Southwest, on Cedar Creek, known during the 19th Century as the Col. Frye homestead, is doubtless still standing, but none of the citizens of that section can identify it. The building was pointed out to the writer many years ago, who at this date recognizes the building as that occupied by Mr. ——— Fauver.

Hayfield, once known as the John White Fort, now occupied by Lee M. Orndorff, is near the post-office of that name, where will be seen an old brick house. This was built by Major Robert White prior to 1780—the preceise date not obtainable. This was where Dr. White, son-in-law of Wm. Hogue, first settled in 1739. This property remained in the possession of his descendants until about 1850, when it was purchased by Robert Brown, father of our popular stock-dealer Albert Brown, Esq. Later on it became the property of J. Howard Cather, son of James Cather, Esq.

Falling away to the Eastward, we enter the territory famous for colonial homesteads, but as that section is now embraced in Warren, Clarke and Jefferson Counties, only brief mention will be given.

The most notable was Greenway Court, the home of Lord Fairfax, and for many years has been the home of the Kennerly family, the residence buildings seen there at this writing, were not the Greenway Court residence used by Lord Fairfax. The Rev. Kennerly about 1830 erected the brick mansion so prominently seen at Greenway Court at this time. His lordship seemed disposed to adopt simple methods for his American home. There is little to be seen now that was used as his residence. For many years, the Greenway Court office building was well preserved. Originally it was a long one-story stone building standing on a sloping hill-side, as described by Washington Irving: "One story in height, with dormer windows with two wooden belfries, chimneys studded with swallow and martin coops, and a roof sloping down, in the old Virginia fashion, into low, projecting eaves that formed a verandah the whole length of the house. It was probably the house originally occupied by his steward or land-agent, but now devoted to hospitable purposes and the reception of guests. As to his lordship, it was one of his many eccentricities that he never slept in the main edifice, but lodged apart in a wooden house not much above twelve feet square." This building made of logs hewn square and fitted closely upon each other, with corners mortised into square logs as corner posts, produced a cabin that endured all encroachments of changing seasons, as well as the relic hunter. The old limestone building became dilapidated long before the log-cabin showed any signs of decay. Portions of the historic building still remain. Capt. Jos. M. K. Kennerly's father erected the comfortable residence long before the Civil War, and as near the site of the old Colonial buildings as possible. Greenway Court was occupied by Thomas Bryan Martin nephew of Lord Fairfax prior and subsequent to the Revolutionary War. The old Colonial building referred to, was a wooden building in three sections, as described by Mr. William C. Kennerly, son of Rev. Thomas Kennerly who erected the brick house in 1833. Mr. K. says that "the first section was built by Lord Fairfax when he came to reside at the Court, was a room 20 feet square and used as a banqueting hall" and that Col. Thomas Bryan Martin his nephew added 20 feet more, and that 20 feet was added to this by Mr. Kennerly's grandfather, making a long one-story building; and in this house Lord Fairfax died, and he, William C. Kennerly was born. Mr. K. also says: "There were lodging offices for the guests of my Lord scattered about in the yard." He also says: "When I was a boy, there was an old wooden building used by my father as a blacksmith shop. This was the arsenal and powder magazine used by Lord Fairfax when he was County Lieutenant."

Carter Hall, the home of the Burwell family during the Colonial period and throughout the 19th Century, had no equal in the class of Colonial homesteads. Located near Millwood, in a natural forest, the magnificent palatial mansion has always attracted attention, and has become famous for its architecture and princely equipment. All the environments suggest to the visitor beauty and grandeur, harmonized by a master genius with lavish expenditure. The splendid homestead was designed and erected by Nathaniel Burwell, who came from the renowned Carter's Grove near Williamsburg, and spent his long life on this estate, where his descendants have ever maintained the reputation of the family for hospitality. About 1904 a Mr. Richardson of St. Louis purchased the homestead; he never occupied it however. At this writing it is going back to the Burwell family, Mr. Townsend having purchased this remnant of his ancestry for $60,000. About 500 acres of the old grant goes with the purchase.

Saratoga the home of Powell Page, Esq., has its Colonial history. The writer will briefly mention this renowned place, lest he weary the reader with repetition of an oft-repeated story: This *Morgan building,* as it was once called, was erected by Genl. Daniel Morgan; and, as often stated, the work was done by prisoners during the time he was commandant of the prison camp. He first built a stockade containing four acres, and there "exercised" the prisoners daily, so his report says. Conveying the stone material for building this house, among the prisoners, were many stonemasons and good workmen. The General reports that "His own health was improved and the condition of the camp was free from epidemic diseases." The General's health had given way from hard service, and he was assigned to the command of the *Convention* prison.

The brief notice given the two prominent Colonial establishments in that section of the Old County, distinguished as three counties, is only intended to call the reader's attention, to what he must behold to fully appreciate. We find dotted here and there in the beautiful country lying between the Opecquon and the Shenandoah River, many magnificent places full of historic interest. A few may be seen with well-preserved Colonial styles, but the conspicuous homesteads are those that were built subsequent to the Revolutionary War.

The Page, Burwell, Randolph and Nelson families have occupied well known places—Saratoga, Pagebrook, Whitehall, Fairfield, New Market; Clifton, home of the Allen family; Shenstone and Sherwood, were built in latter part of the 18th Century.

Willow Brook. There are several old homesteads in Warren County, which must remain unnoticed here. Before leaving this section, there is an old Virginia homestead the writer has long known, deserving special mention. And many readers of this volume of reminiscences will doubtless associate some incidents of their lives with Willow Brook, the home of the Cook family for about one hundred years. The writer knew Willow Brook as the home of Mr. Samuel Cook, son of William, who laid the foundation for this celebrated old Virginia home in 1810. As the name indicates, the weeping willow trees in their majestic grandeur lined the banks of the brook leading from the famous Springs of pure water that unceasingly gush from the limestone ledges. The old mansion is of the type adopted immediately after the Revolutionary War by the gentry of the country. Substantial, unique in architecture, occupying well-chosen site, with landscape so varied, the Blue Ridge so impressive, just to the East, with its great oaks and rock-ribbed pinnacles—presented the appearance of a long line of sentinels; while the sighing cedars were in the intervening plain stretching out from the homestead toward the Shenandoah. While this old estate presented so much for admiration, while wandering along the shady brook, the hospitable old Virginian was ever ready to give hearty welcome and good cheer to those who crossed the threshold of *Willow Brook,* and none left its spacious precincts without comfort. Mr. Cook and his family were well qualified for all that was needed to impress their guests that they had been in the presence and companionship of a Virginia family of the old-school type. From his birth in 1818 to his death in 1893, Mr. Cook knew no other home than Willow Brook. His only child, Mary Evelyn, survived him until within the last few years. All gone—but the old homestead still governed by one of the old family name, Judge Giles Cook of Front Royal being its present owner.

New Market, as seen to-day a short distance West of Old Chapel, shows woeful decay. This was once a famous Colonial homestead of the Burwell family. Inscriptions on many tombs at Old Chapel connect it with the families who lived at the quaint old place, which appears to the modern eye as never possessing attractive features, unless we except the surrounding landscape. The building was made of logs from the forests nearby, immense in dimensions. The place is barely habitable, owing to its long use by persons holding short leases.

Tulyries. This magnificent property is not one of the Colonial homesteads, though it has become familiar to many readers of magazine articles as such; nor can we give it place as one of the few notable edifices established in that part of Old Frederick in the latter part of the 18th Century; but it has been one of the landmarks of that section so long, that we will mention it in connection with those above named. The present owner of this princely estate, Mr. Graham Blandy, found it several years since with neglect and decay destroying the once attractive environments of the mansion; while the great building itself needed skill, taste and money to reclaim it from ruin; and its present appearance shows no radical changes from the original plans and designs, while the transformation is wonderful. The gentleman who has produced it, is to be congratulated for preserving the type in vogue in the early part of the 19th Century. The original Tulyries was familiar to the writer while Col. Joseph Tuley, the founder, enjoyed it in all its grandeur. The Colonel was an immensely rich man as regarded in that day, and delighted in his position as a Virginia gentleman, though he was not to the manor born. Coming from New Jersey with his father, they together amassed a fortune. Kercheval, who wrote of this place in 1833, says: "Col. Tuly has just built a fine brick house on his beautiful farm near Millwood which he has named Tulyries." When the writer was familiar with the old homestead, the splendid mansion, with its imposing portico supported by pillars about thirty feet high, marble slabs for floors and steps, was not the most attractive feature to him. The *Park* enclosed with stone walls, where herds of elk and deer roamed the forest, while the great oak and walnut trees were alive with squirrels. Col. Tuly was a large slaveholder; and thus was able to maintain all the attractive features of this magnificent estate. But the writer saw the time when the slaves were no more; the founder in his grave, and others on the ground, but helpless by reason of changed conditions to maintain the dignity of old Tulyries. The property descended in part to Col. Uriel Wright his son-in-law, who came from St. Louis after the Civil War, where he and U. L. Boyce dispensed liberal hospitality for many years.

Annefield, about two miles N. E. from Old Chappel, now the home of Mr. Edward Gay Butler, is of the Colonial type pure and simple, that is stamped with the features of ye olden time. This "great house," as it was known in that period, built of blue limestone, forty feet square, with capacious halls, staircases, large rooms with lofty ceilings, heavily carved wood-work finishings, singles out this place as one of note. This is and has been often pointed out as the home of "King" Carter. As is well known, Robert Carter of James City County, Virginia, held a grant for a large area of country on both sides of the Blue Ridge. He himself is not traceable in any way for residence in the new country. It was his son Robert, who came at an early day and virtually covered the country from the Opecquon to the River as assignee of his father King Carter; and it was he who settled and founded the Annefield and New Market places,—principally the former, and for several years acted as agent for Lord Fairfax. Holding a power of attorney, he was enabled to create a number of leases, and more than once did he contest the claims of other settlers. He was succeeded by William Fairfax as agent for Sir Thomas. The Carter, Burwell and Randolph families had intermarried, and members of the family interchangeably held and occupied the places referred to and also the homesteads near the Chapel known as Chapel Green. Mr. Philip C. Burwell was the last of the name who lived there. This he had by deed from Nathaniel Burwell of Carter Hall, dated 1804. The conveyance embraces 814 acres, together with thirty-four negroes and horses, cattle, etc., belonging to the Chapel Green Homestead. This is now the home of Madison Hite Baker and sister.

Federal Hill has been too prominent to pass by without a brief notice. It was established prior to the Revolutionary War by Samuel Baker the agent and attorney in fact of Col. Nathaniel Burwell of James City County, Va. Succeeding him, were three generations of the Baker family,—the last being Major Alexander Baker. The building was of that unpretentious character that has escaped notice of those seeking Colonial mansions. The old log structure was in good repair when last seen by the author. At one time the walls were covered with what is now called *pebble* finish;—then it was known as *rough-cast* style—coarse sand and lime plastered over the entire building, after the walls had been lathed. Such finish made attractive exteriors, and very cool houses in Summer. This style preserved the old log-houses erected by early settlers. Federal Hill can be seen near Stone Bridge in Clarke County.

Guilford near Stone Bridge (now in Clarke Co.) was the home of James Madison Hite son of Major Isaac Hite of Bell Grove, and famous for many years for its handsome appointments. While it was not Colonial, it had the attractive style adopted by men of wealth in latter part of the 18th Century. Mr. Hite was a man of ample riches, and his natural taste led him to erect the handsome homestead on such lines that its beauty was marvellous. The writer often heard in his boyhood days, how the gentry were entertained at Guilford. The exact date cannot be given when the mansion was built, but it was prior to 1820. It was once the home of the Ashby family.

While observing many interesting features belonging to the two homesteads Federal Hill and Guilford, the stone-bridge feature was peculiar. For many years, the two homesteads had been separated by an impassable chasm. Though the families were closely allied by marriage; they were compelled to traverse a long, rough route in their daily visits. The two owners at last devised a plan to bridge the barrier that nature had placed between them: This was that each should employ his slaves in utilizing the vast piles and ledges of limestone and hurling the great blue rocks into the yawning gulch, and so in time meet each other midway. Tradition has it that much rivalry existed between the working negroes,—each party excited by a desire to reach mid-stream first. After several years of such work, the stone bridge as now seen was finished, and as Major Baker told the writer, visiting between the families was much enjoyed by the younger members, he being one. From his home over the bridge to Mr. Hite's mansion Guilford, he one day went to claim his bride, Miss Caroline M. Hite.

Mountain View, for many years the well known home of Bishop Meade, passed from his estate to one of the Baldwins, then to Mr. Jos. M. Barton of near Bartonsville, and from him to its present owner, Wm. Powers, Esq.

Wheatland the home of Mr. Joseph A. Miller, was established in the early part of the 19th Century by Maj. Seth Mason. His son J. William Mason and his accomplished wife who was Miss Martha Cook daughter of Wm. Cook, for many years dispensed such hospitalities, that the fame of Wheatland was known to many. The writer knew the highly cultured family when nothing but joy and prosperity crowned the splendid home. He also knew it when war devastated and spoiled the beauty of the former Wheatland; and when the family reunited and endeavored to meet the struggles of the new life, the same refinement and culture was there, but the ability to meet the changed conditions was weakened; and the sad day came when the hospitable home was turned over to others. This estate can be seen on the Front Royal turnpike North of Nineveh, where under the good care of Mr. Miller and his highly esteemed family, friends still enjoy Virginia hospitality.

Highlands, for many years the home of Dr. Oliver R. Funsten, now owned by Mr. Thos. S. Chamblin, situated North of Wheatland, was regarded as one of the finest estates established early in the 19th Century. All that was needed for a Virginia homestead could be seen—superb plantation, grand scenery, solid buildings, extensive lawns, and imposing surroundings, marked it as the home of the old-time Virginia gentleman. The Reconstruction period meant much to such places. Mr. Chamblin and his family have revived the drooping appearance of the old home; and, as seen to-day, it gives the impression that ease and comfort reign within its walls, while prosperity is seen in the broad rich acres. This and Mr. Miller's homestead are near the dividing line of Frederick and Clarke.

We must here fall back again to Frederick and briefly mention other places prominent after the Revolutionary period.

Belle Grove. This historic homestead was designed by Major Isaac Hite, Jr. and his young bride Nelly Conway Madison, sister of President Madison, while they occupied the original Hite building called in some deeds "Hite Hall" and often "Old Hall." The site was well chosen, commanding a perfect view of all the mountain scenery fringing the border of the Lower Valley. The prospective mansion was to spring as if by magic hands up among the virgin oaks of wonderful size. It was a dream to the happy young people. Their plans were so stupendous that several years passed before they could see their completion. When the Spring of 1793 came, they announced to friends far and near, that the dream had been fulfilled, and all must come and see the former belle in a grove of her choice; and from that announcement, the name of the princely establishment was forever settled; and since that eventful day, the regal home has known no other name than Belle Grove. Very briefly the dimensions are given to render some idea to the reader what the guests beheld: The structure, of pure limestone hewn with minute precision, 160 feet in length and forty feet in breadth, had four porticoes, with pillars of such pattern and size as to excite wonder over their origin. The many ornamental blocks of marble filling their respective positions, were curious. Major Hite had drawn upon every quarry in the land to furnish the finishings. Family tradition helps our description of the interior: We can only mention in an irregular way what was seen by guests who have left written descriptions which are well preserved by members of the family: The furniture was mahogany inlaid with satin wood imported from England; the "side-boards" and sofas were heavy with hand-carving in exquisite style and figure; solid mahogany "table-board"—as the great dining-tables were called—were large enough to seat sixty guests; the rare oil paintings, hung so profusely on the walls, occasioned comment which, to read the quaint descriptions now, causes surprise. Visitors to Belle Grove subsequent to the death of the beautiful woman who had planned the palatial homestead, found Major Hite's second wife, Anne Tunstall Maury, whom he married Dec. 1, 1803—less than one year after his attractive Nelly had died—fully installed as mistress of the splendid home; and her life proved her fitness for the responsible position. Extended sketches of the Hite family show who her numerous descendants were; some of whom related to the writer the tender regard she always had for one of the oil paintings that occupied a conspicuous place in the drawing-room. This was the portrait of Major Hite and Nelly his wife and their son. Other fine paintings adorned the walls in the latter days of Major Hite. He prized highly one of Thomas Jefferson, and one of Dolly Madison wife of President Madison, who had been a frequent visitor to Belle Grove. Maj. Hite died in 1836; his wife survived him until Jany. 6, 1851. After her death, the famous furnishings of this noted place were distributed among such of her descendants as cared to possess them. Some of the paintings were lost. The large landed estate had been subdivided among the children; and the remnant of several hundred acres with the bare mansion, passed into the hands of strangers. Mr. J. Wilson Smellie, a Scotchman, is the present owner, having purchased it in 1874.

The celebrated Battle of Cedar Creek centered around this place; and Genl. Sheridan had his headquarters there for a few hours.

Belle View, now the home of Dr. Samuel McCune, was once part of the Belle Grove tract. Hugh H. Hite son of Major Isaac Hite, settled there and made it his home for many years. This estate changed hands several times. Solomon Heater sold it to the present owner in 1867. Genl. Custer's celebrated Division of Cavalry camped on this farm in the Autumn of 1864. Want of space forbids further mention of the other well known subdivisions of the Belle Grove grant, which embraced at one time at least eight thousand acres of land lying in every direction around Middletown.

The Meadows was once a notable estate on the Opecquon, and became more so after it passed into the Magill family. The boundaries extended from the Opecquon far South, taking in several tracts of land that have become prominent farms. The large brick mansion house occupied by Mr. John S. Magill for many years, was chiefly the work of Col. Charles Magill in his lifetime. His death in 1827 found the buildings unfinished. Later on, John S. Magill was ambitious to adorn the great structure and have it compare with other noted homesteads. The large interior, however, was never finished according to his plan;—the death of his young daughter and subsequently his wife (who was Miss Mary Ann Glass) going down in the bloom of her splendid womanhood, changed all of Mr. Magill's plans; and the old place that Col. Charles Magill had named "Gillhall" never arose to the distinction he intended. The old house, from some defect, grew unsafe in recent years, but has been properly repaired by its present owner, Dudley L. Miller Esq. The large estate was purchased by Aaron Bright about 1870, who came from Pennsylvania with ample means and a large family, and for twenty-five years kept the farm up to a high standard. Mr. Bright was highly esteemed. One of his daughters, Mrs. Grove, is the only one of the large family that has any part of the old place. She and her husband have one of the sub-divisions.

Carter Hall the handsome property South of the Magill estate, now owned by B. M. Carter and wife, was the home for many years of Wm. A. Carter its founder. The splendid residence was erected in 1833, and with the thirteen hundred acres of fine land, made this an estate equal to any in the County. In the division of the estate between eight children, the mansion-house tract became the property of B. M. and Geo. H. Carter, subject to the dower of their mother, by whose remarkable ability and their energy, Carter Hall recovered from the waste and destruction wantonly made by Federal troops.

The old Rust property, a large brick house South of the Carter homestead, was erected about 100 years ago, and was celebrated in its day for old time Virginia hospitality. It was a large plantation. Within the last twenty years it has passed to other farmers of that vicinity. Dudley L. Miller and David Miller, relatives of the family, purchased the mansion-house part.

Other old places in this section, found on the road to Marlbo, where well known families lived in the early days, have long since changed owners, and old landmarks gradually disappeared. Leaving this section, going West, we find one place in the vicinity of St. Paul's Church, an old homestead noted for its antiqueness. This for nearly a century was known as the Bengie Fry place.

Buffalo Marsh has often appeared in the old records as the home of more than one old family. This occasioned considerable confusion. Only one estate was entitled to the name. This was for many years mentioned as the Baldwin estate. The name was applied by old settlers to a marshy district constantly supplied with great springs. The marsh was slightly impregnated with salt, and was a famous resort for buffalo that roamed through the Lower Valley during the 18th Century. The old Miller homestead was once called Buffalo Marsh. Joseph Miller the pioneer settled first in this section, and his large family owned splendid homesteads. But what became the Miller homestead of the section, has for many years been the property of D. L. Miller Esq., where he made his home until his removal to his present residence at Stephens City. Mr. Thomas C. Miller, son of the pioneer, and father of D. L. Miller, also lived there during his entire life; his father Joseph coming from Maryland just prior to 1800, laid the foundation for the old home, which was famous for its hospitality during the period when Mr. Thos. C. Miller's family of four sons was unbroken.

Deerfield known in early days as the Ash homestead, was one of a number of old settlements found on what has been long termed the Middle Road, terminating at Old Forge. Franklin Ash was the founder; and as the writer was informed many years ago by Mr. Alec. Newman a very old man, he and his brother Hiram, only surviving male members of that once large family who lived in that section. The homestead was one of the Colonials; and when he was a boy, the plantation swarmed with negro slaves. Mr. Newman was a pensioner of the War of 1812. Deerfield is now the home of Mr. Harvey A. Richard. The writer while gathering material for this volume, visited the delightful home Deerfield; and while scarcely a vestige of the old buildings remain, the old time Virginia hospitality has not disappeared in the new order of things. Mr. Richard became the owner in 1878—the first time to leave the Ash family. The old log-house was occupied by his family until he was able to erect the handsome property now situated on the old site. The old logs, when removed, were found well preserved;—many of them can be seen now on the place. Mr. Richard told the writer many interesting incidents concerning the change, and exhibited a veritable curiosity that he found 'neath the old cellar foundation—a large bone about thirteen inches long, perfectly preserved, and evidently that of some human being of that early day. The words "Nig Bone 1754" plainly written in black, gives it place among the curious finds. The writing is of very durable color. Mr. R. feels sure that it has some interesting history. The writing was there when he unearthed it.

Deerfield farm at this writing contains 110 acres of rich land; and with its fine culture, presents an attractive feature. The home is presided over by a lineal descendant of the first settlers, she being daughter of Samuel Rust, son of Thomas on one side, and the granddaughter of Capt. Joseph Long. Mr. and Mrs. Richard are in the prime of life and derive real enjoyment from their possessions,—their children being one of their chief joys, whose names are Joseph T., Chas. A., Mary E., Rosa B., and Harvey A. Jr.

The District School building within sight, bears the name of Deerfield School. Old Forge is distant about 1-½ miles S. W.

The writer in traveling over the road to this point, was impressed by the marvellous changes going on. When he recalls the lonely stretches on the old road before the War—for instance, from Huck's Mill to this point, only three houses were on the roadside, the first being the Barley place, then the Geo. T. Massie, and John W. Ridings. Now the same roadside is lined with homes of every style—two churches, the handsome M. E. Church at the junction of the old Newtown road, and Sunrise Chapel (U. B.) partly hidden by a grove of oaks—the feeling comes with strong force that we have evidence all around to prove that the period embraced in the last thirty years, surpasses any three decades in the history of this section of old Frederick.

On the Cedar Creek turnpike leading from Opecquon Creek to Cedar Creek, are a few places that retain their early features. This section was well known in the early part of the 19th Century for its historic homesteads. Nearly all have undergone such modern changes, that the originals are about forgotten. We will mention several to save them from oblivion.

Paxton, which has been the property of John Buncutter and wife, now dead, for about fifty years, was owned by Genl. James Singleton who lived there for many years with his large family. Paxton the large stone building was erected by him about 1814. Genl. Singleton removed to Winchester just prior to his death which occurred in 1828. The property continued in the name for several years after. The house was in an unfinished state when the writer saw it in 1850. The building then was regarded as an old place. Mr. Buncutter did what was necessary to make the old stone structure a comfortable home.

For several miles immediately South of Paxton were several old homes in good repair until about 1850. One was the Lukens place now owned by heirs of Jacob R. Crabill deceased and others. The original building was pointed out to the writer when a boy, as being the home of "Lazy Lawrence." This term was applied to the owner who was famous for his desire to hail all persons passing his way, and endeavor to have them spend an hour under the shade of the oaks, and give him the news. This habit became so annoying, that persons shunned the road that led by his house; and it was a common saying that "Lazy Lawrence was in the air." And to this day, we often hear it repeated when the first hot Springtime sun falls across our pathway.

"The Snapp Neighborhood" had its origin in a settlement made by Henry Snapp on a grant by Lord Fairfax about 1750. This grant was for a full century occupied by sons, sons-in-law, and two brothers of the old settler. Large families have come and gone, distinguished for their thrift and good citizenship. One of the descendants, Mr. John A. R. Snapp, has his home at the old homestead.

CHAPTER LI

Homesteads of Frederick County

The Glebe, often called the Glade, was a celebrated tract of land lying on the West side of the old Cartmell and Froman roads. One part of it is now owned by Mr. Andrew Brumback. This tract occasioned much trouble. When the first Vestry was formed in Frederick County, a certain survey was designated as the Glebe land, to be known as the property of the Established Church (Episcopal). All revenues to be for the use of the Vestry towards the "living of the Minister." In 1754, Nathaniel Carr obtained a grant from Fairfax, and located where the old Pitman property is now seen. Later on he built a house where Mr. Jacob Brumback now lives. Carr's grant lapped over into the Glebe. He and the vestry compromised, Carr paying a nominal rent, and was virtually owner. He sold a portion of his grant and included part of the Glebe, to Peter Gilham in 1777. At this time the Vestry was so demoralized by changed conditions in their Church, brought about by the war then in progress, that the tenants were forgotten; and the Glebe was regarded for many years as the property of Gilham's estate. Titles to the Glebe tract were disputed for many years. Col. Carr, as he was called, retained over 1200 acres of land at a cost of one dollar per acre. Several well-known homesteads were formed from this tract.

The Old Quaker School House property was famous in the olden time. Martin Cartmell set aside five acres of his land for this purpose in 1748. This grove of majestic oaks made this a land-mark for a century. A spot West of the Old School House was chosen for a graveyard; and this is where a number of the old Cartmells were buried until 1841. Nothing to mark a single grave. Long since the burial plot was filled by other families, the Carr, Longacre, Funkhouser, Fawcett, Snapp, etc., being of the number. The original five acres has been mysteriously reduced in size. The writer has never been able to find any trace of a conveyance from trustees or others to any coterminous owner. Doubtless gradual encroachments account for the depletion. The writer has always had a tender regard for the Old Quaker School House Graveyard. The last of the "Homespun" Cartmells to go there was Martin Cartmell, a great uncle. His son Thomas K. Cartmell had preceded him by one year. He requested his name be given the writer at his birth, 1838, and, as his namesake and kinsman, he has repeatedly tried to locate the graves. This is a sad commentary on the lives of the ancestors. With all the vast property they owned, not one felt the need of preserving this important bit of history! Quite a number of marble slabs dot the old graveyard; but none are more than 50 years old, the oldest legible inscription being that of Isaac Watson Longacre, born 1793, died 1860. Robert Stephenson died 1864, aged 72 years; Anthony Funkhouser 1796—1871. The Fawcett family is largely in evidence. Doubtless old hidden graves contain the dust of prominent ancestors of this family, who were among the first settlers in this section. It is well known that the old families of Carr, Gilham, Baylis, and Sexton gave up many of their number to take the long sleep in the old place. Quite a number of old graves have stone markings, but no inscription to tell who they were. The old schoolhouse erected in the Colonial period has disappeared, and the site has been added to the graveyard proper. It is gratifying to see the grounds under good care and attention. The graveyard now enclosed comprises about one acre, while the old grove of 1-½ acres protected by wire fence, makes a long and attractive front entrance to the sacred place up on the hillock to the West. North of this point and in sight on same side of the pike, is Mt. Zion U. B. Church, erected several years before the Civil War. To the Eastward is a fine scope of country running North from the Glebe lands, embracing the splendid farms now the property of the estates of Jos. P. Richard, Joshua Lupton and Joseph O. Bywaters, deceased, and the farm of Henry C. Glaize. This large tract was for many years called the Snapp Property, but was not part of the Snapp-Fairfax grant. Where Mr. Bywaters lived, there was an old house erected by the Gordon family about 1740. This family had litigation with Fairfax; they based their claim upon the so-called *Tomahawk* right. The boundary lines were marked by girdled trees; and they stood upon the claim that they had come to this country at the instance of a promulgation from the English Crown, that such settlers could thus secure titles. Investigation of such claims proved that the Gordons held the same views entertained by the Morgan and Sheperd immigrants at their settlements near the Packhorse Ford. The Gordons lost, for the Tomahawk right did not apply to the Valley Section. Their old log houses remained, however, as landmarks for many years after Snapp acquired the property. Then Nash Gordon purchased land adjoining the Glebe, near where Joseph E. Funkhouser lived for many years, and finally absorbed by the Sexsmith tract, known for many years as the Hollingsworth Farms.

Winter Hill, the large brick house now occupied by N. B. Clagett's family, standing near the Cedar Creek Grade, was erected about 1811 by Capt. Charles Brent, who owned a large tract of land extending towards the Creek. This was the home of his large family during the first half of the 19th Century. His widow survived him for many years. She and one single daughter were the last of the immediate family to hold the property. Henry M. Brent, cashier of the Old Valley Bank, a son of Capt. Brent, became the owner at the death of his widowed mother. Later on his son Edwin S. Brent became the owner until his removal to his present residence near the Big Spring. Casper Rinker Esq. having purchased Winter Hill, lived there until his death, and there his widow resided until her death a few years ago. The property was devised by Mr. Rinker to his daughter Mrs. Anne Clagett, subject to her mother's dower. Mr. Clagett took charge of the large farm during Mrs. Rinker's life, and successfully conducted its many interests.

Leaving Winter Hill, going South, we come to the well-known locality "Old Forge," "Marlboro," or "Cedar Creek" as it is variously called. The principal attraction nature presents is the "Big Spring," gushing out great volumes of cold water from the many prominent limestone ledges of enormous proportions. Casting a glance over the wild, romantic surroundings, the beholder is apt to feel that there can be nothing here but a rock-ribbed surface resisting all efforts of cultivation. Soon, however, the eye falls upon the many comfortable homes comprising the scattered village of Old Forge. In approaching this point from Winter Hill, we pass near by the once hospitable home of Mr. Elijah Shull, where he and his happy family dispensed old Virginia hospitality long before the Civil War. His daughter, Mrs. Dr. Cherry, became the fortunate possessor of the homestead in the partition of the estate. One of her nephews, Elijah Shull, is the village merchant. A short distance South from the Spring, can be seen the remains of the once celebrated Marlboro Iron Works, commonly called The Forge,—a term applied when Isaac Zane the owner, undertook to utilize the product of his smelting-furnace in the manufacture of stoves, and also small cannon for the army in 1777. We have very reliable traditionary history to establish this claim. Previous to this, "Stephen Fort" stood near the site of the iron works. The large stone mansion standing on the roadside about one-fourth mile North, now the property of Briscoe C. Shull and family, formerly the home of Eben T. Hancock, was built by Philip Swann in 1850, where he lived with his large family until it passed to Mr. Hancock. The mill on the Creek nearby, is an important feature of Old Forge, occupying the site of one of the first mills in the country, once known as Froman and Hites. Prior to 1755, Indians in their raids, annoyed the owners by taking corn-meal. Prior to the Civil War it became the property of Henry Wisecarver Sr. Passing from his family, Mr. Geisleman purchased it, and used it in connection with his large distillery. Mr. Dorsey Brill, the present owner, has wrought a revolution by using all modern mill appliances, resulting in satisfactory profits far beyond his expectations.

Spring Hill the home of Edwin S. Brent and wife, with its large lawn extending to the wall of "Big Spring," is rich in historic incidents of the 19th Century, including the Civil War and *Reconstruction* periods. Of the latter, fuller notice will be given in family sketches.

Capt. Chas. Brent was its founder. Passing from him to Capt. R. M. Sydnor his son-in-law, in 1826, when from that time it was popularly known as "Captain Sydnors;" his office as commissioner of revenue bringing him into constant intercourse with people in every section, made his home familiar to all tax-payers and to the large family connection and numerous friends who gathered there to enjoy the well-known hospitality of Spring Hill—before the family circle was broken, or the war-clouds had lowered over this peaceful hamlet. The old residence has undergone many desirable changes since Mr. E. S. Brent's grandfather laid the foundation. The major part of the old structure remains. The writer, in the sketch of Cedar Creek Church, has given brief mention of the grounds, etc.

Want of space forbids further notice, not only of the old place, but of several others belonging to the early part of the 19th Century, that have been pointed out between Cedar Creek and Opecquon.

In sketch of Paul Froman and family, it will be seen that the property occupied by J. H. Cleaver—for many years the home of Dr. Hite

Baldwin—was an important point in the Colonial period. In sketch of the Snapp family, it will be shown where the pioneer settled.

Greenfield, now known as the Greenfield Farm of Mr. Thos. N. Lupton, is entitled to special mention. In the partition of the old Cartmell grant between the sons, this tract embraced about 600 acres, and was assigned to Thomas Cartmell about 1770 by his father Nathaniel in his lifetime, where he raised a large family and died in 1808. The widow and several unmarried children remained there until Sept., 1811, when the farm was sold. John Lupton a son-in-law, purchased *26* acres off the North end at 219 pounds and 14 shillings; and Isaac Hite of Belle Grove purchased 400 acres, including the old residence, and paid $25 per acre. From this place went the Cartmells who settled in Kentucky and Ohio. John Lupton acquired the whole tract later on and raised his first set of children there—John, Nathaniel and a daughter. After his death, the property was sold in 1835 under decree of court, when Jonah Lupton the father of the present owner, became the purchaser. There he lived for several years prior to his death. During that period, Thos. N. Lupton built an addition to the old Colonial building, the former occupied by his father and the old building as his own residence until about 1855.

The Cartmell family set apart a small plot of ground due West from the homestead, for a family burial-ground. There Thomas the founder, his wife, and several unmarried children lie in unmarked graves, as well as quite a number from the neighboring families. The place was crowded when the writer saw the last interment there, a Mrs. Wright, in 1850. Since then it has been abandoned, and for many years has nothing to mark the sacred place but a clump of trees standing in an open field, that sometimes reminds the ploughman that the place represents something of the past; and he leaves it, doubtless with some wonder as to what it means. Formerly the old graveyard was enclosed with a durable fence, but for the last fifty years, all has gone. In sketches of the Cartmell family, "Greenfield" branch will more fully appear. Lest there be some confusion, the writer will state here that Mr. Jonah Lupton spent nearly all his life at Rock Harbor, now the property of Rev. Dr. Jonah Lupton, to whom he gave this farm when he removed to Greenfield.

Retirement, the home of Mr. John Wesley Larrick, was founded by Nathaniel Cartmell in 1769. This was part of the old Cartmell grant. He acquired title for 200 acres from his father Nathaniel of "Homespun." The tract adjoined Greenfield on the South and East. Nathaniel Jr. subsequently purchased other tracts, enlarging the boundaries to embrace about 1200 acres at one time. This was reduced, however, to about 600 acres prior to 1820. Since then, *no* transfers occurred. The writer's father, M. B. Cartmell, being the only child, inherited the estate at his father's death, and there reared his large family. The devastation of the War 1861-65, denuded it of many natural attractions, as well as all fencing and some out-buildings. Changed conditions induced the family to part with the old homestead. Mr. Abram Polhamus of Pennsylvania, purchased the entire estate in 1868, where he and his large family lived for upwards of twenty years. When his estate was closed, Mr. Larrick became the owner. During his incumbency, the once famous estate has been restored to its former beauty. Under Mr. Larrick's good management and successful operation, the pristine features have been eclipsed. Large and attractive additions to the Colonial building increase the charm of Retirement; and travelers over the Northwestern Turnpike have a full view of this magnificent estate. The mansion-house, surrounded by the vast acreage of well-tilled lands, with several fruit orchards laden with blossoms in Spring-time and luscious fruit in Summer and Autumn,—produces a picture grateful to the only survivor of the Cartmell generations who enjoyed the homestead for more than a century. And in this connection, he is pleased to state that in all the renovation, the Colonial structure was not demolished. Mr. Larrick is to be congratulated for preserving the walls and other features that point to days of the 18th Century. The property has many natural advantages: Sheltered from Western storms by the brow of Little North Mountain, the numerous springs of good water—flowing rivulets that find their way through the large tract from every direction, and the "Cluster Springs" near the mansion house—ever ready in themselves to cheer the thirsty ones of bygone days—the old stone dairy built before the Revolutionary War, give out tender memories. It is hoped this landmark will remain, and that maybe some pilgrim will come and revive some incidents of the shadowy past.

During the writer's life, old Retirement was known for its unlimited hospitality and happy family circle. These conditions changed after the *soldier's bier* rested in her halls. Sadness and gloom would creep in! Out towards the great highway is seen a memorable spot that was considered as part of the life of the old family. There is the *Family Graveyard,* founded before the old brick church was erected. Just to the North of this plot, is the site of the old School-House, which afforded ample opportunity to the youth of the neighborhood for many years. The old building was razed during the Civil War, and every vestige of it carried to the camps of Genl. Custer's Cavalry Command during the Winter of 1864-5, then in winter quarters in the vicinity of Dr. Jno. S. Lupton's residence on the Northwestern Turnpike. The old foundation can only be traced by a very few,—the writer being one. Few are the survivors of the school-day life at Old Round Hill. The old masters have long since passed to the Beyond; and memory of the birch-rod and rigid discipline has grown dim! The Presbyterian Church standing nearby the places just mentioned, and the old grove of oaks, received attention in the Church Sketches, and those of the Civil War. The School-house lot embraced one-half acre, conveyed to trustees Jany. 24, 1835, by M. B. Cartmell and wife. No consideration, except that the ground be used for no other purpose than for school purposes, and that the grantor reserved all trees standing on the lot. The deed for the Church lot of ¼ acre was executed Aug. 22, 1845, by same parties, and work on the church building started promptly; and in the Autumn of 1846, the large brick building now seen was dedicated. The family graveyard was dedicated October 19, 1833, when Wm. C. Cartmell, infant son of M. B. and Eliza Cartmell was placed in the first grave. The next interment was that of Ann Eliza, another infant from Retirement, May 14, 1846. The next was a grandsire, Wm. Campbell, April, 1838.

In December, 1863, Capt. M. B. Cartmell was the next from Retirement to be interred here. This gallant young soldier had been killed in battle Dec. 17th, and carried from the field by his faithful comrades to the East bank of the Shenandoah at Berrys Ferry, and thence borne to his old home by the writer and his brother N. M. Cartmell, where a few friends had gathered to await the arrival near the midnight hour. The next day, Dec. 22nd, solemn services were held, undisturbed, at the Old Church and graveyard, though the country near Winchester was within the lines of the Federal army. The family circle—now so rudely broken—yielded to increasing trials, and one by one were laid away in the sacred spot. Modest marble slabs show their resting places. The other mounds in this plot will receive notice in Personal Sketches of the families represented here.

Aspen Shade, the home of Perry C. Gore during the latter part of his life, was founded by William Campbell about the close of the 18th Century. About that time he built the stone house as an addition to the wooden building still standing, but added to by Mr. Gore and family. The writer's mother was born in the stone house May 8, 1805. The location was chosen by its founder because it resembled his old home in County Derry, Ireland, where the landscape was similar. The Round Top and Smoky Mount in Derry had their counterpart in old Round Hill and Little North Mountain. The young Irishman brought with him sufficient means to purchase his home; and his energy and intelligence soon made him a conspicuous figure as a prosperous business man, becoming the owner of several good farms, and leaving a valuable estate at his death in 1838, consisting of several families of negroes and other property. This landed estate was parceled out between his sons, his widow and youngest son James Harrison Campbell taking this homestead, where they spent their lives. During that period, the old homestead was a great gathering place for the large connection. Many grandchildren enjoyed the warm hospitality of "Ole Mistus," as the young negroes called the grandmother. After her decease, the Uncle endeavored to maintain the reputation of the old place; his early death and the Civil War wrought serious changes, but the estate has never passed out of the family. Mr. Gore married Laura C., the oldest daughter of James H. Campbell. She inherited the property after the death of her mother Elizabeth C. Campbell. After Mr. Gore's death Jany. 19, 1904, the widow and her two children Thomas Walter and Lena C., removed to Winchester, where the mother died June 26, 1905, thus leaving two of the great-great-grandchildren of William Campbell the founder, owners of the homestead.

CHAPTER LII

Homesteads and Biographical Notices

Walnut Grove (so called in 1804) is now the property of Jno. S. Lupton, who purchased it from his father-in-law Mr. Patrick Smith, who was son-in-law of the founder Joshua Lupton, who died about 1845 at the age of eighty-six. Tradition, however, gives this place an interesting antiquity: That the founder was Joshua's father, John Lupton, who settled the place in 1750, and that he was on friendly terms with the Indians who frequently visited his fine spring, and never molested him during all the Indian massacres. Be this as it may, Joshua spent his entire life at this place, and had the credit of being the builder of the stone house which was an addition to the Colonial log house that was in good repair in 1880. The present owner removed the old log building and erected on its site the handsome stone addition with bow windows. John the father of Joshua, lived on this tract which he acquired in 1754. His *mansion-house* that is mentioned in his will, was situated near a spring "on the edge of a meadow" just Northeast from the present barn. The old house has long since disappeared. It was pointed out to the writer as one of the old land-marks. The will disposed of a large tract of land; Joshua falling heir to the homestead in 1805, which embraced nearly 600 acres, *upon which he then resided* with his family. In 1845, Joshua by his will, divided his estate between his three children, Amos taking the stone house and 259 acres, John (familiarly known as Quaker John) taking the tract of 143 acres where he resided during his long life, N. W. from the homestead; the daughter Sarah, wife of Patrick Smith, taking 176 acres to the Southeast. Mr. Smith was then living on the Cloverdale farm, but removed to their own place and there lived until he acquired the home tract after the death of Amos Lupton. The latter, in his incumbency of the home place, erected a large barn West of his residence, and entered largely into the production of silk. His many mulberry trees, cocoons and silk-worms, were the wonder of the neighborhood for many years after his untimely death. He was survived by his wife and four young children, viz: Mary Janney, afterwards the wife of Thos. N. Lupton, Joshua, Nathan and Henry. The sons when young men found homes in Ohio. We are not sufficiently informed to give details of their families. Thomas N and his wife Mary Janney had two children, Jonah and Alice. Jonah died when a child; Alice married Rev. W. H. Woods, D.D., and is the mother of the following children: Leslie, Mary and Joseph.

Mr. and Mrs. Smith reared an interesting family of five daughters on the old homestead: One daughter Margaret married Dr. Jno. S. Lupton the present owner. She has been dead for several years. They had four sons; only two survive: Lucien S., and Edward Lupton. Lucien S. represented this District in the Virginia State Senate two terms. Dr. John S. the father is a confirmed invalid at this writing, about 79 years old. Lydia the second daughter married H. R. Lupton. Both died several years since. Two children survive, Harry and Nellie. Both live in Winchester. Harry is married. Mr. Smith after the marriage of his two daughters and the death of his wife, changed his residence in 1861, to the home opposite the Cumberland Valley R. Rd. station, where his two lovely daughters Sarah and Mary died with dyphtheria shortly thereafter. Mr. Smith soon followed, and the other daughter Elizabeth married Jno. W. Brown. Both died many years ago, leaving no children. In this connection, we may properly extend a sketch of this branch of the Lupton family. The name has been so numerous in the County, that much difficulty meets the enquirer. The most reliable information gathered, places the family name in the Valley about 1743. Joseph Lupton coming from Pennsylvania, secured what has been termed a *minor grant* for a large tract of land West of the Village of Winchester, and then brought his wife and eight children and settled near the homestead before mentioned; and from this family has sprung all the Luptons found in the Lower Valley. A brother of Joseph settled on Capon River a few years later. Joseph had a son John, who was the founder of the branch we have already mentioned, married Sarah Frost. By this marriage he had seven children. We have already mentioned his son Joshua, who married Lydia Reese. John the son of Joshua married Margaret Smith sister of Patrick. They had the following children: Joshua S., John R., Margaret B. and Thomas. All are now deceased except Thomas; he owns the father's homestead. The three sons were faithful soldiers, members of the 39th Batt., scouts, guides and couriers at Genl. Lee's headquarters. Only one of the family married; this was Joshua S., who married Margaret daughter of Genl. Josiah Lockhart. She died many years ago, leaving three children: Ida, married James Cather, no children; John E., married Mamie daughter of M. Harvey Albin. They have one child Bessie. Charles married a sister of John's wife.

Having briefly mentioned all of Joshua's branch, we will take next his full brother John Lupton, who married Elizabeth daughter of Thomas Cartmell, as already shown in notes on Greenfield Farm, and where he lived. By this marriage were John, Nathaniel C. and one daughter.

John lived on the hill near the Round Hill Presbyterian Church; married Rebecca daughter of Wm. Campbell. They had six sons. Only one member of this family is living to-day: Wm. M. the oldest was a successful physician; married Josephine Kerfoot—both long since dead. Three children survive: Madge, William and Kerfoot; 2nd, Hal. R., married Lydia Smith, both dead; two children survive, Nelly and Harry. 3rd, John C., died in Richmond Hospital during Civil War, buried in R. H. Graveyard. He was member of 39th Batt. at Genl. Lee's headquarters. 4th, Nat C., died from heart trouble about 1863. 5th, J. Frank, married Emily Shull and moved to Missouri. She died leaving one son. Her husband was a member of the 39th Batt.—has been an inmate of the Confederate Veteran Home in Mo. 5th, Robert M., died several years ago.

Nathaniel C. Lupton married Elizabeth Hodgson. They lived and died at their home on the Northwest Turnpike about two miles from Winchester. They had eight children, all dead: 1st Rebecca A., married and died childless; 2nd, Abner W., died when about 30 years of age; 3d, Samuel R., practiced his profession in Romney and died there many years since. Two children survive him, Fred and Mrs. Kate Shaffer. 4th, Elizabeth C., married Jas. H. Campbell; two grandchildren survive, Thos. W. and Lena Gore. 5th, Nathaniel C., married Ella Allamong; both died several years ago leaving two children. 6th, Dr. Frank, married Louise Blue—both dead. John of Greenfield Farm was married three times. After the death of his first wife (Miss Cartmell) his second wife, Miss Williams, was the mother of Joshua, William and Marinda. Joshua married Mary Hodgson. Marinda married Thomas Morrison. They left four children, Silas, Mick, Snowden and a sister, who married Henry C. Glaize. The three sons married three sisters daughters of Martin Snapp. 2nd: William son of John, married Miss Snapp; both dead many years ago; two sons survive them: John and Joseph. Both were good soldiers in the 39th Batt. at Genl. Lee's headquarters. John married; left one William Lupton surviving him. Joseph is a highly-respected citizen of Winchester. The third wife of John was Mary Williams. She was the mother of two sons and three daughters, none of whom married; and only one, Thomas, is living; he is about 80 years old. John the father of Joshua and John, mentioned above, after the death of his first wife Sarah Frost, married Mrs. Ann Rees. By this marriage they had two children Elizabeth and Jonah. Elizabeth married Joseph Carter and lived North of Winchester; they had three children: Jonah, married Miss Smith, sister of Patrick Smith. It will be understood that Jonah was the half-brother of Joshua and John, and lived at his home Rock Harbor. Children of Jonah and Mary (Smith) Lupton were (1) Margaret A., (2) Sarah J., (3) Thomas Neil, (4) Mary, (5) John S., (6) Millicent, and (7) Jonah W., Thomas N. and John S. have been mentioned in this connection. Margaret A. married Clark Cather. Their home West of Winchester is now owned by their son James Cather. The latter married Ida Lupton as previously stated. Next son Jonah married Fanny Cather. They have several children, John, Howard and Russell. Annie, married Jno. W. Lupton son of Nathaniel C. Lupton; Betty married James W. Whetzel; they have several children. Clark married twice—two sisters, daughters of David Shaull. One son by first marriage, David, is a surgeon in the U. S. Navy. Harry his other son is home. William Cather a brother of James died recently. Sarah Cather married Mr. Leatherman; live in Winchester, and have two sons and one daughter. Another brother Howard died several years ago. Sarah J. and Mary, daughters of Jonah and Mary A. Lupton, married two brothers, J. Richard, and John H. Simpson, of Loudoun County. Children of Sarah J.—Jonah L., Blanche, Jno. S., Emily, and Sarah wife of Dr. Jennings of N. Y.; Margaret married J. Wesley Larrick. They live at Retirement, where they have raised a large family. Children of Mary: Jonah, Lucy, Julia Henley, and Floyd. Millicent, the fourth daughter, married J. Howard Cather son of James Cather—both long since dead; no children. Jonah W. the youngest child, married Julia R. daughter of Rev. John McCluskey, D.D., of Penn. He is familiarly known as Rev. Jonah Lupton, D.D., a Presbyterian Minister. His first service was rendered to the Old Round Hill Church during the closing period of the Civil War and Reconstruction years, also assisting Rev. A. A. H. Boyd, D.D., in the Loudoun Street Church; next a long term at Leesburg; then at Clarkesville; then returned to Leesburg, and now, having retired from active work, resides in Winchester with his second wife who was Mrs. Lottie Eichelberger. Dr. Lupton with his highly-esteemed wife Julia, spent several years of their early-married life at Rock Harbor the home mentioned in connection with Greenfield Farm. There several of their children were born. Children of Rev. Jonah W. and Julia Lupton: (1) Mary Hall now the wife of Rev. J. T. Cannon, D.D., Pastor of Grand Ave. Pres. Church, St. Louis, Mo. They have three children, Julia, now the wife of James Smith of Ill. (the mother of Elizabeth) and John and Mary. (2) Wm. Bailey, married Mary Henderson of Tenn., and live at Franklin. (3) Carrie L. now the wife of Rev. Walter L. Caldwell, pastor of 3rd Presbyterian Church, Memphis, Tenn.; have one child Paul. (4) James S. married Imogene Smith of Clarksville, Tenn. (5) Henry McC., married Emma Higgins; live in Clarksville, Tenn; have one son Henry 12 years old. (6) Stuart K., unmarried; in Consular Service in Chile. (7) Millicent L., now the wife of Rev. C. T. Caldwell, D.D., pastor of 1st Presbyterian Church, Waco., Texas. (8) Julia L., died at the age of 25 years. (9) Lydia McC., at the age of 5, and John McCluskey at the age of 3.

This brief sketch is intended to embrace that branch of the Lupton Family commonly called the Presbyterian Luptons, often mentioned as the Round Hill branch. The other branch was designated as the Applepie Ridge Luptons and known as the Quaker Luptons. This family will appear in separate sketch.

Cloverdale. This well-known plantation has been in the Miller family for full sixty years. It has the reputation that its owner never at any time lived on the estate; and this accounts for the indifferent dwelling-house seen there at this time,—supposed to be, and do doubt is, the house built there about 1744. The original grant for this land was to Branson and Thomas in 1735, who assigned it to Martin Cartmell Jany. 14, 1740, who bequeathed it to his two sons Nathaniel and Edward. The great grant embraces the farms adjoining,—the Stribling farm on the Northeast (now Walter A. Miller's), and the Greenfield farm on the West. The tract was divided into several farms when Gerard Briscoe became the owner. He never lived there, however. His heirs, Mrs. Elizabeth Holmes, Mrs. Alex. G. Baldwin and others, sold their undivided interests to Abraham Miller. Hugh Holmes owned and controlled Cloverdale for a number of years prior to 1825; and tradition gives him the credit for building the largest barn then in Frederick County. He also held some shares in the Stribling farm in 1813. Financial embarrassment compelled a sale of all his interests; and in 1827 the two farms became the property of the Miller family, and it has never changed owners since. The writer has been informed that Judge Hugh Holmes lived in the old house, the remnant of which is now habitable.

Robinson's Spring was the Lyles Robinson farm, now owned by Mr. James B. Russell. The old stone mansion-house about one mile West from Winchester, in full view from the Northwestern Turnpike which is the Northern boundary of the magnificent estate, was erected by Mr. Robinson about 1800. (This must have been the father, since Lyles was only 45 at the time of his death.) He there reared his large family of ten children, their mother being the daughter of Dr. Richard Goldsborough of Maryland. After his death in 1834, the estate passed to the Merryman family. One of his sons, Richard A. Robinson, who by his liberality and tender regard for his native county, endowed the present Shenandoah Valley Academy,—had not attained the period of manhood. The family disposed of the large real and personal estate and sought homes elsewhere. Several of the sons became prominent in business circles in Louisville, Ky., and elsewhere. At this writing (1908) one of the name is enquiring for authentic incidents pertaining to the history of this family while residents of Frederick County. We may add that Mr. Russell has divided the large tract into two farms; and has erected a dwelling house, etc., near the turnpike, directly opposite the site of the large mansion-house erected by Alexander Tidball about 1840, afterwards the well-known property of Geo. W. Ward, deceased,—"Elmwood." The latter notable structure was destroyed by fire during the latter years of Mr. Ward's life. The large farm is now the property of his two sons, Dr. Julian F. Ward and State Senator Robert M. Ward.

Wending our way towards Winchester, the traveller finds himself on historic ground as he stops to slake his thirst at the Old Town Spring; for on his right is an old brick mansion-house almost hidden from view by vine-clad walls, and a miniature forest of tall trees, of the Colonial period, while out on yonder hill above the Spring to the left, standing out in bold relief, is seen a large square brick-house. Fifty years ago it was surrounded by a beautiful grove of ornamental trees. Both these places have an interesting history;—the old homestead first mentioned, hoary with age, and of Ye Olden Style, impresses the beholder. This is *Glen Burnie,* now the home of Col. William Wood Glass. This property has been known to the generations which have come and gone for one hundred years as the *Old Wood* estate. At some point on the great lawn lived James Wood the first owner to build habitations on the virgin soil. No white man had trodden there who could call it his. Lord Fairfax had not then seen what he afterwards claimed. Wood came with his order from the *Virginia Council* "to measure out and settle families on such tracts that *he surveyed* of lands on a branch of the Opeckon Creek, not heretofore settled." As Mr. Wood failed to make report of surveys, he lost his right to many thousand acres of the ungranted land. He was content to take what he reported as tracts he had chosen for his *settlement,* estimated to be 1200 acres. (In 1758 Fairfax gave him title to 1241 acres within the survey.) This embraced the present site of Winchester; and extending Westward, included what are now known as the Edward M. Tidball and Aulick farms, and what has been known as the *Steele Lot Company* land, starting from the Spring and extending West to the Tidball farm.

We find James Wood living at this place in 1743, when he qualified as Clerk of the first court held in Frederick County; and evidence has been shown in this volume that the Court held its first sessions "at the house of Mr. Wood," and also that the Clerk's Office was there for about two years; as it appears from orders of court that James Wood had allowances for use of his house for court purposes, and also an order for him to "transfer the records of the Court to the Clerk's Office *at the Court House.*" The Glen Burnie mansion-house was erected by James Wood the Clerk prior to 1755—exact date unknown. The brick were brought from England to Alexandria as ballast on sailing ships, thence by wagons to the plantation. The structure has durability stamped on every feature; the style is Colonial in everything, lacking the portico and large pillars. The porch now over the front was erected by the present owner. The old doorway, of antique style, was familiar to many dignitaries of the 18th Century. The old justices composing the Old County Court, had right of way to Col. Wood's spacious hall and dining-rooms. Their Clerk had their profound regard; Lord Fairfax and Col. Wood had many transactions, and much evidence appears of their intimate relations; and he, too, enjoyed the hospitality of Glen Burnie; and many eminent men assembled there in council—aspirants for political office. George Washington, with his first military commission, deemed it wise to counsel with the Glen Burnie politician, when a candidate for the House of Burgesses, and securing favor, he was elected. Col. Wood was well versed in the arts and tactics of bold leaders in civil and military life. He was no novice. When he first appeared in the Court of 1743, the announcement was made to the Court that he desired to dedicate a portion of his land to the new county, as a site for her public buildings. We have already shown how well he succeeded. This in itself, made him ever after a conspicuous figure in the Lower Valley. Upon this first act, he erected an imperishable monument, marking him the founder of Winchester. The Colonel was prominent in Orange County affairs; and previous to his settlement on his Frederick County tract, was the owner of several tracts of lands elsewhere. Mentioned in the Court Order books as *Col. of horse and foot* in the Colonial Line, "and as County Surveyor in 1734;" special order appears in the minutes of 1742 in connection with Col. John Lewis, Major Morgan Morgan, Captains Andrew Campbell, Thos. Rutherford, Lewis Neill, Lt. Jacob Hite, Thos. Swearingen, and many others who became prominent in Frederick County when the first court was organized. Col. Wood was a conspicuous figure during his entire life. As clerk of the celebrated Court for about seventeen years, his official life was of high order, as the records of the old office fully attest. As County Surveyor, and as one of the commission to ascertain and settle claims of officers and men of the French and Indian Wars, he left a record of marked ability. He is also credited with service in the House of Burgesses, acting as proxy for Washington when engaged in the French and Indian War. (See Hayden's Virginia Genealogy.) Family records show that he came to his new home with his wife and four children of tender age. As he states in his will, written in 1746, "they are under age." The writer, being aware that the name of Wood appears often in records, in connection with several other families long resident of Frederick County and the Lower Valley, deems it desirable to show in this sketch, who comprised the Glen Burnie Wood family and their descendants.

James the founder married Mary the daughter of Captain Thomas Rutherford, the first Sheriff of Frederick; and as Col. Wood and Capt. Rutherford were living in Old Orange County in 1738, we assume the marriage was solemnized in that County. The following is copied from an old note-book of James Wood, now in possession of one of his descendants, daughter of Col. Glass:

Children of James Wood Jr. and Mary Rutherford—

(1) Elizabeth, born Sept. 20, 1739
(2) James " Jany. 28, 1741
(3) Mary " Sept. 23, 1742
(4) John " Jany. 1, 1743—44
(5) Robert, " July 27, 1747.

The following is taken from the family records: Elizabeth married Hon. Alexander White —no children.

James married Jane Moncure, leaving no descendants. He was Col. of a Regt. during the Revolutionary War; promoted Brig. Genl. for gallant services, and Governor of Virginia 1799—1802. At that date he was president of the Virginia Society of Cincinnati at Richmond (See Va. Mg. of Hist., Vol. 1, pp. 95—6—7.)

Mary Wood married Col. Mathew Harrison, an officer in the Revolutionary Army. They have many descendants. The writer regrets his inability to give an intelligible list, owing to the failure on the part of some well-known descendants to furnish their respective lines. We can at present give in part the line of one daughter, Mary Ann Harrison, who married Obed Waite, a prominent official in Winchester for many years. Their daughter Maria Antoinette, married Washington G. Singleton, member of the Winchester Bar in its palmy days. Their town residence was on Cork Street between Washington and Stewart Streets. It has been shown in Gleanings from the Old Courts, that during the War of 1861—65, court was held in Mr. Singleton's residence. The writer knew the sons Obed W., Caldwell, and Wm. Allen, during their school days, at the old Winchester Academy. There were several daughters, one, Miss Mary Singleton, married Henry St. George Offutt; and their daughter, Eleanor Offutt, is now Mrs. Eleanor Barton, of Flushing, New York.

John Wood, son of James was a physician; he married Susannah Baker, and left many descendants.

Robert Wood, youngest son of James Wood and Mary Rutherford, married Comfort Welch. List of their children as follows:

James, Mary, Robert, William, Sarah Ann, Comfort, Catherine, Harriet and Julia. This large family lived at Glen Burnie. Mary Rutherford, widow of James, held her dower in the homestead as provided for in the will of her husband, which was probated 1760; and at her death, about forty years thereafter, her son Robert became sole owner. Only three of the nine children married:

Mary married Lawrence A. Washington.

Comfort married Robert Dailey, of Romney, W. Va., their children being: Doct. Robert, who married a Miss Taylor, his children, Benjamin, James, Judge Robert, C. Wood, Doct. Griffin, Howland and Thomas. Doct. Griffin is located in Romney. C. Wood is a lawyer; he has several children; Judge Robert Dailey lives in Romney—has several children. Doct. Robt.'s daughter Jane married Chas. Lobb. Thomas died single. One daughter married Mr. Baird. She left several children, one of her daughters is a teacher at Fort Loudoun.

Catherine married Thomas Glass, son of Samuel Glass and Elizabeth Rutherford. There were two children by this marriage, Ella and Wm. Wood Glass. The daughter died many years ago in blooming womanhood. William Wood married Nannie R. Campbell, daughter of R. Madison Campbell of Stony Meade. They lived for many years at his father's old homestead Rosehill on the Opecquon. Later on, Col. Glass inherited Glen Burnie by the will of his Aunt Julia, the survivor of the large family; but during her latter years he removed his family to the old ancestral home; and there his family of seven children were reared, viz:

(1) Katherine R., the owner of Fort Loudoun Seminary. Her accomplishments are of that high order and attractive style, that as principal of this renowned institution of learning, she is favorably known to a large circle at home and abroad.

(2) Thomas is married, and at present resides in the new State, Oklahoma.

(3) Hattie W. G., now the wife of Mr. Davis, an official in one of the Departments at Washington, D. C.

(4) William married Miss Louise Baker of Winchester; is a lawyer and lives in Waynesboro, Va.; has one son Wm. Wood, Jr.

(5) Susie married Harry Strider of Jefferson County, W. Va. She and her daughter survive her husband.

(6) Robert McC. is a prominent physician; resides in Winchester—married Miss Kate Cover, daughter of Thomas Cover, Esq. They have one child.

(7) Wood married Mrs. Embrey; lives in Indian Territory, a lawyer in active practice.

This brief sketch gives only an outline of the activities of Glen Burnie life. The old homestead has afforded a resting place to many members of the several generations, as these activities ceased. We find a small plat of ground sheltered from storms by ancient cedars—the family burial place of the Wood family. Here may be found the graves of Robert Wood and his wife Comfort Welch Wood, and their children Dr.

James, Dr. Robert, Sarah Ann, Harriet, William and Julia Wood. Mrs. Comfort Dailey and Mrs. Catherine Glass, and her husband Thomas Glass. Two granddaughters of Robert have their mounds here, Ella Glass and Harriet Dailey. His daughter Mrs. Lawrence Washington, the record shows, was buried in Wheeling, W. Va. Gov. James Wood was buried at Chelsea near Richmond. There is no positive evidence that James, the first Clerk, and his wife Mary are in the unmarked graves seen in the family plot. Some have thought that his prominence and vast possessions would have prevented his grave being unmarked by those who placed him there; and for this reason, some doubt has fallen over his last resting place. This should not be; for it was not the custom in that early day to distinguish graves as is now done. For instance, the Old Episcopal graveyard once on Main Street: if those graves were marked, what has become of the marks? The same can be said of the Old Lutheran and Presbyterian graveyards on the hill; also that Old Chapel in Clarke, where it is well known that wealthy and distinguished persons were buried prior to 1760. But where are the slabs to distinguish them? Family tradition in the Judge White family says that Hon. Alex. White, son-in-law of James Wood was in one of the unmarked graves. Governor James Wood must have been a frequent visitor to his old home; for the deed books from 1796 to 1811 make frequent mention of his presence to acknowledge instruments of writing. His last appearance was in 1811, when he released a mortgage held by him on the Lawrence A. Washington farm, when Alfred H. Powell purchased 350 acres adjoining the Town Spring, from Lawrence A. Washington and wife, then living in Jefferson County, Va. She was daughter of Robert Wood. Tradition says he presented her the Hawthorne homestead as a bridal present. Washington had in 1803 placed a mortgage of $13,420.00 on 570 acres of this tract in favor of Genl. James Wood of Chelsea, Henrico County, Va. This fixes his residence at that point; and there it may be he was laid to rest.

The writer will add in this connection that the Washington tract was part of the Wood tract; also the old Academy tract of 5 acres due West from the Memorial Hospital, and the Judge Hugh Holmes lot or square, now the old Byrd property.

Governor Wood, while Colonel in the Virginia Line, was ordered to Charlottesville to "superintend the Convention prisoners" and was there June 14, 1780. In 1781, his accounts for provisions and care, were settled.

Col. James Wood, as already stated, held his commission as Colonel and County Surveyor in Orange County in 1734. In 1758 he was acting as County Lieutenant in Frederick, though no record of this fact appears in our Order Books. The Secretary's Office has the original of the following copy: "Williamsburg, Sept. 28, 1755. To Col. James Wood: The Bill for adding your lotts to Winchester, has been and I make no doubt will pass into law, Thomas Rutherford is sick * * * 20,000. is voted for payment of yr. Regimt. to ye first of Dec. Yr. Humble Servt., Thos. Walker, Secy."

This proves clearly that he was regarded as the *County Lieutenant*. The law required this officer to receive the pay for the County Regiments, and to disburse the fund; and there is nothing to show that his commission as Colonel was withdrawn. The Colonel was a favorite, it seems; for we find that Gov. Gooch issued him a commission dated April 28, 1739, as Collector for Orange and Prince William Counties. This embraced duties on all skins and furs exported and liquors imported,—to hold the office *at pleasure*. This might imply that Col. Wood was yet a resident near the Orange Court House. As Surveyor of Orange County, he surveyed a tract of land for Abram Hollingsworth in 1735, and signs the report, and that he was on the tract—the number of acres being 1250—being within the limits of Alexander Ross's patent for 100,000, and that it adjoined the tract where Hollingsworth lived. We find him again in 1736 making a survey for John Lilley (or Tilley) for 293 acres on West side of Opecquon, on *Lick Run*, part of Ross tract. Again we find him in 1738 surveying lands in Augusta County, for Reuben Rutherford, 400 acres, adjoining Jno. Bell and others. At this time he was locating the numerous tracts for which he had obtained orders for himself, six of these being styled the New River Patent, aggregating 934 acres. He also had several large tracts on South Branch. The latter gave him trouble with Fairfax. This will be shown in Chapters on Fairfax suits.

Col. Wood accomplished much in his *short* life, for he was only 52 years old when he died Nov. 6, 1759. This is proven by an interesting incident, being an inscription on a *mourning ring* possessed by the family through the after years.

Hawthorn, familiarly known as the home of Thomas Allen Tidball, the third clerk of the county court. As previously stated, it was part of the Glen Burnie plantation, passing from that estate to Alfred H. Powell, who sold 331-½ acres to Joseph Tidball the father of Thomas A. Subsequently Alexander S. and Thomas A. purchased this tract from their father, and Thomas A. having purchased his brother's interest, became sole owner, and after his marriage in 1813, Hawthorn was his residence until his death in 1856. In Sept., 1856, his executors sold the mansion house and 60 acres to Col. Angus W. McDonald, who became a prominent officer in the Confederate States Army. During the Civil War the old homestead was shorn of its beauty—the buildings became a wreck, and the handsome lawn despoiled by wanton destruction of the great ornamental trees, and the magnificent estate was left a dilapidated ruin. The vandalism of certain well-known Federal Brigadiers and their commands, was without the pale of civilized warfare. After the war, the McDonald family sold it to Henry Laughlin of St. Louis, who did much to reinstate what had been destroyed. Passing from his estate to Wm. R. Alexander, a member of the Winchester Bar, it subsequently passed to the present owners, Mr. Edmunds and wife. Under their artistic treatment, we see the *New* Hawthorn. May it never cease to attract the admiration of the small number who knew and admired the old homestead. The Old Town Spring on the roadside, with brick house and walls, became the property of Winchester by a deed from Mr. Tidball June 15, 1840, with reservations for the use of owners of Hawthorn.

Thomas A. Tidball was Deputy-Clerk for James Keith from 1804 to 1824. Upon the death of Judge Keith, Mr. Tidball was appointed Clerk. When the office was made elective by popular vote, he was elected, and continued his long term of 52 years as deputy and clerk without opposition. His official life has been a guide to his successors. None, however, ever felt they could equal their model. The systematic and perfect work found in the old office is easily recognized as that of the man who had the confidence and esteem of all who knew him. Mr. Tidball married Susan Hill, a daughter of Rev. William Hill, D.D., Nov. 18, 1813. They had three children, Joseph, Scott and Bettie. Mr. Tidball was elected and ordained a ruling elder in the Loudoun Street Presbyterian Church, Winchester, Va., the 14th day of Jany., 1855. While the writer knew Mr. Tidball and his family, and could draw from memory many incidents of interest, he prefers to insert here the language of another, taken from a sketch published in "Memorials of Virginia Clerks," written by James Carr Baker, Esq., member of the Winchester Bar, and Mr. Tidball's deputy for many years. "Indulge the writer in a reminiscence of the family of Mr. Tidball. When the writer, in his fourteenth year, entered the family, it consisted of Rev. William Hill and wife, Mr. Tidball and wife, and their three children: Joseph, Alexander Scott, and Bettie Morton. William Marshall of Happy Creek and Lewis Armstead of Fauquier became members soon after. Bettie Morton (now Mrs. Thurston) of Cumberland is the only living member of the family. Joseph was an accomplished scholar; became a lawyer; removed to California, and left the impress of genius on the country of his adoption. Alex. Scott had gone to the same State before his brother, and became in that new country an artist of some note. William Marshall died before completing his education. Lewis Armstead graduated at West Point, and espoused the cause of the Confederacy, and at the Battle of Gettysburg was killed in his saddle."

The author must add that the writer just quoted and Mrs. Thurston, have long since gone beyond the River to join the family circle referred to. Mrs. Thurston's daughter, Miss Helen, married Edward M. Tidball. One daughter (now Mrs. Samuel Barton) survives both parents. One other daughter—is now Mrs. Hunter Boyd of Cumberland, wife of the Judge of the Supreme Court of Maryland.

Joseph married Mary M., daughter of Dr. Stuart Baldwin. Two children survive them: William A. Tidball, of Texas, married Miss Swartzwelder; and Susan married Ed. M. Tidball.

Alex. Scott married in California, and had an interesting family when the writer visited them in 1879.

Selma, the palatial home of Alex. R. Pendleton, Esq., a retired member of the Winchester Bar, located on the lofty eminence just East of Hawthorn, occupies the site of Senator James M. Mason's old home Selma. The old mansion was destroyed during the War by Federal troops, because of Mr. Mason's mission abroad as representative of the Confederate States Government, to secure recognition of the Confederacy. This was known as the Mason and Slidell mission. Senator Mason had sons and daughters: James M., Jr., who has been prominent as a lawyer and politician in West Va., his home being at Charlestown, Jefferson County, being one.

John, another son, also lived in the new State. The oldest son, George, lived in Galveston many years, where the writer saw him last. One of the daughters married the Hon. John Ambler; the other daughters removed to Alexandria, and established a seminary for young ladies.

Judge Edmund Pendleton and his wife erected the present mansion, and lived there in regal splendor during their latter days. They are survived by their only son, A. R. Pendleton.

Hollingsworth Homestead. On the Southeast

side of Winchester can be seen an old homestead known as the first settlement of the Hollingsworth family. Tradition gives a much earlier date than is justified by any evidence recorded concerning their arrival. The writer has been assured by the survivors that very much that has been written about this family is without foundation. Suffice it to say, however, that their first grants fix the family at the old place about 1736. The three survivors, Mary, Jonah and Anna Hollingsworth are children of David, who lived in the stone house now occupied by his children—the oldest being full seventy-five years of age. David the father died many years ago (1859). He was the son of Jonah Hollingsworth. The house was erected prior to 1800. The Hollingsworths intermarried with the Parkins, Lytle, Jolliffe, Robinson, Houghton, Lupton, Griffith and many other families, which makes the lines so intricate and the descendants so numerous, that it would require a large volume to enumerate them;—it being positively asserted that the name appears in Census Reports of every State in the Union save three. The old mill, the remains of which are now used for the power house and pumping station of the new water works, was operated by David and doubtless by his father. The family were reputed as good millers. The large stone mill on the Valley Turnpike one mile South of Winchester, was erected by Isaac Hollingsworth in 1827; who always took pleasure in stating that he himself was the stonemason who built the corner next the water-wheel. This was the mill site for a mill that stood there many years before the stone building went up. The proof of this is interesting to the antiquarian citizens of Winchester; for it establishes two important facts, as will be seen: There is a deed recorded in the County Clerk's Office dated 1746 from William Dobbins, for a lot of ground in Winchester, using this language: "South of Cork Street out towards Mr. Isaac Parkins residence and mill, upon which there is a stone house and other buildings, and the said Dobbins reserves a room in said stone house for his own use." This shows that Winchester had *one* stone house as early as 1746, and the Parkins mill was a landmark near the village that was slowly rising in the virgin forest. Until recently, the date of erection of the present mill was plainly seen from the Valley Turnpike. The old house on the hill, part stone and part logs, was the residence of Isaac Parkins when he operated the mill in 1746, and later on was a member of the House of Burgesses. This property passed from the old Isaac Hollingsworth estate to Festus Hahn subsequent to the Civil War. He built the substantial brick residence East of the Pike now owned by R. M. Henry. After Mr. Hahn's death, the mill and old house property on the hill became the share of Robert Hahn; and, by some misunderstanding with two purchasers, R. M. Henry and Saml. M. Chiles, the old "Milltown Mills" was worn to a frazzle in our courts, so far as Robert was concerned. Mr. Chiles prevailed finally, and is now the owner of the historic mill site. The brick house on East side of the Pike was Mr. Hahn's residence during his latter years. Festus Hahn was miller at this mill during the Civil War; and often told the writer his experiences and observations of the movements of both armies passing this place, and of several severe engagements in the old mill yard between cavalry scouting parties. Mr. Hahn amassed a snug little fortune subsequent to the war, when milling was profitable. The large brick mansion, just South of the mill, now the home of Mrs. Annie Hack and daughter, was the residence of Isaac Hollingsworth, and was built by him long before he built the stone mill. He operated the old Parkins mill, which stood closer to the mill dam; his widow and son Isaac surviving him many years. The son married Aleinda Gibson, of Clarke; and there at Willow Lawn reared their family. Mrs. Hollingsworth and her family removed to Cumberland after they sold the property to Andrew Hack, of Baltimore. Isaac, Jr., in his lifetime, gave the old homestead a reputation for Virginia hospitality; and his accomplished wife was fitted for any of its demands. Willow Lawn during the incumbency of its present owners, has had many attractions added; and their guests' enjoyment while under its roof-tree, affords pleasure to the mother and daughter, who know so well how to bring out all the charms of their typical Virginia home.

Isaac Hollingsworth, son of Zebidae and Lydia Allen, born Nov. 6, 1771; died Nov. 24, 1842. He married (first) Hannah Parkins, Jany. 10, 1799. She was born 1781, died 1824. Their children were: Eliza, born 1800; died 1860—married Alfred Parkins March 14, 1820.

(2) Joseph P., born 1802; died 1870; married (first) Louise Holliday, 1823; second wife Ann E. Osborne, 1856.

(3) Eleanor, married David Hollingsworth 1833; died 1846.

(4) John, born 1807; died 1860; married Dorathea Ayres.

(5) Mary P., born 1809; married Aaron H. Griffith.

(6) William, married Caroline Tuck; died 1878.

(7) Lydia Ann, married James Richards in 1835; died 1845.

(8) Isaac Milton, is mentioned elsewhere.

(9) Cyrus, died 1860—no issue. Charles, Henry C. and Alexander, unmarried, and long since deceased.

Isaac Hollingsworth had two sons by a former marriage; one Joseph, who lived on his farm near the Glebe lands mentioned. He married, and by said marriage had a daughter and son. Harriet was adopted by Mrs. Isaac Hollingsworth, Sr. She married twice,—first, Mr. Sowers, second, Mr. Culler. Joseph married a second wife. She and her two daughters survive him and resided in the large stone dwelling on South Main Street, Winchester. James the son married Miss Gibbons, of Dayton, Ohio.

Isaac Milton, the other son, married Mary Pritchard, and lived for many years near his father, as fully shown in sketch of the Cartmell family.

Isaac Hollingsworth married a second wife, Harriet Holliday in 1828. She died May, 1873. She had one son Isaac, born 1831; died 1873; married Alcinda Gibson, as shown elsewhere—six children by this marriage, viz: Hattie, Gibson, Boyd, Ida, Delia and Holliday. Hattie married Glisson Porter, 1877; Gibson married Chloe Birch, 1880; Boyd married G. Lemley.

The writer has on his table a genealogical memoranda of the Hollingsworth family prepared especially for family use, that is remarkable for its systematic plan; and the traditions of the family are adhered to,—that the son of Valentine Hollingsworth the emigrant, who settled in Pennsylvania, and who first appeared in Frederick County, Va., was Thomas; and that he died near Winchester in 1732 or 1733. This is only given as family tradition. No record evidence appears of this. The location of the mill just described, is mentioned in other pages of this volume as being on Abrams Creek. A short distance below stood what was commonly called the Nathan Parkins Mill. Nathan was the youngest son of the Isaac who founded the mill mentioned. His home, now occupied by Geo. W. Hillyard, is one of the oldest buildings to be found South of Winchester—certainly the old stone part. Mr. Parkins was an honorable and upright man; and attained an old age, leaving two children surviving him, Jany. 5, 1830: John Henry, died in Augusta County, Dec. 26, 1901; left eight grown children, seven of whom are now living, as follows: (Children of John Henry Parkins and Ella Moorman his wife.)

(1) Nathan Parkins, farmer and lawyer, Staunton, Va.

(2) Thomas M. Parkins, physician, Staunton, Va.

(3) Rosabelle, wife of Ernest Keesel, of Richmond, Va. They have one child, Thomas, born Aug. 10, 1905.

(4) C. V. Parkins, Fort Defiance, Va.

(5) Mary E. Parkins.

(6) Roberta Parkins.

The two daughters live with their mother near "Willow Spout" farm, the home of their father at his death.

(7) John H. Parkins, Jr., Chemist with Comr. of Agri., Richmond, Va.

The Nathan Parkins Mill was destroyed by Genl. Hunter during the Civil War; rebuilt by Jacob Keckley 1872—3, with turbine wheel power. This failed, and system changed to present style.

Thomas T. T. Fauntleroy lived in the old Parkins house for a number of years. There he and his happy family enjoyed the many advantages of the old homestead until his elevation to the Bench of the Court of Appeals of Virginia.

On the Opecquon Creek, several miles below, was the home of Alfred Parkins, known as "Parkins Mill," though the homestead name has always been Frederick Hall, where he reared a large family. All are now dead except Milton, who married a sister of the late Capt. Van Fossen. Had only one daughter, who married Freeman Birthright, living in Washington.

One of his sons, Rev. Alexander, died from wounds received in Battle of Bull Run. He was a brave Confederate soldier. A daughter Caroline, married David J. Miller, long since dead. A son, Parkins Miller, lives in St. Joseph, Mo., with a large family.

Second daughter Maria, married Capt. J. Harvey Bitzer, who organized a company of scouts for Genl. Jackson, but was disbanded before seeing much service. The writer knew Capt. Bitzer well. He and his wife died many years ago. Their young family struggled with broken fortunes for several years. At this writing, however, the surviving children are well-to-do. Rev. Geo. L. Bitzer, pastor of Presbyterian Church, Corsicana, Texas; Dr. J. Harvey Bitzer, a dental surgeon, in Alexandria. The former married Miss Ralston, and after by second wife had three children. Dr. J. H., married Miss Turner, and has two sons and one daughter. The two daughters of Capt. Bitzer, the Misses Annie F. and Eliza P. never married; live at Tacoma Park. The latter conducts a profitable stenographic business in Washington City.

One son, J. William Parkins, lived and operated the Parkins Mill for many years, ending his upright life near the old place not many years since. He had two daughters and one son: Maggie was the first wife of Jno. M. Silver; died several years ago; the other, Carrie B., is the wife of Jesse R. Bailey, 1880, who purchased the old mill property—all of which is so changed that the passer-by could scarcely realize that the writer remembers when it was one of the most profitable mill properties in the County. J. Walter Parkins survives both parents, and lives in Loudoun County, and married.

Joseph, second son of Alfred, died with lockjaw; left widow and two children. The widow married Mr. Heironimus, merchant, in Winchester. Both dead.

Alfred, son of Alfred, Sr., married Miss Walter, 1867. Children: Robert B.; Geo. W.; Alfred; Henry D.; Eliza H.; Albin L. and Neil R. The father died in 1887, at Tacoma Park, D. C., their home.

Want of space forbids further mention of this family, who belonged to the first settlers.

Greenwood Mills, the home of the McCalister family, located on Abrams Creek, has been mentioned in previous pages. The large woolen mills in this vicinity, have also received attention. Here was the residence of Aaron H. Griffith, who intermarried with the Hollingsworth family, his wife being Mary P. Hollingsworth. The attractive old homestead bears its early name "Brookland."

The residence and part of the plantation is owned by the family.

Aaron Griffith was a Quaker of the strictest class; maintained his enviable reputation for integrity and charitable acts throughout his long life. The writer recalls many of his generosities. He rigidly adhered to the customs and style of the Sect of Friends. Friend Griffith reared a large family.

(1) Elizabeth B. became the wife of H. B. Bailey, of Ohio, 1856.

(2) Hannah P., died 1839. J. Clarkson, married Mary R. Dilks of Philadelphia, 1859.

(3) Martha, became the wife of Henry O. Ott, of Wheeling, W. Va., 1864.

(4) Harriet H., became the wife of Wm. T. Ellis, of Massachusetts, 1865.

(5) Isaac H., married Katie Cochran, 1879.

(6) Aaron H., born 1843, died 1863.

(7) Richard Ed., married Viola Hunt, of Ind., 1887. One son Richard Edward, born Dec. 24, 1886.

(8) Mary A., unmarried.

(9) John, unmarried. The Griffith family have innumerable relations in Frederick County, in direct lines of descent from brothers and sisters of Aaron H.; and by the marriage in the Hollingsworth family. They start with the celebrated Steer family, that filled the Lower Valley with their descendants. Joseph Steer appeared in Frederick County with the first settlers. His children intermarried with the Jackson, Saxton, Parkins, Lupton and Hollingsworth families; and we find in studying the genealogy of this family, the second generation produced men and women who became important factors in the development of the material resources of the old County. We find the second generation intermarrying with the Baldwin, Burnett, McVeigh, Walker, Brown, Robinson, Taylor, Sowers, Richie, Harlan, Rood, McPherson, Moore, Hough, Wood, Russell, Haines, Whitacre, Lovett, Williams, Roberts, Shields, Burden, Randall, Patterson, Wright, Clevenger, and many other well-known families. Want of space forbids fuller mention of these families. They show a good history. The voluminous notes of the writer may tempt him to furnish sketches of the second and third generations of the families referred to.

Mr. R. Ed. Griffith, son of Aaron H., resident of Winchester, has in his possession some valuable genealogical matter;—so much so, that he has been urged to contribute it to the Handley Library Collection, when its shelves are ready. Mr. Griffith is a graduate of Swarthmore College, once *Old Haverford*, and has considerable literary talent. He has been identified with Winchester affairs for nearly 55 years, and was City Postmaster at one time. Although he had the misfortune to lose an arm when a lad, he has never ceased from the activities of the busy man. He resides in Winchester.

CHAPTER LIII

Old Homesteads and Families in and North of Winchester

Hackwood Park, is now the property of Mr. L. R. Fay, formerly of New York State. Since his purchase, the famous old homestead has been improved during the few years of his ownership; the old style of the 18th Century having been well preserved, while the delightful transformation proceeded. The massive stone structure was always imposing; and sixty years ago was one of the most attractive homesteads in Frederick County. The natural wonders of rock and water added much to its curious style, and the surrounding acreage entitled it to the early name of "Smiths Spring Park." The present owner, with the aid of ample means in money and skill, has utilized every bit of vantage ground to produce the magnificent home he now enjoys. May his spirit of improvement never wane—while his many friends and neighbors partake freely of his hospitality. This old property became famous during the Revolutionary War, as the palatial home of Genl. John Smith. Kercheval, in his quaint History of the Valley, likens him to "Nestor of old;" and dedicates his book to him. The exact date of the building of this huge stone structure has been a matter of conjecture by several writers; and some confusion results from the difference in dates; and this applies to the date of the General's birth. Norris, in his History of the Lower Valley gives the date of his birth "being in the year 1747;" while another fixes 1744 as the date. This discrepancy led the writer to diligently seek what might be a solution. The copy of the family register made by Genl. Smith, is now on the writer's table, kindly loaned by Miss Jacquiline Davison, a lineal descendant, who has carefully preserved the Augustine Smith and Sarah Carver records of Shooters Hill, as well as the ***Purton*** register found in the Bible of the General's niece. Genl. John Smith states that the copy is made by himself. The line of John Smith and Mary Jacquelin of Shooters Hill, copied by Mr. Edward Jacquelin Davison, of Kansas City, from the old Shooters Hill Bible, is before the writer. They all state that John Smith was born ye 7th of May, 1750, about 5 in the morning. Old Common Law causes in the County Office show that Col. John Smith had litigation with two men who had contracted to ***build the stone house by the square foot.*** This suit was in the courts several years, during the period embracing the Revolutionary War. The building was ready for occupancy in the Summer of 1777, for then he signed his reports to the Governor "In my stone Hall in Hackwood Park." Lt. John Smith was member of House of Delegates from Frederick County 1779—83. Col. John Smith was State Senator 1792—95; re-elected 1796; was Member of Congress 1801—1815. In previous pages it is shown that he was in active service, and held the commission of Brig. Genl. in 1801 and 1811, promoted and held commission of Major General until his death, and received large land grants for his services. It has been shown that as County Lieutenant, he received the exiled Quakers and held them as prisoners, and also the Hessians and other military prisoners, and removed the latter to Fort Frederick in Maryland.

Genl. Smith married in Berkeley County, Feby. 10, 1781 Animus Bull, second daughter of Genl. John Bull. The author has in hand an interesting sketch of Genl. Bull and this daughter, written by Miss Jacquelin Davison. Miss Davison, now in her 80th year, told the writer that this comprehensive manuscript is not intended for publication. The descendants of these illustrious families mentioned, should hasten to preserve the valuable work that she has spent twenty years in preparing. The scope of this volume will not admit it fully, else the writer would gladly produce it *verbatim*. The date is reliable, and the style unique and attractive. Norris says Genl. Smith died in 1837 in his ninetieth year. The family record says he died in 1842, and that "he and his wife were buried at the family burying ground at Hackwood Park," which was desecrated by Federal troops during the Civil War. In 1890, their great-grandson, Edward Jaquelin Davison, of Kansas City, had them, with others buried there, removed to a lot in Mt. Hebron Cemetery, Winchester, Va.

The children of Genl. John Smith were:—

(1) Martha Maria, born Jany. 23, 1782.

(2) Eliza Barnwell, born Feb. 10, 1784.

(3) John Augustine, born Jany. 30, 1786; died 1806.

(4) Edward Jaquelin, born Dec. 30, 1787; died in infancy.

(5) Augustine Charles, born Apl. 5, 1789.

(6) Peyton Smith, born 1792.

(7) Edward J. H., born 1793.

(8) John Bull Davison, born 1803.

Martha Maria married Maj. William Davison July 21, 1800. Chas. Augustine Smith, 5th child of Genl. Smith, married Elizabeth D., daughter of Col. Charles Magill; died 1843; was prominent as a lawyer, soldier, educator and citizen; served in the War of 1812; obtained rank of Major and Colonel; prior to 1836 was principal of the Old Winchester Academy; resigned to accept charge of the Female Seminary of Columbia, S. C., returned to Winchester in 1840. He reared 11 children, all of whom became well known in several states. Those of whom the author had personal knowledge will be mentioned. Drs. John Augustine and Chas. Magill Smith became prominent physicians in Louisiana; Augustine J. Smith was President of the Maryland Agricultural College. Archie Magill Smith was once principal of the Winchester Academy, when it occupied the site of the Winchester Inn; succeeded Rev. Dr. Wheat as principal of the Episcopal Female Institute, Winchester. Va., which he resigned, yielding later to Mr. Marshall a few years ago. Professor Smith retired to his stock farm in Fauquier County. One of the daughters of Col. Augustine C. Smith became the mistress of Belle Grove as Mrs. C. B. Hite; one married Dr. L. E. Swartzwelder; one married John Marshall, Esq., of Fauquier County; one became Mrs. William A. Morgan of Jefferson County, Va.; and one was Mrs. G. W. Jackson, of Waco, Texas.

Jordans White Sulphur Springs. This popular resort was originally in the Littler grant. The sulphur springs were carefully guarded by the Catawba Indians. Annually they gathered at that point, and performed many mysterious drills, dances, and used the water. It was during one of these annual dances, that our old friend (previously mentioned) Patrick O'Riely, the Opecquon tavern-keeper, appeared, and being denied his usual privilege to use the sulphur pool for one of his guests, resented the Indians' insult. The altercation grew serious, calling for the attention of the Court in 1747. The Indians from that time abandoned their old trysting place, with its mystic spells. The Sulphur Spring tract became the property of Rezin Duvall, who enlisted the services of Dr. Williams to develop its medicinal properties. This resulted in considerable patronage of the place. Several cabins were erected, and the pool or *dam* as it was called, was enlarged; and invalids from various sections found relief. The property was purchased by Allen Williams, a brother of the Doctor. Branch Jordan, being one of the early visitors, saw in the place a prospect of increasing its patronage. He became the purchaser in 1834, and erected the first brick house, and bath house and several cottages; and for many years the place became famous as Jordan's White Sulphur Springs. Succeeding him later on came Edwin C. Jordan as the purchaser from Robt. M. Jordan, etc., heirs at law of Branch Jordan. When Williams sold to Branch Jordan, he reserved several lots that had been previously sold to Robert Page, Burr Harrison and others. E. C. Jordan, Sr., was the proprietor prior to his purchase in 1867; then he refurnished the houses and conducted the resort in an attractive style until his death in 1889. Mr. Jordan and his accomplished wife were popular with their guests. E. C. Jordan, his only son, conducted the business on a larger scale; and erected the present large hotel after the old brick house had been destroyed by fire. While the accommodations had been increased, the patronage fell off; and Mr. Jordan, after serving the County in the Virginia Legislature for two terms, sold out to his brother-in-law, Harry H. Baker, now Mayor of Winchester, and removed his family to Cape Charles, Va., where he is profitably engaged in oyster planting in that vicinity.

Burnt Factory was once known as a village, laid out in town lots. The factory was known then as "Carters Paper Mill." James Carter, son of Joseph who owned the Spout Spring property, manufactured a good grade of what was known as "printer's paper." The enterprise proved unprofitable, and it was subsequently converted into a woolen mill. Arthur Carter, a nephew, succeeded James. The paper mill and factory are unknown to the present generation.

Glengary was the home of John R. Cooke, the accomplished lawyer who practiced in all the courts of the Lower Valley. He was father of thirteen children. Private letters reveal the interest he had in his large family and estate, and his desire that his sons should "learn the arts of the husbandman during vacation days, and roam daily over the fields and through the woods." Doubtless the life he desired for his gifted sons in their school-days, laid the foundation for that inspiration we find in their literary work. These sons, Philip Pendleton and John Esten Cooke—the former at the age of 17, while a student at Princeton, found time to write of the "Forest and Glen", the green heather, and his steed *Silver Main;* while the latter gradually developed the genius of literature that was destined to sparkle as a rare gem amid the vales of the Shenandoah!

The Glengary of to-day is the property of John Nicodemus, a notable farmer. He has largely planted apples and other fruit, and is successful in his efforts. While the original Cooke plantation has been reduced by several subdivisions, the old dwelling-house has undergone very little change. There is some evidence that it is one of the old Colonial houses. The homestead was owned at one time by Rev. A. H. H. Boyd, D. D. He succeeded the Cooke family. Dr. Boyd never lived there, however, and sold it to James Lewis, who held it until his death after the Civil War. It changed hands temporarily until purchased by its present owner. Its location, two miles North of Winchester on West side of the Martinsburg Turnpike, made it a mark for desolation by the Armies as they camped and fought over every acre from 1861 to 1865.

We could enumerate many more old homesteads in the County, and then not include some places of interest to many readers; but we must for the present turn aside and mention a few old landmarks in Winchester. If the writer were to follow his inclination, he would make free use of the volume of notes prepared by Mr. W. G. Russell about twenty-five years ago, which now lies before him. But the scheme of the present work is not to give minutely such evidences of old buildings as have withstood the ravages of time and the fad for modern changes; but simply to point out here and there some places in which the passer-by may have some interest.

Bell's Corner, at the intersection of Main and Water Streets, became the property of John Bell, Sr., the grandfather of the Bell Bros. of to-day, in 1815. At that time there was a long one-story building in which the elder Bell had conducted his mercantile business for some years, as his old advertisement of "fine dry goods, books, stationery, &c.," indicates. John L. Bowen inherited the property. Mr. Bell, the new owner, erected the present building, which in all these years, has undergone very little change. In the rear of this store on Water Street, Richard Bowen had his printing office;—later on used by Collett, Haas, John Heiskell, Freeland Eichelberger, Judge Sherrard and others. These offices were in two long buildings. Mr. Bell married a daughter of Robert Sherrard. She was the mother of John N., and Rev. Robert Bell, a Presbyterian minister, who lived in Rappahannock County; also of several daughters, one of whom married Rev. Mr. Brown, and one William H. Streit, the merchant. John N. Bell, previously mentioned in this volume, was one of the old Kent Street Presbyterian elders. His father was one of the elders in the Old Presbyterian Church on the hill. John N. married twice. His first wife, Miss Miller, was the mother of John and Samuel Bell, the well-known occupants of the old store, Dr. Wm. A. Bell, the physician, and Robt. Bell, the young Confederate soldier who was killed. Mr. Bell's second wife was Marguerite Brown, of Baltimore. She was the mother of Stewart, Harmon, and the Misses Maudie and Sarah Bell.

The old stone house on West side of Loudoun Street, nearly opposite the old Presb. Church, was the home of Robert Sherrard. He erected it prior to 1800, and lived there. He was a merchant and soldier of the Revolutionary War. His children were Mrs. Bell, Robert B. who removed to Bloomery. Robert was Genl. Sherrard, the father of Robert B. and other children. Genl. Sherrard's widow married Rev. Mr. Harris, and was the mother of Rev. Joseph Sherrard and probably Jno. B.

Passing from Loudoun to corner of Cameron and Piccadilly Streets, we find on the corner a large stone house occupied by Chas. F. Eichelberger at the time of his death. The writer knew this as the home of Dr. Robt. T. Baldwin long before the Civil War. The previous owners were, first, Dr. Grayson who moved to one of the Eastern counties; then it became the property of the distinguished lawyer Jonathan D. Carlisle, ancestor of the well-known John S., a member of President Cleveland's cabinet. The old stone structure has undergone many changes, but the old walls remain. South from this corner was the home of Rev. Dr. Hill; then of Lemuel Bent. The next for many years was known as the home of David W. Barton and his large family, now the Lutheran Parsonage. This was once the property of Alfred T. Magill, whose father erected the first house on the site, part of which comprises the large building now seen,—the addition being made by Mr. Barton. South of this was the home of Col. Chas. T. Magill, the lawyer, and for many years president of the old Valley Bank.

South of the houses last mentioned are two situated on high ground, that deserve mention—the first the home of the Bell family. John Bell built the house about one hundred years ago; and there lived and died. He was succeeded by his son John N. His son Stewart Bell purchased the property in 1905, where he, his mother and sisters have always lived. Mrs. Bell died in 1907.

The other house has been known as the Conrad property for a full century; and doubtless was erected by Dr. James Conrad about

1790. The Farmers Bank was moved into this house about 1813, where it remained until 1820, when it moved into its new building on corner of Loudoun and Water Streets. For several years the property was occupied by John E. Cooke. Succeeding him was a Mrs. Scott, who used it for several years as a young ladies seminary. When she vacated, Mr. Robert Y. Conrad began his residence there about 1827, and made it a cherished home for his large family, all of whom were reared under its rooftree. Major Holmes Conrad, his son, is the present owner, and has always resided there.

The large property on the corner of same lot, where Capt. Geo. W. Kurtz has his handsome furniture warerooms, is an enlargement of a brick building erected there about 1830 by a joint-stock company, composed of Roland Heflebower and others. Thomas Latham succeeded this company; Harrison Bowers next, and then its present owner.

Leaving this section, with many old houses worthy of mention if space permitted, we pass Westward, to several of the old places that have been landmarks throughout the Nineteenth century. These are found on Washington Street. The old homestead seen on the West side, between Clifford and Cecil Streets, was at one time the home of Judge Hugh Holmes; and once the home of Mrs. Estelle Green and her daughters, who conducted a select school for young ladies. This property was owned by E. C. Breeden and Branch Jordan respectively. The latter was one of those who purchased slaves and sold them to Southern cotton planters. Some old citizens now living can tell incidents relating to the "slave-trader," as he was called. Mr. Jordan fitted up the basement with prison cages for the unruly negroes.

From the Green heirs, it passed to Judge Richard Parker, the just judge who tried John Brown. Judge Parker and his amiable and lovely wife, enjoyed the social life of Winchester in the olden times, when society was of that select type not familiar to-day. The original design of the mansion was modeled after "Monticello." The property was purchased after Judge Parker's death by one of his nephews, Mr. David McCormick, who has spared nothing in effort and money to beautify and adorn the old mansion. His sisters, Misses Libbie and Charlotte, reside in the old home of their father, the late Dr. McCormick. Their brothers are identified with large enterprises in Chicago and elsewhere.

On the same side of Washington Street, South of Cecil, is seen the home of the late Col. Wm. Byrd, who lived and died there. On this site Judge Robert White lived for many years. The old house erected by him was destroyed by fire.

On the corner of Washington and Cork Streets, an old house of note—now the home of Maj. Robt. W. Hunter—was in the early part of the Nineteenth Century the home of Obed Waite, prominent in his day, a noted lawyer, who held many offices of trust,—Mayor of Winchester, and one of the old soldiers. He had four sons and one daughter, viz: Harrison, Franklin, William, and Hugh Holmes, the daughter married Washington G. Singleton. Mr. Singleton lived on the same lot directly West, fronting on Cork Street, now the property of James B. Russell.

On the South side of Cork Street, stands an old house in a large lawn extending out to Washington Street—the home of Senator R. M. Ward. This was known in former years as the home of Col. Richard E. Byrd, grandfather of our R. E. Byrd.

Marvelous changes have taken place on Washington Street since the Civil War. The handsome home of Mr. R. T. Barton was first to appear—no pavements then. Opposite his residence was a large lot known as the Holliday nurseries. On this we find the handsome homes of Wm. H. Baker, John Stephenson, Harry H. Baker (mayor), Mrs. M. H. G. Willis, and Chas. W. Heller. On the East side of Washington, North of Mr. Barton, are the residences of A. M. Baker and W. C. Graichen; the latter's house was built by H. C. Krebs, and was his delightful home until adversity overtook him. Standing on same side of the street, but South of Cork, are the handsome homes of James B. Russell and Dr. Julian F. Ward. These modern places are mentioned to show the development of Washington Street; while out on S. Stewart Street, can be seen many attractive homes, and the Memorial Hospital, all having sprung up within recent years, and with the colossal Winchester Inn overlooking all. This section is making rapid strides. Passing from it to the Northern suburbs, the writer contrasts the present with what he knew of that end of Winchester in the past. Starting on Fairmont Avenue, the Alfred H. Powell house, now the home of Dr. P. W. Boyd, Sr.,—every one of the handsome homes seen there (North Frederick Turnpike) going North, have been built since the Civil War. Not a house on either side out to Folk or Potters Hill, was there then, except an old stone house in bad repair, near the home of Walter Barr, and the large brick house now the home of Edward Fries, formerly the Brannon Thatcher property. On Loudoun Street extended, North, the old Magill house—home of Geo. W. Keller, who has added modern style, and the brick house on West side of the street, erected by P. C. L. Burwell, were the last houses seen on the Winchester and Martinsburg Turnpike until "Neffstown" was reached. Braddock Heights and the handsome homes seen there being a creation of recent years. We may add, that the extension of Braddock Street, from Peyton, North, is just being completed, opening an avenue through a formerly dismal section, to what was once the North Common, now the "Heights", where many handsome houses have grown up since 1900. Over on the East side, we find National Avenue, instead of the Berryville Pike, along which many houses are filling the space from East end of Piccadilly Street and Fairfax Lane, to the entrance of the old John F. Wall homestead, now the property of Mr. Latham. No house there prior to the Civil War but the old toll gate, which stood near the end of Fairfax Lane. These changes are mentioned to establish dates for the new landmarks, as the city extends her suburbs.

On the four corners of Loudoun and Piccadilly Streets, are seen at this writing fine buildings. The S. V. N. Bank on the site of a lot owned by Daniel Gold about 1800, where he kept a general store, prior to which it was one of the old tavern stands. Jacob Farra obtained license several times as tavern keeper. About 1816, the first Valley Bank building was erected. Diagonally opposite, where the Evans Hotel stands, was the residence of Lewis Hoff, the first cashier of the Valley Bank. Prior to the Civil War, the old wooden building was used by Randall Evans, father of Wm. Evans, the well-known colored hack-man. The Kremer Bros. conducted there a general grocery after the war, until it gave place to the hotel erected by Henry Evans and Bro., tobacconists. Across Loudoun Street was the place known as Dunbar's Corner for one hundred years. It was the home of Dr. Dunbar. His widow occupied this corner house until her death. Her daughter was the second wife of Phillip Williams. This old landmark was removed by Mrs. Williams' heirs a few years ago, to give place to the modern store-rooms and Dunbar Flats in the rear. Grove Bros. occupy the store-rooms. Diagonally opposite, where the Cooper Bros. conduct their wholesale trade, Capt. Wm. Throckmorton carried on a large business. He was succeeded by Josiah Fawcett. Henry W. Baker succeeded him, whose son, J. Milton Baker erected the present building and conducted a large mercantile business. Passing West on Piccadilly Street, other old landmarks are disappearing. Where the Handley Library is slowly assuming proportions of grandeur, was the old Jacob Mesmer property, a well-remembered old log structure. Jacob's sons: John Jacob and Peter lived there. John was the one-armed Confederate, Chief of Police for years. The old Mackey property on the opposite corner, where Dr. Stewart Baldwin lived and died, is now having the ground broken for the new Government building, to be used for the city postoffice—the old buildings all removed. It would be interesting to the writer and possibly to some readers, to dwell longer on the subject of changed conditions in the old town; but limited space admonishes us.

Handley Library, December 1908

CHAPTER LIV

THE JOHN BROWN RAID

The Capture, Trial and Execution of Brown and His Party

The story of John Brown's raid has been told in every home in America, and even in the countries beyond the Great Oceans. The circumstances have stirred emotions that can never be understood. Old and young in millions of American homes have, from some strange influence of fanaticism, regarded John Brown as their patron saint. Children have been taught to revere his memory. His name and deeds have been woven into song and story, that tell of martyrdom and of his "spirit still marching on," Other millions regarded him as the one chosen to break the shackles of slavery and give freedom to the oppressed slaves; but misguided by his zeal, and plunged into the vortex of ruin—Though he kindled the flame that was never quenched, until his every dream had been fully realized—That the man had come, but not the hour. It is but just to the American people to add, that many other millions regarded his whole life, with its bloody exploits—whether on the plains of Kansas or along the banks of the Potomac—as one to be condemned, to suffer as a traitor. His capture and execution met their approval. Others were seized with the same desire for bloodshed that prompted Brown to do and dare so much. But when the hour came for the blow, they were crouching out of sight, and lacked the courage of their long-cherished convictions. They withheld their promised aid, and allowed the Kansas ruffian to become a hero of his kind, while their names have been held in execration by every other class.

However, there were other millions who differed in their view of this raid, as it has been termed, and regarded it in the true light that shone in upon his attempt to murder, pillage and destroy. Brown's name and his deeds have become familiar in every home in the Southland; and no crime ever committed by the most besotted wretch, was considered so heinous as the hellish designs of John Brown and his murderous gang. The English language fails in attempting to express their full intent and purpose. He had deliberately counseled with well-known abolitionists of the North and West for two full years. Aid was freely given to collect weapons to destroy every life that stood in their pathway through Virginia. The campaign was mapped out and explained to those who furnished the necessary equipment; and the point for rendezvous and attack was well chosen.

For months their emissaries had virtually environed the quiet and peaceful village of Harpers Ferry, at the confluence of the Shenandoah and Potomac. The United States Arsenal in operation at this point was to be their base, where several thousand stands of arms, once captured, added to those they had in convenient storage, would equip an army they hoped to form from the plantation slaves. The hour was well chosen, being about 10 o'clock Sunday night, October 16, 1859. At that hour, the watchman on the railroad bridge, William Williams, was surprised to find twenty-two armed men confronting him, who declared him their prisoner. They were armed with pistols and short rifles, and came from the Maryland side. Williams regarded it as a joke; but he soon discovered they were strangers, and their movements betokened trouble to someone. He was ordered to keep quiet. The party stationed two guards at the bridge, and then marched to the Armory, where the guard—half asleep—was made prisoner. About half their number took possession of the arsenal; the remainder moved rapidly up the Shenandoah River to the rifle factory, where they found a guard, who was also taken in custody. A detachment was left at the rifle works; and their leader marched back to the arsenal. They now had three prisoners. It was then about midnight, the hour for changing the watchman on the railroad bridge. Patrick Higgins, the relief, coming from Sandy Hook, entered the bridge to relieve watchman Williams, when he, too, was taken in custody and led to the Virginia side. But the plucky Irishman, when he discovered the situation, broke from his captors and fled; whereupon the strange guard fired his gun to bring him to a halt. The noise attracted the attention of a negro named Hayward, who was watchman at the railroad agent's office; and when he went out to see what caused the shot, he, too, was halted by the bridge guard, and becoming alarmed, started back to the office, but before reaching the office, he was shot by the guards. It has been stated by some writers that he was killed in the office. This is not true. He was picked up by some persons attracted to the spot by the shooting, and carried into the office, where he died during the night. This was a bad start for the Liberator of the Slave—the first victim being a negro. Brown by this time felt firmly established for the bloody work in hand, for none knew better than he, that he must expect an attack from some quarter. So he conceived the idea of securing some prominent citizens and holding them as hostages for the safety of his gang in case they were captured. Parties were sent to secure such prisoners; and by early dawn, Col. Lewis W. Washington, John M. Alstadt, and several others were brought in as prisoners and placed in the arsenal with the other three. The villagers were astir and bewildered at the strange occurrences—everything so mysterious. Some remembered seeing several strangers wandering around the country during the preceding months, who announced they were expert miners, and were prospecting for minerals in the Blue Ridge.

When morning came, the guards at the bridge and arsenal, and prisoners in custody of armed strangers, were discovered. Government employees were refused admittance to the works; some of them were made prisoners. The little village became panicky. Alarming messages were sent out into the surrounding country, to stir the people to arm in self-defense; for many believed an insurrection was on foot, headed by unknown outlaws who were firing upon every citizen daring to show himself. The second victim was Thomas Boerly, killed in his own doorway. The next was George W. Turner; then Mr. Fontain Beckham, the mayor of the town, was shot unarmed in the street. After Beckham was shot, one of the outlaws named Thompson who had been captured and confined in a room in the old Fouke Hotel, was dragged out by Beckham's nephew, Henry Hunter, aided by one Chambers, taken to the bridge, and there riddled with bullets. The wretch on his way to the bridge said: "Though you take my life, eight millions will rise up to avenge me and carry out my purpose of giving liberty to the slaves." This came out at the Brown trial in the testimony of Hunter.

Col. Robt. Baylor and Col. Jno. T. Gibson hurriedly gathered all the available militia companies and had them assemble at Harpers Ferry. The following report from Col. Gibson to the Virginia Governor, will better illustrate the situation in Jefferson County than any form the author could adopt, and is given to preserve a record of what troops, etc., took part in crushing the invasion from the North. Many members of the companies here named fell in the next invasion, two years later:

Harpers Ferry, Oct. 18, 1859.

"Henry A. Wise, Gov. of Va.

Sir—your order per telegraph dates &c. received.

On the morning of the 17th inst. I received information at Charlestown that a band of abolitionists from the North had taken possession of the Arsenal and workshops of the Government located there; that they had killed several of our citizens, taken others and held them as prisoners. and that they had in possession a large number of slaves, who on the night of the 16th inst. were forcibly taken from their masters.

I immediately ordered out the *Jefferson Guards* and the citizens of Charlestown, which order was quickly responded to, and by 10 o'clock A. M. they were armed and *en route* for this place. We left Charlestown with about one hundred men, and on reaching Halltown (midway between Charlestown and Harpers Ferry) we learned that the insurgents were in large numbers, and we at once despatched orders to Col. L. T. Moore, of Frederick County, and to the *Hamtramack Guards* and *Shepherdstown Troop* to reinforce immediately. We reached Harpers Ferry about half past eleven o'clock A. M., and took our position on Camp Hill. We immediately despatched the Jefferson Guards commanded by Capt. J. W. Rowan, and Lts. H. B. Davenport, E. H. Campbell and W. B. Gallagher, to cross the Potomac River about a mile West of the Ferry, and march down on the Maryland side and take possession of the Potomack bridge; and a company of the citizens of Charlestown and the vicinity, commanded by Capt. Lawson Botts and Lt. F. Lackland, to cross the Winchester and Potomac Railroad, by way of Jefferson's Rock, to take possession of the Galt House, in the rear of the arsenal, and commanding the entrance to the Armory Yard. Capt. John Avis and R. B. Washington, Esq., with a handful of men, were ordered to take possession of the houses commanding the yard to the Arsenal. All these orders were promptly executed.

"Between three and four o'clock P. M., the Hamtramack Guards, Shepherstown Troop and a Company from Martinsburg, commanded by Capt. E. Alburtis, arrived on the ground. The Company from Winchester commanded by R. B. Washington, arrived in the evening. All the insurgents save those who were killed and wounded through the day, retired with their prisoners into the guard-house and engine room, Just inside the gate of the Armory yard, which was firmly locked. About 3 o'clock the enemy, with the most prominent of their prisoners, concentrated in the engine room, leaving a large number of their prisoners fastened up in the guard house. At this point, and after the arrival of the reinforcements from Shepherdstown and Martinsburg, Col. R. W. Baylor assumed the command, and will furnish you with the details of what followed.

(signed) Jno. Thos. Gibson, Comdg. 55 Regt."

Col. Baylor, continuing the report, states the details as follows:

"* * * The Hamtramack Guards and the Shepherdstown Troop, dismounted and armed with muskets, under my command, proceeded down High Street to the center of the town, in front of the Arsenal. During this march, the insurgents having secreted themselves in the Armory Yard, opened a brisk fire on Captain Alburtis' Company * * * The firing was heavy, and the insurgents could not have retained their position many minutes, when the door of the engine house was opened and they presented a white flag. The firing thereupon ceased, and I ordered the troops to draw up in line in front of the Arsenal. During this engagement and the previous skirmishes, we had ten men wounded, two I fear mortally. The insurgents had eleven killed, one mortally wounded, and two taken prisoners, leaving only five in the engine-house, and one of them seriously wounded. Thirty of our citizens were rescued from the guard-house, and they still held in the engine-house ten citizens and five slaves."

In the conference which took place (during the truce) between Brown and Col. Baylor, the terms were stated by the bearer of the flag: Brown with survivors and his prisoners, to be permitted to cross the bridge to the Maryland side, and after his arrival at a point by him selected, the prisoners to be released, and then he to take his chances to escape, whether by "flight or fight". Such terms of capitulation were promptly refused; but in order to save further bloodshed, Col. Baylor offered the reckless old leader the most generous terms that he could afford. Brown was to release what prisoners he held; give them liberty to march out unmolested; and he and his party were to await the action and demand of the Washington Government, for his forcible entrance and occupation of the United States Arsenal. Brown refused all terms offered him, and sullenly retired; broke off all truce relations, and awaited the next movements of the troops.

Returning again to Col. Baylor's report, he says:

"Night by this time had set in, and the weather being very inclement, I thought it best for the safety of our citizens whom they held as prisoners, to cease operations for the night. Should I have ordered an attack at that hour, and in total darkness, our troops would have been as likely to have murdered our own citizens as the insurgents, all being in the same apartment. Having concluded to postpone another attack until morning, guards were posted around the Armory, &c. * * * About 12 o'clock, Col. Lee (afterwards Genl. R. E. Lee of the Confederate Army) arrived, having under his command eighty-five marines from Washington. The Government troops took possession of the Government property, and formed inside the Armory in close proximity to the engine-house. In this position Col. Lee thought it best to remain until morning. The night passed without serious alarm, but not without intense excitement. It was agreed between Col. Lee and myself, that the volunteer forces should form around on the outside of the Government property and clear the streets of all citizens and spectators, to prevent them firing random shots, to the great danger of our soldiers, and to remain in that position whilst he would attack the engine house with his marines. As soon as day dawned, the troops were drawn up, in accordance with the above arrangement, after which Col. Lee demanded of the insurgents to surrender upon the terms I had before proposed to them, which they still declined. The marines were then ordered to force the doors. The attempt was made with heavy sledges, but proved ineffectual. They were then ordered to attack the doors with a heavy ladder, which was lying a short distance off. After two powerful efforts, the door was shattered sufficiently to obtain an entrance. Immediately a heavy volley was fired in by the marines, and an entrance effected, which soon terminated the conflict. In this engagement, the Marines had one killed (Luke Quinn) and one slightly wounded. The insurgents had two killed and three taken prisoners. The firing ceased, and the imprisoned citizens walked out unhurt."

Col. Lee saw no reason why Brown and the few survivors of his gang, were entitled to recognition as prisoners of war; though Brown claimed to be the head of a *provisional government* having for its ultimate object, to free the slaves, and launch a new order of government in the South; and that he was commander-in-chief of all the forces that were then concentrating in many places. The authorities of Virginia were present in the person of Governor Wise, who arrived that morning at 10 o'clock with two volunteer companies from Richmond. Mr. Andrew Hunter, the Commonwealth's attorney for Jefferson County, claimed the prisoners for the offenses of murder and invasion of the State by armed desperadoes, representing that, as a matter of course, their trial must be before the civil tribunal of the county wherein the offenses had been committed. Mr. Hunter, in a most interesting narrative, prepared by himself with great care, has furnished much valuable information concerning the affair. The author has it on his table at this writing, and would be glad to give it space in this work, but its great length forbids. Some important features will be given, however.

Mr. Hunter says that "After Brown was captured, he was carried into the Superintendent's Office wounded, as also Stephens. It was then that he and Gov. Wise went in to see Brown. The Governor recognized in Brown the celebrated 'Ossawotamie murderer, and asked him if he was Ossawotamie Brown of Kansas. His reply was: 'I endeavored to do my duty there.' When Brown was washed of the grime of dust and blood, Mr. Hunter recognized him as the *John Smith* he had seen at Harpers Ferry and Charlestown during the Summer, on several occasions. Mr. Hunter then details the plan adopted to convey the prisoners to the Charlestown jail. He says that when Governor Wise informed him that the time had come for their removal, and that Capt. Rowan's Company could form the guard, he informed the Governor that such a course was unwise; that the soldiers of that Company would massacre the whole batch, and that it would be better to have Col. Lee and his marines take them to the Charlestown jail. The Governor adopted this plan; and he with Col. Lee as officer of the guard, conducted the Governor and prisoners to the county jail. Perhaps no similar incident has ever occurred. The Governor of a State surrounded by the volunteer companies of his State, yet calling upon an officer of the regular army to furnish safe conduct to prison of the remnant of the *provisional army* that had so recklessly invaded the Old Dominion.

Mr. Hunter says further that on the day of Brown's capture, he was informed "that a large number of arms were secreted in a house on the nearby mountain." The Independent Grays of Baltimore were detailed to make the search. They returned in the evening, having found 200 Sharp's rifles, 200 revolvers, 23,000 percussion caps, 100,0000 percussion pistol caps, ten kegs of gunpowder, 13,000 ball cartridges for Sharp's rifles, one Major General's sword, 1,500 pikes, and a large assortment of blankets and clothing of every description.

The writer recalls the appearance of the collection referred to, and the feeling of horror that pervaded the homes throughout the Lower Shenandoah Valley. For months the collecting had been stealthily going on in this peaceful hamlet; and its people were rudely aroused from their quiet, peaceful life, as they realized how barely they had escaped destruction.

If Brown's dream of negro insurrection had culminated as he thought it would, the uprising would have meant butchery, rapine and every other crime known to brutal men; and the *monster* would have gloated over his success. But he miscalculated his strength. The allies upon whom he staked his all, failed him. He believed the negro would rush to arms and gladly use the *steel-headed spear* that he had secreted, and was ready to place in the hands of the poor down-trodden slave that would come to him; and then go forth to murder in the most barbarous way, the sleeping inmates of the thousand homes in the lovely Valley—Homes that in that day were as dear to the slave as the master. The down-trodden slave never answered his call. A few were dragged from their homes, and efforts made to persuade, and even force, them to join the outlaw; but they shook with fear and disgust at every approach made by the ruffian. The negroes of that day could not be tempted by what meant evil to those with whom they had mingled from infancy—forming a relation between the races that can be never understood by those unfamiliar with slavery as it existed at that time. The writer knew hundreds of those grand specimens of *slavery* days. For their tender regard and concern for the welfare of the families in whom they had a part, they are entitled to the heartiest tribute we can give them. Nearly all of that old class have passed out of sight; but the memory of their devotion and good deeds, is cherished by many of us who have survived the great conflict. Peace to their ashes! But for their loyalty, the story of John Brown's raid would be differently told.

Returning to Mr. Hunter's narrative, he says: That the preliminary examinaton was before the old Justices' Court, Braxton Davenport presiding; and on the morning of the 25th of October, 1859, the prisoners, John Brown, Aaron C. Stephen and Edward Coppie, white, and Shields Green and John Copeland, colored (These two negroes came with Brown in the original party), at the close of the examination were delivered to Mr. Campbell, the Sheriff, who returned them to the jail. Cooke and Hazlett had not then been captured. The Circuit Court for Jefferson County for the year 1859, by law commenced its term on the 20th day of October. The Grand Jury was impaneled that day; —was adjourned over until the 25th by the examining Court which had disposed of the preliminary work. The Grand Jury was again adjourned until the 26th, when a joint indictment was found against Brown, Stephens, Shields,

Green, Coppie and Copeland. They were arraigned at the bar the next day, the 27th, and pleaded "not guilty." The indictment charged the prisoners with "feloniously and traitorously making rebellion and levy of war against the Commonwealth of Virginia * * * and did forcibly capture, make prisoners of and detain divers good and loyal citizens of said Commonwealth, to wit: Lewis W. Washington, John M. Alstadt, Archibald M. Fitzmiller, Benjamin J. Mills, John E. P. Dangerfield, Armstead Bell, John Donoho, and did then and there slay and murder, by shooting with firearms, called Sharpe's rifles, divers good and loyal citizens of said Commonwealth, to wit: Thomas Boerly, George W. Turner, Fontain Beckham, together with Luke Quinn a soldier of the U. S., and Hayward Shepherd a free negro * * * and did then and there * * set up without authority of the Legislature of the Commonwealth of Virginia, a government, separate from and hostile to, the existing government of said Commonwealth, and did then and there hold and exercise divers offices under said usurped government, towit: the said John Brown, commander-in-chief of the military forces; the said Aaron Stephens as Captain, the said Edward Coppie as Lieutenant; and the said Shields Green and John Copeland as soldiers * * ."

Mr. Hunter says: "The trial of Brown and his fellow prisoners was perfectly fair from beginning to end. The counsel that appeared for them were at all times courteously received, and had the free use of his office and library."

Brown was first tried, and on Nov. 4th, 1859, the jury returned a verdict of guilty on every count. Brown's counsel, Messrs. Thomas C. Green and Lawson Botts, were assigned him; but on the second day, certain counsel appeared for Brown from Boston. Brown began then to feign sickness. The Court being satisfied from the report of Dr. Mason who had made the examination, that Brown's condition was not such as to justify an adjournment of his trial, on motion of the Atty. for the Commonwealth, he was brought into court on a cot. The Court, however, adjourned over until the Monday following. Hon. Richard Parker was Judge of this Circuit, and presided throughout the trying scenes with such dignity, and firmness and fairness to the prisoners, that he received complimentary mention through the press in every section of the country. It is true, fanatics in the abolition centers, charged unfairness; but their cavil was in keeping with their promised support to old Brown in his attempt to raise insurrection among the slaves. A charge of unfairness in the trials of the John Brown raiders, appears in the famous publication of the distinguished German author Baron Von Holst, "A Constitutional History of the United States." The treatment he has given of the "John Brown Invasion," is so unfair in itself, that the author should not be entitled to credit for impartiality, when he recklessly departs from his regular line of historical incidents—expressed so graphically and attractively—to cast a shadow upon the court that patiently disposed of the criminals, and to charge unfairness in their trials. And this when he knew of the historic fact that the Governor of Virginia, supported by every officer present, civil or military, gave unstinted aid to protect the criminals and secure them a fair trial, who otherwise would have been annihilated by the exasperated citizens. Unfortunately, the history mentioned is studied in the schools of the North and West, and will create impressions that will do infinite harm.

Brown was executed on the 2nd day of December, 1859. Mr. Hunter says: "I had the body sent to Brown's wife who was at Harpers Ferry." So he was not maltreated after death, as has been often stated.

The first five prisoners were tried by Judge Parker. The prisoners Stephens and Hazlett were tried by Judge Kenney of the Rockingham Circuit,—all of whom were condemned to suffer the death penalty. Four of the number were executed on the same scaffold and at the same hour—two whites and two negroes, the white men being Cooke and Coppie; the negroes Green and Copeland.

The trial of John E. Cooke who was the brother-in-law of Governor Willard of Indiana, was very sensational. Daniel W. Vorhees was his counsel. His arguments before the jury produced an impression upon all who heard it (the writer being one of that number). His eloquence, style and diction won sympathy for his young, misguided client; and when his execution came, the writer saw many stout men sigh over the sad ending of the youth that Vorhees had so adroitly created sympathy for, from the multitude that watched the close of the first Act in the Drama of Subjugating the South, so that Slavery should become extinct.

CHAPTER LV

Civil War 1861-65
How the Shenandoah Valley Met the Issues

The Shenandoah Valley, as has been shown, having furnished her volunteers for the United States army that invaded Mexico in 1846; was left in repose from war-like struggles long enough to feel content with the peaceful avocations pursued by her inhabitants. In this lapse, however, the flurried political pulse of the United States betokened trouble. The people were sufficiently informed of the political battles waged in her forum,—as the giant leaders from all sections, continuously struggled in the arena to fan the flame that must ultimately set ablaze the great American Union, and advertise to the world the fanatical weaknesses, jealousies and inabilities of those who had flaunted the Banner of *E Pluribus Unum* in more than one port, and witnessed its influence on the people of many nations. The exciting periods were becoming so strenuous, that the attention of the peaceful and contented citizens of the quiet valley was attracted by the mutterings heard during the Presidential campaign of 1860. An awkward state of affairs existed. The two old political parties, Whig and Democratic, were overwhelmed with dissensions, leaders divided in their views of the chaotic situation brought about by the reckless battles they had fought for years, puzzled the brains of voters. The old Whig party, nearly absorbed in the North and West by an old enemy the Abolitionists, or Free Soil party; a new name was taken in this campaign, *National Republican*—which attracted the dissenters from the old Whig party by the vote the Abolitionists had polled in the previous Presidential election (1856), being nearly one million four hundred thousand, and they rallied under the new standard. These dissenters found a congenial home with their new party. The Democratic party was divided on many questions, which resulted in that party nominating two tickets. Here were two wings—one headed by Stephen A. Douglass, of Illinois, for President and H. V. Johnson, of Ga., for Vice-President, which denied the right of Congress to legislate for or against Slavery in any new territory,—the question to be controlled by the white people of each territory.

The other wing nominated John C. Breckenridge, of Kentucky, for President, and Joseph Lane, of Oregon, for Vice President. This wing held that Congress should protect every citizen of the U. S. who desired to enter any territory with all property, *including slaves;* and if such territory at any time desired Statehood,—their constitution should be so formed, and adopted by the white inhabitants of said territory, they to decide whether they would allow Slavery or not. The remnant of the Whig party hoisted its standard with its new name, The American Party. This party nominated John Bell, of Tenn., for President, and Edward Everett, of Mass., for Vice President. It declared for good principles;—For the constitution of the country, the union of states and the enforcement of the law. It failed to mention the question that disturbed the country, and in the campaign exerted very little influence.

The Republican party gathered up the old Free Soilers, Abolitionists and dissenters from the old parties, who were attracted to the simple but effective device on their standard; "We declare it to be the duty of Congress to prohibit Slavery in the Territory." Abraham Lincoln, of Ill., was nominated for President and Hannibal Hamlin, of Maine, for Vice President. As will be seen by the following statement, the people were swept from their old mooring, demagogues went howling through the land—sections arrayed against section; waves of fanaticism swept through the North and West. The South was driven to desperation by the danger that lurked in the tide that sent breakers up to her two borders,—threatening destruction to all guaranteed rights. She divided her strength, and wasted it on three leaders; the result being what was predicted by many conservative men of that day—defeat for the section that saw nothing but gloom in the election of the Abolitionists.

Lincoln received 1,857,610 votes, Douglass 1,365,976, Breckenridge 847,963, Bell 590,630. Mr. Lincoln was elected by a sectional vote; and his success brought the South face to face with the issues that had been joined in the great political battle. The alarm that seized the South at that time, seems to many of this day as unnecessary; but to many (the writer being one) who stood in full view of the great drama as it was played, thought it perfectly natural. The

Southern People knew the new party meant more than the device on their banner indicated; they knew the rank and file of that party were only interested to the extent of prohibiting Slavery in any new territory. Their minds were easily inflamed, however, as will be shown later on. The South knew what ominous words had fallen from the lips of their open and avowed enemies, who thought of nothing but the "Irrepressible" Conflict; and now since they had come to power, rule or ruin would be the watchword. It was well known that the most gifted orators and very eminent men of the North, had often shown their disregard for the Union of States, if anything stood in their way; they had announced more than once that Slavery must go. Abolitionists of the radical class of Wm. Lloyd Garrison, of Mass., "declared that there ought to be no *union with slave holders;"* and pronounced judgment against the Constitution of the United States, and declared the Federal Constitution to be, "A covenant with death and an agreement with hell;" New England and other Northern States had produced men who often in legislative halls, had proclaimed their abhorrence of a union that permitted "A *master,* the *lash* and the *slave;"* and introduced measures to be adopted to cut away from the slave holding states; others believed it their duty to invade the South with emissaries of their ilk, and work uprising among the slaves and enable them to shake off their yoke. The student of history will some day unfold the actions of both sections, and hold them up before future generations for their study and decision. The South knew that Mr. Lincoln had the reputation for conservatism; and they also knew that he might be powerless, fronting the avalanche that had pressed him to the edge of the precipice. One of the first steps taken, satisfied many wise men of the South, that he was ready to execute the Abolitionists behests—selecting, as he did, Wm. H. Seward for Secretary of State, and knowing that he still adhered to his radical views concerning the South. He it was who uttered language in 1858 in the U. S. Senate, that put Chas. Sumner, of Mass., to shame. He had recently announced from his seat in Congress speaking of Abolitionism: "It has driven you back from California and Kansas; it will yet invade your soil of Sunny South." The South was alarmed, and was doubtless unduly inflamed; but she confronted grave issues. The Author is not called upon at this point to do more than show some reasons why the people in Shenandoah Valley, as the autumn months of 1860 passed so gloomily by, should stop to enquire what these strange happenings were to bring them. The portentous clouds that had arisen in South Carolina, emitted a flash along the horizon that betokened grave conditions. A Convention of the people of that State had assembled on the 20th of Dec., 1860, and passed an Ordinance of Secession, declared all relations off between South Carolina and the other States. It was hoped by many, that the hotheaded State, as she had often been called, could be reconciled. Congress was in session since 3rd of Dec. All of the States were represented in both houses except South Carolina's Senators;—they resigned when it was known the Abolitionists had elected their ticket. Many of the able men in Congress endeavored to get compromise measures adopted, and save the Union. Of such, too much cannot be said; but the writer will leave this to others. Indeed, the reader need only go to the Congressional records of that session, and he will see such men as Crittenden of Kentucky, Jefferson Davis of Miss., Stephen A. Douglass of Ill., Toombs of Ga., and every member from Virginia struggling for days to save the Union; and continuing the struggle until the 21st of Jan., 1861. When Davis received his official information that Miss. had passed the Ordinance of Secession on the 9th day of Jan., it now became his duty to withdraw from the Senate and await the further action of his State. Mr. Davis's speech on that occasion should be handed down to posterity to let them judge him by the sentiments expressed. Florida took the same step Jan. 10th, 1861; Alabama followed on the 11th, Georgia on the 19th, Louisiana on the 26th, and Texas on the 1st Feb., 1861.

The inauguration of Mr. Lincoln took place 4th of March, 1861. One thing occurred at that time, which gave evidence of the temper of the new President. In his address, he gave out no uncertain sound;—said he intended to collect the revenues at every Port, and would recover all arsenals, forts and other property previously held by the General Government. This was an open declaration of War; and to maintain his position, the President must have an army. The regular army posts in the South had been abandoned, except Forts Sumter, Pickens and several smaller places along the Coast. He had no available force in the South; and the country awaited anxiously to see how he intended to recover them. The question was feverishly asked, would he attempt to march troops through the States, to not only retake the forts and collect the port taxes, but to coerce the Seceded States? The country was soon apprised. On the 15th of April, 1861, the President issued his first call for troops—"Give me seventy-five thousand men and I will crush the rebellion." He also called an extra session of Congress for 4th of July.

Events are crowding now. The Seceded States had organized a Government of Confederate States at Montgomery, Alabama, Feb. 4th,—formed a Constitution; elected Jefferson Davis, President and Alexander H. Stephens, of Ga., Vice President. The other Southern States took no action as to secession, until after Lincoln issued his call for troops; and when they were called upon to furnish their quota of troops to coerce their sister States, the reluctant step was taken, and Virginia, the old mother State, who had struggled so hard to maintain her place in the Union, answered with no uncertain sound, April 17th, 1861, having passed her Ordinance of Secession, and then warned the invader that she was ready to meet the struggle. From mountain to sea, the folds of her banner as they opened to the breeze, *"Sic Semper Tyrannis,"* told all comers how Virginia would take her place with the Sister Southern States. Arkansas followed May 6th, North Carolina May 20, Tennessee June 8th. These States took this course, not because they desired a separation from the Old Union, but believed the general government was assuming a right to coerce the dissatisfied States, which was not in accordance with the principles embodied in the old Declaration,—"To be free and independent States." No one ever doubted the right of any of the Original Thirteen States to withdraw from the original compact, that had always been called *The Union.* Many people doubted the propriety of such an act, and deplored the necessity; but the right of Secession, which was guaranteed them when the Union was formed, was a sacred right that they could not allow to be wrested from them under any pretense. And thus Virginia was plunged into the fratricidal strife, and the four years of rapine and carnage which well nigh stripped her of all but her glory. The hundreds of battles fought on her plains, made their soil sacred to the memory of those who survived the desolation and recall the gallant deeds of the chivalry of the Southland, where her noble sons went down on the ensanguined field. Survivors have reared monuments, and never cease to recount the deeds of valor of the fallen; but nothing can assuage the grief and disappointment that struck every heart when they *furled that banner,* and turned their weary foot-steps toward the desolate hearthstones.

Virginia was destined to be the theater of the War in the East. Richmond was chosen as the capital of the New Confederacy. President Davis hastened to establish the Government there; and volunteers for service came from every quarter. Virginia had called her Militia Brigades to rendezvous at different points, and prepare for active service. The Old Valley responded cheerfully—her Militia Regiments were soon on their way to places designated.

The Country, comprising many tracts of well cultivated land, was rich with its approaching harvest; but when that tocsin of war rang through her valleys that the invader was on Virginia soil, the writer recalls with deep emotion at this late day the consternation that was produced one night when the town bells burst forth to ring the news that had just arrived,—that the enemy was in Romney, Bloomery and other points along the border—pressing on towards the Valley. Men went scurrying through the country, to spread the alarm—and 'ere night-fall of the next day, hundreds of men old and young rushed to Winchester to offer their services. There were some odd munitions of war—old rifles and shot pouches that were brought forth, many without powder or bullet;—no preparation at the county seat to supply the deficiency,—no provision made to quarter the unorganized parties. The Old Market House was thrown open, and the citizens of the old town called on for the first time to contribute what they could in food from their homes. Several Regiments and Battalions under command of Gen. James H. Carson, had already marched several days previous to meet the enemy, not knowing the Yankees had really dared to invade Virginia. The Militia encountered them at Bloomery in the Eastern part of Hampshire County about thirty miles N. W. from Winchester. Who can recount the incidents of that march and encounter, without relating the experience of one Militia Regiment. Their Colonel mounted on a superb stallion, of immense size, the two unwieldy bodies were placed at great disadvantage in the effort to maneuver the troops in a narrow defile in Bloomery Gap; and catching a glimpse of the approaching Bluecoats, the Colonel cried out his command in such tones as to startle the enemy, and put new life into the ranks of his brave followers. His command was—and lest it be forgotten the writer gives it a place at this point—"Be quick men—give way to the enemy—but save your Colonel." This big Dutch Colonel, and his big horse, escaped capture;—but his fright clung to him for years. This was his last charge and retreat,—for Virginia had issued orders to disband the Militia and afford the men an opportunity to enter Volunteer companies or reorganize new companies and elect officers from their ranks.

It had been determined to use Harpers Ferry as the strong strategic point to concentrate the numerous independent companies of infantry, cavalry and about one dozen cannon. Many officers were trying to discover who was ranking officer; but all went well, and all agreed to hold the point, without much discipline; and it was during this independent military occupation, that a strangely awkward figure appeared on the scene, producing his commission as Colonel from Gov. Letcher of Virginia, with orders to assume command and proceed to organize an army at that point. The stranger was Col. Thomas J. Jackson, the eccentric military attache at the military Institute at Lexington, Virginia. He soon impressed the Regimental and Company officers with the feeling that a master disciplinarian was in their midst, and their disorder would disappear; never dreaming they were destined to share in the renown of the man who, in a few months, shocked the Washington Government by his first contact with their boastful army; and won fame and name among such comrades as the immortal General Bee on the hills of Manassas.

Col. Jackson found nearly five thousand raw soldiers, composed of volunteer companies and Militia detachments under Gen. Harper, making some show as a garrison. He inaugurated a system that was soon apparent to all; that he would have an army organized for some military genius. Forming battalions, regiments, etc., he used them in several exploits without contact with Federal troops. Lincoln's seventy-five thousand men were assembling at points no nearer than Washington City, fifty miles away, and Chambersburg, Penna., about forty-five miles North of Harpers Ferry. At the latter place Gen. Patterson was organizing an army of about twelve thousand; Jackson had possession of the Baltimore and Ohio Railroad from the point of Rocks in Maryland, twelve miles East and for about one hundred and twenty miles on the Virginia side of the Potomac towards Cumberland. Jackson protected the traffic over this road for more than a month, allowing the mails and all freights to pass unmolested. A desire seized the Garrison to capture the heavily laden trains, quantities of grain, cattle and coal seemed on a rush to the Washington Government, yet the strange Colonel forbade interference; at last it was whispered through the camps that such action was one of President Davis's schemes to induce Maryland to join the Confederacy. Jackson, however, conceived a plan to conciliate all parties, he argued that the enormous shipments of coal was a menace to the Confederacy—in as much as it was intended for Naval supplies. Mr. Davis was in a quandary, and permitted Jackson to use discretion in any protests he made to the Federal Government. This could be easily done through the President of the Railroad company. Jackson had several interviews, which resulted in a change of schedule. He was now planning for his first strategic move on the New Chess Board. He stationed one regiment at Martinsburg and a battalion at Point of Rocks. The new schedule provided that heavy freights must pass both ways in the day time, and none in the night, as the night trains disturbed the rest of his troops. The railroad authorities were glad to make any change so as to save the right to use the roadway. Jackson also demanded tolls from the Railroad which were promptly paid. The day came when he gave orders to his detachments at Martinsburg to allow no trains to pass West of that point; and the Point of Rocks post to allow nothing to pass that point going East. This tie up for one day was all Jackson desired. Thus he caught all the trains on the tracks between the points, and hurriedly transferred them with their locomotives to the Winchester and Potomac road and soon landed his first capture in Winchester, thirty miles South from Harpers Ferry. From Winchester, they were taken by horse power to Strasburg, and transferred to the Manassas Gap Railroad. Shortly after this first surprise to the Washington Government, he was relieved by Gen. Joseph E. Johnston (May 24, 1861), and many soldiers regarded this as a reproof to Jackson for his seeming disregard of previous instructions. Col. Jackson in his skill and knowledge of military tactics, had proven himself capable for organization of the many separate and independent forces concentrating at Harpers Ferry. General Johnston found the army fully up to his expectations; all in perfect harmony with his old discipline; no changes were made. The camps were in perfect military condition, and he soon recognized that he had in Jackson a Lieutenant worthy of further notice by the Confederate Government; and proceeded at once to secure his promotion and service in his new army; Jackson had with some pride no doubt, grouped the regiments made up of men from West of the Blue Ridge, and formed his first Brigade, composed as follows:

The Second Virginia Regiment of Infantry, Col. Allen.

The Fourth Virginia Regiment of Infantry, Col. Preston.

The Fifth Virginia Regiment of Infantry, Col. Harper.

The Twenty-seventh Virginia Regiment of Infantry, Col. Echols.

The Thirty-third Virginia Regiment of Infantry, Col Cummings.

The Rockbridge Artillery, Capt. Rev. Dr. Pendleton.

This combination became the famous Stonewall Brigade; and added to this, was the

Cavalry under the command of Turner Ashby. This company, together with other Cavalry companies appearing at Harpers Ferry, constituted the 7th Virginia Cavalry, which was organized by Lieut. Col. Angus W. McDonald of Winchester, Virginia, June 17th, 1861, the companies composing this Regiment being:

Company A—Capt. Dick Ashby, of Fauquier County, Va.

Company B—Capt J. Q. Wingfield, of Rockingham Co., Va.

Company C—Capt. S. D. Myers, of Shenandoah County, Va.

Company D—Capt. Macon Jordon, Page County, Va.

Company E—Capt. Walter Bowen, Warren County, Va.

Company F—Capt. George F. Sheetz, Hampshire County, Va.

Company G—Capt. Frank Mason, of Maryland.

Company H—Capt. A. Harper, Shenandoah County, Va.

Company I—Capt. E. H. Shands, Rockingham County, Va.

Company K—Capt. Wm. Miller, of Shenandoah County, Va.

Regimental Officers:

Angus W. McDonald, of Winchester, Virginia, Colonel.

Turner Ashby, of Fauquier County, Lt. Col.

Oliver M. Funsten, Warren County, Maj.

A. W. McDonald, of Romney, Adjutant.

Dr. A. P. Burns, Surgeon.

Rev. James D. Avirett, of Frederick County, Chaplain.

Thornton P. Pendleton, of Clarke, A. Q. M.

John D. Richardson, of Clarke, Commissary.

While no company appears from Frederick in this branch of the service, many of her sons were members of the companies named. Col. Jackson was assigned to command the 1st Brigade, which did much to make it possible for him to accomplish the military wonders that won distinction for the General and his Valley men. Both were of that type that had distinguished their ancestors in the French and Indian Wars; and produced such heroes as Morgan and his Valley Riflemen, who stormed the impregnable walls of Quebec.

As we recall the personnel of the Valley army, a strange admixture of people appears. The gray-haired sire and beardless boy from the Shenandoah vales, mingling with the hardy men who had left their Mountain home,—all seeking an opportunity to defend their homes from the invader. We know that pure patriotism caused this assemblage of bold spirits at Harpers Ferry in the Spring of 1861. And the world is learning slowly to appreciate the patriotism that was quenched at Appomattox in 1865. No single class is entitled to distinction above the other; the cabin along the slopes of the Blue Ridge, and the fastnesses of the Alleghany and Massanutten, sent rugged men who became renowned for their adaptation to any duty. Their stern sense of right won the affection of their new associates; and the lowlander was glad to jostle the elbow of the mountaineer while on the battle line. These men were not battling to perpetuate slavery, but more to maintain State's Rights,—a doctrine that was instilled in their forefathers by Jefferson; and will be never abandoned as long as true patriots live. The day is at hand when the States which disregarded this doctrine in 1861, are clamoring for its security; and are looking to the Southern States for help. Colonel Jockson with his zeal and energy, soon found work for his Brigade, the cavalry was distributed along the border line, with Col. McDonald's base at Romney, this line extending from far away points on the upper Potomac, distant from Harpers Ferry full one hundred and thirty miles—was bound to attract the attention of Patterson from his base at Chambersburg. Detachments of Cavalry were dispatched to points on the Potomac beyond Martinsburg. Jackson had gone to the Maryland side and secured the Maryland Heights, and had fortified the position without orders, and wrote Gen. Lee a letter that impressed him with the importance of holding such a strategic position. Only part of this letter is quoted: "I am of opinion that this place should be defended with the spirit which actuated the defenders of Thermopylae; and if left to myself such is my determination. The fall of this place would, I fear result in the loss of the Northwestern part of the State; and who can estimate the moral power thus gained to the enemy and lost to ourselves?" (See O. R. Volume 2, page 814). Operations in the lower valley later on, throw some doubt on Jackson's judgment, though he was sustained by Gen Lee. Gen. Johnston regarded the place as untenable, and prepared for evacuation. Gen. Lee advised to the contrary. Johnston urged that his troops were unprepared for offensive action, and that his line was too long for such ventures. As Patterson had then passed from Penn., into Maryland with fourteen thousand men, heading for Williamsport.

An expedition was sent from Cumberland in the direction of Romney, which was held by Militia detachment. Col. McDonald kept his small detachments of Cavalry busy on the border. His lines were too thin; and when the Federals appeared at Romney, he was compelled to evacuate after stubborn resistance. This investment of Romney by Federal troops and the near approach of Patterson to the Potomac above, and continued demonstrations beyond the Point, by a large force of Federal Cavalry, caused Johnston to hasten the work of evacuation. On June 1st, 1861, he destroyed the railroad bridge at Harpers Ferry, removed all the old arsenal machinery available; burned the government buildings, and on the 15th fell back to Winchester. The work of destruction was entrusted to Capt. Charles Fauntleroy. The author witnessed the conflagration. Jackson's Brigade was left in front of Patterson's, and succeeded, from his new base at Martinsburg, in keeping the latter on the North side of the Potomac until Johnston had all his wagon trains, troops, etc., safely located around Winchester. While he was removing all the engines and cars from Martinsburg that could be found, he finally on June 20th burned the workshops at the B. & O. R. R.

This was accomplished while Patterson waited at Williamsport, ten miles away. Just previous to the evacuation, Lieut. Col. J. E. B. Stuart, appeared at Harpers Ferry, and was assigned by Johnston chief of cavalry. Under his immediate command, however, he could scarcely muster four hundred men; and they were scattered from Point of Rocks to Martinsburg. At first he was regarded by the troopers as a freak—something between the real soldier and a dashing cavalier. He rode gaily along the front with plumes falling from his three-cornered hat over his shoulders. His equipment as a soldier was odd,—uniform somewhat worn, but a distinct style that attractively set off his manly form. He was a fine horseman, and elicited admiration from the men who had witnessed feats of the Ashby brothers. Within ten days, the gallant Four hundred were at his heels wheresoever he went; eager to catch the strains of the war song he so often sung. Not long after, they had ample opportunity to follow Gen. Jeb Stuart in his numerous raids. Jackson and Stuart became close friends. In one of his dashes along the picket line, he discovered Patterson's movement of preparation to cross the Potomac, and he reported this to Jackson. On the second of July, when Patterson was fairly over on the Virginia side, Jackson prepared for his first contact with the Union Troops. He had been instructed by Johnston to avoid general engagements;—to only discover their strength and intentions. This he entrusted to Stuart; while he, with a battery supported by the 5th Virginia under Col. Harper, moved out near the little village of Falling Waters, about five miles South of the Potomac, and near this point the Valley Army fired their first guns. Patterson's van guard was surprised and thrown into confusion. Then was heard the rebel yell as the detachment of the 5th Virginia charged after them; but Jackson called them off to form on the original line. The enemy came back in great style with superior numbers; but at the opportune moment one single gun sent a telling shell into the pursuing column, which produced such confusion that the gay column was in full retreat. Then the Confederate battery was in action to dislodge the Federal battery which they soon drove from their position. Jackson held the field, and gathered up the wounded; and received the first prisoners captured by the Valley army. Stuart had the credit of this capture. He was out on Patterson's right flank with a squad of Troopers; and saw in a field a bunch of Federal Infantry. He was alone at the time; dashing up to the fence, he ordered one of the men to remove the rails, so that he could reach the lost company. He, wearing the old United States uniform, they were taken unawares; and as he shouted, "Throw down your arms or you are all dead men," the order was obeyed; and at this juncture the Confederate troopers came up and marched the prisoners (50) to Jackson's position, where he gave the order to march them to Winchester. (O. R. Vol. 2, P. 157.) Patterson was deceived regarding Jackson's strength; for in his official report, he places the Virginia force at 3,500, when as a matter of fact, not over 500 men had gone out to reconnoitre. While this movement was proceeding, the loss to both armies did not exceed twenty men killed and wounded; but this was their first blood; and old comrades of to-day are glad to meet some of the men who were with Jackson and Stuart in their first and last battle. The next day, July 3rd, Jackson received his commission as Brigadier General in the Confederate army. Jackson fell back in the vicinity of Bunker Hill or about seven miles South of Martinsburg; and remained four days waiting for Patterson to attack. But this prudent Chieftain was content to remain in Martinsburg. Johnston had reinforced Jackson with his entire command; and doubtless Union men gave information of this preparation. On the 8th day of July, Johnston fell back to Winchester; and abandoned that end of the Valley. Men fairly groaned over Johnston's apparent tardiness, if not unfitness; but the old hero knew of his scanty supply of ammunition,—the Infantry had fourteen cartridges apiece, and the Cavalry deficient in arms; while the batteries had meager supplies. He also knew that his services might be called for from the army over the Blue Ridge. Gen. Beauregard was then at Manassas Junction with 20,000 Southern soldiers to stay the advance of Gen. McDowell from Washington, with 50,000 volunteers and regulars, and scores of batteries. West of Staunton, 20,000 of Federals were heading for the Valley. The small force on Rich Mountain was not expected to do more than prevent the occupancy of the upper Valley. After the unfortunate killing of Brigadier General Robt. S. Garnet, and defeat of that small army on the 11th of July, the Valley people began to realize then that Gen. Johnston had more than one point to consider. We now have three points of invasion on Virginia soil; the entire force being about 80,000, not including the column at Romney. To meet these formidable columns, were about 30,000 Confederates all told. The two detachments of militia stationed at Bloomery and Romney,—the former commanded by Col. Robt. F. Baldwin, with the regiment from Berkeley County, Col. Sincindiver, occupying the North Gap, and Col. W. H. Harness with his militia Regiment at Romney, supporting Col. McDonald's 7th Cavalry, then on the line of the B. & O. R. R., met with losses during the period treated in former pages. One incident deserves special notice;—this was the loss of Capt. Dick Ashby, brother of Lieut. Col. Turner Ashby, who was then Northwest of Romney. The two brothers were familiar figures in Winchester;—always prominent at the County fairs and popular tournaments of the Lower Valley where the skill of horsemanship was severely tested. The brothers were inseparable. On the morning of the 26th of June (1861), Capt. Dick was informed by his brother, that he had discovered many citizens living along the border line who were secretly giving information to the enemy, of every movement the Confederates made; and they were organized and controlled by one man, who was a pronounced enemy of the South. From his home in that section he conducted a secret service, helpful to the Federal commander at Cumberland. Col. Turner instructed his brother as to a plan for the capture of this man; and left the rest to Capt. Dick and his small squad of trusted followers. While seeking for clues that would lead to the capture of the leader of the gang of spies, he suddenly entered the Federal line formed in picket posts along the B. & O. R. R. The Federals had been apprised of his whereabouts, through these secret agencies; and lay in ambush. Ashby crossed the Railroad at an unguarded point and entered this ambuscade, which poured forth a deadly volley. Strange to say, all escaped injury, but discovering a large body of Federal Cavalry charging upon them from a nearby wood, the Ashby party of 11 men hurriedly left the scene. Capt. Ashby made several unsuccessful attempts to recross the Railroad over a cattle stock, the only place possible, and there his horse fell the third time. Before he could recover himself, the Federals were upon him. Realizing they meant his brutal murder, he fought with desperation after they had wounded him twice. His shots had telling effect, several men were wounded, one of whom is yet alive, and recounts the encounter as the most desperate he witnessed during the war. About forty men were eager to shoot the prostrate man, and when he had fired his last shot, one man dismounted and plunged a bayonet through his side, and then left him dead as they thought. Col. Turner Ashby the same day, in one of his scouts along the Railroad, had learned that his brother had passed that point in the morning, and shots had been heard in a certain direction. He hastened on to find the battle ground; but not his brother. He easily followed the trail of the retreating Federals, and encountered them at Kelly's Island in the Potomac. A dash was made to surprise the foe. Through a swift current they rode, but 'ere they gained a footing on the bank, two of the gallant fellows fell from their horses, wounded by a volley from the enemy who were preparing for a fight. Turner Ashby was now desperate, he believed this party had murdered his brother, and he was eager to avenge his death; and in his desperation, he cried, "At them with your knives men," the Federals were over-awed by such desperation; and as one of their number in recent years said, "They were demons in our eyes, and their yells paralyzed every man." Ashby and his gallant band fought like demons, and drove all who escaped injury from the Island. The Col. found among the captured spoils, his brother's horse, saddle, spurs, and one pistol. He started a search for the Captain's body, who was found under a tree, not far from where he had received the eight desperate wounds. The pitiable picture tried the strength of every trooper. Turner, the brother, was speechless. While all dwelt upon the vengeance wrought in the force at Kelly's Island, this could not assuage the grief of Turner Ashby. He always regarded this as a brutal murder, and fixed the blame upon the element of would-be Union men found on the border during the war, who would betray friend or foe to protect their miserable existence.

The fight at Kelly's Island, a skirmish at Bloomery, where Col. Baldwin and several of his command were captured, had all occurred before Johnston retired to Winchester. From the time Johnston went into camp around Winchester on the 8th, it was noticeable that he was preparing for some movement. For six days, every officer was busy with his several duties.

Some felt that a sudden attack would be made on Patterson—whose army must give way to the invincible little army led by Johnston—and that he would march into Maryland, and offer her people an opportunity to join the Southern cause. Many hallucinations were afloat. The Confederates felt their prowess, and boasted that Southrons could drive ten times their number across the Potomac, and that the Northerners who had enlisted for ninety days, would not stand the rush of Confederates. Alas, such fallacies were dissipated like the morning mist. It is safe to say that Gen. Lee understood the situation and counseled strategy and concentration of small forces to meet any column then seeking conflict. Events of the war show that the Federal leaders failed to divine the plan of Lee's warfare. They were confused and startled often to find reinforcements on the battle line, coming from sections that seemed to require the presence of every soldier. The first lesson taught the Washington authorities, was near at hand. Patterson was instructed to threaten Winchester and thus hold Johnston, and prevent the withdrawal of his regiments to support Beauregard, while he with his main force would hasten to join McDowell, and completely crush the Confederates at Manassas. Lee, however, divined their plan, and held out inducements for McDowell to advance. Beauregard and Johnston were informed of his plans; and the delicate task of eluding Patterson was assigned to Gen. Johnston, who ordered all the cavalry from the outer posts and concentrated them under Stuart's command, he to use his judgment to make a feint for invasion. Pickets were driven across the Potomac above Martinsburg, while Patterson was at Charlestown; and citizens within his lines were told of the Northern invasion, and the first great battle would be fought North of Mason and Dixon's line. Patterson had left Martinsburg on the 15th, taking his line of march to Winchester. He halted for two days at Bunker Hill. Not being able to draw Johnston out, he moved across country to Charlestown, where we find him on the 17th with an army of ninety-day men, and their term about expired. They were not inclined to be enthusiastic. Patterson's letters to Washington revealed the situation. He told his men that Mr. Lincoln expected every man to stand by the colors; and reinforcements would come, and they would secure Johnston's capture if he crossed the Potomac. Stuart kept the dissatisfied Pennsylvanians in great terror. They needed a man with more energy and ambition than Patterson possessed, to stimulate them. Here was an opportunity lost. Patterson should have forced Johnston to battle, and not given him time to mature plans for reinforcing Beauregard.

McDowell was on the march and actually engaged the Confederate General late in the day July 16th. Patterson claimed that he had not been informed of this movement, and that had he been, he could have made sufficient demonstrations in Johnston's rear, so that his delay in reaching Manassas would have produced different results. In the night of July 17th, Johnston received a telegram from President Davis that McDowell was advancing. The General knew what this meant, he was fully prepared for his part of the campaign. Couriers and staff officers dashed through the camps, circulating orders for the army to prepare for marching. The morning of the 18th, soldiers and citizens were bewildered when the head of the column turned South. Regiments filed through the streets, heading for the Front Royal Turnpike—Artillery and wagon trains bringing up the rear. By eleven A. M., the army was out of sight. The militia under Gen. Carson, once more were in evidence, to hold the post and care for about sixteen hundred sick men; while Stuart and the Cavalry appeared so often among the hills in front of Patterson, that his entire army was in mortal terror. The army was halted near the Opecquon ford, and for the first time the men learned the object of this dispiriting movement. The army was marching in two columns—one via Millwood, the other via Front Royal This order was read by officers along the line: "Our gallant army under Gen. Beauregard is now attacked by overwhelming numbers. The commanding General hopes that his troops will step out like men and make a forced march to save the country."

A letter from Gen. Jackson says: "The effect of this stirring appeal was instantaneous; the soldiers rent the air with shouts of joy, and all was eagerness and animation." The lines of march were well defined now; the soldiers pressing every effort to scale the Blue Ridge. The first Brigade was led off by Jackson, and headed for Berry's Ferry Gap, where they halted for an hour to give time for supper. At ten o'clock that night the Brigade bivouacked at Paris, on the East side of the Ridge, seventeen miles from Winchester. The troops forded the river. The other Brigade, Bee's, Bartow's and Elzey's took the Front Royal Turnpike, and camped that night on the Shenandoah about fourteen miles from Winchester. The next morning (Friday) the 19th, Jackson marched to the Railroad station at Piedmont, six miles distant. The Brigade was there at eight o'clock, and were then thirty-four miles from Manassas Junction. Trains were ready, and by ten o'clock the Brigade was aboard and started for the Junction, where they arrived at 1 o'clock with about twenty-six hundred men. The other Brigades reached Piedmont Station in the afternoon of the 19th. Here was an unfortunate delay. Johnston had arranged for the Railroad to land the four brigades in Manassas early Saturday morning the 20th,—no cars for more than two additional Regiments. The 7th and 8th Georgia, Bartow's Brigade, were sent off—about 1,400 men. The remaining Infantry Regiments were compelled to wait for two days with scant supply of rations. Stuart and part of his Cavalry overtook the command at this time; and as they trotted by, Stuart sang his old song to the Infantry—"If you want to have a good time, come jine the Cavalry."

The Artillery continued their march, and made good time by their arrival at Manassas on the 20th. Johnston went with the 4th Alabama, the 2nd Mississippi, and two companies of the 11th Miss.,—about eleven hundred in all. This force arrived in time for the opening battle. During Saturday night, 20th, Kirby Smith and Elzey got transportation, and with the 6th N. C., 10th Va., 3rd Tenn., and 1st Md.,—about 2,000 men, arrived at Manassas about 1 o'clock on Sunday, and were hurried away for the battle field, six miles distant. They have the credit for saving the day. The 9th Ga., 2nd Tenn., 13th Va., 1st Ky., and part of the 11th Miss., for some reason, were the last of Johnston's 11,000 to arrive; and missed the battle by one day. The men were chagrined at their failure.

The reader must not expect to find in these pages a complete history of the battle of Manassas. Others have given this; and it is not within the scope of this work to do more than to follow the Valley men, as they took position on the fields; and to briefly show how the First Brigade was handled by Jackson. Their first appearance is on the banks of Bull Run, between Blackburn's and Mitchell's fords, near where Bee and Bartow were stationed with their Brigades, between the Blackburn and McLean fords. This position was in the rear of the center, and regarded as reserves. The Confederate battle line, about six miles long, extended from the stone bridge over Bull Run to the Ford at Union Mills on the extreme right. McDowell was well on the ground in the vicinity of Centerville with flanking columns—all in good shape for a drawn battle on the 18th, which he could have precipitated on Beauregard before Johnston's arrival; and with his overwhelming force could have dealt a blow to the South with staggering results, and saved the morale of his army. He was content, however, to only feel his way with his army of 35,000 men. Many were old soldiers—and with his superior Artillery, this formidable array at one time promised victory for the Federals. The firing, started on the 18th, came from this army; ending in nothing more than a skirmish, compared with what followed on the 21st. The losses, while small on both sides, sent a thrill through both armies, the Confederates held the ground with a loss of 15 killed, 53 wounded; none missing.

The Federals lost 19 killed, 38 wounded and 26 missing. On the night of the 18th, McDowell changed his plans of flank attack to a direct one on the Confederate center. This change made it possible for Johnston to enter the arena unobserved by McDowell's column on his right. On Johnston's arrival, he courteously yielded to Beauregard, his seniority of rank, and trusted him to dispose the positions among the various Brigades, while he took observations from the field. From that moment, they worked in harmony with Johnston in command. Sunday the 21st day of July, 1861, was eventful. The day dawned with a clear sky, and tokens of a hot sun. Feverish feeling pervaded both armies;—for all realized that a great conflict could not be postponed. In the early morning, Col. Evans, who had been on the extreme Confederate left at Stone bridge for two days, found a heavy column in his front making such demonstrations, that he felt sure the main attack was to be from that quarter, and prepared to meet the heavy odds against him. Musketry and artillery firing by the Federals under Gen. Tyler, opened shortly after 6 A. M., when skirmish lines fell back to give way for regular battle. Evans won recognition for his ability shown that morning. He saw the intention of the enemy to turn his left, and hastened to take position to meet the column of dust seen in the direction of Sudley Springs. He, however, left several companies to hold the bridge, and sent for other brigades at the other Ford, to reinforce the Stone bridge detachment. About 8 o'clock, Johnston and Beauregard secured information by signals from Capt. Alexander, what the situation was on the left. They at once hastened to the brigades of Bee, Jackson and Cocke; and rushed them to the left flank. This change put Bartow and the Hampton Legion in the column then marching to save Evans. McDowell had held to his original plan to turn the Confederate left; and virtually withdrew his designs upon the center. This enabled Johnston to take the Brigades at the fords on Bull Run and concentrate them at the crucial point on the left. The Federals Evans saw on the Sudley Springs Road, had found fords beyond stone bridge, and were rapidly passing to the South side,—but keeping up a continuous fire from their Artillery upon flank and rear of the Confederates, in their efforts to head off flanking columns. Tyler and the first division were hammering away at stone bridge, to give time for two divisions, 2nd and 3rd under Hunter and Heintzleman, which formed the flanking column then crossing the ford in the vicinity of Sudley Springs, to complete their flank movement; while another division threatened the fords below stone bridge, from which reinforcements must go to save the left flank, as already shown. At Centerville, McDowell had in reserve the 5th division, while the 4th division was on the railroad East of his headquarters, to protect his communication with Washington and the hundreds of spectators from the city, that accompanied his army to witness the *sport;* (see O. R. Vol. 2.) Confronting this formidable army, whose divisions had taken the positions briefly stated, the Confederates, as partly shown, were lined up in Brigade positions on South side of Bull Run at 6 A. M., Sunday, 21st. One exception, however. This was D. R. Jones on the Centerville side a short distance from the McLean ford. Ewell and Holmes were at the Union Mills ford. Early, Bartow and Jackson on the road leading to McLean and Blackburn's fords; while Longstreet was at Blackburn's ford; Bonham and Bee and Mitchell's ford; Stuart's Cavalry between the latter ford and Island ford,—where Hampton's Legion was guarding this and Ball's ford; Cocke just above at Lewis' ford, and Evans on the Warrenton Turnpike where it crosses the Bull Run over the stone bridge. Beauregard and Johnston were together at Mitchell's ford at 11 A. M. The constant firing on the extreme left, led them to believe that Bee and Bartow were on the ground, and likely there would be the place where the Federals would make their supreme effort. Johnston tells in his reports that at 11:30 A. M., he was convinced, and said: "Beauregard, the battle is there, I am going." Then it was that orders were given by Beauregard for Holmes, Early, Bonham, with Walker's and Kemper's batteries, to double quick to the firing point, while D. R. Jones was withdrawn to the South side to do his best to hold the fords. During this time, the battle had drifted somewhat. The Federals who crossed Bull Run at the Sudley Springs Ford, marched a full mile in the direction of Manassas Junction. This brought them almost in the rear of the Confederates at Stone bridge, where Tyler was trying to force his way through. The Confederates were now taking position on the celebrated *Henry Hill,* to intercept the divisions coming from Sudley, and to secure strong positions for a general engagement that seemed imminent. Some writers have criticised the two generals for trusting so much to their Brigadiers, who chose positions and fought their brigades without general supervision. On this field they immortalized themselves. Bee, Bartow and Hampton were with Evans on this Henry Hill at 11 A. M. Evans had been driven from the stone house near the Warrenton Pike, and joined the reinforcements near the Henry house that had taken position there. Bee and Evans were in dire straits. Wade Hampton made an earnest effort to rally their retreating regiments upon his command. Here he made the memorable fight that resulted in losing 121 men out of 600. He caused a delay in the Federal advance for two hours. At this time the Confederates fell back under a seething fire from the Federals. At this juncture a fresh brigade appeared on a high point near the Henry house, drawn up in line of battle. Bee galloped up to the Commander, and recognized General Jackson with his Valley Virginians, cried out: "General, they are driving us." "Then, sir," said Jackson, "We will give them the bayonet." Jackson had received orders to march from Mitchell's ford to the firing line. As he proceeded on this march, his wonderful genius began to develop. As he approached the Henry house, he soon saw at a glance the points that should be held; and selecting his position there, he lined up the Brigade that was to become famous from that hour. Bee hastened back to his retreating men and called out to them: "See Jackson standing like a stone wall. Rally behind the Virginians." Up to that moment, the day seemed lost. Imboden's battery, in great disorder, was rushing to the rear, and was crossing Jackson's line, when he was halted for an explanation of the apparent rout. Imboden roughly answered that his battery had been left without support. Jackson curtly replied: "I'll support your battery. Unlimber right here." Imboden recovered his composure; and with Jackson's suggestions, much havoc was made in the charging ranks of the Federals. Many times they wavered; but still they came. At Noon, Johnston and Beauregard appeared on the scene. The latter galloped along the lines, and infused new life into all the troops. His horse was killed and one of his staff officers. At this time he placed in position two splendid batteries, Pendleton's and Alburtiss's. This was the hour that tried the courage of the broken ranks of the Confederates. The enemy they had fought all morning, were continually reinforced. The broken ranks were soon filled. The two generals seemed so confident of victory, the men soon became enthused, and once more they were ready for the fray. The Federal battle lines shifted; and as they turned several positions, the Confederates apparently gained ground.

During these changes, a point was exposed on the Federal right. This was about 2 o'clock. Stuart, who had been helpless with his cavalry, made a dash for the position; and a regiment of Zouaves in regiments of blue and scarlet, was virtually destroyed, and the Federal right was thrown into confusion. The 33rd Va. under Col. Cummings, succeeded about this hour in destroying two Federal batteries that had been pouring a deadly fire along the hill-side of Jackson's left. Cummings, without orders, could hold out no longer; and deploying to cover among stunted trees and bushes, suddenly appeared in front of these batteries. The Federals were deceived in the regiment advancing. The dust on the gray and blue uniforms, made them all appear alike. Cummings marched up boldly to a fence 70 yards distant, and poured such a volley into men and horses, that nearly everything in sight sank, and the batteries were put out of further action. For thirty minutes there was a lull in the din of battle. Col. Cummings saw from his advanced position great columns of blue infantry lines forming for renewed attack from the Stone Bridge quarter. The divisions that had forced their way *via* Sudley Springs and had struck the Confederates' rear near Stone Bridge, were now recrossing Bull Run and forming for renewed attack on the Henry house hill. Johnston and Beauregard were then on the firing line, busy assigning the new brigades positions on the right and left. This was barely effected, when the Federals charged the line under cover of their batteries. The attack was furious; and it was readily seen that the advancing lines were men enthused with the successes they had achieved in their flank and rear movements, officered by experienced and brave men; and had McDowell given them the divisions he held back at and near Centreville, they would have swept the Confederate lines from their strong position, and victory would have been theirs. Official reports now reveal the shortsightedness of the commanders of both armies. McDowell had planned a successful attack which was now about to culminate on the crest of the famous *Hill;* but failing to send in one of his divisions to support those that had been marching and fighting all day, he saw his mistake too late. While Johnston and Beauregard had galloped away from the Mitchell ford, where they left Longstreet and D. R. Jones to loiter and waste their strength in marching and counter-marching across Bull Run, and were never called upon to fire a gun all day, we see now that had Longstreet been at work either on the center, or called to Stone Bridge by 2 o'clock, the right flank of the Federals would have been beaten back and routed in great disorder, and thousands of prisoners captured before they could reach Centreville. The routed army would in itself have swept McDowell from his base; and the Confederates would not only have gained an easy victory, but could have pursued the enemy far out on the road to Washington. As it was, McDowell and the two Confederate generals were unprepared for the unexpected situation viewed by them at 4 P. M., brought about by heroic efforts of the Confederate brigade under the leadership of Jackson, Bee, Bartow and others. The two heroes of Manassas, Bee and Bartow, had just been killed, as Bonham appeared on Jackson's right; and Kirby Smith and his splendid brigade, arrived from the Valley, was coming up in fine order. This brigade was thrown against the right wing of the advancing Federals. Before this brigade reached their position, the Federals had gained the crest of the hills, driving back every Confederate position except Jackson's, whose brigade was screened from view as they lay flat on their faces. They had not fired a gun, excepting what had been delivered by the 33rd. The moment had come for victory or rout. Jackson about 3 o'clock, approached the center of his line, where the 2nd and 4th Va. lay waiting, and coolly but firmly gave them this order "Reserve your fire until they come within fifty yards; then fire and give them the bayonet; and when you charge, yell like furies." The long line of Virginians who had virtually been inactive for three hours under the hot rays of the July sun, with bursting shells falling around their strained position, was ready for any service that would relieve them of this terrible discipline. They had not long to wait, for the Federal infantry and artillery swept all from their approaches to the crest. The first brigade arose as one man, and poured a volley of destruction into the Federal line then within forty yards of their line, which broke the center and produced such confusion, that they were caught unawares by the gleam of bayonets and Rebel yells. For the first time the elated Federals felt the terror of the bayonet; and demoralized by the shouts heard above the sound of musketry, the hitherto victorious lines gave way, never to reform on that field during the day. Up to that time, they had things their own way by good fighting and overwhelming numbers; but now with their centre broken, Bonham hammering their left flank, and Kirby Smith falling upon their right with about 2,000 fresh men, nothing short of defeat awaited them. No Confederate dreamed it would end in a rout. Genl. Kirby Smith being wounded on the firing line, when victory was in sight, was a severe blow, but Col. Elzey, the ranking Colonel, assumed command and executed Smith's design. At this juncture, the broken regiments composing the commands of Evans, Bee and Hampton, formed on Jackson's right. The whole Confederate line was then advanced by order of Beauregard, and the Federals were swept from the Henry Hill and over the slopes. The rout was well on, when the division that had been lying inactive about Centreville, came sweeping in to take part in a battle now lost. McDowell has been severely criticized by experienced officers for his inability to grasp the situation. Genl. Howard at the head of a fresh brigade, met the routed army, and fought his men well; but they soon became demoralized by stories told them by retreating comrades, of how the Rebels had fought with bayonet, and nothing could stay them now. Howard gave way; a new position was secured, and other reinforcements under McDowell formed on a small creek, with a battalion of regulars in the centre. While they were forming, Jubal Early came up with a fresh brigade and struck their right flank a terrific blow. Beauregard left Jackson to hold the commanding hill positions, with what he could collect from his scattered battalions, and together with captured artillery, to await orders; while he galloped over the Mathews hill in time to see the Federals give way in disorder, ending in a rout. The regular soldiers have been given credit by survivors of both armies, for their splendid order of retreat. When the retreating army was full under way towards Centreville, Stuart and his cavalry were sent to harrass their rear, with Early's brigade for support. The main body of fugitives rushed their own lines that were crossing Stone Bridge in great disorder, and swept on towards Sudley, where they were overtaken by the cavalry, which before 6 P. M. had more prisoners than they could guard; while Early's infantry followed in their wake, gathering up thousands of muskets and other accoutrements the "Yankees" had thrown away. Back on the Confederate battle line, the Confederate banners were hoisted in evidence of their victory. Waiting in fairly good order were the surviving brigadiers, with remnants of their brigades, expecting every moment orders from Johnston or someone, to follow the retreating foe, that had now become a confused mass of infantry, artillery, cavalry, wagon trains, ambulances and everything possessed by the splendid army that had maintained its claim for prestige full eight hours. While in this disorder and confusion, what was the victorious army doing! Surely, none can say it was demoralized and in confusion. It is true many wounded men and stragglers were wandering over the plateau, seeking help; but the lines were intact by 4 P. M. Official reports show this; and they also show in part why that line waited until 6 P. M. for orders to move. The dead and wounded of both armies lay on the field all around, and men were maddened beyond endurance. Surely the fighting lines were not expected to break ranks and perform field hospital service. This had been already amply provided for by the medical corps. It was simply impossible to restrain men from individual effort to find missing comrades and friends; and this caused the scene witnessed by President Davis when he arrived at Manassas that afternoon. He was overcome with the impression that the Confederates had been routed. It has been frequently asked why Johnston and Beauregard did not pursue the retreating army and reap such results as the demolition of Mr. Lincoln's first army and the capture of Washington. This has been answered with some claim for sufficient reasons,—that pursuit would have ended in disaster. Thousands, however, know now and so express themselves, that the Southern leaders there committed their first great war blunder. Genl. Johnston and Beauregard endeavored for many years to shift the responsibility to the shoulders of President Davis; but careful study of the correspondence and official papers, prove that Davis offered no restraint, and they were free to close the day according to their own plans, and were not hampered by Genl. Lee or the President. Students of this military question never hesitate to hold these two generals solely responsible for the inactivity of the victorious Confederates. We have evidence that the brigade commanders not only advised but urged pursuit; and pointed to the fresh troops of Longstreet and D. R. Jones, who had wasted the entire day as already shown, within three miles of Centreville. Longstreet in his "Manassas to Appomattox," makes it clear that he was crossing Bull Run at Blackburns ford all day, and never saw the time when he could use a platoon of soldiers to any good purpose. The battle was over when Mr. Davis appeared on the field; but seeing so many stragglers, he made himself known and urged them to rally and follow him to the front, and endeavor to save the day. Genl. Jackson was at that time undergoing treatment for a wound in his hand; and not understanding the President's language, asked his surgeon Dr. Hunter McGuire, for an explanation. When he understood Mr. Davis' fears, Jackson cried out "We have whipped them; they ran like sheep. Give me 5,000 fresh men and I will be in Washington City tomorrow morning." Subsequent events proved that Jackson could have gained fresh laurels that day, had the two commanders showed a like spirit of venture. Here was the man and here the hour. The "fresh men" were at hand; and the fleeing army could never make a successful stand. The Federals were fully convinced that superior numbers had met and overwhelmed them with defeat; and they were hastening on to tell the Washington government of their disaster and that the capital was in danger. The pursuing columns could have occupied Arlington Heights by Noon of the 22nd; and from this point, so shelled the city, that evacuation must have come within twelve hours. Writers on this situation who were in Washington during those days, have asserted that Confederate Cavalry could have ridden through the streets of the capital any time during that week unmolested. The place had not been fully fortified; and these few positions were not manned by men who would likely be in the way of a victorious army. This is no reckless statement. McClellan says in his narrative of the first battle and the situation at the capital when he succeeded McDowell, says: "When I arrived in Washington July 26th and rode around the city, I found no preparations *whatever* for defense, not even to putting troops in military positions. Not a single avenue of approach guarded. All was chaos, and the streets, hotels and barrooms were filled with drunken officers and men, absent from the regiments without leave. * * * There was really nothing to prevent a small cavalry force from riding into the city * * * If these cessionists attached any value to the possession of Washington, they committed their greatest error in not following up the victory of Bull Run."

It must not be supposed that the army of conquering Confederates laid down on the field they had won with heavy loss, and there gloated over their spoils. Longstreet gives an account of what his division did after 7 o'clock the night after the battle, and how he was cautioned not to bring on another battle. Beyond Centreville he dislodged the division that was covering the retreat; and then he was called off; while Kemper, Kershaw and Elzey out in the vicinity of Bulls ford, Stone Bridge and Sudley Springs, were pressing the fugitives and capturing scores of them, they were called off and received orders through Col. Ferguson, member of Beauregard's staff, for all the Confederates to retire to the South side of Bull Run. Col. E. P. Alexander Chief of Signal Service during the battle, and afterwards Chief of Artillery in Longstreet's Corps, says in his "Military Memoirs," p. 49, "That he was present when these orders were given at 7 P. M., and demanded the reasons, and the answer was that Beauregard and Johnston had been informed that a force of the enemy had been seen South of Bull Run in rear of our flank, and both staff officers regarded the report as the story of some excited men who mistook our force for that of the enemy." Some minor movements were made the next day, which resulted in capturing a score or two of stragglers. Genl. Johnston declined to advance on Washington, and gave his attention to the care of wounded and dead men, and as he says, "reorganized his army." The Confederate Army received a greater shock for the failure to follow up their victory, than from the shock of battle; and the *morale* of the entire command suffered from inactivity. While they loved their leaders, and tried to feel they knew best, they chafed under the situation. Their losses had been severe in killed and wounded,—about equal to that of the Federals—

Federal killed ....460; wounded..1,124
Confederates killed 387; wounded..1,582

The Confederates captured 1,560 prisoners, 26 cannon and their equipment in caissons, and many artillery horses, many battle flags, nearly 4,000 rifles, muskets, large quantities of ammunition, and much needed hospital stores, wagons, ambulances, etc. The wagon trains were never in reach of the Confederates during the day, and McDowell sent them towards Washington. Hundreds of them broke down in the rout and were burned.

The Stonewall Brigade suffered most of all. Out of its 3,000 officers and men, 488 were killed or wounded. We could name a number of the Valley men who were found on the battle field, but will mention only a few at this time, hoping to give a complete list later on: Capt. Wm. L. Clark, of the Winchester Rifles, fell with a wound that affected him for nearly 40 years thereafter; Col. L. T. Moore, likewise, with his limping gait; while Isaac Glaize, Young Powell, Gilbert, Streit, Barton and others of Winchester were killed. Peyton Harrison and the Conrad brothers of Martinsburg were among the slain. The old Valley began to feel the distress of war; and the sorrowful homes could be numbered then, when every heart had sympathy and concern for the first losses. But as times went on and battles more numerous, the days came when the muster roll had to be examined to know who had fallen, and thus learn of other broken home-circles.

The 7th Va. Cavalry, Col. A. W. McDonald, commanding, arrived too late to take part in the Manassas campaign. Col. McDonald and his regiment were sent to Staunton to reconnoitre the Western Virginia thoroughfares leading into Staunton, and report if any demonstrations were made from the mountain regions. The McDowell failure caused all Federal lines to be contracted along the Virginia border. The 7th Cavalry was again sent to Romney, to keep in touch with the B. & O. Railroad. Ashby, with several companies, was sent to Charlestown, Jeff. County. Patterson had disappeared from Virginia along with McDowell. During the month of August, both armies were disposed to cease active operations. New levies were added to both, and divisions were formed into corps. Drill and discipline were practiced. Army supplies, wagon trains, etc., increased the appearance of war at every point. The militia under Genl. James H. Carson, had become very efficient as the home guard of the Lower Valley, with McDonald and Ashby out on the border.

September brought out from their retreats on the North side of the Potomac, numerous Federal expeditions, and caused some interest at Harpers Ferry and Romney. Ashby with Baylor's and Henderson's companies of Cavalry and about 500 militia, met Genl. Geary at the former place; and McDonald with his companies of cavalry and several hundred militia, held a Federal force back from Romney for two days. They finally compelled McDonald to retire. Federals entered the town, but were driven out the next day, after the Virginians learned that the surrounding country was being pillaged by the invaders. A desperate charge was made by the cavalry, supported by the Hampshire militia under Cols. E. H. McDonald and Alex. Monroe. The Federals were driven out and pursued to New Creek station on the B. & O. Railroad, losing many of their men and horses. No further effort was made by the Federals to retake Romney until the latter part of October. During the interval, the Confederates frequently appeared along the B. &. O Railroad, taking observations as to the use of the railroad for transportation for troops, etc. Much valuable information was thus obtained, and the Richmond government fully apprised of the concentration of troops to points on the Lower Potomac. The Federals saw the necessity for their occupation of so strategic a point as the South Branch Valley; and determined to renew their efforts. On the 26th October, the lower end of the little Valley was occupied, but they made no effort to retake Romney; but their position protected the railroad for about 50 miles. On the 24th of November, Genl. Kelly marched into Romney with a large force. Col. McDonald met them at Mechanicsburg Gap, but was driven back to Romney, where he made a gallant stand. Major O. R. Funsten was left at the Bridge over the river with one piece of the "Flying Artillery." When the enemy appeared at the West end of the bridge, Maj. Funsten opened fire into the advancing column, killing horses and men, producing wild confusion. Federal cavalry found a ford, and suddenly struck the weak flank of the daring Confederates, who were forced to retire to Cemetery Hill, then occupied by McDonald, who with one rifled gun was delivering a telling fire in the ranks of the Federal column as they crossed the bridge. Col. McDonald allowed his command to be placed at great disadvantage. The wagon trains were East of the town, with a long mountain road before them, while the militia and cavalry were unequal to the strength of Kelly's force and unable to take care of themselves, much less protect the wagons. It is needless to say that a rout ensued; the men were scattered everywhere. McDonald and Funsten barely escaped capture, and abandoned everything. Every wagon was captured, also the two guns that had been the pride of the old Ashby Command. Several company officers made an ineffectual attempt at Blue's Gap to rally the fugitives who were freely alarmed, and recklessly fled to Winchester. This portion of the 7th Virginia cavalry never heard the last of the Romney defeat during the War.

Col. McDonald at his own request, was relieved from command of the Seventh, and later on was made Commandant of the Post at Winchester. The writer was provost marshal during his incumbency, and takes pleasure in testifying to his efficiency respecting his new office. This office he filled with satisfaction to Genl. Jackson, and to every faithful officer with whom he had official relations. The Colonel was a strict disciplinarian; and if his age and health had not interfered with his active service, doubtless the Confederacy would have felt the effect of his military genius, undaunted courage and spotless integrity. He was a graduate of West Point, but spent the most of his 62 years a private citizen in the Virginia Valley, and was unfitted for the hardships of field service. Turner Ashby was promoted to Colonel of the Seventh. Many of the young men had been clamoring for this promotion; they regarded Ashby as the brilliant flower in all the collection of Virginia chivalry. He possessed in his person every attribute of the ideal cavalryman—Young, handsome, brave and athletic, with perfect health and a burning desire to avenge the wrongs of his native State. No wonder, then, that men rejoiced when general orders were read, announcing him as their leader. He established his headquarters near Charlestown. The Western part of Hampshire had been abandoned to the Federals. The Confederate line extended from Bath (Berkeley Springs) to Harpers Ferry. This was guarded by the Ashby Cavalry. The Valley Cavalry was thus distinguished until his death in 1862; and many old cavalrymen at this writing will tell you they "belonged to Ashby's Cavalry."

Ashby felt the need of light artillery, and efforts were made to organize a battery company. Thirty-three men so organized, received authority Nov. 11, 1861, to elect officers. R. P. Chew was elected Captain; Milton Rouss, 1st Lieut.; J. W. McCarty and James Thompson, Second Lieuts. They were furnished with three guns; the men, their own saddle horses; and as the Mounted Artillery—often called the "Flying" Artillery, the celebrated Chew's Battery was thus started, developing the larger battery as the War progressed. We may add here that Capt. Chew was given command of Stuart's Horse Artillery in 1864; and the *world* was astonished at the destruction they wrought until their guns were surrendered at Appomattox. Of course, old artillerymen know that this battery saw its first service in the Valley with Ashby, and protected Jackson's rear as he fell back from Winchester, and was at the front when he returned. We could relate many noble deeds if space allowed. It was during the Summer and Autumn of 1861 that Harvey L. Bitzer and several other Frederick County men were given authority to recruit a company from the militia regiments, to serve as scouts and messengers. Bitzer was elected Captain. The company was ready for service when Genl. Jackson assumed command of the Valley District the same Autumn; and for several months rendered efficient service. The company was disbanded when authority was given by the Confederate government for the organization of a company from the Lower Valley to serve at Genl. Lee's Headquarters as "scouts, guides and couriers." This being done, A. P. Pifer was elected Captain. This was known as Company A. of the 39th Batt., commanded by Col. Richardson. This branch of the service was very important to Genl. Lee. Every section of the border was represented, and the battalion could furnish competent guides and couriers on all occasions. Genl. Lee took great pleasure in mingling with several of the companies, and always looked after their comfort. Indeed, the "Scouts, Guides and Couriers" were a favored lot, as other soldiers would frequently say; but on the battle fields as they were seen speeding with orders to corps commanders through shot and shell, many would ask, how can those fellows escape? The following named men were from Frederick County: Capt. Pifer, Joshua S. Lupton and his two brothers Jno. R. and Thomas, R. M. Cartmell, Granville Harper, Charles Forsythe, Jno. C. Lupton and brother J. Frank Lupton, B. C. Campbell, Robert M. Campbell, Frank Lupton, J. E. Baker, G. Wash. Pifer, Charles Houck, Chas. I. Sloat.

CHAPTER LVI

Jackson at Winchester, Bath Campaign, Jackson and Loring

The Autumn found the Confederate Army around Centreville enjoying the same passive and monotonous life that August and September brought. Malaria was in the air; and scores of soldiers sank under its insidious invasion—worse even than that of the enemy. In the latter case, the dull camp life would have been broken, and men could have thrown off their lethargy. They had spent nearly three months in idleness. Though the routine of camp life embraced drill and dress parade, this was not the kind of life the men longed for. An epidemic of measles appeared in the camps, sending hundreds of men to the hospital. Johnston was organizing his army into divisions, and preparing for the enemy. Jackson was rigid in the drill service for his brigade, and it was thoroughly equipped for duty. The new camps around Manassas Junction by the first of October, betokened plainly nothing but quiet camp life. Mr. Davis paid another visit to Genl. Johnston about this date; and then discussed the plans for this army of 40,000 men to adopt. When he discovered so much sickness and furloughs, he expressed himself freely. Johnston wanted at least 15,000 men; and assured the President that if he could furnish this number, he would cross the Potomac and conduct a campaign in Maryland. The president said he was not averse to such a movement, but that he had neither troops nor arms to offer; and besides the enemy had been given *too long time to recruit their wasted forces*; "and that the army at Manassas was not able now to make an invasion, if it was not able to follow McDowell on the 22nd of July and cross the Potomac on the heels of a routed army." One of Mr. Davis' biographers, in speaking of this incident, says Mr. Davis told him that Genls. Johnston and Beauregard were offended at his language. It is useless to say the invasion scheme was abandoned. McClellan was then in command of the Federal Army; and he, too, seemed content to let the *Rebels* rest, while he completed his organizations. One of his division commanders asks this pertinent question in a narrative he wrote about the war: "When *did* McClellan complete his organization?" About the middle of October, McClellan began to feel the pressure from Washington for him to do something. He avoided anything like a general engagement; but October 19th, he sent Genl. Baker with about 3,000 men to see what the Confederates were doing at Leesburg under Genl. Evans. (Hero of the Stone Bridge engagement.) This was reconsidered by McClellan, fearing it would alarm Evans and cause him to retire beyond his reach. So he ordered Genl. Stone who was stationed on the Maryland side, to cross over and send out a strong reconnaissance toward Leesburg, hoping to entrap Evans. (See McClellan's report of the Skirmish at Balls Bluff.) On the 20th, Stone was ordered by wire to cross the river at two points—Edwards Ferry and Balls Bluff, two miles apart. Genl. Evans with three regiments and several guns, gave his attention to the Edwards Ferry party, while the 18th Miss. watched the Balls Bluff detachment. They soon were engaged in battle, and drove the Federals back on their main force to the Bluff. There Genl. Baker threw his whole reserve force against the Mississippians. Evans hastened to their relief with the 8th Va. and 17th Miss. regiments, and a desperate fight ensued. Genl. Baker was killed and his entire force driven over the bluff. Many were drowned. The Federal loss reported by McClellan was, killed 49; wounded 158; missing 714. Total 921. The Confederate loss as reported by Evans was: killed 36; wounded 117; missing 2. Total 155. McClellan was denounced by the Northern press, while Evans and his little brigade received the plaudits of the South. In justice to Genl. McClellan, we will add that subsequent events proved that he instructed Genl. Baker to confine his movement to a reconnaissance of the enemy's position, and under no circumstances to bring on a general engagement.

November 1st had come; and the army encamped along the murky waters of Bull Run, was preparing for Winter quarters. Rumors had been afloat for several days that Jackson was to leave for other fields; and many conjectures arose as to what his old brigade would do. All expected it to follow the General; but on the 4th November, the order was read that he had been assigned to the Shenandoah Valley District, embracing all the country between the Blue Ridge and the Alleganies. He ordered the brigade to assemble; and taking position in their midst, he addressed them in these memorable words: "I am not here to make a speech, but simply to say farewell. I first met you at Harpers Ferry, and I cannot take leave of you without giving expression to my admiration of your conduct from that day to this, whether on the march, in the bivouac, or on the bloody plains of Manassas, where you gained the well-deserved reputation of having decided the fate of battle. Throughout the broad extent of country through which you have marched, by your respect for the rights and property of citizens, you have shown that you are soldiers not only to defend, but able and willing to defend and protect. You have already won a brilliant reputation throughout the army of the whole Confederacy; and I trust in the future, by your deeds in the field, and by the assistance of the same kind Providence who has hitherto favored our cause, you will win more victories and add lustre to the reputation you now enjoy. You have already gained a proud position in the future history of this our Second War of Independence. I shall look with great anxiety to your future movements; and I trust whenever I shall hear from the First Brigade on the field of battle, it will be of still nobler deeds achieved, and higher reputation won." Men who were present on that occasion tell us now, that no pen can picture the scene as the General cast the reins of his bridle upon his horse's neck, and waved his long arm over his head, and uttered with deep emotion these closing words: "In the Army of the Shenandoah you were the First Brigade; in the Army of the Potomac you were the First Brigade; in the second corps of the Army you are the First Brigade; you are the First Brigade in the affections of your general, and I hope by your future deeds and bearing, you will be handed down to posterity as the First Brigade in this our Second War of Independence. Farewell!" With a wave of the hand, he seized the bridle rein and galloped out of sight, followed by cheers mingled with tears. The Brigade was left to learn a new lesson of submission to fate.

We will follow Jackson to Winchester and briefly tell what he found and what he did, to lay the foundation of the historic Valley campaigns. One might suppose that the General would have felt affronted by this transfer, having witnessed the transformation of Brigades into Divisions, and then into two corps, forming the Army of Northern Virginia, with Genl. Joseph E. Johnston as Commander, and sent to a district to command the remnants of militia regiments and a few companies of cavalry, that had roamed with free rein for months, knowing no master but their peerless Ashby. But a study of the situation shows that Jackson felt otherwise, judging from his letters to Mrs. Jackson. He was pleased at the prospect of being in closer touch with the Western mountains, where he longed for an opportunity to afford relief to the oppressed people. Word had reached the General that all Southern sympathizers found in the march of Federals through Western Virginia, were persecuted, and hundreds were fugitives from homes he had known from his childhood. It must be remembered that several repulses had been given the Confederate forces defending the country from the Potomac to the Kanawha. Genl. R. E. Lee had gone to infuse his spirit into the dispirited forces and sections, and stem the tide of invasion. He had barely inaugurated a system of defense after the Confederates had been driven from their positions, when Mr. Davis recalled him to Richmond to assume command of the situation near the Confederate capital, and also to go to the army in South Carolina. Jackson's new field was attractive, by reason not only of the grandeur of the Great Valley stretched out in its placid communities of patriotic women and loyal old men, reaching far away into the mountain sections clamoring for relief, but for the gateway offered to the South for the threatening invasions of the country bordering the West lines of Washington. Jackson saw this, and urged Genl. Johnston to spare him a detachment to form a nucleus for the army he proposed to organize for such demonstrations. About the middle of November, Genl. Johnston assented and sent the First Brigade to Winchester, where they arrived on the 18th and formed their camps around the old town. Officers and men took advantage of their close touch with the enthusiastic citizens, and mingled too freely to conform to the ideas of discipline held by their inflexible commander. War was no sport for him; and he required the old Brigade to obey an order issued, requiring officers and men to procure passes to and from the town, under penalty of arrest. The regimental officers joined in a protest, which resulted in such reproofs from Headquarters, that perfect discipline soon held sway. While the Brigade had been a *pet* with Jackson, they learned slowly how necessary for the spoiled child was correction. Jackson on his arrival in Winchester, stopped at the old Taylor hotel on Main Street. He was assigned two rooms for Headquarters: One, No. 23, he chose for his private use, the adjoining room for his official family, yet to be formed. Col. Preston his Adjutant General, was in strict harmony with his Chief; Capt. A. S. Pendleton, Chief of Staff and *Sandy* Jackson aide, with bluff Major Mike Harmon Quarter Master, and the quiet but untiring Maj. C. S. Hawks, Commissary, and with Rev. Dr.

Pendleton, Colonel and Chief of Artillery. The official board was complete. Many applications poured in for positions on the staff; many were unnoticed; others were pigeon-holed for consideration. The Adjutant General's office was transferred to Col. L. T. Moore's residence on North side of Peyton Street, situated on the hill due West from old Fort Loudoun. The General followed and had his official office in the room on the right of the main entrance across the hall, where the Adjutant General's office was held until the Spring of 1862. Genl. Jackson changed his home after the arrival of Mrs. Jackson and child, and found a more congenial abode in the delightful home of Rev. Dr. James R. Graham on N. Braddock Street, who was pastor of the Kent Street Presb. Church. The Quarter Master's Department was on East side of Market Street, the present site of the Baker & Co. warehouses. On the opposite side, in the old Krebs property, Maj. Hawks established the commissariat. Every member of this board applied himself to aid the commander in every effort for organization of the army, that was destined to perform imperishable deeds of valor. Everything seemed in harmony. The Autumn was exceptionally good for such work. December brought no evidence of approaching Winter, except in the varied hues of foliage adorning every wooded hill-top. With such favorable conditions, none should wonder at the desire which took hold upon the General commanding the Valley District, and prompted active movements for a Winter campaign. The border line West of Bath, reaching out towards Cumberland was inviting. By a surprise, that whole section might be recovered from the grasp of the enemy, Kelly be captured at Romney, and possibly Cumberland taken,—thus striking dismay to the hearts of President and cabinet at Washington, resulting in alarm to McClellan, and putting him on the defensive; while Johnston could enter Maryland West of Washington, and with Jackson to join him, the North would be plunged into a vortex of despair, that possibly would end the war by foreign nations recognizing the Southern Confederacy as entitled to rights as a successful belligerent power. This comprehended a prodigy, it is true; but Mr. Davis and Genl. Lee agreed as to the scheme, although doubting its feasibility. Yet they were willing for this bold spirit to test his pinions in the proposed flight, and readily acquiesced in his request for the withdrawal of Loring's Army from Monterey, Western Virginia, and Col. Edw. Johnston from Camp Allegany. Jackson, so authorized, hastened to put in shape the border from Romney to the Southwest, by replacing the volunteer troops with militia, so that all experienced soldiers could concentrate at Winchester. To this end, the writer was dispatched with necessary orders to Brig. Genl. Boggs, residing at Franklin, Pendleton County; and having delivered sealed orders as well as verbal instructions, to proceed to Genl. Loring's and Edw. Johnson's Headquarters and deliver them sealed orders relating to their retirement from their positions. This done, to return by way of the picket lines from Franklin via Petersburg and upper end of Patterson Creek Valley, and report in person to Genl. Jackson if the outposts were guarded by the militia in compliance with his orders. (This is more fully mentioned in personal sketch of T. K. Cartmell.) Pending the transfer of the Western Virginia troops to Winchester, and prior to the issue of these orders, much correspondence passed between Jackson and Johnston, all of which was submitted to the government at Richmond, and fully considered. This is interesting reading, but must be passed by for the present. During the first week in December, a detail was made from the Stonewall Brigade, to accompany Ashby and a squadron or two of his cavalry to make a night raid on Dam No. 4 of the Chesapeake and Ohio Canal, where it was expected that great artery from the coal fields could be destroyed, and transportation of grain and coal seriously interrupted. The undertaking was hazardous and fruitless. One man was killed and several wounded. While the Confederates were hammering away on the locks, the constant fire of the Federals from protected positions, forced Ashby to abandon the effort, and the command returned to Winchester. The next two weeks, Federal scouting parties were routed near Shepardstown and N. Mountain Depot West of Martinsburg, and a brisk fight occurred between the cavalry and an infantry post near Sir John's Run. The Federals were all safely fortified on the North side of the Potomac at every picket post. Genl. Banks was at Frederick City, Md., with his army of 16,000 men, occupying every important point as far West as Cumberland; but seldom did any venture on the Virginia side East of Green Spring Station on the B. &. O. Kelly was at Romney with about 5,000, and Genl. Rosecranz at Clarksburg with an army of at least 20,000, disposed by divisions and brigades from that point to the roads leading to Staunton, some of which were being guarded and held by Loring and Col. Edw. Johnson. Genl. Jackson was satisfied his proposed advance along the lines of the upper Potomac would check all movements of Rosecranz, and thus relieve that portion of Western Virginia, and make it safe for Col. Edw. Johnson to leave his post to militia; and he relied on this gallant officer and his seasoned brigade to lend much aid in his mountain movements. But at the last moment, he was informed from Richmond that Col. Johnson could not leave his position. Genl. Loring arrived at Winchester on Christmas Day, with a depleted division. Men had been furloughed and sick leaves granted, that reduced the fighting strength of this brave band. Splendid soldiers came with Loring, and seemed satisfied at their reception. The General appeared sullen and pompous. The Valley men were suspicious of him. He acted more like the commanding general than did the austere Jackson; and some thought he might rank the latter, and dreaded the consequences. But a few days determined the question. Orders still emanated from Jackson's Headquarters. Regimental officers were informed a movement was on foot, and must be conducted with great secrecy. Banks had been reinforced from Washington, with instructions to reconnoitre the Lower Valley via Williamsport, and ascertain what was intended by Jackson and his reinforcements. Rosecranz was instructed to contract his lines and be ready for some new move of the Rebels in the Valley. Jackson being apprised of these changes, prepared to strike the enemy's line at some weak point, and send a shock to Washington that would disturb all their well-laid plans. The first of January, 1862, found Jackson's army of 9,000 all told (See O. R.) fully equipped for a march. The columns headed towards Bloomery over the Gainsboro Turnpike. Many wild conjectures went through the lines. Ashby and his cavalry were in advance to clear the roads of spies, and to keep a line of communication open from the front. The day was one that can never be forgotten by those who saw the grand column move away. The skies were clear, the air soft and warm like the June days—having continued so for ten days. Men felt burdened with their uniforms; overcoats and blankets were discarded; and away they went. The General and his staff mounted their horses on the lawn near the Col. Moore house. The writer handed him several private letters after he had mounted, and received from him further orders concerning the care of the loose papers left in his office, and directions to send official mail through the regular channels; but to send his private mail not *marked official*, by courier. The writer returned to the Provost Marshal's Office (now occupied by Mr. A. J. Tavenner, atty., in the Bantz building near the C. H.) which was the office of Capt. Wm. L. Clark when he entered the service. There he read instructions from the General to provide *ample accommodation for prisoners of war*, guarding them with details from the militia detachments, and "to separate civilians from captured soldiers." Some of these old war papers have been preserved; and at no distant day the writer hopes to publish them in connection with sketches that cannot appear in this volume, owing to the personal features pertaining to individual actors.) The history of this campaign has been often told in attractive style; and the incidents are fresh in the memory of hundreds of the survivors. We will briefly state the prominent features, and make no effort to enumerate the mistakes of the sorely-tried men on that wintry march in the mountains. The first day's setting sun found the columns scaling the sandy ridges over three roads—all to converge near Bath or Hancock on the Potomac. On those mountain ranges, the troops began to feel that June air was changing to that of November; and without tents or rations, bivouacking on Big Sandy was a dismal performance. A night of discomfort followed, with a dawn black with snow-clouds; and fierce winds rushing through pine forests, gave promise of suffering. Another day of struggle passed; and when the 3rd of January came, it found the army in bad plight, and unable to get their wagon trains up. The enemy having discovered their advance, the General grew impatient; and it could be seen he felt the disappointment. Old soldiers who returned from that campaign, said people must not think *Old Jack* never loses his temper; for when he and old Mike Harmon met in the road, and explanations were demanded why Harmon failed to get the wagon trains up with rations, etc., for the suffering men, the old cap was raised from the brow, his face flashed fire through the snow-flakes, and for once the cussin' quarter master was subdued. Until late in the day of Jany. 3rd, Jackson felt sure he would surprise the large post at Hancock on the North side of the Potomac. But an unfortunate incident occurred. A squadron of cavalry struck a new picket post near Berkeley Springs (Bath), and routed instead of capturing them, as had been planned for the regular post on the South side of the river. The alarm was given; Hancock was apprised, and prepared for a cavalry skirmish, not knowing yet that an army was coming. Jackson urged men forward as soon as he discovered the enemy flushed; but it was impossible to get the infantry and artillery up in time to carry out his plans. Another night had to be spent in the open, without blankets and rations. All efforts to surround the large post that night had to be abandoned. Even yet the enemy was not fully apprised that an army was near at hand. Three regiments of Federal infantry on the South side felt undisturbed until morning, when they discovered Confederate infantry on both flanks, and at once took in the situation. Their post was abandoned with a goodly supply of stores. The large garrison crossed the river on boats, and virtually escaped without loss, save 21 prisoners. They were the *only prisoners* the provost marshal at Winchester received from that expedition. All of this was done in a blinding snow-storm. Confederates bewildered by the storm, wandered aimlessly over strange roads, and utterly failed to reach the post in time to fire a gun on the retreating foe. As the converging lines entered the post, they found a glad surprise—supplies of rations, blankets and *Winter quarters* full of *nick-nacks* of the Federals who had just left. The capture was regarded by the men with great delight. Here they reveled all day and during the night. Not so with the General. He was suffering from the failure of one of his plans. Of course, the Hancock defeat electrified every other post from Banks' Headquarters at Frederick to Kelly's at Romney, and the post at Cumberland. General Jackson realized what this meant; but the tired and hungry men were engrossed with the unexpected spoils.

Early the next morning, the 5th, the Confederate camps were called to arms, and marched through the deep snow to the river, to take action to overawe the large force in and around the village of Hancock on the opposite side. Jackson demanded surrender. The Federals refused, whereupon the Federal commander was given two hours to remove women and children. Then several guns were put in position and the town was thrown into confusion by some shells landing in their streets. This shelling was greatly exaggerated by the Federal commander in his report, and of how he returned the fire, compelling the Confederate fire to cease. The truth is, he simply held on without firing a gun until reinforcements poured in from every quarter that night. Jackson reopened fire next morning, and several infantry regiments were sent to destroy the railroad bridge over Great Capon, and the railroad track. This was all accomplished, and all communication cut between outlying posts. This was too late, however, for Romney had been informed before the telegraph line was cut; and large scouting parties were sent from that point, which fell upon some militia picket posts on the Northwestern Turnpike and routed them. This enabled Kelly to frame a report for his war department that out-rivals any that went from that border line. Jackson left Bath on the 7th, having sent the wagon trains ahead loaded with the spoils, all taking a Southwest course, halting at Unger's Store. The icy roads required a change in the shoes of the teams, and several days were spent in fitting the horses for further movement. On the 10th a line of march was taken up in the direction of Romney; the army dragging its way over the worst roads it had encountered. For miles the ice and snow were barriers; and when the head of the column scaled the last mountain and beheld the deserted Valley below, word was sent back to Jackson. Romney was evacuated—Kelly gone. The column was allowed to bivouac on the mountain sides, for nightfall was near, and the descent to Romney was dangerous. The cavalry was sent on to occupy the place, which they found full of abandoned stores. The next five days were used up in efforts to put new life into the troops, so that detachments of artillery and infantry could support the cavalry in raids on other points of the great line of communication over the B. & O. Railroad, to Washington, and inflict untold damage to the Federal forces on their line for full 150 miles. But Jackson soon discovered that Loring's sullen obedience to orders from the commanding general, had produced discontent in the Loring squadrons, bordering on mutiny. Hundreds of them had been allowed, if not encouraged, to desert the expedition. This state of feeling found its way around the camp-fires; and it was hazardous to proceed further in execution of the original plan. Subsequent events proved that had he been loyally supported by soreheaded Loring, grand results would have followed. Writers of war history give Jackson credit for conceiving the first strategic movement on Washington. By this one feint upon the enemy's long line, the Washington government was compelled more than once to weaken the army of the Potomac on the eve of impending battle, by the withdrawal of troops to watch reported movements in the Shenandoah Valley. Jackson saw the effect on his old brigade, of their contact with the depleted regiments of Loring, and determined to cease active operations. On the 24th of Jany., he summed up his losses and his captures, and sent his official report to Richmond, giving a concise review of his expedition and causes of failure. Never once did he charge Loring's lack of service as a cause. Some friends of the latter have striven to show that Jackson had been discourteous, and forgot that Loring was entitled to command by right of seniority of rank. The expedition only lost 4 men killed and 28 wounded.

Jackson left Loring and his regiments to hold the post at Romney, while he returned to Winchester with the First Brigade, his artillery, and Ashby with three-fourths of his cavalry. This was necessary to make demonstrations on the Potomac near Martinsburg, where Banks had sent a threatening force. Several companies of seasoned militia and two companies of cavalry were left at Romney, subject to his orders. Loring soon proved his unfitness to hold such an outpost subject to the orders of Jackson, who was now practically disregarded by Loring and his demoralized remnants of what had been a splendid brigade before disaffection took hold upon them. The truth must be told—Loring and his men were not at Bull Run and Manassas. They could not appreciate the genius of Jackson, that soon eclipsed such men as Loring.

The old Brigade went into tents North of Winchester, and soon began to make themselves comfortable. Stragglers and sick-leave men were coming in, and the First Brigade men were in a mood to tell stories of their hardships on the famous Winter march. Not a word of censure ever escaped their lips. The old town of Winchester hailed their return with shouts of joy. No blame for any. The post was assuming its old war-like appearance. The militia welcomed the return; for Genl. Carson with two independent companies of cavalry, felt the burden of defending the border growing too heavy for comfort.

Loring was left at Romney with all the comforts the grand little mountain city could bestow, his men occupying the warm Winter quarters Kelly's men had left, besides abundance of supplies of every kind; we find in O. R., Vol. V., p. 1053, one of his letters, dated Jany. 26, 1862, addressed to Mr. Benjamin, Secretary of War, full of complaint of the "hardships found in maintaining a dangerous and useless post, liable to be retaken by the enemy, who had appeared in his front." Jackson had no intimation of this, until the 30th, when he received this message from the Secretary of War: "Our news indicates that a movement is making to cut off General Loring's command: order him back immediately." Naturally Jackson was affronted by this preemptory order; and he hastened a reply dated Headquarters Valley District, Winchester, Va., Jany. 31, 1862, "Hon. J. P. Benjamin, Secretary of War,

"Sir:—Your order, requiring me to direct Genl. Loring to return with his command to Winchester immediately, has been complied with.

"With such interference in my command, I cannot expect to be of much service in the field, and, accordingly, respectfully request to be ordered to report for duty to the Superintendent of the Virginia Military Institute at Lexington, as has been done in the case of other professors. Should this application not be granted. I respectfully request that the President will accept my resignation from the army." (O. R., Vol. V., 1053.) Loring and his officers who had filed complaints against their commander, betrayed their weakness and unfitness for the positions they held, and should have been courtmartialed for inciting mutiny, and contempt for their superiors. No excuse can ever be given for their conduct, and none for the unmilitary and undignified action of the Secretary of War, who knew less about military campaigns than the militia on the border. Jackson's self respect demanded prompt action; and his letters on this painful subject to Genl. Johnston, which found their way to Mr. Davis, are marvels in their line. He pointed out the harm to the discipline of the army, if such orders were passed without censure, and declared such action more harmful than could be conceived by the Secretary of War; that disintegration would be the result; and the Confederacy would be struggling with commanding officers who would not submit to such interference, and chaos would find place in the grand columns then ready for battle under leaders who might be censured and criticized by some inferior officer. Later on Jackson also wrote to Genl. Johnston, his superior in command, and to Gov. Letcher, stating the case with much force. Governor Letcher gave quick response, and urged Jackson to withdraw his resignation for the good of the service; and then called upon the Secretary of War and President Davis, pointing out to them the damage that would result to the country if Jackson were allowed to resign, and made it clear that Jackson was right and the Richmond authorities were wrong. Everything was done to restore harmony; and Genl. Jackson withdrew his resignation, and was never afterwards interfered with. Genl. Loring and his command went into camp near Winchester, making his headquarters in the camp. While he became the guest of Mr. Robert Y. Conrad, feeling ran high in the camps of Jackson's old men, and the people excitedly discussed the incident, and severely condemned what had been done to force Jackson to resign. The writer takes the liberty to mention his connection with the affair. As already stated, he was provost marshal of the army at the time. The town was full of officers and soldiers every day, and much confusion existed. Genl. Jackson observing this, issued this order (the original is preserved):

Headquarters, Valley District,
"January 27, 1864.

"Genl. Order No. 22.

"To T. K. Cartmell, *Capt. and Asst. Provost Marshal.*

"You are hereby commanded to instruct the provost guard, to require every officer and soldier to produce his license for absence from his command. Those failing to produce proper passes, shall be dealt with in accordance with orders this day issued to each Brigade commander; no person, civilian or soldier, shall be allowed to go beyond the lines of this post without a pass from the provost marshal. No officer above the rank of Colonel shall go beyond the picket lines on a pass unless countersigned by the provost marshal, and a record made of his name, rank and road.

"By command of T. J. JACKSON,
"Major Genl.
A. S. PENDLETON, *A. A.*

This stringent order was posted in the office, and an effort made to enforce it. A strong detail was furnished for guard duty. Lt. Eakin of the Liberty Hall Guards from Rockbridge, was assigned for duty, subject to call from the provost's office. The provost guard in strong force appeared on the streets demanding passes. The first day was full of unpleasant incidents. Batches of old soldiers were sent to their camps under guard. Some who had the proper leave from camp, appeared late in the day, with scores of citizens who had been sent back by the post pickets, all clamoring for passes; and not a few blamed the provost marshal for all their troubles. The next few days brought unexpected trouble. To better understand the situation, it may be said that the only mode of travel for persons going South by public conveyance, was by the old style stages drawn by four horses over the Valley Turnpike to Strasburg, connecting there with the railroad. These stages started from the old Taylor Hotel, and were generally crowded. On the Valley Pike, these stages were halted by pickets, and every passenger not supplied with the required pass, would be required to return to Winchester, secure passes and wait the next stage. This caused so much trouble, that to avoid it, provost guards were directed to notify all stage passengers at the stage office that passes would be required of them by the pickets. On the 5th of February, Lt. Eakin and his guard, saw several officers enter the stage, and respectfully approached them and gave the usual notice, when the answer came: "This is General Loring and part of his staff." They were told that they would be embarrassed at the picket post, and to avoid this they could in a few minutes obtain passes at the provost's office. One of the officers in a few minutes stood in the doorway of the office and *demanded* passes for General Loring and staff, at the same time expressing his opinion of "young officers assuming too much authority for the positions they held." Major ——— was informed that proper credentials must be shown before passes could issue from that office, and referred him to the *posted order*. This delay was too much for John Taylor the veteran stage driver. He started his team. At the court-house gate the Major hailed him. General Loring and party left the stage and returned to Mr. Conrad's. The young provost hastened to headquarters, at the Col. Moore house, to know if he had assumed too much in refusing passes to a general officer and his staff. Genl. Jackson was in his office and alone. The case was briefly stated; the General wore a troubled expression as he answered: "Unfortunate, *very* unfortunate. *Continue to execute that order."* Leaving the General's office, the Adjutant General's office was visited, where the incident was gravely discussed. A feverish state of feeling pervaded the official family. They knew letters and resignation had gone to Richmond, and dreaded the results. This was an official secret, however; and it was understood by the parties present as the writer left for his office, that it should so continue, until Jackson authorized its announcement. It appeared later on, that General Loring had been corresponding with the Secretary of War; and desiring to go in person, obtained an order by telegraph to report in Richmond. When Loring received this, he was informed by some friend, that he could not *pass the picket on that order.* Once more the Provost hastened to enquire of Genl. Jackson what should be done. His reply was in his usual calm manner: "Issue passes upon what you consider an order from the Secretary of war, and record the fact." This was probably the 7th or 8th of February (the date not being preserved.) An officer appeared at the provost's office and handed over a large official envelope, remarking: There are the credentials. The envelope contained the telegram and a list of names of officers. Genl. Loring in terst style said: "Please issue, provost Marshal, passes for the above-named officers." Here the incident closed. Though 45 years have passed, the experiences of the days briefly mentioned are easily recalled, without reference to the fading notes of those stirring times.

When it became known that General Jackson had, by his firmness, won a victory over the parties who had trampled upon his military rights, rejoicings were heard all over the land. The Confederate generals like Jackson would not submit as easily to their War Secretary as Federal Generals did to their War Secretary, E. M. Stanton.

Loring and his regiments had gone to more congenial fields. Jackson and his small army of about 5,000 men all told, spent the remainder of February in quiet preparations awaiting the arrival of Spring and the *Yankees*. Genl. N. P. Banks was placed in command of a district that comprehended the Shenandoah Valley. His headquarters were supposed to be at Frederick, Md., and his army of about 45,000 men, stretched from that point to Cumberland, embracing Romney; while McClellan with 200,000 men lay around Washington, waiting for Spring, when he could move against Johnston's army of 32,000, wintering at Centreville. And it was plain to Jackson, no doubt, that he could not hope for victory if he waged battle in his present position, while his little army and people in the town and country believed him invincible and that he would never yield a foot. As it turned out, Jackson was maturing his plans for strategy, and expected to defeat his foes by strategy and good fighting. When Banks began crossing his army over his pontoon bridge at Harpers Ferry the 27th of February, 1862, and landed on the South side of the Potomac with 38,000 men, including 2,000 cavalry and 80 pieces of artillery (See O. R.), the Winchester people had good cause to be apprehensive; but they had their fears changed to joy when they learned Jackson was fortifying his position. Banks' demonstrations showed his desire to engage the Confederates. He had not at that time made acquaintance with Stonewall Jackson. Jackson's letter to Genl. Johnston dated March 8, '62, urging the necessity for General Hill to reinforce him, gave evidence of his great desire to hold the Lower Valley, and for an opportunity to so startle Washington, that McClellan would delay his attack on Johnston. Mr. Davis was not willing to risk his capital any more than Lincoln was his. So Hill was not sent; but an order came for Jackson to use his own judgment in his Valley campaign, but to avoid all danger of defeat by the overwhelming force marching against him. So we find him on the 10th of March preparing to evacuate the town and fall back. Then went up the wail that tried even Jackson's nerves. The Valley men reluctantly yielded to the inevitable and obeyed orders, but with sad hearts; for many mothers, wives, sisters and sweethearts were to be left to the horrors of the first invasion. It may be interesting to show what comprised the Valley Army that Jackson had gathered around him and who were to become so prominent in the terrible struggles. While it looked formidable and grand to those who loved gray soldiers, it was insignificant as compared to the brilliant host closing up towards the gates of Winchester. Briefly told, Jackson had 3,600 infantry, 600 cavalry, and six batteries of 27 guns. Though not all Valley men, they were Virginians. They were divided into three brigades:

First Brigade (or Stonewall)—Brigadier Genl. Garnett—2nd, 4th, 5th, 33rd Virginia Regiments.

Second Brigade—Col. Burks, commanding—21st, 42nd, 48th, 1st, Regular Irish Battalion.

Third Brigade—Col. Fulkerson, commanding—23rd, 27th Virginia Regiments.

McLaughlin's Battery .... 8 guns.
Waters' Battery .... 4 "
Carpenter's Battery .... 4 "
Mayre's Battery .... 4 "
Shumaker's Battery .... 4 "
Ashby's Regiment of Cavalry.
Chew's Horse Artillery Battery.... 3 "

This little army would have presented a strange picture to English or French military critics. The plain gray uniform, slouch hat, all carelessly worn; the marching outfit: one blanket,—rubber blanket (captured at Manassas) folded in a roll that was slung over one shoulder and the two ends tied together under the arm of the other, with a frying pan and skillet stuck in the belt, gave a grotesque appearance to the lines of the old gray soldiers, while it betokened endurance of any fatigue or hardship. The familiar way they handled the muskets, would impress the critic that a gun was no new thing in their hands. They always wore a jaunty, careless look while on the march; but when the enemy was sighted, the lines tightened, muskets more firmly grasped, muscle and brain more active, they were instantly ready to go where Jackson sent them. This applied as well to the artillerists; the only difference being, they had field pieces that were revered for the work they had already done, and were carefully handled now for what they were expected to do. Noble, grand men they were who manned those old-style smooth-bores, The cavalry and its immortal Ashby, were not long enough in one place for the fastidious critic to describe. Mounted on superb horses that were common in the Valley at that time; displaying such horsemanship as singled them out from all other cavalrymen, they were to be seen at all times in scouting squads, watching and annoying the large detachments of Banks' cavalry, now in sight of the spires of Winchester. Ashby and his gallant *Six Hundred* were ready to guard the rear of Jackson's army when it turned away from the old town on the 11th of March, 1862.

In the next chapter will be briefly shown where they went and what they did.

CHAPTER LVII

Jackson's Evacuation of Winchester, March 11, 1862
Retirement to the Upper Valley

The Valley Army briefly mentioned in close of last chapter, we now view in the three brigades as they were in line on March 11th, 1862, with the head of the column towards the South. The wagon trains had been sent to the Valley Turnpike and halted in two sections, one at Kernstown, the other at Newtown; and everything was ready for the march, when an order came for a halt. Col. Burks and the 2nd brigade were wheeled to the right and headed North. Ashby had been skirmishing with cavalry during the night and all morning. About 10 o'clock, a brigade of bluecoats appeared as support to the cavalry. Genl. Jackson was apprised, and sent Burks to meet them. The Federal infantry fell back without firing a shot. Banks had two columns, one camped at Bunker Hill and the other near Charlestown, showing no disposition to come out and gage battle. Burks was recalled; and Ashby left in their front. The little army was soon in motion; and as they marched through the streets and beheld the sad faces of the splendid women who waved their adieus, the old-time spirit spurred them to cry out words of encouragement: "We will be back soon." Some old comrade caught the words and sang out—"Yes, in the sweet by and by." One by one, they took up the refrain, until the pathetic words and music were heard through all the lines, amid the cheers constantly ascending from the gray battalions, dying away as the last squadron passed beyond the southern borders of the town. They pressed on and spent the night with their respective trains. During the night of the 11th, many non-combatants followed the army, seeking refuge beyond the Confederate lines. The public records of the county were sent off at the same time; also bank officers went off with the treasures of their institutions. The entire community was alarmed, and many sank in despair as they contemplated the impending ruin. They had not long to wait. Banks was promptly on hand the next morning, the 12th. A large force of cavalry, supported by two brigades of infantry and 7 pieces of artillery, cautiously entered the town. The cavalry scoured every street, looking for Ashby. Learning that chieftain might be found South of Winchester, Capt. Cole hurried his "Bucktails" out on the Valley Pike. Ashby who had espied the Company, sought a place to give them a surprise. He chose the bend in the turnpike South of the old Parkins' Mill (now Keckleys), where his small squad could not be seen until Cole made the turn by G. W. Hillyard's residence. With wild shouts the gray troopers followed their leader, firing into the front of the column, which recoiled upon the line, which was fired into by several Confederates on their flank. The showy Bucktails were stampeded, and scurried back to Winchester. Two men desperately wounded were carried into Hahn's Mill; three fell from their horses and were picked up; three were killed and carried into the yard of Mr. Nathan Parkins (now Hillyards). Eight or ten horses were captured, and a number of pistols picked up along the line of retreat. Ashby trotted to the edge of the town and gave Cole another chance to come out. That evening the heavy picket line was planted across the country near the mills. Ashby fell back and established a line of vedettes from the Front Royal Turnpike across country, by the old toll-gate and up over the hills due West. Screened from view, they were to give signals to reserve couriers who would hasten to inform Ashby what had been seen of any advancing Federals. Jackson slowly retired to Strasburg, and went into camp, awaiting Banks' movement. The latter delayed so long, that Jackson practiced a ruse on the Federals. Ashby was ordered in; and he hurried away, as if in retreat, halting only at Mt. Jackson. There he bivouacked a few days. Banks seemed content to hold the defenseless town of Winchester until he was ordered to move. Receiving such orders on the 18th of March, Banks sent Shields forward with 11,000 men and 27 guns, with orders to hold Strasburg. All this was in accordance with McClellan's chess-board plan, to move all lines South. (See O. R., Vol. XI, part iii, p. 7). Of this, mention at this time is only made to show why Banks sent a portion of his army to Manassas *via* Castlemans Ferry on the 18th. On the 20th he started with the remainder, and ordered Shields to fall back to Winchester and protect the Lower Valley approaches to Washington. Jackson was informed on the 21st that baggage trains were seen leaving

Winchester with troops, going in the direction of Castlemans Ferry on the Shenandoah; and that Shields falling back to Winchester, meant that he must do something to compel Banks' return and not allow him to appear on Johnston's left. So he at once pushed forward towards Winchester. On the 22nd, Ashby was sent forward; and rushing into Shields' pickets South of Winchester, drove them; but stirred up infantry and artillery, and a severe skirmish ensued. Shields was wounded during the engagement by a stray shell from Chew's Flying Artillery. Ashby was deceived; and reported to Jackson that only a small force was at Winchester; for Shields' whole division was near at hand, but obscured by a range of hills. Jackson arrived at Strasburg March 23rd; and at once proceeded in his march, arriving near Kernstown about 1 P. M. Jackson at that hour discovered the presence of the large force of Federals lying West of the village. The three brigades, now worn out by the two days' hard marching, were in bad condition for an open fight with superior numbers. They were ordered to their positions, however; and although rest was badly needed, Jackson was compelled to open the battle, fearing that reinforcements would come to Shields, if battle were postponed until morning. The cavalry was divided. Major Funsten was sent with half the regiment to cover the left flank. The Federal lines were soon formed, extending to the East side of the Valley Turnpike. Genl. Kimball who had succeeded Shields, was there, and held the heaviest part of his army then visible; while to the West, along the ridge near the old Pritchard homestead, was a line of infantry and two batteries. Jackson determined to assault that West line and turn the enemy's right, and secure a strong position in the cover of a ridge of woodland. Ashby was expected to hold the main body to the East of the turnpike. Jackson hoped by this movement to cut retreat to Winchester. He also believed that the force now in his front was small, and could not be reinforced before he gave the stunning blow. He was not informed of the heavy force concealed all day on the line he expected to take. As the battle progressed with great fury, and he had used his last regiment, and assured that he could complete his plan, he saw from his position that Kimball had crossed the turnpike and was making for strong ground to meet the Stonewall brigade coming up with Garnett at the front. The latter saw the hidden brigade move out on Jackson's position, and with three fresh regiments bearing down on the 27th and 21st Va., over-running Fulkerson's detachment; and two regiments and a battery hurrying up to the right of the old brigade, he deemed it best to fall back and save them from carnage, hoping to find better position. Jackson rode to the new position, and ordered Garnett to move forward; but discovering the heavy line moving to the position he had just left, he took in the situation, and ordered all to fall back. This was about dusk. He had been battling all afternoon against Shields' division of 9,000 men, while he had only 2,000 all told. This battle has been written down in official reports as a victory over the Confederates. A study of the situation, proves the contrary, if the disparity of numbers is considered, the loss in killed and wounded, and the failure of the Federals to follow up their advantage and capture more of Jackson's men.

Want of space forbids further description of this battle. All the regiments fought with desperation against great odds, although worn out on their arrival on the battle field. One incident must be mentioned. When the 27th stirred up the concealed Federals in the Pritchard woods, in its attempt to turn the right of a line of cavalry and infantry, they were repulsed with heavy loss. Part of the 23rd regiment came up in time to see a full regiment sweeping through a field towards an old stone fence. Both regiments made a rush to secure the fence for a barricade. The Confederates landed first, and caught the advancing Federals unprepared to fire, who were then within twenty steps of the fence and under the terrible volley from the Virginians. The splendid regiment went down, banners and all. This was the 51st Ohio. The Colonel was desperately wounded, and related the affair afterwards. He said "when he arose from the ground, he looked along the line to see the effect on his regiment, and out of his 1,100 men, all were on the ground excepting about 100 men who were just delivering a deliberate fire on the Virginians as they arose to fire another volley. When he looked again, part of the 100 had gone down. Those who were not struck, started back and some of the wounded scrambled to their feet and sought shelter. The Confederates then retired; and he, later on, was taken off the field and carried to the Taylor Hotel, where he was tenderly cared for by the proprietor." Men who gathered up the Confederate dead that night, found several Confederates behind the stone fence, every one being shot in the head. The losses as reported in official reports by the Federals, fix the number of killed and wounded at 1,200, one-half being Rebels. This seems strange, when we remember distinctly that 81 dead Confederates were all that could be found, and they were buried in one trench, and about 180 wounded men were accounted for and carried off the field by Jackson's army. This would make *Rebel* loss in killed and wounded 260 instead of 600, and the Federal loss 940. No effort was made to follow the slowly retreating regiments, which were anxious to fall down in some place and rest from the hardships of the last two days. The infantry halted at Newtown, and were sound asleep in less than an hour. Ashby's cavalry bivouacked at Bartonsville, about 1½ miles from the battlefield. (Col. Wm. Allan's Jackson's Valley Campaign.) War reports show that Shields sent couriers for the troops that had crossed the Shenandoah, to return to Winchester by forced marches and reach him in time to meet the expected engagement. This brigade was posted in the woods and held in reserve, and stirred up by Col. Grigsby's 27th regiment. Same reports show that Banks also ordered the Genl. Williams Brigade; and the counter-march was approved by McClellan, although it was done without consulting him. He telegraphed Banks: "Your course was right; as soon as you are strong enough, push Jackson hard and drive him beyond Strasburg. The very moment the thorough defeat of Jackson will permit, resume the movement on Manassas, always leaving the whole of Shields' command, at and near Strasburg and Winchester. Communicate fully and *act vigorously.*" Later on the official reports, War dept., show that the Kernstown battle caused not only the retention of the Williams Brigade, but also that Blenker's division of 9,000 Germans was taken from McClellan and sent to Strasburg to join Fremont, who was marching from Western Virginia towards the Valley; and the first army corps under McDowell then at Manassas, who had been ordered to go to McClellan on the Peninsula, was now ordered to remain at Manassas and act in concert with Banks' army and protect Washington. Thus it will be seen that Jackson's Kernstown campaign, wrought many changes that tended to weaken McClellan's army. Jackson, as soon as the wounded had arrived at the camps, left Newtown with wagon trains and ambulances in front, and leisurely marched to Woodstock, spending the night of the 24th at that point. Banks slowly followed, and camped the same night on Cedar Creek. The next day he camped at Strasburg and sent his cavalry as far as Woodstock. There they found Ashby's cavalry and the 42nd and 48th regiments under Col. Burks. After several skirmishes with Ashby, they retired to Toms Brook and there established a line of pickets. Jackson had gone to Mt. Jackson with the other brigades. Banks remained passive until the 2nd day of April, and then moved Southward to Woodstock. It is useless to say that Ashby kept the Federal cavalry busy every day. The former fell back beyond Edinburg, and was able to stay further movement up the Valley. Jackson was in the vicinity of Mt. Jackson, and determined that his vantage ground justified another engagement with the Federal force now under the personal command of Banks. The latter in his letters to Washington, began to show anxiety about his position; and instead of driving Jackson out of the Valley as McClellan ordered him to do, he began to write about the Luray Valley affording a way of flank movements, that might *annoy his communications.* He also discovered that roads found their way through the Blue Ridge, and that over these, reinforcements might come to Jackson. Thus he whined until the 17th of April, when he put his army in motion. By a flank movement, his cavalry took possession of New Market and captured one of the new companies that had reported to Ashby, whose force had now swelled to about 2,000. This forward movement of Banks', was the most serious of any yet made, so far as the Confederate armies of the Valley and Ewell's army East of the Ridge, were concerned. Their communication was in danger. Jackson taking in the situation, acted promptly to secure the pass through the Blue Ridge known as Swift Run Gap. But to do this, he must go to the Luray valley; and the only way was to take a long march by falling back to Harrisonburg, and there swing around to the South end of the Massanutton Mountain. This required a forced march, in order to reach the desired point in the Elkton Valley before Banks' detachment could secure the pass. On the 18th, the army was in rapid march to accomplish this object, and we find him at a point 5 miles East of Harrisonburg in the evening, having made 31 miles. The next morning, the 19th, he crossed over the mountain road leading to Conrad's store on the East side of South River, which he crossed on a bridge that he strongly fortified; then moved further East and took possession of the Swift Run Gap pass, camping on the Elk Run. Banks was not idle. He sent detachments over the Massanutton from New Market to Luray; and there found the Confederates in the act of destroying two bridges. They were driven off, and the bridges secured by a strong guard. Banks had gone to Harrisonburg, discovering that Jackson had flown. But the cautious General began to take in the situation. Jackson was then on his left flank, where he *might* secure reinforcements from Ewell and recross the mountain in his rear, cut his retreat, and endanger his army equipment. Should he move on to Staunton, with the hope of a juncture with Fremont who was pressing Genl. Edw. Johnson somewhere West of Staunton? Nothing lay between his lines and Staunton. But advices from Washington gave him excuse for not moving further South; and in no sense was he to rely on Fremont joining him at Staunton. (O. R., Vol. XII, p. 104.) Also the latter was not to rely on Banks, as he might be recalled to a base nearer the Lower Valley. Jackson was not content with the simple check given to Banks, by his appearance on his flank; and was corresponding with Genl. Johnston in reference to one of his plans to produce marvelous changes in the Valley. But Johnston disapproved of any movement that would prevent his immediate reinforcement of Ewell, ostensibly reinforcing the former. At this critical juncture, Genl. Lee was assigned control of all armies in Virginia; and he wrote Jackson on the 21st April a very confidential and agreeable letter—"I have no doubt that an attempt will be made to occupy Fredericksburg and use it as a base of operations against Richmond. Our present force there is very small (2,500 men under Genl. Field), and cannot be reinforced except by weakening other corps. If you can use Genl. Ewell's division in an attack on Banks, it will prove a great relief to the pressure on Fredericksburg." (O. R., Vol. XII, part iii, p. 859.) This was the plan that Jackson had *vaguely* submitted to Johnston, which the latter declined. Jackson and Ewell had been in correspondence on this plan, and both were prepared, had Johnston permitted them, to unite. Jackson upon receipt of Genl. Lee's letter, hastened to apprise Ewell and have him prepared for any emergency. Jackson wrote Lee on the 23rd more fully of his plans; and suggested that Ewell remain quiet a few days, so as to be used by Lee if necessary. On April 25th, Genl. Lee wrote Jackson again and expressed his appreciation of Jackson's forethought, as the situation had developed his need of Ewell. On the 28th of April, Jackson wrote Lee that Banks had 21,000 men within one days' march of his position, and that Blenker was at Winchester on the 20th with 7,000 men. "I propose to attack Banks if you will send me 5,000 more men. * * * Now, as it appears to me, is the golden opportunity for striking. Until I hear from you, I will watch an opportunity for striking some exposed point." Subsequent events proved that Jackson had secured the confidence of Genl. Lee at this early period, and he was one, if not the closest, adviser he had. Jackson submitted three plans to Genl. Lee, showing fully what he proposed to do, if any one would meet his approval. These plans embody too much to unfold them in this volume. If the reader desires to study them, he will be edified by a careful reading of their comprehensive treatment by Henderson in his Life of Stonewall Jackson, Vol. I, pp. 283-4. Genl. Lee answered that he had carefully considered the three plans proposed, and that he was satisfied Jackson would select the *"one that promised the most good to the cause in general."* Jackson chose the one that would take him West of Staunton to surprise and defeat Milroy, who was then hammering Genl. Edw. Johnson, who being thus relieved, could return with him to the Valley and cripple if not destroy Banks' Army.

Jackson's army was in motion by the time Lee's letter was read; and everything hastily preparing for an advance to some point, none knew where. He kept his own secrets at that time;—held no counsel with staff or others. Three roads lay out before him: one by Harrisonburg; the second, by Port Republic, Cross Keys and Mt. Sidney; the third, the river road by Port Republic and Staunton. The first of these was already occupied by the Federals. (Henderson, Vol. 1, p. —) Jackson chose the river road; and by Noon of May 30th, he was on his march to McDowell *via* Staunton, going by Port Republic, and arriving at Mechem's Station on the Virginia Central on May 3rd, after a march over almost impassable roads and through Spring rains. All the streams were at flood; wagons and gun carriages sank in quagmires to the axle. The army had spent days of toil over a route that under ordinary circumstances the *foot cavalry* could have traversed in one.

We left Ashby making demonstrations in Banks' front, greatly to the annoyance of the latter. On the 30th, Ewell with 8,000 men glided through Swift Run Gap and camped on Jackson's old camp ground. This led Banks to believe that Jackson was still in the *bottle,* waiting unconsciously for him in his own time to cork and seal. May 4th was Sunday. Jackson had heard from Genl. Edw. Johnson, who needed help. Infantry was put aboard the long train of cars and hurried away to Staunton. Artillery and wagons went by wagon road. By the 6th, all were up and formed a juncture with Johnson. The Staunton people had heard that the Valley Army had crossed the Blue Ridge and Edw. Johnson had fallen back from Milroy's front, and felt disheartened. But when Jackson's men marched through the streets that Sunday morning, they rejoiced to know that their dear old Valley had not been abandoned to the invader. The 6th was spent in resting the troops after their eight days' march. Banks knew nothing of this movement, and continued to interest his Washington authorities with his attractive letters, which afford good reading even now after the lapse of 45 years. One of them written May 30th, '62, is so full of gross ignorance of the situation, that a few quotations are given to show the trend of his intentions, etc. He says: "There is nothing to be done in the Valley this side of Strasburg * * * and if permitted to do so, would cross the Blue Ridge and sweep the country North of Gordonsville. * * * Jackson's Army is reduced, demoralized, on half rations, they are all concentrating for Richmond. * * * I am now satisfied that it is the most safe and effective disposition for our corps. I pray your favorable consideration. Such order will electrify our force." Subsequent events show that his force *was* electrified, but not in the way he predicted. Jackson apparently understood his adversary well enough to know that he would not move to Staunton as long as he could threaten his rear from the Elkton Valley; and that he had not discovered the change from that point, which put Jackson's army in his front at Staunton and Ewell ready to strike when told.

When Jackson left Staunton on the 7th, Banks informed Washington that the "Jackson Army was preparing to attack Harrisonburg." This would mislead his authorities to believe that he held that place, when it is an actual fact that Ashby had been holding that vicinity steadily since the 5th of May. We have it from Dabney, (Vol, 3, p. 65,) how the march was started from Staunton to look after Milroy and others in the Monterey or McDowell section—"Edw. Johnson's regiments led the way, several miles in advance; the Third and Second Brigades followed; the 'Stonewall,' under Genl. Winder, a young West Point officer of exceptional promise, bringing up the rear. The corps of Cadets of the Virginia Military Institute, was also attached to the expedition."

Eighteen miles West of Staunton, they encountered the first line of pickets, some of whom were captured. Johnson halted and bivouacked on a deserted camp after his march of 14 miles. Jackson moved 6 miles further on, when night forced a halt. Milroy learned from the escaped pickets, of Johnson's return. He gathered in his outposts, and soon had his force of about 3,700 men at McDowell, a village at the base of Bull Pasture Mountain. Fremont was known to be somewhere in the South Branch Valley, to whom Milroy looked for help when he needed it. The force nearest to him was a brigade about Franklin, Pendleton County, 34 miles North. To this force Milroy dispatched for reinforcements. This proved to be Genl. Schenck's force, and the messenger found him so near at hand that he easily marched up and took position on the morning of the 8th. Jackson and Johnson were disappointed when they beheld the extent of Milroy's lines, and their strong positions. Milroy had heard through scouts and Union men that Jackson had joined Johnson; and he had sent such word to Schenck, who at once started towards McDowell. The Valley men had come to fight, and Jackson opened battle from several strong positions. The Federal force was composed of Western Virginia and Ohio troops chiefly, and fought desperately; but after repeated assaults, were compelled to retire under cover of the night that had come. Genl. Johnson was wounded, and losses on both sides were heavy. Confederate losses killed and wounded was 498, including 454 officers. The Federals owing to their strong natural defenses—hills, ridges and crests, sustained but slight loss—256 killed, wounded and missing. The Federals kept their camp fires burning brightly all night where they halted about three miles North; but when morning came, they were not to be seen. All had gone in the night, and Jackson had accomplished what he had come so far to do—force the Federals to retire. The McDowell campaign has often been mentioned with Jackson's other victories, and comparing its results with his other battle of Kernstown, it is safe to conclude their strongest feature was the destruction of the enemy's plans rather than his army.

On the morning of the 9th, a cavalry detachment was sent on Milroy's trail, while the infantry tarried in McDowell to be supplied with rations. Then they started in pursuit; but the cavalry reported Milroy twenty miles ahead and pushing on to Franklin. Jackson endeavored to overtake them, but was hindered by forest fires that had been kindled by the retreating foe; and through the dense smoke Jackson's men plunged on, making forced marches on the 10th and 11th. By this time the rear guard was overtaken, and from every vantage ground the Federals planted cannon and shelled the approaching column. At Franklin, Fremont and Blenker had come up, and Jackson prudently started back on the 12th on his return to the Valley. The Federal army offered no resistance, and Jackson and his army continued their march *via* McDowell; but we find he waited long enough to give his men time to hold divine service the day he left Franklin. On May 15th the Valley Army was on the road to Harrisonburg, and going into camp at Lebanon Springs. The 16th was spent in camp, to observe the day set apart by President Davis for fasting and prayer. On the 17th the line of march was once more taken up. Dabney mentions an incident in his biography of Stonewall Jackson that occurred during this day's march that some old comrades may recall. He says: "A mutiny occurred in the 27th Virginia among some companies who had volunteered for twelve months, and whose time had expired and who demanded their discharge. On this being refused, they threw down their arms. Col. Grigsby referred to the general for instructions. Jackson's face, when the circumstances were explained, set hard as flint. "Why," he said, "does Col. Grigsby refer to me to learn how to deal with mutineers? He should shoot them where they stand." The rest of the regiment was ordered to parade with loaded muskets. The insubordinate companies were offered the choice of instant death or instant submission. The men knew their commander, and at once surrendered. This was the last attempt at disobedience in the Valley Army."

Genl. Ewell met Jackson at Mt. Solon, having ridden over from his camp to consult with the General and post him as to the situation in the Valley. Banks had gone to Strasburg, and Ashby was busy with his cavalry, falling trees across the roads through the mountains to prevent Fremont's easy march to reinforce Banks. Fremont says in his official report, (Vol. XII, part I; p. 11) "that in one instance trees were felled along the road for one mile, and culverts torn up and heavy rocks rolled from the mountain sides in many places."

Banks was now in danger. Jackson, Ewell and Johnson were meditating an attack while he was virtually cut off from Fremont's support.

CHAPTER LVIII

Battle of Winchester—Jackson and Banks

The return of Jackson to the Valley with his gallant little army, was destined to produce changes in the war arena, that the Northern government did not expect; and the Southern government had but faint hope that the ray of light held out from the distant Valley could in any event blazon out to encourage the whole Southland. To better appreciate the situation in May, 1862, it may be well to briefly sum up the conditions that perplexed the Southern government and encouraged the Northern. New Orleans had fallen. This virtually filled the Mississippi River with Federal gunboats. Richmond was seriously threatened by McClellan, who had changed his base from West Point—or North of York River—to the White House within twenty miles of Richmond, with 112,000 men; McDowell with 40,000 on the Rappahannock, within four days' march; gunboats in the James River, subject to McClellan's call. To meet this forward movement was the grand army of Joe Johnston, but with less than one-third the strength of the great host that seemed to be pressing from every point. Richmond was so hard pressed, that precautionary measures had been taken. Military stores had already gone to a place of greater safety; President Davis and his family were ready to leave at a moment's notice. His cabinet, with their chests packed, and probably the Confederate government, would have been on wheels in a short time, had they not waited to consider the protests of Virginia through her General Assembly and the City Council of Richmond. The President, however, deemed it best for the general good, to carry out his original plans. Fortunately, Robert E. Lee was at the front, and his military eye saw a gleam of light off in the Shenandoah Valley sky, which a genius for strategy had kindled. Stonewall Jackson held the beacon; and Lee grasped the situation as no others had, and was willing to flash this back to the Valley sentinel: "Whatever movement you make against Banks, do it speedily; and if successful, drive him back towards the Potomac, and create the impression, as far as possible, that you design threatening that line." Genl. Lee had been considering a long letter Jackson had written him on May 16th, after he and Genl. Ewell had consulted at Mt. Solon. Briefly stated, Jackson pointed out Banks, cut off from reinforcements, so unaware of the close proximity of a threatening Confederate army, that he was contemplating a move by way of Gordonsville to join the Federal hosts then closing in on Richmond; that if two brigades were sent him promptly, he could relieve Richmond, by not only crushing Banks and checking his movement, but would tend to withdraw from McClellan, troops to reinforce efforts being made to clear the Valley by Fremont and Milroy, temporarily bottled up in the South Branch Valley. We find Jackson in a dilemma on the 17th. Instead of reinforcements, Ewell had received orders to recross the Blue Ridge, leaving the cavalry to simply watch Banks. Genl. Joe Johnston had interposed objections to anything that would weaken his force. Ewell and Jackson hastily consulted, and a telegram to Lee resulted, to wit: "I am of opinion that an attempt should be made to defeat Banks; but under instructions from Genl. Johnston, I do not feel at liberty to make an attack. Please answer by telegraph at once." This telegram brought the foregoing telegram from Lee. By the morning of the 18th, Jackson felt free to act. Banks was fortifying at Strasburg, whether of his own will, or by order from Washington, need not appear now. Jackson sent Ashby to New Market to establish a picket line near Woodstock, to conceal if possible his own movements. Jackson then moved to the former place on the 20th. Ewell was already in Luray; but had detached one brigade and sent it over to Jackson. This gave Jackson and Ewell a combined strength of 17,000 men and 11 batteries, (according to Col. Wm. Allan's estimates in his *Valley Campaign*, pp 92-3.) The two armies were considered as two divisions; and in order to show to enquirers, who the men were who participated in the celebrated Valley Campaign, the following table is given of regiments composing the divisions; and old soldiers can readily identify their respective companies; and thus company officers and men may be traced through tables that may appear in this volume.

Jackson's Division.

First (Stonewall) Brigade—Genl. Winder—2nd Va., 4th Va., 5th Va., 27th Va., 33rd Va.

Second Brigade—Col. Campbell—21st Va., 42nd Va., 48th Va., 1st Regulars (Irish.)

Third Brigade—Col. Taliaferro—10th Va., 23rd Va., 37th Va.,

Ashby's Cavalry, 7th Va. and several new companies.

Five batteries—22 guns.

Ewell's Division.

First Brigade—Genl. Dick Taylor—6th Louisiana, 7th Louisiana, 8th Louisiana, 9th Louisiana, Wheat's Battalion of Louisiana Tigers.

Second Brigade—Genl. Trimble—21st N. Ca., 21st Ga., 15th Ala., 16th Miss.

Third Brigade—Genl. Elzey—13th Va., 31st Va., 25th Va., 12th Ga.

Fourth Brigade—(Johnson's)—44th Va., 52nd Va., 58th Va.

Maryland—1st Md.

Cavalry—Genl. G. H. Stuart of Md.; 2nd Va., Col. Munford; 6th Va., Col. Flournoy.

Six Batteries, 26 guns.

Inclination is strong to attempt a portrayal of the two chiefs as they appeared in grotesque figure at the head of the two little armies, as well as the brigade, regimental and other officers and men, that were now prepared to enter upon the campaign of unfaded glory. Many of them were familiar figures to the writer. Jackson and his lemons; Ewell with his boiled wheat; Winder with his *tactics;* Taliaferro with his dignity; Dick Taylor and his Louisiana curiosities of Creoles, Tigers and Planters; Elzey with his Maryland men, ever singing "Maryland, My Maryland," until stilled by the New Orleans band, playing superb music to the dancers, of whom Dick Taylor makes mention in his *"Destruction and Reconstruction."* Then we have Trimble, "the nimble," as he was called; A. P. Hill, the inimitable Ashby, Munford, and a host of others. So many of those brave men seem to be flitting before the writer as he pens these lines. But we must hasten to follow them on their march and through their battles, though in briefest manner possible.

May 21st, 1862, the early morning saw Jackson's army astir and the column heading North, with Genl. Dick Taylor in the lead. All now expected to sweep down the Valley Pike and suddenly strike Banks. They were set to wondering what "Ole Jack" was adoin', when the column turned to the right and was soon crossing the Mountains, and went into the vicinity of Luray that night. The next day, 22nd, the whole army was in motion, quietly moving towards Front Royal, stopping that night within ten miles of that place, which was occupied by a considerable force from Banks' command, to fill the place of Shields who had gone across the Ridge to reinforce McDowell. The Washington government felt easy; and waited to hear of glowing victories from the various plans well inaugurated to crush the Rebellion; and were in total ignorance of Jackson's real position. Had they known that he had 17,000 men on the flank of the only Federal force in the Valley, say ten miles to the East and a less distance to points on the Valley Pike, someone in Washington would have spent a restless night. Bank's army was reduced to 10,000, and this scattered. Col. Kenly of the 1st Federal Maryland (of whom we will hear more later on) was at Front Royal with 1,100 men and several cannon. He occupied the low ground between the town and the river, guarding the two bridges and all approaches, but unaware that Jackson was in camp within a few miles of *his* camp. On the morning of the 23rd he was surprised by a rush of Confederates from the woods upon his pickets and through the town. Kenly bravely undertook to stay the charge, and for some time made a gallant stand, using two pieces of artillery with such effect, that he had time to burn his camp equipment before retiring to Guard Hill, and later on to Cedarville. Jackson had taken part of the 6th Va. Cavalry, and finding a fording place, landed on the North side of the river, and recklessly joined in a charge that drove the enemy from their strong positions on the hill. Jackson sent the cavalry forward and waited for the infantry and artillery;—then all advanced on the Cedarville position. Kenly boldly held out until he fell, seriously wounded. The cavalry handled by brave and competent officers, performed the service that eventually produced a Federal rout, and crowned themselves with glory, with the fruits of their victory in hand—250 Confederates overpowered and brought in 600 Federals, including 15 officers and part of a battery. 32 men were killed at that point and 122 wounded, while the Confederate loss was 11 killed and 15 wounded. Ashby had not been idle with his Seventh all this time. He was at his old tricks, tearing up the railroad at Buckton (Riverton,) cutting the telegraph line and intercepting a message just going to Banks, who was yet in blissful ignorance of what was happening at Front Royal. He believed firmly that Jackson was marching down the Valley Pike, from demonstrations in his front by three companies of Ashby's Cavalry that had been left at Woodstock. Capt. Wm. N. McDonald, author of the History of the Laurel Brigade, says, "That Capt. Sam Myers, Capt. E. H. McDonald and Capt. Wm. H. Harness (the writer's Company) drove in the pickets and erected breastworks on the hills near Strasburg in sight of Banks' army. Moving his troops from point to point, partly in view of the Federals, created the impression that he was supported by a large force." It was during these maneuvres, that a detail from the writer's company was posted on the high jutting point of the Massanutton Mountain, overlooking both positions—Banks' quiet camp at Strasburg, and the smoke and shifting firing at Front Royal; beholding later in the day, Banks' break in his camp.

Ashby in destroying the railroad communication at Buckton, encountered a garrison strongly fortified in an old log house near an embankment, which withstood frequent attacks, but was finally overcome and part of two companies captured, who were trying to escape on two freight cars. Ashby accomplished much, but he lost much. At this spot two gallant captains were killed: Capt. Geo. F. Sheetz, of Company F., 7th Va. Cavalry, and Capt. John Fletcher who had succeeded Turner Ashby in command of Company A., 7th Regt. Splendid men they were; fearless leaders, always up with their companies. Several of their men fell beside them. Jackson halted his advance at Cedarville and sent dispatches for infantry and artillery in the rear, to take up line of march for Middletown and Newtown, with the view to cutting Banks' retreat; but owing to the inefficiency of young and inexperienced cavalrymen who were couriers, orders went astray, and much delay and unnecessary hard marching ensued, frustrating some of the general's plans. This occasion induced him to plan his special messenger and scout service.

Jackson had started for Middletown before Banks could be persuaded that he was virtually cut off; and when he came to a full knowledge of the situation, he seemed frightened and unable to understand that this was one volt only of the electric shock that was yet to come. Ashby was sent towards Middletown to keep the left flank covered, and get that point in readiness for the infantry brigades that were closing up on the captures at Front Royal and Buckton, which were estimated at the value of $300,000. Jackson had nearly worn out men of all branches of the army; and the night found all in need of rest. So far, the movement was successful, not only in the loss to the post at Front Royal, but he was now in camp within the enemy's lines, and felt secure in taking a few hours for rest, knowing that Banks must come out or be compelled to see the Confederates go on towards the Potomac. At early dawn of the 24th, Geo. H. Stewart with the 2nd, were off for Newtown, while the infantry did not get into full line before 7:30 A. M. Ashby had stirred up Banks' scouts as they came out towards the Cedarville roads, and had severe skirmishing with them. They were convinced that a heavy force was trying to cut Banks' retreat, and finally succeeded in convincing that general, that retreat must be made at once. Genl. George H. Gordon, one of Banks' prominent field officers, in his attractive description of the situation to be seen in his "Brook Farm to Appomattox," gives out some valuable information. He says: "Banks was obstinate, and waited late in the night before he ordered his personal effects to be packed and sent away;" and then orders were given to fall back. This movement was going on, when Jackson started in the morning. Two brigades were far in the rear of the Ed. Johnson command, who failed to reach the Front Royal camps until the morning of the 24th, being foot sore from their long tramp from Franklin; and this was the case with several regiments of Jackson's old men. Banks' fresh troops had this advantage, and were thus enabled to pass in haste beyond Middletown and Newtown without serious interruption. This only applied to the main body of infantry. The road from Strasburg was lined with wagons, stragglers and army equipments. Stewart on reaching Newtown, saw within his grasp a rich wagon train, which he soon put to confusion; but he in turn was overrun by infantry and artillery and several thousand cavalry. Ashby was at Middletown by 12:30, supported by one of the Louisiana regiments, where they struck the retreating column. Wagons were piled up in the road, and retreat hindered long enough for Chew's Battery to give the line a broadside, while the Louisianians poured a deadly volley into the frightened mass. The panic at this time was fearful. The road was jammed with dead horses, men and riderless horses. 200 prisoners were left in the hands of the Confederates at this point. Surviving squadrons tried to escape towards Winchester. Some turned back; and hundreds dashed towards the mountains, hoping to escape the furious Southrons. Genl. Hatch with two brigades of cavalry, infantry and artillery, rallied on the ridges West of Middletown. By that time, 2 P. M. Jackson was up. Ashby was sent after the flying squadrons down the Valley Pike. At 3 P. M. there was every reason to believe that Banks was fully routed. Ewell was on his way to Winchester over the Front Royal road, proceeding slowly to await news from Jackson. It is well known that both infantry and cavalry were loath to hurry away from the spoils of the camp; and they have been criticized by several of Jackson's staff officers. But it must be remembered that hundreds of the cavalrymen had worn out their horses and needed fresh mounts; and loose horses were at hand among the prisoners and captured wagons; and who can complain if they exchanged their jaded horses for those the prowess of their arms had secured; and who can blame them for filling up on captured bread and meat, when they had been in their saddles since 6 o'clock in the morning; and who can censure them for leading off their broken-down horses to places of safety—horses they had brought from their homes. It may be, some were seen with more than one led horse. The writer knows whereof he speaks when he states some of these horses led away to farms nearby, were those from which some gallant comrade had fallen, and the effort made to save the Boy's horse and trappings, that might later on find their way to those who perhaps would never see the lost rider again. Dabney in his strictures on such incidents, was not justified in using this language. Not content to brand them as horse thieves, he says: "Nor did the men pause until they carried their illegal booty to their homes which were, in some instances, at the distance of one or two days' journey. That such extreme disorders could occur, and that they could be passed over *without a bloody punishment*, reveals the curious inefficiency of officers in the Confederate Army." If so many of these cavalrymen had gone to distant homes, how did they return in time to take part in all the work of the next few days Brigade officers report none missing save those *killed and wounded*. Genl. George H. Gordon says: "When we arrived at Bartonsville late in the afternoon, an effort was made to rally the *fleeing* army, and Genl. Banks in order to save his wagon trains that had not come up, placed at my disposal three regiments of infantry and two batteries, to check further attack from the Confederates; that I went back as far as Newtown and drove Ashby and a detachment of infantry out of Newtown. Genl. Hatch then came up with part of his brigade (cavalry) from a back road and together they held the rear safely." Stewart, it appears, had gone to meet Ewell, after Ashby came down from Middletown. Gordon says further, that about sunset, finding Confederate infantry and artillery pressing *his rear*, in such numbers that he could not check, he burned such wagons that he could not move, and then fell back on Winchester about dark. Jackson followed closely, but found some resistance at Bartonsville. Several guns well posted and supported by some infantry regiments, disputed every inch of ground. Some prisoners captured at that point were Massachusetts men, and said they belonged to the 2nd Mass. then immediately in front. If all of Banks' regiments had been such as this regiment, Jackson's Valley campaign might have ended in disaster; for reinforcements were already hurrying from Washington, and Fremont was cutting his way through the blockaded mountain roads. Jackson knew he could not tarry, and proceeded to force a flank movement through the fields, with hope of halting Banks' main army long enough for battle, instead of skirmishing with a rear guard. The 5th regiment had several companies who knew the lay of the land, and served as good pilots that night. Surviving comrades of that hour have told the writer that nothing but the thought of home kept them on their feet. Men were dropping down in dead sleep. Jackson forged ahead, however, until he arrived at a point West of Kernstown. The Federal rear guard had fallen back, and had again taken position across the fields near the old Opecquon Presbyterian Church. They soon gave way. This was now about an hour before daylight, May 25th. Jackson ordered a halt, and instantly the men were in a deep sleep; and it has been said, that the General was the only sentinel. He and his men knew they would not de disturbed. Sleep was all they had to refresh the worn-out body. From this they were aroused quietly by word passing along the line, as soon as it was light enough to select the routes of march. Word was sent out to the division strung out from the Valley Turnpike to the Pritchard hill; and they, too, were on their feet. All now were in motion, marching in several columns, the West column hugging the range of hills until they arrived at a point due West from the writer's residence on the Valley Turnpike, when a strong Federal position was encountered on the ridge over which the Middle Road passes. Several men were killed on the ground known as the "Beutell property." The Federals retired to another high point Southwest from the old stone mill (Hahn's.) Some casualties occurred at several points due West from the residence of Mrs. Annie R. Hack. The ground was stubbornly held by the skirmishers, falling slowly back upon the strong position the Federals held on the ridge running from Abrams Creek towards Winchester. We must remember that Ewell was on the Front Royal Turnpike, and also had some skirmish lines to overcome. When darkness settled down, his column was within 2½ miles of Winchester. When the next morning came, Ewell was in motion as promptly as Jackson; but he had with him only one brigade. This was Trimble's, with ten guns. The Federals held strong positions; and many of their officers and men displayed as much bravery as veterans of the Stonewall brigade cared to encounter; while over on the Front Royal Road just West of the Rouss (Hollingsworth) Spring, Genl. Donnelly had posted his brigade, with one regiment behind the old stone fence on that part of the road where it turns towards the old Spring. Just as Jackson with the Stonewall brigade, had forced the Federals across Abrams Creek, above Hahn's Mill, and the reserves under Taliaferro and Elzey were coming in from the turnpike to take position on the left of the Stonewall Brigade, Johnson's old Brigade under Scott, began to scale the high hill above the old woolen factory. The column on the Front Royal Road moved up under Trimble. Ewell intended to move up the Town Run hollow, sweep past the cemetery, and strike Banks on flank and rear; but when Trimble ascended that point of the Front Royal Road where the stone fence made the curve towards the spring, the Federal regiment concealed by the fence, arose and poured a deadly volley into his ranks at short range. Eighty officers and men went down; the column was driven back, but soon rallied and swept forward in time to see the Federal regiment hastening towards Cemetery Hill. At this time, the firing from Jackson's advancing army, sweeping the ridge with canister and musketry, struck the ear of Genl. Donnelly, and he hastened to seek a place of safety. But while they hesitated in the hollow North of F. A. Shryock's gardens, Ewell had his guns in position, and catching the range, shelled the demoralized regiments with deadly effect; while Trimble charging with the infantry at a double-quick, overtook the Federals, who were forced to capitulate, and were left by Ewell as prisoners under care of Trimble, while he and the cavalry and artillery, swept around to the Senseny Ridge and caught the fleeing brigade on their flank. Many of them went down as they ascended from the Shawnee hollow, while scores threw down their arms and sought shelter behind the limestone ledges. (Polk Miller, while in Winchester a few years ago with his minstrel troupe, had the writer and some friends accompany him to the scene of the stone-fence engagement, and there pointed out the spot where he saw men of his command go down with the unfortunate *Eighty;* and traced the charge of Trimble's Brigade, and found where the Federals had given up.)

While Ewell was thus engaged, the battle was waging hotly over on the ridge where Jackson's men had obtained a footing on the hillside. There they met Gordon and his Massachusetts men, supported by a large force of cavalry, who made an effort to charge part of Dick Taylor's Louisianians. The 10th Va. caught them on the flank, and sent many troopers to the ground. Then the Louisianians and Virginians rolled over the rocky cliffs and charged with full force into Gordon's plucky Brigade. The shock was too great; they gave way, and Taylor wheeled his men into line alongside the Stonewall Brigade, just as Elzey's Brigade appeared on the summit, when the whole pressed forward with shots and yells. Nothing left now of Banks' Army could stand that avalanche, as it swept towards the streets of the old town, where they had sung their farewell in March *"we'll be back in the Sweet By and By."* Men tell the story to each other to-day, of how they saw Jackson rushing headlong with his troops, waving his old cap, shouting at the top of his voice: "Press forward to the Potomac." The reserves followed the fugitives into and through the town. Some squads of Federals held their ground, and gallantly tried to stay the rout. Banks had gone; and along the highways, through field and lane, his infantry, artillery, cavalry and *all* rushed madly after him. Some organized bodies boldly tried to burn the military stores and other buildings. The pursuing armies pushed through the town, the streets lined with patriotic women. This spurred the old Valley men to press on; but the men were exhausted. Cavalry horses were jaded; and all the available cavalry had gone in pursuit under Ashby. The cavalry had been so hard-pressed for days, that their horses were now unfit for pursuit; and the infantry, too, was worn out. In vain did the General try to rally the men, to press forward to the Potomac. They got out on the Martinsburg Pike in time to see the fugitives everywhere rushing wildly away; but the old Valley Army was worn out. They got as far as the old Carter (now Jackson) farm, where they gave up the chase. Genl. Geo. H. Stewart had under his command about 700 cavalry that should have been profitably employed, working on the regiments that Trimble and Ewell had thrown into confusion. He was ordered to perform one movement which he declined to do, giving as his reason that his orders had not come from Genl. Ewell, thus ignoring Genl. Jackson's order. Jackson, it is said, exhibited temper and impatience at his tardiness in joining in the pursuit with his fresh horses and men. Stewart felt the force of it, and tried to redeem himself; but he was not forgiven by the General. Stewart went forward and overtook Ashby and Chew's battery below Stephensons; and together they pressed the enemy wherever they found opposition. They picked up many fugitives and sent them to the rear. Unfortunately, Genl. Jackson was imposed on by reports coming to him that Ashby, who had been with him on the extreme left, had gone off without orders to Berryville. This was enough to worry the General. We would doubt very much this statement about Jackson, were it not for the statement made by his aide Major Dabney in his "Life of Jackson." But under the excitement of the hour, Jackson failed to consider how unreasonable, if not impossible, it was for such a thing to occur. Why should, and how could Ashby have withdrawn his cavalry from the West side of the battle lines, and reached the Berryville Turnpike Avirett in his "Ashby and his Compeers," p. 249, proves by Col. Chew that the charges cannot be sustained. It is to be regretted that Col. Henderson, who wrote that most attractive work "Stonewall Jackson and the American Civil War," was so often misled in following Dabney in his unfair criticisms of the cavalry arm of the service, and especially in the case just mentioned. Ashby had very few of his men with him at Winchester. They were watching gaps and roads from

Franklin to the Valley, and every mountain crossing from the South Branch country. One company had been sent from Middletown to watch the gaps in the Blue Ridge This was Capt. Sam. Myers'. Harness had been left at Cedar Creek to watch the road from Wardensville. It was a victory complete enough; and the result should have been accepted in the same spirit that one other victor has exhibited—"There is glory enough for all;" and such incidents not carped over, when neither Jackson nor Ashby can raise a voice. We all must acknowledge that the cavalry arm of the service had been neglected up to the period mentioned, so far as the Valley District was concerned. Ashby was Colonel of the Seventh; but no officer of his grade was in the Upper Valley to organize the new companies that were coming in to *join Ashby's Cavalry,* and they were allowed to scout where they pleased. Genl. Jackson was too much absorbed with his strategic plans, to give the matter the attention it deserved. Ashby had no power; and it was not until Major Funsten of the Seventh, made personal application to the Secretary of War, that permission to organize some of the new companies into a battalion was granted; and he had barely taken the initiative in forming the 17th Battalion, when Jackson was on the wing, and no time was allowed for strict Battalion drill. The companies were again sent off upon independent expeditions. The 17th later became the nucleus of the celebrated 11th Virginia Cavalry.

Old cavalrymen who were in the pursuit over the Martinsburg Turnpike, have often told the true story. Banks' main army was shattered and flying to Martinsburg; but while this was the case, stubborn resistance was offered at sundry places by several thousand cavalry supported by artillery, and were hard to dislodge. Genl. Jackson in his pursuit of the enemy from Bartonsville up to 6 o'clock next morning, found them slowly yielding only to his superior numbers. Banks might have taken new courage and collected an army in support of his rear guard, that would have detained Jackson too long in the Lower Valley, and thus miss his opportunity to get beyond Fremont's objective point. Banks made a short halt at Martinsburg, and then hastened on to Williamsport and crossed over the remnant of his army on pontoons. On the 26th, all were on the North side. Then Banks sent on his historic report, which has afforded amusement to every student of that campaign. Banks and his army *had been electrified;* and so had Washington, and all the States North of the Potomac. McClellan caught the alarm as the news flashed over the wires from Washington. Shields with two divisions and one brigade of cavalry—21,200 officers and men—was ordered to turn towards the Valley and discontinue his march towards Richmond. Truly the victory was assuming vast proportions, but not beyond Genl. Jackson's hopes and expectations. For nearly two days after the rout, the Valley army enjoyed a much-needed rest, while congratulations poured in from all sections. On the 28th, the Stonewall Brigade was on its march towards Harpers Ferry, where the Federals under Genl. Saxton, had a force of 7,000 men and 18 guns. Genl. Winder's skirmishers struck a force in the vicinity of Charlestown, two regiments of infantry, artillery and a large force of cavalry. A spirited attack was made by the Confederate advance guard only, when the imposing force fled in disorder, throwing away guns, accoutrements, blankets, etc. They were pursued to Bolivar Heights. The main force appeared on the high ground with artillery. Winder waited for Ewell, who came upon the 29th, and at Halltown they arranged for an attack. The 2nd Virginia crossed the Shenandoah and seized Loudoun Heights. The Federals withdrew to the Potomac for shelter, and were preparing to abandon the post, which was within easy grasp of Winder and Ewell, who were ready to make the final stroke the next morning. But during the night something had occurred that caused Jackson to call a halt. Word had come from his cavalry scouts that Fremont was on his way from Wardensville and Shields was coming too near Manassas Gap to pass unheeded. Jackson had already collected every wagon, both army and private property, and had been loading them with captured stores and sending them up the Valley. May 29th found Ewell and Winder somewhat puzzled over the order from Jackson: "March main force to Winchester, after one brigade and two batteries are left in position to hold enemy in check." Jackson was then at Charlestown, but was taking the train for Winchester. On his arrival, he was informed that Shields had already seized Front Royal, 12 miles from Strasburg, and with his division only could seriously interfere with Jackson's efforts to pass Strasburg; and if Fremont could arrive in time with his 15,000 men, this meant fierce battle and a loss of all his captures. Banks with reinforcements at Williamsport, and the Harpers Ferry garrison in his rear, put Jackson to his best work. To reap the benefits of his wonderful campaign, he must retire in good order, and carry his 2,000 prisoners and captured stores to some safe place beyond Strasburg, which was seriously threatened on the evening of the 29th. Jackson gathered his forces near Winchester on the 30th, and set everything to work for his evacuation; and when night came, the whole army was ordered to move in the early morning. On the 31st, the head of the column was taken by the 21st Virginia guarding the 2,000 prisoners. Next went the wagon trains in double lines, extending from Winchester to beyond the bridge at Bartonsville. Genl. Winder was then ordered up to take the rear. Nothing interfered with the march except a few broken wagons which were cast aside, left to be repaired and put in the rear. The principal portion of the army went into camp that night beyond Strasburg. The Stonewall Brigade bivouacked at Newtown. Jackson felt sure that Fremont and Shields would over-estimate his strength; and as they had no communication, neither was willing to come on an uncertainty to strike his flanks, lest they should be demolished. Official reports now show that this was true in both cases. Fremont was within 6 miles of Strasburg and believed that Jackson had 30,000 men; Shields at Front Royal placed them at 25,000.

Ashby was on the Cotton Town road with his cavalry, holding Fremont's advance in check. On June 1st Ewell went out to support him, and give time for the Stonewall Brigade to get up. Early in the morning, heavy picket firing was heard out towards Cedar Creek. Then it was that Ewell got his artillery in position and sent shot after shot into the advance guard. Infantry regiments poured several volleys into the confused column. Then Ashby and his cavalry did the rest. Fremont was content to fortify against Jackson, not knowing what had occurred during the last few days. In the evening, a brigade under Genl. Bayard tried the roads from Front Royal, and came up in time to see the rear guard of Jackson's army winding its way over Fishers Hill. Fremont stood aghast while his dead and wounded Germans of Blenker's division were gathered up, viewing the gray troopers trotting off to the rear of Jackson's army. Jackson was safe in camp at night of June 1st, with captured stores sufficient to equip his army, of clothing, shoes, etc., and thousands upon thousands of good rations, medical and ordnance supplies in untold quantities, 9,354 small arms and some fine pieces of artillery,—all of which went safely through to Staunton. This was all done, according to official reports with a loss to the Valley Army of 68 killed, 386 wounded, 3 missing, and 156 captured.

Jackson felt sure that he must prepare for these armies in his rear and on his left flank; for he knew Shields would push up the Luray Valley, and with his heavy reinforcements, be able to reach the upper gaps in the Blue Ridge and hold them against Jackson's escape to reinforce Johnston's army. Shields started his advance on the 1st, and waited for the morning to go to hold the bridges at Luray, and then to move rapidly up to Conrads Store and hold the bridge across South River, near the present village of Elkton at the mouth of Swift Run Gap. When Shields' advance got to the two bridges near Luray, they found them burned. The Confederate cavalry had anticipated them by four hours. This cut Shields off from Newmarket. This was June 2nd; and seemed to frustrate his plans. While Shields had been maturing his plans for work in the Luray Valley, Jackson was somewhat annoyed by Fremont's pursuit, who evidently felt sore over his failure to "bag Jackson" at Strasburg. One of his officers, speaking of this failure, writes in a spicy way about the "Pathfinder." He says: "When the General surveyed his army of Hungarians, Germans, etc., that formed the advance guard (the one of honor) recoil before the Rebel cavalry and a detachment of infantry, and learned of Jackson's achievements, there was a perceptible sigh, but it was one of relief."

The Valley Army was called upon to do some good marching, so as to keep out of the way of skirmish lines continually forming between Ashby's Cavalry and the splendid brigade under Bayard—a detachment from Shields' army. The men who composed that brigade were good horsemen and hard fighters. Bayard showed his efficiency every day. Ashby's splendid dashes with his gray troopers, were always met by cool men, with light artillery. It was on the 2nd of June that a desperate encounter occurred about Maurertown North of Woodstock, between the cavalry commands; and then it was the Chew Battery barely escaped with the Flying Artillery. Ashby was driven back in disorder, losing some of his men. Jackson's rear guard, was not disturbed, however, but the army hastened on to Mt. Jackson, and crossed the North fork of the Shenandoah,—culverts and small bridges being destroyed in their rear. The army was in camp South of the river in the afternoon of the 3rd of June. On the 4th, Ashby and his cavalry who were up with him, crossed the river and fired the bridge. Bayard was close at hand, and made desperate efforts to save the bridge; but Ashby, who was equal to a squadron in any battle, was on the bridge, and succeeded by the help of about twenty men, all that could find standing room, in beating back the head of the Federal column, until the work was assured. The fire soon made the bridge dangerous for the heavy body of horses, which backed in confusion. Ashby had his beautiful white horse killed, and a number of the gray troopers were wounded. A swollen river was now between the armies, with no hope for the Federals of using their pontoons, though they made several ineffectual attempts. Jackson was then moving rapidly to gain Port Republic. The army made good use of the 5th and 6th, but was compelled to halt at Cross Keys, a small village on Mill Creek, about S. W. from Harrisonburg. On the night of the 5th, Jackson had his wagon trains and prisoners with the army. The sick and wounded had been sent to Staunton. The Federals wasted no time in pursuit. The burned bridge was all that stood in the way of Fremont and Shields heading off Jackson. The lion was now at bay; and he was ready for Fremont, who came first. He alone, without Shields' help, opened the battle of Cross Keys on the 6th of June, 1862. Bayard dogged every step of the Confederates, and seemed determined to cross swords with Ashby. He recklessly rode in with about 1,000 cavalry upon a long wooded ridge, about 2½ miles from Harrisonburg. The Confederates had chosen their position well, knowing that the Federals would follow, being sure of their game they had been hunting for nearly a week. Believing they outnumbered the Confederates, and that the time must soon come when they could boast of their prize of having killed or captured Ashby, the Bluecoats came charging to the point on the hill that had been prepared for them. Their drawn sabres proved a fatal error. The gray line advanced to the crest of the hill and poured volley after volley into their ranks. The line gave way; and then it was the Confederate cavalry, following with blazing guns and yells, stampeded the whole command, who ran back nearly to Harrisonburg, losing 4 officers and 30 men killed and a number wounded, besides many horses carried back by the Confederates and several well-mounted officers. Subsequent events showed that the Federals had been led by an English officer who was seeking fame on an American battlefield. He was Percy Wyndham who commanded the First New Jersey Cavalry. He had frequently declared that he would capture Ashby. One of the mounted officers proved to be this Wyndham. Wm. McKeever and Jim Baker of Harness' Company, who brought the Englishman in, said he was the most crestfallen prisoner they ever captured. This repulse brought Genl. Bayard out with a heavy force, which consisted of cavalry, several regiments of infantry, and batteries. Bayard was persistent and skillful. Throwing his entire cavalry into line in good order, well supported by steady lines of infantry, they boldly marched to good positions and planted their artillery. Being fully ready, they made a desperate charge, seeming determined to annihilate the cavalry that had annoyed their advance up the Valley, and had an hour before repulsed them with such vigor. Ashby had gone out to the two regiments Ewell had sent him, the 58th Virginia and the 1st Maryland, and there led a charge that was to break the force of the Federal charge now bearing down on the thin line of gray troopers. The onset was terrific. The thin line was outnumbered, and was beaten back upon the two regiments which Ashby was leading with all his old-time spirit, urging the men to meet the shock. Dashing to the front, his horse was killed and he was thrown. For a moment he seemed stunned, but was on his feet at once, and rushed into the open space where some Confederates were cross-firing. His voice was heard above the din of battle, crying: "Charge, men; for God's sake, charge." They seemed to heed his cry; swept into the Federal lines, and drove them back. But their idolized chieftain had fallen with a bullet through his heart. The Federals could no longer hold out against that charge of brave men, now animated to avenge the death of the hero stretched out near the skirt of timber. When the cavalry fell back, they soon rallied and gave place for the infantry regiment to deliver their terrible volley. The gray cavalrymen rushed to a position in the rear of the Federals, taking with them the light-horse artillery; and from their new position, rattled shot into the confused Federals, who broke up in disorder and fled from the field. During the night, they returned to Harrisonburg, leaving a number of dead and wounded on the field.

The news of Ashby's death soon found its way to his old squadrons, who rushed headlong to the place where he lay, surrounded by scores of men lamenting his death. But when his own men came, who had followed him through so many tight places and over a hundred fields, through mountain and stream, the scene was painfully pathetic. Some of his old comrades tenderly bore the lifeless warrior away. They knew not what to do. Finally it was determined to send his body to Port Republic. Jackson relaxed his discipline enough to direct several of his followers to accompany their dead chief. He was temporarily buried in the old graveyard at that place the next morning, where he remained until his removal to Stonewall Cemetery at Winchester, where the tomb of the Ashby Brothers on each recurring Sixth of June is covered with flowers.

Jackson's main army remained in camp during the 6th and 7th of June, resting and waiting for new developments. During both days, however, large detachments of cavalry were required to picket and guard the approaches to the Massanutton Mountain—Shields on the East and Fremont on the West—Jackson's bivouac camp was immediately South of the South end of the Massanutton range, in full view of the peak known as Peaked Mountain or Signal Mountain. Up to this time, neither Shields nor Fremont knew Jackson's position. In the evening of the 7th, a large infantry force while scouting, stumbled over one of Ewell's picket posts, near Cross Keys. This was one of Fremont's reconnoitering parties, which retired after firing a few wild shots. The Stonewall Brigade had been sent to Port Republic. The 7th of June was remembered as a day of extreme quiet. Wagon trains parked in the valley between the two rivers, extending South to Weyer's Cave. But Jackson had his eye on Shields in the Luray Valley, as well as Fremont's large camps around Harrisonburg. The two armies were now planning for his capture. Shields was at Luray on the 6th, and sending word to Fremont that Jackson must now be bottled up, as he was moving up the Valley and expecting to join him (Fremont) and surround the Rebel camp. The situation of Shields was well known to Jackson. He knew he had had trouble with the bridges at Luray and bad roads all through the Valley; that his army was stretched out in several sections, and that he could never get his entire army in position to give regular battle, without exposing one of his sections to attack. But the two armies were slowly coming together. Jackson had chosen the strongest position he ever held. Port Republic is situated at the point where two small rivers form the South River. One is the North Fork and the other the South Fork. Over the North Fork is a bridge for the road leading to Cross Keys and Harrisonburg.—No bridge over the South Fork. Just North of the bridge is high land, commanding the little valley lying out towards the base of the Blue Ridge. Through this valley Shields must come to make his attack. Artillery from the hills above the bridge could rake an army from every point; besides, the river was unfordable. But Fremont was coming; and he must be crippled before damaging Shields. Ewell was on the ground at Cross Keys on the 8th, with part of his division, about 6,000 men, 5 batteries and 500 cavalry. Fremont soon appeared, at 10 A. M., and opened 8 batteries on Ewell's position, which was strong. Ewell's reserves were 4 miles in the rear. Jackson had not left Port Republic. A large force of cavalry was known to be at Conrads Store, and they could work along under cover, and possibly reach Port Republic unexpectedly. So he remained long enough to get a glimpse of the advance guard which suddenly appeared with a large force of cavalry and two batteries. This was a surprise to the Port Republic camp. They were soon repulsed, however. The whole force, losing heavily, fell back on the main army struggling through the mud towards Luray. Jackson placed two brigades in position near the bridge and then hastened away to Ewell, taking the remainder of his army. Ewell's guns were plainly heard about four miles distant, where Fremont was pressing his Germans to their doom. Fremont failed to grasp the situation; for his official reports show that he sent only 5 regiments of Blenker's Dutch out of his 24 full regiments of infantry, large cavalry force and splendid batteries. Part of Trimble's Brigade was in ambush (3 regiments); and at the proper time the Germans were swept from the field, and Ewell occupied the ground that night in full view of Fremont's beaten army. But it must not be accepted that the victory had been easily won. The losses indicate that some of the Federal battalions fought bravely. The 8th New York lost nearly all of its men, while Trimble lost over 200 men. Federal official reports give their loss as 684 killed, wounded and missing. While Fremont was content to remain passive through that night, Ewell was preparing to withdraw and place himself in position to execute what Jackson would have for him on the morrow. It will be shown later on how Fremont regarded the situation after his two unsuccessful attempts to whip Jackson and form juncture with Shields at Port Republic. Following Jackson from Ewell's front, we find him fully apprised of Shields' presence South of Conrads Store, marching on Port Republic. During the night, the Confederates were assembling for an attack on the army now taking positions in full view from the ridge above the bridge. The South Fork was now swollen and dangerous to ford, and required temporary pontoon bridges. This was supplied by collecting wagons and boards from citizens, and a rough but successful one was provided. Old citizens of the village pointed out to the writer the exact spot where this crossing was made, and the remnants of one of the *old wagons* used for that purpose that was dragged to the East side of the Fork and afterwards preserved. The army was astir at 5 o'clock the next morning; and by the time the Stonewall Brigade was over, Genl. Dick Taylor followed, and struck squarely towards level land on the Lewis farm. Ewell was also crossing the impromptu bridge, leaving one regiment of infantry and part of Ashby's old cavalry under Col. Munford on the West side of North Fork to watch Fremont. Col. Munford later on destroyed the bridge in time to prevent Fremont's advance column crossing in Jackson's rear. Jackson with bold and fearless men, routed the Shields army before the main body appeared, as will be shown later on.

CHAPTER LIX

Battle of Port Republic, Etc.

Shields had been delayed in his march up the Luray Valley—his intention being to cross the Massanutten at Luray and join Fremont at New Market—leaving a small force South of Luray to intercept Jackson when he should attempt to escape through Swift Run Gap. His first plan was, as he dispatched Fremont, for the latter to press from Harrisonburg, and he Shields to cut his retreat about Port Republic. But Jackson had retarded Shields' movements, by burning the bridges North of Luray, causing enough delay to enable Jackson to formulate his plans to defeat both in detail.

June 8th, while Ewell was engaging Fremont, Shields was at Luray, struggling with the bridges, but preparing to move on Port Republic. Early in the morning, a splendid body of cavalry under Genl. Carroll, two regiments of mounted infantry, and several pieces of light artillery, left Conrad's Store and made a forced march of 16 miles to Port Republic; and there unexpectedly surprised themselves by surprising Jackson—the latter having depended upon a weak detail of cavalry to keep him posted as to Shields. This detail was on the West side of the river North of McGaheysville, when Shields' advance went sweeping South. Some were dispatched to inform Jackson, arriving about the time the Federal column struck him near the bridge at the North fork of the South River, —Jackson barely escaping capture. Shields' two Brigades, Tyler's and Carroll's, with about six pieces of light artillery, seemed to be everywhere; but Jackson soon brought order out of confusion; and with Carrington's battery, several detachments of cavalry and one company of infantry, a vigorous effort was made to stem the tide that threatened destruction. Reinforcements dropped in on their way to join Ewell, and a rout was skillfully produced in Shields' advance guard, who left every gun and many straggling prisoners and horses. Many troopers, throwing away their arms and accoutrements, returned to Conrad's Store in much disorder, where the two commanders endeavored to reorganize their commands and patch up a report to send Genl. Shields, who had made a bluff start to bring up his main army and reinforce Fremont. But he had sore difficulties to meet, Jackson had made the approach by Port Republic unsafe; and upon the return of his column to Conrad's store, they found the wooden bridge over South River, about ½ mile West from the store (Millers Bridge) had been burned by the straggling cavalry, thus closing the only avenue from this point to Harrisonburg. An incident occurred at Conrad's Store, while this advance guard was stationed there for several days. The author gives it as related to him during the preparation of this work, by a gentleman who in 1862 was a half-grown boy and saw all that transpired. Genl. Carroll, he says, occupied the old Miller brick homestead. Miller being a Southern man, was not around. A notorious Union man from the nearby mountain appeared at Headquarters and desired to see Mr. Miller or some member of his family. Mrs. Miller answered his call, whereupon he proceeded to inform her that the secesh property had been confiscated, and he had come to give the family notice that he had been told by the Union General that he could have the Miller farm as a reward for his services, and that he now would take possession in a few days, and the family must vacate at once. Mrs. Miller hastened to inform Genl. Carroll (who was in an adjoining room with several members of his staff) of the situation and asked what she should do. The General pointed to a pistol lying on the table, and calmly said: Take that and go to the door and shoot him and I will protect you. Mrs. Miller executed the order by firing two shots, the last striking the gate post as the man went over the fence at one bound. It is well to preserve the name of this Loyalist.

Shields' war blood was up, and he crowded everything he had to the front; and was on the plain around Conrad's Store when he received his dispatches. Tradition of the village, as related to the author, gives Shields credit for making military matters breezy for an hour, as he stood in his stirrups ejecting language that made his Irish veterans quail. The American vets so recently driven back from Port Republic, took their share of censure; and all rallied with new courage, as the glowing language fell from the lips of the hot-headed Irishman, who had been chafing under such restraints as bottomless roads, burnt bridges and other drawbacks. But now the crush must come, and with Jackson out of the way, he and his victorious army could press on to Charlottesville. The 9th of June found the three armies in such positions, that if Fremont and Shields could only have divined Jackson's tactics, and that morning hurriedly forced a combined attack, Jackson's army would have been crushed. But Fremont, unable to comprehend the engagement that ended the previous evening, magnifying Jackson's forces and attack, was content on the memorable 9th to take time to consider. Jackson had long since measured the Pathfinder; and felt sure he could keep him in one position with a small force. So leaving Trimble and Patton with their brigades, to keep Fremont at safe distance, he himself during the night planned to have Ewell rejoin him at Port Republic, and then with his combined force meet Shields, on some well chosen ground. Though Jackson was apparently at times endowed with superhuman intelligence, as he determined the plans his foe would likely adopt, an experienced soldier surveying and studying these battle fields at this day, must conclude the wonderful results were due to the masterful mind of a military genius. Fremont South of Harrisonburg, with his 10,000 infantry, 2,200 cavalry and twelve batteries—all perfectly equipped—held in check by the two weak brigades of not over 3,000 men all told—allowed Ewell to withdraw on the morning of the 9th and cross the river on impromptu bridges, rickety and dangerous to the host crowding over, to where Jackson was concentrating his available force to meet Shields' army, as it presented itself on the ridges and plains about four miles North of Port Republic—many positions on what was known as the Lewis farm. The Federal force engaged up to 10 A. M. on the 9th has been variously estimated. Jackson's report gave them 4,400. Shields says the forward movement was conducted by skilled officers—1,200 cavalry, 4,000 infantry, 22 pieces artillery. Civilians encountered during the day gave the force as 12,000. With his reserves between Conrad's Store and the battle ground, why Shields was not up with his entire force, and why Fremont with his legions did not sweep Trimble and Patton out of his way and force his march over the river, as by 11 o'clock he was well supplied with pontoon bridges and every available means to cross the narrow river and strike Jackson while he was engaged with Shields. Why this was not done, can never be explained. Shields blundered in separating from his *forward movement,* and inability to give support. Had he given this support, it is doubtful if Jackson could have held his position; for he had already found it necessary to withdraw Trimble and Patton from Fremont's front. Then if Fremont had followed their withdrawal, as he could so easily have done with half of his well equipped army, they could have saved the bridge that Patton took his last man over and then burned, in full view of the scouting cavalry who hastened back to report the situation to Fremont. This was about 9:30 A. M.—the battle raging on the East side of the river, with odds against the Confederates at that hour—not too late then for Fremont to hasten with his battalions of artillery and strike Jackson in the rear. But he, with apparent composure, moved his columns—but arrived too late. He had shown some pretence of a forward movement during the early morning, while the Confederates were retiring. His reports show that he was wary—believing that Jackson was preparing an ambuscade for his command. He knew that Shields needed him. The administration after the campaign, proved in their correspondence that Shields had informed him as early as 10 o'clock that he had engaged Jackson and needed his support. His official reports state that his advance was stubbornly resisted, when it has been proven by many students of this campaign, that not a shot was exchanged during the withdrawal of Trimble and Patton—the whole forenoon having been consumed in marching 7 miles. Carl Schurz says in his magazine articles that one of Fremont's staff officers told him, when he joined the command a few days later, that when the General beheld the burnt bridge and groups of Federal prisoners and wounded in the plain beyond, he ordered his artillery to fire upon the retreating foe, killing several Federal prisoners, who had hoisted signals of distress. Fremont apparently chagrined at the dismal failure he and Shields made in their imbecile efforts to bag Jackson, fell back to his easy quarters at Harrisonburg, and sent in his famous report of the Valley Campaign. His unfitness to command an army had become well known to Lincoln and Stanton, and a change of commanders was desired by them; but Mr. Lincoln who often played politics, avoided Fremont's displeasure. Later on will be shown the scheme Lincoln adopted to bag Fremont, since he could be of so little use in bagging Jackson.

Shields' "forward movement force" was leaving the field in disorder, When Fremont hove in sight, which soon ended in a rout, which was followed by cavalry and light artillery for about 8 miles, to a point South of Conrad's store between the mountain and South River, where Shields had hastily barricaded roads and thrown up some show of defence. And there the boastful General awaited the arrival of the mysterious Jackson. His official report of this battle must amuse as well as disgust the survivors of the two splendid brigades commanded by Generals Tyler and Carroll, who distinguished themselves in two attacks on Jackson. The Stonewall Brigade under Winder and the Louisianians under Genl. Dick Taylor, met soldiers and not Blenker's Dutch, when they struck the regiments of these brigades. Some of their own blood was in the Ohio and West Virginia troops—men who had fought bravely at Kernstown and won the distinction of holding the battlefield while Stonewall Jackson withdrew from the only field on which he was not victor. Jackson having accomplished his great object, called off his pursuit of the Shields Army, and proceeded to bring his own brigades out of the confusion of this active campaign.

Fremont, as some old veterans may recall as they read this brief sketch of the Valley Campaign in 1862, will remember how incessantly Fremont's guns sent shells over the river to lodge *somewhere,* in the hope of helping some if sent home from his safe ridges overlooking the little valley. Jackson's orders sent out to officers, were for all troops to report at Browns Gap.

The most of this concentration was made during the night. The author could mention many tired, hungry and wounded men who fell on the grass when orders came to cease pursuit; and, forgetful of all else, slept until the next morning's sun was high in the heavens, when the haversack was overhauled once more, and farm houses sought.

The army was soon in good shape; rigid discipline enforced, and repairs to ragged and worn uniforms, as well as broken wagons, caissons, harness and lame horses, made. The cavalry saw no rest—watching Fremont across the mountain, and Shields at Luray. The army soon grew alert to some new movement of their vigilant commander.

Jackson and his hard-worked army enjoyed their few days rest, while Genl. Munford with the old Ashby Cavalry, pressed flank and rear of Fremont, as he fell back on his old place Harrisonburg, leaving the vicinity of Port Republic June 10th. Not one picket could be seen on the morning of the 11th, when the Cavalry crossed the river. Scouting parties were soon on the trail, and not long in discovering the beaten General strengthening his position. General Munford distinguished himself that day and won the confidence of Ashby's followers. While not the dashing horseman of the Knight of the Black Plume, he displayed such skill in maneuvering his men in front of Fremont, that the latter became alarmed and fell back to Mt. Jackson, leaving valuable stores in camp, hospital supplies, and about 250 wounded. Munford seemed inspired as a leader, to divine the thoughts and actions of his antagonist. He harassed the retreating forces on every road, boldly declaring that Genl. Jackson was in close support, and Fremont must fight, run or be captured; that the Federals should have no respite until driven beyond the Potomac. The men caught his fervor and zeal; and when the morning of the 12th dawned upon the old tactician and his foot cavalry crossing the South River, and pressing toward a camp forming on Meridian Ridge, the whole Upper Valley was ablaze with new hope that Jackson was massing for a forward movement on the enemy's country, that he and his army regarded invincible. Besides officers and men declared that Genl. Lee was sending large reinforcements. This news spread like wildfire, reaching Fremont's camp. He was seized with his old pain of consternation, and hastily withdrew to Strasburg. The reader should see his official reports to be able to appreciate his predicament. The great leader was deceived by a ruse practiced by Jackson, in this feint to cover his prearranged plan to leave the Valley and succor General Lee.

On the 14th, Fremont halted at Strasburg, not knowing what course to pursue. Banks was in Middletown, and he could not ignore him. He was doubtful about the route via Front Royal, for Shields—where was he. So the General contented himself with an effort to repair his losses and hold favor with Washington, where Lincoln and Stanton were maturing plans that would revolutionize the Valley Campaigns.

This being the last stand made by this General, who had entered the Shenandoah country in May to capture Jackson, it may be well to briefly sum up a few incidents of his military career, as gathered from official records.

Carl Schurz, as Brig. Genl., joined Fremont at Harrisonburg June —, 1862. Fremont had been ordered from West Virginia to cooperate with Banks and McDowell's troops and effectually "bag Jackson," expecting to cooperate in the vicinity of Strasburg, or Front Royal, as Jackson fell back from his pursuit of Banks to the Potomac. Those Generals failed to meet at the given point until after Jackson had safely moved his army, trains, captured supplies, prisoners, etc.; and when the "Pathfinder" appeared in the Valley at Cotton Town near Cedar Creek, he was disappointed. Many thought at the time that when the General surveyed his army of Hungarians, Germans, etc., and learned of Jackson's achievements, there was a sigh—but it was one of relief.

Blenker had been detached from the army of the Potomac, 1st April, and sent off on a wild march through the mountains to reinforce Fremont at any point. He wandered from place to place, and finally overtook Fremont at Harrisonburg, in time to be slaughtered at the battle of Cross Keys. The Dutch legions were in bad repute. They had been badly handled; and came to Fremont badly demoralized. Many were captured, and they told pitiful stories of hard marches and starvation. They stripped the country through which they marched. Blenker was a Prussian officer. At this point in the campaign, Carl Schurz reported for duty—a young German political friend of Mr. Lincoln, who had commissioned him Brig. Genl. as a reward for services rendered in a Convention of Abolitionists, to ascertain if the bold step could be taken to proclaim freedom to the slaves; and at Harrisonburg we find him placed in command of a Division, taking rank above old experienced officers, and becoming prominent as a confidential correspondent of the President. As a young diplomat in Spain, he had been a success in creating prejudice against the South—having been sent there for that purpose. Genl. Blenker's Brigade was under Schurz. This gave offence. The President about this time, June 26, took the bridle in his hands, consolidated the forces of Fremont, Banks and McDowell, and placed Major Genl. Pope in command. To this Fremont took offence and resigned. This ended his career as a military man. Two years later he appears as the nominee for President of a party that was opposed to the Lincoln administration. His defeat retired him from the public eye. Genl. Franz Seigel succeeded Genl. Fremont; and his branch of the service was distinguished from the other two, and called the Mountain Department. This army was kept busy until about the 1st of August defending the approach to Washington, under the belief that Jackson was gathering strength to make a final rush and drive the large Federal Army before him, invade Maryland, enter Washington, capture the President and cabinet, and thus end the war. Such fallacy appears ludicrous and absurd to the Confederates who participated in the Valley skirmishes in July, 1862. Prisoners captured by Confederate cavalry, told the story; and we find it verified by the official reports and letters written by officers and since published, including Carl Schurz, Lincoln's confidential correspondent, as he styles himself after forty years of mature reflection.

While this well equipped army, composed of men whose war cry "Me fights mit Seigel" kept busy watch over the Valley, Jackson glided through the mountains, landing on Genl. Lee's left, and ready to strike in either direction. The renowned Seigel, who had been so alert in the City of St. Louis in guarding the Union sentiment, and suppressing the Southern, with his hordes of Germans, whom he inflamed with wild zeal, and who finally rode the city streets, relentlessly driving out or imprisoning the latter, and placing in power the friends of the Union cause,—found on the 8th of August, through orders from Washington, that Jackson was not in the Valley, and his army of the Mountain Department must hasten to the relief of Pope, going via Sperryville to Culpeper. This movement resulted in the celebrated battle of Cedar Mountain. It is recorded that this army was utterly demoralized from hard marching, and never took part in this battle. This will be more fully treated in another chapter. The Valley was virtually abandoned for this great campaign.

While Jackson was busy inspecting his battalions in camp, and keeping up constant correspondence with Genl. Lee in reference to completing the great strategy which they had fully planned, and so marvelously executed up to the present stage—for it must be well known to all students of the great campaigns, that Jackson, as Lee's star Lieutenant, was to conduct a campaign in the Great Valley on such a scale of warfare as to deceive the enemy; strike frequent and heavy blows on any and every column operating along the northern border West of the Blue Ridge, and to keep those columns busy in their effort to protect Washington from some hurried movement through the Valley and across the Potomac, thus preventing any one of these columns from swinging off to reinforce McDowell, which meant McClellan. It will be seen that by Jackson's execution of plans created by him alone, he with his army not exceeding at any one time over 15,000 men, held McDowell at Fredericksburg from May to June 24, with an army of 50,000, waiting to either defend Washington from Jackson's direct movement, or to reinforce Genl. Shields, Banks, and Fremont—three well-known Division commanders, with splendidly equipped armies, any one of which exceeded the strength of Jackson's in all his engagements. And it must be borne in mind that these Federal columns had Brigade Commanders who had won fame in other campaigns—Ricketts, Tyler, Carroll, Bayard, etc., with Shields; Donnelly, Gordon, Hatch, etc., with Banks; Milroy, Schenk, Blenker, etc. All were kept busy, to prevent Jackson from swooping down upon Washington. Genl. Lee hoped that Jackson could enliven the upper country sufficiently to alarm Washington, and thus prevent reinforcements hurried away to McClellan, while he, Lee, hoped to strike the latter at some weak spot, and whip his great army in detail. But the over-cautious little Mack waited too long. While Jackson was resting his command in the Upper Valley, his fighting spirit prompted him to write Genl. Lee touching the propriety of making a dash towards the Potomac. To this Genl. Lee was induced to entertain the thought of sending Jackson such reinforcements as to make an advance formidable, and thus strike terror to the administration at Washington; and as McClellan would likely halt to await orders, Lee could rush such weak points along the Chickahominy, that might produce a panic, and send the whole plans of the Federals to the four winds. Either this scheme or—for Jackson, after his first severe blow to the defeated Valley columns, to leave the Valley guarded by detachments of men unfit for the long march; then Jackson to swing away to the Chickahominy without attracting attention, with his whole force, cut all communications, and be prepared for any emergency, while Genl. Lee would attack McClellan. Jackson, in taking another view of the situation, suggested that while the Federal columns were waiting for his attack nearer the Potomac, Lincoln would allow nothing to go from Washington defenses to support McClellan; and it was suggested that he, Jackson, hold himself in readiness in some of the Blue Ridge gaps or hiding places, and await a call from Richmond. The reinforcements, Whiting's and Lawton's Brigades, had arrived in Staunton on the 17th. Genl. Jackson ordered them to report to his camp headquarters on Meridian Ridge, 14 miles North of Staunton near Weyer's Cave. This gave glowing color to the rumor of a great movement down the Valley. Pending this, matters had taken a turn. Genl. Lee presented a new plan for Jackson to join him at once. So Lawton and Whiting found on their arrival in the Valley, that Jackson, Ewell, and all the available forces were then on their way through the gaps of the Blue Ridge. They also found orders directing them to retire to Staunton in such way as to leave Fremont impressed with the belief that they were in camp and preparing to move on him. At Staunton, these Brigades took rail for Gordonsville. (O. R., Wash., D. C., Vol. III, pp. 913, etc.)

Jackson's Campaign, here just closing, has become famous the world over for strategem. With a small but effective force, he had riveted the attention of friend and foe. Distinguished military men have given to the world stories of his brilliant successes, placing him alongside of war heroes of ancient and modern times; comparing his sudden blows, rapid changes, wild marches, to the campaigns of Alexander and Frederick the Great, Napoleon, Von Moltke, etc. The author, in his brief sketch, has only aimed to give the route of marches, locations of engagements, and their dates and general results, with whom engaged, etc.; and has not attempted a complete history of the campaign. At the proper places, notes will appear, giving number of troops engaged, names of commanders, etc. The writer at this late day, in summing up the incidents of the Valley campaign, and beholding the wonderful military genius with his splendid little army disappearing through defiles of the Blue Ridge, leaving the Valley to rest under the glow of his immortal fame,—reluctantly gives him up, and can appreciate the wailings of the Valley people when they realized on that memorable day that their loved army had left the Upper Valley and her blue mountains far behind them, perhaps never to reappear amid the rivers and vales. Coming events were casting their shadows rapidly. One Shadow that fell across their way, was that of Jackson's next appearance in the Upper Valley—on his bier—with guard of honor composed of details of his old Cadet Class, seeking a place at historic Lexington, where he could rest under the shade of trees that crowned the hilltop, overlooking the river as it unceasingly rolled to the sea.

The reader must bear in mind that it is not in the scope of this work to follow that army and its intrepid leaders, after they passed through the Blue Ridge, their columns pointing towards Richmond; for this would conflict with the original design—to study incidents of the Valley, and briefly and accurately collate them.

CHAPTER LX

Civil War Incidents After Close of Jackson's Valley Campaign

The author feels justified in departing from the scheme of his work, so far as to show where Jackson and his Valley soldiers reappeared East of the mountains, where increased fame awaited their heroic efforts.

June 17, 1862, Ewell at the head of the column, took a direct route for Charlottesville; then followed Jackson with all the Valley troops available. As already stated, the two brigades were to follow via Staunton and go to Gordonsville. The utmost secrecy was observed by officers and men as to their movements. Generals Lee and Jackson kept their own secrets. Many conjectures prevailed on that historic march, as to the objective point. At every place where the army camped, the opinion frequently expressed around the camp fires was, that the next morning Old Jack would head North. An old Stonewall Brigade group were asked by some Texans at Gordonsville, what they thought about the direction the army would take. One of the old vets replied: Can't tell the direction; but I know this, that whenever Old Jack goes nosin' around in the night when a fellow is on picket, and talks kind and gentle like, this is a sign that we see plenty of Yanks in the next day's march; and this is what he done last night." It was from Gordonsville that Jackson went virtually alone to Richmond, to confer with Genl. Lee. Major Dabney has made this incident interesting; showing the difficulties the General and one orderly had in their way, needing a relay of horses, passes, etc., so the trip could be made with expedition as well as secrecy; for it must be borne in mind that the Federals, from Commander-in-Chief down, were to rally ignorant of Jackson's whereabouts; and the plan was, to keep the Confederate forces in the vicinity of Richmond, equally ignorant of the proposed flank movement from Jackson.

The author avails himself of the privilege granted, for the benefit of the reader, to quote fully from the admirable history of Stonewall Jackson and the Civil War, presented in all its features in most attractive form by Col. Henderson, of the British Army. This will show when and with whom Genl. Lee held the much talked of council of war, which is supposed to have occurred on June 23rd. Some have written it the 24th.

"At three o'clock in the afternoon, after passing rapidly through Richmond, he reached the headquarters of the Commander-in-Chief. It is unfortunate that no record of the meeting that took place has been preserved. There were present, besides Lee and Jackson, the three officers whose divisions were to be employed in the attack upon the Federals, Longstreet, A. P. Hill, and D. H. Hill. The names of the two former are associated with almost every Confederate victory won upon the soil of Virginia. They were trusted by their great leader, and they were idolized by their men. Like others, they made mistakes; the one was sometimes slow, the other careless; neither gave the slightest sign that they were capable of independent command, and both were at times impatient of control. But, taking them all in all, they were gallant soldiers, brave to a fault, vigorous in attack, and undaunted by adverse fortune. Longstreet, sturdy and sedate, his 'old war-horse' as Lee affectionately called him, bore on his broad shoulders the weight of twenty years' service in the old army. Hill's slight figure and delicate features, instinct with life and energy, were a marked contrast to the heavier frame and rugged lineaments of his older colleague.

"Already they were distinguished. In the hottest of the fight they had won the respect that soldiers so readily accord to valor; yet it is not on these stubborn fighters, not on their companion, less popular, but hardly less capable, that the eye of imagination rests. Were some great painter, gifted with the sense of historic fitness, to place on his canvas the council in the Virginia homestead, two figures only would occupy the foreground: the one weary with travel, white with the dust of many leagues, and bearing on his frayed habiliments the traces of rough bivouacs and mountain roads; the other, tall, straight and stately; still, for all his fifty years, remarkable for his personal beauty, and endowed with all the simple dignity of a noble character and commanding intellect. In that humble chamber, where the only refreshment the Commander-in-Chief could offer was a glass of milk, Lee and Jackson met for the first time since the war had begun. Lee's hour of triumph had yet to come. The South was aware that he was sage in council; he had yet to prove his mettle in the field. But there was at least one Virginia soldier who knew his worth. With the prescient sympathy of a kindred spirit, Jackson had divined his daring and his genius, and although he held always to his own opinions, he had no will but that of his great commander. With how absolute a trust his devotion was repaid, one of the brightest pages in the history of Virginia tells us; a year crowded with victories bears witness to the strength begotten of their mutual confidence. So long as Lee and Jackson led her armies, hope shone on the standards of the South. Great was the constancy of her people; wonderful the fortitude of her soldiers; but on the shoulders of her twin heroes, rested the burden of the tremendous struggle.

To his four major-generals Lee explained his plan of attack, and then, retiring to his office, left them to arrange the details. It will be sufficient for the present to state that Jackson's troops were to encamp on the night of the 25th East of Ashland, fifteen miles North of Richmond, between the village and the Virginia Central Railway. The day following the interview, the 24th, he returned to his command, rejoining the column at Beaver Dam Station."

The author indulges the hope that some of the survivors of the stupendous conflict outlined in this work, may some day chance to see these pages, and, as the scene of that council unfolds, and in the picture, the four distinguished major-generals appear, where their invincible and immortal Lee had called them to consider and mature plans to make it possible to strike a blow that would not only stagger McClellan, but force him to recoil with the grandest army that had as yet been marshaled on the battlefields of America. Old Veterans! as you contemplate this picture, take pride in the emotions welling up from your soul, for generations that follow you as long as history is read, will strive to prove their descent from the men who once followed such leaders in battles which have become renowned the world over. The fame of Lee and his generals, won by the devotion and aid of those dauntless battalions, has been and will be the theme of song and story, so long as the human soul sees beauty and pathos in glorious deeds of brave men. If such feelings should come to the reader, perhaps after the author and a great majority of the old Confederate soldiers shall have rested under the dust, the hope is that he may be inclined to gather around some camp-fire and take comfort in recounting the movements of his command in the days around Richmond, when Jackson fell upon McClellan's flank and saved A. P. Hill from annihilation, and tell of the thunderous cheers that were heard above the din of battle, when the Valley Army plunged into the thickest of the fray, "in Stonewall Jackson's way."

The student of this campaign should study the official reports, carefully preserved and accessible when fully compiled from the originals, as the author has studied them; and from the copious notes now on his table, he is tempted to place before the reader the situations of the two contending armies, as fully shown, from the mountains to the sea.

The disparity of the numbers engaged was simply appalling; but we must pass this and briefly show how the Washington government had been deceived by Lee and Jackson, and that their strategy balanced several Divisions of their foe. To appreciate the situation, we must remember that Jackson left his Blue Ridge camp June 17-18; and after a march with his whole army, along his enemy's front, until he halted at Ashland 15 miles above Richmond on June 25th, and prepared for his attack—and actually fought McClellan for two days,—before it was discovered that he was not at some point threatening Washington City. We have dispatches filed with the official reports, which show the spirit of the times and the stress on several large columns stretching from the Valley to Fredericksburg, watching the phantom Jackson, who never appeared in form until his guns broke the stillness on McClellan's flank.

On June 20th, Fremont announced in his dispatches that Jackson's main army was moving down in two columns upon the points held by his army and Shields'. The latter had just received orders to reinforce McDowell at Fredericksburg. Banks' opinion was that Jackson was making forced marches through the mountain valley West of the Big North, to enter Maryland below Cumberland, capture great army supplies, destroy the B. & O. and rush on to Washington. It is not strange, then, that the Washington government was alarmed and deceived. But who can excuse those Generals on the border for their imbecility. Same official reports have dispatches showing that on June 24th, McDowell was threatened the same day that Fremont and Banks fell back for safer positions—Jackson then within 35 miles of Richmond. Same official papers contain the official correspondence of the Federal generals, responding to personal letters from the President and his Secretary of War. During these days Jackson was changing his base. The President discloses his dilemma. He evidently suffered anxiety for his personal safety and that of his capital. The generals are apprised of reports reaching Washington, crediting Jackson with depleted ranks and dispirited troops, and again with an army ranging from fifteen to sixty thousand men. One enterprising officer, in very close relation with the President, Carl Schurz, describes Jackson as the most determined and enterprising of all Lee's generals. That while he was only expected to conduct a guerilla warfare along the border, he at times was able to gather a marauding host and strike some vulnerable point. Mr. Lincoln was impressed with his friendly suggestions that he immediately recall his order to McDowell, to stay his movements, and be prepared to receive an attack from Jackson, who was reported as being at Gordonsville with 60,000 men. It appears strange that Lincoln did not at once order McClellan to force an entrance to Richmond over Lee's depleted ranks; for if he believed Jackson had such an army, he must have drawn from Lee his reinforcements, and McClellan with his 85,000 men, could have taken every line around Richmond, and McDowell, Shields, Banks, Fremont and the Washington garrison could unite and overwhelm Jackson.

The same official reports, (in Vols. XI and XII,) will repay the student for an examination; and he will see disclosed much more than the author has space to give here, that will show the great deficiency among the U. S. government officials. McClellan has been censured for his lack of action—for his months of preparation; but it is a well known fact that Mr. Lincoln retarded his movements, though he frequently expressed dissatisfaction at his tardiness. The President was never willing up to that time for any of his generals to lose sight of their first duty—"Save Washington at all hazards."

Some military critics excuse McClellan thiswise: 1st, that McDowell could withstand any attack Jackson could make, by concentration of the scattered columns of Rickett, Shields, Banks, Fremont, etc., so that an army of such magnitude could not only protect Washington, but overwhelm Jackson; and thus so cripple Lee, that McClellan would have Richmond in his grasp. Little Mack probably figured this out on his chessboard before he had fully learned of the strategy Lee and Jackson had so successfully wrought out. It is useless to add that the entire Federal line was illy supplied by its bureau of information, for the first two years of the war. The Federal Secret Service was also a failure. Nothing reliable was ever reported through such channels. The generals of columns, as well as the authorities in Washington, relied often upon the wild statements given by fugitive slaves, and from whites who lacked judgment in estimating numbers, and in locating them. The celebrated Jesse Scouts, named in honor of General Fremont's wife, amounted to nothing as reliable scouts The information furnished was oftener misleading than otherwise. The very license given them to scout the border without let or hindrance, resulted in disaster to many of the campaigns. False reports given their leaders, confused them as to much of the celebrated Jackson campaigns, so that it was found necessary to curtail their privileges. But the organization was composed of the worst class of men found on the border. Many were deserters from the Confederates, who never dared venture near enough the Confederate lines to obtain information. Many were of the men found along the Virginia border who were Union men, not for the love they bore the Union, but because it gave them license to plunder their neighbors and insult and maltreat old men, women and children, as no regular Union soldier did. The Lower Valley had its full share of this despicable class, who as horse-thieves and murderers and other villains, left behind them a most infamous record. Many were killed during their dare-devil escapades by the men of Moseby's and White's battalions. Some survived the war, and with their ill-gotten gains became owners of good property, and posed for years as citizens among the people they had robbed and betrayed. The author knew many of this class, and saw them often wince under the scathing glances of those they had wronged. One by one they have disappeared, until nearly all are gone; but their infamy can never be effaced from memory. The withered remnant of that band who once rode the country down, arrayed in gray uniforms, is a pitiable wreck. Property gone, life miserably spent, and conscious of the execrations that silently start from those who pass them by,—they drag their way down to graves that must be welcome asylums. The author could give the names of scores of the band; but inasmuch as some have left offspring that may chance become useful citizens, he refrains; and they may never know the bitter sting that attaches to their parentage by reason of the infamy mentioned.

It must not be wondered that the Federals were so imperfectly supplied with good scouts, the most of them being of the class mentioned, and the remainder hirelings, to perform a service hazardous in the extreme. Consequently the Confederates were able to move and change base without detection. Not so with General Lee and his generals. Every man was not only a hero but a patriot. Many of them had left home and fireside within the Federal lines; and when information was desired, the Confederate general could entrust the mission to hundreds of such brave fellows, who took delight in flanking pickets, entering the enemy's lines, visiting the old home, and in many ways contriving to obtain information of inestimable value. They were trained soldiers; they had reason for being accurate in estimating numbers, for they well knew that 'ere many days they would be pitted against those bluecoats they were sizing up; and besides, they were experts as to what troops did on the eve of marching, and whether for marches or engagements, and the direction to be taken. The author made such surveys frequently. So, from such causes the two great armies stood strangely apart on the 28th of June, 1862. The Federals knew nothing definite. Here is Secy. Stanton's exact language found in the O. R. addressing McClellan: "As to numbers or position of Jackson's force, we have no definite information. Within the last two days the evidence is strong that for some purpose the enemy is circulating rumors of Jackson's advance in various directions, with a view to conceal the real point of attack. Neither McDowell nor Banks nor Fremont have any accurate knowledge of the subject." What an admission of inefficiency! And this dispatch was received by McClelland after Jackson had been on his flank for 12 hours.

Not so with the Confederates. Genl. Lee knew every position, and went to battle on plans marked out; and found the field notes correct. The battle opened on the 26th, and for the first time Jackson failed to occupy ground at the time he had himself fixed during the council, and consequently did not take the part contemplated in the Beaver Dam Station battle; and some critics have argued that Jackson was only obeying orders of his superior, and failed to take the same interest he would have done if it had been his independent campaign. This is unfair, for a careful study of the official orders of Lee and Jackson of this great battle, prove that the blow struck by Jackson on the 28th made greater terror and came at a time when McClellan was unprepared and had no time to change front, and was compelled to witness all his plans frustrated, his army defeated, and no hope for reinforcements within four days march from McDowell; and this he knew had passed beyond his control; for Stanton had informed him in the dispatch mentioned, which he received during the engagement, that a new army corps had been organized with Genl. Pope as commander. This would embrace the columns of McDowell, Fremont, Banks, etc.,—he to operate against the troublesome Valley Army under Jackson and Ewell, and henceforth McClellan would not have Jackson to reckon with. This seems absurd now, when we read of Jackson coming in on a bloody field of the 28th.

To appreciate and understand in part this great battle, the famous orders of Genl. Lee relating to this battle, and issued as a result of the council referred to, is copied from the official reports of the battle.

"Headquarters, Army of Northern Va.

June 24, 1862.

Genl. Orders No. 75.

I. Genl. Jackson's command will proceed tomorrow (June 25) from Ashland towards the Slash Church, and encamp at some convenient point west of the Central Railroad. Branch's Brigade of A. P. Hill's Division, will also, tomorrow evening, take position on the Chickahominy, near Half Sink. At three o'clock Thursday morning 26th, Genl. Jackson will advance on the road leading to Pole Green Church, communicating his march to Genl. Branch, who will immediately cross the Chickahominy and take the road leading to Mechanicsville. As soon as the movements of these columns are discovered, Genl. A. P. Hill, with the rest of his Division, will cross the Chickahominy at Meadow Bridge and move direct upon Mechanicsville. To aid his advance the heavy batteries on the Chickahominy will at the proper time open upon the batteries at Mechanicsville. The enemy being driven from Mechanicsville and the passing of the bridge being opened, Genl. Longstreet with his divisions, and that of Genl. D. H. Hill, will cross the Chickahominy at or near that point; Genl. D. H. Hill moving to the support of Genl. Jackson, and Genl. Longstreet supporting Genl. A. P. Hill; the four divisions keeping in communication with each other and moving *en échelon* on separate roads if practicable; the left division in advance, with skirmishers and sharpshooters extending in their front, will sweep down the Chickahominy, and endeavor to drive the enemy from his position above New Bridge, Genl. Jackson bearing well to the left, turning Beaver Dam Creek, and taking the direction towards Cold Harbor. They will then press forward towards the York River R. R., closing upon the enemy's rear, and forcing down the Chickahominy. An advance of the enemy towards Richmond will be prevented by vigorously following his rear and crippling and arresting his progress.

II. The divisions under Genls. Huger and Magruder will hold their position in front of the enemy against attack and make such demonstrations, Thursday, as to discover his operations. Should opportunity offer, the feint will be converted into a real attack.

IV. Genl. Stuart with the 1st, 4th and 9th Va. Cavly. The Cavly. of Cobb Legion and the Jeff Davis Legion will cross the Chickahominy tomorrow (Wednesday 25th) and take position to the left of Genl. Jackson's line of march. The main body will be held in reserve with scout well extended to the front and left. Genl. Stuart will keep Genl. Jackson informed of the movements of the enemy on his left, and will cooperate with him in his advance. * * *"

The foregoing is given to show Genl. Lee's plan of the great battle. If the reader will study this together with the official reports of Jackson, the two Hills and Genl. Stuart, good reasons will appear why Jackson was not at his place at the appointed time. His supply train from Richmond failed to connect with him on the 25-6, and while thus unavoidably detained, Jackson was supplied with such information on the 26th as required material changes in his plan for attack. It is true A. P. Hill must have suffered without his support. Genl. Lee's orders plainly indicate that Jackson must be regarded with peculiar privileges. He must determine without conference with Genl. Lee, what changes of position or attack would be desirable; and Genl. Jackson was to supply Lee with information, and to protect his flanks. Jackson had soon divined the intentions of the enemy in his front and flank. The official reports show that staff officers in filling up the general orders, committed blunders that Jackson soon discovered; and to extricate his army from tangled, marshy forests, turbid streams and damaged bridges, he was compelled to rely upon his own staff and the vigor of his guides to unravel the threads of his approach to the arena. Hill's struggle was desperate, his loss heavy; and if Jackson could have taken his position at the crucial moment, the Federals would have been driven from the field with great slaughter. But the impetuous Hill could not restrain his gallant spirit long enough to open communication with Jackson; so he plunged into what seemed to him an inviting field. The enemy changed base during the night, and at 5 A. M. June 27th, Jackson had crossed Beaver Dam Creek, and arranged to form a juncture with Longstreet, Old Cold Harbor being the objective point. Jackson was compelled to abandon the direct route and take a more circuitous one, which caused several hours delay. The battle opened early in the day; and gradually the lines opened for attack for a great distance, covering ridges, swamps and boggy creeks, one of the latter running from Cold Harbor near the McGehee house. Along this line was to be the battle to determine the fate of the two leaders, McClellan and Lee. During the afternoon, when Genl. Lee was near the front to witness the concentrated charge of every available arm of his army—knowing that Jackson was striking at the same moment, and the fate of Richmond if not the Confederacy, depended upon the result of this great struggle, he gave out the word—"The Valley men are here." Henderson says—"with the cry of Stonewall Jackson for their slogan, the Southern army swept across ravine and morass into the galling fire of deadly batteries, which had turned their canister into the ranks of the rushing Southerners;" and the battle of Gaines Mill and Cold Harbor passed into history as a victory to the Confederates, but at what sacrifice! Official Reports show a loss of at least 8,000 officers and men, killed and wounded. The Federals left on the field 4,000 dead and wounded, and several thousand prisoners.

The Little Napoleon was compelled to change his base and act on the defensive, and to urgently call on Washington for more troops. He already had more men than he could use to advantage. The next day Jackson received orders from Genl. Lee to make a forced march to the Long Bridge Road, by way of White Oak Swamp, and from his new position guard Lee's left flank from the enemy who would force the bridges and fords of the Chickahominy, and to hold positions on that road until further orders. Some have thought he should have joined Longstreet and not wait "for further orders." It must be admitted that this was Genl. Lee's campaign. His was the master mind; and if a failure to destroy McClellan's army occurred, the fault should not be laid at the door of his subordinate who obeyed orders. The battle of Frayser's farm did not result as McClellan feared it would he was in better condition when he fell back on Malvern Hill July 1st, than he expected, though his army left evidences along the line of march that the retreat resembled a rout. It is hard to understand how a young Napoleon with 95,000 men, could be routed and forced to abandon all his plans by an army of 75,000, many of whom were exhausted before the campaign opened; but it is not the writer's province to criticize this General, but to briefly follow Jackson and his Valley army, and point out the engagements, leaving the study of the campaign to readers who may desire to know the features of the Seven Days battle around Richmond.

Jackson was at Malvern Hill, but his Valley army did not bear the brunt of the fearful day. D. H. Hill and Magruder's forces, about 30,000, suffered heavy losses in beating against the strong positions held by the best troops under Genl. Porter, that McClellan commanded to the front. The havoc in the Confederate ranks failed to hold McClellan to the field. The morning revealed a fearful condition to the Confederates. Official reports from General Trimble of Genl. Ewell's Division, say—"I went off the next morning to ask for orders, when I found the whole army in the utmost disorder—thousands of straggling men were asking every passerby for their regiments; ambulances, wagons and artillery obstructing every road, and altogether in a drenching rain, presented a scene of the most woeful and distracting confusion." Here seemed McClellan's opportunity to rout Lee's army. But we find by the official reports that he left the field early in the day and rode away to Harrison's Landing on the James, but wrote his famous letter to Washington before he left the field—"that his men were exhausted, and dreaded an attack from fresh troops under Stonewall Jackson." Continuing, he says: "I will retire tonight to Harrison's Landing under cover of the gunboats;" and begs for time, and reinforcements. "My men have proved themselves the equals of any troops in the world, but they are worn out." (See O. R., Vol. XI, part III, pp. 282, etc.) This proves an overwhelming defeat of the commander, whether his army had the same fear or not; and this, too, after such generals as Jackson, Magruder and D. H. Hill had recoiled from their disastrous attack on Genl. Porter's strong position. Henderson, in his intensely interesting review of this campaign, presents the scene at Genl. Jackson's headquarters next morning: "The condition to which McClellan was reduced, seems to have been realized by Jackson. The crushing defeat of his own troops failed to disturb his judgment. Whilst the night still covered the battlefield, his divisional generals came to report the condition of their men, and to receive instructions. 'Every representation,' says Dabney, 'which they made was gloomy.' At length after many details of losses and disasters, they concurred in declaring that McClellan would probably take the aggressive that day, and that the Confederate army was in no condition to resist him. Jackson had listened silently, save when he interposed a few brief questions to all their statements; but now he replied: No; he will clear out in the morning. Jackson was correct in his view; for when morning fully dawned, Malvern Hill was found deserted, but on the field were scores of surgeons at work among the wounded, and everywhere hundreds of dead Federals were lying uncared for. One of McClellan's generals, Hooker, gave as his evidence on the conduct of the War, (O. R. p. 580) "We retreated like a parcel of sheep, and a few shots from the enemy would have panic-stricken the whole command." A committee of Congress which took evidence on the conduct of the war, state that "Nothing but a heavy rain, thereby preventing the enemy from bringing up their artillery, saved the army from destruction."

Jackson, in the early morning, discovered after riding through the same rain to the front, the apparent rout; ordered his staff to form three lines of battle and be prepared for an advance that Genl. Lee would certainly expect to order. But a council of war held at Genl. Jackson's headquarters (Willis's Church) on the 2nd of July—Genl. Lee, President Davis, Longstreet and others being present,—decided not to advance in force. Major Dabney writing to Col. Henderson on this feature, says: "Jackson favored vigorous action. He knew McClellan was retreating with a defeated and demoralized army, which could be virtually destroyed if pressed that day; but Mr. Davis opposed a general engagement lest the enemy would turn towards Richmond and ultimately defeat Lee. A compromise was effected, and the army allowed to advance on the 3rd, but this delay was disastrous." Dabney further states: "That the Valley army, crawling in rear of Longstreet, marched only three miles that day, and such sluggish progress put the climax to Jackson's discontent; and the morning of the 4th he exhibited much anger at the slow movement of his staff, and ordered the mess chest locked and put into the wagon. Thus the staff lost their breakfast and incurred the displeasure of their chief." The day was spent waiting, watching the enemy. No fierce fighting. McClellan had time to gain an impregnable position on heights, under cover of his gunboats. The next three days were spent in securing the spoils, arms, stores, etc., the Federals had left on their lines of retreat—52 guns and 35,000 rifles told the story of the plight of McClellan's host on the 2nd and 3rd; and shows that Jackson's view of the situation was correct, and that someone erred when the advance was stayed. Students of the seven days campaign may conclude for themselves where the blame should rest. On the 8th of July, Genl. Lee fell back to Richmond. McClelland had been frustrated in all his plans, but the Confederates suffered the heavy loss of 20,000 men, while the Federal loss was 16,000. (The student in his study of McClellan's report to his government, will be confused somewhat by his declarations, and may desire fuller explanation that he gives in O. R., Vol. XI, part III, pp. 299, etc. This will be found in Report of Congressional Com. on Conduct of the War, pp. 27—580, etc.) It will be seen that reinforcements were drawn from every possible point to recruit McClellan. Lincoln called earnestly for 300,000 recruits; but all the States were disheartened, and regarded the management of the war as a dismal failure; and Congress was urged to investigate. The country seemed on the verge of revolt. Regarding the Seven Days Battle from this standpoint, the Southern people arose in their might and proclaimed Lee and Jackson invincible; and although thousands of her bravest had gone down in woeful carnage, and sorrow was in every home, yet the verdict was: a glorious victory, and Richmond safe. The grand armies of the North, combining the reinforcements with the original 95,000, presented to the world an armed host numbering full 150,000 (See O. R.) to stem the invasion threatened by Lee. What a spectacle! And this at a time when Lee with his depleted 75,000 should have been overwhelmed by this mighty host.

Major Dabney in his careful study of the situation after the battles, says that Genl. Jackson advised an advance at once of the Valley Army towards the Northern border, to invade the enemy's country, expressing as his opinion that McClellan was beaten and had no intention to move on Richmond. This view he presented to Mr. A. R. Boteler, member of congress from the Valley District, "and insisted that the horrors of war should be transferred across the border—throw 60,000 men into Maryland, and it was the only way to bring the North to its senses and end the war;" and added he was not seeking leadership, but would follow Lee or anyone *who would fight.*" Mr. B. asked, why do you not urge your views on Genl. Lee? I have done so, replied Jackson. And what does he say to them? "He says nothing," was the answer. "But do not understand that I complain of this silence; it is proper that Genl. Lee should observe it. He is wise and prudent. He feels that he bears the responsibility, and he is right in declining a hasty expression of his purpose to a subordinant like me."

It is apparent that Jackson's suggestions were considered by either Davis or Lee, for we find in O. R., C. S. A., that Jackson received an order July 13th to march westward; and we find him at Gordonsville on the 16th, where he found Pope's Cavalry near that point in large numbers. The Valley Army now 11,000 to check Pope and his Army of Virginia with 47,000, composed of Fremont's command, now Seigel's, 13,000; Banks 11,000; McDowell's 18,000, and Bayard's and Buford's Cavalry 5,000 (O. R., Vol. XI, part III, p. 334, etc.) This was an army of veterans, with leaders well known to Jackson, all commanded by the braggart Pope. These columns or corps, were dispersed over a long line from Sperryville near the Blue Ridge to Fredericksburg. Here was another field for old Stonewall and his strategy. McClellan in his correspondence with Washington (O. R., Vol. XI, Part III) discloses his ignorance of Lee's strength; for he says, "we believe that Jackson has started towards the Valley with 60,000 to 80,000 troops." Strange he did not move on Lee and crush him. He calls for 30,000 reinforcements, to enable him to move on Richmond. Jackson's plans were submitted to Genl. Lee; and were promptly approved. (See his letter of July 27, among army files.) A. P. Hill and the 2nd Louisiana Brigade sent as reinforcements, arrived at Gordonsville, and all remained for several days, making full preparations for the celebrated battle that was imminent; for Pope's order, with Headquarters in the Saddle, was so famous, that the whole section was familiar with his boastful intentions. To preserve it for convenient reference, it is given here in full as taken from O. R., Vol. XII, part III, pp. 474, etc.)

"I have come to you" addressing his soldiers, "from the West, where we have always seen the backs of our enemies—from an army whose business it has been to seek the adversary, and beat him when found, whose policy has been attack and not defense * * * I presume that I have been called here to pursue the same system, and to lead you against the enemy. It is my purpose to do so, and that speedily. Meantime I desire you to dismiss from your minds certain phrases, which I am sorry to find in vogue amongst you. I hear constantly of taking strong positions and holding them—of lines of retreat and of bases of supplies. Let us discard such ideas * * * Let us study the probable line of retreat of our opponents, and leave our own to take care of ourselves. Let us look before and not behind. Success and glory are in advance. Disaster and shame lurk in the rear."

Jackson was well supplied with such information, and was studying the braggart's weak places. Pope had ordered his corps commanders to subsist on the country; and he has the credit of being the first Federal commander to issue such an order, which meant devastation of every vestige of food supply. Many battalions of his army had in other sections, without orders, pillaged the country on their marches. The helpless home people were enraged at this brutal warfare, and vied with each other in conveying to Jackson and his brave men, intelligence of the atrocities. And thus the Valley Army became aroused to strike a telling blow. Jackson through the same source, knew every movement of the enemy, as well as of the hellish acts of his soldiery; and has left on record evidences of his determination to annihilate such foes, or be extinguished forever from war's arena. Pope and his mode of warfare, was a new feature on the Virginia border. A bristling activity in his cavalry betokened activity in the grand army, massing for the complete overthrow of Jackson. This genius of war and adept in strategy, realized that no ordinary antagonist was in his front; and besides he knew that many thousands in the divisions preparing to engage him, were no longer raw recruits, but were seasoned soldiers, and had given evidence in the Valley campaign of being foemen worthy of respect, when on the battle line led by competent leaders. Jackson could not conceal his movements as readily as was his wont. The Federal cavalry had become a power, under the leadership of Bayard of the Valley Campaigns, an officer of rare ability, aided by the veteran Genl. Buford. They had trained their cavalry for the last three months to become bolder; and they were soon discovered near Gordonsville, watching Jackson. While his cavalry was alert, they were unable to penetrate the neutral ground far enough to obtain much information regarding the main army. Genl. Stuart finally made a dash towards Fredericksburg, and learned enough to cause Jackson to shift positions; and this induced Pope to make a dash, under the impression that Jackson was retreating. But the famous strategist was preparing for his greatest achievement.

All the old Valley combinations, joined by McDowell and commanded by the hitherto invincible Pope, pitted against him an army of about 50,000, supplied with munitions of war truly appalling. Against this serried host, were opposed about 24,000 worn-out men, with limited munitions, and other supplies. The scene was one stupendous array of men and steel. Army trains were on every road leading towards Culpeper C. H., led by great columns—Banks sweeping down from Sperryville—Part of McDowell's fine corps heading for the same point; while two other columns were coming from Warrenton and Falmouth. This was Jackson's supreme hour. He determined to take them in detail, as usual. The Old Stonewall Division, under Genl. Winder, 3,000; Ewell, 7,550; A. P. Hill, with his flying division of 12,000; and Stuart, 12,000 cavalry. Every command had lost heavily in the terrific struggles; and the depletion of their ranks was perceptible. Brigades had dwindled to small regiments; and as the eye ran along their lines, many famous leaders were missing. But the same old spirit shone out from every squadron; and their General knew he had the men near him to undertake the great work. Washington hoped that Genl. Pope would strike a telling blow; and at his suggestion, a large force of 11,000 men under Genl. Cox, was ordered to march across country from Lewisburg (a point S. W. from Staunton) and threaten Jackson's flank and rear. Jackson knew this; and Genl. Lee informed him that McClellan was preparing for another move on Richmond, and the hour had come for their old tactics of strategy. And as Jackson and his tried soldiery once more breathed the pure mountain air and drank from the limpid Blue Ridge streams, the old war-like spirit was manifest. The feeling that MacGregor was on his native heath. Every soul was inspired; and as the light-hearted Stuart whirled through the skirmish lines of the advancing columns, he was able to apprise Jackson of the position of each advancing column. Their old antagonist Banks was in the lead, and gave evidence of his desire to redeem his flagrant blunders. We must remember that forced marches were required, under the beating rays of an August sun. The 7th of August brought only a portion of the army to Orange C. H., 20 miles distant from Culpeper, which all were struggling to reach. Ewell and A. P. Hill were far in the rear, contending with mixed orders. Jackson in his reports, complained of Hill's tardiness in this march, and of his lack of interest; but we must throw no blame upon the fair name of that gallant and magnificent chieftain, which can never be tarnished. Jackson doubtless failed to enlighten Hill of his bold designs upon the enemy. Strange but true. This was his weakness. He derived comfort from the hazy mystery of his strategic movements, and was selfish enough to withhold them from such grand leaders as Ewell and Hill. The situation on the 8th must have revealed this weakness to Jackson; for if his main supports had understood his scheme, they doubtless would have been enthused; their columns would have lined up, and the smoke of their camp-fires mingled on the same plain that night, no such insinuations would have found place in his celebrated official reports. But Jackson was not the general to be disconcerted and thrown from his base,—although his orders had gone astray and the much-needed columns were not up. He doggedly set to work to strike some column of the enemy before concentration on Culpeper could be effected. The early dawn of August 9th saw Hill on the road, and the whole army gaining their lost advantages. Army trains were on other roads guarded by Gregg and Lawton's brigades. Ewell led the march; and along the West side of Slaughter Mountain discovered a large force of cavalry in line of battle on Cedar Run, awaiting his approach. The old war-horse, waiting a moment to unlimber his guns, opened fire; the Federal batteries replied, and regiments supported. It soon became apparent that a general engagement was imminent at a point 7 miles from Culpeper, the place Jackson had planned to reach on the 8th. Col. Henderson says Banks reached Culpeper on the 8th, and sent his advance brigade to Cedar Run, and he followed on the 9th. Banks in his report does not mention Culpeper; but says he intercepted Jackson at Cedar Run on the 9th, and immediately engaged his advance columns and urged

Pope to send him reinforcements. Be that as it may, Jackson had divined the movement, and met Banks' column in fighting mood. Survivors of the Stonewall Brigade will remember when Early moved to the front, Ewell to the right—all heading for Slaughter Mountain; Winder swung to the left, and the battle was thus opened. Hill was held in reserve. We lack space for a description of this battle. The Federals fought bravely and held their position tenaciously—both sides losing heavily. Genl. Winder had fallen, mortally wounded. The fighting was intense after 5 o'clock. The old Stonewall Brigade suffered severely—Garnett's Brigade went down in the carnage, losing nearly all of the regimental leaders under the withering fire. Banks' old soldiers had learned to fight. Early's Brigade was driven asunder. Old men describe this conflict as the hardest in their experience. The Stonewall Brigade rallied and sailed into the left; then Jackson came to the front with Hill and Ewell; other brigades which had suffered severely and were partly routed, took new courage, and 'ere 7 o'clock came, Slaughter Mountain was in the grasp of the Confederates, and once more Banks was routed. But 3,000 men lay dead and wounded on the field. All this carnage occurred within two hours. Jackson immediately rallied his scattered battalions, to organize them for other serious work. Pope's other corps were near at hand to be reckoned with; the fighting Siegel and wary McDowell were in his front; and we find Jackson resuming his march to Culpeper. Within two miles, he was confronted by a large force. Guns were unlimbered, and a heavy fire poured into the large camp of Federals who retreated in disorder. Prisoners were captured, who proved to be those who had boasted in the Valley that "me fights mit Siegel." Jackson ordered a halt for the night; and the next morning fell back to Cedar Run, having learned that Pope was in his front with his full force. No fighting on the 10th. On the 11th, both armies under flags of truce gathered up their dead. On the night of the 11th, Jackson once more changed his base and fell back on Gordonsville.

In his official reports, Vol. XII, part III, p. 185, he explains this retreat, which caused anxiety at Washington; for we have Genl. Halleck's letter to Pope (O. R., Vol. XII) with this language: "Beware of a snare; feigned retreats are Secesh tactics." Also same record, containing letter from McClellan to the Commander-in-Chief, using this language: "I don't like Jackson's movements; he will suddenly appear when least expected." We can gather from such language enough to show that the Federals were becoming better acquainted with the great tactician, and preparing for his strategems; and recent battles had disclosed to the Confederates an improved *morale* in the Federal Army. And now both sides were lining up for stupendous efforts. The North seemed fairly beaten at times, judging from the tone of the press; but at no time did their President relax. He had cast the die; and had faith in the results. Though the Summer of 1862 was overwhelming in its demand for brainy work and tireless faith, Lincoln exhibited more determination and unalterable purpose with each succeeding episode, whether defeat or victory. Certainly he occupied a position before the world never approached, much less attained, by any of his predecessors. On the night of the 15th, Jackson moved three divisions from Gordonsville to a suitable point near Clark Mountain, and there waited for reinforcements. Genl. Lee had joined Jackson on the same day; and the latter submitted his plan of engaging the enemy. The plans were approved, and Genl. Lee was hastening what troops he could spare from Richmond to this point. The Valley Army crossed the Rapidan in the early morning of the 18th at Somerville Ford; Longstreet crossed at Raccoon Ford; and we find the whole Confederate forces concentrated under the shadow of Clark Mountain on the morning of the 18th. Pope with his 52,500 men was on the plain beyond. He was evidently unaware of Jackson's near approach on his flank, and ignorant of his movements.

His main army massed on the Culpeper road waiting for an attack. The boaster was doomed to ruin. But an unforeseen incident occurred that postponed his sudden overthrow. Genl. Stuart on the night of the 17th, endeavoring with his escort to escape capture, while near Verdiersville, lost his plumed hat and a package of dispatches. The hat was well known; the package contained dispatches from Genl. Lee, which revealed his presence and that of his reinforcements to aid Jackson in his attack. Pope gathered enough from the dispatches to put him on his guard; and we have it from his official correspondence that he, having learned through a trusted scout on the 18th, the real situation, he deemed it wise to change his base to the Rappahannock. The attack was held up by Genl. Lee. He has been severely criticized for thwarting Jackson's plans. These views coupled with opinions expressed by Federal generals who were present at the time, strongly support the claim that Jackson was prevented in executing the scheme that would have annihilated Pope's Army. Genl. Geo. H. Gordon, a Federal General we have had occasion not only to mention in this work, but to study his very fair narrative of the army of Virginia, says: "It was fortunate that Jackson was not in command of the Confederates on the night of

Aug. 17th, for the superior force of the enemy would have overwhelmed us, if we could not have escaped, and escape on that night was impossible."

It is said that Jackson chafed under this restraint; and viewing his great work at this day, we are constrained to admit that Jackson had cause to chafe. He had his plans completed, and doubtless could have executed them on the 18th to the overthrow of Pope's unsuspecting army lying beyond his undiscovered rendezvous, in three separate columns, if Genl. Lee had not appeared. We must, however, leave this to the military critics. Genl. Lee late in the afternoon, discovered too late that Pope was retreating. Whatever was to be done, must be quickly conceived and executed before McClellan, who was changing his base, could reinforce Pope. The army was put into forward movement during the night of the 19th, fording the Rapidan at the Raccoon and Somerville Fords; Stuart followed Pope; rapidly encountered the Federal Cavalry at Brandy Station, where the first Brandy Station battle occurred. On the 21st the Confederates were well up on the Rappahannock front, and seeking attack. Jackson with Stewart had cautiously moved to the fords near Warrenton Springs; Early's Brigade crossed about a mile below, near an old mill, and took position on a ridge; the Valley army proper remained on the West bank. Another brigade crossed the river next morning the 23rd. The 24th was spent in skirmishing and changing position; the Federals were driven back by the Valley Army. Stuart had on the 22nd used his cavalry on their flanks, and swooping down upon Catlett's Station, succeeded in capturing large trains and camp supplies and many provisions, and secured a prize in one of Pope's staff, with his horses, treasure chest, clothing and official papers. This sufficed for the loss of his "plumed hat." Stuart's raid resulted in the destruction of much army supplies and the capture of 330 officers and men. Pope was deceived by Stuart falling back, and concentrated his force on the Old Pike from Warrenton to Alexandria. He now had, including reinforcements from McClellan on the 25th, about 80,000 men. The captured dispatches disclosed his strength and position, and that he had promise of 75,000 more if they could be used to defeat Jackson. Genl. Lee who was on the ground, saw an immense problem before him, and that Jackson's plan to fight on the 18th was a golden opportunity lost. Lee and Jackson held their famous council on the 24th, when it was decided to fight Pope in detail. Jackson swung towards Thoroughfare Gap, to strike in the rear and flank; Lee remained to operate in the front and occupy Pope. The old Valley Army was off with the old Stonewall Brigade or Division under Genl. Taliaferro—Ewell and Hill pressing Northwest on the 25th. The old divisions knew not whether their destination was the dear old Valley or Washington; all felt that a surprise was in store; and each man tightened his old belt; ate green apples and stepped lively, following their old leader without halt until midnight, near Salem. Some old survivors of this famous march may recall incidents of that day, if he perchance follows the author in his outline of this campaign; and will remember how the Bull Run mountains loomed up before their bivouac the morning of the 26th. The men divined their leader's movement now; and as the word went through the camp "fall in men," no warning was needed to hush into silence this grand body of men, every one of whom was a hero in the eyes of their commanders and of their country. Old Manassas plains lay out before them; and by noon they were full 14 miles in rear of Pope's Headquarters. He had not detected this movement. Bristoe Station was seized; tracks and bridges destroyed, and good positions chosen for fear Pope would fall suddenly back and find the small force, and overwhelm it with sheer weight. With the railroad bridge gone, Pope was cut off from his great stores at Manassas. At Bristoe Station, Munford and Ewell surrounded several companies, cavalry and infantry, and secured them as prisoners. Then a rush on Manassas Junction, where prisoners, stores and batteries were captured. Pope's supplies of ammunition, stores of flour, bacon, etc., fell in the hands of the hungry troops. In this attack, the twin regiments, 21st Ga. and 21st N. C. received the plaudits of their fellow soldiers. On the 27th, when Hill and the Old Stonewall rolled in from Bristoe Station, and beheld the new town sprung up since they had last seen the place, and every building crowded with army supplies, besides several miles of freight cars standing on the tracks—acres covered with barrels of flour, pork, etc., wagons, ambulances by the hundreds, artillery munitions in huge stacks—no wonder then the Confederates yelled until they fell from sheer exhaustion. Many deemed this victory enough to repay all the hardships endured. But other matter of serious import was occupying the attention of Jackson; for the magnificent army of Genl. Pope was in fighting trim, and stood directly between this Jackson wing and Genl. Lee. No time to lose, for Pope could easily throw 50,000 men upon him in a few hours, and have a sufficient force on the Rappahannock to check Lee, if not defeat him. But Jackson with scarcely 20,000 men held a strong card—a good position—all the supplies for Pope's army, and the most enthusiastic soldiery the world has ever seen.

On the 27th of August, Old Stonewall could be excused if he indulged in a little self-glory; but none have ever told that he exhibited such feelings. The author fain would give extracts from many private letters, as well as official reports, picturing the scenes of the soldiers when given license to partake of such things as they desired out of the wondrous stores all around them, but lack of space forbids. Jackson had learned that Pope had sent a large force in his direction, and that Longstreet was heading for Thoroughfare Gap, and it was wise for him to form a juncture with Longstreet at that point. Consequently the stores must be destroyed before the Federals could occupy Manassas. Ewell had already had an engagement at Bristoe Station during the day; and it was plain the Federals were feeling their way in considerable force. So it will be seen a complete change must occur in Pope's plans, to be able to entrap Jackson. He changes from his original plan to concentrate at Warrenton, after he learned that Jackson and Ewell had been driven from their recently acquired positions and captures. And the Official Reports (Vol. XII, part II, p. 72) show that on the 28th he has an army moving cautiously towards Manassas Junction, with a small cavalry force under Genl. Buford to watch Thoroughfare Gap. Coming in full view of Jackson's recent position, and not a vestige of the Confederates left to tell the way of their going; and hearing just at that time, 4:30 P. M., that the railroad station 12 miles out from Alexandria had been destroyed by Confederate Cavalry, he was in confusion. He believed that the Confederates were between that point and his headquarters in large numbers; and he hastened a concentration at Centreville. He was at a loss to know the whereabouts of the impudent foe that dared destroy his army stores; he had come in person to "bag the whole crowd." (See O. R.) These show that our old acquaintances seen in the Mountain and Valley campaigns, rapidly formed around Centreville that evening—Banks, Siegel, Rickett, Reynolds, lining up next to McDowell—Hooker's, Kearney's, Reno's and other distinguished Divisions. While these were forming, Pope discovered new complications—rumbling of artillery far away to the Southwest, beyond some wooded ridges or mountains, caught his ear. The battle had opened where he least suspected. He also saw battle smoke in Thoroughfare Gap. He was bewildered. Was this McDowell who had overtaken Jackson, and would he be crushed? We shall see that Jackson executed his change of position so as to produce this impression. While moving Northward to concentrate at Centreville, Jackson moved West, in order to get in closer touch with Lee. Col. Henderson, in his graphic account of this maneuvre, explains the situation so plainly, that we adopt his language: "While his enemies were watching the midnight glare above Manassas, Jackson was moving North by three roads; and before Morning broke, A. P. Hill was at Centreville. Ewell had crossed Bull Run by Blackburns ford, and Taliaferro was North of Bald Hill, with a brigade at Groveton, while Stuart's squadrons formed a screen to front and flank. Then as the Federals slowly converged on Manassas, Hill and Ewell, marching unobserved along the North bank of Bull Run, crossed the stone bridge. Taliaferro joined them, and before Pope found that his enemy had left the Junction, the Confederates were in bivouac North of Groveton hidden in the woods, and recovering from the fatigue of their long midnight march." (Hill had marched 14 miles, Ewell 15, and Taliaferro with the wagon trains, etc., about 10 miles.)

Jackson's new position was well chosen; he was within 12 miles of Thoroughfare Gap, giving him a line of retreat if needed, and especially to make it easy for Genl. Lee to reach him by courier or in person, or with reinforcements. The plan seems now to have been well formed—Jackson to allow Pope to follow him, or beat a retreat and wait for McClellan; and 'ere the hour came for his arrival with reinforcements via Aquia Creek, Jackson was to attack and hold Pope until Genl. Lee came to complete his overthrow. Pope was defiant; he had not yet felt the sting of defeat; he had witnessed losses of army stores and many men, but these could be replaced in a short time. Pope had sent Siegel to find Jackson; and after several skirmishes near Gainsville, Siegel pressed on to Manassas; and while he gazed upon the ruin, he dispatched to Pope the information that "Jackson had escaped." Jackson during that afternoon had become fully informed through a captured dispatch from Genl. McDowell, of the disposition of his Divisions. This was for Siegel to go to Manassas Junction, Reynolds to follow Siegel, King to follow Reynolds, and Rickett to follow King; but to halt at Thoroughfare Gap if the Confederates were in force there. Jackson, possessed of this knowledge, immediately sent the Stonewall Division under Taliaferro to attack at once—Ewell to support; and the whole army was moving as if by magic, in close range of the Washington Turnpike. No Federal force was encountered. One of the Federal Divisions under King turned from their original course to Manassas, and started back to Centreville via Groveton and Stone Bridge, not knowing that Jackson occupied ground on his line of march. Longstreet in the interval, had come in contact with Rickett at Thoroughfare Gap; Stuart had been harassing the Federals near Haymarket all day. This situation on that afternoon, if fully understood, would have shown to the contending leaders that their men were strangely seated on the military chessboard. Genl. Rickett ran headlong into Longstreet at Thoroughfare Gap, where he had been informed the way was clear except a small force of cavalry; Genl. King executing a strategic countermarch to Centreville by way of Groveton and Stone Bridge, the sheltered little vale where Jackson and his main force awaited developments. Surprises awaited all parties. The Federals were learning many of Jackson tactics, and Old Stonewall was not prepared for the visitors that afternoon. He had every reason to believe that McDowell was near him in great force, for he deferred his attack to be sure who his opponents were and also if Longstreet could reach him under cover of night, if he should be driven back by McDowell's superior force. Had he known that only one division was approaching on the Groveton Road, he assuredly would have made a rush and demolished King's Division. Ewell and Taliaferro in a woodland due North, were ready for action and in battle line; other brigades were in convenient location under Ewell, to the left—Lawton's, Trimble's, Early's—giving this force near Groveton the strength of 8,000 men and several batteries; while according to McDowell in O. R., King's Division composed of good fighting brigades, numbered 10,000 infantry and artillery—no cavalry. This army totally unconscious of their close proximity to an enemy, marched carelessly along the road in full view of Jackson's hidden veterans, at this time anxious for the tilt that must soon come. The battle opened by a Confederate battery, startling the Federals; but being veterans, they were reformed, and desperation seized both armies. For two hours the struggle ensued. Being at close range and with Enfield rifles, the losses were severe. Jackson's old brigades once more were pitted against Western men, who, handled by skillful officers, fought with desperation. Genl. Ewell fell badly wounded, losing his leg. Then quickly fell Genl. Taliaferro and many other officers. The Old Stonewall Brigade lost one-third of their number, killed and wounded. Ewell's Division lost over 700 out of the 3,000 he led into the galling fire. The gallant 21 Ga. lost more than half its number. The Federal loss was heavy, but no accurate report was ever made, but from private sources their dead and wounded is estimated at 1,300. As the shades of night settled down, the Valley Army saw no evidence of victory, and were barely able to hold their position. Pope was emboldened; and in the night planned for a general advance from every point at break of day. He was reckless in his conception of the situation, and was ignorant of the positions of many of his columns, and equally so of Jackson's strategy; which was to draw all the fire in his direction, and thus give time for Longstreet to work his way through Thoroughfare Gap, which he did by scaling the mountain on both sides, and struck Rickett on both flanks, compelling him to leave the Gap and field entirely clear. Pope's orders all went astray; and receiving no information from his division commanders, his whole army was left without a head on the morning of the 29th. King had disappeared from Jackson's front. Genl. Lee failed to receive word of the true situation when night closed down on the battle field of the 28th, for he knew that three distinct fields were well marked:—Jackson at Groveton, Longstreet at the Gap, and A. P. Hill holding out against Siegel. It has been said that when Lee and Jackson had their first interview after the battle of the 29th, both expressed satisfaction that their plans had not been changed, and on the morrow the world would be astonished at the results. Be this true or otherwise, the 29th *has* been remembered by survivors of those terrors, as one of such horror, that doubt has often arisen whether the first day's victory of the Second Manassas justified the carnage suffered by the entire command. The old Valley Army had been used in several counter-strokes that saved the day; but many of their veteran comrades lay stark and stiff on hard-fought lines that had shifted to the old Manassas field. No bugle could call them to their bivouac circles now. Genl. Lee with Longstreet's Corps, lay off to the left, observing the scene, until in the afternoon, when the latter sent two of his brigades to reconnoitre; but they were not in the battle. Both armies were content to take night for recuperation, each holding the positions gained at nightfall. The 30th revealed to Genl. Lee, who was now on the ground with reins in hand, what led him to believe that McClellan's heavy reinforcements had arrived during the night; and Pope was strengthening his positions. The scene that morning was impressive to the bravest men. Yonder over ridges and vales was a great host numbering full 65,000 men and about 30 splendid batteries, with reinforcements at no great distance, pressing forward. On the Confederate side was scarcely 50,000; but all were heroes, and guided by such men as Lee, Jackson and others, they felt they were invincible, and that this day must forever reveal to the world the possibilities of an army of patriots battling for a sacred principle under the guiding hand of born leaders. On the other hand, brave men fighting desperately to subjugate one section of their common country, to preserve a union of States. The difference may appear to the student of the great questions involved; and he may comprehend the Confederate soldier's tenacious efforts, and learn why he fought for the cause that was finally lost. Some ascribe the numerous victories lost by the Federals, to deficiencies in their commanders—lack of skill and genius.

The forenoon of the 30th was oppressive in its stillness. Two great armies were in full battle array, but neither seemed disposed to reopen the deadly engagement the previous night had closed. Pope's official dispatches to Washington during the morning, show his ignorance of the entire field over which his imagination ran. He was unaware that Jackson was lying in wait for the first advance, and totally at sea as to several of his own splendid brigades. He had fixed his plan to follow Jackson's retreating army, to overtake and destroy it—not knowing that Lee's and Longstreet's corps were ready to take a hand in the game. Several of his leading division commanders, Porter, Reynolds, Ricketts, Buford, had apprised him of the presence of Confederates on well chosen ground, who were stubbornly awaiting attack, and were not in retreat; but Pope disregarded all warnings, and sent a dispatch to Washington—"August 30th, 1862, high noon—Headquarters in the Saddle, Manassas Plains, Va. A forward movement of the entire army is now being executed, and the retreating enemy will be pressed vigorously." As our effort is chiefly to follow the Valley Army, and not give details of the great battle, we will turn to Jackson and his Valley Army. which had been concealed in the strip of woodland near Groveton village, a position he had evidently chosen, to meet what he supposed would be an advance by Pope to overtake the retreating Confederates. This seems to have been the scheme that he suggested to Genl. Lee:—that possibly, the Federals being now broken into scattered columns, he with Longstreet near, might crush them in detail. Genl. Jackson in his report says it was 12:30 when he saw a large force of about 20,000 on his front, extending their line to within a half mile of Bull Run, while in the rear over the ridges was a force in his estimate of 35,000, with batteries taking positions in the imposing line. Pope no doubt was sincere in his conception of the situation, and felt assured that the crushing blow was now being dealt. If his position was such as some writers have given him, which was high ground near the celebrated stone house, he could readily see how the crushing blow was dealt. Three of his columns were in swift motion, one entering the Groveton woodland, one rushing along Bull Run, and Porter's corps in two columns, endeavoring to get the high ground "and sweep the field of retreating Rebels,"—when suddenly the signal for attack was sounded along the Confederate lines up and over the ridges near the railroad; and then the master mind of Jackson shone out why he had hugged that woodland so silently, and his old Valley army caught the spirit of their leader, and burst forth with terrific yells. Securing the natural defences, they opened such a destructive fire into flank and face of the unconscious foe, that a panic was imminent. But the Federals soon rallied and formed; and if a great Captain had been present with them, the Confederate stories of this battle would have a sad shading. Many an old soldier remembers when Genl. Porter wheeled his Division into three battle lines and marched across the flat land with perfect military precision, not firing a gun though under heavy fire, until when within a few hundred steps, one line rushed upon Jackson's right, and opened fire deliberately; pressing on, repeated their fire with every forward step. Then it was that the Valley men got in one of their telling cross-fires that virtually swept the field. Natural breastworks protected the old Stonewall men, but many of them were laid low. The author spent much effort to discover who of the Federals made this desperate charge, and can only say that Genl. Morrell was in command; but what regiments he commanded, and who any of the regimental leaders were who gallantly rode with their lines to be swept to death, he has nothing to give; but will add that old survivors of the Valley Army often speak of the brave men who charged their lines that day, and of one officer who rode over their breastworks, when horse and rider went down 'ere he could be rescued from the galling fire; and hundreds of Confederates who witnessed the feat, would gladly have saved his life. Frequently deadly assaults were made along the Jackson lines, but were repulsed with great loss. It was on this line the Confederates used stones at close quarters, to save ammunition, which was rapidly reduced. The whole of Lee's army was now engaged in striking the Federal columns in detail, thus enabled to throw superior numbers against the weaker Federal column, while Pope stood afar off, watching the breaks in his lines, whereas if he had marched out that morning in more solid phalanx, he possibly would have held sway over the entire field, frustrated the plans of Lee, and ended the day with a dispatch to Washington that he had met and overcome Lee and all his hosts. But the fates had decreed otherwise, and Lee seemed chosen to execute the decree. Jackson and his Valley Army resisted all attacks from their strong position, with infantry, supported by several batteries well posted on the ridges in the rear; and finally Fitz John Porter went staggering back fully defeated. Orders went along the lines in every direction from General Lee, for the whole army to advance. The old warriors, Jackson, Longstreet and Hill had already taken in the situation, and were making their forward movement when the orders were received. It is related by survivors of both armies, that the intense excitement of the Confederates in that solid forward movement upon the broken ranks of Pope's Army, is well remembered. The lines swept on, and Pope's great army was beaten, but not routed, as some have written. When night closed the struggle, the Confederates were victors, but the Federals held the "Henry Hill," which was a strong key to the situation. But Pope was fairly beaten, and *retired* to Centreville, 4 miles distant, during the night, leaving the battlefield strewn with his dead and wounded. Pope's official dispatches to Washington still snapped of spirit and bravado; and boasted that having fought Lee's entire army throughout the day, he was in a strong position, and when Franklin and Sumner with 20,000 fresh troops, were in position during the night, "the morrow would witness Lee's complete overthrow." Strange commentary! The morrow witnessed Lee's overthrow of Pope's magnificent army. The day's battle had closed with intense darkness and torrents of rain—the whole face of the country deluged with water—the heavens full of every element of the most terrific storm that ever lowered over a battlefield. Both armies were compelled to await the morrow's dawn, to learn fully their peculiar situation; when we find Jackson and his Valley Army had swung around by the Sudley ford of Bull Run, and was 10 miles in Pope's rear, preparing for one of his counter-strokes. Pope learned during that fearful night that Lee was not beaten; his own army had found cover in the ample earthworks around Centreville, never supposing that Lee would decline a front attack, and would prefer to use his strategy by threatening his rear. If he were the Great Captain he so frequently boasted being, why, it may be asked, did he not divine Jackson's plan to pass around at some point and embarrass him in his fortified position? Pope was fully satisfied by 1 P. M., that Jackson was hurrying down Little River Turnpike. He then saw he must evacuate Centreville; and fell back of Fairfax C. H. Jackson with Hill and Stuart were on the Turnpike, and landed on Pope's flank, resulting in a two hours battle late in the afternoon. The Federals in fighting mood, handled by Genl. Reno, finally gave way with heavy loss; but they had changed Jackson's plans, and with the night and a heavy storm, the battle was called off. This engagement was called the Battle of Chantilly. Old veterans will recall the day and the place.

The 2nd of September brought Pope to a standstill; and he was forced to acknowledge his helplessness, and after stating his situation to the Washington authorities, was instructed to fall back, as he requested, to the fortifications at Washington and Alexandria. Pope was beaten and unstrung. He soon hurried away to shelter, although he had full 80,000 men, including the reinforcements arriving every hour. He allowed himself to be driven from his chosen positions by an army that did not exceed 55,000 men of all arms during the entire campaign. O. R. Federal, show that Pope lost 7,000 as prisoners, 13,500 killed and wounded, 30 pieces of artillery, 20,000 Enfield rifles, and army supplies that could not be estimated in quantity or value.

The Confederates could not accomplish such wonders without great loss; and their O. R. fix the total at 10,000 officers and men. Genl. Lee's official report says: "It was found that the enemy had conducted his retreat so rapidly, that the attempt to interfere with him was abandoned, the proximity of the fortifications around Alexandria and Washington rendering further pursuit useless." We may properly add this ended Pope's connection with the War. Genl. McClellan assumed command of the army and defences. Pope was sent to the frontier to play with Indian forays, where he had ample opportunities to review his failures, the unsurpassed strategy of Lee, and the maneuvres of Jackson.

War critics have written fully of this historic campaign, and some are inclined to attribute Jackson's success to chance; but when the shadows are cast aside, good reason is given why Jackson chose so many perilous positions—isolating his command from the main army—that seemed hazardous. Such were parts of the great plan studied out before he turned the head of his column towards the mountains. Lee's object was not only to defeat Pope by fighting Federal columns in detail, but to turn McClellan from the James, where he was banging on the gates of Richmond, and compel him to rush to the Potomac in front of Washington. The reader will see from this outline, how completely Lee accomplished his object, for he sees Pope beaten and relieved of his command, and McClellan and his mighty host making a grand stand to save the capital. Many startling events since the early Spring have been briefly stated in these pages. We must now follow the Valley Army. President Davis, as a result of the Summer's mighty work, consented to invasion—a step that, according to his opinions and desires of the fighting Southrons, should have been taken in the early Summer, 'ere the flower of the Army of Northern Virginia had been withered. Mr. Davis had delayed too long. The army on this memorable 2nd of September, 1862, was enfeebled by terrific losses. At this day we can name hundreds of gallant leaders and thousands of the bravest of the brave who had gone down in many battlefields, stretching from the mountains to the sea. Genl. Jackson and his Valley Army was chosen to take the head and form the advance guard of the army of invasion. This he urged during the previous Summer, when the prospect for success was clearer than it now appeared to this old warrior. But many remember how eagerly he set his army in motion, and remember too well how the men began to straggle to seek their homes that had been within the lines of the enemy so long. They hoped to see the loved ones, gather some needed outfit and overtake the army before the Potomac was reached. The whole army needed shoes, clothing, and a chance to recuperate; but the situation required prompt action; and it must be recorded here by one who witnessed the forward movement, that the rank and file were in sore straits, and lacked the vigor and strength that an invading army must have to bring success. However, Old Stonewall and his depleted divisions struck out for Leesburg, where on the 5th they rested a full day, while D. H. Hill's Division was transferred to the front. On the 6th Jackson, now forming the rear guard, crossed the Potomac at White's Ford. When once on the Maryland side, Jackson pressed forward, and bivouacked around Frederick City. The Marylanders were either stilled by surprise or awed by fear. They kept aloof and failed to exhibit their feelings. Many of the noble women, however, were profuse in their warm greetings, but recruits came neither from town or farm; and it was soon discovered that a majority of the men did not desire the presence of the ragged Southrons. The Frederick people were generous, and gave of their abundance, which went far towards resuscitating the tired army. While this was grateful to the troops, they well knew they had come for work. It was also soon discovered that the lower end of the Valley was occupied by Federals. Genl. Lee's reports fix the force at Winchester at 3,000, Martinsburg 3,000, and Harpers Ferry at 8,000; and there was every indication that Harpers Ferry was to hold out for reinforcements. The force at Winchester commanded by Genl. White, abandoned that place on the 2nd of September, after firing numerous buildings near the old W. & P. R. R. depot. Some contained army supplies. The magazine was blown up. White hurried away, and was found at Harpers Ferry. The force at Martinsburg was driven into the net at Harpers Ferry. Jackson and Hill were started on the 10th with a large force, 25,000 to scoop up the Valley points. Eagerly they plunged forward, leaving about an equal number of troops to contend with any attacks made by McClellan. Several writers on this campaign say that Genl. Longstreet and several other generals, opposed this division of the army in the enemy's country; but Lee seemed so well acquainted with McClellan's mode of warfare, that he tried to assure his generals that McClellan would be slow and cautious as usual, and there need be no fear. When Jackson started for Harpers Ferry, Lee moved to Hagerstown. Jackson and Hill marched 14 miles; halted for the night near the village of Boonesboro. Next morning they moved in two lines for Martinsburg, Jackson via Williamsport and Hill by the direct road. On the 12th, Martinsburg was invested, and the Federals there decamped for Harpers Ferry. The Confederates received ovations in Martinsburg that cheered them for their unfinished work. Jackson hurried away in the afternoon, and halted on historic Opecquon. On the 13th he hurried around to Halltown and halted just North of the village, where a solid line of pickets and sharpshooters were thrown out to connect with other Confederate positions, for the old ferry was completely surrounded before the commanding officer was aware that he had anything but detachments of cavalry to contend with. Sunday morning, Sept. 14th, found the Confederates in position as follows: Jackson in front and to the West of Bolivar, McLaws on Maryland Heights, Genl. Jos. G. Walker on Loudoun Heights, Genl. A. P. Hill on the Shenandoah River. All had received the following orders by 11 o'clock:

"Headquarters, Valley Dist.
"Sept. 14, 1862.

"1. Today Maj. Genl. McLaws will attack so as to sweep with his artillery the ground occupied by the enemy, take his batteries in reverse, and otherwise operate against him as circumstances may justify.

"2. Brigadier Genl. Walker will take in reverse the battery on the turnpike, and sweep with his artillery the ground occupied by the enemy, and silence the batteries on the island of the Shenandoah should he find a battery there.

"3. Maj. Genl. A. P. Hill will move along the left bank of the Shenandoah and thus turn the enemy's left flank and enter Harpers Ferry.

"4. Brigadier Genl. Lawton will move along the turnpike for the purpose of supporting Genl.

Hill, and otherwise operating against the enemy to the left of Genl. Hill.

"5. Brig. Genl. Jones will with one of his brigades and a battery of artillery, make a demonstration against the enemy's right; the remaining part of this division will constitute the reserve and move along the turnpike.

By order of Major General Jackson.

Wm. L. Jackson,
Acting Asst. Adjt. Genl."

The author was requested to supply information concerning the capture of Harpers Ferry, so that the positions could be better understood; and is pleased to give copies from the original orders found in Confederate Official Reports and from these reports comes answer to the question frequently asked: Why did the Christian soldier Stonewall Jackson open fire on the helpless civilians before demanding surrender? He says that "during early morning a dispatch from McLaws stated that McClellan had threatened the rear and he had sent three detachments to detour in the rear." This accounts for the cannonading heard in the early morning far to the northward, and this was near Genl. Lee's position; so there was no time to be lost. The work in hand must be disposed of, so this army could go to his relief. Orders were given to open fire on the *enemy's works*, and not on the village, as has been so often stated, though during the afternoon of Sunday, some shells demolished several buildings occupied by Federals. The cordon tightened hourly, and the heavy garrison was doomed. When night closed, the Federals had hopes that Little Mack would send promised relief. The next morning, the 15th, found both armies ready for battle. The Federals handled their artillery handsomely, but it availed them but a short respite, for as Jackson closed in, he gave the word for quick work; and every gunner sprang to his place. For one hour every Confederate battery poured the bursting shells upon front, flank and rear of the Federals. There were brave men who stood by their guns that morning, but nothing could hold out against the network of destruction that had been so adroitly woven around their position. Hill's infantry was ready to charge in conjunction with Walker. But when the river breeze had swept away the smoke and mist, a white flag had taken the place of the Starspangled Banner that had withstood shot and shell for twenty hours. The work was done, and the infantry failed to get in their counterstrokes. The Federals proposed surrender, and turned over their entire army, except the Cavalry that had escaped in the darkness—12,520 prisoners, 13,000 muskets, 73 pieces of artillery, and nearly three hundred wagons. Genl. White of Winchester fame, was in command, he having taken rank over Genl. Miles who had held Harpers Ferry for several months, feeling safe.

The author has talked with Federal soldiers who stated "they were surrendered at Harpers Ferry, and Saw Genl. Jackson ride along the streets that morning," and expressed great pleasure that they could say that they had seen Stonewall Jackson.

Genl. Jackson immediately notified Genl. Lee of the capture, and was ready to receive further orders; that Genl. Hill would dispose of the prisoners, captured arms, etc. Genl. Longstreet, in his interesting account of the Maryland Campaign, says that "Genl. Lee was forced back from his position at South Mountain to Sharpsburg, and that late in the afternoon, Jackson, Walker and McLaws were ordered to rejoin without further delay." And thus the terrific Sharpsburg battle was initiated; and since Genl. Longstreet has criticized Jackson for not moving sooner from Harpers Ferry and attacking McClellan East of South Mountain and shocking his rear, thus giving him time to get into position,—Jackson's old soldiers have often asked why Longstreet did not join D. H. Hill earlier in the day! In Battles and Leaders, (Vol. II, p. 666,) we have this criticism by a writer who was amply supplied by observation, while on the same field: "The order for the march had been given the night before, and there seems to have been no good reason, even admitting the heat and dust, that Longstreet's command should not have joined Hill at Noon. The troops marched at daylight (5 A. M.), and took ten hours to march 13 miles; and owing to their late arrival, only four brigades took part in a very disjointed fashion." We may add that this was not the first time that Longstreet was too slow. We will not discuss these points, but hastily follow the Valley Army from Harpers Ferry. We find Jackson once more with Lee on the 16th, anxious to execute any plan. Lee's army, now reduced to 45,000 men (O. R.) were pitted against McClellan's 90,000. The night of the 16th, lines were completed; positions fixed; and the great Federal host made ready for the morrow. The Confederates knew that they were outnumbered, but not outgeneraled; and though the odds were against them, the brave men slept through the night, and hoped to be in line for the terrible conflict that hung over their way. Hooker and Mansfield with their two corps, First and Twelfth, had crossed the Antietam, and were in powerful battle lines facing South, on the North of Sharpsburg, hidden from Jackson's left by a dense forest. On the 17th, before sunrise, Hooker's pickets appeared along the line protected by woodland, with infantry pressing forward. Jackson was apprised of an early attack and was already prepared to receive them. Hooker's leading generals were tried men, like Meade, Doubleday, Ricketts and others, with their veteran troops. Had McClellan seized this opportunity and entered the wave of battle in spirit equal to that exhibited by his subalterns, Jackson's corps would have been demolished. As it was, the losses were heavy, and the Confederate line was barely maintained. Hooker in his official report says: "Over thirty acres of corn was cut as close by the bullets as if it had been reaped by the sickle, and the dead lay piled in regular ranks along the whole Confederate front." Genl. Jones in command of the Valley troops, fell in this action and was carried from the field. The gallant and intrepid Genl. Starke assumed command, and led the old Valley Army once more into the plain. The onslaught between Federal and Confederate battle lines is beyond description. The old regiments led by the dauntless Starke, checked the advance of Hooker, and then rushed upon Doubleday's Division now exposed, and struck a stunning blow both to his front and flank, causing the Federals to turn in great confusion. In this last charge Genl. Starke was killed. Stuart with his cavalry was doing good service, using his artillery on Doubleday's flank, distracting his attention, and compelling several detachments to leave Jackson's front and protect the Federal flank from Stuart's threatened advance. Doubleday was forced to fall back on new lines. It was about 8 A. M. when Hooker realized that his well laid plan had been demolished by Jackson, and acknowledged a repulse that compelled a cessation of battle. The Valley Army was badly shattered; and Jones' and Lawton's Divisions which had withstood the brunt of the three hours storm, could not reasonably expect to hold out against a renewal of attack. Jackson's official report says: The troops actually engaged in the two divisions numbering 4,200 infantry at the opening attack, lost 1,700 of their number, every brigade and regiment having lost their commanders who led the charge; the remnant of the two hard-fought divisions who had again elicited admiration for their unfaltering courage and fearful blow dealt Hooker's avalanche of Western men, were not left alone in their perilous position. Early's Brigade was soon hurried across fields to the woodland. Hood was up now with his 1,800 Texans to support Lawton; part of D. H. Hill's division also came up. Hooker was also receiving reinforcements. Mansfield's corps of 8,500 were rapidly taking position to support Hooker. The battle opened again in deadly style, with fearful loss to both sides. Jackson's front was broken, and new lines were formed. But according to official reports, the Federals paid dearly for what they had won. The celebrated Hooker Corps, (1st) had been handled by Jones and Lawton, who had literally cut it to pieces. The field was covered by their slain, exceeding by vast numbers the heroes in tattered gray who also sank in the terrible carnage and lay on the same ground, in hundreds of instances touching elbows with their gallant foemen—all noble sacrifices for their chosen principles. This battle told heavily on both sides. Many homes were saddened both North and South, for be it known none but American heroes were strewn on that plain. No hireling soldiery on that field. The Federal loss was 2,500 officers and men left on the field; and stragglers by thousands were seen rushing towards Antietam Creek. Genl. Hooker was severely wounded; and Mansfield's 12th Corps, while not defeated, suffered a loss of 1,500 men, and were unable to move forward, while he, an old grizzled hero of many hot engagements, went down mortally wounded. While there was a lull in the infantry attacks, the artillery never ceased firing; and old artillery men serving on that day with the contending batteries, have given the author thrilling accounts of the great duel. Full three hundred guns kept up incessant roar, and the experiences of that afternoon can never be forgotten. The artillerists in both armies were in constant and fearful conflict, and the result must have seemed to be the destruction of both armies. When the smoke had cleared, the field presented the scene of conflict, for lying on the ground were thousands of dead and wounded. It appeared that during the lull of infantry firing, McClellan had hurried reinforcements to aid Hooker. Jackson who had occupied a position which enabled him to survey the whole field, divined McClellan's plans, and he was prepared to meet the army that he believed would come in on his flank. He had notified Genl. Lee and asked for reinforcements to move to certain points, under Walker, McLaws, Anderson and Early, and he would further instruct them to fall upon the flank of the new army that he believed would pass a certain point. General Lee answered promptly, and urged each general to press forward. Sedgewick with a splendid corps, was observed bearing down upon Jackson's weak front and flank; when suddenly Walker and McLaws *double-quicked* through a woodland, striking Sedgewick's flank. Early at that moment with his fresh troops appeared, and with the vigor usual to this famous command, plunged into the thickest of the fight. Jackson from his position, saw his plans fully executed, and remarked to one of his aides that a Federal rout would occur. Federal official reports show that Sedgewick lost 2,000 killed and wounded within eight minutes. Jackson's official report says: "Sedgewick's Division was defeated and driven from the field in confusion; and when a Brigade was sent from the 12th Federal Corps to support Sedgewick, McLaws met and overwhelmed the reinforcements, and this cleared the field of all save dead and wounded." The Confederates jubilant over their victory, were soon called upon to meet fresh troops that McClellan was rushing to strong positions to save his army. The First and Twelfth Corps were completely disabled, and no more appeared in line that day. But Meade and his Pennsylvania Reserve Corps was coming into action, and supported by the Veteran Sixth Corps, with over 100 guns, was a formidable army to engage troops that had borne the storm of the entire day; for A. P. Hill had not yet arrived, and there were no new troops to send to meet the fresh Federals. At 1 P. M., the Confederates hastened to new positions. The Federals were supported by artillery that never ceased to fill the air with screaming shells and crashing timber; the cavalry of both armies were skirmishing on all exposed flanks, and possibly every available man in both armies had been engaged in the hottest strife for more than 7 hours. The Dunkard Church, Roulette Farm, Piper House, Bowman's Woods, Sunken Road and Bloody Lane, West Wood, The Corn Field, Antietam Creek and Heights, are places that can never be forgotten by the survivors of that terrible day; and only the veterans of the contending armies could ever appreciate the slaughter and deeds of valor wasted on the battlefield of Sharpsburg Sept. 17, 1862. The afternoon was spent in maneuvres. Genl. J. E. B. Stuart called for reinforcements to aid him to turn the Federal right wing, which was swinging around toward the Potomac. Jackson started the Valley Army, and gave orders for other troops to move in same direction. But by 4 o'clock, Stuart was compelled to give way, and thus McClellan's right rested on the Potomac. Stuart declined a general engagement, and night settled down upon both armies—the tired survivors sleeping restfully, as only worn-out soldiers can. 21,000 dead and wounded were lying on the nearby fields. Whole regiments were entirely wiped out. The Virginia regiments suffered beyond recognition; but as the groups were found the next morning, they had place under other commanders, and answered the call to duty once more. The reorganized forces waited patiently all through the day (18th), expecting an engagement; but McClellan was inactive. Genl. Lee devised several plans to attack the Federals on their right, but was discouraged by Genls. Jackson, Stuart and others. Genl. Jackson and Col. Stephen D. Lee commanding the Artillery division, at the request of Genl. Lee, had reconnoitred that formidable *right,* and found evidences of the terrific struggle Genl. Stuart and his cavalry had experienced the day before in their effort to prevent Hooker and the 12th corps reforming there after the battle. Dead and disabled horses, caissons and guns were on every hand, but the gallant riders had been compelled to give way; and Genl. Jackson reported that it would be unwise to make any effort to force that right. Genl. Lee then decided to recross the Potomac that night. All day, however, Lee from several positions challenged McClellan to reopen battle; but at no time did the Federals show any disposition to attack, preferring to await reinforcements that were hourly arriving. Couch's division of veterans from the vicinity of Harpers Ferry, no longer needed there, Genl. Humphrey's division from Frederick City—all fresh troops—were hastily forming on the Antietam; and the Pennsylvania militia were coming from every point in the State to resist the further march of Lee. Looking at the situation to-day, from many positions, in company with both Federal and Confederate officers, the opinion expressed to the author was "That McClellan should have rushed upon Lee on the 18th, and crippled him to such an extent that he could not have possibly recrossed the Potomac except in a disorganized condition;" and further, "if Genl. Lee on the 18th could have mustered such an army as he had before it was so badly decimated by the battle of the previous day, that nothing could have withstood his attack on McClellan's right, the front would have given way and a veritable rout ensued." As it was, we find McClellan inactive and actually allowing Genl. Lee to change his base and transfer his army, trains and all, over the Potomac near Shepherdstown, without the slightest interruption. The Federals certainly could not have been ignorant of this. Their front and both flanks must have been aware of a change, and doubtless gave Genl. Lee credit for some new strategem; and were surprised on the 19th to find that he had not appeared elsewhere—then safely seated on the South bank of the Potomac, with every wagon, gun and soldier, except the wounded who had been left in Sharpsburg carefully cared for and a few stragglers. Jackson and the remnant of the Valley Army forming the rear guard, crossed the river about 9 o'clock that morning. Stuart's cavalry skirmish line later in the day were driven in, and then, his division retiring under heavy fire, still threatened McClellan's flank and even rear. That gallant Stuart and his brave riders were fighting on an abandoned line, for he had not yet received orders from Genl. Lee to fall back and cross the river at Williamsport 15 miles above; consequently he was ignorant of Lee's situation, when late in the evening several Federal brigades crossed the river and made a desperate attack on what they now believed a retreating foe. The Confederates had carelessly disposed their commands for bivouac and rest after their night's work, and the rear guard was surprised and driven from their position, losing four guns. Genl. Pendleton then in command of the rear guard, apprised Genl. Lee of the situation, who at once ordered Jackson to take charge. This was about 1 o'clock at night. The messenger found Genl. Jackson in his saddle and far to the front, giving orders for A. P. Hill and Early (who had succeeded Lawton) to march from their camp near Martinsburg and proceed to Shepherdstown and clear the South side. On the morning of the 20th, the Federals were driven back and the forward movement checked. The Federal artillery from the opposite side of the river shelled the advancing Confederates under Hill. Soon, however, the Federals were driven over the bluffs and hastily returned to their main line, suffering some loss. The Confederate loss was less than 300 in killed and wounded; but the loss they sustained by this vigorous check was great; for had the Federals poured their hosts across the river and rushed upon the scattered camps of Confederates, the story of Lee's change of base might have been sadly different. But McClellan was deceiving himself again—over-estimating Genl. Lee's strength,—and failed to discover the careless camps of the Confederates. He also was annoyed by the unceasing encounters from Genl. Stuart on the lines of his rear, which led him to believe that Genl. Lee had some counter stroke in store for him. For in his official reports, he complains that his cavalry rendered very little service, and failed to discover Lee's retreat and misconstrued Stuart's movements. They reported that a heavy force threatened his rear. Thus it appears that the cavalry handled by Stuart and his famous subalterns, prevented McClellan's pursuit of Lee. On the evening of the 21st of September, Stuart sent the *Laurel Brigade,* composed of the 6th, 7th, 11th and 12th regiments, and White's battalion, to give the great Northern army his parting salute, which was accomplished by a brilliant charge on the enemy's flank, bringing away prisoners and horses, without the loss of a man. The gallant warrior, with his long black plume hanging over his shoulder, rode gallantly away, across the Potomac, and fell in on the rear of the Army of Northern Virginia, thus ending a series of battles embracing six months of the Spring and Summer of memorable 1862. The great armies having changed their positions from the country near Richmond to the country overlooking Washington City; the Summer campaign closing on the North bank of the Potomac within thirty miles of the fortifications of the Capital. The outlines of the movements of Jackson and the Valley Army thus briefly given, has required more space than was contemplated by the author; but he had been importuned by many veterans and their descendants to outline if possible the movements of the Valley men; and the foregoing may interest many readers to search the sources of information referred to, and obtain much that not only relates to individual divisions, brigades, regiments and companies, but to individual deeds of valor rendered by the heroes in gray or blue, that may be dear to the reader of these pages, long after the actors in that great campaign have answered the last reville.

The following statement is subjoined for easy reference, to show what Confederate troops were engaged in the battle at Sharpsburg (or Antietam,) and losses. This has been taken from the official reports:

General Jones Division, 1,800

	Loss
The Stonewall Brigade 260	88
Taliaferro's Brigade	173
Starke's Brigade	287
Jones' Brigade	152
	700

General Ewell's Division, 3,600

	Loss.
Lawton's Brigade, 1,180	569
Early's Brigade, 1,240	204
Trimble's Brigade, 740	237
Hays' Brigade, 550	336
	1,346

A. P. Hill's Division, 3,000

	Loss.
Branch's Brigade	104
Gregg's Brigade	165
Archer's Brigade	105
Pender's Brigade	30
Field's Brigade (not engaged)	
Thomas's Brigade (at Harpers Ferry)	
Artillery	67
	472

Genl. D. H. Hill's Division, 3,500

	Reported Loss.
Rodes' Brigade	203
Anderson's Brigade	302
	Estimated Loss.
Garland's Brigade	300
Ripley's Brigade	300
Colquitt's Brigade	300
	1,405

Genl. McLaw's Division, 4,500

	Estimated Loss.
Kershaw's Brigade	355
Cobbs' Brigade	156
Barksdale's Brigade	294
Semme's Brigade	314
	1,119

Semme's four regiments engaged in Jackson's counterstroke, reported percentage of losses as follows: 53rd Ga., 30 p. c.; 32nd Va., 45 p. c.; 10th Ga., 57 p. c.; 15th Va., 58 p. c.; (Henderson, Vol. II, pp. 371, etc.)

FIRST CORPS—LONGSTREET

Genl. D. R. Jones' Division, 3,500

	Estimated Loss.
Toombs' Brigade	125
Drayton's Brigade	400
Kemper's Brigade	120
	O. R. Estimated Loss
Anderson's Brigade	87
Garnett's Brigade	99
Jenkins' Brigade	210
	1,041

Genl. Walker's Division, 3,500

	O. R. Loss
Walker's Brigade	825
Ransom's Brigade	187
	1,012

Genl. Hood's Division, 2,250

	O. R Loss.
Laws' Brigade	454
Hood's Old Brigade	548
Evans' Brigade, 250	200
	1,202

Genl. R. H. Anderson's Division, 3,500

	O. R. Loss
Featherston's Brigade	304
Mahone's Brigade	76
Bruor's Brigade	182
Armstead's Brigade	35
Wright's Brigade	203
Wilcox's Brigade	221
	1,021

Artillery

	O. R. Loss
Col. S. D. Lee's Battalion	85
Washington's Artillery (N. Orleans)	34
	Estimated Loss
Cavalry	143
	262
Total Conf. loss, killed and wounded	9,566

ARMY POTOMAC—FEDERAL ARMY

(McClellan)

	O. R. Loss
First Corps, Hooker	2,590
Second Corps, Sumner	5,138
Fifth Corps, Porter	109
Sixth Corps, Franklin	439
Ninth Corps, Burnside	2,349
Twelfth Corps, Mansfield	1,746
Cavalry Division, Etc.	39
Total Federal killed and wounded	12,401

Genl. McClellan in his official reports of the recent campaign, complains bitterly of his depleted ranks; and insists that he must be allowed time for reorganization; that his supply trains were badly crippled, and that every arm of the service required recuperation and rest; and believed it wise to allow the army to enjoy rest after the arduous campaign from the Peninsula to South Mountain, where they had *won brilliant victories, but with great loss.* This extract from his correspondence with President Lincoln, indicates the condition of himself and his army. He says on the 27th: "The Army is not now in a condition to undertake another campaign nor to *bring on another battle* unless great advantages are offered by some mistake of the enemy, or pressing military exigencies render it necessary." This shows plainly that he was expecting Genl. Lee to renew his invasion. He therefore was content to remain on the North side of the Potomac, sending an occasional cavalry scout to the South side, to ascertain Lee's intentions. The vigilant Stuart with his dashing horsemen, filled them with such dismay, that they hurried back to inform McClellan that Lee was gathering his strength for a vigorous movement. How strange this appears to the student of this fierce campaign; for he will discover that Genl. Lee was endeavoring to reorganize his army in camps from Winchester to Bunker's Hill, struggling to bring back his stragglers who were swarming by thousands through the Lower Valley, seeking old homes, to relate the trials through which all had passed. Thousands of their comrades had been left dead or dying on the slaughter fields from Malvern Hill to Sharpsburg; and the dispirited and broken-hearted survivors desired to tell their story to some sympathetic ear. These stragglers were not deserters. They knew as well as Genl. Lee that they had inflicted a blow to McClellan; that he would not likely cross the river to renew battle; they knew the spirit of the army they had vanquished; they knew that thousands of the Federals had broken ranks and fled, and that both armies had endured too much to make battle probable. We find Genl. Lee complaining to President Davis in his letter of the 25th of September, of the temper and spirit of his army, and that stragglers were everywhere, including officers. Every arm of the service seriously affected, and that he had established a system to arrest them and return them to camp. Genl. Jones had been sent to Winchester with about 300 cavalry to execute the order. The reader will bear in mind that this straggling extended from Leesburg to North Mountain, a territory too great to cover with small provost guards. We find, however, in Genl. Jones' report to Genl. Lee that he had sent back to their commands about 6,000 men within five days. The ragged but brave and loyal stragglers needed only to be reminded that Genl. Lee required them at once. Many survivors of that old provost guard,—the author being one, recalls with pleasure, how cheerfully these stragglers received their notices, and how promptly they responded and reported to their commands; and in none but a few flagrant cases, were men treated as deserters. Poor fellows! the temptation was irresistible. With the old firesides and loved ones to listen to the fate of their boy left on some far-away plain,—the last good bye to the aged and helpless, and the other adieus—too tender to mention and only told by wistful glances from sad-eyed maiden, as she watched her ragged soldier disappear over the copse in the direction of the bivouacs of the Old Stonewall Brigade.

The author dare not state here that the invasion was a mistake; for many military critics have regarded this as a master-stroke of General Lee and his great lieutenants. But it must be said, though the Sharpsburg-Antietam battles were won by the Confederates with great loss of life, the *morale* of the Army of Northern Virginia had suffered fearfully; and if the Army of the Potomac had not suffered to a greater extent in this respect, Genl. McClellan could have forced his way into the Lower Valley, and given Genl. Lee such an encounter as would possibly have shattered his entire army.

But it may be said the Confederates never felt that the blow inflicted on McClellan's army, accomplished profitable results. The army of Northern Virginia had thrown the Federals on the defensive; and for the time being, the Washington authorities were in confusion, and compelled to take up the old question how to take Richmond and save Washington. The Confederates felt, furthermore, that their last engagement was with seasoned veterans, supported by every army equipment, led by experienced and brave officers, like Hooker, Porter, Sumner and others, and with numbers far in excess of the Southern forces. They felt justly proud of the tremendous effort made to save the honor and reputation of the Army of Northern Virginia. The Little Napoleon (McClellan) was removed, and Burnside installed as Commander of the Army of the Potomac. The Confederates hailed this as part of their great victory, and felt confident that any successor to McClellan would result favorably to them. They knew McClellan had become familiar with the strategems of Lee and Jackson; and with the great army he had trained, his strength was more perceptible in every battle; and though wary and slow, he had become more active and alert; and his defeat in the campaign around South Mountain, Antietam and Sharpsburg, considering the relative strength and position of the contending armies, must go down in history, a stupendous victory for the Confederates.

Burnside prepared for a change of base, and chose the Rappahannock. The army was soon reorganized; the nearby States poured in the reinforcements urgently called for. Longstreet had been sent to Culpeper C. H. Burnside moved towards Falmouth, passing through Warrenton, arriving in the vicinity of Aquia Creek on the 17th and 18th of November. At this point his army was easily supplied by waterway transports. Jackson was left in charge of the Lower Valley, to threaten another invasion. About this time there seems to have been a mixing-up of the armies. The Federals were massing troops along the Manassas Gap Railroad, endeavoring to form a new line from the Blue Ridge to his Aquia Creek supply station. Genl. Lee found that his stragglers had once more given him a most formidable army on their return to their new commands, greatly recuperated and rested; and they cheerfully took up the arduous march. On the 17th, Longstreet sent part of his corps to Fredericksburg. Jackson had been hovering in the Valley, hoping to see his way clear to make a feint along the Potomac, to check Burnside in his headlong career along the Rappahannock. But the new commander felt impelled to strike Genl. Lee as soon as possible; and to prepare for this, Jackson was ordered to bring his army through the Blue Ridge and quietly camp at Orange C. H. The old Valley had enjoyed the presence of Genl. Jackson and the Valley Army for a full month. McClellan was content to remain on the Maryland side during all this time, recruiting his strength and courage to cross swords with Lee once more; and while thus waiting, Genl. Stuart, with Genl. Hampton, Col. Wm. E. Jones and W. H. F. Lee and about 1,200 picked men crossed the Potomac near Darkesville (Oct. 9th,) capturing pickets wherever found; marched due North through Mercersburg and Chambersburg, then swept around the rear of the Union Army, through Emmitsburg; crossed the Monocacy near Frederick City, then through Hyattstown; headed for the Potomac and crossed to the Virginia side at White ford, without the loss of a man killed, having encountered in his ride of 126 miles, many detachments of Federals who were routed and captured—wagon trains broken and destroyed, and bringing out at least 800 horses, etc. Strange to say, this command was sailing gaily around McClellan for about 60 hours, and part of the time within 30 miles of Harpers Ferry, near to which McClellan had his headquarters. The reader must not be deceived and take for granted that McClellan was ignorant of this raid. Not so; he knew of it, and rushed every horseman he could muster in pursuit, and made great efforts to head Stuart off and capture the entire force. But men were with the raiders who knew every road and path through field or forest that led to the Potomac. Genl. Stuart and his fearless riders never forgot the hardships of that famous ride. Genl. Lee received more intelligence of McClellan's position and apparent inactivity than he hoped from the adventure. It is shown in Federal official reports that the entire cavalry forces under Pleasanton and Averill were completely disabled by their forced marches. It is recorded that Averill's command rode 200 miles in four days, and Pleasanton marched 78 miles in twenty-four hours. This crippled the Federals and interfered with the forward movement. The correspondence between McClellan and Washington shows this raid caused the sudden change of commands.

Nov. 22nd, '62, Genl. Jackson had his army in motion heading South. Many sad farewells were said on that memorable day. The General, like many of the men of his Valley Army, never returned to the historic old town. Out the Valley Pike the line of march took its way, passing Kernstown, Strasburg and on to New Market; then through the Massanutton to the Luray Valley; then into Fishers Gap over the Blue Ridge, stopping at Madison C. H. on the 26th. After a day's rest, the whole corps was in camp at Orange C. H., 36 miles from Fredericksburg. Jackson reports that the army had marched 120 miles with no straggler reported. This should convince the reader that this celebrated army was composed of patriots; and the statements made in former reports, of their desertion in the close of the last campaign, were unjust and should never have been published. The old Valley Army was again in close touch with Genl. Lee. This increased Genl. Lee's strength to 78,500 officers and men of all arms, exceeding largely his numbers that fought the Maryland campaign.

Genl. Lee had already divined Burnside's intentions. He knew the pressure put upon him to do battle, and of his burning desire to show the Washington authorities that no mistake had been made by placing him in command of McClellan's splendid army, now thoroughly reorganized. This work had been accomplished by the latter before his removal. In fact, McClellan had already planned a new campaign, and had his advance columns crossing the Potomac below Harpers Ferry, when Burnside appeared and changed the whole plan. Genl. Burnside was well known to Genl. Lee and his lieutenants, and also to many of the rank and file. They knew he was a fighter, and also knew him as a blunderer. Many remembered his dismal failure when, with his splendid corps on the Federal left at Sharpsburg, he maneuvered an attack on the Confederate right, which resulted in terrific slaughter to his detached columns; and the same Burnside was now laboring to maneuvre the entire army of the Potomac along the North bank of the Rappahannock, feeling his way for an easy crossing. Genl. Lee disposed his divisions on the South side, and awaited the hour when the new commander would appear on his front for battle, believing that he could crush any force that would venture. Longstreet was on the ridges West of Fredericksburg, called

Mayre's Hill. Jackson was in control lower down the River; Early with Ewell's division was at Skinner's Neck about 12 miles below Fredericksburg;—D. H. Hill at Port Royal; A. P. Hill and Jackson's old Valley Army under Taliaferro, were in the vicinity of Guinea Station. Survivors of Stuart's cavalry may recall their first experience in fighting *gunboats*. They had been called upon to attack everything they found in their front, on land; but when Genl. Stuart called for experts with long range guns, they were sent to the water line, and from ambush they were to pick off the prominent figures on deck as the monster boats turned their prows up stream. The troops from the ridges viewed with amazement the results of this effort. The gunboats with great difficulty, changed their course, and finally drifted down stream beyond the range of the troopers' guns. Federal official reports show that these gunboats had been ordered "to appear in the river at Port Royal, and shell the Confederates on the ridges, while a crossing was effected at Skinners Neck;" but the enemy appeared in great numbers along the river, and with long-range guns, killed officers, seamen and gunners on board, the gunboats being helpless to protect themselves." Their guns could not get the range on the low grounds. Burnside wrestled with his plans for days and nights, making several efforts to cross the river, but he never abandoned his original plan, which was to bring Lee to battle before he could strengthen his army.

Dec. 12, '62, four army corps crossed the river on pontoons, led by Hooker, Sumner and Franklin. Genl. Lee concentrated his forces and waited for the crucial moment. Lord Wolseley, in the North American Review, Vol. 149, pp. 282, etc., says: "Once more the Army of Northern Virginia was concentrated at exactly the right moment on the field of battle." We find the Valley Army as usual, well up and well protected by natural formations, as likewise were the entire Confederate lines. Heavy guns opened early in the day; and at 9 A. M., the Federal battle lines were well defined. One of the survivors of that battle says: "The Army moved in three lines, with scores of batteries—full 80,000 men coming with great precision—bayonets glittering—banners waving—bands playing. The scene was one of supreme grandeur; and the mighty host seemed invincible, as they bore down on the lines in gray." Major Dabney graphically describes the opening of the battle, saying "that Stafford Heights, where the Federal reserves were posted in dense masses, sent a storm of shot and shell into the Confederate lines; and for once War unmasked its terrible proportions with a distinctness hitherto unknown in the forest-clad landscapes of America; and the plain of Fredericksburg presented a panorama that was dreadful in its grandeur." From 11 A. M. to 1 P. M. official reports show that over 400 cannon continuously poured shot and shell into the contending lines. Fredericksburg had been shelled by the Federal guns and burned. At this hour the engagement was open to all. The Federals were mostly veterans and fought tenaciously to gain and hold positions The Valley men once more were in the thickest of the fight; for at a time when Genls. Archer and Gregg had their lines broken by the division under Meade, Jackson coolly ordered Early and Taliaferro to advance with the bayonet and clear the front; and well did they do the work; for at this point where Meade, Gibbon and Birney made repeated assaults, their loss in killed and wounded was 5,000 (See O. R.) The old Stonewall Brigade was complimented by Genl. Jackson in his report, who says, the success of his corps was beyond his expectations. The entire lines of Burnside's grand army of nearly 100,000, were driven from every position. A rout ensued in many places—Burnside was beaten. Official reports show his incompetency to handle an army of such magnitude. The Southern soldiers once more beheld a beaten foe, but were unable to force the pursuit, owing to the peculiar topography of the country. Burnside sent his flag of truce, asking permission to bury his dead and care for his wounded, on the field now held by Lee, numbering 12,647, including 877 officers—all of whom had been uncared for for two days. This was on the 15th of December, when men of both armies mingled in gathering the dead and wounded. Burnside had effected a strong line near the South side of the Rappahannock, and gave evidence of his readiness to reopen battle, after the humane work was completed. While Burnside was fully defeated and begged for time to bury his dead, his army seemed invincible. The men had rallied from their rout, and seemed anxious to renew work and redeem their losses. But it has been disclosed by Federal writers, who were present and participated in the battle, that they were unwilling to risk battle with Burnside as commander; and it is related that Genl. Franklin refused at one time to move the First Corps to an attack ordered by Burnside. The commander realized the danger, and did what has been questioned by men of both armies as a violation of the truce. During the night of the 15th, before the truce had expired, he effected a most marvellous retreat; crossed the river on his six bridges; and when the morning of the 16th dawned upon the Rappahannock, his grand army had vanished, and a new army, apparently, appeared on the North side of the river, safely sheltered from Lee. But they had left a gruesome scene along the South side. For several miles, the fallen men lay scattered in groups and piles among dead and wounded horses. Guns, broken caissons, small arms—every accompaniment of an army were everywhere in profusion—old Fredericksburg in ruins, and hundreds of the wounded stowed away in the ruins for treatment. Burnside's "On to Richmond" brought tremendous slaughter and loss of life; and he was the loser.

The appendix will show what troops were engaged on both sides and their respective losses.

The Confederates prudently declined to pursue the retreating foe. We glean from the mass of official matter and correspondence, that Genl. Lee urged President Davis to allow him to invade Maryland again and keep the campaign alive before another change of leaders would be made for the Army of the Potomac; but Mr. Davis opposed such action, stating that hostilities would cease in sixty days; that the Confederacy would be recognized by foreign powers, etc. It appears now that both Mr. Davis and Genl. Lee may have been wrong in their estimate of the situation. Foreign powers, however, had come to regard the American struggle with a change of feeling, and were in no mood to interfere. They had until recently shown but little sympathy with the Northerners in their effort to save the Union from dissolution. But when Europe learned through Washington sources, that *saving the Union* was no longer the prime object to be attained, the great secret was disclosed. When Mr. Lincoln proclaimed his intention to wage war on a destructive scale—"The Rebels must be conquered," and that the slaves should be freed from the galling yoke, foreign powers were at a standstill; and Mr. Davis found before the expiration of sixty days, all hope for recognition gone; and he also discovered that thousands of Northern people were inflamed by the new order of warfare. Tens of thousands welcomed the opportunity to take part in the struggle to liberate the negro and humiliate the Southrons. This class cared nothing for a Union while slavery existed in any section. The fighting soldiery up to this period, were Union men, and fought for their love of that Union. The Abolitionists who deserted John Brown, were never of that class of Unionists;—they never felt satisfied with the mode of warfare in vogue, and clamored for their fanatical principle,—one they had cherished for years. The *freedom of the negro and annihilation of the South;* and although Mr. Lincoln kept them down for nearly two years for political reasons, not daring to do that which might offend the real Union men then in the army, yet we find he was not only willing but anxious to put in execution that which would secure sympathy in Europe, and captivate the ultra-abolitionists. It was a bold stroke; but a fearless man stood between the forces of disaffection; and he believed that his personal magnetism could control the desperate situation. The North was becoming stirred by the repeated failures to subdue the South. Great armies had been driven back along all lines; the best men of the Northland were sacrificed to save the Union, and failed to gain promised victories; and it was not surprising that mutterings of complaint stirred the people. The public press was in many cases, demanding a cessation of hostilities and to let the South go. Something must be done. Lincoln and his cabinet had been supplied with all the sinews of war. The several States had sent their quotas without a murmur—all eager to crush the rebellion by sustaining their President; but the splendid armies he had sent to the front had failed; and his policy was condemned by many who spoke in such tones, that he was compelled to resort to some change, for a few more blunders would show him a dismal failure. Lincoln was a man of courage and iron will. He has been called the "National Joker;" but he was capable of executing any measure; and we find him driven to this strait after the Sharpsburg campaign. The declaration of his purpose produced consternation everywhere. Many Northerners were affected and predicted grave disaffection in the ranks of the army. Lincoln never wavered, but hastened to put the machinery in motion; and although he had blundered again through Burnside's failure, the country recognized his desperate earnestness, and gave evidence of their willingness to try this new project. Pending this change of conditions, had General Lee carried out his plan to invade Maryland, he would have found the Army of the Potomac stronger by reinforcements constantly pouring in. It was too soon after the last terrible campaign; and approaching Winter was too forbidding, to carry any hope of success to his worn soldiers, who needed rest, and here was the opportunity. Both armies settled down for Winter quarters; and both had ample opportunity to study the proposed change in conducting the war.

But it may be argued that, had Genl. Lee headed an invading army at this critical juncture, when the Army of the Potomac was without a competent leader and while the disaffection was so apparent among the original Union men, who were ready to let the South go rather than adopt the new mode and risk of further conflict under the scheme adopted by Lincoln and his cabinet,—the discontent would have increased and an armistice might have resulted, procuring peace. Under the light of revelation, Lee's plan for invasion was sound; and Mr. Davis saw too late his error in refusing Lee the right to invade at such a critical moment. At this point it may be well to give the full text of this new policy, which must be forever regarded as unnecessary and in complete violation of the Constitution of the United States. It has been called a war measure, and therefore necessary. The Federal government had millions of men and boundless resources to subdue the South. Why then, it may be asked, did Lincoln so eagerly grasp the first safe opportunity to execute the unfinished work of John Brown, when Brown had been executed as a traitor and murderer, and his small party supposed to have gone down justly to their doom as fanatics. Brown was promised help, to place arms in the hands of the slaves and let them do the work of rapine and murder. But the negroes of that day were loyal and true to their life-long friends. Lincoln conceived his plan to do what Brown had attempted—to arm every able-bodied negro in the South, and encourage him to pillage, murder and destroy the families who had nurtured them and the generations before them; and this, too, when the white men were absent in the army, fighting to protect their homes. And it will be seen that the slave population was to be protected and aided in the hellish work that Lincoln thought they would gloat over. And thus the poor, deluded negroes were encouraged to do what the whole Northern government had failed to accomplish—subjugate and destroy the South. Orders and instructions were promulgated throughout the entire army;—officers were required to render such service necessary for the execution of this plan to liberate the slave and overrun the South.

CHAPTER LXI

(THE EMANCIPATION PROCLAMATION)

By the President of the United States of America:

A PROCLAMATION

Whereas, on the twenty-second day of September, in the year of our Lord one thousand eight hundred and sixty-two, a proclamation was issued by the President of the United States, containing, among other things, the following, to-wit:

"That on the first day of January, in the year of our Lord one thousand eight hundred and sixty-three, all persons held as slaves within any State or designated part of a State, the people whereof shall then be in rebellion against the United States, shall be then, thenceforward, and forever free; and the Executive Government of the United States, including the military and naval authority thereof, will recognize and maintain the freedom of such persons, and will do no act or acts to repress such persons, or any of them, in any efforts they may make for their actual freedom.

"That the Executive will, on the first day of January aforesaid, by proclamation, designate the States and parts of States, if any, in which the people thereof, respectively, shall then be in rebellion against the United States; and the fact that any State, or the people thereof, shall on that day be, in good faith, represented in the Congress of the United States by members chosen thereto at elections wherein a majority of the qualified voters of such State shall have participated, shall, in the absence of strong countervailing testimony, be deemed conclusive evidence that such State, and the people thereof, are not then in rebellion against the United States."

Now, therefore, I, ABRAHAM LINCOLN, President of the United States, by virtue of the power in me vested as Commander-in-Chief, of the Army and Navy of the United States in time of actual armed rebellion against the authority and government of the United States, and as a fit and necessary war measure for suppressing said rebellion, do, on this first day of January, in the year of our Lord one thousand eight hundred and sixty-three, and in accordance with my purpose so to do publicly proclaimed for the full period of one hundred days, from the day first above mentioned, order and designate as the States and parts of States wherein the people thereof respectively, are this day in rebellion against the United States, the following, to-wit:

Arkansas, Texas, Louisiana, (except the Parishes of St. Bernard, Plaquemines, Jefferson, St. John, St. Charles, St. James, Ascension, Assumption, Terrebonne, Lafourche, St. Mary, St. Martin, and Orleans, including the City of New Orleans) Mississippi, Alabama, Florida, Georgia, South Carolina, North Carolina, and Virginia, (except the forty-eight counties designated as West Virginia, and also the counties of Berkley, Accomac, Northampton, Elizabeth City, York, Princess Ann, and Norfolk, including the cities of Norfolk and Portsmouth,——— and which excepted parts are, for the present, left precisely as if this proclamation were not issued.)

And by virtue of the power, and for the purpose aforesaid, I do order and declare that all persons held as slaves within said designated States, and parts of States, are, and henceforward shall be free; and that the Executive Government of the United States, including the military and naval authorities thereof, will recognize and maintain the freedom of said persons.

And I hereby enjoin upon the people so declared to be free to abstain from all violence, unless in necessary self-defence; and I recommend to them that, in all cases when allowed, they labor faithfully for reasonable wages.

And I further declare and make known, that such persons of suitable condition, will be received into the armed service of the United States to garrison forts, positions, stations, and other places, and to man vessels of all sorts in said service.

And upon this act, sincerely believed to be an act of justice, warranted by the Constitution, upon military necessity, I invoke the considerate judgment of mankind, and the gracious favor of Almighty God.

In witness whereof, I have hereunto set my hand and caused the seal of the United States to be affixed.

Done at the City of Washington, this first day of January, in the year of our Lord one thousand eight hundred and sixty-three, and of the Independence of the United States of America the eighty-seventh.

[SEAL] ABRAHAM LINCOLN.

By the President:
William H. Seward,
Secretary of State.

This proclamation failed to appall the Southrons, as the President had hoped. On the contrary, it stimulated them to greater efforts. Every available man stood ready to avenge the wrong that was to be perpetrated. They knew desperate measures must be resisted with desperation. The negro who accepted the offer to take up arms against the South was doomed. From the Potomac to the Mississippi, negroes were urged by every measure available, to organize; and soon negro regiments were turned loose in every section, supported by Lincoln's chosen military, to pillage and destroy. The Abolition element was enthused at the prospect. Their humane President was now their idol. They hoped, and so wrote for the public press, that the down-trodden slave in breaking his shackles, would crush his owners; and that the arrogant Southrons were doomed to annihilation unless they threw down their arms and repented.

Such a monstrous crusade as thus proposed, should have no place in warfare between civilized races. The flagrant usurpation of right, and the bitter and barbarous warfare proposed by its author, has no equal in all the annals of history, unless it were some blood-thirsty monster who gratified his passion by destroying some helpless community. The names of such have received the execrations of all civilized peoples. The pertinent question may be asked by succeeding generations: Why Lincoln's name should not be associated with such usurpers? He is known to the world as the "Martyred President!" His biographers have presented him in many attractive forms; and his wonderfully interesting and complex character is well worth careful study; and the student may do what the Southern people have in great measure done long since—throw the mantle of charity over the great wrong he dealt the people he had urged to remain in the Union. To the credit of many thousands in the armies forming the circle to crush the Confederates, the brutality of the act was condemned by them. Hundreds of brave officers resigned; and but little sympathy was given by the old veterans. But the impetus given by the Abolition element, could not be stemmed.

This digression is allowable, because it must be shown as part of the Winter campaign of 1862-3. Both armies had ample time to study the new plan to subjugate the South. The Army of the Potomac chafed under their new leader, and also under the new plans; while the Confederates were preparing for whatever should appear. Some activities occurred on both sides. The cavalry, under Genl. Hampton (one brigade) raided the country as far as Occoquon, and was rewarded with captures of prisoners and supplies. This was started on the 18th of December; and the day after Christmas, Genl. Stuart reviewed his divisions of cavalry, and announced that he desired to celebrate the festive season by paying his respects to the Washington authorities and gathering in some luxuries of the season. Starting out in his usual gay style, he led 1,800 of his bold riders to the rear of the splendid army across the river, passing within twenty miles of Burnside's headquarters; then North towards Washington, stopping 15 miles from Alexandria. There he sent a telegram to the Quartermaster General in Washington, that the mules furnished Burnside's army were so indifferent, that he was unable to haul away the wagons he had captured, and desired him to furnish a better article hereafter, for he would call again. He returned to the South side via Warrenton and Culpeper. The raid was successful. Many prisoners were captured, and a large amount of army supplies were gathered for the festive season. He covered 150 miles in about 4 days. About 30 officers and men were lost by falling into Federal scouting parties. Several gallant men were killed. Genl. Stuart frequently related incidents of this march. How he had intercepted telegrams, answering same in such manner that the Federal cavalry rode their horses down on wild chases.

On the 26th of January, '63, Burnside was goaded to make a movement against Lee, which proved a failure. He was then superceded by Genl. Hooker. The two armies proceeded to make Winter quarters their chief object. Hostilities were not looked for by either side. The Rappahannock was the separating line, both sides patrolled by unbroken lines of pickets, who soon grew communicative with each other. The severe wintry weather forced the unemployed to remain in their rude huts and tents and around the camp fires. Camp life became wearisome at times, though visitors to the Confederate camps were impressed with the systematic schemes adopted by the various regimental camps to break the monotony and make pleasure and mirth, and thus minimize the plague *ennui,* which naturally exists among such hosts, settled down for a long Winter. Many interesting incidents of army life in "winter quarters" could be mentioned here from personal recollections of the author, and many more as related to him by the survivors. The Valley Army being our chief subject, it is only necessary to locate it, while waiting for the opening Spring. Genl. Jackson's Corps (2nd) was assigned to the slopes and ridges of the country overlooking the deep and silent river, with his headquarters at Moss Neck, about 10 or 11 miles East from Fredericksburg. The place occupied by the General was an old homestead owned by a rich Virginia planter named Corbin. The General preferred a large vacant building on the lawn to the sumptuous apartments offered in the mansion; and the mistress of the latter hastily and tastefully furnished the building for the use of the General and his staff This position pleased him, being in easy contact with the contested points stretching away towards Port Royal—the Valley Army in camp about 7 miles distant in the vicinity of Guinea Station. A large proportion of the officers were allowed to visit their homes on short leave; and the cavalry were seeking rest and forage far to the rear, where their wants were more easily supplied. There seemed to be a mutual understanding that hostilities should not reopen until the stern Winter had relaxed its icy grasp. The men who remained in camp took advantage of the resources of the tide-water streams, and revelled in the enjoyment of fish and oysters. The old Stonewall Brigade erected a rude log structure for public worship. The numerous chaplains made almost daily use of it during the Winter. The author hopes to mention in personal sketches some incidents that will show more fully how the camp life was endured and even enjoyed.

It was late in the Spring of 1863 before the armies showed any disposition to cast aside their lethargy; and old soldiers were speculating about peace and when all would go home. We must add at this point, that Genl. Lee's Army had been much weakened by the withdrawal of Genl. Longstreet's Corps, by order of President Davis to reinforce weak points—D. H. Hill's and Ransom's divisions going away about the first of January. About the middle of February, Hood and Pickett were called to protect Richmond from some fancied attack by gunboats, etc. Full 20,000 seasoned fighting men withdrawn from the Army of Northern Virginia, produced a feeling of anxiety in the army. Old soldiers well knew if peace could not come without further conflict, that when hostilities reopened, desperation would predominate in the two recruited armies. Officers had been active with the regiments during the Spring days, drilling and preparing for active work. Genl. Jackson had abandoned his Winter quarters, changing headquarters to several tents near Guinea Station, being in closer touch with his Old Valley men. April weather encouraged Genl. Hooker to get the Army of the Potomac in motion. Old soldiers could easily divine his intentions. They knew that the hosts on the North side of the Rappahannock were preparing for an effort to overwhelm the depleted army on the South side. Hooker was eager to cross the river and try his skill. The Valley Army was not surprised when the great crossing was announced by the roar of Hooker's cannon in the early morning of April 29th, '63. For several days they had been making ready for the grand opening. All during the previous night and day, the Army of Northern Virginia had been on the alert; and when the advancing columns of that magnificently appearing army fell into battle lines on the South side to crush Lee and his divisions in gray, they found solid lines to encounter. Veterans were to meet veterans—Americans struggling to emphasize a principle,—Hooker with his 134,000 crossed the river in three columns and at different points. The army to receive the three columns, according to official reports, barely numbered 61,800 and 176 cannon, some of the latter being siege guns and not available if flank movements were made by the enemy. And thus the world-renowned Battle of Chancellorsville received its initiation. It is not within the province of this work to give any description of this historic battle. This has been done by partial and impartial writers; and their comprehensive compilations are available to any reader who desires to study them. The work in hand is briefly to recount the general movements of the Valley Army. Genl. Hooker and his lieutenants displayed admirable traits as leaders in their effort to change Lee's front and drive him from his base. Every column moved swiftly to their positions, and gave no evidence of their old-time tardiness and delay. The great host seemed eager for the fray. Hooker appeared wary and cared not to attack the center, but bore out towards the flanks and especially Lee's left. The Valley Army, comprising part of Jackson's (the 2nd corps), forming a line from their Winter quarters to Port Royal, was brought promptly into action with Sedgewick's 6th Corps, with the possibility of the 2nd and 3rd closing in at a moment's notice. The Valley Cavalry was with Genl. J. E. B. Stuart at Culpeper, who had then about 2,500 of his fearless riders to meet an attack from Genl. Stoneman with full 10,000 cavalry (O. R., Vol. XXA, pp. 268, etc.) then concentrating at Warrenton Station. It will be seen that the Valley soldiers were still conspicuous and in position to become famous in the campaign, which had again opened. Old strategems practiced in the Valley, did not apply here. Maneuvreing and hard fighting was their only hope, guided by their immortal Stonewall and his trusted lieutenants; for remember, Genl. Lee had sent early word to Jackson to do as he thought best. All felt the need at that early hour of reinforcements; but strange to say the Richmond government failed to grasp the situation so plainly presented by Genl. Lee, who had urgently called for more cavalry to aid Stuart in his arduous work, and that Longstreet should be returned immediately. Mr. Davis has been properly censured for his course in connection with the Spring campaign of 1863. On the evening of April 30th, three Federal army corps had swung around and assembled at and near the Chancellorsville house, having marched nearly fifty miles in three days, over roads almost impassable; fording rivers and fighting over every mile; and at the twilight hour the situation appeared perplexing to the rank and file of the Confederates; and while other columns were hastening to the same point, all in the rear of Genl. Lee, the question was frequently asked: Why has Genl. Lee allowed this apparent success to attend the Federal Army, and how can he extricate his army from such a net-work? Hooker was sending dispatches to Washington, glowing with enthusiasm, promising a complete annihilation of Lee's Rebel army. (See official reports.) But it appears from these O. R. that Genl. Stuart was accomplishing wonders out on Stoneman's flanks, not only impeding his progress, but accumulating information relative to the flank and rear movement of Hooker; so that he was able to report the situation to Genl Lee, who in after years referred to Stuart's exploits as the most useful ever afforded a Commander-in-Chief by the cavalry arm of the service. Stuart had by his bold dashes deceived Stoneman and caused him to deflect from his original plan, and to divide his 10,000 horsemen into fragmentary columns uselessly marching to intercept phantom brigades; while he, Stuart, threw his effective force upon the flanks of infantry corps, who were astonished by their appearance. May 1st was chosen by Hooker for all his lines to close in, believing that Lee had not made and could not make any changes that would prevent the execution of his matured plans. But Lee and Jackson had become fully apprised of the location of the great fighting host, and also knew the topography of the intervening country, which has become familiarly known as The Wilderness. To reach that point without being observed by the outposts at Fredericksburg, where balloons and signal corps were expected to keep Sedgewick posted, Jackson took advantage of the dark night and morning's fog, to hurry away to points that might lead to an attack at the Chancellorsville House; and long before the darkness and fog cleared away, Jackson had landed his corps at the Little Cross Roads Church, not far East from Chancellorsville, where Genl. Anderson had taken position to check the Federal Genl. Anderson; and with his small force, had made good use of their time, by throwing up entrenchments along the lower ridge hidden from view by the dense forest that resembled a jungle more than a forest. Though seemingly interminable, several roads had been cut through this wilderness of trees, underbrush and every imaginable vine and scrubby growth. This dense growth covered a space of full twenty miles in length from West to East, and about twelve or fifteen miles in width from North to South. It was in this forest where the Federals were in tremendous force—masses of infantry and artillery holding every avenue leading to the central point, the Chancellorsville House. Genl. Jackson upon his arrival at Genl. Anderson's position, immediately decided upon an offensive movement, and not to wait for an attack. He had then about 45,000 infantry, 100 guns, and Fitz Hugh Lee's Brigade of cavalry; and by 11 A. M. this army was in motion, heading for the scene of the coming struggle. One road was called a pike—Genl. Anderson led the command on this road, with a regiment of cavalry in advance as scouts and skirmishers; then McLaws' division; following this, two brigades of Anderson's Division. Genl. Jackson with three divisions and the artillery, took what was called the plank road. The Federals were encountered on the Pike after a march of one mile—an infantry force who fought stubbornly and yielded slowly. Federals also appeared on the plank road. They gave way to the Valley men, falling back to their positions near the Chancellorsville House; and by 5 P. M. Federal artillery poured a galling fire into the columns marching through the forest. The cavalry suffered in all these approaches. The forests were so dense that the columns made slow progress, and produced but little effect in the use of the artillery, failing to get positions for the batteries. It is related by surviving staff officers of Generals Jackson and Stuart, that in the afternoon when they had gone well to the front with several pieces of artillery, to find the positions of the Federal guns, several masked batteries opened from the Federal lines and killed a number of horses and men who had ridden to the front with them; and that Jackson's and Stuart's escape was nothing short of miraculous. The gloom of the dense forest was heightened by clouds of smoke, added to which the dim light of day was entirely shut off by the first hours of the dark night. Genl. Jackson, however, had full knowledge of Hooker's position, whose strong lines stretched along the plank road that followed the Chancellorsville ridge running to the Southward. We have a reliable description of Hooker's position in the language of Genl. Lee in his report of this approaching battle: "Genl.

Hooker had assumed a position of great natural strength, surrounded on all sides by a dense forest, filled with a tangled undergrowth, in the midst of which breastworks of logs had been constructed, with trees felled in front, so as to form an almost impenetrable abattis. His artillery swept the few narrow roads, by which the position could be approached from the front, and commanded the adjacent woods. The left of his line extended from Chancellorsville towards the Rappahannock, covering the Bark Mill (U. S.) ford, which communicated with the North bank of the river by a pontoon bridge. His right stretched westward along the Germana Ford road (the pike) more than two miles. As the nature of the country rendered it hazardous to attack by night, our troops were halted and formed in line of battle in front of Chancellorsville at right angles to the plank road extending on the right to the Mine road, and to the left in the direction of the Catherine Furnace." We understand from Genl. Lee's statement, that Genl. Hooker held a position in the rear of the original position of the Confederates, and so strongly held by his tremendous army, with breastworks facing North and West, that the Southern army was compelled to storm the fortified front. Official reports show that both Hooker and Lee held war councils in the night of May 1st—Hooker confident in the success of his plan to head off the retreat and virtually destroy the Army of Northern Virginia;—Lee and Jackson considering plans to flank the enemy, hoping thereby to surprise and virtually destroy the Army of the Potomac. The student of military history will be impressed with the boldness of Hooker in planting his army where he was on May 1st, 1863, and equally impressed with the boldness of Lee and Jackson in executing the plans agreed upon during the night, with Sedgewick's 35,000 on the river near Fredericksburg, awaiting orders to harass and attack the Confederates under Jackson, with only Genl. Early to offer resistance. The two great armies were on the verge of victory or overthrow. We are indebted to Major Hotchkiss, in his valuable description of this campaign, for preserving an incident relating to the last interview between Genl. Lee and Jackson. Maj. Hotchkiss says: "About daylight on May 2nd, Genl. Jackson awakened me, and requested that I would at once go down to Catherine Furnace, which is quite near, and where a Col. Welford lived, and ascertain if there was any road by which we could secretly pass around Chancellorsville to the vicinity of Old Wilderness Tavern. I had a map, which our engineers had prepared from actual surveys of the surrounding country, showing all the public roads, with but few details of the immediate topography." Major Hotchkiss obtained satisfactory information, and returning to Headquarters at 3:30 A. M., he says: "I found Genls. Lee and Jackson in conference, each seated on a cracker box, from a pile which had been left there by the Federals the day before. In response to Genl. Jackson's request for my report, I put another cracker box between the two Generals, on which I spread the map; showed them the road I had ascertained, and indicated, so far as I knew it, the position of the Federal Army. Genl. Lee then said: "General Jackson, what do you propose to do?" He replied: "Go around here," moving his finger over the road which I had located upon the map." Genl. Lee said: "What do you propose to make this movement with?" "With my whole corps" was the answer. Genl. Lee then asked: "What will you leave me?" "The divisions of Anderson and McLaws,'' said Jackson. Genl. Lee, after a moment's reflection, remarked: "Well go on;" and then pencil in hand gave his last instructions. The whole corps (2nd) marched out in single column, Fitzhugh Lee with the 1st Va. Cavalry, taking the front; Rodes' Division next; then A. P. Hill's. This movement was started between 4 and 5 A. M. Col. Henderson mentions this march in the early morning as the hour when Genls. Lee and Jackson held their last interview. Official papers indicate that the last meeting was at a later hour. Col. Henderson says that while the column was pressing rapidly forward, Genl. Lee stood by the roadside to watch them pass; and while there, Genl. Jackson appeared at the head of his staff and drew rein when opposite the Commander-in-Chief, and the two conversed for a few moments. An eye-witness has written of this incident as one that impressed all who saw the last interview between Lee and Jackson.

McLaw's and Anderson's Divisions were kept busy to distract attention from Jackson's march of ten miles through the forest and broken country, where he expected to fall upon Hooker's flank and rear. The Federals being in great force, were encountered frequently after the first 8 miles. The moving column was discovered by Federals from a strong position near Catherine Furnace, where, about Noon, the Federals forced an engagement with Genl. Anderson, which threatened a serious interruption to Jackson's general movement. He, however, moved on, sending several requests to reinforce Anderson; and while the latter was expected to check all attacks on the flank, he was expected to keep in touch with the main column. Genl. Fitz Lee, in his carefully prepared account of this flank movement, says that after using every means his dashing riders could adopt, he was far in the front of Genl. Jackson, and saw the Federals in such positions that would be interesting to Genl. Jackson. He galloped back and met the General about 2 P. M., where he had just reached the Plank road—the point from which he expected to move rapidly Eastward and strike Hooker's flank. Fitz Lee had discovered Genl. Howard's Division not a mile distant from the point where he beheld the Federals, entirely oblivious to danger of attack. When he approached Genl. Jackson, he said: "General, if you will ride with me, halting your columns here out of sight, I will show you the great advantage of attacking down the Old Turnpike instead of the Plank Road, the enemy's lines being taken in reverse. Bring only one courier, as you will be in view from the top of the hill." Jackson followed Genl. Fitz Lee to a high point overlooking the country occupied by the Federal General Howard. There he beheld a scene that compensated for many of the struggles during the heat and dust attending his project for a flank attack. Howard's army, the 11th corps, lay at his mercy. He was where he could strike him unaware. Genl. Fitz says he addressed him several times, without answer; though after studying the situation, he turned to his courier and said: "Tell Genl. Rodes to move across the Plank Road and halt when he gets to the Old Turnpike. I will join him there." This was 2 o'clock; and at 4 P. M. Genl. Rodes was on the turnpike. The cavalry and the old Stonewall Brigade occupied places along the Plank Road, to conceal the movement on the turnpike, to within one mile of Howard's breastworks. There they halted, prepared for battle. While this change was in progress, Genl. Jackson sent his last dispatch to Genl. Lee. It is given here:

" Near 3 P. M., May 2, 1863.

"General—The enemy has made a stand at Chancellor's (Dowdall's Tavern) which is about two miles from Chancellorsville. I hope as soon as practicable to attack. I trust that an ever kind Providence will bless us with great success. "Respectfully,

T. J. JACKSON,
Lieutenant General.

"The leading division is up, and the next two appear to be well closed. T. J. J."
"General R. E. Lee."

Official reports and historical sketches from Federal sources, show that Hooker as late as 4:10 P. M., May 2nd, was entirely mistaken in his estimates of the situation. At that hour he learned for the first time that Confederates had appeared on his right, but believed that Lee was actually in retreat, and the demonstration at Catherine's Furnace between the Confederates under Genls. Archer and Thomas, and Federals under Genl. Sickles, was an effort to save the wagon trains of Genl. Lee. A study of the battle field reveals the weakness that always prevailed among the Federals, when preparing for great battles. Large divisions were in position, remote from each other, always inviting attack from the strategic generals, thus allowing a large army to be whipped in detail. At 6 P. M. when Jackson was at the front, giving his orders to Genl. Rodes, Genl. Howard was totally unprepared for the impending attack. The Federals had allowed an army of men, artillery, etc., to march a distance of about 16 miles during the day, and take position within a mile of his breastworks without his knowledge. Federal writers have censured Howard for his surprise, claiming that he had been importuned by several brigadiers to prepare for an attack. When the Rebel yell fell upon his ear late that evening, the General was dazed. The sudden attack from an unexpected source appalled others besides the General in Command at that point. Some brave Federal officers stood to their posts, and were gallantly supported by veteran regiments, who held their ground until outnumbered. Many more were panic-stricken and sought refuge in the black Wilderness, throwing away arms, etc. Confederate artillery thundered shot and shell into their fleeing ranks. One brigade with wonderful coolness and bravery, stood in position along the edge of the front, in some old fields on the South side of the turnpike, and received a shock of battle not often seen. Here the loss of life was terrific. Genl. George H. Gordon in his "From Brook Farm to Appomattox," says not a mounted officer survived the first charge. The field was won, and Genl. Howard's former position was a scene to gratify the victorious Jackson and his gallant hosts. Nearly all the accoutrements of the Federal Army lay strewn on the field, with dead, dying and droves of prisoners. Other brigades caught the infection of disaster, and were fleeing towards Hooker's Union Army. The old Plank Road could not contain them. The fields were covered with fleeing men, horses and cattle. The 11th Army Corps apparently routed, and divisions and brigades panicky. Yet to the credit of brave men, several hotly contested positions yielded slowly. The last stand made was near Dowdall's Tavern and on the Talley Farm. Then it was Jackson personally called upon his old Valley men commanded by Genl. Colston, to charge in conjunction with Genl. Rodes, and sweep the last vestige of the 11th Army Corps into confusion and rout. The official reports show the result of their deadly work. 7 P. M. found the remnant of the right wings of the Army of the Potomac, shattered and rushing pell mell into Hooker's centre, who was still unconscious of his danger; his left occupied by his 2nd and 5th Corps, had been vigorously attacked by Genl. Lee, with the McLaws' and other troops left with him when Jackson and he parted. Sickles and his 3rd Corps had early in the day been checked and confused by Genl. Anderson's Divisions at Hazel Grove; while Hooker's Headquarters at Chancellorsville had no force to protect his fortified centre, which Genl. Jackson now rushing from the rear, could easily sweep, for the boasted strength of the fortifications were useless now. Guns pointing in the wrong direction, and no men to stand by them. In the edge of the forest, the Federals had some protection, and stubbornly held to their fortified places. Genl. Jackson sent to Genl. Rodes to clear the front and occupy the barricades. A. P. Hill was ordered to relieve Genl. Colston and prepare for a night attack; and Genl. Jackson set to work in person to reform his old Command that had suffered heavy loss and was scattered in confusion in the tangled forests. When this was accomplished, Colston with the Valley Army reformed on the roads leading to Hazel Grove. Many readers of this brief outline will be interested in all of Stonewall Jackson's expressions and movements on that fateful night. The writer will quote freely from Col. Henderson, who so zealously gathered every incident from the surviving staff officers who were at his side during the entire evening. When Genl. Colston was in position, and other plans for further movements made, Genl. Jackson proceeded to his advance line, then heading for the open, that would rout Hooker from his Chancellorsville Headquarters. At the point where the road to the White House and United States ford strikes the Plank Road, he met Genl. Lane, seeking his instructions for the attack. "Push right ahead, Lane, right ahead." His next command was to Genl. A. P. Hill. "Press them; cut them off from the United States ford, Hill; press them." Jackson directed his Chief Engineer, Capt Boswell, to act as guide for Genl. Hill, he having said he was not sufficiently acquainted with the topography of the country to move with safety; and then, turning to the front, rode up to the Plank Road, passing quickly through the ranks of the 18th North Carolina, of Lane's Brigade. Two or three hundred yards eastward the General halted, for the sound of axes and words of command were plainly heard in the enemy's lines. During the last hour, while the Confederates were reforming, Hooker had diligently urged his reserves to come to his relief. The General from his advanced position, learned that he was losing too much time, and grew impatient for Hill's advance. On his return to press the troops forward, an officer who was with him said: "General, you should not expose yourself so much." "There is no danger, sir, the enemy is routed. Go back and tell Genl. Hill to press on." Changing his route somewhat, he together with his entire staff then present and several couriers, found they were near the 18th North Carolina Infantry, who were standing in the trees, the General halted at sounds of voices coming from that quarter,—the General's party also hidden from view by the dismal shades of the forest. At this moment a single rifle shot rang out on the stillness. A detachment of Federal Infantry groping their way through the thickets, had approached the Confederate lines. Skirmishing at once opened on both sides; and the lines of battle in rear became keenly alert. Some mounted officers galloped back to their commands. The sounds startled the Confederate soldiers; and an officer of the 18th North Carolina, seeing a group of strange horsemen riding towards him through the darkness—for Genl. Jackson hearing the firing, had turned back to his own lines—gave the order to fire. The volley was fearfully effective. Men and horses fell dead and dying. Jackson himself received three bullets, one in the right hand and two in the left arm, cutting the main artery and crushing the bone below the shoulder; and as the reins dropped upon his neck, "Little Sorrel," frantic with terror, plunged into the woods and rushed toward the Federal lines. An overhanging bough struck the General violently in the face; tore off his cap, and nearly unhorsed him; but recovering his seat, he managed to seize the bridle with his bleeding hand, and turned into the road. Here Capt. Milbourne, one of his staff officers, succeeded in catching the reins; and as the horse stopped, Jackson leaned forward and fell into his arms. Capt. Hotchkiss, who had just returned from a reconnoissance, rode off to find Dr. McGuire, While Capt. Milbourne with a small penknife, ripped up the sleeve of the wounded arm. As he was doing so, Genl. Hill, who had himself been exposed to the North Carolinians, reached the scene, and throwing himself from his horse, pulled off Jackson's gauntlets, which were full of blood, and bandaged the shattered arm with a handkerchief. "General," he said, "are you much hurt?" "I think I am," was the reply; "and all my wounds are from my own men. I believe my right arm is broken." The group of officers decided that the General must be carried to the rear, the point now occupied being in front of the lines he had so recently formed.

Two Federal skirmishers just then appeared in the edge of the thicket, halting only a few steps from the party. Genl. Hill with remarkable self-possession, turned to his escort saying: "Take charge of those men," and two soldiers sprang forward and seized the rifles of the Federals. Lieut. Morrison who had gone down the road to reconnoitre, reported that he had seen a section of artillery unlimbering close at hand. Hill gave orders that the General should be removed, and that no one should tell the men that he was wounded. Jackson lying on Hill's breast, opened his eyes and said: "Tell them simply that you have a wounded Confederate officer." Lieuts. J. P. Smith and Morrison and Capt. Leigh of Hill's staff, now lifted him to his feet, and with their aid he walked a few steps through the trees. But hardly had they gained the road, when the Federal batteries along their whole front, opened a terrible fire of grape and canister. The storm of bullets, tearing through the foliage, was too high; and the three young officers laying the General down by the roadside, endeavored to shield him by lying between him and the leaden hail. The author has known Capt. Jas. P. Smith, the young officer mentioned, intimately since the day he was assigned to Genl. Jackson's staff; and has often heard him relate the historic incidents of that terrible night. The hour of removal was full of all the horrors that actual battle could produce. Shot and shell from Federal batteries near at hand, answering the Confederate guns only a few yards distant, produced a scene indescribable. The Federals in their last desperate effort to cover their retreat, fought like demons. At this moment Genl. Pender met the group, and recognizing Jackson, was instantly on the ground beside his General, to not only express his grief, but to be instructed what he should do, as his lines were scattered through the thickets by the terrific fire from the Federal artillery, and he feared it would be necessary to fall back. At this moment, says Capt. Smith, "the scene was a fearful one. The air seemed to be alive with the shriek of shells and whistling bullets: horses riderless and mad with fright, dashed in every direction; hundreds left the ranks and hurried to the rear, and the groans of the wounded and dying mingled with the wild shouts of others to be led again to the assault." Almost fainting as he was from loss of blood, desperately wounded, and in the midst of this awful uproar, Jackson's heart was unshaken. The words of Pender seemed to rouse him to life. Pushing aside those who supported him, he raised himself to his full height and answered feebly but distinctly enough to be heard above the din: "You must hold your ground, General Pender; you must hold to the last sir."

His strength by this time had fully given way and he was helpless. Capt. Leigh had procured a litter upon which he was carried to some safer place. While they were yet in the forest one of the litter bearers was shot in the arm. He loosened his hold so suddenly that the General was thrown to the ground falling on his crushed arm. Capt. Smith quickly raised his head and said: "General are you seriously hurt?" "No, Mr. Smith, don't trouble yourself about me," he replied quietly, and added something about winning the battle first and then giving attention to the wounded. He was again lifted to the litter and carried several hundred yards with no cessation of the shells falling along their pathway. Dr. Hunter McGuire, his medical director, was there with an ambulance to meet him. Dr. McGuire knelt down beside him and said: "I hope you are not badly hurt, General." He quietly replied: "I am badly injured, Doctor, and I fear I am dying;" and then added, "I am glad you have come; I think the wound in my shoulder is still bleeding." After rearranging the bandage, he was placed in the ambulance beside a wounded officer, Col. Crutchfield. The ambulance was slowly driven through the fields from which he had so recently driven Hooker's right wing. Arriving at the field hospital, Dr. McGuire administered necessary stimulants to bring reaction, the General having suffered serious collapse from loss of blood, suffering, and the trying strain. Dr. McGuire says in a letter on this subject, written shortly after he amputated the General's arm: "That after reaching the hospital, he was carried to a tent and placed in bed, covered with blankets, and another drink of whiskey and water given him. Two hours and a half elapsed before sufficient reaction took place to warrant an examination; and at 2 o'clock on Sunday morning chloroform was administered and the left arm amputated about two inches below the shoulder. About half-past three Col. Pendleton arrived at the hospital. He stated that General Hill had been wounded and that the troops were in great disorder. General Stuart was in command, and had sent him to see the General. At first I declined to permit an interview, but Pendleton urged that the safety of the army and success of the cause depended upon his seeing him. When he entered the tent, the General said: "Well, Major, I am glad to see you; I thought you were killed." Pendleton briefly explained the position of affairs; gave Stuart's message, and asked what should be done. Jackson was at once interested and asked in his quick way several questions. When they were answered, he remained quiet, evidently trying to think. He contracted his brow; set his mouth, and for some moments lay obviously endeavoring to concentrate his thoughts. . . . He presently answered, very feebly and sadly "I don't know—I can't tell. Say to Genl. Stuart he must do what he thinks best," soon after this he slept."

We must leave the stricken General in his sleep, while we trace the din of battle for the Old Valley Army. Some of Hooker's corps commanders deserve unstinted credit for their efforts to save the day to the Union arms; and their work on the night of May 2nd told fearfully on Genl. Lee's army. The loss of Jackson and Hill, who alone knew the plan of battle, was heightened by the distance that lay between the scene in the forest that night and General Lee who was then contending with Sedgewick's Army and the reinforcements intended to march from Fredericksburg to succor Hooker. Genl. Stuart, who had been watching Ely's Ford, was suddenly called to take command of Jackson's army at a most critical juncture. He found it on the verge of a great victory, or, it might be, disaster. Desperation had seized the Federals who stood to their guns; and the night's battle seemed to be in their favor. The Confederates, deprived of their master spirit, were in confusion. Jackson had won the battle but was stricken too soon to complete the rout. The Federals gathered courage while the Confederates waited for orders and leaders; and when Genl. Stuart arrived, he found Rodes and Colston reforming in good order out in the open fields near Dowdall's Tavern, and Hill's Division reforming in the forest. Stuart knew that not a moment should be lost; he had come from points where he had observed furious preparation on the part of the Federals to sweep along the line of the wilderness and strike a blow that might save the day. His experience as a cavalry leader, enabled him to grasp the situation in time to meet and check the avalanche of Federals coming from the quarter where Anderson with four small brigades had all day and into the night, held in check Genl. Sickle's Corps, Pleasanton's Cavalry and Bering's and Whipple's divisions. (See Genl. Carl Schurz's magazine articles, and Gen. Geo. H. Gordon in "Brook Farm to Appomattox.")

We find Genl. Stuart calling for the Old Valley Army. Genl. Colston moved to the rude log breastworks in the timber, and with Rodes' Division, was in strong position to meet the surging foe. Hill's old division was in support; and when the shock came, about Midnight, Stuart was ready with artillery and musketry, held in reserve until the Federal lines were in easy range. Then belched forth the terrific fire that convinced the Federals that they must seek shelter or be destroyed. It has been told by Old Valley men that never before did the Old Stonewall men shot with such calmness and accuracy. They were simply invincible. The night's battle subsided then until morning. The scene then was shifting. Stuart had planted guns on the ridge called Hazle Grove; and as the morning dawned, the Federals were surprised when the attack came from that quarter; and believing that General Lee had reached that point with his contingent, the Federals formed a new base, only to be driven from it after several hours of fearful slaughter. Genl. Stuart excelled himself in the conduct of this day's work. Federals sought shelter in the forests, and endeavored to move in some show of order along the narrow Wilderness roads. Much of the forest was in flames; the Chancellorsville House was destroyed; added to this the debris of both armies, the dead and wounded,—all made a scene that beggars description; and in the afternoon of May 3rd, when the Old Valley men rallied under the reveille call, their decimated ranks told where they had been and of their loss. The question may be asked: What was accomplished by all this havoc? Valor displayed; heroes made and chivalry theirs! But what of the firesides over their Valley? We may in other chapters tell something of those firesides and of individual valor. The Battle of Chancellorsville—covering several days of fierce fighting resulted in victory to the Army of Northern Virginia and humiliating defeat to the Army of the Potomac. Had Jackson been spared those fatal shots from his own men, the defeat of Genl. Hooker would have been overwhelming. And if Mr. Davis had acceded to Genl. Lee's request and returned a portion of Longstreet's Corps, so they could have been on the field on the fourth of May, Hooker and his great army would have been in a panic; and instead of retreating in disorder on the 5th and 6th to the North side of the Potomac, seeking shelter from his pursuing foe, rout and capture would have destroyed the demoralized corps, as they hurried from the scene of their overthrow. The Federal loss in killed and wounded, according to O. R., amounted to 16,844, 13 guns and 6,000 officers and men supposed to have been captured.

The Confederate loss, killed and wounded, 10,277, and 2,000 officers and men missing.

The Federals sustained the crushing blow of a dispirited army; while the Confederates were buoyed by their ability to defeat the grand army and force its broken ranks to seek refuge under their siege guns and gunboats. Once more the two armies occupy their old positions on the Rappahannock—to form new plans—The Northern Army to change commanders, while the Confederates lamented the loss of their hero chieftain. Genl. Lee sought in vain for one to fill the place; for Stonewall Jackson succumbed to his unfortunate injuries, and passed beyond the din of battle and plaudits of men on Sunday, May 10th, and entered the Eternal Rest.

We will not linger here with the recitals of incidents attending the change. In a personal sketch of Genl. T. J. Jackson, a fuller account will be given.

CHAPTER LXII

WITH THE VALLEY ARMY
After Jackson's Death

After the storm and strife had ceased at Chancellorsville, Genl. Lee found it necessary to reorganize the army, so many changes had occurred. Three Corps now composed the army—Longstreet's, the 1st Corps; Ewell to take Jackson's old Corps, the 2nd, and A. P. Hill, the third.

The divisions of the 2nd corps were, Early's, 6,943 men—Brigadiers: Hays, Smith, Hoke and Gordon.

2nd Division, Johnson's, 5,564 men—Brigadiers: Stuart, Walker, Nichol, Jones.

3rd Division, Rodes', 8,454 men—Brigadiers: Daniel, Doles, Iverson, Ransome and O'Neal.

1,000 Artillerists—Total, 21,961.

This 2nd Corps contained many of the Valley soldiers, principally in Early's Division. Of course, the reader recalls the notice given in former pages, that the writer would only endeaver to follow the Valley men, and briefly show their lines of march and positions in battle by division, brigade or regiment. We will now adhere to this line, while we follow them under their new corps commander, Genl. Ewell. As they begin the march that ultimately takes them to Gettysburg, on June 6th 1863, Ewell started with the 2nd Corps for Culpeper C. H. Hooker, who had discovered the change in Genl. Lee's front, sent a large force of cavalry under Buford and Gregg with two brigades of infantry, to attack the cavalry camps along and near the Rappahannock. They were checked, however, by discovering a large Confederate force marching across their proposed line. When they returned, Genl. Pleasanton, the Chief of Federal Cavalry at the time, ordered out three divisions of cavalry and two of infantry, and moved away again. Ewell's Corps had arrived at Culpeper and was ready to leave on the 9th of June, but delayed on account of heavy firing in the direction of Brandy Station; and did not get away until the 10th.

We must enquire about the Brandy Station affair. Stuart had been instructed by Genl. Lee that he contemplated an invasion of Pennsylvania, and that the cavalry should be concentrated at some convenient point.

The Genl. Wm. E. Jones' raid through West Virginia, taking over thirty days, had just been terminated, and the brigade had settled down at Mt. Crawford to enjoy much needed rest. The camp on the 26th of May presented a scene well remembered by old troopers. Men were dividing the captured horses and stuff they had jointly brought in from that celebrated raid, which had touched every prominent point on the border from New Creek Station on the B. & O. railroad around to the Kanawha River, taking in Cumberland, Rowlesburg, Clarkesburg and all other points; gathering up in their 700 mile ride nearly 800 prisoners, about 1,200 cattle and same number of horses, and every sort of article found in sutlers' and government stores, from tooth-brushes and calico to heavy cloths, clothing, shoes, boots, etc. The prisoners were sent on to where they could be cared for, and the cattle to Genl. Lee's army, while the horses, etc., were substituted for the broken-down privates' horses. The men were entitled to remounts and given liberty to find places for the worn-out steeds, where they could be revived for future use. One regiment noticeably had an extra supply of variegated calico. This was the 12th; and from that day on it was distinguished as the Calico Twelfth. The brigade, while strictly respecting private property in its hard ride, gave strict attention to public property wherever found, including railroad bridges. Sixteen of these had been destroyed. The loss of the brigade as summed up by Genl. Jones in his O. R., was 10 killed and 42 wounded. None missing. No definite report of the Federal loss; but it was well known that several had been killed and wounded. Space may be given later on to show some of the experiences of certain officers and men.

While the brigade was indulging itself during the last days of May and the first of June, orders were received one evening for all commands to prepare for marching. Much private booty was distributed among the homes nearby, to await the return of the troopers. Alas! Many of these never returned. The bright June morning came when the brigade was seen winding its way down the Eastern slopes of the Blue Ridge, to join the Cavalry near Brandy Station, that could be seen coming from Culpeper Court House and other points. When the 5th of June,

1863, came, with Stuart's grand review, old troopers looked on the picture with strange emotions. Stuart and his staff came dashing through the lines, as they were drawn up with gleaming sabres at *present arms*. The General, bedecked with flowers presented by scores of fair Virginia women who had taken position on one of the hills; and with his plume in constant motion, some thought *Jeb was entertaining the ladies*, with no thought of practical uses. No invidious distinction can be made in singling out any of the grand array of horsemen and according to them the honor of conspicuous military appearance. But the writer may be pardoned if he says, that the Brigade which had just returned from the recent raid along the border, attracted special attention from Stuart, as they passed in review, with grim Billy Jones in the lead, and was given the post of honor at the end of a long ridge. This was the first time the cavalry arm of the service had been in Grand Review. It was a grand scene—8,000 horsemen on the ground at one time—Wade Hampton leading the Palmetto and Tar Heel Brigades. Fitz Lee with all his youthful vigor, prancing his superb horse along the lines of the Tidewater Virginians. Every trooper gave evidence of their familiarity with spirited horses, and reflected credit on the cavalry that was destined for the great work near at hand. It was noted by hundreds of the best riders, that none bore resemblance of the Cavalier Ashby, who had gone from the nearby plains at his country's first call, and who had one year before yielded his all as a sacrifice upon his country's altar.

On the 8th, Genl. Lee was present, and reviewed the Corps. Old soldiers began to conjecture as to what all this meant. They had but little time to wait and know; for the Army of Northern Virginia was moving towards the North. The Federal commander sent out Genl. Pleasanton with a large force of cavalry to make reconnoissance of such movement, and to strike every point in the flank of the advance. This force was in motion on the 8th, when Genl. Lee made the only and last review of the Cavalry. Pleasanton crossed the Rappahannock in two columns, one at Beverly's ford, the other at Kelly's ford. O. R. show that he had three divisions of cavalry and two of infantry. They started towards Culpeper Court House. The advance was met by Company A. of the 6th Va. This one Company, led by Capt. Bruce Gibson, dashed headlong into what turned out to be the 8th New York. The Company was compelled to retire to favorable ground and awaited their regiment to come to their support. Part of this regiment on very short notice was on hand, and soon found themselves in front of the heavy column in a country road. After a desperate charge, the 8th withdrew and waited for the 7th to come up. The 6th had now lost about 30 men. When the 7th got up, some of the men were without saddles, so quickly had they been rushed by Genl. Jones. The fighting was desperate, holding out long enough for the wagon trains to safely get away, and the remainder of the Confederate regiments to get in line, with the artillery in good position at St. James' Church. The Federals under Gregg now swept forward and many hand to hand struggles occurred. The lines fell back over ridges to Brandy Station, with Genl. W. F. Lee on the Federal right and Hampton on the left—the 6th, 7th, 11th, 12th and White's battalion fighting desperately in the front. The great battle of Brandy Station was now at flood tide. The fighting continued until evening, when the Federals were content to withdraw and seek the Rappahannock. Many brave men went down. Stuart's loss was 523 officers and men; Federal killed and wounded 936 officers and men, 486 prisoners, 3 pieces of artillery and small arms. Genl. Jones in his report says his brigade bore the brunt of battle. The writer's brother Capt. M. B. Cartmell of Company B, 11th Va. Regt., had three horses killed. The reader is referred to a graphic account of this battle as given by Capt. W. N. McDonald in "History of the Laurel Brigade," and to "The Campaigns of Stuart's Cavalry," by Maj. H. B. McClellan, Chief of Staff. The Federals fought well, but not wisely, making their usual mistake of fighting only a portion of their great host at a time. Had Pleasanton hurled Buford in along with Gregg, Stuart's cavalry might not have rested on the battle ground that night, where they had the day before been in grand review before Genl. Lee.

Returning now to the 2nd corps, we find after they left Culpeper on the 10th, they struck boldly for the Valley. Men of old Stonewall Brigade sniffed the air of Winchester, as they defiled through the Blue Ridge. Early and Johnson went to Winchester, while Rodes went to Berryville. When Early and Johnson struck the Valley, it was their desire to surprise Milroy, who had held high carnival at Winchester for some time. He was regarded as the lowest type of that class of commanders whose mode of warfare was to persecute women and children, declaring often that it was the sure way to break the Rebellion. The brutalities of this ruffian and braggart, so well remembered to this day, were a disgrace to the soldiery of America; and his name is never mentioned except to point to his infamy and ultimate overthrow. Early was the man for the work; and securing good guides, he left the main thoroughfares at Bartonsville, and followed defiles through field and forest to the West of Kernstown, where he was completely hidden from view by the great ridge running West of Winchester North and South. Passing through the Cloverdale Farm, he struck the Northwestern Turnpike at Dr. John S. Lupton's residence. The whole column then disappeared through the woodlands of the Lupton farms, and took position in the edge of heavy timber near the Parish farm, about two miles in an air line from the big Milroy Fort near where is seen the residence of Mr. Fred Strother. Early soon had a good position for his heavy guns, which were timed to fire in quick succession. The guides—the writer being one and Mr. James Carr Baker the other—were then relieved of the responsibility for undertaking to place the command in the position described to Genl. Early on the banks of the Shenandoah, and ordered to proceed in haste to the brigades on the Valley Pike, and direct them not to enter the town until he ceased firing. The writer must acknowledge a disobedience of this order. He had two reasons: one was that he must linger long enough to see the big guns belch forth and see if possible where the shells landed. Having waited long enough for the third volley, he hastened away to meet the column on the Valley Pike that had kept up a desultory fire for several hours to distract Milroy's attention while Early was getting into position. No juncture could be formed that evening between the scout and the brigade South of Winchester. Early fired his first gun between 5 and 6 P. M., and continued to cannonade until dark, while his infantry charged through the lowlands to the slopes of the ridge West of the fort. The garrison kept up a heavy fire with siege guns, but did no harm. Several pieces, however, got the range on the charging infantry and killed some men. Milroy packed his trains in the hollows N. E. from the fort, and galloped away at early dawn with about 500 cavalry, overtaking several regiments of his infantry near Stephensons, he put them in line, and had them charge the Confederate batteries stationed at the road crossing; and after several volleys were poured into the artillerymen and their weak support, Milroy and all the cavalry that could follow, literally rode over his own infantrymen and over the dead men and battery horses, and escaped. Pursuit was impossible at that hour. Later on, mounted infantrymen followed him for several miles, but losing his trail, returned to Stephensons, where many prisoners were surrendering. The Stonewall Brigade was sent from Early's position the evening before to reach Stephensons, and there meet Rodes marching via Berryville. A juncture was thus formed, with flanks well guarded and Ewell with two other brigades pressing the rear. It was believed Milroy's command "would be scooped up," as Genl. Early curtly said. Some one East of town was to blame. Rodes passing through Berryville on time, drove all before him in such shape, he mistook his orders and never stopped until he reached Martinsburg, capturing guns, stores, and a few prisoners. Had he halted at some point under cover of timber near old Hackwood, until the Stonewall appeared, there would doubtless have been a complete surrender. As it was, over 1,600 men were taken from the fort the next morning and confined in the Court House yard that was enclosed with a high iron fence. The writer was detailed to take the names of men, regiments, etc.; and in recent years has met some of the men who were of that number. One incident occurred to cause all to remember the day and place: After guards were thrown around the yard, the prisoners complained of extreme hunger; and when told that the Confederates were in the same strait and would be until the rations could be issued, several of the prisoners stated they knew where there was a big lot of sutlers' supplies. Taking two of the prisoners and a detail of Confederates, the stores were found in an old storeroom nearly opposite the Taylor Hotel—barrels of crackers, canned stuffs, cheese, etc., were carried to the Court House yard and freely distributed among the prisoners, many of whom have told the writer of their gratitude. About this time prisoners came from Stephensons' swelling the number captured to nearly 4,000, with about 30 guns all told, siege and other cannon, besides a rich wagon train a mile long. Genl. Lee's Reports show that 250 wagons, 400 horses and 20 ambulances and a lot of ammunition, etc., was captured, together with the prisoners and sutlers' outfits. The marches made by this corps under Ewell, and the rout of Milroy with the fruits of victory, compare well with some campaign work the old Corps did for Stonewall Jackson 13 months before. Early and Johnson in their advance upon Winchester, marched 70 miles in three days.

Rodes speaks of his march to the Potomac, as "the most trying march we have yet had; most trying because of the intense heat, the character of the road (stony and dusty) and the increased number of barefooted men in the command."

Hooker's demonstrations caused Genl. Lee to retain Longstreet and Hill for any emergency. Strange to say Fighting Joe Hooker allowed politics to enter and interfere with an attack on Lee at some point in the vicinity of Manassas, that most surely would have overthrown the latter, and gained renown for Hooker that no politicians like Stanton, Halleck and Chase could have wrested from him. Genl. Lee certainly knew the weakness of the man and felt sure he would not come out into the open, so disregarded Hooker entirely; for on the 15th Longstreet was marched away from Culpeper to the eastern base of the Blue Ridge, while A. P. Hill went via Front Royal and entered the Valley to unite with Longstreet near Snickers and Ashbys Gaps, which was effected on the 20th. A large force of cavalry protected Longstreet's flank and front, and fought three severe battles worthy of notice, beginning at Aldie, Loudoun County, then Middleburg, and on the slopes of the Blue Ridge near Upperville. It was at this last place where Capt. Chas. T. O'Ferral was seriously injured and carried from the field by one of his comrades Mr. Alfred Fergusson, now living in Winchester. The old Ashby Brigade under Brig. Genl. Wm. E. Jones, distinguished itself again in this battle, fighting over every foot of ground from Aldie and over the hills about Middleburg. Stuart had been fighting Genl. Gregg on the 19th, and was barely able to hold his ground, while Longstreet was crossing the mountain. In the evening, Jones appeared and succeeded in securing a good position about 4 miles from Upperville; and being reinforced the next day, kept in close touch with Stuart; and this afforded protection to the infantry and trains. On the 21st, Gregg and Buford came up with a brigade of infantry, and headed for Jones out on the road to Middleburg. This brought the whole cavalry into action, resulting in the Upperville battle. The cavalry had gradually given way, and retired slowly to the long line of hills near the village. Artillery was brought into action, Chew's battery doing great service. The Valley regiments, the 6th, 7th, 11th and 12th were conspicuous, and fought several pitched engagements, and held the ground despite the good fighting of the Federals, who lost heavily in the day's work. The Confederates met many men that day who fought fiercely. The 7th had 5 men killed and 16 wounded; the 11th 7 killed and 24 wounded; the 12th 2 killed and 11 wounded. The Federals were forced to retire and left Upperville to the Confederates. Old soldiers regarded the three days' fighting well sustained by both sides.

On the 24th Stuart started on his raid. Jones' and Robertson's Brigades were left for other duties. Jones marched from Snickersville to Berryville, and then took up an interrupted line of march to join the army in Maryland. The 6th, 7th and 11th crossed the river at Williamsport; and bravely they rode where Genl. Lee ordered. General Stuart's raid around the rear of the Federal Army after he crossed the Potomac, has been lamented by the Cavalry, for their fruitless ride; and Genl. Lee had cause to lament that Stuart had not joined Jones; as from the combined force he could have drawn what he needed during the terrible three days spent on that raid. Stuart had started on the 24th, and from the 26th to the 2nd of July, Genl. Lee had not seen him, though needing him every day. None can blame the gallant Stuart, for he undertook the expedition with the knowledge and consent of Lee and Longstreet, and he had endured trying hardships.

CHAPTER LXIII

GETTYSBURG

On July 1st, 1863, we find the preliminary movements in the Army of Lee indicating an engagement in the vicinity of Gettysburg. Several other positions had been chosen; but the Federal armies were appearing at so many points, that Genl. Lee had the Gettysburg field forced upon him. He saw some strategic points on the field that should be held by him; and this is why Ewell was directed to change positions of Early and Rodes from the Cashtown Road, and head for Gettysburg. Meade had discovered Ewell's Corps between York and Carlisle, and had on the 29th turned his whole army in that direction. General Lee discovered this movement barely in time to extricate the corps from Meade's meshes.

The Battle of Gettysburg which opened July 1st, 1863, was the result, it appears, of incidental movements—demonstrations and skirmishes between outlying divisions. Meade had relieved Hooker; and was on the field more to inspect positions than to join battle with Lee. Every road leading towards the general field, was lined with troops hastening to repel further invasion. The first day's battle developed the positions around which the powerful legions of both armies were to test the valor and ability of their soldiers, from the chiefs in command to the foot-sore private. The stupendous Battle of Gettysburg, that appalled nations in their study of the American Soldier, and immortalized the "Blue and the Gray," has been an exhaustless theme for historians, novelists and poets; and the reader must be referred to the vast collections found in the public libraries for pen pictures of that famous field, reeking with the blood of heroes for days, and then abandoned on the Fourth of July. Lee with his shattered divisions, quickly withdrew towards the Potomac, while Meade with his crippled corps, stood aghast at the carnage, and withdrew to positions beyond the awful spectacle, where the medical corps of both armies were gathering up the wounded, and details were hastily covering the slain with the earth their blood had drenched. It is not within the scope of this work to do more than show briefly where the Valley men were in the desperate struggle.

It will be remembered that Ewell's Corps embraced the Stonewall Brigade and other Virginia troops; and in tracing the movement of Ewell, Early and Edw. Johnson, the Shenandoah Valley troops are included; while the J. E. B. Stuart cavalry embraced the Brigades of Jones and Imboden of the Cavalry, and Chew and others of the artillery. The writer feels his inability to do justice to any of the splendid battalions handled by the leaders mentioned; and lack of space forbids personal mention of individual heroism. All have heard how and why Lee failed to occupy Cemetery Ridge. Longstreet comes in for his share of criticism for failure to appear at the right moment; while he and his personal friends have sought to shift the blame to Genl. Ewell, charging that the impetuosity of Genl. Early with his invincible Valley Army, storming impregnable positions with terrific loss, enlightened the Federals as to Lee's desperate condition. A careful study of the battle and subsequent reports from all commanders, reveals the lamentable fact that Early could have been supported by Longstreet with his fresh divisions at 5 P. M. the first day; but for some reason the support was withheld, and Early forced to retire from the very key of the field. Genl. Lee expected Genl. Longstreet to use his discretion in supporting any effort made to seize the crest of the historic ridge; and certainly did not contemplate his failure to move to some point. Ewell was in position at 4 P. M. to join any effort made to take Culp's Hill, a strong point from which heavy cannonading was bearing upon A. P. Hill's position on Seminary Ridge. Genl. Edw. Johnston was struggling to maintain a foothold under the brow of the hills. Ewell dispatched Early for his support, expecting Longstreet to join not later than 6 o'clock. On the right, Early and Johnson did not have their full brigades. Other regiments had been used for rear guards of two columns. Early's official report agrees with that of Johnson. They passed over all obstacles—two ridges and several batteries—and across the long deep hollow bordering Cemetery Ridge, and finally scaled the crest, beating down everything before them with heavy loss to the charging Virginians. The enemy's breast-works were taken, where two batteries were in position; and while holding this position in the face of strong divisions in their front, were overwhelmed with astonishment that no attack had been made on the right by Longstreet or any of the brigades they expected to move that way. Their position was plainly untenable; for the heavy force that should have been attacked on the right, meeting nothing from that quarter, immediately turned against their position on the crest; and they prudently fell back under heavy fire, "but with comparatively slight loss." Even the gallant Rodes failed to appear. His report shows he was engaged at two important points. We dare not attach blame to any of the brave men who were on that field. All doubtless, did their duty as they saw it. The first day was a victory for the Confederate brigades engaged, but ended with no good results. The second day was full of preliminaries for the next day's battle. Longstreet fought several engagements with the enemy during the forenoon, and held his positions. The afternoon was spent in a drawn battle between part of the 1st Corps and a large force of the enemy, who fought fiercely to recover what they had lost in the morning. Longstreet yielded at dark, and fell back. In his reports, he intimates that Ewell and Hill were to blame *for failure to cooperate;* while his Chief of Artillery, Genl. E. P. Alexander, in his attractive history of this battle, states the case in these words: "Co-operative attacks by Ewell and Hill *ordered* by Lee, failed to be effective because both Ewell and Hill had failed to have their divisions in proper positions for the charge long before the moment arrived, although each had ample time." We have no comment to make. The curious can see the O. R. and judge the case from *all the evidence.*

The third day at Gettysburg found both armies fully prepared for the final struggle. Meade was proving his ability to command the hosts that surrounded him. His corps commanders were all experienced leaders, and many of his division and brigade commanders had shown enough skill and bravery to justify the impression that prevailed in Lee's camp during the night. All felt that the third day must be the last, and all were keyed up for the supreme effort. Genl. Lee in his official report ending with the accounts of the second day's battle, uses this language: "The result of the (second) day's operations induced the belief that with proper concert of action, and with the increased support that the positions gained on the right would enable the artillery to render the columns, we should unltimately succeed, and it was accordingly determined to continue the attack."

The general plan was unchanged. Longstreet reinforced by Pickett's three brigades, was to attack in the morning, and Ewell was ordered to assault the enemy's right at the same time. The latter during the night, reinforced by Johnson with two brigades from Rodes' and one from Early's division.

The plans of Lee started off favorably at early dawn, with several brigades from Ewell's Corps, under the impression that Longstreet was to attack at the same hour. The latter says in his "Memoirs," that he received no orders during the night, and his troops could not be gotten into their positions before Noon. This sounds strangely, when we have it from Genl. Lee plainly that "Longstreet was to attack the next morning." Some staff officer probably failed to find Genl. Longstreet. So we have the Virginians in the thickest of the fray nearly all day, repulsing heavy divisions of Federal infantry and artillery without support, which compelled the brave Confederates to fall back from every position they had taken at such heavy cost. Official figures show that the loss that morning to Edw. Johnson's command was *1,873*. Ewell and the other brigades of his corps, were hotly engaged until after 2 P. M. Then the terrific cannonading was at its height—several hundred guns sending death and destruction every moment for several hours. Then there was a lull—a fitting prelude to the sacrifice about to be offered by the immortal Pickett and his men. An ominous silence seemed to pervade the two great armies, foretelling, as it were, that some event would occur that day which would live for ever. The awful drama was well set, and the actors were ready; General George E. Pickett being the star, while his veteran brigade was his support. Well did they enter the arena that hot July afternoon, to the music of cannon and yells from friend and foe. The story of Pickett and his charge for the possession of Round Top has been told at every fireside in the land; yet none can ever become familiar with the deeds of heroism immortalized on the slopes and summit of that hill side. And strange to say, none were there to sustain and hold the prize he at one time held. Every other feat performed by brave men on the field of Gettysburg, did and will ever pass into obscurity under the blaze of glory that shone around the pinnacle of fame of Pickett's Brigade.

Why say more! The final sacrifice seemed to satisfy friend and foe. Lee's broken columns were more closely drawn to lines for either attack or defence. Meade and his great army seemed stunned by the spectacle, and patiently waited for hours, giving no appearance of a victorious army. After nightfall, Lee formed his lines on Seminary Ridge, with the flank extending far off to Willoughby Run. Here he was on the morning of the 4th of July, in sullen silence waiting for attack. This was a masterly movement under the circumstances. His army was in condition for battle. He had already in the afternoon of the 3rd, prepared for retreat, let the battle be won or lost. He sent for Genl. Imboden, who arrived with about 2,100 men and one battery, whom he instructed to collect all wagons, etc., into a train and accompany to Williamsport without halt. Here he was to stop only to feed; then ford the Potomac and proceed to Winchester. Imboden gives a graphic account of this huge undertaking. At least 1,800 vehicles were to be collected, and all safely and secretly conducted to Virginia. He says: "His column would be at least 17 miles long." About 4 P. M. on the 4th, the head of the train was moving past Cashtown. Very shortly after the train was in motion, Imboden says: "A heavy rainfall suddenly came, and probably 4 inches of water fell within 12 hours, and this was sure to make the Potomac unfordable for a week." (See his Battles and Leaders.) A brigade of cavalry was to guard the rear. Provision was made to take all the wounded who could bear handling, in the empty wagons and ambulances. The first and third corps were started about 5:30, while the second corps under Ewell remained in the vicinity of Gettysburg until 12:30 on the 5th. How all this could be done in the face of an army that claimed a victory, has never been sufficiently explained. Surely Meade could have surrounded this corps and compelled surrender. Doubtless Lee had an object in leaving the Shenandoah men in his rear; and beyond doubt Meade knew who they were. Imboden and the trains moved on roads far to the right of the infantry and artillery, and were thus protected from cavalry attacks; while out on the right was Genl. Wm. E. Jones' cavalry brigade of Valley men, who knew the country roads. Many skirmishes occurred between this brigade and the cavalry from the upper Potomac district.

We hasten on to the Potomac where Imboden had landed his advance wagons loaded with wounded men. Williamsport was called upon to prepare provisions for the wounded; the river was forbidding, in its muddy rush of water, past fording; and only two small ferry boats were at his disposal. During the night the trains drew in and found place to halt for feed, etc. The next morning, a large cavalry force appeared, 7,000 strong with a battery. Imboden armed teamsters and convalescents; and with his own cavalry presented such an array of soldiers, that the Federal commander withdrew just in time to escape a fight with Stuart's and Jones' cavalry that came thundering down the roads in fine style. The infantry columns were making deliberate marches by several other roads—all leading to Williamsport, where they began to arrive on the 5th and 6th; and by the 8th all divisions were up and going to suitable bivouac stations. The river had fallen somewhat, and a crossing was expected for the 7th, but another two days' rain interfered; and besides, some demonstrations were made on the leading roads by large bodies of cavalry. Genl. Lee immediately put his army in position to receive battle in case Meade made an attack. Good lines of defence were chosen; and the old Army of Northern Virginia seemed ready for either defense or attack. But fortunately the latter was not attempted. Imboden was busy pushing the ambulances over by ferry; then came the turn of the 5,000 prisoners, which required hours; and then came the wagons, some of which were now crossing on the pontoon bridge that had been made out of lumber torn from some old warehouses. A crossing was effected during the night of the 13th (July). The river had fallen enough to justify fording by the infantry. Longstreet's and Hill's corps crossed via the bridge, while Ewell's corps passed by the ford. The river was on another rise. The routes from the camps to the ferry and bridge, were through water-soaked fields. Through the dark night, large fires were kept burning to light the columns on their way. All night was consumed in efforts to pass the entire army. Many wagons stalled in the quagmire roads. This delay prevented Hill reaching the South side until about 1 o'clock on the 14th—all being safely over, save a few stragglers and disabled horses and men. Stuart remained on the North side to skirmish with any advancing lines. It is natural for some to ask where was Meade from the 4th of July until the 15th. Eleven days frittered away with an army of untold numbers, half of which should have been able to inflict sufficient damage to Lee's retreating squadrons, that would have turned an orderly retreat into a rout; and the other half have sailed in and gathered up the broken regiments. Meade has undertaken to answer this through his official reports. But the Washington government had their faith shaken.

Meade felt the censure; and consulted some of his officers; but nothing was done until the 12th, when it was determined to move forward the next day. Had they done so, they would have caught Lee's army in the worst plight it had ever been—all in the mud, or in the Potomac on pontoons or ferry boats—with nothing to offer in return for shells from 200 guns that could have been planted to sweep the river by front or enfilade; and 15,000 cavalry to sweep by every obstacle offered by Stuart's worn-out horses and men.

Meade waited until the 14th before he got

away; and moved cautiously, allowing the advance to be halted several times, owing to some cavalry skirmishes between Kilpatrick and Stuart. During the retreat to Williamsport, the Confederate cavalry desperately fought over every foot of ground with the Federal cavalry under Fitzpatrick, whose men deserved the support that Meade could so easily have given. Very often the wagon trains were in the grasp of Kilpatrick's numerous brigades, that seemed to be everywhere. The service rendered by the Confederate Cavalry during that retreat must go down in history as an example to men of this branch of any army, of what cavalry can accomplish when handled by such leaders as Jeb Stuart and his veteran brigadiers. From Fairfield to Williamsport had been their battleground; through forest and glen, over fences, swollen streams, through clouds of dust, ending in quagmire on the Potomac in their final struggle, when Kilpatrick was beaten back and foiled in his persistent effort to capture the trains and produce rout in the Confederate infantry. In the numerous battles, Jones' brigade did valiant work. The 11th Virginia led by Col. Lomax, made some of the most desperate charges horsemen ever made with drawn sabres. They often bore down on many times their number, losing many brave men. Near Williamsport this regiment charged headlong into two Federal regiments; drove them from the field and brought back 100 prisoners. The 7th Virginia Cavalry, led by the gallant Col. Marshall, fought and overpowered the 6th U. S. Regulars, bringing back 60 prisoners. On this long battle line, all the cavalry under Stuart and Imboden, nobly did their part in this retreat—unparalleled in history for orderly movement under most trying circumstances.

On the 13th, Jones crossed the Potomac to take the front of Lee's Army and keep the General informed of any attempt to intercept his further movements South. When the infantry corps left the defences on the North side, Stuart entered them and held back all night any advance of the enemy. The next day he withdrew and crossed his entire command to the Virginia side. The 12th regiment was not in the campaign, but was left at Harpers Ferry, and performed good service at that point. They were compelled to give way on the 14th, when a Federal force recaptured the place. This shows why Lee had Jones to cross into Virginia on the 13th and at once march to Charlestown, where he was in position to do such picket service as the situation required.

Genl. Rodes says in his report: "My division waded the river just above the acqueduct over the mouth of the Conococheague. The operation was a perilous one. It was very dark, rainy and excessively muddy. The men had to wade through the acqueduct. The water was cold, deep and rising; and the lights on either side of the river were dim, just affording enough light to mark the place of entrance and exit. The cartridge boxes of the men had to be placed around their necks. The water was up to the arm-pits of a full-sized man. We crossed without loss except of some 25,000 or 30,000 rounds of ammunition, unavoidably wetted and spoiled. After crossing, I marched a short distance beyond Falling Waters and then bivouacked; and there ended the Pa. Campaign."

A study of Genl. Lee's official reports indicates clearly that he intended to cross the Blue Ridge into Loudoun County, where he hoped to oppose Meade's crossing into Virginia; but the Shenandoah was impassable by the floods. Meade did cross the Potomac below Harpers Ferry, and seized several of the passes, and moved along the eastern base of the ridge. This was intended to cut Lee off from Gordonsville and the railroad. Longstreet was sent forward; crossed the Shenandoah with great difficulty, and prevented the Federals from occupying Manassas and Chester Gaps, through which Longstreet passed July 24th and on to Culpeper Court House. Hill's Corps soon followed, and Ewell's crossed at Thornton's Gap further South.

August 4th, 1863, found the Army of Northern Virginia along the South side of the Rapidan; while the cavalry under Stuart remained at Culpeper.

Meade with the Army of the Potomac, formed his lines along the Rappahannock.

To answer, what was the result of the terrible campaign? We subjoin the following tables. The totals given are from the official returns of both armies; but the Confederate returns are known to be very incomplete. The table was prepared by Genl. Edward P. Alexander, which the writer now takes the liberty to copy and enter at this point. It will preserve a convenient plan to show what brigades fought in the great battle; and some old comrades will be able to review memories, and associate themselves once more with the fighting squadrons.

GETTYSBURG

Confederate Casualties. Approximate. By Brigades.

McLaws' Division.

Commands	Killed	Wounded	Missing	Total
Kershaw	115	483	32	630
Semmes	55	284	91	430
Barksdale	105	550	92	747
Wolford	30	192	112	334
Cabell's Artillery...	8	29	....	37
	313	1,538	327	2,178

Pickett's Division

Commands	Killed	Wounded	Missing	Total
Garnett	78	324	539	941
Armistead	88	460	643	1,191
Kemper	58	356	317	731
Dearing's Artillery	8	17	....	25
	232	1,157	1,499	2,888

Hood's Division

Commands	Killed	Wounded	Missing	Total
Laws	74	276	146	496
Anderson, G. T.	105	512	54	671
Robertson	84	393	120	597
Benning	76	299	122	497
Henry's Artillery	4	23	....	27
	343	1,504	442	2,289
Alexander's Artillery	19	114	6	139
Washington's Artillery	3	26	16	45
Reserve Artillery	22	140	22	184
Aggregate of 1st Corps	910	4,339	2,240	7,539

Early's Division

Commands	Killed	Wounded	Missing	Total
Hays	36	201	76	313
Hoke	35	216	94	345
Smith	12	113	17	142
Gordon	71	270	39	380
Jones' Artillery	2	6	....	8
	156	806	226	1,188

Johnson's Division

Commands	Killed	Wounded	Missing	Total
Steuart, G. H.	83	409	190	682
Nichol	43	309	36	388
Stonewall	35	208	87	330
Jones'	58	302	61	421
Latimer's Artillery	10	40	....	50
	229	1,269	375	1,873

Rodes' Division

Commands	Killed	Wounded	Missing	Total
Daniel	165	635	116	916
Iverson	130	328	308	820
Doles	24	124	31	179
Ramseur	23	122	32	177
O'Neal	73	430	193	696
Carter's Artillery	6	35	24	65
	421	1,728	704	2,853
Brown's Artillery	3	19	....	22
Nelson's Artillery	....	....	....	....
Reserve Artillery	3	19	....	22
2nd Corps Totals	809	3,823	1,305	5,937

Anderson's Division

Commands	Killed	Wounded	Missing	Total
Wilcox	51	469	257	777
Mahone	8	55	39	102
Wright	40	295	333	668
Perry	33	217	205	455
Posey	12	71	....	83
Lane's Artillery	3	21	6	30
	147	1,128	840	2,115

Heth's Division

Commands	Killed	Wounded	Missing	Total
Pettigrew	190	915	....	1,105
Brockenbrough	25	123	....	148
Archer	16	144	517	677
Davis	180	717	....	897
Garnett's Artillery	....	5	17	22
	411	1,905	534	2,850

Pender's Division

Commands	Killed	Wounded	Missing	Total
Perrin	100	477	....	577
Lane	41	348	....	389
Thomas	16	136	....	152
Scales	102	323	110	535
Poague's Artillery	2	24	6	32
	262	1,312	116	1,690
McIntosh's Artillery	7	25	....	32
Pegram's Artillery	10	37	1	48
Reserve Artillery	17	62	1	80
3rd Corps Totals	837	4,407	1,491	6,735

Cavalry

Commands	Killed	Wounded	Missing	Total
Hampton	17	58	16	91
Lee, Fitz	5	16	29	50
Jones	12	40	6	58
Jenkins' Artillery	....	....	....	....
Total Cavalry	36	140	64	240
Aggregate Losses	2,592	12,709	5,150	20,451

The foregoing table does not embrace Imboden's Cavalry, who sustained losses on the extreme left; nor does it include Jenkins' Cavalry, nor the N. C. Brigade of Chambliss, nor White's Battery, nor Chew's Battery. These commands sustained heavy losses, which will receive attention in another chapter. These omissions partly account for the discrepancy between Genl. Alexander's Table of Casualties, and what is found in "Numbers and Losses in the Civil War," collected by Livermore, whose estimate is as follows:

Total killed 3,903; Wounded 18,735; Missing 5,425; Total 28,063.

GETTYSBURG

Federal Casualties. Approximate.

Command	Killed	Wounded	Missing	Total
1st Corps..........	666	3,131	2,162	6,059
2nd Corps..........	797	3,194	378	4,369
3rd Corps..........	593	3,029	589	4,211
5th Corps..........	365	1,611	211	2,187
6th Corps..........	27	185	30	242
11th Corps.........	369	1,922	1,510	3,801
12th Corps.........	214	812	66	1,082
Artillery and Cavalry Total	....	....	....	1,098
Aggregate	3,155	14,529	5365	23,049

A revision of losses now being made in the War Department, estimates an increase of losses at 55 per cent. Adding this to the aggregates above, show a large excess of loss over the Confederates, as given by Livermore.

CHAPTER LXIV

LEE AND MEADE ON THE RAPIDAN

Gen. Early in the Shenandoah Valley

The Army of Northern Virginia had ample time to reorganize while in camps along the Rapidan; and it was marvellous to see how rapidly it rallied. No evidence of a defeated army. Officers and men regarded the Pennsylvania campaign a failure; but never doubted the ability of their great commander to lead them in any campaign he chose to map out. Meade seemed contented with the situation, and there rested with his many corps for several days; allowing Genl. Lee to send Longstreet to Tennessee to reinforce Genl. Bragg, while being pressed by Rosecrans. Lee, in summing up the situation as reported to the War Office, says he was called to Richmond the 23rd of August by the President; and there remained for two weeks in consultation regarding proposed changes; and that Sept. 9th, the first effort was made to get Longstreet away with five brigades. Some pertinent questions have been asked the writer, for reasons of Meade's refusal to attack Lee; and in many cases has referred such to the pithy writings of Northern historians. We have not space for further notice of these historical facts, nor for mention of the historic slaughter at Chickamauga.

While the infantry divisions and batteries were quickly recruiting on the Rapidan, there was no rest for the cavalry under Stuart. He had reorganized his command, forming two divisions, with Generals Fitzhugh Lee and Wade Hampton in command. Ashby's old brigade, Wm. E. Jones, Col., was assigned to Hampton. About the middle of September, this old brigade was dispatched towards the old Rapidan bridge, where a large force of Federal cavalry was crossing, with Col. Lomax of the 11th in command. (Genl. Jones had been placed under arrest some two weeks previous by Genl. Stuart. This will be more fully noticed later.) Lomax had the 11th, 7th, 12th and 6th regiments and Chew's Battery. It was not long before the brigade encountered their old antagonists Kilpatrick and Buford; and held their two divisions in check for two hours near Culpeper C. H.; Chew and his famous battery doing great service with its well-timed shots. An infantry corps coming up to the support of Kilpatrick, Lomax fell back to another position, where he was joined by W. F. H. Lee's brigade, and for hours these two brigades held the powerful forces in check. It amuses survivors of the old brigade to read Kilpatrick's report of this *battle,* as he terms it. He says: "The enemy appeared in force, making a desperate resistance, with a battery of artillery and a large force of cavalry. . . I rode over to a *wood,* and found Custer heavily engaged, with Second New York flanked and extreme right driven in. We were overpowered by numbers." Capt. Wm. N. McDonald in history of the 'Laurel Brigade,' speaking of this engagement, says: "When it is remembered that the two brigades of Lomax and Lee were confronted by two divisions of Federal cavalry, the numerous repulses of the Federals must be attributed rather to the valor and skill of the Confederates than to their superiority in numbers." The Federal O. R. show now that the movement was made to capture Lee's wagon trains on their way from Culpeper C. H. to the Rapidan. This unsuccessful expedition terminated in a withdrawal of the infantry; but Kilpatrick continued to entertain Stuart and his men all through the Autumn of 1863. One engagement must be briefly mentioned. Col. Funsten of the 11th, who had been promoted, took the brigade hastily to Madison C. H., where he at once began a series of scout and picket work, intended to protect and screen a flank movement of Genl. Lee towards Bristoe Station. The object of Funsten's movement was to distract Meade's attention from Genl. Lee's move on Bristoe Station. Consequently every trooper felt the responsibility for keeping secret the object of their appearance out on the road from Sperryville to Culpeper. The 11th was sent to the Warrenton Turnpike, Lt. Col. Ball in command; and at Rixeyville drove in the Federal pickets, and rode through a deserted infantry camp. The regiment followed the trail, and struck the rear guard a heavy blow. The 7th and 12th were busy at other points. Kilpatrick with about 4,000 of his cavalry, was at the Court House, and drawn up in battle line. Stuart had gone to the head of the column; and saw that his 1,500 men could not hope to force a change in position. He turned to the left; Col. Funsten led the way, all marching rapidly towards Brandy Station. The Federals poured over the dusty roads on the right, heading for the same point, only a skirt of woods separating the columns. Evidently Kilpatrick expected to cut the Virginians off and attempt their capture. Had he succeeded, he could have boasted a rich haul, for Stuart, Fitz Lee, Cols. Marshall, Lomax, Massie, Funsten, Ball and Gordon were all there, not to mention the veteran captains with their hard-fought companies. But Stuart was equal to the occasion; and with rapid orders, our companies were assigned to such positions as would annoy Kilpatrick, who virtually wasted his strength by fighting in detail the scattered companies, who rallied around Stuart at a given signal; and with one grand charge, Brandy Station fell to the men in gray; while Kilpatrick's forces withdrew when he discovered Fitz Lee on his flank; and by sunset the Federals had recrossed the Rappahannock, beaten and baffled by vastly inferior numbers. The loss to the Brigade was about 40. A number of Federals were killed and 200 missing. The latter were taken to the rear by Company B. of the 11th, Capt. Cartmell commanding.

Shortly after this, Stuart made a dash towards Catlett's Station, barely escaping capture; and was compelled to remain in one position in a heavy woodland skirting the roads where two Federal Infantry columns were falling back. Stuart in his report, says his escort spent the night near the roadside, and distinctly heard the troopers talking. As soon as it was light enough, he succeeded in reaching the main body not far away; and at once opened fire on the astonished body of infantry, who had halted and stacked arms, and made coffee. When his seven guns belched forth so suddenly, it struck panic in their ranks; but Stuart was dealing now with old soldiers, who soon rallied and assaulted the battery. But the dismounted cavalry was at hand. Vainly did the Federals assail every point; and at last they gave way, losing heavily. The cavalry regiments engaged, lost several gallant men. The 1st N. C. cavalry came up on the left flank; and made a charge that confounded all in their front. The Federals fled, but the Carolinians suffered severe loss. Col. Ruffin, who led them, was killed. This charge enabled Stuart to move away and retire towards Warrenton, Col. Funsten with the 11th, protecting the rear. The brigade went into camp at Manassas to recuperate. While there, sometime late in October Genl. Thos. L. Rosser was installed commander. This young officer made a favorable impression on the men. They admired his dashing style. He was unlike all others who had led them. Rosser was at West Point when the War came in 1861; and when he found the government was preparing to send cadets to active service, he resigned and made his way South, where he entered the Confederate service with a Lieutenant's commission. He gradually worked up for promotion, which came to him; and now he stood at the head of the celebrated Ashby Brigade. This title the men clung to, little dreaming the new commander would have them win such distinction that 'ere long they would be crowned *The Laurel Brigade.*

By the 1st of November, Genl. Lee went into Winter quarters. The Federals seemed inclined to abandon further demonstrations on his lines. He had offered them every inducement to come out and attack his lines. The cavalry of Stuart had satisfied Meade that he was not yet prepared for general engagement. His cavalry had brought such exaggerated accounts of the *overwhelming numbers* lining every avenue of approach, that he too concluded that Winter quarters, on the Rappahannock, would be a safe place to handle his chessboard. We must here leave the armies until Spring blossoms come again, and not encumber this narrative with the monotony of Winter-quarters life among the soldiers along the Rapidan in the Winter of 1863-4.

Genl. Jubal Early and a portion of the Valley men, during the latter part of November, '63, had been assigned to the Valley District, and was expected to secure supplies to maintain his army while it recruited its strength for the Spring campaigns, and secure if possible supplies for Lee's Army. But he soon grew restless; and stimulated by Fitz Lee's raids into Western Virginia, he figured out his first campaign. This was early in January, 1864. At New Market he organized his little army for the expedition, composed of Rosser's Brigade, one brigade of infantry and all the men of Harry Gilmore's command that had been furloughed to subsist in nearby neighborhoods, and with Capt. McNeil's Mountain Rangers, and four pieces of McClanahan's Battery, he started for Moorefield on the 28th of January, 64. He had no doubt forgotten the January campaign of Jackson and its hardships. However, he and Rosser were over the mountains and in Moorfield the next day, and ready for action. The infantry brigade and artillery got into bivouac near Moorefield that evening. Early was then preparing to capture a wagon train that scouts had seen on the road from New Creek to Petersburg, Hardy County, Rosser started the next morning to accomplish this task, taking his brigade and two pieces of artillery over the Moorefield and Allegany Turnpike. He found the train, and also obstructions in the road, at a gap in the mountain, and an infantry regiment on guard. The 12th regiment was dismounted, and broke through the fallen trees, driving the Federals down the road towards the train. The wagons were rushed together and made a formidable breastwork. The Federals had about 900 men, Rosser only about 450 men. Col. Massie with the 12th, got in the rear of the train, and made an unsuccessful attempt to rout the heavy guard. One of the cannon came up at this time and went into action. The Federals were unprepared for this, and began to waver. Then a joint charge was made, and the prize was won, with the loss of 25 Confederates. 90 wagons and about 50 prisoners were captured. Some of the mules and horses were ridden away in the stampede by the drivers. A number of dead and wounded Federals were left on the field.

Rosser's next move was to Petersburg; but nothing was found there but large quantities of ammunition and commissary stores. From there he proceeded down Patterson's Creek Valley, to forage the country for cattle and strike the railroad. The 7th regiment was sent to Mechanicsburg Gap, there to check Averill's Cavalry, while the main body proceeded to the railroad, where he destroyed the bridges, damaged the canal, and cut the telegraph wires. Averill appeared on the flank several times, but was easily driven to cover in the mountain gaps. The expedition was a success. A large drove of cattle and other supplies were gathered and safely landed in Moorefield, and there met by Capt. John McNeil and his Rangers, with several hundred cattle they had brought from the western side of the Alleganies. This celebrated raid cost the loyal people of the Moorefield Valley untold troubles in retaliation. But such is the fate of War. All must suffer!

Genl. Early started on the return march over the mountains to the Shenandoah Valley, where were landed 1,500 cattle, 500 sheep, the captured wagons full of rich supplies, and a good batch of prisoners. Genl. Stuart in his report, speaking of this expedition in the dead of Winter, 1864, (Feby.) says: "The bold and successful enterprise herein reported, furnishes additional proof of Genl. Rosser's merit as a commander, and adds fresh laurels to that veteran brigade so signalized for valor already."

The Brigade went into camp in the Luray Valley near Port Republic, where they recuperated, and enjoyed the fruits of their captures, until the 1st of March, when they were in line for a march through the Blue Ridge, hastening towards Richmond, in obedience to a call from Stuart. That forced march through sleet, rain and dark nights must be well remembered by every surviving trooper, even now after the lapse of forty-three years. By this forced march, it was intended to join in the capture of the celebrated Dahlgren, in his attempt to raid Richmond, murder the citizens, and destroy the city. The old brigade was stimulated by stories told on their near approach to the section where the Federal raiders were supposed to be. A halt was finally made within 5 miles of Richmond, for the men to recover from their two weeks' hunt for the raiders. Dahlgren had been killed, and a number of his followers killed and captured. The remainder escaped. Lack of forage compelled the brigade to change camps. They marched to Gordonsville; and while there, horses and men were on short rations. They were rejoiced on the 16th of March, when orders came to move slowly towards Staunton, subsisting as best they could, chiefly on the drained resources of the country. About the 1st of April, they were in camp near Lexington, Va. No surviving trooper can forget April of 1864, when the old brigade enjoyed its only rest. While rations were light, the social charms of old Rockbridge were abundant and glorious. Many a disheartened wanderer from home was cheered to take up his burden again with renewed vigor. The women of that end of the old Valley did much towards recruiting the depleted regiments. Many have crossed the river—the fair women and brave troopers—unconscious of these tender recollections, or of the garlands that betimes bedeck their graves!

About the 1st of May, the old brigade was put under review. It was noticeable how the ranks had filled up. Stragglers came with fresh looks, old uniforms cleaned and repaired by some fair hands. New recruits were added; and all betokened answer to the appeal that General Lee had made for help. General orders were read, ordering the Brigade to break camp and march to Stuart's relief, for *Grant was crossing the Rapidan*. All knew what this meant. The command after a quick march, found itself in camp on the East side of the Blue Ridge, all in good condition. May 4th they were called for, and hastily took position near Mine Run, close to Genl. Lee's lines. The next morning (5th) found the brigade on *Cat-hoppin* road. This was the route to the "Todd Tavern." It was not long before the head of the column ran into Wilson's strong division of cavalry. Rosser, nothing daunted, sent in Col. Massie with the 12th supported by the 11th, 7th and White's battalion. Something must give way—for the gray troopers felt good that day, although the heat was intense. Pistols, sabres and Rebel yells shocked the head of the Federal column, which gave way after a hand-to-hand struggle in that narrow road. The Federals fell back, and crossing the river, made a stand, but nothing could stay the gray veterans now. Recklessly they charged over the river and again drove their enemies back. This time Wilson found cover for his artillery; and for a while the Confederates suffered under a galling fire. The artillerists were supported by several battalions. The 12th again made a bold dash. They were twice repulsed, but never wavered. The 11th and 7th went to the support in fine style. The 11th was led by Maj. Ed. McDonald, as brave a man as ever led a charge; and well did his men follow him to the victory. The 7th joined in the grand charge with yells, shots and strokes that ended in a route "of the enemy." Many prisoners were captured. White's Battalion (35th Va. Cavalry) which had been nick-named "The Camanches," made a desperate charge with sabre alone, for they had no ammunition. Gregg was on his way to aid Wilson. They rallied and moved forward in such force, that the renewed attack on Rosser was fierce, resulting in considerable loss to both sides. Rosser, however, held the ground until he fell back to stronger positions. Gregg's official reports show that his force added to Wilson's comprised seventeen regiments of cavalry and six batteries. It was this great victory of Genl. Rosser's that gave them the name of the Laurel Brigade; and many men rode away with sprigs of laurel in their hats. The Confederate loss in killed, wounded and missing was 114. Gregg's O. R. show the following loss to his command: 94 men killed, 27 officers and 389 men wounded, and 187 missing. Yet the infantry in both armies claimed the cavalry avoided battle! An impartial study of the different arms of the service, show they not only rendered more days of hard service, but also that the cavalry losses were larger in proportion to numbers engaged than that of the infantry.

The 6th of May, '64, was one of awful experience to the old Brigade; but, gaining some ground, they were ready for the 7th. The infantry and artillery of both armies were not so active. The cavalry bore the brunt of frequent attempts of Federal Cavalry to strike weak points. Stuart and Wade Hampton were on the ground, and met them at every point. The next morning (the 8th) the Laurel Brigade was assigned to Hampton. Rosser and the brigade formed part of Hampton's command all that Summer. Hampton succeeded General Stuart when the latter was mortally wounded on the 11th, and was Chief in Command from the 16th. Genl. Butler of S. C. assumed command of the division. The brigade did splendid service during the previous week. Sheridan with his powerful force of cavalry, swept around Lee's right on the 9th. At *Yellow Tavern* on the 11th, Stuart met him with his gallant troopers; but the odds were so great that the gray lines felt a shock was coming, and nerved themselves. After severe fighting, the Confederate cavalry escaped from the avalanche, by forming new lines on Sheridan's flank, and forced him to change his route to Richmond. Heavy losses to both commands was the result. Many brave men went down from the Laurel Brigade that day, never again to answer to the bugle-call. The survivors retired gloomily from the field, for their gallant leader and his plume had been carried to the rear. When it was known that Stuart was mortally wounded, heads were bared; the spirits of his brave men who had been cheered by his battle-cry, drooped; and grizzled warriors wept like children. They heeded his last words of entreaty—"*Go back; go back and do your duty as I have done mine, and our country will be safe.*" Genl. Stuart, the hero of many battles, had fought his last. The next day his noble spirit took its flight to another realm, where glories never fade.

Sheridan's tremendous effort to march into Richmond, was an utter failure. His divisions swept the defenceless sections along his line of march, clean of everything. The Confederate cavalry defeated many of his plans. As is well known, he was glad to get back to Grant's lines.

CHAPTER LXV

THE CIVIL WAR

THE WILDERNESS

The Shenandoah Valley Men in the Battle of The Wilderness, Shown Only by their Commands

The first week in May, 1864, with its Spring atmosphere and early blossoms, brought also roadways, that had been impassable for the two great armies that had wintered along the Rappahannock and Rapidan. Both had grown restless. Especially was this true of the Army of the Potomac, whose new commander had stirred the great host from its Winter's sleep. Genl. Grant had assumed control, and much was expected from the hero of Vicksburg and the southwest. "On to Richmond" was the cry. It was plain to old cavalrymen that unusual commotion existed on the North side. Genl. Lee had for some time been apprised that the great army was preparing for action, but Genl. Lee was ready for developments. Possibly students of the situation will question the latter statement; for they will find that plans had matured during the Winter to exterminate the Southern armies. But confining our studies to the Virginia field, we have Genl. Grant commanding the entire line along the Virginia border, with forces at his command of (1st) Grant's individual force (by his own official reports) comprising the four great army corps, viz: the 2nd, 5th, 6th and 9th, and legions of cavalry, giving a total of 102,869 present for duty, with 242 guns, then his siege trains of 106 guns and mortars, all manned with experts.

In the Shenandoah Valley were 15,000 men and 40 guns, under Siegel. Genl. Crook was coming towards Staunton from Western Virginia with 9,000 men and 24 guns; Butler was at Fortress Monroe with monitors and a fleet of gunboats. He had 30,000 men and 79 guns. Besides these armies, the army at Washington or vicinity numbered 40,000 and strong defences. The 19th corps of 12,000 arrived about the 1st of July.

Genl. Lee was commanding the forces to oppose the 156,000 men Grant had at his disposal; and here is the official list in Grant's immediate front, viz:

Ewell's Corps	17,079
Hill's Corps	22,199
Longstreet's Corps	10,000

Longstreet arrived May 5th with this portion of his corps.

Artillery	4,854
Cavalry	8,497
Miscellaneous	1,355

Total about 64,000 men and 274 guns.

Breckenridge was expected to meet the armies of Siegel and Crook in the Valley with 9,000 men and 24 guns.

Beauregard was at Petersburg with 22,000 infantry, 2,000 cavalry and about 50 guns. These included Pickett's Division of Longstreet's Corps, and about 5,000 men, which joined Lee June 1st.

This gives Lee about 95,000 all told, to meet Grant's armies of 156,000.

The 4th of May, Grant started for battle, crossing the Rapidan at Ely's and Germana fords. Lee sent Longstreet to Todd's Tavern, Ewell to the Wilderness Tavern, the center of Grant's line. On the 5th, Grant's 5th corps met Ewell's whole corps within two miles of the Tavern, about 7 A. M.; and then the famous battle of the Wilderness opened, with the Valley men on the firing lines. The Fifth Corps numbered about 24,000, reinforced with 12,000 from the 6th. Ewell's 17,000 met this superior force with the coolness and bravery that always distinguished him in battle. Night closed the battle in the dark forest, with Ewell holding his ground. Two of his generals had been killed: J. M. Jones and Stafford, and Pegram severely wounded.

Hill's corps was also engaged on the Plank road; but his position was not so severely assailed. Night closed all down. The next morning, the battle against Ewell was renewed, and Longstreet was on his way to assist Hill. All that day the battle waged at every available spot. The Wilderness is well remembered by both armies, for its tangled growth. Many brave men went down that day on both sides. Grant fought his divisions in distinct military order, using his great numbers to crush Lee by sheer weight. But Lee and his veteran lieutenants met all such avalanches, and turned the tide of battle by skillful movements and hard fighting. Longstreet was wounded, General Jenkins and several other prominent officers killed. About 4:30 a lull in the great battle occurred; and men had time to look upon the horrors around them, which were increased by the roaring flames. The woods were burning; and wounded men lay helpless. Many were never seen after the fire. Night again closed the battle, and Grant tried other places to defeat Lee. The losses to Grant for the two days was 2,246 killed, 12,037 wounded, 3,383 missing. Total 18,366. No returns can be found showing the Confederate loss. Some estimates have been made that place the killed and wounded at 14,283. The next morning, the 7th, Grant started his army to turn Lee's right flank. His advance was met by Hampton and Fitz Lee's Cavalry, who rendered great service. Lee discovered Grant's design in time to meet his columns at Spottsylvania C. H. The numerous engagements occuring on the 7th, 8th and 10th must be passed without any attempt to give a tracing of the Valley men. Official reports show their valorous deeds, and war histories are replete with accounts of the great battles of the Wilderness and Chancellorsville. The reader can be enlightened and entertained by reading them, written by men who shared the dangers of the famous battles, and have since made careful study of their incidents.

Official reports of this campaign, made by some Federal officers, are regarded by military critics as fairly impartial. The renowned "Bloody Angle," which received its baptism of blood and title, that Ewell had designedly or accidentally created, has been criticized by all and condemned by some for its terrible slaughter. All have agreed that the position Ewell took at that point in the Wilderness with his corps—where the Valley men were conspicuous—where Hancock vainly endeavored with part of the 6th Corps to overwhelm and hold, was the strategic point in the battle; and Genl. Grant so regarded it, and renewed his attack on the 18th with fearful odds. But his great numbers were not available, owing to the surrounding woods and undergrowth. Ewell had been reinforced and strengthened by log breastworks; and as Grant rushed his divisions of brave men into this Angle, they sank in heaps. The slaughter apparently whetted Grant's appetite for blood; but he was compelled to call a halt and change his plans of destruction. His own account shows that he started to pierce Lee's centre, cut his army asunder, and then overpower the two wings with his immense host. His failure only stiffened Grant's determination to crush Lee; for we find him massing his army to turn Lee's right flank by a rush in that direction; and when he received admonitions from Washington, his defiant reply was "That he would fight it out on this line, if it took all Summer."

The battles of the Wilderness and Spottsylvania, started on the 5th of May, were continued without cessation *via* City Point and Petersburg, to finally culminate at Appomattox. We must not attempt to follow the great leaders through these desperate struggles. The losses of the Federals at Spottsylvania, as shown by O. R., were 28,202 killed and wounded, missing 4,235. The Confederate losses may never be known in these battles to the surrender, as very few reports could be made while the regiments were constantly engaged. The following is given as an estimate: Confederate loss 17,250. (See Humphrey, Livermore, and others.)

The battles now were shifting to the North Anna, Chickahominy, Cold Harbor, the James, and Petersburg, with the siege of Petersburg during the Winter of 1864-5.

Leaving the great armies, the reader will be called to that theatre of the terrible conflict between the North and South, as seen in the Shenandoah Valley.

During the Summer of 1864, as already mentioned, Genl. Breckenridge was in the Valley. He had fought a victorious battle at Newmarket, May 15th. It was there the cadets from Lexington Military Institute distinguished themselves, when Genl. Siegel had been overwhelmed with disaster and driven down the Valley in great confusion. This called for Grant's strong will. He sent one of the most bitter haters of the South that he could find at his disposal—for plans were matured for dastardly work—and *David Hunter* had proved himself sufficiently infamous to undertake the devastation of the Valley. Genl. Hunter entered upon his work about the 1st of June, 1864; and gathering the scattered forces, he found himself at the head of an army of about 15,000 men, with no Valley army to stay his march to Staunton, where he was joined by Crook and Averill with their large forces of cavalry and infantry. Genl. Breckenridge with his two brigades, had been ordered to join Lee. This army of Hunter's took a line of march for Lynchburg via Lexington, and left ruin in its wake. Genl. Wm. E. Jones, who had been transferred from the old brigade to Southwest Virginia, met Averill first and repulsed him with heavy loss, but was unable to cope with the infantry force. Genl. Lee knew of the intended campaign of Hunter, and had dispatched Genl. Early with the old Valley troops to intercept the movement, but allowed Hunter to get from his Staunton base before any attempt was made to engage him. Hunter finding himself outgeneraled, endeavored to escape into West Virginia. His army was completely stampeded, but escaped capture. Early then established his post in the Upper Valley and prepared for a move down towards the Potomac. The latter part of June he had a small but resolute army, and began feeling his way North. July 1st he crossed Cedar Creek and rested for one day, when he made a rapid march to Martinsburg, where he landed July 3rd, hoping to surprise Siegel; but the latter made such hasty exit that only a few stragglers and abandoned army supplies were captured. Early continued his march, crossing the river; struck the Old National Turnpike and marched boldly on to Frederick City, where he learned that a Federal force under Genl. Lew Wallace, was on the Monocacy about 5 miles distant. He fearlessly attacked the Federals, inflicting heavy loss before they fled towards Baltimore. Rockville was his next objective point, where he arrived just at nightfall, July 10, 1864. They then struck a bee-line for Washington, but halted only long enough to give his command time to see the capitol plainly. Many rumors were afloat as to the object of this campaign. The capture of the city seemed easy; but he deliberately turned his column towards the Valley, where he arrived somewhat refreshed by his visit. Genl. Lee had pointed out the misfortune that might result from an engagement. All that was desired was to make demonstrations on Washington, strong enough to require the withdrawal of troops from Grant's Army, so as to relieve Lee. This was done; the 6th and 19th Corps hurried away to the capital. This proved a serious interruption of Grant's plans, for he had planned for these corps to harrass Lee's rear and flanks, while he was changing his base to the James. Lee was free to follow his movements; and waged battle at every available point, until Grant was compelled to make City Point his base. We will not stop to consider if this was not really advantageous to Grant in carrying out his general plan. Early when safely in camp in Winchester, summed up his captures and embodied them in his official report, which bubbles over with humor and sarcasm. He had stirred up the Washington authorities. Their loss of several thousand horses and beef cattle, and train loads of rich army stores, was small, calculating the ease with which it was done. This gateway to Washington must be closed, and vigorous measures were made ready. Sheridan was preparing for the command of the District. Hunter was ordered to raid the Valley again, and was given authority to collect the scattered forces. This required a full month. During this time, Early was hovering over the Lower Valley without any serious interruption. Imboden's command was doing duty as cavalry. To this was added a brigade commanded by Genl. McCausland, of West Va. Early sent this brigade on a raid to stir up a little interest across the Potomac, and to turn Hunter's attention in that direction. McCausland proceeded as far as Chambersburg, and burned part of that town on the 30th of July, in retaliation, as many believed, for the wrongs done to his people in Western Virginia by Federal scouting squadrons. McCausland says it was done because the citizens refused to comply with a levy made on them to furnish supplies for his hungry troopers. The raid ended in disaster to this command, which endeavored to escape to the Valley by a circuitous route. Overtaken at Moorefield when they felt secure, they were surprised and routed. Many condemned this fruitless raid. McCausland was not equal to such work as Stuart and others successfully accomplished. This stirred up strife among the Federals. Hunter was urged to move, which he did about the 1st of August, '64. Early met him near Winchester, very nearly on the same ground where Genl. Ramseur had a pitched battle on the 20th of July with Averill's large force of cavalry, supported by artillery. Ramseur had made a gallant fight, losing many of his men and such officers as Genl. Lilly, Lewis and others. He was compelled to fall back on Genl. Early, who was then at Newtown 8 miles South of Winchester. For the first time Early failed to render proper support to one of his subalterns—Ramseur had been left to fight the battle alone. It is true Early had given some support on the left, as the lines extended over the Martinsburg Turnpike; but why he fell back to Newtown without notice to Ramseur, none will ever know. In an interview between himself and a correspondent for one of the large newspapers, Genl. Early said: "It was part of the plan of strategy; that the Federals would be flushed with victory and would recklessly rush into one of his chosen positions." Subsequent events show this was not his last misconception of the intentions of his adversaries.

On the 4th of August, Hunter and his new army appeared at Winchester. Early was then beyond Cedar Creek. The cavalry met in skirmishes. Averill came to redeem himself with a large force of cavalry, with Genl's Torbett and Wilson Chiefs in Command. South of Winchester several severe engagements took place, as Hunter slowly advanced and Early slowly retired. Both Generals seemed willing to avoid collision. Hunter had already applied the torch in several sections. As his infantry covered the ground, his two columns of cavalry—one towards Front Royal and the other on the Valley Turnpike and the two back roads—moved cautiously, spending several days on their way South, foraging and pillaging every hamlet and home through the country. The infantry and artillery seemed disinclined for fight. Hunter in this style of advance, proceeded far enough to disclose Early's lines near Strasburg. The column of cavalry that entered Front Royal on the 15th, met stubborn resistance from a quarter they regarded as clear. They waited to get communication with Hunter at Strasburg. The cavalry of the back roads had been repulsed several times, yet they pressed on. The central column planted two heavy pieces of artillery on a high ridge South of Middletown, and fired some harmless shells in the direction of Early's lines. The latter supposing Hunter's army to be Sheridan's, declined battle on the 16th, and fell back on the highlands near Woodstock; the indications being that the flanking column at Front Royal intended to cut off his retreat while he fought on the centre. He again fell back; and before he learned that reinforcements were at Front Royal, and the Federals were at a standstill at that point, word was sent Hunter during the night of the 16th, that Lee and his whole army were entering the Valley at Front Royal. Hunter immediately ordered the army to retire, but to sweep the country clean of every barn, mill, hay or wheat stack, and to gather all cattle, horses and sheep into herds and drive them out of the Valley, and to kill all hogs and any broken-down horses. Details were made from each regiment, of men who would faithfully execute this order. When daylight came, the whole army was in motion and the work of destruction had begun. The cavalry detachments were scouring the country for hours before the army started, and the herds were forming on every road, all hurrying towards the Potomac, then nearly 50 miles away. When day dawned, the poor war-stricken country presented a strange scene to the citizens, as they beheld the numerous cavalcades hastening on, increasing every mile as the last cow or horse disappeared from the home. Their amazement was soon to take the form of fear, for at 6 A. M. the torches were applied; and from the Shenandoah to the Little North Mountain, the volumes of smoke that rose high in the air, betokened destruction of their homes. Steadily the tide rolled. Hunter rode to the front, leaving the infantry and artillery to protect the rear of the vandal hordes. When Early learned that Kershaw's division of infantry and Fitz Lee's division under Genl. R. H. Anderson, had arrived at Front Royal and were seeking a juncture with him at Strasburg, he was astounded. He had expected reinforcements, but looked for them by way of Luray and New Market, and expected their arrival in time to make a grand stand and stem the tide of Sheridan's army as it rolled South. Caught unawares, he waited until the 18th before he changed his base. Moving down to Strasburg, he found Kershaw and Fitz Lee exasperated over the situation. Their long march had ended amid heaps of desolation, instead of the oasis full of plenty they had longed to see once more. The 17th of August, 1864, will go down in history as the blackest day the Lower Valley has ever seen. By 11 o'clock the atmosphere was stifling with smoke; the lurid flames that shone in the early morning from river to mountain, were obscured by the increasing pall of darkness that rested on the once beautiful landscapes. The besom of destruction swept on to the gates of Winchester. The Valley troopers of their own accord, plunged through the smoke and ruins, seeking to avenge the terrible wrongs perpetrated by demons who gladly obeyed the hellish order of the insatiate wretch who claimed the right to wear the uniform of an officer in the United States Army, and also the right to bear the name of a family Virginia has honored through successive generations. His deeds of infamy will never stain the name of the Hunter family of Virginia. Not to the manor born, he will go down to posterity as an alien to the Commonwealth of the Old Dominion.

Many startling incidents occurred that day that may not be told here. Lest some be confused as to the date of that day of gloom, we add there were two burnings of the Valley; the other will appear in its proper place.

Early hastened to redress these wrongs, and if possible atone for his tardiness. The main body of reinforcements under General Anderson, left Front Royal on the 17th, marching over the Front Royal Turnpike. Kershaw and Fitz Lee joined them later. Early started his army in motion, and on the 18th formed a juncture at Winchester. A sharp engagement ensued between Kershaw's advance and a division of Federal infantry. Some captures were made; and the enemy driven towards Stephensons, where a stand was made. Early continued his pursuit to Harpers Ferry; the Federals gradually fell back, and finally sought the North side of the Potomac for a new base. Early also halted. This was not in accordance with Genl. Lee's plans. When he sent reinforcements, he expected Early with his strong force to boldly cross at Williamsport, and march towards Pennsylvania, hoping this would change all of Grant's plans. But the old fighter was not Stonewall Jackson. He could not or would not appreciate Lee's strategy; and wasted time in skirmishes, showing no disposition to advance. Lee ordered Kershaw and Fitz Lee back to Culpeper C. H. This was on the 15th of September. Early had wasted a month of valuable time; for Sheridan was ordered to proceed in person to the Valley with all the army he needed, and wage a war that would exterminate the Valley armies. Early had fallen back to Winchester before the departure of Kershaw; and for the first time it suited Sheridan to enter the Lower Valley with great pomp and show, and truly with an army of banners. He came *via* Harpers Ferry; and boldly extended his lines along the Shenandoah as far as Berryville. Aside from Hunter's scattered forces, Sheridan came with the 6th and 19th corps of infantry, the two divisions of cavalry under Torbett and Wilson, and the West Virginia division under Crook and Averill, and many batteries. Truly it was a grand army; and was destined to be a bolt of destruction to the Confederacy. Genl. Early congratulated himself during his entire life that he had so conducted his campaign in the Valley, as to compel Grant to yield to the demands from Washington and allow the 6th and 19th corps to remain in easy call to defend the city from his attacks. Be this as it may, General, military critics find you in a precarious position on the 14th, 15th and 16th of September, '64.

Some doubt arises in the study of this campaign as to the withdrawal of Kershaw and Fitz Lee from the Valley, in obedience to the order from Genl. Lee, dated Sept. 15th. We will give the benefit of the doubt to the critic and treat the battle of Winchester as if they had not gone before the order was countermanded.

Genl. Early's forces including his reinforcements, consisted of about 9,000 infantry and about 2,800 cavalry and three batteries of artillery, to meet the great army stretching itself along his right flank. The fighting old Jubal, as his men delighted to style him, showed a bold front; but the movement he first made advertised his blunder. The official map of the battlefield places Early's men about in the following positions: Ramseur's Division (about 1,500 men) and Wickham with Fitz Lee's Cavalry at Winchester, while Wharton with the remnant of the once grand division, and Lomax with the Valley Cavalry, went to Stephensons five miles North, the terminal of the W. & P. R. R., while he, the General, Chief-in-Command, marched away to Martinsburg with Rodes' and Gordon's divisions, to destroy the railroad. (So stated in his reports.) This places Early at the North end of his line of battle, 22 miles long, while Sheridan with his immense army—five times Early's combined strength—occupied the country from Charlestown to White Post, within an eight mile march, to cut off retreat on the Valley Turnpike at any point South of Winchester. Any student of battlefields must conclude that Genl. Early was either over-confident or had become incompetent. There is nothing to prove that Genl. Early, when he left Martinsburg on the 18th of September and deliberately camped at Bunkers Hill 12 miles from Winchester, had any knowledge of Sheridan's moving from Berryville towards Winchester and his column in motion early in the morning of the 19th. The writer and other scouts (now living) informed Genl. Early before he left Winchester for his march to Martinsburg, and also in the night of the 17th apprised him of Sheridan's forward movement, and that it was believed he was seeking a point on the Valley Turnpike South of Winchester to form a line in his rear. Nothing in his reports of this campaign indicate that he suspected such movement. The situation was plain to every scout. They informed every outpost of cavalry, and the officers commanding the two positions at Winchester and Stephensons Station knew, that heavy forces of cavalry were pressing every point held by Lomax and Wickham. Clearly Genl. Early was outwitted by Sheridan, and allowed the enemy to attack Ramseur Southeast of Mt. Hebron Cemetery at 5 A. M. on the 19th, before he made any effort to support him. Fitz Lee's cavalry were on the ridges overlooking the Opecquon. Ramseur and this cavalry won laurels of glory on that morning. About 11 A. M., Early got Rodes' division to the field, when desperate fighting ensued. Gordon arrived about this time, and took position on the left, extending over what is known as the old Hackwood farm. About this time the gallant Rodes, who had distinguished himself so often on other fields, was killed. Wharton fell away from Stephensons and entered the battle, after the memorable fight made to prevent two full divisions of cavalry and three batteries under Genl. Torbet, from cutting off Early in his march from Bunker Hill. Lomax's cavalry had been sent South of Winchester to join Fitz Lee who had swung to the right after the infantry forces met on the Berryville Pike. Willson with his large column of cavalry, was sweeping towards the Valley pike to strike a point about two miles South. It now looked like Early was bagged. Fitz Lee, with the dash and daring he always exhibited when occasion demanded, fell upon the Federal advance from Vantage ground, so that the whole column was brought to a standstill. Gray troopers fired from copse and cover. Willson seemed bewildered; and his column felt that some great disaster was near; and instead of forming his line of battle and sweeping the Confederates aside, he turned the head of the column East and trotted off, exposing a weak point that Lee attacked with such fury, that the trot march ended in a veritable rout. The cavalry then hastened to give aid to the fighting infantry under Gordon, where he was hard pressed. For one hour before Wharton arrived, Genl. Gordon fought a famous engagement. He charged repeatedly over strong lines of the enemy, but was too weak to hold his positions, and was driven back. It was during this hour, that Major James Breathed with his battery of 6 guns, won renown by masking his battery and allowing Torbett's line to sweep around Gordon's left and form on his rear and flank. He then rushed his guns to a position on high ground and swept the entire line. Men and horses went down in great numbers, and the enemy gave way in great disorder. Gordon again charged; and a rout occurred that left him master of the field. About this time Crook loomed up with the 8th corps in such force, the Confederates fell back to new positions, believing the day had been saved. Breckenridge's division under Wharton appeared and reopened the battle. Then the two divisions of cavalry under Averill and Merritt, with two light batteries, swept around to the old Carter place on the Martinsburg Turnpike; and here for one hour a few weak companies of Lomax's cavalry and a small regiment of infantry under Col. Patton, held in check the flanking cavalry. It has been often said that for one hour every Confederate that could stand, was hotly engaged.—No Reserves, no support, and confronted by overwhelming numbers at every point on front, flank and rear—so seriously threatened at that hour were they, it seemed impossible to escape capture. And if Sheridan possessed great skill as a general, he failed to show it. With his immense army, and the advantage he had on the morning of the 19th of September, as shown, he should have compelled the surrender of Early's whole command. It was a sad scene to behold. Men never fought better than did the Confederates of every arm. They were stimulated by love of the old town and country-side that had so recently cheered them to their work. Now after such heroic struggles, they were driven through the streets to seek shelter. Early in his official report says he retired to Fishers Hill. Brave men who fell in the battle of the 19th of September, and those who survived and retired to Fishers Hill, would never have suffered such disaster under the leadership of their old Stonewall Captain. 2,500 prisoners and several pieces of artillery were left in the hands of Sheridan, along with the many dead stretched along that long battle line. Fitz Lee had been desperately wounded, and many other well-known officers.

The retreat to Fishers Hill was made in good order, although the powerful force of Federal cavalry beat upon the rear, protected by part of the Confederate cavalry. Early's army arriving at Fishers Hill, immediately formed lines of defence and awaited Sheridan's advance. The new position was a tempting one, but it proved untenable. Flanking columns could pass it on either side and not engage Early. The Lower Valley was open, and heavy columns could by way of Luray Valley cross over to New Market and join a column that could march up the Back Road near the North Mountain and thus cut off his further retreat up the Valley. The middle column remained on the Valley Pike and made a feint on Early's front. Early soon found himself in the above position. Torbett tried the Luray Valley, and but for Wickham's appearance at Front Royal with a small force of worn-out cavalry, he would have cut the retreat, as a large body of infantry and cavalry did take the back road, while Sheridan was at his front on the 22nd to force battle. Genl. Early hastened his retreat after having barely escaped the net.

Sheridan should have pressed the retreating army from Winchester on the 20th with his large force, and a rout of ruin to Early would have occurred. No; "Fighting Phil" was content to move slowly and allow the Confederates to keep out of the way, saving wagon trains, etc.

Sheridan again allowed Early to move slowly off, while he lingered to enjoy the fruits of pillage his men perpetrated on the helpless communities. Federal cavalry pursued Early to Harrisonburg, and then returned to the main army that had encamped on the North side of Cedar Creek in the vicinity of Middletown. From this camp, a systematic plundering of the country set in. Foraging parties extended their raids for miles East and West of the Little North Mountain, and swept every home in that section clean of every particle of food that fell in their way—wearing apparel, bedding and many other articles held sacred by families, were ruthlessly carried away. This also prevailed in all the country as far away as the Northwestern Turnpike East of the Mountain. The horrors of such warfare can only be compared to the terrors inflicted by brutes on the helpless palatinates of old, that ultimately drove the refugees to seek homes in America; and here we see their descendants gloating over similar brutalities. This was not war; but hellish treatment of the helpless.

Early went into camp in the vicinity of Harrisonburg and Bridgewater; and proceeded to reorganize his remnants. It was not long before he had rallied around him the scattered men. The camps took on new life; and it was observed that this army was not yet beaten; and old Jubal had fight in him yet. We find by the first of October he was planning for another move down the Valley. On all the roads leading South, Sheridan's cavalry could be seen daily; and frequent skirmishes occurred. Often brave men went down; but this warfare went on. On the 5th of October, late in the day, all were surprised and delighted to see the Laurel Brigade come into the camp near Bridgewater to reinforce the Fitz Lee and other cavalry. The Laurels had marched from Petersburg in less than eight days, and needed rest; but their old enemy Genl. Custer was in sight, and had been giving them trouble for several days. Rosser assumed command of all the cavalry; and proceeded without delay to cross sabres once more with the long-haired chieftain. The reader will remember Custer and Rosser met at Trevillian Station; and there the former made acquaintance with the gray troopers for the first time. On the 6th, the Laurel Brigade led off; and the cavalry, under the impression that they would encounter Custer and his gaily attired troopers, spruced up, and tried to look their best. Custer was encountered, and after brisk fighting at many points, the Federal cavalry fell back towards their main army. As the Valley men pursued the retreating legions, they beheld their country groaning under the destruction the Federal cavalry had inflicted. Barns were burning, and ruin seemed complete in many homes. This was only a foretaste of what the Valley would be called upon to endure, as will be shown later on.

Early now felt strengthened for another effort. More reinforcements came in. The Valley, from his positions to the plains beyond Woodstock, was clear. Confederate cavalry and scouts were bringing word that the Federals had settled down on the North side of Cedar Creek, with their lines stretching from the Cedar Creek Turnpike to Front Royal. The Confederates prepared for a forward movement; and many wondered what Early could do to justify any attempt to re-open battle with Sheridan's great host. On the 17th, the army was put in motion. It has been estimated that his force all told did not exceed 9,000 men. When he arrived at Woodstock, a halt was ordered; heavy scouting squadrons were kept busy all day long, skirmishing with bands of cavalry found on the South side of the river below Strasburg and also along the roads leading to Cedar Creek above Strasburg. Rosser kept Early informed. They had planned to surprise the enemy in the night; but finding this impracticable, owing to the constant appearance of Federals on the South side, it was decided to wait until early morning and strike before the camps were astir, or the daily patrols had started. Early moved slowly down the roads, and put himself within a short march of his coveted prize, and then waited for the darkness to cover his further movements. Rosser's cavalry kept up a slight movement all day. The camps on the North side were reported as being entirely unconscious of danger. There lay the great army. Immediately in Early's front was the 19th corps, and the 6th and 8th corps on the right and left. Here they had an encampment that will be remembered by every mortal who lived in the territory North for fifteen miles, and the horrors of those times are told today by survivors, with trembling lips.

The Old Valley men now waiting in grim silence, had heard of the outrages, and they were eager to go into the heart of that camp and avenge the wrongs.

Rosser had fought a severe battle on the 9th by rushing into a full division of cavalry near Strasburg, and lost prisoners and one piece of light artillery; and though compelled to retreat in disorder, he rallied; and the day after continued to annoy the picket line. When the Federals heard firing on their left in the night of the 18th, they felt sure it was of no importance. Scouts had been busy for two days seeking routes to satisfy General Early. His desire was to cross some ford between Strasburg and Marlboro, that was not heavily guarded. This seemed impossible; but at midnight the line of march was taken up. About seven miles of rough road lay out there in the darkness. Old soldiers speak of the scramble over rock and brush as a thing they will never forget. Early aimed to cross the creek, while the not infrequent picket firing was plainly heard on the right. Gordon's Division was in front, Ramseur's next, and Pegram in reserve. At daylight, the column was over the ford and prepared to surprise the great camps. The 8th received the first shock. None were prepared. The Confederates made good use of every moment. Men were over-run, killed and wounded; and prisoners were in confused masses. Several thousands surrendered; others fled, and rushing through the 19th corps, which was making some effort to form, produced a panic by their yells. The 19th soon wavered, and fled as only scared men can. The two camps were entirely abandoned; and their late occupants were rushing past Middletown before they were partly checked by the 6th corps under Genl. Wright. This was of short duration; for when the Confederate reserves began to swing around a flank movement was feared, and everything gave way to rout and confusion. Genl. Early called off the pursuit, and the scattered Confederate battalions returned to the rich camp and feasted on their spoils. While this indulgence was in progress, Genl. Wright rallied his 6th corps, and gallantly undertook to retrieve the terrible losses; and it is well known that he did the work well. The Confederates were unfortunate in the end. They failed to appreciate the disparity in numbers; and felt they were secure from attack. Genl. Wright's corps, the 6th, was composed of fighting men, and he was a brave and competent officer. He was soon in line of battle; and at 2:20 P. M. disaster to the Confederates was in sight. They were unorganized and totally unprepared for the magnificent line of battle moving down upon them, capturing hundreds of small squads of Confederates as they made for the pillaged camp. By 3 o'clock the well-disciplined line of the 6th corps was on the old camp ground. In vain did Gordon try to stay the uneven attack. Ramseur and Kershaw hastened away; Pegram and the artillery held on at the ford, and checked the charge for a moment; but from this ford to Fishers Hill a fearful rout ensued; and it was this that Genl. Sheridan styled *his* victory. Guns, medical and ordnance stores were abandoned, 23 pieces of artillery and 1,500 prisoners captured; and the Federals occupied the camps they had deserted in the morning. A heavy column of cavalry crossed the Creek and wrought havoc among the retreating Confederates. Wagon trains and more prisoners were captured. Sheridan in his official report of the affair, gives himself the credit for reforming his army and routing Early, and for many marvellous feats performed by his orders; and fails to give Genl. Wright and his brigadiers any credit.

Sheridan and his black horse, and the ride of twenty miles, was an incident to fire the drooping spirits of the masses, and a theme for maudlin verse and war stories for many years. But the day came when participants in the two routs of the 19th of October, 1864, could meet in reunions of the Blue and the Gray, and the battle-scarred veterans comparing notes, told the true story. Then it was agreed that the self-styled hero and his dramatic story, was a myth. His ride of twelve miles instead of twenty, ended after 3 o'clock, the hour when Genl. Wright in person and his 6th corps, had driven Gordon and other Confederates from the camp and across the ford.

Genl. Early, during the time between 1 and 3 o'clock, had been aroused from his lethargy, and vainly endeavored to save his army. It may be asked, where had Genl. Early been for five hours. It was well known at the time that he, too, had been enjoying the pillage rather than the fruits of his victory; and when his broken-hearted troops read his address of censure—when he charged disaster to their misconduct, they sullenly expressed their disapproval, and boldly asserted his incompetency resulted from causes they had discovered in two other campaigns; and from that hour the troops sought every just means to change commanders. They saw the need of change. The Richmond authorities, doubtless, were well aware that a mistake was made when Early was entrusted with the work that Stonewall Jackson inaugurated. The defeat of Early's Army was a death blow to the Valley. No hope for holding out. The Valley Army virtually disbanded. Breckenridge was sent to the South; Gordon rejoined Lee; the Cavalry were allowed to shift for themselves—Forage all gone—!

We find Early—the Lieutenant General who had performed wonderful feats under the guidance of master spirits—now stranded. His genius as a Brigadier; his fighting qualities so much admired by his followers, can never be forgotten. And may all who read this brief notice of his last battles, throw the mantle of charity over his mistakes, and retain a regard for his service, such as Genl. Lee exhibited in his letter of condolence, of which we give space for a copy:

Head Quarters, C. S. Armies,
March 30, 1865.

Lt. General J. A. Early,
Franklin C. H., Va.

Dear sir:

My telegram will have informed you that I deem a change of commanders in your department necessary; but it is due to your zealous and patriotic services that I should explain the reason that prompted my action. The situation of affairs is such that we can neglect no means calculated to develop the resources we posses to the greatest extent, and make them as efficient as possible. To this end it is essential that we should have the cheerful and hearty support of the people and a full confidence of the soldiers, without which our efforts would be embarassed, and our means of resistence weakened. I have reluctantly arrived at the conclusion that you cannot command the united and willing co-operation which is so essential to success. Your reverses in the Valley, of which the public and the army judge chiefly by results, have, I fear, impaired your influence both with the people and the soldiers and would add greatly to the difficulties, which will, under any circumstances, attend our military operations in South-western Virginia. While my own confidence in your ability, zeal and devotion to the cause is unimpaired, I have nevertheless felt that I could not oppose what seems to be the current of opinion without injustice to your reputation and injury to the service. I therefore felt constrained to endeavor to find a commander who would be more likely to develop the strength and resources of the country, and inspire the soldiers with confidence, and, to accomplish this purpose, thought it proper to yield to my own opinion, and defer to that of those to whom alone we can look for support. I am sure that you will understand and appreciate my motives, and that no one will be more ready than yourself to acquiesce in any manner which the interests of the country may seem to require, regardless of all personal considerations. Thanking you for the fidelity and energy with which you have always supported my efforts, and for the courage and devotion you have ever manifested in the service of the country,

I am, very respectfully and truly your obedient servant, R. E. LEE,
General."

We need not follow Early through the Valley after his disaster on the 19th of October, 1864, when he made several ineffectual stands to save the dissolution of his army. Sheridan inflicted a yet more complete disaster at Fishers Hill on the 22nd, when Gordon by tremendous efforts, held the advancing columns in check; but all finally gave way. The Valley was abandoned. Early retired with his remnants to mountain passes beyond Staunton; and Sheridan filled the Upper Valley with horrors, but finally returned to Strasburg, where he summed up his campaign in a letter to the Washington authorities, which tells the story of his devastations. Sheridan chose to fall back and destroy the country, rather than march boldly on and swing around to the rear of Lee's Army, and enable Grant with his colossal equipments to crush the tattered remnants of the Army of Northern Virginia. This letter can be found among the files of the War Department, a copy of which is here given to show his vicious temperament:

"In moving back to this point, the whole country has been made untenable for a rebel army. I have destroyed over two thousand barns filled with hay and farm implements, over 70 mills, filled with flour and wheat; have driven in front of the army 4,000 head of stock, and have killed and issued to the troops not less than three thousand sheep. The destruction embraces the Luray Valley and Little Fort Valley as well as the main Valley."

Some writers have confounded this burning with that of Hunter's fires on the 17th of August; and some have confounded it with the fires in the Bridgewater neighborhood, about the last of September. The latter was done by Sheridan in retaliation for the killing of Col. Meigs, his chief of staff; and at the same time he had several prisoners brutally shot who had no part in the affair. The man who killed the staff officer is living in Rockingham County at this writing; and several citizens of that section furnished the writer with a full account of it. Sheridan ordered the town to be destroyed. His men extended the fires; and other property was burned.

We have not space to recount the deeds of the Valley Cavalry during the calamitous day mentioned in connection with the Valley Campaign. They never faltered; and on many occasions fought detachments of cavalry that patrolled the Valley, until December. The reader will find graphic accounts of the service rendered by the cavalry, in the History of the Laurel Brigade, already referred to.

CHAPTER LXVI

FALL OF RICHMOND

Appomattox and Surrender

In connection with the notice of the Valley campaign, the culmination of which seemed to foreshadow the fall of Richmond, it seems proper to briefly mention the situation in Grant's front.

Genls. Grant and Lee scarcely allowed a day to pass during the last Winter of the War, without testing their siege guns—Grant bombarding the trenches around Petersburg, and the defences of Richmond; Lee answering in a thunderous roar that can never be forgotten by the men in the celebrated trenches. The compass of this volume prevents any narration of the incidents of that Winter. We may say, however, that General Lee, about the last of March, made a demonstration on the South side of the Appomattox. Genl. Gordon commanded the expedition, which promised good results; but overwhelming numbers forced him to retire, and realize the sad lesson, that the day had passed for offensive movements for the Army of Northern Virginia. Grant now ordered Sheridan to sweep through the Valley by way of Waynesboro. On the 27th of February, 1865, he was on the March. He found Genl. Early at Waynesboro March 2nd, with all that was left of the Valley Army, about 1,200 men, unorganized and in distress, having suffered many privations during the Winter. Sheridan's powerful cavalcade soon rode everything down. About 1,000 worn-out Confederates were captured, and Genl. Early barely escaped with a few humiliated staff officers. Charlottesville fell into Sheridan's hands next day. He found the James impassable, and his course was changed. He swung around Genl. Lee's left, and crossed the Pamunkey River near the White House; and on the 25th of March joined Grant. While he was unable to obtain a position that Grant had indicated, he was on hand with an effective force of cavalry that performed an important part in the final drama. Sheridan in his march to Lynchburg, destroyed more public property in the shape of railroad bridges, canal locks, etc., than it is possible to describe here, and private property melted away. The desolation was complete.

March 29th Grant threw his 5th and 2nd corps and Sheridan's 1,200 cavalry against Lee's right. This was the beginning of the final overthrow. To meet this, Genl. Lee sent the divisions of Wise, Pickett and Johnson (Bushrod), with Fitz Lee's Division and Rarsome's Brigade—about 16,000 men. Sheridan was at Dinwiddie C. H., the same evening; and there he brought on a severe but short fight between his forces and Pickett's and Johnson's. The Federal cavalry were driven back, but held out until the 5th corps came up on the 1st of April; and then occurred the surrender of full 5,000 Confederates.. The remainder fled in great confusion. It has been related by officers who were near Genl. Lee when he discovered that his right wing was routed and his whole position in danger, that he exhibited much impatience, and ordered all stragglers put under guard; and censured some of the officers with much feeling.

Perhaps officers and men were impressed with the feeling that a new base was forced upon the army; and they lost the spirit of further resistance. But why should we linger over what Capt. Chew and others did at Fort Gregg, when brave men uselessly gave up their lives! The heroic deeds of that garrison will ever be recounted with fervor by Confederates who survived the conflict. No incident of the War has elicited as vivid descriptions as has this glorious struggle. Writers on both sides have illumined pages of their histories with the halo over Fort Gregg. With its fall, the Army of Northern Virginia was cut in twain. Genl. Lee had notified the War Office at Richmond to prepare for evacuation that night. Richmond's people were unconscious of the impending fate. The first Sabbath and Monday of April, 1865, saw her in the throes of desolation. The city was virtually abandoned when the Federal General Weitzel marched his troops in her streets. Negro regiments seemed to hold the place of honor in the column. The retiring Confederates obeyed orders that should never have been issued, and committed useless and wanton acts of destruction that were condemned then, and that the lapse of time has not palliated. Fire brands and explosions were deadly in their work. The entire business part of the city was destroyed; acres of warehouses, stores, factories, mills, bridges, etc., all in ruins; and the captors found no captives and no prize.

While this scene was witnessed at Richmond, Genl. Lee was forming new lines, which led from Petersburg; and it was a memorable morning, that of the 3rd of April. Great batteries and earthworks had been blown up; and a lurid light from Petersburg to Richmond told full well that Genl. Lee was seeking the Appomattox hills for a new base. Grant's untold thousands were in front and flank. When the first halt was made at Amelia C. H. on the 4th, for the broken army to take rations, nothing was found for the famishing men. Grant was in pursuit; and Genl. Lee was bent upon two things only: one to secure food for his starving men; the other to escape. On the 5th he moved once more, hoping to reach the hills near Farmville. Men were dropping from the ranks by hundreds; and it was plainly seen that the remnant of the army that still held out, must soon succumb to a soldier's worst enemy—exhaustion from hunger.

April 6th, Sheridan was in flank and rear, where he met Ewell and Pickett. Some deadly work checked the advance of the enemy. Ewell was captured; Curtis fell and most of his command surrendered. Once more the line of march was attempted. The morning of the 7th found the shattered army near Farmville, having recrossed the Appomattox. Gordon remained at High Bridge. The morning of the 8th Gordon was drawn into a severe fight, and many brave men were sacrificed, Capt. Hugh McGuire being one.

Longstreet gave battle on the hills near Farmville. Gordon joined in the lines around that town, and a show of battle was made at this point. A skirmish occurred over an effort to Capture Lee's wagon train. The Federals were repulsed and 200 prisoners captured by the Confederates.

On the 8th, the army was working its way over bad roads that ran through scrubby pines and oaks. In the afternoon, they emerged from the tangled woods and struck a good road and marched rapidly until dark. When the head of the army reached Appomattox Court House, the rear was only four miles distant. The whole column was a picture of distress—and this was the remnant of an army that had held the combined forces of the old Union, recruited from every civilized nation of the world, in check for four long years!

The name of Lee and his generals and the grand Army of Northern Virginia, had startled the world with their victories.

The line of retreat to Lynchburg, twenty miles off, was cut by Sheridan. The country between the Appomattox and James was only about eight miles wide. Meade was pressing the rear; and a corps was Southwest of the Court House. Here the great Lee was confronted with hosts of victorious divisions on every side. He must give battle or succumb, as thousands of his followers had done for four or five days. An effort was made by Gordon on the 9th to march through the town, and make one more effort to dislodge Sheridan. The wagon trains followed, with sick and starving men clinging to the wagons. One vain effort was made to break through the Federal lines. Genl. Lee was ordering up more men to support Gordon,when he was driven back; and while the artillery was firing some fatal shots, a white flag was seen approaching Genl. Lee's Headquarters; and the enemy then ceased firing. The flag meant a truce between the armies, pending a correspondence between the two Generals. We give it place, thinking it may interest readers who have not seen it elsewhere.

"April 7, 1865.

Gen. R. E. Lee, Commanding C. S. A.;

General: The result of last week must convince you of the hopelessness of further resistance on the part of the Army of Northern Virginia in this struggle. I feel that it is so, and regard as my duty to shift from myself the responsibility for any further effusion of blood, by asking of you the surrender of that portion of the Confederate Southern Army known as the Army of Northern Virginia.

Very respectfully,
Your obedient Servt.,
U. S. GRANT,
Lieutenant Genl. Commanding Armies of U. S.

"April 7, 1865.

General: I have received your note of this day. Though not entirely of the opinion you express of the hopelessness of further resistance on the part of the Army of N. Va., I reciprocate your desire to avoid useless effusion of blood, and therefore, before considering your proposition, ask that the terms you will offer on condition of its surrender.

R. E. LEE, *General.*

To Lieut. Genl. U. S. Grant,
Commanding Armies of the United States."

" April 8, 1865.

To Genl. R. E. Lee, Comdg. C. S. A.,

General: Your note of last evening, in reply to mine of same date, asking the conditions on which I will accept the surrender of the Army of North Virginia is just rec'd.

In reply, I would say, the peace being my first desire, there is but one condition that I insist upon, viz:

That the men surrendered shall be disqualified for taking up arms again against the Government of the United States, until properly exchanged.

I will meet you, or designate officers to meet any officers you may name for the purpose of arranging definitely the terms upon which the surrender of the Army of Northern Virginia shall be received.

Very respectfully,
Your obedient servant,
U. S. GRANT, *Lieutenant General,*
Commanding Armies of U. S."

"April 8, 1865.

General: I received at a late hour your note of to-day in answer to mine of yesterday.

I did not intend to propose the surrender of the Army of Northern Va., but to ask the terms of your proposition. To be frank, I do not think the emergency has arisen to call for the surrender.

But as the restoration of peace should be the sole object of all, I desire to know whether your proposals would tend to that end.

I cannot, therefore, meet you with a view to surrender the Army of Northern Virginia; but so far as your proposition may affect the Confederate forces under my command and tend to the restoration of peace, I should be pleased to meet you at 10 A. M. to-morrow, on the old stage road to Richmond, between the picket lines of the two Armies.

Very respectfully,
Your obedt. servt.,
R. E. LEE, *General,*
C. S. A.
To Lieut. Genl. Grant,
Commanding Armies of U. S."

"Apl. 9, 1865.

To Genl. R. E. Lee, Commdg., C. S. A.

General: Your note of yesterday is received. As I have no authority to treat on the subject of peace, the meeting proposed for 10 A. M. today could lead to no good. I will state, however, General, that I am equally anxious for peace with yourself; and the whole North entertains the same feeling. The terms upon which peace can be had are well understood. By the South laying down their arms they will hasten that most desirable event, save thousands of human lives, and hundreds of millions of property not yet destroyed.

Sincerely hoping that all difficulties may be settled, without the loss of another life, I subscribe myself,

Very respectfully,
Your obdt. Servt.,
U. S. GRANT,
L. Genl. U. S. Army.

"April 9, 1865.

General: I received your note of this morning on the picket line, whither I had come to meet you and ascertain definitely what terms were embraced in your proposition of yesterday with reference to the surrender of this army. I now request an interview in accordance with the offer contained in your letter of yesterday for that purpose.

Very respectfully,
Your obdt. Servt.,
R. E. LEE, *General.*
To Lieut. Genl. Grant, Commdg. Armies of U. S."

"April 9, 1865.

Gen. R. E. Lee, Comdg. C. S. A.

Your note of this date is but this moment—11:39 A. M. received.

In consequence of my having passed from the Richmond and Lynchburg road to Farmville and Lynchburg road, I am at this writing, about four miles West of the Walters' Church, and will push forward to the front for the purpose of meeting you.

Notice sent me on this road where you wish the interview to take place, will meet me.

Very respectfully, Your obdt. Servt.

U. S. GRANT,
Lieut. Genl."

"Appomattox Court House,
Apl. 9, 1865.

Genl. R. E. Lee, Comdg., C. S. A.

In accordance with the substance of my letter to you on the 8th inst. I propose to receive the surrender of the Army of North Va. on the following terms, to-wit:

Rolls of all the officers and men to be made in duplicate, one copy to be given to an officer designated by me, the other to be retained by such officers as you may designate.

The officers to give their individual parole not to take arms against the Govt. of the U. S. until properly exchanged; and each company or regimental commander to sign a like parole for the men of their commands.

The arms, artillery, and public property to be parked and stacked, and turned over to the officers appointed by me to receive them.

This will not embrace the side arms of the officers, nor their private horses or baggage.

This done, each officer and man will be *allowed to return to their homes not to be disturbed by United States authority,* so long as they observe their parole and the laws in force where they may reside.

Very respectfully,
U. S. GRANT, *Lieut. Genl."*

"Head Qrs. Army Nor. Va.,
Apl. 9, 1865.

Lt. Gen. U. S. Grant, Commdg. U. S. A.

General: I have received your letter of this date, containing the terms of surrender of the Army of North Va., as proposed by you. As they are substantially the same as those expressed in your letter of the 8th inst, they are accepted. I will proceed to designate the proper officers to carry the stipulations into effect.

Very respectfully, Your obdt. Servt.

R. E. LEE, *General.*"

The interview of the two Commanders took place at the house of Mr. Wilmer McLean. It was simple. Genl. Lee was attended by one of his aides, Col. Marshall.

On the 12th, all terms having been completed, the Army of Northern Virginia formed in columns, by divisions; marched to the spot near Appomattox Court House, and stacked arms. About 7,500 men laid down their arms, while about 18,000 stragglers who had lost their arms from exhaustion, appeared and accepted their paroles. Genl. Grant was not present at this final act in the great drama, and was not seen by Genl. Lee after his first interview on the 9th.

On the 10th, Genl. Lee bade his farewell to his army in well chosen language; and rode away towards Richmond.

The disbanded army was bewildered by the scenes around them. The hungry and worn-out men were virtually the guests of the victorious army. Genl. Grant had commanded officers and men to relieve the wasted Confederates, and with good will the order was obeyed. Within three days, the remnant of the Army of Northern Virginia could be seen wending their way towards the desolate homes. To many, this was the dreariest march of all. Of others, whose homes lay in the great Virginia Valley, their spirits were lightened as they scanned the blue mountains in the distance. Their work was done. They were obeying the last order of their beloved Commander. They were disappointed, but they were submissive; and never broke their parole. Genl. Grant's magnanimity was fully appreciated. His army had virtually closed its career; and when disbanded, many old soldiers returned to their distant homes, and entered into more congenial pursuits.

The Southern Armies under Johnston and others, soon effected terms of surrender; and thus, the great drama of 1861-65 closed with no blare of trumpets.

CHAPTER LXVII

Biographical Sketches

Benjamin Borden.—Some mystery is attached to this old settler. He first appears at the Jan. court, 1734, Orange County, with a commission as Justice of the Peace. At the Oct. Term, 1740, same court, Benjamin Borden, the justice, answered a summons to court. 1743 he was living on his Spout Run Plantation, North of Winchester. Executed a deed to his son Benjamin for tract of land on the Bullskin, being part of his grant of Oct. 1, 1734. This grant embraced several thousand acres of land on the James River in Orange County (later Augusta) and other tracts, from the Potomac Southward. In 1744, his widow, Zeuriah, was living in N. Jersey;—executed a power of attorney to her son Benjamin to sell any lands of the estate except the 5,000 acres on James River, and mentions him as residing in Augusta County. Benjamin shortly thereafter made deed to Arthur Barrett for a plantation on lower Opecquon Creek. The will gives names of widow and sons: Benjamin, John, Joseph, and daughters.

He also says: "This plantation where I live, on *Spought Run* on Opeckon may be sold, etc."

The widow says in the power of attorney, that she is in New Jersey, and her age and sickness prevents her leaving N. Jersey. Benjamin, Jr., located on the Burden (Borden) grant on the James; and proceeded to execute title to land to the settlers as they appeared. His brother Joseph joined him, and did much to attract the Scotch-Irish settlers. Benjamin died 1753. Joseph and John have descendants throughout the Valley.

David Vance. (often written Vaunce by the first co. clk.) The first of the name was one of the Hite party—settled South of where Winchester now stands; reared a large family, who intermarried with many prominent families: Glass, Hoge, White and others. Their descendants are found in Virginia, Kentucky, Tennessee, N. Carolina, and several Western States—some becoming prominent in affairs of State and church. David was one of the justices forming the first court, 1743.

Old county records show numerous transactions in land—in the old county office fully one hundred entries made from the arrival of the emigrant to 1840. Several of the descendants left wills: Andrew Vance in 1743, David, 1745; Elizabeth, James, John, James (2), Robert and William—all of which are recorded in county clerk's office, and show names of children, etc., and much that can be learned of the location of many of them. In 1753 Samuel son of Andrew "sold his land and settled in Ky." Joseph C., son of David, settled on 450 acres of land in Hampshire Co., devised to him by his father. David and John inherited the home farm, which embraced part of the farm near Hillman's Toll Gate on the Valley Pike. The old stone mansion stood on the East side, a few hundred yards South of the gate, and was in good condition prior to the Civil War, when it was destroyed by Federal Soldiers in 1863, to avenge the killing of a number of a scouting party, in a skirmish with the writer's Company of Cavalry. A score of dismounted Confederates used the house as an impromptu fort, and wrought havoc on the advancing cavalry, while the main body of Confederates engaged the Federals on their flank. The old house was regarded as an historical landmark,—it being held as one of the numerous places where the youthful Washington frequently visited his friend James Vance, who in 1778 enlisted in Company No. 7 under Daniel Morgan; and later held a commission. James married Eliza, second daughter of Samuel Glass the emigrant. We have some evidence that three brothers came with Hite: Samuel, James and Andrew, though it has been considered by many of the descendants that James and Andrew were the sons of David. Andrew died in 1753, and owned land as early as 1742. James also had settled on his land in 1742.

Hon. Zebulon Vance, the distinguished North Carolinian, was a descendant of the emigrant; likewise two prominent Presbyterian divines, now in active service in their church.

William Hogue (Hoge) was of the Hite party, and settled on a branch of the Opecquon and called it Hogue Run. He erected his cabin at the fountain head, and continued to live there until his death. He claimed title through a grant independent of Hite; and controlled a large tract, and sold parcels therefrom without question as to his title. The homestead was due West from the Opeckon Memorial Church, and in full view. It changed hands several times after the emigrant's death—Stephen Pritchard and family one of the first owners—the home now of Chas. H. Grim family. The brick mansion now on the old site, was built about 1850 by the Pritchard family. Stephen Pritchard's wife was Mary Cartmell. William Hoge settled on his grant about 1735. They were living in Chester County, Penna., in 1734. His wife was Barbara Hume. They had five sons: John, William, Alexander, James and George. John remained in Pennsylvania, and died at Hogestown 9 miles West of Harrisburg. The other sons and daughters accompanied the father to his Virginia home. William J. afterwards married a quakeress, and removed to what is now Loudoun County, and left many descendants. James settled near Middletown. Alexander became a lawyer; lived near Winchester; was a member of the first Congress of the U. S., and also of the Virginia Convention that adopted the first Constitution of the U. S. James the fourth son, was the father of the first Rev. Moses Hoge, who was direct ancestor of several preachers of that name—found afterwards in many parts of the country—Notably Rev. Moses D. Hoge, D.D., of Richmond, Va. Rev. John Hoge, who has been mentioned as the first regular pastor of Opecquon Church, was the son of John. George the fifth son, was a member of the first courts of Frederick County; subsequently he changed his residence to N. Carolina. One of the daughters, Margaret, married Dr. Robert White a surgeon in the British Navy. A grandson of Solomon Hoge married Mary Glass, granddaughter of Samuel Glass the emigrant. Through this line, the Hoge family of Berkeley County, Va., descends. No attempt will be made to follow the line fully. The other daughters of the emigrant Wm. Hoge, intermarried in prominent families. (Want of space forbids fuller mention of this family.)

William the emigrant, was a Presbyterian, and donated the land for the first "meeting-house" at Opeckon, Feb. 19, 1745. The Opecquon Memorial Church stands on the same site. (See chapter on churches.)

John Willson. It is not claimed that John Willson came with Hite. He left the record of his arrival in Frederick County from Ireland, July 6, 1737. He was one of many composing the Scotch, English and Irish emigration in 1737, induced to seek homes in the Shenandoah Valley, through the agency of Joist Hite; and on their arrival, sought the old pioneer, who accorded them such welcome that they chose homes along and near the Opecquon. It has been well established that John Willson was the first school teacher for the infant colony, and for years was the teacher at the first meeting-house at Opeckon, and doubtless was a leader in Gospel services on the Sabbath, until visiting ministers appeared from Donegal Presbytery. Mr. Willson tells a pathetic story on the old tombstone in Opeckon graveyard, in relation to his family, which doubtless is the oldest marked grave in the Shenandoah Valley. It appears that Robert Willson a brother came at the same time and settled on his plat of ground near the railroad station at Kernstown; erected a stone and log dwelling combined; lived there and reared a family, who intermarried with the Glass and McDowell families. The Willson family removed to Kentucky and Tennessee.

Peter Stephens, the emigrant, located on a tract of land South of the Opeckon, for which he obtained an order of the Colonial Council, to have it surveyed and laid off for himself and several families. This was subsequent to the order granted Hite for his large grants. Stephens failed to comply with the conditions of his order; and allowed it to lapse. Hite's order covered all unsurveyed and ungranted land in that vicinity. When his survey and report was returned, he conveyed and caused to be made a transfer of a large tract to Peter Stephens, who for some reason failed to have it recorded. He was never disturbed in his title as will be seen elsewhere. Hite conveyed to Lewis Stephens Apl. 28, 1738, a large tract of land on Crooked Run, a small stream having its source in the vicinity of the New Town that was thereafter incorporated by Lewis Stephens as Stephensburg. The Stephens family was of the German contingent to the Hite party. Lewis Stephens was given a charter to erect his town, by the General Assembly, 1758, on part of his 900 acres; and referring to the Act (appearing elsewhere) it will be seen he represents that all of the lots with the outlots annexed "are purchased by different persons who are now settling and building thereon." This proves that Lewis Stephens was fully alive to the development of his section, and his energy and intelligence made it possible to secure recognition from the county court; and it was in doubt for several years whether his influence, supported by that of Lord Fairfax, would not result in the selection of his town for the county seat. He has the credit of fixing the site and donating the lot for the first Methodist Church erected West of the Blue Ridge. On this lot John Hite and his sister Mrs. Phelps, erected the church mentioned in Sketch of the Methodist Church. This Lewis Stephens and his family acquired riches, consisting of farms, town lots in Stephensburg and Winchester, five families of slaves, and other property; and in the early part of the 19th Century, we find the accumulations had become immense. The will of Mary Stephens, widow of Lewis (2nd), in 1829, disposing of a large estate, does not mention any children, but devises property to her nephew Wm. Hening and his sister Elizabeth, and to James Hening, and to Col. Henry Beaty husband of her deceased sister Sarah Hening, and to her sister Shannon of Kentucky; devises slaves to Wm. Hening; provides for their maintenance, he to pay her aged sister Joanna McChesney; also legacies to nieces and nephews of her husband, the children of Robert Hening of Kentucky. In a clause of her will may be found several interesting matters. "To carry out the intentions of my husband which he was prevented by the suddenness and nature of his last sickness, I devise to Thos. A. Tidball, Alex. S. Tidball and John R. Cooke, Esqs.," certain valuable property, etc., "for them to hold in trust for the use of the Theological Seminary of the Presbyterian Church located in Princeton, N. Jersey, for the purpose of endowing a scholarship in said Seminary, etc." "I also direct that the Presbytery of Winchester shall have the right to select and appoint the beneficiaries who are to profit by this charitable fund." She makes some changes in this bequest by a codicil to her will, which is: "Whereas the Theological Seminary at Princeton has acquired large funds, and is in successful operation, I direct this fund to be used for the benefit of the Theological Seminary *lately* established at Hampden Sydney College in Prince Edward County, Virginia, and surplus to be kept until sufficient sum is realized for the endowment of a second scholarship at same Seminary."

Query: Did Hampden Sydney and Winchester Presbytery get the benefit of this endowment?

The Lewis Stephens referred to, was the son of Lewis the founder of Stephensburg, who by his will, probated 1805, devised the bulk of his fine estate to his son Lewis. His will mentions among other things, that he devises to his son "the piece or parcel of land commonly known as the *muster ground* on the West side of the town." This parcel of land has been a subject for litigation for two years—Some citizens of the town regarding it as waste land, secured a grant from the Commonwealth and surveyed what was termed ungranted land. The people are contesting this right. The family name is fast disappearing from the records of the present day. Many descendants, however, by intermarriage, are citizens of the Lower Valley.

The Glass Family

Dr. William H. Foote, author of Sketches of Virginia, published in 1855, in its first pages, introduces his readers to the first settlers of the Shenandoah Valley, giving prominence to this Scotch-Irish family in this language: "Samuel Glass and Mary Gamble his wife, who came in their old age, from Ban Bridge, County Down, Ireland, and were among the early settlers, taking their abode on the Opecquon in 1736. His wife often spoke of "her two fair brothers that perished in the siege of Derry." Mr. Glass lived like a patriarch with his descendants. Devout in spirit, and of good report in religion, in the absence of the regular pastor, he visited the sick, to counsel and instruct and pray. His grandchildren used to relate in their old age, by way of contrast, circumstances showing the strict observance by families—Mr. Glass, in the midst of wild lands to be purchased at a low rate, thought sixteen hundred acres enough for himself and children."

The writer has been requested to write a sketch of this emigrant and his numerous family. The reader would be appalled at the outset, if he thought this request would be complied with. The scope of this volume can only embrace the foundation for sketches of the various lines emanating from the founder of Greenwood. To this task the writer will devote willingly his best efforts to unfold an intelligent tracing of every generation of this family from the emigrant down to the present date. This is all that can be done. This tracing can be regarded as reliable, taken as it is, from the only known genealogical chart of this family, kept by the Glass family of Frederick County for ages, and finally descending to one member of this family who kept in touch with the scattered tribe, and year after year added to each line the additions she gathered. This was the wife of the writer, who now holds it in sacred trust for his only child Annie Lyle Randolph. The knowledge of this chart caused numerous members of this family to make the request referred to. In sketches of Opeckon and other Presbyterian churches, found in this volume, the Glass family is necessarily mentioned. Ireland in the early part of the 18th Century, furnished many families renowned for their thrift and love of freedom, and a desire to try their fortunes beyond the narrow confines of their Emerald Isle. The Ulster people were the first to organize for emigration. Consulting Marmion's Maritime Ports of Ireland, we find that one hundred families sailed from Lough Foyle in 1718. They settled in New Hampshire. This colony became as famous in America as the Plymouth Colony. More distinguished men descended from this first Ulster emigration, than from the latter. In 1727, three thousand people sailed for the North American colonies from Belfast Lough. The following year seven ships took one thousand more; and in the next three years as many as forty-two hundred. These emigrants were for the most part of Scotch origin. Their success in securing good "seatings" in the New World, induced many more to follow. We find that between the years 1720 and 1742, over three thousand emigrants annually left Ulster County alone. (Gordon's History of Ireland). The golden prospect in America was one reason for this. The oppressive land laws and the restrictions placed on all Irish industries, were the main causes, doubtless, for this desertion of the Island homes—Venturing the perilous voyage across the Atlantic in sail ships, with all the discomforts known to exist aboard the best of them, and requiring in many cases six months before they could land on American shores. It was during this great upheaval, that the subject of our sketch, severed every tie that bound him to his native land and, together with his sons and daughters and grandchildren, sought the Valley of the "Sherrandore." The writer has on his table "The Belfast Witness" bearing date March 19, 1877, which gives a comprehensive review of the periods mentioned, furnishing the names of many prominent families that left Ireland at that date. A clipping from the Belfast paper says: In 1736 a number of families emigrated from Benbridge and neighborhood, amongst them were members of the Glass, McDowell, Magill, Mulholland, Linn and other families. These people settled in the Shenandoah Valley on the banks of the Opeckon, Virginia" * * * This from the same paper: "Samuel Glass had six children: John, Eliza, Sarah, David, Robert and Joseph, all born at Benbridge." It is this Samuel Glass and his family that we now propose to trace after their arrival on the Opeckon. The family chart says: "Samuel Glass and his wife Mary Gamble, came from Ireland 1735, settled on the Opeckon 1736. They were advanced in life when they came, with children and grandchildren. He purchased 1,600 acres of land from Joyce Hite and Lord Fairfax, whose grants were divided by the Opeckon."

(1) John Glass mar. Miss Bicket in Ireland. He settled in Augusta County, Va. His children removed to Tenn., and did not keep up communication with the family—names unknown.

(2) Eliza Glass, mar. James Vance in Ireland. They had two children, Samuel and William. Samuel mar. Miss Rannells. William mar. twice, first wife Miss Gilkeson: Issue by this union reported: James Vance, mar. Catherine Heiskill. They had two sons, William and John Thomas. The three children of Wm. Vance and his wife Miss Colville: William married Margaret Myers; six children by this union, Mary Catherine, Edwin, Susan E., Wm. Alexander, James Henry, and Sarah Emily. Elizabeth dau. of William Vance and Miss Colville, mar. Dr. Tilden, no children of this union reported. John Vance one of three children of William Vance and Miss Colville was married four times, 1st wife Emily McNeill, three children by this union, Mary, Sally, Cary, and Laura. 2nd wife Susan Myers, 3rd wife Eliza Hoge, 4th wife Catherine Williams.

(3) Sarah dau. of the emigrant, mar. Mr. Beckett, 5 children by this union, to-wit: Robert, Sarah, Mary, Elizabeth and Joseph.

(4) David, son of Samuel Glass, mar. Miss Fulton; his children removed to Ky.—names unknown.

(5) Robert, son of Samuel, was born in Ireland 1716. He mar. Elizabeth Fulton; from this union sprang many descendants. This branch comprised many families who were known in Frederick County for several generations. They reared 13 children. The 1st, Samuel, mar. Elizabeth Rutherford; 7 children by this union, to-wit: Samuel, Sarah, Benjamin, Robert, Thomas, Elizabeth and James. Thomas mar. Catherine Wood, grand dau. of James Wood the first Clerk of Frederick Co. Two children by this union, Ella, died unmarried; William Wood Glass; mar. twice; 1st wife Nannie Lucket, no issue; 2nd wife Nannie R. Campbell; children by this marriage Katherine R., Hattie, mar, W. B. Davis, Susan Louise, mar. Harry Strider. She and one child survive her husband. Other children of William Wood Glass: Thomas, William, Robert and Wood. This branch is more fully mentioned in the sketch of the James Wood family. Mary, 2nd child of Robert, mar. James David Vance, their children being James David, Robert Chambers, Mary and Martha Cornelia.

Elizabeth, 3d child of Robert, mar. John Cummings and removed to Illinois.

Sarah, 4th child of Robert and 5th Susan, not married.

Martha, 6th child of Robert, mar. Henry Sherrard. Their daughter Sarah mar. (first) Mr. Barbee and, (second,) Col. Sowers.

Ann 7th child of Robert, mar. (first) Wm. Vance, one child Mary; 2nd husband Robert Gray of Winchester, two sons by this union, to-wit: Wm. Hill and Joseph Gray; her granddaughter, dau. of Wm. Hill Gray, mar. Capt. Wm. N. McDonald.

Ruth, 8th child of Robert Glass, mar. Rev. James Vance, three sons by this union, to-wit: Robert, David and William.

Margaret, 9th child of Robert Glass, mar. Thomas White, three children: Robert, James and Sarah.

Robert David, 10th child of Robert Glass, mar.

Greenwood Homestead, founded by Samuel Glass, 1738

Old Mill; erected by Samuel Glass, 1740
(Only one of the kind in the County)

Elizabeth Rust; they reared 5 children, to-wit: Elizabeth mar. James M. Glass son of Rev. Joseph Glass, Robert Jeremiah mar. Louisa Bryarly; two children survived them, Robert mar. Belle Taylor; he and his daughter Mary Louise survive the mother. This Robert lives at the old homestead *The Meadows,* where Robert the 1st settled in 1736. This estate has never gone out of the family. The other child of Robert J. is Sarah mar. Dudley L. Miller; they have 2 daughters Louise and Cecelia, young ladies of rare attractions.

Mary A., 3d daughter of Robert David, mar. John S. Magill of Long Meadows, no child surviving. Susan another daughter mar. Thomas Bryarly. James V. Glass the 5th child of Robert David, died unmarried. John the 11th child of Robert Glass, Sr., died unmarried.

James, 12th child of Robert Glass, Sr., mar. twice, 1st wife, Elizabeth Sowers, 2 children by this issue: Lewis mar. Miss McCormick. Lewis was clerk of courts in Clarke Co., Va., from 1865-1869. His son George succeeded him and held office until 1875. Children of Lewis: George, Isaac James and 2 daughters. This has been known as the Glass family of Clarke Co., Va. Several of this family reside in that county. Elizabeth, sister to Lewis, mar. Wm. N. Thompson; their descendants live in Florida.

James, mar. Isabella Catlett for second wife; one daughter, Isabella, by this union.

Joseph, the 13th child of Robert Glass, Sr., mar. Miss White; their children, Robert. Sarah, Mary, Elizabeth and Joseph.

(6) Joseph, the 6th child of Samuel Glass the emigrant, was born in Ireland 1722; lived at Greenwood; died June 12, 1794. He mar. Eliza Wilson. This is the most numerous branch of all the Glass family. While many families lived in Frederick Co., hundreds of the descendants may be found in a half dozen States. Joseph is buried at Opeckon graveyard. He reared 12 children, several of whom had large families; many of their descendants were and are now distinguished men and women. The 1st child, Mary, mar. Solomon Hoge; they had 8 children, to-wit: James, Moses, Harvey, Arabella, Eliza, Juliet, Mary and Mertilla. 2nd child, Samuel, mar. twice; name of first wife unknown; one child, Eliza, survived her mother. She mar. Mr. Campbell. Samuel's 2nd wife was Miss McCormick; 6 children by this union, to-wit: Eliza, Catherine, Samuel, Hugh and Mary. She married twice, a Mr. Robinson and Mr. Harbison. Robert, the 3rd child, mar. Sarah Owens, their children being Joseph, Owen, Robert, Elizabeth, Samuel, David, Mary Nancy, Martha, and Sarah Ann.

Georgetta, 4th child of Joseph Glass, mar. Robert Wilson—names of their children not given.

Sarah, 5th child of Joseph, mar. Rev. John Lyle. (See sketches of Presb. churches in Hampshire Co., wherein full mention of his services.) Their children were John Newton, Eliza, Joseph Glass, Daniel, Jane, John, Wilberforce, and Sarah.

Elizabeth, 6th child of Joseph, Sr., mar. Robert Marshall, and removed to Ky., and reared 5 children near Lexington: Joseph, Elizabeth, Robert, Sarah, and Glass Marshall. The writer visited Mr. Glass Marshall and family many years ago, at his old homestead near Paine's Depot West of Lexington. Glass Marshall was widely known, a prominent ruling elder in the Presb. Church. He possessed much knowledge covering its early history in Ky. Several of his sons live near their old home.

Joseph Glass, Jr., 7th child of Joseph, was born 1774; died Oct. 27, 1821, at Greenwood. This was Rev. Joseph Glass. (more fully mentioned in Notes on Presb. Churches.) He married Ann McAllister Mch. 13, 1799; ten children by this union, to-wit: Eliza Wilson Glass, the first child, mar. Rev. Wm. Henry Foote, D.D., a minister of great prominence in the Presby. Church, also author of much literary work—Foote's Sketches of Virginia, and also of N. Carolina, comprising part of his published works; one child by this union, Anne Waterman, mar. Hon. Jas. D. Armstrong of Romney, W. Va., a lawyer of ability; represented Hampshire County in the Genl. Assembly prior to the Civil War; served as Judge of the Circuit Ct. of Hampshire and adjoining county for many years; resigned on account of failing health. Judge Armstrong died shortly thereafter, regretted by all. His widow of advanced age, lives in Romney. One child was born to them, Eliza Wilson, who died in early girlhood. Mrs. Armstrong and her half-sister, Miss Mary Belle Foote, daughter of Dr. Foote by his 2nd marriage, are companions in Mrs. Armstrong's home, famous, not only for its hospitality, but for the intellectual enjoyments found there. There the writer met the most distinguished divines of the Presbyterian Church.

Elizabeth, 2nd daughter of Rev. Joseph Glass, mar. James McAllister.

Sarah Ann, 3rd daughter of Rev. Joseph, was the Poetess of the Opeckon; died in the bloom of her beautiful womanhood. Her tomb is to be seen among her Glass Ancestors at Old Opeckon.

Mary McKnight, daughter of Rev. Joseph, died at an advanced age in 1879, unmarried; spent her long life at Greenwood.

Hester Sophia, another unmarried daughter, lived and died at Greenwood.

Susan E., another daughter, married James Carr Baker, a lawyer; owned Greenwood farm for many years, and there reared his 4 children, to-wit: Annie G., who became the wife of T. K. Cartmell, the author of this volume, in 1866. By this union were two children: Robbie, who died in infancy, and Annie Lyle, who is married to D. C. Randolph, of Cumberland County, Va.

Samuel, 2nd child of Jas. C. Baker and his wife Susan E., was twice married, first wife Jennie Taylor; children by this union, Harry Carr, Joseph G., Alexander, and Jennie. The latter died in infancy. Harry C. mar. Edmonia Stine; they have 3 children, Harman, Elizabeth and an infant daughter. Joseph G. married—no children. Samuel's 2nd wife was Maggie Heist, their children Emily H., Graham, and George T., all of whom survive the father, Capt. Samuel Baker.

Eliza G., the 3rd child of Jas. C. and Susan E., married Charles K. Bowers, their children being Chas. Carr, now dead; Etta, a lovely girl of 17 summers, died in Richmond, Va.; Edgar, a prominent druggist in Richmond, Va.; James C., mar. daughter of Dr. Geo. B. Steele of Richmond; they have one child. Gamble, another son, now a civil engineer, and Eugene who lives with his mother in Richmond, Va. Mr. Chas. K. Bowers was killed in a railroad accident several years ago.

James Carr, the youngest child of James C. and Susan E., mar. Ada Keene of Maryland, a lawyer by profession; was Commonwealth's atty. for Shenandoah for a number of years; became Col. of the 2nd Va. Regt., and ordered to Cuba during the Spanish-Am. War; this regiment formed the reserve forces in Florida, where he was ranking officer. His children are Ann Lewelyn, Sue G., who married Mr. Mitchell, an Episcopal minister, Ada C., mar. Alfred Walton of Norfolk; they have one child, Francis, adopted daughter of Col. Baker; William and James C., unmarried, Mrs. Susan E. Baker died in 1885, aged 71 years; her husband James Carr Baker, died in 1889, aged 75 years. Both lie in Mt. Hebron.

Sidney Ormsby, another daughter of Rev. Joseph Glass, mar. John McDowell; they had one child, Woodie, mar. Mr. Tabb of Romney; they left several children, Lelia, mar. Rev. Mr. Vandevender, a Presb. minister; Anna, unmarried, and two sons survive both parents.

Joseph, the youngest son of Rev. Joseph, mar. Kate Maynard, who died in Georgia many years ago. No children; he was an artist; some of his paintings are held by members of the family.

Emeline Marshall, another daughter, never married; died in 1867; interred in Mt. Hebron.

Anne McAlister, another daughter, mar. Philip B. Streit; both died many years ago; one child, Mary G.; raised by her aunts in the Greenwood home; married Wm. F. Rinker; they have several sons and daughters, two of the latter professional nurses.

Martha, the 8th child of Joseph Glass, mar. Dr. Chas. McPheters, six children by this marriage: Joseph, Elizabeth, Rebecca, Martha, Harvey and Mary.

Ruth, 9th child of Joseph, Sr., mar. David McClure; six children by this union: Joseph, Alexander, William, Martha, Samuel, David and Robert Marshall.

David, 10th child of Joseph, Sr., mar. Sarah Steele; ten children by this union, to-wit: Elizabeth Ann mar. Mr. Irwin; Joseph; Mary mar. Mr. J. White, 2nd husband Mr. Venable; James Robert Thompson, David, Ella mar. Rev John Mathews, Henry Marshall, Sarah Agnes. No fuller report of this family; the descendants may be found in Tenn. and Ky.

Mary, 11th child of Joseph, Sr., mar. Lee Bird; 5 children by this union: Elizabeth mar. Mr. Lee, Catherine mar. Mr. Dunlap and lived in St. Louis; Emily mar. Mr. Owen; Sophia mar. Joseph Lyle. No further report.

Sophia, 12th child of Joseph, Sr., mar. Rev. Francis Montfort of Ky., 7 children by this union; 4 of the sons became distinguished ministers of the Presb. Church; Joseph Glass Montfort for many years a forceful preacher and editor of the strong church paper published in Louisville, Ky., and conducted now by his sons; Elizabeth 2d child; Lawrence 3d child; next Rev. Francis P.; next Sophia C.; then Rev. Isaac Watts, and Rev. David Montfort. This completes the line of Samuel Glass the emigrant and those of his six children, so far as the chart shows.

The writer will add that his correspondence with descendants of this family, shows their residence in many States of the Union; many of whom hope to supply the close of several lines that appear here unfinished, and thus bring every line to the present generation. If such data be received, an effort will be made to show it in an appendix.

The Cartmell Family

The name Cartmell is from Kert, a camp or fortification, and Mell a fell. The family had its origin in the ancient Shire of Northumberland, England. "The township of Cartmell is situated in Lancashire." The writer several years ago, in his investigation of this origin, found two descendants of the original stock residing in the township or Parish of Cartmel: they being George E. Cartmell, Treasurer of Westmoreland County, England, and his brother James, who cheerfully undertook to produce historical evidence of their relationship to the Cartmell family found in America in 1724. A large

Cartmell Parish Church, England

The name CARTMELL is from Kert, a camp or fortification and mell a fell. It means "The fortress among the fells." The church dates back to 677, and Egfred, King of Northumberland, gave St. Cuthbert the land and all the Britons in it. A priory was founded in 1188, which was destroyed, but the site was regranted by Henry VIII. Cartmell township is 15 miles long and 4 or 5 wide, and indeed it is difficult to imagine that even Adam, in all the beauty of Paradise, looked upon a much fairer landscape than that which meets the eye, when from the summit of Hamps Fell, the Valley of Cartmell is seen lit up with the setting lustre of an autumn sun. In the south the sea, in the north the valley, in the east the Fell, in the west Howbarrow and tree-clad St. Bernard.

The organ was erected in 1780. The stalls of choir are in Grecian style, surmounted by Corinthian capitals, with sculptured heads.

A grant of the rectory of Cartmell was made to Cuthbert, a bishop of Chester, in the fourth or fifth year of the reign of Philip and Mary, 1554.

family of this name was living at that date in New Jersey, having purchased two tracts of land from the Lord Proprietors. The head of the family was Nathaniel. After long and careful research, it was found among the Shire records, that a Nathaniel Cartmell sold his belongings and "took sail with his family and certain others of the Sect of Friends," to seek homes in the North American Colonies. In order to establish proof of the relationship, Mr. George E. Cartmell sought out the old *Church Yard,* where many of the name had been entombed for several centuries. There he found such family names as have been adopted by all the generations in America; and from this we jointly concluded that the connection was fully established. Later on, the author of this volume procured a photograph of the Cartmell Church and its history, which, for its antiquity and quaint architectural features, he embodies in this sketch; as doubtless it will be a revelation to the American members of this family who may chance to see this history. The following description accompanied the photograph:

"The Church dates back to 677; and Egfred, King of Northumberland, gave to St. Cuthbert the land and all the Britons in it. A priory was founded in 1188, which was destroyed, but the site was regranted by Henry VIII. Cartmel town is 15 miles long, 4 or 5 wide, and indeed it is difficult to imagine that even Adam, in all the beauty of Paradise, looked upon a much fairer landscape than that which meets the eye, when from the summit of Hamps Fell, the Valley of Cartmel is seen lit up with the setting lustre of an Autumn sun: In the South the sea, in the North the Valley, in the East the Fell, in the West Howbarrow and tree-clad St. Bernard.

The organ was erected in 1780. The stalls of choir are in Grecian style, surmounted by Corinthian capitals, with sculptured heads. The grant of the rectory of Cartmel was made to Cuthbert, a bishop of Chester, in the fourth or fifth year of the reign of Philip and Mary, 1554."

It is the American Cartmells that the author will endeavor to trace; and lest some of the name may expect a connected chain, he announces now, that after most diligent search and correspondence, and personal visits, he can give only what may seem partial history. One or two lines are reliably traced; while other lines that have unmistakable identity with the emigrant family, have many broken links in the chain. Possibly from these broken chains—that one of the *tribe* submits for study—some of the present generation may take up and supply the missing links.

We are unable to account for the large family found in New Jersey in 1724 and for several years thereafter. We know that the name appeared in the records there for a brief period after the family sold out in New Jersey and followed the fortunes of Hite, in the Virginia Valley, though they came not with Hite. A *minor grant* was secured which placed a family within the 100,000 acre grant of Hite. This family consisted of the widow of Nathaniel, and her sons Martin, Nathaniel, Nathan, and Edward, and several daughters, names not mentioned. The date of their order for survey of several large tracts was 1735. No report of survey, however, until March, 1737. These surveys locate the widow with her son Edward and his sisters on a tract of land South of the Opeckon. This was the land in the old Quaker Graveyard vicinity. Adjoining this tract of unknown quantity, her son Martin was seated on a tract of over 700 acres. He also had a survey for 1,100 acres on North side of Opeckon Creek, adjoining on the West the *Thomas* grant. This evidently was the tract which became known as Homespun. The other brothers, Nathaniel and Nathan, must have been minors, for no survey was at that time made in their names. *All* surveys in name of Martin. There were two other tracts surveyed near the site of Middletown, and there Edward was seated. Nathaniel and Nathan lived at some point on the big survey North of the Opeckon. Martin lived and died near his aged mother's home. In his will dated 1749, he makes provision for his mother and his wife Esther, and then wills his lands to his sons Nathan, Edward and Nathaniel. Same old family names. And this makes it difficult to separate the second generation from the first. Martin must have been an old man, although his mother was still living. Her three grandsons were certainly of lawful age, for Martin charges them to provide for his mother, out of the lands he devises to them. We have no evidence that Martin's brothers, Edward and Nathan were married, and none of their death. We have evidence that Edward, whom we find living with his mother and subsequently *settling* on the survey near Middletown, was succeeded by his nephew Edward, and that he himself plunged deeper into the wilderness and traded with the Indians. No trace of him after that. Thus the two Edwards, uncle and nephew, have caused much confusion. After Martin's death, 1749, we find his son Nathan continued to live with his mother until his death, 1755. His will shows he was unmarried; that he bequeathed his property to his brothers Edward and Nathaniel, and charges them to give good support to his mother Esther. Martin's will shows that his sons Nathaniel and Edward remained on tracts South of the Opeckon.

Here we will leave them and trace their uncles, Nathaniel and Nathan, who had settled North of the Opeckon, at some point in the 1,100 acre survey. These holdings gave them trouble with Fairfax; for although they were seated on the survey, it was not in their name. Nathan was for years in evidence as owning the large tract known as Cloverdale and Greenfield farms. Nathaniel remained near Opeckon Creek, and held adverse possession of a large tract until 1747, when he secured by lease a tract of 200 acres from Nathaniel Thomas. This tract is described as being "at the head of South Branch of Opeckon" beginning at Joist Hite's corner "This adjoined said Cartmell's other lands." The Thomas tract was always called the Old Meadow tract (a portion of which is now owned by the writer.) We may safely assume that this the first Nathaniel, who claimed the large tract known as the Cartmell Spring Tract, afterwards known as Homespun, was married at the time he came with Martin and the mother, for subsequent to his purchase, he appears as assignee of other small tracts, and assigned them to his sons Thomas and John. Nothing to show that they were married or that they lived on the tracts; and we must conclude they were not married, and died or departed to parts unknown. This being the case, we find that Nathaniel and his son Nathaniel were the Cartmells of the Homespun tracts, and that they also inherited their share of the Cloverdale and Greenfield farm tracts, and subsequently Nathaniel 2d acquired the interests of Martin's sons, if they had any, in this large landed estate. This Nathaniel died about 1765 at an advanced age, leaving no will. Much difficulty arises as to who were his sons. We have positive proof, however, that his son Nathaniel, the only one to survive, succeeded the father in the ownership of the large Homespun tract; and he it was who built the stone house in 1771, and lived there at the time of his death in 1795. His will names all his children, towit: Thomas, Nathaniel, Nathan, John, Jacob, Elijah, Elizabeth, Sarah, Rachel, Mary and Solomon. This family of eleven children married prior to the death of their father, and several of them sought homes outside of Virginia. Their lines are difficult to trace correctly. Nathan and Jacob were in Kentucky prior to 1800;—they and their wives acknowledged deeds there in 1802-3, for their interests in lands in Frederick County. Elijah and John removed to Ohio at a later day. Elijah subsequently took his family to Kentucky. Elizabeth married Dr. Michael Archdeacon. Their line cannot be ascertained; neither can that of Sarah, who married James Cochran; nor Rachael, who married Thomas Crist. Mary married Nathaniel Willis of Martinsburg, Berkeley County, Va.

Thomas, the oldest child, was living at the Greenfield Farm in 1770. Nathaniel, who married Paul Froman's daughter, was living at Retirement in 1780, at the time his wife died. Family history places them there in 1769—the homestead a bridal present from his father. Solmon, who married a Miss Raife (or Ralph as the name often appears), was settled on a tract due West from Homespun,—the property now owned by Enos Jackson, formerly owned by Bell and Miller, James Ginn, Morrison and L. F. Campbell, respectively.

Thomas, son of Nathaniel 2d, was found on the Greenfield farm in 1770, with his young wife Ann Hite. (Family tradition says she was the daughter of Maj. Isaac Hite of Belle Grove. This is erroneous, as Maj. Hite was not married until just prior to the erection of Belle Grove in 1793.) She might have been a daughter of Isaac Hite of Long Meadows, father of Major Isaac. The recital of a deed recorded in 1790, speaks of Thos. Cartmell's wife Anne the daughter of Joseph Hite. This must be the Thomas that tradition says married a cousin of Dolly Madison; and was the 5th child of the owner of Greenfield farm. The children of Thomas, Sr., by his will probated in 1808, were two married daughters Rachel Nutt and Sarah Morris, John, Eleanor, Thomas, Wm. Hite, Jacob, Nathaniel, and a daughter Betsy wife of John Lupton. It will be observed that one son is mentioned as Wm. Hite,—evidently there was some Hite connection, and it is safe to assume that the widow named in the will as Nancy, was Ann Hite. This Thomas, Jr., died in Virginia; left a widow and 2 children, one daughter Sarah married —— Hamilton and settled on the Ohio, near Cincinnati; the son died at an early age. The writer often heard the family mention his two children, but is unable to report anything more. The widow Ann Hite removed to Ohio with her brother-in-law Nathaniel Cartmell in 1805, and died Aug. 10, 1821. The writer is informed that her tombstone in Vernon Cemetery near Catawba, fixes the date and says she was the "consort of Thomas Cartmell." The widow of Thomas, the father, was living in Frederick County, Va., in 1811, and died soon thereafter, advanced in years.

Following Nathaniel, family record says he married Rebecca D. ManMeter, Mch. 27, 1801. She was born Aug. 9, 1784, died Aug. 1, 1858, was the daughter of Jacob Van Meter, who died 1803. Nathaniel was born 1773, died near Catawba, Ohio, Feb. 1, 1854. Family record shows that he, his wife and party made the journey on horseback, carrying two sons, John and

"Homespun"
Homestead of Nathaniel Cartmell 2nd; erected 1771

Thomas. The rifle that was used on the long trip for protection and to furnish game for sustenance, has been carefully preserved by the family, and is now in possession of Mr. Perley Cartmell of Springfield, Ohio. After their settlement in Ohio, two other sons were born, Jacob Van Meter Cartmell and Nathaniel Madison Cartmell, the latter born Nov. 24, 1817, died Apl. 4, 1889. He married Mary Lofland, Jany. 2, 1844, dau. of David Holmes Lofland, and born in the Blockhouse at Marietta, Sept. 20, 1799. Children by this marriage were Perley, William M., Marietta, Henry Clay, Chas M., Ann Eliza, who married Wm. H. Narr, owned the farm the family settled on in Bucks Co., 1805. Other children of Nathaniel Cartmell and Rebecca D. Van Meter were John, Thos. J., Mary A., Ellen M., and Martin R. Jacob Van Cartmell married in Ohio. He lived on the old National Turnpike, near Springfield, during the latter part of his life. His sons have been connected with the Springfield Engine and Thresher Company for years, viz: Joseph, John, Van and Dawson; they have three sisters.

Elizabeth (Betsy), the daughter who married John Lupton, and her children are fully mentioned in the sketch of Round Hill Lupton family.

John, the son of Thomas, Sr., mar. Chestina Fry, Apl. 23, 1782. She was the daughter of Capt. Frye who lived in southwest part of Frederick County, and had many encounters with Indian raiders. Kercheval says in relation to an Indian raid on the Greenbrier River "that two of John Cartmell's daughters were taken by the Indians and remained with them several years. Their brother went to the Indian country, obtained their release and brought them home." As this was one of the raids the Indians made about 1795, we may infer that John was living in that section; and, from disconnected lines, the writer is of the opinion that it was this branch that furnished the bachelor brothers James, John and Thomas Cartmell, who lived in Botetourt County, Va., from about 1830 and for many years after, and died there leaving large bodies of mineral and other lands, which the survivor devised to his housekeeper. We have nothing further about John.

William Hite, the youngest son of Thomas, Sr., after his mother's death, was East of the Blue Ridge for several years, and executed papers that were filed in the Chancery Court at Winchester, Va., pertaining to the settlement of his mother's estate. He was afterwards in Western Virginia, near the Kanawha River, and executed similar papers. William H. was married, but when is not known. He left a widow and minor children. There was a David Cartmell in the vicinity of Charleston, Kanawha County, Va., in 1817, who had trouble with land titles, known as the Gov. James Wood grant. This suit in Old Chancery Court terminated in 1820. After David's death, an effort was made to reinstate it in the name of his widow and next friend of David—Minor children—No other proceedings found and our enquiry is estopped. The writer however, has some evidence that this may have been the origin of what is known as the Cartmell family of Maysville, Ky., and will submit some family history furnished by a member of this family, Miss Elizabeth M. Cartmell. She says that her father was Dr. Simon Morgan Cartmell, born in Charleston, Va., Jany. 2, 1818, and brought to Kentucky in 1822, and that he was named for Capt. Simon Morgan, his grandfather, and that her grandfather was David, and that David's mother was Sarah Wallace, but does not know with any degree of certainty what his father's given name was, but thinks her father said *William.* She also says that her father's oldest sister, Eliza Ann, married Rowan Hardin, son of Ben. Hardin, the celebrated Kentucky jurist; she also says that Genl. Joe David was a first cousin of her grandfather David, and that Genl. David married Nancy Marshall, sister of Chief Justice Marshall. David married Nancy Morgan, daughter of Capt. Simon Morgan, of Fauquier County, Va., about 1812 or 1813; their child, a daughter, married Dr. Thos, Tebbs; died without children. Doctor Simon Morgan Cartmell married Miss Lucretia Taylor Wood; died in Maysville, Ky., 1896; eight children by this union, five of whom are living: Dr. John W., Robert M., Jennie L., Charlotte, and Elizabeth. Mrs. Hardin's surviving children are Ben. Hardin, and Nancy Hardin Rowan, of Bardstown, Ky.

Four sons of Nathaniel mentioned in his will, 1795, *i. e.,* Nathan, Jacob, John and Elijah, two of whom, as previously stated, were in Ky. and Ohio prior to their father's death; and the other two, Nathan and Jacob, were there in 1802. Most diligent effort has been made to follow these four sons. We have every evidence of their residence in those two States, and of three large families; and many descendants of those families have in many ways assured the writer of their connection, yet in no case has it been possible to trace the lines to a conclusion. He has visited families of this name in several States, and finds all trace their descent back to the Virginia Cartmells. The writer found an interesting family of Cartmells in Santa Rosa County, Cal., many years ago—Father, two sons and three daughters—Father an old man; had traveled abroad often and was an intellectual man; and this family was the subject of the attractive little book entitled "Travels of the

Cartmell Family." This old gentleman believed he was from the Kentucky branch. The family of brothers in North Carolina trace their line to Kentucky, but can furnish nothing more. It is much regretted that the chain is so incomplete.

Mary, daughter of Nathaniel, as previously stated, married Nathaniel Willis Jany. 13, 1789. They lived in Martinsburg, Va., for many years. Mr. Willis was owner of a newspaper published there, and also published several books and did considerable printing of other matter. They had born unto them two children that were distinguished literary persons of the 19th Century: Nathaniel P. Willis, the author of several publications both prose and poetry, perpetuated his name and fame in many of his accomplishments. His home was Idlewild, located on the West bank of the Hudson River a short distance above West Point—an attractive and romantic spot. The homestead is now controlled by a society in New York and held by similar regulations governing Mount Vernon. The writer was a frequent visitor to Idlewild in the Summers of 1877-8, while N. P. Willis had fame as a writer. His sister, Mrs. James Parton, gained note as "Fanny Fern." Her facile pen never hesitated in touching any subject; and her magazine articles were eagerly read. Her intellect was ever alert for the prominent questions disturbing the *body politic;* and her scathing criticisms in prose or verse made interesting reading for those good old times. Her sister married Mr. Ferguson and removed to Ohio, and for years this family could be found in the vicinity of Columbus. The writer knew two of her daughters: One was Mrs. Julia Ware, of Columbus, the other Mattie Dodridge, married Dr. Joseph P. Bywaters, of Groveport, Ohio, a physician of rare ability. They visited the *Retirement* family several times prior to the Civil War. Mrs. B. was conspicuous for her ministrations to the wants of suffering Confederate prisoners at Camp Chase. Her memory is revered by hundreds who still live. After the War and death of her husband, she changed her residence to Winchester, where she educated her only child, an invalid daughter; and becoming the wife of Capt. Milton McVeigh, of Loudoun County, purchased an old homestead at Aldie, and there lived, surviving her daughter and husband. At this writing she is a confirmed invalid. Some readers will remember her as *Cousin Mattie.*

Solomon Cartmell, son of Nathaniel, 2d, was one of the sons who remained in Virginia, and settled near his old Homespun home. As previously stated, he married Elizabeth Raife (Ralph) Jany. 26, 1792, Rev. Christian Streit officiating. Solomon died, leaving widow and five children, just prior to 1804. His widow married James Leach, March 5, 1805. The children of Solomon were: Nathan, Nathaniel, Martin, Henry R., and Mary—all being minors. Their Orphans Accounts were settled in the courts of Frederick County, 1816 and 1819. Their mother we will not undertake to follow further, except to state that the second marriage was not agreeable to the children. The sons at an early age forsook mother and home, and for something better, sought homes in Tennessee. We find Nathaniel and Nathan in Wilson County, Tenn., in 1816, and Martin in same State in 1819, when their guardian settled with the Court. Henry R. wandered off to the wilds of Texas before she ran up the *Lone Star.* Mary remained with her uncles in Frederick County. We will now endeavor to trace these five children through one generation.

Nathaniel married Isabella Gleaves, and lived at Lebanon, Tenn., until his death about 1880, having acquired a fortune. A son, William M., became somewhat prominent, by a large bequest made by him to the Vanderbilt University. He has been dead many years. The other children were James, Thomas, Mary, Rachael, Sophia and Eliza.

Nathan married ——— ——— and he, too, lived at or near Lebanon, Tenn., and there reared several children. He had one daughter, Tennie, the writer saw in Tenn. in 1860, the bride of ——— Goodmyer. He had five other children. Robert C., served in a Tenn. Regiment in Army of Northern Virginia, where the writer saw him in 1863. H. M. Cartmell , now in Lebanon, Tenn., 82 years old, Thomas, long since dead. Mary Cartmell married ——— Barrow; their children live in Wilson County, Tenn. Several other daughters died young. Martin, son of Solomon Cartmell, married twice; first wife Miss Neal, left two children Sallie and Ann; second wife Jemima Sharp, was living in Jackson, Tenn., in 1860, when the writer enjoyed a brief visit to his happy and unbroken family. He was a striking type of the Virginia gentleman in the palmy days. Though intensely Tennessean, he was attached to his native State; and twice he and his daughter, Mary Bond, and brothers from Lebanon, visited Homespun and Retirement. Martin had been very successful in his struggle with Tennessee life; his possessions were large and remunerative; and after his forty years of strenuous effort, the writer found him keenly alive to all his enjoyments. The family by his second wife consisted of (first) his son Robert, lawyer by profession, but living near the town on a magnificent farm. His wife, Mary J. Baldwin and four children, made his home happy.

Names of children: Lizzie, Gooton, Robert and Harry.

Mary daughter of Martin, was the happy wife of Mr. J. D. Bond. He is survived by his wife and several children. One daughter, Mary, is the wife of A. H. Plant, auditor of the Southern Railroad system. They live in Washington, D. C.; their children being Helen, Alfred, George and Ollie. The writer enjoys frequent visits to their palatial home on Euclid Place, where the happy family joyfully extends the Tennessee hospitality. Mrs. Mary Bond spends much of her time as she grows more feeble, with her daughter.

The other children of John D. Bond and Mary E. Cartmell are Sydney S., Helen, Martin, Anna T.

Sydney S. married Mr. Mayo, one child. Helen married Hugh C. Anderson, one son, Bond. Martin married Nannie Mayo, children John, Martin and Mary.

Anna T. Bond married Findlay Snider; one child, Nettie May.

Martin, second son of Martin Cartmell, Sr., married (first) Sophia Williams; children Lena and Martin; and of second wife, J. Reid, Robert and A. D. Cartmell.

William Cartmell, son of Martin, Sr., was killed in battle, aged 21 years.

Henry Reif (Ralph) Cartmell, son of Solomon, as previously stated, went to Texas at an early day. The writer saw him in 1860, at his home in the town of Washington, Texas, then apparently an old man. His life had been full of adventure. He was active in the struggle for independence, and was allotted a large body of land for his service, and possessed many tokens from the young Republic in recognition of his loyalty and devotion to the cause. He also served as an officer during the war between the U. S. and Mexico; and was known far and near as Major Cartmell. He spent a small fortune in his efforts to operate steamboats on the Brazos River. The writer saw his beautiful little steamboat, Belle Sulphur, lying fast along the murky shores of the river, going to decay in the insurmountable mud. Maj. Cartmell had two children by his first wife, one Mary, the wife of Mr. ——— Willson; one son, Tom Cartmell, spent many years in Austin City. His popularity was remarkable. The writer arrived in Austin a short time after his sudden death; and when presented to many of the citizens by his friend, Col. William Byrd, then a brilliant lawyer in the city, as his friend Tom Cartmell,—the writer was impressed by their warm reception.

Major C. had his second wife and several sons and daughters around him in 1860.

Mary, the only daughter of Solomon, married Mr. Stephen Pritchard, a prosperous farmer near Kernstown, Va. Their home was for many years in the old house built by Wm. Hoge, later on the large brick mansion now owned by Chas. H. Grim's estate, was occupied by them. Their large family was reared in the old house. They had 7 children: Reese, Cornelius, Elizabeth R., Mary, Ann, James Henry, and Solomon. Reese was a man of many parts. For many years before the railroads penetrated Tenn. from the Virginia Valley, he kept two large six-horse teams and the old-time covered wagons constantly on the great highway, carrying supplies for merchants at Knoxville and border towns. At that time, prior to 1855, it was not unusual to see many such teams on the Valley Turnpike. Reese married and continued to live at the home place; raised a family there. His son, Frank Pritchard, owns a comfortable home on the Cedar Creek Turnpike, is married and is a worthy young man. The other children have left the country.

Cornelius, the second son, removed to some point in Page County; operated a profitable business; was married, unable to give any report of his family. Elizabeth R. married John M. Miller and lived near Middletown on his fine estate until his death, where they reared three sons and one daughter, viz: John, Reese, Anna Mary and William; the latter died unmarried. Anna Mary married J. Miller Long and lived at Vaucluse. John married and moved to Missouri. Reese married Miss ——— Fitch, of Winchester, where they have their home; one child, John, by this marriage. Mary married I. Milton Hollingsworth many years ago, and lived at the stone house East of and near the Keckley Mill; a magnificent farm attached, embracing what is now known as the Wickersham or Steck Orchard Farm, and extended across the Valley Turnpike, taking in the hillside, where the Beutell, John H. Campbell and Affleck houses now stand, which were all built since 1869. The field lying on the Valley Pike between the Toll Gate Road and the Keckley Mill, did not belong to the old farm, but was a part of the Nathan Parkins farm. The Civil War made havoc with the Hollingsworth homestead—barn and outbuildings burned by the Federal troops, and the mansion house rendered unfit for habitation. Mr. Hollingsworth removed his large family to Shenandoah County, where Mrs. Hollingsworth, now feeble with age (87 years), and several members of her family reside. Mr. H. died several years ago. One of the daughters, Harriet, married Mr. Hannon; her children: Nettie mar. Otto Hollis; Mary mar. Rothwell Vashion, by this husband two children, George and Maud; 2nd husband, Wm. Timberlake, one child, Frank G. Mary Hollingsworth married Capt. Jno. H.

Grabill, of Woodstock; and, as shown in this volume, has been editor and proprietor of the Shenandoah Herald. Children are: Elizabeth G., Jno. D., Frank, Holmes (dead), Mary C., Lucy, Catherine (dead), Anna M., David W., Henry E., and Ella H. John D. Grabill married Maud Grandstaff; David W. married Annie Magruder.

Clark Hollingsworth (dead), married Mrs. Mary Mossier. His daughter, Bessie, married Wm. Russell.

Stephen P. married Artie Hisey. His son, Alfred R., married Elizabeth Hockman and have seven children, viz: Grace, Lula, Harrison, Mary, Lloyd, Nina and Ruth.

Charles M. Hollingsworth was a physician (dead), mar. Josephine Roller; children: Francis, Marie, Pritchard, Charles and Joseph.

Edwin Hollingsworth mar. Francis Coffelt. Children: Lucy, Milton, Charles, and Martha Pritchard. The other three children of I. Milton and Mary Hollingsworth are unmarried, viz: Alfred R., Annie and Lucy.

Ann, the third daughter of Mrs. Mary Cartmell Pritchard, married Francis Carter of Loudoun County, where she spent the remainder of her life. She was noted for her beauty. Children by this union were: John, Lizzie, Maggie and Kate.

James Henry, son of Mrs. Mary C. Pritchard, whereabouts unknown.

Solomon the youngest son, was married and assigned a portion of the old homestead; built the house a short distance West, where Dr. T. Yardley Brown lived for many years, now occupied by a relative of his family.

Martin Cartmell, son of Nathaniel 2nd, by the will of his father inherited the Homespun farm. He was the youngest child. His mother, Sara Cartmell, continued her control of the mansion house and curtilage, slaves, etc., until her death in the spring of 1815. Her will probated May court, mentions several of her children—special legacies to Martin and her daughters, Elizabeth Louise (this must have been the widow of Archdeacon), Mary Willis, Sarah and Rachael. Martin married Ann Ball July 10, 1808, Alexander Balmaine officiating. A son and daughter were born to them: Thomas K. Cartmell, for whom the writer was named—never married. He was always mentioned by his relatives as very handsome and graceful, and a gentleman of the pure Virginia type. His portrait, which hung on the wall of the old drawing-room at Homespun, fully sustained the statement so frequently made to his namesake, who was taught from infancy to call him *Uncle Tom.* His untimely death Sept. 16, 1842, in his thirty-third year, was a severe blow to his many friends and relatives, especially so to his father, who only survived him until Feby. 3, 1843—71 years old. Both were laid away in the Old Quaker School House Graveyard, already referred to in other pages. Strange to say, their graves are unmarked. Their magnificent estate was ample to have given them a durable monument. The writer sought in vain to discover their nameless graves, so that he could erect some mark; but, alas, none could distinguish where they were placed.

The daughter, Eliza Ball, married Wm. Reed Campbell (brother of the writer's mother) May 30, 1832. They lived at Bellville (mentioned elsewhere as the home of the Tavenner and Levi G. Miller families) for a few years, when they went to Homespun and there reared three sons: Wm. Martin, Thomas K. and L. Franklin Campbell. They survived mother and father and also a brother James, who was killed by a fall from his horse Jany. 28, 1853, when quite young. The three sons married and had children (fuller mention of whom will be seen in the Campbell Family Sketch.)

Nathaniel Cartmell, the second son of Nathaniel of Homespun, married Elizabeth Froman, daughter of Paul Froman, and settled at his future home Retirement in 1775, which was allotted to him by his father. As stated elsewhere, he secured grants for other tracts. With these, together with several purchases, he owned a large landed estate. His wife died about 1789. No children left by this union. It has been asserted by some that she was the daughter of John Paul Froman, son of Paul; but the writer must stand by the traditions of his family without better proof to the contrary. Nathaniel's first matrimonial venture apparently discouraged him, for his second marriage did not occur until April 27, 1807, when he married Sarah Bean, daughter of Major Mordecai Bean, a contemporary of Isaac Zane in the manufacture of iron. He was a large holder of valuable ore land, and undertook their development prior to the Revolutionary War, when he and Zane operated two smelting furnaces.

Nathaniel Cartmell, born Nov. 20, 1753; died Aug. 4, 1826.

Sarah Bean, his wife, born Sept. 19, 1781, died Feby. 7, 1830.

Children of Nathaniel and Sarah, his wife:

Mordecai B., born Feb. 13, 1808; died Jany. 20, 1870.

Martin was born Jany. 29, 1809; died July, 1815.

Mordecai B. married Eliza Campbell April 5, 1827; eight children by this union.

Mary E. R., born Dec. 26, 1827—unmarried; died June 22, 1896.

Nathaniel M., born March 23, 1829; married Ellen Moore Sydnor Dec. 5, 1854. Dr. A. H. H. Boyd solemnized rites. Children by this union:

"Retirement"
Homestead of Nathaniel Cartmell 3rd; 1780

Fannie S. married three times, first John Cartmell of Springfield, Ohio, one child Jack; "her daughter, Sarah, died Jany. 25, 1891, buried in Mt. Hebron." 2nd husband, Mr. Clark, died after a lingering sickness; 3d husband, David Shanks, of Lexington, Va. No children by the last marriages. Fannie S. and her husband live in California. She is the authoress of several books and numerous magazine articles.

Robertina K. married Horace G. Browne. Three children by this union: Nellie, married Alexander Baker, son of Wm. H. Baker of Winchester, Va. Two children by this union: Katherine and Ellen. They live in Winchester, Va. Boyer B., second son, and Horace G. Browne, two young men of bright prospects, are now in Lima, Peru. Boyer B. has charge of the electrical plant of W. D. Grace & Co. Horace G. holds a position in same.

Nellie F., 3rd daughter of N. M. and E. M. Cartmell married Capt. Anderson. One son survives them.

William C., oldest son of N. M. and E. M., married. (Now dead). He left several children. They live on the Pacific coast.

Lidie, 4th daughter of N. M. and E. M. Cartmell, died at Capon Springs.

Katherine, 5th daughter, married John Graham, of Wilkesbarre, Penna. They reside at Newville, Penna. Mr. Graham was the promoter and owner of several trolley railroads; amassed a large fortune.

Nathaniel, the youngest son, is a Lieutenant in the Regular Army, stationed in the Philippines; saw active service in the Spanish-Am. War, with Col. Roosevelt at San Juan, etc. He has been twice married: 1st wife, Mrs. Nora Gentry; 2nd wife, Annita La T. Collins. They have two children: Nathaniel M., Jr., and Katharine.

Nathaniel M. Cartmell, father of the above-named children, born Mch. 23, 1829, died in California July 7, 1898, while on a visit to his daughter Fannie. He now lies in Mt. Hebron. He was Sheriff of Frederick County prior to the Civil War; then proprietor of the Taylor Hotel, Capon Springs, and partner of Col. Peyton, of the White Sulphur Springs—all famous hostelries in that day. His wife, Ellen M., died Feby. 21, 1901, while temporarily a guest in the Taylor Hotel.

Sallie R. Cartmell, 3d child of Mordecai B. and Eliza, born June 24, 1830—unmarried; died in Winchester after a lingering sickness. Her life was a beacon light to many pilgrims. The furnace of her afflictions refined every emotion and thought of her beautiful life. She laid down her burden with no word of weariness. Her grave can be found in the sacred plot at the Round Hill Church.

William C., 4th child, born Aug. 24, 1832; died in infancy.

Robert M. Cartmell, 5th child, born March 7, 1834; unmarried; died at Evans Hotel, Winchester, Dec. 17, 1902; interred in family lot at Round Hill. He was Deputy Sheriff for several terms prior to 1858; entered the Army in early part of Civil War as 1st Sergeant of Co. A, 39th Batt., stationed at Genl. R. E. Lee's Headquarters. This branch of the service was styled "Scouts, Guides and Couriers." He saw much of the historic campaign of the Army of Northern Va.; and grew in much favor with his comrades and with Genl. Lee and his military family; was honored by promotion to Lieut. He was familiar with many unwritten incidents of several campaigns, but his comrades frequently remarked that his reticence, so well maintained during his close contact with the principal in the great drama, clung to him, although no longer bound to secrecy. The writer induced him on one occasion to describe his meeting with Genl. Longstreet during the terrible scenes on the field of Gettysburg. It will be recalled by many readers, that Longstreet was charged by military critics with lack of interest in the great struggles made by Pickett and his famous command, thus causing a derangement of Genl. Lee's plans. Lt. Cartmell carried the celebrated dispatch from Lee to Longstreet. The latter took the dispatch and wrote these words on the back: "Too late to execute," and handed it back. This was shown Genl. Lee, who, crumpling it in his hand for a moment, returned the paper to Lt. Cartmell, who carefully preserved it. The writer may some day use it in a suitable publication, together with what Lt. Cartmell said concerning the episode, and other incidents of that day, so full of unparalleled carnage.

Ann Eliza, the 6th child, born May 4, 1836; died in infancy.

Thomas K. Cartmell, 7th child, born 28th day of Jany., 1838; married Annie Glass Baker, daughter of James C. and Susan E. Baker, at Greenwood, Nov. 22, 1866, Rev. W. H. Foote, D.D., officiating. Two children by this union, Robbie M., born Apl. 7, 1868, died in infancy, interred at Round Hill; Annie Lyle, 2nd child, married D. Coupland Randolph Nov. 7, 1904, at Ingleside, Rev. J. R. Graham officiating. Her mother died at the Evans Hotel, Winchester, Va., Jany. 18, 1907, interred in Mt. Hebron. Thomas K. Cartmell, now in his 71st year, enjoys good health and strength, and is the last of the name living in the Lower Valley, where at one time eleven Cartmell families were located on large tracts. The old deed books show over 100 conveyances recorded in the name. The subject of this sketch has had an eventful life. At this time he is serving his twenty-eighth year as Clerk and Deputy of the County Court of Frederick County. Prior to the Civil War he was assistant U. S. Marshal for the Southwestern District of Texas; superintended the taking of the Census in 1860. Returned to Virginia early in 1861. Was in Alexandria when Jackson killed Col. Ellsworth, whose Zouaves killed him in his hotel. Arriving in Winchester, was immediately commissioned Asst. Quartermaster, with Col. W. L. Willson, whom he knew in Texas. Was the officer who took the first wagon train, horses, caissons and cannon to Genl. Johnson's Army at Harpers Ferry. Reported to Col. Thomas J. Jackson, commandant of the post, forming an acquaintance which strengthened into friendship, that continued through the General's life. Was appointed by him Assistant Provost Marshal in Fall of 1861, and, with Col. Lawson Botts, conducted the first military execution, being that of Miller for shooting Capt. Henderson. Was sent as special messenger to order Genl. Boggs, of Pendleton County, to use his Brigade of Militia to picket that frontier. Proceeding thence to the headquarters of Genl. Loring in the Allegany Mountains, delivered dispatches, ordering his command to report to Genl. Jackson at Winchester. Received confidential orders from Genl. Jackson when he started on his Bath campaign, Jany. 1, 1862; executed his rigid orders that led to the necessity of Genl. Loring securing a pass from the Provost Marshal, when he desired to visit Richmond, pending the conflict of authority between them. Resigned as Provost Marshal when Winchester was evacuated March 11, 1862. Enlisted as a private in a cavalry company just organized, with Col. Wm. H. Harness as Captain. With this Company under Genl. Turner Ashby, as rear guard of Genl. Jackson's Army as it fell back from Genl. Banks, in frequent skirmishes in that march. Detailed at Woodstock to enter the mountains to the West and report the movements of Genl. Fremont. Reported to headquarters at Lacy Springs, with information, and several prisoners. The detail was composed of men from Capt. Harness' Company. With many escapades of this and subsequent service rendered by this Company, known as Campany B. of the 17th Batt., and 11th Virginia Regiment, while it followed such leaders as Ashby, Jones, Lomax, Rosser and others. (Which may receive fuller notice elsewhere.) Was badly disabled on Linville Creek in a Cavalry fight, and lay helpless for weeks; then detailed by Genl. Ashby for special scout service, approved by Genl. Jackson. This resulted in formation of the *Bureau of Information,* with the writer in charge of the Valley District, until the War closed. Of this service it is not proper to write in this volume. Some other day it may appear in another form. Some papers relating to this detail and service, have been preserved. He is now writing a History of Frederick County.

Mordecai B. Cartmell, eighth and youngest child of M. B. and Eliza, was born Dec. 23, 1839. Was killed at Sangsters Station, a point between Fairfax C. H. and Manassas, Dec. 17, 1863. He was then Capt. of Co. B., 11th Va. Cavalry, Rosser's Brigade. He enlisted as private in this Company, with the writer, Mch., 1862; was made orderly sergeant, and soon recognized for efficiency. His gallant conduct in such severe cavalry battles as Trevillians, Brandy Station, Upperville, and many others, won the admiration of officers and men; and when Capt. Harness resigned, he was promoted to the Captaincy of his Company, B., that he loved. Survivors of the great battles, hard marches, West Virginia raids, and his last, the Rosser raid around Genl. Meade's Army, can recall many deeds of valor and bravery. Falling in the last raid at the head of his squadron, he gave up his young life 'ere the hour came when the Lost Cause was known—and never knew the pathetic poem of the *Furled Banner*, or the anguish and gloom that hovered over his old Retirement home. In the sketch of the latter, it is shown how and when he returned to this home. Capt. Cartmell was a superb horseman—fearless in battle, generous and affectionate in temperament, he was beloved by all. Gallant comrade and brother; your survivors are answering the Roll Call every day, as they wearily wend their way to the river where they must soon cross over, hoping "to rest under the shade of the trees."

Mordecai B. Cartmell, the father of this large family, spent his entire life at Retirement, until 1869, having sold the property, he removed to Winchester with the two daughters and their mother, where he and Sallie R. died. The mother and daughter Mary E. shortly thereafter removed to Ingleside, the writer's home, and there ended their days. The father and mother reared their family at Retirement in old time style familiar in those days in that class of homestead. Many festal occasions could be mentioned, that are recalled by hundreds who were guests under the famous old rooftree. M. B. Cartmell belonged to the old school class; was a gentleman by native instinct and practice. In politics an old time Whig, he was one of the old Justices when Virginia enjoyed their courts. The mother was peculiarly fitted for her position as mother and housewife in such a homestead. Children and grandchildren always delighted to recount the lovely deeds and influences flowing from her generous heart. She lived a life beautifully adorned with charitable acts. Of cheerful temperament, she made life at Retirement precious to all. Both parents lie in the Old Church Yard at Round Hill.

Having disposed of the Homespun branch, it is in order to take up Edward, the son of Martin Cartmell, who died in 1749, and nephew of Nathaniel 1st. We left him seated near Middletown to pursue the lines of Nathaniel. (See first pages of this sketch.)

Edward Cartmell was a large land-owner, and sold several tracts of land in his lifetime. He was twice married. His first wife, Miss Bailey, left several children—name of his second wife not mentioned. She too had children. In settling his estate after his death about 1806, we find names of his children as follows: George, Harrison, Martin, Regina, Elizabeth, Jane, Parthenia and Rachael. Hannah Bevens and Rebecca Weaver are also named; and it is likely they were his sisters, for Rebecca Cartmell married John Weaver Aug. 8, 1790. She could not have been his daughter. Parthenia Cartmell married John Maxwell June, 1807. This must have been his daughter, though some evidence indicates she was his widow. Edward owned a large lot in Winchester (Martin and Nathaniel also owned lots in Winchester) and also owned the "Big Woods" tract near the Southern boundary of Winchester. His children by his second marriage were minors in 1812. The first set gradually disappeared from the records. Harrison was located in some Western county. No trace of others except as to George, who was living in Berkeley County, Va., in 1815, owning land there and holding an interest in his father's estate in Frederick. These children seem to have lost their identity with their Frederick County kin. They have been traced to Ill., Missouri, Kansas, California, and into several Northern States; but their descendants are unable up to this time to give anything definite. This is to be regretted, for Edward was a man of large interests in the County from 1750 to his death, having spent an active life for about sixty years.

The Campbell Family

The Campbells found in the Old County at an early day, became prominent in the development of the new country. They were soldiers and statesmen. Capt. Andrew Campbell won reputation as a member of the Justices Court, and distinction as the leader of Hibernians and other troops during the wars of the 18th Century, as waged in Valley territory. Of him, or those who were here prior to the days of 1776, it is not our purpose now to speak. It is of the large family of that name which sprang from William Campbell of Londonderry, whose name is briefly mentioned in the sketch of his old homestead near Round Hill, that we desire to trace. This appears here in this volume, by reason of the intermarriage of the Cartmell and Campbell families; so that references can be more easily made.

William Campbell sought his home in the Shenandoah Valley just as the great war closed in 1782. It was not the first time he touched the soil of Virginia. He had had some interest in certain sailing craft, and shipped large quantities of Virginia and Maryland tobacco to his native country, making many voyages. He evidently found his enterprise profitable, for when he appears in Frederick County, he was prepared to buy land and build good houses. He was twice married; his first wife was Miss ——— Buchanan of Penna. He died April, 1838, aged 73 years. Three children were born of this marriage: Jane, Mary and James. His second wife was Mary Johnson, of Frederick Co. 7 children by this marriage: Wm. Reed, Rebecca, Eliza, Robt. M., Jno. Chambers, James Harrison and L. Franklin Campbell.

Jane, daughter by the first marriage, married Patrick Denver, Jr., Jany. 2, 1817. They removed to Clinton County, Ohio, October, 1830. Their children were Elizabeth, James W., Frank, Arthur St. C., Rosalie, Mary, Jane, Harrison, Josephine and Cornelia, all of whom were born in Frederick County except the last two. Elizabeth married Samuel Johns, of that County, who died in 1881. She died at the age of 83. They reared the following children: Jennie, Harry D., and Samuel Johns.

James W. Denver, the oldest son, has been so familiar to the American people, that his history is well known. Born in Frederick County, he attended school near Gainsboro, until the family left for Ohio. He became a lawyer; and while in practice at a town in Missouri, the war clouds between the United States and Mexico began looming over the Southern horizon. He became enthused; and, as he told the writer, addressed a communication to the President, expressing his views of the exciting question, and requested to be sent a colonel's commission by next post, so that he might take command of the regiment he proposed to raise. This was long before mail facilities were good in that country. He timed the probable arrival of the stage coach with Eastern mails; then he watched the arrivals with much interest. His calculation missed by one arrival only. He received his commission as a matter of every-day occurrence. The General was always amused in telling this incident, remarking that simplicity and candor attended the actions of great men in that day.

The Colonel had his share of that war; returned with a Brigadier's commission, and visited Retirement and Stony Meade relatives. His uniform produced lasting impression on his young cousins. The General crossed the *Plains* with the *Forty-Niners,* and tried his fortunes in California. Was Secretary of State. During his term, resented an insult to the Governor, culminating in a duel, in which his antagonist fell mortally wounded (the ground was pointed out to the writer when in California in 1880.) He was member of Congress from California; then Commissioner of Indian Affairs; appointed by President Buchanan Provisional Governor of Kansas, when ruffianism ruled that great Territory. His stern character taught that element that law and order must prevail; revolutionized the lawless government, and laid the foundation for the great States that have been carved out of Kansas; laid out a village, which has grown into the magnificent city bearing his name—Denver City frequently honored him with marked attentions. Entering the Union Army as Brigadier General, he served with distinction, until Lincoln issued his Emancipation Proclamation, when he resigned. Became prominent before the Supreme Court at Washington in the practice of his profession, amassing a large fortune. He was supported by large delegations for the nomination of President, when Cleveland was first nominated at Chicago. He died in Washington. Genl. Denver married Miss Lou Rombach, of Wilmington, Ohio. A woman of rare accomplishments, she advanced every walk of his life, and was the mother of his four children: Katherine, James W., Mary and Matt R. Katherine became the wife of a Southern planter, Hon. James C. Williams, of Natchez, Miss., and there resided until her husband's death. She with her two children have temporary residence at Northampton, Mass., where every effort is made to secure the education of the children.

J. W. Denver, known as Col. Will Denver, was born Dec. 16, 1863. After his father's death, he assumed control of the vast estate; and was remarkable for his ability as a financier. His life was above reproach. Truly it can be said of Will Denver: "None knew him but to love him; none named him but to praise." He died in the full bloom of his splendid manhood, Nov. 26, 1898.

Mary married Mr. Lindley, of Cincinnati. Their home is in New York City; they have two children. The charms of her beautiful girlhood, while visiting the writer's family at Ingleside, are well remembered.

Matt R. is married and is now the Hon. Matt R. Denver, Member of Congress from the Wilmington District. His election as a Democrat in a District overwhelmingly Republican, is a marvel among politicians. This attests his popularity and integrity. He is married and has one child.

Arthur St. C., second son of Patrick Denver and Virginia Campbell, married in California and lived there for many years. Removed to Washington City, and there died. His wife and daughter Cornie survived him.

Rosalie married Mr. Dacon, of Ohio—two children, Frank and Jennie, survive their parents.

Mary C. and Jane were twin sisters, noted for perfect resemblance to each other. Both were gifted, as their sweet poems will forever attest. Every trait in their beautiful lives was an adornment noticeable by all who knew them. Jane died in mature girlhood, while Mary survived her sister many years. Her sad expression of voice and eye plainly told of the ineffaceable sorrow. Mary was a frequent visitor at old Retirement. Her death occurred at her home in Clinton County, Ohio.

Harrison C. Denver was born in Frederick County, Va., July 31, 1829. He married Rose B. Telfair October 25, 1872. The writer enjoyed a visit to their lovely home, Oak Ridge. This splendid gentleman and his beautiful Rose are no longer at that homestead so famous for its prodigal hospitality. He died Feb. 28, 1890. She survived him until Jany. 5, 1894.

Frank was born in Frederick County; went to California to seek its goldfields; and spent the remainder of his days on the Pacific Coast. He was prominent in its affairs. His wife and daughter Jennie survive him.

Josephine married Rev. Norman Jones, a Presbyterian Minister.

Cornelia or Cornie, as she was called, the youngest child of Patrick Denver and Virginia Campbell, was born in Ohio, married Mr. James, a prominent lawyer of Coshocton, Ohio, where they lived until his death. She has two daughters Mary and Rosalie, both highly accomplished, and are well known for their attainments in higher education. All are living in New York City. Mary married Mr. Arthur Sullivan of that city.

Mary Campbell, second daughter of William Campbell, married Wm. Wood, and they too removed to Ohio at an early day. Both long since dead. Their children are widely scattered.

James Campbell, oldest son of William, has been mentioned elsewhere as Lt. Campbell, who died at Point Comfort during War of 1812.

William Reed, son of Wm. and Mary Campbell, has also been mentioned as the husband of Eliza Cartmell. He died at Homespun Apl. 13, 1851, aged 44 years. Three sons survive these parents: Wm. Martin, married a Miss Kern of

Newtown. He died many years ago. His widow and only daughter survive him.

Thomas K. married Miss Grim of Winchester. They live in Washington City. Their children are Edward, William. They had a brother, now deceased, this was Hunter.

L. Franklin is a physician; lived in Point Pleasant, W. Va., from 1867 until recently, when the family removed to Birmingham, Ala. He was reared by his uncle, R. M. Campbell; served during the Civil War in Company H., 13th Va. Infty.; received injuries by explosion of shell. Captured and a prisoner at Camp Chase for many months. Dr. Campbell married Miss Barbee. They have four children: Louis R., Archie, L. F. and daughter Cornie, married and lives at Point Pleasant, W. Va.

Eliza Campbell has been mentioned in the Cartmell Sketch as the wife of M. B. Cartmell. By reference to it, the names of her children appear. She was born May 8, 1805.

Rebecca, daughter of Wm. and Mary Campbell, and wife of John Lupton. For list of her children, reference may be had to the Cartmell sketch.

Robert Madison, son of Wm. and Mary Campbell, married Rebecca A. Lockhart, daughter of Genl. Josiah Lockhart; twelve children born of this union, all of whom survive the parents except one, Maggie, an infant, died 1853. Robert M. rounded out his long and busy life at the head of Opeckon, where he had spent the greater part of it. His large family was reared at *Stony Meade,* heretofore mentioned. He saw them all as men and women go out into the world well equipped for its affairs. The writer will now briefly show who they were, where they went, and what they have done. His life was closely entwined with this family, and he therefore feels competent to compile a few facts, though he may fall far short of producing a pen picture that will do justice to this large and interesting family.

Names of children: Josiah L., Mary E., William H., Nannie R., Bean C., Robert M., Emma, Roberta, J. Edwards, Herbert and Allan W.

Josiah L. Campbell born in 1834, was a physician with a large practice at Woodstock, Va. Married Annie Walton, a woman remarkable for her pure life. She was survived by her husband and two sons, Willie and Harry; both are dead. Dr. Campbell married a second time. They have one daughter, Bertie. The Doctor retired from practice several years ago; present residence is in Norfolk, Va. He was one of the organizers of the first military company of Shenandoah, for service in the Civil War, called the "Muhlenburg Guards." He was one of its officers; later was Regimental Surgeon; served Shenandoah County in the General Assembly, the first session held under the Reconstruction règime, when nearly every Southern county of the State sent negro men to the Assembly. During his term, the floor of the Assembly hall fell, injuring many members, the Doctor being one.

Mary E. Campbell, born 1837—unmarried—spent her life with parents through every stage of their long life, in prosperity, adversity and trial; and tenderly cared for them as the shadows lengthened in the glorious sunset of their lives. A few years thereafter, she yielded to the generous and earnest solicitations of her brother, and removed to Prairie Grove, Arkansas.

William H. Campbell spent his boyhood at Stony Meade, and there formed habits of industry and frugality; learned lessons of social life, and imbibed the religious doctrines daily taught in that large household. During all this youthful period "Will" as he was called, acquired sufficient education in good schools—old Winchester Academy, etc., to fit him for commercial life. He chose the profession of medicine. At this time he was interrupted by his prompt offer to serve his State in her first effort to repel the invader. His war record was untarnished; his service was faithful, and after the four years struggle, he was spared to return home to start afresh. His useful life since then has much in it to show the merits of the man and skill of the physician. His marriage to Miss Jessie Gorsuch, of Baltimore, led him to finally settle at McDonough Institute, Md., where he has enjoyed a lucrative practice, reared seven children. John, his oldest son, is married and principal at "St. James School," Md.; another son, Robert M. Campbell, successfully passed the schools of West Point, and is now an officer in the Regular Army. His sister, Francenca, an accomplished young lady, is unmarried. The other four are Thos., Douglas, Allan and Elizabeth.

Bean C., 3rd son, and Robert M. Campbell, 4th son, entered the army while yet in their teens; became active members of Company A., 39th Batt., Scouts, Guides and Couriers, stationed at Genl. Lee's headquarters; served faithfully until his surrender; returned home; embarked in farming with their cavalry horses; later on removed to Missouri. Bean C. Married in Virginia Bessie Walker, daughter of Dr. Walker, of Va. After some experiences with his brother, J. Edward, in the Indian Territory, he now lives in Arkansas. He has children. Dorothea and one son.

Robert M. married in Missouri, and there lived for some time, rearing his family of children. His oldest daughter Rebecca is married. Their home now is in the new State of Oklahoma.

Nannie R. became the wife of Col. W. W. Glass, during the Civil War. She and her children are fully mentioned in the Sketch of the Wood and Glass families.

Emma married Lincoln Maupin, of Rockingham County, where their children were reared, being Bessie, Carrie (who died in Frederick County), Emily, Lincoln and Richard. Subsequently they spent several years near Clearbrook, Fredk. County, Va. In about 1900 the family removed to Arkansas, near Prairie Grove.

Roberta married Henry Magruder, of Woodstock, Va.; lived in that vicinity, rearing several children: Annie, Emma, Margery, Robert and Henry. They, too, removed to Arkansas, and formed a new family circle near Prairie Grove. Mr. Magruder was for many years a Ruling Elder in the Presb. Church. He died a few years after settling in the S. Western home. The two sisters briefly mentioned, are well remembered as the two young daughters of Stony Meade, possessing rare charms.

J. Edward Campbell was a beardless boy during the Civil War; and at its close, grew restless with the crippled condition of his native State, and soon cast his fortunes on the Western borders of Missouri, to embark, later on, into the Indian Territory. He soon ingratiated himself into favor among the friendly tribes; was virtually adopted by the Delawares; married an educated daughter of their chief. Was soon recognized for his ability and integrity; secured the confidence of those new and peculiar citizens of the country; grew in influence, acquiring considerable means, and ultimately became the J. E. Campbell so well known throughout the Southwest. At this writing, he enjoys a prominent position of large wealth and generous in nature, he held out his helping hand to his aged parents, his brothers and sisters, and was instrumental in securing to them the comfortable homes they now enjoy. As he rounds out his useful and active life, we predict his new State will take a just pride in bestowing high honors to crown his remarkable career. He has two married children, Roberta J. and Herbert.

Herbert grew tired of farm life at Stony Meade, and graduated in the Baltimore Schools of Medicine; but realizing that such professional life was not in accord with his temperament, he cast his diploma aside, and sought the home of his brother in the Indian Territory. There he found a life congenial to his tastes—roaming over those beautiful prairies, he became one of the cow boys familiar in the eighties. His success has been marvellous. He represents and owns banking interests, promoter of oil projects, of untold riches, his possessions extend into Texas, where he owns farms and stock ranches of immense value. Herbert has never married. He lives at *No Wata,* Ind. Territory, where his brother, J. E. Campbell, has lived for many years.

Allan W. was the last of the Campbells to leave Stony Meade. He remained there after the farm went to its present owner, John G. Miller. For several years he was its successful farmer. He married Lucy Walker, sister of Bean C's wife. Allan was prominent in church affairs—a Ruling Elder in the Round Hill Presb. Church. After the death of his father and mother, he removed his family to the Indian Territory, where he now lives. His energy and economy have secured him gratifying success in his new field. He has two children: Leslie and Jessie.

We can scarcely afford to close this brief sketch without touching some of the incidents in the life of Robert Madison Campbell, the Patriarch of Upper Opecquon. His influence in that vicinity for well nigh two-thirds of a century, was of that character which commanded respect from all. His sincerity as a Christian gentleman was never doubted. Being a Ruling Elder, first in the Loudoun St. Presb. Church, with such pastors as Dr. Hill and Dr. A. H. Boyd; later on he held same office in Round Hill Church, when it had separate organization through the help of Rev. Henry M. White, D.D. Mr. Campbell was a tower of strength. His enjoyment of the Old Grove meetings at Round Hill, they were rich places in his religious experiences. Then those old time services were attended by gathering in new converts, some of whom as old men and women, delight to mention those never-to-be-forgotten sermons. Mr. Campbell could tell the day, hour and spot in the old Grove, where he a thoughtless listener was first awakened. This was long before the church was erected. The old school house afforded a place for occasional services. The old school house near the Greenwood home was used by Mr. Campbell and Mr. James Carr Baker for a half century, for prayer services. The whole neighborhood gathered there every Sunday night for those services. Their influence and the untiring efforts of those Godly men, saved the community from threatened ruin at one time. A new-comer started a distillery near the place; the youths began to yield. When discussing the best mode to adopt to force its removal, the two elders arrived at the same conclusion: they would resort to special prayer, as one of them told the writer. He said "the surest way was to pray it down." The operator became converted and all his household; the objectionable enterprise disappeared, never to return; the wanderers were gathered into the fold, and to-day the community is celebrated for good order. It must be stated that in all of Mr. Campbell's struggles (which as the writer knows were numerous and heavy) he had the loyal support of his wife,—a woman scarcely equalled in the land for her superb endowments. Her intellect was of high order and under good cultivation. Her gentle influence went out with great power. These two were happily joined for their great life work, the record of which cannot be read now; but some day the Book will be open. In Mt. Hebron can be seen suitable memorials on the slabs that mark their graves:

John Chambers, son of Wm. and Mary Campbell, while a young man engaged in the mercantile business in Winchester, occupying the store on Main Street now the business place of Russell and Green. He then removed to Clarksburg, W. Va., where he married Ann Wilson, and made that place his home for many years, rearing several children: Louisa, Rebecca, Ann, John and Augustine. Mr. Campbell for several years prior to the Civil War, was one of the County Clerks in that section; and when West Virginia became a State, he was chosen County Clerk for ——— County, and held the office up to his death.

J. Harrison Campbell. (See Campbell Homestead sketch for whom he married.) Mr. Campbell remained at the homestead with his mother, who became an invalid and great sufferer. Previous to her death and his marriage, he was the prince among bachelors, popular and wonderfully attractive to his numerous nephews and nieces, who enjoyed many visits to the *Old Place*, as it was generally called. He was passionately fond of horses and hounds, and all the sports in which they could take part. He had in his possession the accoutrements of his brother Lt. James Campbell; and the sword and belt, horse pistols, cocked hat, etc., were curious things for the youngsters to look upon and hear their history. He died in his 46th year; and left his widow and young children to struggle through the trying period of the closing years of the Civil War and the other hard years that followed. Nobly did she battle with the problem of living, finally succeeding in providing a comfortable home out of the wreck, and there reared four of her children to mature years. The two sons, Wm. Albert and Mortimer, died just as they entered manhood. Mortimer died in Missouri; Wm. Albert was on crutches all his life, from some spinal trouble. His district elected him Commissioner of the Revenue. He was very popular—handsome and attractive. This left the mother and two daughters, Laura and Minnie. The latter survived her mother several years; Laura had previously become the wife of Mr. P. C. Gore, as previously stated. She was stricken in the prime of her admirable life, leaving many to mourn the loss of a warm-hearted friend. Her two children, Walter and Lena, are mentioned in the sketch of the homestead.

L. Franklin Campbell, youngest son of Wm. and Mary Campbell, grew to be a man of immense proportions—very tall. He became a student at the Winchester Medical College, receiving his diploma about 1852. He located at Morgantown, West Va., and there spent the remainder of his days.

The Baker Family.

This name has for many years been applied to four distinct families in Frederick County, during the 18th, 19th and 20th Centuries. The most numerous family bearing this name for nearly one hundred years, was the German family who came to the Valley of Virginia about 1756. For many years they were distinguished by the German name of Baechter (which will appear in another sketch.) One other family, claiming to be Huguenots, settled on Capon River. One other was a Baker family found with the German Mueller settlement near Woodstock, and was mentioned as the Moravian family. The writer after careful investigation, fails to find any trace of German in their line, and is led to believe they were of the family once numerous on Lost River. And further, the three briefly mentioned, had no connection with the Baker family the subject of this sketch. The first appearance of this family in Virginia was in the early part of 1700, when a family of this name came from England and settled in James City County. This was James Baker. His name frequently appears in leases made by Nathaniel Burwell as early as 1733, attesting signatures as James Baker, scribe. This relation existed apparently during the lifetime of James. We have no evidence that this James Baker removed from James City County to Frederick County. We have, however, evidence that his two sons, James and Samuel, were living on part of the Col. Burwell estate in what is now Clarke County about 1760. In a mass of old Burwell papers, are found a number of letters from the two sons. James writes for the boundaries of the tract upon which he resides; complains of encroachments from other lessees. None of these leases were recorded; and doubtless the holdings of James were simply permits for him to enjoy the uses of that portion of the Burwell grant, while Samuel seems to have acted as agent, to collect and forward tobacco, rents. There is a family tradition, however, that James, the father, was the James who had the leasehold. Samuel, a son, was old enough in 1773, to write

Col. Burwell concerning the Old Chapel Graveyard. About this time, Hugh Nelson gave permission to have a church erected on the Old Chapel lot; and, as will be seen in Church sketches, a survey was made 1791, by request of Samuel Baker agent for Col. Nathaniel Burwell, of James City County, for two acres of land on Old Chapel run, etc. In this connection it may be proper to state that a Charles Baker was living on a small tract of land on Crooked Run in Frederick County, prior to 1740 "part of the Joist Hite survey." He conveyed 25 acres of this tract to Samuel Earle 1743. He was there in 1756, and in 1759 conveyed more land to Charles Baker, Jr.,—41 acres, and in 1761 Charles Baker, Jr., conveyed 69 acres on Crooked Run to Branson. He evidently was of the English family, and doubtless a brother of James found in James City County in 1710. All records concerning this Charles Baker clearly show he was an Englishman; and, as it will appear later on, he was located in Frederick County nearly twenty years before the German family settled in the county. It may interest some descendants of this English family to take up the investigation where the writer must leave it.

The genealogical chart of the family now in possession of the writer can be relied on as authentic. The writer has given the suggestions for what they are worth.

The chart says James Baker and wife settled in Frederick County (now Clarke) at a very early day. They had three children: Samuel, James and Elizabeth.

Samuel married twice; first wife Miss Ship. She was the mother of Ewell and Matilda Baker. Ewell was known in Warren County as Capt. Ewell Baker. He was Clerk of Courts from 1865 until his death, May 26, 1881, except about one year during the Reconstruction period. He never married. Matilda married twice; first husband Dr. Fletcher, who had one daughter Mary L., who married Mr. Garnett; two children, Tillie, died, Mollie B. Garnett who married Dr. Steele of Richmond, Va. Children by these marriages, Maude, Louise, Bessie, Albert, Thomas and Edith. Matilda's second husband was Mr. Slaughter. Samuel Baker married the 2nd time Eliza Gamble; children by this marriage: Ann Gamble, James Carr, Eliza H., Joseph Gamble, Mary Lisle. Ann G. married Lloyd Logan. Children by this union: Eliza, wife of Thomas D. Spindle, Maria wife of Charles Worthington, Mary wife of Lou Davisson, Sarah wife of Dr. J. Arnold, Lloyd D. married Elizabeth Mackey, Samuel B. married Jeannette Thruston, Charles married ———.

James Carr Baker married Susan E. Glass. (The Glass family sketch gives names of their 4 children.)

Eliza Hamilton married D. K. Pitman of Missouri. She was his second wife; two children, Anna E. wife of Wm. T. Glanville: one child Annie, married Mr. Carter; son John married twice; lives at Kirkwood, Mo.

Joseph Gamble, son of Samuel Baker and Eliza Gamble, married Lavinnia Massey of Winchester, Va. Twin daughters by this union, Emma dec'd, and Lavinia married Samuel Neel: five children, Carr, Louise, Sam, Lavinia, Elsie.

Mary Lisle, wife of B. A. Alderson of Mo., 6 children: Bettie G. wife of Mr. Watkins, Fannie wife of Charles Durell, 3 children Albert, Bessie and James Carr. Samuel B., now Rev. S. B. Alderson, D.D., married Miss Barbee of Ky. Children by this union: Frank, Mary Lisle, Lottie O., Howard, Porter, and Lizzie B.

David P. Alderson married Miss Witting of Miss.; Robert F. Alderson married Elsie Kirk of Ohio. William Alderson married **Mabel** Haines of Mo.

James Baker, son of James Baker and Elizabeth Brown, married Nancy Campbell. 10 children by this union: 1st John (Capt. Jack Baker) married Mary Morgan; no children. (2) Samuel married Eliza Reed; their children being James married Elizabeth Forsyth; their children were Forsyth, Samuel and Louise McIntyre. Ann R. daughter of Samuel Baker married Wm Morgan, his children: James, Anna K., Mary C., Samuel, Lilly and William. Mr. Morgan married twice, his other wife being Mary Cooper, and the three children last named appear to have been her children.

Alexander C., son of Samuel Baker and Eliza Reed; his children were Samuel Colin and Louise Collin; grandchildren: Alfred, Eliza R., Ella W., S. Colin, Ellen H., Louisa W., Elizabeth, Anita Blanche. The writer hesitates to submit this list of children and grandchildren in the order named, since the entry on the chart is confusing, hoping, however, that those of Alexander Cooper's branch may understand the complication.

William, son of Samuel Baker and Eliza R., his daughter Maria Cooper, married Rev. Edgar Wood, D.D., a distinguished Presb. minister, Pastor of the Charlottesville Church for many years. Dr. Wood aided by his accomplished wife, exerted an influence in his church work, that became a monument to them in their declining years. They established the celebrated Pantops Academy. The name of this institution was familiar throughout the Union, and mentioned with veneration in the faraway heathen lands. They lived long and well, to see grand results. The patient wife and loving mother answered the summons recently: "Come up higher, the earthly work is ended." Their union was blessed with 5 children, whose lives reflect the precepts and examples that emanated from the parents. Their only daughter Annie E. married John R. Sampson, who succeeded Dr. Woods at Pantops. Mr. and Mrs. Sampson took the institution when it was ready for the new life they infused into its every channel; additional buildings were erected; an increase of students set in, many distant climes sending young men to become part of the Pantops life. When reaching the crest of the wave, Mr. Sampon's health gave way and his grand work was called off. He is survived by his wife and Anne Russell and Merle his children. Mrs. Sampson is well known for her church work. Samuel B. son of Edgar Woods and Maria C. married Lucretia Gilmore. Children Edgar, Gilmore, Samuel, Henry, Lucretia and Maria.

Henry McK., son of Dr. Edgar Woods, married Josephine Underwood, now missionaries in China; their children are Henry, Josephine, Edgar.

Edgar, son of Dr. Edgar Woods, married Francis Smith, daughter of Dr. Jas. P. Smith. They and their two children, Mary Barclay and Sue S., are engaged in Chinese missionary work.

James B., son of Dr. Edgar Woods, married Elizabeth Smith; have one child Agnes Lacy; are in China.

William, James and Corlein Baker, sons of James Baker and Nancy Campbell. No report from these branches.

Alexander Baker, son of James Baker and Nancy Campbell, was born in what is now Clarke County, May 16, 1814. He was married in 1837 to Caroline, daughter of James M. Hite. He served as Quartermaster in the Confederate Army, with rank of Major. He possessed all the traits of the old Virginia gentleman. Ten children were born to them, four of whom died in infancy. Maria married Dr. Thomas M. Lewis; Nancy married D. Cockey; Lelia H., Alexander C. (dec'd), Carrie M. (dec'd), and James Madison Hite Baker. He and his sister Lelia live near Old Chapel.

Elizabeth married Cyrus Murry.

Nancy, dau. of James Baker and Nancy Campbell, mar. George Brown; one daughter mar. Robert Bently.

Maria, daughter of James Baker, wife of Thomas Ingram.

Sophia G., another daughter of James Baker, mar. Buckner Ashby; had three sons, William, James Lewis and Buckner Ashby, all dead.

Elizabeth Baker, daughter of James Baker and Elizabeth Brown, married Wm. Cook. She was always mentioned by the family as Betsy Baker of Federal Hill. She was married while yet a child; born Aug. 19, 1783, married March 5, 1797. She became the mother of ten children, to-wit:

Eliza, married Jos. Gamble, no children.

Lucy Davenport—unmarried—died 1878.

Mary, mar. Winterton Murphy, and left 8 children.

Lina died young; her brother William died in Indiana, 1866. His wife was Sarah Kelly.

Giles, son of Betsy Baker and William Cooke, born June 22, 1812; died Sept. 29, 1891, in Front Royal, Va., where he practiced law for 55 years. His legal knowledge was recognized in the Virginia courts; his splendid life ornamented the community that always accorded him their admiration. Was commonwealths Attorney for Warren County many years. Was a member of the celebrated State Convention of 1850. His wife was Elizabeth Lane. They had five children.

(1) Giles, Jr., born Mch. 28, 1845; married Alice Woodward. This is Judge Giles Cook of Front Royal, president of Front Royal Nat. Bank. Judge Cook is Ruling Elder in the Presb. Church. He is well known in his church courts for his sound judgment and unvarying integrity. The writer values the warm friendship that has always existed between Giles Cook and himself. He entered the Army a mere boy; but his service during the trying days of 1862-65, made him a conspicuous hero.

George Wythe, second son of Giles, Sr., born Oct. 28, 1846, mar. Rebecca Lloyd of Alexandria. This line is in Washington. He is the well known Dr. Wythe Cook of that city.

Henry Lane, 3d son of Giles, Sr., born Aug. 30th, 1850, married Alice Slemmer.

Martha, 4th child of Giles, Sr., born May 11, 1852, married Dr. W. S. Roy.

Mary, 5th child of Giles, Sr., born March 3, 1854, married C. A. Macatee. He was Clerk of Courts for Warren County for several years.

The writer regrets his inability to give names of the grandchildren of Mr. Giles Cook, no lists having arrived. Nannie, dau. of Betsy Baker and William Cook, married James Beale, surviving this husband. Her children were Bertie, Giles and Josephine. The latter married Capt. Joseph McK. Kennerly of Greenway Court. Mrs. Nannie Beale married 2nd time Garland T. Wheatley; they had one dau. Nannie, who died in Memphis with yellow fever in 1878.

Sarah, dau. of Betsey Baker and Wm. Cook, married Garland T. Wheatley—no children.

Martha, dau. of Betsey Baker and Wm. Cook, born Mch. 11, 1816, died Apl. 1, 1893; married James W. Mason; they had 6 children: (1) Laura mar. Wm. T. Morrill; both died without children; (2) George, mar. Fannie Lewis; (3) Gertrude, unmarried; (4) Joseph, mar. Gertrude Carr of W. Va.; (5) Douglas, married Lula Clark, of Dermopolis, Ala; lived in Philada.; (6) Florence, mar. Benjamin T. Fendell, civil engineer, of Balto.

Samuel, son of Betsey Baker and Wm. Cook, Born Oct. 10, 1818; died Oct. 29, 1893; they had only one child, Evelyn Cook. This branch is mentioned in sketch of Willow Brook.

A word may properly be added in this connection, relating to the progenitor of William Cook, the subject of this sketch. William was born Feby. 1, 1768; he was the son of Giles Cook, Jr., who removed from Gloucester County, Va., to Old Frederick County and settled near Charlestown (now) Jefferson County. This was previous to the birth of this son William, who lived at Willow Brook from 1810 until his death Apl. 22, 1843. He was presiding Justice of the Old County at one time, and by virtue of his seniority in office, was also High Sheriff. Was Quartermaster for Genl. Morgan during the Whiskey War in Penna., 1794. His widow Betsey (Baker) died in 1866, 83 years old, at Willow Brook, where she had lived for nearly sixty years.

The Baker Family, originally the German Baechter Family.

This family had for its founder in the Shenandoah Valley Heinrich Baechter. This name was always signed by him in German. Scribes who wrote from their knowledge of the language, caused the name to appear differently in authography, but not materially. Thus we have the name Bechter, Bechther. Beekter, Bacher—all relating to the same person. The sons of the founder adopted the simpler way of disposing of this confusion of sounds, and wrote the names Baker. The old emigrant had one branch of his family to adhere strictly to the old style Baecher for many years. This branch was known as the Hillary W. Baker family in Northwest part of the County. The family history of the family says Henry Baker was born in Germany in 1731; came to this country about 1755, and married Maria E. Fink in Winchester 1759, and died in Winchester, 1807. His sons were Henry W., Joseph, Isaac, John, Abraham, Jacob and one daughter, Elizabeth; and it is assumed by tradition in this family that he was the first of his German family to settle in Frederick County. The writer submits, however, a few brief facts which conflict with old history: First, we find that John Nichos Baker was living on his own plantation in Frederick County prior to 1755; his will probated in 1762, written in Dutch as the translator states in his deposition—mentions his second wife and her sons who *are of age,* Melchior, John N. and Philip. In one recital he says his children by his first wife are provided for by the legacy they will receive from Germany; mentions several tracts of land near the North Mountain. The writer was led to think at one time this was the family that settled on the South Branch, the family names being similar; but upon reflection, this could have hardly been true, for the Hampshire County Court would have been the court to probate his will in 1762. Then, again, we find Joshua Baker in Frederick County in 1764, on his land at the North of Warm Spring. His will mentions one son, Joshua. And some will enquire who was that brilliant lawyer in active practice in Berkeley County about 1800, and the fearless Federalist in 1810, and elected to Congress upon his well known principles, where he made a record for his activity, 1812. This was John Baker. The writer associates him with the James Baker English family. It must not be expected for this volume to embrace full tracings of this numerous family; indeed, it would be a prodigious task to follow Heinrich Baechter and his seven children through the mazes of as many generations. Some of the branches springing from the old tree planted in Winchester in 1755 are unable to give definite data; therefore we lose much of this family history that should be preserved. The large family in Winchester, familiarly known as the Jacob Baker family has been so prominently before the public in a business and social way, that their history is well known to many who may chance to see this volume. The writer has always enjoyed the friendship of this family, and feels that he must add a word, not, however, to give a connected line of descent, nor even a brief sketch of the splendid men and women of this family. Mr. Jacob Baker, the head of this family, was a grandson of Heinrich Baechter, the emigrant, and son of Henry W., who was born in Winchester in 1760. Jacob was born in Frederick, Md., in 1789, the former home of his mother, Catherine Miller. It has been shown elsewhere that he served as Quartermaster in the War of 1812. He married Catherine B. Streit, dau. of Rev. Christian Streit, in 1814; became a partner with his father in business on Main Street, succeeding his father at his death. He then began the great general business which he and his sons and their sons have maintained well into the 20th Century, thus covering periods of three centuries. The large family referred to consisted of eight sons and six daughters: Henry S., William B., Camillus S., Augustus (died in infancy), Geo. P., Jacob E., Robert M., Christian S., Susan C., Harriet E., Mary Virginia,

Julia E., Emma F. (died at age of 13 years), and Portia B. About 1837, Mr. Baker changed his place of business and opened a large wholesale and retail house near the W. & P. R. R. depot, being virtually the site of the present wholesale establishment of W. H. Baker. In the new enterprise he had as partner his brother, George Baker, amassing a handsome fortune, he retired from the active part of the large business about 1850, and looked to his sons to maintain its reputation. The three sons: Henry S., Wm. B., Camillus S. Baker and his son-in-law, Oliver Brown, successfully continued the business for many years. The Civil War wrought havoc among the business men of the town. The old building, badly damaged by fire, was unfit for use at the close of the War, when the three sons gathered courage from their venerable father and started the business in a small way in the house now occupied by Miss Portia Baker. Marvellous success crowned every effort they made. The writer recalls an incident in a conversation he had with Mr. Jacob Baker on the first day's opening of the new store. Mr. Baker asked him to look at the large stock and form some idea of the capital required to start the business. He then said: Every article was purchased on credit. We had no money to make a start; and on my suggestion Pully (his son William) went to Baltimore to see the old business men with whom he had formerly dealt, and see what could be done to renew business on a small scale. Baltimore firms volunteered to supply all that was required, and what you see now we expect to pay for as we reduce the stock, saving to each firm a percentage of their several lines." This incident is one of many that could be mentioned to show the integrity of the father and sons as they stood in the business world. Mr. Baker lived to see Baker & Company re-established in the large property they now occupy, he having rebuilt and added warehouses, etc., for their accommodation. He died March 10, 1874, aged 84 years.

Henry S. Baker, the son, was born 1814, married Catherine Price in 1840 (died in 1851), and in 1858 he married Aletta W. Hunt. They are survived by two sons and two daughters, Mayor Harry H. Baker of Winchester, and Dr. Robert Baker of Washington, D. C., Mrs. Robt. T. Barton and Miss Lilly Baker. Mr. Baker lived to see his son H. H. Baker and his nephews, successors of the old firm.

William B. Baker, son of Jacob, was born 1818; married Elizabeth Mantz, of Frederick, Md., in 1842. She and their five children survive him. Wm. H. Baker, one of the successors of the old firm, is the proprietor of the Wm. H. Baker Chocolate manufactory, located in New York State; owns the Baker & Co. wholesale establishment, having purchased Harry H. Baker's interests several years ago. His two brothers, Albert and Alexander M. Baker, succeeded their father as owners and operators of the large Steam Flouring Mill established by him in 1872, near the old warehouse. This is known by the firm name of W. B. Baker Sons. Wm. H. Baker married Miss Ginn; they have 4 sons and several grandchildren. Alexander M. married Miss Gilkeson; they have a daughter Virginia. Albert is unmarried.

Camillus S. Baker, the other son referred to as a member of the firm organized in 1850, was born in 1822, and carries his 86 years with a light step; enjoys good health, and social intercourse with his host of friends. He married Miss Annie E. Gaither of Frederick, Md., in 1849. They have four daughters.

The family record of Mr. Jacob Baker's family, enables the writer to embody the following brief memoranda in this sketch. The same appears in Norris' History, in relation to those not so fully mentioned. The two sons, Geo. P., and Christian S. Baker, together with W. B. Baker, established a general business in Martinsburg in 1856, and in Staunton in 1866. In 1869, Geo. P. and Christian S. succeeded to the business. Geo. P. was born in 1828; married Miss Lyle McCleary in 1861, and in 1868 married Hattie Cook. By the latter he had seven children. Christian S. was married in 1867 to Fannie Baylor, and had three children. Jacob. E. Baker was born in 1828; was a twin brother of Geo. P. He lived on a fine farm West of Winchester, being part of the original tract purchased by Heinrich the emigrant; married in 1867 to Mary Ellen Miller. She and her six daughters and one son survive him, he having died in 1907. His son Jacob married Miss Mary Willis, and resides in Winchester. Robert M. Baker was born in 1834; became a minister in the Episcopal Church, married Louisa F. Davidson in 1862; his widow and eight children survived him. He died in 1883, while Rector of a Church in Georgetown, D. C. Susan C. married Oliver M. Brown in 1836, and died in 1850; seven children survived the parents; a son, J. Few Brown, is assistant cashier of Shen. Valley Bank in Winchester. One daughter married Rev. Mr. Smith, a Lutheran minister, one married Mr. Kagey. Miss Fannie Brown and sisters live in Winchester.

Harriet E., another daughter of Jacob Baker, married Henry M. Brent in 1848; died in 1873; had one child; parents and child long since dead. Mary Virginia married Rev. C. P. Krauth, D.D., in 1855. A son became a minister in the Lutheran Church. Julia E. married A. McK. Boyd in

1857; she died in 1859. leaving two children. Miss Portia B. Baker, the youngest daughter, resides in Winchester, Va.

Joseph Baker, son of Heinrich Baechter, was born June 14, 1762, at Winchester. He was twice married; first wife Miss Sarah Weaver, daughter of a pioneer who owned a large property and kept a well-known tavern situated on the old Braddock Road near the old Homestead of Joseph Baker. She was the mother of five children, viz: B. Franklin, Stern, Clarissa, Isabinda and Juliet. One of the daughters became the wife of Thomas Philips a merchant of Winchester. Rebecca, the 2nd wife of Joseph Baker, was a daughter of Robert Lockhart of Back Creek Valley. His children by Rebecca Lockhart were Robert L., Caroline, Rebecca, Edwin S. and Alcinda. About 1810 he settled on a large tract of land about 3 miles N. W. from Winchester, which has been known for three-fourths of a century as the farms of Col. Robt. L. and Edwin S. Baker. Joseph and his two sons spent their entire lives on these splendid homesteads. Joseph died in 1833, and was laid to rest in a tomb of his own design and making. The huge stones used in the foundation, walls and capstone of this rude mausoleum, suggest to the spectator, that its occupant had dreams of eternal durability, while completing the massive walls of this unique structure. But we find now, after the lapse of 75 years only, that what was regarded then as imperishable, shows marks of gradual ruin. Another cycle of time may find the old monument a confused mass, with the great stones tumbled in upon the dust of the eccentric old ancestor.

Robert L., son of Joseph, married his cousin, Julia A. Baker: three children by this union: Scott (died when young), M. Catherine and Roberta. Col. Baker, as he was always called, lived and died at the old homestead occupied by his father. As shown elsewhere, he was in the Genl. Assembly of Virginia, president of the old Farmers Bank for many years, president of the old Agricultural Society prior to the Civil War; was a man of affairs generally, successful in his pursuits. He was regarded as one of the wealthiest farmers in the county; once owned the farms owned by Scott Grant, the site of the Kernstown R. R. station, the Stayman farm now occupied by Jacob Crisman. On this farm he grazed large herds of cattle, and indulged his taste for handling well-bred short-horns. Col. Baker's oldest daughter married Genl. Robert L. Wright of Loudoun County, in 1858. She is now known as Mrs. Kate Wright, and resides in the old homestead. She inherited part of this property, and removed from Loudoun County after her father's death in 1871. Her husband had died in 1865. She and her four young children met with all the trials incident to the War and Reconstruction periods. Her loss of property, while great, was small compared with the loss of father and husband. She very successfully combatted changed conditions. Two of her sons married and left Frederick County. Robert B. lived on his father's farm in Loudoun County for a number of years. J. Carter married Miss Barnewell of Alabama, and resides in that State. Miss Julia B. and Arthur S. continue to live with their mother, whose gentle influence has been enjoyed by them, making a home valued by mother and children. Arthur S. is an enterprising farmer, inherits from his grandfather the taste and skill for handling high grades of stock, and has been an active member of the Board of Directors of the Shen. Valley Agri. Society for many years. Col. Baker's other daughter married Doct. Wortham, both dead—likewise his son, Scott Baker.

Edwin S. Baker, son of Joseph, was born in 1816, at the old homestead four miles N. W. from Winchester; was married in 1845 to Martha A., daughter of William Wood, whose home was near Pughtown. By this union three children were born: Selina G., who became the wife of Capt. John Glaize; both were survived by sons and daughters.

Julian W. oldest son of Edwin S., married Miss Kate Stump, of Hampshire County, W. Va. Their children are Lelia, now the widow of Dr. J. E. Janney, Julian W., Jr., now Deputy County Clerk of Frederick County, Edwin S., Frank W. and Wm. Wood.

Julian W. the father, owns the homestead of his father, and is a prosperous farmer. He and his wife enjoy life in their comfortable home noted for its genuine hospitality. They have hosts of friends. Mr. Baker is Superintendent and Treasurer of the North Frederick Turnpike, member of the Board of Directors of the Shen. Val. Agr. Society, and a Democrat from principle.

Thomas B., the other son of Edwin S., married Miss Stine, dau. of Isaac Stine; his widow and daughter survive him; he died in 1889. He was county surveyor, succeeding his father.

Edwin S. Baker was a remarkable man in many ways. Having had a first-class academic education, and being a man of unusual mental capacity, he gradually imbibed much useful knowledge; his intelligence on many subjects was unsurpassed. He was regarded as an authority on matters of importance. Being a county surveyor for twenty-eight years, he possessed a thorough knowledge of the topography and people of the county. In 1851, Mr. Baker was a member of the House of Delegates. It has been stated that he was a Republican in politics when the War closed. This needs an explanation. Mr. Baker was an old time Democrat, voted with his party, and was Chairman of the Democratic Executive Committee until 1880. During Gov. Holliday's term, 1880-81, the Virginia Debt question was becoming serious; the Readjuster movement started with Genl. Mahone as leader, a new party came to the front. This was known as the Readjuster-*Democratic* party. Mr. Baker was in sympathy with this movement, and gave his large influence. He was berated by indiscreet would-be leaders of the regular Democratic party, until his proud spirit was driven to seek redress. He lived to see the day when many of his views were adopted as compromise measures; but in doing this, he was affiliated with the Republican party; and the writer can say that this old Jeffersonian Democrat deplored the necessity of the break between partizan friends, and never enjoyed being called a Republican. He had no objections to the term Readjuster Democrat. The daughters never married. Miss Alcinda died many years prior to Miss Rebecca's death, which came in old age.

George W. Baker, son of Henry W. and grandson of the emigrant, was born in 1800; was a merchant on Main Street, until he and his brother Jacob established the large business referred to in this connection. He married Emily S. Streit, Jan. 15, 1829. She was born June 16, 1809. They had the following children: Camillus W., married Miss Baugher—no children. Fannie E., became the wife of Edwin S. Brent—no children. Virginia, mar. James H. Thompson, children: Mary H., married John F. Sowers; Emilie S., married Chas. H. Gibbs.

Emily C. married Rev. L. M. Siebole—no children. Emily S., died Jany. 17, 1843.

George W. Baker married second wife Sarah Hartman Dec. 14, 1843, and had children by this marriage: William H., married Mary R. Pierce of N. C., children Sarah R., married Thos. J. Holt, of Ga., children Norma, Mary R., Sara B., and Harrietta. Louisa P. married Wm. W. Glass. Mary P. Baker unmarried.

Franck, married Elizabeth Wyatt; their children: Martha S., Lewis L., Elizabeth S., mar. Dr. Thos. M. Jones, of Ind., Carrie V., Eloise and Laura Virginia.

Rosalie H. mar. J. E. Valk; children Eugene, Arthur, Leslie P., Rosalie B.

Louis H., died aged 9 years.

Harriet A., daughter of Henry W. Baker, born 1796, mar. William Miller. His son was W. "Bake" Miller. Father and son were merchants in Winchester; place of business site of Baetjer and Co.'s store; residence on Market Street, now the residence of Marion Bantz. His son "Bake" Miller lived where the Misses Wall kept a boarding house for years.

Nathan Camillus, son of Henry W. Baker, born 1803, married Mary Ann Roberts, of Winchester, Va., daughter of George Roberts, Aug. 2, 1825. Children by this union Henry Camillus Baker born 18th Dec., 1826, George Luther born Oct. 29, 1829, died 1847, Nathan Camillus, Jr., died 1832, Henry Camillus Baker being the only child after 1847. His mother, Mary Ann Roberts, was the only daughter of a very distinguished man—George Roberts, Commander of the Colombia Navy, during the war period when the noted Boliver so inspired military men with his successes, they called him the Washington of South America. Commander Roberts, while his daughter was a young girl, was a prisoner of war in Spain, under condemnation of death as a rebel and traitor; so that for nine years his family heard nothing from him, and concluded he had been wrecked and lost. During this period, the daughter was under the care of her uncle in Delaware, who subsequently sent her to Winchester, where she was placed under the care of Col. Beaty and Col. Roberts, where she met Nathan Camillus Baker and, as we have shown, became his wife. Her father, Commander Roberts, abandoned ocean life, and died in Winchester. Henry Camillus Baker, the only surviving child, now 82 years old, lives in Baltimore, well preserved. He had a poetic nature, and indulged in many effusions, some of which found their way to the public. The writer has before him now his poem "Night Scene—The Ruined Chapel," in which he pictures the ruins of the old Lutheran Church, and recalls scenes of his childhood in lines of such pathos that, if it were possible, they would apepar in this volume. The writer remembers Mr. Baker as he appeared on the streets of his native town when a young man. His general appearance and peculiar style commanded attention wherever seen. His tall, graceful figure, and long black hair, stamped him as quite different from several others of the Baker family bearing the name of Camillus—all to be called *Mick*. The writer has been asked many times, who was *Spanish Mick Baker*; and has tried in this brief way to unravel what has often been intimated was a mystery. This Henry Camillus Baker married Francis Marie, daughter of James Tucker, of Baltimore County, Md. By this union they had the following children: Claude, born Sept. 29, 1856, died 1858; twins Carl and May Day, born Sept. 17, 1860. Carl died Aug. 21, 1861; May Day died May 10, 1862. Camille, born Apl. 30, 1858, died Jany. 1, 1907; Sallie Tucker Baker, born Jany. 27, 1862; Henry Southworth Baker, born Aug. 25, 1864; Julia Monroe, born July 3, 1867, died June 28, 1872. Henry

Southworth Baker mar. Lulu B., daughter of Samuel H. Higinbotham, of Wheatland, near Charlestown, W. Va., June 27, 1903. They have two sons: Henry S., born May 2, 1904, Samuel H. born Jany. 24, 1907. Mr. Baker is a merchant in Winchester, an active member of the Board of Deacons of the Presb. Church, and is an ardent worker in the home mission field near the city.

Maria C., daughter of Henry W. Baker, born 1805, married Rev. Mr. Kurtz.

Henry M., son of Henry W. Baker, born Dec. 24, 1809; was known as Lame Henry Baker, to distinguish him from several others of the same name. He married and reared a large family at his splendid home, Glendobbin. His children were Flora, married Jos. T. Hiett, who was a gallant Confederate soldier, (now dead.) They have several children.

H. William, married Miss Hillary—lives in Berryville and has one daughter.

B. West Baker, married Miss Lutie Hiett. His life has been spent at Glendobbin, having purchased it from his brothers and sisters. Their children are Love, only daughter, and Henry, now in full manhood. "West," as he is familiarly called by his host of friends, is an up-to-date farmer; his magnificent farm, with its orchards and fine stock, is profitably managed. Mr. Baker has been an active member of the Board of Directors of the S. V. A. Society.

George, the other son of Henry M., never married, and died several years ago.

Hallie Baker married Roland Bryarly and removed to Texas. Subsequent to his death, Mrs. Bryarly returned to Winchester with her three children Henry R., Roland T., and Eva. The latter died a few years ago, just as she had rounded out her sweet girlhood. Henry is married; Roland unmarried, and lives with his mother.

Florence, daughter of Henry M., married John S. Miller, hardware merchant on Main Street.

Katherine, married W. Spottswood White, son of Rev. George White, D.D., Presb. Minister at Moorefield, W. Va.

Mr. Baker the father of the children briefly mentioned, was a farmer, and always active as a member of The Farmers Club a society formed many years ago before the Civil War, composed of about twenty of the most intelligent farmers in the County. Mr. Baker was an artist of considerable reputation, and many valued specimens of his brush are distributed among his friends. The writer has a portrait of his brother which Mr. Baker painted as a token of his friendship. Mr. B. was one of those happy and jolly men that made him exceedingly popular in his large circle of friends, though compelled to appear on his crutches. His widow, now advanced in years, carries their weight with seeming ease.

The Zane Family

It seems appropriate to mention this family, as brief notices are given the families living along Cedar Creek and the North Mountain during the 18th Century. But we cannot claim the family for these sections exclusively; for we find Isaac Zane in Winchester at one time, dispensing lavish hospitality. He owned several desirable properties, and, as shown elsewhere, was a substantial friend of the old Winchester Academy in its early history. At one time he lived in Stephensburg. He had temporary residence at his Marlboro Iron Works, and spent some time with his friend Maj. Mordecai Bean, while engaged in testing the ores of the North Mountain in a smelter which they started on Bean's large tract. There is some confusion about this name. Some writers fix Isaac Zane's first appearance as one of the first pioneers, and also as Genl. Isaac Zane of the Revolutionary War period; and Col. Isaac Zane one of the Burgesses, 1773; and member of the Virginia Convention, 1775; and member of the first House of Delegates, 1784. The father and son were confounded. Isaac Zane Senior came first. It was in 1767 that he purchased 350 acres of land along the North Mountain from Henry Secrist, adjoining Michael White and Jacob Cackley. He was then a resident of Philadelphia; and it is doubtful if he ever lived in Virginia. Isaac Zane, Jr., obtained from Lewis Stephens in 1771, a large tract of land on Cedar Creek. The language of the deed points to two facts worth notice: "To Isaac Zane Junr. Iron Master, for land on Cedar Creek, includes the land where the *Dutch Chapel* stands and adjoins John Stickley, Craybill and Henry Piper." This was the tract where he conducted his iron works, and other business. In 1776 he acquired more land near Stephensburg, where he had resided. Part of this tract he sold to Joseph Holmes a merchant in the same village. Subsequent to this period, we find him living near his Marlboro Iron Works, and taking an active part in politics, as shown elsewhere. While a member of the house of Burgesses, he was commissioned Colonel in the Virginia Line. In the new organization, after the Revolutionary War, he was commissioned Brigadier-General of Militia, and was not a Brigadier during the war. He died in his Frederick home in 1795, possessed of great wealth for that period, owning large landed estate (9,000 acres), some of which consisted of many lots lying on South Washington and Stewart Streets, Winchester. He also owned the land where the old Winchester Academy stood. His will, recorded in the old District Court, mentions two sisters, Hannah Pemberton and Sarah Zane, to whom he left the bulk of his estate in Frederick County, with annuity to Isaac Zane McFarlane. He further provided for the gradual emancipation of his twenty-one slaves. The inventory of his personal estate shows he was a merchant, distiller, miller and founder. He was doubtless an educated man. His library contained many rare volumes. These and his valuable furniture naturally found places in many homes after the sale of his effects, which required several days. We cannot follow his name further. The family were prominent in reclaiming the country from the Indians, as already shown in this volume. He was granted several thousand acres of land along the Ohio and Monongahela Rivers, which was inherited by his family. One branch of this family were pioneers of the South Branch Valley. During the Indian Wars, Wm. Zane and his family were carried away as prisoners by the Indians in 1753. One of his sons has been previously mentioned in connection with Ohio settlements.

Genl. Zane lived in his stone mansion—as he termed it in his letters. This was near his iron works and mill, and a short distance North of the site of the present mill of D. S. Brill. Near by was his large warehouse or store, the walls of which were of heavy stone. The ruins of these buildings were to be seen until about 1890. The ruins of the old iron works can be seen at this writing.

The Bean Family

This name has been frequently mentioned in this volume. Mordecai Bean, who appeared in Frederick County with Isaac Zane, Sr., about 1767-8, had applied for a patent for ungranted lands lying along the North Mountains; but his claim was held up by caveat filed by Lord Fairfax who, by a compromise, executed a lease to Bean in 1777 for land on Paddy Mountain, being mineral land. This lease was recorded in the Proprietor's Office, Book No. 2, page 201 (Land Office, Richmond, Va.). In 1779, Mordecai Bean purchased a tract of "300 acres from Evan Thomas, being part of the Ellis Thomas grant at the head of Hogg Creek." This, then, was the seating of a family that for nearly a century held large sway in that section. He was interested in several of the Zane projects for making iron from the rich ores found on his land. Of the many shipments of foundry produced by Zane, mention is made that the iron was produced at "Bean's Smelter." This afterwards became known as the Taylor Furnace.

The family is of English origin. The name has been found in Pennsylvania, Maryland, N. Carolina, Virginia, Kentucky and several Western States. In recent years, one of the name died in Texas, after having amassed a large fortune which has been partly distributed, the Bean family of Washington, D. C., having received their portion. This once numerous family has but one household that bears the name in Frederick County—that of Joseph F. Bean and his family. Many descendants, however, by intermarriage, are well-known citizens of the County. Mordecai Bean married Judith Hammond, daughter of an old settler along Cedar Creek, and one of the pioneer names, that disappeared from that section long since. She was the mother of James and Isaac, Betsy Frye, Margaret Richards and Sally Cartmell, all of whom are mentioned in Major Bean's will, probated in 1814. He left a large estate of land, slaves, etc.

His son Isaac removed to Kentucky, and there raised a large family, which has representatives in prominent affairs of that and other States. His other son was Major James Bean, who married Judith Frye. She was the mother of Mordecai, Nathan, James, Eliza and Rebecca. Nathan made his home in Ohio. James married Miss Fawcett, dau. of Joseph. They lived and died in the brick house at Taylor Furnace, now the home of his daughter, Mrs. J. Harvey Williams. Mordecai, brother of James, became one of the largest land owners in the county. He was a noted litigant at every term of court. He was an ardent Union man at the outbreak of the Civil War. He committed some overt act; and was so pronounced in his enmity to the Confederate government, that he was arrested and carried to some Southern prison, where he died. He was offered his freedom, to return to his home when the Lower Valley was abandoned by the Confederates; but the stiff-necked old man refused all offers. Some of his descendants are to be found, but none that bear his name. His sister Eliza married Jonathan Jenkins; and was the mother of the James Jenkins who sold his fine property, now owned by Isaac H. Faulkner and M. H. Rosenberger, and removed to Nebraska about 1890.

Rebecca married Samuel Hodgson, who lived

near the Round Hill. She was the mother of a large family: Abner W. Hodgson (father of James B. Hodson, so well known to Winchester for the past twenty years as a contractor), John Robert who married Miss Shearer, Henry Clay, Ann Eliza. These last two moved to Missouri. Clay is one of the prosperous men of that country. Mrs. Florence Willis lives in Winchester. Her sister Mary and her aged mother live with her. Their mother has attained the age of 96 years, with good health and memory. She is doubtless the oldest person in Winchester.

The Pifer Family

This family, represented by two brothers, Maj. Elijah and 'Squire John W. Pifer, who were identified with the affairs of that seciton of Frederick County mentioned above, from about 1830,—was an old family found on Cedar Creek near the Marlboro Iron Works, as one of the pioneers. The name was German, and when signed by Henry, the emigrant in German, was so tortured in its translation by others, as to be hard to connect it with the present pronunciation, being often written Peoffer, Pepher, Piper.

The two brothers were sons of John W. Pifer, who owned a large estate about the vicinity of Capon Roads. Part of this old homestead is owned by his descendants. Elijah Pifer lived out a long and useful life. He was often chosen for trusted positions. His sons and daughters survived him. One was Capt. A. P. Pifer, Co. A., 39th Batt., mentioned elsewhere as serving at Genl. Lee's Headquarters. Capt. Pifer survived the war; spent many years in North Carolina, in educational work, but died in Norfolk, 1907. His brother, G. Wash. Pifer, lives at Gravel Springs, where he has reared a large family. Silas B., Elijah, one daughter, Kate, who married Rev. Mr. Shenk, now of Newport News. Bettie married Dr. Cover; one married Luther Brill, the owner of the mill at that point. One daughter remains single. Their mother, Margaret Honaker, can trace her line to the old Revolutionary Honaker soldier mentioned elsewhere.

John W. Pifer married three times. His first wife, Mary Rudolph, was the mother of Randolph, Harriet and Ella. Randolph is known as Capt. Ran Pifer; who saw service as a Confederate soldier; was county treasurer, farmer, school teacher, and held other offices. Harriet married Josiah Rinker, mother of A. R. Rinker and sisters. Capt. Ran. P. lives on his farm near Stephens City. He has a large family. His father married Margaret Ritenour in 1847. She was the mother of Cyrus, Laura, Stanley and Clarence. His third wife was Miss Langley, of Winchester, 1880. 'Squire Pifer, as he was called, was born 1809.

Capt. Jacob Pifer who died at Capon Roads many years ago, was a brother. One of his daughters is Mrs. John W. Rice, of Winchester. She has one son, Warren Rice, a lawyer. In other sections of the County, the name appears. The bearers are doubtless descendants from Henry the pioneer, who has been associated by tradition with the Hite emigration; but of this there is no record evidence.

Michael White, mentioned in the foregoing, belonged to an English and Scotch emigration that tried the *tomahawk* title plan to secure land, in 1735. Surveys lapped over such claims; and the squatter generally lost his claim. The White family still has its representatives in that section. Anderton L. White and his family, Benjamin F. White, and one other branch in that section, and James W. White of Opecquon, and his brother of Maryland, maintain the good reputation of this old honest family.

On the Southern end of Little North Mountain is a well-known spring that the writer remembers. One branch of the White family living at that place, it bears the name of the old lady, Ginnie White's Spring. Her son Mordecai lived there. He was a member of the 39th Battalion, Genl. R. E. Lee's body-guard. Several sons survived him: Thomas W. lives in Winchester.

The Larrick Family of the North Mountain section, have very little trace of their connection with the family in vicinity of Middletown. Henry Larrick was on the ground at an early day. Asa, John Henry and David W. Larrick were well known to the writer. They were upright, honorable men, industrious and successful farmers, and the owners of comfortable homes. They have left large families, who have been widely scattered by death, marriage and removals. David W. and John Henry's homes are owned by members of their families; while Asa's old homestead passed into the hands of the Hedrick brothers of Washington, D. C. One of Asa's sons was Capt. James W. Larrick of the Militia line, now dead. John Wesley, another son, mentioned elsewhere, has reared a large family at Old Retirement, viz: Maude M., Hugh, Howard, Richard, John, Jonah, Ada, Carl, Margaret and Meryilles. One sister, Nancy, is Mrs. Jacob Crisman, of Kernstown. She is the mother of a large family. Mrs. Emma Pifer, Asa P., Asa R., Geo. O., Mrs. Ollie Smith, Mrs. Bertha Hockman, Jacob L., Fred A., Minnie and Etha. Their father, Jacob Crisman, was a private in Co. C., 12th Va. Cavly., he claims credit for capture of Percy Wyndham, an Englishman in command of a Union regiment.

The Kercheval Family

The first appearance of this family as one of the pioneers of the County, near Wheeling, was prior to the Revolutionary War. John Kercheval settled on Buffalo Creek, about twenty miles above its junction with the Ohio River. There quite a number of families took possession of tracts of land under the supposed *Tomahawk right,* in 1773, just in time to suffer from the Dunmore War, started the next Spring. The settlers erected cabins and forts. The section was adapted to easy cultivation; and several families crossed the high mountains to the East every Spring, and raised crops of corn and potatoes on land where there was less timber and more sunshine. In the Fall they would return and spend the Winter in their Cabins and near their forts. John Kercheval's was one of these families. When the Indian outbreak occurred in 1774, the families deserted the first settlement, to find better security at Morris's Fort in Sandy Creek Glade. We find this family at Dodridge's Fort also, during the historic siege. Samuel Kercheval, the Valley historian, says he was about fourteen years old at the time and "ranked as a fort soldier." John Kercheval and his family in 1782 drifted slowly through the mountains, and took up their abode on the Opecquon, a few miles from Berryville; and in 1784 purchased the farm where he died in 1788, leaving a large family and his wife Winifred, the step-mother of his four oldest children. He devised his plantation to the following ten children: Sukey, John, Peggy, Samuel, Winney, Lydia, Sally, Frances, Betsy and James. He willed four negroes to his widow. His sons John and Samuel were his executors. Thomas Barry, J. Milton and Wm. Kercheval his grandson, witnessed the will. John lived in Winchester and purchased two tracts of land in 1791 on Abrams Creek. Samuel purchased a tract of land in 1790 from Lewis Stephens, located on Buffalo Marsh. Part of this he sold in 1792 to Lee. He then established a home a few miles N. West, adjoining lands of Elisha Fawcett and others. There he lived out the remainder of his days. During the latter part of his life, he traveled extensively through the Shenandoah Valley, gathering material facts and incidents, which he wove into what has been known as "Kercheval's History of the Valley of Virginia," which he published in 1833. Although three editions of this quaint, peculiar and valuable history have been published, the book is rarely seen, and is highly prized by those who are fortunate enough to have preserved a copy.

The Wigginton Family

This name appeared West of the Blue Ridge at the dawn of the 19th Century, coming from the pioneer family of Old Orange. Though not strictly speaking a pioneer of the Valley, James Wigginton, who was for a half century so closely identified with Frederick County families, the writer feels it is a duty we owe the memory of this man, to have him mentioned in connection with the early settlers of the section between the Little and Big North Mountains. Mr. Wigginton was one of the old time *school masters.* Scarcely a community in the Southwest section of Frederick County can be found, where he did not appear as teacher of those who learned good lessons. His territory extended from the Round Hill neighborhood to Cedar Creek. He married a daughter of the historic Whetzel family. She was Christina, daughter of John and Barbara Whetzel; married Feby. 18, 1818. Their children were: Sarah, James Bean, Harriet, Mary A., Andrew J., Jane, Joseph H., and George W. Sarah married Elijah Williams, and was the mother of a large family. Bean started a tanyard that became the Star Tannery under Thomas Cover. Mary A. married (first) Isaac Tevalt; 2nd husband is the venerable John McIntire, already mentioned. Andrew J. married Mary E. Morrison. Jane married (first) Martin Whetzel who died in the Confederate service. She then married Martin Hodgson who started the first store at Opecquon. Joseph H. married Miss Dispanet a descendant of the pioneer mentioned elsewhere. Their children were: A. J. Wigginton, one of the constables of the county at this writing, J. R., Laura C., Geo. A., Francis M., Lillian B., Newton J., and J. Ed.—one son being the well-known nurseryman and orchardist near the Round Hill Presb. Church. George W. son of James married and went West.

James had one brother William, and two sisters Mary and Lucy. One of William's sons was Isaac W. Wigginton who was at one time owner of the old Fizer tavern property. His brother Harrison lives in Winchester. One son James spent his life in Kansas.

Mary spent nearly forty years of her life in the family of the writer's father. She was familiarly called *Aunt Polly* by the young members of several families, who were benefited by her care and benign influence. Her sister Lucy married Jacob Good, a miller. She was the mother of Mary, Catherine and Joshua Good.

Jacob Whetzel, brother of Mrs. James Wigginton, was a man of intelligence and integrity. Two of his sons live in the Northern section of the county: James W., who has been mentioned as the husband of Miss Cather. The Whetzel family can trace their line back to the famous John and Lewis Whetzel, the *Indian fighters.*

The Whissen Family

John Whissen, who died in 1907, about 90 years old, belonged to the family of this name who first appeared in Frederick County during the Revolutionary War. His home was in the neighborhood of the families last mentioned. He was widely known in the county as a man of exemplary habits. He married late in life, Miss Copp of Shenandoah County, and was the father of one son and several daughters. One daughter married Amos E. Marker; another is Mrs. Scott Sherman in the Round Hill neighborhood. Both have promising families. One daughter Ada is the wife of Ashby Graves, of near Relief P. O. This name has been subjected to much criticism for its various ways of pronunciation. The first time the name appears is in a deed signed by John Wessant and wife, 1785. She was the widow of Henry Lockmiller, and derived title to the land from her first husband. We find in 1779, Jos. Wessant's estate was settled. In 1809, John signs by his mark, Whissen—name written by the clerk of the court. In 1828 the name is signed John Whissent; in 1837 signed Whissen, and as such attaches to the family wherever it appears in the Valley of Virginia.

There are so many descendants of the pioneers who settled along the southern drains of Hogue Creek, so well known to the author, that he finds it difficult to pass them by. The old families left interesting traditionary history that may be used in independent sketches.

With English and Scotch-Irish emigrants who settled on the upper drains of Hogue Creek, was William Hall., who secured a grant for 2,236 acres; and proceeded to locate several families; but was hindered by Lord Fairfax, who finally compromised and executed release deed, 1764. The old pioneer died in 1768 and was succeeded by his son William. He and his brothers James, Thomas and Bennett established homes at various points in the great survey. With Hall was a Scotch-Irishman who wrote his name as David Mulelcuro; by others written Mucklewee. This was the pioneer of the *McIlwee* family, which has held sway in that section for about one hundred years. For it was in 1808 the name of this family was first written McIlwee. David, the pioneer, and his two sons, William and Daniel, were with Capt. William Hall in his raid on a band of marauding Indians, 1788.

Col. James B. Hall owned the property where the Wotring families now live. The Halls have all disappeared save Jno. W. a grandson of Col. Hall. In this section we find at this writing A. J. McIlwee and family, mentioned elsewhere; James T. McIlwee and his family, whose father was William, who died in 1895, an aged man. His father was David who died in 1806. There were a David and John who purchased land from Jacob Turner and others 1847-55. James T. who has been mentioned as one of the supervisors of the county, served several terms as Justice of the Peace, Commissioner of Roads, etc. He married a daughter of Wm. P. Gardner, one of the most famous *mill-wrights* of his day. One of his sons, Dr. Silas Gardner of Capon Bridge, was a member of the General Assembly of West Virginia. The children of James T. McIlwee are: Wm. F., Charles A., Minnie, Bertha, Mary, Danl. W., Edna, Eva, Branson.

The Wotring Family

Strictly speaking, this is a Western Virginia family. They were pioneers in that part of the old Colony when it was known as Frederick County. In 1850 Daniel E. Wotring made his first entry into the great Valley. He came as Superintendent of repairs to the Northwestern Turnpike. In 1857 he married Nancy V. daughter of Col. James B. Hall. He soon acquired the fine homestead he now occupies. Being a public-spirited man, he soon became identified with the best interests of the County. When the Civil War opened he was Major of Militia. He served two years in the 51st Virginia Regiment; was taken prisoner in 1863, and confined in Camp Chase and Fort Delaware for six months. Since the War he has held important positions of trust. His long life of 78 years has been well spent. Though feeble from ill health and age, he takes a lively interest in politics. He is a Democrat. His children are: James A., Robert L., Daniel E., Cora P., Inez and Blanche. James A. lives in Hampshire County on his attractive mountain farm, highly esteemed by his many friends. Robert L. lives in Morgantown, W. Va. He was at one time deputy county treasurer for his uncle Lt. John H. Wotring, who married Martha daughter of Col. Hall. Lt. Wotring was a gallant member of the 33rd Va. Infantry; he lost his arm at the 2nd Battle of Manassas. He was county treasurer from 1883 until his death in 1888. His children were: Minnie L., Thos J., Lillian R., Edmund P. D., Felton H., and Mary A. The Wotring family has the distinction of having furnished five brothers for the Confederate service: Joshua B. was 2nd Lieut. in the 33rd Va. Infty.; he died in 1863 from wounds received in the 2nd Battle of Manassas. Benjamin was a member of Capt. McNeill's Cavalry.

The Rosenberger and Clowser Families

These were old families belonging to the early

Colonial Homestead of Major Robert White

life of the County. The Clowsers have been mentioned as one of the pioneers who suffered from Indian raids. The writer remembers two old men of this name, Henry and Joseph. They owned good homes on Hogue Creek, and left large families. The same can be said of the Rosenbergers, except, however, they first appeared West of the Blue Ridge about the first of the 19th Century, coming from Orange and Rappahannock. The old men of this family the writer knew when a boy: William, the father of Jacob H. Rosenberger, the prominent farmer of that section, had arrived at that milestone in his long and active life where he could see success at almost every turn. He had a large family. M. H. and Jacob Rosenberger, the well-known distillers near Hayfield, who have now retired from business to their farms, are grandsons of William and sons of Henry. Their brother John Rosenberger is the well-known carpenter and contractor of Winchester. Charles is the storekeeper at Rosenberger.

The Ramey Family

This was a prominent family during the 19th Century. The two brothers Presley and John W. were well known to the writer. They came from the pioneer family who were found near Strasburg in the Colonial period. Many descendants can be found; but few bear the name. Boyd P. Ramey and his brother John C. represent the Presley branch. They are sons of John W. Ramey who was born in 1837; and lived his entire life at the old homestead of his father Presley. This is now the home of Robert Worsley and family. The old house belongs to the Colonial days. The old house referred to, is an old stone structure. Tradition gives this homestead as the home of Dr. Robert White, the pioneer. It is thought his son Robert H. White built the old stone house about 1763, where he lived until the brick house called "Hayfield" was ready for habitation about 1790. The old stone building is still in very good condition, after its long battle with nearly 150 years. It was formerly surrounded with a stockade for protection to the settlers, as shown elsewhere. John Ramey, brother of Presley, died many years ago. He left a small family.

Passing around the North Mountain from the Ramey, White, Jenkins and Blackhard neighborhood, to enter upper Back Creek, we pass an old homestead once the property of William Seemer, the pioneer glove-maker and dresser of deer skins, mentioned in notes of Winchester. This is now the home of Jacob H. Rosenberger. Beyond this point, where the turnpike suddenly rounds the North Mountain, we pass over the spot where a son of Westfall Frye, of Wardensville, was killed by the Federals. Passing up Back Creek, we soon enter one of the old mill yards, now the property of Chas. W. Parish. The Sibert family lived there and operated a profitable mill prior to the Civil War. This mill is mentioned elsewhere. Passing up this stream, we find the Hook, Scrivener, Pool, Elliott, Dunlap, Good, Anderson, Capper, Triplett and other families; while far up on the Creek, the Larricks were found. Crossing to the West, we enter Timber Ridge section, noted in the long ago, as now, for the sturdy, well-to-do families there. We have only space to point out who were the pioneers. The Andersons, Dunlaps, Giffins, Johnstons, Garvins, Fletchers, Parishes, Murphys, Farmers, and several others were the founders of the homes, schools and churches of this prosperous section; while the Householders, Morrisons, Herrells and Lockharts entered during the 19th Century.

The Muse Family need have no difficulty in tracing their lines back to Lt. Col. George Muse of the 1st Virginia Regiment, mentioned in connection with Indian Wars, or to Brig. Genl. Muse of the Revolutionary War, their names being found in the military archives of Washington and Richmond, and mentioned in Hennings statutes. The writer remembers Major Edward Muse of the Virginia Militia, as he appeared in *general muster* prior to the Civil War; and his brothers Martin and Robert Muse. They were influential men in their day; owned good homes, and held many offices of trust. Capt. R. Bruce Muse, living at one of the old homesteads, has been mentioned elsewhere. He was a son of Edward R. Muse, was born 1836; never married. He entered the Confederate Army as Lieut. in the Capt. Holliday Company of the 33rd Va. Regt.; was promoted Captain before the surrender. One of his sisters married Rev. Wm. G. Eggleston. She was the mother of Mrs. Isaac W. Russell, Robert B. Eggleston and brother and sisters. The name in the old section is also represented by Wm. J. Muse. A. Wade Muse lives near Vaucluse Station. He is the father of sons and daughters who give good promise of maintaining the good reputation of the family. Jno. W. Muse removed Westward with his family many years ago. Two of his sons revisited their former home in 1906.

The Muse family of Caroline and other Eastern counties, from which the Muse family came during the Revolutionary War period, had its foundation in two brothers, Robert and John Muse, who were landowners then. Robert leased land in 1812, and was required to plant 100 apple trees by his brother John. In 1838, a George Muse of Caroline County appears in court and executed a mortgage on 31,304 acres partly on the Great Kanawha, and the Shenandoah Rivers, for 1,800 pounds sterling, due Rev. Chas. Mynn Thruston. This may have been Col. Geo. Muse.

The Dunlaps that figured as old war veterans, sent their sons to the help of Virginia at the outbreak of the Civil War. The writer would like to mention a few incidents relating to the older set, and on down to the old men he knew: Archibald, John and William; but he must pass them by at present. William was famed as a Democratic leader in his day. He died at his mill property near Rock Enon Springs, leaving a large family. Capt. Henry Herrell married one of his daughters. His son Turner A. lives near the old place. Sons of the brothers that lived on Timber Ridge are Jerry, of Winchester, Joel, in the old section. They and their married sisters are likely to maintain a good line of descendants.

The old *Capper Family* has none of the name in the old section that can tell of the struggles of their Colonial ancestors. Meredith Capper who was a long-time resident of Winchester, survived now by his family, was once a merchant and farmer in the old neighborhood. Several of his sons are prominent business men of Winchester. Two are connected with the two railroad offices; M. Lohr being the well-known implement dealer.

Of the old *Giffin Family,* that have descendants, whom the writer knew prior to the Civil War, he might name Bartholomew, James and John. Several of this name have been mentioned in connection with old wars. The name was also familiar in the Confederate service. Many of the residents of Timber Ridge remember John Giffin the constable and auctioneer of Western Frederick. He erected the house now the property of Edgar L. Hook. The latter established the mill on that place.

The Good Family represented in the early days by Felix, already mentioned, with James W., Jacob and brothers, with their large families, are still numerous in Back Creek Valley. The sons are largely engaged in the lumber trade, etc. F. D. Good, Jacob and other sons of the old stock are prominent men.

The *Householders* and *Herrell*s belong to families who came from Loudoun County during the 19th Century.

The *Scrivener Family* were old pioneers. They intermarried with many of the best families of that section. Edwin H. Scrivener, the constable, was an important resident of the community.

The Lockharts of Timber Ridge and Upper Back Creek, are the children and descendants of Josiah Lockhart by his second wife. They have been identified with that section in many ways. Beverly N., mentioned as one of the Supervisors of the county, was a Justice of the Peace for many years, and highly regarded for his integrity. One of his sons James W. is constable, and other children live in that section. Algernon, of Back Creek Dist., and James of Kansas, are brothers of 'Squire Beverly Lockhart.

The Parish Family belongs to the early days. The name is well represented at this writing by three brothers, Jno. W., Charles W. and George W. Parish, sons of Daniel Parish, the prosperous country store-keeper of Timber Ridge for about thirty years subsequent to the Civil War. He amassed considerable property. John W. has been mentioned as one of the County Supervisors. He lives at Gore; has a handsome home, and recently built the commodious store building he now occupies. Chas. W. has been registrar of Gore precinct for several years. Geo. W. lives on the N. W. Turnpike to the West, where he has a country store and good residence.

Up on Timber Ridge we find C. N. Garvin, the successful merchant and general business man, to represent the old stock who first settled in that part of old Frederick County, now Hampshire. This family living along the Hampshire line, has been claimed by both counties. The old Anderson tavern, mentioned elsewhere as *Number Six Voting Precinct,* marks a place where the family lived prior to the Civil War. The old stock, Paul, Michael, James and Jacob were descendants of pioneers, who have been mentioned as old war soldiers.

The Morrisons belong properly to the Morrisons who lived along the Eastern base of the Little North Mountain. Thomas E. Morrison who lives several miles South of Gore on Timber Ridge, has been mentioned as one of the County Supervisors. His father James Morrison, moved to that section prior to the Civil war. Thomas married a daughter of Joseph Smoke. Lemuel C. Johnston and brother, high up on the Ridge, represent the old stock. "Lem" was one of the young men who joined the Confederate forces when the first call was made.

We must for the present leave Timber Ridge. Passing by Gore, we feel justified in taking a moment to interview one of the residents who first appeared there subsequent to the Civil War. This is Joseph Potts, a Union veteran, who has spent nearly forty years among the people of that section, and claims that he has no known enemy. He was the wagon-maker of the section until recently; is now postmaster, and retired from active business. Mr. Potts has the distinction of being the only Republican voter who voted against Samuel J. Tilden. Since then, he has gained some strength for his party. He has a large family. His sons are in business in Winchester and Washington.

Along the Turnpike to Winchester, we pass through Petticoat Gap, where on either side of the road lived several families that belong to the Colonial period. Leonard McFarlane and Benjamin Cubbage the writer remembers as queer characters. The former was a very old man in 1850; and often displayed a musket and war trappings that he claimed were used by him at the Battle of the "Cowpens." This was treated as a joke; but since then, the name has been found in lists of old soldiers.

Benjamin Cubbage was designated as the *water witch,* using a certain branch from a peach tree, he claimed he could find water for the many wells he and others dug in the early days. The old man is still remembered for his ability to work out any example in arithmetic, without pencil or pen, he not being able to write.

Ephraim Hawkins, so well remembered for his integrity, spent the last fifty years of his life in this section, that was uncongenial to his tastes and habits. He could tell a sad story about a business man of Winchester, who had swindled him out of his property when he was a prosperous resident there prior to 1840. The old man and his sons for many years conducted a wagon-maker's shop and saw-mill on the roadside, about a half-mile West from the Wardensville Grade. All now have disappeared; nothing but the site where the buildings once stood is left. But one son is left. This is John Hawkins, an old man, whose son can be seen as the mail carrier from the B. & O. station to the city postoffice. The other sons of Ephraim: George, Charles, Owen and Joseph, were highly esteemed. Their children are scattered. George has a son Joseph living in Gainsboro District, who maintains the good reputation of this family.

The *Cochran Families*—Elijah on the South and William on the North side of the Turnpike, belong to the pioneers. James W., Amos, John H. and sisters, children of Elijah; and Henry, John and sisters, children of William, are well-known in the county.

On the North side of the Turnpike, not far from the old Hawkins shops, were three families of the pioneer period. Two of these when mentioned, will sound strange to most readers, because they have been extinct in this region for many years. The ProBasco and Sidebottom families were well represented in the old wars. Lt. Sidebottom and two brothers gained honors that many persons of this day have no claim to. The Pro-Basco, or as it was often written Basco family, disappeared about 1850. Previous to this, one of the family, Rhyan ProBasco, settled on the Ohio, and grew up with Cincinnati, and through his family the city enjoys the most unique water fountain to be found, called the ProBasco Memorial. The writer's curiosity led him to trace the lineage to the old family in Petticoat Gap. The Harper family living hard by, intermarried with the ProBascos. This family was noted for several huge men. They were Levi, Elijah, Robert, Hiett and several others. They were sons of old pioneer families. Hiett was noted for his great strength. He left a large family: John R., Benjamin, William and Franklin Harper, and several daughters. Franklin is the father of John W. Harper. William was a merchant in Winchester, corner of Water and Braddock Streets. His family removed to Washington, D. C., several years after his death.

George Johnston and *Samuel Carter* were pioneers in that section bordering the Chambers Mountain and Round Hill. The name has become extinct in Frederick County, as relates to these two settlers. The William Johnson family found near head of Opecquon, had its origin on the site of the old Bayliss Tavern. As we approach the East side of Round Hill, the homes of the Hodgson family were found about 1800. The writer knew the old men Robert and Abner Hodgson. The latter married in the Johnson family. He was an old man in 1844; was the father of Elizabeth wife of Nathaniel Lupton; Samuel, and Mary Ann wife of Joshua Lupton, Marinda wife of Thomas Morrison. Samuel married Miss Bean, as stated elsewhere. Robert Hodgson who lived where Elijah Hodgson's Heirs still own the remnant of his tract, was the father of Robert, Elijah, Rev. William, John and Abner Hodgson; and the wife of John Milhorn. Robert, Jr., lived at the old Paxton farm; married Sally Renner. She was the mother of Rebecca J., second wife of Jonathan Jenkins; Isaac who has a family in a Western State; Laban F., H. Martin; two daughters, one Virginia, wife of Marion Cooper; and Scottie who has a family in West Virginia. Elijah, father of Robert, the father of Charles and brother who own the old property. Rev. William Hodgson spent his useful life under the shadows of the Round Hill. His wife, still living, is the mother of Mrs. Martha A. Yeakley, Mrs. Elizabeth Fling, and Dr. Watson Hodgson of Cumberland. John was a brick-mason; he lived in Winchester, the father of Luther Hodgson and other children. Abner married the daughter of N. C. Lupton—no children. His second wife was Miss Crum, sister of John and Charles Crum, of Winchester, sons of Henry Crum. One daughter by second marriage became the wife of Mason Robinson who moved to Missouri. Abner lived where the Scott Sherman family now live. The old house was brick, and was destroyed by fire several years ago. The present brick house stands on the old site. The Robert, Sr., mentioned, ended his days in the home of his son Abner.

The first Hodgson to appear in the neighborhood mentioned was John. This was prior to 1800. In 1762, a Robert Hodgson obtained land from Hiland, "Adjoining lands of Hogue on drains of Opeckon." In 1780, Robert Hodgson and Jacob Lindsey held joint interest in a large tract on Long Marsh; conveyed part thereof to Edward Clare. Some enterprising members of this generation may be able to trace the relationship, and supply links between these families.

The Ball Family

The first appearance of this family in the old county was in 1772, when Jasper Ball came from Loudoun County, and purchased a tract of 86 acres. The following year he purchased an adjoining tract on Morgan's Marsh. He doubtless was the father of William Ball who died in 1796, who by his will disposed of his estate between his children, viz: Wm. Payne, Thomas Kemp, Judith Throckmorton, Betsey, Henry and Nancy Ball. The latter was the wife of Martin Cartmell, of Homespun, 1808. Judith T. was the wife of Genl. Singleton, 1797. Betsey married Geo. Smith, 1790. Other marriages appear, evidently of same family, and are mentioned for the benefit of some descendants: Sally Ball married Samuel Connor, 1789; Wm. Ball married Drucilla Singleton, 1790. Phebe Ball married Wm. Morgan, 1795; Frances married M. Fauntleroy, 1809; Lavinia Ball married Josiah Massie, whose daughter married Mr. Gamble Baker.

The Massie Family

The first appearance of this family in the Valley, was in 1780, when Major Thomas Massie, of New Kent County, Va., came to take possession of a large tract of land of 1,548 acres which he had purchased of Joseph L. Savage, then a resident of Gloucester County. The Major had seen service in the War then in progress; and it is thought he was here with his regiment, the Fifteenth, when it was organized. He disposed of his 2,080 acre tract before he left New Kent, where he had mills and good plantations. He was the progenitor of the large family that have held to a residence in Frederick for more than a hundred years, some of whom saw service in Virginia regiments in all her wars,—Col. Tom Massie of the 12th Virginia Cavalry being one. The writer knew George Tom Massie and his family, Thomas W. Massie, John Buckner and Robert F. Massie, all of whom are now dead. The first named was a cousin of the three last, who were brothers, and sons of Thomas Duncan Massie and Sidney Ashby, daughter of Lewis Ashby. Thomas D. was a son of Asa Massie; they were married in 1825. Thomas W. married Jennie Whissen, 1860. One of his sons John B. is a member of the Winchester Police force. One daughter Lucy C. married Wm. R. Hillyard; they have several children. Thomas B. Massie of Relief, son of George T., is a well-known farmer of that section.

The Triplett Family

There seems to be no known connection between the family of this name on Back Creek, and the family at Kernstown. J. R. Triplett and family live in a remodeled Colonial house, originally the home of Adam *Kearnes*. They belong to the Triplett family of Fauquier County. Jeremiah Triplett came to Kernstown in the early part of the 19th Century; lived in that vicinity, and there reared his family. J. Reuben his son, moved into his present home about 1885. He married Miss Jones, a niece of Edward and Marcus Jones, daughter of Joseph. They have several daughters and one son Irvin. Mr. Triplett has filled several important offices in his district. He is a good citizen and a staunch friend.

The Gilkeson Family

This family has been mentioned in connection with Old Opecquon Church. They may be classed with the pioneers of the Lower Valley, though they first appeared about 1765. William seems to have been the first to own land. He leased 220 acres South of Kernstown in 1769. The recital says he was late of Pennsylvania. In 1788, his will was probated in the County Court of Frederick County. He mentions his sons: John, Hugh, William, Samuel, Isaac and Ebenezer, and daughters Susana, Arnol, Martha Galt and Jannett Marshall. The reader is referred to sketch of Opecquon Church graveyard, where he will see the line of John the son mentioned above, who was the father of Col. John who died in 1856, age 76 years. Col. Gilkeson owned the farm where Jos. M. Barton lives. His children were Wm. D., James, Lucy who married Mr. Wood of Staunton; her daughter Janet survives her; John of St. Louis, and probably more. William married Miss Baker who was the mother of William, James, Frances and another son. James, son of Col. John, moved to Missouri when well advanced in years. Isaac and Ebenezer inherited the farm near the head of Opecquon, spoken of elsewhere as the Samuel and Robert Beckett homestead. They sold it to John Gilkeson in 1792. The same property later on passed by sale to Amos Pierce. His son Hugh O. is the present owner. The writer remembers Mr. James Gilkeson, who inherited through his father John G. the Beckett farm mentioned above; and knew his two sons John Bell and J. Smith Gilkeson. Both were merchants in Winchester. Mr. Bell Gilkeson spent the latter part of his life in Moorefield, West Virginia, and left several daughters who intermarried with families in that section. Mr. Smith Gilkeson married Miss Cabell; left two children, one Mrs. A. M. Baker of Winchester, and Henry Gilkeson who lives in a Western State. Mr. Robert B. Gilkeson, for many years a prominent merchant of Romney, was a brother of John Bell and J. Smith. His family is represented by well-known sons, Henry B. Gilkeson, the lawyer of Romney, and Edward, of Moorefield.

The McKays, Meades, Earles, Hamiltons, Ashbys, Greens, Duffs, and many more of this class, were the pioneers who settled in that section of Frederick County, now Clarke and Warren Counties, at the birth of the old County, several coming into their sections while it was yet part of Spottsylvania, then Orange, some of whom have received notice elsewhere. They were known for many years as the English immigrants. This is misleading; for though they shipped from the English coast, the emigrant ships carried families of every nationality. We find in those lists, Germans such as Sowers and Nisewander—the pioneer of the one being Jacob Sowers who is found on land in 1737, where Winchester village arose. One of the descendants has been mentioned in connection with Federal Hill. The McKays of Warren, now reduced to two small families—all that are left of the once numerous family. Some of the name drifted to other States; some intermarried with many Warren and Clarke families. We need say nothing of the Meade family. They can refer to Bishop Meade's Sketches of Old Churches and Families, and there find tracings of their many lines. The name has always been identified with the Clarke County section.

The Earle Family had its origin in England. The first to come to the Shenandoah Valley was Alex. A. Earle, who was in the Indian Wars. Then came Esaius Earle, who seems to be the direct ancestor, the grandfather of John B. Earle, the father of Capt. A. M. Earle, so well known to generations from 1850 until his death a few years ago. Jno. B. Earle left a large family, besides Capt. A. M. There were Archibald and Bayliss. Two daughters married respectively Hiram Evans and John Burns. Capt. Earle born in 1819, was one of the old Justices from 1851 for many years. He was a member of the Legislature when the Civil War opened; enlisted in the Confederate Army, and was Quartermaster of the Twelfth Va. Cavalry. At the close of the war he married a cousin, Miss Burns, of Missouri, 1867: Children of this union were John B., Alexander M., Paul B., Virginia M., and Elizabeth K. In 1881 he was State Senator from the Clarke and Warren District. His homestead was called Mount Zion, a colonial home once owned by Col. Chas. Mynn Thruston, who was so distinguished for his remarkable life as a Minister of the Gospel and a Revolutionary War officer. Col. Thruston left many descendants through the lines of his twelve children. His first wife was a Miss Buckner; second wife, Miss Alexander. The children intermarried with many distinguished families such as George Rogers Clark, Norton, Dangerfield, Huston, etc. Sidney married Alfred Powell the Winchester lawyer. One married Edmond Taylor, of Louisville, Ky. One daughter became the wife of Frederick Conrad, uncle of the late Robert Y. Conrad, of Winchester. Another daughter, Mary B., was the wife of Col. Charles MaGill whose children intermarried with the prominent families of this and other sections. The writer hopes to mention several of Col. Thruston's lines of descent. They are found in many States.

Col. Thruston has been mentioned in connection with the Old Courts during the Colonial Period, as one of the Presiding Justices. In 1809, he removed to Louisiana, and died there in 1812, and was buried on his own plantation, where the Battle of New Orleans was fought in 1815 by Genl. Andrew Jackson.

The Hamiltons and Ashbys have special history; but brief notices already given them must suffice. When we contemplate the numerous settlements made by the pioneers along the Shenandoah and Opecquon, we are amazed at their gigantic success; but we must not forget that many other pioneers were following the North and South forks of the Shenandoah in the Valleys to the East and West of the Massanutten range. Near the site of Woodstock, long before the *Muellerstadt* village was started, the English, Scotch and Irish had founded their homes, and have maintained a foothold through all the passing generations. We can barely mention a few: Benjamin Allen, Reily Moore, Wm. White, Jno. Branson, Levi Fawcett, Briscoe, Calvert, Crawford, Newman, Walker and Sibert were on the ground about 1734-36; while in the Massanutten we find an Englishman, Powell, who held adverse possession of a large mountain tract, which he and his two sons gave the name of "Fort Mountain." Many traditions attach to this man and his natural fort. Some claim that he was there when that section was discovered, and declined to give any account of his arrival or antecedents. We have nothing to verify this. Some evidence can be produced that the pioneers on the North Fork disputed all claims which the German pioneers presented for settlement, and they were thus hindered for some time. Many passed further South, and peopled the rich sections of what became Rockingham County.

For the settlement of the Upper Valley, we have reliable data prepared by two gifted sons of Augusta. (See Waddel's "Annals of Augusta," and "The History of Augusta County" by Col. J. Lewis Peyton,) the latter a descendant of the founder of Augusta. John Lewis, who settled on a grant in the Western Part of Orange County prior to 1735, was the father of Samuel, Thomas, Andrew, William and Charles B. Lewis. These sons won immortal fame as citizens and soldiers. Several of them have been mentioned by the author in connection with the early history of the Valley. The Madison family was among Augusta's pioneers. John Madison was clerk of the first court, held Dec. 9, 1745. This first court, tradition says, was held at his home near the site of Port Republic. The old homestead and what has been regarded as the old clerk's office, was pointed out to the writer recently in good condition. The oldest inhabitants of that section have faith in the story. In this old house Bishop Madison was born August 27, 1749. This indicated that this place was probably the county seat until the court house was built in Staunton at some date subsequent to 1748.

So also the Givens, Campbells, McClenahans, Stuarts, Robertsons, McDowells, Bells, Craigs, Pattons, and several others are strictly pioneers; while the Peytons, Breckenridges, Prestons and others follow later.

John Patton was the first sheriff of Augusta. We find our Gabriel Jones on hand as one of the attorneys, together with Wm. Russell, James Porter, John Quinn, Thomas Chew who qualified to practice law, and aid the new court to set the ball of justice rolling. John and Thomas Lewis were two of the Justices. The Lewis family has representatives on part of the original Lewis tracts near Port Republic. While in the Upper Valley, taking a hasty glance over the historic places of interest, where the old English and Scotch-Irish pioneers had laid the foundation, amid difficulties akin to what Frederick County experienced,—the writer was tempted into this digression. The undulating landscapes, adorned with homes, are full worthy of their reputation for thrift, hospitality and elegance. The refined and sturdy population must have imbibed many of their distinguished traits in drinking deeply from the gushing springs and rivulets that form the North and South forks of the Shenandoah. As we follow the flow of the South Fork, it finds its way through mountain and Valley, passing Weyer's Cave ("Grottoes"), forming new strength at Port Republic, we reach the Southern verge of Luray Valley, where the German element has always predominated. In this Valley between Port Republic and Luray, we find the Adam Miller family, and others mentioned in the Joist Hite Sketch. The writer visited the splendid property of Miss Lizzie Miller, a lineal descendant of Adam Mueller, Hite's rival. She owns a large body of land embraced in the original survey. Her old Colonial house is in full view of the site where the pioneer built the first house in 1729, remnants of which remain, and the site is owned by Miss Miller. This property is near the river, on the East side, and slightly North of the mouth of Swift Run Gap, through which reliable traditions claim the German emigrants came on their way from the Germana Iron Works after their rupture with Alexander Spottswood. The family possesses much unwritten history pertaining to the settlement. They were beyond doubt the pioneers of that section, and the first white people who had actual residence West of the Blue Ridge. This section is now traversed by the Norfolk and Western, or Shenandoah Valley, Railroad. The thriving village of Elkton is the trading station, near which is located the celebrated Elkton Hotel, near Elk Run mentioned in the original survey. Here is found the Elk Lythia Springs famed for their medicinal properties. The hotel, conducted by A. C. Drawbaugh and his accomplished wife, entertains a large number of guests every Summer; the writer being one who there found recreation and comfort, and where he has prepared much matter for this volume.

Following the flow of this South River, we pass

Luray and the caverns near by. In this section we find the Ruffner family had its origin. The Linebergers, Jordans, Maucks, the Bare family (Bear) near Elkton and the Snapps, Jarvis and others were pioneers. Much could be said of them; but we lack space, not the inclination. The student of the early history of this beautifully valley lying East of the *Massanutting*, and extending Southward from the river that forms a junction with South River West of Front Royal, would never tire at his task. The majestic Blue Ridge on the East, has its rival in the Massanutton on the West, with her three mountain ranges extending for about forty miles.

The Overall Family

The South River, or Luray, Valley has never seen the time in its history when this pioneer family was not represented; yet very few persons can be found in this section of Virginia, who can tell you of the historical incidents that belong to the Overall family. The name has been prominent in England for several centuries. Bishop Overall and Bishop Cosen compiled the Book of Common Prayer of the Established Church. The American Overalls are in direct descent from Bishop Overall who was also author of the Convocation Book, mentioned by McCauley in his History of England. The first settlement made by this family in America, was in Stafford County, Va., about 1700. One member of this branch came to the Shenandoah Valley as soon as it was open for settlement. This was John Overall, who married Maria Christina Froman, granddaughter of Joist Hite; settled on South River, and there reared seven children, viz: John, William, Nathaniel, Mary, Nancy, Robert and Christina.

John married Elizabeth Waters in 1773. She was the mother of Abraham, Isaac and Jacob.

John married his second wife, Mrs. Mary Byrne (nee Earle) in 1783, and reared six children, viz: Elias E., Elizabeth, Marion, John Froman, and Christina W. Overall. Abraham the oldest son of John, married Hannah Leathe in Virginia, and then moved to Tennessee in 1805. He was the father of ten children, who intermarried with distinguished families, whose descendants are numerous in Tenn., Kentucky, Texas and other States.

Isaac Overall, second son of John, married Miss Carson and settled in what is now Page County, Va. He was known as Col. Isaac; was the father of seven children. This has been called the Virginia branch. The first daughter Maria Louisa married Andrew Pitman. Mary Ann, second daughter, married Gibson N. Roy; they had four children: Mary C., Thomas Benton, Gibson E., and Walter Scott. Thos. Benton served on Genl. Hardee's staff during the Civil War, and married Miss Sarah Hardee. William Carson Overall, seventh child of Col. Isaac, married Selina Jolliffe. He was captain in the Confederate Army; died in 1885. They had six daughters, viz:

(1) Julia, married Capt. Milton Hopper, of Confed. Army.

(2) Mary, married P. H. Hoff; and have 8 children.

(3) Lucy M., married Thos. D. Keyes; and have 2 children.

(4) Selina, married Clarendon Smith; issue 2 children.

(5) Harrie Tyson, lives at the old home, "Overall," Page Co., Va.

(6) Fanny L., married Wm. G. Burns; issue one child.

Jacob Overall, third son of John, married Nancy Lawrence and moved to Tennessee in 1805; and had eight children, whose descendants are too numerous for this sketch. Some of them are in Kentucky, Texas and Tennessee, Jno. W. Overall, U. S. Marshal at Nashville, being one.

Elias Earle Overall, son of John by second marriage, married the widow of Rev. Geo. H. Reynolds. One daughter by this union, Fannie Brent, married Geo. W. Dellinger (dentist) now of Front Royal.

William B. Overall, son of John, moved to Miss. in 1788.

Marian Overall, daughter of John, married James Hadley (or Headly) and went to Kentucky in 1824. They left eight children and many grandchildren; Jno. W. Headley, Secy. of State, 1904-5, and Wm. O. Headly, of Louisville, being descendants. This family is related to the Headleys of Frederick County, Va.

Nancy A. Overall, daughter of John, married Abraham Bowman, Jr., son of Col. Abraham Bowman of Revolutionary War fame. This branch of this family lived near Louisville, Ky. Four sons, John W., Jos. L., Isaac G., and Abram Hite Bowman by this marriage. Some of their children are found in Missouri and Texas.

John Froman Overall, son of John, married Teresa Young, 1820, and moved from Virginia to Mississippi. They reared nine children. Several of the sons were distinguished for their learning. John W. practiced law, and was also editor of several papers in New Orleans and St. Louis. He finally moved to New York, and was literary editor of the Sunday Mercury. Opie P. Read styled Mr. Overall as "a typical journalist."

The other sons, Gibson T. and Elias E. were found in Alabama and Texas.

Christena W. Overall, youngest daughter of

John and Mary A., married Nicholas W. Yager, and reared a family of six children in what is now Warren County, Va.

William Overall, son of John and Maria Christina, was born in Frederick County, Va., 1754. In 1776 this man is found in East Tennessee, where he joined others in planting a settlement on the Cumberland River, where he and his two brothers Nathaniel and Robert and two married sisters, Mary Espey and Nancy Thomas, became fully identified with Tennessee and her struggles with the Indians. Tennessee history shows their great work and sacrifices and subsequent lives of their descendants. We must refer the reader to such reliable publications for fuller accounts of their deeds.

In Rutherford County, Tenn., was a celebrated place called "Overall Camp Ground," where the first settlement was made. Near this place, Robert Overall, second child of Nathaniel above named, settled about 1810, having married Mary Espey. He served in the War of 1812. Reared twelve children,—seven sons and five daughters. Their descendants are so numerous, we must pass them without further notice, excepting, however, the third son, James G. Overall, who was born 1814; married Rachel W. Davis in 1837; his three surviving sons being Asbury M. Overall; L. C., of Murfreesburg, Tenn., and N. D. Overall, of Nashville, Tenn. The writer is indebted to Mr. Asbury M. Overall for a most comprehensive genealogy of this remarkable family, which will be carefully preserved for future reference.

The Berry Family

Joseph Berry has been mentioned elsewhere in connection with the Ferry bearing his name. He and his brother Thomas came from Northumberland County, Va., during the early part of the 18th Century. They evidently belonged to the Berry family of Maryland, and are found in King George County, Va., the latter part of the 17th Century. We find the name of Berry in the Shenandoah Valley at several points. Old Augusta County records show that Thomas and William Berry were vestrymen in 1748, and George in 1751. John, Francis and David had land grants in 1774. They intermarried with the Bowmans, Crawfords, Wilsons, Walkers and other old Valley families. At this writing, however it is difficult to say more, as the various lines are not prepared with satisfactory data. We also find the name in other States,—all claiming this section of Virginia as the home of their ancestors.

Capt. Thomas Berry, an officer in the Revolutionary War, was the father of James E. Berry, who married the granddaughter of Col. Patrick Crawford. She was the daughter of James McChesney and Sarah Crawford. Thomas Berry son of James E., removed to Georgia. His daughter, Miss Maria Berry, is founder and principal of the celebrated Berry School at Rome, Ga., one of the most successful industrial schools known to the writer. She is in direct line from the Berry family who incorporated the town of Berryville, Va., in 1798.

The McCormick Family

This name has been mentioned in connection with the pioneers of Applepie Ridge. There is no evidence of family connection between the families. The McCormick family found in Clarke County, are certainly of the pioneer type. The first appearance of the name was about 1736; John McCormick being one of the Irish emigration mentioned elsewhere. Francis McCormick, a large land owner in old Frederick about 1760, it is thought was a son of the John who lived in the region now known as Summit Point. This family is too well known and too numerous to justify a full sketch in our limited space.

William McCormick's son Province, was one of the old lawyers in practice from 1822 to 1870. Two members of this family prominent in Clarke County at this time, are Province and Marshall McCormick. The former being a large landowner, the latter being not only possessor of large real estate, but has fame as a lawyer, his services being in demand as counsel in many celebrated cases. The reader is referred to Norris's History of the Lower Valley for full and complete sketch of the McCormick family.

The Jolliffe Family

This family has been mentioned in other connections in this volume. Mr. William Jolliffe, the author of a family history of the Jolliffe Pioneers and their descendants, preserves in this way what is of great value to this family and their large connection. To this we refer the reader.

The Huck Family

This family has close connection with the Jolliffes and Neills; and in this way are descendants of the pioneers. Thomas Van Horne Huck married Mary Neill, and reared three children, viz: Richard Saunders, Mary, and Lewis Neill Huck. Capt. Lewis Huck, the brave Confederate officer, was well known in the Lower Valley. He won the esteem of all; he was a lawyer of the peculiar type that made the Winchester Bar famous from 1850 to 1885. The old law firm of Byrd and Huck enjoyed a lucrative practice, until declining health overtook Col. Byrd. Capt. Huck was noted for his courage and personal attractions. The writer enjoyed his sincere friendship. The Captain and his sister, Miss

Mary, owned what was familiarly known as the Neill-Huck farm on the upper Opecquon. Adjoining this farm, was the home of their brother, Richard S. Huck. He married Sarah Stabler, daughter. of Edward Stabler, of Alexandria They reared six children, viz: Harriet S., Lewis N., Lydia N., Charlotte M., Frank S., and Richard S. Huck. Charlotte became the wife of Mr. George Jolliffe, son of Joseph N. Jolliffe, previously mentioned. Frank and his sister, Miss Hallie (as she is called), occupy the old homestead.

The Byrd Family

While we may not claim them as one of the pioneer families of the Shenandoah Valley, the State of Virginia claims the ancestor, Col. William Byrd of Westover, as a prominent pioneer of the Colony. His history has been told by several historians; and the archives of the Colonial government contain much valuable information relating to the struggles of the infant colony, with Col. Byrd as one of the most prominent figures. The progenitor of the Frederick County branch was Richard E. Byrd, a prominent lawyer in the Shenandoah Valley for the first half of the 19th Century. The writer in his earliest recollections, associates Mr. Byrd with the Winchester Bar. He was tall and slender, dignified, and austere in manner at times. A forceful advocate before a jury, his knowledge of law secured the respect and attention of the courts. He represented the County in the House of Delegates for several terms. In the War of 1861 65, he was staff officer to Genl. James H. Carson, Commander of the Militia Brigade. Genl. Jackson appointed him Provost Marshal for the army post in Nov., 1861, with commission as Colonel. At his request, the writer was detailed for service in his office as assistant provost, when the ties of friendship grew stronger between the austere Colonel and his youthful assistant. This service is mentioned in connection with the Civil War. Col. Byrd's health gave way before the war closed; and in a few years thereafter, death ended his career. The writer knew his three sons: George, William and Alfred. The latter died at full manhood. George established a large and profitable business in New York City; married there and reared his family. He has one son living in Clarke County at this writing.

William was a scholarly man; chose the law for his profession, and commenced its practice in Austin City, Texas. The writer found him there in 1859-60, prominent in politics, and one of the leaders of the legal fraternity, but ready to promote the interests of his young friend, who has ever cherished the recollections of his warm friendship. It was during one of the writer's official visits to Austin in the Spring of 1860, that Mr. Byrd's first son was born—Richard Evelyn Byrd, whose mother was a daughter of Judge Rivers, of Austin. Her other children were: Mary, Susie, Ann, Margaret, William and George R. During the Summer of 1860, Mr. Byrd was drawn into the celebrated political campaign that stirred the country. He was a Breckenridge Democrat, and canvassed the State. The writer saw him at one of the Texas *barbecues,* in hot debate with Genl. Sam Houston, who was speaking for Bell and Everett. Mr. Byrd at that time had a strong, clear voice, and was a popular speaker. The contrast between the speakers amused the great concourse of people, who came from adjoining counties. Genl. Houston's giant figure, partly covered with queer apparel, looked immense, as he towered over the lithe figure sitting near by. Mr. Byrd's power lay in ridicule. The old General had never felt such darts; and was greatly overbalanced at times. During one of his passionate appeals to the crowd—whom he addressed as children—he turned his full force upon the young man, and demanded what right he had to attempt to mislead the people. In the excitement, the General, as was his habit, tugged at his favorite *cat-skin* vest, and unconsciously rolled it up from the bottom; and when he asked the second time for a reason, Mr. Byrd quietly said: "General, pull down your vest." The old hero stood speechless. Then ringing out from that lithe figure went the cry: "General, pull down your vest; pull down your vest." The people took it up; and the hero of many battles wilted. Byrd was called; and for twenty minutes the crowd was convulsed over the humorous ridicule that he poured forth. After the November elections, Mr. Byrd was made Adjutant General of Texas troops. Later on he saw active service as Colonel, at the head of a Texas Regiment, and again as staff officer. At the close of the war, he removed to Winchester, to be near his father in his last lingering sickness. Col. Byrd and Capt. Huck formed a law partnership which continued for years. His war experience resulted in weakened vocal organs, and he never recovered the strength of his clear voice. His family have resided in Baltimore since 1900.

Richard E., the oldest son, has his home in Winchester; and is the Hon. Richard Evelyn Byrd mentioned elsewhere in this volume. His wife was Miss Flood, granddaughter of Hon. Charles J.Faulkner, ex-Minister to France. They have three sons, familiarly known as Tom, Dick and Harry. The latter gives promise for a successful business man; has headed several important enterprises, that heretofore were conducted by men of maturer years. His friends predict good results to follow his intelligent efforts.

He is president of the Evening Star Publishing Co., and also of a similar enterprise in Martinsburg.

The Magill Family

This name has frequently appeared in this volume in connection with the courts, war records and the General Assembly of Virginia. While representatives of the family have no claim that their progenitor was one of the pioneers, he is found in active life in Frederick County in 1767. This was John Magill, mentioned in the minutes of Court December 4, 1768, when he was recommended to the "Gentlemen appointed to examine into the capacity of Persons applying for License to practice as Attorney, as a Person of Probity, Honesty and good Demeanor."

Mr Magill and his two brothers, Charles and Arthur, came from near Belfast, Ireland, about 1740, and settled at Middletown, Conn. Where the subject of this sketch spent the intervening years previous to his appearance in Frederick County, we are unable to say. He was born in 1722. The family record fixes his marriage with Magdaline Dickson, Jany. 9, 1755. His biographer, Dr. Jas. R. Graham, says the issue of this marriage were eight children; and all died before the family removed to Virginia except Charles and Archibald. Charles, the oldest son, was born in Ireland, 1760. When he was 17 years of age, he had enlisted in the War of 1777. For his zeal and efficiency, Genl. Washington appointed him on his staff with rank of Major of Cavalry. This is the Col. Charles Magill mentioned elsewhere in this volume; and as already shown, he became a distinguished member of the Winchester Bar under the new State government, and active in politics. Col. Magill was twice married:—first, Apl. 22, 1789, in Spottsylvania County, Va., to Miss Elizabeth Dangerfield. His 2nd marriage was May 24, 1792, to Miss May Buckner Thurston; and had residence on North Market Street, Winchester, known as the Governor Holliday residence. (See notes on Winchester.) It has been stated by Norris in his "History of the Lower Valley," that Col. Magill spent his closing years on his magnificent estate called the "Meadows," surrounded with elegance, comfort, etc." This is explained in notes on Old Homesteads. Col. Magill never lived in the country; though he erected the mansion house at the "Meadows," he never completed it. He mentions this fact in his will dated March 21, 1827. His widow survived her husband twenty-three years, spending much of that time at the Meadows, which is mentioned in several writings as Gill Hall. Dr. Graham says she died in Washington City, while visiting her daughter Mrs. Fannie Thruston.

The children of Col. Charles Magill and Mary B. Thruston were: Charles T., Elizabeth D., Ann M., Archibald, John S., Alfred T., Henry D., Mary B. T., Augustine S., Frances C., Buckner T., all dead.

1. *Charles T. Magill.* This son of John the pioneer of 1767, has been mentioned as one of the members of the Winchester Bar. His wife was Miss Bronaugh of Loudoun County. His children by this marriage were Wm. B., Sarah S., Virginia F., Mary and Alfred T. Virginia F. married John W. Sommers. She was the mother of nine children. Mary Magill, her sister, married a Federal soldier after the Civil War named Clark Nason. Alfred T. born 1838; died 1862. The writer knew this family when they lived on part of the Meadows plantation.

2. *Elizabeth D. Magill.* This oldest daughter of Col. Magill, married Oct. 30, 1811, Augustine Chas. Smith, son of Genl. John Smith, of Hackwood. This is Major Augustine Chas. Smith mentioned elsewhere as one of the State Senators of Virginia. He resided in Winchester, and for many years in the stone house on N. Main Street, corner of Baker, given them by Mrs. Smith's uncle Archibald, and now owned by Lohr Capper. They had fifteen children, eleven of whom reached maturity, and all, except the oldest of these, married. (See Magill History, by Dr. Graham.) For brief mention of this branch, see Sketch of Hackwood. One daughter, Josepha N. Smith, married in 1844, Leonard E. Swartzwelder, a merchant of Winchester. Their daughter Elizabeth S. married July 11, 1867, Rev. W. C. Meredith, Rector of Christ Church, Winchester. Mary Jacquelin, her sister, married Willie H. Tidball, now of Fort Worth, Texas. Another sister, Augusta, married in 1885, John Scott, now of Waco. One other sister, Rebecca B., married John Marshall, U. S. Army, 1850. Another sister, Mary A., married Dr. Adam C. Swartzwelder, 1853, and removed to Ohio. He was a volunteer surgeon in the Union Army during the Civil War. Archibald Magill, son of Col. Chas. A. Smith, born 1835, married, 1867, Mary D. Meredith; eight children by this union. They are found in various sections of the country, prominent in business. Prof. Smith was a Confederate soldier, mentioned elsewhere in that connection and also with the educational features of Winchester.

3. *Ann M. Magill,* daughter of Col. Chas. Magill and Mary B. Thruston, born 1798, married Thomas T. Fauntleroy, a lawyer of Warrenton, Va., about 1820. This was Genl. Fauntleroy, mentioned elsewhere. He served as Lieut. in the volunteer army, 1812. In 1836 he was com-

missioned Major in the Regular Army. His service in the Seminole and other Indian Wars belongs to National history. He was Col. of the 1st Regiment of U. S. Cavalry in the Spring of 1861; and when Virginia seceded, he resigned and offered his services to his native State. He was commissioned Brig. Genl. Genl. Fauntleroy felt aggrieved at something Prest. Davis said about ranking officers, and resigned his commission. He survived the War, and lived a retired life until his death, Sept. 12, 1883. He had five children, viz: Charles M., who was in the U. S. Navy. He resigned in 1861 and entered the Confederate service; was promoted to a colonelcy. He reared a large family.

Thomas T. Fauntleroy, Jr., second son of Genl. F., born 1823, died in St. Louis Oct. 1, 1906. This was Judge Fauntleroy of the Court of Appeals, already mentioned together with his family.

Mary Thruston Fauntleroy, mar. Dr. Jos. K. Barnes in 1844. He was Surgeon in the U. S. Army, and was Surgeon Genl. during latter part of the Civil War. Mrs. Barnes was the mother of several children.

Catherine Knox Fauntleroy, married Major Jos. H. Whittlesey, of U. S. A. Their three children went to Western cities.

Archibald M. Fauntleroy, was Dr. Fauntleroy who was commissioned Asst.-Surgeon in U. S. Army in 1860, and resigned in 1861. He entered the Confederate Army; and served on Genl. Joe Johnston's staff; survived the war, and was superintendent of the Western Lunatic Asylum from 1877 to 1886. His wife was Miss Sallie H. Conrad (See Conrad family sketch).

4. *Archibald Magill.* This fourth child of Col. Chas. Magill, married Mary Jane Page, daughter of Mann Page of Gloucester County, Va. He spent most of his married life near Bartonsville, on his farm, Barleywood. No issue to survive.

5. *John S. Magill.* This son of Col. Charles has been fully mentioned elsewhere. He died March 8, 1877. His wife was Mary Ann Glass, whom he married in 1840. She was the daughter of Major Robt. Glass.

6. *Alfred Thruston Magill, M. D.* Born in Winchester, Va., 1804; died at "Woodbury," Jefferson County, June 13, 1837. He practiced medicine in Winchester until 1833, when he filled the chair of Practice of Medicine in the University of Virginia for about four years. He married Nov. 1, 1827, Miss Ann E. Hunter Tucker, daughter of Henry St. George Tucker, Presiding Judge of the Court of Appeals of Virginia. Their home in Winchester was on North Market Street, in the house built for them by Judge Tucker, which is now the Lutheran Parsonage. Their children are:

1. Fanny T. Bland Magill, born Dec. 17, 1828; died May 13, 1901; married Oct. 3, 1853, Rev. James R. Graham, Pastor of the Kent Street Presb. Church, Winchester, and now Pastor Emeritus of the Presbyterian Church. He was born in Montgomery, N. Y., July 16, 1824. His pastoral charge during the 58 years of his ministry, has been in the Winchester Church. Mrs. Graham endeared herself to the entire community; and had the affectionate regard of a large circle. The writer and his family enjoyed her friendship. She was the mother of eight children, viz: William, died in infancy; Ann Magill, died 1889, unmarried. Rev. Alfred T. Graham, D.D., graduated at Hampden-Sydney College, 1878, the Union Theological Seminary 1883—Pastor at Rockville, Md., 1883-89; at Davidson, N. C., 1889-1907; at Lexington, Va., 1907. Married Nov. 16, 1886, Isabelle Irwin, of N. C. Three children by this union.

William Graham took the law course at the University of Virginia, 1880-82; removed to St. Louis; entered a wholesale drug house; married 1905 Mrs. Sarah Hopkins. They reside in St. Louis. No children.

The fifth child of Dr. and Mrs. Graham is Miss Evelina Tucker Graham. She and her father reside at the Parsonage on North Braddock Street, Winchester.

Rev. James R. Graham, Jr., was ordained to the Foreign Mission work June 5, 1889; married same year Miss Sophie C. Peck, dau. of Rev. Dr. Peck, Professor in Union Theo. Seminary; sailed same year for China, and stationed ever since at one of the missions. They have three living children.

Rev. Henry Tucker Graham, the 7th child, graduated at Union Theo. Seminary, 1891; married Aug. 12, 1891, Lillian dau. of Col. Wm. Baskerville of Virginia; sailed next month for Japan, where they spent five years in that country in the missionary service. On his return to America, was pastor at Fayetteville, N. C., 1897-1905, and at Farmville, 1905. They have one child.

The 8th child of Dr. Graham is John Randolph Graham, M.D.; graduated at Princeton University, 1896, and at Missouri Medical College, 1899; practices his profession in New York City. He married Belle Knight Ward, dau. of William Ward of Maryland. Their only child, John Randolph, Jr., died March 23, 1908.

Dr. Alfred T. Magill's other daughters, Miss Mary T., Evelina H., and Virginia Louise have been mentioned elsewhere. The former was the teacher, authoress, etc. Miss "Eva" H. married Capt. W. L. Powell in 1872. One child survives both parents—Dr. Wm. Leven Powell, Jr., of Roanoke, Va. He married Oct. 23, 1907, Ellen Kerr, of Philadelphia.

Virginia Louise married Major Edwards, of Kentucky. Both died in Atlanta, Georgia.

Henry D. Magill, M.D., 7th child of Col. Charles, married in 1833, Ann E. Mason, dau. of Wm. Temple Mason, of Loudoun County. Their only son, Thomas H. Magill, was one of Moseby's Men, was wounded and taken prisoner. He now resides in Louisiana; married Agnes Torian. Dr. Graham says he is the only living descendant of Col. Charles Magill, male or female, whose surname is Magill. His sister, Ann E. T. Magill married in Baltimore, 1877, Leonard K. Sparrow. He now resides in Richmond, Va., and has three children, viz: Ann E. S., Carroll M. S., and Leonard Kip S.

8. *Mary B. Thruston Magill* married June 10, 1830, Robert Lee Randolph, of Fauquier County. Their children are: Rev. Alfred Magill Randolph, now Bishop of the Southern Diocese of Virginia. He married Apl. 27, 1859, Sallie G., dau. of Dr. Wm. W. Hoxton, of Alexandria. Their children are Robert Lee, Eliza L., married James Ambler, Alfred Magill, married Miss Pace, of Richmond. They reside in Europe.

Evelyn B., Eleanor C. married Theodore S. Garnett, Jr.

Francis H. married Richard C. Taylor, Jr.

William Fitzhugh Randolph, brother of the Bishop, married Miss Carter; now lives in Miss., and has eight children. His sister Mary M. married Edward C. Turner. There are three children by this union: Beverly Randolph, born 1839; lives at the old homestead, Fauquier County and unmarried. His brother, Rev. Buckner M. Randolph, was the well-known minister who spent eighteen years in church work in lower Virginia. His wife was Miss Hoxton. His large family of children live in various sections.

Augustine Smith Magill, born 1811, married Miss Weeks,, granddaughter of Col. Charles M. Thruston; removed to Louisiana. After his death in 1851, his surviving family was swept away by the Tidal wave at Last Island on the Gulf Coast, when over 400 persons lost their lives.

10. *Frances C. Magill* married in 1834 Thomas G. Gordon, of Florida. One of her daughters, Mary M. Gordon, married July 17, 1866, Rev. Geo. A. Long. They had eight children. Mrs. Gordon after the death of her husband in Texas, married her cousin Alfred Thruston. By this marriage there were three children: (1) Jeanette P. who married Saml. B. Logan, of Winchester, Dec. 11, 1867. After his death, she married Dr. Wm. H. Rader, of Broadway, Va., by whom she had three children.

Alfred Buckner Thruston born 1848, is well remembered by the writer. He was familiarly called Buck, and was a warm-hearted young man. He spent many days at "Greenwood," as a temporary member of Mr. James C. Baker's family. He now resides at Sedalia, Mo.; married in 1881 Mary L. Washington, of Tenn. They have five children. Mr. Thruston is a civil engineer. Sidney F. Thruston, sister of Buckner, married in 1873 Chr s R. Branner, of Rockingham County, Va. (now deceased). Six children by this union.

11. *Buckner Thruston Magill* was Asst. Surgeon in U. S. Navy. Died at sea some time in 1841, unmarried. He was youngest child of Col. Charles Magill.

James Magill owned land on Hogue Creek in 1768; and was still in that country as late as 1777. It is thought he was not a brother of John Magill who first appears in Frederick County in 1768.

The Moore Family

The first appearance of this family in the Shenandoah Valley was in 1824, when Thomas A. Moore came from Alexandria and opened a law office in Charles Town. In 1840 he became Clerk of Jefferson County Court and held the office until his death in 1889. He reared four sons: S. J. C. Moore, who practiced law in Clarke County. He was Major Samuel J. C. Moore of Confederate War fame. Cleon Moore became a member of the Charles Town bar. His brother, B. W. Moore, a lawyer, removed to Fayette County, West Virginia. The remaining son is Rev. J. Harry Moore mentioned elsewhere as the accomplished Presbyterian divine. Cleon Moore, of Alexandria, was the ancestor of this family. We find that one of his sons, Thomas Moore, was a commissioned officer in the Virginia Line at the close of the Revolutionary War. Several of the Moore generations are found in other States, Texas and Mississippi.

Mr. A. Moore, Jr., the prominent attorney of Berryville, has won success in his profession. His ancestors were of the pioneer class in South Carolina, but removed to Virginia about 1760, and remained in Westmoreland County. Mr. Moore's father removed to the Shenandoah Valley early in the 19th Century. The subject of this notice was born in Clarke County, May 30, 1846, where he received his academic education; entered the Confederate Army when only fifteen, and served to the surrender. His law course at the University of Virginia, closed in 1870, when he commenced the practice of his profession in Berryville. In 1889 he represented Clarke and Warren counties in the House of Delegates. Mr. Moore's splendid library contains valuable collections of Colonial history. The author here acknowledges Mr. Moore's courtesy for the use of his library.

The Lupton Family of Applepie Ridge

Generally distinguished as the Quaker branch, this family had its origin in David Lupton, son of Joseph and Rachael Lupton. David was born 1757; died 1822.

Children of David, son of David, Sr., and Mary Hollingsworth:

(1) Ruth, wife of Phineas Janney; died 1804.
(2) Joseph Lupton; died 1825.
(3) Isaac Lupton; died 1820.
(4) David Lupton; died 1814.
(5) Nathan Lupton; died 1843.
(6) Jonah Lupton, born July 20, 1795; died 1870.
(7) Lewis, born Oct. 16, 1797; died 1859.
(8) Joel Lupton, born Mch. 28, 1804; died 1883.

Joel Lupton married Sarah G., dau. of John and Rebecca Haines. She died 1863. Was the mother of Wm. G., Nathan, Mary Ann, Rebecca H., Joseph, Rachael, Susan A., Joel, Jr., Sarah Jane, and Maria C. Lupton.

Joel, Jr., married Ellen Hough, 1869. The children by this issue were Mary Wood, Charles Littler, Hugh, Jr., and Anna Lupton. Wm. G., married E. Virginia Donnelley, issue: Sarah E. and Mary S. Wm. G. became prominent in Phila. Miss Mary S. is the only survivor of this family, her travels abroad and liberal education gives her distinction in the Lupton connection. One of her father's sisters is the wife of Mr. John Jolliffe.

The writer hoped to follow the line of Joel to date; but the branches have failed to respond in time.

The brothers Lewis and Joel Lupton were extensively engaged in the lumber business. They furnished the sawed lumber for making and equipment of the Winchester and Potomac Railroad. During the time referred to, Lewis invented, made and used the first road scraper seen in this section. Some enterprising machinists of Kennet Square, Penna., seeing it in use, took advantage of their opportunity, and soon had this useful piece of road machinery in general use, claiming exclusive rights. These brothers also have the credit of inventing and making the first cylinder threshing machine known to be in use in this section. It was Joel Lupton who first advanced the idea that to mow grass successfully, the motion of shears must be used; and invented a mowing machine with this improvement, which he sold to a man named Hubbard in New Jersey. McCormick, then working on the same line, assisted Hubbard, and secured the right to take the machine to Chicago, and proceeded to control its use. Hubbard instituted suit to recover his rights; then it was the celebrated law suit relating to patents was instituted. Joel Lupton was an important witness; he identified the machine. The suit resulted in a verdict favorable to Hubbard. What Joel received in return is not known.

Jonah H. Lupton, son of David, was married to his first wife, Martha A. Sidwell, dau. of Richard and Charity Sidwell, Apl. 17, 1817. She died 1836, leaving one daughter Thomasin M. Lupton, born 1818; died 1897. She was the wife of Jacob Rees, and was the mother of the following children: Jonah L., Martha A., Ruth E., Samuel D., and Jane S.

Jonah H. Lupton married his second wife Lydia Walker. She was the daughter of Edward and Mary Walker; was born Jan. 20, 1804; died Jany. 29, 1829, and was the mother of Ann Lupton, Mary Walker Lupton, Edward W., Hugh Sidwell, David P., and Rebecca Jane.

Ann M. Lupton married John L. Bond; she was the mother of Howell M., Walker M., Allen B., Edward L., Anna S., and Mary E. Bond.

Mary Walker Lupton married William L. Irish; died 1890; was the mother of Rachael S., Edward L., and Lydia W. Irish.

Edward Walker Lupton married Mary E. Janney; issue, E. Janney, William Taylor and James McSherry Lupton.

Hugh S. Lupton married Mary R. Speekman, Jany. 1, 1880. Issue: Daniel Walker, born Nov. 27, 1881; Carrie D., born Nov. 5, 1883; James R. born Oct. 16, 1892; Hugh Sidwell, Jr., born Dec. 24, 1895.

Rebecca J. Lupton married Seneca P. Broomell Sept 23, 1884; was the mother of G. Lupton Broomell, Arthur Wm., and Margaret.

David Lupton, mentioned as the progenitor of the Applepie Ridge branch, was a nephew of John the father of Joshua, who have been fully mentioned in connection with the Round Hill, or Presbyterian Lupton branch. The pioneer of both branches was Jos. Lupton who died 1758, leaving 8 children, several of whom were then married. Their names will appear in this connection.

David Lupton and his aged father Joseph, son of Joseph the pioneer, lived on a large tract at the head of Babb's Marsh, devised by the pioneer. They soon acquired other tracts, aggregating about 1,700 acres. On this tract David built the brick house in 1795, at a cost of $5,000. This house has been mentioned elsewhere as the home of Mr. Ruble. Strange to say, this house at that early day, gained notoriety for two features in its construction: one being the windows were hung with cords and weights—the first used in the Shenandoah Valley beyond a doubt. The wine vault built in the cellar, was one of the most complete attachments the old Friend had to offer his guests. This vault was in its original style when the writer saw it many years ago (minus the wine). The large tract was subdivided between the three sons, Jonah, Lewis and Joel. They owned and maintained well known homesteads up to and during the Civil War. All were conscientious Union men and unmistakable Quakers. The old homesteads have somewhat lost their identity with the old period.

Joseph Lupton the pioneer, in his will, probated in 1758, mentions the following children: William, Sarah Pickering, Joseph, Elizabeth Paxon, Ann, Mercy Haines, Jonathan and John. The last named must have been the youngest child. He is mentioned fully elsewhere as the father of Joshua. Joseph the third child of the pioneer, died at his home on Applepie Ridge, 1791. His father mentions this son in connection with his personal effects in this wise: "I desire my son Joseph shall have my Gold-headed cane." This is mentioned to verify a tradition concerning the cane, held by some members of the family. This Joseph died in 1791. By his will he left a large estate to his family, which consisted of Rachael his wife, son David, Ann Updegraff, Hannah Lupton, and David and Rachael Wood, his grandchildren.

David only son of Joseph, has been fully mentioned. David the only son of Joseph, died 1805. His uncle John, father of Joshua and brothers, constituted the Presbyterian branch. John in his will, leaves his large estate to his wife Ann, and his minor children, viz: Joshua, Nathan, Grace Steer, John, Jr., Joseph, Mary Baley, Sarah Russell, and Elizabeth Lupton.

Nathan and Joseph with their lines, drifted into other States; and at this writing no definite reports come to close the large connection.

The John Lupton family found in Clarke County, the writer has been informed, descended from the David Lupton branch. This John's sister Mary married Jos. S. Jackson. John's wife was Miss Milton, mother of Rebecca, wife of Rev. Mr. Lingamphleter, and John, now of Louisville, Ky.

There is a tradition in the family that three persons bearing this name (Lupton) were deported from England in 1635; landed at Boston, where there is a record of their arrival. This may be doubted, since we have no evidence that Boston or its harbor had a place on any map at that early day.

Mr. Hugh S. Lupton, mentioned as the grandson of David, lives near Clearbrook, in one of the most modern and complete houses found in the country, which he built in 1897 at a cost of $5,000. One hundred years after his grandfather erected his at the same cost. Mr. Lupton owns a well-cultivated farm, and has successfully managed an insurance business, with offices in Winchester.

The Huntsberry Family

This family is well known in the section North of Winchester as belonging to that sturdy class of citizens who developed the resources of the country, Augustine Huntsberry being of that number. He left a large estate and a large family of children, viz: Henry, Jacob, John, Edward C., Mrs. Robt. T. McVicar, and Mrs. James H. Faulkner (his first wife). Henry and family live in Washington, D. C. His children are: George, Harry, Lucy, William, Augusta, and Melly. Jacob lives in Rockingham County; John married Miss Grant. Edward C. married dau. of Oscar Barr.

Augustine had two sisters, Mrs. Catharine Kyle, and Mrs. Cain. The latter's husband is of the highly-respected family found along the Opecquon in early days.

The Hardesty Family

The first of this name appears in what is now Jefferson County, and settled in vicinity of Smithfield, in 1791. This was Richard Hardesty. He reared a large family, having married twice. His first wife was a Miss Smith. She was the mother of John, Isaac, Lee, George, Ephraim, Reese, Franklin, Moses and Mary. His second wife was a Miss Pierce, the mother of Richard S., Adrian D., Thomas P., James M., Lucy C., Catherine, Charles W., Joseph E., Elijah and Matilda. From these have sprung many prominent men and women, mostly to be found outside of Frederick. George Hardesty represented Clarke County for two terms in the General Assembly. William G. was one of the Justices of Clarke, 1852-60. One brother was a merchant in Berryville, and several others were noted farmers and stock-dealers.

A daughter of Reese Hardesty married U. S. Senator Daniel W. Vorhees. Mr. Jones J. Hardesty is a well-known farmer and stock-dealer, residing in Frederick.

The Colston Family

This name has been familiar to Shenandoah

Valley history from the days of the Revolution in 1776. Long before this period it was widely known in Eastern Virginia. We find William and Armstead in Old Frederick County in the early part of the 19th Century. Their ancestor was John Colston, of Jefferson County, Va. Then we have Col. Raleigh Colston in Winchester in 1778. In 1798 he purchased Maidstone Manor in Berkeley County, to which he moved and spent the remainder of his life. There he died in 1823. His wife was a sister of Chief Justice Marshall. Their son Edward inherited the homestead, who married Sarah J., daughter of Judge Wm. Brockenbrough, of the Court of Appeals of Virginia. He has been mentioned as one of the soldiers of the 1812 War. His brother Thomas Colston settled in Loudoun County. His son Raleigh married Gertrude Powell, of same county. He was in the Auditor's Office in Richmond when the writer saw him last.

The Colstons intermarried with many prominent families in several states. Their lines are too numerous to mention in this limited space. Some of these families are Minors, Blackfords, Thomases, Gordons, Leighs, Robinson, Stephensons, and Taylors. The Colstons of Clarke, Jefferson and Berkeley County are descendants of the old line.

The Dearmont Family

This name appears in the list of Irish emigrants that found their way into the Shenandoah Valley prior to the Revolutionary War, among whom were William and Michael Dearmont. William is found in Fauquier County in 1771. Michael enlisted in one of the Valley Companies in 1773, and received pay for two months service. William was in Col. Fry's Regiment; and his name was carried on the rolls through the War from 1778 to 1783. He had a son Michael in Prince William County in 1827. He then appears in Frederick County in vicinity of White Post the following year. Michael's wife was a Miss Furguson of P. William County. Col. Washington Dearmont was one of their six children reared in Clarke County. He married a daughter of Strother Bowen. She was the mother of Ernest, William A., Charles O., and Mamy J. Their father was one of the Militia Colonels when the Civil War came. He then enlisted in the Col. Jno. S. Moseby's First Company of Guerillas, and served through many raids of this noted chieftain.

The Lucas Family

This name is associated with the pioneers in many ways. Old records point to their prominence from 1743 all down through the eventful vista to the present time. The author has no intention to write even a scrap of history of the family, which has been well told in many forms by others; and we need no more than a note at this time.

We find the Lucas name prominently mentioned in connection with every war period from the Indian massacres to and through the Civil War, 1861-65.

We find Edward Lucas in the War of 1812, and in Congress in 1833-37, as the representative from the Valley District. We find his brother William Lucas, from the same district, in Congress from 1839-43. He was the father of Hon. Daniel B. Lucas, the gifted lawyer, orator and poet, whose mother was the daughter of Capt. Daniel Bedinger, of Revolutionary War fame. Mr. Lucas has gathered renown from his countrymen in various ways. His services as legislator, judge, lawyer and citizen, have been of high value to his State. In 1869, he married Miss Lena Brooke.

Alexander R. Boteler

The name of "Alec" Boteler was familiar to the people of the Lower Valley during the heated political campaign of 1851-59, while he was contending with such men as Ran. Tucker, Charles J. Faulkner, and Wm. L. Lucas, for honors. Mr. Boteler was an old line Whig; and his stump speeches were notable specimens of oratory, captivating voters and winning fame. His opponents, being men of marked ability, made those campaigns memorable. The writer heard them gladly on every occasion possible. He was defeated by Mr. Faulkner in 1852, by a small majority, and also in 1857. In 1859 they were again in the field. This time he defeated Mr. Faulkner, and took his seat in the 36th Congress. His short term of service was distinguished for its activity and oratorical effect upon the Congress that was confronted with the dissolution of the Union in 1860. Mr. B. saw service in the Confederate Army, and was at one time member of the Confederate Congress. Mr. Boteler was born in Shepherdstown in 1815. His father was Dr. Henry Boteler. Several of the ancestors were in the Revolutionary War. Their homes were near the border line of Maryland and Virginia.

The Lewis Family of Clarke and Jefferson

The writer can only mention this distinguished family to show their presence in the Valley about the Revolutionary War period. They have a direct line from Col. Fielding Lewis, whose marriage with his two cousins, Kate and Bettie Washington, has always given the Lewis family prominent notice by historians of the Washingtons of Westmoreland.

One of Col. Lewis's sons, Major Lawrence Lewis, married Eleanor Parke Custis, the adopted daughter of Genl. Washington; and Major Lawrence became the grandfather of the Lewis families found in Clarke and Jefferson within the last thirty years. One of his sons was Lorenzo Lewis, who married a Miss Coxe of Philadelphia. Two of his daughters, Frances Parke, and Angela, married respectively Genl. Butler, of Louisiana, and Hon. Charles M. Conrad, of the same State. (President Fillmore's Secretary of War.)

Mr. Lewis had six sons, three of whom were familiar figures in the Lower Valley. They were J. R. C., Edward P. C., and H. L. Dangerfield Lewis. The former was an officer in Commodore Perry's expedition to Japan, and also an officer in the Confederate Army, 1861-65. After this service, he retired to his farm in Clarke County. Edward P. C. became prominent in business in Hoboken, N. Y. The youngest son, Dangerfield Lewis, has been mentioned in this volume as the president of the S. V. Agricultural Society. His home was in Clarke, the old Audley homestead. After his death, his widow and children removed to New York.

General Adam Stephen has been mentioned as a compatriot of Genl. Morgan. Genl. Stephen must not be confounded with the Peter Stephens family, for no trace of family relation can be found. He was one of the prominent pioneers of the extreme Northern section of Frederick County; and his family intermarried with the pioneer families of that section. He was a brother of Alexander Stephen, whose will was probated Aug. 3, 1768. Adam and his brother Robert inherited part of his estate. Genl. Adam Stephens' will was probated Sept., 1791, in the District Court of Frederick County. He devised lands, slaves, etc., to his family; mentions his daughter Mrs. Dandridge and son Robert Stephen.

The Baylor Family

The Baylors of Jefferson County, West Virginia, may not be classed with the pioneers of the Shenandoah. They belong to the John Baylor family found in Gloucester County in the latter part of the 18th Century, who had two sons John and Gregory in Caroline County, 1640 to 1760. Their descendants are to be found in Jefferson County and also in Augusta County. We find Richard the oldest son of Gregory in Jefferson County, about 1786. His sons have been prominent in military and civil life. One was Capt. Robert Baylor mentioned in connection with the Laurel Brigade. Two of his sons were killed during the Civil War. Judge R. E. B. Baylor, the founder of the Baylor University, Texas, was a son of Capt. Walker Baylor of the Revolutionary War. At this writing, three of his grandchildren live in Frederick County, viz: Frances Courtenay Baylor (Mrs. Barnum) the authoress, Mrs. Genl. John B. Walker, and Major Eugene Baylor. Mrs. Walker's son, Capt. Philip M. Walker, U. S. Army, maintains the military spirit of the Baylor and Walker families.

The Gibson Family

Braxton D. Gibson, of Charles Town, son of Col. Jno. T. Gibson of Confederate War fame, belongs to the Scotch-Irish emigration that came through Pennsylvania and settled in the vicinity of Winchester about the beginning of the Revolutionary War. The Gibsons of South Branch and those of Jefferson County, West Virginia, are all of this stock. They have been previously mentioned in this work. The good name of this prominent family has been well sustained by the gentleman first named, Col. B. D. Gibson. He has served his State in the General Assembly of West Virginia; is a lawyer in good practice, and one of the wealthy citizens of his county. He married Miss Mason a niece of the late Governor Holliday. Her father was Dr. Mason of Charles Town.

The Timberlake Family

This family first appeared as one of the pioneers in 1733. Coming from England, they made settlement in Tidewater Virginia. Two grandsons of this first family, William and David, are found on large tracts of land in what is now Clarke County, about the middle of the 18th Century. From this settlement, numerous branches grew, until the name was found in various localities in the Valley. Want of space prevents a satisfactory sketch of several lines that have been familiar to many readers. The writer remembers the brothers Stephen D. and Washington Timberlake who owned splendid estates in the Northern part of Frederick County, prior to the Civil War, both of whom sent gallant sons into the Confederate Army. Some were slain in battle. Mr. Stephen D. was a splendid type of the old Virginia gentleman. His old homestead in recent years passed to James T. Clevenger. When the war closed, Capt. Seth M. Timberlake returned to the old place, and for several years he and his attractive family did much to restore much of its old-time appearance. Finally he and his brother Joseph went to New York and spent many years with Charles B. Rouss.

Mr. Wm. Timberlake, of Brucetown, Fredk. Co., is well known in Frederick County for his integrity. He is the son of William and grandson of Benjamin, related to the families mentioned.

Washington Timberlake had two sons who survived the Civil War, both are Confederate veterans. George was badly wounded; Harry lives in Winchester. The Timberlakes of Clarke County were always distinguished as the "Hill and Dale" family. Capt Dick Timberlake was associated with this place for many years. He was born near Berryville in 1801. Mr. Thos. W. Timberlake who lived at "Milldale," was his son, whose intermarriage connected him with the Griggs, Harfield, Sherman and Bee families.

The Douglas Family

This name appears among the pioneers of Northern Frederick. This was William Douglas. He came from Delaware; was of the Douglas Clan, so prominent in Scottish history. He reared a large family in what is now Jefferson County, West Virginia. Several of his sons became distinguished men in other States. One son, who remained in his native county, was Judge Isaac R. Douglas, mentioned elsewhere in connection with Old District Courts. He reared a large family; but so far as known to the writer, not one of the name is to be found in the Lower Valley at this writing. One son, Dr. Wm. A. Douglas, was an eminent physician in San Francisco a few years ago. One daughter became the wife of Judge White, of St. Louis. Her sister is the wife of Dr. W. McPherson Fuller, of Winchester, and mother of "Doug" Fuller, Cashier of the Farmers and Merchants Nat. Bank of Winchester. One of Mrs. Fuller's brothers, Archibald M. Douglas, was living in West Virginia a few years ago.

Judge Parker

We have frequently mentioned Judge Richard Parker in connection with old law suits, criminal trials and other subjects. He succeeded Judge Douglas in 1849; and presided as Judge of the District Courts until his service was closed by the Civil War. He belonged to an old line of jurists. His great-grandfather, Richard, was Judge of the East Virginia Circuit; died 1813. He had five sons in the Revolutionary War. Judge Parker's father, Judge Richard E. Parker, was a Judge of the General Court in the Norfolk Circuit, 1817-31; and then moved to the Shenandoah Valley and lived in Winchester; was elected U. S. Senator, 1836; afterwards appointed Judge of the Supreme Court of Appeals of Virginia. Judge Richard, the son, was M. C. in 1848. His old home on Washington Street, Winchester, has been mentioned elsewhere. The quaint old house has the credit of being planned by Thomas Jefferson, for Judge Hugh Holmes. The Parker residence was noted for true hospitality. Mrs. Parker was an accomplished woman, and had a large circle of relatives and friends, who saw many days of pleasure in her quiet home. The Judge survived her for several years, and then in 1888 he, too, was carried away to Mt. Hebron; and the old mansion virtually closed its doors. During the latter part of his life, he had frequent interviews with persons from various sections of the country, seeking information concerning the John Brown trial. Judge Parker's name at that time had national renown as the trial judge.

Judge Edmund Pendleton

Properly speaking, Judge Pendleton succeeded Judge Parker. At the close of the Civil War, the courts were reorganized, as shown elsewhere. This left Frederick County, as the 13th Judicial District. Judge Pendleton held his first term June 10, 1869. He was succeeded by Judge Robert H. Turner June 10, 1870. Judge Pendleton continued to reside in Winchester, but gave little attention to his profession; and enjoyed the ease and comfort of a retired lawyer. He purchased the Senator Mason property, where he erected a splendid mansion. There he and his small family—his wife and son Alexander R., maintained a royal establishment. This was sadly interrupted by the untimely death of the Judge. His widow survived him for several years, but she never resumed her social life, which had been a charm to Winchester society. She had the sympathy and affection of sincere friends. Surviving both parents, was their son Alexander R. Pendleton, the lawyer of whom we have had occasion to make mention. Mr. Pendleton was the law partner of Edmund P. Dandridge for about twenty years. He survived his partner; closed the business of the firm, and retired to his palatial home, where he enjoys rural life sublimely. Mr. P's scholarly attainments, untiring energy, and high regard for business principles, fitted him for any sphere. The writer has always enjoyed his friendship.

The Pendletons are associated with the early history of the old Colony. They came from England about the middle of the 17th Century, and settled in Caroline County, Virginia, where we find Philip Pendleton and his large family in 1700. His sons and daughters intermarried with prominent families. Their descendants are found in Lower Virginia and many other sections. We find William and Philip Pendleton in the North end of Old Frederick County, about 1750. From Philip descended many lines—he being the father of fourteen children, who intermarried with the

Hogues, Hunter, Strother, Brooke, Mathews, Kennedy and other prominent families.

Col. Philip Clayton Pendleton of this family, married a daughter of Genl. Elisha Boyd, of Berkeley County. His children were Philip, Dr. E. B., and Judge Edmund Pendleton, of Winchester, Va. His two brothers lived at Berkeley Springs. Col. Pendleton's brother Edmund, lived in Berkeley County and reared a large family. His children were: Isaac P., Serena P. (Mrs. Dandridge), Sarah wife of Adam Stephen Dandridge, whose son Adam Stephen lives in Jefferson County; Philip P., Mrs. R. M. T. Hunter, Dr. A. S. Dandridge, of Cincinnati; Mrs. Buckhannon, and Mrs. Kennedy; Maria, another daughter, married John R. Cooke, the Winchester lawyer. He and his children are mentioned elsewhere.

The Lee Family

No attempt will be made to sketch the life and movements of this well known family. The writer could mention several of the name found in the Shenandoah Valley alongside the pioneers.

Mr. Chas. S. Lee, living near Berryville, Clarke County, and Col. Hugh Lee, found in Winchester as an old resident in 1850, were descendants of Edward Jennings Lee, Sr. Others could be named; but the history of this family has been often written, because of the connection with Genl. Lee and Light Horse Harry Lee.

Mr. Chas. S. Lee has two sons in Norfolk, Va.; one Daughter, Mrs. Garrett, in Baltimore, and Mrs. Nancy Lee Coble, of Winchester.

The Page Family

This name appeared in the Shenandoah Valley during the 18th Century. We find John Page, of Pagebrooke, and Mathew Page at Annefield about 1780. These famous homesteads have been mentioned elsewhere. The brothers came from Broadneck, Hanover County. They were sons of Robert Page, whose father was Mann Page, of Rosewell, Gloucester County, Virginia. It has been said that from Mann Page and his three sons, Mann, John and Robert Page, all the Virginia Pages have sprung.

Eastern Virginia has produced notable men and women of this name. They intermarried with the Randolphs, Lees, Carters, Nelsons, Harrisons, Couplands, and others in that section; while the Pages of Clarke County have family connection with the Burwell, Whiting, Byrd, Mayo, Atkinson, McGuire and other well-known families.

Judge John E. Page had two sons, John Y. and Dr. Robert Page. This family has been prominent in Clarke County. So also were other lines from John Page of Pagebrooke. R. Powell Page, of Saratoga, is the only son of Dr. Robert P. Page, who was a cousin of the Pagebrooke family. The writer knew Mr. Mann Randolph Page. His two sons, George R. and William Byrd Page have been well-known residents of Clarke County. The Pages, Couplands, and Randolphs of Cumberland County, Va., have close connection with the Pages of this Valley.

The Funsten Family

The writer has had occasion to mention frequently the name of Col. O. R. Funsten in the foregoing pages,—the gallant Major of the 17th Batt. and Col. of the 7th and 11th Regiments. This brief sketch will not embrace his military record. The Colonel's Home was the Highlands, near the Clarke County line, (now the home of Thos. S. Chamblin). He was a man of liberal education for a country gentleman. His home was noted for its hospitality and fine equipment. He was the son of Oliver Funsten and Margaret McKay—daughter of Andrew McKay, one of the pioneer families mentioned elsewhere.

When the writer first knew the Highlands, Dr. O. R. Funsten (Col. Funsten) was very popular as a physician and citizen. He was then entering a political campaign that resulted in his election to the State Senate. The Doctor married a daughter of David Meade for his first wife. After her death, he married a daughter of James Bowen, of Albemarle County, Va.

Many old Confederate Cavalrymen remember the Colonel's son, Lt. "Bos" Funsten, the Adjutant. His sister married Mr. Fletcher, of Rappahannock County.

Col. Funsten had one sister, Margaret, who married Major Richard Bennett, U. S. Army, after whose death, she married Richard E. Byrd. Another sister, Julia Anne Funsten, married George W. Ward, the lawyer and State Senator, previously mentioned. Children by this union were George W., Minna, Julian F. and Emily Funsten Ward, who died a missionary in China. Robert M. and David F. The oldest son was Judge Geo. W. Ward (deceased.) The second son is Dr. Julian F. Ward, of Winchester. Robert M. has been mentioned as the State Senator. The other son, Rev. David F. Ward (now deceased).

Col. Funsten had one brother David, who was a lawyer in Alexandria. He married Susan C. daughter of David Meade. He had two daughters, one being wife of Rev. Wm. Dame, D.D., the other is the wife of Hon. Robt. M. Ward. Mr. Funsten was a Confederate soldier, and represented the 7th District in the Confederate Congress.

The Harmer Family

While we may not claim this as one of the pioneer families of the Shenandoah Valley, Winchester history points to many periods when the name was identified with her growth and prosperity. Jacob Harmer, Sr., the old Revolutionary soldier, first appeared in this section early in the 19th Century. This was perhaps merely a visit; for we find him subsequent to this period in Germantown, Penna., with his application to the court for license to conduct his line of business. Such applications had to be supported by affidavits of persons well-known to the court as to the character and fitness of the applicant. The Court announced that Mr. Harmer should produce such testimony. Then it was that the most distinguished member of the Bar addressed the Court—saying that he held in his hand a paper signed by Genl. Washington, which certified to the character and faithful services of Jacob Harmer. This was his honorable discharge from the Continental Army. The lawyer asked if additional voucher would be required. The court immediately directed that Mr. Harmer be granted such privileges as he desired.

In 1801, we find him in Winchester, when he witnesses Genl. Morgan's will. They were doubtless comrades in the Northern campaign. He was a man of many parts. An architect of good reputation, he planned a number of the old buildings which still attest his skill. His son, Jacob Harmer, was born in Philadelphia Jany. 23, 1794. He married Eliza Tyson, daughter of Peter Ham. Jacob, Jr., had two brothers: Samuel and Joseph. The latter became prominent as the editor and proprietor of the New York Citizen, a popular newspaper in its day. Jacob, Jr., raised the following named children: Benjamin Tyson, who went to Western Virginia and there reared his family. The Harmers of West Virginia, who were his sons, have been distinguished men.

Peter Ham Harmer, 2nd son, married and reared a small family in Front Royal.

J. Albert was the well known tobacconist, who died in Winchester, 1893, unmarried.

Theoderick S., 4th son, married Mary daughter of Simeon and Charlotte Hillman, so well-known as the Tollgate keepers who demanded toll from General Jackson, Banks, and Sheridan's armies. Mrs. Harmer and her two sons, William and Tyson, were well-known figures at the old toll-gate on the Valley Pike. William married Miss Chrisman, and is a farmer in Carpers Valley. Tyson is at the old gate, receiving tolls. The father died when they were children. The mother survived her husband.

John R. Harmer, the 5th son, married Miss Steele, and left two children: Marian, and John J., the well known young business man of this county. His father was called Captain Harmer, being at one time Captain of one of the Winchester Fire Companies. He was a member of Company A, 39th Batt. Virginia Cavalry.

Edgar R. Harmer, the 6th son of Jacob, Jr., married Miss Groves, of Rappahannock County, Va.; has four children: Lizzie A., Stanley E., Annie G., and Ivy L. Stanley has been connected with the W. & P. and B. & O. Railroads, and has made the run from Winchester to Baltimore for many years. He is in the line of promotion, which he justly merits. His father Edgar R. was a tobacconist in Winchester for many years. Since the Civil War, his health has been somewhat impaired. His outdoor life as Winchester's newsdealer, brought improved conditions. Many business men welcome his daily appearance. His fund of anecdote and narrations seems inexhaustible. Mr. H. often indulges his poetic vein. Several of his poems have been published. His father was engaged in several enterprises during the 19th Century. The beaver hats of his manufacture, and his unadulterated tobacco are well-remembered by the writer.

The Affleck Family

This family made its first appearance in Frederick in the early part of the 19th Century (1818). We find several brothers and sisters of this name living with their aged mother on what was known as the old Holmes farm in 1843. The mother evidently was the widow of James, who had married Marion Gladstone. James Affleck and Marion Gladstone were married in the County of Peebles, Scotland, July 19, 1799. (Extracts from the Session Record of Drumelzier). Children by this union were James Affleck, John G., Robert F., Christiana, Alexander Gladstone, Jean Twedeep, Betty, William, Nancy Glass, and Marion Holmes.

After their arrival in America, a sister, Mrs. Jane Affleck Tait, husband and family came to this country and settled in Washington City. Their descendants still reside there. James Affleck, the emigrant, was born in Scotland 1776, and died Nov. 16, 1828. His wife was born 1779 and died 1844.

James Affleck, their oldest child, married Miss Hotzenpeller. Children by this union were: John H., James, Betsy J., Nannie, Margaret and Ellen. John married Miss Keckley; their children are James R., married Hannah, dau. of Thomas Cook, an Englishman. His sister Mary married James R. Koontz. Her brother William married Mrs. Rosenberger; Sally, another daughter, married Mr. Hottle. Her sister Susan married

George W. Hillyard, Jr. J. Edward is married and lives in Winchester. Dick, the youngest, is at home with his mother.

James Affleck, brother of John H., married Miss Baker, of Shenandoah County; lived and died in that county; left two children: Arthur who lives in South end of Winchester, and his sister who married a son of Wesley J. Carper. Both have children.

Margaret Affleck, dau. of James and Catherine Hotzenpeller, married Jonathan M. Gibbons. They left several children.

Nanny V., her sister, married Manson P. Smith in 1871. Mr. S. is a prosperous farmer and miller on Cedar Creek; and is the father of Mary B., Catherine A., and James R. Smith.

Ellen Affleck, sister of Mrs. Smith, married John Campbell, near Stephens City. He has one son living at that place.

Alexander Gladstone Affleck, son of the emigrant, married Ann E. Hoover, of Kernstown, Oct. 13, 1835. He was the father of six children, viz: Philip J. Affleck, married and lived in Berryville. He was a well-known bugler in the Confederate Army.

Marion L., Ann V., Scott A., married, and is the well-known farm implement dealer in Winchester.

John William, married, and associated with his brother.

Francis R., unmarried.

One of the daughters married Col. Solomon Pritchard; his daughter has his sword and vest. She lives with her aunt Miss Fannie Affleck (Francis R.), who has many interesting matters of history pertaining to their distinguished relative, William E. Gladstone, Prime Minister of England under Queen Victoria.

Ann Hoover mentioned in this connection, was a descendant of John Hendrick Hober, who came from Holland in 1766. His passport issued by that government, written in Dutch, and certified under seal, is well preserved and shows he was a native of Switzerland.

The Grant Family

The progenitor of this family was William Grant. He first appears as general collector of quit rents for Lord Fairfax in 1762; executed his bond in Fauquier for 1,000 pounds sterling, and was empowered to collect the rents at any place in the Northern Neck (See Fairfax's Court records). William settled on the "Bullskin," Berkeley County, about 1770. His sons were Stewart, Robert, Jacob and John. Stewart is mentioned elsewhere as one of the old merchants in Winchester, and a veteran of the War of 1812. He married Miss Fridley. Children by this union were: William, Sally, Susan, Charles and John L. Grant. William married Miss Gano; he had two sons William and Ward, who live in Ohio. Sally Grant married Wm. Heterick, who became the father of Rev. Edward Heterick of Welltown, this county, and Robert M. Heterick, county clerk of Rappahannock County, 1859-87. His son Edward C. succeeded him for one term. Several children of William and Sally lived in Ohio. Susan Grant married William Lupton, second wife—no issue. Charles Grant married sister of George S. Pine near White Hall, this county. Stewart, one of the sons, operates a livery and sales stable in Winchester, where his brother Paul resides. Lee and William, two other sons, are non-residents. John L. Grant, the youngest son of Stewart, married Miss Sarah E. Swartz. Their children are Fannie, wife of John Huntsberry. John G. is a physician; lives at Manassas, married Miss Smith. Robert R. is a physician; lives at Rosedale, La.; married Miss Talbot; they have two children: Rob. E. and Ed. T.

Scott T. Grant is an extensive farmer and stock-dealer, near Kernstown, unmarried. Edward is a farmer. James, the youngest son, lives in Winchester, manufacturer of fruit sprayers, etc. Bettie is single; lives with her father in his old Colonial home on Fort Hill. His wife died several years ago. Mr. Grant owns a large farm North of Winchester.

The Kern Family

It has been an accepted fact that Adam Kern gave his name to the village known to the pioneers as Opecquon, and later on as Hoge's Tavern. The name has clung to the village for more than a century; but the "Kernstown" of to-day has none of the name as an inhabitant. Once the Kern family was numerous in the Lower Valley; now the lines are widely scattered, and difficult to trace. At this writing we can only briefly mention the Nimrod Kern family. The writer enjoyed the friendship of this gentleman for many years. He owned a valuable mill property on Abrams Creek, and also a productive farm. His family was well known for their intelligence. Mr. K. always encouraged a spirit of education, manifested by his children. The Rev. John A. Kern, D.D., mentioned elsewhere, is one of the family. Another son, Bentley R. Kern, the postmaster of Winchester, has been identified with Winchester business men in various ways. He married the daughter of Ben Brooke mentioned in connection with the M. E. Church, as the orator and preacher. Their children are: Harry R., the lawyer; Hunter, assistant postmaster; John, connected with the same office; Asbury, the talented young lawyer, who has recently commenced the practice of law in a Western State; and Brooke. One daughter resides with her parents on Amherst Street.

The Kern family of Kernstown vicinity, intermarried with the Steele and Shryock families. Some of the name lived in Romney and other places. Some of the old stock drifted far up the Valley, sending descendants to other States.

Hon. John W. Kern, candidate for Vice President with W. J. Bryan in the election of 1908, being one.

Nimrod Kern had two daughters, Miss Lonie being one. The mother of his children was Miss Bentley. Adam Kern was his grandfather. We find the name written in various ways. The pioneers being German, the name by its English translation produced Karns, Carens, Karnes, Kearne. But about 1800, the family adopted the simple name of Kern. The first appearance of the name in our County records was in 1770, where we have Michael and Henry Kearn as litigants in one of the old suits. Doubtless they were brothers of Adam, who built several good houses, and operated a large distillery East of the village, where the terraced grounds which formed part of his lawn, are well preserved at this writing. (Now the property of the author).

It is not known what, if any, family connection, exists between the Adam Kern family and those found in Western Frederick. The writer recalls the Benjamin F. Kerns family, of Rock Enon, and that of Sydnor Kerns West of Pughtown. They were not brothers. Benjamin F. was a son of Nathan Kern, who was the father of eight children.

Benjamin F. married Miss Triplett. She was the mother of 12 children, all of whom are widely scattered; several live in Frederick County. He died in 1885.

Rev. D. H. Kern, pastor of the Braddock M.E. Church, is not able to trace his line to the old emigrants just mentioned.

Mr. Kerns, the well known wagon manufacturer on Martinsburg Turnpike, belongs to another family.

The Gold Family

While it is not claimed that, strictly speaking, this family was one of the pioneers, it is known that a family of this name was in Frederick County in 1754. This was John Gold, who was served with a writ of ejectment. Shortly thereafter, Thomas Gold leased land near Charlestown. Still later, his son John Gold was on his own farm near Berryville. This was in 1815. His family then consisted of his wife Lucy McBride, and three children: Daniel, Nancy and Catherine. His second wife was Lucy Easton. She was the mother of Calvin, John, Washington, Thomas E., Elizabeth (Mrs. Ballinger), Mary (Mrs. McMahon), and James.

Daniel, the oldest son, was a prominent business man in Winchester. The writer remembers seeing him at his home on Braddock Street (now the home of Mrs. Dandridge). He died in 1852. At one time he was an elder in the Presb. Church. He was thrice married; his first wife was Sarah Duffield. She was the mother of but one daughter, Emeline, who became the wife of Mr. Spindle; and she was the mother of Thomas D. Spindle who married Eliza daughter of Lloyd Logan of Winchester. Mr. Gold's second wife was Mary Floyd; she was the mother of Selina (Mrs. Boswell), William Henry, Sarah (Mrs. Kurtz), and Daniel Lewis. His third wife was Mrs. Scott. No children.

Wm. Henry Gold, son of Daniel, was born 1820. His first wife was Margaret R. Wood, youngest dau. of Wm. Wood of Western Frederick. Children by this marriage were: Alice M., (Mrs. Whiting of Clark, and both dead); Edward T., Henry L., Emma S., Mary F., Margaret R., and William Wood. The mother died during the Civil War. Mr. Gold married his second wife in 1868, Miss Viola L. Pitman, of Shenandoah County, dau. of Philip Pitman. Her children are Philip H. Gold, Julian B. and Laura W., (twins), Hunter Boyd, and John Calvin, (twins). Julian died at the age of nine years. Philip H. has been previously mentioned as county clerk. He married Miss Rebecca Clayton. They have two children.

Laura W. became the wife of Frank Crawford in 1908, son of Rev. Wm. A. Crawford, deceased.

Mr. Wm. Henry Gold was widely known in Frederick County, where he spent his entire life, which ended Jany. 26, 1898. He held several offices of trust; was County School Supt. for several years. He had a liberal education, and possessed many noble traits of character. He was a ruling elder in the Presb. Church for many years, and devoted much of his time to church work.

Calvin Gold, when a young man, settled in Illinois; married a Miss Marshall of that State. He had three children: Lucy, Achsah, and George.

James Gold had several children who went to Missouri.

Washington Gold lived in Berkeley County. He left three daughters: Page, Sally and Margaret, and one son, Samuel.

John and Thomas E. Gold remained on the old homestead near Berryville. John never married. Thomas E. married Lucy M. Allen. Only one son survived, Thomas D. Gold, now living on the old homestead, Ellwood. Mr. Gold entered the Confederate Army when 16 years old;

served in the 2nd Va. Infty. In 1866 he married Sarah Helm Barnett. She was the mother of five children: Henry S., Mary W., Edward Barnett, Thomas E., and Lucy Nevill.

The Wall Family, of Winchester

This name has been mentioned frequently in this volume. There seem to be three distinct families of this name, that have no known connection. The well known brothers Wm. W. and Thomas T. Wall, are the sons of Wm. T. Wall, who came to Winchester from Maryland about 1825. He married Elizabeth Vanhorn, related to the Vanhorn family mentioned elsewhere as living West of Winchester 1795. The same family probably that lived on the farm in 1830, now owned by James B. Russell. Mrs. Vanhorn left as children William W. Wall, the grain merchant of Winchester; Thomas T. Wall, the book and stationery merchant; Elizabeth, who married James W. Barr; the Misses Mattie and Virginia lived on N. Market Street for many years; died unmarried. William W. married Miss Barr (see sketch of that family). Thomas T. married Miss Sallie Huffman, dau. of Mr. Edward Huffman, well known for his integrity.

One other family of this name, was known as the John F. Wall family. He had two brothers, Gracchus and Jacob. John F. Had two sons, Dr. Thomas Wall who married Miss Pancoast. Several children survived the parents; none, however, live in this county. The other son is Dr. Asa Wall, was once a surgeon in the U. S. Navy, but resigned to enter the Confederate Army.

Jacob Wall lived on Potato Hill, where Marcus Spotts now lives. Mrs. Spotts, John, and Treadwell were children of Jacob Wall. Gracchus died an old man, unmarried.

The Tavenner Family

The first appearance of this name in Frederick County was shortly after 1833. This was Stacey J. Tavenner, who had married Pleasant P. Purcell in Loudoun County, and removed to Ohio, where he remained only a few years. There his son Jonah was born. He returned to Virginia in 1840, and lived for several years on Applepie Ridge; then removed to Bellville near the head of Opecquon, where he reared a large family, viz: Newton who joined the 1849 gold-hunters, and started to California, but died before reaching the "gold diggings." The next child was Mary E. who became the wife of Jonah J. Lupton and died at Cloverdale; left two children, who are mentioned in the Lupton Sketch.

The next was Jonah, the well known and highly esteemed resident of Gainsboro District. He has two children, Judge Frank Tavenner, of Woodstock; and Minnie, who became the wife of Mr. Eastham. They live in Texas and have several children.

The fourth child was Miss Rebecca Tavenner, mentioned elsewhere in connection with the Bryarly homestead.

The fifth child was Joseph, who moved to Missouri many years ago. His brother Albert followed later on.. Both married, and were prominent business men in their section.

The 7th was Emma, who married her cousin, Brown Tavenner. Their son, Alvin J. Tavenner, lives with his aunt Rebecca. A brother of Alvin's lived in Ill. at one time.

The 8th child was John V. Tavenner, married and lived in Loudoun County, and then returned to Frederick; purchased the old Cather farm on Flint Ridge, and there reared his family. He is mentioned elsewhere as the representative of Frederick County in the House of Delegates. He is now living in Norfolk, Va. The Tavenners have numerous connections—through the Janneys of Loudoun and other families.

Mr. Stacey Tavenner is mentioned elsewhere as one of the old time school-masters. The writer can testify that he was a "tutor" in the strictest sense 1849-50.

The Myers Family

This name appears among the pioneers, and were of that class who stood by their "clearings," when Lord Fairfax instituted suits of ejectment. The settlements made by them in what became Hampshire County, still later Morgan County, were of the "Tomahawk" claim; but as they were good sentinels on the outposts, they escaped serious litigation, but were subjected to Indian forays. Henry Myers came to Frederick County about 1840, and purchased a farm near the Hackwood Spring. He had married Mary Sherrard daughter of Robert Sherrard, a sister of Judge Sherrard of Winchester. While Henry lived in Morgan County, he had born to him the following children: Mary S., who became the wife of C. Lewis Brent; Betty B. who married J. Chap Riely; and Wm. H. Myers, born 1831. He married in 1857 Mary J. dau. of John Harman. Children by this union: Mary, (now Mrs. J. W. Taylor), John H., Henry, Ann Lee, Wm. M., Florence and Elizabeth. Mrs. Taylor is the mother of several sons and daughters, James W. the young merchant on West Water Street, being one of her sons. John H. and Henry are successful farmers of the home farm. Their father was Capt. Wm. H. Myers a gallant officer in the Laurel Brigade; has been dead several years.

The Silver Family

This family came to the Valley early in the 19th Century, and settled in Berkeley County. This was Francis Silver and family. He had one son Zepheniah, who was born in Berkeley County. He married a daughter of Hiram Henshaw, of English origin. Mr. Silver purchased a fine property on Applepie Ridge and spent the remainder of his life in Frederick; died in 1875, at the age of 74. He had several sons who served in the Confederate Army, Capt. Frank Silver being one. His son Gray is now State senator in the West Va. legislature.

The only one of the name in Frèderick today is John M. Silver, son of Zepheniah. He has been twice married; first wife Miss Parkins; she left one son Byard. The second wife was a daughter of Dr. Daniel Janney, and sister of Drs. J. E. and Mac Janney. She is the mother of several children. Mr. Silver lives at the Daniel Janney homestead (Welltown). John M. Silver has been mentioned elsewhere as one of the county supervisors and member of the House of Delegates from Frederick County.

The *Silver family* of the Valley came from Silver Spring, Penna. They might be considered as English-Scotch-Irish origin, as the name has been identified with these countries. The Henshaw family, with whom Zepheniah Silver intermarried, is one of great antiquity, found in England when two men of the name took shipping from that coast in the 17th Century, and landed in Massachusetts. From those two brothers, came the Henshaws of America, so far as known, —certainly those found in Penna., Maryland and Virginia.

This name must not be confounded with the splendid German family Hancher, so well represented by James, Thomas and others on Applepie Ridge.

Col. Frank Silver married Mary, a daughter of James W. Gray, Esq. Their children are Martha (named for her grandmother Martha Henshaw), familiarly known as Miss Georgie, the trained nurse. Her sister Odelia is the wife of J. W. S. Boyd son of John Boyd the scout—one child John E., Jr.; another sister, Anna Beall, married Lester C. Hoffman; another Mary Llewellyn Silver. Their brother, Senator Gray Silver married Miss Kate Bishop recently.

Augustine Huntsberry left a large family of children, viz: Henry, Jacob, John, Edward C., Mrs. Robt. T. McVicar and Mrs. James H. Faulkner (first wife). Henry and family live in Winchester. His children are George, Harry, Lucy, Wm. Augustine and Melly.

Jacob lives in Rockingham County.

John married Miss Grant.

Edward C. married daughter of Oscar Barr, and is mentioned elsewhere.

Augustine had two sisters, Mrs. Catherine Kyle and Mrs. Cain. The latter's husband is of the highly respected family found along the Opecquon in early days.

The Steck Family

In connection with the sketch of the Greenwood Homestead, (the home of Samuel the emigrant), this family has been briefly mentioned. Dr. M. Steck, son-in-law of Thomas Wood, of Penna., came to Virginia with his family in 1880, and occupied the old homestead, as already shown. His family consisted of his wife and three children: John M., Thomas W., and Rachael.

Dr. Steck was a man of sterling character, and immediately commanded the respect and esteem of the entire community. His sudden death within one year of his arrival, was deeply deplored by his new friends. The Doctor held several important offices under President Fillmore, and was nominated for Lieut. Governor of Pennsylvania in 1878; received a large vote, but not sufficient to elect his ticket over the Republicans, whose numerical strength was great.

His son Thomas W. is one of the leading fruit growers in the county; and takes pleasure in showing what the modernized Greenwood farm has done under his management; while his accomplished mother dispenses the hospitalities of the old homestead in such manner worthy the approval of those she has succeeded. Her son John M. married Miss Cover and has been mentioned elsewhere.

The Coe Family

This was a well-known family in the early part of the 19th Century. Three brothers, William, Craven and John Coe came to Winchester from Maryland by way of Loudoun County. John remained but a short time; sold his interest in a lot of ground to his brother William, where they started the celebrated Coe's Tavern mentioned in this volume. John, after accumulating considerable property, including a farm near Winchester, sold out and went, first to Baltimore, and then to Tennessee. The tavern went into the hands of Robert Brannon for many years.

William purchased a large farm in the N. West part of Frederick, where he and his brother Craven Coe lived for many years. Craven survived his brother and, as the writer knew him, he commanded the respect of the entire community. His son Charles lives in that section, and other descendants by intermarriage.

John C. Coe, son of John Coe and Louisa Fenton, born 1836, has been known to Winchester people for thirty years as the proprietor of the Coe Dairy, of Jersey cows. He owns a fine farm two miles East of Winchester, and in all these years has maintained a high reputation for his famous dairy. In his early days, he sought fortune in the West;—was once a conductor on the Illinois Central Railroad. He married Celia Collins, of Toledo, Ohio, in 1858. They have two children. The son, De Soto Coe, was an officeholder in the Internal Revenue Department, under President Cleveland, and so efficient, that the Harrison administration did not remove him for some time. He again returned to the Department under Cleveland's second term, and held important places as inspector of storekeepers, etc. He married Miss Savage, of Kernstown. He is now living in Frederick County—a good farmer and an ardent Democrat.

The Brannon Family

This family name has been familiar to Winchester and Frederick County during the 18th, 19th, and 20th Centuries. The first to appear in the land records was John Brannon. He obtained a grant from the Commonwealth June 26, 1789, for 552 acres of waste land on drains of Back Creek. He sold portions off in 1791, and from that day to the present, the Brannon family has had some of the name living in that section. John, however, had resided in Winchester previous to that date, and was in business on Cameron Street. The John Brannon found in the list of Revolutionary Soldiers, possibly was this man, though we have nothing to prove it. Perhaps none of the name was so generally known prior to 1850 as Robert Brannon, the famous old tavern keeper of Winchester. For fifty years he had been before the public, and owned large interests in every enterprise. He was a leading politician in his day. His tavern stands have received attention in other chapters. He died 1851. His executors in March, 1852, report an inventory of great length, enumerating the articles and furniture used in his tavern business; his horses and vehicles in great numbers indicate a large livery business; and his farm products and implements would mark him a farmer, while from his list of "*likely young negroes,*" he might be taken for a slave dealer. The writer has often heard him mentioned as an all-around man. A race track East of town, bore his name for a full century.

The family history credits John Brannon, the Irish emigrant, with twelve children, most of whom went West; and their descendants live in Kentucky and Ohio. Among those who remained in Frederick County, were three of his children: Robert, Levi, and Rachael who married Evan Thatcher. All three of these men served in the War of 1812, and drew pensions, as already shown.

Robert Brannon's children were: John, born 1821, Harriet, Stewart, Morgan, Henry and Rachael. John became the famous lawyer of West Virginia. Harriet was the wife of Henry McDaniel (already mentioned). Their only son, Lieut. McDaniel, died in a Northern prison in 1863. Stewart died in Clarke County in 1859; Morgan died in Winchester, Va., 1900. He had been one of the trusted friends and employees of Chas. B. Rouss. Henry, the only living child of Robert, is Judge Brannon of the Supreme Court of West Virginia, with 18 years service. He was born in 1837. Rachael married Evan Thatcher in 1817; had 5 children: John, Catherine, Mary, Brannon and Evan R. The latter was one of the Supervisors of Frederick County. Brannon lived on the North Frederick Turnpike, near the Fair Grounds; built the brick house where Ed. Frieze now lives, and there reared his family. He was one of Winchester's famous butchers in the good old times when the market-house had well arranged meat stalls, and all families visited their favorite stall every Wednesday and Saturday—the regular market days— and laid in a supply.

A brother of Robert was killed by Dr. Bull who was a brother of Mrs. Genl. John Smith, of Hackwood. This occurred about 1818. Bull committed suicide.

Levi Brannon, brother of Robert, lived on the Brannon farm in the Pughtown section, and raised a large family. He married Ruth Gray and had 12 children. His son *Will* was killed at the Wilderness in 1864—one of the gallant young members of the Boomerang Company from Winchester. L. Gray Brannon, another son, married a daughter of Craven Coe; they had several children. One son, J. William, is in the mercantile business at Whitacre and owns part of the old home tract. R. Bruce is a prosperous farmer. His other son, C. Coe Brannon, is now Comr. of the Revenue for the Northern Dist. of Frederick. All worthy young men, and are maintaining the good name of their father.

John Brannon, son of Robert, who owned the old tavern, corner Fairfax Lane and Loudoun Street, sold out and moved West between 1830 and 1840. He had several sons: James, Stephen, William and Reese.

The Hoover Family

This is one of the oldest families to settle in Winchester, about 1766. Many lines have run down from this family. They have been noted for their integrity and unassuming lives. Frequently, however, they filled posts of honor in the town, and the name always appears with respectable and commendable enterprises. They can be strictly classed with the best Yeomanry of the early days. Those of the name have become few. Charles E. Hoover, superintendent of water and streets, and his family, are well known. He was born in 1845; married twice. First wife was Alice V. Grim, who died in 1872, four years after her marriage. Second wife was Miss Ramey, of Penn. Mr. Hoover's father, grandfather and great grandfather bore the name of John; and his son John, who has been connected with newspaper business, beginning with the Evening Item, is endowed with the peculiar talent that local editors require to make their articles and criticisms please all readers. His cheery salutations gain him many friends as well as *items* for his paper.

The Haymaker Family

This family belongs to the Colonial period, and Winchester has never been without good representatives of this family since that period. We find Adam Haymaker the gunsmith of the early war period, very much in evidence. His services were greatly in demand, making and repairing the old-time Flintlock guns. He had several assistants who had been apprenticed to him to learn the trade. The old fellow seemed to have things his own way. For example, we give the tenor of indenture papers between Henry Brinker and himself, when the son, George Brinker, entered the shops on Cameron Street. George was then 17 years 9 months and 14 days old. He was bound to Haymaker to serve his time until he was 21 years old. Henry Brinker signed his name in German, he being one of Joist Hite's emigration. Brinker was to furnish his son good wearing apparel, hat and shoes, pay doctor's bills, etc.; and agreed that his son "should neither buy nor sell any article, nor go to taverns, nor play cards or throw dice, nor go to race-tracks, nor absent himself, nor commit fornication, without his master's permission." Adam was simply to get the boy's time and service for the "meat and drink he chose to give him."

There was a John Haymaker who bought a lot from Philip Bush on Cameron Street, and also a lot on the common. This was in 1778. The family intermarried with Winchester families; and although we find very few of the name in the town at this writing, many descendants are here. William Haymaker who died since the Civil War, was a man of property; left a large family. Several sons have been well-known mechanics, brick-masons, carpenters, cabinet-makers, plasterers, etc. Capt. James M. Haymaker, who has been member of the City Council and Captain of the Friendship Fire Company for many years, is in active business, although he experienced four years of faithful service as a Confederate soldier. His father was a son of Adam, the son of Adam the gunsmith. James M. married Lucy E. Davis and has the following children: Mrs. Frank Anderson, Mrs. Wm. Breckenridge and James C. Haymaker.

When the writer was a boy, he knew an old man of this name who lived on the N. W. Turnpike four miles from Winchester, near a fine Spring. The walls of the spring-house are in good condition now and the water just as cold. This was Henry Haymaker. He was highly respected by his neighbors. He had a large family, three sons: John, Charles and George—all married and moved westward. He had one daughter who married John Barr who raised a large family: Sons Robert and James. His daughters married H. Wigginton, A. W. Hodgson and M. Ritchcreek. They all left families. The A. W. Hodgson family live in and about the town. This name Haymaker has often been confounded with the Hammakers and Hamichers—the first being English. The latter bears evidence of German descent in early conveyances.

George Haymaker, the well-known cabinetmaker, a great-great-grandson of Adam and son of Jno. W. Haymaker and Sophia Grim, lives on part of the lot where Adam had his shop. This was lot No. 202 on S. Market Street, described in deed from Lord Fairfax, dated 1753. Part of this lot has never changed name of owners. Geo. Haymaker was born 1844; married Rebecca, daughter of Levi Grim; their children being Annie, William, Cora, Minnie and Louella. George had several brothers and sisters, all now dead. The daughters of John W. Haymaker were Rebecca, married James Hoey—no children.

Hannah Haymaker married William C. Langley, father of Philip Langley who lives near Stephenson, the oldest representative of the name. William C. came from Ohio; married his wife Feby. 15, 1826, and returned to Ohio. After a short residence there, he returned to Frederick County, where he rented a farm on Applepie Ridge, the property of Wm. L. Clark. When the Winchester & Potomac Railroad was under construction, Mr. Clark selected his tenant to purchase certain materials for its equipment. Philip, who was born in 1840, was conductor on this railroad for 14 years, and had four sons to serve as engineers and conductors for many years. Three are now on the Valley Division. Philip has in his possession the old family flesh-fork, nearly two feet long, with the words "1804, made by Adam Haymaker," graved on this old-time cooking utensil. The lettering is brazed and is perfect now. Philip had several brothers and sisters. Rebecca married Henry V. Willis, father of William Willis, husband of Florence Hodgson.

A cousin was Lisle Langley, single, who died an old man. His sister Harriet married Mr. Marsttella. A daughter by this marriage is the wife of City Justice Wilson. Mary, a sister of Lisle Langley, was the wife of William Lauck, the machinist and gunmaker.

The Barr Family

The first appearance of this name in the County records, is that of George Peter Barr, who came from Loudoun County, and acquired an interest in land through his wife, which they sold to Martin Frieze. This was in 1766; and in 1770 he settled on 100 acres adjoining Major Maxwell's grant. This was in the western part of Frederick. This was the Jacob Morgan tract which Geo. Peter Barr's executors sold in 1816. Robert B. and John Barr appear in the Western part of the county at this time, and James purchased a tract from John Brannon West of Pugh's Town. Hugh Barr was then living in Winchester, one of the old-time brickmakers. He conducted business on a large scale. Many old buildings show his peculiar brick. Orders of court show he furnished brick for the present court house and jail.

Robert B. Barr, third son of George Peter Barr, removed his large family from Frederick County to Winchester about 1812, and purchased property on South Loudoun Street. His wife was Ariminta Avery, of Fairfax County. Their children were: James, John Hugh, Robert, William, Cornelius B., Ann and Elizabeth. James moved to Staunton and married. His children Were Robert, John and Elizabeth. They continued to live in that section, and intermarried with families of the Upper Valley.

John Barr married Ann, daughter of Henry Haymaker (as already shown in Haymaker Family Sketch.)

Hugh Barr married Elizabeth Arnold; their children being Ellen, Ann, Oscar, Hugh, William and Clinton. Ellen married Robert Kurtz; Ann married Richard O'Roak.

Oscar Barr married (first) Lucy J. Kerrell, daughter of Dempsey Kerrell, of Loudoun County. Children by this marriage were Virginia who married C. E. Huntsberry. Their children are:

Walter E., married Miss Stine.

Thomas M., married Miss Seal.

Mary E., married A. E. Dabney, of Staunton, Va.

Oscar's second wife was Miss McKinster, 1885. They have one daughter Rebecca, unmarried. Oscar Barr, one of the retired merchants of Winchester, was born July 1, 1835, in Winchester. He has been identified with the best interests of the city during his entire life, save his four years of service in the Confederate Army, and a few years' residence as a merchant in Hampshire County, West Va. While resident in Hampshire County, prior to the Civil War, he was Captain of Company in Col. Monroe's 114th Regt. Va. Militia; and was with the Colonel in his disastrous engagement at Blue's Gap. He then enlisted in Company A., Marion Rifles; served three years and was then transferred to the 23rd Va. Cavalry. During the war he was frequently detailed to assist surgeons in field hospitals, because of his nerve, and knowledge and experience with wounded men. After the War, Mr. Barr controlled a large mercantile business on North Main Street, until he was succeeded by his son Walter E., who retired later by reason of ill-health. The father entered business again, to be succeeded by his son Thomas M. Mr. Barr has filled many posts of trust under the City government.

Hugh Barr, brother of Oscar, was Drum Major of the 5th Reg. Va. Infantry. William and Clinton the other brothers, made their homes in Texas, and are men of prominence and wealth. William was a gallant soldier in Capt. Jack Adams' Cavalry Company, which won distinction.

Robert Barr, son of Robert Barr and Araminta Avery, his wife, was born June 27, 1811. His first wife was Mary, daughter of Peter Kreemer. Their five children were: Julia, married Charles Correll. They had children, one being J. E. Correll, who has been Commissioner of the Revenue for Winchester for several terms.

James W., son of Robert, married Miss Wall; children being Willie and Frank (twins). Owen (dead), Elizabeth, married Samuel Atwell. The father died several years ago. He was well known for many noble traits; and filled places of trust with signal ability. He was a member of the mercantile firm of Kern, Barr & Co., doing business on corner of Market and Piccadilly Streets for many years subsequent to the Civil War.

Edward M. Barr, son of Robert, has been for many years the well-known brick manufacturer. He married Emma, daughter of James Kiger. Their children are Charles, Frederick S., Mary Jackson and Edward Mitchell.

Elizabeth Barr, daughter of Robert, married W. W. Wall. Issue, 3 daughters and 2 sons. Mary married Fred S. Barr; Grace married Dalgetty Kerr; Julia, unmarried. One son, Dr. Harry Wall, lives in Norfolk; Taylor lives in Winchester.

Rebecca Wall, daughter of Robert, married Newton A. Swartz. They have several children.

Robert Barr married Sydney Jackson for his

second wife; their children being: Lewis, Virginia, Frank and Robert. Lewis married twice, his first wife a Miss Jackson, second wife Miss Julia Spurr. He lives in Washington, and is one of the city engineers. Robert married Miss Sumption, and has been connected with steam laundry work in Winchester.

Mr. Robert Barr owned and operated the large farm near the Paper Mill, and also was a contractor and builder; being an expert brick mason, and highly esteemed for his many good deeds. He left a handsome estate, the result of his own skill and efforts.

William Barr, son of Robert, 2nd, married Miss Brown. No issue. He was a member of the Old Continental Morgan Guards, that was engaged in the first battle of Manassas. He was stricken with fever after the battle, and died in Winchester.

Cornelius B., 6th son of Robert, married a daughter of Henry Grim and moved to Delaware. Their issue was Henry, Charles, John, Bettie and perhaps one other.

Ann Barr, daughter of Robert, 2nd, married Samuel Trenary. They had the following children: Jas. M., R. Ed., Henry C., Saml., Chas. H., Ann E (Mrs Myers), Katie G (Mrs. Grim), A. B., Ida V. (single). R. Ed. was a gallant Confederate soldier.

Samuel Trenary deserves more than a passing notice. He was a brick-mason prior to the Civil War, and lived on North Braddock Street, the present home of Oscar Barr. He was a man of rough exterior, large frame and loud voice; but he had noble qualities, and was ever willing to lend a ready hand to the helpless. He was a Union man during the War. The writer was in a helpless condition as a prisoner during the War, and was refused assistance by a man who should have offered help. At this severe juncture in the case, which meant death to the prisoner, Mr. Trenary appeared on the scene, and in his bluff manner *demanded* to know what was meant by the prisoner's sad plight, who was suffering from extreme disability and charged with being a spy. When answer was made, and a request that he receive surgical attention and be paroled to accept quarters with friends in the town, this man promptly replied to the provost marshal: "Colonel, give him to me, and I will report him every morning at nine o'clock;" while the man who refused all sympathy, sat speechless but with venom in his eye. For the one, the writer has grateful remembrance; for the other, a desire to forget the man of evil passions. His name has been necessarily mentioned in this volume. Mr. Trenary was sheriff during the Reconstruction period.

Elizabeth Barr, sister of Saml. Trenary's wife, married Adam Haymaker.

The Chenowith Family

This family was one of the pioneers of the Valley, and settled in what is now Berkeley County. Sons and daughters intermarried with many well-known families. Their descendants lived along the Opecquon Creek and on Applepie Ridge. Several of the name served in the Indian Wars as Minute Men, and several in the Revolutionary War. Of this number was John Chenowith, who lived and died in Frederick County. He enlisted in 1776, while temporarily in Hampshire County, entering as a private in Capt. Able Westfall's Company, which was assigned to Col. Peter Muhlenburg's Regiment. He was assigned to Capt. Cresap's Company of Col. Rawlings' Maryland Regiment in August, 1776; and was made a sergeant. His wife was Mary Pugh. She applied for a pension June 28, 1837, when she was 75 years old, while living in Randolph County, Virginia. The Pension Bureau, Washington, D. C., shows that the widow of John Chenowith lived in Kentucky later on, and received pension payable to Mary Buskirk. This indicates that she had remarried or that there were two John Chenowiths. Descendants of this family will find much to interest them in the old records of Frederick County, and also in the Pension Bureau.

The Faulkner Family of Berkeley County

We may not claim this family as one of the pioneers; but their prominence in the Lower Valley and identification with Frederick County, justifies a brief notice at this point. Hon. Chas. J. Faulkner, Sr., at one time claimed the old County as his birthplace. He was elected to Congress prior to the Civil War from this District. The writer remembers his campaign, with the eloquent A. R. Boteler as his opponent. He was minister to France in 1859; returned in 1861, was arrested by the Washington government; afterwards served as staff officer during the War. As shown elsewhere, he was a son-in-law of Genl. Boyd. His two sons, Senator C. J. Faulkner and E. Boyd Faulkner, have been identified with the best interests of West Virginia. The former lives at the ancestral home (Boydville, near Martinsburg. They are lawyers and statesmen of acknowledged ability. A sister married Dr. Love of Winchester. Mrs. Elizabeth Love is widely known as the President of the Winchester Chapter "Daughters of the Confederacy." She has two married daughters living in Hampton, Va., and another, Mrs. Bessie Latane of Winchester, wife of Dr. Latane.

It may be possible to find space for fuller

notice of this and other distinguished families of Berkeley, as well as Jefferson Counties. In the early days the Bedinger, Pendleton, Lucas, Gray, Lewis, Tabb, Cunningham, Harrison, Bell, Bryarly, Burnett and many other families of this class, were identified with the settlements. Many others have been mentioned elsewhere in this volume.

The Griffith Family

No effort will be made to write a sketch of this large family, whose many lines are found in almost every State in the Union; nor is it necessary to trace the family that came from Chester County, Penna., in 1777 and settled in Frederick County. The comprehensive genealogy, recently published and now found in the Griffith families, covers the period from their first arrival in America to the present date; and space will only admit of a bare mention of those who were numerous in Frederick County in the latter part of the 18th and during the 19th Centuries. The Griffiths were of Welsh origin. Three brothers emigrated from Wales because of their oppressions, and settled in Pennsylvania about 1716. One of the brothers named John was the ancestor of the Frederick County families of this name, which was spelled at the time of his arrival in America, in Welsh, Gruffydd; and then for the first time the name of Griffith or Griffiths, became established as a surname with the succeeding generations. John, 2nd, son of the John Griffith just mentioned, was born in Chester County, Penna., June 13, 1737; died in Frederick County, Virginia, Jany. 22, 1833. He married his first wife Oct. 11, 1768, in York, Penna. She was Mary, daughter of Jesse and Martha Faulkner. He married his second wife, Mary Ellis, who lived on Crooked Run East of Stephensburg, Frederick County, Va. No issue by this marriage. Children by his first wife were:

(1) Martha, born 1769, mar. Jos. Morgan, no issue.

(2) Mary, born 1771, mar. Asa Hoge.

(3) Jesse, born 1776; died 1777.

(4) John, born 1778, is the John Griffith in whom we are now interested. He was born in Frederick County, Va.; spent his long life of 92 years in the County, surrounded by his large progeny of several generations. His will is recorded in the County Clerk's Office, wherein he mentions his children, and devised a sum to be used by his son Aaron H., towards the repairs and improvement of the Hopewell Graveyard. He married Rachael, daughter of Joseph and Martha Hackney, Apl. 15, 1801. She died 1863. He had children by this marriage:

(1) Aaron H., born March 11, 1802.

(2) Mary, born May 27, 1804; mar. David Wright; no issue.

(3) Martha Ann, born Feb. 22, 1807; mar. Samuel F. Balderson. They reared a large family.

(4) Joseph H., born Dec. 14, 1809; died Mch. 3, 1870, unmarried.

(5) James H., born Feb. 3, 1812; mar. June 6, 1841, Jane R., daughter of David and Ann Lupton. He died 1899, and she in 1905. Issue: David L., Virginia, John McPherson, Rachael Anna, mar. Edwin Griffith in 1882; had several sons and daughters. Hannah, married Geo. D. Stone in 1875.

(6) Lydia H., born 1814, married Jesse Wright, 1842. Issue: John D. Wright, mar. Anne Cochran (two daughters by this marriage: Alice, mar. Benjamin Byers; Nellie, mar. Wilmer T. Hoffman). Rachael, unmarried. Mary Susan, mar. Frederick A. Cochran; his only son, Dr. F. A. Cochran, mar. Etha Clevenger. Martha E., mar. Wm. D. Bishop, 1887, Rebecca T., married Samuel R. Baldwin. Issue: Wm. W., Mary, Saml. R., and Joseph R. Joseph Richard married Annie E. Clagett. Samuel B. Wright, born 1859; died Sept. 29, 1893; married Elizabeth, daughter of Daniel Mellinger (Issue: Daniel. Jesse and Frederick C.)

(7) John W. Griffith, born Oct. 17, 1816, mar. Keziah, dau. of Seth and Mary Smith. He left several children.

(8) Richard Sidwell Griffith, born 1819, mar. Mary L. Newbold, of New Jersey; one daughter, Anna T.

(9) Robert D. Griffith, born 1821, never married.

(10) William P., born Mch. 8, 1824; mar. Mary V. Barnny. Issue: Fannie L., mar. E. T. Holt in 1887 (Issue son Harry); John B., Lulu, mar. Wm. McCarroll, and Anna T., mar. ——— Dunn.

(11) Aaron Hackney Griffith, born in Frederick County, Va., Mch. 11, 1802; died there in his old home Brookland, Feby. 8, 1877; married Apl. 15, 1830, Mary Parkins, dau. of Isaac and Hannah (Parkins) Hollingsworth. She was born July 15, 1809; died July 23, 1896. She became the mother of ten children, five sons and five daughters and lived to see several great-great-grandchildren. Mrs. Griffith was spared many of the infirmities of old age. She enjoyed unusual health and strength, and was thus enabled to maintain her reputation for good deeds, and a living example of the Virginia matron of *ye Olden time*. May her large posterity emulate her well-spent life. The names of the children of this family may be found under the head of Colonial places. See Brookland, etc.

The Griffith name once so numerous in the County, at this writing has been reduced to two children of Aaron H., viz: Richard Ed. and his sister Mary Ann (and Richard Ed. son of

Richard Ed., Sr.) The name was identified with the Applepie Ridge section. They were all Quakers and non-combatants in time of war. But in the study of the family history, the writer has found several of the family doing good service in the Union and Confederate Armies: one being H. H. Griffith, Capt. 1st Iowa Battery, which signalized itself in the 15th Army Corps, Genl. John A. Logan, commander.

On the Confederate side, several of the name distinguished themselves as soldiers; of this number perhaps Joseph T. Griffith, who has made Berryville his home since the War, may be mentioned as an example. He lived in Maryland until 1858, when he moved to Duffield, Jefferson County. When the storm of 1861 came, he forsook business and entered the Confederate Army, under Genl. Joseph E. Johnston, and served in the campaigns of Tenn. and Miss. This indicates that all the Griffiths were not non-combatants.

The Snapp Family

John Snapp, the progenitor of the large families found in the well-known "Snapp Neighborhood," about 7 miles S. W. from Winchester, owning their own homes, where many of the name have lived since John number 1 settled there about 1747 on one of the *Minor* Grants. He had three sons, John, Joseph and Henry. We find a lease from Lord Fairfax dated July 23, 1750, to John Snapp (No. 2) for 400 acres of land on the "East side of Little North Mountain, adjoining the tract of his father John Snapp on the South." (Known in later years as the Bengie Frye place). John, Jr., had three sons and two daughters, viz: John (3rd), Samuel, Joseph, Leah and Sally. Leah married Henry Wisecarver; Sally married ——— Saunders. Henry Snapp's children were: John, Edward, Elisha and Henry. John went to Ohio and raised a family. Edward's sons were: Joseph, Camillus and Henry. Elisha's children: Joseph H., Camillus, James W., Mary J. who married Eli Ashwood.

Henry's sons were: Cornelius, John E., Camillus and James. Joseph Snapp, grandson of John, Sr., was the father of John William, Joseph H., Morgan and Amanda who married John Henry Snapp; Catherine married Elijah Rudolph (no children). Jno. Wm.'s only child, Charles W. Snapp, lives on his father's homestead on the Cedar Creek Grade.

Joseph H. Snapp's children were Edward J., Benton, Tilden, Laura, Christina and Caroline.

Morgan W. Snapp's children were: Milton, Simon, Lloyd (dead), Albert, Alberta, Harriet and Jerusha. Alberta married H. C. Womeldorff. Harriet married Jno. Lamp. Jerusha married E. Smoke.

Children of John Snapp No. 3: John Henry, Martin, Mary who married Wm. Wilson, Catherine became the wife of Wm. Lupton. She had two sons, Joseph and John. The latter married and left one son, Wm. Lupton of Winchester, Va. Jane died single. John Henry's children were: Joseph (Dody), Josephine mar. Henry White, Victoria mar. Francis Peery. She lives at the old place of John Snapp, Sr. Dody married Martha, daughter of Joseph P. Richard, and lives at the home of his father, who died many years ago.

Martin Snapp, the great grandson of John, Sr., married Elizabeth Rudolph and was the father of Joseph M., who married Irene Cunningham. Issue: Catherine, Robert and Ethel. Jno. A. R., son of Martin Snapp, mar. Helen Snapp, daughter of Sydnor Snapp—no children. Martin's daughters were: Catherine mar. Silas Lupton; Mary B., mar. Mick Lupton: issue, son Charles; Jane mar. Snowden Lupton: issue, daughter, Vernon, mar. Jno. B. Bywaters; Mary, unmarried.

Alice, daughter of Martin, married Ed. Lupton; issue: Bettie, Harry and Rebecca.

Samuel Snapp, grandson of John No. 1, was the father of John William, Addison, Sydnor, Elizabeth, who became the second wife of Amos Pierce; no children; Rachael, married Wm. Tevalt; issue Strother and Morgan.

Joseph Snapp, grandson of John No. 1, was the father of Jacob and James, who has one son, Harvey.

Leah Wisecarver, daughter of John Snapp No. 1, had born by her marriage with Henry Wisecarver, the following children: Samuel, Abram, Joseph, Henry, Martin. Samuel and Abram were unmarried and died many years ago. Henry was twice married, leaving children by both wives.

Joseph was the father of William Henry, Jos. T., and James W. Wisecarver.

William Henry died in prison, having been captured by Federal scouts the night of his marriage.

Joseph T. and James have large families.

Martin, son of Henry Wisecarver, Sr., married Miss Bayliss; their one son S. Marion, married Miss Cuningham; now living in Campbell County, Va., and have children. Martin married for his second wife Miss Frye, daughter of James Frye, the gallant Confederate veteran who conducts a profitable market garden on South Main Street. Martin owns the old Wisecarver homestead in the "Snapp Neighborhood," but has retired from business and lives in his handsome home on Amherst Street. Mrs. Sally Saunders, granddaughter of John Snapp No. 1, had one son, Joseph, who moved to West Virginia. One daughter married Hiram Roe; her sister married

Robert Roe; both left children. Henry Wisecarver, Sr., died in 1858, aged 74 years. Considerable effort has been made to enumerate all the descendants of John Snapp, the first settler; but so far one line is not complete.

The Snapp family of Winchester will receive attention under another sketch, as it is believed the two families have no known connection. Neil, John B., James and Cornelius Snapp in the Rosenberger P. O. neighborhood, and the Snapps West of Middletown, are descendants of the pioneer Snapp family.

The Calmes Family

The founder of this family in the Shenandoah Valley when it was embraced in the territory of Spottsylvania County, was Marquis Calmes, who was forced to leave France in 1724, together with several hundred persons, by reason of their pronounced views on religious questions. This and other similar emigrations were known as Huguenots, who sought temporary asylum in England. Two colonies sailed for America in 1726; landed at Old Point Comfort, Virginia, and sought homes in that section. There was at that time a small colony of French emigrants in North Carolina, who induced a number of families to join their colony. Calmes and others founded homes near the James River below Richmond. The low lands, however, proved unhealthy for the French; and in 1734 they disposed of their holdings, some going to the mountain regions of Carolina, while others chose the mountain section of Virginia. Marquis Calmes secured one of the *Minor Grants* for land West of the Great Mountains, which Lord Fairfax confirmed by a deed, when he took up his abode at Greenway Court. As shown in the first chapters of this volume, Calmes was one of the justices composing the first court held in Frederick County, and is shown elsewhere as an officer of the Virginia Line Militia. He died just prior to the Indian and French War, and is supposed to have been buried on his farm known to this day as the Vineyard Plantation. His wife was Winifred Waller, of Lower Virginia. An old slab in Old Chapel Cemetery, bears this inscription: "Here lies the body of Winifred, the wife of Major Marquis Calmes. They were joined in wedlock 26 years and had six children. . . . She departed this life Oct. 6th, 1751."

One of the sons, William, married the daughter of Capt. George Neville. From this marriage, sprang a number of distinguished descendants. One of his sons, Marquis, was a distinguished officer in the Revolutionary War. Many persons have confounded this Marquis Calmes with his grandfather. Another son, Harry, was an officer in the War of 1812. Both of these brothers removed to Kentucky. One brother, Fielding Calmes, lived and died in Old Frederick County, Va. (now Clarke). He was born Aug. 30, 1766; married the daughter of William Helm, the son of Meredith Helm, an old settler. His homestead was known as "Helmly," which remained the home of succeeding generations. One of the sons, Geo. F. Calmes, died there in 1873; two of his sons, Fielding H. and Marquis, both were Confederate soldiers—Marquis a private in Company D., Sixth Va. Cavalry, was killed 1864. Fielding H. was born at the old Homestead 1832; was twice married. His first wife was the dau. of A. Moore, of Clarke County: two sons by this marriage are George G. and A. M. Calmes. Their father was the well-known Major Fielding Calmes who was a familiar figure to those who so often saw him with his lame arm, the result of a wound received in service. He enlisted as a private in Company D., First Va. Cavalry; was wounded near Charlestown, 1863; was then promoted Major and assigned to the 23rd Va. Cavalry. Major Calmes died a few years ago. Other branches of the Calmes family will receive notice, if data is received in time.

The Helm Family

This name appears in Virginia about 1700, when we find Leonard Helm in the territory that was soon to be known as the Shenandoah Valley. His will was probated in Frederick County, Va., Dec. 5, 1745. He mentions his children: Meredith, Leonard, Mayberry, Joseph, Christopher and his youngest daughter, Bridget Madison. Meredith and Leonard qualified as executors. Doubtless the founder of the Valley family left his native country, England, with other members of the older set, landing on Long Island 1675. Thomas Helm was a resident there for several years, and is supposed to be the father of the Leonard named. "A history of the Parochial Chapelry of Goosnargh, Lancashire, England, by Henry Fishnick, F. H. S." gives interesting facts relating to the Helm family, who were prominent during the 16th and 17th Centuries. The family names, appearing in America far into the 18th and 19th Centuries, bear unmistakable evidence that this Leonard Helm was one of this English family. Meredith Helm who appears as one of the Justices of the first court held in Frederick County, 1743, and Sheriff in 1753, and who frequently appears in public life until his death in 1768, lived near Winchester at one time. His plantations were in that part of the county known at this writing as Clarke. He died intestate; but the settlement of his estate shows two of his sons, Meredith and Thomas, as his administrators. Meredith married Margaret Neill; and Thomas married Elizabeth Neill. The descendants of these marriages are too numerous to mention in this connection. The author is in correspondence with the line of Thomas Helm, the co-admr. of Meredith. He was a Justice of the Peace when the Revolutionary War began. Thomas had four sons, and probably more: William, Joseph B., Thomas and Meredith. One of Joseph's descendants, Mrs. John T. Doneghy, lives in Macon, Mo. Many of the name live in Kentucky.

Capt. Leonard Helm commanded a company in the George Rogers Clarke expedition to old Fort St. Vincent, and obtained land bounty for his services. (See list of Companies in this Vol.)

The Glaize Family

The first recorded evidence we have of this family in Frederick County, was in 1784, when the pioneer George Glaize—name written in German "Kloess" was "listed a resident who desired to become a citizen, he having been administered the oaths." He was the son of Frederick Kloess of Pennsylvania. He purchased a tract of land West of Winchester in 1786, on what was known then as "Title Bond," which guaranteed a deed of conveyance when the last payment was made. The tract was what has been referred to several times in this volume as the *Hessian Prisoners* farm. The pioneer was settled there in 1790, as a taxpayer. He was married to Catherine Hetzel before he left Pennsylvania. They lived at this place until his death in 1823, and there raised five sons and one daughter, viz: Sampson, Henry, Solomon, George, John H. and Joannah. Sampson married Elizabeth Renner, having three sons and several daughters by this marriage. George F., the oldest son, was born 1827. He entered the Confederate Army in 1861; was 1st Lt. in the 23rd Va. Cavalry, serving faithfully through the entire war; then resumed the lumber business that he had started in 1854, which he successfully conducted up to his death. He married Alice E., daughter of Henry Stine, of Fredk. County, in 1875. One son by this marriage, Frederick L., born 1876, succeeded his father and conducted business at his father's well-known place near the B. &. O. Railroad station. His thrift, energy and intelligence has been rewarded in extensive improvements showing at this writing—planing mills, sash and door factory, and all ornamental work for modern buildings, and heavy stock of lumber.

George F. Glaize's two brothers were Isaac N. and Henry W. Isaac N. Glaize entered the Confederate Army in the 2nd Va. Infantry, and was killed in the first battle of Manassas, July 21, 1861. He was found dead after Stonewall Jackson's first bayonet charge, lying dead beside two dead Union soldiers—all three having fatal bayonet thrusts, telling the mute story that he had killed his two antagonists before he fell. Isaac was a fine specimen of the Valley soldier—a large muscular man and an adept in bayonet drill. Henry W. was a member of the 12th Va. Cavalry, serving faithfully until Lee's surrender. He was wounded in the Battle of the Wilderness, May 5, 1864.

Solomon Glaize, the second son of the pioneer, was born Jan. 21, 1796. He was twice married; his first wife being Elizabeth Streit, in 1825; she died in 1837. His second wife was Elizabeth Fries, married 1839; she died July 6, 1875. He had 7 children. We can recall the following who survived him: John W., Mrs. Henry Stine, Mrs. Isaac Stine, Miss Rachael and David S. Glaize. The last named was born Aug. 23, 1842. He was a Confederate soldier; was captured in Feby., 1862; was a prisoner in Camp Chase, Ohio, for 7 months, when he was exchanged at Vicksburg, Miss. He was deputy Sheriff for two years after the war, deputy county treasurer for about 10 years, and was appointed Treasurer in 1888 to succeed John H. Wotring who died in office. He married Elizabeth B. Baker, daughter of J. Milton Baker, Feb. 26, 1885. One son was born to them May 31, 1888, David Brevitt Glaize, whose life-sized statue marks his grave in Mt. Hebron Cemetery.

Henry Glaize, the third son of George the pioneer, was born 1794. His wife was Miss Yeakley. They had a large family, only three of whom can be recalled by the writer, viz: John Glaize, George F. and Mrs. Vance Bell. John was the Capt. John Glaize, the well-known Quartermaster of Stonewall Jackson's Corps. He was largely engaged in the steam sawmill business before the war, which he resumed after peace was declared. He was a Justice of the Peace prior to the War, and Sheriff 1867-68. At one time he was President of the City Council of Winchester. He married Selina G., daughter of Edwin S. Baker, issue by this marriage, five children. One son is now clerk in the Winchester postoffice.

George F. Glaize, brother of Captain John, was a successful farmer, and lived for years near Gainsboro. He was the father of several children. One son, Henry C., a prosperous farmer lived South of Opecquon postoffice. One daughter became the wife of Joseph O. Bywaters; one is the wife of W. S. Hiett; and one the wife of Albert Williams. Two sons, Luther and Jefferson left Frederick County several years ago.

Henry C. married Ellen, daughter of Joshua

Lupton: two sons by this marriage are Conly and Harry Glaize.

Henry Glaize, the father, was a soldier in the War of 1812.

The Fries Family

This family boasts of unnumbered descendants. The "Family Reunions" have their long list increased by the reports from the scattered tribe. They have been noted for their thrift and industry. The pioneer of this family was Martin Fries, a German, who emigrated from Pennsylvania during the latter part of the Revolutionary War, bringing with him sons and daughters, viz: Elizabeth, Mary, Michael, Catherine, David, Rebecca, Anne, and Jacob. From this family have sprung many branches; intermarrying with numerous other families, their progeny is too extensive to follow. The writer has repeatedly solicited many of the name to furnish him data to comprise an intelligent sketch of the family. The old records show the names of Martin, Jacob, John, Abraham, Isaac, George of the older set; while the familiar names of the next generation show that Martin, Josiah, George Y., David, Jesse and others figured; while another gives the names of some of their children: David A., George M., John B., sons of Josiah. J. Courcy and brothers, sons of George Y.; and also sons of George C., Edward, etc. This family was noted for their loyalty to the Union cause during the Civil War, Josiah being a single exception. He lived and died an ardent friend of the South, and also a Democrat in politics, as was also his son David A. The son owned the large brick house near Back Creek on the North side of the N. W. Turnpike. On his way home a few years ago, he was drowned in attempting to ford "Gap Run," where the turnpike crossed it. About two years thereafter, the roadway was changed to the North bank of the stream, to avoid the crossing.

The old pioneer settled near the site of the present village of White Hall; and the numerous families have chiefly lived in what is known as the Applepie Ridge section, gradually extending towards Winchester. Some of them own splendid farms, Jesse being one of the largest landowners in that section.

The Branson Family

Three brothers of this name, viz: David W., Nathaniel B. and Jonathan W. were well known to the writer. They were honorable and upright men; who lived on their own farms near Clearbrook, Frederick County, and were prosperous farmers. They and their ancestors were members of the Old Hopewell Meeting, where the Society of Friends have held their service since 1755. Their grandfather Abraham Branson resided in Stafford County, Virginia, where he was born in 1754. He married Catherine Reese, daughter of Henry Reese, of Frederick County, Oct. 22, 1779, where the pair lived and died. One son by this marriage Reese Branson (his mother dying a few years after his birth). His father Abraham afterwards married a Miss White, of Frederick County. Issue by this marriage: Mary (who became the wife of Joseph Fawcett) and six sons: William, Nathaniel, Isaac, Thomas, Joseph and Benjamin, all of whom removed westward except Thomas and Joseph. Thomas lived and died in Frederick in his eighty-third year. Joseph married Tacy, daughter of Jonathan and Hannah Wright, of Frederick County, Apl. 11, 1827. They lived and died in the home their father had enjoyed so long, and became the parents of the three brothers first named above. David W. married Ann, daughter of Wm. E. and Sarah Bailey of Chester County, Penna., and spent their lives in the old home. One son, William E., survives the parents and lives on the old homestead. David W. made many surveys of lands for his neighbors.

Nathaniel B. Branson married Nancy, daughter of Elijah and Elizabeth Holmes, of Loudoun County, Va. Two children survive the parents, Joseph H. and Mary E. The son is a successful physician in Washington, D. C.

Jonathan W. Branson married Caroline, daughter of Edward L. and Elizabeth R. Cunningham, of Harford County, Md. They had two children, Tacy and Lillian. This surviving brother lives on part of the old homestead, and while in good health and prospering in business, has had his full share of sorrow and trials.

These brothers had one sister, Ruth Hannah, who married Samuel H., son of Joshua and Mary Mathews, of Baltimore City, Sept. 11, 1860. The issue of this marriage: Tacy B., Joshua H., and Mary M. Mathews.

The Adams Family

This was one of the families to settle on Back Creek, Frederick County, about 1755, the pioneer being William Adams, who came from West Jersey with several sons and daughters. We can trace but one son, Thomas Adams, who was born in Virginia in 1772. There is evidence that he was a son of the second marriage. He became the father of the well-known men who have been enterprising farmers in the section where the grandfather settled; they were W. Wash Adams, Martin M., James H., Thomas J., and John Dean. They had two sisters, Ellen A. and Albena. Wm. Wash. was born Mch. 6, 1815, and married Sarah C., daughter of Wm. Brown: issue from this union, T. Carson Adams, who married Bertie, dau. of Wm. H. Anderson. T. Carson is the well known J. P. who has served in this office for several terms. Martin M., son of Thos. Adams, was born July 30, 1817. He never married until 1862, when he married daughter of Alfred Garrett, of Fredk. County, who came from Loudoun County, Va., and lived on Back Creek. Mr. Garrett was one of the *Old Ironside* Baptists, and took pleasure in expressing his views on religious subjects. Two sons, Ernest W. and Thomas G., survive their father, Martin M. May they emulate his good principles and deeds. The writer was associated with Mr. Adams when he was a member .of the Board of Supervisors of Frederick County, and could point to many of his splendid traits. Martin M. was a prisoner with the Rev. Dr. Boyd (notice of which has been made).

John Dean Adams, one of the sons of Thomas, was born in 1832. He married Hannah, daughter of Gideon Zirkle of Shenandoah County: issue by this union, Wm. Z., Chas R., Gertrude M. and John S., who survive their father, who died about 1905 on his fine farm near Whitehall, Frederick County. The Adams brothers were ardent sympathizers in the South's great struggle, Capt. Jack Adams attesting this in many severe engagements. He was Captain of Company K, 23rd Regt. of Va. Cavalry. His home for many years after the war was in Shenandoah County, where he died in 1906. His grave is in Stonewall Cemetery, Winchester, where his remains were placed by his surviving comrades with military honors.

Cotemporary with the Adams family, were the Jackson, Robinson, DeHaven, Clark and other well-known families. If space will permit, special notice will be given them, as being of the number who have been found on Back Creek below Gainsboro for 150 years.

The Jackson Family

This once numerous family in Back Creek section, has gone with other changes. Mr. Jonathan Jackson and his son now living near the Gainsboro village, are holding on as landmarks of their busy ancestors of that name. The pioneer of the family was Josiah Jackson, the same who married into the family of Joseph Steer, already mentioned as one of the first settlers. There were six sons and four daughters born of this union. The descendants became numerous; and several of the name found along the Opecquon and vicinity of Winchester, trace their lines from Josiah.

Samuel Jackson, oldest son of Josiah, born on Back Creek in 1760 and died 1845, spent nearly his entire life in the same section. He married Miss McVeigh of Loudoun County, Va. Issue of this union: Benjamin F., Margaret A., Jonathan and Ruth G. Jonathan married Janie S., dau. of Archibald and Lydia Robinson, in 1873. One child by this marriage is the well-known Llewellyn Jackson—farmer, merchant and telephone operator. To his enterprise is largely due the good service their line gives to the Back Creek and other sections. Jonathan Jackson was born June 27, 1832; consequently he may be regarded as an old man, but he is still hale and hearty, and has his second wife. Mr. Jackson has always taken an interest in politics, being a Democrat. His parents were Friends, and enjoyed the esteem of the community.

The Robinson Family

From the very earliest settlement of the Valley, this family name appears. Some trace of their entrance to this Shenandoah section, from the head springs of Robinsons River, which are found East of the Blue Ridge, referred to in Lord Fairfax's grant as his starting point. The family is of Irish origin; and some have thought they came with the immigration that came direct from Ireland through the influence of the Scotch-Irish element that settled in the Valley in 1734-8. The ancestor of this branch of the family was James Robinson, who was a noted Irish weaver. There are so many descendants of this old emigrant, that we will only mention a few names familiar in the Back Creek section during the 19th Century, commencing with Andrew A. Robinson, who was born in this section 1781. He was father of Archibald, Jackson, James, Jonathan, Mary Jane, David, Josiah, Joseph, Andrew A., and William, and perhaps more. Following the various lines, we find the name quite numerous. Nearly all those named are dead, having filled out their useful lives principally as farmers, noted for their good management. Their homes were attractive and unstinted hospitality prevailed. Connected with the Society of Friends, they were non-combatants during all wars, though several of this name appear during the Revolutionary War as soldiers. During the Civil War, they were for the Union. Mr. A. A. Robinson was an exception. He died at an advanced age in 1907. He had served several terms as Commissioner of the Revenue for the Northern District, and Assessor of Lands. The neatness of his work as found in the records of the County Clerk's Office have often attracted attention. The generation following, show some very enterprising men as farmers, fruit-growers and merchants. Wm. T. Robinson the well-known farmer near Clearbrook being one; James W. Robinson living near Winchester on the Pughtown Turnpike, so well known for his marvelous success as an orchardist, with his fine apple orchards on either side, which tell of great results accomplished. His orchards in 1907 yielded full $20,000 in gross receipts. This family intermarried with the Steer, Jackson, Clevenger and other well-known families. Several years ago Mr. Frank Clevenger, of Wilmington, Ohio, a well-known lawyer, married Miss Robinson, daughter of Jonathan Robinson. Her two brothers, D. A. and J. W., live in Frederick County.

The Clevenger Family

This family, though not one of the oldest, has continuously resided in Frederick County for over one hundred years. They have been found in several sections of the county, chiefly in what is now known as Stonewall Magisterial District. The Gainsboro District had the John Clevenger branch. East of Stephens City may be found at this writing John W. Clevenger and his family. The well-known families of Alfred, Thomas, Asa and others North of Winchester, are well represented. James T. Clevenger, son of Alfred, and his sons, are large land-owners, and very successful farmers. James T. married Constance, dau. of Chas. E. Evard, in 1861. His wife inherited one-half the Hackwood farm; their children being Louie R., Robt. G., Ernest B., and Carrie I. Mr. J. T. Clevenger's sister married John W. McKown.

Chas. E. Clevenger has been mentioned as one of the Supervisors of Frederick County. He lives on the Opecquon, as does his brother, B. Frank. Both have been successful farmers. The home of the former was formerly owned by Mr. Richard Hardesty.

The McKown Family

This well-known family was one of the old Irish families to settle in Old Frederick, now Berkeley County, West Va. There the name grew numerous; and large influential families have been prominent residents in the rich farming sections of that county. The monuments standing in the old Gerardstown Churchyard show where many of them lived and died. Mr. John W. McKown the highly esteemed citizen at the village of Grimes, represents the Frederick County family. His father was Warner McKown, who removed from Berkeley County and lived on one of the celebrated Applepie Ridge farms. He was the son of Samuel McKown, whose father was one of the Irish immigrants prior to the Revolutionary War.

John W. was born in Berkeley County in 1838, and came to Frederick with his father when two years old. He married Fannie, dau. of Alfred Clevenger: issue by this marriage, Wm. A., Clara A. and Ada G. Mr. McKown rendered efficient service as Commissioner of Roads in Stonewall District for several terms.

The Bailey Family

This name comprises the three families of John W., Jesse R., and Charles P. Bailey, and their children, all well known in Frederick. John W. lives near Whitehall; Charles P. at Greenspring, merchant and farmer. His two sons are popular merchants conducting the store on the Hitching Yard property; while Jesse R. owns the Alfred Parkins property on the Front Royal Turnpike. All are prosperous men and highly esteemed by their friends. They are sons of William Bailey, whose father was Wm. P. Bailey, who came from Loudoun County in the early part of the 19th Century. He was the owner of the Greenspring Woolen Factory, and there conducted a thriving business up to the time of his death in 1834. Then William conducted the factory until 1861, when it was destroyed by fire.

The Barrett Family

The Barrett name has been familiar in the county records since 1749, when Arthur Barrett, an English Quaker, settled on Applepie Ridge. The farm has never gone out of the Barrett family. This was the home of Joel Barrett at the time of his death a few years ago. The writer knew the splendid old men of the third generation, Jonathan, Joel and Benjamin—all now dead. Some of their sons and daughters are well-known citizens of the county.

The Yeakley Family

The progenitor of this family was John Yeakley, who settled in Frederick County at the close of the Revolutionary War, in 1783; then declared his intentions to become a citizen of the county; took the oaths required, and was listed for taxation. He married a daughter of Michael Fries; issue six daughters and three sons. One of the sons, George, married a daughter of Abner Babb: children by this union were John A., James H., Wm. R., Rees B., Martin F. Among those who married and left children we mention Wm. R. who married Rachael dau. of Martin Fries: issue, Laura V., Geo. H., Martin L., Molly C., John W., Robt. D., and Taylor B. He lived and died on his farm North of Winchester, adjoining the old Cooke "Glengarry" farm on the West. He was a Confederate soldier, and was wounded. Mr. Yeakley was an honorable, upright man. He was born 1831. John A. and James H. Yeakley left children. Martin F. Yeakley was born 1835. He was a Confederate soldier. In 1872 he married Martha A. daughter of Rev. William Hodgson (see mention of his life in connection with sketch of Round Hill M. E. Church). By this union they have William Holmes, a popular physician in Cumberland, Md., who married Miss Ransom, of Staunton, and Catherine E. who is now the wife of Dr. J. A. Richard, a dentist in Winchester.

The Bond Family

The first of this family to appear in Frederick County was John Bond, who was living on Cacapon River about 1816. He previously lived in Shenandoah County, where his son Abner was born Oct. 10, 1801. They settled on what has been known as the Lost Stream farm, taking its name from two streams flowing from springs near the house. These streams suddenly disappear, following a subterranean channel to an outlet a half mile distant. John L. Bond, son of Abner, owns the fine place, where he enjoys all the comforts that his splendid home affords. He married Ann M., dau. of Jonah H. and Lydia Lupton, in 1873. Mr. Bond has been one of the Commissioners of Elections for many years. The members of the Bond family have always been consistent members of the Society of Friends. John L. Bond's only sister, Rachael, married Jacob Harman and removed to Indiana many years ago. The old homestead was settled by Wm. Lupton. His son Samuel built the Colonial house which stands near the modern structure of brick.

George Ruble lives in the large brick house about one mile North, built by David Lupton prior to 1800.

In this connection we will add that George Ruble's ancestor, Peter, 1st, was one of the oldest settlers in the North end of Frederick, and controlled large tracts of land. He saw service in the Revolutionary War.

It may be of interest to many readers to mention in this connection, that a great many tracts of land were parceled out by Alexander Ross for settlement of a number of families; and as he was a Quaker, that section lying North of Winchester became known as the Quaker settlement. This does not imply that all such settlers were Friends or Quakers; for we find the names of such old families as Babb, Mercer, Gerard, Bryan, Bryant, O'Farrell, O'Roke, Chenowith, Beeler, Rouse, McCormick, Beesons, Haines, Littler, Bowen, Quinn, Daugherty, Denton and many others—none of whom had any connection with the Society of Friends. It has been asserted by several writers—Hawks in 1836, and Norris in 1890, that Ross had a grant for 40,000 acres of land dated 1730. This statement is not sustained by any record. This matter has been fully treated elsewhere; but it may be well to say here that the first grant received was dated 22nd November, 1734, for 2,373 acres (See MS Journal of Governor's Council, Land Office, Richmond, Va.) And Ross was not fully prepared to legally seat families for about ten years after he secured his order to make surveys, etc. The first deed made by Ross to any settler was to Joseph Bryan for 214 acres, dated Apl. 13, 1744. Many of his surveys were contested by Lord Fairfax; and some of the settlers paid the quit rents demanded rather than litigate the claims. Ross obtained several other grants for such land upon which he could seat settlers, but very few ever matured, as he was enjoined by Joist Hite.

The Hackney, Jolliffe, Neil, Rees and other old families of this section referred to, may receive fuller notice if space permits. We turn aside for the present to mention a few families in Gainsboro District. The Smith family of Back Creek Valley has been given space to show their large connection with other families. Many of the old families living in that section prior to 1800, are well represented at this writing by their descendants, while others have entirely disappeared. Of the former we have the Whitacres, Rinkers, Braithwaites, Bakers, Browns, Allemongs, Brannons, McIntyres, Pughs, Shades, DeHavens, Heironimous and McIlwees.

Conrad Heironimous was there in 1758, though he did not become a land owner until 1767.

There was a time in the history of that section and within the memory of the writer, when names that are now silent exerted great influence in shaping the affairs of that section of the county, and whose names 'ere another decade is gone, will seldom be mentioned there, or their splendid traits and acts be recalled by the rising generation—a sad commentary upon the families that continually fall away after their strength is spent!

The Cather Family

James Cather who lived and died at his home "Flint Ridge" situated in Western Frederick, was well known to the writer and enjoyed his hospitality often. Mr. Cather was largely above the average farmer in intellect. Possessed with rare physical strength and wonderful energy,—these qualities gave him many advantages over weaker men. Always informed on the current topics of the day, his conversational qualities were admirable. Young men were always benefited by having him as a friend. Mr. Cather was born in 1795, in Frederick County, of Scotch-Irish parents, in the house where he spent his long life of eighty years. He married Ann Howard, a daughter of that Irish family so well known in that section a half century ago. From the old home, they sent out into the world a large family of sons and daughters, well equipped for the affairs of life, some of whom became prominent in their several walks and struggles in life. All are now gone; their places are fast becoming shadows of the past. But it is a pleasure to be able to record here, that some of the descendants are maintaining the principles taught by their elders, and have adhered to lessons of integrity that went with them from the old home. The children were: Perry, John, William, Clark, J. Howard, Adaline, (who was Mrs. John Purcell) and Sidney (who was the wife of Mahlon Gore.)

John Cather once lived on Hogue Creek, but removed to Missouri; and there reared several children. His two daughters returned to Frederick County after the father's death, and received their education in Winchester. One, Fannie, married her cousin, Jonah Cather. Miss Addie was the well-known teacher in Fairfax College. She afterwards became the second wife of Dr. John S. Lupton. William the third son lived in Frederick County until about 1880, when he and his family removed to Nebraska. He was appointed Sheriff by the Military government after the Civil War. His two sons George and Charles were his deputies. William erected the large brick house on the N. W. Turnpike near Back Creek, and there lived for several years.

Clark Cather the fourth son of James, married Margaret A., daughter of Jonah Lupton (see Lupton Sketch). He was a prosperous farmer, and lived and died in the brick house where his son James now lives. He was a consistent Christian gentleman; was an Elder of the Loudoun Street Presb. Church and Round Hill Church. Two of his sons James and Clark, as stated elsewhere, are members of the Board of Supervisors of Frederick County. J. Howard, the 5th son, married Millicent Lupton, and lived for many years on the old Major White property near Hogue Creek. No children. He was an Elder and devout member of the Hayfield Presb. Church.

Mrs. Sidney Gore, widow of Mahlon Gore, who was the merchant of the only store in Back Creek Valley prior to his death in 1860, was one of the most remarkable women in her day. She was left with three young sons, dependent upon her own resources, which comprised intellect, endless energy and unswerving integrity. She chose her task to support the young family and fit her sons for the future—both as to this life and that beyond. How well she did the work is attested by the "Valley Home" and its many adjoining acres, and the useful lives of her sons, who adorned their professions. Two of them became scholars of national reputation. Prof. Joshua W. Gore, of the University of North Carolina, where he died in 1907, after long years of service. Professor J. Howard Gore, the other, of Washington, D. C., well known for his literary work, as author of text book on Geological and Geodesy Surveys, "Handbook of Technical German," etc. He married in 1889 Miss Sarrendahl, of Sweden, having one child, now dead. Perry C. Gore, the oldest brother, for many years during the latter part of his life, was identified with the affairs of the county. He served several terms as high sheriff, filling his office acceptably to all. His life was an example for good. His courteous manners, firm purpose, strong will, supported by his integrity and Christian life, reflected credit upon the Mother for whom he bore the tenderest filial affection. In 1877 he married Laura C. Campbell. (See Old Homestead Sketch.)

Mrs. Sidney Gore's work embraced every walk in life—helping the needy; educating young men who became prominent ministers of the Gospel.

Adaline J. dau. of James Cather married John Purcell, of Frederick County, upon his return from the gold fields of California, he being one of the old Forty-Niners who made the overland trip with wagons and pack mules. Mr. Purcell's family is not one of the old settlers; but a brief sketch at this point may properly appear in connection with the Cather family.

The Purcell Family

This family came from Loudoun County, Virginia. Purcell brought with him his young children: Pleasant, Mary, Joseph, Mordecai, Thomas, "Lott," Lydia Ann, Rosanna, Priscilla, John, Rebecca and Elias. Possibly several of the younger children were born in Frederick. Their mother was Mary Jane dau. of Joseph Janney, of Loudoun County. The Purcell ancestors were Irish. Not one of the children named are living. As already stated, John married Adaline Cather, whose Christian life should be as "bread cast upon the waters." Her family and the community in which she lived, may find it as their days roll by; and it is hoped they may emulate her example. Mrs. Purcell was a devout Presbyterian. She was the mother of six children, four of whom are living: Anna L. wife of Edw. Foreman, Mary I., wife of Dr. *Mac* Janney, Clark H., and J. Perry. Both parents died several years ago.

Clark H. is one of the most prosperous business men in Frederick County, owning several fine farms, orchards, etc. His home was one of the Colonials; became the property of the Byrarly family, known as "Long Green." This is in the Applepie Ridge section. There Clark's father lived and died, who was noted for his unbounded hospitality. Being a prosperous man, he indulged his generosity to such an extent, that it became known as the *Wanderers Home*. The writer had many persons to tell him of the kind acts of John Purcell and his estimable wife. His son Clark continues to keep the latch string on the outside; and as his acquaintance is large, his guests are numerous and of all types. Clark has been High Sheriff since the death of Perry C. Gore, and is an efficient officer. His wife was Miss Bertha Siler. No children.

J. Perry, at this writing, is in business in Winchester. He married a daughter of J. H. Clayton and has two children. Pleasant P. daughter of John Purcell married Stacy J. Tavenner, who will be mentioned as one of the old citizens on the Opecquon. Lott married and his children and their children are well known in the county. Mr. T. V. Purcell and his family live East of Winchester, engaged in trucking, etc. He was once a merchant in Winchester. Samuel M. Purcell of Brucetown has been the "undertaker" for that section for many years. Mordecai never married. Rebecca became the wife of William Lodge. Elias was married. His only dau. married Dr. J. E. Janney, who left two children, Elias and Rose to inherit the two estates.

The Wood Family of Back Creek

William Wood who once owned the farm the home of Jonah Tavenner, was a prominent man in the early part of the 19th Century. He was one of the old Justices; and when Senior Justice, became High Sheriff of the county. It is not known what connection he was to several other families who bore his name. One of his daughters Martha A. married Edwin S. Baker in 1845. One Selena became the first wife of Wm. H. Gold. Algernon was a lawyer and moved further South. Mary Jane married Capt. Pugh of Hampshire County. There were three other sons, David, William and Joseph. All died years ago, single.

The Lovett Family

This name has been familiar to the writer his entire life; for he knew Mahlon S. Lovett the county surveyor prior to the Civil War. He was 6 feet 8 inches in height with a large muscular frame. Mr. Lovett's home was near the ford where the old Indian Hollow Road crosses Back Creek. The large brick house seen there to-day was where Mr. Lovett delighted to entertain the dignitaries of the County. He had quite a literary vein; wrote many interesting articles on politics, agriculture, etc., and wrote many poems of rare sentiment and choice expression. Mr. Lovett's wife was Miss Muse, who became the mother of a large family, all of whom are probably dead. The sons were Byron, Julian, Winfield S., Fannie, Cornelia and Ida E. Fannie was the wife of Capt. Hatcher, of Loudoun. Their children were R. Fred, lives in Washington City, engaged in the real estate business. His wife was Miss Hall. Lind another brother, and Ada, married and lives in Washington.

Ida E. became the wife of James C. Pugh, 1886.

Byron Lovett married Miss Bryarly. They had two children, James B. Lovett, principal of the Shen. Valley Academy for several years. His sister married and removed South.

The Denver Family

This family has been fully mentioned in sketch of Wm. Campbell's family, Patrick, Jr., having married his daughter in 1817. Within a few years thereafter, they established a home on Hogue Creek and named it "Selma" (The home mentioned in the Mahlon S. Lovett Sketch); and there continued to live until their removal to Ohio about 1840. Patrick Denver, Jr., was a son of Patrick Denver who was one of the leaders in the Irish Rebellion in the latter part of the 18th Century; and for this reason, doubtless, he emigrated to America, landing in 1799, on the day that witnessed the funeral of George Washington. He loitered some time along the Atlantic coast; for his first appearance in Frederick County was not until 1803. He located his family on a farm now known as the old Nathaniel Lupton farm on the N. W. Turnpike. There he lived until his death March 31, 1831, when his body was laid to rest in the Old Catholic Cemetery at the East end of Piccadilly Street, Winchester, Va. His remains were removed a few years ago to the New Catholic Cemetery, South Market and Kent Streets. What composed his family, is not definitely known. He had three sons, however, who were Arthur, Daniel and Patrick. Arthur was a seafaring man. The writer was informed by his father when a boy, that Arthur was always called Captain Denver on his occasional visits to his father; and was regarded by those who knew him as one of the *privateers,* who sailed the ocean from 1812 to 1824, and found the trade profitable. The Captain's last visit was just before his father's death. At that time he furnished *cash* to pay a mortgage on the farm. He was never heard from after this visit. Daniel the other brother, lost his eyesight as he grew older, and was amply provided for by his nephew General Denver. He resided in the neighborhood of Mr. James Cather, who was the General's agent to look after his uncle until his death. The writer knew Daniel Denver. He was an intelligent man, and remembered his arrival in Virginia, and why the family left their home in

County Down, Ireland. Such recollections call to mind many incidents pertaining to the lives of the families mentioned in this sketch, but they do not properly belong to this work.

The Lockhart Family

This was once a large family in Gainsboro District; but the name no longer appears in that part of the county. The old homestead of this family as known by the writer, was where two very old buildings now stand on the West side of the N. W. Turnpike near Gore; the store of John W. Parish being the next building on the same side of the road. This old group of buildings was the celebrated Lockhart Tavern. Here the writer saw Genl. Josiah Lockhart. In later years after the marriage of his children and death of his wife, he turned over the tavern and farm to his son Robert, and removed his home to another farm Southward on Timber Ridge, now the home of Thomas E. Morrison. Two of his sons John and Thomas went to Missouri; Samuel to Western Virginia. Two daughters married and moved to Ohio. One was Emeline who married Mr. Lovett; the other, Margery, married Mr. Gore, an engineer who assisted in the survey of the N. W. Turnpike. As already stated, Rebecca A. married R. M. Campbell; and the youngest Margaret B. married Joshua S. Lupton. Mary Jane married Sydnor McDonald.

Robert V. Lockhart continued the tavern business until his death. He was a man of remarkable traits; was intelligent, generous, and wielded a large influence in the neighborhood. He was true to principles and friends; but having general intercourse with all classes, he occasionally incurred the displeasure of some evil-minded men who never dared confront him on equal footing. Two such bided their time, and securing the services of a gang of Yankee soldiers and scouts, hunted him down during the Civil War and shot him to death in his ice house, where they found him secreted. These two men whom he had helped in many ways, were strongly condemned by their neighbors for the dastardly act; and after the war sought other places to end their days. Robert V. married Mary dau. of Col. James B. Hall, and was the father of a large family, that are too scattered to attempt further mention. Genl. Lockhart was a tall, muscular man, of dignified style and manners. He was at one time General of the Militia Brigade of this District; and was an officer of the War of 1812, as was also his brother Samuel Lockhart, who was commissioned Captain May 22, 1811. They were the sons of Robert, Sr., who had a grant for large tracts.

Turner Scrivener, who lives in Back Creek Dist. married a daughter of Bev. Lockhart, Esq.

The Bywaters Family

This family became first known to Back Creek Valley about the beginning of the 19th Century, when the ancestor of the family came from the East side of the Blue Ridge, where can now be found relatives of the family. They selected a limestone farm West of Pughtown, and there the family the writer knew, was raised, only three of whom he will mention: Robert C., Joseph P., and Asenath Bywaters who married Alfred Garrett. Robert C. succeeded the father as head of the family. There he lived until about 1884, when he sold out to Jacob Emmart and removed to Kentucky. Two of his children remained in Frederick County. One was Joseph O., already mentioned as living on the Cedar Creek Grade. Robert was a man of exemplary character. His brother Jos. P. was a physician; he went to Ohio and first practiced at Groveport, becoming very successful. He married Miss Mattie Fergusson of that place. She has been previously mentioned in the Cartmell Sketch. They frequently visited Frederick County previous to the Civil War. He and his wife ministered to the wants of Confederate prisoners at Camp Chase, Ohio. The Doctor survived the War only a few years. His grave may be found in the family lot at the old homestead, with suitable monument marking the place. Other graves show who were the ancestors. The old house occupied now by Edward Emmart, son of Jacob F., deceased, is supposed to have been erected by the Curlett family prior to the Revolutionary War. His brother Clinton Emmart lives adjoining him. Mr. Bywaters made some changes in the house during his incumbency. Back Creek flows through the farm. A celebrated spring at this place has been known as the Bywaters Spring for a century; and traditionary history gives this as a place of settlement by the Smith family at an early day. We give the statement made by Mr. Wm. R. Smith for what it may be worth to others, who may probe the mysteries of the past with more success than the writer, who is unable to substantiate the statement from any recorded evidence.

The Smith Family of Back Creek Valley, as given by Mr. Wm. R. Smith.

Jeremiah Smith was the pioneer settler of this Valley. He came from New Jersey in company with two other men (names not known) about 1730, before the settlement of the Shenandoah Valley. They camped at what is now known as Bywaters Spring, on the banks of Back Creek, just below the historic Back Creek Valley. After staying there three months, they returned to New Jersey. Smith remarried in

New Jersey and returned to Virginia. While in Virginia the first time, he marked out a farm, which afterwards was subdivided and became what was William Smith's farm, Samuel Smith's farm, the Old Home Farm, just North, and running down to the tollgate at Back Creek, the Jo. Davis farm, the Seibert farm, and the Sampson Frum farm. The tract comprised all of the little valley that lies before the traveler, when he passes through the mountain going West, and comes in sight of Back Creek. When Smith returned with his wife, he took possession of this tract of land; built a house just a little Northwest of where the turnpike crosses Back Creek in going to Romney; where he raised a large family, and divided his land among his children.

Jeremiah Smith had born to him one child, a son, by his New Jersey wife. She died. The son grew to manhood; went with his mother's people to the Carolinas; volunteered in the Revolutionary Army, and died in the struggle for Independence. George Smith, son of Jeremiah Smith by his second wife, came in possession of the old homestead where he was born, and later, of the greater portion of the land owned by his pioneer father,— his brothers and sisters selling their interests and moving to the West.

George Smith married Frances Curlett, dau. of Nicholas Curlett. They raised a large family of children, all of whom have passed over to the great unknown. Samuel Smith, son of George and Frances Smith, was born Mch. 6, 1802. He married Maria Tidings. To them were born the following children: Frances, Lucy, George, K., Giles K., Wm. R., Granville, Algernon W., and John T.—four of whom are dead. George K. lives in Colorado. Giles J. lives at the home where he was born, in Back Creek Valley; William R. lives in Winchester, Va. Dr. John T. Smith lives in Baltimore, Md.

Back Creek Valley was the name given to the postoffice in that vicinity by the P. O. department more than one hundred years ago. In my earliest recollection, it was kept by Genl. Lockhart. In going to and returning from school, we had to pass by his house, and would get the mail. I remember having to pay ten cents in coin to have a letter mailed, the amount paid at that time for mailing a letter, which now costs two cents. The name of the postoffice has been changed, and is now known as Gore. I have to feel sorry every time I write the name, that they did not retain the ancient and historic name of *Back Creek Valley*.

In 1777, Harrison Taylor bought land of Jeremiah Smith on Back Creek. Again in 1787 Harrison Taylor bought land lying on Back Creek "on the great road leading from Winchester to Romney," from the same Jeremiah Smith. On this tract he, Harrison Taylor, built what was then known as "The Big Mill" on Back Creek, which was then on the road known as the Great Road leading from Winchester to Romney.

Later, when the North Western Turnpike was built, they changed the location of the road at the crossing of the creek, running it more to the West, leaving the mill to the South. This mill did the grinding for that community and for all the surrounding country for many miles.

Harrison Taylor was known as *"Honest old Taylor at the Mill."* He married Margaret Curlett, daughter of Nicholas Curlett, and sister to Frances Curlett, who married George Smith, above named. Later they sold their property in Virginia and moved to Kentucky. Harrison Taylor came East to Winchester when it was a frontier village, from central Virginia. His parents were of Welsh and English origin.

At the present time Mr. Charles W. Parish owns and occupies the old Mill property and farm, Mr. Ott Kerns operating the Mill.

William Smith, grandson of the pioneer, inherited a large tract of land which descended to his grandchildren, the homestead passing to Wm. C. Smith, whose children now enjoy it as their home, which lies on the creek below the ford. William, Sr., reared a large family, five sons and several daughters. The oldest, Thomas B. Smith, once owned the old mill, mentioned by Wm. R., which was once known as the Sibert Mill. Thomas B. married Miss Harris of Culpeper County, about 15 years ago he removed his family South. If living, he is the only survivor of the family of brothers and sisters. Robert B. Smith, his brother, married Sarah E., daughter of Nathaniel C. Lupton, living in full view, just West of the Northwest Turnpike ford. After raising his family, he removed to Kansas; later on to Oklahoma. His son, Dr. Nat. Smith living at Gainsboro village, is the only survivor of this family. Dr. A. J. Smith, the well-known physician who lived on the West side of the pike beyond the ford going West, died there a few years ago. The son William and daughter Jennie survive the parents and inherited his fine estate. Dr. George Smith removed to Ohio. Jennie is the wife of Mr. Calvin Garvin, of Loudoun County. William C. Smith, the youngest son, lived and died at the old homestead. He married Miss Harris, sister to Thomas B.'s wife. His widow and children maintain the splendid property successfully.

The other branches of the pioneer's family are not traceable at present. One of William Smith, Sr.'s, daughters married Wm. Cather;

and one of his sisters was the mother of Robt. C. and Dr. Bywaters.

The Whitacre Family

This family is now so numerous in Western Frederick, that it is difficult to trace every family line. The name appears in several of the Virginia counties East of the Blue Ridge. Joshua the first of the name found in Frederick County, lived at one time in Loudoun County; he probably is the Joshua Whitacre who figured as a soldier during the Revolutionary War. His son George was born in Loudoun County, but was in Frederick County with his father about 1800. George married Rachael Wilson, of Loudoun County; issue by this union: Nimrod, Asbury, Annette, Robert, Phineas, Zedwell, Richard and Aglen. George died in 1853 on Timber Ridge, Frederick County, an old man, the owner of large tracts of land, which were divided among his children, the major part of which is now held by his grandchildren. Their name is legion, and like the ubiquitous Smiths, precludes the possibility of bringing them into line. The first and second generations have intermarried with nearly every family in Western Frederick. Some moved to other counties and other States. The oldest son of George, Nimrod born in 1822, married Elizabeth A. dau. of Peter Mauzy, of Hampshire County, Va., in 1844. As stated elsewhere, he served as Justice of the Peace, and one term in the Virginia Legislature. There were born to them Harrison P., L. C., James P., George S., Wm. Clark, Turner A., Robt. E. L., and Herbert D. Harrison P. is the well-known merchant at Gainsboro, who has been a member of the Board of Supervisors of the county for several terms. He married Mary V., daughter of Richard Johnson: issue Effie A., Elizabeth J., Sophia A., and Nimrod S. James P. Whitacre has prospered in the practice of the law in Winchester for nearly thirty years. He also has a law office in New York City, where he spends part of his time. He married a lady of that city. No children.

George S. is a prosperous farmer, married, and has a family. W. Clark, the widely known merchant and miller at Whitacre P. O., married a daughter of John Giffin.

Turner A., Robt. E., and Herbert D. are active business men. Robert and the other sons of George are all dead, but they have many representatives, who rank among the best men in that Western section. O. C. Whitacre the Justice of the Peace, Charles the widely-known auctioneer and stock-dealer, and his brothers Joshua, Hiram, Isaac and others in the North end of the District are men respected and esteemed by all. John R. Whitacre was Commissioner of the Revenue for the Northern District for two terms and a well-known school teacher. Ira C. Whitacre, an old Frederick County school teacher, is now in charge of the prosperous Academy at Fairfax C. H. We must here leave this family for the present, hoping to receive later on a fuller memo. of the family lines.

The Braithwaite Family

This family can feel proud of their origin. They come of old English stock, where the name is honored now as it was 200 years ago, where the Civil, Army and Navy Gazettes, show the name in many stations. The pioneer of the family so far as Frederick County is concerned, was William Braithwaite who was in the vicinity of Middletown, Va., at the close of the Revolutionary War, in which he served as a soldier, produced proof of this to the courts, and was listed as a tax-payer. Tradition fixes his birth in England about 1760, and that he was in America when only 16 years of age, and must have enlisted very soon after his arrival. He married Miss Brookover, of Frederick County, where he continued to live until his death July 13, 1831. His grave is in the old Heironimous graveyard, now known as Redland. He was one of the *ante bellum* school-teachers—a class of men well remembered by the old people of to-day. He was the father of thirteen children, who intermarried with so many families, we are unable to give much at this writing. His oldest son Benjamin was born Aug. 28, 1787; then came William, Jacob, John and Emory, the eight daughters made up the 13 children. The old marriage record in the County Office will show whom they married. One of the sons John, enlisted in Capt. Van Horn's Company when 18 years of age, and served in the War of 1812, as shown elsewhere. He married Susan Farmer May 8, 1828, and died in 1864. His widow was entitled to a pension until her death at the age of 94 years. The four children by this union were: William F., born May 1, 1830, John A., 1832; Lydia, 1835, and Hannah, 1839. William F. Braithwaite was one of Gainsboro's most enterprising citizens. He prospered in farming and milling at Cross Junction. He was a gallant Confederate soldier; served as Justice of the Peace for many terms, and was Commissioner of Elections as long as his health would admit. He married Mary S. Grove and had eight children. His son, O. D. Braithwaite the merchant at Cross Junction, served several terms as Commissioner of the Revenue for the Northern District. The writer recalls with sincere pleasure his many visits to the Clerk's Office in connection with his office. His affable manners as an official and his efficient service, made him agreeable in his important work. Florence C., Verena D., and Clara were the daughters. Jackson S. and Edward W., the other sons, are highly respected young men. Samuel (Jackson S.) operates mills and threshes in connection with his farming. Edward W. is well known among the educational interests of his section, and is a successsful teacher. Their father Wm. F. died several years since; and Edward W. was one of his executors to settle his estate.

The DeHaven Family

The writer regrets his inability to produce a full record of this family; and having had considerable experience in tracing this and the *Mercer* family in connection with some *mystic fortune,* his efforts to name any, would not do justice to those not mentioned.

Jacob, John and Caleb were among very early settlers; and their descendants are numerous, and many of them well-known business men in the vicinity of the post office and mill, stores, etc., of this name. The sons of James W. lived for many years; Turner A. and his brothers. Alexander, Thomas and Isaac N. on Back Creek, and their sons, are all active and useful citizens.

Dorsey DeHaven, one of the oldest men of the name, lives on Lower Back Creek, and owns what was known for many years as the old Abm. Haines property. His estate is very noticeable. His sons James R., Bradley T. and Caleb D. are prosperous farmers. His three daughters are Mrs. A. B. Braithwaite, Mrs. C. E. O'Roke, and Mrs. Jos. Barney.

Harvey D. DeHaven's children are Jos. T., William, and Mrs. Geo. Whitacre.

The Mercer Family (once called Messer)

The family were of the Caleb, Joshua and Job Mercer stock,—all distantly related to Genl. Mercer of Revolutionary War fame. None of the name is in the county to-day. They were once numerous. Many other families that intermarried with the Mercers, have numerous progeny that have been seeking for clues to a claim the Mercers had at one time against the U. S. Government and also to a deposit in the Bank of England. Some of the descendants have faith in the statements made by shrewd agents; and some of the best business men of this family are spending money in their effort to recover these fortunes.

The Pugh Family

This is one of those families that settled on Back Creek far back, in the 18th Century. Job Pugh who founded Pugh's Town (Gainsboro) in 1797, had a large family. Some of the married sons and daughters founded homes on Timber Ridge, and gradually crossed Bear Ridge, and branches of the family settled on Capon River, becoming permanent citizens of Hampshire County. Several of the name have been very prominent men in that county, one being the present sheriff; two of the name have served as members of the Virginia House of Delegates. The most prominent in Frederick County for the last twenty years is Malachi Pugh, who owns several farms near the Hampshire line. By his thrift and industry he has accumulated quite an estate. One daughter married George Fletcher; and one son is married and lives near his father; likewise another daughter.

The McIntire Family is represented now by Mr. John McIntire, 92 years old, hale and hearty —a good sample of this sturdy family—all others now gone. Mr. McIntire was one of the old-time school teachers.

The Fletcher Family was once quite numerous. George and John are good business men.

The Mauzy Family is one of the oldest families in that section. Robert Mauzy and his family maintain the good reputation of their ancestors.

The Heironimous Family was numerous at one time, but in later years the name has become few in number.

The Bageant Family. This family still maintains its good name. Andrew Jackson Bageant was well known during his long life. His sons John W. and brother are farmers in comfortable circumstances. Sons of the former live in Washington, and are young men of ambition and merit success. Mr. Ed. Bageant is a prominent farmer of this section; he married a daughter of Mrs. Siler, who makes her home with him.

The *Bakers Mill* voting precinct takes its name from the Baker family who lived in that section for more than a century (See sketch of the Baker family.) Erastus B. Baker and his brother Dr. I. N. Baker are good representatives of the old stock. The former has been Registrar at that precinct for many years. Dr. Baker was a Confederate soldier.

Robert Luttrell represents an old family of that name.

The Collins Family

This family now represented by Chas. P. Collins and his brother, sons of Daniel Collins, whose father emigrated from Ireland the latter part of the 18th Century, are all good types of that class of Irish emigrants who found homes in the Shenandoah Valley.

The Shade Family is not so numerous as it once was; but such men as Philip, Robert and Edward are good descendants of the old stock, that was probably founded by Jacob and brother.

The Peacemakers, Omps, Shanholtzes, Browns, Strothers, Darlingtons, Howards, Hinckles, Rinkers (see sketch of this family) and many others, are well-known families and entitled to fuller notice; but we have devoted more space to Gainsboro District than this volume will justify.

The writer remembers Benedict Omps, the father of Gore, Chris. and Benj. F.—the last two were soldiers in the Stonewall Brigade. Richard L. Omps one of the grandsons of Benedict, is one of the most prominent and successful men in that section. Jacob Hinckle the old Justice, Patrick Howard the old miller, Wm. Grove and son-in-law Daniel Gano, the Place, Peacemaker, Largent, Ziler (Siler) Shockey, Strother and the well-known Heironimous family—all have interesting connection with the early days of N. West Frederick. Families who were prominent in Frederick County during the 19th Century, are so numerous, that we can only mention a few, and as briefly as possible. Starting the limited number with the old country doctors, who so faithfully traversed the country day and night with *saddle pockets* full of medicine bottles and instruments, that the modern physician in his rubber tire or automobile would not deign to handle. Then microbes and the appendicitis had not been discovered.

Dr. Robt. McCandless was found near the site of Clear Brook; Dr. Z. Brown at Pughtown; still later, Dr. Danl. Janney at Welltown; Dr. J. W. Best at Brucetown, who first started at Whitehall; Dr. Cochran, Sr., at Welltown, before Janney; Dr. E. B. Smoke at Whitehall; Dr. J. E. Janney, Dr. Tom Hinckle at Cross Junction, and Dr. W. Hollis. Dr. Peter Senseny; Dr. Peter Ridings, at Middletown; following him came Drs. Guyer, Davisson and Larrick.

At Newtown we find Drs. McLeod, Jno. W. Owen, T. M. Miller and S. M. Stickley.

At Cedar Creek was Drs. Hite Baldwin, Chas. W. Sydnor and E. D. Cherry. On the Cedar Creek Grade, Dr. I. M. Brumback.

Along the Big North Dr. Keffer, Dr. Hollis, and Dr. Jack Smith in Back Creek Valley; Dr. Wm. M. Lupton at the Round Hill. Some old country doctors who preceded these mentioned, have been noticed elsewhere in this volume.

Of the younger class we have Drs. P. B. Stickley and Montgomery at Stephens City; Dr. Cover at Mountain Falls, Drs. R. W. Gover and Chas. Anderson at Gore; Dr. Nat. Smith at Gainsboro, and Dr. Weaver at Middletown.

The Stephenson Family

We find three families of this name in the County early in the 19th Century. No relationship is recognized between them. Stephenson Station on the Winchester and Potomac Railroad, five miles from Winchester, was started by William Stephenson, who owned a large tract of land. His highly cultivated farms were landmarks in that section. His two sons John W. and Henry inherited the landed estate, which they found at the close of the Civil War, swept clean of fences and outbuildings. The old mansion-house, "Kenilworth," was spared. Henry occupied this and a large farm adjoining until his death about 1904. He married Miss Marbury, of Georgetown, D. C., in 1878. His widow and two sons survive him. John W. lived for many years on his portion; his residence being East of the railroad. He also erected good tenant houses, and donated the land for the Methodist Church. His wife was Miss Mason. They have one son, W. Roy Stephenson, the well-known member of the Winchester Bar. The family has resided in Winchester for several years in their handsome property on Washington Street. The other children of William were: one brother and three sisters.

William was the son of James W. Stephenson, of Burnside, County Donegal, Ireland, and came to Virginia in 1794, with his family and settled in Charlestown, Jefferson County. His son William was then eleven years old.

James W. Stephenson, who has been mentioned as one of the Supervisors of Frederick County, lived in the vicinity of Brucetown, until his death a few years ago. He was very successful in his quiet farm life. His son-in-law Luther A. Huyett, occupies the splendid property. Mr. Stephenson and his brother Samuel, came from Shenandoah where the family had settled in the early days. Samuel died in Frederick County, leaving one daughter who is the wife of Dr. Henkel, of Winchester.

Mention is made elsewhere of the third family of this name, whose ancestor was Robert Stephenson, settling near the old Quaker Graveyard.

The Isaac Wood Family

To distinguish this family from that of James Wood, the old Clerk, we find they first settled in Pennsylvania, coming from Lancashire, England. Thomas seems to have been the pioneer of this family. He is found in Chester County, Penn., with his wife and two sons, William and Joseph, in 1725 and 1750. About this time Joseph the second son of William was born, who removed to Frederick County and died in 1816. His son Isaac was born in this county in 1787, and died 1855. He married Maria Littler, of Frederick County; and through his wife inherited part of what was known in early days as the Yorkshireman's Branch farm, afterwards Red Bud. This was about 4 miles from Winchester, near the Opecquon. The property passed to his son Charles L. Wood. Isaac was the father of eight children, all dead but one, who is Daniel T. Wood, known to all for his splendid traits, maintained throughout his long life of 86 years. Mr. Wood owns the fine property on the Opecquon about 5 miles from Winchester, where we find one of the mills, near the Spout Spring ford on the Opecquon, where a substantial and much needed bridge has been built. Mr. Wood married Miss Nichols, and had eight children by this union, only four of whom are now living, viz: Mrs. Lucretia Eley, Mrs. Margaret Talbott, of Ohio, Mary and Clara at home. The old homestead, once known as Spout Spring, was first settled by Joseph Carter, who erected a good-sized stone house, used as a Tavern stand. This became a favorite camp ground for the Indians. The writer has many traditions of that period—1747-56, but lacks space for them. The old stone house served as fort and tavern; and guests felt secure when stopping with Joseph Carter and his son John.

Charles L. Wood the oldest son of Isaac, had only one child to survive him—Nannie, who married George W. Bowly, of Winchester. Mr. Bowly has lived in Atlanta for several years. They are the parents of several children. One son Charles L. Bowly is a frequent visitor to Winchester, where his mother temporarily resides.

Isaac left two other sons, Robert and Thomas. Robert Married Miss Hollingsworth, of Ohio. He was in business in Winchester for several years. He left three children: Florence, Effie (Mrs. Cartright of Winchester), and Charles, who married Miss Fishpaw.

Thomas B. Wood erected a fine woolen mill on Red Bud, and there conducted a profitable business until his untimely death. He married (first) Miss Vass, and had one son William, who lives in Oregon. One daughter, Leslie, by his second wife, became the wife of E. C. Jordan, Jr.

The Clayton Family

David L. Clayton who lived and died near Cedar Grove, Frederick County, erected the large brick mansion now occupied by his son John. Mr. Clayton came to the County from Western Virginia in 1817, when only 16 years old. For many years he was a ruling elder in the old Kent Street Presb. Church. He was highly respected and had a wide acquaintance. He taught vocal music in several neighborhoods. The writer remembers Mr. Clayton, and the losses he sustained as surety on a sheriff's bond. He died in 1854, leaving six children. One son, Elisha P., married and removed to Ohio about 1861. One daughter is the wife of Capt. George W. Kurtz; one son, David L. Clayton, lives in Cumberland, Md. The others died many years ago. John H. C. Clayton has served his section as Justice of the Peace, Commissioner of Roads and other offices of trust. He married Mary George daughter of Lewis George, of Frederick County. Five children were born of this union. The three sons died several years ago. One daughter became the wife of J. Perry Purcell (now dead). Rebecca J. is the wife of Phil. H. Gold.

The Littler Family

This family that Isaac Wood intermarried with, was one of the old English colony that secured a minor grant Nov. 12, 1735. This grant was to John Littler and Thomas Rees for 1735 acres; and the survey describes the tract as extending up the Yorkshireman's branch, sometimes called Littler Run.

A similar grant embraced the land where the Stephenson station is. One of the grandsons lived at that point, and is credited with the erection of "Kenilworth" prior to 1800. The name frequently appeared during the 18th Century. Several members were of that old class known as the Tavern Keepers; several were millers; some farmers—all active business men. But 'ere the first quarter of the 19th Century closed, the name was extinct; some finding homes in Ohio and other Western *free soil* States. They owned slaves in Virginia, but were opposed to the extension of slavery, as one of the name stated to the writer many years ago. John Littler the founder died in 1748, and left a will. His sons were: John, Samuel, Nathan. Samuel died in 1778. He mentions son Elijah and daughters in his will. John, Jr., died in 1818, leaving sons Elisha, John, Joshua, Laban, Nathan, and daughters Mary, Rosanna and others. He owned land also in Ohio.

The Hott Family

This family made its first appearance in the Shenandoah Valley just prior to the Revolutionary War. This was George Hott, who leased a tract of land from John Painter, 1772; and in 1776 he purchased the whole tract from Painter;

and this farm has never passed out of the Hott family. There they raised a large family. From the many children we can trace lines of Jacob F. Hott and his wife Jane. Mr. Hott was a Minister of the Gospel, a member of the U. B. Church. One of his sons was Bishop James W. Hott, whose brother Elkana Hott was a minister in the same church. One other son Charles Martin was also a Minister; one son-in-law M. F. Keiter who was also a minister. One son George P. has been principal of Shenandoah Institute, at Dayton, Va. One other son Jacob W. is a merchant in Frederick County. Another line of the old stock brings us to David F. Hott, living near White Hall and owning a handsome estate. He is an intelligent and prosperous farmer; was born 1830, a son of Jacob Hott. The Hott family of this branch lived at one time in Berkeley County. His wife was a daughter of Joseph Hancher. They had born of this union nine children, viz: Mrs. Fannie Sincindiver, Mrs. Ann R. Randall, Lucy E., Laura L., John T., Arie A., David F., and Franklin E. They have always been classed with the German immigrations. This was because the original French family had been driven from their native country, escaping into Germany; followed the emigrations to America, and settled in Pennsylvania sometime about 1700. David F. is a devout member of the U. B. Church.

The Brown Family

One of the well-known old homesteads North of Winchester is Mulberry Grove, where we find two unmarried sisters, Elisan and Catherine Brown, who are very familiar with the history of their family. Their brother Wilson L. Brown died a few years ago. The trio made one of the quaint pictures such as we sometimes read about in Dickens, but seldom see. They are *Friends* in the strictest sense. The two sisters are conducting their affairs as their Quaker ancestors did from 1774, and at the same place. Their great-grandfather was Daniel Brown, who settled at this point about 3½ miles from Winchester. Isaac Brown their grandfather was born in Chester County, Penna., in 1746. He came with his father to this farm, and there lived and died, following out in detail his father's mode of living. Family history says he married Margaret, daughter of Col. John Hite, granddaughter of Joist Hite. One son by this union, viz: John Brown. Isaac's second wife was Sarah Ballinger, of Maryland. She lived 90 years, and died 1842. They had five children by this marriage: Wm. H., Isaac, Samuel, Margaret, Esther and Cassandra.

Wm. H. Brown was the father of Jane C., Rebecca W., Eliza, Wilson L., Elisan and Catherine. He died at the old place in 1865. He was twice married. His first wife was Sarah, dau. of Lewis and Rachael Neill, with two daughters by this marriage, long since deceased. His second wife was Martha Rees, dau. of Thomas and Jane. She was the mother of Wilson L. and the sisters above named.

The Jolliffe Family

This is one of the old families. They have a complete family history, prepared by Mr. William Jolliffe, of Buchannon, Va., several years ago. The writer recommends this to the Jolliffe family and numerous connections, for study. He remembers when several families of the name owned fine farms. Joseph N. has been mentioned elsewhere. Meredith H. lived on the Martinsburg Turnpike; Dr. E. C. Jolliffe near the site of Clear Brook. One sister married Samuel Hopkins, brother of Johns Hopkins. Then there were John, Amos and James, all long since dead. Very few of their descendants can be found in the old County. This family have generally adhered to the Society of Friends. In sketches of several other families, this name will appear.

The well-known Tanquary family belongs to the 19th Century class; also the Timberlakes, and old Daniel Wright family of brothers and their descendants. Daniel Wright at one time was the owner of more fertile farms than any other person in the county. He parceled them out between his nephews and nieces. The Swimleys, Cunningham, Jefferson, Shaull, Duvall, Chamberlaine, Jordan, Smoke, Silver, Hancher, Seevers, Horton, Jobe, Harman, Boyles, Daugherty, Hiett, Randall, Pitzer, Ebert, Payne, Lewis, Myers, Stine, Hardesty, Huntsberry, Heterick, McCormack families were all in active life during the period that witnessed the wonderful development of the county. The Throckmorton, Hackney, Rees, Bryarly, Bruce, Berry, Doster, Fitzsimmons, Dumas, Farrell, Daugherty, Silver and McCormick names belong to the 18th Century, and may receive special notices.

John Bruce, mentioned above, was the founder of Brucetown; he died there in 1748, leaving a large family. Several children lived near his home,—two sons, George and James, and two daughters, Mrs. Margaret Allen and Mrs. Richard Carter; and thus the settlement became known as Bruce's village. Many descendants of the Irish emigration can be found. Very few, however, bear the names of the old ancestors.

The Ebert Family

This family became part of Frederick County during the 19th Century, when Martin Ebert came from Adams County, Penna., in 1841 and settled near Greenspring. His family comprised his wife, Mary Myers, two sons and three daughters. John E. died Dec. 5, 1841; William H. married Anna R. Ridgeway, dau. of Jonas Ridgeway of Berkeley County, whose ancestors came from Berks County, England, about 1750. William H. lived and died in an old Colonial house, the site of the present handsome home of his son John Ebert on the Welltown Turnpike. His other two sons, Martin and Charles, are successful farmers and live on farms near the old homestead. The father of these sons died in 1900, respected by his neighbors. He and his sons accumulated valuable property. Two daughters, Mary and Rebecca, died respectively in 1848 and 1867. The other daughter, Harriet, became the wife of George W. Brent in 1844. She survived her husband who died in 1899, and died Feby. 5, 1908. Martin the father, died 1862; his wife in 1870. The Ebert ancestry came from Wurtemburg, Germany, early in the 18th Century, and settled near York, Penna.

After the din of battle ceased, and the Civil War clouds had drifted by, the Northern part of the county derived much advantage from an emigration from Maryland and Pennsylvania, composed of well-to-do farmers, most of whom became splendid citizens, many of them holding places of trust. Of this number can be mentioned Jas. K. McCann, the Byers, Metz, Zinn, Mellinger, Staddon and other families. James K. McCann served one term in the Virginia Legislature, and was Chairman of the Board of Supervisors of the County for several terms. He is also a large landowner.

The author feels inclined to extend these personal sketches over the section of the county North of Winchester, among the people with whom he has had such intimate acquaintance and warm friendship; but we must now briefly mention some of the pioneers South of Winchester.

The Kline Family

The pioneer of this family was Jacob Kline, who always signed his name in German. We find it frequently translated as Clyne, Cline, Klein, Klyne. He was one of the German immigration who landed in Pennsylvania 1735; and then in 1764 joined several other families and settled in Frederick County East of Middletown, erecting a large flax-seed oil mill where Kline's Mill now stands. After about twenty years of experience, this was abandoned, and the building enlarged and used for making flour, and serving as a residence for the family, where his twelve children were reared. Anthony, who was born in 1777, erected the present log mill in 1794, while his father was living. He married Jemima, dau. of James Russell, of Fredk. County. Children by this union were: James R., Eliza, Anthony M. and Martha. James R. was born May 1, 1805. One of his sons, James O. Kline, has a large clock made by Anthony and started to run on his son's birthday. The date May 1, 1805, is legibly written on the inside by the maker. This clock keeps perfect time at this writing, giving days of week and month, changes of moon, etc. We may add at this point that the maker was doubtless one of the famous clockmakers found in Middletown in 1797 and probably connected with the manufacture of wheat threshers. James R. Kline's children were James O., Samuel A., Francis, Alcinda, Mary, Ellen. James O. married Ann Dinges: children, Hugh B., Clara (Mrs. Wise), Harvey married Miss Stickley; Octavia and Howard, single. F. Estes married Miss Stickley.

Samuel A. Kline's children: Russell and Elizabeth (Mrs. Gruber).

Francis Kline married Wm. Powers, of Fredk. County. Their son, William Powers, lives in Clarke County.

Alcinda married Rev. Daniel Baker: children, Quinter, Daniel.

One daughter married Edward Stickley, another married L. R. Dettra; one is Mrs. Kimble; Effie is single.

Mary Kline married C. Milton Peery; children: Lloyd, Charles, Lulu and Fannie. Lloyd married Miss McLeod; Lulu married Saml. Miller; Fannie is Mrs Frazier.

Ellen Kline married Amos Guard: one son, Atwell.

Anthony M., son of James R., born 1816, married Emily B. Muse, dau. of Major Robert B. Muse, of Back Creek, in 1836. Children by this union: Snowden B., Charles O., Petara J., Mary, Rigdon, Lucy, Thomas L., and Martin Trone.

Olivia V. married Jno. Sperry, of Middletown. Anthony M. has been mentioned elsewhere as Chairman of the Board of Supervisors.

Daniel W. Kline, who was well-known as the faithful superintendent of the Court House, etc., during the latter part of his life, was the son of John I. Kline, of Middletown, who died in Martinsburg. Daniel served in one of the fighting Confederate batteries, and treasured a memory of his war experiences. He was a great sufferer from a serious malady, and underwent trying operations that produced no permanent relief. He died 1907. His mother Eliza Kline, brother C. N. Kline and sister Mrs. Kilmer survive him; also his widow and several children. She was a daughter of Harry Hoover.

John G. Senseny married a daughter of James

R. K. One daughter Ann married Rev. J. Spessard.

Much confusion has arisen concerning this name. Another family always bearing the name of Cline, living chiefly in Hampshire County, are sometimes regarded as a branch of the Klines who preceded them. The well-known gun and locksmith Cline, of Winchester, doing business in the old building of John I. Baker on South Main Street until his death some years ago, knew no connection between the families.

Anthony Kline and Kezziah Russell emancipated negro *Sam*, in 1823 (see Deed Book). We also find an Adam Kline at an early date. He mentions his children John, Mary Gilham, Barbara Grapes, Susana Green, Michael, Elizabeth Evans, and two other daughters.

The Senseny Family

This family belonged to the sturdy people who did so much during the 18th Century to develop the Southern section of Frederick County. Dr. Peter Senseny was the progenitor. He was born 1738; and settled in that section when a young man. From him we trace several branches, who chiefly lived in and around Middletown. His daughter Catherine married George Wright. Of this family who entered the Confederate Army was, C. W. Senseny, found in Co. D, 18th Va. Cavalry, now resides in Bloomington, Ills. Jacob Senseny, mentioned frequently in Sketches of Winchester, was a son of Dr. Peter. He lived in Winchester from his boyhood until his death in 1860. He owned the land South of Mt. Hebron Cemetery, and erected the large brick house at the East end of Cork Street, for many years occupied by M. and T. Conway, now the home of Geo. W. Haddox. He was the father of George E. Senseny, Editor of the Winchester Republican for many years prior to his death in 1869, and also father of Edgar Senseny who has lived in Missouri for forty years, and of Mrs. Kate Needles, whose tomb can be seen in Mt. Hebron.

The Wright Family (Middletown)

Geo. Wright was the first of his family to appear in Middletown, which was in the Summer of 1819. He was born in England, near York, Sept. 11, 1792. On his arrival, he soon set his skill and genius to improve upon the machines made by Ridings and McKeever; and produced a threshing machine that won favor with the wheat growers. He married Catherine daughter of Dr. Peter Senseny, Oct. 17, 1820.

Peter Senseny Wright, a son by this marriage, was born in Middletown March 21, 1834; died Feby. 16, 1885. He was by education and temperament well fitted for his life work, which was devoted to the growth of fruit and ornamental trees, shrubbery, etc. His well-kept nursery was one of the institutions of the Middletown section for years. His love for plants and flowers, was gratified by his intelligent knowledge of them, having made botany his careful study. He married his cousin Maud Wright. She was the daughter of John and Sarah Wright. John Wright came from England in 1827, and became a successful farmer. He married Sarah Kercheval (daughter of Samuel Kercheval, author of the History of the Valley). Their only child was Ethel, who became the wife of Jos. Watson a few years ago.

The Larrick Family

The pioneer of this family was George Larrick, who first appeared in Frederick County about 1755. His name appears in a lease assigned by Hite and McKay. The name is written in the body of the paper as Laruck. Fairfax's agent reported a list of persons unlawfully occupying his lands, George Laruck being one. Processes for ejectment were served, and rents demanded. Some of the parties compromised with Fairfax and paid their rents, George Laruck being one; and in 1760 Fairfax made them lease and release deeds. The pioneer secured part of the tract where he had erected his buildings; and it is claimed by the descendants, that the original homestead was preserved and additions made from time to time. This name has undergone several changes. The family that landed at New Castle, Delaware, came over with what was designated as an Irish emigration. They were registered in the ship's lists as Laroque, natives of France. By the grace of her Majesty Queen Anne, their abode was Ireland. The ships were met by agents, who escorted a large number to the new country. The identity seems clear. The writer has been informed by members of the family, that family tradition claimed them as Huguenots. One son of the pioneer was George Larrick, who was born 1770. He married Rebecca Brinker, dau. of George Brinker, whose wife, as will be seen in the Hite Sketches, was the grand-daughter of Joist Hite. Their children were: Rebecca, Asaph, Manly, Pamelia, Catherine, Mazey, George B., Killesta, Elizabeth, Cealta, Rachael, Isaac, Mary Ann and Jacob B.

Catherine married Alfred Rust, Cealta wife of Silas Simmons of Ill. Isaac moved to Missouri, and served in a Missouri Company during the Mexican War. From the lines of the children named, could be traced large families, for which we have not room; but we will mention briefly the names of the well-known family of Jacob B. Larrick, who was born Mch. 12, 1826, in the old homestead, and spent his useful life there, dying Oct. 22, 1887. He married in 1851 Mary Ann dau. of George B. and Sarah Scaggs, of Maryland. Their children were: Geo. W., Lucy B., (widow of James F. Faulkner, of Winchester), Sarah E. (wife of Samuel Williams), E. Olin, James I., Jacob B., Cora L. (married P. A. Scaggs), Robert A., and Herbert S. George W. became a prominent physician in the Middletown section. He first practiced at Toms Brook; but forming a partnership with Dr. John S. Guyer, he returned to Middletown in 1879. Although suffering with a diseased leg, he held out under his large practice for more than twenty years, when he was compelled to succumb to the inroads of his old enemy. Dr. Larrick was a genial-hearted gentleman, very pronounced in his opinions, a Democrat in politics and a Methodist in religion. His widow was M. Louise McGee, of Baltimore. E. Olin and James I. compose the widely known firm of Larrick and Larrick, at their large warehouses near the railroad station. E. Olin has been very active for several years as member of the School Board. J. B. lives in Washington, D. C. Robert A. lives at the old homestead. Herbert S., now Commonwealth's Atty. for the County, has resided in Winchester for several years, enjoying a lucrative practice with his partner, Senator Robt. M. Ward. The father, Jacob B. Larrick, was prominent in his church (M. E. South) and always took an active part in the old campmeeting experiences of the Methodist Church. The writer recalls with pleasure the unbounded hospitality Mr. Larrick offered to visitors at his splendid tent during those seasons at the old camp ground near Stickley Springs. Mr. Larrick was a Confederate soldier.

Another branch of the Larrick family found in the vicinity of Middletown, during the writer's knowledge, were the three brothers, Jacob H., Geo. B., and James S. Jacob H. Larrick was the proprietor of the Larrick Tavern for many years. George B. was sargeant of Company B., 11th Va. Cavalry. While this company was in the 17th Battalion, he was desperately wounded near the Yellow House North of Winchester. He survived the War; married Miss Briggs of Winchester and removed to Lexington, Va., where he died about two years ago.

The other brother, Capt. James S. Larrick, living near Middletown and generally known in the county as a surveyor of lands, was one of the Cadets at the Virginia Military Institute during the early part of the Civil War, and participated in the celebrated Battle of New Market. The three brothers have children, but the writer has been unable to secure their names.

The Ridings Family

Some confusion has arisen as to the date when this family settled in Southern Frederick. Some writers claim they were in that section prior to 1800. This seems to be a mistake. James Ridings and two sons were on the tax lists in 1817; but James became a landowner for the first time in 1829, when he purchased a house and lot in Middletown. It appears, however, that he was a mechanic of the village some time prior thereto, having come from Baltimore. He later on established a factory and fullers mill East of Middletown, and organized what was known as Ridings Chapel. There was a Dr. Peter Ridings near Winchester in 1812; who took the oath of allegiance to the United States and renounced his allegiance to England, he being a native of that country. What relation he was to James, if a brother, is not definite. He, too, is found later on living East of Middletown, having married in England prior to 1800. They reared a large family. John W. Ridings who lived on his fine estate on the Middle Road, was of this line. It is well known that Dr. Ridings was connected with a woolen factory in that section. Edwin B. Ridings son of Dr. Peter and father of John W. Ridings, was born in England 1798; and died in Frederick County, 1878. He owned the old woolen factory, grist mills, etc. Though a member of the M. E. Church, he gave the ground for the U. B. Chapel (mentioned elsewhere). His first wife was Lydia Rhodes, the mother of Jacob, Peter and John W. In 1828 he married his second wife Susan Painter, who died in 1834, leaving James R. (a mute), Sarah A. and George E.

During the Civil War, this family suffered, as did many others; but two instances of specially brutal treatment may be mentioned: Peter was taken from his home and family and shot dead by a squad of Union soldiers, within a half mile of his home; while at another time, John W. Ridings' wife was killed in her own home on the Middle Road, West of Newtown. A large squad of Sheridan's Cavalry, led by ——— Brown, a renegade Frederick County man, made a rush upon the house, firing many volleys. Mrs. Ridings was killed. Both cases were without excuse. William Ridings, her son, lives in the vicinity at this writing; and several other children survive. E. C. Ridings, James W. (now Notary Public) and other members of the two families mentioned, live at Middletown and vicinity. The writer hopes to receive matter from them pertaining to their lines.

In connection with the Ridings family, we will mention for convenience the Smith family, found in the same section and intermarried with them. Isaac N. Smith, it has been shown, served in the War of 1812. He was the father of John W. Smith, Thomas Smith, Benjamin F. and several other children. Benjamin F. served through the Civil War, a member of Company A., First Virginia Cavalry. He married Mary C. Ridings. The brothers are all dead. John W. was a prosperous farmer and a most honorable man. His daughter Mrs. Hiram O. Craig, lives on his old homestead near the Front Royal Turnpike; while his son James W. Smith lives on part of the home farm, which he has improved with handsome buildings, orchards, etc. One of James' sons, Clark, is in the S. V. N. Bank; Arch lives on Dr. Bell's farm. Isaac N. a brother of James lives in the county. Several other families of this name are found in other parts of Frederick County. Manson P. Smith on Cedar Creek, the prosperous farmer and miller, while a son of Benjamin Smith and family names similar, connection is not traceable. The latter will be mentioned in connection with the Affleck family.

The Stickley Family

This is one of the German families that emigrated from Pennsylvania in the latter part of the 18th Century. The first of the name to appear in the Shenandoah Valley was David Stickley, who made large purchases of land on both sides of Cedar Creek. Several large tracts were owned by his descendants in Shenandoah County, through several generations. The progenitor, however, fixed his home on the Frederick side, where the old mansion can be seen in good repair.

David married Miss Harman, and was the father of three sons and two daughters. One son Levi lived on a large tract in Shenandoah County; he married Eliza Dosh. She was the mother of Dr. Silas M. Stickley, who is the popular physician at Stephens City. He married Lucy J. Jenkins. They had 7 children. ***Abram Stickley,*** his youngest son, was born in 1792. His wife was Rachael Murphy who was the mother of four children: Benj. F., Wm. M., Annie E. and David A. They were all raised at what was called the Chrisman Spring place, the old *stone* house built by Chrisman, which Abram purchased in 1816 together with 600 acres of land. The neighborhood is now designated as Vaucluse Station. The sons all married and lived in the vicinity. The old house where Abram lived, was known at one time as the homestead of George Chrisman, son-in-law of Joist Hite, which was erected near the once celebrated spring. The great mass of limestone rock that the first settler found surrounding the spring, is being reduced by the extensive limekilns operated near the spring. This necessarily transforms the scenery once so wild and attractive. The present owner is David A. Stickley.

Benjamin F. married a dau. of David Dinges, Sr., and reared his family at his splendid farm, which is still in the family. His two daughters married brothers, Harvey and F. Estes Kline. The son Edward married Miss Baker. All are prosperous and highly esteemed families in the old neighborhood.

Levi Stickley (mentioned above) was the father of E. E. Stickley. This is Col. Stickley, of Woodstock. Another son, John H., married a Miss Margaret Stickley.

Dr. P. B. Stickley, of Stephens City, married a daughter of Justice Downing.

The Stickley family intermarried with the Boyer, McInturff, Jenkins, Browning, Fisher, Helm and Cutler families. The two last named were wives of Col. E. E. Stickley, of Woodstock. Ann E., the only daughter, remained single. She inherited about 200 acres of her father Abram's large estate.

The Brinker Family

This family has been associated with the Southern part of Frederick for many years, and was regarded as having first settled in that section. This is a mistake. Henry Brinker the pioneer, first lived in the village of Winchester prior to 1750, and died on his farm N. E. of Winchester in 1772. In 1754, this minute appears in the Order Book of the Court: "Henry Brinker a German Protestant, proved to the Court that he had been an inhabitant of the Colony seven years and not absent two months at any time and had a certificate from Rev. John Gordon, that he had received the rites of Sacrament of the Lord's Supper according to the rites and ceremonies of the Church of England." Henry Brinker purchased 381 acres of land from Lord Fairfax in 1763, located on Opecquon N. E. of Winchester. He mentions his wife Catherine in his will, and also his children, Elizabeth Haas, Henry and George. George was then living on a plantation near Winchester on East side of Potomac Road, and in his will he mentions his wife Rebeccana and his children Catherine M., Abram, Isaac., J., Rebecka and George. This last son later on owned land near Middletown, and resided there and raised a large family.

It will be seen in Sketches of the Hite Family, that Benjamin Brinker married a grand-daughter of Isaac Hite. This was Louisa Ann Lodor. Three children by this union were George, Eltinge who married her cousin Oland Brinker, and Madison Brinker. The writer remembers Major Ben Brinker as one of the most prominent men of that section, and prior to the Civil War was a large property holder. Suffering reverses during that period, he was induced to dispose of his farm and try his fortunes in one of the Western States. Having disposed of all their landed estate at various times between 1874 and 1880, he and his brother George finally ended their days in Denver City. The latter was city treasurer at one time, and both were connected with the State government of Colorado. The Brinkers intermarried with several families in Southern Frederick, but at this writing the name of Brinker does not appear in the Lower Valley.

The Dinges Family

This family appeared in Frederick County in 1831 for the first time, though a family of this name was in the Shenandoah Valley among the pioneers, but their lineage is not traceable. David Dinges, Sr., who purchased the farm where Wm. H. Dinges now lives, was born in Woodstock in 1788, where he married Catherine a daughter of Philip Miller in 1822. She was born in 1820. Her father was the son of Jacob Miller the founder of Mullerstadt, afterwards Woodstock. Children by this union were: Ellen G., Elizabeth, and Francis were born in Woodstock. The family then removed to Frederick County, 1831, where Wm. H., Ann R., Virginia, America, Mary Catherine and David B. were born. Seven of them married and lived in Frederick County within two miles of the homestead. All are now dead except Wm. H. and Davis B. The former lives on part of the old homestead and is a successful farmer, a ruling elder in the Cedar Cliff Presb. Church, and has been Chairman of the Board of Supervisors of Frederick County for several terms. David B. is a merchant in Middletown. He retired from farming several years ago, having sustained a serious fracture of his leg. He, too, is one of the elders of the Presbyterian Church. Philip Miller is mentioned as having served as Major in the War of 1812. He was born in 1760. David Dinges, Sr., served in the same war. He had five brothers and two sisters. Wm. H. Dinges married (first) Miss Smith, daughter of William Smith, of Back Creek. One son George survives his mother. Wm. H. married his second wife in Shenandoah County. She was Miss Whissen. Children by this union are Roy W., and William D., (dead) and the Misses Nellie H., Edna M., Vista Grove, and Mary G. Dinges.

David B. Dinges married Ida Reely, children: Harold, Edith and Ida M.

Henry A. and his brother David C. are related distantly to the Dinges family just mentioned. Henry married a daughter of Mager Steele, without issue. He is one of the retired merchants of Stephens City; an old Confederate soldier, and at this writing, in declining health. David C. his brother is a farmer, living East of Stephens City. His other brother George has been mentioned elsewhere.

The Steele Family of Stephensburg

The writer knew Mager Steele, Esq., as one of the prominent men of his section. He filled several offices of trust prior to the Civil War; was one of the old Commissioners of the Revenue, Justice of the Peace, etc. Mr. Steele was the father of Milton B. and Mager B. Steele, who composed the well-known firm of Steele Brothers. Both are now dead. Their widows and several children survive them, Boyd Steele of Stephens City being one, and Elmer Steele, dentist, son of Milton B. Steele another.

John M. Steele, son of Mager, Sr., once of the firm of Steele and Dinges, merchants, is now retired. Mr. Steele and his family live in Stephens City. One of his sisters is Mrs. Henry A. Dinges. He has two other sisters, the Misses Inez and Ida Steele. The latter is authoress of Methodism in Newtown, a valuable history of the M. E. Church of that place.

The Willey Family

We find three brothers of this name at a very early day in active life near Middletown, viz: Achilles, Alfred and William. Alfred left his three sons Atwell, Jacob W. and George and several daughters. Their descendants are well known in their neighborhood. William was the father of John W. Willey, Lawson, Jacob, Edward a gallant Confederate killed at Gettysburg. Three daughters were the wives respectively of the well known citizens Messrs. Yates, Mathews and Venable. Capt. Jacob was the guide for Genl. Early when he crossed Cedar Creek near Bowman's Mill to attack Sheridan's Army.

The Hammack Family

Joseph Hammack now 90 years old, lives due East from Middletown on the same tract of land his father purchased from ——— ————, who tradition says was one of the Hessian prisoners. This family was of Welsh origin. Ashby Hammack and several sisters live in the same section. Others of this name are living in Hampshire County. Daniel Hammack lived on Hogue Creek and was one of the honest millers in his day. He died an old man many years since.

The Heater Family

Solomon Heater came from Loudoun County in 1845, and purchased "Cedar Grove" near Middletown. He then married Caroline daughter of Dr. Henry Winder, of Penna. They had three sons, John P., member of the 7th Va. Cavalry; wounded at Pattersons Creek and died there Jany. 5, 1864; Henry, also of the 7th, captured and died in prison at Fort Delaware 1865, and Chas. W. Heater, who lives South of Middletown, in one of the handsomest homes in the Valley. He has been president of the State Board of Agriculture for several years. Their mother was a remarkable business woman, an ardent Presbyterian. She enjoyed nearly 80 years of active life. Charles W. has but one son, Chas. W., married and without children.

The Rhodes Family

It has already been shown that one of the old mills on Cedar Creek West of Middletown, was erected by Valentine Rhodes, who had several brothers. Their ancestor was one of the pioneers. From this family sprung the family of this name found in the vicinity of Middletown during the 19th Century. We may mention the names of Isaac, Jacob, Valentine, Jr. From these lines we find some of the name still prominent in that section—James W. Rhodes and his family, whose son is now a merchant in Middletown.

The Edmondson Family

This name appears about the Revolutionary War period. The Sketch of Winchester mentions Thomas Edmondson, the Tavern Keeper. The name has been connected with the South end of the county since that period, C. E. Edmondson the merchant of Middletown, being one of the descendants of this family.

The Danner Family

Jacob Danner has been mentioned elsewhere as one of the clockmakers prior to 1800; and Danner has been mentioned as a tavern keeper in Winchester, showing this family to be one of the 18th Century pioneers The writer knew Jacob S. Danner, of Middletown, long before the Civil War. He was an active man during his long life; owned several tracts of land; and he too conducted the jewelry business of the village for many years. His wife was a daughter of Joseph Miller, sister to John M. Their children were Atwell, William and three sisters, Martha, Bernice and Mary Ellen. Bernice became the wife of Rev. David Harris, of Middletown. Mary Ellen married (first) David Walton, a lawyer of Woodstock, and afterwards, as his widow, became the second wife of Rev. Harris. Rev. Mr. Harris, now of Baltimore, is the son of Bernice. The three sisters were noted for their attractions. One of the brothers married Miss Lodor, and one Miss Carson; they live in Richmond. The name of Danner is now extinct in the Valley.

The Dellinger Family

This family has beeen mentioned previously as one of the pioneers of the Valley. The writer knew several members of the later generation. David was the father of James H. Dellinger and Dr. George E. and other members. James H. held several important offices subsequent to the Civil War, in which he had been a gallant Confederate. His death about 1890 was lamented by many of his old comrades and friends.

The Everly Family

Wm. H. Everly, the widely known coach and wagon maker of Middletown, maintains the good reputation of this family. He is now and has been the efficient registrar of the Middletown election precinct. Mr. Everly's family belongs to the 19th Century. So also such families as the Ewings, Ridenours, Braggs, Hottles, Cooleys, Wilkinsons, Hensells and Yates. To the East, we find the Orndorffs, Guards, Lockes, Gollidays and many others that started the wave of progress after 1830; while to the West we find the Headleys, Chiles, Rusts, Carsons, Massies, Newmans, Grimms, Watsons, Barleys, Afflecks, Ogdens, Mathews, Mahaneys, Pangles, Tablers—busy with their farms, shops and other enterprises, starting with the early part of the 19th Century. Still Westward towards the mountain, we find the population changed in name and condition, since Zane started his Marlboro Iron Works. The Carrs, Longacres, Baldwins, Briscoes, Hogues and others of the 18th Century, have long since disappeared, and their places filled by a class of people that belong to the history of the 19th Century. We find the old Brent family represented by one of the descendants of a name that has been familiar in that section for more than 100 years.

The Brent—Sydnor Families

These families have been mentioned in Old Homestead Sketches. Charles Brent having survived the Revolutionary War, and settled down on his large tract of land already mentioned, was again in 1812 serving his country in that war. He reared a large family. Of his sons we mention Henry M., John G., Charles Innes. He had several daughters. One was Mrs. Jas. P. Riely, Mrs. Emily O'Bannon (of whom see other sketches); one daughter Susan lived in Winchester about 90 years. Mary A. became the wife of Capt. R. M. Sydnor; the children being Charles W. (Dr. Sydnor), Ellen Moore, Ann H., Richard M., Silas, Fauntleroy, and Kate. Ellen Moore married N. M. Cartmell (See Cartmell Sketches). Ann married Capt. S. G. Jamison; no children living. The sons all served in the Confederate Army. Dick, as he was familiarly called, was in some famous scouting service. He and Silas died in Texas several years ago. Fauntleroy died near his old home. Kate married a Mr. Wilkes of Washington. She survives her husband. Dr. Sydnor's widow and several children survived him. His widow is now dead. Carrie married G. W. Bragg. Ann married and left the county. One son Dr. Wm. Sydnor, lives near Richmond, Va. Capt Sydnor has been mentioned in connection with Spring Hill, his homestead near Old Forge. Capt. Sydnor was captured by the British on the high seas in 1811; the ship looted, and all the crew impressed in the naval service. The writer heard him recount his experiences and of the merchant seamen who were so unfortunate as to fall into the hands of the British Navy. Such outrages ended with the War of 1812-14. Capt. Sydnor and several of his old crew escaped after two years imprisonment and brutal treatment, and finding his way to one of the privateer vessels of the American Navy, did good service for his country until peace was declared. He bore marks of the flogging punishment he received at the hands of the British officer. The last year of the War, he was given command of a privateer vessel; and he always believed his crew sank the very vessel that had been his place of torture for two years. This was off the coast of Cuba in 1815. After his return to the Valley, he and his brother William lived in what was then called Syndor's Gap, West of Winter Hill. After his marriage with Miss Brent, he purchased Spring Hill.

Henry M. son of Col. Charles Brent, has been mentioned as one of the prominent citizens of Winchester. He was the father of C. Lewis Brent, Edwin S. and Henry M., Jr., all of whom have been mentioned in other pages. One daughter Carrie, by a second marriage, died young. Col. Charles died in 1830, an old man. He owned the large spring and provided for its continuance in the Brent family. He also provided for his wife Rachael, and directed that a plat of ground at Winter Hill be set apart for the burial of himself and family. He also provided for the support of his aged father and mother who lived in his homestead. Whether this was the aged and distinguished lawyer George Brent, who was a member of the Winchester Bar in 1772, is not known to the writer.

The Sperry Family

This family found at Middletown during the 19th Century, is traceable from the Sperrys of Winchester, who possibly built the first cabins along the old town run, before they had their deed, found among the old Spottsylvania records in the land office at Richmond, which mentions the existence of a house on the land lying on a branch of the Opecquon. When the town was laid out, the Sperry lots were recognized, showing their first location may have been on the run when they had two small tanyards in 1739. We find them ever afterwards in the town and county, taking part in civil and military activities. John Sperry and his family of Middletown, are all that bear the name to-day, though many descendants are found in the Valley. The author knew two old men many years ago, Peter E. and Peter G. Sperry residents of Winchester, Va. They were distantly related. One child of Peter, Lottie, is the wife of Rev. J. W. Lupton; another daughter was Mrs. Doct Chris Reed. Two prominent business men of N. York City, Joseph and Thomas Sperry, are of this line. We find the name often written Speary, Spirey, Sparry. Admiral Sperry of the American Navy, traces his line to the Valley poineers.

The Beatty Family

This family first appeared in the town of Winchester at an early day as one of the pioneers, sending its branches Southward into the County, and intermarrying with many prominent families. The Beatty families found at this day about Stephens City and country East, viz: the late Capt. John W. Beatty, R. S. Beatty, J. C. and several others, are traceable from Capt. Henry Beattie who has been mentioned in these pages as an officer in the Revolutionary War and other war periods. The name has suffered some changes by scribes during the periods mentioned. Beatty Carson who was prominent in the early part of the 19th Century, points the connection with this family. Col. Henry Beattie died in 1840, eighty years old. He was in command of a Va. Regiment at Crainey Island in 1813. Congress presented him a sword for gallant services. He had a son Dr. Stephen Rittenhouse Beatty, and a daughter Juliet who married John Shipe. Their tombs are in Mt. Hebron. Three brothers of this name came from Ireland when young, and settled East of the Blue Ridge. Two of these are found in the regiments during the Indian Wars. They secured land in Frederick County, near where Front Royal now stands; and their descendants are found in Warren County now, on part of the same land.

The large family mentioned, living in Frederick County, are chiefly the children of Robert Beatty who died in 1888, aged 88.

Capt. Jno. W. Beatty's two sons Atwell and Charles, live in Stephens City.

Henry C. Beatty's children are: J. C., Minnie, Frank and David. R. S. Beatty's children are: James R., John S., Harry E., Chas. C., Lloyd

W., Atwell S., Guy T., Ida B. wife of Wm. Lewin, and Flora B. wife of A. R. Woods.

Samuel W. Beatty, at Strasburg, sons: Howard, Frank and Roy.

Irvin Beatty has sons at Pittsburg.

Four of Robert's sons were Confederate soldiers.

Samuel Beatty, a brother of Robert, lived in Ohio for years, with a large family.

The Bucher (Booker) Family

This family found about Newtown as one of the pioneers, also in the Western section of the county, often spelled the name Boogher. They furnished soldiers for all the wars during the history of the county. Many old citizens living near the old Russell Precinct, remember old Capt. Jacob Bucher; and those about Stephens City remember the old Buchers of that section. The name is familiar in Tidewater Virginia, and prominent in St. Louis. Old records of the County afford much valuable information relative to this family. If space permit, fuller notice will appear.

The Lemley Family

The first of this name was John Lemley who lived in Winchester prior to 1755. From him is traceable the old Newtown Lemleys, and the well-known families found in Stephens City at this writing. Jacob Lemley and his sons Robert T. and Frank, well-known merchant tailors; James M., married Miss Barr and several other members of this family are well known business men and have been identified with the best interests of this historic town.

What is said of the Lemleys, may also be said of the Weaver, Young, Grove, Adams, Shryock, Guard, and Steele families, prominent about the old Stephens Town from its earliest history. Several of those families had branches in Winchester; and several representatives were well-known Confederate soldiers.

The Cadwallader Family

James W. Cadwallader is the representative of this pioneer family which settled in the neighborhood of Stephensburg. He was a Confederate soldier of the Civil War. Mr. Cadwallader was left a widower while his large family of boys were quite small; and they have all turned out a credit and comfort to him in his declining years. They are John, who is the agent and store-keeper at Vaucluse Station, married and has a family. Floyd, who is married and in business in Stephens City, and Milton.

The Shryocks, Gibsons, Barnes, Drakes, Argenbrights, Samsells, Mayers and Allamongs, are all part of the 19th Century. The writer hopes to find space for fuller mention of them. To the East of the Village, the Wise, Walter, Hale, Nelson, Albin, Cornwell, Grimm, Perry, Mumaw and several other families belong to old periods.

The McLeod families found around Stephens City, belong to the family of that name found far back in the early history of the county. They have been mentioned elsewhere.

Wm. Albin obtained a reward for taking up a runaway slave in 1754. Old court orders mention many of the above names.

Samuel Newman was a Justice of the Peace in 1754.

Associated with the Newtown section, were two well-known officials, no doubt forgotten by the population of to-day—Jas. Johnston and Watson Peery, the efficient constables. Johnston had a brother who removed to Mississippi many years before the Civil War. He has recently visited his nephew, B. C. Shull, hale and hearty at 94 years.

Watson Peery (not Perry as often called) was of the old family found in Carr's Gap (now Fawcett's) in the pioneer days. His brother James died near the old settlement since the Civil War. both were men of fine traits. C. Milton Peery and C. W. Peery were sons of Watson. We could name many other well known families; but the reader must now be referred to the old records of the County.

The Chipley Family

This was one of the pioneer families. They were on the ground long before their first deed was recorded in 1775. Several lines started from this original stock, and descendants bearing the name are found in several States. The ancestors of James and L. J. Chipley, who took prominent part in the affairs of the county, were buried at Opecquon in a small lot on the South side of the old stone church. Prior to the Civil War, this lot was surrounded by a stone wall, and graves were marked by marble slabs,—all of which went along with other devastation. The only mark of the lot now is the wall foundation under the shade of old aspen trees. L. J. C. Chipley was a lawyer. James a farmer lived in the house of his ancestors near old Newtown, on the N. E. side of the Valley pike. It was the home of Thos. Harrison, an Englishman, subsequent to the Civil War. Capt. John Chipley, who died in Hardy County a few years ago, and W. D. Chipley of Stephens City, were sons of James.

The Carson Family

This family has been incidentally mentioned in other pages. Genl. Jas. H. Carson and his brother lived due West from Newtown. This family was connected with Anderson and other families of that section.

The Carter Family

Much has been said in other pages about the Carter family. This, however, related to the Carters found North of Winchester, as pioneers. From this family came Wm. A. Carter, who was the founder of the family living West of old Newtown. He was born in 1799; died 1857. He was a son of Arthur Carter mentioned as the paper manufacturer. He was twice married. His first wife Miss Beeler, was the mother of two children: Wm. A. and Mary E. Carter. Both moved to Missouri. The latter became the wife of James Taylor Mitton. The second wife of Wm. A., Sr., was Mary C. daughter of Lawrence Pittman, of Shenandoah County. Their children were John L., Robert K., Joseph M., Charles, Berryhill M., Geo. H., and Anna L. B. M. married Miss Caldwell of Fredericksburg. She has been very prominent in educational work. Her essays on various subjects testify to her accomplishments. Geo. H. married Eva C. daughter of Chas. Castleman. She is the mother of several well known children. Geo. H. is now connected with farm implement manufacturers.

The Shull Family

This family has been mentioned already, but the writer feels inclined to add something more. He knew Elijah Shull long before the Civil War, when he lived on the high point North of the Cedar Creek Spring, now the home of his daughter Mrs. Dr. Cherry. Mr. Shull's father was Jonathan Shull, whose ancestor was one of the pioneers of the Cedar Creek country, and left a large family. Elijah married Harriet Johnson. She became the mother of Edmonia (Mrs. Cherry), Godfrey, a large land holder of Missouri. He married Miss Vic. Baker of Hardy County. Briscoe C., served in Company C., 12th Va. Cavalry; married in 1871 Emma Hancock, now the mother of a large family. One daughter is the wife of Mr. Sowers; one the wife of Mr. Clagett; one son, Dr. Shull, lives in Oklahoma. Herbert is Comr. of the Rev. for the Southern District.

Emily, sister of Briscoe C., married J. Frank Lupton. Bertie became the second wife of Capt. S. G. Jamison. Charles lives in Missouri, Dr. E. D. Cherry, husband of Edmonia Shull, was a South Carolinan; he served 4 years in the Confederate Army as Surgeon, and practiced medicine in Southern Frederick from 1866 until his death in about 1904.

The Rinker Family

This family mentioned in connection with the Brent homestead as already stated, was founded by Casper Rinker, who moved from the old stone mill property at the head of Opecquon, when he purchased the Winter Hill property. His wife was Sarah Keckley. They lived at the mill property for about forty years. There they reared their family, viz: Belle, Anna, Wm. F., and Frederick. Belle married Hugh O. Pierce, and is the mother of Blanche, Conley and Gus.

Anna married J. Norton Claggett. They live at Winter Hill. She is the mother of several children.

William F. married Mary Streit—several children by this union.

Fred became a physician, and lives at Upperville, Va. Casper Rinker's father was Casper Rinker who lived near Pughtown, and had several children by his first wife, viz: Casper, Mrs. James Pangle, Josiah and Jacob. Also raised a family by his second wife. Josiah left several sons: one son, A. L. Rinker, lives on his father's old homestead, and has two children. This family can trace their lines through the old records from Gaspar Rinker, who owned land West of Winchester. He was appointed Apl. 2, 1771, overseer of a road from Hunting Ridge to the county line, in room of James McGill. The old pioneer had several brothers and sisters. William Rinker owned several large tracts of slate land West of Winchester, the father of John G. Rinker and George W. Rinker, was a grandson of one of the brothers. Henry Rinker brother of Gaspar, lived in Winchester in 1770.

The Pittman Family

This family has been mentioned several times, and is entitled to fuller notice. The writer remembers several of the old stock: Solomon, Andrew, Jacob and John. They could trace their lines from the earliest settlements. The family is dwindling in numbers, and indications are, the name like other old families, may become extinct. The three brothers Joseph, John W. and Philip, hold on to the old homestead. Joseph died long since, unmarried, and the other two are single. Their old homestead is one of the colonials, and once owned by Rev. Nash Legrand.

The Brumback Family

The handsome estate adjoining the Pitman home, owned by this family, justifies a brief mention of this family at this point. The family belongs to the Colonial settlers; but their first settlement was in old Frederick County, now Page. Joseph Brumback came from Page County about 1840, and made his home where his son

Jacob now lives, being the old Carr homestead. There he reared his family and spent a long and useful life. He was Justice of the Peace for several terms. His oldest son Andrew has been previously mentioned. Dr. Isaac M. Brumback, a brother, living in same neighborhood, is well known. He has one son a physician, and also several other children.

The Funkhouser Family

This family also came from the upper section early in the 19th Century. Anthony Funkhouser, the head of the large family, has been mentioned elsewhere. He reared a large family, Joseph H. being one, whose death occurred about 1906. One of his sons Chas. E. Funkhouser, is a prosperous farmer of Clarke County; one lives in Maryland. Daniel C. lives at the old homestead, a prosperous farmer, with a large family. Chas. Wesley lives on part of the old Glebe Tract. He has a son and daughter.

The Fawcett Family

Thomas Fawcett the pioneer who settled in the part of Frederick County now Warren County, and started the old homestead in 1797, was the father of fourteen children, his son Joseph being one. He inherited the homestead where his son Elkanah spent his long life, having married a daughter of Martin Funkhouser. They left a large family: Benjamin F., Joseph, Wm. P., T. F., and several daughters. The old stone homestead is retained by one of the sons. The older set were Quakers. The family came from Belfast, Ireland, among the early immigrations. The family has been mentioned as intermarrying with well-known families. Joseph Fawcett died 1862.

The Bayliss Family

This name appears elsewhere. John Bayliss was one of the old county surveyors,—cotemporary with the Hites, Briscoes, Baldwins, etc. His son Henry Bayliss was an officer in the Revolutionary War. One of his sons Thomas, was one of the 1812 War pensioners. He was the father of eleven children, Marshall H., and Milton E. Bayliss being his sons. One of his daughters was Martin Wisecarver's first wife, who was the mother of Marion M. Wisecarver, now resident in Campbell County, Va. One of Henry Bayliss' sons was John Bayliss, father of Harrison T. Bayliss, one of the old tavern-keepers on the Northwestern Turnpike. His wife was Ann Jane Fizer, daughter of Michael Fizer who kept the old tavern on same road. Afterwards his son-in-law John Wilson, conducted the well-known establishment. Harrison Bayliss left a large family, his sons being Joseph H., M. Conley, John E. and Wm. H.

The Stephenson Family

Robert Stephenson, the first of the family in the Southern part of Frederick, married a daughter of Casper Rinker. She was a sister of Casper of Winter Hill, and had two sons by this marriage; Joseph C., now living at the old homestead.

Passing from this neighborhood, up the drains of Cedar Creek, we find many descendants of old pioneers of that section, seated on the old homesteads. The Fryes, Goughs, Williams, Keckleys (Cackleys), Brills, Orndorffs, Milhorns. Still further, we find the Russells, Richards, Richard, Beans, McIlwees, Coopers, Whites, Turners; while towards the South are found the Vances, Kellars, Findlays, Himelrights, Orndorffs, Wilsons, Pifers, and many others; while to the North, on the East side of North Mountain are the Clowsers, Halls, Rameys, Cochrans, Kerns, Crabills, Larricks, Whissens, Spellmans, Ryans, Perrys, Wiggintons, Whetzels, Linaburgs, Lamps, Tevalts.

Many old pioneers have none to represent their name in the Valley.

The Richards Family

For many years there has been some confusion about this name. Some regarding this and the *Richard* family as the same. It will be seen from the following brief notice, they were distinct, one family being altogether English, the other purely German.

The pioneer of the Richards family was John Richards, who located his grant for a large tract of land along upper Cedar Creek and its drains. This was in 1735. He proceeded to settle other families who followed the first Hite immigration. Such leases or deeds were recorded in Orange County. In 1744 he sold part of his patent tract to Benjamin Fry, an Englishman. John Richards was an Englishman. By his will in 1749, he devises his lands to the children of his deceased brother Peter. They were then living in England. A provision of his will was: "If one of Peter's sons come to this country, then he to have half the estate; in case of his death, then to his brother Henry and sister Hannah." In 1770 "Peter Richards, County of Devon, Kingdom of Great Britain, Yeoman, Mary Richards of East Budleigh same county, and Alice wife of John Lee of Haspford same co., Yeoman, Jonathan R. of same county, and Henry Richards late of Philadelphia but now of Frederick County, Virginia, children of Peter Richards the elder brother of John late of Frederick County," executed a power of attorney to John Lee to settle their affairs in America. Henry had been on the land and held one-half the estate as the will provided. On Lee's arrival, Henry sold a tract of land on Cedar Creek to John Lee. This was the ancestor of the John C. Lee family found in that section during the 19th Century. In 1778, Henry and Jane his wife and brother Jonathan of England, conveyed a tract of land to Jacob Huffman. In 1793, Henry by his will devised his property to his widow Jane, and to his sons John and Henry, and daughter Elees wife of John Shriver, Mary wife of Archibald Hamilton, Hannah wife of Frederick Cooper, and Ann his single daughter. His estate consisted of several tracts of land, mills and large family of slaves. We will not follow the lines of his married daughters. John died in 1860, 90 years of age, leaving three sons, Henry M., Moses and James M. Richards and several daughters.

The children of Henry M.; Mary C. Ginn, Henry G. and Lewis W. Richards received portions of the estate—$1,000 to James M. and the home farm to Moses after the death of his stepmother, Sarah Richards. Henry M. died in Winchester in 1861. He devised property to Henry M., Eva and Sally C., children by his second wife.

James M. Richards the other son, married twice, first, Miss Hollingsworth. By this marriage was born a son and daughter. His second wife was Margaret Fry, who was the mother of A. B. Richards, a prosperous farmer, and Comr. of Roads for Shawnee District for several terms. Mordecai another son is a farmer living in Frederick County. John and Morict are non-residents. A. B. Richards has a large family of sons and daughters. His farm was part of the Glass estate. His children are: Clara, L. Adolph. This son is a young man of rare promise. After taking his academic course, he graduated at the University of Virginia; he also took honors at Columbia College and Johns Hopkins. He now has a classical school in Washington, D. C. Emma E., mar. Charles Cooper, Sadie L., Harry A., Boyd R., Alva C., Augusta, Nelson and Roy reflect credit on the old family.

Henry Richards son of Henry who died in 1793 and brother of John, lived in the old neighborhood. He owned a large estate—land, mill and slaves. S. B. Sale owns the homestead at this writing. Henry died prior to the Civil War. His wife Lydia died at an advanced age. A son Col. James Richards lived and died in Front Royal, a man of culture and wealth. He was once Sheriff of Frederick County. His sister Harriet married Capt. George R. Long. One daughter survived her. This was Mary wife of Dr. Godfrey S. Miller of Winchester.

The Richard Family

This name was written many ways for several years. Being German, scribes differed as to the translation—Reichert, Richet, Rickart, finally adopting Richard, as written. The first appearance we have of this German name was in the early part of the 19th Century. This was Henry who settled near the North Mountain. He was an old man in 1833 when he made his will, which was not probated until 1847. This will is signed in German. He wills several tracts of land to his oldest son Joseph, including a lot of one-fourth acre at Pembroke Springs, together with his slaves, stills, blacksmith tools, etc., Joseph to pay legacies to his sister Sarah Frye, to brothers, Isaac, Henry, Jacob, Elijah and John. Several sons were then married. Jacob lived near the old home, and had sons Henry P., Joseph P., Isaac and Uriah. Their mother was Margaret Pifer. All are now dead. Henry P.'s children were Rev. Dr. Richard, Rev. Asa Richard, a Lutheran Minister.

Rev. Asa has one son in the ministry.

Joseph P. Richard's first wife was Nancy C., daughter of Casper Rinker, Sr., mother of William, Harvey A. and one sister. William lives near White Post. The sister moved West.

Harvey A. has been previously mentioned. Joseph P.'s second wife was Susan Larrick, she was the mother of Dr. J. A. Richards, dentist in Winchester, Mrs. Joseph Snapp, Wesley, J. Luther, Julius W.

Dr. Wm. H. Keffer who built the Pembroke Springs building, married Miss Richard. He was born in Woodstock 1830. He had two brothers John and Jacob, who went West; and two Addison and James lived in Frederick County. Dr. Keffer had several sons: John W., a Justice in Back Creek District. James and brother live in West Virginia.

The Foreman Family

This name has sometimes been confounded with that of Froman. There is no occasion for this. The latter distinctly belongs to the Hite immigration; while the Foremans belong to a subsequent period, the name being found in Berkeley County in 1770. From this branch came John Foreman about 1820. He was employed by Benjamin Keckley as an expert distiller. Prior to the Civil War he operated his own stills in the Western part of Frederick County; and there reared a large family. His two sons Amos and Josiah reside in that section. Another son John removed to Cumberland.

Amos married a daughter of Edward Snapp, and raised a large family. The writer recalls with sincere gratitude valuable services rendered to him during the Civil War by Amos Foreman.

The Barley Family

This was not a pioneer family; but the large family of men and women who lived near what is now Relief postoffice, deserve notice. Adam Barley who died in 1825 near Winchester, was the father of John, Margaret, Peter, Mary Harriet, Louise, William and Adam. All are now dead. Adam left a large family. One of his sisters married Mr. Gordon, father of John P. Gordon, who has a large family of children. The Barleys were noted farmers.

The Pritchard Family

The writer has known several families of this name. They are distantly related. Some have been previously mentioned. One family lived near Kernstown for many years prior to the Civil War, extending back to the Revolutionary War period. Stephen Pritchard has been mentioned in connection with the Cartmell sketch. His father preceded him as a farmer in that section. A family of this name lived in Winchester during this period. Mr. Housen Pritchard who lives in the old stone house corner of Main and Cork Streets, is a descendant of the Winster branch. His single sister lives with him. Another sister is Mrs. Charles Ward, living near Stephens City. Housen has been mentioned in connection with the old Winchester News. He is a man of remarkable intelligence; has been in failing health for several years. He was an old Confederate soldier.

Another family of this name lived on South Main Street.

The Faulkner Family of Winchester

The first appearance of this family in Winchester was in 1836, when Isaac H. Faulkner established his business as manufacturer of ladies' shoes. This was satisfactory. He was a Marylander. The year following his arrival, he married a Miss Frederick. Mr. Faulkner had six sons, who became prominent citizens in Winchester since the Civil War, several of whom were Confederate soldiers. Of the brothers who remained in Winchester, were James F., Isaac H., Jr., Walter W., and Ollie F. Faulkner.

John W. the third son of Isaac H., Sr., located in Lynchburg since the War, and there conducted a large wholesale and retail drug business. Isaac H. and Ollie F. live in Winchester and have retired from business in comfortable circumstances. One of their sisters became the wife of Dr. Maynard, who died in Winchester about 1896.

The Kreemer Family

This is one of the old families found in business in Winchester in the early part of the 19th Century. The writer is unable to trace their line fully. Members of the family have failed up to this time to furnish details. We can recall the names of George Kreemer, whose home is on South Market Street. He was one of the town officers for many years. On South Main Street, lived another George Kreemer. He intermarried with the Coburn family. Israel Coburn and brother have been mentioned elsewhere as school-teachers, surveyors, etc. This George Kreemer was the father of James Kreemer. The other George was the father of Merton Kreemer and other children. John Kreemer had several sons who engaged in the grocery and supply business after the war, on the corner where the Evans Hotel now stands. They have since conducted a similar business at several other points. George has a meat store; Charles and Brothers have a large grocery on Main Street. John and Tom also conduct a grocery on South Main near Water St. Another member of the older generation, was Coonrod Kreemer the tailor.

The Burgess Family

This family, once prominent in business in Winchester, has become almost extinct in the Lower Valley. James H. Burgess once owned a farm on the East suburb of Winchester, now the property of the Harris Brothers. For many years he was identified with the Shenandoah Valley Agricultural Society. Mr. B. had two sons to enter the Confederate Army. Both were killed. One of his daughters was Miss Virginia Burgess, a teacher well-known in Winchester. Her sister was Mrs. Dr. Simms. Her daughter is Mrs. Calmes of Winchester.

Capt. James B. Burgess, who has been mentioned elsewhere, was a son of James Burgess who built the octagon house on the N. W. Turnpike just East of the Town Spring.

The author finds he lacks space to pursue the line he had mapped out for this volume; and can do no more than barely mention a few names as they occur to him. Several families they represent, would otherwise receive fuller notice. Of this number, the numerous Carper families, of Carpers Valley, would fill a chapter; likewise the Fords. Three well-known men of this name were prominent millers: Benjamin F., William and John T. All three left children. Capt. John Ford, of Co. C., 12th Cavalry, son of William, is now a resident of Winchester. John

T.'s sons are promising young men. Luther is in the U. S. Railway Mail Service; Benjamin a farmer, and Cromwell in dairy and fruit business. One daughter is the wife of John Bacher, a lawyer in Norfolk; another married Calvin Kater, the nurseryman. The Carpenter family is now represented by Newton A., James H. and David Carpenter. They all have families. The Pelters were numerous at one time in the vicinity of Kernstown. One of the sons, John W., purchased a farm near Pughtown since the Civil War. He left several children; James Pelter being now the sole representative of the name in this section. His sister is Mrs. Robinson, of near Opecquon postoffice. In this connection, we will mention David Watson, whose wife was a sister of John W. Pelter. The Watsons of Southern part of Frederick, have been previously mentioned. Joseph and family live West of Middletown. Benjamin Watson his brother was a famous scout, as the writer can personally testify. They were not brothers of David. The Deans came to Frederick County from Penna. early in the 19th Century. William and his large family settled near Kernstown, and were harness and saddle makers. He owned the property now occupied by his youngest son Henry—a brick house on West side of the Valley Turnpike. This was once part of the old Pritchard and Hoge plantation. Adam Dean, one of William's sons, married a Miss Kern, and lived in Newtown for many years. He now lives on his farm West of that place. His sons, A. W., M. K. and brother are well known. William Dean, Jr., lives in Youngstown, Ohio. His sister is the widow of Thomas McCardell, and lives with her single brother Henry. The Gibson Brothers, well-known wagon makers of Stephens City, are descendants of pioneers. So also was the Marks family. James Lemley married Miss Barr. This family came from Penna. since the Civil War. The Barr brothers operated a steam flour mill near the Railroad station. The McLeods have been mentioned elsewhere. B. T. Argenbright, another of Newtown's good mechanics, may not be classed with the pioneers of Frederick, but it is well known that his ancestors were in the Valley at one time early in the 19th Century; and he may trace his line to them. The Painters West of Newtown belong to the 19th Century and own the property formerly occupied by Martin R. Kauffman until after the Civil War. Still to the West was Jonas Chamberlain, one of the most successful farmers in that section. His son Charles was drowned in the Shenandoah River. The father had been accidentally killed by his son. Mr. Chamberlain's only daughter married James B. Streit. In this neighborhood was the family of Thomas W. Chapman, the blacksmith, who had the credit of shoeing horses for Stonewall Jackson, Ashby and the Cavalry command. Mr. C. had several sons: George W., Thomas, Jr., James W., and one other. Still West was James W. Ginn, on a large tract of land called Sunnyside. Mr. Ginn was a successful farmer; reared his large family on this place. He afterwards moved to Clarke County. His wife was a Miss Hardy. Charles, Samuel, Richard and Holmes were his sons. He had several daughters. Lucy married Mr. Ginn of Maryland. She was the mother of Mrs. Wm. H. Baker. Mrs. Ginn married for second husband Mr. Charles B. Meredith. One of Mr. James Ginn's sons—Samuel, married a sister of Amos Marker. Amos was the son of John Marker, who belonged to one of the old families of the county. He was an old Confederate soldier, and has been deputy sheriff of the county. Harlan P. Tabb, who owns fine farms in the Opecquon neighborhood, came to Frederick from Hampshire County after the Civil War; he is a descendant of the large and influential family found in Berkeley County in the early days. He has three children: Edward, son by his first marriage, whose mother was a Miss Vandiver. His second wife was a Miss Manuel; she is the mother of his twin daughters, Madge and Molly. West of the Little North Mountain, lived several families the writer knew to be pioneers, which he intended to embody in a special sketch—Tilberry Goff and Nicholas Perry being of the number. They were 1812 soldiers. The former has one son T. F. Gough (so written by him) who lives on the homestead. He has a large family of sons and daughters. Mr. Perry died an old man many years ago, and left several sons and daughters, Elijah and John being of the number. Elijah left a large family. Several of his grown children moved to Martinsburg and are highly respected. While in this section, the writer will mention briefly a family which was very prominent at one time—Lewis V. Shearer, who owned and operated Mt. Vernon tannery. This was a notable place for many years prior to the Civil War. Mr. S. conducted a successful business. The leather vaults were often used as a rendezvous by Confederate scouts during the time when Milroy and Sheridan occupied the Lower Valley. There they could safely meet and mature plans for penetrating the Federal lines. Mr. Shearer was a true friend to the venturesome scouts. The writer bears testimony to this fact. His large family of sons and daughters, viz: Susan wife of John R. Hodgson, A. L. Shearer, the well-known business man of Winchester who married Nina daughter of Wm. G. Kiger; Robert, now of Cumberland, George of California. Two of their sisters moved to

Charleston, West Va., with their father where he died several years ago. Mr. Shearer was an upright and useful man. During the prosperous days of the tannery, he had the benefit of the services of an expert tanner. This was A. L. Elosser, who spent 27 years at that point; and after the war conducted a tannery on the Romney road, about 5 miles from Winchester. He is now an old man; makes his home in Winchester with his daughter Mrs. Haines on Water Street. Mr. E. has a competency as the result of his energy and faithful service. He has one son L. H. W. Elosser, who is now a retired tanner, having accumulated ample means. We may add that the Mt. Vernon Tannery has been a thing of the past for thirty years or more. In this connection, Wm. G. Kiger has been mentioned. He was one of the old firm of merchants in Winchester, known as Taylor, Kiger and Seevers. Mr. Kiger lived in the house known as Fort Loudoun during the Civil War. His daughter Susie married Capt. J. C. Van Fossen. Another daughter married and lived in Clarke County. Mr. James B. Taylor, of the firm, has one son living in Winchester; who has been city sergeant for several years. One of Mr. Taylor's daughters married Capt. Samuel Baker. One is the wife of Mr. Black, of Penna. Miss Annie, another daughter lives in Winchester. In this connection we may add that Capt. Baker's second wife was Miss Maggie Heist. She was a daughter of Mr. Geo. Heist, who was identified with the W. & P. Railroad for at least thirty years. After the Civil War, he removed to Baltimore, and was a trusted office clerk for the B. &. O. R. R. until his death. Mr. Heist had two other daughters; one was the wife of Granville Harper, and the other is Miss Mamie Heist. Their brother is the well-known dentist Geo. K. Heist. His son George is also a dentist, whose sister is Miss Mae Heist.

The Conway Brothers, Nathan T. and William G., are descendants of a pioneer family. Their father was Hugh Conway, who married a Miss Haines, of Berkeley County. He was one of the Forty-Niners, who went to California, and there died. His father was James Conway, who lived and died in Jefferson County. He owned the farm known now as the Charles B. Rouss farm. Hugh Conway lived at one time on Applepie Ridge on the farm known now as Mr. Green's large apple orchard farm. William G. his son was a member of Company H., 13th Va. Infty. Regt. Stonewall Brigade; was a merchant in Winchester for years. He is now Deputy County Treasurer. Nathan has always lived in Winchester. The Conways emigrated from Wales at an early day, and settled in Northern part of old Frederick. (There is no known connection between them and the two railroad contractors, Michael and Timothy Conway.)

Mrs. Richard Sidwell is a sister of Nathan and William G. Conway. She now lives in Baltimore with her daughter, and has attained the age of 85 years. Richard Sidwell was a son of Hugh Sidwell. His mother was a Miss Haines. He has two sisters living in Loudoun County,—Mrs. Philips and Miss Martha Sidwell.

Many years ago there lived in Frederick County Mr. Wm. B. Walter, a man prominent in his day, but remembered by but few of the present population. He was the father of the three brothers William B., Jr., Dorsey and Frank Walter, so well known to Winchester business men. Dorsey was a well-known figure in the courts, acting as a Commissioner in Chancery. He had the respect and confidence of the Winchester Bar. His death occurred in 1908. He left a large family. Two sons give promise to maintain the good name of their father. One is cashier of a Georgia bank; Carroll is a young lawyer. Dorsey was a Confederate soldier. William B. has been previously mentioned as one of the clerks of the Corporation Court. Frank was a merchant in Winchester for several years. He is now a clerk in the Farmers and Merchants Bank. He has several children. He, too, was a Confederate soldier.

The Aulick Family

Charles Aulick, the progenitor of the Shenandoah Aulicks, had four children: One son Charles went to Kentucky. Henry another son, was Commodore Aulick of the U. S. Navy during the early part of the 19th Century. He had several children, all dead, one being Richmond Aulick, who was Lieut. Comdr. in the Navy when he died. Frederick Aulick, the third son, lived and died in Winchester an old man. His wife was a Miss Smith. She was the mother of James and Alberta. The latter became Mrs. Kuhnert, the wife of a German professor of music. She survives her husband. George Aulick, the fourth son, married Mary Crebs (Crepts). Her father was Conrad Crepts. He was a native of Hesse-Cassell, Germany; and claimed that he was one of the Hessian soldiers connected with the British Army. Geo. Aulick's children were Eliza, Cordelia, Edwin, George who married and went to California, was the founder of the town Modesta, the citizens of which honored his memory by the erection of an imposing monument. The next son Charles E., is Mr. Eugene Aulick, the extensive florist, living in the handsome property on South Braddock Street. He married Miss "Reb" Kreemer, daughter of James and Annie Kreemer. They have two children, Mary C. and Charles E.

Another son of George Aulick, was Hendren Aulick, generally known as Ernest, Surgeon in the U. S. Navy. He had won distinction for his services, when his untimely death in 1881 cut short his career.

Conrad Crepts, father of Mrs. George Aulick, married a Miss Bruner, of Maryland. His children were Conrad, Berry, Lewis, Harry and Mrs. Smoke, mother of Dr. E. B. Smoke of Frederick County.

Berry Crebs went to Illinois; married and lived in Carmow; left several children. His family became prominent in that section. His son John Crebs was M. C. from that District, and also Colonel of an Illinois Regiment during the Civil War.

Harry Crebs was the father of two well-known men John H., one of the police justices in Winchester, and Joshua N. Crebs of Kernstown, whose son Jack is a well-known hotel man in St. Louis.

Old records show that old Conrad Crepts could not have been a poor man when he chose to remain in Winchester and not return with the Hessian prisoners to his old country. His savings of gold coin, paid by England for his three years services, must have been hoarded by him; and when the war closed, he was virtually a rich man among the people who had nothing but worthless scrip for money. This man prior to 1820, had built several good houses on Potato Hill. The old stone house on the corner of Main and Leicester Streets, known for many years as the Washington South corner, was one of these; thence Southward, he owned nearly all the lots out to the Common. These facts are mentioned to remove the impression formed concerning all the Hessian prisoners.

The Nulton Family

This family name appeared in the Valley early in the 19th Century. The writer has always known two distinct families of this name in Winchester, who are unable to show any family connection.

Abraham Nulton was largely engaged in the stove and tinware business for many years—located on Main Street. He owned a large building and lot. His wife was a Miss Carson, one of the Beatty-Carson family already mentioned. Their children were Beatty Nulton, Emily wife of John Dixon; Hattie wife of Geo. Haines; Kate, wife of a Mr. Hubbard, of Baltimore.

Joseph A. Nulton has been mentioned elsewhere as the clerk of the circuit court. This was Col. Nulton of the 2nd Va. Regiment organized after the Civil War. He had a good record as a soldier in the Stonewall Brigade. Joseph A. succeeded his father and conducted the business at the old stand until he was elected clerk in 1881. He died during his second term, and was succeeded by his son J. Howard, for a short time. He married Miss Virginia Clark, dau. of James Clark, a farmer of good reputation who lived West of the Hahn Mill on Abrams Creek. Their children are Louis McCoy Nulton, Lt. Commander, U. S. Navy; at this writing, on the Battleship Ohio, forming part of the Naval Fleet sailing around the world. The writer has before him, in this connection, a long letter written aboard the Ohio, mailed on the coast of Turkey. The features of this letter indicate the vast amount of information Naval officers are supposed to have concerning the many countries and seaports of the world. Commander Nulton married Miss Evans, dau. of Edward Evans, the well-known tobacconist, of Winchester. They have two children, Virginia Adams, and Dorothy Evans.

Bessie C. Nulton, dau. of Joseph A., married John B. Hoffman; no children. J. Howard, her brother, is prominent as an official in the insurance business. His sister Miss Nanny, is connected with educational work.

The Nulton name had some struggles in the 18th Century, to become simplified. We have seen the name in Penna. records spelled (1) Noltonne; then Nultone; then Knoultone, and Knolton. About 1790, the same family signed writings simply Nulton. It has been thought "by some" the name is of French origin, though it is generally conceded that John Nulton, the father of Abraham, came from *Hesse-Cassel,* Germany, just prior to 1800.

The other Nulton family found in Winchester, was John H. Nulton, Superintendent of Streets, Water, etc. He was a familiar figure to the town for forty years, holding this and other responsible offices. He was competent, faithful and just. Mr. Nulton believed the two families were related, but could not trace the line. Two of his grand-daughters live in Winchester, and his grandson is in the Navy.

The Jones Family

From the writer's earliest recollection, a family of this name lived on the Opecquon in the Glass neighborhood. The venerable James Jones lived there on a large plantation in a brick house said to have been erected by his father. On this same tract was an old fort in good repair in 1850. Mr. Jones married in 1817 Eleanor Marquis. Their sons Edward H., Marquis, William, and Joseph were active business men and have been previously mentioned. A younger brother, James Harvey, moved West when a young man. William and Joseph died many years ago. Both had sons and daughters, who married and reared families. William Jones was the father of Laura, Alice and Annie. (Mrs. A. G. Rudolph.) Their three brothers are James, Albert and Luther. Joseph Jones' children are James B., Mrs. J. R. Triplett, and Mrs. Massie. Mr. E. H. Jones died recently, leaving a large estate. His brother Marquis lives at the old homestead, the last survivor of the five brothers. William, Joseph and Marquis rendered service to the Confederate Army. Their grandfather was James Jones, one of the pioneers in the Valley.

In the section East of Newtown, near the Clarke line, there were several families well known to the writer. Of this number were three men, James F. Leach, Geo. L. Stephens, and Benjamin Hicks. They were sterling men; always active in every political battle; fought under the old election laws. Magnus Leach son of James, lives in Warren County; one of his sisters married Park Strode, both have promising sons and daughters. The old men died long since. Mr. Hicks has one son Gilbert. He and his sister live at the old home near Nineveh.

In that section are found the Cornwell and Gardner families, descendants of pioneer families.

The Orndorff family has been quite numerous in that section; they are unable to trace their lines to the Orndorffs in the Northwest part of the County, where Isaac, William, Benjamin, Solomon and several others were heads of large families. They can trace their lines back to the pioneers. The writer has known many of the name. Some are found in Shenandoah, Hardy and Hampshire Counties.

Many persons in Frederick for years have known Joseph B. Orndorff, now an old man, who was one of the constables prior to the Civil War. In more recent years, he was one of the Justices in the Western section. He married a daughter of Abraham Keller, whose father was one of the Revolutionary War soldiers. At one time this family owned large tracts of land along upper Cedar Creek. Mrs. Orndorff is the mother of a large family of sons and daughters, viz: Lee, Morgan, Marion, Archie, Ellen and two sisters, one of whom married Asa Rosenberger. These children are prospering in business. We find in that section several other families who belong to the pioneers. Of these we may name briefly, the Himelrights. The well-known farmers John Y., and Joseph maintain the good name of their ancestors.

The Coopers are of the old stock. The writer knew Samuel and Watson C. when they were prosperous men. Both left small families. Their brother Jackson once owned a farm near Hillman's Tollgate; he sold his property and went to the wild country of the *Canaan,* West Virginia, and accumulated wealth. He has several sons and daughters.

The Huffs of that section, John and Joseph, are sons of an enterprising father, who spent money in prospecting for silver in that section many years ago.

The Windles, found along Cedar Creek, have been in that section since its first settlement. The Windles of Winchester, Adam and Theo., belong to the same family.

The Cooper family just mentioned, had no connection with another family of this name. Abraham Keller, had two sons-in-law, one was Ignatius Cooper, father of a large family; three of his sons being Newton A., Cornelius N., and Marshall, well-known to the present generation. They have several sisters. Their uncle was the father of Marion, Salem and Hiram Cooper. In the North Mountain section may be found several families who are descendants of the old men the writer knew when a boy. They were Isaac, Solomon and Jacob Brill. All three were 1812 soldiers. Their father, Hezekiah was a soldier in Col. Fry's Regiment of Minute Men. The Frys living in that same section, are descendants of Col. Fry.

Benjamin Williams lived in that section during the early part of the 19th Century, and together with his two sons, Philip B. and James W. Williams, operated one of the old-time fulling mills in the vicinity of Mountain Falls, now the property of S. B. Sale. After the Civil War, they built a large woolen mill on Abrams Creek West of the Valley Pike. His grandsons Hunter and James Williams, have been mentioned as owners of the large woolen mills South of Winchester. Their father Philip B. Williams, is mentioned in the list of Delegates in the Virginia Legislature. There is no known connection between this and the families of same name previously mentioned.

The Russell family, once so prominently known in the northwest section, have disappeared. We have mentioned James A. Russell and family elsewhere. His cousin William Russell lived in that section. They married sisters, the Misses Baker, of Hardy County. William was the father of Mrs. James Cover, Mrs. Zepp and one son John. Mr. James A. Russell lived to be an old man. His father was one of the Minute Men, as shown elsewhere. Mr. Russell's gallant son, Stanley, was killed during the early part of the Civil War,—a brave Confederate, well-known to the writer. His sister Mrs. Annie Hack and her brothers, have been previously mentioned.

The author's scheme included among other subjects, one to embody a roster of Confederate Soldiers, who had enlisted as Frederick County men; but abandons this now for two reasons: one is that he has reached the limit of his space; the other, that ample provision has been made by the State of Virginia to maintain a record of all Virginia soldiers. This is being done by recording in each Clerk's Office rosters of all companies mustered into service for their respective counties. This will be of inestimable value for the future generations. We have had occasion to mention incidentally many of the gallant fellows who gave up all to answer the call of Virginia in her great effort to check invasion of her soil and defend her sacred rights.

Sketch of the Williams Family in Shenandoah Valley—Now Shenandoah

The second Clerk of the County Court of Shenandoah County was John Williams, Jr., serving as such from 1784 to 1789. (The first clerk was Marshall, 1772-1784.)

John was the son of William Williams and Lucy Clayton. He was a Revolutionary soldier; enlisted August, 1777, and served until Feby., 1781. He attained the rank of Major in the State service March 3, 1785. In 1770 he married Eleanor Hite, third daughter of Isaac Hite, of Long Meadows, Frederick County. The author will add at this point that some question has arisen as to John Williams, Jr., (the second county clerk) being the son of William Williams. That John Williams the oldest son of William, was never clerk;—that John, Jr., was not related to the family. Be this as it may, the genealogy of this family has been carefully studied; and the author gives the benefit of a doubt to the statement made that he was the son of William and the second clerk of Shenandoah County.

This Major John Williams had three children to survive him:

1. Isaac Hite Williams.
2. John C. Williams.
3. Eleanor Eltinge Williams.

Isaac Hite Williams was a brilliant lawyer; lived in Fredk. County, Va.; married Lucy Coleman Slaughter. Seven children by this marriage:

1. Ophelia Ann, mar. Rev. Geo. Archibald Smith.
2. Margaret F., mar. John Mercer Patton.
3. Mary Eleanor, mar. Dr. Walker Maury Hite.
4. Isaac Hite Williams; never married.
5. Eliza, unmarried.
6. Lucy Ann, unmarried.
7. John James, married Francis T. Thompson.

John C. Williams, second son of Major John, married Mary Tutt. Their children:

1. Mary Stevens Williams, mar. Rev. Henry Porter.
2. John W. Williams, mar. Francis Mason.

Eleanor Eltinge, third child of Major John Williams, mar. Capt. Reuben Long of Culpeper County, Va., who has credit for distinguished services in the Revolutionary War. Their children were:

1. Reuben Long, mar. Elizabeth R. Miller.
2. Mary Evans Long, mar. Chas. U. Lovell.
3. Lucy Green Long, mar. Col. Robt. Turner.

Children of Reuben Long and Elizabeth R. Miller:

1. J. Miller Long, mar. (1) Anna Mary Miller, dau. of John M. and E. R. Miller, 1878. His second wife was Jane Vivian Lewis.

Children of Chas. U. Lovell and Mary E. Long, 7 in number:

1. Janet U., mar. Dr. I. N. Buck.
2. Wm. Yates Lovell, mar. Miss Allen.
3. Eleanor U., mar. Saml. C. Richardson.
4. Lucy Ann, mar. Thos. C. Randolph.
5. Mary Julia, mar. Thos. W. Kiger.
6. John T. Lovell, mar. Lucy Ann Williams, 1859; was a Confederate soldier; practiced law in the West and also at Front Royal; Judge of Old County Court of Warren County for four terms; member of House of Delegates; State Senator, 1882; Editor of Warren Sentinel. The writer was familiar with his useful and active life.
7. Sarah E., mar. Col. Mandly Taylor.

The children of Col. Robt. Turner and Lucy G. Long:

1. Robert H. Turner, mar. Anna M. Davison; practiced law in Front Royal; member of State Convention that passed Ordinance of Secession. A private in Warren Rifles when the Civil War began; then Lieut.; then Major of Staff of Genl. Corse; surrendered at Appomattox. 1869 was appointed Judge of the old 12th Circuit, filling this office for nearly 25 years. His wife was grand-daughter of Major Isaac Hite, of Belle Grove.
2. James H. Turner; married twice. First wife Annette Tyler; second, Mary Jackson; married 1867. A physician in Front Royal for years.
3. Smith S. Turner, mar. Louisa Bird, dau. of Judge Mark Bird, of Woodstock; practiced law in Front Royal; member of Congress from his Dist.; suffered serious injuries in the Confederate service, from which he never entirely recovered. His wife was a grand-daughter of Major Hite, of Belle Grove.

John W. Williams, only son of Capt. "Jack" Williams, and Mary Tutt wife of John W., left his native county, Rappahannock, in 1840 for Buchannan, Va., and established a large business. He had two children:

1. James W. Williams, mar. Mary Easley; served in Army of Northern Virginia; lived at Pearisburg, Va.; member of the House of Dele-

gates from his and Pulaski Counties. His son John W. Williams was clerk in 1906.

2. Mary Ellen, married (1st) Capt. Wm. H. Payne, 1863. Second husband, Capt. David A. French, 1869.

Philip Williams, the third clerk of Shenandoah County, was the third son of William Williams and Lucy Clayton. He was born near Culpeper C. H., Va., in 1771; came to the Valley when 18 years of age, and settled in Woodstock. Shenandoah at that time embraced the greater portion of Page and Warren County territory. He soon won the esteem and confidence of his new friends. In 1789, Aug. 27, he was chosen Clerk of the County Court, which office he held continuously until June, 1845, when he declined re-election Mr. Williams enjoyed an enviable reputation in the 54 years of his service, for his efficiency as clerk of the court. In all the changes of legislation, he was ever ready to meet any requirement of service in connection with his responsible and onerous office. His long experience made him familiar with all statute laws—all technicalities of the court, and adroitness of the most distinguished lawyers. He grew so closely interwoven with law practice, that he was regarded by the Bench and Bar alike, as an authority in the rules of practice; and his profound knowledge of human nature and the people of his large county was so great, that his advice was often sought by contending litigants. His biographer, in the work of Mr. Johnston styled "Memorials of Virginia Clerks," says: "That he was an adherent of the Episcopal Church, as his family had been in every generation," and that he was an official member of the congregation when Rev. Peter Muhlenberg preached his celebrated patriotic sermon—an event that he remembered so well, that his description of the scene in the old church, stirred quicker emotions than any other incident he could recall. His political life was as true and firm as any other of his convictions an any subject. He was a Democrat of the old school, and was a leader in all campaign efforts. Through his zeal and administration, Shenandoah was known far and near as the "Tenth Legion of Democracy." When in the 75th year of his age, he laid down the burden, his well-spent life entitled him to the epitaph his many friends inscribed on the slab that marks his grave, to be found in the old Episcopal graveyard at Woodstock. Here it is—well worth the study of the passer-by: "He was Clerk of the County of Shenandoah for fifty-four years, and lived and died without an enemy."

Mr. Williams married Sarah Croudson, in 1791. She was the only daughter of John Croudson and Elizabeth Warrington, County Lancaster, England. They had ten children:

1. Lucy Clayton, married (1) John W. Bayliss, 1811. After his death, she married Capt. Ambrose Powell Hill, Mch. 30, 1830. He had the honor of commanding the Culpeper Minute Men in 1812. No children by either marriage.

2. Elizabeth, born 1795; mar. Col. Rob. Turner, 1813. She died 1820, childless.

3. Ann Jane Williams, born 1797, mar. Philip De Catesby Jones, 1817.

4. John Croudson Williams.

5. Philip Williams, married (1) Ann Maury Hite, 1826. (2) Mary Louise Lillie Dunbar, 1834.

6. James Clayton Williams, mar. Amandy C. Ott, 1828.

7. Mary Susan, mar. Dr. Wm. W. Magruder, 1825.

8. Samuel Croudson Williams, mar. Sarah C. Ott, 1833.

9. Sarah Frances, mar. Travis J. Twyman, Sept. 14, 1830. He was son of Col. Wm. Twyman of the Revolution, and his wife was Bettie Garnett.

10. Eleanor Francis, mar. Rev. Andrew Hunter Holmes Boyd. (See sketch of Boyd family.)

The children of Philip C. Jones and Ann J. Williams:

1. John Wm. Jones, mar. Elizabeth W. Chipley. Mr. Jones is a Baptist minister, distinguished for his active services during the Civil War, and his prominence in all Confederate Reunions since; is author of "Christ in the Camp."

2. Lewin T. Jones, mar. Lydia C. Russell, of Loudoun County.

3. Elizabeth Sarah Jones, mar. Gerard M. Effinger, 1861. Son of John F. and Mary Hite, dau. of John Hite, Jr., of Rockingham Co.

Philip Williams, son of Philip and Sarah Croudson, was a lawyer of such distinction in the Shenandoah Valley as entitles him to more than the brief notice accorded many others in this work. He was a student of law in the office of his uncle, Wm. Clayton Williams, of Richmond, Va. His first experience as an attorney was in Woodstock, Va., where he was admitted to the Bar about 1824. His reputation as an attorney in his native county, can be measured somewhat by an examination of the old dockets of the courts in the first few years of his practice. Hundreds of suits were instituted and skillfully handled by him. He was soon made Commonwealth's Attorney for the county, and also elected to the Virginia Legislature. Later on, he changed his residence to Winchester; but his extensive practice in Shenandoah and other Counties, was successfully handled. Perhaps no other lawyer in the Virginia Valley was so well known. He was associated with Mr. David W.

Barton, also one of the great legal lights in his day; and together they were interested in hundreds of suits in all of the adjoining courts. Mr. Williams, though not of the oratorical style, was regarded as a forceful speaker. His adroitness as a cross-examiner, gave him great power in conducting his cases. He was an earnest advocate before a jury—winning their closest attention, and generally their verdict. His name and fame usually attracted crowds to the court room in *ye olden* times. This always enthused him. His wiry frame often quivered with delight as he glanced over the listening multitude. Then it was that his listening brethren of the bar, felt his weight with the masses. He was a born lawyer. Mr. Williams was well known for his devotion to the Southern cause. Though never in the service as a soldier, his aid went out fully to the cause He suffered unjust imprisonment in a loathsome place in Wheeling, W. Va.; his fellow prisoners from Winchester being Rev. Dr. Boyd, Robert Y. Conrad and others. The Federals held them as hostages for some Union men who had been arrested by the Confederates. The author was always familiar with the life of Mr. Williams in the many years he knew him previous to the war. No incident ever impressed him as much as what he witnessed during the period of Reconstruction. Mr. Williams was employed by some Virginians who were members of the author's old Cavalry Regiment, that made a celebrated scout along the B. & O. Railroad, capturing prisoners and securing horses and cattle, bringing them all safely to the Army headquarters. A number of suits for damages were brought against the old soldiers who went back to their homes after the war, some of whom were arrested. The case came up for hearing in the U. S. District Court at Kingwood, West Virginia. Many of the old Regiment soldiers living in the Valley, were summoned to assist their friends. The author accompanied Mr. Williams. His nervousness attracted attention; and when asked the cause, replied that this was to be the supreme effort of his life; that he had learned that —— Stanton, brother of Edward M. Stanton, Lincoln's Secretary of War, who was a terror to all who knew his bitterness, was to prosecute these cases; and he knew there would be an effort made to crush every Southern man involved;—that this brother was equal to the Secretary for his bitterness of feeling.

The court-room was a scene never to be forgotten. The few old soldiers huddled in a corner of the room, under guard—the hard countenances of the West Virginia prosecutors—the towering form of that Stanton, standing near the lithe figure of Mr. Williams, cast a gloom over the litigants and witnesses from the Valley. Stanton seemed to be all the court; and insisted on judgments and summary punishment, without the usual formalities of trial by jury. At the critical moment, Mr. Williams announced that inasmuch as the court had admitted him to practice before the high tribunal, he felt himself the equal of Mr. Stanton before this court; and raised the question of jurisdiction. The offences charged, having been committed before the new State was formed, why should these charges be tried in the United States Court? Arguments on points of law continued for two days. Mr. Williams met the stalwart Stanton at every point, and overwhelmed him with confusion, until he yielded to Mr. Williams' motion, that the Court take time to consider the grave question, and allow all contestants leave to depart upon their own recognizances. The learned Judge announced that the further hearing of these cases would be postponed until after the Christmas season, then two days off. The cases never came to a conclusion.

Mr. Williams never fully recovered from the effects of his prison life; but continued in active practice of his profession until the moment of his death, which occurred in Woodstock April 2, 1868. By a remarkable coincidence, he died stricken with apoplexy in the court-room, the scene forty-five years before of his maiden speech.

There were two children by his first marriage:

1. Philip C. Williams, who was a prominent physician in Baltimore during his long and useful life. (For his line, see the sketch of Maj. Isaac Hite and family.)

2. Ann Hite Williams, mar. T. T. Fauntleroy, 1850. (For this line see the Maj. Isaac Hite Sketch.)

The children by the second marriage of Philip Williams and his wife Mary Louise Dunbar:

1. Mary Louisa Dunbar Williams, mar. Rev. Jas. B. Avirett, 1862. Mr. Avirett has been widely known as the Chaplain of Ashby's Brigade during the Civil War, and as the biographer of the gallant chieftain.

2. Philip Williams Avirett.

2nd child of Philip and Mary Williams: John James Williams, married Emilie W. Gray. He was a gallant soldier. Later on further mention will be made of him. His children are:

1. R. Gray Williams, succeeding his father to a good law practice in Winchester; now City Counsel to the City Council of Winchester. He married Elizabeth Reid King.

2. Ann Douglas Williams.

3. Philip Williams.

3rd child of Philip and Mary Williams: Thomas Clayton Williams, mar. Louisa Chilton Baker. He served as a soldier in Chew's Battery, and later was a physician in Winchester; no issue.

4. Lucy Dunbar Williams—unmarried.

5. Sarah Ellen Williams—unmarried.

James Clayton Williams, second son of Philip and Sarah Croudson Williams, lived and died in Woodstock. One child survived him, Sally Clayton Williams, married Richard H. Miller, 1849. Five children by this marriage:

1. Mary Katherine, mar. Chas. Sweet Johnson; no issue.

2. Hunter Boyd Miller.

3. Eleanor Williams Miller.

4. Sallie Dunbar Miller, mar. Dr. Wm. Virginius Giddings; no children.

5. Frank Washington Miller, mar. Mary Francis Gill. They live in Chicago and have two sons.

Samuel Croudson Williams, youngest son of Philip and Sarah (Croudson) Williams, succeeded his father as Clerk of Shenandoah County, which position he held for seventeen years, until his death. Like his father, he was universally esteemed and trusted; but, unlike him, he had a genius and liking for politics. Trenchant in debate and subtle in the management of party machinery, he was invariably successful in his campaigns. He was delegate to the National Conventions of 1844, '48, 52, and '56, member of the Constitutional Conventions of 1850-51; for two terms member of the Virginia Legislature; and in the memorable State Convention of 1861, he signed the minority report in favor of secession. When Virginia at last seceded, Samuel C. Williams at the head of his Company, the Muhlenburg Rifles, was among the first to respond to his State's call for troops. He reported for duty at Harpers Ferry; but owing to rapidly failing health, he was forced to return home, where after a lingering illness, he died in the fiftieth year of his age.

His wife, Sarah Carpenter Ott (daughter of George Ott) and others of her family, were largely instrumental in founding the Woodstock Presb. Church, of which all her children save one became members, that one remaining in the church of many of his ancestors—the Episcopal. Their ten children were:

1. Lucy Ann, mar. Judge John T. Lovell (See sketch of Major John Williams' family.) Their children were:

(1) Mary Julia Lovell, mar. Enoch Marshall Jeffries. They have six children.

(2) Sally Williams Lovell, mar. Dr. Philip Taylor. They have one daughter.

2. James Harrison Williams (son of Saml. C. Williams) married Cora De Novelle Pritchartt. He had an eventful life. Was a lawyer, legislator, soldier, politician; graduate of the Law School of the Virginia University; first practiced in Dubuque, Iowa; elected to the Iowa Legislature, as a Democrat. When Virginia seceded, he abandoned his adopted home and returned to his native State; enlisted in Chew's Battery; was made Lieut.; promoted for gallant services, and given a captain's commission near the close of the war. He resumed his profession after the war, in Winchester, forming a partnership with his cousin Jno. J. Williams. He soon ranked with the foremost lawyers at the celebrated Winchester Bar; enjoyed a lucrative practice, and won admiration from hosts of friends. He was an orator of considerable reputation. His ability as a stump speaker was recognized by such shrewd politicians as Mahone of Readjuster fame. Capt. Williams was drawn into that vortex which ultimately shattered his fortune and his health. He went in on the Mahone wave, and served one term in the Virginia Legislature, and became an able ally of that boastful demagogue, who had made himself U. S. Senator; and to Capt. Williams went the empty honor of a Brigadier-Generalship of the State Militia. Genl. Williams should have been the senator, or one of the Judges of the Supreme Court of Virginia. He finally removed his office to Woodstock, and formed a partnership with his brother, Wm. T. Williams. This firm enjoyed a large practice; but the pressure of such an eventful life was too much, even for this robust man; and for several years prior to his death, his many friends in the Lower Valley were saddened by his failing health. His widow and daughter, Miss Nannie W. Williams, survive him, and reside in Woodstock, Virginia.

3. Elizabeth Sarah Williams, mar. Thomas Marshall. He was Lieut. of Co. E., 12th Va. Cavalry, and killed at Brandy Station, Oct. 12, 1863. Three children.

(1) Saml. Williams Marshall, mar. Mary N. Williams; 8 children.

(2) Lucy Williams Marshall, mar. James W. Luke. No issue.

4. Philip Green Williams; died unmarried.

5. Virginia L. Williams, dead.

6 Saml. Croudson Williams (dead), mar. Sarah F. Clower. Their children:

(1) George Brandon Williams.

(2) Julia C.

(3) Lucy Lovell.

(4) James Marshall.

(5) Wm. Newman, mar. Mary H. Rhodes.

(6) Samuel Jacob.

(7) Louis W., mar. Elizabeth V. Rhodes.

(8) Charles Winfield (dead).

7. George Henry, member of Co. E., 12th Va. Cavalry. Killed at Brandy Station.

8. Mary Julia Williams, mar. Louis Wagner; no issue.

9. William Twyman Williams, mar. Sarah Madison Bird, daughter of Judge Mark Bird and his Wife, Sarah Clark Hite, who was a daughter of Major Isaac Hite of Belle Grove and his wife Ann Tunstall Maury. Mr. Williams is one of the prominent lawyers of the Valley. His cases are docketed in several Judicial Districts. He is widely known for his integrity and legal accomplishments. Mr. Williams has been for a number of years ruling elder in the Woodstock Presb. Church, and on several occasions represented the Winchester Presbytery in the higher Church Courts. Four children, viz:

(1) William Twyman Williams, Jr. After his successful college course, he is now a student of Theology in the Union Theological Seminary (Presbyterian) at Richmond, Va. The author is indebted to him for many genealogical notes, of great value, in connection with these sketches. The collection so carefully compiled and so comprehensive, gives evidence of a studious mind. May his collection of Gospel truths be such, that large audiences may be edified in the near future.

(2) Anna Hite Williams.

(3) Philip Williams.

(4) Clayton E. Williams.

10. Charles Clayton, 10th child of Samuel Williams, died unmarried.

The children of Dr. Wm. W. Magruder and Mary Susan Williams, his wife, were:

1. Geo. Wm. W. Magruder, mar. Catherine Powell, 1861. For a number of years he was a physician of Woodstock, Va.; later, he removed to Fort Worth, Texas, where he died, leaving 5 children.

2. Philip W., married Anna Ott; is a lawyer, and resides in Woodstock; has seven children.

3. Mary Ellen Magruder, married Holmes Conrad, 1864; no issue.

4. John Wm. Magruder, mar. Mary Ellen Donaldson; resides in Woodstock; has eight children.

5. Henry Clay Magruder, married Roberta B. Campbell, 1873, dau. of R. M. and Rebecca A. Campbell, of Frederick County, Va., He resided on his farm near Woodstock for a number of years; removed in 1903 to Prairie Grove, Arkansas, where he died Jan., 1906, leaving 5 children.

Margaret French Williams, dau. of Isaac Hite Williams, son of Major John Williams, married John Mercer Patton, who for many years was a brilliant lawyer in Richmond, Va., and Member of Congress. They had nine children:

1. Robt. W. Patton, died unmarried.

2. John Mercer, married (1) Sally L. Taylor; next Lucy Crump. Was Colonel of 21st Va. Infantry.

3. Isaac Williams Patton, married Fanny Meredith. Was Col. of a Louisiana Regiment in the Civil War.

4. George Smith Patton, mar. Susan T. Glassell; was Col. of 22nd Regt. of Va. Infty., killed while in command of his brigade at Winchester, Va.

5. Waller Tazwell Patton, Col. of 7th Reg. Va. Infty. Mortally wounded in the charge with Pickett at Gettysburg. He and his brother George are buried in the same grave in Stonewall Cemetery at Winchester, Virginia.

6. Eliza Patton, married John Gilmer.

7. Hugh Mercer Patton, married Fanny Bull; was a Lieut. in C. S. A., and now resides in Lynchburg.

8. James French Patton, married Malinda Caperton; Lieut. of C. S. A.; and was Judge of the Supreme Ct., West Virginia.

9. Wm. McFarlane Patton, married Annie Jordan; died May 27, 1905.

Ophelia Ann Williams, daughter of Isaac Hite Williams, who was the son of Maj. John, and by some supposed to be the John Williams who was the second clerk of Shenandoah, married Rev. Archibald Smith, who for years was head of a school for boys near the Episcopal Seminary, Alexandria, Va. Eight children:

1. Isaac Williams Smith.
2. Mary Watson Smith.
3. Eliza Smith.
4. Lucy E.
5. George Hugh.
6. Eleanor Eltinge.
7. Isabella Keightley.
8. Henry Martyn.

Thomas Cover. The author has adhered closely to his scheme through the foregoing pages of this volume, and shown who many of the pioneers were who laid the foundations for civilization of the Shenandoah Valley, when it was held by the Aboriginees; and followed the development to the present writing, giving full credit to the descendants of the pioneers. We have found along the line now and then, conspicuous figures filling vacant places in all the march of enterprise, as some of the descendants would disappear.

The subject of this brief sketch has been one of the most prominent of those figures. Mr. Cover came to Frederick County in 1868, and immediately entered upon his career. He was endowed with extraordinary mental and physical strength; and possessed unlimited energy and a thorough knowledge of the business he proposed to conduct in the mountain country. His finances gave but little promise for planting a great enterprise. Having settled on upper Cedar Creek with his small family, he is soon found successful in establishing the Star Tannery, which secured a reputation at home and abroad; and was called upon to ship its products beyond the Atlantic. Mr. Cover with his large plant, dominated all of Western Frederick; but the demand for his stock required more plants. In a few years, his tanneries at Capon Bridge, Lost City and the Narrows in Giles County, Va., and Moorefield, West Va., gave evidence of accumulating wealth, and increase of mental capacity. At this juncture, he had the valuable assistance of his son, Loring A. Cover, with his university education and splendid business traits, inherited from his father, and with lofty principles of character instilled by his faithful mother, such timely aids did much towards the great results which followed.

The great enterprise attracted the attention of the Leather Trust. Agents pressed every point, to compel Cover and Son to yield to their demands; but they found in Mr. Cover courage and self reliance, with ample means to dictate terms. He fixed his price, and never swerved from his original plan. His wonderful knowledge of human nature and the power of his holdings, made it possible for his retirement as more than a millionaire.

Surrounded by his family and hosts of friends, he and Mrs. Cover are to be congratulated upon what they have done and are continuing to do. Their munificence has been felt by public and private objects of their attention.

Their children are: Mrs. Harrison, wife of Judge T. W. Harrison; Mrs. Steck, wife of John M. Steck, of the Winchester Bar; Mrs. Kern, wife of Harry R. Kern, Commonwealth's Attorney for the City of Winchester, for several years; Mrs. Russell, wife of Harry Russell, the well-known business man; Mrs. Glass, wife of Dr. Robert Glass. These families live in their attractive homes near the homestead, Angerona. One daughter was the wife of Lewis N. Barton. Both died when their three sons, Tom, Louie and Joie were quite young.

Loring A. married Miss Grace Stayman, and lives in Baltimore. He is largely interested in the manufacture of concrete cement.

Thomas Cover, his brother, is married and lives in Philadelphia, and is prospering in business.

The Covers are of English origin. The subject of our sketch is the son of Tobias Cover, a prominent citizen of Maryland. He was one of the electors on the Democratic ticket that voted for James K. Polk for president in 1852.

William H. Baker

In the sketch of the Winchester Baker family, this gentleman has had frequent mention. We now regard him as one of the figures, the age of enterprise has developed. Mr. B. has always been prominent in the old Baker and Company firm. During that period, he became interested in the manufacture of chocolate; and entered that arena of enterprising men, having his plant in New York, which he conducted as a collateral branch of his large wholesale business, under the name of W. H. Baker Company. His increasing business attracted the attention of the old Walter H. Baker Company, which had up to that time monopolized the manufacture of chocolate. Serious litigation resulted, upon that firm instituting suit for damages, by reason of the new firm using their trade mark. The suit involved Mr. Baker in perplexing efforts and expenditure of large sums of money, to maintain his position. The contest attracted wide attention; several courts exercised jurisdiction; able lawyers confronted each other in the interests of their clients—Mr. R. T. Barton, of the Winchester bar being chief counsel for Mr. Baker. Several years were spent dragging the case through the courts. Finally W. H. Baker Company triumphed over the Walter H. Baker Company; and to-day we find Mr. Baker not only fully recovered from his temporary embarrassment, but established in the business that has already yielded large returns. His success has become marvelous; and his friends are predicting that Winchester will become the home of a multi-millionaire in the near future. Mr. Baker is still a young man. May he be spared with health and strength to maintain the position he has held for many years, as one of the best business men found in the Shenandoah Valley, and a man ever ready to enhance the material interests of his native city. His palatial residence corner of Water and Washington Streets, was erected several years prior to his manufacturing enterprise.

German Smith

This gentleman is fully entitled to distinction as one of the figures which now and then are found prominently in new enterprises. Mr. Smith often expressed satisfaction over two of his ventures: the first being the general store he opened in Winchester in 1865. This was the first to appear in Winchester after peace was declared. (Several army sutlers remained with the army post for about one year after the war.) Mr. Smith started the first sumac factory in the valley, which he maintained on an extensive scale until his death about 1895. This plant was located on Braddock Street nearly opposite the M. E. Church. The new enterprises benefited thousands of poor people in every section of the Valley; affording opportunities to dispose of the branches of the sumac shrub that hitherto had been useless. The product was known in the commercial world as quercitron, used for tanning purposes in foreign countries. Mr. Smith realized a handsome sum. Within a few years after his death, the business was abandoned by his family. Mrs. Smith and her son German Smith live in Winchester at their handsome home on Fairmont Avenue. The son married Miss Virginia Jack, daughter of Mr. and Mrs. C. P. Jack, proprietors of the Evans Hotel. The Jack family trace their line back to Revolutionary heroes. They spelled the name at that period Jacques, often abbreviating it, until it finally became the present name. They settled as pioneers near the Potomac River West of Martinsburg; and one or more of the name figured prominently in one of the forts already mentioned. James Jack who lived in Morgan County in 1850, inherited large tracts of land from the old Revolutionary ancestor.

Albert Baker

We find substantial evidence in Winchester of Mr. Baker's enterprising spirit.. He contributed freely of his time, talent and money to establish a knitting mill on North Kent Street, which has been in successful operation since about 1895. He is a brother of Wm. H. Baker and unmarried. His health gave way several years ago; and he no longer manages his large properties. This enterprise suggested another: which resulted in the profitable woolen mills standing just north of the Knitting Factory, Mr. Leafe being manager. Shirley Carter and other business men of Winchester organized and established the plant.

CHAPTER LXVIII

Pioneers of the Upper Valley

In the tracings given of many pioneers, the writer confined his notices to such as properly belonged to the Lower Valley, known as Frederick County. He will now briefly mention the names of pioneers who settled in the Shenandoah Valley chiefly South of the line between the Augusta and Frederick Counties, whose deeds were recorded in Orange County between the years 1738 and 1744. This class of pioneers purchased large tracts from what has been called the Beverly Grant, which was issued 12th of August, 1736, to William Beverly of Essex County, Sir John Randolph of City of Williamsburg, Knight, Richard Randolph of Henrico County, and John Robinson of King and Queen, "for 118,491 acres, being in Orange beyond the mountains." This grant extended from the Augusta line Southward towards the head springs of the Shenandoah River. Prior to this settlement, there is no doubt but that the historic Lewis family had seated themselves in the lower section near what is generally known as Port Republic. Thomas Lewis, the pioneer, and several sons were there about 1733. He obtained his grant for a large tract of land. His sons, Andrew, William and Charles were settled near by. This family have their historic names associated with events mentioned in this volume. The pioneers who had deeds, represent a large class of the English, Scotch and Irish immigrations, who were not willing to contend with the Fairfax and Hite prospective litigations, on their arrival in the Lower Valley, pressed further South beyond the Fairfax line, and began to settle all over the Valley South of a line from Swift Run Gap beyond the mountains North of Harrisonburg. Among this class a few names will be recognized as Germans, Hollanders, etc. John Lewis, William Cathey, Samuel Givens, George Hutchinson, Thomas Black, James Caldwell, George Robinson, James Davis, Daniel Mahahan, Patrick Campbell, Thomas Henderson, John Wilson, Wm. Smith, John Trimmell, John Anderson, Samuel Guy, John and Samuel Davison, James McClure, Andrew and Fra McClure, Joseph Tees, Martha Mitchell, George Home, John Moffett, John R. and Wm. Weysties, John Mills, James Deeper, Robert Turk, William Sedgwood, James Carr, Findley McClure, Robert King, Alexander and John Breckenridge, Samuel Hughes, Thomas Kirkpatrick, James Fulton, Sarah Ramsey, Wm. Johnston, Robert Page, Pat Martin, John Seabright, Wm. Wright, David Edmiston, John Hart, James Risk, Pat Cook, Robert Campbell, M. Patterson, James Robinson, Moses Thompson, Wm. Vance, Joseph Reid, George Caldwell, Robert McDonald, D. Byre, Geo. Anderson, Robert Patterson, John Pickens, Robert Crockett, James Lesley, David Campbell, Robert McClenehan, John McCutchen, James Patton, Wm. Hutcheson, Robert Young, Pat Hays, Samuel Doag, Frederick Beatty, Abraham Hambreton, J. McUllock, Robt. Black, Andrew Russell, Wm. Skillian, Geo. and Robt. Breckenridge, Jacob Lockhart, John Craig, Robert Cunningham, A. Campbell, Wm. Thompson, Henry Ruffner, Jordan Grays, Bare, Madison, Weyer, Harrison, Linville, Crawford, Roller, Gratton, Hanger and many more of this class settled in Augusta about the time the first court was held in December, 1745, and have their records in that court.

Rev. John Craig, a Presb. Minister, was preaching at a meeting house in 1740, (now Tinkling Spring Church). About this time came the Prestons, Waddells, Allens and Browns. Later on, the McCues and Stuarts; while down towards the old county line were the Harnsborough, Sprinkle, Steinberger, Rude, and other families.

CHAPTER LXIX

Frederick County at This Writing, Showing the Advantages of Her Soil and Climate

In the foregoing chapters we have traced many developments of the County for one hundred and seventy years. We may now properly consider what has been done with her thousands of acres, celebrated for fertility and location.

Situated in the heart of the Shenandoah Valley, shut in by the Allegany ranges on the West, which afford almost a perfect barrier against cyclonic and tornado storms that sweep from the Great Lake region, the prosperous population contentedly strove through all the years to develop its great variety of soils. Consequently Frederick County makes a showing along agricultural lines unsurpassed in any section. The highly improved farms found in every section, attract the attention of everyone. Especially is this true in the middle or limestone section, running entirely through the County North and South. The well-kept homes, where are seen large farm buildings of every class, the neat farm houses, immense barns, good fencing and well-tilled lands, produce the impression that the agricultural classes are prosperous and happy. This is true;—they have become independent from their intelligent management of such a splendid belt of country. The horticultural feature is no longer an experiment. The numerous apple orchards in full bearing, and thousands of apple and other fruit trees planted every year, give the County marvellous returns. The limestone belt referred to produces wheat, corn, oats, rye and hay in quantity and quality far above the average. Many farmers adopt the diversified plan; cultivate the cereals, and successfully handle from five to fifty acres in orchard, and graze large herds of sheep and cattle, selecting the improved breeds which thrive on the rich pasturage and well-watered ranges. Horse raising has been an important factor with the farmers for a number of years, many of the best being heavy draft, such as the Percheron and Clydesdale; for light draft, the French coach. Thoroughbreds of the Kentucky strain supply a demand for the saddle and harness. The Shenandoah Valley Agricultural Society, with its annual exhibitions, offers inducements to the enterprising farmer to display his choice stock, and sell thereof to the visiting dealers.

The hay crop has become important since the baling process was introduced; and many thousand tons are shipped to Southern markets, yielding large returns. It is not infrequent for the farmer to receive from $12 to $18 per ton. Timothy is chiefly the commercial variety. Red clover grows to perfection,—the hay affording choice food for the farm stock and a fertilizer on worn soils. *Blue grass* is indigenous to the soil and climate of Frederick. The slate-soil farms found in the Western and Eastern sections of the County, make a good showing. While in many cases the land is not so fertile as the limestone region, we find many highly improved and productive farms, making the old adage good "There is more in the man than in the land." We will take occasion to mention some such farms and their successful owners. We find large portions of the two slate belts interspersed with good red clay subsoils, a few ridges of limestone in the Western section, and red slate veins in the Eastern. Such diversity of soil has offered inducements to fruit men—the highly-colored apple growing to perfection in the Western, and the popular varieties of peaches in the Eastern section,—always demanding good prices. Considerable attention has been given to stock-raising in the Western section. The mountain ranges afford early spring grazing, and the well-tilled farms afford ample Summer grass and hay to finish their herds for market. Farmers have found considerable profit in raising hogs for the last twenty years; large numbers are cheaply handled and sold to shippers at paying prices. While the farmers generally pursue the regular line of agriculture, hundreds of them have turned their attention to raising apples for the increasing demand. Of this number, many notable cases are prominent, where the old-time farm has been transformed;—it not being uncommon to see the 100 acre orchard taking the place of the large areas of waving wheat, and the farmer in his new avocation realizing large sums of money. During the fruit season of 1907, many orchardists sold their products at prices varying from One thousand to Twenty thousand dollars—the minimum being for small archards from eight to ten acres, while the maximum sum was obtained from orchards not exceeding thirty acres This gives a slight idea of what the revenues will be when the larger orchards are ready for market. The varieties are York Imperial, Ben Davis, Grimes Golden, Winesap, Black Twig, Newtown or Albemarle Pippin, such being chiefly commercial orchards, while other splendid table sorts are in abundance for home consumption.

The forests of Frederick were famous for several years,—some being well-known virgin forests, where the gigantic oaks were found in abundance,—the pride of the County. Walnut, chestnut, locust, hickory and other varieties attracted the attention of the lumbermen; and for several years the hum of the steam sawmill could be heard in every neighborhood. Millions of feet of first-class lumber were shipped in every direction, giving to owners of the timber belts handsome profits. While the present owners derive large sums from this wholesale depletion of the splendid woodland and mountain forests, we may well enquire what the succeeding generations will have as a substitute. Many thousand acres of this virgin soil, however, are gradually converted into areas for the cereal crops and orchards.

Frederick County has had ventures in handling ores. Several furnaces at one time smelted the rich iron ores; and operators found profit, until the railroads brought bar iron to the consumer at less cost than the pig iron could be delivered by the local furnace in Winchester, compelling abandonment of the industry many years ago. In the Western parts of the County, mountains of rich ore abound, and only await the railroads to penetrate those sections, but twelve miles distant, to be rekindled.

Much could be said about hidden veins of coal, which are known to exist in several distant sections of the County. The day is not far distant when paying quantities of coal will be mined; and some predict that oil-wells will follow such development. However, the careful observer regards the present developments of the County sufficient for the home-seeker and fortune hunter. The citizenship of this great country, being above the average, insures social advantages to the new-comers. At this writing, many large tracts of land are being subdivided; and new homes appear in every section.

The climate is inviting. The crisp Virginia Winter, and mild Summers, with a balmy Spring and Indian-Summer Autumns, give this section the advantages of four distinct seasons,—all of which tend to invigorate, and not enervate, the spirits of the happy dwellers in this land flowing with milk and honey, and free from the lowland fevers and epidemics that prevail West of the great mountains. Frederick County continues to maintain the reputation the Old County had one hundred and fifty years ago, when the first settlers found an Eden with untold attractions, whose descendants by unstinted efforts, have made a garden spot famous from ocean to ocean.

Celebrated mineral springs abound in every section. These and other springs of delicious water, may receive fuller notice if space admit.

As will be seen in other pages of this work, good and numerous roads have been an interesting feature in the history of the County. Since the introduction of road machinery,—the road-plow, scraper and stone-crusher—many miles of the common roads have been permanently improved. In the limestone region, especially is this true. Nothing unusual to find the *MacAdam* plan in active operation. Thus the ledges of limestone are utilized greatly to the advantage of the general public, while to enterprising parties, large lime plants have sprung up in several sections; and thousands of barrels of pure, white lime find ready sale in the Southern markets. The raw material is inexhaustible, while the demand increases.

The Fruit Industry

It is estimated that fully five hundred farmers are engaged in fruit culture, and that at least two thousand acres of land are planted in apples, the orchards ranging from 10 acres to 150, while many thousand trees are planted every year. This fruit development is one of the wonders of the age, when we consider that the change has occurred within twenty years; for previous to that time, the orchard for commercial purposes, was regarded as a doubtful experiment. The writer remembers well the comments made as to the folly of one man who planted the first pippin orchard near the Northwestern Turnpike, about two miles from Winchester, and waited full fifteen years before there was a crop of apples; and when this occurred, none supposed it possible to find a market. When this crop was sold, however, for about $5,000, all were astonished; and several farmers ventured to plant small orchards. But the majority held back; and some of this number are still holding out, predicting failure, while those who followed the example of the promoter of this enterprise, have gathered in many thousand dollars.

To give some idea of what this industry has done for this section, we subjoin the following, as furnished by the agents for the two railroads:

Number of barrels of apples shipped from Winchester over the Cumberland Valley Railroad for the season of 1907, 65,000 barrels, and over the B. & O. Railroad, 17,000.

The area of Frederick County as of to-day is four hundred and twenty-one square miles, comprising two hundred and sixty-nine thousand three hundred and sixty-six acres (269,366).

Population, including Winchester, about 20,000.

The elevation above sea-level an average of 1,200 feet.

APPENDICES

APPENDIX NO. 1

List of Burgesses from Frederick County

Samuel Earle	1743-1747
Andrew Campbell	1745-1747
George Fairfax	1748-1750
Gabriel Jones	1748-1754
Geo. Wm. Fairfax	1752-1755
Isaac Parkins	1754-1755
Hugh West	1756-1758
Thomas Swearingen	1756-1758
Geo. Washington	1758-1761
Thos. Bryan Martin	1758-1761
George Mercer	1761-1765
Robert Rutherford	1766-1772
James Wood	1766-1775
Isaac Zane	1773-1775

It may be of interest to show how the Burgesses were elected. The suffrage rights were not liberal in the colonial period. None could vote but freeholders. This freeholder was supposed to be of the *gentry* class and owner of valuable estates. When the General Assembly convened at the capitol, power was vested in the Royal Governor to prorogue the assembly—extending the sessions or dissolving same. These prorogations continued for three years prior to 1762. At a session held November, 1762, the General Assembly by Royal authority, increased the electorate. The freeholder clause was more liberally construed. Those who proved they owned not less than fifty acres of unimproved land, or 25 acres with a house thereon at least twelve feet square, or a lot in town with house thereon, were allowed to vote, and to vote in any other county where they had similar holdings. The General Assembly was to be holden once in three years at least.

Delegates to the Colonial Convention Held in Richmond, Virginia, Monday, July 17, 1775

Isaac Zane and Chas. Mynn Thruston, Frederick Co.

Robert Rutherford and Adam Stephen, Berkeley Co.

James Mercer, Hampshire Co.

No delegate present, Shenandoah Co.

When the name of Adam Sttphen was called, a protest from many citizens of Berkeley County was presented and considered by the Convention: the complaint being that a fraudulent election had been held in Berkeley County. Col. Stephen was charged with using his office of Commander-in-Chief of the Militia of that County, to secure his election; and that it was accomplished in this wise. The Colonel ordered the several companies to appear on election day for muster, and were then marched to the polls and requested to vote for their Colonel. The charge was vigorously supported by the contestants. The Convention refused him a seat; and a new election was ordered. Stephen quietly submitted; and from some cause the election was not held. Stephen loitered in Richmond for several months, and mingled with the delegates; and from this, he has been accredited by some writers as a member of the first Convention.

The Convention elected delegates to represent the Colony of Virginia in General Congress then assembling in Philadelphia, to-wit: Peyton Randolph, George Washington, Patrick Henry, Richard Henry Lee, Edmund Pendleton, Benjamin Harrison, and Richard Bland.

Rev. Chas. Mynn Thruston, delegate from Frederick, read the prayers and preached for the Convention the first Sunday, May 23rd.

We find the Convention was much disturbed in the Autumn of 1775 by reason of British war vessels appearing in the Lower James; and in December adjourned, to meet promptly at Williamsburg.

This Convention took charge of necessary legislation, supplanting the House of Burgesses. The question of protecting the Western border and enlisting men for the new general government, was taken up. Six regiments were ordered to be raised in the Counties of Augusta, Dunmore, Frederick, Berkeley, Hampshire, Culpeper and Fincastle. One of the regiments to be raised in the Valley to be called the German regiment. General Congress to appoint general officers. The Convention to appoint field officers, and the several county courts to appoint captains, etc., upon recommendation of the general committee.

State Senators, 1776-1800

Senator for the District composed of Frederick, Berkeley and Hampshire

	Session
Robert Rutherford	1776
Continued in office to	1791
Col. John Smith	1792-1795
Hugh Holmes	1795

	Session
Col. John Smith	1796
Hugh Holmes	1797-1798
Chas. McGill	1799-1800
No record of Session of	1800
No member for	1801

Frederick, Berkeley, Hampshire and Hardy

	Session
Lewis Wolf	1804
Lewis Wolf	1805
Lewis Wolf	1807
Lewis Wolf	1810
Lewis Wolf	1811
A. H. Powell	1813
A. H. Powell	1814
A. H. Powell	1815
A. H. Powell	1816

Frederick and Jefferson

	Session
A. H. Powell	1817
A. H. Powell	1818
H. St. G. Tucker	1818
H. St. G. Tucker	1821
H. St. G. Tucker	1822
William B. Page	1823
William B. Page	1824
William B. Page	1825
William B. Page	1826
Augus'e C. Smith	1827
Augus'e C. Smith	1828
Augus'e C. Smith	1829
Hierome L. Opie	1830
Hierome L. Opie	1831
Hierome L. Opie	1832
Hierome L. Opie	1833
Hierome L. Opie	1834
Hierome L Ppie	1835
Hierome L. Opie	1836

Frederick, Jefferson and Clarke

	Session
Hierome L. Opie	1837
Hierome L. Opie	1838
Hierome L. Opie	1839
Robert Y. Conrad	1840
Robert Y. Conrad	1841
Robert Y. Conrad	1842
Robert Y. Conrad	1843
John S. Gallaher	1844
John S. Gallaher	1845
John S. Gallaher	1846
John S. Gallaher	1847
H. L. Opie	1848
H. L. Opie	1849
H. L. Opie	1850

Frederick, Warren and Clarke

	Session
Oliver R. Funsten	1851
Oliver R. Funsten	1852
Oliver R. Funsten	1853
Oliver R. Funsten	1854
Oliver R. Funsten	1855
Oliver R. Funsten	1856
Oliver R. Funsten	1857-'58

Frederick Va. State Convention (Secession)

	Session
Robert R. Conrad	1861
James Marshall	1861

State Senators Since Civil War

Frederick, Clarke and Warren

	Session
James H. Carson	1862
James H. Carson	1863
S. W. Thomas	1864
Nathaniel B. Meade	1865
Nathaniel B. Meade	1866
Nathaniel B. Meade	1867

Frederick, Clarke and Shenandoah

	Session
William D. Smith	1869
William D. Smith	1870

Frederick, Clarke and Warren

	Session
G. W. Ward	1871
G. W. Ward	1872
G. W. Ward	1873
G. W. Ward	1874
G. W. Ward	1875
G. W. Ward	1876
G. W. Ward	1877
G. W. Ward	1878
John T. Lovell	1879
John T. Lovell	1880
John T. Lovell	1882
J. M. McCormick	1883
J. M. McCormick	1884
J. M. McCormick	1885
Marshall McCormick	1886
Marshall McCormick	1887
T. W. Harrison	1888-'90
T. W. Harrison	1890-'92
T. W. Harrison	1892-'94
Thomas D. Gold	1895-'96

Frederick and Shenandoah

	Session
J. G. McCune	1896
S. L. Lupton	1900
F. S. Tavenner	1904
R. M. Ward	1908

Members of the House of Delegates from Frederick County

	Session
James Wood and Isaac Zane	1776
Isaac Zane and John Smith	1779

Session

Joseph Holmes....1781
Alexander White and Chas. Mynn Thruston, 1785
Chas. Mynn Thruston and Sher. Woodcock, 1787
Joseph Holmes and Robert White....1789
Joseph Holmes and Mann Page....1790
Mathew Page and Robert White....1792
Mathew Page and Archibald McGill....1794
Archibald McGill and Robert Page....1795
Wm. McGuire and James Singleton....1796
Wm. McGuire and Archibald McGill....1797
Wm. McGuire and Archibald McGill....1798
Wm. McGuire and George Eskridge....1799
Wm. McGuire and George Eskridge....1800
George Eskridge....Jan. and Dec. 1800-Jan, 1801
Archibald Magill....
....1800-01-12-13-14-15-17-18-19-20-21
Hugh Holmes....January, 1802
James Singleton......December 1806-Jany., 1807
Charles Brent....1808-9-10-11
Jared Williams....1812-13-14-15
William B. Page....1822-23
Richard W. Barton....1823-25-32-33-34-35-39
James Ship....1824-25-26-27-28
James M. Mason....1826-27-28-29-30-31
William M. Barton....1827-28
William Castleman, Jr....1828-29-30-31
William Wood 1830-31-32-38-40-41-42-43-44
John B. D. Smith....1831-32-33-34-35-36-37
James G. Bryce....1831-32
James Gibson....1833-34-35
John S. Davisson....1835-36
James Bowen....1835-36
Edgar W. Robinson....1836-37
Robert L. Baker....1839-40
Richard E. Byrd....1839-40-41-42-43-44-50-51
James Cather....1840-41 and 1845-46
James H. Carson....1844-45-46-47-59-60-61
Jonathan Lovett....1844-45
John F. Wall....
1845-46-47-48-49-50-51-65-66 (an extra session)
Algernon R. Wood....1847-48-49-50
R. M. Sydnor....1848-49-50-51
Lewis A. Miller....1852-53-54
Edwin S. Baker....1852
John B. McLeod....1853-54
Thomas T. Fauntleroy....1857-58
M. R. Kaufman....1857-58-59-60 (Ex. 61)
George W. Ward....
........1859-60-(Ex. 61)-62-63-(Called 64-65)
M. R. Kaufman........1862 (called 63) 63-64-65
J. S. Magill....1865-66-67 (67 extra)
David J. Miller....1869-70
John F. Wall....1867-70-71-72-73-75-76-77
*William D. Smith....1869-70-71
E. M. Tidball....1871-(72-extra)-73
Geo. W. Ward....1871-(72-extra)-73
R. W. Hunter....1874-75
James H. Williams....1874-75
P. B. Williams....1876-77

Session

Nimrod Whitacre....1877-78
T. T. Fauntleroy, Jr....1877-78
E. P. Dandridge....1879-80
Holmes Conrad....1881-82
Robert T. Barton....1883-84
John V. Tavenner....1886-87
Jno. M. Silver....1888-91
Joseph A. Miller....1892-93
Chas. F. Nelson....1894-95
Jas. K. McCann....1896-97
E. C. Jordan....1898-1905
Richard E. Byrd..1906-08 (Speaker of House '08)

---

*W. D. Smith represented Frederick, Clarke and Shenandoah Counties.

APPENDIX NO. 2

GOVERNORS OF VIRGINIA

Colony and State

"It is difficult to make a clear and comprehensive list of the Governors of Virginia, for the reason that the person bearing the title of Governor often resided in England, while the real official head, residing in Virginia, was a deputy." So says the Hon. Secretary of State, in his effort to compile a list. The author submits the following as a subject for reference.

The history of Virginia executives divides itself into nine heads, including the period of attempted colonization in the time of Elizabeth, though the real history of Virginia begins with the London Company, whose rule lasted for eighteen years, under two presidents or treasurers—Sir Thomas Smith and Sir Edwin Sandys—neither of whom visited the colony. Therefore, the early government of Virginia was intended to be a colonial council, with a president, often spoken of as governor. The first man ever to have the title of Governor was Lord Delaware, appointed by the London Company, in 1609, to hold office for life. He held the office for nine years, dying in 1618. He resided in Virginia only nine months; and for the balance of the nine years was represented by a deputy. In 1624, the London Company lost its charter; and Virginia then passed into the hands of the King, who from time to time appointed Royal Governors. These governors often resided in England, and were represented in Virginia by deputies. Virginia still retained a resident council; and if, for any reason, the governor or deputy governor was absent from the colony, the president of the council was the acting governor. In 1652, the appointive power passed under the Commonwealth (Cromwell's); and the General Assembly by its own authority, elected four governors.

From 1660 to 1776, Virginia was again under the rule of the King, who appointed the governors. During this period, there were only ten governors of Virginia and a great number of deputies. Of these governors, Sir William Berkeley, Sir Herbert Jeffries, Lord Culpeper and Sir Edmond Andros, were residents of Virginia the greater portion of their terms. But the Earl of Orkney, the Earl of Albemarle, the Earl of Loudoun, and Sir Jeffrey Amherst, governors from 1697 to 1763, never came to Virginia, and were represented by deputies. The last two governors to be appointed by the King, Lord Botetourt and Lord Dunmore, resided in Virginia during their terms of office.

I. *Virginia in the Time of Elizabeth*

Sir Walter Raleigh, Lord Proprietor of Virginia, 1584-90.

Ralph Lane, Governor of Raleigh's First Colony, on Roanoke Island, N. C., 1585-1586.

John White, Governor of Raleigh's Second Colony, 1578-1590.

II. *Virginia Under the London Company, 1606-1624*

Sir Thomas Smith, President and Treasurer of the London Company. As Treasurer of the Company, Smith (or Smythe) was President of the Company, and the real Governor of Virginia, though resident in England, 1606-1618.

Edward M. Wingfield, President of the Council, resident in Virginia, May 13, 1607 to Sept. 10, 1607.

John Ratcliffe, President of the Council, resident in Virginia, 1607-1608.

Capt. John Smith, President of the Council, resident in Virginia, 1608-1609.

Capt. George Percy, President of the Council, resident in Virginia, 1609-1610.

Thomas West, Lord De La Warr, Governor and Captain General, 1609-1618.

Sir Thomas Gates, Lieutenant General and Deputy Governor, May to June, 1610.

Thomas West, Lord De La Warr, Governor, resident in Virginia, June, 1610-Mch., 1611.

Captain George Percy, Deputy Governor, March to May, 1611.

Sir Thomas Dale, High Marshal and Acting Governor, May to August, 1611.

Sir Thomas Gates, Acting Governor, 1611-1613.

Sir Thomas Dale, Acting Governor, 1613-1616.

Capt. George Yeardley, Deputy or Lieutenant Governor, 1616-1617.

Sir Edwin Sandys, President and Treasurer of London Company, 1618-1624.

Capt. Samuel Argall, Deputy Lieutenant Governor, 1617-1619.

Capt. Nathaniel Powell, President of the Council in Va. and Acting Governor, April 9 to Apl. 19, 1619.

Sir George Yeardley, Gov. and Captain General, 1619-1621.

Sir Francis Wyatt, Governor and Captain General, 1621-1624.

III. *Virginia Under the King, 1624-1652*

Sir Francis Wyatt, Gov. and Captain General, 1624-1626.

Sir George Yeardley, Gov. and Captain General, 1626-1627.

Capt. Francis West, President of the Council and Acting Governor, 1627-1629.

Sir John Harvey, Gov. and Captain General, 1628-1629.

Doctor John Pott, President of the Council and Acting Governor, 1629-1630.

Sir John Harvey, Governor and Captain General, 1630-1635.

Capt John West, President of the Council and Acting Governor, 1635-1636.

Sir John Harvey, Governor and Captain General, 1626-1639.

Sir Francis Wyatt, Governor and Captain General, 1639-1642.

Sir William Berkeley, Governor and Captain General, 1642-1644.

Richard Kempe, President of the Council and Actg. Gov. while Gov. Berkeley visited England, 1644-1645.

Sir William Berkeley, Governor, 1645-1652.

IV. *Virginia Under Cromwell's Commonwealth, 1652-1660*

Richard Bennett, Governor, elected by the Assembly, 1652-1655.

Edward Diggs, President of Council and Governor, elected by the Assembly, 1655-1658.

Capt. Samuel Mathews, Governor, elected by the Assembly, 1658-1660.

Sir William Berkeley, Governor, elected by the Assembly, March to July, 1660.

V. *Virginia, a Royal Province, 1660 to 1676*

Sir William Berkeley, Governor, 1660-1677.

Col. Francis Morryson (or Morrison) Deputy or L. Gov., acting while Berkeley visited England, 1661-1662.

Sir Herbert Jeffries, Lt. Governor and Governor, 1677-1678.

Sir Henry Chicheley, Deputy Governor, 1678-1680.

Thomas Lord Culpeper (Baron of Thorsway), Governor, 1680-1683.

Nicholas Spencer, President of the Council and Acting Governor, 1684-1688.

Nathaniel Bacon, President of the Council, 1688-1690.

Sir Francis Nicholson, Lt. Governor, 1690-1692.

Sir Edmond Andros, Governor, 1692-1698.

George Hamilton Douglas, (Earl of Orkney) Governor in Chief, (never in Virginia), 1697-1737.

(NOTE.—During his long term, 34 years, the following named eight Lt. Governors resided in Virginia and served the following terms):

Sir Francis Nicholson, Lieut. Governor, 1698-1705.

Edward Nott, Lieut. Governor, 1705-1706.

Edmund Jennings, President of the Council and Acting Governor, 1706-1710.

Robert Hunter, Lieut. Governor, commissioned 1707, but being captured by the French, never reached Virginia.

Alexander Spottswood, Lieut. Governor, 1710-1722.

Hugh Drysdale, Lieut. Governor, 1722-1726.

Robert Carter, President of the Council and Acting Governor, 1726-1727.

William Gooch, Lieut. Governor, 1727-1737.

William Anne Keppel, (Earl of Albemarle), Governor in Chief (never came to Va.) 1737-1754.

William Gooch, Lieut. Governor, 1737-1740.

Commissary James Blair, President of the Council and Acting Governor, 1740-1741.

John Robinson, President of the Council, and Acting Governor, 1749-1749.

Thomas Lee, President of Council, 1749-1751.

Lewis Burwell, President of Council, 1751 1751.

Robert Dinwiddie, Lieut. Governor, 1751-1756.

John Campbell, Earl of Loudoun, Governor General of all the American Colonies, never came to Virginia, 1756-1763.

Robert Dinwiddie, Lieut. Governor, 1756-1758.

John Blair, President of the Council and Acting Governor, January to June, 1758.

Francis Fauquier, Lieut. Governor, 1758-1768.

Sir Jeffrey Emherst, Governor in Chief, never in Virginia, 1763-1768.

John Blair, President of the Council and Acting Governor, Mch. to Oct., 1768.

Norborne Berkeley (Baron de Botetourt), Governor in Chief, 1768-1770.

William Nelson, President of the Council and Acting Governor, 1770-1771.

John Murray (Earl of Dunmore), Governor in Chief, 1771-1776.

VI. *Virginia in Revolt—The Convention Period*

Peyton Randolph, President of Virginia, Conventions of 1774-Mch., 1775, and July, 1775.

Edmund Pendleton, President of the Conventions, May, 1776 and Dec. 1778.

VII. *Virginia as an Independent Commonwealth*

Patrick Henry.............	Governor	1777-1779
Thomas Jefferson..........	"	1779-1781
Thomas Nelson, Jr..........	"	1781-1781
Benjamin Harrison.........	"	1781-1784
Patrick Henry, (2nd term)..	"	1784-1786
Edmund Randolph.........	"	1786-1788
Beverly Randolph..........	"	1788-1791
Henry Lee.................	"	1791-1794
Robert Brooke.............	"	1794-1796
James Wood...............	"	1796-1799
James Monroe..............	"	1799-1802
John Page.................	"	1802-1805
William H. Cabell..........	"	1805-1808
John Tyler................-	"	1808-1811
James Monroe...............	Jan. to Nov.	1811

(Resigned to become Sec. of State to Madison.)

Geo. William Smith as Sen. Member of the Council of State, Actg. Gov. Nov. to Dec.,1811

From 1776 to 1852 the Governors were elected by the Legislature, and were assisted in their executive duties by a Council of State. On the resignation or death of a governor, the senior councilor acted as governor until the election of one by the legislature. Therefore on the resignation of Monroe, George William Smith acted as Governor; but when he was burned to death in the Richmond Theatre, he in turn was succeeded by Peyton Randolph until the Legislature elected James Barbour (see files in office of Sec. of State.)

Peyton Randolph as Senior Member of the Council of State, Actg. Gov. Dec. 26, 1811 to Jan. 3................................1812

James Barbour.............	Governor,	1812-1814
Wilson Carey Nicholas......	"	1814-1816
James P. Preston...........	"	1816-1818
Thomas Mann Randolph.....	"	1819-1822
James Pleasants, Jr.........	"	1822-1825
John Tyler.................	"	1825-1827
William B. Giles............	"	1827-1830
John Floyd................	"	1830-1834
Littleton Waller Tazwell.....	"	1834-1836

(Resigned)

Wyndham Robertson as Senior Member of Council, Actg. Governor, Apl.-Mch., 1836-1837

David Campbell............	Governor,	1837-1840
Thomas Waller Gilmer......	"	1840-1841

Gilmer resigned by reason of disagreement with the Legislature, which was unable for 21 months to elect a Governor; so the senior members of council, Patton, Rutherford and Gregory, were Acting Governors.

John Mercer Patton, Senior Member of Council, Actg. Governor, Mch. 18 to 31, 1841

John Rutherford, Senior Member of the Council, Acting Governor, Mch.-Jany, 1842-1843

James McDowell,............Governor, 1843-1846
William Smith.............. " 1846-1849
John Buchanan Floyd....... " 1849-1852
Joseph Johnson............. " 1852-1856
Henry Alexander Wise...... " 1856-1860
John Letcher............... " 1860-1864
William Smith.............. " 1864-1865

VIII. *Virginia Under Federal Rule*

Francis H. Pierpont, Governor........1865-1868
Genl. J. M. Schofield, Military Com., 1867-1869
Henry H. Wells, Provisional Governor, 1868-1869
Genl. E. R. S. Canby, Military Com., 1869-1870
Gilbert C. Walker, Provisional Gov. Apl.-Jany 1869-1870

IX. *Virginia Again in the Union*

Gilbert C. Walker...........Governor, 1870-1774
James Lawson Kemper...... " 1874-1878
Frederick W. M. Holliday.. " 1878-1882
William E. Cameron........ " 1882-1886
Fitzhugh Lee................ " 1886-1890
Philip W. McKinney........ " 1890-1894
Charles T. O'Ferrall........ " 1894-1898
James Hoge Tyler.......... " 1898-1902
Andrew Jackson Montague.. " 1902-1906
Claude A. Swanson......... " 1906-

APPENDIX NO. 3

List of Members of Board of Supervisors from their First Meeting held July 26, 1870

Anthony M. Kline, (elected Chairman) 1870-1886
James W. Stephenson.................1870-1882
Josiah Rinker..........................1870-1878
A. Wade Muse........................1870-
James A. Russell......................1872-
Jacob W. Richard.....................1874-1880
M. M. Adams.........................1879-1896
Martin Wisecarver, (Shawnee Dist. added) 1879-1881
E. R. Thatcher........................1881-1891
A. W. Dunlap.........................1881-1884
Chas. E. Clevenger....................1882-1884
Jno. M. Silver.........................1884-1886
James K. McCann (Chairman from '89) 1887-1897
Joseph A. Miller (Chairman '87-'89)...1887-1892
Martin Wisecarver....................1891-1897
Wm. H. Dinges........................1892-1897
R. Bruce Muse........................1884-1893
Jas. T. McIllwee.......................1893-1895
Ran Pifer.............................1897-1901
Wm. H. Dinges, (Chairman since 1901) 1901-1908
T. E. Morrison........................1895-1897
Jas. T. McIlwee.......................1897-1901
John W. Parish........................1901-1904
H. P. Whitacre........................1896-1908
James Cather 1897-1908
Clark Cather 1897-1908
Jas. T. McIlwee.......................1904-1907
Bev. N. Lockhart......................1908-

APPENDIX NO. 4

Colonial Soldiers and Pensioners

The General Assembly held at Williamsburg Sept. 24, 1758, realizing that the border counties needed encouragement from the Colonial government, to insure greater protection to the settlers who were required to render unceasing service to protect their homes from the ravages of Indian warfare, enacted a law that stimulated the Valley counties, to not only maintain their independent warfare, but to furnish enlistments in the Colonial Regiments then being recruited for general purposes. Up to this date the border counties were expected to protect their homes at their own expense, and also to furnish their quotas for the Line regiments. This was found unjust to the Valley settlers, who for twenty years had formed a bulwark of defense for the country East of the Blue Ridge. At no time did they allow Indian forays to extend Eastward beyond their own settlements. The General Assembly recognized this, and appropriated a large sum to pay the Home Guards—or Minute Men, as they were called—for their services, equal to that paid the Line soldiers; and being furnished with lists from all the border counties, named them in the Act and fixed the amounts then due, and made provision for all who should thereafter secure certificates from their courts.

The author will give names of soldiers from Old Frederick, only to show who were the old defenders. Some of these names will appear in the Sketches of Indian Wars; but the repetition here is not undesirable, and will serve as an index to the reader to single out, if he can, his old ancestor.

The amounts will be given as found in the record of that period, in pounds, shillings and pence, only in a few instances, to show the general scheme for payment.

Frederick County

	£	s	d
To Archibald Ruddall, Lieutenant....	3	6	..
" Henry Selser, Sergeant..........	1	9	4
" John Jones......................	1	1	
" Jeremiah Odle, Moses Job, Rendy Mauk, George Bennett, Jonathan Odle, and James Thruston, each 17 s, ...	5	2	
" Patrick Kenney..................	1	2	
" Richard Mauk, Henry Mauk and Daniel Mauk, each 17 s, ...	2	11	

To Henry McKenney................ 1 2
" Nathaniel Bailey, Peter Bailey and William Cross, 15 s each.......... 2 5
" Richard Murphy................. 0 17
" Thomas Speak, as ensign,
" Charles Littleton, Sergeant,
" Daniel Johnston, Stephen Southard, Edward Linsey, Josiah Springer, Jacob Prickett, Stephen Stradler, Chas. Colston, John Hampton, Samuel Mason, Peter Petanger, Francis McCormack, Thos. Alfort, Richard Stearman, Thos. Linsey, Robert Pearis—
To Thos. Speake, Lieutenant,
" John Horden, Ensign,
" Wm. Mathews, John Stephenson, John Vance, James Meamick, James Morris, William Hall, Wm. Miller, Bang Foolam, Wm. Lockard, Thos. Linsey.

To Levi Jones, Edward Martin, Mark Hardin, Solomon Burkem, Samuel Stubbs, Gilbert Gordon, George Bell, James Grigson, Geo. Rice, Jno. Miller, Wm. Jacobs, Joshua Ewings, Thos. Conaly, Isaac Linsey, David James, Edward Tummens, Owen Wingfield, Walter Shirley, Robert Gooseberry, Jarvis Shirley, Jno. Parke, Isaac Thomas, James Jack, Hugh Johnston, James Jones, Francis Maginis, Joseph Lyon, Thos. Allen, Andrew Blackburn, William Stephenson, John M'Gill, Benj. Blackburn, Isaac White, Mathew Harbinson, Wm. Blackburn, Bryan Money, James Hughes, Joseph Fleming, Wm. White, John Young, Joseph Faucett, John Capper, David Williams, Leonard Cooper, Joseph Carroll, John Cook, Wm. Wilson, Samuel Vance, Andrew Vance, James Huston, Wm. Hughes, John Cooper, Daniel Johnson, S. Suthard, Thos. Price, Robert Stewart, Stephen Johnson, Isaac Linsey, John Regan, Ed. Timmons, Sol. Littleton, Thos. Robinson, Edward Degell, Francis McCrimas, Gasper Bewtoole, Hugh Stephenson, Edward Haven, John Hudson, Benj. Fulhone, John Vance, John Stephenson, Josiah Combs, Jno. Morris, John Laman, James Legat, John Dickson, Holoway Perry, Jos. Pierce, Henry Vanmeter, Lawrence Lender, Ed. Mergee, Jos. Vanmeter, Jacob Mergee, Remembrance Williams, Jos. Polson, Wm. Fiell, Nicholas McIntire, Edward Lucas, Robert Buckus, Benj. Sweet, John Taylor, Anthony Turner, John Magill, James Hugh, James Huston, James Camp, Richard Hawkins, John Duckworth, Joseph Greenway, Joseph Wallbroke, Anthony Dunlevy, Jesse Jackson,—Privates.

To Joseph McDowell, Lieutenant,
" John Allen, Ensign,
" James Treson, Sergeant,
" Thomas Speak, Captain,
" John Hardin, Lt.
" Magnus Tate, Ensign,
" Chas. Littleton, Sergt.,
To John Champain, Sergt.,
" George Wright, Sergt.,
" James Treson, Ensign,
" Will Elimus Ghink, Doctor.

The following list shows who furnished provisions, etc., to the Minute Men, when in need:
To John Blackburn's admrs., for provisions.
" John Mendenall, "
" James Jack, "
" John Shearer, "
" James Magill, "
" Edward Sningers, "
" Robt. Stockdale, "
" Van Swearingen, "
" Isaac Pearce, "
" Wm. Nealy's Estate, "
" Edward Stroud, "
" Lewis Stephens, for provisions and horse hire.
" Isaac Parkins, " " " "
" John Philips, " " " "
" Robt. Cropper, for horse hire.

This list is taken from Henning's Revised Statutes, Vol. 7. As previously stated, Congress by three Acts, directed the Secy. of War to publish a list of all Revolutionary Soldiers entitled to pensions or Bounty Land Warrants, then living, which he accordingly did in 1835. From the Virginia list, the author submits the following, as the soldiers of Frederick County:

James Beckman, John Bageant, Wm. Braithwaite, Dennis Bush, Saml. Cox, Thos. Crawford, Danl. Haley, James Hamilton, John Haney, John Harris, John Hefferlin, John Kiger, Wm. Kingore, A. McDonald, Alexander McMullin, Daniel Miller, Richard Murray, James Oliver, Moses Perry, Geo. Seifert, Jeremiah Sargeant, James Thompson, Geo. Van. Landengham, Geo. Wright, Jas. Barr, Henry Beatty, Geo. Black, Geo. Blakeman, Humphrey Brook, Phil. P. Buckner, John Campbell, Jno. Colbert, Peter Edwards, James Foster, John Grim, Geo. Hensell, Michael Humble, Henry Knipe, Conrad Kramer, Peter Lauck, Geo. Lonas, John Schultz, Geo. Lonas, Basil Lucas, Jas. M. Marshall, Wm. Monroe, Hugh Parrall, Wm. Philips, John Piper, Andrew Pittman, James Riely, Jacob Shade, John Smith, Col. of Va. State Line, Jacob Sperry, Andrew McGuire, Robert White, Owen Campbell, Reuben Cave, Richard Jenkins, Andrew Keyser, Joseph Sampson, Thos. Tharp.

The following are supposed to be those living in Shenandoah County:

Daniel Anderson, Philip Barr, Jno. Bly, Geo. Clowser, Leonard Cooper, captain, and died in Fredk. County, Joachim Fetzer, Archibald Finley, Joseph Golloday, Wm. Grady, Danl. Gray, Peter Grim, Drury Jackson, Benj. McKnight, Lewis Miller, Collin Mitchum, Abner Newman, Thos. Purdour, John Rolls, John Smith, Elias

Turner, Jeffrey Collins, Geo. Fletcher, Joshua Foltz, Jacob Helsey, Moses Henry, Thomas Hudson, Jacob Kepps, John Larey, Jacob Lineweaver, Christian Miller, David O'Rourke, Henry Roarer, Robt. Russell, Martin Zea, John Berry, Jesse Brown, Dennis O'Ferrell.

The foregoing lists have never appeared so fully in any other history of the Valley counties. Prof. Jno. W. Wayland of the University of Virginia, has recently given many of the last mentioned in his valuable and instructive book, entitled "The German Element of the Shenandoah Valley." The author has found it very useful as a text book in his studies of the German settlers.

The Secretary of War in his lists of 1832-35, gives many names familiar in Berkeley, Jefferson and Hampshire Counties; but there is not space for fuller mention of them in this work. The reader is referred to publications of writers of West Virginia history, and especially to the exhaustive work of Virgil A. Lewis.

APPENDIX No. 5

Fairfax and Hite Suit

The most famous suits of original action in the Shenandoah Valley, have generally been mentioned as the Hite-Fairfax suits.

The author promised in his opening chapters to give a comprehensive sketch of the suit instituted by Joist Hite et als. vs. Fairfax et als. He finds now that limited space will not admit of more than a note of reference.

This celebrated suit makes its first appearance 10th Oct., 1749, when Hite and his associates filed a bill in chancery in the general court against Lord Fairfax and those claiming under him, "setting forth the circumstances * * * praying that Lord Fairfax might be decreed to make deeds to the plaintiff for the surveyed lands * * * " (See 4 Call. 42-52.) Lord Fairfax in his answer, ignored all rights of Hite and his associates, and erroneously claimed that the right to convey lands to settlers in the Northern Neck, existed in him alone; and thus denied the rights granted through what has been termed Minor Grants. This class of grants is mentioned elsewhere in this volume. Some conflict of opinion existed in the courts; and considerable delay occasioned by reason of the general caveat entered by Lord Fairfax against all orders of council and patents from the Crown office, for lands in his proprietary. The courts finally, 1786, five years after the death of Fairfax, confirmed the grants to Hite and his associates, where it had been shown that settlers had complied with orders of council by retaining surveys of their individual tracts.

The General Court had on the 15th October, 1771, made a decree that virtually settled the rights of Hite and those to whom he had sold land and executed conveyances within the boundaries of the Van Meter grants, and also of the Hite and McKay grants; Hite having seated fifty-four families, pursuant to orders of Council 1730-31.

Had Fairfax been sustained, every lot owner in Winchester who derived his right under James Wood, would have suffered a loss of his holding. Fairfax seemed determined to stand upon his rights as the Lord proprietor of the Northern Neck; and although he had an agreement with Wood, Hite, Rogers and others, that he would make them quit-rent deeds without payment of the usual fee, yet he declined to withdraw from the contest; and allowed the suit to drag along until all the original litigants were dead. This left Denny Martin Fairfax, his nephew, to contend as an alien for his title to Lord Fairfax's estate, with quit-rents and other holdings sequestered by Acts of Assembly passed in 1782 (II Hen. Stat. 128). The court held that Fairfax had no claim against settlers who held Minor Grants for land West of the Blue Ridge prior to 1738. This virtually determined that Wood had good cause, and need not submit to any demand made by Fairfax for the site of Winchester. Much more could be written concerning these titles; but we must refer the student of such history to Henning's Statutes, Vols. 2, 3-4.

More than five hundred settlers were affected by these ejectment suits instituted by Fairfax.

APPENDIX NO. 6

The Hession Prisoners

In the preparation of the foregoing chapters, the author had occasion to mention the Hession Prisoners. It may be well to condense scraps of their history for future reference.

At the battle of Saratoga, Genl. (Baron) Riedesel surrendered to the American Army the remnant of his command, about 8,000 men of every class and grade. All were the Hesse-Darmstadt contingent of the British Army. From the battle-field, these Hessian prisoners marched to Boston. Efforts were made at once by Genl. Washington to have them exchanged. A convention was held, composed of officers from both armies, to consider the terms. An agreement was effected; the prisoners were allowed to return to their native country, on conditions that they should not be re-hired to fight against the Americans. Pending these negotiations, an alliance was formed between France and the United States. France protested against their return, giving the reason that these prisoners would be employed against France on the continent. Congress annulled the cartel, and disregarded protests of Genl. Washington and other officers. At the suggestion of Mr. Jefferson, Governor of Virginia, the entire Hessian command was sent to Williamsburg, Virginia. On their march, the inhabitants were greatly disturbed, but no serious trouble occurred. At that time every American patriot detested the hireling. When Williamsburg was reached, they found ample provision had been made by the Governor for their safe and comfortable imprisonment. Stockades had been made for the rank and file; and quarters secured for the general officers. Many of the men desired permanent residence in that section, and were allowed to remain under certain conditions. From Williamsburg, the main body marched in three detachments: one to Charlottesville, one to Winchester, and one to Frederick, Maryland. This has been previously mentioned. The first batch to arrive in Winchester, numbered 710; and were quartered in the town temporarily; and, as others arrived, swelling the number to nearly two thousand, they were gradually transferred from tents to cabins, on the farm West of Winchester now the property of Mr. Glaize, as already stated.

During his imprisonment in Virginia, the Hessian General seems to have enjoyed many liberties under his parole; for Mr. Jefferson's well preserved papers show a correspondence between the Governor and the General; while the latter with his wife sojourned at Berkeley Springs.

The writer is well aware that some historians state with authority that no Hessian prisoners were allowed to remain in America, when the command was released by articles of peace. He, however, could name quite a number who remained in the Shenandoah Valley. Several families in Winchester and Frederick County of to-day, have been traced to certain Hessians with odd names.

The Governor of the State was regarded as the Commissioner General of the Convention Prisoners. We have shown elsewhere who several of his deputy commissioners-general were.

APPENDIX NO. 7

James Rumsey, Inventor of the First Steamboat

While we may not properly claim James Rumsey as one of the pioneers, or a descendant of one who figures in the Shenandoah Valley in its early development, yet we can claim him as one of the Revolutionary War soldiers. He was born in Maryland in 1743; but was South of the Potomac in 1767; in 1783 he was engaged in business in the Village of Bath, Berkeley County, Virginia, when he exhibited portions of his invention to several friends, who subsequently made sworn statements to that effect. In the same year he is on record in the General Assemblies of Maryland and Virginia as inventor of generators of steam. In 1788, we find him well on the way with his steamboat propelling power. We have evidence that the boat had been built in 1783, and a test made of the steam in the Potomac River near Bath in the night of October ——, 1783. Two friends assisted in getting the apparatus on board and in position—Jos. Barnes and Nicholas Orrick. This experiment was made with great secrecy. In 1786, Genl. Washington wrote Rumsey from Mt. Vernon, expressing his desire that the claim as inventor of the mechanical boat should be made public without further delay; suggesting that "some genius might anticipate you (Rumsey), and thus gain credit for the invention." In March, 1786, another trial was made in the night, in the presence of Jos. Barnes, Charles Morrow, Dr. McMechin, and F. H. Hamilton. The trial was made against the current and proved satisfactory, excepting as to size of boiler. In 1787, the boat was taken to Shepherdstown, and notice given that public exhibition would take place Dec. 3, 1787.

We are indebted to writings of A. R. Boteler for an account of this first public exhibition of the first steam-boat. Mr. B. says "I knew many of those who witnessed Rumsey's success, and conversed with them about Rumsey and his invention." The following are named by Mr. Boteler as composing this number of witnesses: Mrs. Ann Baker, Mrs. Eleanor Shepherd, Major Henry Beddinger, Jacob Haines, Michael Fouke, and Peter Fisher. Mr. Boteler says many groups of ladies and gentlemen were near by and witnessed the wonder of the age, namely: Genl. Gates, Rev. Robert Stubbs, Capt. A. Shepherd, Col. Swearingen, Genl. Darke, Philip Pendleton, John Kearsley, Cato Moore, John Mark, Thomas White, David Gray, Benoni Swearingen, and many others. Mr. B. says the boat continued to steam up and down the river for the space of two hours, between the two points, Swearingen Spring and where the Shenandoah Valley Railroad bridge spans the Potomac, keeping up an average rate of speed of three miles an hour. Upon the second trial the following week, Dec. 11, 1787, the rate of speed was four miles per hour. During the winter of 1788, Rumsey went to Philadelphia. He found the city excited over his invention. "The Rumseyan Society" was organized with Benjamin Franklin as president. This Society was instrumental in Rumsey's visit to London the following May. There he proceeded to secure patents from the British government for his invention. He constructed a boat and launched it in the Thames in the Spring of 1790. There he met Robert Fulton. The two became warm friends. After Rumsey's sudden death in Dec., 1772, in London, Fulton took up the work and spent nearly 20 years in constructing a steamboat, virtually on the plans of the original inventor. In 1839, Congress awarded "to James Rumsey Jr., the son and only surviving child of James Rumsey, deceased, a gold medal as a token of his father's services in giving to the world the benefits of the steamboat." The Shenandoah Valley claims James Rumsey as one of its most renowned citizens.

APPENDIX NO. 8

The Negro

No discussion of what is so often called the Negro Problem, can nor ever will accomplish much good to the two races as they exist in the South. If left alone, they will work out their own destiny to their own satisfaction. No two races ever lived in such harmony as the White and Black races enjoyed in *ye olden times,* before the negro was taught by the fanatics that slavery was a yoke that must be removed, and *he must do his part.* We have seen that no uprising could be produced; and when great armies stood ready to receive them if they would desert their firesides, they stood aghast; and nine-tenths of the negroes on the Northern border refused to cross over when there was nothing to hinder. When Bank's Army came in the Summer of 1861, it is a well-known fact that officers with men and wagons visited many homesteads and urged the negroes to accompany them. The writer can testify to this from his personal knowledge. Three negro families were thus taken from his old home, not one of whom desired to go. Many noble specimens of the race clung to the fortunes of their former masters, protecting and supporting the helpless women and children of the old home, who felt secure when thus guarded. No insults or outrages then, except from that class of soldiers who thought of nothing else but liberty to the slave. How sad the change in this race! When a slave, he was a trusted friend; now we are taught that the rising generations have many monsters to be hounded by mobs and destroyed. Under the old conditions, no monsters or frenzied communities disturbed the country. The two races knew each other. Vicious people were punished without unjust criticism. We have the right to enquire for the cause which has apparently transformed the natures of the two races. Southern people remember no trouble between the two races until after the emancipation proclamation, and subsequent schemes adopted by the Washington government to make allies of the negro race. The negro was then encouraged to take weapons of destruction in his hands and wreak vengeance on his old oppressors; even then he hesitated, and no wholesale crime was committed, until the negro regiments were organized and marched alongside Union columns that led the way for pillage and ruin. While many vile-tempered negroes took advantage of their license to commit crime, only a very small per cent. accepted the offer of Mr. Lincoln. Several millions of the race remained in their old communities; and there died since the war; and millions of their descendants still hold on to their Sunny South. Others have been enticed away, to learn new ideas; and then, when too late, to realize that the true friend to his race is to be found in the South. Southerners have often asked the question, was President Lincoln's act justifiable as a war measure? This may be answered: that he had untold resources in men and munitions of war, on the increase every day; while the South suffered depletion from every source. Her brave men fast disappearing, and army supplies lessening; certainly there was no need to encourage the poor deluded negro to conduct a war of rapine and slaughter against the people with whom he had lived in harmony—they and their ancestors, from the time they landed on the Southern shores as African heathen. This never seemed necessary to secure success to the Union armies. The sacrifices made by this act were a fearful offset to what was gained. The confederates, whenever opportunity offered, tried to annihilate every negro regiment, stimulated to do so by the same motives that now lead them to hunt for the monster who brutishly commits an outrage on some helpless woman. It could in no sense better the condition of the race. Their freedom was not hastened; nor could any good result to those who remained within the Confederate lines. The act produced discord between the races that a half century has not removed.

Mr. Lincoln was noted for his kind heart and humane feelings, but this one act of his has cast a shadow over his life. His desire to be humane and helpful to the race, caused him to weigh lightly the horrors of a race-war he inaugurated, and which was sustained through the reconstruction period by the military acting in concert with an element composed of Northern adventurers and renegade natives of the South. Had Lincoln been spared to witness the results of his dangerous experiment, he doubtless would have striven to atone for his direful blunder. The two races have suffered in all these years.

The white race had cause for animosity; but the history of their legislation proves they have produced wonderful results in the improved conditions of the other race. They have verified their good will toward the negro; they have spent millions in establishing and maintaining negro schools; they have always aided in building their churches, educating their ministers and teachers, and liberally providing for the destitute and helpless. They are bound to each other by mutual friendships and ties of interest that should never be sundered. Away with all the wild schemes of deportation and segregation in some other territory! Let the ten millions of negroes alone. No feasible plan of removal can be suggested. The American nation, even with its tremendous transportation facilities, could never land them on any foreign shore; and it is well known that ninety-nine per cent. of the race would never willingly abandon the Southern States. Many have tried the States North and West in the vain hope that they would find more congenial homes. Experience has proven they are not wanted there.

The writer has never known the time when he was unfamiliar with the habits and wants of this peculiar race. The old slaves were his companions and friends; and the few of this class who have survived the wreck and ruin of old cherished institutions, spend many hours recounting happy reminiscences; and together we live the old life in memory. The old Christmas reunions, and two weeks of *holiday,* with all the *doin's around the great house,* where roast pig, turkeys, plum puddings, etc., was liberally dispensed, the old Mammies, Aunties, and Uncles with their several generations, made relations between the races possible, that can never be understood by those who never enjoyed such experiences. These old landmarks are passing rapidly out of sight. Frederick County never was a large slave-holding community. Some of the old homesteads mentioned in this volume, were famous for splendid negro families. Very few are left of those the writer knew sixty years ago. The Glass, Magill, Cartmell, Campbell, Jones, Carson, Gilkeson and other families, owned many splendid men and women. Some of their descendants are here. During the early part of the 19th Century, many slaves were emancipated. They afterwards became known as *free negroes.* The Virginia laws required their removal to a free State. A large majority refused to change their homes. The clerks of county courts were required to register all such. This class was required to produce proof annually that they were constantly employed by some responsible white man, who would be responsible for their taxes and good behavior. By this mode, they were annually before the court; their cases called and continued; and in this evasive way, they spent the remainder of their days in their old communities. This old Register, the writer, while clerk, found several years ago. It may now be seen on file in the old clerk's office. A study of it will repay many of our old negro families. When the Civil War came, we had quite a number of this class in Winchester, viz: Edmund Kean, Randall Evans, Sawnee Bell, Robert Orrick's father, Beverly Tucker, Joe Branson, Robert, John and Sim Tokes, Jim Sisco, several of the Walker family, Parson Bob Robinson, William Layton, Parson John Garrison, John Marshall, Hutton Lovett; while in the county could be named Sandy Scott, Frank Whetz, Sam Toles, and others near Round Hill; the Careys and Robinsons in South end of the County, Ben Watson, Jim Allen and others North of Winchester. All were respected by their white friends. Hutton Lovett was a slave of Judge Tucker. His wife belonged to Mr. Tidball, the old clerk. Hutton purchased her freedom for $1200.00,—a fair price for so good a wife. She was the mother of Mont Lovett the well-known barber.

It may be well to say that slavery and the slave trade existed in the North as long as profitable. Then the negroes were driven in gang lots and sold to the planters in Virginia and other Southern States. More negroes were emancipated in Virginia than in all the New England States combined. Virginia was the first State to enact a law to suppress the slave trade. The writer could name several old Quaker families, and clergymen of the several churches, who owned negroes. The former gave gradual emancipation; the latter educated their slaves to some extent. Of this number we name Rev. Alex. Balmain, Dr. Wm. Hill, Dr. A. H. H. Boyd. Two well-known women of Winchester still living, Ann and Susan Robinson, belonged to the family owned by Dr. Balmain.

The Negro race has always exhibited considerable interest in church work. For seventy-five years they had their separate organization. The Methodist branch have occupied a building on East Cork Street, distinguished as the John Mann Church. Prior to the Civil War, their services were conducted by their local preachers. Since that time, the congregation has increased and the building improved. This church and the Free Will Baptist Church on South Braddock Street, are well supplied with ministers from time to time, having regular services on every Sabbath.

In the North end of the city are two churches—one an old Ironside Baptist type. Visitors will find there the same class of preachers that figured in the long-ago. Their style of service and old-time doctrines, remind one of the antebellum days. This building is on North Market Street.

The church on North Main has quite a congregation, and a good building.

The two churches—one at Newtown and one at Middletown—have fairly good village congregations.

There are several other churches in Frederick County.

We can add that the white and colored churches in the Valley have always worked in harmony towards the betterment of the race.

L'ENVOI

Farewell, Old Pioneers! I pen these words with reluctance. You and your descendants have been my companions in the study of the volume just laid aside. Much benefit has been derived in following many of your number into Tennessee, Kentucky, Ohio, Illinois, Indiana, Missouri, Texas, and other great States, where your mighty work was done, that has grown familiar to the nation. In many cases, your descendants have been traced to this day. This has been wonderfully true of the Lower Valley. Many were found occupying good homes on the site of the pioneer's cabin. We must not forget that Frederick County of to-day has a large number of splendid citizens who had no part in the pioneers' work in the Shenandoah; they, however, had ancestors who had pioneers elsewhere. But as this was intended as a history of the Shenandoah Valley pioneers and their descendants, I reluctantly adhered to the scheme, and only made a departure when unavoidable. My inclination was to embrace all; but the volume grew so bulky, this had to be abandoned.

Farewell! All my work has been a pleasure. I have enjoyed every moment in my efforts to trace you. During that time, several hundreds of our well-known men and women have been called hence. Their vacant places will be filled, however, and the grand old Valley will continue to hold her place in the line of progress.

During the latter years of this work, the author was subjected to severe trials. The dark shadow that fell across his pathway, well nigh ended all efforts to complete what he had undertaken. The constant contact with the pioneers and their descendants in the study of their interesting lives during the last three years, has been a solace through many dark days. May the perusal of this volume afford pleasure and instruction to the reader, as its preparation has given—

THE AUTHOR.

ADDENDUM

Pending the publication of the "Shenandoah Valley Pioneers and Their Descendants," Winchester made some important history. The author has been requested to mention two prominent features. The Handley Library photo found in the book exhibits the building in course of construction. The magnificent structure is now completed, and efforts being made to equip the attractive interior so as to reflect credit to the impressive memorial of Judge John Handley in evidence of his philanthropy.

Sewerage System in Winchester

The summer of 1909 produced commotion in the streets of the city while the eight miles of sewerage pipes were laid, traversing all the principal streets. Excavations were made generally through solid limestone rock, ranging in depth from eight to seventeen feet. At the intersection of Water and Market streets the large tiles were laid on solid rock foundations, fully fifteen feet below the surface. The installation of this system, at a cost of about $50,000, will doubtless redound to the name and fame of the city as a summer resort for the hundreds of visitors who annually enjoy the advantages of historic Winchester; while her citizens will enjoy a much-needed comfort. Chief engineer, N. Wilson Davis, of Harrisonburg, Va.; contractors, Irwin Bros.

The casual reader of this book may find what appears many inconsistencies in spelling names of places and persons. The author in many cases conformed to the style adopted in the various periods of early history of the Old County. This is gradually explained and styles changed as the book advanced through the Colonial Stages.

INDEX

A

B

C

D

E

F

G

H

I

J

K

L

M

N

O

P

Q

R

S

T

U

V

W

Y

Z